CONTENT AREA 3: PRINCIPLES, PROCESSES AND CON[...]

#	TASK
3-1	Define and provide examples of behavior/response/response class.
3-2	Define and provide examples of stimulus and stimulus class.
3-3	Define and provide examples of positive and negative reinforcement.
3-4	Define and provide examples of conditioned and unconditioned reinforcement.
3-5	Define and provide examples of positive and negative punishment.
3-6	Define and provide examples of conditioned and unconditioned punishment.
3-7	Define and provide examples of stimulus control.
3-8	Define and provide examples of establishing operations.
3-9	Define and provide examples of behavioral contingencies.
3-10	Define and provide examples of functional relations.
3-11	Define and provide examples of extinction.
3-12	Define and provide examples of generalization and discrimination.
3-13	Describe and provide examples of the respondent conditioning paradigm.
3-14	Describe and provide examples of the operant conditioning paradigm.
3-15	Define and provide examples of echoics and imitation.
3-16	Define and provide examples of mands.
3-17	Define and provide examples of tacts.
3-18	Define and provide examples of intraverbals.
3-19	Define and provide examples of contingency-shaped and rule governed behavior and distinguish between examples of each.

CONTENT AREA 4: BEHAVIORAL ASSESSMENT

#	TASK
4-1	State the primary characteristics of and rationale for conducting a descriptive assessment.
4-2	Gather descriptive data.
a.	Select various methods.
b.	Use various methods.
4-3	Organize and interpret descriptive data.
a.	Select various methods.
b.	Use various methods.
4-4	State the primary characteristics of and rationale for conducting a functional analysis as a form of assessment.
4-5	Conduct functional analyses.
a.	Select various methods.
b.	Use various methods.
4-6	Organize and interpret functional analysis data.
a.	Select various methods.
b.	Use various methods.

CONTENT AREA 5: EXPERIMENTAL EVALUATION OF INTERVENTIONS

#	TASK
5-1	Systematically manipulate independent variables to analyze their effects on treatment.
a.	Use withdrawal designs.
b.	Use reversal designs.
c.	Use alternating treatments (i.e., multielement, simultaneous treatment, multiple or concurrent schedule) designs.
d.	Use changing criterion design.
e.	Use multiple baseline designs.
5-2	Identify and address practical and ethical considerations in using various experimental designs.
5-3	Conduct a component analysis (i.e., determining effective component(s) of an intervention package).
5-4	Conduct a parametric analysis (i.e., determining effective parametric values of consequences, such as duration or magnitude).

continued on back inside cover

Teacher Preparation Classroom

TEACHER PREP

MERRILL

PRENTICE HALL

Your Class. Their Careers. Our Future. Will your students be prepared?

We invite you to explore our new, innovative and engaging website and all that it has to offer you, your course, and to-morrow's educators! Preview this site today at www.prenhall.com/teacherprep/demo. Just click on "go" on the login page to begin your exploration.

Organized around the major courses pre-service teachers take, the Teacher Preparation site provides media, student/teacher artifacts, strategies, research articles, and other resources to equip your students with the quality tools needed to excel in their courses and prepare them for their first classroom.

This ultimate on-line education resource will provide you and your students access to:

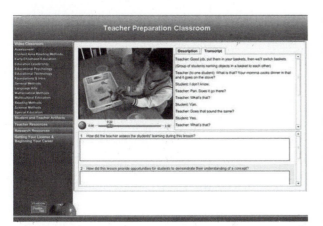

Online Video Library. More than 250 video clips—each tied to a course topic and framed by learning goals and Praxis-type questions—capture real teachers and students working in real classrooms.

Student and Teacher Artifacts. More than 200 student and teacher classroom artifacts—each tied to a course topic and framed by learning goals and application questions—provide a wealth of materials and experiences to help your students observe children's developmental learning.

Lesson Plan Builder. Step-by-step guidelines and lesson plan examples support students as they learn to build high-quality lesson plans.

Articles and Readings. Over 500 articles from ASCD's renowned journal Educational Leadership are available. The site also includes Research Navigator, a searchable database of additional educational journals.

Strategies and Lessons. Over 500 research-supported instructional strategies appropriate for a wide range of grade levels and content areas.

Licensure and Career Tools. Resources devoted to helping your students pass their licensure exam; learn standards, law, and public policies; plan a teaching portfolio; and succeed in their first year of teaching.

How to ORDER *Teacher Prep* for you and your students:

For students to receive a *Teacher Prep* Access Code with this text, the instructor **must** provide a special value pack ISBN number on their textbook order form. To receive this special ISBN, please email: **Merrill.marketing@pearsoned.com** and provide the following information:

- Name and Affiliation
- Author/Title/Edition of Merrill text

Upon ordering *Teacher Prep* for their students, instructors will be given a lifetime *Teacher Prep* Access Code.

Applied Behavior Analysis

Second Edition

John O. Cooper

Timothy E. Heron

William L. Heward

All, The Ohio State University

PEARSON

Merrill
Prentice Hall

Upper Saddle River, New Jersey
Columbus, Ohio

Library of Congress Cataloging in Publication Data

Cooper, John O.
    Applied behavior analysis / John O. Cooper, Timothy E. Heron, and William L.
Heward. -- 2nd ed.
        p. cm.
    Includes bibliographical references (p.   ) and indexes.
    ISBN 0-13-142113-1
    1. Behaviorism (Psychology)--Textbooks. 2. Human behavior--Textbooks. I. Heron,
Timothy E. II. Heward, William L. III. Title.

BF199.C65 2007
150.19'43--dc22   2006052490

Vice President and Executive Publisher: Jeffery W. Johnston
Executive Editor: Ann Castel Davis
Editorial Assistant: Penny S. Burleson
Senior Production Editor: Linda Hillis Bayma
Production Coordination: Linda Zuk, WordCraft, LLC
Design Coordinator: Diane C. Lorenzo
Cover Designer: Keith Van Norman
Production Manager: Laura Messerly
Director of Marketing: David Gesell
Marketing Manager: Autumn Purdy
Marketing Coordinator: Brian Mounts

This book was set in Times Roman by Pine Tree Composition. It was printed and bound by Courier Kendallville, Inc. The cover was printed by The Lehigh Press, Inc.

Photo Credits: Jack Michael, May 23, 1998, at the 24th annual convention of the Association for Behavior Analysis, p. v; Jill C. Dardig, p. vii; B. F. Skinner Foundation, p. 10 (left); Julie S. Vargas/B. F. Skinner Foundation, p. 10 (right).

Pearson Education Ltd.   Pearson Education Australia Pty. Limited
Pearson Education Singapore Pte. Ltd.   Pearson Education North Asia Ltd.
Pearson Education Canada, Ltd.   Pearson Educación de Mexico, S.A. de C.V.
Pearson Education—Japan   Pearson Education Malaysia Pte. Ltd.

10 9 8 7 6 5 4 3 2 1
ISBN-13: 978-0-13-142113-4
ISBN-10:   0-13-142113-1

This book is dedicated to Donald M. Baer,
whose extraordinary contributions to applied behavior analysis
are evident in every aspect of the science.

Donald Merle Baer (1931–2002)

*"That there could be a science of behavior, of what we do, of who we are?
How could you resist that?"*

About the Authors

John Cooper (left), Tim Heron (right), and Bill Heward (center)

John O. Cooper, Ed.D., Professor Emeritus of Education, The Ohio State University. John's research interests include precision teaching, inner behavior, fluency building, and verbal behavior. His many publications include the text *Measuring Behavior,* Second Edition. He served as the president of The Standard Celeration Society and as the Applied Representative to the Executive Council of the Association for Behavior Analysis.

Timothy E. Heron, Ed.D., Professor Emeritus of Education, The Ohio State University. Tim's research interests include tutoring systems, inclusion of students with disabilities in general education classrooms, consultation, and self-correction approaches to instruction. Tim is co-author of the text *The Educational Consultant: Helping Professionals, Parents, and Students in Inclusive Classrooms,* Fourth Edition (2001).

John Cooper, Tim Heron, and Bill Heward were faculty members at The Ohio State University for a combined 88 years. Together they trained classroom teachers and leadership personnel for special education whose work is guided by the philosophical, scientific, and technological principles of applied behavior analysis. The Ph.D. program in special education and applied behavior analysis that they and their colleagues created at Ohio State University was the first doctoral program to be accredited by the Association for Behavior Analysis. During their careers John, Tim, and Bill each received the Alumni Award for Distinguished Teaching, The Ohio State University's highest honor for teaching excellence.

William L. Heward, Ed.D., BCBA, Professor Emeritus of Education, The Ohio State University. Bill's research interests include promoting the generalization and maintenance of newly learned skills, increasing the effectiveness of group instruction, and improving the academic success of students with disabilities in general education classrooms. He has authored or coauthored five other books, including *Exceptional Children: An Introduction to Special Education,* Eighth Edition (Merrill/ Prentice Hall, 2006). Bill is a Fellow of the Association for Behavior Analysis, and in 2006 he received the American Psychological Association's Division 25 Fred S. Keller Behavioral Education Award.

Chapter Contributors

Thomas R. Freeman, M.S., BCBA, is the District Behavior Analyst and chair of the Local Behavior Analysis Services Plans Review Committee for the Florida Agency for Persons with Disabilities, an instructor in the applied behavior analysis graduate program at Florida Institute of Technology, and president of Praiseworx, Inc. Tom has more than 25 years of behavioral experience and has held various supervisory and clinical positions in community-based and residential settings in Florida and Massachusetts. Tom also participated in long-term animal behavioral studies with orangutans in Borneo and spinner dolphins in Hawaii, and was Field Director of the University of Hawaii's Humpback Whale Research project. Tom's interests include legal and professional issues, program development tactics based on consumer involvement and interdisciplinary team building, and the coordination of psychiatric and behavioral services.

Brian A. Iwata, Ph.D., BCBA, is Professor of Psychology and Psychiatry at the University of Florida. He and his students have published more than 200 articles and chapters on research methodology, developmental disabilities, and the functional analysis and treatment of severe behavior disorders. Brian is a former editor of the *Journal of Applied Behavior Analysis* and past president of the Association for Behavior Analysis, Division 33 of the American Psychological Association, the Society for the Advancement of Behavior Analysis, the Society for the Experimental Analysis of Behavior, and the Florida Association for Behavior Analysis. Brian has chaired study sections for both NIH and NIMH and is a fellow of the American Association on Mental Retardation, the Association for Behavior Analysis, the American Psychological Association, and the Association for Psychological Science.

Jose Martinez-Diaz, Ph.D., BCBA, is Associate Professor and Chair of the applied behavior analysis graduate program at the Florida Institute of Technology and president of ABA Technologies, Inc. Jose is a member of the executive council of the Behavior Analyst Certification Board and a member of the Florida Behavior Analysis Certification and Peer Review Committees. He is past president of the Florida Association for Behavior Analysis and recipient of the Charles H. Cox Award for Outstanding Service and Advancement of Behavior Analysis. Jose's main interests are professional and legal issues, supervision, administration, conceptual and philosophical issues, verbal behavior, and the role of motivating operations in behavioral treatment. He completed his doctorate at West Virginia University.

Jack Michael, Ph.D., is Professor Emeritus in the Department of Psychology at Western Michigan University, where he taught for 38 years. His primary scholarly interests are verbal behavior, basic theory regarding motivation, and the technical terminology of behavior analysis. Jack contributed to the founding of the Association for Behavior Analysis and served as its third president. His publications include a text that all behavior analysts should read, *Concepts and Principles of Behavior Analysis* (2004). He currently serves as editor of the journal *The Analysis of Verbal Behavior.* A Fellow of the Association for Behavior Analysis and the American Psychological Association, Jack's many honors and recognitions include the Distinguished Service to Behavior Analysis Award from the Association for Behavior Analysis, the 2002 Don Hake Award for research that bridges the gap between experimental and applied behavior analysis from Division 25 of the American Psychological Association, and both of Western Michigan University's top two honors for faculty: the Distinguished Faculty Scholar Award and Distinguished Teaching Award.

Nancy A. Neef, Ph.D., is Professor of Special Education at The Ohio State University. She has served as editor of the *Journal of Applied Behavior Analysis,* as president of the Society for the Experimental Analysis of Behavior, and on the Executive Council and as chair of the publication board for the Association of Behavior Analysis. Nancy has published more than 60 articles and chapters in the areas of developmental disabilities, research methodology, and instructional technology. Much of her recent research has focused on extensions and applications of basic research in the assessment and treatment of attention deficit hyperactivity disorder. Nancy was the recipient of the first Distinguished Alumnus Achievement Award in Psychology from Western Michigan University and the 2006 Award for Outstanding Research in Applied Behavior Analysis from Division 25 of the American Psychological Association.

Matthew Normand, Ph.D., BCBA, is Assistant Professor in the applied behavior analysis program at the Florida Institute of Technology. He received his B.A. in psychology from Western New England College, his M.A. in behavior analysis from Western Michigan University, and his M.S. and Ph.D. in psychology from the Florida State University. Matt serves on the editorial boards of *The Analysis of Verbal Behavior* and the *Journal of Early and Intensive Behavior Interventions.* As a clinician, he works with schools and families on a variety of child behavior problems. As a researcher, his primary interests are the application of basic behavioral principles to problems of social significance (including autism, obesity, and other community health issues) and verbal behavior.

Stephanie M. Peterson, Ph.D., BCBA, is Associate Professor of Special Education at Idaho State University. Her primary research interests are choice and concurrent schedules of reinforcement in the treatment of severe problem behavior and in the functional analysis of problem behavior. Stephanie also has interests in applications of behavior analysis to educational interventions and teacher training. She has served on the editorial boards of the *Journal of Applied Behavior Analysis* and *The Behavior Analyst* and currently serves as one of the senior editors for *Education and Treatment of Children.*

Richard G. Smith, Ph.D., BCBA, is Professor and Chair of the Department of Behavior Analysis at the University of North Texas. Rick received his master's and doctoral degrees at the University of Florida. His primary research interest is in the assessment and treatment of behavior disorders in persons with developmental disabilities, with specific areas of focus in motivational variables, advances in functional analysis procedures, and the use of complex research designs to investigate basic principles underlying the effects of behavioral interventions. A former associate editor for the *Journal of Applied Behavior Analysis,* Rick received the 1997 American Psychological Association's Division 25 B. F. Skinner Award for Innovative and Important Research by a New Researcher, and the 2000 Texas Association on Mental Retardation's Research Award.

Mark L. Sundberg, Ph.D., BCBA, is a Licensed Psychologist in private practice. He specializes in language research and the development of language assessment and intervention programs for children with autism. Mark is founder and past editor of the journal *The Analysis of Verbal Behavior,* a past president of The Northern California Association for Behavior Analysis, and former chair of the Publication Board of the Association for Behavior Analysis. Mark is the co-author of three books: *Teaching Language to Children with Autism or Other Developmental Disabilities, The Assessment of Basic Language and Learning Skills: The ABLLS* (with James W. Partington), and *A Collection of Reprints on Verbal Behavior* (with Jack Michael). Mark has received several awards, including the 2001 Distinguished Alumnus Achievement Award in Psychology from Western Michigan University.

Foreword

The "White Book." It is like the "White Album" of applied behavior analysis (of course, that reference dates the author and any readers who understand its significance). It is almost like an icon for students in applied behavior analysis. Or, as my students tell me, "You do not read the White Book, you live the White Book" (Stevens, 2006). It is only fitting that Cooper, Heron, and Heward have written the only text that could take the place of the original 1987 edition, the second edition of the White Book, with some very important and timely additions.

The first time I met John Cooper, Tim Heron, and Bill Heward was at an Association for Behavior Analysis conference. I remember being very nervous about meeting the authors of what I considered then and still consider the definitive textbook in applied behavior analysis (ABA). At the time I met them I was a graduate student. I had been a practitioner of ABA for some years, but I was attempting to learn about the historical, conceptual, and empirical foundations of the discipline through my graduate studies. I was at the stage of my academic development at which you could politely say that I was a behavioral groupie (a less polite colleague might say I was a fanatic). I had found an academic discipline that made sense to me. It helped me be more effective with the children with disabilities with whom I worked, it valued data and empiricism, it was pragmatic, it had multiple applications in everyday life, and my mentors would answer questions with phrases such as, "It's an empirical question," "We need to see what the data say," "It will work or it won't work; we will learn something either way," and "You will know that you have solved the problem when the person who made the referral in the first place stops complaining."

Meeting Coop, Tim, and Bill did not disappoint. In fact you could say it helped to fuel the fire. Here were three eminent scholars in ABA who were accessible, brilliant, and fun. They were phenomenally generous with their time and they seemed to genuinely enjoy spending time with students (their own and others), answering questions and telling stories. They appeared to be truly interested in helping new generations of behavior analysts learn about the discipline and how to be good stewards of the science. Their deep understanding of ABA that is so apparent in the book was even more apparent in person. But what struck me about all three of them from that meeting was their commitment to the role of being a professor: helping their students understand behavioral principles and learn to apply them to address important social issues.

That commitment to teaching others about behavior analysis was evident in the first edition of *Applied Behavior Analysis,* and it is evident in the second edition. Cooper, Heron, and Heward have taken a complex academic discipline and made it accessible to students, teachers, parents, and other consumers. Although I know many people who will be reluctant to give up their copies of the first edition, I am confident that they will find the second edition an even better definitive source to use in their teaching, writing, and research.

I envision students poring over the second edition of the White Book with their professors, discussing definitions, examples, and applications of the principles. Clearly, this edition will be a standard for every student preparing to become a Board Certified Behavior Analyst (BCBA®). Cooper, Heron, and Heward have even made this goal more easily accessible for students by including the most current BACB® Task List in the text.

The idea of helping more people learn about ABA fits well into the practice of this discipline. It is important, as behavior analysts, that we take the time to teach about the principles rather than proselytize about the possible outcomes. Teaching prospective users and consumers about behavioral principles will perhaps lead to better and more widespread applications of those principles; and as Baer, Wolf, and Risley (1968) taught us, "Better applications, it is hoped, will lead to a better state of society. . ." (p. 91).

Teaching consumers about the behavioral principles may help to make them better consumers of their application. It will minimally help the consumers and, in return, the users to be aware of the process of the application of the principles, rather than focusing on outcomes alone. As Don Baer (1970) said, "In my opinion, it is the process of development, not merely the outcome of development, which should be our subject matter" (p. 241). He went on to say that "a particular learning procedure [a.k.a. behavioral intervention strategy] may not produce its expected effect in an organism, *unless it occurs at the right time*" (p. 243). This statement begins to make the strong argument about the contextual nature of applied behavior analysis. This importance of understanding the context in which a behavior occurs is essential to both understanding and effectively changing behavior. This dependence on context is often misunderstood by naïve consumers of ABA, but it will not be misunderstood or overlooked by the readers of Cooper, Heron, and Heward's second edition.

Applied behavior analysis is in the midst of some interesting times. On the one hand, the field is experiencing an explosion in numbers of potential practitioners and consumers. One factor contributing to this growth is the increase of the prevalence of autism and the effectiveness of behavioral programming for young children with autism; applied behavior analysts are more in demand than ever before. Another contributing factor may be the growth and wide-scale adoption of positive behavior support (PBS). PBS, an approach to dealing with challenging behaviors, was developed and evaluated by behavior analysts (e.g., Horner, Sugai, Carr, and Dunlap). More than any other behavioral intervention, PBS has been adopted widely by public schools and integrated fully into public law and funding priorities. Functional behavior assessments (FBA), a cornerstone of PBS, are required by federal law (Individuals with Disabilities Education Act–IDEA) for students who demonstrate challenging behaviors at school. Behavioral intervention plans, informed by FBAs, are also now required by federal law for students who demonstrate challenging behavior. In other words, school districts are being required to implement components of ABA to be in compliance with federal special education law.

On the other hand, the increased need for behavior analysts has led to some unscrupulous behavior on the part of some practitioners. Some people with little more experience than a weekend workshop hang shingles in communities, selling their services to families who have young children with autism. Although the behavior analysis community has risen to the occasion by developing a certification program to ensure quality, more needs to be done to ensure that all consumers of behavioral practice receive high quality and ethical services. We are also experiencing a potentially dangerous divide within the field of applied behavior analysis. While PBS has widespread acceptance in the U.S. Department of Education and public schools across the country, it has not been accepted with open arms by all behavior analysts.

It is extraordinarily important that we resolve the challenges that are facing the behavior analysis community quickly and in an amicable manner. These challenges are issues of quality control, training, and definition of the field. One could make the argument that they are issues related to social validity. As the readers of this volume know, social validity is the process of asking consumers of an intervention about its acceptability and how that acceptability affects the sustainability of the intervention. Although social validity is never considered a primary dependent variable—that is, it should not be considered in determining the effectiveness of an intervention—it may be a major predictor of the sustainability of an intervention. That is, it may assure that the intervention will be maintained after the experimenter leaves the setting. The literature, unfortunately, is replete with examples of effective interventions that were not sustained (e.g., Project Follow Through; see *Effective School Practices,* 1995-6, Volume 15, No. 1, for an entire issue dedicated to this topic). We have an equal number of examples of interventions that have no effectiveness data and yet remain perennial favorites in education and other aspects of human service (e.g., whole language, psychoanalysis). As behavior analysts, we have been reticent to use social validity data to examine our own behavior. It is my hope that the readers of this volume will embrace data on the social validity of their practices and use those data to make decisions about the appropriateness of the target behaviors selected, the acceptability of the intervention as implemented, and the degree to which the outcomes of the intervention are satisfactory.

Thinking about social validity leads to thinking about Don Baer, to whom this volume is dedicated. I had the honor and the great pleasure of studying with Don when I was a graduate student at the University of Kansas. Don, for me, was the perfect graduate advisor. He was the ultimate academic. He looked like a professor, he talked like a professor, and he treated me (and his other graduate students) as colleagues. Don never told me that an idea I had was not very well thought out (although that was the case much of the time) or that I should have prepared more thoroughly before a meeting (although that was the case much of the time). He would simply ask a series of questions, listening intently to my answers, with his head cocked to the side just a bit and the tips of his fingers pressed together. He would listen, he would nod, and without saying too much he would teach.

In this edition Cooper, Heron, and Heward have created an opportunity for all of us to learn important material from great teachers. I look forward to sharing this book with my students and, while I am doing that, I will be thinking of Don and trying to remember that some-times you can teach more by listening than by talking and that the best answers to most questions can be found in the data.

Ilene S. Schwartz
University of Washington

Preface

Our goal in writing the second edition was to produce an accurate, comprehensive, and contemporary description of applied behavior analysis. The result is a book whose size, scope, and treatment of various concepts, principles, procedures, and issues suggest that it is intended for concentrated and serious study.

In spite of its size, scope, and in-depth treatment, *Applied Behavior Analysis* should be viewed as an introductory text for two reasons. First, the reader need not possess any particular prerequisite knowledge to understand the content. Second, the attainment of a full understanding of applied behavior analysis requires considerable study and application beyond this text. There is no topic presented within these pages that has not been treated elsewhere. Serious students of applied behavior analysis will build upon what they learn from this book by reading other works. How much reading is needed to fully grasp and appreciate applied behavior analysis? Donald M. Baer (2005), one of the co-founders of applied behavior analysis and the person to whom we have dedicated the second edition, estimated that

> [T]he cost of knowing well the basic principles and paradigms of the theoretical and experimental aspects of behavior analysis would require about 2,000 pages and some laboratory experience. ABA shares the same basic principles with the theoretical and experimental branches of behavior analysis and adds to them an even larger number of secondary principles, strategies, and tactics for making those basic principles work in the real world as they do in the laboratory. ABA also adds a set of principles about ethical and humane practice, prominent among which is the need to be certain, through constant and extensive measurement and experimentation, that the particular case in hand is going well and will continue to go well—because it will change as it progresses. The cost of knowing all that is, I estimate, about 3,000 pages of reading and several years of supervised practical experience. (pp. 27–28)

We hope that this book will provide 700 pages of Baer's reading assignment for many future behavior analysts. Specific suggestions for other essential readings in applied behavior analysis can be found in Saville, Beal, and Buskist (2002) as well as the conceptual, basic, and applied primary-source works cited throughout this text.

Again, while our objective is to provide a complete description of the principles and procedures for systematically changing socially important behavior, mastery of this book's content represents the beginning, not the end, of one's study of applied behavior analysis. If our efforts are successful, the serious and dedicated student will come away with a fundamentally sound repertoire of knowledge about applied behavior analysis that will serve as the foundation for more advanced study and supervised practicum opportunities that, in turn, will lead to independent efforts to change and understand behavior that are socially significant, scientifically sound, and ethically appropriate.

Terminology

A standard set of technical terms is prerequisite to the meaningful description of any scientific activity. Effective communication about the design, application, and/or outcomes of an applied behavior analysis relies upon the accurate and careful use of the discipline's terminology. Throughout this text we have made every effort to define and use the terminology of behavior analysis in a conceptually systematic and consistent manner. Mastering the technical vocabulary of applied behavior analysis is an important initial step in embracing the science and participating effectively as a behavioral researcher or practitioner. We encourage students to study the field's technical terminology with diligence. Toward that end, we have added a glossary of more than 400 technical terms and concepts to the second edition.

Graphs, Extracts, and References

One important function of any introductory text to a scientific discipline is to expose students to the empirical and conceptual literature of that field. Therefore, the second edition contains more than 1,400 citations to primary-source publications, including historically important experiments (e.g., the first set of data presented by B. F. Skinner in his 1938 book *The Behavior of Organisms*), and classic and contemporary examples of applied behavior analysis research—most of which were published in the field's flagship journal, the *Journal of Applied Behavior Analysis*. We have also made extensive use of extracts and quotations from key publications representing the conceptual literature. We have done this not only for the historical and/or technical authority that these authors provide, but also because their inclusion increases students' exposure to and appreciation for the field's rich primary-source literature.

The second edition includes more than 100 graphs displaying original data from peer-reviewed research, many of which are accompanied by detailed descriptions of the procedures used in the study. We have a fourfold purpose for including so many descriptions of procedures, graphs, and references. First, to the extent possible, we want to illustrate behavior analysis principles and procedures with actual applications and real data, not hypothetical examples. Second, reading the procedural descriptions will help students begin to appreciate the high degree of technical precision and control of complex environments that researchers and practitioners must achieve to solve problems and show functional relations between variables. Third, the references provide students whose interests are piqued by the descriptions or graphs with directions to the original studies so that more in-depth study can be pursued. And finally, the graphs provide students with multiple opportunities to develop—through practice and discussion with their instructors and mentors—their skills in visually analyzing graphic data displays.

New Content and Features of the Second Edition

The second edition is a thorough and extensive revision and update of the original text. Though still a young and developing science, behavior analysis has become more mature and sophisticated in the 20 years that have passed since the first edition was published. Although the basic principles of behavior have remained unchanged, advances in all three interrelated domains of the science of behavior—theoretical, basic research, and applied research—

have improved our understanding of those principles and led to increased effectiveness in developing and applying effective and humane behavior change interventions. These developments are reflected in the nearly 1,000 new references to the conceptual, basic, and applied literatures of behavior analysis that have been added to this edition.

Five New Chapters by Contributing Authors

The second edition includes chapter-length treatments of five topics that have become increasingly important in applied behavior analysis over the past two decades. The new chapters are authored by some of the most prominent scholars in behavior analysis, including two former editors of the *Journal of Applied Behavior Analysis*, the current and past editors of *The Analysis of Verbal Behavior*, and two former presidents of the Association for Behavior Analysis. Many of the most significant advances in behavior analysis over the past two decades were first reported in publications by this well-known and prolific group of behavior analysts.

Negative Reinforcement

In Chapter 12, Negative Reinforcement, Brian Iwata and Rick Smith present an authoritative account of this commonly misunderstood and misapplied form of reinforcement. In addition to dispelling misconceptions about negative reinforcement, Iwata and Smith provide specific guidelines for how this basic principle of behavior can be incorporated into behavior change interventions.

Motivation

Until recently, motivation, a major topic in psychological theories and everyday explanations of behavior, has been an assumed, but inadequately understood, topic in behavior analysis. Today, due largely to the work of Jack Michael, behavior analysts have a much better understanding of motivation and its role within applied behavior analysis. In Chapter 16, Motivating Operations, Michael explains how certain antecedent events have dual motivating effects: a behavior-altering effect, which makes certain behaviors more (or less) likely; and a value-altering effect, which makes certain events more (or less) effective as reinforcement.

Functional Behavior Assessment

In Chapter 24, Functional Behavior Assessment, Nancy Neef and Stephanie Peterson describe one of the most significant developments in applied behavior analysis in recent years. Functional behavior assessment has become a well-established method for discovering the function that a problem behavior serves for a person (e.g., to obtain social attention, to avoid assigned work, to provide sensory stimulation), information that enables a practitioner to design interventions that target adaptive replacement behaviors that serve the same function.

Verbal Behavior

In Chapter 25, Verbal Behavior, Mark Sundberg contrasts B. F. Skinner's functional analysis of verbal behavior with traditional, structural approaches to language, defines and gives examples of basic types of verbal operants (e.g., mands, tacts, textuals, intraverbals), and describes implications and applications for these concepts in designing and implementing language intervention programs.

Ethics

In Chapter 29, Ethical Considerations for Applied Behavior Analysts, Jose Martinez-Diaz, Tom Freeman, and Matt Normand help us to understand what ethical behavior is, explain why ethical behavior must be a necessary part of the applied behavior analyst's repertoire, review ethical codes of conduct for behavior analysts, and describe specific procedures for ensuring and assessing ethical practice.

Text Content Related to the Behavior Analyst Certification Board® BCBA® & BCABA® Behavior Analyst Task List© – Third Edition

The Behavior Analyst Certification Board (BACB) is an international body that certifies individuals to offer behavior analysis services. To be recognized as a Board Certified Associate Behavior Analyst (BCABA) or a Board Certified Behavior Analyst (BCBA), a person must complete a specified number of classroom hours of instruction across six content areas (e.g., ethical considerations in behavior analysis, basic behavior analytic principles and concepts, behavioral assessment and selecting intervention strategies, experimental evaluation of interventions, measurement of behavior, and interpreting behavioral data), acquire a minimum number of hours of supervised fieldwork and practicum experience, and pass a certification examination. Detailed information on the requirements for taking the examination is available on the Behavior Analyst Certification Board's website, www.BACB.com.

The BACB conducted an extensive occupational analysis and developed the Behavior Analyst Task List–Third Edition, which specifies the minimum content that all behavior analysts should master (Moore & Shook, 2001; Shook, 1993; Shook, Johnston, & Mellichamp,

2004; Shook, Rosales, & Glenn, 2002). The complete BCBA® & BCABA® Task List©–Third Edition is printed inside the front and back covers of this text.

Through an agreement and in consultation with the BACB, we have integrated the content of this text with the tasks that the BACB determined are necessary to function as a behavior analyst. We have done this in two ways. First, a chart at the beginning of each chapter identifies the Task List items that are covered within that chapter. Due to the complex nature of applied behavior analysis in which the concepts and principles and their application are interrelated and not easily or effectively presented in a linear fashion, some Task List items are treated in more than one chapter. Second, to assist students in studying for the BACB examinations, the appendix shows the page numbers where relevant information about each item in the BACB Task List–Third Edition can be found.

This text presents the basic knowledge that a qualified behavior analyst must possess. Although mastering this content will help you obtain a passing score on the Behavior Analyst Certification Board examination—which is the final step in becoming a Board Certified Associate Behavior Analyst (BCABA) or a Board Certified Behavior Analyst (BCBA)—two important qualifiers must be recognized. First, each of the Behavior Analyst Certification Board examinations requires knowledge *beyond* that included in this, or any, introductory text. Therefore, we encourage students to study original sources, engage in supervised practica, and discuss areas of personal interest with trusted and competent mentors in further preparation for the Board examination. Second, no matter how accurate, extensive, and current the textbook, and no matter how thoroughly a student masters its content, he or she will not be fully qualified to *function* as a behavior analyst. Successful completion of the required course work in behavior analysis is but one step in the preparation to become a BCBA and BCABA. For the most recent information on the requirements for becoming a BCABA or BCBA, go the Behavior Analyst Certification Board's website at www.BACB.com.

Text Organization and Structure

The book's 29 chapters are organized into 13 parts. The two chapters in Part 1 describe some tenets that are fundamental to all scientific endeavors, outline a history of behavior analysis as a natural science approach to understanding behavior, define applied behavior analysis, and describe some principles and concepts of that science. Parts 2 and 3 examine the elements necessary for an applied behavior analysis. Part 2 presents considerations, criteria, and procedures for selecting, defining, and measuring *applied behavior.* The five chapters in Part 3 examine the logic and operation of specific tactics for the experimental *analysis* of behavior-environment relations, and some issues in planning, replicating, and evaluating analyses of behavior.

Parts 4 through 8 consist of chapter-length treatments of the major principles of behavior (e.g., reinforcement, punishment, extinction) and procedures derived from those principles (e.g., shaping, chaining) for increasing the frequency of existing behavior, obtaining desired patterns of stimulus control, developing new behaviors, and decreasing the frequency of behavior with nonpunishment procedures. Part 9 describes functional behavioral assessment, sophisticated methods for determining the function that problem behavior serves for a person, and important information that leads to the design of treatments that replace the problem behavior with adaptive replacement behavior that serves the same function.

Part 10 examines B. F. Skinner's analysis of verbal behavior and some of its implications and applications for language development. The two chapters in Part 11 detail the rationale, uses, implementation procedures, and considerations for four special applications of behavior change technology: contingency contracting, token economy, group contingencies, and self-management. Part 12 outlines a set of strategies and tactics for increasing the likelihood that the behavior analyst's efforts to change behavior will yield lasting and useful behavior change in the form of generalized outcomes; that is, changes in behavior that are maintained across time, occur in appropriate settings and situations beyond the training setting, and spread to other useful behaviors. The book's final part describes ethical considerations and practices for applied behavior analysts.

Supplements and Resources for Students and Instructors

BACB Task List Appendix

This appendix enables the reader to locate the page numbers where each item in the Behavior Analyst Certification Board® Task List©–Third Edition is explained in the text. A complete listing of the BCBA® & BCABA® Be-

havior Analyst Task List©–Third Edition is printed on the inside front and back covers of this text.

Companion Website

A user-friendly Companion Website (www.prenhall.com/cooper) designed to complement this text enhances learning by giving students access to the following study aids and resources:

- *Interactive Chapter Quizzes* help students gauge their understanding of chapter content.
- *The Special Assignments* module houses different types of assignments to help students through the topics studied in the text, and includes Templates and Resources for Completing Activities/Assignments.
- *The In-Class Activities* module offers different types of activities for each chapter, including Group Activities and Response Card Activities.
- *Resources Related to Chapter Topics* provides Web links in each chapter to help students access additional information on chapter topics and areas of study.

Instructor's Manual with Test Questions

The Instructor's Manual includes numerous recommendations for presenting and extending text content. The manual consists of chapter objectives and overviews of essential concepts; connections to the BACB Task List standards; class discussion and essay/position paper topics; in-class activities such as cooperative group activities, response card activities, and ideas for application exercises and homework assignments. The Instructor's Manual also includes example course outlines suggesting how different parts of *Applied Behavior Analysis* can provide the primary reading for several courses in a program preparing behavior analysts (e.g., a first course on basic principles, a second course on applications, a course on behavioral research methods). For each chapter, the Instructor's Manual also includes test questions tied to chapter content. The Instructor's Manual is available by going to www.prenhall.com and clicking on the Instructor Resource Center.

Acknowledgments

The second edition of *Applied Behavior Analysis* is the product of the collective and cumulative efforts of many people. Although space limitations prevent us from thanking everyone by name, we would like to acknowledge those who made substantial contributions to the book's content or production during the four years we spent revising the text. First and foremost, we are deeply grateful to the authors of the five contributed chapters: Jack Michael (Motivating Operations); Brian Iwata and Rick Smith (Negative Reinforcement); Nancy Neef and Stephanie Peterson (Functional Behavior Assessment); Mark Sundberg (Verbal Behavior); and Jose Martinez-Diaz, Tom Freeman, and Matt Normand (Ethical Considerations for Applied Behavior Analysts). Because of their efforts, readers of the second edition will be introduced to topics whose significance in applied behavior analysis has evolved greatly since the first edition was published 20 years ago by some of the scholars whose research has helped to define and develop those areas.

We thank the Behavior Analyst Certification Board (BACB) for allowing us to integrate the Behavior Analyst Certification Board® BCBA® & BCABA® Behavior Analyst Task List©—Third Edition throughout the revised edition of our text. We are especially grateful to Gerald Shook, Ph.D., BCBA, Chief Executive Officer of the Behavior Analyst Certification Board. Jerry helped us develop the arrangement with the BACB and provided helpful suggestions throughout the revision process.

A content-rich discipline such as applied behavior analysis presents difficult challenges to instructors and students. There are literally hundreds of concepts, terms, and techniques to be taught and learned. Thanks to Stephanie Peterson and Renee Van Norman, instructors and students using the second edition can turn to a comprehensive set of ancillary materials to help them teach and learn the content. With the able assistance of Lloyd Peterson, Shannon Croizer, Megan Bryson, Jessica Frieder, Pete Molino, and David Bicard, Stephanie and Renee produced the Instructor's Manual and Companion Website materials that accompany this text. Stephanie and Renee are supremely qualified to develop these important materials: each is a knowledgeable and skilled behavior analyst and an outstanding teacher.

We thank Ilene Schwartz for writing the Foreword. Although suspicious of our being worthy of her extremely kind observations, we are nevertheless humbled and honored by them. We are grateful to Julie Vargas and the B. F. Skinner Foundation for providing the two classic photographs of Skinner that appear in Chapter 1, and to Jack Michael for providing the photograph of Don Baer, to whom this book is dedicated. A special note of thanks goes to Kathy Hill, Business Manager of the *Journal of Applied Behavior Analysis,* for her always-prompt and gracious assistance in processing our many requests for permissions to reprint graphs, tables, and extracts from JABA. Michael Preston also provided invaluable assistance with accommodating our requests to reprint material copyrighted by the Association for Behavior Analysis.

Turning more than 2,000 pages of manuscript into the book you are reading required the support and contributions of a talented team of publishing professionals at Merrill/Prentice Hall. We are grateful to former Acquisitions Editor Allyson Sharp, who was instrumental in convincing us to tackle this project. Senior Production Editor Linda Bayma worked closely and patiently with us throughout. Copyeditor Patsy Fortney improved the manuscript immeasurably. Her talent in turning rough prose into clear and understandable text is evident on every page. Any bumpy spots that remain are our responsibility. Production coordinator Linda Zuk, ultimate multi-tasker, used her considerable behavior management skills to pull everything together. We also wish to acknowledge Merrill's Jeff Johnston, Vice President and Executive Publisher, and Ann Castel Davis, Executive Editor, for their long-standing commitment not only to this title but also to publishing books on behavior analysis and evidence-based practices.

Last, but certainly not least, among those we wish to thank for important contributions to the production of the second edition is Keith "Dutch" Van Norman, who designed the creative and captivating cover.

Throughout our careers, we have been fortunate to have mentors, colleagues, and students who provided us with the instruction, models, and inspiration needed to attempt to write a book like *Applied Behavior Analysis.* To the extent that our goals in writing this book are achieved, each of them will have played a role. To the professors who first taught us about applied behavior analysis—Saul Axelrod, Vance Cotter, Todd Eachus, Dick Malott, Jack Michael, Joe Spradlin, and Don Whaley—we will be indebted always. For more than 30 years our faculty colleagues at Ohio State helped to create and sustain an academic environment in which work of this kind is valued and can be accomplished. The many enthusiastic and dedicated students who we have been lucky enough to teach and learn with and from over the years have also encouraged and motivated us.

Finally, we want to acknowledge the immediate members of our families: Bunny, Chris, Sharon, Greg, Brian, and the memory of Carroll and Vera Cooper; Ray, Bernice, Marge and Kathy Heron, and Christine and Matt Harsh; and Jill Dardig, Lee and Lynn Heward, and Joe and Helen Heward. Without their love and support we would never have attempted, let alone completed, this book. And to each of them, we pledge to redouble our efforts to fulfill the promise we made when dedicating the first edition.

Brief Contents

Contents

PART 13

Ethics   657

29 Ethical Considerations for Applied Behavior Analysts   658

Jose A. Martinez-Diaz, Thomas R. Freeman, Matthew Normand, and Timothy E. Heron

Appendix   Textbook Coverage of the Behavior Analyst Certification Board® BCBA® & BCABA® Behavior Analyst Task List© – Third Edition   679

Note: Every effort has been made to provide accurate and current Internet information in this book. However, the Internet and information posted on it are constantly changing, and it is inevitable that some of the Internet addresses listed in this textbook will change.

PART 1

Introduction and Basic Concepts

We believe that, prior to learning specific principles and tactics for analyzing and changing behavior, the student of applied behavior analysis should be introduced to the conceptual and historical foundations of the discipline. A basic knowledge and appreciation of the scientific and philosophical underpinnings of behavior analysis are requisites to a thorough understanding of the discipline's nature, scope, and potential. We also believe that a preliminary overview of basic concepts, principles, and terminology helps make the in-depth study of behavior analysis more effective. The two chapters in Part 1 respond to these two beliefs. Chapter 1 explains the scientific and philosophical roots of applied behavior analysis and identifies the discipline's defining dimensions, characteristics, and overall goals. Chapter 2 defines the field's fundamental elements—behavior and the environmental events that influence it—and introduces key terms and principles used by applied behavior analysts to describe the relationships among those elements.

CHAPTER 1

Definition and Characteristics of Applied Behavior Analysis

Key Terms

applied behavior analysis (ABA)
behaviorism
determinism
empiricism
experiment
experimental analysis of behavior
   (EAB)

explanatory fiction
functional relation
hypothetical construct
mentalism
methodological behaviorism
parsimony

philosophic doubt
radical behaviorism
replication
science

Behavior Analyst Certification Board® BCBA® & BCABA® Behavior Analyst Task List©, Third Edition

	Content Area 2: Definition and Characteristics
2-1	Explain behavior in accordance with the philosophical assumptions of behavior analysis, such as the lawfulness of behavior, empiricism, experimental analysis, and parsimony.
2-2	Explain determinism as it relates to behavior analysis.
2-3	Distinguish between mentalistic and environmental explanations of behavior.
2-4	Distinguish among the experimental analysis of behavior, applied behavior analysis, and behavioral technologies.
2-5	Describe and explain behavior, including private events, in behavior analytic (nonmentalistic) terms.
2-6	Use the dimensions of applied behavior analysis (Baer, Wolf, & Risley 1968) for evaluating interventions to determine if they are behavior analytic.
	Content Area 3: Principles, Processes, and Concepts
3-10	Define and provide examples of functional relations.

Applied behavior analysis is a science devoted to the understanding and improvement of human behavior. But other fields have similar intent. What sets applied behavior analysis apart? The answer lies in its focus, goals, and methods. Applied behavior analysts focus on objectively defined behaviors of social significance; they intervene to improve the behaviors under study while demonstrating a reliable relationship between their interventions and the behavioral improvements; and they use the methods of scientific inquiry—objective description, quantification, and controlled experimentation. In short, applied behavior analysis, or ABA, is a scientific approach for discovering environmental variables that reliably influence socially significant behavior and for developing a technology of behavior change that takes practical advantage of those discoveries.

This chapter provides a brief outline of the history and development of behavior analysis, discusses the philosophy that underlies the science, and identifies the defining dimensions and characteristics of applied behavior analysis. Because applied behavior analysis is an applied science, we begin with an overview of some precepts fundamental to all scientific disciplines.

Some Basic Characteristics and a Definition of Science

Used properly, the word *science* refers to a systematic approach for seeking and organizing knowledge about the natural world. Before offering a definition of science, we discuss the purpose of science and the basic assumptions and attitudes that guide the work of all scientists, irrespective of their fields of study.

Purpose of Science

The overall goal of science is to achieve a thorough understanding of the phenomena under study—socially important behaviors, in the case of applied behavior analysis. Science differs from other sources of knowledge or ways we obtain knowledge about the world around us (e.g., contemplation, common sense, logic, authority figures, religious or spiritual beliefs, political campaigns, advertisements, testimonials). Science seeks to discover nature's truths. Although it is frequently misused, science is not a tool for validating the cherished or preferred versions of "the truth" held by any group, corporation, government, or institution. Therefore, scientific knowledge must be separated from any personal, political, economic, or other reasons for which it was sought.

Different types of scientific investigations yield knowledge that enables one or more of three levels of understanding: description, prediction, and control. Each level of understanding contributes to the scientific knowledge base of a given field.

Description

Systematic observation enhances the understanding of a given phenomenon by enabling scientists to describe it accurately. Descriptive knowledge consists of a collection of facts about the observed events that can be quantified, classified, and examined for possible relations with other known facts—a necessary and important activity for any scientific discipline. The knowledge obtained from descriptive studies often suggests possible hypotheses or questions for additional research.

For example, White (1975) reported the results of observing the "natural rates" of approval (verbal praise or encouragement) and disapproval (criticisms, reproach) by 104 classroom teachers in grades 1 to 12. Two major findings were that (a) the rates of teacher praise dropped with each grade level, and (b) in every grade after second, the rate at which teachers delivered statements of disapproval to students exceeded the rate of teacher approval. The results of this descriptive study helped to stimulate dozens of subsequent studies aimed at discovering the factors responsible for the disappointing findings or at increasing teachers' rates of praise (e.g., Alber, Heward, & Hippler, 1999; Martens, Hiralall, & Bradley, 1997; Sutherland, Wehby, & Yoder, 2002; Van Acker, Grant, & Henry, 1996).

Prediction

A second level of scientific understanding occurs when repeated observations reveal that two events consistently covary with each other. That is, in the presence of one event (e.g., approaching winter) another event occurs (or fails to occur) with some specified probability (e.g., certain birds fly south). When systematic covariation between two events is found, this relationship—termed a *correlation*—can be used to predict the relative probability that one event will occur, based on the presence of the other event.

Because no variables are manipulated or controlled by the researcher, correlational studies cannot demonstrate whether any of the observed variables are responsible for the changes in the other variable(s), and no such relations should be inferred (Johnston & Pennypacker, 1993a). For example, although a strong correlation exists between hot weather and an increased incidence of drowning deaths, we should not assume that a hot and humid day causes anyone to drown. Hot weather also correlates with other factors, such as an increased number of people (both swimmers and nonswimmers) seeking relief in the water, and many instances of drowning have been found to be a function of factors such as the use of alcohol or drugs, the relative swimming skills of the victims, strong riptides, and the absence of supervision by lifeguards.

Results of correlational studies can, however, suggest the possibility of causal relations, which can then be explored in later studies. The most common type of correlational study reported in the applied behavior analysis literature compares the relative rates or conditional probabilities of two or more observed (but not manipulated) variables (e.g., Atwater & Morris, 1988; Symons, Hoch, Dahl, & McComas, 2003; Thompson & Iwata, 2001). For example, McKerchar and Thompson (2004) found correlations between problem behavior exhibited by 14 preschool children and the following consequent events: teacher attention (100% of the children), presentation of some material or item to the child (79% of the children), and escape from instructional tasks (33% of the children). The results of this study not only provide empirical validation for the social consequences typically used in clinical settings to analyze the variables maintaining children's problem behavior, but also increase confidence in the prediction that interventions based on the findings from such assessments will be relevant to the conditions that occur naturally in preschool classrooms (Iwata et al., 1994; see Chapter 24). In addition, by revealing the high probabilities with which teachers responded to problem behavior in ways that are likely to maintain and strengthen it, McKerchar and Thompson's findings also point to the need to train teachers in more effective ways to respond to problem behavior.

Control

The ability to predict with a certain degree of confidence is a valuable and useful result of science; prediction enables preparation. However, the greatest potential benefits from science can be derived from the third, and highest, level of scientific understanding—control. Evidence of the kinds of control that can been derived from scientific findings in the physical and biological sciences surrounds us in the everyday technologies we take for granted: pasteurized milk and the refrigerators we store it in; flu shots and the automobiles we drive to go get them; aspirin and the televisions that bombard us with news and advertisements about the drug.

Functional relations, the primary products of basic and applied behavior analytic research, provide the kind of scientific understanding that is most valuable and useful to the development of a technology for changing behavior. A **functional relation** exists when a well-controlled experiment reveals that a specific change in one event (the *dependent variable*) can reliably be pro-

duced by specific manipulations of another event (the *independent variable*), and that the change in the dependent variable was unlikely to be the result of other extraneous factors (*confounding variables*).

Johnston and Pennypacker (1980) described functional relations as "the ultimate product of a natural scientific investigation of the relation between behavior and its determining variables" (p. 16).

> Such a "co-relation" is expressed as $y = f(x)$, where x is the independent variable or argument of the function, and y is the dependent variable. In order to determine if an observed relation is truly functional, it is necessary to demonstrate the operation of the values of x in isolation and show that they are sufficient for the production of y. . . . [H]owever, a more powerful relation exists if necessity can be shown (that y occurs *only if* x occurs). The most complete and elegant form of empirical inquiry involves applying the experimental method to identifying functional relations. (Johnston & Pennypacker, 1993a, p. 239)

The understanding gained by the scientific discovery of functional relations is the basis of applied technologies in all fields. Almost all of the research studies cited in this text are experimental analyses that have demonstrated or discovered a functional relation between a target behavior and one or more environmental variables. However, it is important to understand that functional relations are also correlations (Cooper, 2005), and that:

> In fact, all we ever really know is that two events are related or "co-related" in some way. To say that one "causes" another is to say that one is solely the result of the other. To know this, it is necessary to know that no other factors are playing a contributing role. This is virtually impossible to know because it requires identifying all possible such factors and then showing that they are not relevant. (Johnston & Pennypacker, 1993a, p. 240)

Attitudes of Science

> Science is first of all a set of attitudes.
> —B. F. Skinner (1953, p. 12)

The definition of science lies not in test tubes, spectrometers, or electron accelerators, but in the behavior of scientists. To begin to understand any science, we need to look past the apparatus and instrumentation that are most readily apparent and examine what scientists do.[1] The

---

[1]Skinner (1953) noted, that although telescopes and cyclotrons give us a "dramatic picture of science in action" (p. 12), and science could not have advanced very far without them, such devices and apparatus are not science themselves. "Nor is science to be identified with precise measurement. We can measure and be mathematical without being scientific at all, just as we may be scientific with these aids" (p. 12). Scientific instruments bring scientists into greater contact with their subject matter and, with measurement and mathematics, enable a more precise description and control of key variables.

pursuit of knowledge can properly be called *science* when it is carried out according to general methodological precepts and expectations that define science. Although there is no "scientific method" in the sense of a prescribed set of steps or rules that must be followed, all scientists share a fundamental assumption about the nature of events that are amenable to investigation by science, general notions about basic strategy, and perspectives on how to view their findings. These attitudes of science—determinism, empiricism, experimentation, replication, parsimony, and philosophic doubt—constitute a set of overriding assumptions and values that guide the work of all scientists (Whaley & Surratt, 1968).

Determinism

Science is predicated on the assumption of **determinism.** Scientists presume that the universe, or at least that part of it they intend to probe with the methods of science, is a lawful and orderly place in which all phenomena occur as the result of other events. In other words, events do not just happen willy-nilly; they are related in systematic ways to other factors, which are themselves physical phenomena amenable to scientific investigation.

If the universe were governed by *accidentalism,* a philosophical position antithetical to determinism that holds that events occur by accident or without cause, or by *fatalism,* the belief that events are predetermined, the scientific discovery and technological use of functional relations to improve things would be impossible.

> If we are to use the methods of science in the field of human affairs, we must assume behavior is lawful and determined. We must expect to discover what a man does is the result of specifiable conditions and that once these conditions have been discovered, we can anticipate and to some extent determine his actions. (Skinner, 1953, p. 6)

Determinism plays a pivotal dual role in the conduct of scientific practice: It is at once a philosophical stance that does not lend itself to proof and the confirmation that is sought by each experiment. In other words, the scientist first assumes lawfulness and then proceeds to look for lawful relations (Delprato & Midgley, 1992).

Empiricism

Scientific knowledge is built on, above all, **empiricism**—the practice of objective observation of the phenomena of interest. Objectivity in this sense means "independent of the individual prejudices, tastes, and private opinions of the scientist. . . . Results of empirical methods are objective in that they are open to anyone's observation and do not depend on the subjective belief of the individual scientist" (Zuriff, 1985, p. 9).

In the prescientific era, as well as in nonscientific and pseudoscientific activities today, knowledge was (and is) the product of contemplation, speculation, personal opinion, authority, and the "obvious" logic of common sense. The scientist's empirical attitude, however, demands objective observation based on thorough description, systematic and repeated measurement, and precise quantification of the phenomena of interest.

As in every scientific field, empiricism is the foremost rule in the science of behavior. Every effort to understand, predict, and improve behavior hinges on the behavior analyst's ability to completely define, systematically observe, and accurately and reliably measure occurrences and nonoccurrences of the behavior of interest.

Experimentation

Experimentation is the basic strategy of most sciences. Whaley and Surratt (1968) used the following anecdote to introduce the need for conducting experiments.

> A man who lived in a suburban dwelling area was surprised one evening to see his neighbor bow to the four winds, chant a strange melody, and dance around his front lawn beating a small drum. After witnessing the same ritual for over a month, the man became overwhelmed with curiosity and decided to look into the matter.
>
> "Why do you go through this same ritual each evening?" the man asked his neighbor.
>
> "It keeps my house safe from tigers," the neighbor replied.
>
> "Good grief!" the man said. "Don't you know there isn't a tiger within a thousand miles of here?"
>
> "Yeah," the neighbor smiled. "Sure works, doesn't it!" (pp. 23–2 to 23–3)

When events are observed to covary or occur in close temporal sequence, a functional relation may exist, but other factors may be responsible for the observed values of the dependent variable. To investigate the possible existence of a functional relation, an experiment (or better, a series of experiments) must be performed in which the factor(s) suspected of having causal status are systematically controlled and manipulated while the effects on the event under study are carefully observed. In discussing the meaning of the term *experimental,* Dinsmoor (2003) noted that

> two measures of behavior may be found to covary at a statistically significant level, but it is not thereby made clear which factor is the cause and which is the effect, or indeed whether the relations between the two is not the product of a third, confounded factor, with which both of them happened to covary. Suppose, for example, it is found that students with good grades have more dates than those with lower grades. Does this imply that high

grades make people socially attractive? That dating is the royal road to academic success? That it pays to be smart? Or that financial security and free time contribute both to academic and to social success? (p. 152)

Reliably predicting and controlling any phenomena, including the presence of tigers in one's backyard, requires the identification and manipulation of the factors that cause those phenomena to act as they do. One way that the individual described previously could use the experimental method to evaluate the effectiveness of his ritual would be to first move to a neighborhood in which tigers are regularly observed and then systematically manipulate the use of his antitiger ritual (e.g., one week on, one week off, one week on) while observing and recording the presence of tigers under the ritual and no-ritual conditions.

> The experimental method is a method for isolating the relevant variables within a pattern of events. . . . [W]hen the experimental method is employed, it is possible to change one factor at a time (independent variable) while leaving all other aspects of the situation the same, and then to observe what effect this change has on the target behavior (dependent variable). Ideally, a functional relation may be obtained. Formal techniques of experimental control are designed to make sure that the conditions being compared are otherwise the same. Use of the experimental method serves as a necessary condition (sine quo non) to distinguish the experimental analysis of behavior from other methods of investigation. (Dinsmoor, 2003, p. 152)

Thus, an **experiment** is a carefully conducted comparison of some measure of the phenomenon of interest (the dependent variable) under two or more different conditions in which only one factor at a time (the independent variable) differs from one condition to another. Strategies and tactics for conducting experiments in applied behavior analysis are described in Chapters 7 through 10.

Replication

The results of a single experiment, no matter how well the study was designed and conducted and no matter how clear and impressive the findings, are never sufficient to earn an accepted place among the scientific knowledge base of any field. Although the data from a single experiment have value in their own right and cannot be discounted, only after an experiment has been replicated a number of times with the same basic pattern of results do scientists gradually become convinced of the findings.

Replication—the repeating of experiments (as well as repeating independent variable conditions within experiments)—"pervades every nook and cranny of the experimental method" (Johnston & Pennypacker, 1993a,

p. 244). Replication is the primary method with which scientists determine the reliability and usefulness of their findings and discover their mistakes (Johnston & Pennypacker, 1980; 1993a; Sidman, 1960). Replication—not the infallibility or inherent honesty of scientists—is the primary reason science is a self-correcting enterprise that eventually gets it right (Skinner, 1953).

How many times must an experiment be repeated with the same results before the scientific community accepts the findings? There is no set number of replications required, but the greater the importance of the findings for either theory or practice, the greater the number of replications to be conducted. The role of replication in behavioral research and replication strategies used in applied behavior analysis are described in Chapters 7 through 10.

Parsimony

One dictionary definition of *parsimony* is great frugality, and in a special way this connotation accurately describes the behavior of scientists. As an attitude of science, **parsimony** requires that all simple, logical explanations for the phenomenon under investigation be ruled out, experimentally or conceptually, before more complex or abstract explanations are considered. Parsimonious interpretations help scientists fit their findings within the field's existing knowledge base. A fully parsimonious interpretation consists only of those elements that are necessary and sufficient to explain the phenomenon at hand. The attitude of parsimony is so critical to scientific explanations that it is sometimes referred to as the Law of Parsimony (Whaley & Surratt, 1968), a "law" derived from *Occam's Razor,* credited to William of Occam (1285–1349), who stated: "One should not increase, beyond what is necessary, the number of entities required to explain anything" (Mole, 2003). In other words, given a choice between two competing and compelling explanations for the same phenomenon, one should shave off extraneous variables and choose the simplest explanation, the one that requires the fewest assumptions.

Philosophic Doubt

The attitude of **philosophic doubt** requires the scientist to continually question the truthfulness of what is regarded as fact. Scientific knowledge must always be viewed as tentative. Scientists must constantly be willing to set aside their most cherished beliefs and findings and replace them with the knowledge derived from new discoveries.

Good scientists maintain a healthy level of skepticism. Although being skeptical of others' research may be easy, a more difficult but critical characteristic of scientists is that they remain open to the possibility—as well as look for evidence—that their own findings or interpretations are wrong. As Oliver Cromwell (1650) stated in another context: "I beseech you . . . think it possible you may be mistaken." For the true scientist, "new findings are not problems; they are opportunities for further investigation and expanded understanding" (Todd & Morris, 1993, p. 1159).

Practitioners should be as skeptical as researchers. The skeptical practitioner not only requires scientific evidence before implementing a new practice, but also evaluates continually its effectiveness once the practice has been implemented. Practitioners must be particularly skeptical of extraordinary claims made for the effectiveness of new theories, therapies, or treatments (Jacobson, Foxx, & Mulick, 2005; Maurice, 2006).

> Claims that sound too good to be true are usually just that. . . . Extraordinary claims require extraordinary evidence. (Sagan, 1996; Shermer, 1997)
>
> What constitutes extraordinary evidence? In the strictest sense, and the sense that should be employed when evaluating claims of educational effectiveness, evidence is the outcome of the application of the scientific method to test the effectiveness of a claim, a theory, or a practice. The more rigorously the test is conducted, the more often the test is replicated, the more extensively the test is corroborated, the more extraordinary the evidence. Evidence becomes extraordinary when it is extraordinarily well tested. (Heward & Silvestri, 2005, p. 209)

We end our discussion of philosophic doubt with two pieces of advice, one from Carl Sagan, the other from B. F. Skinner: "The question is not whether we *like* the conclusion that emerges out of a train of reasoning, but whether the conclusion *follows* from the premise or starting point and whether that premise is true" (Sagan, 1996, p. 210). "Regard no practice as immutable. Change and be ready to change again. Accept no eternal verity. Experiment" (Skinner, 1979, p. 346).

Other Important Attitudes and Values

The six attitudes of science that we have examined are necessary features of science and provide an important context for understanding applied behavior analysis. However, the behavior of most productive and successful scientists is also characterized by qualities such as thoroughness, curiosity, perseverance, diligence, ethics, and honesty. Good scientists acquire these traits because behaving in such ways has proven beneficial to the progress of science.

A Definition of Science

There is no universally accepted, standard definition of science. We offer the following definition as one that encompasses the previously discussed purposes and attitudes of science, irrespective of the subject matter. **Science** is a systematic approach to the understanding of natural phenomena—as evidenced by description, prediction, and control—that relies on determinism as its fundamental assumption, empiricism as its prime directive, experimentation as its basic strategy, replication as its necessary requirement for believability, parsimony as its conservative value, and philosophic doubt as its guiding conscience.

A Brief History of the Development of Behavior Analysis

Behavior analysis consists of three major branches. **Behaviorism** is the philosophy of the science of behavior, basic research is the province of the experimental analysis of behavior (EAB), and developing a technology for improving behavior is the concern of applied behavior analysis (ABA). Applied behavior analysis can be fully understood only in the context of the philosophy and basic research traditions and findings from which it evolved and remains connected today. This section provides an elementary description of the basic tenets of behaviorism and outlines some of the major events that have marked the development of behavior analysis.[2] Table 1.1 lists major books, journals, and professional organizations that have contributed to the advancement of behavior analysis since the 1930s.

Stimulus–Response Behaviorism of Watson

Psychology in the early 1900s was dominated by the study of states of consciousness, images, and other mental processes. Introspection, the act of carefully observing one's own conscious thoughts and feelings, was a primary method of investigation. Although the authors of several texts in the first decade of the 20th century defined psychology as the science of behavior (see Kazdin, 1978), John B. Watson is widely recognized as the spokesman for a new direction in the field of psychology.

---

[2]Informative and interesting descriptions of the history of behavior analysis can be found in Hackenberg (1995), Kazdin (1978), Michael (2004), Pierce and Epling (1999), Risley (1997, 2005), Sidman (2002), Skinner (1956, 1979), Stokes (2003), and in a special section of articles in the fall 2003 issue of *The Behavior Analyst*.

Table 1.1 Representative Selection of Books, Journals, and Organizations That Have Played a Major Role in the Development and Dissemination of Behavior Analysis

Decade	Books	Journals	Organizations
1930s	*The Behavior of Organisms*—Skinner (1938)		
1940s	*Walden Two*—Skinner (1948)		
1950s	*Principles of Psychology*—Keller & Schoenfeld (1950)	*Journal of the Experimental Analysis of Behavior* (1958)	Society for the Experimental Analysis of Behavior (SEAB) (1957)
	Science and Human Behavior—Skinner (1953)		
	Schedules of Reinforcement—Ferster & Skinner (1957)		
	Verbal Behavior—Skinner (1957)		
1960s	*Tactics for Scientific Research*—Sidman (1960)	*Journal of Applied Behavior Analysis* (1968)	American Psychological Association - Division 25 Experimental Analysis of Behavior (1964)
	Child Development, Vols. I & II—Bijou & Baer (1961, 1965)		Experimental Analysis of Behaviour Group (UK) (1965)
	The Analysis of Behavior—Holland & Skinner (1961)		
	Research in Behavior Modification—Krasner & Ullmann (1965)		
	Operant Behavior: Areas of Research and Application—Honig (1966)		
	The Analysis of Human Operant Behavior—Reese (1966)		
	Contingencies of Reinforcement: A Theoretical Analysis—Skinner (1969)		
1970s	*Beyond Freedom and Dignity*—Skinner (1971)	*Behaviorism* (1972) (became *Behavior and Philosophy* in 1990)	Norwegian Association for Behavior Analysis (1973)
	Elementary Principles of Behavior—Whaley & Malott (1971)	*Revista Mexicana de Analisis de la Conducta* (1975)	Midwestern Association for Behavior Analysis (MABA) (1974)
	Contingency Management in Education and Other Equally Exciting Places—Malott (1974)	*Behavior Modification* (1977)	Mexican Society of Behavior Analysis (1975)
	About Behaviorism—Skinner (1974)	*Journal of Organizational Behavior Management* (1977)	Association for Behavior Analysis (formerly MABA) (1978)
	Applying Behavior-Analysis Procedures with Children and Youth—Sulzer-Azaroff & Mayer (1977)	*Education & Treatment of Children* (1977)	
	Learning—Catania (1979)	*The Behavior Analyst* (1978)	
1980s	*Strategies and Tactics for Human Behavioral Research*—Johnston & Pennypacker (1980)	*Journal of Precision Teaching and Celeration* (originally, *Journal of Precision Teaching*) (1980)	Society for the Advancement of Behavior Analysis (1980)
	Behaviorism: A Conceptual Reconstruction—Zuriff (1985)	*Journal of Organizational Behavior Management* (1977)	Cambridge Center for Behavioral Studies (1981)
	Recent Issues in the Analysis of Behavior—Skinner (1989)	*Analysis of Verbal Behavior* (1982)	Japanese Association for Behavior Analysis (1983)
		Japanese Journal of Behavior Analysis (1986)	
		Behavior Analysis Digest (1989)	

Table 1.1   *(continued)*

Decade	Books	Journals	Organizations
1990s	*Concepts and Principles of Behavior Analysis*—Michael (1993)	*Behavior and Social Issues* (1991)	Accreditation of Training Programs in Behavior Analysis (Association for Behavior Analysis) (1993)
	Radical Behaviorism: The Philosophy and the Science—Chiesa (1994)	*Journal of Behavioral Education* (1991)	Behavior Analyst Certification Board (BACB) (1998)
	Equivalence Relations and Behavior—Sidman (1994)	*Behavioral Interventions* (1986)	Council of Directors of Graduate Programs in Behavior Analysis (Association for Behavior Analysis) (1999)
	Functional Analysis of Problem Behavior—Repp & Horner (1999)	*Journal of Positive Behavior Interventions* (1999)	
		The Behavior Analyst Today (1999)	
2000s		*European Journal of Behavior Analysis* (2000)	First Board Certified Behavior Analysts (BCBA) and Board Certified Associate Behavior Analysts (BCABA) credentialed by the BACB (2000)
		Behavioral Technology Today (2001)	European Association for Behaviour Analysis (2002)
		Behavioral Development Bulletin (2002)	
		Journal of Early and Intensive Behavior Intervention (2004)	
		Brazilian Journal of Behavior Analysis (2005)	
		International Journal of Behavioral Consultation and Therapy (2005)	

In his influential article, "Psychology as the Behaviorist Views It," Watson (1913) wrote:

> Psychology as the behaviorist views it is a purely objective experimental branch of natural science. Its theoretical goal is the prediction and control of behavior. Introspection forms no essential part of its methods, nor is the scientific value of its data dependent upon the readiness with which they lend themselves to interpretation in terms of consciousness. (p. 158)

Watson argued that the proper subject matter for psychology was not states of mind or mental processes but observable behavior. Further, the objective study of behavior as a natural science should consist of direct observation of the relationships between environmental stimuli (S) and the responses (R) they evoke. Watsonian behaviorism thus became known as stimulus–response (S–R) psychology. Although there was insufficient scientific evidence to support S–R psychology as a workable explanation for most behavior, Watson was confident that his new behaviorism would indeed lead to the prediction and control of human behavior and that it would allow practitioners to improve performance in areas such as ed-

ucation, business, and law. Watson (1924) made bold claims concerning human behavior, as illustrated in this famous quotation:

> Give me a dozen healthy infants, well-formed, and my own specified world to bring them up in and I'll guarantee to take any one at random and train him to become any type of specialist I might select—doctor, lawyer, artist, merchant-chief and, yes, even beggar-man and thief, regardless of his talents, penchants, tendencies, abilities, vocations, and race of his ancestors. I am going beyond my facts and I admit it, but so have the advocates of the contrary and they have been doing it for many thousands of years. (p. 104)

It is unfortunate that such extraordinary claims were made, exaggerating the ability to predict and control human behavior beyond the scientific knowledge available. The quotation just cited has been used to discredit Watson and continues to be used to discredit behaviorism in general, even though the behaviorism that underlies contemporary behavior analysis is fundamentally different from the S–R paradigm. Nevertheless, Watson's contributions were of great significance: He made a strong

B. F. Skinner *(left)* in his Indiana University lab circa 1945 and *(right)* circa 1967.

case for the study of behavior as a natural science on a par with the physical and biological sciences.[3]

Experimental Analysis of Behavior

The experimental branch of behavior analysis formally began in 1938 with the publication of B. F. Skinner's *The Behavior of Organisms* (1938/1966). The book summarized Skinner's laboratory research conducted from 1930 to 1937 and brought into perspective two kinds of behavior: respondent and operant.

Respondent behavior is reflexive behavior as in the tradition of Ivan Pavlov (1927/1960). Respondents are elicited, or "brought out," by stimuli that immediately precede them. The antecedent stimulus (e.g., bright light) and the response it elicits (e.g., pupil constriction) form a functional unit called a *reflex*. Respondent behaviors are essentially involuntary and occur whenever the eliciting stimulus is presented.

Skinner was "interested in giving a scientific account of all behavior, including that which Descartes had set aside as 'willed' and outside the reach of science" (Glenn, Ellis, & Greenspoon, 1992, p. 1330). But, like other psychologists of the time, Skinner found that the S–R paradigm could not explain a great deal of behavior, particularly behaviors for which there were no apparent antecedent causes in the environment. Compared to reflexive behavior with its clear eliciting events, much of the behavior of organisms appeared spontaneous or "voluntary." In an attempt to explain the mechanisms responsible for "voluntary" behavior, other psychologists postulated mediating variables inside the organism in the form of hypothetical constructs such as cognitive processes, drives, and free

will. Skinner took a different tack. Instead of creating **hypothetical constructs,** presumed but unobserved entities that could not be manipulated in an experiment, Skinner continued to look in the environment for the determinants of behavior that did not have apparent antecedent causes (Kimball, 2002; Palmer, 1998).

> He did not deny that physiological variables played a role in determining behavior. He merely felt that this was the domain of other disciplines, and for his part, remained committed to assessing the causal role of the environment. This decision meant looking elsewhere in time. Through painstaking research, Skinner accumulated significant, if counterintuitive, evidence that behavior is changed less by the stimuli that precede it (though context is important) and more by the consequences that immediately follow it (i.e., consequences that are contingent upon it). The essential formulation for this notion is S–R–S, otherwise known as the three–term contingency. It did not replace the S–R model—we still salivate, for instance, if we smell food cooking when we are hungry. It did, however, account for how the environment "selects" the great part of learned behavior.
>
> With the three-term contingency Skinner gave us a new paradigm. He achieved something no less profound for the study of behavior and learning than Bohr's model of the atom or Mendel's model of the gene. (Kimball, 2002, p. 71)

Skinner called the second type of behavior *operant behavior*.[4] Operant behaviors are not elicited by preceding stimuli but instead are influenced by stimulus changes that have followed the behavior in the past. Skinner's

---

[3]For an interesting biography and scholarly examination of J. B. Watson's contributions, see Todd and Morris (1994).

[4]In *The Behavior of Organisms,* Skinner called the conditioning of respondent behavior Type S conditioning and the conditioning of operant behavior Type R conditioning, but these terms were soon dropped. Respondent and operant conditioning and the three-term contingency are further defined and discussed in Chapter 2.

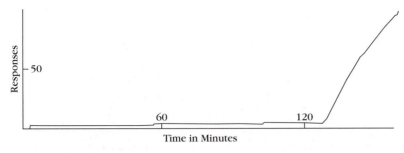

Original Conditioning
All responses to the lever were reinforced. The first three reinforcements were apparently ineffective. The fourth is followed by a rapid increase in rate.

Figure 1.1   The first data set presented in B. F. Skinner's *The Behavior of Organisms: An Experimental Analysis* (1938).
From *The Behavior of Organisms: An Experimental Analysis* by B. F. Skinner, p. 67. Original copyright 1938 by Appleton-Century. Copyright 1991 by B. F. Skinner Foundation, Cambridge, MA. Used by permission.

most powerful and fundamental contribution to our understanding of behavior was his discovery and experimental analyses of the effects of consequences on behavior. The operant three-term contingency as the primary unit of analysis was a revolutionary conceptual breakthrough (Glenn, Ellis, & Greenspoon, 1992).

Skinner (1938/1966) argued that the analysis of operant behavior "with its unique relation to the environment presents a separate important field of investigation" (p. 438). He named this new science the **experimental analysis of behavior** and outlined the methodology for its practice. Simply put, Skinner recorded the rate at which a single subject (he initially used rats and later, pigeons) emitted a given behavior in a controlled and standardized experimental chamber.

The first set of data Skinner presented in *The Behavior of Organisms* was a graph that "gives a record of the resulting change in behavior" (p. 67) when a food pellet was delivered immediately after a rat pressed a lever (see Figure 1.1). Skinner noted that the first three times that food followed a response "had no observable effect" but that "the fourth response was followed by an appreciable increase in rate showing a swift acceleration to a maximum" (pp. 67–68).

Skinner's investigative procedures evolved into an elegant experimental approach that enabled clear and powerful demonstrations of orderly and reliable functional relations between behavior and various types of environmental events.[5] By systematically manipulating the arrangement and scheduling of stimuli that preceded and followed behavior in literally thousands of laboratory experiments from the 1930s through the 1950s, Skinner and his colleagues and students discovered and verified the basic principles of operant behavior that continue to provide the empirical foundation for behavior

analysis today. Description of these principles of behavior—general statements of functional relations between behavior and environmental events—and tactics for changing behavior derived from those principles constitute a major portion of this text.

Skinner's Radical Behaviorism

In addition to being the founder of the experimental analysis of behavior, B. F. Skinner wrote extensively on the philosophy of that science.[6] Without question, Skinner's writings have been the most influential both in guiding the practice of the science of behavior and in proposing the application of the principles of behavior to new areas. In 1948 Skinner published *Walden Two,* a fictional account of how the philosophy and principles of behavior might be used in a utopian community. This was followed by his classic text, *Science and Human Behavior* (1953), in which he speculated on how the principles of behavior might be applied to complex human behavior in areas such as education, religion, government, law, and psychotherapy.

Much of Skinner's writing was devoted to the development and explanation of his philosophy of behaviorism. Skinner began his book *About Behaviorism* (1974) with these words:

> Behaviorism is not the science of human behavior; it is the philosophy of that science. Some of the questions it asks are these: Is such a science really possible? Can it account for every aspect of human behavior? What

---

[5]Most of the methodological features of the experimental approach pioneered by Skinner (e.g., repeated measurement of rate or frequency of response as the primary dependent variable, within-subject experimental comparisons, visual analysis of graphic data displays) continue to characterize both basic and applied research in behavior analysis. The five chapters in Part III provide detailed descriptions of how applied behavior analysts use this experimental approach.

[6]Skinner, who many consider the most eminent psychologist of the 20th century (Haagbloom et al., 2002), authored or coauthored 291 primary-source works (see Morris & Smith, 2003, for a complete bibliography). In addition to Skinner's three-volume autobiography (*Particulars of My Life,* 1976; *The Shaping of a Behaviorist,* 1979; *A Matter of Consequences,* 1983), numerous biographical books and articles have been written about Skinner, both before and after his death. Students interested in learning about Skinner should read *B.F. Skinner: A Life* by Daniel Bjork (1997), *B.F. Skinner, Organism* by Charles Catania (1992), *Burrhus Frederic Skinner (1904–1990): A Thank You* by Fred Keller (1990), *B. F. Skinner—The Last Few Days* by his daughter Julie Vargas (1990), and *Skinner as Self-Manager* by Robert Epstein. Skinner's contributions to ABA are described by Morris, Smith, and Altus (2005).

methods can it use? Are its laws as valid as those of physics and biology? Will it lead to a technology, and if so, what role will it play in human affairs? (p. 1)

The behaviorism that Skinner pioneered differed significantly (indeed, radically) from other psychological theories, including other forms of behaviorism. Although there were, and remain today, many psychological models and approaches to the study of behavior, **mentalism** is the common denominator among most.

> In general terms, *mentalism* may be defined as an approach to the study of behavior which assumes that a mental or "inner" dimension exists that differs from a behavioral dimension. This dimension is ordinarily referred to in terms of its neural, psychic, spiritual, subjective, conceptual, or hypothetical properties. Mentalism further assumes that phenomena in this dimension either directly cause or at least mediate some forms of behavior, if not all. These phenomena are typically designated as some sort of act, state, mechanism, process, or entity that is causal in the sense of initiating or originating. Mentalism regards concerns about the origin of these phenomena as incidental at best. Finally, mentalism holds that an adequate causal explanation of behavior must appeal directly to the efficacy of these mental phenomena. (Moore, 2003, pp. 181–182)

Hypothetical constructs and explanatory fictions are the stock and trade of mentalism, which has dominated Western intellectual thought and most psychological theories (Descartes, Freud, Piaget), and it continues to do so into the 21st century. Freud, for example, created a complex mental world of hypothetical constructs—the id, ego, and superego—that he contended were key to understanding a person's actions.

Hypothetical constructs—"theoretical terms that refer to a possibly existing, but at the moment unobserved process or entity" (Moore, 1995, p. 36)—can neither be observed nor experimentally manipulated (MacCorquodale & Meehl, 1948; Zuriff, 1985). Free will, readiness, innate releasers, language acquisition devices, storage and retrieval mechanisms for memory, and information processing are all examples of hypothetical constructs that are inferred from behavior. Although Skinner (1953, 1974) clearly indicated that it is a mistake to rule out events that influence our behavior because they are not accessible to others, he believed that using presumed but unobserved mentalistic fictions (i.e., hypothetical constructs) to explain the causes of behavior contributed nothing to a functional account.

Consider a typical laboratory situation. A food-deprived rat pushes a lever each time a light comes on and receives food, but the rat seldom pushes the lever when the light is off (and if it does, no food is delivered).

When asked to explain why the rat pushes the lever only when the light is on, most will say that the rat has "made the association" between the light being on and food being delivered when the lever is pressed. As a result of making that association, the animal now "knows" to press the lever only when the light is on. Attributing the rat's behavior to a hypothetical cognitive process such as associating or to something called "knowledge" adds nothing to a functional account of the situation. First, the environment (in this case, the experimenter) paired the light and food availability for lever presses, not the rat. Second, the knowledge or other cognitive process that is said to explain the observed behavior is itself unexplained, which begs for still more conjecture.

The "knowledge" that is said to account for the rat's performance is an example of an **explanatory fiction,** a fictitious variable that often is simply another name for the observed behavior that contributes nothing to an understanding of the variables responsible for developing or maintaining the behavior. Explanatory fictions are the key ingredient in "a circular way of viewing the cause and effect of a situation" (Heron, Tincani, Peterson, & Miller, 2005, p. 274) that give a false sense of understanding.

> Turning from observed behavior to a fanciful inner world continues unabated. Sometimes it is little more than a linguistic practice. We tend to make nouns of adjectives and verbs and must then find a place for the things the nouns are said to represent. We say that a rope is strong and before long we are speaking of its strength. We call a particular kind of strength tensile, and then explain that the rope is strong *because* it possesses tensile strength. The mistake is less obvious but more troublesome when matters are more complex. . . .
>
> Consider now a behavioral parallel. When a person has been subject to mildly punishing consequences in walking on a slippery surface, he may walk in a manner we describe as cautious. It is then easy to say that he walks with caution or that he shows caution. There is no harm in this until we begin to say that he walks carefully *because* of his caution. (Skinner, 1974, pp. 165–166, emphasis added)

Some believe that behaviorism rejects all events that cannot be operationally defined by objective assessment. Accordingly, Skinner is thought to have rejected all data from his system that could not be independently verified by other people (Moore, 1984). Moore (1985) called this operational view "a commitment to truth by agreement" (p. 59). This common view of the philosophy of behaviorism is limited; in reality, there are many kinds of behaviorism—structuralism, methodological behaviorism, and forms of behaviorism that use cognitions as causal factors (e.g., cognitive behavior modification and social learning theory), in addition to the radical behaviorism of Skinner.

Structuralism and methodological behaviorism do reject all events that are not operationally defined by objective assessment (Skinner, 1974). Structuralists avoid mentalism by restricting their activities to descriptions of behavior. They make no scientific manipulations; accordingly, they do not address questions of causal factors. Methodological behaviorists differ from the structuralists by using scientific manipulations to search for functional relationships between events. Uncomfortable with basing their science on unobservable phenomena, some early behaviorists either denied the existence of "inner variables" or considered them outside the realm of a scientific account. Such an orientation is often referred to as **methodological behaviorism.**

Methodological behaviorists also usually acknowledge the existence of mental events but do not consider them in the analysis of behavior (Skinner, 1974). Methodological behaviorists' reliance on public events, excluding private events, restricts the knowledge base of human behavior and discourages innovation in the science of behavior. Methodological behaviorism is restrictive because it ignores areas of major importance for an understanding of behavior.

Contrary to popular opinion, Skinner did not object to cognitive psychology's concern with private events (i.e., events taking place "inside the skin") (Moore, 2000). Skinner was the first behaviorist to view thoughts and feelings (he called them "private events") as behavior to be analyzed with the same conceptual and experimental tools used to analyze publicly observable behavior, not as phenomena or variables that exist within and operate via principles of a separate mental world.

Essentially, Skinner's behaviorism makes three major assumptions regarding the nature of private events: (a) Private events such as thoughts and feelings are behavior; (b) behavior that takes place within the skin is distinguished from other ("public") behavior only by its inaccessibility; and (c) private behavior is influenced by (i.e., is a function of) the same kinds of variables as publicly accessible behavior.

> We need not suppose that events which take place within an organism's skin have special properties for that reason. A private event may be distinguished by its limited accessibility but not, so far as we know, by any special structure of nature. (Skinner, 1953, p. 257)

By incorporating private events into an overall conceptual system of behavior, Skinner created a **radical behaviorism** that includes and seeks to understand all human behavior. "What is inside the skin, and how do we know about it? The answer is, I believe, the heart of radical behaviorism" (Skinner, 1974, p. 218). The proper connotations of the word *radical* in radical behaviorism

are *far-reaching* and *thoroughgoing,* connoting the philosophy's inclusion of all behavior, public and private. *Radical* is also an appropriate modifier for Skinner's form of behaviorism because it represents a dramatic departure from other conceptual systems in calling for

> probably the most drastic change ever proposed in our way of thinking about man. It is almost literally a matter of turning the explanation of behavior inside out. (Skinner, 1974, p. 256)

Skinner and the philosophy of radical behaviorism acknowledge the events on which fictions such as cognitive processes are based. Radical behaviorism does not restrict the science of behavior to phenomena that can be detected by more than one person. In the context of radical behaviorism, the term *observe* implies "coming into contact with" (Moore, 1984). Radical behaviorists consider private events such as thinking or sensing the stimuli produced by a damaged tooth to be no different from public events such as oral reading or sensing the sounds produced by a musical instrument. According to Skinner (1974), "What is felt or introspectively observed is not some nonphysical world of consciousness, mind, or mental life but the observer's own body" (pp. 18–19).

The acknowledgment of private events is a major aspect of radical behaviorism. Moore (1980) stated it concisely:

> For radical behaviorism, private events are those events wherein individuals respond with respect to certain stimuli accessible to themselves alone. . . . The responses that are made to those stimuli may themselves be public, i.e., observable by others, or they may be private, i.e., accessible only to the individual involved. Nonetheless, to paraphrase Skinner (1953), it need not be supposed that events taking place within the skin have any special properties for that reason alone. . . . For radical behaviorism, then, one's responses with respect to private stimuli are equally lawful and alike in kind to one's responses with respect to public stimuli. (p. 460)

Scientists and practitioners are affected by their own social context, and institutions and schools are dominated by mentalism (Heward & Cooper, 1992; Kimball, 2002). A firm grasp of the philosophy of radical behaviorism, in addition to knowledge of principles of behavior, can help the scientist and practitioner resist the mentalistic approach of dropping the search for controlling variables in the environment and drifting toward explanatory fictions in the effort to understand behavior. The principles of behavior and the procedures presented in this text apply equally to public and private events. Radical behaviorism is the philosophical position underlying the content presented in this text.

A thorough discussion of radical behaviorism is far beyond the scope of this text. Still, the serious student of applied behavior analysis should devote considerable study to the original works of Skinner and to other authors who have critiqued, analyzed, and extended the philosophical foundations of the science of behavior.[7] (See Box 1.1 for Don Baer's perspectives on the meaning and importance of radical behaviorism.)

Applied Behavior Analysis

One of the first studies to report the human application of principles of operant behavior was conducted by Fuller (1949). The subject was an 18-year-old boy with profound developmental disabilities who was described in the language of the time as a "vegetative idiot." He lay on his back, unable to roll over. Fuller filled a syringe with a warm sugar-milk solution and injected a small amount of the fluid into the young man's mouth every time he moved his right arm (that arm was chosen because he moved it infrequently). Within four sessions the boy was moving his arm to a vertical position at a rate of three times per minute.

> The attending physicians . . . thought it was impossible for him to learn anything—according to them, he had not learned anything in the 18 years of his life—yet in four experimental sessions, by using the operant conditioning technique, an addition was made to his behavior which, at this level, could be termed appreciable. Those who participated in or observed the experiment are of the opinion that if time permitted, other responses could be conditioned and discriminations learned. (Fuller, 1949, p. 590)

During the 1950s and into the early 1960s researchers used the methods of the experimental analysis of behavior to determine whether the principles of behavior demonstrated in the laboratory with nonhuman subjects could be replicated with humans. Much of the early research with human subjects was conducted in clinic or laboratory settings. Although the participants typically benefited from these studies by learning new behaviors, the researchers' major purpose was to determine whether the basic principles of behavior discovered in the laboratory operated with humans. For example, Bijou (1955, 1957, 1958) researched several principles of behavior with typically developing subjects and people with mental retardation; Baer (1960, 1961, 1962) examined the effects of punishment, escape, and avoidance

contingencies on preschool children; Ferster and DeMyer (1961, 1962; DeMyer & Ferster, 1962) conducted a systematic study of the principles of behavior using children with autism as subjects; and Lindsley (1956, 1960) assessed the effects of operant conditioning on the behavior of adults with schizophrenia. These early researchers clearly established that the principles of behavior are applicable to human behavior, and they set the stage for the later development of applied behavior analysis.

The branch of behavior analysis that would later be called applied behavior analysis (ABA) can be traced to the 1959 publication of Ayllon and Michael's paper titled "The Psychiatric Nurse as a Behavioral Engineer." The authors described how direct care personnel in a state hospital used a variety of techniques based on the principles of behavior to improve the functioning of residents with psychotic disorders or mental retardation. During the 1960s many researchers began to apply principles of behavior in an effort to improve socially important behavior, but these early pioneers faced many problems. Laboratory techniques for measuring behavior and for controlling and manipulating variables were sometimes unavailable, or their use was inappropriate in applied settings. As a result, the early practitioners of applied behavior analysis had to develop new experimental procedures as they went along. There was little funding for the new discipline, and researchers had no ready outlet for publishing their studies, making it difficult to communicate among themselves about their findings and solutions to methodological problems. Most journal editors were reluctant to publish studies using an experimental method unfamiliar to mainstream social science, which relied on large numbers of subjects and tests of statistical inference.

Despite these problems it was an exciting time, and major new discoveries were being made regularly. For example, many pioneering applications of behavior principles to education occurred during this period (see, e.g., O'Leary & O'Leary, 1972; Ulrich, Stachnik, & Mabry 1974), from which were derived teaching procedures such as contingent teacher praise and attention (Hall, Lund, & Jackson, 1968), token reinforcement systems (Birnbrauer, Wolf, Kidder, & Tague, 1965), curriculum design (Becker, Englemann, & Thomas, 1975), and programmed instruction (Bijou, Birnbrauer, Kidder, & Tague, 1966; Markle, 1962). The basic methods for reliably improving student performance developed by those early applied behavior analysts provided the foundation for behavioral approaches to curriculum design, instructional methods, classroom management, and the generalization and maintenance of learning that continue to be used decades later (cf., Heward et al., 2005).

University programs in applied behavior analysis were begun in the 1960s and early 1970s at Arizona State

---

[7]Excellent discussions of radical behaviorism can be found in Baum (1994); Catania and Harnad (1988); Catania and Hineline (1996); Chiesa (1994); Lattal (1992); Lee (1988); and Moore (1980, 1984, 1995, 2000, 2003).

Box 1.1
What Is Behaviorism?

Don Baer loved the science of behavior. He loved to write about it, and he loved to talk about it. Don was famous for his unparalleled ability to speak extemporaneously about complex philosophical, experimental, and professional issues in a way that always made thorough conceptual, practical, and human sense. He did so with the vocabulary and syntax of a great author and the accomplished delivery of a master storyteller. The only thing Don knew better than his audience was his science.

On three occasions, in three different decades, graduate students and faculty in the special education program at Ohio State University were fortunate to have Professor Baer serve as Distinguished Guest Faculty for a doctoral seminar, Contemporary Issues in Special Education and Applied Behavior Analysis. The questions and responses that follow were selected from transcripts of two of Professor Baer's three OSU teleconference seminars.

If a person on the street approached you and asked, "What's behaviorism?" how would you reply?

The key point of behaviorism is that what people do can be understood. Traditionally, both the layperson and the psychologist have tried to understand behavior by seeing it as the outcome of what we think, what we feel, what we want, what we calculate, and etcetera. But we don't have to think about behavior that way. We could look upon it as a process that occurs in its own right and has its own causes. And those causes are, very often, found in the external environment.

Behavior analysis is a science of studying how we can arrange our environments so they make very likely the behaviors we want to be probable enough, and they make unlikely the behaviors we want to be improbable. Behaviorism is understanding how the environment works so that we can make ourselves smarter, more organized, more responsible; so we can encounter fewer punishments and fewer disappointments. A central point of behaviorism is this: We can remake our environment to accomplish some of that much more easily than we can remake our inner selves.

An interviewer once asked Edward Teller, the physicist who helped develop the first atomic bomb, "Can you explain to a nonscientist what you find so fasci-

nating about science, particularly physics?" Teller replied, "No." I sense that Teller was suggesting that a nonscientist would not be able to comprehend, understand, or appreciate physics and his fascination with it. If a nonscientist asked you, "What do you find so fascinating about science, particularly the science of human behavior?" what would you say?

Ed Morris organized a symposium on just this topic a couple of years ago at the Association for Behavior Analysis annual convention, and in that symposium, Jack Michael commented on the fact that although one of our discipline's big problems and challenges is communicating with our society about who we are, what we do, and what we can do, he didn't find it reasonable to try to summarize what behavior analysis is to an ordinary person in just a few words. He gave us this example: Imagine a quantum physicist is approached at a cocktail party by someone who asks, "What is quantum physics?" Jack said that the physicist might very well answer, and probably should answer, "I can't tell you in a few words. You should register for my course."

I'm very sympathetic with Jack's argument. But I also know, as someone who's confronted with the politics of relating our discipline to society, that although it may be a true answer, it's not a good answer. It's not an answer that people will hear with any pleasure, or indeed, even accept. I think such an answer creates only resentment. Therefore, I think we have to engage in a bit of honest show business. So, if I had to somehow state some connotations of what holds me in the field, I guess I would say that since I was a child I always found my biggest reinforcer was something called understanding. I liked to know how things worked. And of all of the things in the world there are to understand, it became clear to me that the most fascinating was what people do. I started with the usual physical science stuff, and it was intriguing to me to understand how radios work, and how electricity works, and how clocks work, etcetera. But when it became clear to me that we could also learn how people work—not just biologically, but behaviorally—I thought that's the best of all. Surely, everyone must agree that that's the most fascinating subject matter. That there could be a science of behavior, of what we do, of who we are? How could you resist that?

Adapted from "Thursday Afternoons with Don: Selections from Three Teleconference Seminars on Applied Behavior Analysis" by W. L. Heward & C. L. Wood (2003). In K. S. Budd & T. Stokes (Eds.), *A Small Matter of Proof: The Legacy of Donald M. Baer* (pp. 293–310). Reno, NV: Context Press. Used by permission.

University, Florida State University, the University of Illinois, Indiana University, the University of Kansas, the University of Oregon, the University of Southern Illinois, the University of Washington, West Virginia University, and Western Michigan University, among others. Through their teaching and research, faculty at each of these programs made major contributions to the rapid growth of the field.[8]

Two significant events in 1968 mark that year as the formal beginning of contemporary applied behavior analysis. First, the *Journal of Applied Behavior Analysis (JABA)* began publication. *JABA* was the first journal in the United States to deal with applied problems that gave researchers using methodology from the experimental analysis of behavior an outlet for publishing their findings. *JABA* was and continues to be the flagship journal of applied behavior analysis. Many of the early articles in *JABA* became model demonstrations of how to conduct and interpret applied behavior analysis, which in turn led to improved applications and experimental methodology.

The second major event of 1968 was the publication of the paper, "Some Current Dimensions of Applied Behavior Analysis" by Donald M. Baer, Montrose M. Wolf, and Todd R. Risley. These authors, the founding fathers of the new discipline, defined the criteria for judging the adequacy of research and practice in applied behavior analysis and outlined the scope of work for those in the science. Their 1968 paper has been the most widely cited publication in applied behavior analysis, and it remains the standard description of the discipline.

Defining Characteristics of Applied Behavior Analysis

Baer, Wolf, and Risley (1968) recommended that applied behavior analysis should be *applied, behavioral, analytic, technological, conceptually systematic, effective,* and capable of appropriately *generalized outcomes.* In 1987 Baer and colleagues reported that the "seven self-conscious guides to behavior analytic conduct" (p. 319) they had offered 20 years earlier "remain functional; they still connote the current dimensions of the work usually called applied behavior analysis" (p. 314). As we write this book, nearly 40 years have passed since Baer, Wolf, and Risley's seminal paper was published, and we find that the seven dimensions they posed continue to serve as the primary criteria for defining and judging the value of applied behavior analysis.

Applied

The *applied* in applied behavior analysis signals ABA's commitment to affecting improvements in behaviors that enhance and improve people's lives. To meet this criterion, the researcher or practitioner must select behaviors to change that are socially significant for participants: social, language, academic, daily living, self-care, vocational, and/or recreation and leisure behaviors that improve the day-to-day life experience of the participants and/or affect their significant others (parents, teachers, peers, employers) in such a way that they behave more positively with and toward the participant.

Behavioral

At first it may seem superfluous to include such an obvious criterion—of course applied *behavior* analysis must be *behavioral.* However, Baer and colleagues (1968) made three important points relative to the behavioral criterion. First, not just any behavior will do; the behavior chosen for study must be *the* behavior in need of improvement, not a similar behavior that serves as a proxy for the behavior of interest or the subject's verbal description of the behavior. Behavior analysts conduct studies *of* behavior, not studies *about* behavior. For example, in a study evaluating the effects of a program to teach school children to get along with one another, an applied behavior analyst would directly observe and measure clearly defined classes of interactions between and among the children instead of using indirect measures such as the children's answers on a sociogram or responses to a questionnaire about how they believe they get along with one another.

Second, the behavior must be measurable; the precise and reliable measurement of behavior is just as critical in applied research as it is in basic research. Applied researchers must meet the challenge of measuring socially significant behaviors in their natural settings, and they must do so without resorting to the measurement of nonbehavioral substitutes.

Third, when changes in behavior are observed during an investigation, it is necessary to ask whose behavior has changed. Perhaps only the behavior of the observers has changed. "Explicit measurement of the reliability of human observers thus becomes not merely good technique, but a prime criterion of whether the study was appropriately behavioral" (Baer et al., 1968, p. 93). Or perhaps the experimenter's behavior has changed in an unplanned way, making it inappropriate to attribute any observed change in the subject's behavior to the independent variables that were manipulated. The applied behavior analyst should attempt to monitor the behavior of all persons involved in a study.

---

[8]Articles describing the histories of the applied behavior analysis programs at five of these universities can be found in the winter 1994 issue of *JABA*.

Analytic

A study in applied behavior analysis is *analytic* when the experimenter has demonstrated a functional relation between the manipulated events and a reliable change in some measurable dimension of the targeted behavior. In other words, the experimenter must be able to control the occurrence and nonoccurrence of the behavior. Sometimes, however, society does not allow the repeated manipulation of important behaviors to satisfy the requirements of experimental method. Therefore, applied behavior analysts must demonstrate control to the greatest extent possible, given the restraints of the setting and behavior; and then they must present the results for judgment by the consumers of the research. The ultimate issue is believability: Has the researcher achieved experimental control to demonstrate a reliable functional relation?

The analytic dimension enables ABA to not only demonstrate effectiveness, but also to provide the "acid test proof" of functional and replicable relations between the interventions it recommends and socially significant outcomes (D. M. Baer, October 21, 1982, personal communication).

> Because we are a data- and design-based discipline, we are in the remarkable position of being able to prove that behavior can work in the way that our technology prescribes. We are not theorizing about how behavior *can* work; we are describing systematically how it *has* worked many times in real-world applications, in designs too competent and with measurement systems too reliable and valid to doubt. Our ability to prove that behavior can work that way does not, of course, establish that behavior *cannot* work any other way: we are not in a discipline that can deny any other approaches, only in one that can affirm itself as knowing many of its *sufficient* conditions at the level of experimental proof . . . our subject matter is behavior change, and we can specify some *actionable* sufficient conditions for it. (D. M. Baer, personal communication, October 21, 1982, emphasis in original).

Technological

A study in applied behavior analysis is *technological* when all of its operative procedures are identified and described with sufficient detail and clarity "such that a reader has a fair chance of replicating the application with the same results" (Baer et al., 1987, p. 320).

> It is not enough to say what is to be done when the subject makes response R_1; it is essential also whenever possible to say what is to be done if the subject makes the alternative responses, R_2, R_3, etc. For example, one may read that temper tantrums in children are often extinguished by closing the child in his room for the duration of the tantrums plus ten minutes. Unless that

procedure description also states what should be done if the child tries to leave the room early, or kicks out the window, or smears feces on the walls, or begins to make strangling sounds, etc., it is not precise technological description. (Baer et al., 1968, pp. 95–96)

No matter how powerful its effects in any given study, a behavior change method will be of little value if practitioners are unable to replicate it. The development of a replicable technology of behavior change has been a defining characteristic and continuing goal of ABA from its inception. Behavioral tactics are replicable and teachable to others. Interventions that cannot be replicated with sufficient fidelity to achieve comparable outcomes are not considered part of the technology.

A good check of the technological adequacy of a procedural description is to have a person trained in applied behavior analysis carefully read the description and then act out the procedure in detail. If the person makes any mistakes, adds any operations, omits any steps, or has to ask any questions to clarify the written description, then the description is not sufficiently technological and requires improvement.

Conceptually Systematic

Although Baer and colleagues (1968) did not state so explicitly, a defining characteristic of applied behavior analysis concerns the types of interventions used to improve behavior. Although there are an infinite number of tactics and specific procedures that can be used to alter behavior, almost all are derivatives and/or combinations of a relatively few basic principles of behavior. Thus, Baer and colleagues recommended that research reports of applied behavior analysis be *conceptually systematic*, meaning that the procedures for changing behavior and any interpretations of how or why those procedures were effective should be described in terms of the relevant principle(s) from which they were derived.

Baer and colleagues (1968) provided a strong rationale for the use of conceptual systems in applied behavior analysis. First, relating specific procedures to basic principles might enable the research consumer to derive other similar procedures from the same principle(s). Second, conceptual systems are needed if a technology is to become an integrated discipline instead of a "collection of tricks." Loosely related collections of tricks do not lend themselves to systematic expansion, and they are difficult to learn and to teach in great number.

Effective

An effective application of behavioral techniques must improve the behavior under investigation to a practical degree. "In application, the theoretical importance of a variable is usually not at issue. Its practical importance, specifically its power in altering behavior enough to be socially important, is the essential criterion" (Baer et al., 1968, p. 96). Whereas some investigations produce results of theoretical importance or statistical significance, to be judged *effective* an applied behavior analysis study must produce behavior changes that reach clinical or social significance.

How much a given behavior of a given subject needs to change for the improvement to be considered socially important is a practical question. Baer and colleagues stated that the answer is most likely to come from the people who must deal with the behavior; they should be asked how much the behavior needs to change. The necessity of producing behavioral changes that are meaningful to the participant and/or those in the participant's environment has pushed behavior analysts to search for "robust" variables, interventions that produce large and consistent effects on behavior (Baer, 1977a).

When they revisited the dimension of effectiveness 20 years later, Baer, Wolf, and Risley (1987) recommended that the effectiveness of ABA also be judged by a second kind of outcome: the extent to which changes in the target behaviors result in noticeable changes in the reasons those behaviors were selected for change originally. If such changes in the subjects' lives do not occur, ABA may achieve one level of effectiveness yet fail to achieve a critical form of social validity (Wolf, 1978).

> We may have taught many social skills without examining whether they actually furthered the subject's social life; many courtesy skills without examining whether anyone actually noticed or cared; many safety skills without examining whether the subject was actually safer thereafter; many language skills without measuring whether the subject actually used them to interact differently than before; many on-task skills without measuring the actual value of those tasks; and, in general, many survival skills without examining the subject's actual subsequent survival. (Baer et al., 1987, p. 322)

Generality

A behavior change has *generality* if it lasts over time, appears in environments other than the one in which the intervention that initially produced it was implemented, and/or spreads to other behaviors not directly treated by the intervention. A behavior change that continues after the original treatment procedures are withdrawn has generality. And generality is evident when changes in targeted behavior occur in nontreatment settings or situations as a function of treatment procedures. Generality also exists when behaviors change that were not the focus of the intervention. Although not all instances of generality are adaptive (e.g., a beginning reader who has

just learned to make the sound for the letter *p* in words such as *pet* and *ripe,* might make the same sound when seeing the letter *p* in the word *phone*), desirable generalized behavior changes are important outcomes of an applied behavior analysis program because they represent additional dividends in terms of behavioral improvement. Strategies and tactics for promoting desirable generalization of behavior changes are detailed in Chapter 28.

Some Additional Characteristics of ABA

Applied behavior analysis offers society an approach toward solving problems that is accountable, public, doable, empowering, and optimistic (Heward, 2005). Although not among ABA's defining dimensions, these characteristics should help increase the extent to which decision makers and consumers in many areas look to behavior analysis as a valuable and important source of knowledge for achieving improvements.

Accountable

The commitment of applied behavior analysts to effectiveness, their focus on accessible environmental variables that reliably influence behavior, and their reliance on direct and frequent measurement to detect changes in behavior yield an inescapable and socially valuable form of accountability. Direct and frequent measurement—the foundation and most important component of ABA practices—enables behavior analysts to detect their successes and, equally important, their failures so they can make changes in an effort to change failure to success (Bushell & Bear, 1994; Greenwood & Maheady, 1997).

> Failure is always informative in the logic of behavior analysis, just as it is in engineering. The constant reaction to lack of progress [is] a definitive hallmark of ABA. (Baer, 2005, p. 8)

Gambrill (2003) described the sense of accountability and self-correcting nature of applied behavior analysis very well.

> Applied behavior analysis is a scientific approach to understanding behavior in which we guess and critically test ideas, rather than guess and guess again. It is a process for solving problems in which we learn from our mistakes. Here, false knowledge and inert knowledge are not valued. (p. 67)

Public

"Everything about ABA is visible and public, explicit and straightforward. . . . ABA entails no ephemeral, mystical, or metaphysical explanations; there are no hidden treatments; there is no magic" (Heward, 2005, p. 322). The transparent, public nature of ABA should raise its value in fields such as education, parenting and child care, employee productivity, geriatrics, health and safety, and social work—to name only a few—whose goals, methods, and outcomes are of vital interest to many constituencies.

Doable

Classroom teachers, parents, coaches, workplace supervisors, and sometimes the participants themselves implemented the interventions found effective in many ABA studies. This demonstrates the pragmatic element of ABA. "Although 'doing ABA' requires far more than learning to administer a few simple procedures, it is not prohibitively complicated or arduous. As many teachers have noted, implementing behavioral strategies in the classroom . . . might best be described as good old-fashioned hard work" (Heward, 2005, p. 322).

Empowering

ABA gives practitioners real tools that work. Knowing how to do something and having the tools to accomplish it instills confidence in practitioners. Seeing the data showing behavioral improvements in one's clients, students, or teammates, or in oneself, not only feels good, but also raises one's confidence level in assuming even more difficult challenges in the future.

Optimistic

Practitioners knowledgeable and skilled in behavior analysis have genuine cause to be optimistic for four reasons. First, as Strain and Joseph (2004) noted:

> The environmental view promoted by behaviorism is essentially optimistic; it suggests that (except for gross genetic factors) all individuals possess roughly equal potential. Rather than assuming that individuals have some essential internal characteristic, behaviorists assume that poor outcomes originate in the way the environment and experience shaped the individual's current behavior. Once these environmental and experiential factors are identified, we can design prevention and intervention programs to improve the outcomes. . . . Thus, the emphasis on external control in the behavioral approach . . . offers a conceptual model that celebrates the possibilities for each individual. (Strain et al., 1992, p. 58)

Second, direct and continuous measurement enables practitioners to detect small improvements in performance that might otherwise be overlooked. Third, the more often a practitioner uses behavioral tactics with positive outcomes (the most common result of behaviorally based interventions), the more optimistic she becomes about the prospects for future success.

> A sense of optimism, expressed by the question "Why not?" has been a central part of ABA and has had an enormous impact on its development from its earliest days. Why can't we teach a person who does not yet talk to talk? Why shouldn't we go ahead and try to change the environments of young children so that they will display more creativity? Why would we assume that this person with a developmental disability could not learn to do the same things that many of us do? Why not try to do it? (Heward, 2005, p. 323)

Fourth, ABA's peer-reviewed literature provides many examples of success in teaching students who had been considered unteachable. ABA's continuous record of achievements evokes a legitimate feeling of optimism that future developments will yield solutions to behavioral challenges that are currently beyond the existing technology. For example, in response to the perspective that some people have disabilities so severe and profound that they should be viewed as ineducable, Don Baer offered this perspective:

> Some of us have ignored both the thesis that all persons are educable and the thesis that some persons are ineducable, and instead have experimented with ways to teach some previously unteachable people. Those experiments have steadily reduced the size of the apparently ineducable group relative to the obviously educable group. Clearly, we have not finished that adventure. Why predict its outcome, when we could simply pursue it, and just as well without a prediction? Why not pursue it to see if there comes a day when there is such a small class of apparently ineducable persons left that it consists of one elderly person who is put forward as ineducable. If that day comes, it will be a very nice day. And the next day will be even better. (D. M. Baer, February 15, 2002, personal communication, as cited in Heward, 2006, p. 473)

Definition of Applied Behavior Analysis

We began this chapter by stating that applied behavior analysis is concerned with the improvement and understanding of human behavior. We then described some of the attitudes and methods that are fundamental to scientific inquiry, briefly reviewed the development of the science and philosophy of behavior analysis, and examined the characteristics of ABA. All of that provided necessary context for the following definition of applied behavior analysis:

Applied behavior analysis is the science in which tactics derived from the principles of behavior are applied systematically to improve socially significant behavior and experimentation is used to identify the variables responsible for behavior change.

This definition includes six key components. First, the practice of applied behavior analysis is guided by the attitudes and methods of scientific inquiry. Second, all behavior change procedures are described and implemented in a systematic, technological manner. Third, not any means of changing behavior qualifies as applied behavior analysis: Only those procedures conceptually derived from the basic principles of behavior are circumscribed by the field. Fourth, the focus of applied behavior analysis is socially significant behavior. The fifth and sixth parts of the definition specify the twin goals of applied behavior analysis: improvement and understanding. Applied behavior analysis seeks to make meaningful improvement in important behavior and to produce an analysis of the factors responsible for that improvement.

Four Interrelated Domains of Behavior Analytic Science and Professional Practices Guided by That Science

The science of behavior analysis and its application to human problems consists of four domains: the three branches of behavior analysis—behaviorism, EAB, and ABA—and professional practice in various fields that is informed and guided by that science. Figure 1.2 identifies some of the defining features and characteristics of these four interrelated domains. Although most behavior analysts work primarily in one or two of the domains shown in Figure 1.2, it is common for a behavior analyst to function in multiple domains at one time or another (Hawkins & Anderson, 2002; Moore & Cooper, 2003).

A behavior analyst who pursues theoretical and conceptual issues is engaged in behaviorism, the philosophical domain of behavior analysis. A product of such work is Delprato's (2002) discussion of the importance of countercontrol (behavior by people experiencing aversive control by others that helps them escape and avoid the control while not reinforcing and sometimes punishing the controller's responses) toward an understanding of effective interventions for interpersonal relations and cultural design.

The experimental analysis of behavior is the basic research branch of the science. Basic research consists of experiments in laboratory settings with both human and nonhuman subjects with a goal of discovering and

clarifying fundamental principles of behavior. An example is Hackenberg and Axtell's (1993) experiments investigating how choices made by humans are affected by the dynamic interaction of schedules of reinforcement that entail short- and long-term consequences.[9]

Applied behavior analysts conduct experiments aimed at discovering and clarifying functional relations between socially significant behavior and its controlling variables, with which they can contribute to the further development of a humane and effective technology of behavior change. An example is research by Tarbox, Wallace, and Williams (2003) on the assessment and treatment of elopement (running or walking away from a caregiver without permission), a behavior that poses great danger for young children and people with disabilities.

The delivery of behavior analytic professional services occurs in the fourth domain. Behavior analysis practitioners design, implement, and evaluate behavior change programs that consist of behavior change tactics derived from fundamental principles of behavior discovered by basic researchers, and that have been experimentally validated for their effects on socially significant behavior by applied researchers. An example is when a therapist providing home-based treatment for a child with autism embeds frequent opportunities for the child to use his emerging social and language skills in the context of naturalistic, daily routines and ensures that the child's responses are followed with reinforcing events. Another example is a classroom teacher trained in behavior analysis who uses positive reinforcement and stimulus fading to teach students to identify and classify fish into their respective species by the shape, size, and location of their fins.

Although each of the four domains of ABA can be defined and practiced in its own right, none of the domains are, or should be, completely independent of and uninformed by developments in the others. Both the science and the application of its findings benefit when the four domains are interrelated and influence one another (cf., Critchfield & Kollins, 2001; Lattal & Neef; 1996; Stromer, McComas, & Rehfeldt, 2000). Evidence of the symbiotic relations between the basic and applied domains is evident in research that "bridges" basic and applied areas and in applied research that translates the knowledge derived from basic research "into state-of-the-art clinical practices for use in the community" (Lerman, 2003, p. 415).[10]

---

[9]Schedules of reinforcement are discussed in Chapter 13.

[10]Examples and discussions of bridge or translational research can be found in the winter 1994 and winter 2003 issues of *JABA;* Fisher and Mazur (1997); Lattal and Neef (1996); and Vollmer and Hackenberg (2001).

Figure 1.2   Some comparisons and relationships among the four domains of behavior analysis science and practice.

	Behaviorism	Experimental Analysis of Behavior (EAB)	Applied Behavior Analysis (ABA)	Practice Guided by Behavior Analysis
	◄——— The Science of Behavior Analysis ———►			
		◄———The Application of Behavior Analysis ———►		
Province	Theory and philosophy	Basic research	Applied research	Helping people behave more successfully
Primary activity	Conceptual and philosophical analysis	Design, conduct, interpret, and report basic experiments	Design, conduct, interpret, and report applied experiments	Design, implement, and evaluate behavior change programs
Primary goal and product	Theoretical account of all behavior consistent with existing data	Discover and clarify basic principles of behavior; functional relations between behavior and controlling variables	A technology for improving socially significant behavior; functional relations between socially significant behavior and controlling variables	Improvements in the lives of participants/clients as a result of changes in their behavior
Secondary goals	Identify areas in which empirical data are absent and/or conflict and suggest resolutions	Identify questions for EAB and/or ABA to investigate further; raise theoretical issues	Identify questions for EAB and/or ABA to investigate further; raise theoretical issues	Increased efficiency in achieving primary goal; may identify questions for ABA and EAB
Agreement with existing database	As much as possible, but theory must go beyond database by design	Complete—Although differences among data sets exist, EAB provides the basic research database	Complete—Although differences among data sets exist, ABA provides the applied research database	As much as possible, but practitioners must often deal with situations not covered by existing data
Testability	Partially—All behavior and variables of interest are not accessible (e.g., phylogenic contingencies)	Mostly—Technical limitations preclude measurement and experimental manipulation of some variables	Mostly—Same limitations as EAB plus those posed by applied settings (e.g., ethical concerns, uncontrolled events)	Partially—All behavior and variables of interest are not accessible (e.g., a student's home life)
Scope	**Most** ◄———			———► **Least**
	Wide scope because theory attempts to account for all behavior	As much scope as the EAB database enables	As much scope as the ABA database enables	Narrow scope because practitioner's primary focus is helping the specific situation
Precision	**Least** ◄———			———► **Most**
	Minimal precision is possible because experimental data do not exist for all behavior encompassed by theory	As much precision as EAB's current technology for experimental control and the researcher's skills enable	As much precision as ABA's current technology for experimental control and the researcher's skills enable	Maximum precision is sought to change behavior most effectively in specific instance.

The Promise and Potential of ABA

In a paper titled, "A Futuristic Perspective for Applied Behavior Analysis," Jon Bailey (2000) stated that

> It seems to me that applied behavior analysis is more relevant than ever before and that it offers our citizens, parents, teachers, and corporate and government leaders advantages that cannot be matched by any other psychological approach. . . . I know of no other approach in psychology that can boast state-of-the-art solutions to the most troubling social ills of the day. (p. 477)

We, too, believe that ABA's pragmatic, natural science approach to discovering environmental variables that reliably influence socially significant behavior and to developing a technology to take practical advantage of those discoveries offers humankind its best hope for solving many of its problems. It is important, however, to recognize that behavior analysis's knowledge of "how behavior works," even at the level of fundamental principles, is incomplete, as is the technology for changing socially significant behavior derived from those principles. There are aspects of about which relatively little is known, and additional research, both basic and applied, is needed to clarify, extend, and fine-tune all existing knowledge (e.g., Critchfield & Kollins, 2001; Friman, Hayes, & Wilson, 1998; Murphy, McSweeny, Smith, & McComas, 2003; Stromer, McComas, & Rehfeldt, 2000).

Nevertheless, the still young science of applied behavior analysis has contributed to a full range of areas in which human behavior is important. Even an informal, cursory survey of the research published in applied behavior analysis reveals studies investigating virtually the full range of socially significant human behavior from A to Z and almost everywhere in between: AIDS prevention (e.g., DeVries, Burnette, & Redmona, 1991), conservation of natural resources (e.g., Brothers, Krantz, & McClannahan, 1994), education (e.g., Heward et al., 2005), gerontology (e.g., Gallagher & Keenan, 2000), health and exercise (e.g., De Luca & Holborn, 1992), industrial safety (e.g., Fox, Hopkins, & Anger, 1987), language acquisition (e.g., Drasgow, Halle, & Ostrosky, 1998), littering (e.g., Powers, Osborne, & Anderson, 1973), medical procedures (e.g., Hagopian & Thompson, 1999), parenting (e.g., Kuhn, Lerman, & Vorndran, 2003), seatbelt use (e.g., Van Houten, Malenfant, Austin, & Lebbon, 2005), sports (e.g., Brobst & Ward, 2002), and zoo management and care of animals (e.g., Forthman & Ogden, 1992).

Applied behavior analysis provides an empirical basis for not only understanding human behavior but also improving it. Equally important, ABA continually tests and evaluates its methods. The remainder of this text will present a foundation of knowledge that can lead to a full understanding of applied behavior analysis.

 # Summary

Some Basic Characteristics and a Definition of Science

1. Different types of scientific investigations yield knowledge that enables the description, prediction, and/or control of the phenomena studied.

2. Descriptive studies yield a collection of facts about the observed events that can be quantified, classified, and examined for possible relations with other known facts.

3. Knowledge gained from a study that finds the systematic covariation between two events—termed a correlation—can be used to predict the probability that one event will occur based on the occurrence of the other event.

4. Results of experiments that show that specific manipulations of one event (the independent variable) produce a reliable change in another event (the dependent variable), and that the change in the dependent variable was unlikely the result of extraneous factors (confounding variables)—a finding known as a functional relation—can be used to control the phenomena under investigation.

5. The behavior of scientists in all fields is characterized by a common set of assumptions and attitudes:

   • Determinism—the assumption that the universe is a lawful and orderly place in which phenomena occur as a result of other events.

   • Empiricism—the objective observation of the phenomena of interest.

   • Experimentation—the controlled comparison of some measure of the phenomenon of interest (the dependent variable) under two or more different conditions in which only one factor at a time (the independent variable) differs from one condition to another.

   • Replication—repeating experiments (and independent variable conditions within experiments) to determine the reliability and usefulness of findings

   • Parsimony—simple, logical explanations must be ruled out, experimentally or conceptually, before more complex or abstract explanations are considered.

   • Philosophic doubt—continually questioning the truthfulness and validity of all scientific theory and knowledge.

A Brief History of the Development of Behavior Analysis

6. Behavior analysis consists of three major branches: behaviorism, the experimental analysis of behavior (EAB), and applied behavior analysis (ABA).

7. Watson espoused an early form of behaviorism known as stimulus–response (S–R) psychology, which did not account for behavior without obvious antecedent causes.

8. Skinner founded the experimental analysis of behavior (EAB), a natural science approach for discovering orderly and reliable relations between behavior and various types of environmental variables of which it is a function.

9. EAB is characterized by these methodological features:
   - Rate of response is the most common dependent variable.
   - Repeated or continuous measurement is made of carefully defined response classes.
   - Within-subject experimental comparisons are used instead of designs comparing the behavior of experimental and control groups.
   - The visual analysis of graphed data is preferred over statistical inference.
   - A description of functional relations is valued over formal theory testing.

10. Through thousands of laboratory experiments, Skinner and his colleagues and students discovered and verified the basic principles of operant behavior that provide the empirical foundation for behavior analysis today.

11. Skinner wrote extensively about a philosophy for a science of behavior he called radical behaviorism. Radical behaviorism attempts to explain all behavior, including private events such as thinking and feeling.

12. Methodological behaviorism is a philosophical position that considers behavioral events that cannot be publicly observed to be outside the realm of the science.

13. Mentalism is an approach to understanding behavior that assumes that a mental, or "inner," dimension exists that differs from a behavioral dimension and that phenomena in this dimension either directly cause or at least mediate some forms of behavior; it relies on hypothetical constructs and explanatory fictions.

14. The first published report of the application of operant conditioning with a human subject was a study by Fuller (1949), in which an arm-raising response was conditioned in an adolescent with profound retardation.

15. The formal beginnings of applied behavior analysis can be traced to 1959 and the publication of Ayllon and Michael's article, "The Psychiatric Nurse as a Behavioral Engineer."

16. Contemporary applied behavior analysis (ABA) began in 1968 with the publication of the first issue of the *Journal of Applied Behavior Analysis (JABA).*

Defining Characteristics of Applied Behavior Analysis

17. Baer, Wolf, and Risley (1968, 1987) stated that a research study or behavior change program should meet seven defining dimensions to be considered applied behavior analysis:
    - Applied—investigates socially significant behaviors with immediate importance to the subject(s).
    - Behavioral—entails precise measurement of the actual behavior in need of improvement and documents that it was the subject's behavior that changed.
    - Analytic—demonstrates experimental control over the occurrence and nonoccurrence of the behavior—that is, if a functional relation is demonstrated.
    - Technological—the written description of all procedures used in the study is sufficiently complete and detailed to enable others to replicate it.
    - Conceptually systematic—behavior change interventions are derived from basic principles of behavior.
    - Effective—improves behavior sufficiently to produce practical results for the participant/client.
    - Generality—produces behavior changes that last over time, appear in other environments, or spread to other behaviors.

18. ABA offers society an approach toward solving many of its problems that is accountable, public, doable, empowering, and optimistic.

A Definition of Applied Behavior Analysis

19. Applied behavior analysis is the science in which tactics derived from the principles of behavior are applied to improve socially significant behavior and experimentation is used to identify the variables responsible for behavior change.

20. Behavior analysts work in one or more of four interrelated domains: behaviorism (theoretical and philosophical issues), the experimental analysis of behavior (basic research), applied behavior analysis (applied research), and professional practice (providing behavior analytic services to consumers).

21. ABA's natural science approach to discovering environmental variables that reliably influence socially significant behavior and developing a technology to take practical advantage of those discoveries offers humankind its best hope for solving many of its problems.

CHAPTER 2

Basic Concepts

Key Terms

antecedent
automaticity of reinforcement
aversive stimulus
behavior
behavior change tactic
conditioned punisher
conditioned reflex
conditioned reinforcer
conditioned stimulus
consequence
contingency
contingent
deprivation
discriminated operant
discriminative stimulus (S^D)
environment
extinction

habituation
higher order conditioning
history of reinforcement
motivating operation
negative reinforcement
neutral stimulus
ontogeny
operant behavior
operant conditioning
phylogeny
positive reinforcement
principle of behavior
punisher
punishment
reflex
reinforcement
reinforcer

repertoire
respondent behavior
respondent conditioning
respondent extinction
response
response class
satiation
selection by consequences
stimulus
stimulus class
stimulus control
stimulus–stimulus pairing
three-term contingency
unconditioned punisher
unconditioned reinforcer
unconditioned stimulus

Behavior Analyst Certification Board® BCBA® & BCABA® Behavior Analyst Task List,© Third Edition

Content Area 3: Principles, Processes, and Concepts	
3-1	Define and provide examples of behavior/response/response class.
3-2	Define and provide examples of stimulus and stimulus class.
3-3	Define and provide examples of positive and negative reinforcement.
3-4	Define and provide examples of conditioned and unconditioned reinforcement.
3-5	Define and provide examples of positive and negative punishment.
3-6	Define and provide examples of conditioned and unconditioned punishment.
3-7	Define and provide examples of stimulus control.
3-8	Define and provide examples of establishing operations.
3-9	Define and provide examples of behavioral contingencies.

(continued)

Content Area 3: Principles, Processes, and Concepts (*continued*)	
3-13	Describe and provide examples of the respondent conditioning paradigm.
3-14	Describe and provide examples of the operant conditioning paradigm.

This chapter defines the basic elements involved in a scientific analysis of behavior and introduces several principles that have been discovered through such an analysis. The first concept we examine—behavior—is the most fundamental of all. Because the controlling variables of primary importance in applied behavior analysis are located in the environment, the concepts of environment and stimulus are defined next. We then introduce several essential findings that the scientific study of behavior–environment relations has discovered. Two functionally distinct types of behavior—respondent and operant—are described, and the basic ways the environment influences each type of behavior—respondent conditioning and operant conditioning—are introduced. The three-term contingency—a concept for expressing and organizing the temporal and functional relations between operant behavior and environment—and its importance as a focal point in applied behavior analysis are then explained.[1] The chapter's final section recognizes the incredible complexity of human behavior, reminds us that behavior analysts possess an incomplete knowledge, and identifies some of the obstacles and challenges faced by those who strive to change behavior in applied settings.

Behavior

What, exactly, is behavior? Behavior is the activity of living organisms. Human behavior is everything people do, including how they move and what they say, think, and feel. Tearing open a bag of peanuts is behavior, and so is thinking how good the peanuts will taste once the bag is open. Reading this sentence is behavior, and if you're holding the book, so is feeling its weight and shape in your hands.

Although words such as *activity* and *movement* adequately communicate the general notion of behavior, a more precise definition is needed for scientific purposes. How a scientific discipline defines its subject matter exerts profound influence on the methods of measurement, experimentation, and theoretical analysis that are appropriate and possible.

Building on Skinner's (1938) definition of behavior as "the movement of an organism or of its parts in a frame of reference provided by the organism or by various external objects or fields" (p. 6), Johnston and Pennypacker (1980, 1993a) articulated the most conceptually sound and empirically complete definition of **behavior** to date.

The behavior of an organism is that portion of an organism's interaction with its environment that is characterized by detectable displacement in space through time of some part of the organism and that results in a measurable change in at least one aspect of the environment. (p. 23)

Johnston and Pennypacker (1993a) discussed the major elements of each part of this definition. The phrase *behavior of an organism* restricts the subject matter to the activity of living organisms, leaving notions such as the "behavior" of the stock market outside the realm of the scientific use of the term.

The phrase *portion of the organism's interaction with the environment* specifies "the necessary and sufficient conditions for the occurrence of behavior as (a) the existence of two separate entities, organism and environment, and (b) the existence of a relation between them" (Johnston & Pennypacker, 1993a, p. 24). The authors elaborated on this part of the definition as follows:

Behavior is not a property or attribute of the organism. It happens only when there is an interactive condition between an organism and its surroundings, which include its own body. This means that independent states of the organism, whether real or hypothetical, are not behavioral events, because there is no interactive process. Being hungry or being anxious are examples of states that are sometimes confused with the behavior that they are supposed to explain. Neither phrase specifies an environmental agent with which the hungry or anxious organism interacts, so no behavior is implied.

---

[1] The reader should not be overwhelmed by the many technical terms and concepts contained in this chapter. With the exception of the material on respondent behavior, all of the concepts introduced in this chapter are explained in greater detail in subsequent chapters. This initial overview of basic concepts is intended to provide background information that will facilitate understanding those portions of the text that precede the more detailed explanations.

Similarly, independent conditions or changes in the environment do not define behavioral occurrences because no interaction is specified. Someone walking in the rain gets wet, but "getting wet" is not an instance of behavior. A child may receive tokens for correctly working math problems, but "receiving a token" is not behavior. Receiving a token implies changes in the environment but does not suggest or require change in the child's movement. In contrast, both doing math problems and putting the token in a pocket are behavioral events because the environment both prompts the child's actions and is then changed by them. (Johnston & Pennypacker, 1993a, p. 24)

Behavior is movement, regardless of scale; hence the phrase *displacement in space through time*. In addition to excluding static states of the organism, the definition does not include bodily movements produced by the action of independent physical forces as behavioral events. For example, being blown over by a strong gust of wind is not behavior; given sufficient wind, nonliving objects and organisms move similarly. Behavior can be accomplished only by living organisms. A useful way to tell whether movement is behavior is to apply the dead man test: "If a dead man can do it, it ain't behavior. And if a dead man can't do, then it is behavior" (Malott & Trojan Suarez, 2004, p. 9). So, although being knocked down by strong wind is not behavior (a dead man would also be blown over), moving arms and hands in front of one's face, tucking and rolling, and yelling "Whoa!" as one is being blown over are behaviors.[2]

The *displacement in space through time* phrase also highlights the properties of behavior most amenable to measurement. Johnston and Pennypacker (1993a) referred to these fundamental properties by which behavior can be measured as *temporal locus* (when in time a specified behavior occurs), *temporal extent* (the duration of a given behavioral event), and *repeatability* (the frequency with which a specified behavior occurs over time). The methods used by applied behavior analysts to measure those properties are detailed in Chapter 4.

Acknowledging that the last phrase of the definition—*that results in a measurable change in at least one aspect of the environment*—is somewhat redundant, Johnston and Pennypacker (1993a) noted that it emphasizes an important qualifier for the scientific study of behavior.

Because the organism cannot be separated from an environment and because behavior is the relation between organism and environment, it is impossible for a behavioral event not to influence the environment in some way. . . . This is an important methodological point because it says that behavior must be detected and measured in terms of its effects on the environment. (p. 27)

As Skinner (1969) wrote, "To be observed, a response must affect the environment—it must have an effect upon an observer or upon an instrument which in turn can affect an observer. This is as true of the contraction of a small group of muscle fibers as of pressing a lever or pacing a figure 8" (p. 130).

The word *behavior* is usually used in reference to a larger set or class of responses that share certain physical dimensions (e.g., hand-flapping behavior) or functions (e.g., study behavior).[3] The term *response* refers to a specific instance of behavior. A good technical definition of **response** is an "*action of an organism's effector. An effector is an organ at the end of an efferent nerve fiber that is specialized for altering its environment mechanically, chemically, or in terms of other energy changes*" (Michael, 2004, p. 8, italics in original). Human effectors include the striped muscles (i.e., skeletal muscles such as biceps and quadriceps), smooth muscles (e.g., stomach and bladder muscles), and glands (e.g., adrenal gland).

Like stimulus changes in the environment, behavior can be described by its form, or physical characteristics. *Response topography* refers to the physical shape or form of behavior. For example, the hand and finger movements used to open a bag of peanuts can be described by their topographical elements. However, careful observation will reveal that the topography differs somewhat each time a person opens a bag of snacks. The difference may be significant or slight, but each "bag opening response" will vary somewhat from all others.

Although it is sometimes useful to describe behavior by its topography, behavior analysis is characterized by a *functional analysis* of the effects of behavior on the environment. A group of responses with the same function (that is, each response in the group produces the same effect on the environment) is called a **response class.** Membership in some response classes is open to responses of widely varying form (e.g., there are many ways to open a bag of peanuts), whereas the topographical variation among members of other response classes is limited (e.g., a person's signature, grip on a golf club).

Another reason underscoring the importance of a functional analysis of behavior over a structural or

---

[2]Odgen Lindsley originated the dead man test in the mid-1960s as a way to help teachers determine whether they were targeting real behaviors for measurement and change as opposed to inanimate states such as "being quiet."

[3]Most behavior analysts use the word *behavior* both as a mass noun to refer to the subject matter of the field in general or a certain type or class of behavior (e.g., operant behavior, study behavior) and as a count noun to refer to specific instances (e.g., two aggressive behaviors). The word *behavior* is often implied and unnecessary to state. We agree with Friman's (2004) recommendation that, "If the object of our interest is hitting and spitting, let's just say 'hitting' and 'spitting.' Subsequently, when we are gathering our thoughts with a collective term, we can call them behaviors" (p. 105).

topographical description is that two responses of the same topography can be vastly different behaviors depending on the controlling variables. For example, saying the word *fire* while looking the letters, *f-i-r-e,* is a vastly different behavior from yelling "*Fire!*" when smelling smoke or seeing flames in a crowded theatre.

Behavior analysts use the term **repertoire** in at least two ways. *Repertoire* is sometimes used to refer to all of the behaviors that a person can do. More often the term denotes a set or collection of knowledge and skills a person has learned that are relevant to particular settings or tasks. In the latter sense, each person has acquired or learned multiple repertoires. For example, each of us has a repertoire of behaviors appropriate for informal social situations that differs somewhat (or a lot) from the behaviors we use to navigate formal situations. And each person has repertoires with respect to language skills, academic tasks, everyday routines, recreation, and so on. When you complete your study of this text, your repertoire of knowledge and skills in applied behavior analysis will be enriched.

Environment

All behavior occurs within an environmental context; behavior cannot be emitted in an environmental void or vacuum. Johnston and Pennypacker (1993a) offered the following definition of **environment** and two critical implications of that definition for a science of behavior:

"Environment" refers to the conglomerate of real circumstances in which the organism or referenced part of the organism exists. A simple way to summarize its coverage is as "everything except the moving parts of the organism involved in the behavior." One important implication . . . is that only real physical events are included.

Another very important consequence of this conception of the behaviorally relevant environment is that it can include other aspects of the organism. That is, the environment for a particular behavior can include not only the organism's external features but physical events inside its skin. For instance, scratching our skin is presumably under control of the external visual stimulus provided by your body, particularly that part being scratched, as well as the stimulation that we call itching, which lies inside the skin. In fact, both types of stimulation very often contribute to behavioral control. This means that the skin is not an especially important boundary in the understanding of behavioral laws, although it can certainly provide observational challenges to discovering those laws. (p. 28)

The environment is a complex, dynamic universe of events that differs from instance to instance. When be-

havior analysts describe particular aspects of the environment, they talk in terms of stimulus conditions or events.[4] A good definition of **stimulus** is "an energy change that affects an organism through its receptor cells" (Michael, 2004, p. 7). Humans have receptor systems that detect stimulus changes occurring outside and inside the body. *Exteroceptors* are sense organs that detect external stimuli and enable vision, hearing, olfaction, taste, and cutaneous touch. Two types of sense organs sensitive to stimulus changes within the body are *interoceptors,* which are sensitive to stimuli originating in the viscera (e.g., feeling a stomach ache), and *proprioceptors,* which enable the kinesthetic and vestibular senses of movement and balance. Applied behavior analysts most often study the effects of stimulus changes that occur outside the body. External stimulus conditions and events are not only more accessible to observation and manipulation than are internal conditions, but also they are key features of the physical and social world in which people live.

The environment influences behavior primarily by stimulus change and not static stimulus conditions. As Michael (2004) noted, when behavior analysts speak of the presentation or occurrence of a stimulus, they usually mean stimulus change.

For example, in respondent conditioning the conditioned stimulus may be referred to as a tone. However, the relevant event is actually a change from the absence of tone to the tone sounding . . . , and although this is usually understood without having to be mentioned, it can be overlooked in the analysis of more complex phenomena. Operant discriminative stimuli, conditioned reinforcers, conditioned punishers, and conditioned motivative variables are also usually important as stimulus changes, not static conditions (Michael, 2004, pp. 7–8).[5]

Stimulus events can be described formally (by their physical features), temporally (by when they occur with respect to a behavior of interest), and functionally (by their effects on behavior). Behavior analysts used the term **stimulus class** to refer to any group of stimuli sharing a predetermined set of common elements in one or more of these dimensions.

---

[4]Although the concepts of stimulus and response have proven useful for conceptual, experimental, and applied analyses of behavior, it is important to recognize that stimuli and responses do not exist as discrete events in nature. Stimuli and responses are detectable "slices" of the continuous and ever-changing interaction between an organism and its environment chosen by scientists and practitioners because they have proven useful in understanding and changing behavior. However, the slices imposed by the behavior analyst may not parallel naturally occurring divisions.

[5]Respondent conditioning and the operant principles mentioned here are introduced later in this chapter.

Formal Dimensions of Stimuli

Behavior analysts often describe, measure, and manipulate stimuli according to their formal dimensions, such as size, color, intensity, weight, and spatial position relative to other objects. Stimuli can be nonsocial (e.g., a red light, a high-pitched sound) or social (e.g., a friend asking, "Want some more peanuts?").

Temporal Loci of Stimuli

Because behavior and the environmental conditions that influence it occur within and across time, the temporal location of stimulus changes is important. In particular, behavior is affected by stimulus changes that occur prior to and immediately after the behavior. The term **antecedent** refers to environmental conditions or stimulus changes that exist or occur prior to the behavior of interest.

Because behavior cannot occur in an environmental void or vacuum, every response takes place in the context of a particular situation or set of antecedent conditions. These antecedent events play a critical part in learning and motivation, and they do so irrespective of whether the learner or someone in the role of behavior analyst or teacher has planned or is even aware of them.

> For example, just some of the functionally relevant antecedents for a student's performance on a timed math test might include the following: the amount of sleep the student had the night before; the temperature, lighting, and seating arrangements in the classroom; the teacher reminding the class that students who beat their personal best scores on the test will get a free homework pass; and the specific type, format, and sequence of math problems on the test. Each of those antecedent variables (and others) has the potential to exert a great deal, a little, or no noticeable effect on performance as a function of the student's experiences with respect to a particular antecedent. (Heward & Silvestri, 2005, p. 1135)

A **consequence** is a stimulus change that follows a behavior of interest. Some consequences, especially those that are immediate and relevant to current motivational states, have significant influence on future behavior; other consequences have little effect. Consequences combine with antecedent conditions to determine what is learned. Again, this is true whether the individual or someone trying to change his behavior is aware of or systematically plans the consequences.

Like antecedent stimulus events, consequences may also be social or nonsocial events. Table 2.1 shows examples of various combinations of social and nonsocial antecedent and consequent events for four behaviors.

Behavioral Functions of Stimulus Changes

Some stimulus changes exert immediate and powerful control over behavior, whereas others have delayed effects, or no apparent effect. Even though we can and often do describe stimuli by their physical characteristics (e.g., the pitch and decibel level of a tone, the topography of a person's hand and arm movements), stimulus changes are understood best through a functional analysis of their effects on behavior. For example, the same decibel tone that functions in one environment and set of conditions as a prompt for checking the clothes in the dryer may function as a warning signal to fasten a seat belt in another setting or situation; the same hand and arm motion that produces a smile and a "Hi" from another person in one set of conditions receives a scowl and obscene gesture in another.

Stimulus changes can have one or both of two basic kinds of functions or effects on behavior: (a) an immediate but temporary effect of increasing or decreasing the current frequency of the behavior, and/or (b) a delayed but relatively permanent effect in terms of the frequency of that type of behavior in the future (Michael, 1995). For example, a sudden downpour on a cloudy day is likely to increase immediately the frequency of all behavior that has resulted in the person successfully escaping rain in the

Table 2.1   Antecedent (Situation) and Consequent Events Can Be Nonsocial (Italicized), Social (Boldface), or a Combination of Social and Nonsocial

Situation	Response	Consequence
Drink machine	*Deposit coins*	*Cold drink*
Five cups on table	*"One-two-three-four-five cups"*	**Teacher nods and smiles**
Friend says "turn left"	Turn left	*Arrive at destination*
Friend asks "What time is it?"	"Six-fifteen"	**Friend says "Thanks"**

From "Individual Behavior, Culture, and Social Change" by S. S. Glenn, 2004, *The Behavior Analyst, 27,* p. 136. Copyright 2004 by the Association for Behavior Analysis. Used by permission.

past, such as running for cover under an awning or pulling her jacket over her head. If the person had decided not to carry her umbrella just before leaving the house, the downpour may decrease the frequency of that behavior on cloudy days in the future.

Respondent Behavior

All intact organisms enter the world able to respond in predictable ways to certain stimuli; no learning is required. These ready-made behaviors protect against harmful stimuli (e.g., eyes watering and blinking to remove particles on the cornea), help regulate the internal balance and economy of the organism (e.g., changes in heart rate and respiration in response to changes in temperature and activity levels), and promote reproduction (e.g., sexual arousal). Each of these stimulus–response relations, called a **reflex,** is part of the organism's genetic endowment, a product of natural evolution because of its survival value to the species. Each member of a given species comes equipped with the same repertoire of unconditioned (or unlearned) reflexes. Reflexes provide the organism with a set of built-in responses to specific stimuli; these are behaviors the individual organism would not have time to learn. Table 2.2 shows examples of reflexes common to humans.

The response component of the stimulus–response reflex is called respondent behavior. **Respondent behavior** is defined as behavior that is elicited by antecedent stimuli. Respondent behavior is induced, or brought out, by a stimulus that precedes the behavior; nothing else is required for the response to occur. For example, bright light in the eyes (antecedent stimulus) will elicit pupil contraction (respondent). If the relevant body parts (i.e., receptors and effectors) are intact, pupil contraction will occur every time. However, if the eliciting stimulus is presented repeatedly over a short span of time, the strength or magnitude of the response will diminish, and in some cases the response may not occur at all. This

Table 2.2   Examples of Unconditioned Human Reflexes Susceptible to Respondent Conditioning

Unconditioned stimulus	Unconditioned response	Type of effector
Loud sound or touch to cornea	Eye blink (lid closes)	Striped muscle
Tactile stimulus under lid or chemical irritant (smoke)	Lachrimal gland secretion (eyes watering)	Gland (duct)
Irritation to nasal mucosa	Sneezing	Striped and smooth muscle
Irritation to throat	Coughing	Striped and smooth muscle
Low temperature	Shivering, surface vasoconstriction	Striped and smooth muscle
High temperature	Sweating, surface vasodilation	Gland, smooth muscle
Loud sound	Contraction of tensor tympani and stapedius muscles (reduces amplitude of ear drum vibrations)	Striped muscles
Food in mouth	Salivation	Gland
Undigestible food in stomach	Vomiting	Striped and smooth muscle
Pain stimulus to hand or foot	Hand or foot withdrawal	Striped muscle
A single stimulus that is painful or very intense or very unusual	Activation syndrome—all of the following:	
	Heart rate increase	Cardiac muscle
	Adrenaline secretion	Gland (ductless)
	Liver release of sugar into bloodstream	Gland (duct)
	Constriction of visceral blood vessels	Smooth muscle
	Dilation of blood vessels in skeletal muscles	Smooth muscle
	Galvanic skin response (GSR)	Gland (duct)
	Pupillary dilation (and many more)	Smooth muscle

From *Concepts and Principles of Behavior Analysis* (rev. ed.) by J. L. Michael, 2004, pp. 10–11. Copyright 2004 by Society for the Advancement of Behavior Analysis, Kalamazoo, MI process of gradually diminishing response strength is known as **habituation.**

Respondent Conditioning

New stimuli can acquire the ability to elicit respondents. Called **respondent conditioning,** this type of learning is associated most with the Russian physiologist Ivan Petrovich Pavlov (1849–1936).[6] While studying the digestive system of dogs, Pavlov noticed that the animals salivated every time his laboratory assistant opened the cage door to feed them. Dogs do not naturally salivate at the sight of someone in a lab coat, but in Pavlov's laboratory they consistently salivated when the door was opened. His curiosity aroused, Pavlov (1927) designed and conducted an historic series of experiments. The result of this work was the experimental demonstration of respondent conditioning.

Pavlov started a metronome just an instant before feeding the dogs. Prior to being exposed to this **stimulus–stimulus pairing** procedure, food in the mouth, an **unconditioned stimulus (US),** elicited salivation, but the sound of the metronome, a **neutral stimulus (NS),** did not. After experiencing several trials consisting of the sound of the metronome followed by the presentation of food, the dogs began salivating in response to the sound of the metronome. The metronome had thus become a **conditioned stimulus (CS),** and a **conditioned reflex** was established.[7] Respondent conditioning is most effective when the NS is presented immediately before or simultaneous with the US. However, some conditioning effects can sometimes be achieved with considerable delay between the onset of the NS and the onset of the US, and even with backward conditioning in which the US precedes the NS.

Respondent Extinction

Pavlov also discovered that once a conditioned reflex was established, it would weaken and eventually cease altogether if the conditioned stimulus was presented repeatedly in the absence of the unconditioned stimulus. For example, if the sound of the metronome was presented repeatedly without being accompanied or followed by food, it would gradually lose its ability to elicit salivation. The procedure of repeatedly presenting a conditioned stimulus without the unconditioned stimulus until the conditioned stimulus no longer elicits the conditioned response is called **respondent extinction.**

Figure 2.1 shows schematic representations of respondent conditioning and respondent extinction. In this example, a puff of air produced by a glaucoma-testing machine is the US for the eye blink reflex. The opthalmologist's finger pressing the button of the machine makes a faint clicking sound. But prior to conditioning, the clicking sound is an NS: It has no effect on eye blinking. After being paired with the air puff just a few times, the finger-on-the-button sound becomes a CS: It elicits eye blinking as a conditioned reflex.

Conditioned reflexes can also be established by stimulus–stimulus pairing of an NS with a CS. This form of respondent conditioning is called **higher order** (or *secondary*) **conditioning.** For example, secondary respondent conditioning could occur in a patient who has learned to blink at the clicking sound of the button during the glaucoma-testing situation as follows. The patient detects a slight movement of the ophthalmologist's finger (NS) just before it contacts the button that makes the clicking sound (CS). After several NS–CS pairings, movement of the ophthalmologist's finger may become a CS capable of eliciting blinking.

The form, or topography, of respondent behaviors changes little, if at all, during a person's lifetime. There are two exceptions: (a) Certain reflexes disappear with maturity, such as that of grasping an object placed in the palm of the hand, a reflex usually not seen after the age of 3 months (Bijou & Baer, 1965); and (b) several unconditioned reflexes first appear later in life, such as those related to sexual arousal and reproduction. However, during a person's lifetime an infinite range of stimuli that were previously neutral (e.g., the high-pitched whine of the dentist's drill) can come to elicit respondents (i.e., increased heartbeat and perspiration).

Respondents make up a small percentage of the behaviors typically of interest to the applied behavior analyst. As Skinner (1953) pointed out, "Reflexes, conditioned or otherwise, are mainly concerned with the internal physiology of the organism. We are most often interested, however, in behavior which has some effect upon the surrounding world" (p. 59). It is this latter type of behavior, and the process by which it is learned, that we will now examine.

---

[6]Respondent conditioning is also referred to as classical or Pavlovian conditioning. Pavlov was not the first to study reflexes; like virtually all scientists, his work was an extension of others, most notably Ivan Sechenov (1829–1905) (Kazdin, 1978). See Gray (1979) and Rescorla (1988) for excellent and interesting descriptions of Pavlov's research.

[7]*Unconditioned stimulus* and *conditioned stimulus* are the most commonly used terms to denote the stimulus component of respondent relations. However, because the terms ambiguously refer to both the immediate evocative (eliciting) effect of the stimulus change and its somewhat permanent and delayed function-altering effect (the conditioning effect on other stimuli), Michael (1995) recommended that the terms *unconditioned elicitor* (UE) and *conditioned elicitor* (CE) be used when referring to the evocative function of these variables.

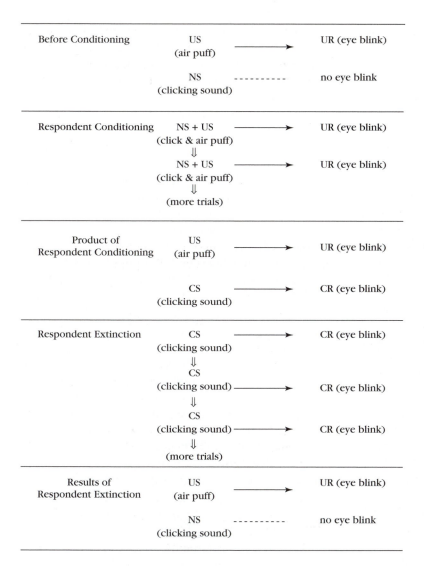

Figure 2.1 Schematic representation of respondent conditioning and respondent extinction. The top panel shows an unconditioned reflex: a puff of air (unconditioned stimulus, or US) elicits an eye blink (an unconditioned response, or UR). Before conditioning, a clicking sound (a neutral stimulus, or NS) has no effect on eye blinking. Respondent conditioning consists of a stimulus–stimulus pairing procedure in which the clicking sound is presented repeatedly just prior to, or simultaneously with, the air puff. The product of respondent conditioning is a conditioned reflex (CR): In this case the clicking sound has become a conditioned stimulus (CS) that elicits an eye blink when presented alone. The bottom two panels illustrate the procedure and outcome of respondent extinction: Repeated presentations of the CS alone gradually weaken its ability to elicit eye blinking to the point where the CS eventually becomes an NS again. The unconditioned reflex remains unchanged before, during, and after respondent conditioning.

Operant Behavior

A baby in a crib moves her hands and arms, setting in motion a mobile dangling above. The baby is literally operating on her environment, and the mobile's movement and musical sounds—stimulus changes produced by the baby's batting at the toy with her hands—are immediate consequences of her behavior. Her movements are continuously changing as a result of those consequences.

Members of a species whose only way of interacting with the world is a genetically determined fixed set of responses would find it difficult to survive, let alone thrive, in a complex environment that differed from the environment in which their distant ancestors evolved. Although respondent behavior comprises a critically important set of "hardwired" responses, respondent behavior does not provide an organism with the ability to learn from the consequences of its actions. An organism whose behavior is unchanged by its effects on the environment will be unable to adapt to a changing one.

Fortunately, in addition to her repertoire of genetically inherited respondent behaviors, our baby entered her world with some *uncommitted behavior* that is highly malleable and susceptible to change through its consequences. This type of behavior, called operant behavior, enables the baby over the course of her life to learn novel, increasingly complex responses to an ever-changing world.[8]

Operant behavior is any behavior whose future frequency is determined primarily by its history of consequences. Unlike respondent behavior, which is elicited by antecedent events, operant behavior is selected, shaped, and maintained by the consequences that have followed it in the past.

[8]The verb *emit* is used in conjunction with operant behavior. Its use fits in well with the definition of operant behavior, allowing reference to the consequences of behavior as the major controlling variables. The verb *elicit* is inappropriate to use with operant behavior because it implies that an antecedent stimulus has primary control of the behavior.

Unlike respondent behaviors, whose topography and basic functions are predetermined, operant behaviors can take a virtually unlimited range of forms. The form and function of respondent behaviors are constant and can be identified by their topography (e.g., the basic form and function of salivation is always the same). By comparison, however, the "meaning" of operant behavior cannot be determined by its topography. Operants are defined functionally, by their effects. Not only does the same operant often include responses of widely different topographies (e.g., a diner may obtain a glass of water by nodding his head, pointing to a glass of water, or saying yes to a waiter), but also, as Skinner (1969) explained, the same movements comprise different operants under different conditions.

Allowing water to pass over one's hands can perhaps be adequately described as topography, but "washing one's hands" is an "operant" defined by the fact that, when one has behaved this way in the past, one's hands have become clean—a condition which has become reinforcing because, say, it has minimized a threat of criticism or contagion. Behavior of precisely the same topography would be part of another operant if the reinforcement had consisted of simple stimulation (e.g., "tickling") of the hands or the evocation of imitative behavior in a child whom one is teaching to wash his hands. (p. 127)

Table 2.3 compares and contrasts defining features and key characteristics of respondent behavior and operant behavior.

Selection by Consequences

Human behavior is the joint product of (i) the contingencies of survival responsible for the natural selection of the species and (ii) the contingencies of reinforcement responsible for the repertoires acquired by its members, including (iii) the special contingencies maintained by the social environment. [Ultimately, of course, it is all a matter of natural selection, since operant conditioning is an evolved process, of which cultural practices are special applications.]

—B. F. Skinner (1981, p. 502)

Skinner's discovery and subsequent elucidation of operant selection by consequences have rightly been called "revolutionary" and "the bedrock on which other behavioral principles rest" (Glenn, 2004, p. 134). **Selection by consequences** "anchors a new paradigm in the life sciences known as *selectionism*. A basic tenet of this position is that all forms of life, from single cells to complex cultures, evolve as a result of selection with respect to function" (Pennypacker, 1994, pp. 12–13).

Selection by consequences operates during the lifetime of the individual organism (**ontogeny**) and is a con-

ceptual parallel to Darwin's (1872/1958) natural selection in the evolutionary history of a species (**phylogeny**). In response to the question, "Why do giraffes have long necks?" Baum (1994) gave this excellent description of natural selection:

Darwin's great contribution was to see that a relatively simple mechanism could help explain why phylogeny followed the particular course it did. The explanation about giraffes' necks requires reference to the births, lives, and deaths of countless giraffes and giraffe ancestors over many millions of years. . . . Within any population of organisms, individuals vary. They vary partly because of environmental factors (e.g., nutrition), and also because of genetic inheritance. Among the giraffe ancestors that lived in what is now the Serengeti Plain, for instance, variation in genes meant that some had shorter necks and some had longer necks. As the climate gradually changed however, new, taller types of vegetation became more frequent. The giraffe ancestors that had longer necks, being able to reach higher, got a little more to eat, on the average. As a result, they were a little healthier, resisted disease a little better, evaded predators a little better—on the average. Any one individual with a longer neck may have died without offspring, but on the average longer-necked individuals had more offspring, which tended on the average to survive a little better and produce more offspring. As longer necks became more frequent, new genetic combinations occurred, with the result that some offspring had still longer necks than those before, and they did still better. As the longer-necked giraffes continued to out-reproduce the shorter-necked ones, the average neck length of the whole population grew. (p. 52)

Just as natural selection requires a population of individual organisms with varied physical features (e.g., giraffes with necks of different lengths), operant selection by consequences requires variation in behavior. Those behaviors that produce the most favorable outcomes are selected and "survive," which leads to a more adaptive repertoire. Natural selection has endowed humans with an initial population of uncommitted behavior (e.g., babies babbling and moving their limbs about) that is highly malleable and susceptible to the influence of the consequences that follow it. As Glenn (2004) noted,

By outfitting humans with a largely uncommitted behavioral repertoire, natural selection gave our species a long leash for local behavioral adaptations. But the uncommitted repertoire of humans would be lethal without the . . . susceptibility of human behavior to operant selection. Although this behavioral characteristic is shared by many species, humans appear to be most exquisitely sensitive to behavioral contingencies of selection. (Schwartz, 1974, p. 139)

Table 2.3   Comparing and Contrasting Defining Features and Key Characteristics of Respondent and Operant Behavior

Characteristics or features	Respondent behavior	Operant behavior
Definition	Behavior elicited by antecedent stimuli.	Behavior selected by its consequences.
Basic unit	Reflex: an antecedent stimulus elicits a particular response (S–R).	Operant response class: A group of responses all of which produce the same effect on the environment; described by three-term contingency relation of antecedent stimulus conditions, behavior, and consequence (A–B–C).
Examples	Newborn's grasping and suckling to touch; pupil constriction to bright light; cough/gag to irritation in throat; salivation at smell of food; withdrawing hand from painful stimulus; sexual arousal to stimulation.	Talking, walking, playing the piano, riding a bike, counting change, baking a pie, hitting a curveball, laughing at a joke, thinking about a grandparent, reading this book.
Body parts (effectors) that most often produce the response (not a defining feature)	Primarily smooth muscles and glands (adrenaline squirt); sometimes striated (skeletal) muscles (e.g., knee-jerk to tap just below patella).	Primarily striated (skeletal) muscles; sometimes smooth muscles and glands.
Function or usefulness for individual organism	Maintains internal economy of the organism; provides a set of "ready-made" survival responses the organism would not have time to learn.	Enables effective interaction and adaptation in an ever-changing environment that could not be anticipated by evolution.
Function or usefulness for species	Promotes continuation of species indirectly (protective reflexes help individuals survive to reproductive age) and directly (reflexes related to reproduction).	Individuals whose behavior is most sensitive to consequences are more likely to survive and reproduce.
Conditioning process	Respondent (also called, classical or Pavlovian) conditioning: Through a stimulus–stimulus pairing procedure in which a neutral stimulus (NS) presented just prior to or simultaneous with an unconditioned (US) or conditioned (CS) eliciting stimulus, the NS becomes a CS that elicits the response and a conditioned reflex is created. (See Figure 2.1.)	Operant conditioning: Some stimulus changes immediately following a response increase (reinforcement) or decrease (punishment) the future frequency of similar responses under similar conditions. Previously neutral stimulus changes become conditioned reinforcers or punishers as result of stimulus–stimulus pairing with other reinforcers or punishers.
Repertoire limits	Topography and function of respondents determined by natural evolution of species (phylogeny). All biologically intact members of a species possess the same set of unconditioned reflexes. Although new forms of respondent behavior are not learned, an infinite number of conditioned reflexes may emerge in an individual's repertoire depending on the stimulus–stimulus pairing he has experienced (ontogeny).	Topography and function of each person's repertoire of operant behaviors are selected by consequences during the individual's lifetime (ontogeny). New and more complex operant response classes can emerge. Response products of some human operants (e.g., airplanes) enable some behaviors not possible by anatomical structure alone (e.g., flying).

Operant Conditioning

Operant conditioning may be seen everywhere in the multifarious activities of human beings from birth until death. . . . It is present in our most delicate discriminations and our subtlest skills; in our earliest crude habits and the highest refinements of creative thought.
—Keller and Schoenfeld (1950, p. 64)

Operant conditioning refers to the process and selective effects of consequences on behavior.[9] From an operant conditioning perspective a functional consequence is a stimulus change that follows a given behavior

[9]Unless otherwise noted, the term *behavior* will refer to operant behavior throughout the remainder of the text.

in a relatively immediate temporal sequence and alters the frequency of that type of behavior in the future. "In operant conditioning we 'strengthen' an operant in the sense of making a response more probable or, in actual fact, more frequent" (Skinner, 1953, p. 65). If the movement and sounds produced by the baby's batting at the mobile with her hands increase the frequency of hand movements in the direction of the toy, operant conditioning has occurred.

When operant conditioning consists of an increase in response frequency, *reinforcement* has taken place, and the consequence responsible, in this case the movement and sound of the mobile, would be called a **reinforcer.**[10] Although operant conditioning is used most often to refer to the "strengthening" effects of reinforcement, as Skinner described earlier, it also encompasses the principle of punishment. If the mobile's movement and musical sounds resulted in a decrease in the baby's frequency of moving it with her hands, *punishment* has occurred, and the mobile's movement and sound would be called **punishers.** Before we examine the principles of reinforcement and punishment further, it is important to identify several important qualifications concerning how consequences affect behavior.

Consequences Can Affect Only Future Behavior

Consequences affect only future behavior. Specifically, a behavioral consequence affects the relative frequency with which similar responses will be emitted in the future under similar stimulus conditions. This point may seem too obvious to merit mention because it is both logically and physically impossible for a consequent event to affect a behavior that preceded it, when that behavior is over before the consequent event occurs. Nevertheless, the statement "behavior is controlled by its consequences" raises the question. (See Box 2.1 for further discussion of this apparent logical fallacy.)

Consequences Select Response Classes, Not Individual Responses

Responses emitted because of the effects of reinforcement of previous responses will differ slightly from the previous responses but will share enough common elements with the former responses to produce the same consequence.

> Reinforcement strengthens responses which differ in topography from the response reinforced. When we reinforce pressing a lever, for example, or saying Hello, responses differing quite widely in topography grow more probable. This is a characteristic of behavior which has strong survival value . . . , since it would be very hard for an organism to acquire an effective repertoire if reinforcement strengthened only identical responses. (Skinner, 1969, p. 131)

These topographically different, but functionally similar, responses comprise an operant response class. Indeed, "an operant is a class of acts all of which have the same environmental effect" (Baum, 1994, p. 75). It is the response class that is strengthened or weakened by operant conditioning. The concept of response class is "implied when it is said that reinforcement increases the future frequency of the *type* of behavior that immediately preceded the reinforcement" (Michael, 2004, p. 9). And, as will be shown in later chapters, the concept of response class is a key to the development and elaboration of new behavior.

If consequences (or natural evolution) selected only a very narrow range of responses (or genotypes), the effect would "tend toward uniformity and a perfection of sorts" (Moxley, 2004, p. 110) that would place the behavior (or species) at risk of extinction should the environment change. For example, if the mobile's movement and sound reinforced only arm and hand movements that fell within an exact and narrow range of motion and no similar movements survived, the baby would be unable to contact that reinforcement if one day her mother mounted the mobile in a different location above the crib.

Immediate Consequences Have the Greatest Effect

Behavior is most sensitive to stimulus changes that occur immediately after, or within a few seconds of, the responses.

> It is essential to emphasize the importance of the immediacy of reinforcement. Events that are delayed more than a few seconds after the response do not *directly* increase its future frequency. When human behavior is apparently affected by long-delayed consequences, the change is accomplished by virtue of the human's complex social and verbal history, and should not be thought of as an instance of the simple strengthening of behavior by reinforcement. . . . [As with reinforcement,] the longer the time delay between the occurrence of the response and the occurrence of the stimulus change (between R and S^P), the less effective the punishment will be in changing the relevant response frequency, but not

---

[10]Skinner (1966) used rate of responding as the fundamental datum for his research. To strengthen an operant is to make it more frequent. However, rate (or frequency) is not the only measurable and malleable dimension of behavior. As we will see in Chapters 3 and 4, sometimes the duration, latency, magnitude, and/or topography of behavior changes are of pragmatic importance.

Box 2.1
When the Phone Rings:
A Dialogue about Stimulus Control

The professor was ready to move on to his next point, but a raised hand in the front row caught his attention.

Professor: Yes?

Student: You say that operant behavior, like talking, writing, running, reading, driving a car, most everything we do—you say all of those behaviors are controlled by their consequences, by things that happen *after* the response was emitted?

Professor: Yes, I said that. Yes.

Student: Well, I have a hard time with that. When my telephone rings and I pick up the receiver, that's an operant response, right? I mean, answering the phone when it rings certainly didn't evolve genetically as a reflex to help our species survive. So, we are talking about operant behavior, correct?

Professor: Correct.

Student: All right then. How can we say that my picking up my telephone is controlled by its consequence? I pick up the phone *because* it is ringing. So does everybody else. Ringing controls the response. And ringing can't be a consequence because it comes before the response.

The professor hesitated with his reply just long enough for the student to believe himself the hero, nailing a professor for pontificating about some theoretical concept with little or no relevance to the everyday real world. Simultaneously sensing victory, other students began to pile on with their comments.

Another Student: How about stepping on the brake when you see a stop sign? The sign controls the braking response, and that's not a consequence either.

A Student from the Back of the Room: And take a common classroom example. When a kid sees the problem 2 + 2 on his worksheet and he writes 4, the response of writing 4 has to be controlled by the written problem itself. Otherwise, how could anyone learn the correct answers to any question or problem?

Most of the Class: Yah, that's right!

Professor: (with a wry smile) All of you are correct. . . . So too am I.

Someone Else in the Class: What do you mean?

Professor: That was exactly my next point, and I was hoping you would pick up on it. (The professor smiled a thank you at the student who had started the discussion and went on.) All around us, every day, we are exposed to thousands of changing stimulus conditions. All of the situations you've described are excellent examples of what behavior analysts call stimulus control. When the frequency of a given behavior is higher in the presence of a given stimulus than when that stimulus is absent, we say that stimulus control is at work. Stimulus control is a very important and useful principle in behavior analysis, and it will be the subject of much discussion this semester.

But, and here's the important point: A discriminative stimulus, the antecedent event that comes before the response of interest, acquires its ability to control a particular response class because it has been associated with certain consequences in the past. So it is not just the sound of the phone's ring that causes you to pick up the receiver. It is the fact that in the past answering the phone when it was ringing was followed by a person's voice. It's that person talking to you, the consequence of picking up the receiver, that really controlled the behavior in the first place, but you pick up the phone only when you hear it ringing. Why? Because you have learned that there's someone on the other end only when the phone's ringing. So we can still speak of consequences as having the ultimate control in terms of controlling operant behavior, but by being paired with differential consequences, antecedent stimuli can indicate what kind of consequence is likely. This concept is called the three-term contingency, and its understanding, analysis, and manipulation is central to applied behavior analysis.

much is known about upper limits. (Michael, 2004, p. 110, 36 emphasis in original, words in brackets added)

Consequences Select Any Behavior

Reinforcement and punishment are "equal opportunity" selectors. No logical or healthy or (in the long run) adaptive connection between a behavior and the consequence that functions to strengthen or weaken it is necessary. Any behavior that immediately precedes reinforcement (or punishment) will be increased (or decreased).

It is the *temporal relation* between behavior and consequence that is functional, not the topographical or logical ones. "So far as the organism is concerned, the only important property of the contingency is temporal. The reinforcer simply *follows* the response. How this is brought about does not matter" (Skinner, 1953, p. 85, emphasis in original). The arbitrary nature of which behaviors are reinforced (or punished) in operant conditioning is exemplified by the appearance of idiosyncratic behaviors that have no apparent purpose or function. An example is the superstitious routine of a poker player who taps and arranges his cards in a peculiar fashion because similar movements in the past were followed by winning hands.

Operant Conditioning Occurs Automatically

Operant conditioning does not require a person's awareness. "A reinforcing connection need not be obvious to the individual [whose behavior is] reinforced" (Skinner, 1953, p. 75, words in brackets added). This statement refers to the **automaticity of reinforcement;** that is, behavior is modified by its consequences regardless of whether the individual is aware that she is being reinforced.[11] A person does not have to understand or verbalize the relation between her behavior and a consequence, or even know that a consequence has occurred, for reinforcement to "work."

Reinforcement

Reinforcement is the most important principle of behavior and a key element of most behavior change programs designed by behavior analysts (Flora, 2004; Northup, Vollmer, & Serrett, 1993). If a behavior is followed closely in time by a stimulus event and as a result the future frequency of that type of behavior increases in similar conditions, **reinforcement** has taken place.[12] Sometimes the delivery of just one reinforcer results in significant behavior change, although most often several responses must be followed by reinforcement before significant conditioning will occur.

Most stimulus changes that function as reinforcers can be described operationally as either (a) a new stimulus added to the environment (or increased in intensity), or (b) an already present stimulus removed from the environment (or reduced in intensity).[13] These two operations provide for two forms of reinforcement, called positive and negative (see Figure 2.2).

Positive reinforcement occurs when a behavior is followed immediately by the presentation of a stimulus and, as a result, occurs more often in the future. Our baby's increased frequency of batting the mobile with her hands, when doing so produces movement and music, is an example of positive reinforcement. Likewise, a child's independent play is reinforced when it increases as a result of his parent's giving praise and attention when he plays. Positive reinforcement and procedures for using it to promote desired behaviors are described in detail in Chapter 11.

When the frequency of a behavior increases because past responses have resulted in the withdrawal or termination of a stimulus, the operation is called **negative reinforcement.** Skinner (1953) used the term **aversive stimulus** to refer to, among other things, stimulus conditions whose termination functioned as reinforcement. Let us assume now that a parent programs the mobile to automatically play music for a period of time. Let us also assume that if the baby bats the mobile with hands or feet, the music immediately stops for a few seconds. If the baby bats the mobile more frequently when doing so terminates the music, negative reinforcement is at work, and the music can be called *aversive.*

Negative reinforcement is characterized by escape or avoidance contingencies. The baby escaped the music by striking the mobile with her hand. A person who jumps out of the shower when water suddenly becomes too hot

---

[11]*Automaticity of reinforcement* is a different concept from that of *automatic reinforcement,* which refers to responses producing their "own" reinforcement (e.g., scratching an insect bite). Automatic reinforcement is described in Chapter 11.

[12]The basic effect of reinforcement is often described as increasing the probability or strength of the behavior, and at times we use these phrases also. In most instances, however, we use *frequency* when referring to the basic effect of operant conditioning, following Michael's (1995) rationale: "I use frequency to refer to number of responses per unit time, or number of response occurrences relative to the number of opportunities for a response. In this way I can avoid such terms as *probability, likelihood* and *strength* when referring to behavior. The controlling variables for these terms are problematic, and because of this, their use encourages a language of intervening variables, or an implied reference to something other than an observable aspect of behavior" (p. 274).

[13]Malott and Trojan Suarez (2004) referred to these two operations as "stimulus addition" and "stimulus subtraction."

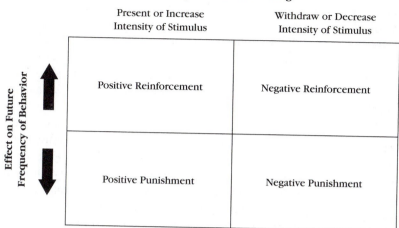

Type of Stimulus Change

	Present or Increase Intensity of Stimulus	Withdraw or Decrease Intensity of Stimulus
↑	Positive Reinforcement	Negative Reinforcement
↓	Positive Punishment	Negative Punishment

(left axis label: **Effect on Future Frequency of Behavior**)

Figure 2.2 Positive and negative reinforcement and positive and negative punishment are defined by the type of stimulus change operation that immediately follows a behavior and the effect that operation has on the future frequency of that type of behavior.

escapes the overly hot water. Likewise, when the frequency of a student's disruptive behavior increases as a result of being sent to the principal's office, negative reinforcement has occurred. By acting out, the misbehaving student escapes (or avoids altogether, depending on the timing of his misbehavior) the aversive (to him) classroom activity.

The concept of negative reinforcement has confused many students of behavior analysis. Much of the confusion can be traced to the inconsistent early history and development of the term and to psychology and education textbooks and professors who have used the term inaccurately.[14] The most common mistake is equating negative reinforcement with punishment. To help avoid the error, Michael (2004) suggested the following:

> Think about how you would respond if someone asked you (1) whether or not you like negative reinforcement; also if you were asked (2) which you prefer, positive or negative reinforcement. Your answer to the first question should be that you do indeed like negative reinforcement, which consists of the removal or termination of an aversive condition that is already present. The term *negative reinforcement* refers **only** to the termination of the stimulus. In a laboratory procedure the stimulus must, of course, be turned on and then its termination can be made contingent upon the critical response. No one wants an aversive stimulus turned on, but once it is on, its termination is usually desirable. Your answer to the second question should be that you cannot choose without knowing the specifics of the positive and negative reinforcement involved. The common error is to choose positive reinforcement, but removal of a very severe pain would certainly be preferred over the presentation of a small monetary reward or an edible, unless the food deprivation was very severe. (p. 32, italics and bold type in original)

Negative reinforcement is examined in detail in Chapter 12. Remembering that the term *reinforcement* always means an increase in response rate and that the modifiers *positive* and *negative* describe the type of stimulus change operation that best characterizes the consequence (i.e., adding or withdrawing a stimulus) should facilitate the discrimination of the principles and application of positive and negative reinforcement.

After a behavior has been established with reinforcement, it need not be reinforced each time it occurs. Many behaviors are maintained at high levels by schedules of *intermittent reinforcement*. Chapter 13 describes various *schedules of reinforcement* and their effects on behavior. However, if reinforcement is withheld for all members of a previously reinforced response class, a procedure based on the principle of **extinction,** the frequency of the behavior will gradually decrease to its prereinforcement level or cease to occur altogether. Chapter 21 describes the principle of extinction and the use of behavior change tactics based on extinction to decrease undesired behavior.

Punishment

Punishment, like reinforcement, is defined functionally. When a behavior is followed by a stimulus change that decreases the future frequency of that type of behavior in similar conditions, **punishment** has taken place. Also, like reinforcement, punishment can be accomplished by either of two types of stimulus change operations. (See the bottom two boxes of Figure 2.2.)

---

[14]For examples and discussions of the implications of inaccurate representations of principles of behavior and behaviorism in psychology and education textbooks, see Cameron (2005), Cooke (1984), Heward (2005), Heward and Cooper (1992), and Todd and Morris (1983, 1992).

Although most behavior analysts support the definition of *punishment* as a consequence that decreases the future frequency of the behavior it follows (Azrin & Holz, 1966), a wide variety of terms have been used in the literature to refer to the two types of consequence operations that fit the definition. For example, the Behavior Analyst Certification Board (BACB, 2005) and textbook authors (e.g., Miltenberger, 2004) use the terms *positive punishment* and *negative punishment,* paralleling the terms *positive reinforcement* and *negative reinforcement.* As with reinforcement, the modifiers *positive* and *negative* used with *punishment* connote neither the intention nor the desirability of the behavior change produced; they only specify how the stimulus change that served as the punishing consequence was affected—whether it was presented (positive) or withdrawn (negative).

Although the terms *positive punishment* and *negative punishment* are consistent with the terms used to differentiate the two reinforcement operations, they are less clear than the descriptive terms for the two punishment operations—*punishment by contingent stimulation* and *punishment by contingent withdrawal of a positive reinforcer*—first introduced by Whaley and Malott (1971) in their classic text, *Elementary Principles of Behavior.* These terms highlight the procedural difference between the two forms of punishment. Differences in procedure as well as in the type of stimulus change involved—reinforcer or punisher—hold important implications for application when a punishment-based behavior-reduction technique is indicated. Foxx (1982) introduced the terms *Type I punishment* and *Type II punishment* for punishment by contingent stimulation and punishment by contingent withdrawal of a stimulus, respectively. Many behavior analysts and teachers continue to use Foxx's terminology today. Other terms such as *penalty principle* have also been used to refer to negative punishment. (Malott & Trojan Suarez, 2004). However, it should be remembered that these terms are simply brief substitutes for the more complete terminology introduced by Whaley and Malott.

As with positive and negative reinforcement, numerous behavior change procedures incorporate the two basic punishment operations. Although some textbooks reserve the term *punishment* for procedures involving positive (or Type I) punishment and describe *time-out from positive reinforcement* and *response cost* as separate "principles" or types of punishment, both the methods for reducing behavior are derivatives of negative (or Type II) punishment. Therefore, time-out and response cost should be considered behavior change tactics and *not* basic principles of behavior.

Reinforcement and punishment can each be accomplished by either of two different operations, depending on whether the consequence consists of presenting a new stimulus (or increasing the intensity of a current stimulus) or withdrawing (or decreasing the intensity of) a currently present stimulus in the environment (Morse & Kelleher, 1977; Skinner, 1953). Some behavior analysts argue that from a functional and theoretical standpoint only two principles are required to describe the basic effects of behavioral consequences—reinforcement and punishment.[15] However, from a procedural perspective (a critical factor for the applied behavior analyst), a number of behavior change tactics are derived from each of the four operations represented in Figure 2.2.

Most behavior change procedures involve several principles of behavior (see Box 2.2). It is critical for the behavior analyst to have a solid conceptual understanding of the basic principles of behavior. Such knowledge permits better analysis of current controlling variables as well as more effective design and assessment of behavioral interventions that recognize the role various principles may be playing in a given situation.

Stimulus Changes That Function as Reinforcers and Punishers

Because operant conditioning involves the consequences of behavior, it follows that anyone interested in using operant conditioning to change behavior must identify and control the occurrence of relevant consequences. For the applied behavior analyst, therefore, an important question becomes, What kinds of stimulus changes function as reinforcers and punishers?

Unconditioned Reinforcement and Punishment

Some stimulus changes function as reinforcement even though the organism has had no particular learning history with those stimuli. A stimulus change that can increase the future frequency of behavior without prior pairing with any other form of reinforcement is called an **unconditioned reinforcer.**[16] For example, stimuli such as food, water, and sexual stimulation that support the biological maintenance of the organism and survival of the species often function as unconditioned reinforcers. The words *can* and *often* in the two previous sentences

---

[15]Michael (1975) and Baron and Galizio (2005) present cogent arguments for why positive and negative reinforcement are examples of the same fundamental operant relation. This issue is discussed further in Chapter 12.

[16]Some authors use the modifiers *primary* or *unlearned* to identify *unconditioned reinforcers* and *unconditioned punishers.*

Box 2.2
Distinguishing between Principles of Behavior and Behavior Change Tactics

A principle of behavior describes a basic behavior–environment relation that has been demonstrated repeatedly in hundreds, even thousands, of experiments. A **principle of behavior** describes a functional relation between behavior and one or more of its controlling variables (in the form of $b = fx$) that has thorough generality across individual organisms, species, settings, and behaviors. A principle of behavior is an empirical generalization inferred from many experiments. Principles describe how behavior works. Some examples of principles are reinforcement, punishment, and extinction.

In general, a behavior change tactic is a method for operationalizing, or putting into practice, the knowledge provided by one or more principles of behavior. A **behavior change tactic** is a research-based, technologically consistent method for changing behavior that has been derived from one or more basic principles of behavior and that possesses sufficient generality across subjects, settings, and/or behaviors to warrant its codification and dissemination. Behavior change tactics constitute the technological aspect of applied behavior analysis. Examples of behavior change procedures include backward

chaining, differential reinforcement of other behavior, shaping, response cost, and time-out.

So, principles describe how behavior works, and behavior change tactics are how applied behavior analysts put the principles to work to help people learn and use socially significant behaviors. There are relatively few principles of behavior, but there are many derivative behavior change tactics. To illustrate further, reinforcement is a behavioral principle because it describes a lawful relation between behavior, an immediate consequence, and an increased frequency of the behavior in the future under similar conditions. However, the issuance of checkmarks in a token economy or the use of contingent social praise are behavior change tactics derived from the principle of reinforcement. To cite another example, punishment is a principle behavior because it describes the established relations between the presentation of a consequence and the decreased frequency of similar behavior in the future. Response cost and time-out, on the other hand, are methods for changing behavior; they are two different tactics used by practitioners to operationalize the principle of punishment.

---

recognize the important qualification that the momentary effectiveness of an unconditioned reinforcer is a function of current **motivating operations.** For example, a certain level of food **deprivation** is necessary for the presentation of food to function as a reinforcer. However, food is unlikely to function as reinforcement for a person who has recently eaten a lot of food (a condition of **satiation**). The nature and functions of motivating operations are described in detail in Chapter 16.

Similarly, an **unconditioned punisher** is a stimulus change that can decrease the future frequency of any behavior that precedes it without prior pairing with any other form of punishment. Unconditioned punishers include painful stimulation that can cause tissue damage (i.e., harm body cells). However, virtually any stimulus to which an organism's receptors are sensitive—light, sound, and temperature, to name a few—can be intensified to the point that its delivery will suppress behavior even though the stimulus is below levels that actually cause tissue damage (Bijou & Baer, 1965).

Events that function as unconditioned reinforcers and punishers are the product of the natural evolution of the species (phylogeny). Malott, Tillema, and Glenn (1978)

described the natural selection of "rewards" and "aversives" as follows:[17]

> Some rewards and aversives control our actions because of the way our species evolved; we call these unlearned rewards or aversives. We inherit a biological structure that causes some stimuli to be rewarding or aversive. This structure evolved because rewards helped our ancestors survive, while aversives hurt their survival. Some of these unlearned rewards, such as food and fluid, help us survive by strengthening our body cells. Others help

---

[17]In addition to using *aversive stimulus* as a synonym for a *negative reinforcer,* Skinner (1953) also used the term to refer to stimuli whose onset or presentation functions as punishment, a practice continued by many behavior analysts (e.g., Alberto & Troutman, 2006; Malott & Trojan Suarez, 2004; Miltenberger, 2004). The term *aversive stimulus* (and *aversive control* when speaking of behavior change techniques involving such stimuli) is used widely in the behavior analysis literature to refer to one or more of three different behavioral functions: an aversive stimulus may be (a) a negative reinforcer if its termination increases behavior, (b) a punisher if its presentation decreases behavior, and/or (c) a motivating operation if its presentation increases the current frequency of behaviors that have terminated it in the past (see Chapter 16). When speaking or writing technically, behavior analysts must be careful that their use of omnibus terms such as *aversive* does not imply unintended functions (Michael, 1995).

our species survive by causing us to produce and care for our offspring—these stimuli include the rewarding stimulation resulting from copulation and nursing. And many unlearned aversives harm our survival by damaging our body cells; such aversives include burns, cuts and bruises. (p. 9)

While unconditioned reinforcers and punishers are critically important and necessary for survival, relatively few behaviors that comprise the everyday routines of people as they go about working, playing, and socializing are directly controlled by such events. For example, although going to work each day earns the money that buys food, eating that food is far too delayed for it to exert any direct operant control over the behavior that earned it. Remember: Behavior is most affected by its immediate consequences.

Conditioned Reinforcers and Punishers

Stimulus events or conditions that are present or that occur just before or simultaneous with the occurrence of other reinforcers (or punishers) may acquire the ability to reinforce (or punish) behavior when they later occur on their own as consequences. Called **conditioned reinforcers** and **conditioned punishers,** these stimulus changes function as reinforcers and punishers only because of their prior pairing with other reinforcers or punishers.[18] The stimulus–stimulus pairing procedure responsible for the creation of conditioned reinforcers or punishers is the same as that used for respondent conditioning except that the "outcome is a stimulus that functions as a reinforcer [or punisher] rather than a stimulus that will elicit a response" (Michael, 2004, p. 66, words in brackets added).

Conditioned reinforcers and punishers are not related to any biological need or anatomical structure; their ability to modify behavior is a result of each person's unique history of interactions with his or her environment (ontogeny). Because no two people experience the world in exactly the same way, the roster of events that can serve as conditioned reinforcers and punishers at any particular time (given a relevant motivating operation) is idiosyncratic to each individual and always changing. On the other hand, to the extent that two people have had similar experiences (e.g., schooling, profession, the culture in general), they are likely to be affected in similar ways to many similar events. Social praise and attention are examples of widely effective conditioned reinforcers in our culture. Because social attention and approval (as well as disapproval) are often paired with so many other reinforcers (and punishers), they exert powerful con-

trol over human behavior and will be featured in later chapters when specific tactics for changing behavior are presented.

Because people who live in a common culture share similar histories, it is not unreasonable for a practitioner to search for potential reinforcers and punishers for a given client among classes of stimuli that have proven effective with other similar clients. However, in an effort to help the reader establish a fundamental understanding of the nature of operant conditioning, we have purposely avoided presenting a list of stimuli that may function as reinforcers and punishers. Morse and Kelleher (1977) made this important point very well.

> Reinforcers and punishers, as environmental "things," appear to have a greater reality than orderly temporal changes in ongoing behavior. Such a view is deceptive. There is no concept that predicts reliably when events will be reinforcers or punishers; *the defining characteristics of reinforcers and punishers are how they change behavior* [italics added]. Events that increase or decrease the subsequent occurrence of one response may not modify other responses in the same way.
>
> In characterizing reinforcement as the presentation of a reinforcer contingent upon a response, the tendency is to emphasize the event and to ignore the importance of both the contingent relations and the antecedent and subsequent behavior. It is *how* [italics added] they change behavior that defines the terms *reinforcer* and *punisher;* thus it is the orderly change in behavior that is the key to these definitions. It is *not* [italics added] appropriate to presume that particular environmental events such as the presentation of food or electric shock are reinforcers or punishers until a change in the rate of responding has occurred when the event is scheduled in relation to specified responses.
>
> A stimulus paired with a reinforcer is said to have become a conditioned reinforcer, but actually it is the behaving subject that has changed, not the stimulus. . . . It is, of course, useful shorthand to speak of conditioned reinforcers . . . just as it is convenient to speak about a reinforcer rather than speaking about an event that has followed an instance of a specific response and resulted in a subsequent increase in the occurrence of similar responses. The latter may be cumbersome, but it has the advantage of empirical referents. Because many different responses can be shaped by consequent events, and because a given consequent event is often effective in modifying the behavior of different individuals, it becomes common practice to refer to reinforcers without specifying the behavior that is being modified. These common practices have unfortunate consequences. They lead to erroneous views that responses are arbitrary and that the reinforcing or punishing effect of an event is a specific property of the event itself. (pp. 176–177, 180)

The point made by Morse and Kelleher (1977) is of paramount importance to understanding behavior—

---

[18]Some authors use the modifiers *secondary* or *learned* to identify *conditioned reinforcers* and *conditioned punishers.*

environment relations. Reinforcement and punishment are not simply the products of certain stimulus events, which are then called reinforcers and punishers without reference to a given behavior and environmental conditions. There are no inherent or standard physical properties of stimuli that determine their permanent status as reinforcers and punishers. In fact, a stimulus can function as a positive reinforcer under one set of conditions and a negative reinforcer under different conditions. Just as positive reinforcers are not defined with terms such as *pleasant* or *satisfying,* aversive stimuli should not be defined with terms such as *annoying* or *unpleasant.* The terms *reinforcer* and *punisher* should not to be used on the basis of a stimulus event's assumed effect on behavior or on any inherent property of the stimulus event itself. Morse and Kelleher (1977) continued:

> When the borders of the table are designated in terms of stimulus classes (positive–negative; pleasant–noxious) and experimental operations (stimulus presentation–stimulus withdrawal), the cells of the table are, by definition, varieties of reinforcement and punishment. One problem is that the processes indicated in the cells have already been assumed in categorizing stimuli as positive or negative; a second is that there is a tacit assumption that the presentation or withdrawal of a particular stimulus will have an invariant effect. These relations are clearer if empirical operations are used to designate the border conditions. . . . The characterization of behavioral processes depends upon empirical observations. The same stimulus event, under different conditions, may increase behavior or decrease behavior. In the former case the process is called *reinforcement* and in the latter the process is called *punishment.* (p. 180)

At the risk of redundancy, we will state this important concept again. Reinforcers and punishers denote functional classes of stimulus events, the membership to which is not based on the physical nature of the stimulus changes or events themselves. Indeed, given a person's individual history and current motivational state, and the current environmental conditions, "any stimulus change can be a 'reinforcer' if the characteristics of the change, and the temporal relation of the change to the response under observation, are properly selected" (Schoenfeld, 1995, p. 184). Thus, the phrase "everything is relative" is thoroughly relevant to understanding functional behavior–environment relations.

The Discriminated Operant and Three-Term Contingency

We have discussed the role of consequences in influencing the future frequency of behavior. But operant conditioning does much more than establish a functional relation between behavior and its consequences. Oper-

ant conditioning also establishes functional relations between behavior and certain antecedent conditions.

> In contrast to *if-A-then-B* formulations (such as S-R formulations), the *AB-because-of-C* formulation is a general statement that the relation between an event (B) and its context (A) is because of consequences (C). . . . Applied to Skinner's three-term contingency, the relation between (A) the setting and (B) behavior exists because of (C) consequences that occurred for previous AB (setting-behavior) relations. The idea [is] that reinforcement strengthens the setting-behavior relation rather than simply strengthening behavior. (Moxley, 2004, p. 111)

Reinforcement selects not just certain forms of behavior; it also selects the environmental conditions that in the future will evoke (increase) instances of the response class. A behavior that occurs more frequently under some antecedent conditions than it does in others is called a **discriminated operant.** Because a discriminated operant occurs at a higher frequency in the presence of a given stimulus than it does in the absence of that stimulus, it is said to be under **stimulus control.** Answering the phone, one of the everyday behaviors discussed by the professor and his students in Box 2.1, is a discriminated operant. The telephone's ring functions as a **discriminative stimulus (S^D)** for answering the phone. We answer the phone when it is ringing, and we do not answer the phone when it is silent.

Just as reinforcers or punishers cannot be identified by their physical characteristics, stimuli possess no inherent dimensions or properties that enable them to function as discriminative stimuli. Operant conditioning brings behavior under the control of various properties or values of antecedent stimuli (e.g., size, shape, color, spatial relation to another stimulus), and what those features are cannot be determined a priori. (Stimulus control is described in detail in Chapter 17.)

> Any stimulus present when an operant is reinforced acquires control in the sense that the rate will be higher when it is present. Such a stimulus does not act as a goad; it does not elicit the response in the sense of forcing it to occur. It is simply an essential aspect of the occasion upon which a response is made and reinforced. The difference is made clear by calling it a discriminative stimulus (or S^D). An adequate formulation of the interaction between an organism and its environment must always specify three things: (1) the occasion upon which a response occurs; (2) the response itself; and (3) the reinforcing consequences. The interrelationships among them are the "contingencies of reinforcement." (Skinner, 1969, p. 7)

The discriminated operant has its origin in the three-term contingency. The **three-term contingency**—*a*ntecedent, *b*ehavior, and *c*onsequence—is sometimes

Figure 2.3 Three-term contingencies illustrating reinforcement and punishment operations.

Antecedent Stimulus	→	Behavior	→	Consequence	Future Frequency of Behavior in Similar Conditions	Operation
"Name a carnivorous dinosaur."	→	"Tyrannosaurus Rex."	→	"Well done!"	↑	Positive Reinforcement
Foul smell under kitchen sink	→	Take trash outside	→	Foul smell is gone	↑	Negative Reinforcement
Icy road	→	Drive at normal speed	→	Crash into car ahead	↓	Positive Punishment
Popup box asks, "Warn when deleting unread messages?"	→	Click on "No"	→	Important e-mail message is lost	↓	Negative Punishment

called the ABCs of behavior analysis. Figure 2.3 shows examples of three-term contingencies for positive reinforcement, negative reinforcement, positive punishment, and negative punishment.[19] Most of what the science of behavior analysis has discovered about the prediction and control of human behavior involves the three-term contingency, which is "considered the basic unit of analysis in the analysis of operant behavior" (Glenn, Ellis, & Greenspoon, 1992, p. 1332).

The term **contingency** appears in behavior analysis literature with several meanings signifying various types of temporal and functional relations between behavior and antecedent and consequent variables (Lattal, 1995; Lattal & Shahan, 1997; Vollmer & Hackenberg, 2001). Perhaps the most common connotation of contingency refers to the *dependency* of a particular consequence on the occurrence of the behavior. When a reinforcer (or punisher) is said to be **contingent** on a particular behavior, the behavior must be emitted for the consequence to occur. For example, after saying, "Name a carnivorous

dinosaur," a teacher's "Well done!" depends on the student's response, "Tyrannosaurus Rex" (or another dinosaur of the same class).[20]

The term *contingency* is also used in reference to the *temporal contiguity* of behavior and its consequences. As stated previously, behavior is selected by the consequences that immediately follow it, irrespective of whether those consequences were produced by or depended on the behavior. This is the meaning of contingency in Skinner's (1953) statement, "So far as the organism is concerned, the only important property of the contingency is temporal" (1953, p. 85).

Recognizing the Complexity of Human Behavior

Behavior—human or otherwise—remains an extremely difficult subject matter.

—B. F. Skinner (1969, p. 114)

The experimental analysis of behavior has discovered a number of basic principles—statements about how behavior works as a function of environmental variables. These principles, several of which have been introduced

---

[19]Contingency diagrams, such as those shown in Figure 2.3, are an effective way to illustrate temporal and functional relationships between behavior and various environmental events. See Mattaini (1995) for examples of other types of contingency diagrams and suggestions for using them to teach and learn about behavior analysis. State notation is another means for visualizing complex contingency relations and experimental procedures (Mechner, 1959; Michael & Shafer, 1995).

[20]The phrase *to make reinforcement contingent* describes the behavior of the researcher or practitioner: delivering the reinforcer only after the target behavior has occurred.

Chapter 2 Basic Concepts

in this chapter, have been demonstrated, verified, and replicated in hundreds and even thousands of experiments; they are scientific facts.[21] Tactics for changing behavior derived for these principles have also been applied, in increasingly sophisticated and effective ways, to a wide range of human behaviors in natural settings. A summary of what has been learned from many of those applied behavior analyses comprises the majority of this book.

The systematic application of behavior analysis techniques sometimes produces behavior changes of great magnitude and speed, even for clients whose behavior had been unaffected by other forms of treatment and appeared intractable. When such a happy (but not rare) outcome occurs, the neophyte behavior analyst must resist the tendency to believe that we know more than we do about the prediction and control of human behavior. As acknowledged in Chapter 1, applied behavior analysis is a young science that has yet to achieve anything near a complete understanding and technological control of human behavior.

A major challenge facing applied behavior analysis lies in dealing with the complexity of human behavior, especially in applied settings where laboratory controls are impossible, impractical, or unethical. Many of the factors that contribute to the complexity of behavior stem from three general sources: the complexity of the human repertoire, the complexity of controlling variables, and individual differences.

Complexity of the Human Repertoire

Humans are capable of learning an incredible range of behaviors. Response sequences, sometimes of no apparent logical organization, contribute to the complexity of behavior (Skinner, 1953). In a response chain, effects produced by one response influence the emission of other responses. Returning a winter coat to the attic leads to rediscovering a scrapbook of old family photographs, which evokes a phone call to Aunt Helen, which sets the occasion for finding her recipe for apple pie, and so on.

Verbal behavior may be the most significant contributor to the complexity of human behavior (Donahoe & Palmer, 1994; Michael, 2003; Palmer, 1991; Skinner, 1957). Not only is a problem generated when the difference between saying and doing is not recognized, but verbal behavior itself is often a controlling variable for many other verbal and nonverbal behaviors. The analysis of verbal behavior is introduced in Chapter 25.

Operant learning does not always occur as a slow, gradual process. Sometimes new, complex, repertoires

appear quickly with little apparent direct conditioning (Epstein, 1991; Sidman, 1994). One type of rapid learning has been called *contingency adduction,* a process whereby a behavior that was initially selected and shaped under one set of conditions is recruited by a different set of contingencies and takes on a new function in the person's repertoire (Adronis, 1983; Layng & Adronis, 1984). Johnson and Layng (1992, 1994) described several examples of contingency adduction in which simple (component) skills (e.g., addition, subtraction, and multiplication facts, isolating and solving for X in a simple linear equation), when taught to fluency, combined without apparent instruction to form new complex (composite) patterns of behavior (e.g., factoring complex equations).

Intertwined lineages of different operants combine to form new complex operants (Glenn, 2004), which produce response products that in turn make possible the acquisition of behaviors beyond the spatial and mechanical restraints of anatomical structure.

> In the human case, the range of possibilities may be infinite, especially because the products of operant behavior have become increasingly complex in the context of evolving cultural practices. For example, anatomical constraints prevented operant flying from emerging in a human repertoire only until airplanes were constructed as behavioral products. Natural selection's leash has been greatly relaxed in the ontogeny of operant units. (Glenn et al., 1992, p. 1332)

Complexity of Controlling Variables

Behavior is selected by its consequences. This megaprinciple of operant behavior sounds deceptively (and naively) simple. However, "Like other scientific principles, its simple form masks the complexity of the universe it describes" (Glenn, 2004, p. 134). The environment and its effects on behavior are complex.

Skinner (1957) noted that, "(1) the strength of a single response may be, and usually is, a function of more than one variable and (2) a single variable usually affects more than one response" (p. 227). Although Skinner was writing in reference to verbal behavior, multiple causes and multiple effects are characteristics of many behavior–environment relations. Behavioral covariation illustrates one type of multiple effect. For example, Sprague and Horner (1992) found that blocking the emission of one problem behavior decreased the frequency of that behavior but produced a collateral increase in other topographies of problem behaviors in the same functional class. As another example of multiple effects, the presentation of an aversive stimulus may, in addition to suppressing the future occurrences of the behavior it follows, elicit

---

[21]Like all scientific findings, these facts are subject to revision and even replacement should future research reveal better ones.

respondent behaviors and evoke escape and avoidance behaviors—three different effects from one event.

Many behaviors are the result of multiple causes. In a phenomena called *joint control* (Lowenkron, 2004), two discriminative stimuli can combine to evoke a common response class. Concurrent contingencies can also combine to make a behavior more or less likely to occur in a given situation. Perhaps we finally return our neighbor's weed trimmer not just because he usually invites us in for a cup of coffee, but also because returning the tool reduces the "guilt" we are feeling for keeping it for 2 weeks.

Concurrent contingencies often vie for control of incompatible behaviors. We cannot watch "Baseball Tonight" and study (properly) for an upcoming exam. Although not a technical term in behavior analysis, *algebraic summation* is sometimes used to describe the effect of multiple, concurrent contingencies on behavior. The behavior that is emitted is thought to be the product of the competing contingencies "canceling portions of each other out" as in an equation in algebra.

Hierarchies of response classes within what was presumed to be a single response class may be under multiple controlling variables. For example, Richman, Wacker, Asmus, Casey, and Andelman (1999) found that one topography of aggressive behavior was maintained by one type of reinforcement contingency while another form of aggression was controlled by a different contingency.

All of these complex, concurrent, interrelated contingencies make it difficult for behavior analysts to identify and control relevant variables. It should not be surprising that the settings in which applied behavior analysts ply their trade are sometimes described as places where "reinforcement occurs in a noisy background" (Vollmer & Hackenberg, 2001, p. 251).

Consequently, as behavior analysts, we should recognize that meaningful behavior change might take time and many trials and errors as we work to understand the interrelationships and complexities of the controlling variables. Don Baer (1987) recognized that some of the larger problems that beset society (e.g., poverty, substance addiction, illiteracy), given our present level of technology, might be too difficult to solve. He identified three barriers to solving such complex problems:

> (a) We are not empowered to solve these bigger remaining problems, (b) we have not yet made the analysis of how to empower ourselves to try them, and (c) we have not yet made the system-analytic task analyses that will prove crucial to solving those problems when we do empower ourselves sufficiently to try them. . . . In my experience, those projects that seem arduously long are arduous because (a) I do not have a strong interim reinforcer compared to those in the existing system for status quo and must wait for opportunities when weak control may operate, even so, or (b) I do not yet have a

correct task analysis of the problem and must struggle through trials and errors. By contrast (c) when I have an effective interim reinforcer and I know the correct task analysis of this problem, long problems are simply those in which the task analysis requires a series of many behavior changes, perhaps in many people, and although each of them is relatively easy and quick, the series of them requires not so much effort as time, and so it is not arduous but merely tedious. (pp. 335, 336–337)

Individual Differences

You did not need to read this textbook to know that people often respond very differently to the same set of environmental conditions. The fact of individual differences is sometimes cited as evidence that principles of behavior based on environmental selection do not exist, at least not in a form that could provide the basis for a robust and reliable technology of behavior change. It is then argued that because people often respond differently to the same set of contingencies, control of behavior must come from within each person.

As each of us experiences varying contingencies of reinforcement (and punishment), some behaviors are strengthened (selected by the contingencies) and others are weakened. This is the nature of operant conditioning, which is to say, human nature. Because no two people ever experience the world in exactly the same way, each of us arrives at a given situation with a different **history of reinforcement.** The repertoire of behaviors each person brings to any situation has been selected, shaped, and maintained by his or her unique history of reinforcement. Each human's unique repertoire defines him or her as a person. We are what we do, and we do what we have learned to do. "He begins as an organism and becomes a person or self as he acquires a repertoire of behavior" (Skinner, 1974, p. 231).

Individual differences in responding to current stimulus conditions, then, do not need to be attributed to differences in internal traits or tendencies, but to the orderly result of different histories of reinforcement. The behavior analyst must also consider people's varying sensitivities to stimuli (e.g., hearing loss, visual impairment) and differences in response mechanisms (e.g., cerebral palsy) and design program components to ensure that all participants have maximum contact with relevant contingencies (Heward, 2006).

Additional Obstacles to Controlling Behavior in Applied Settings

Compounding the difficulty of tackling the complexity of human behavior in the "noisy" applied settings where people live, work, and play, applied behavior analysts are sometimes prevented from implementing an effective behavior change program due to logistical, financial, sociopolitical, legal, and/or ethical factors. Most applied behavior analysts work for agencies with limited resources, which may make the data collection required for a more complete analysis impossible. In addition, participants, parents, administrators, and even the general public may at times limit the behavior analyst's options for effective intervention (e.g., "We don't want students working for tokens"). Legal or ethical considerations may also preclude determining experimentally the controlling variables for an important behavior. Ethical considerations for behavior analysts are discussed in Chapter 29.

Each of these practical complexities combines with the behavioral and environmental complexities previously mentioned to make the applied behavior analysis of socially important behavior a challenging task. However, the task need not be overwhelming, and few tasks are as rewarding or as important for the betterment of humankind.

It is sometimes expressed that a scientific account of behavior will somehow diminish the quality or enjoyment of the human experience. For example, will our increasing knowledge of the variables responsible for creative behavior lessen the feelings evoked by a powerful painting or a beautiful symphony, or reduce our appreciation of the artists who produced them? We think not, and we encourage you, as you read and study about the basic concepts introduced in this chapter and examined in more detail throughout the book, to consider Nevin's (2005) response to how a scientific account of behavior adds immeasurably to the human experience:

> At the end of *Origin of Species* (1859), Darwin invites us to contemplate a tangled bank, with its plants and its birds, its insects and its worms; to marvel at the complexity, diversity, and interdependence of its inhabitants; and to feel awe at the fact that all of it follows from the laws of reproduction, competition, and natural selection. Our delight in the tangled bank and our love for its inhabitants are not diminished by our knowledge of the laws of evolution; neither should our delight in the complex world of human activity and our love for its actors be diminished by our tentative but growing knowledge of the laws of behavior. (Tony Nevin, personal communication, December 19, 2005)

 Summary

Behavior

1. In general, behavior is the activity of living organisms.

2. Technically, behavior is "that portion of an organism's interaction with its environment that is characterized by detectable displacement in space through time of some part of the organism and that results in a measurable change in at least one aspect of the environment" (Johnston & Pennypacker, 1993a, p. 23).

3. The term *behavior* is usually used in reference to a larger set or class of responses that share certain topographical dimensions or functions.

4. *Response* refers to a specific instance of behavior.

5. *Response topography* refers to the physical shape or form of behavior.

6. A response class is a group of responses of varying topography, all of which produce the same effect on the environment.

7. *Repertoire* can refer to all of the behaviors a person can do or to a set of behaviors relevant to a particular setting or task.

Environment

8. Environment is the physical setting and circumstances in which the organism or referenced part of the organism exists.

9. Stimulus is "an energy change that affects an organism through its receptor cells" (Michael, 2004, p. 7).

10. The environment influences behavior primarily by stimulus change, not static stimulus conditions.

11. Stimulus events can be described formally (by their physical features), temporally (by when they occur), and functionally (by their effects on behavior).

12. A stimulus class is a group of stimuli that share specified common elements along formal, temporal, and/or functional dimensions.

13. Antecedent conditions or stimulus changes exist or occur prior to the behavior of interest.

14. Consequences are stimulus changes that follow a behavior of interest.

15. Stimulus changes can have one or both of two basic effects on behavior: (a) an immediate but temporary effect of increasing or decreasing the current frequency of the behavior, and/or (b) a delayed but relatively permanent effect in terms of the frequency of that type of behavior in the future.

Respondent Behavior

16. Respondent behavior is elicited by antecedent stimuli.

17. A reflex is a stimulus–response relation consisting of an antecedent stimulus and the respondent behavior it elicits (e.g., bright light–pupil contraction).

18. All healthy members of a given species are born with the same repertoire of unconditioned reflexes.

19. An unconditioned stimulus (e.g., food) and the respondent behavior it elicits (e.g., salivation) are called unconditioned reflexes.

20. Conditioned reflexes are the product of respondent conditioning: a stimulus–stimulus pairing procedure in which a neutral stimulus is presented with an unconditioned stimulus until the neutral stimulus becomes a conditioned stimulus that elicits the conditioned response.

21. Pairing a neutral stimulus with a conditioned stimulus can also produce a conditioned reflex—a process called higher order (or secondary) respondent conditioning.

22. Respondent extinction occurs when a conditioned stimulus is presented repeatedly without the unconditioned stimulus until the conditioned stimulus no longer elicits the conditioned response.

Operant Behavior

23. Operant behavior is selected by its consequences.

24. Unlike respondent behavior, whose topography and basic functions are predetermined, operant behavior can take a virtually unlimited range of forms.

25. Selection of behavior by consequences operates during the lifetime of the individual organism (ontogeny) and is a conceptual parallel to Darwin's natural selection in the evolutionary history of a species (phylogeny).

26. Operant conditioning, which encompasses reinforcement and punishment, refers to the process and selective effects of consequences on behavior:
    • Consequences can affect only future behavior.
    • Consequences select response classes, not individual responses.
    • Immediate consequences have the greatest effect.
    • Consequences select any behavior that precedes them.
    • Operant conditioning occurs automatically.

27. Most stimulus changes that function as reinforcers or punishers can be described as either (a) a new stimulus added to the environment, or (b) an already present stimulus removed from the environment.

28. Positive reinforcement occurs when a behavior is followed immediately by the presentation of a stimulus that increases the future frequency of the behavior.

29. Negative reinforcement occurs when a behavior is followed immediately by the withdrawal of a stimulus that increases the future frequency of the behavior.

30. The term *aversive stimulus* is often used to refer to stimulus conditions whose termination functions as reinforcement.

31. Extinction (withholding all reinforcement for a previously reinforced behavior) produces a decrease in response frequency to the behavior's prereinforcement level.

32. Positive punishment occurs when a behavior is followed by the presentation of a stimulus that decreases the future frequency of the behavior.

33. Negative punishment occurs when a behavior is followed immediately by the withdrawal of a stimulus that decreases the future frequency of the behavior.

34. A principle of behavior describes a functional relation between behavior and one or more of its controlling variables that has thorough generality across organisms, species, settings, and behaviors.

35. A behavior change tactic is a technologically consistent method for changing behavior that has been derived from one or more basic principles of behavior.

36. Unconditioned reinforcers and punishers function irrespective of any prior learning history.

37. Stimulus changes that function as conditioned reinforcers and punishers do so because of previous pairing with other reinforcers or punishers.

38. One important function of motivating operations is altering the current value of stimulus changes as reinforcement or punishment. For example, deprivation and satiation are motivating operations that make food more or less effective as reinforcement.

39. A discriminated operant occurs more frequently under some antecedent conditions than it does under others, an outcome called stimulus control.

40. Stimulus control refers to differential rates of operant responding observed in the presence or absence of antecedent stimuli. Antecedent stimuli acquire the ability to control operant behavior by having been paired with certain consequences in the past.

41. The three-term contingency—*a*ntecedent, *b*ehavior, and *c*onsequence—is the basic unit of analysis in the analysis of operant behavior.

42. If a reinforcer (or punisher) is contingent on a particular behavior, the behavior must be emitted for the consequence to occur.

43. All applied behavior analysis procedures involve manipulation of one or more components of the three-term contingency.

Recognizing the Complexity of Human Behavior

44. Humans are capable of acquiring a huge repertoire of behaviors. Response chains and verbal behavior also make human behavior extremely complex.

45. The variables that govern human behavior are often highly complex. Many behaviors have multiple causes.

46. Individual differences in histories of reinforcement and organic impairments also make the analysis and control of human behavior difficult.

47. Applied behavior analysts are sometimes prevented from conducting an effective analysis of behavior because of practical, logistical, financial, sociopolitical, legal, and/or ethical reasons.

PART 2

Selecting, Defining, and Measuring Behavior

An applied behavior analysis must achieve and document quantifiable changes in behavior that improve the lives of participants. Therefore, the careful selection and systematic measurement of behavior form the operational foundation of applied behavior analysis. Chapter 3 describes the methods applied behavior analysts use to identify and assess the social significance of potential target behaviors, prioritize target behaviors, and define the behaviors selected to enable accurate and reliable measurement. Chapter 4 explains the role of measurement in applied behavior analysis, identifies the dimensions by which behavior can be measured, and describes the measurement procedures commonly used by applied behavior analysts. Chapter 5 identifies common threats to the validity, accuracy, and reliability of behavioral measurement in applied settings; makes recommendations for combating those threats; and describes methods for assessing the quality of behavioral measurement.

CHAPTER 3

Selecting and Defining Target Behaviors

Key Terms

ABC recording	ecological assessment	reactivity
anecdotal observation	function-based definition	relevance of behavior rule
behavior checklist	habilitation	social validity
behavioral assessment	normalization	target behavior
behavioral cusp	pivotal behavior	topography-based definition

Behavior Analyst Certification Board® BCBA® & BCABA® Behavior Analyst Task List ©, Third Edition

Content Area 1: Ethical Considerations

1-5	Assist the client with identifying lifestyle or systems change goals and targets for behavior change that are consistent with:
(a)	the applied dimension of applied behavior analysis.
(b)	applicable laws.
(c)	the ethical and professional standards of the profession of applied behavior analysis.

Content Area 8: Selecting Intervention Outcomes and Strategies

8-2	Make recommendations to the client regarding target outcomes based on such factors as client preferences, task analysis, current repertoires, supporting environments, constraints, social validity, assessment results, and best available scientific evidence.
8-3	State target intervention outcomes in observable and measurable terms.
8-5	Make recommendations to the client regarding behaviors that must be established, strengthened, and/or weakened to attain the stated intervention outcomes.

Content Area 6: Measurement of Behavior

6-2	Define behavior in observable and measurable terms.

Applied behavior analysis is concerned with producing predictable and replicable improvements in behavior. However, not just any behavior will do: Applied behavior analysts improve *socially important behaviors* that have immediate and long-lasting meaning for the person and for those who interact with that person. For instance, applied behavior analysts develop language, social, motor, and academic skills that make contact with reinforcers and avoid punishers. An important preliminary step involves choosing the *right* behaviors to target for measurement and change.

This chapter describes the role of assessment in applied behavior analysis, including preassessment considerations, assessment methods used by behavior analysts, issues in determining the social significance of potential target behaviors, considerations for prioritizing target behaviors, and the criteria and dimensions by which selected behaviors should be defined to enable accurate and reliable measurement.

Role of Assessment in Applied Behavior Analysis

Assessment is considered a linchpin in a four-phase systematic intervention model that includes: assessment, planning, implementation, and evaluation (Taylor, 2006).

Definition and Purpose of Behavioral Assessment

Traditional psychological and educational assessments typically involve a series of norm- and/or criterion-referenced standardized tests to determine a person's strengths and weaknesses within cognitive, academic, social, and/or psychomotor domains. **Behavioral assessment** involves a variety of methods including direct observations, interviews, checklists, and tests to identify and define targets for behavior change. In addition to identifying behavior(s) to change, comprehensive behavioral assessment will discover resources, assets, significant others, competing contingencies, maintenance and generalization factors, and potential reinforcers and/or punishers that may inform or be included in intervention plans to change the target behavior (Snell & Brown, 2006).[1]

Linehan (1977) offered a succinct and accurate description of the purpose of behavioral assessment: "To figure out what the client's problem is and how to change

it for the better" (p. 31). Implicit in Linehan's statement is the idea that behavioral assessment is more than an exercise in describing and classifying behavioral abilities and deficiencies. Behavioral assessment goes beyond trying to obtain a psychometric score, grade equivalent data, or rating measure, as worthy as such findings might be for other purposes. Behavioral assessment seeks to discover the function that behavior serves in the person's environment (e.g., positive reinforcement by social attention, negative reinforcement by escape from a task). Results of a comprehensive behavioral assessment give the behavior analyst a picture of variables that increase, decrease, maintain, or generalize the behavior of interest. A well-constructed and thorough behavioral assessment provides a roadmap from which the variables controlling the behavior can be identified and understood. Consequently, subsequent interventions can be aimed more directly and have a much better chance of success. As Bourret, Vollmer, and Rapp (2004) pointed out: "The critical test of . . . assessment is the degree to which it differentially indicates an effective teaching strategy" (p. 140).

Phases of Behavioral Assessment

Hawkins (1979) conceptualized behavioral assessment as funnel shaped, with an initial broad scope leading to an eventual narrow and constant focus. He described five phases or functions of behavioral assessment: (a) screening and general disposition, (b) defining and generally quantifying problems or desired achievement criteria, (c) pinpointing the target behavior(s) to be treated, (d) monitoring progress, and (e) following up. Although the five phases form a general chronological sequence, there is often overlap. Part III of this book, "Evaluating and Analyzing Behavior Change," describes the monitoring and follow-up stages of assessment. This chapter is concerned with the preintervention functions of assessment, the selection and definition of a **target behavior**—the specific behavior selected for change.

To serve competently, applied behavior analysts must know what constitutes socially important behavior, have the technical skills to use appropriate assessment methods and instruments, and be able to match assessment data with an intervention strategy.[2] For instance, the remedial reading specialist must understand the critical behaviors of a competent reader, be able to determine which of those skills a beginning or struggling reader lacks, and deliver an appropriate and effective instruction as intervention. Likewise, the behaviorally trained marriage and family therapist must be knowledgeable about the range

---

[1]The behavioral assessment of problem behaviors sometimes includes a three-step process, called *functional behavior assessment,* for identifying and systematically manipulating antecedents and/or consequences that may be functioning as controlling variables for problems. Chapter 24 describes this process in detail.

[2]See O'Neill and colleagues (1997) for their discussion of *competing behavior analysis* as a bridge between functional assessment and subsequent intervention programs.

of behaviors that constitutes a functional family, be able to assess family dynamics accurately, and provide socially acceptable interventions that reduce dysfunctional interactions. In short, any analyst must be knowledgeable about the context of the target behavior.

A Preassessment Consideration

Before conducting an informal or formal behavioral assessment for the purpose of pinpointing a target behavior, the analyst must address the fundamental question, Who has the authority, permission, resources, and skills to complete an assessment and intervene with the behavior? If a practitioner does not have authority or permission, then his role in assessment and intervention is restricted. For example, suppose that a behavior analyst is standing in a checkout line near a parent attempting to manage an extremely disruptive child. Does the behavior analyst have the authority or permission to assess the problem or suggest an intervention to the parent? No. However, if the same episode occurred after the parent had requested assistance with such problems, the behavior analyst could offer assessment and advice. In effect, applied behavior analysts must not only recognize the role of assessment in the assessment–intervention continuum, but also recognize those situations in which using their knowledge and skills to assess and change behavior is appropriate.[3]

Assessment Methods Used by Behavior Analysts

Four major methods for obtaining assessment information are (a) interviews, (b) checklists, (c) tests, and (d) direct observation. Interviews and checklists are *indirect assessment* approaches because the data obtained from these measures are derived from recollections, reconstructions, or subjective ratings of events. Tests and direct observation are considered *direct assessment* approaches because they provide information about a person's behavior as it occurs (Miltenberger, 2004). Although indirect assessment methods often provide useful information, direct assessment methods are preferred because they provide objective data on the person's actual performance, not an interpretation, ranking, or qualitative index of that performance (Hawkins, Mathews, & Hamdan, 1999; Heward, 2003). In addition to being aware of these four major assessment methods, analysts can provide further assistance to those they serve by increasing their skills relative to the ecological implications of assessment.

---

[3]Chapter 29, "Ethical Considerations for Applied Behavior Analysts," examines this important issue in detail.

Interviews

Assessment interviews can be conducted with the target person and/or with people who come into daily or regular contact with the individual (e.g., teachers, parents, care providers).

Interviewing the Person

A behavioral interview is often a first and important step in identifying a list of potential target behaviors, which can be verified or rejected by subsequent direct observation. The interview can be considered a direct assessment method when the person's verbal behavior is of interest as a potential target behavior (Hawkins, 1975).

A behavioral interview differs from a traditional interview by the type of questions asked and the level of information sought. Behavior analysts rely primarily on *what* and *when* questions that focus on the environmental conditions that exist before, during, and after a behavioral episode, instead of *why* questions, which tend to evoke mentalistic explanations that are of little value in understanding the problem.

> Asking the clients why they do something presumes they know the answer and is often frustrating to clients, because they probably do not know and it seems that they should (Kadushin, 1972).

> "Why" questions encourage the offering of "motivational" reasons that are usually uninformative such as "I'm just lazy." Instead, the client could be asked "What happens when . . . ?" One looks closely at what actually happens in the natural environment. Attention is directed toward behavior by questions that focus on it, such as, "Can you give me an example of what [you do]?" When one example is gained, then another can be requested until it seems that the set of behaviors to which the client refers when he employs a given word have been identified. (Gambrill, 1977, p. 153)

Figure 3.1 provides examples of the kinds of *what* and *when* questions that can be applied during a behavioral assessment interview. This sequence of questions was developed by a behavioral consultant in response to a teacher who wanted to reduce the frequency of her negative reactions to acting out and disruptive students. Similar questions could be generated to address situations in homes or community settings (Sugai & Tindal, 1993).

The main purpose of the behavioral assessment interview questions in Figure 3.1 is to identify variables that occur before, during, and/or after the occurrence of negative teacher attending behavior. Identifying environmental events that correlate with the behavior provides valuable information for formulating hypotheses about the controlling function of these variables and for

Figure 3.1 Sample behavioral interview questions.

Problem Identification Interview Form

Reason for referral: The teacher requested help reducing her negative attention to acting out and disruptive students who were yelling and noncompliant.

1. In your own words, can you define the problem behaviors that prompted your request?
2. Are there any other teacher-based behaviors that concern you at this time?
3. When you engage in negative teacher attention (i.e., when you attend to yelling or noncompliant behavior), what usually happens *immediately before* the negative teacher attending behavior occurs?
4. What usually happens *after* the negative teacher attention behavior occurs?
5. What are the students' reactions when you yell or attend to their noncompliant behavior?
6. What behaviors would the students need to perform so that you would be less likely to attend to them in a negative way?
7. Have you tried other interventions? What has been their effect?

---

planning interventions. Hypothesis generation leads to experimental manipulation and the discovery of functional relations (see Chapter 24).

As an outgrowth of being interviewed, clients may be asked to complete questionnaires or so-called needs assessment surveys. Questionnaires and needs assessment surveys have been developed in many human services areas to refine or extend the interview process (Altschuld & Witkin, 2000). Sometimes as a result of an initial interview, the client is asked to self-monitor her behavior in particular situations. Self-monitoring can entail written or tape-recorded accounts of specific events.[4] Client-collected data can be useful in selecting and defining target behaviors for further assessment or for intervention. For example, a client seeking behavioral treatment to quit smoking might self-record the number of cigarettes he smokes each day and the conditions when he smokes (e.g., morning coffee break, after dinner, stuck in a traffic jam). These client-collected data may shed light on antecedent conditions correlated with the target behavior.

Interviewing Significant Others

Sometimes the behavior analyst either cannot interview the client personally or needs information from others who are important in the client's life (e.g., parents, teachers, coworkers). In such cases, the analyst will interview one or more of these significant others. When asked to describe a behavioral problem or deficit, significant others often begin with general terms that do not identify specific behaviors to change and often imply causal factors intrinsic to the client (e.g., she is afraid, aggressive, unmotivated or lazy, withdrawn). By asking variations of *what, when,* and *how* questions, the behavior analyst can

help significant others describe the problem in terms of specific behaviors and environmental conditions and events associated with those behaviors. For example, the following questions could be used in interviewing parents who have asked the behavior analyst for help because their child is "noncompliant" and "immature."

- What is Derek doing when you would be most likely to call him immature or noncompliant?
- During what time of day does Derek seem most immature (or noncompliant)? What does he do then?
- Are there certain situations or places where Derek is noncompliant or acts immature? If so, where, and what does he do?
- How many different ways does Derek act immature (or noncompliant)?
- What's the most frequent noncompliant thing that Derek does?
- How do you and other family members respond when Derek does these things?
- If Derek were to be more mature and independent as you would like, what would he do differently than he does now?

Figure 3.2 shows a form that parents or significant others can use to begin to identify target behaviors.

In addition to seeking help from significant others in identifying target behaviors and possible controlling variables that can help inform an intervention plan, the behavior analyst can sometimes use the interview to determine the extent to which significant others are willing and able to help implement an intervention to change the behavior. Without the assistance of parents, siblings, teacher aides, and staff, many behavior change programs cannot be successful.

---

[4]Procedures for self-monitoring, a major component of many self-management interventions, are described in Chapter 27.

Figure 3.2   Form that parents or significant others in a person's life can use to generate starter lists of possible target behaviors.

The 5 + 5 Behavior List

Child's name: _____

Person completing this list: _____

Listmaker's relationship to child: _____

5 good things _____ does now	5 things I'd like to see _____ learn to do more (or less) often
1. _____	1. _____
2. _____	2. _____
3. _____	3. _____
4. _____	4. _____
5. _____	5. _____

Directions: Begin by listing in the left-hand column 5 desirable behaviors your child (or student) does regularly now; things that you want him or her to continue doing. Next, list in the right-hand column 5 behaviors you would like to see your child do more often (things that your child does sometimes but should do with more regularity) and/or undesirable behaviors that you want him or her to do less often (or not at all). You may list more than 5 behaviors in either column, but try to identify at least 5 in each.

Checklists

Behavior checklists and rating scales can be used alone or in combination with interviews to identify potential target behaviors. A **behavior checklist** provides descriptions of specific behaviors (usually in hierarchical order) and the conditions under which each behavior should occur. Situation- or program-specific checklists can be created to assess one particular behavior (e.g., tooth brushing) or a specific skill area (e.g., a social skill), but most practitioners use published checklists to rate a wide range of areas (e.g., *The Functional Assessment Checklist for Teachers and Staff* [March et al., 2000]).

Usually a Likert scale is used that includes information about antecedent and consequence events that may affect the frequency, intensity, or duration of behaviors. For example, the *Child Behavior Checklist (CBCL)* comes in teacher report, parent report, and child report forms and can be used with children ages 5 through 18 (Achenbach & Edelbrock, 1991). The teacher's form includes 112 behaviors (e.g., "cries a lot," "not liked by other pupils") that are rated on a 3-point scale: "not true," "somewhat or sometimes true," or "very true or often true." The *CBCL* also includes items representing social competencies and adaptive functioning such as getting along with others and acting happy.

The *Adaptive Behavior Scale—School (ABS-S)* (Lambert, Nihira, & Leland, 1993) is another frequently used checklist for assessing children's adaptive behavior. Part 1 of the *ABS-S* contains 10 domains related to independent functioning and daily living skills (e.g., eating, toilet use, money handling, numbers, time); Part 2 assesses the child's level of maladaptive (inappropriate) behavior in seven areas (e.g., trustworthiness, self-abusive behavior, social engagement). Another version of the *Adaptive Behavior Scale,* the *ABS-RC,* assesses adaptive behavior in residential and community settings (Nihira, Leland, & Lambert, 1993).

Information obtained from good behavior checklists (i.e., those with objectively stated items of relevance to the client's life) can help identify behaviors worthy of more direct and intensive assessment.

Standardized Tests

Literally thousands of standardized tests and assessment devices have been developed to assess behavior (cf., Spies & Plake, 2005). Each time a *standardized test* is administered, the same questions and tasks are presented in a specified way and the same scoring criteria and procedures are used. Some standardized tests yield norm-referenced scores. When a *norm-referenced test* is being developed, it is administered to a large sample of people selected at random from the population for whom the test is intended. Test scores of people in the norming sample are then used to represent how scores on the test are generally distributed throughout the population.

The majority of standardized tests on the market, however, are not conducive to behavioral assessment because the results cannot be translated directly into target behaviors for instruction or treatment. For example, results from standardized tests commonly used in the schools, such as the *Iowa Tests of Basic Skills* (Hoover, Hieronymus, Dunbar, & Frisbie, 1996), the *Peabody Individual Achievement Test–R/NU* (Markwardt, 2005), and the *Wide Range Achievement Test—3* (WRAT) (Wilkinson, 1994), might indicate that a fourth-grader is performing at the third-grade level in mathematics and at the first-grade level in reading. Such information might be useful in determining how the student performs in these subjects compared to students in general, but it neither indicates the specific math or reading skills the student has mastered nor provides sufficient direct context with which to launch an enrichment or remedial program. Further, behavior analysts may not be able to actually administer a given test because of licensing requirements. For instance, only a licensed psychologist can administer some types of intelligence tests and personality inventories.

Tests are most useful as behavioral assessment devices when they provide a direct measure of the person's performance of the behaviors of interest. In recent years, an increasing number of behaviorally oriented teachers have recognized the value of criterion-referenced and curriculum-based assessments to indicate exactly which skills students need to learn and, equally important, which skills they have mastered (Browder, 2001; Howell, 1998). Curriculum-based assessments can be considered direct measures of student performance because the data that

are obtained bear specifically on the daily tasks that the student performs (Overton, 2006).

Direct Observation

Direct and repeated observations of the client's behavior in the natural environment are the preferred method for determining which behaviors to target for change. A basic form of direct continuous observation, first described by Bijou, Peterson, and Ault (1968), is called **anecdotal observation,** or **ABC recording.** With anecdotal observation the observer records a descriptive, temporally sequenced account of all behavior(s) of interest and the antecedent conditions and consequences for those behaviors as those events occur in the client's natural environment (Cooper, 1981). This technique produces behavioral assessment data that can be used to identify potential target behaviors.

Rather than providing data on the frequency of a specific behavior, anecdotal observation yields an overall description of a client's behavior patterns. This detailed record of the client's behavior within its natural context provides accountability to the individual and to others involved in the behavior change plan and is extremely helpful in designing interventions (Hawkins et al., 1999).

Accurately describing behavioral episodes as they occur in real time is aided by using a form to record relevant antecedents, behaviors, and consequences in temporal sequence. For example, Lo (2003) used the form shown in Figure 3.3 to record anecdotal observations of a fourth-grade special education student whose teacher had complained that the boy's frequent talk-outs and out-of-seat behavior were impairing his learning and often disrupted the entire class. (ABC observations can also be recorded on a checklist of specific antecedents, behaviors, and consequent events individually created for the client based on information from interviews and/or initial observations. See Figure 25.3.)

ABC recording requires the observer to commit full attention to the person being observed. A classroom teacher, for example, could not use this assessment procedure while engaging in other activities, such as managing a reading group, demonstrating a mathematics problem on the chalkboard, or grading papers. Anecdotal observation is usually conducted for continuous periods of 20 to 30 minutes, and when responsibilities can be shifted temporarily (e.g., during team teaching). Following are some additional guidelines and suggestions for conducting anecdotal direct observations:

- Write down everything the client does and says and everything that happens to the client.

Figure 3.3   Example of an anecdotal ABC recording form.

Student: <u>Student 4</u>   Date: <u>3/10/03</u>   Setting: <u>SED resource room (math period)</u>

Observer: <u>Experimenter</u>   Starting time: <u>2:40 P.M.</u>   Ending time: <u>3:00 P.M.</u>

Time	Antecedents (A)	Behavior (B)	Consequences (C)
2:40	T tells students to work quietly on their math worksheets	Walks around the room and looks at other students	T says, "Everyone is working, but you. I don't need to tell you what to do."
	✓	Sits down, makes funny noises with mouth	A female peer says: "Would you please be quiet?"
	✓	Says to the peer, "What? Me?" Stops making noises	Peer continues to work
2:41	Math worksheet	Sits in his seat and works quietly	No one pays attention to him
	Math worksheet	Pounds on desk with hands	SED aide asks him to stop
2:45	Math worksheet	Makes vocal noises	Ignored by others
	Math worksheet	Yells-out T's name three times and walks to her with her worksheet	T helps him with the questions
2:47	Everyone is working quietly	Gets up and leaves his seat	T asks him to sit down and work
	✓	Sits down and works	Ignored by others
	Everyone is working quietly	Gets up and talks to a peer	T asks him to sit down and work
	✓	Comes back to his seat and works	Ignored by others
2:55	Math worksheet, no one is attending to him	Hand grabs a male peer and asks him to help on the worksheet	Peer refuses
	✓	Asks another male peer to help him	Peer helps him
2:58	✓	Tells T he's finished the work and it's his turn to work on computer	T asks him to turn in his work and tells him that it's not his turn on the computer
	✓	Whines about why it's not his turn	T explains to him that other students are still working on the computer and he needs to find a book to read
	✓	Stands behind a peer who is playing computer and watches him play the game	Ignored by T

Adapted from *Functional Assessment and Individualized Intervention Plans: Increasing the Behavior Adjustment of Urban Learners in General and Special Education Settings* (p. 317) by Y. Lo. Unpublished doctoral dissertation. Columbus, OH: The Ohio State University. Used by permission.

- Use homemade shorthand or abbreviations to make recording more efficient, but be sure the notes can be and are accurately expanded immediately after the observation session.
- Record only actions that are seen or heard, not interpretations of those actions.
- Record the temporal sequence of each response of interest by writing down what happened just before and just after it.
- Record the estimated duration of each instance of the client's behavior. Mark the beginning and ending time of each behavioral episode.
- Be aware that continuous anecdotal observation is often an obtrusive recording method. Most people behave differently when they see someone with a pencil and clipboard staring at them. Knowing this, observers should be as unobtrusive as possible (e.g., stay a reasonable distance away from the subject).

• Carry out the observations over a period of several days so that the novelty of having someone observe the client will lessen and the repeated observations can produce a valid picture of day-to-day behavior.

Ecological Assessment

Behavior analysts understand that human behavior is a function of multiple events and that many events have multiple effects on behavior (cf., Michael, 1995). An ecological approach to assessment recognizes the complex interrelationships between environment and behavior. In an **ecological assessment** a great deal of information is gathered about the person and the various environments in which that person lives and works. Among the many factors that can affect a person's behavior are physiological conditions, physical aspects of the environment (e.g., lighting, seating arrangements, noise level), interactions with others, home environment, and past reinforcement history. Each of these factors represents a potential area for assessment.

Although a thorough ecological assessment will provide a tremendous amount of descriptive data, the basic purpose of assessment—to identify the most pressing behavior problem and possible ways to alleviate it—should not be forgotten. It is easy to go overboard with the ecological approach, gathering far more information than necessary. Ecological assessment can be costly in terms of professional and client time, and it may raise ethical and perhaps legal questions regarding confidentiality (Koocher & Keith-Spiegel, 1998). Ultimately, good judgment must be used in determining how much assessment information is necessary. Writing about the role of ecological assessment for special education teachers, Heron and Heward (1988) suggested that

> The key to using an ecological assessment is to know *when* to use it. Full-scale ecological assessments for their own sake are not recommended for teachers charged with imparting a great number of important skills to many children in a limited amount of time. In most cases, the time and effort spent conducting an exhaustive ecological assessment would be better used in direct instruction. While the results of an ecological assessment might prove interesting, they do not always change the course of a planned intervention. Under what conditions then will an ecological assessment yield data that will significantly affect the course of treatment? Herein lies the challenge. Educators must strive to become keen discriminators of: (1) situations in which a planned intervention has the potential for affecting student behaviors other than the behavior of concern; and (2) situations in which an intervention, estimated to be effective if the target behavior were viewed in isolation, may be ineffective because other ecological variables

come into play. Regardless of the amount and range of information available concerning the student, a teacher must still make instructional decisions based on an empirical analysis of the target behavior. Ultimately, this careful analysis (i.e., direct and daily measurement) of the behavior of interest may be ineffective because other ecological variables come into play. (p. 231)

Reactive Effects of Direct Assessment

Reactivity refers to the effects of an assessment procedure on the behavior being assessed (Kazdin, 1979). Reactivity is most likely when observation is *obtrusive*—that is, the person being observed is aware of the observer's presence and purpose (Kazdin, 2001). Numerous studies have demonstrated that the presence of observers in applied settings can influence a subject's behavior (Mercatoris & Craighead, 1974; Surratt, Ulrich, & Hawkins, 1969; White, 1977). Perhaps the most obtrusive assessment procedures are those that require the subject to monitor and record her own behavior. Research on self-monitoring shows that the procedure commonly affects the behavior under assessment (Kirby, Fowler, & Baer, 1991).[5]

Although research suggests that even when the presence of an observer alters the behavior of the people being observed, the reactive effects are usually temporary (e.g., Haynes & Horn, 1982; Kazdin, 1982). Nevertheless, behavior analysts should use assessment methods that are as unobtrusive as possible, repeat observations until apparent reactive effects subside, and take possible reactive effects into account when interpreting the results of observations.

Assessing the Social Significance of Potential Target Behaviors

In the past, when a teacher, therapist, or other human services professional determined that a client's behavior should be changed, few questions were asked. It was assumed that the change would be beneficial to the person. This presumption of benevolence is no longer ethically acceptable (not that it ever was). Because behavior analysts possess an effective technology to change behavior in predetermined directions, accountability must be served. Both the goals and the rationale supporting

---

[5]Reactive effects of assessment are not necessarily negative. Self monitoring has become as much a treatment procedure as it is an assessment procedure; see Chapter 27.

behavior change programs must be open to critical examination by the consumers (clients and their families) and by others who may be affected (society) by the behavior analyst's work. In selecting target behaviors, practitioners should consider *whose* behavior is being assessed—and changed—and why.

Target behaviors should not be selected for the primary benefit of others (e.g., "Be still, be quiet, be docile," in Winett & Winkler, 1972), to simply maintain the status quo (Budd & Baer, 1976; Holland, 1978), or because they pique the interest of someone in a position to change the behaviors, as illustrated in the following incident:

> A bright, conscientious graduate student was interested in doing his thesis in a program for seriously maladjusted children. He wanted to teach cursive writing to a . . . child [who] could not read (except his name), print, or even reliably identify all the letters of the alphabet. I asked "Who decided that was the problem to work on next?" (Hawkins, 1975, p. 195)

Judgments about which behaviors to change are difficult to make. Still, practitioners are not without direction when choosing target behaviors. Numerous authors have suggested guidelines and criteria for selecting target behaviors (e.g., Ayllon & Azrin, 1968; Bailey & Lessen, 1984; Bosch & Fuqua, 2001; Hawkins, 1984; Komaki, 1998; Rosales-Ruiz & Baer, 1997), all of which revolve around the central question, To what extent will the proposed behavior change improve the person's life experience?

A Definition of Habilitation

Hawkins (1984) suggested that the potential meaningfulness of any behavior change should be judged within the context of **habilitation,** which he defined as follows:

> Habilitation (adjustment) is the degree to which the person's repertoire maximizes short and long term reinforcers for that individual and for others, and minimizes short and long term punishers. (p. 284)

Hawkins (1986) cited several advantages of the definition in that it (a) is conceptually familiar to behavior analysts, (b) defines treatment using measurable outcomes, (c) is applicable to a wide range of habilitative activities, (d) deals with individual and societal needs in a nonjudgmental way, (e) treats adjustment along a continuum of adaptive behavior and is not deficit driven, and (f) is culturally and situationally relative.

Judgments about how much a particular behavior change will contribute to a person's overall habilitation (adjustment, competence) are difficult to make. In many cases we simply do not know how useful or functional a given behavior change will prove to be (Baer, 1981, 1982),

even when its short-term utility can be predicted. Applied behavior analysts, however, must place the highest importance on the selection of target behaviors that are truly useful and habilitative (Hawkins, 1991). In effect, if a potential target behavior meets the habilitation standard, then the individual is much more likely to acquire additional reinforcement in the future and avoid punishment.

From both ethical and pragmatic perspectives, any behavior targeted for change must benefit the person either directly or indirectly. Examining potential target behaviors according to the 10 questions and considerations described in the following sections should help clarify their relative social significance and habilitative value. Figure 3.4 summarizes these considerations in a worksheet format that can be used in evaluating the social significance of potential target behaviors.

Is This Behavior Likely to Produce Reinforcement in the Client's Natural Environment After Treatment Ends?

To determine whether a particular target behavior is functional for the client, the behavior analyst, significant others, and whenever possible the client should ask whether the proposed behavior change will be reinforced in the person's daily life. Ayllon and Azrin (1968) called this the **relevance of behavior rule;** it means that a target behavior should be selected only when it can be determined that the behavior is likely to produce reinforcement in the person's natural environment. The likelihood that a new behavior will result in reinforcement after the behavior change program is terminated is the primary determinant of whether the new behavior will be maintained, thereby having the possibility of long-term benefits for that person.

Judging whether occurrences of the target behavior will be reinforced in the absence of intervention can also help to clarify whether the proposed behavior change is primarily for the individual's benefit or for someone else. For instance, despite parental wishes or pressure, it would be of little value to try to teach math skills to a student with severe developmental disabilities with pervasive deficits in communication and social skills. Teaching communication skills that would enable the student to have more effective interactions in her *current* environment should take precedence over skills that she might be able to use in the *future* (e.g., making change in the grocery store). Sometimes target behaviors are selected appropriately not because of their direct benefit to the person, but because of an important indirect benefit. Indirect benefits can occur in several different ways as described by the three questions that follow.

Figure 3.4 Worksheet for evaluating the social significance of potential target behaviors.

Client's/Student's name: _____ Date: _____

Person completing worksheet: _____

Rater's relationship to client/student: _____

Behavior: _____

Considerations	Assessment			Rationale/Comments
Is this behavior likely to produce reinforcement in the client's natural environment after intervention ends?	Yes	No	Not sure	
Is this behavior a necessary prerequisite for a more complex and functional skill?	Yes	No	Not sure	
Will this behavior increase the client's access to environments in which other important behaviors can be acquired and used?	Yes	No	Not sure	
Will changing this behavior predispose others to interact with the client in a more appropriate and supportive manner?	Yes	No	Not sure	
Is this behavior a pivotal behavior or behavioral cusp?	Yes	No	Not sure	
Is this an age-appropriate behavior?	Yes	No	Not sure	
If this behavior is to be reduced or eliminated from the client's repertoire, has an adaptive and functional behavior been selected to replace it?	Yes	No	Not sure	
Does this behavior represent the actual problem/goal, or is it only indirectly related?	Yes	No	Not sure	
Is this "just talk," or is it the real behavior of interest?	Yes	No	Not sure	
If the goal itself is not a specific behavior (e.g., losing 20 lbs.), will this behavior help achieve it?	Yes	No	Not sure	

Summary notes/comments: _____

_____

_____

Is This Behavior a Necessary Prerequisite for a Useful Skill?

Some behaviors that, in and of themselves, are not important are targeted for instruction because they are necessary prerequisites to learning other functional behaviors. For example, advances in reading research have demonstrated that teaching phonemic awareness skills (e.g., sound isolation: What is the first sound in *nose?*; phoneme segmentation: What sounds do you hear in the word *fat?*; odd word out: What word starts with a different sound: *cat, couch, fine, cake?*) to nonreaders has positive effects on their acquisition of reading skills (National Reading Panel, 2000).[6]

Will This Behavior Increase the Client's Access to Environments in Which Other Important Behaviors Can Be Learned and Used?

Hawkins (1986) described the targeting of "access behaviors" as a means of producing indirect benefits to clients. For example, special education students are sometimes taught to complete their workbook pages neatly, interact politely with the general education classroom teacher, and stay in their seats during the teacher's presentation. These behaviors are taught with the expectation that they will increase acceptance into a general education classroom, thereby increasing access to general education and instructional programs.

Will Changing This Behavior Predispose Others to Interact with the Client in a More Appropriate and Supportive Manner?

Another type of indirect benefit occurs when a behavior change is of primary interest to a significant other in the person's life. The behavior change may enable the significant other to behave in a manner more beneficial to the person. For example, suppose a teacher wants the parents of his students to implement a home-based instruction program, believing that the students' language skills would improve considerably if their parents spent just 10 minutes per night playing a vocabulary game with them. In meeting with one student's parents, however, the

teacher realizes that although the parents are also concerned about poor language skills, they have other and, in their opinion, more pressing needs—the parents want their child to clean her room and help with the dinner dishes. Even though the teacher believes that straightening up a bedroom and washing dishes are not as important to the child's ultimate welfare as language development, these tasks may indeed be important target behaviors if a sloppy room and a sink full of dirty dishes impede positive parent–child interactions (including playing the teacher's vocabulary-building games). In this case, the daily chores might be selected as the target behaviors for the direct, immediate benefit of the parents, with the expectation that the parents will be more likely to help their daughter with school-related activities if they are happier with her because she straightens her bedroom and helps with the dishes.

Is This Behavior a Behavioral Cusp or a Pivotal Behavior?

Behavior analysts often use a building block method to develop repertoires for clients. For example, in teaching a complex skill (e.g., two-digit multiplication), simpler and more easily attainable skills are taught first (e.g., addition, regrouping, single-digit multiplication), or with shoe tying, crossing laces, making bows, and tying knots are taught systematically. As skill elements are mastered, they are linked (i.e., chained) into increasingly complex repertoires. At any point along this developmental skill continuum when the person performs the skill to criterion, reinforcement follows, and the practitioner makes the determination to advance to the next skill level. As systematic and methodical as this approach has proven to be, analysts are researching ways to improve the efficiency of developing new behavior. Choosing target behaviors that are behavioral cusps and pivotal behaviors may increase this efficiency.

Behavioral Cusps.

Rosales-Ruiz and Baer (1997) defined a **behavioral cusp** as:

> a behavior that has consequences beyond the change itself, some of which may be considered important. . . . What makes a behavior change a cusp is that it exposes the individual's repertoire to new environments, especially new reinforcers and punishers, new contingencies, new responses, new stimulus controls, and new communities of maintaining or destructive contingencies. When some or all of those events happen, the individual's repertoire expands; it encounters a differentially selective maintenance of the new as well as some

---

[6]A target behavior's indirect benefit as a necessary prerequisite for another important behavior should not be confused with indirect teaching. Indirect teaching involves selecting a target behavior different from the true purpose of the behavior because of a belief that they are related (e.g., having students with poor reading skills practice shape discrimination or balance beam walking). The importance of directness in target behavior selection is discussed later in this section.

old repertoires, and perhaps that leads to some further cusps. (p. 534)

Rosales-Ruiz and Baer (1997) cited as examples of possible behavioral cusps behaviors such as crawling, reading, and generalized imitation, because they "*suddenly open* the child's world to new contingencies that will develop many new, important behaviors" (p. 535, emphasis added). Cusps differ from component or prerequisite behaviors. For an infant, specific arm, head, leg, or positional movements would be component behaviors for crawling, but crawling is the cusp because it enables the infant to contact new environments and stimuli as sources of motivation and reinforcement (e.g., toys, parents), which in turn opens a new world of contingencies that can further shape and select other adaptive behaviors.

> The importance of cusps is judged by (a) the extent of the behavior changes they systematically enable, (b) whether they systematically expose behavior to new cusps, and (c) the audience's view of whether these changes are important for the organism, which in turn is often controlled by societal norms and expectations of what behaviors should develop in children and when that development should happen. (Rosales-Ruiz & Baer, 1997, p. 537)

Bosch and Fuqua (2001) suggested that clarifying "a priori dimensions for determining if a behavior might be a cusp is an important step in realizing the potential of the cusp concept" (p. 125). They stated that a behavior might be a cusp if it meets one or more of five criteria: "(a) access to new reinforcers, contingencies, and environments; (b) social validity; (c) generativeness; (d) competition with inappropriate responses; and (e) number and the relative importance of people affected" (p. 123). The more criteria that a behavior satisfies, the stronger the case that the behavior is a cusp. By identifying and assessing target behaviors based on their cusp value, practitioners may indeed open "a new world" of far-reaching potential for those they serve.

Pivotal Behavior

Pivotal behavior has emerged as an interesting and promising concept in behavioral research, especially as it relates to the treatment of people with autism and developmental disabilities. R. L. Koegel and L. K. Koegel and their colleagues have examined pivotal behavior assessment and treatment approaches across a wide range of areas (e.g., social skills, communication ability, disruptive behaviors) (Koegel & Frea, 1993; Koegel & Koegel, 1988; Koegel, Koegel, & Schreibman, 1991). Briefly stated, a **pivotal behavior** is a behavior that, once

learned, produces corresponding modifications or co-variations in other adaptive untrained behaviors. For instance, Koegel, Carter, and Koegel (2003) indicated that teaching children with autism to "self-initiate" (e.g., approach others) may be a pivotal behavior. The "longitudinal outcome data from children with autism suggest that the presence of initiations may be a prognostic indicator of more favorable long-term outcomes and therefore may be 'pivotal' in that they appear to result in widespread positive changes in a number of areas" (p. 134). That is, improvement in self-initiations may be pivotal for the emergence of untrained response classes, such as asking questions and increased production and diversity of talking.

Assessing and targeting pivotal behaviors can be advantageous for both the practitioner and the client. From the practitioner's perspective, it might be possible to assess and then train pivotal behaviors within relatively few sessions that would later be emitted in untrained settings or across untrained responses (Koegel et al., 2003). From the client's perspective, learning a pivotal behavior would shorten intervention, provide the person with a new repertoire with which to interact with his environment, improve the efficiency of learning, and increase the chances of coming into contact with reinforcers. As Koegel and colleagues concluded: "The use of procedures that teach the child with disabilities to evoke language learning opportunities in the natural environment may be particularly useful for speech and language specialists or other special educators who desire ongoing learning outside of language teaching sessions" (p. 143).

Is This an Age-Appropriate Behavior?

A number of years ago it was common to see adults with developmental disabilities being taught behaviors that a nondisabled adult would seldom, if ever, do. It was thought—perhaps as a by-product of the concept of mental age—that a 35-year-old woman with the verbal skills of a 10-year-old should play with dolls. Not only is the selection of such target behaviors demeaning, but their occurrence lessens the probability that other people in the person's environment will set the occasion for and reinforce more desirable, adaptive behaviors, which could lead to a more normal and rewarding life.

The principle of **normalization** refers to the use of progressively more typical environments, expectations, and procedures "to establish and/or maintain personal behaviors which are as culturally normal as possible" (Wolfensberger, 1972, p. 28). Normalization is not a single technique, but a philosophical position that holds the goal of achieving the greatest possible physical and social integration of people with disabilities into the mainstream of society.

In addition to the philosophical and ethical reasons for selecting age- and setting-appropriate target behaviors, it should be reemphasized that adaptive, independent, and social behaviors that come into contact with reinforcement are more likely to be maintained than are behaviors that do not. For example, instruction in leisure-time skills such as sports, hobbies, and music-related activities would be more functional for a 17-year-old boy than teaching him to play with toy trucks and building blocks. An adolescent with those behaviors—even in an adapted way—has a better chance of interacting in a typical fashion with his peer group, which may help to ensure the maintenance of his newly learned skills and provide opportunities for learning other adaptive behaviors.

If the Proposed Target Behavior Is to Be Reduced or Eliminated, What Adaptive Behavior Will Replace It?

A practitioner should never plan to reduce or eliminate a behavior from a person's repertoire without (a) determining an adaptive behavior that will take its place and (b) designing the intervention plan to ensure that the replacement behavior is learned. Teachers and other human services professionals should be in the business of building positive, adaptive repertoires, not merely reacting to and eliminating behaviors they find troublesome (Snell & Brown, 2006). Even though a child's maladaptive behaviors may be exceedingly annoying to others, or even damaging physically, those undesirable responses have proven functional for the child. That is, the maladaptive behavior has worked for the child in the past by producing reinforcers and/or helping the child avoid or escape punishers. A program that only denies that avenue of reinforcement is a nonconstructive approach. It does not teach adaptive behaviors to replace the inappropriate behavior.

Some of the most effective and recommended methods for eliminating unwanted behavior focus primarily on the development of desirable replacement behaviors. Goldiamond (1974) recommended that a "constructional" approach—as opposed to an eliminative approach—be used for the analysis of and intervention into behavioral problems. Under the constructional approach the "solution to problems is the construction of repertoires (or their reinstatement or transfer to new situations) rather than the elimination of repertoires" (Goldiamond, 1974, p. 14).

If a strong case cannot be made for specific, positive replacement behaviors, then a compelling case has not been made for eliminating the undesirable target behavior. The classroom teacher, for example, who wants a behavior change program to maintain students staying in their seats during reading period must go beyond the simple notion that "they need to be in their seats to do the work." The teacher must select materials and design contingencies that facilitate that goal and motivate the students to accomplish their work.

Does This Behavior Represent the Actual Problem or Goal, or Is It Only Indirectly Related?

An all-too-common error in education is teaching a related behavior rather than the behavior of interest. Many behavior change programs have been designed to increase on-task behaviors when the primary objective should have been to increase production or work output. On-task behaviors are chosen because people who are productive also tend to be on task. However, as *on task* is usually defined, it is quite possible for a student to be on task (i.e., in her seat, quiet, and oriented toward or handling academic materials) yet produce little or no work.

Targeting needed prerequisite skills should not be confused with selecting target behaviors that do not directly represent or fulfill the primary reasons for the behavior analysis effort. Prerequisite skills are not taught as terminal behaviors for their own sake, but as necessary elements of the desired terminal behavior. Related, but indirect, behaviors are not necessary to perform the true objective of the program, nor are they really intended outcomes of the program by themselves. In attempting to detect indirectness, behavior analysts should ask two questions: Is this behavior a necessary prerequisite to the intended terminal behavior? Is this behavior what the instructional program is really all about? If either question can be answered affirmatively, the behavior is eligible for target behavior status.

Is This Just Talk, or Is It the Real Behavior of Interest?

Many nonbehavioral therapies rely heavily on what people *say* about what they do and why they do it. The client's verbal behavior is considered important because it is believed to reflect the client's inner state and the mental processes that govern the client's behavior. Therefore, getting a person to talk differently about himself (e.g., in a more healthful, positive, and less self-effacing way) is viewed as a significant step in solving the person's problem. Indeed, this change in attitude is considered by some to be the primary goal of therapy.

Behavior analysts, on the other hand, distinguish between what people say and what they do (Skinner, 1953). Knowing and doing are not the same. Getting someone to understand his maladaptive behavior by being able to talk logically about it does not necessarily mean that his behavior will change in more constructive directions. The gambler may know that compulsive betting is ruining his life and that his losses would cease if he simply stopped placing bets. He may even be able to verbalize these facts to a therapist and state quite convincingly that he will not gamble in the future. Still, he may continue to bet.

Because verbal behavior can be descriptive of what people do, it is sometimes confused with the performance itself. A teacher at a school for juvenile offenders introduced a new math program that included instructional games, group drills, timed tests, and self-graphing. The students responded with many negative comments: "This is stupid," "Man, I'm not writin' down what I do," "I'm not even going to try on these tests." If the teacher had attended only to the students' talk about the program, it would probably have been discarded on the first day. But the teacher was aware that negative comments about school and work were expected in the peer group of adolescent delinquents and that many of her students' negative remarks had enabled them in the past to avoid tasks they thought they would not enjoy. Consequently, the teacher ignored the negative comments and attended to and rewarded her students for accuracy and rate of math computation when they participated in the program. In one week's time the negative talk had virtually ceased, and the students' math production was at an all-time high.

There are, of course, situations in which the behavior of interest *is* what the client says. Helping a person reduce the number of self-effacing comments he makes and increase the frequency of positive self-descriptions is an example of a program in which talk should be the target behavior—not because the self-effacing comments are indicative of a poor self-concept, but because the client's verbal behavior is the problem.

In every case, a determination must be made of exactly which behavior is the desired functional outcome of the program: Is it a skill or motor performance, or is it verbal behavior? In some instances, doing and talking behaviors might be important. A trainee applying for a lawn mower repair position may be more likely to get a job if he can describe verbally how he would fix a cranky starter on a mower. However, it is possible that, once hired, he can hold his job if he is skilled and efficient in repairing lawn mowers and does not talk about what he does. However, it is highly unlikely that a person will last very long on the job if he talks about how he would fix a lawn mower but is not able to do so. Target behaviors must be functional.

What If the Goal of the Behavior Change Program Is Not a Behavior?

Some of the important changes people want to make in their lives are not behaviors, but are instead the result or product of certain other behaviors. Weight loss is an example. On the surface it might appear that target behav-

ior selection is obvious and straightforward—losing weight. The number of pounds can be measured accurately; but weight, or more precisely losing weight, is not a behavior. Losing weight is not a specific response that can be defined and performed; it is the product or result of other behaviors—most notably reduced food consumption and/or increased exercise. Eating and exercise are behaviors and can be specifically defined and measured in precise units.

Some otherwise well-designed weight loss programs have not been successful because behavior change contingencies were placed on the goal (reduced weight) and not on the behaviors necessary to produce the goal. Target behaviors in a weight loss program should be measures of food consumption and exercise level, with intervention strategies designed to address those behaviors (e.g., De Luca & Holborn, 1992; McGuire, Wing, Klem, & Hill, 1999). Weight should be measured and charted during a weight loss program, not because it is the target behavior of interest, but because weight loss shows the positive effects of increased exercise or decreased food consumption.

There are numerous other examples of important goals that are not behaviors, but are the end products of behavior. Earning good grades, for example, is a goal that must be analyzed to determine what behaviors produce better grades (e.g., solving math problems via guided and independent practice). Behavior analysts can better help clients achieve their goals by selecting target behaviors that are the most directly and functionally related to those goals.

Some goals expressed by and for clients are not the direct product of a specific target behavior, but broader, more general goals: to be more successful, to have more friends, to be creative, to learn good sportsmanship, to develop an improved self-concept. Clearly, none of these goals are defined by specific behaviors, and all are more complex in terms of their behavioral components than losing weight or getting a better grade in math. Goals such as being successful represent a class of related behaviors or a general pattern of responding. They are labels that are used to describe people who behave in certain ways. Selecting target behaviors that will help clients or students attain these kinds of goals is even more difficult than their complexity suggests because the goals themselves often mean different things to different people. Being a success can entail a wide variety of behaviors. One person may view success in terms of income and job title. For another, success might mean job satisfaction and good use of leisure time. An important role of the behavior analyst during assessment and target behavior identification is to help the client select and define personal behaviors, the sum of which will result in the client and others evaluating her repertoire in the intended fashion.

Prioritizing Target Behaviors

Once a "pool" of eligible target behaviors has been identified, decisions must be made about their relative priority. Sometimes the information obtained from behavioral assessment points to one particular aspect of the person's repertoire in need of improvement more so than another. More often, though, assessment reveals a constellation of related, and sometimes not-so-related, behaviors in need of change. Direct observations, along with a behavioral interview and needs assessment, may produce a long list of important behaviors to change. When more than one eligible target behavior remains after careful evaluation of the considerations described in the previous section, the question becomes, Which behavior should be changed first? Judging each potential target behavior in light of the following nine questions may help determine which behavior deserves attention first, and the relative order in which the remaining behaviors will be addressed.

1. *Does this behavior pose any danger to the client or to others?* Behaviors that cause harm or pose a serious threat to the client's or to others' personal safety or health must receive first priority.

2. *How many opportunities will the person have to use this new behavior?* or *How often does this problem behavior occur?* A student who consistently writes reversed letters presents more of a problem than does a child who reverses letters only occasionally. If the choice is between first teaching a prevocational student to pack his lunch or to learn how to plan his two-week vacation each year, the former skill takes precedence because the employee-to-be may need to pack his lunch every workday.

3. *How long-standing is the problem or skill deficit?* A chronic behavior problem (e.g., bullying) or skill deficit (e.g., lack of social interaction skills) should take precedence over problems that appear sporadically or that have just recently surfaced.

4. *Will changing this behavior produce higher rates of reinforcement for the person?* If all other considerations are equal, a behavior that results in higher, sustained levels of reinforcement should take precedence over a behavior that produces little additional reinforcement for the client.

5. *What will be the relative importance of this target behavior to future skill development and independent functioning?* Each target behavior should be judged in terms of its relation (i.e., prerequisite or supportive) to other critical behaviors needed for optimal learning and development and maximum levels of independent functioning in the future.

6. *Will changing this behavior reduce negative or unwanted attention from others?* Some behaviors are not maladaptive because of anything inherent in the behavior itself, but because of the unnecessary problems the behavior causes the client. Some people with developmental and motoric disabilities may have difficulty at mealtimes with using utensils and napkins appropriately, thus reducing opportunities for positive interaction in public. Granted, public education and awareness are warranted as well, but it would be naive not to consider the negative effects of public reaction. Also, not teaching more appropriate mealtime skills may be a disservice to the person. Idiosyncratic public displays or mannerisms may be high-priority target behaviors if their modification is likely to provide access to more normalized settings or important learning environments.

7. *Will this new behavior produce reinforcement for significant others?* Even though a person's behavior should seldom, if ever, be changed simply for the convenience of others or for maintenance of the status quo, neither should the effect of a person's behavior change on the significant others in his life be overlooked. This question is usually answered best by the significant others themselves because people not directly involved in the person's life would often have

> no idea how rewarding it is to see your retarded 19 year old acquire the skill of toilet flushing on command or pointing to food when she wants a second helping. I suspect that the average taxpayer would not consider it "meaningful" to him or her for Karrie to acquire such skills. And, although we cannot readily say how much Karrie's being able to flush the toilet enhances her personal reinforcement/punishment ratio, I can testify that it enhances mine as a parent. (Hawkins, 1984, p. 285)

8. *How likely is success in changing this target behavior?* Some behaviors are more difficult to change than others. At least three sources of information can help assess the level of difficulty or, more precisely, predict the ease or degree of success in changing a particular behavior. First, what does the literature say about attempts to change this behavior? Many of the target behaviors that confront applied behavior analysts have been studied. Practitioners should stay abreast of published research reports in their areas of application. Not

only is such knowledge likely to improve the selection of proven and efficient techniques for behavior change, but also it may help to predict the level of difficulty or chance of success.

Second, how experienced is the practitioner? The practitioner's own competencies and experiences with the target behavior in question should be considered. A teacher who has worked successfully for many years with acting-out, aggressive children may have an array of effective behavior management strategies ready to employ and might predict success with even the most challenging child. However, that same teacher might decide that he is less able to improve a student's written language skills.

Third, to what extent can important variables in the client's environment be controlled effectively? Whether a certain behavior *can* be changed is not the question. In an applied setting, however, identifying and then consistently manipulating the controlling variables for a given target behavior will determine whether the behavior *will* be changed.

Fourth, are the resources available to implement and maintain the intervention at a level of fidelity and intensity long enough that is likely to achieve the desired outcomes? No matter how expertly designed a treatment plan, implementing it without the personnel and other resources needed to carry out the intervention properly is likely to yield disappointing results.

9. *How much will it cost to change this behavior?* Cost should be considered before implementing any systematic behavior change program. However, a cost–benefit analysis of several potential target behaviors does not mean that if a teaching program is expensive, it should not be implemented. Major courts have ruled that the lack of public funds may not be used as an excuse for not providing an appropriate education to all children regardless of the severity of their disability (cf., Yell & Drasgow, 2000). The cost of a behavior change program cannot be determined by simply adding dollar amounts that might be expended on equipment, materials, transportation, staff salaries, and the like. Consideration should also be given to how much of the client's time the behavior change program will demand. If, for example, teaching a fine motor skill to a child with severe disabilities would consume so much of the child's day that there would be little time remaining for her to learn other important behaviors—such as communication, leisure, and self-help skills—or simply to have some free time, the fine motor skill objective may be too costly.

Developing and Using a Target Behavior Ranking Matrix

Assigning a numerical rating to each of a list of potential target behaviors can produce a priority ranking of those behaviors. One such ranking matrix is shown in Figure 3.5; it is an adaptation of a system described by Dardig and Heward (1981) for prioritizing and selecting learning goals for students with disabilities. Each behavior is given a number representing the behavior's value on each of the prioritizing variables (e.g., 0 to 4 with 0 representing no value or contribution and 4 representing maximum value or benefit).

Professionals involved in planning behavior change programs for certain student or client populations will usually want to weigh some of the variables differentially, require a maximum rating on certain selection variables, and/or add other variables that are of particular importance to their overall goals. For example, professionals planning behavior change programs for senior citizens would probably insist that target behaviors with immediate benefits receive high priority. Educators serving secondary students with disabilities would likely advocate for factors such as the relative importance of a target behavior for future skill development and independent functioning.

Sometimes the behavior analyst, the client, and/or significant others have conflicting goals. Parents may want their teenage daughter in the house by 10:30 P.M. on weekends, but the daughter may want to stay out later. The school may want a behavior analyst to develop a program to increase students' adherence to dress and social codes. The behavior analyst may believe that these codes are outdated and are not in the purview of the school. Who decides what is best for whom?

One way to minimize and work through conflicts is to obtain client, parent, and staff/administration participation in the goal determination process. For example, the active participation of parents and, when possible, the student in the selection of short- and long-term goals and treatment procedures is required by law in planning special education services for students with disabilities (Individuals with Disabilities Education Improvement Act of 2004). Such participation by all of the significant parties can avoid and resolve goal conflicts, not to mention the invaluable information the participants can provide relative to other aspects of program planning (e.g., identification of likely reinforcers). Reviewing the results of assessment efforts and allowing each participant to provide input on the relative merits of each proposed goal or target behavior can often produce consensus on the best direction. Program planners should not commit *a priori* that whatever behavior is ranked first will necessarily be considered the highest priority target behavior. However,

Figure 3.5 Worksheet for prioritizing potential target behaviors.

Client's/Student's name:_____ Date:_____

Person completing worksheet:_____

Rater's relationship to client/student: _____

Directions: Use the key below to rank each potential target behavior by the extent to which it meets or fulfills each prioritization criteria. Add each team member's ranking of each potential target behavior. The behavior(s) with the highest total scores would presumably be the highest priority for intervention. Other criteria relevant to a particular program or individual's situation can be added, and the criteria can be differentially weighted.

Key: 0 = No or Never; 1 = Rarely; 2 = Maybe or Sometimes; 3 = Probably or Usually;
4 = Yes or Always

Potential Target Behaviors

(1) _____ (2) _____ (3) _____ (4) _____

Prioritization Criteria

	(1)	(2)	(3)	(4)
Does this behavior pose danger to the person or to others?	0 1 2 3 4	0 1 2 3 4	0 1 2 3 4	0 1 2 3 4
How many opportunities will the person have to use this new skill in the natural environment? or How often does the problem behavior occur?	0 1 2 3 4	0 1 2 3 4	0 1 2 3 4	0 1 2 3 4
How long-standing is the problem or skill deficit?	0 1 2 3 4	0 1 2 3 4	0 1 2 3 4	0 1 2 3 4
Will changing this behavior produce a higher rate of reinforcement for the person?	0 1 2 3 4	0 1 2 3 4	0 1 2 3 4	0 1 2 3 4
What is the relative importance of this target behavior to future skill development and independent functioning?	0 1 2 3 4	0 1 2 3 4	0 1 2 3 4	0 1 2 3 4
Will changing this behavior reduce negative or unwanted attention from others?	0 1 2 3 4	0 1 2 3 4	0 1 2 3 4	0 1 2 3 4
Will changing this behavior produce reinforcement for significant others?	0 1 2 3 4	0 1 2 3 4	0 1 2 3 4	0 1 2 3 4
How likely is success in changing this behavior?	0 1 2 3 4	0 1 2 3 4	0 1 2 3 4	0 1 2 3 4
How much will it cost to change this behavior?	0 1 2 3 4	0 1 2 3 4	0 1 2 3 4	0 1 2 3 4
Totals	_____	_____	_____	_____

if the important people involved in a person's life go through a ranking process such as the one shown in Figure 3.5, they are likely to identify areas of agreement and disagreement, which can lead to further discussions of target behavior selection and concentration on the critical concerns of those involved.

Defining Target Behaviors

Before a behavior can undergo analysis, it must be defined in a clear, objective, and concise manner. In constructing target behavior definitions, applied behavior analysts must consider the functional and topographical implications of their definitions.

Role and Importance of Target Behavior Definitions in Applied Behavior Analysis

Applied behavior analysis derives its validity from its systematic approach to seeking and organizing knowledge about human behavior. Validity of scientific knowledge in its most basic form implies replication. When predicted behavioral effects can be reproduced, principles of behavior are confirmed and methods of practice developed. If applied behavior analysts employ definitions of behavior not available to other scientists, replication is less likely. Without replication, the usefulness or meaningfulness of data cannot be determined beyond the specific participants themselves, thereby limiting the orderly development of the discipline as a useful technology (Baer, Wolf, & Risley, 1968). Without explicit, well-written definitions of target behaviors, researchers would be unable to accurately and reliably measure the same response classes within and across studies; or to aggregate, compare, and interpret their data.[7]

Explicit, well-written definitions of target behavior are also necessary for the practitioner, who may not be so concerned with replication by others or development of the field. Most behavior analysis programs are not conducted primarily for the advancement of the field; they are implemented by educators, clinicians, and other human services professionals to improve the lives of their clients. However, implicit in the application of behavior analysis is an accurate, ongoing evaluation of the target behavior, for which an explicit definition of behavior is a must.

A practitioner concerned only with evaluating his efforts in order to provide optimum service to his clients, might ask, "As long as I know what I mean by [name of

target behavior], why must I write down a specific definition?" First, a good behavioral definition is operational. It provides the opportunity to obtain complete information about the behavior's occurrence and nonoccurrence, and it enables the practitioner to apply procedures in a consistently accurate and timely fashion. Second, a good definition increases the likelihood of an accurate and believable evaluation of the program's effectiveness. Not only does an evaluation need to be accurate to guide ongoing program decisions, but also the data must be believable to those with a vested interest in the program's effectiveness. Thus, even though the practitioner may not be interested in demonstrating an analysis to the field at large, she must always be concerned with demonstrating effectiveness (i.e., accountability) to clients, parents, and administrators.

Two Types of Target Behavior Definitions

Target behaviors can be defined functionally or topographically.

Function-Based Definitions

A **function-based definition** designates responses as members of the targeted response class solely by their common effect on the environment. For example, Irvin, Thompson, Turner, and Williams (1998) defined hand mouthing as any behavior that resulted in "contact of the fingers, hand, or wrist with the mouth, lips, or tongue (p. 377). Figure 3.6 shows several examples of function-based definitions.

Applied behavior analysts should use function-based definitions of target behaviors whenever possible for the following reasons:

- A function-based definition encompasses all relevant forms of the response class. However, target behavior definitions based on a list of specific topographies might omit some relevant members of the response class and/or include irrelevant response topographies. For example, defining children's offers to play with peers in terms of specific things the children say and do might omit responses to which peers respond with reciprocal play and/or include behaviors that peers reject.

- The outcome, or function, of behavior is most important. This holds true even for target behaviors for which form or aesthetics is central to their being valued as socially significant. For example, the flowing strokes of the calligrapher's pen and the gymnast's elegant movements during a floor

---

[7]Procedures for measuring behavior accurately and reliably are discussed in Chapter 4.

Figure 3.6 Function-based definitions of various target behaviors.

Creativity in Children's Blockbuilding

The child behaviors of blockbuilding were defined according to their products, *block forms*. The researchers created a list of 20 arbitrary, but frequently seen forms, including:

Arch—any placement of a block atop two lower blocks not in contiguity.

Ramp—a block leaned against another, or a triangular block placed contiguous to another, to simulate a ramp.

Story—two or more blocks placed one atop another, the upper block(s) resting solely upon the lower.

Tower—any story of two or more blocks in which the lowest block is at least twice as tall as it is wide. (Goetz & Baer, 1973, pp. 210–211).

Exercise by Obese Boys

Riding a stationary bicycle—each wheel revolution constituted a response, which was automatically recorded by magnetic counters (DeLuca & Holborn, 1992, p. 672).

Compliance at Stop Signs by Motorists

Coming to a complete stop—observers scored a vehicle as coming to a complete stop if the tires stopped rolling prior to the vehicle entering the intersection (Van Houten & Retting, 2001, p. 187).

Recycling by Office Employees

Recycling office paper—number of pounds and ounces of recyclable office paper found in recycling and trash containers. All types of paper accepted as recyclable were identified as well as examples of nonrecyclable paper (Brothers, Krantz, & McClannahan, 1994, p. 155).

Safety Skills to Prevent Gun Play by Children

Touching the firearm—the child making contact with the firearm with any part of his or her body or with any object (e.g., a toy) resulting in the displacement of the firearm.
Leaving the area—the child removing himself or herself from the room in which the firearm was located within 10 seconds of seeing the firearm (Himle, Miltenberger, Flessner, & Gatheridge, 2004, p. 3).

---

routine are important (i.e., have been selected) because of their effects or function on others (e.g., praise from the calligraphy teacher, high scores from gymnastics judges).

• Functional definitions are often simpler and more concise than topography-based definitions, which leads to easier and more accurate and reliable measurement and sets the occasion for the consistent application of intervention. For example, in their study on skill execution by college football players, Ward and Carnes (2002) recorded a correct tackle according to the clear and simple definition, "if the offensive ball carrier was stopped" (p. 3).

Function-based definitions can also be used in some situations in which the behavior analyst does not have direct and reliable access to the natural outcome of the target behavior, or cannot use the natural outcome of the target behavior for ethical or safety reasons. In such cases, a *function-based definition by proxy* can be considered.

For example, the natural outcome of elopement (i.e., running or walking away from a caregiver without consent) is a lost child. By defining elopement as "any movement away from the therapist more than 1.5 m without permission" (p. 240), Tarbox, Wallace, and Williams (2003) were able to measure and treat this socially significant target behavior in a safe and meaningful manner.

Topography-Based Definitions

A **topography-based definition** identifies instances of the target behavior by the shape or form of the behavior. Topography-based definitions should be used when the behavior analyst (a) does not have direct, reliable, or easy access to the functional outcome of the target behavior, and/or (b) cannot rely on the function of the behavior because each instance of the target behavior does not produce the relevant outcome in the natural environment or the outcome might be produced by other events. For example, Silvestri (2004) defined and measured two classes

Figure 3.7   Topography-based definitions for two types of teacher statements.

Generic Positive Statements

Generic positive statements were defined as audible statements by the teacher that referred to one or more student's behavior or work products as desirable or commendable (e.g., "I'm proud of you!", "Great job, everyone."). Statements made to other adults in the room were recorded if they were loud enough to be heard by the students and made direct reference to student behavior or work products (e.g., "Aren't you impressed at how quietly my students are working today?"). A series of positive comments that specified neither student names nor behaviors with less than 2 seconds between comments was recorded as one statement. For example, if the teacher said, "Good, good, good. I'm so impressed" when reviewing three or four students' work, it was recorded as one statement.

Teacher utterances not recorded as generic positive statements included (a) statements that referred to specific behavior or student names, (b) neutral statements indicating only that an academic response was correct (e.g., "Okay", "Correct"), (c) positive statements not related to student behavior (e.g., saying "Thanks for dropping off my attendance forms" to a colleague), and (d) incomprehensible or inaudible statements.

Behavior-Specific Positive Statements

Behavior-specific positive statements made explicit reference to an observable behavior (e.g., "Thank you for putting your pencil away"). Specific positive statements could refer to general classroom behavior (e.g., "You did a great job walking back to your seat quietly") or academic performance (e.g., "That was a super smart answer!"). To be recorded as separate responses, specific positive statements were separated from one another by 2 seconds or by differentiation of the behavior praised. In other words, if a teacher named a desirable behavior and then listed multiple students who were demonstrating the behavior, this would be recorded as one statement (e.g., "Marissa, Tony, and Mark, you did a great job of returning your materials when you were finished with them"). However, a teacher's positive comment noting several different behaviors would be recorded as multiple statements regardless of the interval between the end of one comment and the start of the next. For example, "Jade, you did a great job *cleaning up* so quickly; Charles, thanks for *putting the workbooks away;* and class, I appreciate that you *lined up quietly*" would be recorded as three positive statements.

Adapted from *The Effects of Self-Scoring on Teachers' Positive Statements during Classroom Instruction* (pp. 48–49) by S. M. Silvestri. Unpublished doctoral dissertation. Columbus, OH: The Ohio State University. Used by permission.

of positive teacher statements according to the words that made up the statements, not according to whether the comments produced specific outcomes (see Figure 3.7).

Topography-based definitions can also be used for target behaviors for which the relevant outcome is sometimes produced in the natural environment by undesirable variations of the response class. For example, because a duffer's very poor swing of a golf club sometimes produces a good outcome (i.e., the ball lands on the green), it is better to define a correct swing by the position and movement of the golf club and the golfer's feet, hips, head, and hands.

A topography-based definition should encompass all response forms that would typically produce the relevant outcome in the natural environment. Although topography provides an important element for *defining* target behaviors, the applied behavior analyst must be especially careful not to *select* target behaviors solely on the basis of topography (see Box 3.1).

Writing Target Behavior Definitions

A good definition of a target behavior provides an accurate, complete, and concise description of the behavior to be changed (and therefore measured). It also states what is not included in the behavioral definition. Asking to be excused from the dinner table is an observable and measurable behavior that can be counted. By comparison, "exercising good manners" is not a description of any particular behavior; it merely implies a general response class of polite and socially acceptable behaviors. Hawkins and Dobes (1977) described three characteristics of a good definition:

1. The definition should be objective, referring only to observable characteristics of the behavior (and environment, if needed) or translating any inferential terms (such as "expressing hostile feelings," "intended to help," or "showing interest in") into more objective ones.

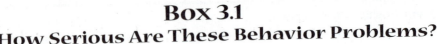

Box 3.1
How Serious Are These Behavior Problems?

Suppose you are a behavior analyst in a position to design and help implement an intervention to change the following four behaviors:

1. A child repeatedly raises her arm, extending and retracting her fingers toward her palm in a gripping/releasing type of motion.

2. An adult with developmental disabilities pushes his hand hard against his eye, making a fist and rubbing his eye rapidly with his knuckles.

3. Several times each day a high school student rhythmically drums her fingers up and down, sometimes in bursts of 10 to 15 minutes in duration.

4. A person repeatedly grabs at and squeezes another person's arms and legs so hard that the other person winces and says "Ouch!"

How much of a problem does the behavior pose for the person or for others who share his or her current and future environments? Would you rate each behavior as a mild, moderate, or serious problem? How important do you think it would be to target each of these behaviors for reduction or elimination from the repertoires of the four individuals?

Appropriate answers to these questions cannot be found in topographical descriptions alone. The meaning and relative importance of any operant behavior can be determined only in the context of the environmental antecedents and consequences that define the behavior. Here is what each of the four people in the previous examples were actually doing:

1. An infant learning to wave "bye-bye."

2. A man with allergies rubbing his eye to relieve the itching.

3. A student typing unpredictable text to increase her keyboarding fluency and endurance.

4. A massage therapist giving a relaxing, deep-muscle massage to a grateful and happy customer.

Applied behavior analysts must remember that the meaning of any behavior is determined by its function, not its form. Behaviors should not be targeted for change on the basis of topography alone.

Note: Examples 1 and 2 are adapted from Meyer and Evans, 1989, p. 53.

---

2. The definition should be clear in that it should be readable and unambiguous so that experienced observers could read it and readily paraphrase it accurately.

3. The definition should be complete, delineating the "boundaries" of what is to be included as an instance of the response and what is to be excluded, thereby directing the observers in all situations that are likely to occur and leaving little to their judgment. (p. 169)

Stated succinctly, a good definition must be objective, assuring that specific instances of the defined target behavior can be observed and recorded reliably. An objective definition increases the likelihood of an accurate and believable evaluation of program effectiveness. Second, a clear definition is technological, meaning that it enables others to use and replicate it (Baer et al., 1968). A clear definition therefore becomes operational for present and future purposes. Finally, a complete definition discriminates between what is and what is not an instance of the target behavior. A complete definition allows oth-

ers to record an occurrence of a target behavior, but not record instances of nonoccurrence, in a standard fashion. A complete definition is a precise and concise description of the behavior of interest. Note how the target behavior definitions in Figures 3.6 and 3.7 meet the standard for being objective, clear, and complete.

Morris (1985) suggested testing the definition of a target behavior by asking three questions:

1. Can you count the number of times that the behavior occurs in, for example, a 15-minute period, a 1-hour period, or one day? Or, can you count the number of minutes that it takes for the child to perform the behavior? That is, can you tell someone that the behavior occurred "x" number of times of "x" number of minutes today? (Your answer should be "yes.")

2. Will a stranger know exactly what to look for when you tell him/her the target behavior you are planning to modify? That is, can you actually see the child performing the behavior when it occurs? (Your answer should be "yes.")

3. Can you break down the target behavior into smaller behavioral components, each of which is more specific and observable than the original target behavior? (Your answer should be "no.").

In responding to the suggestion that perhaps a sourcebook of standard target behavior definitions be developed because it would increase the likelihood of exact replications among applied researchers and would save the considerable time spent in developing and testing situation-specific definitions, Baer (1985) offered the following perspectives. Applied behavior analysis programs are implemented because someone (e.g., teacher, parent, individual himself) has "complained" that a behavior needs to be changed. A behavioral definition has validity in applied behavior analysis only if it enables observers to capture every aspect of the behavior that the complainer is concerned with and none other. Thus, to be valid from an applied perspective, definitions of target behaviors should be situation specific. Attempts to standardize behavior definitions assume an unlikely similarity across all situations.

Setting Criteria for Behavior Change

Target behaviors are selected for study in applied behavior analysis because of their importance to the people involved. Applied behavior analysts attempt to increase, maintain, and generalize adaptive, desirable behaviors and decrease the occurrence of maladaptive, undesirable behaviors. Behavior analysis efforts that not only target important behaviors but also change those behaviors to an extent that a person's life is changed in a positive and meaningful way, are said to have **social validity.**[8] But how much does a target behavior need to change before it makes a meaningful difference in the person's life?

Van Houten (1979) made a case for specifying the desired outcome criteria *before* efforts to modify the target behavior begin.

> This step [specifying outcome criteria] becomes as important as the previous step [selecting socially important target behaviors] if one considers that for most behaviors there exists a range of responding within which performance is most adaptive. When the limits of this range are unknown for a particular behavior, it is possible that one could terminate treatment when performance is above or below these limits. Hence, the behavior would not be occurring within its optimal range. . . .
>
> In order to know when to initiate and terminate a treatment, practitioners require socially validated standards for which they can aim. (pp. 582, 583)

Van Houten (1979) suggested two basic approaches to determining socially valid goals: (a) Assess the performance of people judged to be highly competent, and (b) experimentally manipulate different levels of performance to determine empirically which produces optimal results.

Regardless of the method used, specifying treatment goals before intervention begins provides a guideline for continuing or terminating a treatment. Further, setting objective, predetermined goals helps to eliminate disagreements or biases among those involved in evaluating a program's effectiveness.

 ## Summary

Role of Assessment in Behavior Analysis

1. Behavioral assessment involves a full range of inquiry methods including direct observations, interviews, checklists, and tests to identify and define targets for behavior change.

2. Behavioral assessment can be conceptualized as funnel shaped, with an initial broad scope leading to an eventual narrow and constant focus.

3. Behavioral assessment consists of five phases or functions: (a) screening, (b) defining and quantifying problems or goals, (c) pinpointing the target behavior(s) to be treated (d) monitoring progress, and (e) following up.

4. Before conducting a behavioral assessment, the behavior analyst must determine whether he has the authority and permission, resources, and skills to assess and change the behavior.

Assessment Methods Used by Behavior Analysts

5. Four major methods for obtaining assessment information are (a) interviews, (b) checklists, (c) tests, and (d) direct observations.

6. The client interview is used to determine the client's description of problem behaviors or achievement goals. *What, when,* and *where* questions are emphasized, focusing on the actual behavior of the client and the responses of significant others to that behavior.

---

[8]A third component of social validity concerns the social acceptability of the treatment methods and procedures employed to change the behavior. The importance of social validity in evaluating applied behavior analysis will be discussed in Chapter 10.

7. Questionnaires and needs assessment surveys are sometimes completed by the client to supplement the information gathered in the interview.

8. Clients are sometimes asked to self-monitor certain situations or behaviors. Self-collected data may be useful in selecting and defining target behaviors.

9. Significant others can also be interviewed to gather assessment information and, in some cases, to find out whether they will be willing and able to assist in an intervention.

10. Direct observation with a behavior checklist that contains specific descriptions of various skills can indicate possible target behaviors.

11. Anecdotal observation, also called ABC recording, yields a descriptive, temporally sequenced account of all behavior(s) of interest and the antecedent conditions and consequences for those behaviors as those events occur in the client's natural environment.

12. Ecological assessment entails gathering a large amount of information about the person and the environments in which that person lives and works (e.g., physiological conditions, physical aspects of the environment, interactions with others, past reinforcement history). A complete ecological assessment is neither necessary nor warranted for most applied behavior analysis programs.

13. Reactivity, the effects of an assessment procedure on the behavior being assessed, is most likely when the person being observed is aware of the observer's presence and purpose. Behavior analysts should use assessment methods that are as unobtrusive as possible, repeat observations until apparent reactive effects subside, and take possible reactive effects into account when interpreting the results of observations.

Assessing the Social Significance of Potential Target Behaviors

14. Target behaviors in applied behavior analysis must be socially significant behaviors that will increase a person's habilitation (adjustment, competence).

15. The relative social significance and habilitative value of a potential target behavior can be clarified by viewing it in light of the following considerations:

    - Will the behavior be reinforced in the person's daily life? The relevance of behavior rule requires that a target behavior produce reinforcement for the person in the postintervention environment.

    - Is the behavior a necessary prerequisite for a useful skill?

    - Will the behavior increase the person's access to environments in which other important behaviors can be learned or used?

    - Will the behavior predispose others to interact with the person in a more appropriate and supportive manner?

- Is the behavior a cusp or pivotal behavior? Behavioral cusps have sudden and dramatic consequences that extend well beyond the idiosyncratic change itself because they expose the person to new environments, reinforcers, contingencies, responses, and stimulus controls. Learning a pivotal behavior produces corresponding modifications or covariations in other untrained behaviors.

- Is the behavior age appropriate?

- Whenever a behavior is targeted for reduction or elimination, a desirable, adaptive behavior must be selected to replace it.

- Does the behavior represent the actual problem or achievement goal, or is it only indirectly related?

- A person's verbal behavior should not be confused with the actual behavior of interest. However, in some situations the client's verbal behavior should be selected as the target behavior.

- If a person's goal is not a specific behavior, a target behavior(s) must be selected that will produce the desired results or state.

Prioritizing Target Behaviors

16. Assessment often reveals more than one possible behavior or skill area for targeting. Prioritization can be accomplished by rating potential target behavior against key questions related to their relative danger, frequency, longstanding existence, potential for reinforcement, relevance for future skill development and independent functioning, reduced negative attention from others, likelihood of success, and cost.

17. Participation by the person whose behavior is to be changed, parents and/or other important family members, staff, and administration in identifying and prioritizing target behaviors can help reduce goal conflicts.

Defining Target Behaviors

18. Explicit, well-written target behavior definitions are necessary for researchers to accurately and reliably measure the same response classes within and across studies or to aggregate, compare, and interpret their data.

19. Good target behaviors definitions are necessary for practitioners to collect accurate and believable data to guide ongoing program decisions, apply procedures consistently, and provide accountability to clients, parents, and administrators.

20. Function-based definitions designate responses as members of the targeted response class solely by their common effect on the environment.

21. Topography-based definitions define instances of the targeted response class behavior by the shape or form of the behavior.

22. A good definition must be objective, clear, and complete, and must discriminate between what is and what is not an instance of the target behavior.

23. A target behavior definition is valid if it enables observers to capture every aspect of the behavior that the "complainer" is concerned with and none other.

Setting Criteria for Behavior Change

24. A behavior change has social validity if it changes some aspect of the person's life in an important way.

25. Outcome criteria specifying the extent of behavior change desired or needed should be determined before efforts to modify the target behavior begin.

26. Two approaches to determining socially validated performance criteria are (a) assessing the performance of people judged to be highly competent and (b) experimentally manipulating different levels of performance to determine which produces optimal results.

CHAPTER 4

Measuring Behavior

Key Terms

artifact
celeration
celeration time period
celeration trend line
count
discrete trial
duration
event recording
free operant

frequency
interresponse time (IRT)
magnitude
measurement
measurement by permanent product
momentary time sampling
partial-interval recording
percentage
planned activity check (PLACHECK)

rate
repeatability
response latency
temporal extent
temporal locus
time sampling
topography
trials-to-criterion
whole-interval recording

Behavior Analyst Certification Board® BCBA® & BCABA® Behavior Analyst Task List©, Third Edition

	Content Area 6: Measurement of Behavior
6-1	Identify the measurable dimensions of behavior (e.g., rate, duration, latency, or interresponse times).
6-3	State the advantages and disadvantages of using continuous measurement procedures and sampling techniques (e.g., partial- and whole-interval recording, momentary time sampling).
6-4	Select the appropriate measurement procedure given the dimensions of the behavior and the logistics of observing and recording.
6-6	Use frequency (i.e., count).
6-7	Use rate (i.e., count per unit of time).
6-8	Use duration.
6-9	Use latency.
6-10	Use interresponse time (IRT).
6-11	Use percentage of occurrence.
6-12	Use trials-to-criterion.
6-13	Use interval recording methods.

Lord Kelvin, the British mathematician and physicist, supposedly said, "Until you can express what you are talking about in numbers and can measure it, your knowledge is meager and unsatisfactory." Measurement (applying quantitative labels to describe and differentiate natural events) provides the basis for all scientific discoveries and for the development and successful application of technologies derived from those discoveries. Direct and frequent measurement provides the foundation for applied behavior analysis. Applied behavior analysts use measurement to detect and compare the effects of various environmental arrangements on the acquisition, maintenance, and generalization of socially significant behaviors.

But what is it about behavior that applied behavior analysts can and should measure? How should those measures be obtained? And, what should we do with these measures once we have obtained them? This chapter identifies the dimensions by which behavior can be measured and describes the methods behavior analysts commonly use to measure them. But first, we examine the definition and functions of measurement in applied behavior analysis.

Definition and Functions of Measurement in Applied Behavior Analysis

Measurement is "the process of assigning numbers and units to particular features of objects or events. . . . [It] involves attaching a number representing the observed extent of a dimensional quantity to an appropriate unit. The number and the unit together constitute the measure of the object or event" (Johnston & Pennypacker, 1993a, pp. 91, 95). A *dimensional quantity* is the particular feature of an object or event that is measured. For example, a single occurrence of a phenomenon—say, the response of "c-a-t" to the question, "How do you spell *cat?*"—would be assigned the number *1* and the unit label *correct*. Observing another instance of the same response class would change the label to *2 correct*. Other labels could also be applied based on accepted nomenclature. For example, if 8 of 10 observed responses met a standard definition of "correct," accuracy of responding could be described with the label, *80% correct*. If the 8 correct responses were emitted in 1 minute, a *rate* or *frequency* label of 8 per minute would apply.

Bloom, Fischer, and Orme (2003)—who described measurement as the act or process of applying quantitative or qualitative labels to events, phenomena, or observed properties using a standard set of consensus-based rules by which to apply labels to those occurrences—

pointed out that the concept of measurement also includes the characteristics of what is being measured, the quality and appropriateness of the measurement tools, the technical skill of the measurer, and how the measures obtained are used. In the end, measurement gives researchers, practitioners, and consumers a common means for describing and comparing behavior with a set of labels that convey a common meaning.

Researchers Need Measurement

Measurement is how scientists operationalize empiricism. Objective measurement enables (indeed, it requires) scientists to describe the phenomena they observe in precise, consistent, and publicly verifiable ways. Without measurement, all three levels of scientific knowledge—description, prediction, and control—would be relegated to guesswork subject to the "individual prejudices, tastes, and private opinions of the scientist" (Zuriff, 1985, p. 9). We would live in a world in which the alchemist's suppositions about a life-prolonging elixir would prevail over the chemist's propositions derived from experimentation.

Applied behavior analysts measure behavior to obtain answers to questions about the existence and nature of functional relations between socially significant behavior and environmental variables. Measurement enables comparisons of a person's behavior within and between different environmental conditions, thereby affording the possibility of drawing empirically based conclusions about the effects of those conditions on behavior. For example, to learn whether allowing students with emotional and behavioral challenges to choose the academic tasks they will work on would influence their engagement with those tasks and disruptive behavior, Dunlap and colleagues (1994) measured students' task engagement and disruptive behaviors during choice and no-choice conditions. Measurement revealed the level of both target behaviors during each condition, whether and how much the behaviors changed when choice was introduced or withdrawn, and how variable or stable the behaviors were during each condition.

The researcher's ability to achieve a scientific understanding of behavior depends on her ability to measure it. Measurement makes possible the detection and verification of virtually everything that has been discovered about the selective effects of the environment on behavior. The empirical databases of the basic and applied branches of behavior analysis consist of organized collections of behavioral measurements. Virtually every graph in the *Journal of the Experimental Analysis of Behavior* and the *Journal of Applied Behavior Analysis* displays an ongoing record or summary of behavioral measurement. In short, measurement provides the very basis for learning and talking about behavior in scientifically meaningful ways.[1]

Practitioners Need Measurement

Behavioral practitioners are dedicated to improving the lives of the clients they serve by changing socially significant behaviors. Practitioners measure behavior initially to determine the current level of a target behavior and whether that level meets a threshold for further intervention. If intervention is warranted, the practitioner measures the extent to which his efforts are successful. Practitioners measure behavior to find out whether and when it has changed; the extent and duration of behavior changes; the variability or stability of behavior before, during, and after treatment; and whether important behavior changes have occurred in other settings or situations and spread to other behaviors.

Practitioners compare measurements of the target behavior before and after treatment (sometimes including pre- and posttreatment measures obtained in nontreatment settings or situations) to evaluate the overall effects of behavior change programs (*summative evaluation*). Frequent measures of behavior during treatment (*formative assessment*) enable dynamic, data-based decision making concerning the continuation, modification, or termination of treatment.

The practitioner who does not obtain and attend to frequent measures of the behavior targeted for intervention is vulnerable to committing two kinds of preventable mistakes: (a) continuing an ineffective treatment when no real behavior change has occurred, or (b) discontinuing an effective treatment because subjective judgment detects no improvement (e.g., without measurement, a teacher would be unlikely to know that a student's oral reading has increased from 70 words per minute to 80 word per minute). Thus, direct and frequent measurement enables practitioners to detect their successes and, equally important, their failures so they can make changes to change failure to success (Bushell & Baer, 1994; Greenwood & Maheady, 1997).

> Our technology of behavior change is also a technology of behavior measurement and of experimental design; it developed as that package, and as long as it stays in that package, it is a self-evaluating enterprise. Its successes are successes of known magnitude; its failures are almost immediately detected as failures; and whatever its outcomes, they are attributable to known inputs and procedures rather than to chance events or coincidences.
> (D. M. Baer, personal communication, October 21, 1982)

In addition to enabling ongoing program monitoring and data-based decision making, frequent measurement provides other important benefits to practitioners and the clients they serve:

• *Measurement helps practitioners optimize their effectiveness.* To be optimally effective, a practitioner must maximize behavior change efficiency in terms of time and resources. Only by maintaining close, continual contact with relevant outcome data can a practitioner hope to achieve optimal effectiveness and efficiency (Bushell & Baer, 1994). Commenting on the critical role of direct and frequent measurement on maximizing the effectiveness of classroom practice, Sidman (2000) noted that teachers "must remain attuned to the pupil's messages and be ready to try and to evaluate modifications [in instructional methods]. Teaching, then, is not just a matter of changing the behavior of pupils; it is an interactive social process" (p. 23, words in brackets added). Direct and frequent measurement is the process by which practitioners hear their clients' messages.

• *Measurement enables practitioners to verify the legitimacy of treatments touted as "evidence based."* Practitioners are increasingly expected, and in some fields mandated by law, to use evidence-based interventions. An evidence-based practice is a treatment or intervention method that has been demonstrated to be effective through substantial, high-quality scientific research. For example, the federal No Child Left Behind Act of 2001 requires that all public school districts ensure that all children are taught by "highly qualified" teachers using curriculum and instructional methods validated by rigorous scientific research. Although guidelines and quality indicators regarding the type (e.g., randomized clinical trials, single-subject studies) and quantity (e.g., number of studies published in peer-reviewed journals, minimum number of participants) of research needed to qualify a treatment method as an evidence-based practice have been proposed, the likelihood of complete consensus is slim (e.g., Horner, Carr, Halle, McGee, Odom, & Wolery, 2005; U.S. Department of Education, 2003). When implementing any treatment, regardless of the type or amount of research evidence to support it, practitioners can and should use direct and frequent measurement to verify its effectiveness with the students or clients they serve.

• *Measurement helps practitioners identify and end the use of treatments based on pseudoscience, fad, fashion, or ideology.* Numerous educational methods and treatments have been claimed by their advocates as breakthroughs. Many controversial treatments and proposed cures for people with developmental disabilities and autism (e.g., facilitated communication, holding therapy, megadoses of vitamins, strange diets, weighted vests,

---

[1]Measurement is necessary but not sufficient to the attainment of scientific understanding. See Chapter 7.

dolphin-assisted therapy) have been promoted in the absence of sound scientific evidence of effectiveness (Heflin & Simpson, 2002; Jacobson, Foxx, & Mulick, 2005). The use of some of these so-called breakthrough therapies has led to disappointment and loss of precious time at best for many people and their families, and in some cases, to disastrous consequences (Maurice, 1993). Even though well-controlled studies have shown many of these methods to be ineffective, and even though these programs are not justified because they lacked sound, scientific evidence of effects, risks, and benefits, parents and practitioners are still bombarded with sincere and well-meaning testimonials. In the quest to find and verify effective treatments and root out those whose strongest support is in the form of testimonials and slick advertisements on the Internet, measurement is the practitioner's best ally. Practitioners should maintain a healthy skepticism regarding claims for effectiveness.

Using Plato's "Allegory of the Cave" as a metaphor for teachers and practitioners who use untested and pseudo-instructional ideas, Heron, Tincani, Peterson, and Miller (2002) argued that practitioners would be better served if they adopted a scientific approach and cast aside pseudo-educational theories and philosophies. Practitioners who insist on direct and frequent measurement of all intervention and treatment programs will have empirical support to defend against political or social pressures to adopt unproven treatments. In a real sense they will be armed with what Carl Sagan (1996) called a "baloney detection kit."

• *Measurement enables practitioners to be accountable to clients, consumers, employers, and society.* Measuring the outcomes of their efforts directly and frequently helps practitioners answer confidently questions from parents and other caregivers about the effects of their efforts.

• *Measurement helps practitioners achieve ethical standards.* Ethical codes of conduct for behavior analytic practitioners require direct and frequent measurement of client behavior (see Chapter 29). Determining whether a client's right to effective treatment or effective education is being honored requires measurement of the behavior(s) for which treatment was sought or intended (Nakano, 2004; Van Houten et al., 1988). A behavioral practitioner who does not measure the nature and extent of relevant behavior changes of the clients she serves borders on malpractice. Writing in the context of educators, Kauffman (2005) offered this perspective on the relationship between measurement and ethical practice:

> [T]he teacher who cannot or will not pinpoint and measure the relevant behaviors of the students he or she is teaching is probably not going to be very effective. . . .

Not to define precisely and to measure these behavioral excesses and deficiencies, then, is a fundamental error; it is akin to the malpractice of a nurse who decides not to measure vital signs (heart rate, respiration rate, temperature, and blood pressure), perhaps arguing that he or she is too busy, that subjective estimates of vital signs are quite adequate, that vital signs are only superficial estimates of the patient's health, or that vital signs do not signify the nature of the underlying pathology. The teaching profession is dedicated to the task of changing behavior—changing behavior demonstrably for the better. What can one say, then, of educational practice that does not include precise definition and reliable measurement of the behavioral change induced by the teacher's methodology? It is indefensible. (p. 439)

Measurable Dimensions of Behavior

If a friend asked you to measure a coffee table, you would probably ask why he wants the table measured. In other words, what does he want measurement to tell him about the table? Does he need to know its height, width, and depth? Does he want to know how much the table weighs? Perhaps he is interested in the color of the table? Each of these reasons for measuring the table requires measuring a different dimensional quantity of the table (i.e., length, mass, and light reflection).

Behavior, like coffee tables and all entities in the physical world, also has features that can be measured (though length, weight, and color are not among them). Because behavior occurs within and across time, it has three fundamental properties, or *dimensional quantities,* that behavior analysts can measure. Johnston and Pennypacker (1993a) described these properties as follows:

- **Repeatability** (also called *countability*): Instances of a response class can occur repeatedly through time (i.e., behavior can be counted).

- **Temporal extent:** Every instance of behavior occurs during some amount of time (i.e., the duration of behavior can be measured).

- **Temporal locus:** Every instance of behavior occurs at a certain point in time with respect to other events (i.e., when behavior occurs can be measured).

Figure 4.1 shows a schematic representation of repeatability, temporal extent, and temporal locus. Alone and in combination, these dimensional quantities provide the basic and derivative measures used by applied behavior analysts. In the following pages these and two other measurable dimensions of behavior—its form and strength—will be discussed.

Figure 4.1   Schematic representation of the dimensional quantities of repeatability, temporal extent, and temporal locus. *Repeatability* is shown by a count of four instances of a given response class (R_1, R_2, R_3, and R_4) within the observation period. The *temporal extent* (i.e., duration) of each response is shown by the raised and shaded portions of the time line. One aspect of the *temporal locus* (response latency) of two responses is shown by the elapsed time ($\leftarrow L \rightarrow$) between the onset of two antecedent stimulus events (S_1 and S_2) and the initiation of the responses that follow (R_2 and R_4).

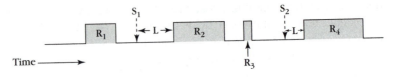

Measures Based on Repeatability

Count

Count is a simple tally of the number of occurrences of a behavior—for example, the number of correct and incorrect answers written on an arithmetic practice sheet, the number of words written correctly during a spelling test, the number of times an employee carpools to work, the number of class periods a student is tardy, the number of widgets produced.

Although how often a behavior occurs is often of primary interest, measures of count alone may not provide enough information to allow practitioners to make useful program decisions or analyses. For example, data showing that Katie wrote correct answers to 5, 10, and 15 long division problems over three consecutive math class periods suggests improving performance. However, if the three measures of count were obtained in observation periods of 5 minutes, 20 minutes, and 60 minutes, respectively, a much different interpretation of Katie's performance is suggested. Therefore, the observation period, or counting time, should always be noted when reporting measures of count.

Rate/Frequency

Combining observation time with count yields one of the most widely used measures in applied behavior analysis, **rate** (or **frequency**) of responding, defined as the number of responses per unit of time.[2] A rate or frequency measure is a ratio consisting of the dimensional quantities of count (number of responses) and time (observation period in which the count was obtained).

Converting count to rate or frequency makes measurement more meaningful. For example, knowing that Yumi read 95 words correctly and 4 words incorrectly in 1 minute, that Lee wrote 250 words in 10 minutes, and that Joan's self-injurious behavior occurred 17 times in 1 hour provides important information and context. Expressing the three previously reported measures of Katie's performance in math class as rate reveals that she correctly answered long division problems at rates of 1.0, 0.5, and 0.25 per minute over three consecutive class periods.

Researchers and practitioners typically report rate data as a count per 10 seconds, count per minute, count per day, count per week, count per month, or count per year. As long as the unit of time is standard within or across experiments, rate measures can be compared. It is possible to compare rates of responding from counts obtained during observation periods of different lengths. For example, a student who, over four daily class activities of different durations, had 12 talk-outs in 20 minutes, 8 talk-outs in 12 minutes, 9 talk-outs in 15 minutes, and 12 talk-outs in 18 minutes had response rates of 0.60, 0.67, 0.60, and 0.67 per minute.

The six rules and guidelines described below will help researchers and practitioners obtain, describe, and interpret count and rate data most appropriately.

Always Reference the Counting Time.   When reporting rate-of-response data, researchers and practitioners must always include the duration of the observation time (i.e., the counting time). Comparing rate measures without reference to the counting time can lead to faulty interpretations of data. For example, if two students read from the same text at equal rates of 100 correct words per minute with no incorrect responses, it would appear that they exhibited equal performances. Without knowing the counting time, however, an evaluation of these two performances cannot be conducted. Consider, for example, that Sally and Lillian each ran at a rate of 7 minutes per mile. We cannot compare their performances without reference to the

---

[2]Although some technical distinctions exist between *rate* and *frequency,* the two terms are often used interchangeably in the behavior analysis literature. For discussion of various meanings of the two terms and examples of different methods for calculating ratios combining count and observation time, see Johnston and Pennypacker (1993b, Reading 4: Describing Behavior with Ratios of Count and Time).

distances they ran. Running 1 mile at a rate of 7 minutes per mile is a different class of behavior than running at a rate of 7 minutes per mile over a marathon distance.

The counting time used for each session needs to accompany each rate measure when the counting time changes from session to session. For instance, rather than having a set counting time to answer arithmetic facts (e.g., a 1-minute timing), the teacher records the total time required for the student to complete an assigned set of arithmetic problems during each class session. In this situation, the teacher could report the student's correct and incorrect answers per minute for each session, and also report the counting times for each session because they changed from session to session.

Calculate Correct and Incorrect Rates of Response When Assessing Skill Development.   When a participant has an opportunity to make a correct or an incorrect response, a rate of response for each behavior should be reported. Calculating rate correct and rate incorrect is crucial for evaluating skill development because an improving performance cannot be assessed by knowing only the correct rate. The rate of correct responses alone could show an improving performance, but if incorrect responding is also increasing, the improvement may be illusionary. Correct and incorrect rate measures together provide important information to help the teacher evaluate how well the student is progressing. Ideally, the correct response rate accelerates toward a performance criterion or goal, and the incorrect response rate decelerates to a low, stable level. Also, reporting rate correct and rate incorrect provides for an assessment of proportional accuracy while maintaining the dimensional quantities of the measurement (e.g., 20 correct and 5 incorrect responses per minute = 80% accuracy, or a multiple of X4 proportional accuracy).

Correct and incorrect response rates provide essential data for the assessment of fluent performance (i.e., proficiency) (Kubina, 2005). The assessment of fluency requires measurement of the number of correct and incorrect responses per unit of time (i.e., proportional accuracy). Analysts cannot assess fluency using only the correct rate because a fluency performance must be accurate also.

Take Into Account the Varied Complexity of Responses.   Rate of responding is a sensitive and appropriate measure of skill acquisition and the development of fluent performances only when the level of difficulty and complexity from one response to the next remains constant within and across observations. The rate-of-response measures previously discussed have been with whole units in which the response requirements are essentially the same from one response to the next. Many important behaviors, however, are composites of two or more component behaviors, and different situations call for varied sequences or combinations of the component behaviors.

One method for measuring rate of responding that takes varied complexity into account for multiple-component behaviors is to count the operations necessary to achieve a correct response. For example, in measuring students' math calculation performance, instead of counting a two-digit plus three-digit addition problem with regrouping as correct or incorrect, a researcher might consider the number of steps that were completed in correct sequence within each problem. Helwig (1973) used the number of operations needed to produce the answers to mathematics problems to calculate response rates. In each session the student was given 20 multiplication and division problems selected at random from a set of 120 problems. The teacher recorded the duration of time for each session. All the problems were of two types: $a \times b = c$ and $a \div b = c$. For each problem the student was asked to find one of the factors: the product, the dividend, the divisor, or the quotient. Depending on the problem, finding the missing factor required from one to five operations. For example, writing the answer 275 in response to the problem $55 \times 5 = ?$ would be scored as four correct responses because finding the missing factor requires four operations:

1. Multiply the ones: $5 \times 5 = 25$.
2. Record the 5 ones and carry the 2 tens.
3. Multiply the tens: $5 \times 5(0) = 25(0)$.
4. Add the 2 tens carried and record the sum (27).

When more than one way to find the answer was possible, the mean number of operations was figured for that problem. For example, the answer to the problem, $4 \times ? = 164$, can be obtained by multiplication with two operations and by division with four operations. The mean number of operations is three. Helwig counted the number of operations completed correctly and incorrectly per set of 20 problems and reported correct and incorrect rates of response.

Use Rate of Responding to Measure Free Operants.   Rate of response is a useful measure for all behaviors characterized as free operants. The term *free operant* refers to behaviors that have discrete beginning and ending points, require minimal displacement of the organism in time and space, can be emitted at nearly any time, do not require much time for completion, and can be emitted over a wide range of response rates (Baer & Fowler, 1984). Skinner (1966) used rate of response of free operants as the primary dependent variable when developing the experimental analysis of behavior. The bar press and key peck are typical free operant responses used in nonhuman animal laboratory studies. Human subjects in a basic laboratory experiment might depress keys on a keyboard. Many socially significant behaviors meet the definition of free operants: number of words read during a 1-minute counting period, number of head slaps per minute, number of letter strokes written in 3 minutes. A person can make these responses at almost any time, each discrete response does not use much time, and each response class can produce a wide range of rates.

Rate of response is a preferred measure for free operants because it is sensitive to changes in behavior values (e.g., oral reading may occur at rates ranging from 0 to 250 or more correct words per minute), and because it offers clarity and precision by defining a count per unit of time.

Do Not Use Rate to Measure Behaviors that Occur within Discrete Trials.   Rate of response is not a useful measure for behaviors that can occur only within limited or restricted situations. For example, response rates of behaviors that occur within **discrete trials** are controlled by a given opportunity to emit the response. Typical discrete trials used in nonhuman animal laboratory studies include moving from one end of a maze or shuttle box to another. Typical applied examples include responses to a series of teacher-presented flash cards; answering a question prompted by the teacher; and, when presented with a sample color, pointing to a color from an array of three colors that matches the sample color. In each of these examples, the rate of response is controlled by the presentation of the antecedent stimulus. Because behaviors that occur within discrete trials are opportunity bound, measures such as percentage of response opportunities in which a response was emitted or trials-to-criterion should be employed, but not rate measures.

Do Not Use Rate to Measure Continuous Behaviors that Occur for Extended Periods of Time.   Rate is also a poor measure for continuous behaviors that occur for extended periods of time, such as participating in playground games or working at a play or activity center. Such behaviors are best measured by whether they are "on" or "off" at any given time, yielding data on duration or estimates of duration obtained by interval recording.

Celeration

Just like a car that accelerates when the driver presses the gas pedal and decelerates when the driver releases the pedal or steps on the brake, rates of response accelerate and decelerate. **Celeration** is a measure of how rates of response change over time. Rate of response accelerates when a participant responds faster over successive counting periods and decelerates when responding slows over successive observations. Celeration incorporates

three dimensional quantities: *count* per unit *time*/per unit of *time;* or expressed another way, rate/per unit of time (Graf & Lindsley, 2002; Johnston & Pennypacker, 1993a). Celeration provides researchers and practitioners with a direct measure of dynamic patterns of behavior change such as transitions from one steady state of responding to another and the acquisition of fluent levels of performance (Cooper, 2005).

The Standard Celeration Chart (see Figure 6.14) provides a standard format for displaying measures of celeration (Pennypacker, Gutierrez, & Lindsley, 2003).[3] There are four Standard Celeration Charts, showing rate as count (a) per minute, (b) per week, (c) per month, and (d) per year. These four charts provide different levels of magnification for viewing and interpreting celeration. Response rate is displayed on the vertical, or *y,* axis of the charts, and successive calendar time in days, weeks, months, or years is presented on the horizontal, or *x,* axis. Teachers and other behavioral practitioners use the count per minute–successive calendar days chart most often.

Celeration is displayed on all Standard Celeration Charts with a *celeration trend line.* A trend line, a straight line drawn through a series of graphed data points, visually represents the direction and degree of trend in the data.[4] The celeration trend line shows a factor by which rate of response is multiplying (accelerating) or dividing (decelerating) across the celeration time period (e.g., rate per week, rate per month, rate per year, rate per decade). A *celeration time period* is 1/20th of the horizontal axis of all Standard Celeration Charts. For example, the celeration period for the successive calendar days chart is per week. The celeration period for the successive calendar weeks chart is per month.

A trend line drawn from the bottom left corner to the top right corner on all Standard Celeration Charts has a slope of 34°, and has an acceleration value of X2 (read as "times-2"; celerations are expressed as multiples or divisors). It is this 34° angle of celeration, a linear measure of behavior change across time, that makes a chart standard. For example, if the response rate were 20 per minute on Monday, 40 per minute the next Monday, and 80 per minute on the third Monday, the celeration line (i.e., the trend line) on the successive calendar days chart would show a X2 acceleration, a doubling in rate per week. A X2 acceleration on successive calendar weeks chart is a doubling in rate every week (e.g., 20 in Week 1, 40 in Week 2, and 80 in Week 3). In most cases, celeration values should not be calculated with fewer than seven data points. Chapter 6 provides more information

---

[3]*Celeration,* the root word of *acceleration* and *deceleration,* is a generic term without specific reference to accelerating or decelerating response rates. Practitioners and researchers should use *acceleration* or *deceleration* when describing increasing or decreasing rates of response.

[4]Methods for calculating and drawing trend lines are described in Chapter 6.

on plotting and interpreting celeration data on the Standard Celeration Charts.

Measures Based on Temporal Extent

Duration

Duration, the amount of time in which behavior occurs, is the basic measure of temporal extent. Researchers and practitioners measure duration in standard units of time (e.g., Enrique worked cooperatively with his peer tutor for 12 minutes and 24 seconds today).

Duration is important when measuring the amount of time a person engages in the target behavior. Applied behavior analysts measure the duration of target behaviors that a person has been engaging in for too long or for too short of a time period, such as a child with developmental disabilities who tantrums for more than an hour at a time, or a student who sticks with an academic task for no more than 30 seconds at a time.

Duration is also an appropriate measure for behaviors that occur at very high rates (e.g., rocking; rapid jerks of the head, hands, legs) or task-oriented continuous behaviors that occur for an extended time (e.g., cooperative play, on-task behavior, off-task behavior).

Behavioral researchers and practitioners commonly measure one or both of two kinds of duration measures: *total duration* per session or observation period and *duration per occurrence.*

Total Duration per Session. Total duration is a measure of the cumulative amount of time in which a person engages in the target behavior. Applied behavior analysts use two procedures for measuring and reporting total duration. One method involves recording the cumulative amount of time a behavior occurs within a specified observation period. For example, a teacher concerned that a kindergarten child is spending too much time in solitary play could record the total time that the child is observed engaged in solitary play during daily 30-minute free-play periods. Procedurally, when the child engages in solitary play, the teacher activates a stopwatch. When solitary play ceases, the teacher stops the stopwatch but does not reset it. When the child drifts into solitary play again, the teacher starts the stopwatch again. Over the course of a 30-minute free-play period, the child might have engaged in a total of 18 minutes of solitary play. If the duration of the free-play periods varied from day to day, the teacher would report the total duration of solitary behavior as a percentage of total time observed (i.e., total duration of solitary behavior ÷ duration of free-play period × 100 = % of solitary behavior in one free-play period). In this case, 18 minutes of cumulative solitary play within a 30-minute session yields 60%.

Zhou, Iwata, Goff, and Shore (2001) used total duration measurement to assess leisure-item preferences of people with profound developmental disabilities. They used a stopwatch to record physical engagement with an item (i.e., contact with both hand and the item) during 2-minute trials. They reported total contact in seconds by summing the duration values across three 2-minute trials of each assessment. McCord, Iwata, Galensky, Ellingson, and Thomson (2001) started and stopped a stopwatch to measure the total duration in seconds that two adults with severe or profound mental retardation engaged in problem behavior (see Figure 6.6).

The other measure of total duration recording is the amount of time a person spends engaged in an activity, or the time a person needs to complete a specific task, without specifying a minimum or maximum observation period. For example, a community planner concerned with the amount of time senior citizens attended a new recreation center could report the total number of minutes per day that each senior spends at the center.

Duration per Occurrence. Duration per occurrence is a measure of the duration of time that each instance of the target behavior occurs. For example, assume that a student leaves his seat frequently and for varying amounts of time. Each time the student leaves his seat, the duration of his out-of-seat behavior could be recorded with a stopwatch. When he leaves his seat, the stopwatch is engaged. When he returns, the stopwatch is disengaged, the total time recorded, and the stopwatch reset to zero. When the student leaves his seat again, the process is repeated. The resulting measures yield data on the duration of occurrences of each out-of-seat behavior over the observation period.

In a study evaluating an intervention for decreasing noisy disruptions by children on a school bus, Greene, Bailey, and Barber (1981) used a sound-recording device that automatically recorded both the number of times that outbursts of sound exceeded a specified threshold and the duration in seconds that each outburst remained above that threshold. The researchers used the mean duration per occurrence of noisy disruptions as one measure for evaluating the intervention's effects.

Selecting and Combining Measures of Count and Duration. Measurements of count, total duration, and duration per occurrence provide different views of behavior. Count and duration measure different dimensional quantities of behavior, and these differences provide the basis for selecting which dimension to measure. Event recording meaures repeatability, whereas duration recording measures temporal extent. For instance, a teacher concerned about a student who is out of her seat "too much" could tally each time the student leaves her seat. The behavior is discrete and is unlikely to occur at such a high rate that counting the number of occurrences would be difficult. Because any instance of out-of-seat behavior has the potential to occur for an extended time and the amount of time the student is out of her seat is a socially significant aspect of the behavior, the teacher could also use total duration recording.

Using count to measure out-of-seat behavior provides the number of times the student left her seat. A measure of total duration will indicate the amount and proportion of time that the student was out of her seat during the observation period. Because of the relevance of temporal extent in this case, duration would provide a better measurement than count would. The teacher might observe that the student left her seat once in a 30-minute observation period. One occurrence of the behavior in 30 minutes might not be viewed as a problem. However, if the student remained out of her seat for 29 of the observation period's 30 minutes, a very different view of the behavior is obtained.

In this situation, duration per occurrence would make an even better measurement selection than either count or total duration recording would. That is because duration per occurrence measures the repeatability *and* the temporal extent of the behavior. A duration-per-occurrence measure would give the teacher information on the number of times the student was out of her seat and the duration of each occurrence. Duration per occurrence is often preferable to total duration because it is sensitive to the number of instances of the target behavior. Further, if a total duration measure is needed for other purposes, the individual durations of each of the counted and timed occurrences could be summed. However, if behavior endurance (e.g., academic responding, motor movements) is the major consideration, then total duration recording may be sufficient (e.g., oral reading for 3 minutes, free writing for 10 minutes, running for 10 kilometers).

Measures Based on Temporal Locus

As stated previously, temporal locus refers to when an instance of behavior occurs with respect to other events of interest. The two types of events most often used by researchers as points of reference for measuring temporal locus are the onset of antecedent stimulus events and the cessation of the previous response. These two points of reference provide the context for measuring response latency and interresponse time, the two measures of temporal locus most frequently reported in the behavior analysis literature.

Response Latency

Response latency (or, more commonly, *latency*) is a measure of the elapsed time between the onset of a stimulus and the initiation of a subsequent response.[5] Latency is an appropriate measure when the researcher or practitioner is interested in how much time occurs between an opportunity to emit a behavior and when the behavior is initiated. For example, a student might exhibit excessive delays in complying with teacher directions. Response latency would be the elapsed time from the end of the teacher's direction and when the student begins to comply with the direction. Interest can also focus on latencies that are too short. A student may give incorrect answers because she does not wait for the teacher to complete the questions. An adolescent who, at the slightest provocation from a peer, immediately retaliates has no time to consider alternative behaviors that could defuse the situation and lead to improved interactions.

Researchers typically report response latency data by the mean or median and range of individual latencies measures per observation period. For example, Lerman, Kelley, Vorndran, Kuhn, and LaRue (2002) used a latency measure to assess the effects of different reinforcement magnitudes (i.e., 20 seconds, 60 seconds, or 300 seconds of access to a reinforcer) on postreinforcement pause. The researchers measured the number of seconds from the end of each reinforcer-access interval to the first instance of the target behavior (a communication response). They then calculated and graphed the mean, median, and range of response latencies measured during each session (see Lerman et al., 2002, p. 41).

Interresponse Time

Interresponse time (IRT) is the amount of time that elapses between two consecutive instances of a response class. Like response latency, IRT is a measure of temporal locus because it identifies *when* a specific instance of behavior occurs with respect to another event (i.e., the previous response). Figure 4.2 shows a schematic representation of interresponse time.

Although it is a direct measure of temporal locus, IRT is functionally related to rate of response. Shorter IRTs coexist with higher rates of response, and longer IRTs are found within lower response rates. Applied behavior analysts measure IRT when the time between instances of a response class is important. IRT provides a basic measure for implementing and evaluating interventions using differential reinforcement of low rates (DRL), a procedure for using reinforcement to reduce the rate of responding (see Chapter 22). Like latency data, IRT

---

[5]*Latency* is most often used to describe the time between the onset of an antecedent stimulus change and the initiation of a response. However, the term can be used to refer to any measure of the temporal locus of a response with respect to any type of antecedent event. See Johnston and Pennypacker (1993b).

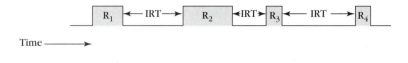

Time ⟶

Figure 4.2   Schematic representation of three interresponse times (IRT). IRT, the elapsed time between the termination of one response and the initiation of the next response, is a commonly used measure of temporal locus.

measures are typically reported and displayed graphically by mean (or median) and range per observation period.

Derivative Measures

Percentage and trials-to-criterion, two forms of data derived from direct measures of dimensional quantities of behavior, are frequently used in applied behavior analysis.

Percentage

A **percentage** is a ratio (i.e., a proportion) formed by combining the same dimensional quantities, such as count (i.e., number ÷ number) or time (i.e., duration ÷ duration; latency ÷ latency). A percentage expresses the proportional quantity of some event in terms of the number of times the event occurred per 100 opportunities that the event could have occurred. For example, if a student answered correctly 39 of 50 items on an exam, an accuracy percentage can be calculated by dividing the number of correct answers by the total number of test items and multiplying that product by 100 ($39 \div 50 = .78 \times 100 = 78\%$).

Percentage is frequently used in applied behavior analysis to report the proportion of total correct responses. For example, Ward and Carnes (2002) used a percentage-of-correct-performances measure in their study evaluating the effects of goal setting and public posting on skill execution of three defensive skills by linebackers on a college football team. The researchers recorded counts of correct and incorrect reads, drops, and tackles by each player and calculated accuracy percentages based on the number of opportunities for each type of play. (Data from this study are shown in Figure 9.3.)

Percentage is also used frequently in applied behavior analysis to report the proportion of observation intervals in which the target behavior occurred. These measures are typically reported as a proportion of intervals within a session (e.g., see Figure 21.4). Percentage can also be calculated for an entire observation session. In a study analyzing the differential effects of reinforcer rate, quality, immediacy, and response effort on the impulsive behavior of students with attention-deficit/hyperactivity disorder, Neef, Bicard, and Endo (2001) reported the percentage of time each student allocated to two sets of concurrently available math problems (e.g., time allocated to math problems yielding high-quality delayed reinforcers ÷ total time possible × 100 = %).

Percentages are used widely in education, psychology, and the popular media, and most people understand proportional relationships expressed as percentages. However, percentages are often used improperly and frequently misunderstood. Thus, we offer several notes of caution on the use and interpretation of percentages.

Percentages most accurately reflect the level of and changes in behavior when calculated with a divisor (or denominator) of 100 or more. However, most percentages used by behavioral researchers and practitioners are calculated with divisors much smaller than 100. Percentage measures based on small divisors are unduly affected by small changes in behavior. For example, a change in count of just 1 response per 10 opportunities changes the percentage by 10%. Guilford (1965) cautioned that it is unwise to compute percentages with divisors smaller than 20. For research purposes, we recommend that whenever possible, applied behavior analysts design measurement systems in which resultant percentages are based on no fewer than 30 response opportunities or observation intervals.

Sometimes changes in percentage can erroneously suggest improving performance. For example, an accuracy percentage could increase even though the frequency of incorrect responses remains the same or worsens. Consider a student whose accuracy in answering math problems on Monday is 50% (5 of 10 problems answered correctly) and on Tuesday it is 60% (12 of 20 problems answered correctly). Even with the improved proportional accuracy, the number of errors increased (from 5 on Monday to 8 on Tuesday).

Although no other measure communicates proportional relationships better than percentage does, its use as a behavioral quantity is limited because a percentage has no dimensional quantities.[6] For example, percentage cannot be used to assess the development of proficient or fluent behavior because an assessment of proficiency cannot occur without reference to count and time, but it can show the proportional accuracy of a targeted behavior during the development of proficiency.

---

[6]Because percentages are ratios based on the same dimensional quantity, the dimensional quantity is canceled out and no longer exists in the percentage. For example, an accuracy percentage created by dividing the number of correct responses by the number of response opportunities removes the actual count. However, ratios created from different dimensional quantities retain the dimensional quantities of each component. For example, rate retains a count per unit of time. See Johnston and Pennypacker (1993a) for further explication.

Another limitation of percentage as a measure of behavior change is that lower and upper limits are imposed on the data. For example, using percent correct to assess a student's reading ability imposes an artificial ceiling on the measurement of performance. A learner who correctly reads 100% of the words she is presented cannot improve in terms of the measure used.

Different percentages can be reported from the same data set, with each percentage suggesting significantly different interpretations. For example, consider a student who scores 4 correct (20%) on a 20-item pretest and 16 correct (80%) when the same 20 items are given as a posttest. The most straightforward description of the student's improvement from pretest to posttest (60%) compares the two measures using the original basis or divisor (20 items). Because the student scored 12 more items correct on the posttest than he did on the pretest, his performance on the posttest could be reported as an increase (gain score) over his pretest performance of 60%. And given that the student's posttest score represented a fourfold improvement in correct responses, some might report the posttest score as a 300% improvement of the pretest—a completely different interpretation from an improvement of 40%.

Although percentages greater than 100% are sometimes reported, strictly speaking, doing so is incorrect. Although a behavior change greater than 100% may seem impressive, it is a mathematical impossibility. A percentage is a *proportional* measure of a total set, where *x* (the proportion) of *y* (the total) is expressed as 1 part in 100. A proportion of something cannot exceed the total of that something or be less than zero (i.e., there is no such thing as a negative percentage). Every coach's favorite athlete who "always gives 110%" simply does not exist.[7]

Trials-to-Criterion

Trials-to-criterion is a measure of the number of response opportunities needed to achieve a predetermined level of performance. What constitutes a trial depends on the nature of the target behavior and the desired performance level. For a skill such as shoe tying, each opportunity to tie a shoe could be considered a trial, and trials-to-criterion data are reported as the number of trials required for the learner to tie a shoe correctly without prompts or assistance. For behaviors involving problem solving or discriminations that must be applied across a large number of examples to be useful, a trial might consist of a block, or series of response opportunities, in which each response opportunity involves the presentation of a different exemplar of the problem or discrimination. For example, a trial for discriminating between the short and long vowel sounds of the letter *o* could be a block of 10 consecutive opportunities to respond, in which each response opportunity is the presentation of a word containing the letter *o*, with short-vowel and long-vowel *o* words (e.g., *hot, boat*) presented in random order. Trials-to-criterion data could be reported as the number of blocks of 10 trials required for the learner to correctly pronounce the *o* sound in all 10 words. Count would be the basic measure from which the trials-to-criterion data would be derived.

Other basic measures, such as rate, duration, and latency, can also be used to determine trials-to-criterion data. For example, a trials-to-criterion measure for solving two-digit minus two-digit subtraction problems requiring borrowing could be the number of practice sheets of 20 randomly generated and sequenced problems a learner completes before she is able to solve all 20 problems on a single sheet in 3 minutes or less.

Trials-to-criterion data are often calculated and reported as an ex post facto measure of one important aspect of the "cost" of a treatment or instructional method. For example, Trask-Tyler, Grossi, and Heward (1994) reported the number of instructional trials needed by each of three students with developmental disabilities and visual impairments to prepare three food items from recipes without assistance on two consecutive times over two sessions. Each recipe entailed from 10 to 21 task-analyzed steps.

Trials-to-criterion data are used frequently to compare the relative efficiency of two or more treatments or instructional methods. For example, by comparing the number of practice trials needed for a student to master weekly sets of spelling words practiced in two different ways, a teacher could determine whether the student learns spelling words more efficiently with one method than with another. Sometimes trials-to-criterion data are supplemented by information on the number of minutes of instruction needed to reach predetermined performance criteria (e.g., Holcombe, Wolery, Werts, & Hrenkevich 1993; Repp, Karsh, Johnson, & VanLaarhoven, 1994).

Trials-to-criterion measures can also be collected and analyzed as a dependent variable throughout a study. For example, R. Baer (1987) recorded and graphed trials-to-criterion on a paired-associates memory task as a dependent variable in a study assessing the effects of caffeine on the behavior of preschool children.

Trials-to-criterion data can also be useful for assessing a learner's increasing competence in acquiring a related class of concepts. For instance, teaching a concept such as the color red to a child could consist of presenting "red" and "not red" items to the child and providing

---

[7]When a person reports a percentage in excess of 100% (e.g., "Our mutual fund grew by 120% during the recent bear market"), he is probably using the misstated percentage in *comparison to* the previous base unit, not as a proportion of it. In this example, the mutual fund's 20% increase makes its value 1.2 times greater than its value when the bear market began.

differential reinforcement for correct responses. Trials-to-criterion data could be collected of the number of "red" and "not red" exemplars required before the child achieves a specified level of performance with the discrimination. The same instructional and data collection procedures could then be used in teaching other colors to the child. Data showing that the child achieves mastery of each newly introduced color in fewer instructional trials than it took to learn previous colors might be evidence of the child's increasing agility in learning color concepts.

Definitional Measures

In addition to the basic and derived dimensions already discussed, behavior can also be defined and measured by its form and intensity. Neither form (i.e., topography) nor intensity (i.e., magnitude) of responding is a fundamental dimensional quantity of behavior, but each is an important quantitative parameter for defining and verifying the occurrence of many response classes. When behavioral researchers and practitioners measure the topography or magnitude of a response, they do so to determine whether the response represents an occurrence of the target behavior. Occurrences of the target behavior that are verified on the basis of topography or magnitude are then measured by one or more aspects of count, temporal extent, or temporal locus. In other words, measuring topography or magnitude is sometimes necessary to determine whether instances of the targeted response class have occurred, but the subsequent quantification of those responses is recorded, reported, and analyzed in terms of the fundamental and derivative measures of count, rate, duration, latency, IRT, percentage, and trials-to-criterion.

Topography

Topography, which refers to the physical form or shape of a behavior, is both a measurable and malleable dimension of behavior. Topography is a measurable quantity of behavior because responses of varying form can be detected from one another. That topography is a malleable aspect of behavior is evidenced by the fact that responses of varying form are shaped and selected by their consequences.

A group of responses with widely different topographies may serve the same function (i.e., form a response class). For example, each of the different ways of writing the word *topography,* shown in Figure 4.3, would produce the same effect on most readers. Membership in some response classes, however, is limited to responses within a narrow range of topographies. Although each of the response topographies in Figure 4.3 would meet the functional requirements of most written communications, none would meet the standards expected of an advanced calligraphy student.

Figure 4.3   Topography, the physical form or shape of behavior, is a measurable dimension of behavior.

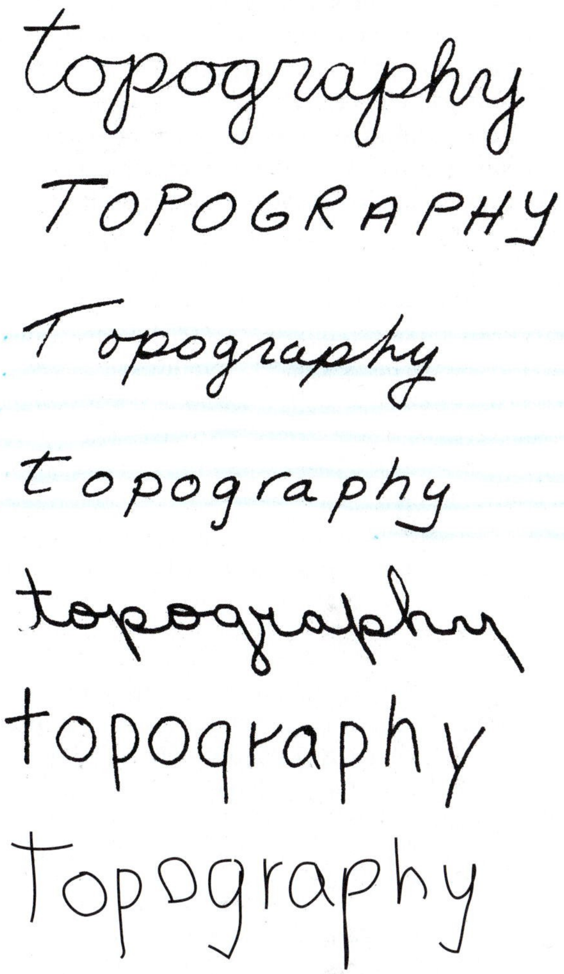

Topography is of obvious and primary importance in performance areas in which form, style, or artfulness of behavior is valued in its own right (e.g., painting, sculpting, dancing, gymnastics). Measuring and providing differential consequences for responses of varied topographies is also important when the functional outcomes of the behavior correlate highly with specific topographies. A student who sits with good posture and looks at the teacher is more likely to receive positive attention and opportunities to participate academically than is a student who slouches with her head on the desk (Schwarz & Hawkins, 1970). Basketball players who execute foul shots with a certain form make a higher percentage of shots than they do when they shoot idiosyncratically (Kladopoulos & McComas, 2001; see Figure 6.3).

Trap, Milner-Davis, Joseph, and Cooper (1978) measured the topography of cursive handwriting by first-grade students. Plastic transparent overlays were used to detect deviations from model letters in lower- and upper-case letters written by the children (see Figure 4.4). The researchers counted the number of correct letter strokes—those that met all of the specified topographical criteria (e.g., all letter strokes contained within the 2-mm parameters of the overlay, connected, complete, sufficient length)—and used the percentage correct of all strokes written by each student to assess the effects of visual and verbal feedback and a certificate of achievement on the children's acquisition of cursive handwriting skills.

Magnitude

Magnitude refers to the force or intensity with which a response is emitted. The desired outcomes of some behaviors are contingent on responding at or above (or below) a certain intensity or force. A screwdriver must be turned with sufficient force to insert or remove screws; a pencil must be applied to paper with enough force to leave legible marks. On the other hand, applying too much torque to a misaligned screw or bolt is likely to

strip the threads, and pushing too hard with a pencil will break its point.

The magnitude of speech or other vocalizations that were considered too loud or too soft has been measured in several studies. Schwarz and Hawkins (1970) measured the voice loudness of Karen, a sixth-grade girl who spoke so softly in class that her voice was usually inaudible to others. Karen's voice was recorded on videotape during two class periods each day. (The videotape was also used to obtain data on two other behaviors: face touching and the amount of time Karen sat in a slouched position). The researchers then played the videotape into an audiotape recorder with a loudness indicator and counted the number of times the needle went above a specified level on the loudness meter. Schwarz and Hawkins used the number (proportion) of needle inflections per 100 words spoken by Karen as the primary measure for evaluating the effects of an intervention on increasing her voice volume during class.

Greene and colleagues (1981) used an automated sound-recording device to measure the magnitude of noisy disruptions by middle school students on a school bus. The recording device could be adjusted so that only sound levels above a predetermined threshold activated it. The device automatically recorded both the number of times outbursts of sound exceeded a specified threshold (93 dB) and the total duration in seconds that the sound remained above that threshold. When the noise level exceeded the specified threshold, a light on a panel that all students could see was activated automatically. When the light was off, students listened to music during the bus ride; when the number of noisy disruptions was below a criterion, they participated in a raffle for prizes. This intervention drastically reduced the outbursts and other problem behaviors as well. Greene and colleagues reported both the number and the mean duration per occurrence of noisy disruptions as measures of evaluating the intervention's effects.[8]

Table 4.1 summarizes the measurable dimensions of behavior and considerations for their use.

Figure 4.4   Examples of outlines on a transparent overlay used to measure inside and outside boundaries of manuscript letters and an illustration of using the transparent overlay to measure the letter *m*. Because the vertical stroke of the letter *m* extended beyond the confines of the outline, it did not meet the topographical criteria for a correct response.

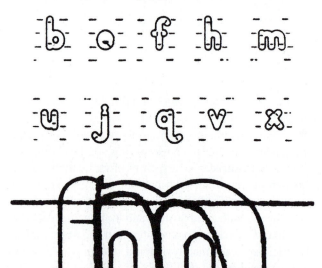

From "The Measurement of Manuscript Letter Strokes" by J. J. Helwig, J. C. Johns, J. E. Norman, J. O. Cooper, 1976. *Journal of Applied Behavior Analysis, 9*, p. 231. Copyright 1976 by the Society for the Experimental Analysis of Behavior, Inc. Used by permission.

---

[8]Researchers sometimes manipulate and control response topography and magnitude to assess their possible effects as independent variables. Piazza, Roane, Kenney, Boney, and Abt (2002) analyzed the effects of different response topographies on the frequency of pica (e.g., ingesting nonnutritive matter that may threaten one's life) by three females. Pica items were located in various places, which required the subjects to respond in different ways (e.g., reach, bend over, get on the floor, open a container) to obtain them. Pica decreased when more elaborate response topographies were required to obtain pica items. Van Houten (1993) reported that when a boy with a long history of intense and high-frequency face slapping wore 1.5-pound wrist weights, face slapping immediately dropped to zero. Studies such as these suggest that problem behaviors may be reduced when engaging in those behaviors requires more effortful responses in terms of topography or magnitude.

Table 4.1 Fundamental, derived, and definitional dimensions by which behavior can be measured and described.

Fundamental measures	How calculated	Considerations
Count: The number of responses emitted during an observation period.	Simple tally of the number of responses observed. Judah contributed 5 comments during the 10-minute class discussion.	• Observation time in which count was recorded should be referenced. • Most useful for comparison when observation time (counting time) is constant across observations. • Used in calculating rate/frequency, celeration, percentages, and trials-to-criterion measures.
Rate/frequency: A ratio of count per observation time; often expressed as count per standard unit of time (e.g., per minute, per hour, per day).	Report number of responses recorded per time in which observations were conducted. If Judah's comments were counted during a 10-minute class discussion, his rate of responding would be 5 comments per 10 minutes. Often calculated by dividing the number of responses recorded by number of standard units of time in which observations were conducted. Judah made comments at a rate of 0.5 per minute.	• If observation time varies across measurements, calculate with standard units of time. • Minimize faulty interpretations by reporting counting time. • Evaluating skill development and fluency requires measurement of correct and incorrect response rates. • Account for varied complexity and difficulty when calculating response rates. • Rate is the most sensitive measure of changes in repeatability. • Preferred measure for free operants. • Poor measure for behaviors that occur within discrete trials or for behaviors that occur for extended durations. • Most sensitive measure of behavior repeatability.

Derived measures	How calculated	Considerations
Celeration: The change (acceleration or deceleration) in rate of responding over time.	Based on count per unit of time (rate); expressed as factor by which responding is accelerating/decelerating (multiplying or dividing). A trend line connecting Judah's mean rates of commenting over 4 weeks of 0.1, 0.2, 0.4, and 0.8 comments per minute, respectively, would show an acceleration of by a factor of times-2 per week.	• Reveals dynamic patterns of behavior change such as transitions from one steady state to another and acquisition of fluency. • Displayed with a trend line on a Standard Celeration Chart (see Chapter 6). • Minimum of seven measures of rate recommended for calculating. *(continued)*

85

Table 4.1 (continued)

Fundamental measures	How calculated	Considerations
Duration: The amount of time that a behavior occurs.	*Total duration:* Two methods: (a) Add the individual amounts of time for each response during an observation period; or (b) record total time individual is engaged in an activity, or needs to complete a task, without a minimum or maximum observation period. Judah spent 1.5 minutes commenting in class today. *Duration per occurrence:* Record duration of time for each instance of the behavior; often reported by mean or median and range of durations per session. Judah's 6 comments today had a mean duration of 11 seconds, with a range of 3 to 24 seconds.	• Important measure when target behavior is problematic because it occurs for durations that are too long or too short. • Useful measure for behaviors that occur at very high rates and for which accurate event recoding is difficult (e.g., finger flicking). • Useful measure for behaviors that do not have discrete beginnings and for which event recoding is difficult (e.g., humming). • Useful measure for task-oriented or continuous behaviors (e.g., cooperative play). • Duration per occurrence often preferred over total duration because it includes data on count and total duration. • Use total duration when increasing the endurance of behavior is the goal. • Measuring duration per occurrence entails counting responses, which can be used to calculate rate of responding.
Response latency: The point in time when a response occurs with respect to the occurrence of an antecedent stimulus.	Record time elapsed from the onset of the antecedent stimulus event and the beginning of the response; often reported by mean or median and range of latencies per session. Judah's comments today had a mean latency of 30 seconds following a peers' comment (range, 5 to 90 seconds).	• Important measure when target behavior is a problem because it is emitted with latencies that are too long or too short. • Decreasing latencies can reveal person's increasing mastery of some skills.
Interresponse time (IRT): The point in time when a response occurs with respect to the occurrence of the previous response.	Record time elapsed from the end of previous response and the beginning of next response; often reported by mean or median and range of IRTs per session. Judah's comments today had a median IRT of 2 minutes and a range of 10 seconds to 5 minutes.	• Important measure when the time between responses, or pacing of behavior, is the focus. • Although a measure of temporal locus, IRT is correlated with rate of responding. • An important measure when implementing and evaluating DRL (see Chapter 22).

Derived measures	How calculated	Considerations
Percentage: A proportion, expressed as a number of parts per 100; typically expressed as a ratio of the number of responses of a certain type per total number of responses (or opportunities or intervals in which such a response could have occurred).	Divide number of responses meeting specified criteria (e.g., correct responses, responses with minimum IRT, responses of particular topography) by the total number of responses emitted (or response opportunities) and multiply by 100. Seventy percent of Judah's comments today were relevant to the discussion topic.	• Percentages based on divisors smaller than 20 are unduly influenced by small changes in behavior. Minimum of 30 observation intervals or response opportunities recommended for research. • Change in percentage may erroneously suggest improved performance. • Always report the divisor on which percentage measures are based. • Cannot be used to assess proficiency or fluency.

- Imposes upper and lower limits on performance (i.e., cannot exceed 100%)
- Widely different percentages can be reported from the same data set.
- To calculate an overall percentage from percentages based on different denominators (e.g., 90% [9/10], 87.5% [7/8], 33% [1/3], 100% [1/1], divide the total numerators of the component percentages (e.g., 18) by the total denominators (e.g., 18 / 22 = 81.8%). A mean of the percentages themselves yields a different outcome (e.g., 90% + 87.5% + 33% + 100% / 4 = 77.6%).

- Provides an ex post facto description of the "cost" of a treatment or instructional method.
- Useful for comparing relative efficiency of different methods of instruction or training.
- Useful in assessing changes in the rate at which a learner masters new skills (agility).

Trials to criterion: Number of responses, instructional trials, or practice opportunities needed to reach a predetermined performance criterion.

Add number of responses or practice trials necessary for learner to achieve specified criterion.

During class discussion training sessions conducted in the resource room, 14 blocks of 10 opportunities to comment were needed for Judah to achieve the criterion of 8 on-topic comments per 10 opportunities.

Definitional measures	How calculated	Considerations
Topography: The form or shape of behavior.	Used to determine whether responses meet topographical criteria; responses meeting those criteria are measured and reported by one or more fundamental or derivative measures (e.g., percentage of responses meeting topographical criteria). The plane of the golf club remained within plus or minus 2 degrees from backswing to follow-through on 85% of Amanda's swings.	• Important measure when desired outcomes of behavior are contingent on responses meeting certain topographies. • Important measure for performance areas in which form, style, or artfulness is valued.
Magnitude: The strength, intensity, or force of behavior.	Used to determine whether responses meet magnitude criteria; responses meeting those criteria are measured and reported by one or more fundamental or derivative measures (e.g., count of responses meeting magnitude criteria). Jill bench pressed a 60-pound bar 20 times.	• Important measure when desired outcomes of behavior are contingent on responses within certain range of magnitudes.

Procedures for Measuring Behavior

Procedures for measuring behavior used most often by applied behavior analysts involve one or a combination of the following: event recording, timing, and various time sampling methods.

Event Recording

Event recording encompasses a wide variety of procedures for detecting and recording the number of times a behavior of interest occurs. For example, Cuvo, Lerch, Leurquin, Gaffaney, and Poppen (1998) used event recording while analyzing the effects of work requirements and reinforcement schedules on the choice behavior of adults with mental retardation and preschool children while they were engaged in age-appropriate tasks (e.g., adults sorting silverware, children tossing beanbags or jumping hurdles). The researchers recorded each piece of silverware sorted, each beanbag tossed, and each hurdle jumped.

Devices for Event Recording

Although pencil and paper are sufficient for making event recordings, the following devices and procedures may facilitate the counting process.

- *Wrist counters.* Wrist counters are useful for tallying student behaviors. Golfers use these counters to tally strokes. Most wrist counters record from 0 to 99 responses. These counters can be purchased from sporting goods stores or large department stores.

- *Hand-tally digital counters.* These digital counters are similar to wrist counters. Hand-tally counters are frequently used in grocery chain stores, cafeterias, military mess halls, and tollgates to tally the number of people served. These mechanical counters are available in single or multiple channels and fit comfortably in the palm of the hand. With practice, practitioners can operate the multiple-channel counters rapidly and reliably with just one hand. These digital counters can be obtained from office supply stores.

- *Abacus wrist and shoestring counters.* Landry and McGreevy (1984) described two types of abacus counters for measuring behavior. The abacus wrist counter is made from pipe cleaners and beads attached to a leather wristband to form an abacus with rows designated as ones and tens. An observer can tally from 1 to 99 occurrences of behavior by sliding the beads in abacus fashion. Responses are tallied in the same way on an abacus shoestring counter except the beads slide on shoestrings attached to a key ring, which is attached to the observer's belt, belt loop, or some other piece of clothing such as a buttonhole.

- *Masking tape.* Teachers can mark tallies on masking tape attached to their wrists or desk.

- *Pennies, buttons, paper clips.* One item can be moved from one pocket to another each time the target behavior occurs.

- *Pocket calculators.* Pocket calculators can be used to tally events.

Event recording also applies to the measurement of discrete trial behaviors, in which the count for each trial or opportunity to respond is either 1 or 0, representing the occurrence or nonoccurrence of the behavior. Figure 4.5 shows a form used to record the occurrence of imitation responses by a preschooler with disabilities and his typically developing peer partner within a series of instructional trials embedded into ongoing classroom activities (Valk, 2003). For each trial, the observer recorded the occurrence of a correct response, no response, an approximation, or an inappropriate response by the target child and the peer by circling or marking a slash through letters representing each behavior. The form also allowed the observer to record whether the teacher prompted or praised the target child's imitative behavior.

Considerations with Event Recording

Event recording is easy to do. Most people can tally discrete behaviors accurately, often on the first attempt. If the response rate is not too high, event recording does not interfere with other activities. A teacher can continue with instruction while tallying occurrences of the target behavior.

Event recording provides a useful measurement for most behaviors. However, each instance of the target behavior must have discrete beginning and ending points. Event recording is applicable for target behaviors such as students' oral responses to questions, students' written answers to math problems, and a parent praising his son or daughter. Behaviors such as humming are hard to measure with event recording because an observer would have difficulty determining when one hum ends and another begins. Event recording is difficult for behaviors defined without specific discrete action or object relations, such as engagement with materials during free-play activity. Because engagement with materials does not present a specific discrete action or object relation, an observer may have difficulty judging when one engagement starts and ends, and then another engagement begins.

Session date: **May 21**   Session no: **16**   Observer: **Jennie**

Target child: **Jordan**   Peer: **Ethan**   IOA day: (**YES**) NO

Target behavior: **Place block on structure**   Condition: **5-sec time delay**

Code: C = Correct   N = No response   A = Approximation   I = Inappropriate

Trial	Target child's behavior				Teacher behavior toward target child		Peer's behavior				Teacher praise
1	Ⓒ	N	A	I	Prompt	⟨Praise⟩	Ⓒ	N	A	I	⟨Praise⟩
2	Ⓒ	N	A	I	Prompt	⟨Praise⟩	Ⓒ	N	A	I	⟨Praise⟩
3	Ⓒ	N	A	I	Prompt	⟨Praise⟩	Ⓒ	N	A	I	⟨Praise⟩
4	C	N	Ⓐ	I	⟨Prompt⟩	⟨Praise⟩	Ⓒ	N	A	I	⟨Praise⟩
5	Ⓒ	N	A	I	⟨Prompt⟩	⟨Praise⟩	C	N	Ⓐ	I	Praise
6	C	N	Ⓐ	I	⟨Prompt⟩	⟨Praise⟩	Ⓒ	N	A	I	⟨Praise⟩
7	Ⓒ	N	A	I	Prompt	⟨Praise⟩	Ⓒ	N	A	I	⟨Praise⟩
8	Ⓒ	N	A	I	Prompt	⟨Praise⟩	Ⓒ	N	A	I	⟨Praise⟩
9	Ⓒ	N	A	I	Prompt	⟨Praise⟩	Ⓒ	N	A	I	⟨Praise⟩
10	Ⓒ	N	A	I	Prompt	⟨Praise⟩	Ⓒ	N	A	I	⟨Praise⟩

No. corrects by target child: **8**   No. corrects by peer: **9**

****

Target behavior: **Place sticker on paper**   Condition: **5-sec time delay**

Trial	Target child's behavior				Teacher behavior toward target child		Peer's behavior				Teacher praise
1	Ⓒ	N	A	I	Prompt	⟨Praise⟩	C	Ⓝ	A	I	Praise
2	C	N	Ⓐ	I	⟨Prompt⟩	⟨Praise⟩	Ⓒ	N	A	I	⟨Praise⟩
3	C	N	Ⓐ	I	⟨Prompt⟩	⟨Praise⟩	Ⓒ	N	A	I	⟨Praise⟩
4	Ⓒ	N	A	I	Prompt	⟨Praise⟩	Ⓒ	N	A	I	⟨Praise⟩
5	C	N	Ⓐ	I	⟨Prompt⟩	⟨Praise⟩	Ⓒ	N	A	I	⟨Praise⟩
6	C	N	Ⓐ	I	Prompt	⟨Praise⟩	C	N	A	Ⓘ	Praise
7	C	N	A	Ⓘ	⟨Prompt⟩	Praise	Ⓒ	N	A	I	⟨Praise⟩
8	C	N	Ⓐ	I	⟨Prompt⟩	⟨Praise⟩	Ⓒ	N	A	I	Praise
9	Ⓒ	N	A	I	Prompt	⟨Praise⟩	Ⓒ	N	A	I	⟨Praise⟩
10	Ⓒ	N	A	I	Prompt	⟨Praise⟩	Ⓒ	N	A	I	⟨Praise⟩

No. corrects by target child: **4**   No. corrects by peer: **8**

Figure 4.5   Data collection form for recording the behavior of two children and a teacher during a series of discrete trials.

Adapted from *The Effects of Embedded Instruction within the Context of a Small Group on the Acquisition of Imitation Skills of Young Children with Disabilities* by J. E. Valk (2003), p. 167. Unpublished doctoral dissertation, The Ohio State University. Used by permission.

Another consideration with event recording is that the target behaviors should not occur at such high rates that an observer would have difficulty counting each discrete occurrence accurately. High-frequency behaviors that may be difficult to measure with event recording include rapid talking, body rocks, and tapping objects.

Also, event recording does not produce accurate measures for target behaviors that occur for extended time periods, such as staying on task, listening, playing quietly alone, being out of one's seat, or thumb sucking. Task-oriented or continuous behaviors (e.g., being "on task") are examples of target behaviors for which event recording would not be indicated. Classes of continuous behaviors occurring across time are usually not a prime concern of applied behavior analysts. For example, reading per se is of less concern than the number of words read correctly and incorrectly, or the number of reading comprehension questions answered correctly and incorrectly. Similarly, behaviors that demonstrate understanding are more important to measure than "listening behavior," and the number of academic responses a student emits during an independent seatwork period is more important than being on task.

Timing

Researchers and practitioners use a variety of timing devices and procedures to measure duration, response latency, and interresponse time.

Timing the Duration of Behavior

Applied researchers often use semi-automated computer-driven systems for recording durations. Practitioners, however, will most likely use nonautomated instruments for recording duration. The most precise nonautomated instrument is a digital stopwatch. Practitioners can use wall clocks or wristwatches to measure duration, but the measures obtained will be less precise than those obtained with a stopwatch.

The procedure for recording the total duration of a target behavior per session with a stopwatch is to (a) activate the stopwatch as the behavior starts and (b) stop the watch at the end of the episode. Then, without resetting the stopwatch, the observer starts the stopwatch again at the beginning of the second occurrence of the behavior and stops the watch at the end of the second episode.

The observer continues to accumulate the durations of time in this fashion until the end of the observation period, and then transfers the total duration of time showing on the stopwatch to a data sheet.

Gast and colleagues (2000) used the following procedure for measuring duration with a foot switch and tape recorder that enables a practitioner to use both hands to present stimulus materials or interact with the participant in other ways throughout the session.

> The duration of a student's target behavior was recorded by using a cassette audio tape recorder with a blank tape in it that was activated by the instructor using her foot to activate a jellybean switch connected to the tape recorder. When the student engaged in the target behavior, the teacher activated the switch that started the tape running. When the student stopped engaging in the behavior, the teacher stopped the tape by activating the switch again. At the end of the session the teacher said, "end" and stopped the tape recorder and rewound the tape. [After the session the teacher] then played the tape from the beginning until the "end" and timed the duration with a stopwatch. (p. 398)

McEntee and Saunders (1997) recorded duration per occurrence using a bar code data collection system to measure (a) functional and stereotypic engagements with materials and (b) stereotypy without interaction with materials and other aberrant behaviors. They created and arranged bar codes on a data sheet to record the behaviors of four adolescents with severe to profound mental retardation. A computer with a bar code font and software read the bar code, recording the year, month, day, and time of particular events. The bar code data collection system provided real-time duration measurements of engagements with materials and aberrant behaviors.

Timing Response Latency and Interresponse Time

Procedures for measuring latency and interresponse time (IRT) are similar to procedures used to measure duration. Measuring latency requires the precise detection and recording of the time that elapses from the onset of each occurrence of the antecedent stimulus event of interest and the onset of the target behavior. Measuring IRTs requires recording the precise time that elapses from the termination of each occurrence of the target behavior to the onset of the next. Wehby and Hollahan (2000) measured the latency of compliance by an elementary school student with learning disabilities to instructions to begin math assignments. Using a laptop computer with software designed to detect latency (see Tapp, Wehby, & Ellis, 1995, for the MOOSES observation system), they measured latency from the request to the onset of compliance.

Time Sampling

Time sampling refers to a variety of methods for observing and recording behavior during intervals or at specific moments in time. The basic procedure involves dividing the observation period into time intervals and then recording the presence or absence of behavior within or at the end of each interval.

Time sampling was developed originally by ethologists studying the behavior of animals in the field (Charlesworth & Spiker, 1975). Because it was not possible or feasible to observe the animals continuously, these scientists arranged systematic schedules of relatively brief but frequent observation intervals. The measures obtained from these "samples" are considered to be representative of the behavior during the entire time period from which they were collected. For example, much of our knowledge about the behavior of gorillas is based on data collected by researchers such as Jane Goodall using time sampling observation methods.

Three forms of time sampling used often by applied behavior analysts are whole-interval recording, partial-interval recording, and momentary time sampling.[9]

Whole-Interval Recording

Whole-interval recording is often used to measure continuous behaviors (e.g., cooperative play) or behaviors that occur at such high rates that observers have difficulty distinguishing one response from another (e.g., rocking, humming) but can detect whether the behavior is occurring at any given time. With **whole-interval recording,** the observation period is divided into a series of brief time intervals (typically from 5 to 10 seconds). At the end of each interval, the observer records whether the target behavior occurred *throughout* the interval. If a student's on-task behavior is being measured via 10-second whole-interval recording, the student would need to meet the definition of being on task during an entire interval for the behavior to be recorded as occurring in that interval. The student who was on task for 9 of an interval's 10 seconds would be scored as not being on task for that interval. Hence, data obtained with whole-interval recording usually underestimate the overall percentage of the observation period in which the behavior actually occurred. The longer the observation intervals, the greater the degree to which whole-interval recording will underestimate the actual occurrence of the behavior.

---

[9]A variety of terms are used in the applied behavior analysis literature to describe measurement procedures that involve observing and recording behavior within or at the end of scheduled intervals. Some authors use the term *time sampling* to refer only to momentary time sampling. We include whole-interval and partial-interval recording under the rubric of time sampling because it is often conducted as a discontinuous measurement method to provide a representative "sample" of a person's behavior during the observation period interval.

Data collected with whole-interval recording are reported as the percentage of total intervals in which the target behavior was recorded as occurring. Because they represent the proportion of the entire observation period that the person was engaged in the target behavior, whole-interval recording data yield an estimate of total duration. For example, assume a whole-interval observation period consisting of six 10-second intervals (a one-minute time frame). If the target behavior was recorded as occurring for four of these whole intervals and not occurring for the remaining two intervals, it would yield a total duration estimate of 40 seconds.

Figure 4.6 shows an example of a whole-interval recording form used to measure the on-task behavior of four students during academic seatwork time (Ludwig, 2004). Each minute was divided into four 10-second observation intervals; each observation interval was followed by 5 seconds in which the observer recorded the occurrence or nonoccurrence of target behavior during the preceding 10 seconds. The observer first watched Student 1 continuously for 10 seconds, and then she looked away during the next 5 seconds and recorded whether Student 1 had been on task throughout the previous 10 seconds by circling YES or NO on the recording form. After the 5-second interval for recording Student 1's behavior, the observer looked up and watched Student 2 continuously for 10 seconds, after which she recorded Student 2's behavior on the form. The same procedure for observing and recording was used for Students 3 and 4. In this way, the on-task behavior of each student was observed and recorded for one 10-second interval per minute.

Continuing the sequence of observation and recording intervals over a 30-minute observation period provided thirty 10-second measures (i.e., samples) of each student's on-task behavior. The data in Figure 4.6 show that the four students were judged by the observer to have been on task during Session 17 for 87%, 93%, 60%, and 73% of the intervals, respectively. Although the data are intended to represent the level of each student's behavior throughout the observation period, it is important to remember that each student was observed for a total of only 5 of the observation period's 30 minutes.

On-Task Recording Form

Date: __May 7__   Group no: __1__   Session no: __17__

Observer: (Robin)_____   IOA session: ___Yes _X_ No

Experimental condition: Baseline   On task   (Productivity)

Obs. start time: __9:42__   Stop time: __10:12__

10-sec intervals	Student 1		Student 2		Student 3		Student 4	
1	(YES)	NO	(YES)	NO	(YES)	NO	YES	(NO)
2	(YES)	NO	(YES)	NO	(YES)	NO	(YES)	NO
3	(YES)	NO	(YES)	NO	YES	(NO)	(YES)	NO
4	(YES)	NO	(YES)	NO	YES	(NO)	(YES)	NO
5	(YES)	NO	(YES)	NO	(YES)	NO	(YES)	NO
6	(YES)	NO	(YES)	NO	YES	(NO)	YES	(NO)
7	(YES)	NO	(YES)	NO	YES	(NO)	(YES)	NO
8	(YES)	NO	(YES)	NO	(YES)	NO	YES	(NO)
9	YES	(NO)	(YES)	NO	(YES)	NO	(YES)	NO
10	YES	(NO)	(YES)	NO	(YES)	NO	(YES)	NO
11	(YES)	NO	(YES)	NO	YES	(NO)	YES	(NO)
12	(YES)	NO	YES	(NO)	(YES)	NO	YES	(NO)
13	(YES)	NO	(YES)	NO	(YES)	NO	(YES)	NO
14	YES	(NO)	YES	(NO)	(YES)	NO	YES	(NO)
15	(YES)	NO	(YES)	NO	YES	(NO)	YES	(NO)
16	(YES)	NO	(YES)	NO	(YES)	NO	(YES)	NO
17	(YES)	NO	(YES)	NO	(YES)	NO	(YES)	NO
18	(YES)	NO	(YES)	NO	(YES)	NO	(YES)	NO
19	YES	(NO)	(YES)	NO	YES	(NO)	(YES)	NO
20	(YES)	NO	(YES)	NO	(YES)	NO	(YES)	NO
21	(YES)	NO	(YES)	NO	YES	(NO)	(YES)	NO
22	(YES)	NO	(YES)	NO	YES	(NO)	(YES)	NO
23	(YES)	NO	(YES)	NO	(YES)	NO	(YES)	NO
24	(YES)	NO	(YES)	NO	(YES)	NO	(YES)	(NO)
25	(YES)	NO	(YES)	NO	YES	(NO)	(YES)	NO
26	(YES)	NO	(YES)	NO	YES	(NO)	(YES)	NO
27	(YES)	NO	(YES)	NO	(YES)	NO	(YES)	NO
28	(YES)	NO	(YES)	NO	YES	(NO)	(YES)	NO
29	(YES)	NO	(YES)	NO	(YES)	NO	(YES)	NO
30	(YES)	NO	(YES)	NO	(YES)	NO	(YES)	NO
Totals	26	4	28	2	18	12	22	8
% Intervals on task	86.6%		93.3%		60.0%		73.3%	

(Yes) = On-task   (No) = Off-task

Figure 4.6 Observation form used for whole-interval recording of four students being on task during independent seatwork time.

Adapted from *Smiley faces and spinners: Effects of self-monitoring of productivity with an indiscriminable contingency of reinforcement on the on-task behavior and academic productivity by kindergarteners during independent seatwork* by R. L. Ludwig, 2004, p. 101. Unpublished master's thesis, The Ohio State University. Used by permission.

Figure 4.7   Portion of a form used for partial-interval recording of four response classes by three students.

	1	2	3	4
Student 1	Ⓐ T S D N	Ⓐ T S D N	Ⓐ Ⓣ S D N	A T S D Ⓝ
Student 2	A T Ⓢ Ⓓ N	A Ⓣ Ⓢ D N	A T S Ⓓ N	Ⓐ T S D N
Student 3	A T S D Ⓝ	A T S Ⓓ N	Ⓐ T S Ⓓ N	A Ⓣ Ⓢ D N

Key:
A = Academic response
T = Talk-out
S = Out-of-seat
D = Other disruptive behavior
N = No occurrences of target behaviors

Observers using any form of time sampling should always make a recording response of some sort in every interval. For example, an observer using a form such as the one in Figure 4.6 would record the occurrence or nonoccurrence of the target behavior in each interval by circling YES or NO. Leaving unmarked intervals increases the likelihood of losing one's place on the recording form and marking the result of an observation in the wrong interval space.

All time sampling methods require a timing device to signal the beginning and end of each observation and recording interval. Observers using pencil, paper, clipboard, and timers for interval measurement will often attach a stopwatch to a clipboard. However, observing and recording behavior while having to look simultaneously at a stopwatch is likely to have a negative impact on the accuracy of measurement. An effective solution to this problem is for the observer to listen by earphone to prerecorded audio cues signaling the observation and recording intervals. For example, observers using a whole-interval recording procedure such as the one just described could listen to an audio recording with a sequence of prerecorded statements such as the following: "Observe Student 1," 10 seconds later, "Record Student 1," 5 seconds later, "Observe Student 2," 10 seconds later, "Record Student 2," and so on.

Tactile prompting devices can also be used to signal observation intervals. For example, the *Gentle Reminder* (dan@gentlereminder.com) and *MotivAider* (www.habitchange.com) are small timing instruments that vibrate at the time intervals programmed by the user.

Partial-Interval Recording

When using **partial-interval recording,** the observer records whether the behavior occurred *at any time* during the interval. Partial-interval time sampling is not concerned with how many times the behavior occurred during the interval or how long the behavior was present, just that it occurred at some point during the interval. If the target behavior occurs multiple times during the interval, it is still scored as occurring only once. An observer using partial-interval recording to measure a student's disruptive behavior would mark an interval if disruptive behavior of any form meeting the target behavior definition occurred for any amount of time during the interval. That is, an interval would be scored as disruptive behavior even if the student was disruptive for only 1 second of a 6-second interval. Because of this, data obtained via partial-interval recording often overestimate the overall percentage of the observation period (i.e., total duration) that the behavior actually occurred.

Partial-interval data, like whole-interval data, are most often reported as a percentage of total intervals in which the target behavior was scored. Partial-interval data are used to represent the proportion of the entire observation period in which the target behavior occurred, but unlike whole-interval recording, the results of partial-interval recording do not provide any information on duration per occurrence. That is because any instance of the target behavior, regardless of how brief its duration, will cause an interval to be scored.

If partial-interval recording with brief observation intervals is used to measure discrete responses of short duration per occurrence, the data obtained provide a crude estimate of the minimum rate of responding. For example, data showing that a behavior measured by partial-interval recording consisting of 6-second contiguous intervals (i.e., successive intervals are not separated by time in which the behavior is not observed) occurred in 50% of the total intervals indicates a minimum response rate of five responses per minute (on the average, at least one response occurred in 5 of the 10 intervals per minute). Although partial-interval recording often overestimates the total duration, it is likely to underestimate the rate of a high-frequency behavior. This is because an interval in which a person made eight nonverbal sounds would be scored the same as an interval in which the person made only one sound. When the evaluation and understanding of a target behavior requires an accurate and sensitive measure of response rate, event recording should be used.

Because an observer using partial-interval recording needs to record only that a behavior has occurred at any point during each interval (compared to having to watch the behavior throughout the entire interval with whole-interval), it is possible to measure multiple behaviors concurrently. Figure 4.7 shows a portion of a form for measuring four response classes by three students using partial-interval recording with 20-second intervals. The observer watches Student 1 throughout the first 20-second interval, Student 2 for the next 20 seconds, and Student 3 for the next 20 seconds. Each student is observed for 20 seconds out of each minute of the observation period. If a student engages in any of the behaviors being measured at any time during an observation interval, the observer marks the letter(s) corresponding to those behaviors. If a student engages in none of the behaviors being measured during an interval, the observer marks N to indicate no occurrences of the target behaviors. For example, during the first interval in which Student 1 was observed, he said, "Pacific Ocean" (an academic response). During the first interval in which Student 2 was observed, she left her seat and threw a pencil (a behavior within the response class "other disruptive behavior"). Student 3 emitted none of the four target behaviors during the first interval that he was observed.

Momentary Time Sampling

An observer using **momentary time sampling** records whether the target behavior is occurring at the moment that each time interval ends. If conducting momentary time sampling with 1-minute intervals, an observer would look at the person at the 1-minute mark of the observation period, determine immediately whether the target behavior was occurring, and indicate that decision on the recording form. One minute later (i.e., 2 minutes into the observation period), the observer would look again at the person and then score the presence or absence of the target behavior. This procedure would continue until the end of the observation period.

As with interval recording methods, data from momentary time sampling are typically reported as percentages of the total intervals in which the behavior occurred and are used to estimate the proportion of the total observation period that the behavior occurred.

A major advantage of momentary time sampling is that the observer does not have to attend continuously to measurement, whereas interval recording methods demand the undivided attention of the observer.

Because the person is observed for only a brief moment, much behavior will be missed with momentary time sampling. Momentary time sampling is used primarily to measure continuous activity behaviors such as engagement with a task or activity, because such behaviors are easily identified. Momentary time sampling is not recommended for measuring low-frequency, short-duration behaviors (Saudargas & Zanolli, 1990).

A number of studies have compared measures obtained by momentary time sampling using intervals of varying duration with measures of the same behavior obtained by continuous duration recording (e.g., Gunter, Venn, Patrick, Miller, & Kelly, 2003; Powell, Martindale, Kulp, Martindale, & Bauman, 1977; Powell, Martindale, & Kulp, 1975; Simpson & Simpson, 1977; Saudargas and Zanolli 1990; Test & Heward, 1984). In general, this research has found that momentary time sampling both overestimates and underestimates the continuous duration measure when time intervals are greater than 2 minutes. With intervals less than 2 minutes, the data obtained using momentary time sampling more closely matched that obtained using the continuous duration measure.

Results of a study by Gunter and colleagues (2003) are representative of this research. These researchers compared measures of on-task behavior of three elementary students with emotional/behavioral disorders over seven sessions obtained by momentary time sampling conducted at 2-, 4-, and 6-minute intervals with measures of the same behavior obtained by continuous duration recording. Measures obtained using the 4-minute and 6-minute time sampling method produced data paths that were highly discrepant with the data obtained by continuous measurement, but data obtained using the 2-minute interval had a high degree of correspondence with the measures obtained using the continuous duration method. Figure 4.8 shows the results for one of the students.

Planned Activity Check

A variation of momentary time sampling, **planned activity check (PLACHECK)** uses head counts to measure "group behavior." A teacher using PLACHECK observes a group of students at the end of each time interval, counts the number of students engaged in the targeted activity, and records the tally with the total number of students in the group. For example, Doke and Risley (1972) used data obtained by PLACHECK measurement to compare group participation in required and optional before-school activities. Observers tallied the number of students in either the required or the optional activity area at the end of 3-minute intervals, and then the number of children actually participating in an activity in either area.

Figure 4.8 Comparison of measures of the on-task behavior of an elementary student obtained by 2-minute, 4-minute, and 6-minute momentary time sampling with measures of the same behavior obtained by continuous duration recording.

From "Efficacy of using momentary time samples to determine on-task behavior of students with emotional/behavioral disorders" by P. L. Gunter, M. L. Venn, J. Patrick, K. A. Miller, and L. Kelly, 2003, *Education and Treatment of Children, 26,* p. 406. Used by permission.

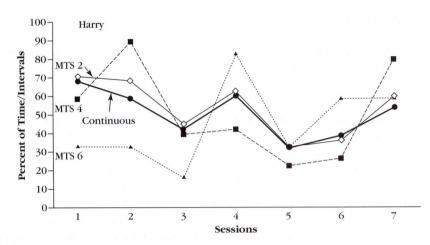

They reported these data as separate percentages of children participating in required or optional activities.

Dyer, Schwartz, and Luce (1984) used a variation of PLACHECK to measure the percentage of students with disabilities living in a residential facility engaged in age-appropriate and functional activities. As students entered the observation area, they were observed individually for as long as it took to determine the activity in which they were engaged. The students were observed in a predetermined order not exceeding 10 seconds per student.

Other variations of the PLACHECK measurement can be found in the literature, though they usually are called time sampling or momentary time sampling. For example, in a study examining the effects of response cards on the disruptive behavior of third-graders during daily math lessons, Armendariz and Umbreit (1999) recorded at 1-minute intervals whether each student in the class was being disruptive. By combining the PLACHECK data obtained across all of the no-response

cards (baseline) sessions, and graphing those results as the percentage of students who were disruptive at each 1-minute mark, and doing the same with the PLACHEK data from all response cards sessions. Armendariz and Umbreit created a clear and powerful picture of the differences in "group behavior" from the beginning to the end of a typical lesson in which response cards were used or not used.

Recognizing Artifactual Variability in Time Sampling Measures

As stated previously, all time sampling methods provide only an estimate of the actual occurrence of the behavior. Different measurement sampling procedures produce different results, which can influence decisions and interpretations. Figure 4.9 illustrates just how different the results obtained by measuring the same behavior with

Figure 4.9

Comparing measures of the same behavior obtained by three different time sampling methods with measure obtained by continuous duration recording.

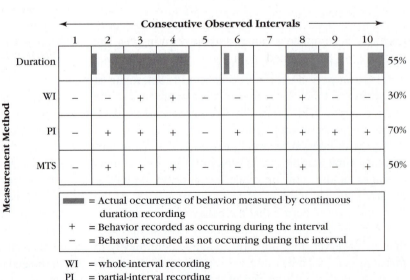

different time sampling methods can be. The shaded bars indicate when the behavior was occurring within an observation period divided into 10 contiguous intervals. The shaded bars reveal all three dimensional quantities of behavior: repeatability (seven instances of the behavior), temporal extent (the duration of each response) and temporal locus (interresponse time is depicted by the space between the shaded bars).

Because the time sampling methods used in applied behavior analysis are most often viewed and interpreted as measures of the proportion of the total observation period in which the behavior occurred, it is important to compare the results of time sampling methods with those obtained by continuous measurement of duration. Continuous measurement reveals that the behavior depicted in Figure 4.9 occurred 55% of the time during the observation period. When the same behavior during the same observation period was recorded using whole interval recordings the measure obtained grossly underestimated the actual occurrence of the behavior (i.e., 30% versus 55%), partial-interval recording grossly overestimated the actual occurrence (i.e., 70% versus 55%), and momentary time sampling yielded a fairly close estimate of actual occurrence of the behavior (50% versus 55%).

The fact that momentary time sampling resulted in a measure that most closely approximated the actual behavior does not mean that it is always the preferred method. Different distributions of the behavior (i.e., temporal locus) during the observation period, even at the same overall frequency and duration as the session shown in Figure 4.9, would result in widely different outcomes from each of the three time sampling methods.

Discrepancies between measures obtained by different measurement methods are usually described in terms of the relative accuracy or inaccuracy of each method. However, accuracy is not the issue here. If the shaded bars in Figure 4.9 represent the true value of the behavior, then each of the time sampling methods was conducted with complete accuracy and the resulting data are what should be obtained by applying each method. An example of the inaccurate use of one of the measurement methods would be if the observer using whole-interval recording had marked the behavior as occurring in Interval 2, when the behavior did not occur according to the rules of whole-interval recording.

But if the behavior actually occurred for 55% of the observation period, what should we call the wrong and misleading measures of 30% and 70% if not inaccurate? In this case, the misleading data are artifacts of the measurement procedures used to obtain them. An **artifact** is something that appears to exist because of the way it is examined or measured. The 30% measure obtained by whole-interval recording and the 70% measure obtained by partial-interval recording are artifacts of the way those

measures were conducted. The fact that data obtained from whole-interval and partial-interval recording consistently underestimate and overestimate, respectively, actual occurrence of behavior as measured by continuous duration recording is an example of well-known artifacts.

It is clear that interval measurement and momentary time sampling result in some artifactual variability in the data, which must be considered carefully when interpretating results obtained with these measurement methods. Some common causes of measurement artifacts and how to avoid them are discussed in Chapter 5.

Measuring Behavior by Permanent Products

Behavior can be measured in real time by observing a person's actions and recording responses of interest as they occur. For example, a teacher can keep a tally of the number of times a student raises her hand during a class discussion. Some behaviors can be measured in real time by recording their effects on the environment as those effects are produced. For example, a hitting instructor advances a handheld counter each time a batter hits a pitch to the right-field side of second base.

Some behaviors can be measured after they have occurred. A behavior that produces consistent effects on the environment can be measured after it has occurred if the effects, or products left behind by the behavior, remain unaltered until measurement is conducted. For example, if the flight of the baseballs hit by a batter during batting practice were not impeded, and the balls were left lying on the ground, a hitting instructor could collect data on the batter's performance after the batter's turn was completed by counting each ball found lying in fair territory on the right-field side of second base.

Measuring behavior after it has occurred by measuring the effects that the behavior produced on the environment is known as **measurement by permanent product.** Measuring permanent products is an ex post facto method of data collection because measurement takes place after the behavior has occurred. A permanent product is a change in the environment produced by a behavior that lasts long enough for measurement to take place.

Although often described erroneously as a method for measuring behavior, measurement by permanent product does not refer to any particular measurement procedure or method. Instead, measurement by permanent product refers to the time of measurement (i.e., after the behavior has occurred) and the medium (i.e., the effect of the behavior, not the behavior itself) by which the measurer comes in contact with (i.e., observes) the behavior. All of the methods for measuring behavior described in this chapter—event recording, timing, and time sampling—can be applied to the measurement of permanent products.

Permanent products can be natural or contrived outcomes of the behavior. Permanent products are natural and important outcomes of a wide range of socially significant behaviors in educational, vocational, domestic, and community environments. Examples in education include compositions written (Dorow & Boyle, 1998), computations of math problems written (Skinner, Fletcher, Wildmon, & Belfiore, 1996), spelling words written (McGuffin, Martz, & Heron, 1997), worksheets completed (Alber, Heward, & Hippler, 1999), homework assignments turned in (Alber, Nelson, & Brennan, 2002), and test questions answered (e.g., Gardner, Heward, & Grossi, 1994). Behaviors such as mopping floors and dishwashing (Grossi & Heward, 1998), incontinence (Adkins & Matthews, 1997), drawing bathroom graffiti (Mueller, Moore, Doggett, & Tingstrom, 2000), recycling (Brothers, Krantz, & McClannahan, 1994), and picking up litter (Powers, Osborne, & Anderson, 1973) can also be measured by the natural and important changes they make on the environment.

Many socially significant behaviors have no direct effects on the physical environment. Reading orally, sitting with good posture, and repetitive hand flapping leave no natural products in typical environments. Nevertheless, ex post facto measurement of such behaviors can often be accomplished via contrived permanent products. For example, by audiotaping students as they read out loud (Eckert, Ardoin, Daly, & Martens, 2002), videotaping a girl sitting in class (Schwarz & Hawkins, 1970), and videotaping a boy flapping his hands (Ahearn, Clark, Gardenier, Chung, & Dube, 2003) researchers obtained contrived permanent products for measuring these behaviors.

Contrived permanent products are sometimes useful in measuring behaviors that have natural permanent products that are only temporary. For example, Goetz and Baer (1973) measured variations in the form of children's block building from photographs taken of the constructions made by the children, and Twohig and Woods (2001) measured the length of fingernails from photographs of nail-biters' hands.

Advantages of Measurement by Permanent Product

Measurement by permanent product offers numerous advantages to practitioners and researchers.

Practitioner Is Free to Do Other Tasks

Not having to observe and record behavior as it occurs enables the practitioner to do something else during the observation period. For example, a teacher who uses an audiotape recorder to record students' questions, comments, and talk-outs during a class discussion can concentrate on what her students are saying, provide individual help, and so on.

Makes Possible Measurement of Some Behaviors That Occur at Inconvenient or Inaccessible Times and Places

Many socially significant behaviors occur at times and places that are inconvenient or inaccessible to the researcher or practitioner. Measuring permanent products is indicated when observing the target behavior as it occurs would be difficult because the behavior occurs infrequently, in various environments, or for extended periods of time. For example, a music teacher can have his guitar student make audio recordings of portions of his daily practice sessions at home.

Measurement May Be More Accurate, Complete, and Continuous

Although measuring behavior as it occurs provides the most immediate access to the data, it does not necessarily yield the most accurate, complete, and representative data. An observer measuring behavior from permanent products can take his time, rescore the worksheet, or listen to and watch the videotape again. Videotape enables the observer to slow down, pause, and repeat portions of the session—to literally "hold still" the behavior so it can be examined and measured again and again if necessary. The observer might see or hear additional nuances and aspects of the behavior, or other behaviors that she overlooked or missed altogether during live performances.

Measurement by permanent product enables data collection on more participants. An observer can look at a videotape once and measure one participant's behavior, then replay the tape and measure a second participant's behavior.

Video- or audiotaping behavior provides data on the occurrence of all instances of a target behavior (Miltenberger, Rapp, & Long, 1999; Tapp & Walden, 2000). Having this permanent product of all instances of the behavior lends itself to later scoring by using the built-in calibrated digital timer (e.g., on a VCR), set to zero seconds (or the first frame) at the beginning of the session, to note the exact time of behavior onset and offset. Further, software programs facilitate data collection and analysis based on exact timings. PROCORDER is a software system for facilitating the collection and analysis of videotaped behavior. According to Miltenberger and colleagues, "With a recording of the exact time of the onset and offset of the target behavior in the observation

Figure 4.10 Data collection form for recording count and temporal locus of three classes of teacher statements from videotaped sessions.

Participant: T1 Date of session: 4/23 Exp. condition: Self-scoring generalization

Observer: Susan Date of observation 4/23 Duration of observation: 15:00 Decimal: 15.0

Transcribe positive and negative statements, corresponding time indexes, and time indexes of repeated statements in the boxes below.

Generic Positive (transcribe first instance)	Time index	Time index of repeats		**Specific Positive** (transcribe first instance)	Time index	Time index of repeats		**Negative** (transcribe first instance)	Time index	Time index of repeats	
Excellent	0:17	1:37	3:36	I like how you helped her.	1:05						
		4:00	4:15								
		7:45	9:11	Thank you for not talking.	1:57	2:10	3:28				
		10:22	10:34								
Beautiful	0:26	1:44	1:59	Good—nice big word.	2:45	6:53	8:21				
		9:01	11:52			9:56					
		13:09		You raised your hand, beautiful job.	3:37	4:33					
Good	0:56	1:22	4:42	Good job, that's a new word.	3:46						
		5:27	5:47								
		6:16	6:38	Thank you for paying attention.	4:56						
		8:44	9:25								
Smart	5:14	7:06	11:59	Thank you for not writing.	7:50						
High five	8:00										
Count: 28	% repeats: 83%			Count: 13	% repeats 46%			0	% repeats:		
No. per min. 1.9				No. per min. 0.9							
All Positives:	Count: 41			No. per min. 2.7	% repeats 71%						

From *The effects of self-scoring on teachers' positive statements during classroom instruction* by S. M. Silvestri (2004), p. 124. Unpublished doctoral dissertation, The Ohio State University. Used by permission.

session, we are able to report the frequency (or rate) or the duration of the behavior" (p. 119).[10]

Facilitates Data Collection for Interobserver Agreement and Treatment Integrity

Video- or audiotapes assist with data collection tasks such as obtaining interobserver agreement data (see Chapter 5) and assessing treatment integrity (Chapter 10). Permanent products of behaviors make possible the repeated measurement of behaviors, eliminating the need to bring multiple observers into the research or treatment setting.

[10]Edwards and Christophersen (1993) described a time-lapse videotape recorder (TLVCR) that automatically records on one 2-hour tape time samples of behavior over observation periods ranging from 2 to 400 hours. A TLVCR programmed to record over a 12-hour period would record for 0.10 of each second. Such a system can be useful for recoding very low frequency behaviors and for behaviors that occur over long periods of time (e.g., a child's sleep behavior).

Enables Measurement of Complex Behaviors and Multiple Response Classes

Permanent products, especially videotaped records of behavior, afford the opportunity to measure complex behaviors and multiple response classes in busy social environments. Schwarz and Hawkins (1970) obtained measures of the posture, voice volume, and face touching of an elementary student from videotapes taken during two class periods. The three behaviors were targeted as the result of operationalizing the girl's "poor self-esteem." The researchers were able to view the tapes repeatedly and score them for different behaviors. In this study, the girl also watched and evaluated her behavior on the videotapes as part of the intervention.

Figure 4.10 shows an example of a recording form used by Silvestri (2004) to measure three types of statements by teachers—generic positive, specific positive, and negative—from audiotapes of classroom lessons. (See Figure 3.7 for definitions of these behaviors.) The movement, multiple voices, and general commotion that characterize any classrooms would combine to make it very difficult, if not impossible, for a live observer to consistently detect and accurately record these behaviors. Each teacher participant in the study wore a small wireless microphone that transmitted a signal to a receiver that was connected to a cassette tape recorder.

Determining Whether Measurement by Permanent Product Is Appropriate

The advantages of measurement by permanent product are considerable, and it may seem as though permanent product measurement is always preferable to real-time measurement. Answering the following four questions will help practitioners and researchers determine whether measurement by permanent product is appropriate: Is real-time measurement needed? Can the behavior be measured by permanent product? Will obtaining a contrived permanent product unduly affect the behavior? and How much will it cost?

Is Real-Time Measurement Needed?

Data-based decision making about treatment procedures and experimental conditions is a defining feature of applied behavior analysis and one of its major strengths. Data-based decision making requires more than direct and frequent measurement of behavior; it also requires ongoing and timely access to the data those measures provide. Measuring behavior as it occurs provides the most immediate access to the data. Although real-time measurement by permanent product can be conducted in some situations (e.g., counting each batted ball that lands to the right of second base as a hitter takes batting practice), measurement by permanent product will most often be conducted after the instructional or experimental session has ended.

Measures taken from video- or audiotapes cannot be obtained until the tapes are viewed after a session has ended. If treatment decisions are being made on a session-by-session basis, this behavior-to-measurement delay poses no problem as long as the data can be obtained from the tapes prior to the next session. However, when moment-to-moment treatment decisions must be made according to the participant's behavior during the session, real-time measurement is necessary. Consider a behavior analyst trying to reduce the rate of a person's self-injurious behavior (SIB) by providing access to a preferred stimulus contingent on increasing durations of time without SIB. Accurate implementation of the treatment protocol would require the real-time measurement of interresponse times (IRT).

Can the Behavior Be Measured by Permanent Product?

Not all behaviors are suitable for measurement by permanent product. Some behaviors affect fairly permanent changes in the environment that are not reliable for the purposes of measurement. For example, self-injurious behavior (SIB) often produces long-lasting effects (bruises, welts, and even torn and bleeding skin) that could be measured after the occurrence of the behavior. But accurate measures of SIB could not be obtained by examining the client's body on a regular basis. The presence of discolored skin, abrasions, and other such marks would indicate that the person had been injured, but many important questions would be left unanswered. How many times did SIB occur? Were there acts of SIB that did not leave observable marks on the skin? Was each instance of tissue damage the result of SIB? These are important questions for evaluating the effects of any treatment. Yet, they could not be answered with certainty because these permanent products are not precise enough for the measurement of the SIB. Behaviors suitable for measurement via permanent product must meet two rules.

Rule 1: Each occurrence of the target behavior must produce the same permanent product. The permanent product must be a result of every instance of the response class measured. All topographical variants of the target behavior and all responses of varying magnitude that meet the definition of target behavior must produce the same permanent product. Measuring an employee's work productivity by counting the number of correctly assembled widgets in his "completed work" bin conforms to this rule. An occurrence of the target behavior in this case is defined functionally as a correctly assembled widget. Measuring SIB by marks on the skin does not meet Rule 1 because some SIB responses will not leave discernable marks.

Rule 2: The permanent product can only be produced by the target behavior. This rule requires that the permanent product cannot result from (a) any behaviors by the participant other than the target behavior or (b) the behavior of any person other than the participant. Using the number of correctly assembled widgets in the employee's "completed work" bin to measure his productivity conforms to Rule 2 *if* the observer can be assured that (a) the employee put no widgets in his bin that he did not assemble and (b) none of the assembled widgets in the employee's bin were put there by anyone other than the employee. Using marks on the skin as a permanent product for measuring self-injurious behavior also fails to meet Rule 2. Marks on the skin could be produced by other behaviors by the person (e.g., running too fast, which caused him to trip and hit his head, stepping in poison ivy) or by the behavior of other people (e.g., struck by another person).

Will Obtaining a Contrived Permanent Product Unduly Affect the Behavior?

Practitioners and researchers should always consider reactivity—the effects of the measurement procedure on the behavior being measured. Reactivity is most likely when observation and measurement procedures are obtrusive. Obtrusive measurement alters the environment, which may in turn affect the behavior being measured. Permanent products obtained using recording equipment, the presence of which may cause a person to behave differently, are called contrived permanent products. For example, using an audiotape to record conversations might encourage the participant to talk less or more. But it should be recognized that reactivity to the presence of human observers is a common phenomenon, and reactive effects are usually temporary (e.g., Haynes & Horn, 1982; Kazdin, 1982, 2001). Even so, it is appropriate to anticipate the influence that equipment may have on the target behavior.

How Much Will It Cost to Obtain and Measure the Permanent Product?

The final issues to address in determining the appropriateness of measuring a target behavior by permanent product are availability, cost, and effort. If recording equipment is required to obtain a contrived product of the behavior, is it currently available? If not, how much will it cost to buy or rent the equipment? How much time will it take to learn to use the equipment initially? How difficult and time-consuming will it be to set up, store, and use the equipment for the duration of the study or behavior change program?

Computer-Assisted Measurement of Behavior

Computer hardware and software systems for behavioral measurement and data analysis have become increasingly sophisticated and useful, especially for applied researchers. Developers have produced data collection and analysis software for observational measurement using laptops (Kahng & Iwata, 2000; Repp & Karsh, 1994),

handheld computers (Saudargas & Bunn, 1989), or personal digital assistants (Emerson, Reever, & Felce, 2000). Some systems use bar-code scanners for data collection (e.g., McEntee & Saunders, 1997; Saunders, Saunders, & Saunders, 1994; Tapp & Wehby, 2000). Most computer software systems require a DOS or Windows operating system. A few software systems have been developed for the Mac OS. Regardless of the computer operating systems, Kahng and Iwata (2000) stated:

> These systems have the potential to facilitate the task of observation by improving the reliability and accuracy of recording relative to traditional but cumbersome methods based on paper and pencil and to improve the efficiency of data calculation and graphing. (p. 35)

Developments in microchip technology have advanced the measurement and data analysis capabilities of these systems, and have made the software increasingly easier to learn and apply. Many of these semiautomated systems can record a number of events, including discrete trials, the number of responses per unit of time, duration, latency, interresponse time (IRT), and fixed and variable intervals for time-sampling measurement. These systems can present data calculated as rate, duration, latency, IRT, percentage of intervals, percentage of trials, and conditional probabilities.

A distinct advantage of computer-based observation and measurement systems is that when aggregating rates, time-series analyses, conditional probabilities, sequential dependencies, interrelationships, and combinations of events, these data can be clustered and analyzed. Because these systems allow for the simultaneous recording of multiple behaviors across multiple dimensions, outputs can be examined and analyzed from different perspectives that would be difficult and time-consuming with paper-and-pencil methods.

In addition to recording behavior and calculating data, these systems provide analyses of interobserver agreement (e.g., smaller/larger, overall, occurrence, nonoccurrence) and measurement from audio and video documents. The semiautomated computer-driven systems, as compared to the commonly used paper-and-pencil data recording and analysis methods, have the potential to improve interobserver agreements, the reliability of observational measurements, and the efficiency of data calculation (Kahng & Iwata, 1998).[11]

---

[11]Descriptions of the characteristics and capabilities of a variety of computer-assisted behavioral measurement systems can be found in the following sources: Emerson, Reever, & Felce (2000); Farrell (1991); Kahng & Iwata (1998, 2000); Repp, Harman, Felce, Vanacker, & Karsh (1989); Saunders, Saunders, & Saunders (1994); Tapp & Walden (2000); and Tapp and Wehby (2000).

The practical value derived from the greater efficiency and ease of use of computer-assisted measurement systems will likely increase their use by applied researchers and practitioners who currently use mechanical counters, timers, and paper and pencil for observational recording.

 Summary

Definition and Functions of Measurement in Applied Behavior Analysis

1. Measurement is the process of applying quantitative labels to observed properties of events using a standard set of rules.

2. Measurement is how scientists operationalize empiricism.

3. Without measurement, all three levels of scientific knowledge—description, prediction, and control—would be relegated to guesswork and subjective opinions.

4. Applied behavior analysts measure behavior to obtain answers to questions about the existence and nature of functional relations between socially significant behavior and environmental variables.

5. Practitioners measure behavior before and after treatment to evaluate the overall effects of interventions (summative evaluation) and frequent measures of behavior during treatment (formative assessment) to guide decisions concerning the continuation, modification, or termination of treatment.

6. Without frequent measures of the behavior targeted for intervention, practitioners may (a) continue an ineffective treatment when no real behavior change occurred, or (b) discontinue an effective treatment because subjective judgment detects no improvement.

7. Measurement also helps practitioners optimize their effectiveness; verify the legitimacy of practices touted as "evidence based"; identify treatments based on pseudoscience, fad, fashion, or ideology; be accountable to clients, consumers, employers, and society; and achieve ethical standards.

Measureable Dimensions of Behavior

8. Because behavior occurs within and across time, it has three dimensional quantities: repeatability (i.e., count), temporal extent (i.e., duration), and temporal locus (i.e., when behavior occurs). These properties, alone and in combination, provide the basic and derivative measures used by applied behavior analysts. (See Figure 4.5 for a detailed summary.)

9. Count is the number of responses emitted during an observation period.

10. Rate, or frequency, is a ratio of count per observation period; it is often expressed as count per standard unit of time.

11. Celeration is a measure of the change (acceleration or deceleration) in rate of responding per unit of time.

12. Duration is the amount of time in which behavior occurs.

13. Response latency is a measure of the elapsed time between the onset of a stimulus and the initiation of a subsequent response.

14. Interresponse time (IRT) is the amount of time that elapses between two consecutive instances of a response class.

15. Percentage, a ratio formed by combining the same dimensional quantities, expresses the proportional quantity of an event in terms of the number of times the event occurred per 100 opportunities that the event could have occurred.

16. Trials-to-criterion is a measure of the number of response opportunities needed to achieve a predetermined level of performance.

17. Although form (i.e., topography) and intensity of responding (i.e., magnitude) are not fundamental dimensional quantities of behavior, they are important quantitative parameters for defining and verifying the occurrence of many response classes.

18. Topography refers to the physical form or shape of a behavior.

19. Magnitude refers to the force or intensity with which a response is emitted.

Procedures for Measuring Behavior

20. Event recording encompasses a wide variety of procedures for detecting and recording the number of times a behavior of interest is observed.

21. A variety of timing devices and procedures are used to measure duration, response latency, and interresponse time.

22. Time sampling refers to a variety of methods for observing and recording behavior during intervals or at specific moments in time.

23. Observers using whole-interval recording divide the observation period into a series of equal time intervals. At the end of each interval, they record whether the target behavior occurred throughout the entire interval.

24. Observers using partial-interval recording divide the observation period into a series of equal time intervals. At the end of each interval, they record whether behavior occurred at any point during the interval.

25. Observers using momentary time sampling divide the observation period into a series of time intervals. At the end of each interval, they record whether the target behavior is occurring at that specific moment.

26. Planned activity check (PLACHECK) is a variation of momentary time sampling in which the observer records whether each individual in a group is engaged in the target behavior.

27. Measurement artifacts are common with time sampling.

Measuring Behavior by Permanent Products

28. Measuring behavior after it has occurred by measuring its effects on the environment is known as measurement by permanent product.

29. Measurement of many behaviors can be accomplished via contrived permanent products.

30. Measurement by permanent product offers numerous advantages: The practitioner is free to do other tasks; it enables the measurement of behaviors that occur at inconvenient or inaccessible times and places; measurement may be more accurate, complete, and continuous; it facilitates the collection of interobserver agreement and treatment integrity data; and it enables the measurement of complex behaviors and multiple response classes.

31. If moment-to-moment treatment decisions must be made during the session, measurement by permanent product may not be warranted.

32. Behaviors suitable for measurement via permanent products must meet two rules. Rule 1: Each occurrence of the target behavior must produce the same permanent product. Rule 2: The permanent product can only be produced by the target behavior.

Computer-Assisted Measurement of Behavior

33. Computer hardware and software systems for behavioral measurement and data analysis have become increasingly sophisticated and easier to use.

34. Developers have produced data collection and analysis software for observational measurement using laptops, handheld computers, personal digital assistants (PDAs), and desktop computers.

35. Some systems allow for the simultaneous recording of multiple behaviors across multiple dimensions. Outputs can be examined and analyzed from different perspectives that would be difficult and time-consuming with paper-and-pencil methods.

CHAPTER 5

Improving and Assessing the Quality of Behavioral Measurement

Key Terms

accuracy
believability
calibration
continuous measurement
direct measurement
discontinuous measurement
exact count-per-interval IOA
indirect measurement
interobserver agreement (IOA)

interval-by-interval IOA
mean count-per-interval IOA
mean duration-per-occurrence IOA
measurement bias
naive observer
observed value
observer drift
observer reactivity
reliability

scored-interval IOA
total count IOA
total duration IOA
trial-by-trial IOA
true value
unscored-interval IOA
validity

Behavior Analyst Certification Board® BCBA® & BCABA® Behavior Analyst Task List,© Third Edition

Content Area 6: Measurement of Behavior	
6-4	Select the appropriate measurement procedure given the dimensions of the behavior and the logistics of observing and recording.
6-5	Select a schedule of observation and recording periods.
6-14	Use various methods of evaluating the outcomes of measurement procedures, such as interobserver agreement, accuracy, and reliability.

 The data obtained by measuring behavior are the primary material with which behavioral researchers and practitioners guide and evaluate their work. Applied behavior analysts measure socially significant behaviors to help determine which behaviors need to be changed, to detect and compare the effects of various interventions on behaviors targeted for change, and to evaluate the acquisition, maintenance, and generalization of behavior changes.

Because so much of what the behavior analyst does either as a researcher or practitioner depends on measurement, concerns about the legitimacy of the data it produces must be paramount. Do the data meaningfully reflect the original reason(s) for measuring the behavior? Do the data represent the true extent of the behavior as it actually occurred? Do the data provide a consistent picture of the behavior? In other words, can the data be trusted?

Chapter 4 identified the measurable dimensions of behavior and described the measurement methods most often used in applied behavior analysis. This chapter focuses on improving and assessing the quality of behavioral measurement. We begin by defining the essential indicators of trustworthy measurement: validity, accuracy, and reliability. Next, common threats to measurement are identified and suggestions for combating these threats are presented. The chapter's final sections detail procedures for assessing the accuracy, reliability, and believability of behavioral measurement.

Indicators of Trustworthy Measurement

Three friends—John, Tim, and Bill—took a bicycle ride together. At the end of the ride John looked at his handlebar-mounted bike computer and said, "We rode 68 miles. Excellent!" "My computer shows 67.5 miles. Good ride, fellas!" Tim replied. As he dismounted and rubbed his backside, the third biker, Bill, said, "Gee whiz, I'm sore! We must've ridden 100 miles!" A few days later, the three friends completed the same route. After the second ride, John's computer showed 68 miles, Tim's computer read 70 miles, and Bill, because he wasn't quite as sore as he was after the first ride, said they had ridden 90 miles. Following a third ride on the same country roads, John, Tim, and Bill reported distances of 68, 65, and 80 miles, respectively.

How trustworthy were the measures reported by the three bicyclists? Which of the three friends' data would be most usable for a scientific account of the miles they had ridden? To be most useful for science, measurement must be valid, accurate, and reliable. Were the three friends' measurements characterized by validity, accuracy, and reliability?

Validity

Measurement has **validity** when it yields data that are directly relevant to the phenomenon measured and to the reason(s) for measuring it. Determining the validity of measurement revolves around this basic question: Was a relevant dimension of the behavior that is the focus of the investigation measured directly and legitimately?

Did the measurements of miles ridden by the three bicyclists have validity? Because the bikers wanted to know how far they had ridden each time, the number of miles ridden was a relevant, or valid, dimension of their riding behavior. Had the bikers' primary interest been how long or how fast they had ridden, the number of miles ridden would not have been a valid measure. John and Tim's use of their bike computers to measure directly the miles they rode was a valid measure. Because Bill used an indirect measure (the relative tenderness of his backside) to determine the number of miles he had ridden, the validity of Bill's mileage data is suspect. A direct measure of the actual behavior of interest will always possess more validity than an indirect measure, because a direct measure does not require an inference about its relation to the behavior of interest, whereas an indirect measure always requires such an inference. Although soreness may be related to the distance ridden, because it is also influenced by such factors as the time on the bike saddle, the roughness of the road, riding speed, and how much (or little) the person has ridden recently, soreness as a measure of mileage has little validity.

Valid measurement in applied behavior analysis requires three equally important elements: (a) measuring directly a socially significant target behavior (see Chapter 3), (b) measuring a dimension (e.g., rate, duration) of the target behavior relevant to the question or concern about the behavior (see Chapter 4), and (c) ensuring that the data are representative of the behavior's occurrence under conditions and during times that are most relevant to the question or concern about the behavior. When any of these elements are suspect or lacking—no matter how technically proficient (i.e., accurate and reliable) was the measurement that produced the data—the validity of the resultant data are compromised, perhaps to the point of being meaningless.

Accuracy

When used in the context of measurement, **accuracy** refers to the extent to which the **observed value,** the quantitative label produced by measuring an event, matches the true state, or true value, of the event as it exists in nature (Johnston & Pennypacker, 1993a). In other words, measurement is accurate to the degree that it corresponds to the true value of the thing measured. A **true**

value is a measure obtained by procedures that are independent of and different from the procedures that produced the data being evaluated and for which the researcher has taken "special or extraordinary precautions to insure that all possible sources of error have been avoided or removed" (p. 136).

How accurate were the three bikers' measures of miles ridden? Because each biker obtained a different measure of the same event, all of their data could not be accurate. Skeptical of the training miles the three cyclists were claiming, a friend of theirs, Lee, drove the same country roads with a Department of Transportation odometer attached to the back bumper of his car. At the end of the route the odometer read 58 miles. Using the measure obtained by the DOT odometer as the true value of the route's distance, Lee determined that none of the three cyclists' measures were accurate. Each rider had overestimated the true mileage.

By comparing the mileage reported by John, Tim, and Bill with the true value of the route's distance, Lee discovered not only that the riders' data were inaccurate, but also that the data reported by all three riders were contaminated by a particular type of measurement error called measurement bias. **Measurement bias** refers to nonrandom measurement error; that is, error in measurement that is likely to be in one direction. When measurement error is random, it is just as likely to overestimate the true value of an event as it is to underestimate it. Because John, Tim, and Bill consistently overestimated the actual miles they had ridden, their data contained measurement bias.

Reliability

Reliability describes the extent to which a "measurement procedure yields the same value when brought into repeated contact with the same state of nature" (Johnston & Pennypacker, 1993a, p. 138). In other words, reliable measurement is consistent measurement. Like validity and accuracy, reliability is a relative concept; it is a matter of degree. The closer the values obtained by repeated measurement of the same event are to one another, the greater the reliability. Conversely, the more observed values from repeated measurement of the same event differ from one another, the less the reliability.

How reliable were the bicyclists' measurements? Because John obtained the same value, 68 miles, each time he measured the same route, his measurement had complete reliability. Tim's three measures of the same ride—67.5, 70, and 65 miles—differed from one another by as much as 5 miles. Therefore, Tim's measurement was less reliable than John's. Bill's measurement system was the least reliable of all, yielding values for the same route ranging from 80 to 100 miles.

Relative Importance of Validity, Accuracy, and Reliability

Behavioral measurement should provide legitimate data for evaluating behavior change and guiding research and treatment decisions. Data of the highest quality (i.e., data that are most useful and trustworthy for advancing scientific knowledge or for guiding data-based practice) are produced by measurement that is valid, accurate, and reliable (see Figure 5.1). Validity, accuracy, and reliability are relative concepts; each can range from high to low.

Measurement must be both valid and accurate for the data to be trustworthy. If measurement is not valid, accuracy is moot. Accurately measuring a behavior that is not the focus of the investigation, accurately measuring an irrelevant dimension of the target behavior, or accurately measuring the behavior under circumstances or at times not representative of the conditions and times relevant to the analysis will yield invalid data. Conversely, the data obtained from measuring a meaningful dimension of the right behavior under the relevant circumstances and times is of little use if the observed values provide an inaccurate picture of the behavior. Inaccurate measurement renders invalid the data obtained by otherwise valid measurement.

Reliability should never be confused with accuracy. Although John's bicycle computer provided totally reliable measures, it was also totally inaccurate.

> Concern about the reliability of data in the absence of a prior interest in their accuracy suggests that reliability is being mistaken for accuracy. The questions for a researcher or someone who is reading a published study is not, "Are the data reliable?" but "Are the data accurate?" (Johnston & Pennypacker, 1993a, p. 146)

If accuracy trumps reliability—and it does—why should researchers and practitioners be concerned with the reliability of measurement? Although high reliability does not mean high accuracy, poor reliability reveals problems with accuracy. Because Tim and Bill's measurements were not reliable, we know that at least some of the data they reported could not be accurate, knowledge that could and should lead to checking the accuracy of their measurement tools and procedures.

Highly reliable measurement means that whatever degree of accuracy (or inaccuracy) exists in the measurement system will be revealed consistently in the data. If it can be determined that John's computer reliably obtains observed values higher than the true values by a constant amount or proportion, the data could be adjusted to accommodate for that constant degree of inaccuracy.

The next two sections of the chapter describe methods for combating common threats to the validity, accuracy, and reliability of behavioral measurement.

Figure 5.1   Measurement that is valid, accurate, and reliable yields the most trustworthy and useful data for science and science-based practice.

Measurement that is . .

Valid	Accurate	Reliable	. . . yields data that are . . .
Yes	Yes	Yes	. . . most useful for advancing scientific knowledge and guiding data-based practice.
No	Yes	Yes	. . . meaningless for the purposes for which measurement was conducted.
Yes	No	Yes	. . . always wrong.[1]
Yes	Yes	No[2]	. . . sometimes wrong.[3]

1. If adjusted for consistent measurement error of standard size and direction, inaccurate data may still be usable.

2. If the accuracy of every datum in a data set can be confirmed, reliability is a moot point. In practice, however, that is seldom possible; therefore, knowing the consistency with which a valid and accurate measurement system has been applied contributes to the level of confidence in the overall trustworthiness of the data set.

3. User is unable to separate the good data from the bad.

Threats to Measurement Validity

The validity of behavioral data is threatened when measurement is indirect, when the wrong dimension of the target behavior is measured, or when measurement is conducted in such a way that the data it produces are an artifact of the actual events.

Indirect Measurement

Direct measurement occurs when "the phenomenon that is the focus of the experiment is exactly the same as the phenomenon being measured" (Johnston & Pennypacker, 1993a, p. 113). Conversely, **indirect measurement** occurs when "what is actually measured is in some way different from" the target behavior of interest (Johnston & Pennypacker, 1993a, p. 113). Direct measurement of behavior yields more valid data than will indirect measurement. This is because indirect measurement provides secondhand or "filtered" information (Komaki, 1998) that requires the researcher or practitioner to make inferences about the relationship between the event that was measured and the actual behavior of interest.

Indirect measurement occurs when the researcher or practitioner measures a proxy, or stand-in, for the actual behavior of interest. An example of indirect measurement would be using children's responses to a questionnaire as a measure of how often and well they get along with their classmates. It would be better to use a direct measure of the number of positive and negative interactions among the children. Using a student's score on a standardized math achievement test as an indicator of her mastery of the math skills included in the school's curriculum is another example of indirect measurement. Accepting the student's score on the achievement test as a valid reflection of her ability with the school's curriculum would require an inference. By contrast, a student's score on a properly constructed test consisting of math problems from recently covered curriculum content is a direct measure requiring no inferences about what it means with respect to her performance in the curriculum.

Indirect measurement is usually not an issue in applied behavior analysis because meeting the applied dimension of ABA includes the targeting and meaningful (i.e., valid) measurement of socially significant behaviors. Sometimes, however, the researcher or practitioner has no direct and reliable access to the behavior of interest and so must use some form of indirect measurement. For example, because researchers studying adherence to medical regimens cannot directly observe and measure patients' behavior in their homes, they rely on self-reports for their data (e.g., La Greca & Schuman, 1995).[1]

Indirect measurement is sometimes used to make inferences about private events or affective states. For example, Green and Reid (1996) used direct measures of smiling to represent "happiness" by persons with profound multiple disabilities. However, research on private events does not necessarily involve indirect measurement. A research participant who has been trained to observe his own private events is measuring the behavior of interest directly (e.g., Kostewicz, Kubina, & Cooper, 2000; Kubina, Haertel, & Cooper, 1994).

---

[1]Strategies for increasing the accuracy of self-reports can be found in Critchfield, Tucker, and Vuchinich (1998) and Finney, Putnam, and Boyd (1998).

Whenever indirect measurement is used, it is the responsibility of the researcher to provide evidence that the event measured directly reflects, in some reliable and meaningful way, something about the behavior for which the researcher wishes to draw conclusions (Johnston & Pennypacker, 1993a). In other words, it is incumbent upon the researcher to provide a convincing case for the validity of her data. Although it is sometimes attempted, the case for validity cannot be achieved by simply attaching the name of the thing one claims to be measuring to the thing actually measured. With respect to that point, Marr (2003) recounted this anecdote about Abraham Lincoln:

> "Sir, how many legs does this donkey have?"
> "Four, Mr. Lincoln."
> "And how many tails does it have?"
> "One, Mr. Lincoln."
> "Now, sir, what if we were to call a tail a leg; how many legs would the donkey have?"
> "Five, Mr. Lincoln."
> "No sir, for you cannot make a tail into a leg by calling it one." (pp. 66–67)

Measuring the Wrong Dimension of the Target Behavior

The validity of behavioral measurement is threatened much more often by measuring the wrong dimension of the behavior of interest than it is by indirect measurement. Valid measurement yields data that are relevant to the questions about the behavior one seeks to answer through measurement. Validity is compromised when measurement produces values for a dimension of the behavior ill suited for, or irrelevant to, the reason for measuring the behavior.

Johnston and Pennypacker (1980) provided an excellent example of the importance of measuring a dimension that fits the reasons for measurement. "Sticking a ruler in a pot of water as the temperature is raised will yield highly reliable measures of the depth of the water but will tell us very little about the changing temperature" (p. 192). While the units of measurement on a ruler are well suited for measuring length, or in this case, depth, they are not at all valid for measuring temperature. If the purpose of measuring the water is to determine whether it has reached the ideal temperature for making a pot of tea, a thermometer is the correct measurement tool.

If you are interested in measuring a student's academic endurance with oral reading, counting the number of correct and incorrect words read per minute without measuring and reporting the total time that the student read will not provide valid data on endurance. Number of words read per minute alone does not fit the reason for

measuring reading (i.e., academic endurance). To measure endurance, the practitioner would need to report the duration of the reading period (e.g., 30 minutes). Similarly, measuring the percentage of trials on which a student makes a correct response will not provide valid data for answering questions about the student's developing fluency with a skill, whereas measuring the number of correct responses per minute and the changing rates of responding (celeration) would.

Measurement Artifacts

Directly measuring a relevant dimension of a socially significant target behavior does not guarantee valid measurement. Validity is reduced when the data—no matter how accurate or reliable they are—do not give a meaningful (i.e., valid) representation of the behavior. When data give an unwarranted or misleading picture of the behavior because of the way measurement was conducted, the data are called an *artifact*. As introduced in Chapter 4, a *measurement artifact* is something that appears to exist because of the way it is measured. Discontinuous measurement, poorly scheduled measurement periods, and using insensitive or limiting measurement scales are common causes of measurement artifacts.

Discontinuous Measurement

Because behavior is a dynamic and continuous phenomenon that occurs and changes over time, continuous measurement is the gold standard in behavioral research. **Continuous measurement** is measurement conducted in a manner such that all instances of the response class(es) of interest are detected during the observation period (Johnston & Pennypacker, 1993a). **Discontinuous measurement** describes any form of measurement in which some instances of the response class(es) of interest may not be detected. Discontinuous measurement— no matter how accurate and reliable—may yield data that are an artifact.

A study by Thomson, Holmber, and Baer (1974) provides a good demonstration of the extent of artifactual variability in a data set that may be caused by discontinuous measurement. A single, highly experienced observer used three different procedures for scheduling time sampling observations to measure the behavior of four subjects (two teachers and two children) in a preschool setting during 64-minute sessions. Thomson and colleagues called the three time sampling procedures contiguous, alternating, and sequential. With each time sampling procedure, one-fourth of the observer's time (i.e., 16 minutes) was assigned to each of the four subjects.

When the contiguous observation scheduled was used, the observer recorded the behavior of Subject 1 throughout the first 16 minutes of the session, recorded the behavior Subject 2 during the second 16 minutes, and so on until all four students had been observed. In the alternating mode, Subjects 1 and 2 were observed in alternating intervals during the first half of the session, and Subjects 3 and 4 were observed in the same fashion during the last half of the session. Specifically, Student 1 was observed during the first 4 minutes, Subject 2 during the next 4 minutes, Subject 1 during the next 4 minutes, and so on until 32 minutes had expired. The same procedure was then used for Students 3 and 4 during the last 32 minutes of the session. The sequential approach systematically rotated the four subjects through 4-minute observations. Subject 1 was observed during the first 4 minutes, Subject 2 during the second 4 minutes, Subject 3 during the third 4 minutes, and Subject 4 during the fourth 4 minutes. This sequence was repeated four times to give the total of 64 minutes of observation.

To arrive at the percentage of artifactual variance in the data associated with each time sampling schedule, Thomson and colleagues (1974) compared the observer's data with "actual rates" for each subject produced by continuous measurement of each subject for the same 64-minute sessions. Results of the study showed clearly that the contiguous and alternating schedules produced the most unrepresentative (and therefore, less valid) measures of the target behaviors (often more than 50% variance from continuous measurement), whereas sequential sampling procedure produced results that more closely resembled the data obtained through continuous recording (from 4 to 11% variance from continuous measurement).

In spite of its inherent limitations, discontinuous measurement is used in many studies in applied behavior analysis in which individual observers measure the behavior of multiple subjects within the same session. Minimizing the threat to validity posed by discontinuous measurement requires careful consideration of when observation and measurement periods should be scheduled. Infrequent measurement, no matter how accurate and reliable it is, often yields results that are an artifact. Although a single measure reveals the presence or absence of the target behavior at a given point in time, it may not be representative of the typical value for the behavior.[2] As a general rule, observations should be scheduled on a daily or frequent basis, even if for only brief periods.

Ideally, all occurrences of the behavior of interest should be recorded. However, when available resources

preclude continuous measurement throughout an observation period, the use of sampling procedures is necessary. A sampling procedure may be sufficient for decision making and analysis if the samples represent a valid approximation of the true parameters of the behavior of interest. When measurement cannot be continuous throughout an observation period, it is generally preferable to sample the occurrence of the target behavior for numerous brief observation intervals that are evenly distributed throughout the session than it is to use longer, less frequent intervals (Thomson et al., 1974; Thompson, Symons, & Felce, 2000). For example, measuring a subject's behavior in thirty 10-second intervals equally distributed within a 30-minute session will likely yield more representative data than will observing the person for a single 5-minute period during the half hour.

Measuring behavior with observation intervals that are too short or too long may result in data that grossly over- or underestimate the true occurrence of behavior. For example, measuring off-task behavior by partial-interval recording with 10-minute intervals may produce data that make even the most diligent of students appear to be highly off task.

Poorly Scheduled Measurement Periods

The observation schedule should be standardized to provide an equal opportunity for the occurrence or nonoccurrence of the behavior across sessions and consistent environmental conditions from one observation session to the next. When neither of these requirements is met, the resultant data may not be representative and may be invalid. If observation periods are scheduled at times when and/or places where the frequency of behavior is atypical, the data may not represent periods of high or low responding. For example, measuring students' being on-task during only the first 5 minutes of each day's 20-minute cooperative learning group activity may yield data that make on-task behavior appear higher than it actually is over the entire activity.

When data will be used to assess the effects of an intervention or treatment, the most conservative observation times should be selected. That is, the target behavior should be measured during those times when their frequency of occurrence is most likely to be different from the desired or predicted outcomes of the treatment. Measurement of behaviors targeted for reduction should occur during times when those behaviors are most likely to occur at their highest response rates. Conversely, behaviors targeted for increase should be measured when high-frequency responding is least likely. If an intervention is not planned— as might be the case in a descriptive study—it is important to select the observation times most likely to yield data that are generally representative of the behavior.

---

[2]Single measures, such as pretests and posttests, can provide valuable information on a person's knowledge and skills before and after instruction or treatment. The use of *probes,* occasional but systematic measures, to assess maintenance and generalization of behavior change is discussed in Chapter 28.

Insensitive and/or Limited Measurement Scales

Data that are artifacts may result from using measurement scales that cannot detect the full range of relevant values or that are insensitive to meaningful changes in behavior. Data obtained with a measurement scale that does not detect the full range of relevant performances may incorrectly imply that behavior cannot occur at levels below or above obtained measures because the scale has imposed an artificial floor or ceiling on performance. For example, measuring a student's oral reading fluency by giving him a 100-word passage to read in 1 minute may yield data that suggest that his maximum performance is 100 wpm.

A measurement scale that is over- or undersensitive to relevant changes in behavior may produce data that show misleadingly that meaningful behavior change has (or has not) occurred. For example, using a percentage measure scaled in 10% increments to evaluate the effects of an intervention to improve quality control in a manufacturing plant may not reveal important changes in performance if improvement in the percentage of correctly fabricated widgets from a baseline level of 92% to a range of 97 to 98% is the difference between unacceptable and acceptable (i.e., profitable) performance.

Threats to Measurement Accuracy and Reliability

The biggest threat to the accuracy and reliability of data in applied behavior analysis is human error. Unlike the experimental analysis of behavior, in which measurement is typically automated and conducted by machines, most investigations in applied behavior analysis use human observers to measure behavior.[3] Factors that contribute to human measurement error include poorly designed measurement systems, inadequate observer training, and expectations about what the data should look like.

Poorly Designed Measurement System

Unnecessarily cumbersome and difficult-to-use measurement systems create needless loss of accuracy and reliability. Collecting behavioral data in applied settings requires attention, keen judgment, and perseverance. The more taxing and difficult a measurement system is to use, the less likely an observer will be to consistently detect and record all instances of the target behavior. Simplify-

ing the measurement system as much as possible minimizes measurement errors.

The complexity of measurement includes such variables as the number of individuals observed, the number of behaviors recorded, the duration of observation periods, and/or the duration of the observation intervals, all of which may affect the quality of measurement. For instance, observing several individuals is more complex than observing one person; recording several behaviors is more complex than recording a single behavior; using contiguous 5-second observation intervals with no time between intervals to record the results of the observation is more difficult than a system in which time is reserved for recording data.

Specific recommendations concerning reducing complexity depend on the specific nature of the study. However, when using time sampling measurements, applied behavior analysts can consider modifications such as decreasing the number of simultaneously observed individuals or behaviors, decreasing the duration of the observation sessions (e.g., from 30 minutes to 15 minutes), and increasing the duration of time intervals (e.g., from 5 to 10 seconds). Requiring more practice during observer training, establishing a higher criterion for mastery of the observational code, and providing more frequent feedback to observers may also reduce the possible negative effects of complex measurement.

Inadequate Observer Training

Careful attention must be paid to the selection and training of observers. Explicit and systematic training of observers is essential for the collection of trustworthy data. Observation and coding systems require observers to discriminate the occurrence and nonoccurrence of specific classes of behaviors or events against an often complex and dynamic background of other behaviors or events and to record their observations onto a data sheet. Observers must learn the definitions for each response class or event to be measured; a code or symbol notation system for each variable; a common set of recording procedures such as keystrokes or scan movements; and a method for correcting inadvertent handwritten, keystroke, or scan mistakes (e.g., writing a plus sign instead of a minus sign, hitting the F6 key instead of the F5 key, scanning an incorrect bar code).

Selecting Observers Carefully

Admittedly, applied researchers often scramble to find data collectors, but not all volunteers should be accepted into training. Potential observers should be interviewed to determine past experiences with observation and measurement activities, current schedule and upcoming

---

[3]We recommend using automatic data recording devices whenever possible. For example, to measure the amount of exercise by boys on stationary bicycles, DeLuca and Holborn (1992) used magnetic counters that automatically recorded the number of wheel revolutions.

commitments, work ethic and motivation, and overall social skills. The interview might include a pretest to determine current observation and skill levels. This can be accomplished by having potential observers watch short video clips of behaviors similar to what they may be asked to observe and noting their performance against a criterion.

Training Observers to an Objective Standard of Competency

Observer trainees should meet a specified criterion for recording before conducting observations in applied settings. During training, observers should practice recording numerous examples and nonexamples of the target behavior(s) and receive a critique and performance feedback. Observers should have numerous practice sessions before actual data collection. Training should continue until a predetermined criterion is achieved (e.g., 95% accuracy for two or three consecutive sessions). For example, in training observers to measure the completion of preventive maintenance tasks of heavy equipment by military personnel, Komaki (1998) required three consecutive sessions of at least 90% agreement with a true value.

Various methods can be used to train observers. These include sample vignettes, narrative descriptions, video sequences, role playing, and practice sessions in the environment in which actual data will be collected. Practice sessions in natural settings are especially beneficial because they allow both observers and participants to adapt to each other's presence and may reduce the reactive effects of the presence of observers on participants' behavior. The following steps are an example of a systematic approach for training observers.

Step 1 Trainees read the target behavior definitions and become familiar with data collection forms, procedures for recording their observations, and the proper use of any measurement or recording devices (e.g., tape recorders, stopwatches, laptops, PDAs, bar code scanners).

Step 2 Trainees practice recording simplified narrative descriptions of behavioral vignettes until they obtain 100% accuracy over a predetermined number of instances.

Step 3 Trainees practice recording longer, more complex narrative descriptions of behavioral vignettes until they obtain 100% accuracy for a predetermined number of episodes.

Step 4 Trainees practice observing and recording data from videotaped or role-played vignettes depicting the target behavior(s) at the same speed and complexity as they will occur in the natural environment. Training vignettes should be scripted and sequenced to provide trainees practice making increasingly difficult discriminations between the occurrence and nonoccurrence of the

target behavior(s). Having trainees rescore the same series of vignettes a second time and comparing the reliability of their measures provides an assessment of the consistency with which the trainees are applying the measurement system. Trainees remain at this step until their data reach preestablished accuracy and reliability criteria. (If the study involved collecting data from natural permanent products such as compositions or academic worksheets, Steps 2 through 4 should provide trainees with practice scoring increasingly extensive and more difficult to score examples.)

Step 5 Practicing collecting data in the natural environment is the final training step of observer training. An experienced observer accompanies the trainee and simultaneously and independently measures the target behaviors. Each practice session ends with the trainee and experienced observer comparing their data sheets and discussing any questionable or heretofore unforeseen instances. Training continues until a preestablished criterion of agreement between the experienced observer and the trainee is achieved (e.g., at least 90% for three consecutive sessions).

Providing Ongoing Training to Minimize Observer Drift

Over the course of a study, observers sometimes alter, often unknowingly, the way they apply a measurement system. Called **observer drift,** these unintended changes in the way data are collected may produce measurement error. Observer drift usually entails a shift in the observer's interpretation of the definition of the target behavior from that used in training. Observer drift occurs when observers expand or compress the original definition of the target behavior. For example, observer drift might be responsible for the same behaviors by a child that were recorded by an observer as instances of noncompliance during the first week of a study being scored as instances of compliance during the study's final week. Observers are usually unaware of the drift in their measurement.

Observer drift can be minimized by occasional observer retraining or booster sessions throughout the investigation. Continued training provides the opportunity for observers to receive frequent feedback on the accuracy and reliability of measurement. Ongoing training can occur at regular, prescheduled intervals (e.g., every Friday morning) or randomly.

Unintended Influences on Observers

Ideally, data reported by observers have been influenced only by the actual occurrences and nonoccurrences of the target behavior(s) they have been trained to measure. In reality, however, a variety of unintended and undesired influences on observers can threaten the accuracy and reliability of the data they report. Common causes of this type of measurement error include presuppositions an observer may hold about the expected outcomes of the data and an observer's awareness that others are measuring the same behavior.

Observer Expectations

Observer expectations that the target behavior should occur at a certain level under particular conditions, or change when a change in the environment has been made, pose a major threat to accurate measurement. For example, if an observer believes or predicts that a teacher's implementation of a token economy should decrease the frequency of inappropriate student behavior, she may record fewer inappropriate behaviors during the token reinforcement condition than she would have recorded otherwise without holding that expectation. Data influenced by an observer's expectations or efforts to obtain results that will please the researcher are characterized by measurement bias.

The surest way to minimize measurement bias caused by observer expectations is to use naive observers. A totally **naive observer** is a trained observer who is unaware of the study's purpose and/or the experimental conditions in effect during a given phase or observation period. Researchers should inform observer trainees that they will receive limited information about the study's purpose and why that is. However, maintaining observers' naiveté is often difficult and sometimes impossible.

When observers are aware of the purpose or hypothesized results of an investigation, measurement bias can be minimized by using target behavior definitions and recording procedures that will give a conservative picture of the behavior (e.g., whole-interval recording of on-task behavior with 10-second rather than 5-second intervals), frank and repeated discussion with observers about the importance of collecting accurate data, and frequent feedback to observers on the extent to which their data agree with true values or data obtained by observers who are naive. Observers should not receive feedback about the extent to which their data confirm or run counter to hypothesized results or treatment goals.

Observer Reactivity

Measurement error resulting from an observer's awareness that others are evaluating the data he reports is called **observer reactivity.** Like reactivity that may occur when participants are aware that their behavior is being observed, the behavior of observers (i.e., the data they record and report) can be influenced by the knowledge that others are evaluating the data. For example, knowing that the researcher or another observer is watching the same behavior at the same time, or will monitor the measurement through video- or audiotape later, may produce observer reactivity. If the observer anticipates that another observer will record the behavior in a certain way, his data may be influenced by what he anticipates the other observer may record.

Monitoring observers as unobtrusively as possible on an unpredictable schedule helps reduce observer reactivity. Separating multiple observers by distance or partition reduces the likelihood that their measures will be influenced by one another's during an observation. One-way mirrors in some research and clinical settings eliminate visual contact between the primary and secondary observers. If sessions are audiotaped or videotaped, the secondary observer can measure the behavior at a later time and the primary observer never has to come into contact with the secondary observer. In settings where one-way mirrors are not possible, and where audio- or videotaping may be intrusive, the secondary observer might begin measuring the behavior at a time unknown to the primary observer. For example, if the primary observer begins measuring behavior with the first interval, the secondary observer could start measuring behavior after 10 minutes have elapsed. The intervals used for comparisons would begin at the 10-minute mark, ignoring those intervals that the primary observer recorded beforehand.

Assessing the Accuracy and Reliability of Behavioral Measurement

After designing a measurement system that will produce a valid representation of the target behavior and training observers to use it in a manner that is likely to yield accurate and reliable data, the researcher's next measurement-related tasks are evaluating the extent to which the data are, in fact, accurate and reliable. Essentially, all procedures for assessing the accuracy and reliability of behavioral data entail some form of "measuring the measurement system."

Assessing the Accuracy of Measurement

Measurement is accurate when the observed values (i.e., the numbers obtained by measuring an event) match the true values of the event. The fundamental reason for determining the accuracy of data is obvious: No one wants to base research conclusions or make treatment decisions on faulty data. More specifically, conducting accuracy assessments serves four interrelated purposes. First, it is important to determine early in an analysis whether the data are good enough to serve as the basis for making experimental or treatment decisions. The first person that the researcher or practitioner must try to convince that the data are accurate is herself. Second, accuracy assessments enable the discovery and correction of specific instances of measurement error. The two other approaches to assessing the quality of data to be discussed later in this chapter—reliability assessments and interobserver agreement—can alert the researcher to the likelihood of measurement errors, but neither approach identifies errors. Only the direct assessment of measurement accuracy allows practitioners or applied researchers to detect and correct faulty data.

A third reason for conducting accuracy assessments is to reveal consistent patterns of measurement error, which can lead to the overall improvement or **calibration** of the measurement system. When measurement error is consistent in direction and value, the data can be adjusted to compensate for the error. For example, knowing that John's bicycle computer reliably obtained a measure of 68 miles for a route with a true value of 58 miles led not only to the cyclists correcting the data in hand (in this case, confessing to one another and to their friend Lee that they had not ridden as many miles as previously claimed) but to their calibrating the measurement instrument so that future measures would be more accurate (in this case, adjusting the wheel circumference setting on John's bike computer).

Calibrating any measurement tool, whether it is a mechanical device or human observer, entails comparing the data obtained by the tool against a true value. The measure obtained by the Department of Transportation's wheel odometer served as the true value for calibrating John's bike computer. Calibration of a timing device such as a stopwatch or countdown timer could be made against a known standard: the "atomic clock."[4] If no differences are detected when comparing the timing device against the atomic clock, or if the differences are tolerable for the intended purposes of measurement, then calibration is satisfied. If significant differences are found, the timing device would need to be reset to the standard. We recommend frequent accuracy assessments in the beginning stages of an analysis. Then, if the assessments have produced high accuracy, less frequent assessments can be conducted to check the calibration of the recorders.

A fourth reason for conducting accuracy assessments is to assure consumers that the data are accurate. Including the results of accuracy assessments in research reports helps readers judge the trustworthiness of the data being offered for interpretation.

Establishing True Values

"There is only one way to assess the accuracy of a set of measures—by comparing observed values to true values. The comparison is relatively easy; the challenge is often obtaining measures of behavior that can legitimately be considered true values" (Johnston & Pennypacker, 1993a, p. 138). As defined previously, a *true value* is a measure obtained by procedures that are independent of and different from the procedures that produced the data being evaluated and for which the researcher has taken "special or extraordinary precautions to ensure that all possible sources of error have been avoided or removed" (p. 136).

True values for some behaviors are evident and universally accepted. For example, obtaining the true values of correct responses in academic areas such math and spelling is straightforward. The correct response to the arithmetic problem $2 + 2 = ?$ has a true value of 4, and the *Oxford English Dictionary* is a source of true values for assessing the accuracy of measuring the spelling of English words.[5] Although not universal, true values for many socially significant behaviors of interest to applied researchers and practitioners can be established conditionally on local context. For example, the correct response to the question "Name the three starches recommended as thickeners for pan gravy" on a quiz given to students in a culinary school has no universal true value. Nevertheless, a true value relevant to the students taking the quiz can be found in the instructor's course materials.

True values for each of the preceding examples were obtained through sources independent of the measures to be evaluated. Establishing true values for many behaviors studied by applied behavior analysts is difficult because the process for determining a true value must be different from the measurement procedures used to obtain the data one wishes to compare to the true value. For example, determining true values for occurrences of a behavior such as cooperative play between children is difficult because the only way to attach any values to the behavior is to measure it with the same observation procedures used to produce the data in the first place.

It can be easy to mistake true values as values that only appear to be true values. For example, suppose that

---

[4]The official time in the United States can be accessed through the National Bureau of Standards and the United States Naval Observatory atomic clock (actually 63 atomic clocks are averaged to determine official time): http://tycho.usno.navy.mil/what1.html. The atomic clock is accurate to 1 billionth of a second per day, or 1 second per 6 million years!

[5]The preferred spelling of a word may change (e.g., *judgement* becomes *judgment*), but in such cases a new true value is established.

four well-trained and experienced observers view a video-tape of teacher and student interactions. Their task is to identify the true value of all instances of teacher praise contingent on academic accomplishments. Each observer views the tape independently and counts all occurrences of contingent teacher praise. After recording their respective observations, the four observers share their measurements, discuss disagreements, and suggest reasons for the disagreements. The observers independently record contingent praise a second time. Once again they share and discuss their results. After repeating the recording and sharing process several times, all observers agree that they have recorded every instance of teacher praise. However, the observers did not produce a *true value* of teacher praise for two reasons: (1) The observers could not calibrate their measurement of teacher praise to an independent standard of teacher praise, and (2) the process used to identify all instances of teacher praise may be biased (e.g., one of the observers may have convinced the others that her measures represented the true value). When true values cannot be established, researchers must rely on reliability assessments and measures of interobserver agreement to evaluate the quality of their data.

Accuracy Assessment Procedures

Determining the accuracy of measurement is a straight-forward process of calculating the correspondence of each measure, or datum, assessed to its true value. For example, a researcher or practitioner assessing the accuracy of the score for a student's performance on a 30-word spelling test reported by a grader would compare the grader's scoring of each word on the test with the true value for that word found in a dictionary. Each word on the test that matched the correct letter sequence (i.e., orthography) provided by the dictionary and was marked correct by the grader would be an accurate measure by the grader, as would each word marked incorrect by the grader that did not match the dictionary's spelling. If the original grader's scoring of 29 of the test's 30 words corresponded to the true values for those words, the grader's measure would be 96.7% accurate.

Although an individual researcher or practitioner can assess the accuracy of the data she has collected, multiple independent observers are often used. Brown, Dunne, and Cooper (1996) described the procedures they used to assess the accuracy of measurement in a study of oral reading comprehension as follows:

> An independent observer reviewed one student's audio-tape of the delayed one-minute oral retell each day to assess our accuracy of measurement, providing an assessment of the extent that our counts of delayed retells approximated the true value of the audio-taped

correct and incorrect retells. The independent observer randomly selected each day's audiotape by drawing a student's name from a hat, then listened to the tape and scored correct and incorrect retells using the same definitions as the teacher. Observer scores were compared to teacher scores. If there was a discrepancy between these scores, the observer and the teacher reviewed the tape (i.e., the true value) together to identify the source of the discrepancy and corrected the counting error on the data sheet and the Standard Celeration Chart. The observer also used a stopwatch to time the duration of the audio-tape to ensure accuracy of the timings. We planned to have the teacher re-time the presentation or retell and re-calculate the frequency per minute for each timing discrepancy of more than 5 seconds. All timings, however, met the 5-second accuracy definition. (p. 392)

Reporting Accuracy Assessments

In addition to describing procedures used to assess the accuracy of the data, researchers should report the number and percentage of measures that were checked for accuracy, the degree of accuracy found, the extent of measurement error detected, and whether those measurement errors were corrected in the data. Brown and colleagues (1996) used the following narrative to report the results of their accuracy assessment:

> The independent observer and the teacher achieved 100% agreement on 23 of the 37 sessions checked. The teacher and the observer reviewed the tape together to identify the source of measurement errors for the 14 sessions containing measurement discrepancies and corrected the measurement errors. Accurate data from the 37 sessions rechecked were then displayed on the Standard Celeration Charts. The magnitude of the measurement errors was very small, often a difference of 1 to 3 discrepancies. (p. 392)

A full description and reporting of the results of accuracy assessment helps readers of the study evaluate the accuracy of all of the data included in the report. For example, suppose a researcher reported that she conducted accuracy checks on a randomly selected 20% of the data, found those measures to be 97% accurate with the 3% error being nonbiased, and corrected the assessed data as needed. A reader of the study would know that 20% of the data are 100% accurate and be fairly confident that the remaining 80% of the data (i.e., all of the measures that were not checked for accuracy) is 97% accurate.

Assessing the Reliability of Measurement

Measurement is reliable when it yields the same values across repeated measures of the same event. Reliability is established when the same observer measures the same data set repeatedly from archived response products such as audiovisual products and other forms of permanent products. The more frequently a consistent pattern of observation is produced, the more reliable the measurement (Thompson et al., 2000). Conversely, if similar observed values are not achieved with repeated observations, the data are considered unreliable. This leads to a concern about accuracy, which is the primary indicator of quality measurement.

But, as we have pointed out repeatedly, reliable data are not necessarily accurate data. As the three bicyclists discovered, totally reliable (i.e., consistent) measurement may be totally wrong. Relying on the reliability of measurement as the basis for determining the accuracy of measurement would be, as the philosopher Wittgenstein (1953) noted, "As if someone were to buy several copies of the morning paper to assure himself that what it said was true" (p. 94).

In many research studies and most practical applications, however, checking the accuracy of every measure is not possible or feasible. In other cases, true values for measures of the target behavior may be difficult to establish. When confirming the accuracy of each datum is not possible or practical, or when true values are not available, knowing that a measurement system has been applied with a high degree of consistency contributes to confidence in the overall trustworthiness of the data. Although high reliability cannot confirm high accuracy, discovering a low level of reliability signals that the data are then suspect enough to be disregarded until problems in the measurement system can be determined and repaired.

Assessing the reliability of behavioral measurement requires either a natural or contrived permanent product so the observer can remeasure the same events. For example, reliability of measurement of variables such as the number of adjectives or action verbs in students' essays could be accomplished by having an observer rescore essays. Reliability of measurement of the number and type of response prompts and feedback statements by parents to their children at the family dinner table could be assessed by having an observer replay and rescore videotapes of the family's mealtime and compare the data obtained from the two measurements.

Observers should not remeasure the same permanent product soon after measuring it the first time. Doing so might result in the measures from the second scoring being influenced by what the observer remembered from the initial scoring. To avoid such unwanted influence, a researcher can insert several previously scored essays or videotapes randomly into the sequence of "new data" being recorded by observers.

Using Interobserver Agreement to Assess Behavioral Measurement

Interobserver agreement is the most commonly used indicator of measurement quality in applied behavior analysis. **Interobserver agreement (IOA)** refers to the degree to which two or more independent observers report the same observed values after measuring the same events. There are numerous techniques for calculating IOA, each of which provides a somewhat different view of the extent and nature of agreement and disagreement between observers (e.g., Hartmann, 1977; Hawkins & Dotson, 1975; Page & Iwata, 1986; Poling, Methot, & LeSage, 1995; Repp, Dietz, Boles, Dietz, & Repp, 1976).

Benefits and Uses of IOA

Obtaining and reporting interobserver agreement serves four distinct purposes. First, a certain level of IOA can be used as a basis for determining the competence of new observers. As noted earlier, a high degree of agreement between a newly trained observer and an experienced observer provides an objective index of the extent to which the new observer is measuring the behavior in the same way as experienced observers.

Second, systematic assessment of IOA over the course of a study can detect observer drift. When observers who obtained the same, or nearly the same, observed values when measuring the same behavioral events at the beginning of a study (i.e., IOA was high) obtain different measures of the same events later in the study (i.e., IOA is now low), one of the observers may be using a definition of the target behavior that has drifted. Deteriorating IOA assessments cannot indicate with assurance which of the observer's data are being influenced by drift (or any other reason for disagreement), but the information reveals the need for further evaluation of the data and/or for retraining and calibration of the observers.

Third, knowing that two or more observers consistently obtained similar data increases confidence that the definition of the target behavior was clear and unambiguous and the measurement code and system not too difficult. Fourth, for studies that employ multiple observers as data collectors, consistently high levels of IOA increase confidence that variability in the data is not a function of which observer(s) happened to be on duty for any given session, and therefore that changes in the data more likely reflect actual changes in the behavior.

The first two reasons for assessing IOA are proactive: They help researchers determine and describe the degree to which observers have met training criteria and detect possible drift in observers' use of the measurement system. The second two purposes or benefits of IOA are as summative descriptors of the consistency of measurement across observers. By reporting the results of IOA assessments, researchers enable consumers to judge the relative **believability** of the data as trustworthy and deserving of interpretation.

Requisites for Obtaining Valid IOA Measures

A valid assessment of IOA depends on three equally important criteria. Although these criteria are perhaps obvious, it is nonetheless important to make them explicit. Two observers (usually two, but may be more) must (a) use the same observation code and measurement system, (b) observe and measure the same participant(s) and events, and (c) observe and record the behavior independent of any influence from one other.

Observers Must Use the Same Measurement System

Interobserver agreement assessments conducted for any of the four previously stated reasons require observers to use the same definitions of the target behavior, observation procedures and codes, and measurement devices. Beyond using the same measurement system, all observers participating in IOA measures used to assess the believability of data (as opposed to evaluating the observer trainees' performance) should have received identical training with the measurement system and achieved the same level of competence in using it.

Observers Must Measure the Same Events

The observers must be able to observe the same subject(s) at precisely the same observation intervals and periods. IOA for data obtained by real-time measurement requires that both observers be in the setting simultaneously. Real-time observers must be positioned such that each has a similar view of the subject(s) and environment. Two observers sitting on opposite sides of a classroom, for example, might obtain different measures because the different vantage points enable only one observer to see or hear some occurrences of the target behavior.

Observers must begin and end the observation period at precisely the same time. Even a difference of a few seconds between observers may produce significant measurement disagreements. To remedy this situation, the timing devices could be started simultaneously and outside the observation setting, but before data collection begins, with the understanding that the data collection would actually start at a prearranged time (e.g., exactly at the beginning of the fifth minute). Alterna-

tively, but less desirably, one observer could signal the other at the exact moment the observation is to begin.

A common and effective procedure is for both observers to listen by earphones to an audiotape of prerecorded cues signaling the beginning and end of each observation interval (see Chapter 4). An inexpensive splitter device that enables two earphones to be plugged into the same tape recorder allows observers to receive simultaneous cues unobtrusively and without depending on one another.

When assessing IOA for data obtained from permanent products, the two observers do not need to measure the behavior simultaneously. For example, the observers could each watch and record data from the same video- or audiotape at different times. Procedures must be in place, however, to ensure that each observer watched or listened to the same tapes and that they started and stopped their independent observations at precisely the same point(s) on the tapes. Ensuring that two observers measure the same events when the target behavior produces natural permanent products, such as completed academic assignments or widgets manufactured, would include procedures such as clearly marking the session number, date, condition, and subject's name on the product and guarding the response products to ensure that they are not disturbed until the second observer has obtained his measure.

Observers Must Be Independent

The third essential ingredient for valid IOA assessment is ensuring that neither observer is influenced by the other's measurements. Procedures must be in place to guarantee each observer's independence. For example, observers conducting real-time measurement of behavior "must be situated so that they can neither see nor hear when the other observes and records a response" (Johnston & Pennypacker, 1993a, p. 147). Observers must not be seated or positioned so closely to one another that either observer can detect or be influenced by the other observer's recordings.

Giving the second observer academic worksheets or written assignments that have already been marked by another observer would violate the observers' independence. To maintain independence, the second observer must score photocopies of unadulterated and unmarked worksheets or assignments as completed by the subjects.

Methods for Calculating IOA

There are numerous methods for calculating IOA, each of which provides a somewhat different view of the extent and nature of agreement and disagreement between observers (e.g., Hartmann, 1977; Hawkins & Dotson, 1975;

Page & Iwata, 1986; Poling, Methot, & LeSage, 1995; Repp, Dietz, Boles, Dietz, & Repp, 1976). The following explanation of different IOA formats is organized by the three major methods for measuring behavioral data described in Chapter 4: event recording, timing, and interval recording or time sampling. Although other statistics are sometimes used, the percentage of agreement between observers is by far the most common convention for reporting IOA in applied behavior analysis.[6] Therefore, we have provided the formula for calculating a percentage of agreement for each type of IOA.

IOA for Data Obtained by Event Recording

The various methods for calculating interobserver agreement for data obtained by event recording are based on comparing (a) the total count recorded by each observer per measurement period, (b) the counts tallied by each observer during each of a series of smaller intervals of time within the measurement period, or (c) each observer's count of 1 or 0 on a trial-by-trial basis.

Total Count IOA.[7]   The simplest and crudest indicator of IOA for event recording data compares the total count recorded by each observer per measurement period. **Total count IOA** is expressed as a percentage of agreement between the total number of responses recorded by two observers and is calculated by dividing the smaller of the counts by the larger count and multiplying by 100, as shown by this formula:

$$\frac{\text{Smaller count}}{\text{Larger count}} \times 100 = \text{total count IOA \%}$$

For example, suppose that a child care worker in a residential setting recorded that 9-year-old Mitchell used profane language 10 times during a 30-minute observation period and that a second observer recorded that Mitchell swore 9 times during that same period. The total

count IOA for the observation period would be 90% (i.e., $9 \times 10 \div 100 = 90\%$).

Great caution must be used in interpreting total count IOA because a high degree of agreement provides no assurance that the two observers recorded the same instances of behavior. For example, the following is one of the countless ways that the data reported by the two observers who measured Mitchell's use of profane language may not represent anywhere close to 90% agreement that they measured the same behaviors. The child care worker could have recorded all 10 occurrences of profane language on her data sheet during the first 15 minutes of the 30-minute observation period, a time when the second observer recorded just 4 of the 9 total responses he reported.

Mean Count-per-Interval IOA.   The likelihood that significant agreement between observers' count data means they measured the same events can be increased by (a) dividing the total observation period into a series of smaller counting times, (b) having the observers record the number of occurrences of the behavior within each interval, (c) calculating the agreement between the two observers' counts within each interval, and (d) using the agreements per interval as the basis for calculating the IOA for the total observation period. The hypothetical data shown in Figure 5.2 will be used to illustrate two methods for calculating count-per-interval IOA: mean count-per-interval and exact count-per-interval. During a 30-minute observation period, two observers independently tallied the number of times each witnessed an instance of a target behavior during each of six 5-minute intervals

Even though each observer recorded a total of 15 responses within the 30-minute period, their data sheets reveal a high degree of disagreement within the observation period. Although the total count IOA for the entire observation period was 100%, agreement between the two observers within each 5-minute interval ranged from 0% to 100%, yielding a mean count-per-interval IOA of 65.3%. **Mean count-per-interval IOA** is calculated by this formula:

$$\frac{\text{Int 1 IOA} + \text{Int 2 IOA} + \text{Int N IOA}}{n \text{ intervals}}$$
$$\times 100 = \text{mean count-per-interval IOA \%}$$

Exact Count-per-Interval IOA.   The most stringent description of IOA for most data sets obtained by event recording is obtained by computing the **exact count-per-interval IOA**—the percentage of total intervals in which two observers recorded the same count. The two observers whose data are shown in Figure 5.2 recorded

---

[6]IOA can be calculated by product-moment correlations, which range from +1.0 to −1.0. However, expressing IOA by correlation coefficients has two major weaknesses: (a) High coefficients can be achieved if one observer consistently records more occurrences of the behavior than the other, and (b) correlation coefficients provide no assurance that the observers agreed on the occurrence of any given instance of behavior (Poling et al., 1995). Hartmann (1977) described the use of *kappa (k)* as an measure of IOA. The *k* statistic was developed by Cohen (1960) as a procedure for determining the proportion of agreements between observers that would be expected as a result of chance. However, the *k* statistic is seldom reported in the behavior analysis literature.

[7]Multiple terms are used in the applied behavior analysis literature for the same methods of calculating IOA, and the same terms are sometimes used with different meanings. We believe the IOA terms used here represent the discipline's most used conventions. In an effort to point out and preserve some meaningful distinctions among variations of IOA measures, we have introduced several terms.

Figure 5.2 Two methods for computing interobserver agreement (IOA) for event recording data tallied within smaller time intervals.

Interval (Time)	Observer 1	Observer 2	IOA per interval
1 (1:00–1:05)	///	//	2/3 = 67%
2 (1:05–1:10)	///	///	3/3 = 100%
3 (1:10–1:15)	/	//	1/2 = 50%
4 (1:15–1:20)	////	///	3/4 = 75%
5 (1:20–1:25)	0	/	0/1 = 0%
6 (1:25–1:30)	////	////	4/4 = 100%
	Total count = 15	Total count = 15	Mean count-per-interval IOA = 65.3% Exact count-per-interval IOA = 33%

the same number of responses in just two of the six intervals, an exact count-per-interval IOA of 33%.

The following formula is used to calculate exact count-per-interval IOA:

$$\frac{\text{Number of intervals of 100\% IOA}}{n \text{ intervals}} \times 100 = \text{exact count-per-interval IOA \%}$$

Trial-by-Trial IOA. The agreement between two observers who measured the occurrence or nonoccurrence of discrete trial behaviors for which the count for each trial, or response opportunity, can only be 0 or 1 can be calculated by comparing the observers' total counts or by comparing their counts on a trial-by-trial basis. Calculating total count IOA for discrete trial data uses the same formula as total count IOA for free operant data: The smaller of the two counts reported by the observers is divided by the larger count and multiplied by 100, but in this case the number of trials for which each observer recorded the occurrence of the behavior is the count. Suppose, for example, that a researcher and a second observer independently measured the occurrence or nonoccurrence of a child's smiling behavior during each of 20 trials that the researcher showed the child a funny picture. The two observers compare data sheets at the end of the session and discover that they recorded smiles on 14 and 15 trials, respectively. The total count IOA for the session is 93% (i.e., 14 ÷ 15 × 100 = 93.3%), which might lead an inexperienced researcher to conclude that the target behavior has been well defined and is being measured with consistency by both observers. Those conclusions, however, would not be warranted.

Total count IOA of discrete trial data is subject to the same limitations as total count IOA of free operant data:

It tends to overestimate the extent of actual agreement and does not indicate how many responses, or which responses, trials, or items, posed agreement problems. Comparing the two observers' counts of 14 and 15 trials suggests that they disagreed on the occurrence of smiling on only 1 of 20 trials. However, it is possible that any of the 6 trials scored as "no smile" by the experimenter was scored as a "smile" trial by the second observer and that any of the 5 trials recorded by the second observer as "no smile" was recorded as a "smile" by the experimenter. Thus, the total count IOA of 93% may vastly overestimate the actual consistency with which the two observers measured the child's behavior during the session.

A more conservative and meaningful index of interobserver agreement for discrete trial data is **trial-by-trial IOA,** which is calculated by the following formula:

$$\frac{\text{Number of trials (items) agreement}}{\text{Total number of trials (items)}} \times 100 = \text{trial-by-trial IOA \%}$$

The trial-by-trial IOA for the two observers' smiling data, if calculated with the worst possible degree of agreement from the previous example—that is, if all 6 trials that the primary observer scored as "no smile" were recorded as "smile" trials by the second observer and all 5 trials marked by the second observer as "no smile" were recorded as "smile" trials by the experimenter—would be 45% (i.e., 9 trials scored in agreement divided by 20 trials × 100).

IOA for Data Obtained by Timing

Interobserver agreement for data obtained by timing duration, response latency, or interresponse time (IRT) is obtained and calculated in essentially the same way as it is for event recording data. Two observers independently time the duration, latency, or IRT of the target behavior, and IOA is based on comparing either the total time obtained by each observer for the session or the times recorded by each observer per occurrence of the behavior (for duration measures) or per response (for latency and IRT measures).

Total Duration IOA. **Total duration IOA** is computed by dividing the shorter of the two durations reported by the observers by the longer duration and multiplying by 100.

$$\frac{\text{Shorter duration}}{\text{Longer duration}} \times 100 = \text{total duration IOA \%}$$

As with total count IOA for event recording data, high total duration IOA provides no assurance that the observers recorded the same durations for the same occurrences of behavior. This is because a significant degree of disagreement between the observers' timings of individual responses may be canceled out in the sum. For example, suppose two observers recorded the following durations in seconds for five occurrences of a behavior:

	R1	R2	R3	R4	R5
Observer 1:	35	15	9	14	17

(total duration = 90 seconds)

	R1	R2	R3	R4	R5
Observer 2:	29	21	7	14	14

(total duration = 85 seconds)

Total duration IOA for these data is a perhaps comforting 94% (i.e., $85 \div 90 \times 100 = 94.4\%$). However, the two observers obtained the same duration for only one of the five responses, and their timings of specific responses varied by as much as 6 seconds. While recognizing this limitation of total duration IOA, when total duration is being recorded and analyzed as a dependent variable, reporting total duration IOA is appropriate. When possible, total duration IOA should be supplemented with mean duration-per-occurrence IOA, which is described next.

Mean Duration-per-Occurrence IOA. Mean duration-per-occurrence IOA should be calculated for duration per occurrence data, and it is a more conservative and usually more meaningful assessment of IOA for total duration data. The formula for calculating **mean duration-per-occurrence IOA** is similar to the one used to determine mean count-per-interval IOA:

$$\frac{\text{Dur IOA R1} + \text{Dur IOA R2} + \text{Dur IOA R}n}{n \text{ responses with Dur IOA}} \times 100 = \text{mean duration-per-interval IOA \%}$$

Using this formula to calculate the mean duration-per-occurrence IOA for the two observers' timing data of the five responses just presented would entail the following steps:

1. Calculate duration per occurrence IOA for each response: R1, $29 \div 35 = .83$; R2, $15 \div 21 = .71$; R3, $7 \div 9 = .78$; R4, $14 \div 14 = 1.0$; and R5, $14 \div 17 = .82$

2. Add the individual IOA percentages for each occurrence: $.83 + .71 + .78 + 1.00 + .82 = 4.14$

3. Divide the sum of the individual IOAs per occurrence by the total number of responses for which two observers measured duration: $4.14 \div 5 = .828$

4. Multiply by 100 and round to the nearest whole number: $.828 \times 100 = 83\%$

This basic formula is also used to compute the *mean latency-per-response IOA* or *mean IRT-per-response IOA* for latency and IRT data. An observer's timings of latencies or IRTs in a session should never be added and the total time compared to a similar total time obtained by another observer as the basis for calculating IOA for latency and IRT measures.

In addition to reporting mean agreement per occurrence, IOA assessment for timing data can be enhanced with information about the range of differences between observers' timings and the percentage of responses for which the two observers each obtained measures within a certain range of error. For example: Mean duration-per-occurrence IOA for Temple's compliance was 87% (range across responses, 63 to 100%), and 96% of all timings obtained by the second observer were within +/–2 seconds of the primary observer's measures.

IOA for Data Obtained by Interval Recording/Time Sampling

Three techniques commonly used by applied behavior analysts to calculate IOA for interval data are interval-by-interval IOA, scored-interval IOA, and unscored-interval IOA.

Interval-by-Interval IOA. When using an interval-by-interval IOA (sometimes referred to as the *point-by-point* and *total interval* method), the primary observer's record for each interval is matched to the secondary observer's record for the same interval. The formula for calculating **interval-by-interval IOA** is as follows:

$$\frac{\text{Number of intervals agreed}}{\text{Number of intervals agreed} + \text{number of intervals disagreed}} \times 100 = \text{interval-by-interval IOA \%}$$

Figure 5.3 When calculating interval-by-interval IOA, the number of intervals in which both observers agreed on the occurrence or the nonoccurrence of the behavior (shaded intervals) is divided by the total number of observation intervals. Interval-by-interval IOA for the data shown here is 70% (7/10).

Interval-by-Interval IOA										
Interval no. →	1	2	3	4	5	6	7	8	9	10
Observer 1	X	X	X	0	X	X	0	X	X	0
Observer 2	0	X	X	0	X	0	0	0	X	0

X = behavior was recorded as occurring during interval
0 = behavior was recorded as not occurring during interval

The hypothetical data in Figure 5.3 show the interval-by-interval method for calculating IOA based on the record of two observers who recorded the occurrence (X) and nonoccurrence (0) of behavior in each of 10 observation intervals. The observers' data sheets show that they agreed on the occurrence or the nonoccurrence of the behavior for seven intervals (Intervals 2, 3, 4, 5, 7, 9, and 10). Interval-by-interval IOA for this data set is 70% (i.e., $7 \div [7 + 3] \times 100 = 70\%$).

Interval-by-interval IOA is likely to overestimate the actual agreement between observers measuring behaviors that occur at very low or very high rates. This is because interval-by-interval IOA is subject to random or accidental agreement between observers. For example, with a behavior whose actual frequency of occurrence is only about 1 or 2 intervals per 10 observation intervals, even a poorly trained and unreliable observer who misses some of the few occurrences of the behavior and mistakenly records the behavior as occurring in some intervals when the behavior did not occur is likely to mark most intervals as nonoccurrences. As a result of this chance agreement, interval-by-interval IOA is likely to be quite high. Two IOA methods that minimize the effects of chance agreements for interval data on behaviors that occur at very low or very high rates are scored-interval IOA and unscored-interval IOA (Hawkins & Dotson, 1975).

Scored-Interval IOA. Only those intervals in which either or both observers recorded the *occurrence of the target behavior* are used in calculating **scored-interval IOA.** An agreement is counted when both observers recorded that the behavior occurred in the same interval, and each interval in which one observer recorded the occurrence of the behavior and the other recorded its nonoccurrence is counted as a disagreement. For example, for the data shown in Figure 5.4, only Intervals 1, 3, and 9 would be used in calculating scored-interval IOA. Intervals 2, 4, 5, 6, 7, 8, and 10 would be ignored because both observers recorded that the behavior did not occur in those intervals. Because the two observers agreed that the behavior occurred in only one (Interval 3) of the three scored intervals, the scored-interval IOA measure is 33% (1 interval of agreement divided by the sum of 1 interval of agreement plus 2 intervals of disagreement × 100 = 33%).

Figure 5.4 Scored-interval IOA is calculated using only those intervals in which either observer recorded the occurrence of the behavior (shaded intervals). Scored-interval IOA for the data shown here is 33% (1/3).

Scored-Interval IOA										
Interval no. →	1	2	3	4	5	6	7	8	9	10
Observer 1	X	0	X	0	0	0	0	0	0	0
Observer 2	0	0	X	0	0	0	0	0	X	0

X = behavior was recorded as occurring during interval
0 = behavior was recorded as not occurring during interval

For behaviors that occur at low rates, scored-interval IOA is a more conservative measure of agreement than interval-by-interval IOA. This is because scored-interval IOA ignores the intervals in which agreement by chance is highly likely. For example, using the interval-by-interval method for calculating IOA for the data in Figure 5.4 would yield an agreement of 80%. To avoid overinflated and possibly misleading IOA measures, we recommend using scored-interval interobserver agreement for behaviors that occur at frequencies of approximately 30% or fewer intervals.

Unscored-Interval IOA. Only intervals in which either or both observers recorded the *nonoccurrence of the target behavior* are considered when calculating **unscored-interval IOA.** An agreement is counted when both observers recorded the nonoccurrence of the behavior in the same interval, and each interval in which one observer recorded the nonoccurrence of the behavior and the other recorded its occurrence is counted as a disagreement. For example, only Intervals 1, 4, 7, and 10 would be used in calculating the unscored-interval IOA for the data in Figure 5.5 because at least one observer recorded the nonoccurrence of the behavior in each of those intervals. The two observers agreed that the behavior did not occur in Intervals 4 and 7. Therefore, the unscored-interval IOA in this example is 50% (2 intervals of agreement divided by the sum of 2 intervals of agreement plus 2 intervals of disagreement × 100 = 50%).

For behaviors that occur at relatively high rates, unscored-interval IOA provides a more stringent assessment of interobserver agreement than does interval-by-interval IOA. To avoid overinflated and possibly misleading IOA measures, we recommend using unscored-interval interobserver agreement for behaviors that occur at frequencies of approximately 70% or more of intervals.

Considerations in Selecting, Obtaining, and Reporting Interobserver Agreement

The guidelines and recommendations that follow are organized under a series of questions concerning the use of interobserver agreement to evaluate the quality of behavioral measurement.

How Often and When Should IOA Be Obtained?

Interobserver agreement should be assessed during each condition and phase of a study and be distributed across days of the week, times of day, settings, and observers. Scheduling IOA assessments in this manner ensures that the results will provide a representative (i.e., valid) picture of all data obtained in a study. Current practice and recommendations by authors of behavioral research methods texts suggest that IOA be obtained for a minimum of 20% of a study's sessions, and preferably between 25% and 33% of sessions (Kennedy, 2005; Poling et al., 1995). In general, studies using data obtained via real-time measurement will have IOA assessed for a higher percentage of sessions than studies with data obtained from permanent products.

The frequency with which data should be assessed via interobserver agreement will vary depending on the complexity of the measurement code, the number and experience of observers, the number of conditions and phases, and the results of the IOA assessments themselves. More frequent IOA assessments are expected in studies that involve complex or new measurement systems, inexperienced observers, and numerous conditions and phases. If appropriately conservative methods for obtaining and calculating IOA reveal high levels of agreement early in a study, the number and proportion of sessions in which IOA is assessed may decrease as the study progresses. For instance, IOA assessment might be conducted in each

Figure 5.5   Unscored-interval IOA is calculated using only those intervals in which either observer recorded the nonoccurrence of the behavior (shaded intervals). Unscored interval IOA for the data shown here is 50% (2/4).

Unscored-Interval IOA										
Interval no. →	1	2	3	4	5	6	7	8	9	10
Observer 1	X	X	X	0	X	X	0	X	X	0
Observer 2	0	X	X	0	X	X	0	X	X	X

X = behavior was recorded as occurring during interval

0 = behavior was recorded as not occurring during interval

session at the beginning of an analysis, and then reduced to a schedule of once per four or five sessions.

For What Variables Should IOA Be Obtained and Reported?

In general, researchers should obtain and report IOA at the same levels at which they report and discuss the results of their study. For example, a researcher analyzing the relative effects of two treatment conditions on two behaviors of four participants in two settings should report IOA outcomes on both behaviors for each participant separated by treatment condition and setting. This would enable consumers of the research to judge the relative believability of the data within each component of the experiment.

Which Method of Calculating IOA Should Be Used?

More stringent and conservative methods of calculating IOA should be used over methods that are likely to overestimate actual agreement as a result of chance. With event recording data used to evaluate the accuracy of performance, we recommend reporting overall IOA on a trial-by-trial or item-by-item basis, perhaps supplemented with separate IOA calculations for correct responses and incorrect responses. For data obtained by interval or time sampling measurement, we recommend supplementing interval-by-interval IOA with scored-interval IOA or unscored-interval IOA depending on the relative frequency of the behavior. In situations in which the primary observer scores the target behavior as occurring in approximately 30% or fewer intervals, scored-interval IOA provides a conservative supplement to interval-by-interval IOA. Conversely, when the primary observer scores the target behavior as occurring in approximately 70% or more of the intervals, unscored-interval IOA should supplement interval-by-interval IOA. If the rate at which the target behavior occurs changes from very low to very high, or from very high to very low, across conditions or phases of a study, reporting both unscored-interval and scored-interval IOA may be warranted.

If in doubt about which form of IOA to report, calculating and presenting several variations will help readers make their own judgments regarding the believability of the data. However, if the acceptance of the data for interpretation or decision making rests on which formula for calculating IOA is chosen, serious concerns about the data's trustworthiness exist that must be addressed.

What Are Acceptable Levels of IOA?

Carefully collected and conservatively computed IOA assessments increasingly enhance the believability of a data set as agreement approaches 100%. The usual convention in applied behavior analysis is to expect independent observers to achieve a mean of no less than 80% agreement when using observational recording. However, as Kennedy (2005) pointed out, "There is no scientific justification for why 80% is necessary, only a long history of researchers using this percentage as a benchmark of acceptability and being successful in their research activities" (p. 120).

Miller (1997) recommended that IOA should be 90% or greater for an established measure and at least 80% for a new variable. Various factors at work in a given situation may make an 80% or 90% criterion too low or too high. Interobserver agreement of 90% on the number of words contained in student compositions should raise serious questions about the trustworthiness of the data. IOA near 100% is needed to enhance the believability of count data obtained from permanent products. However, some analysts might accept data with a mean IOA as low as 75% for the simultaneous measurement of multiple behaviors by several subjects in a complex environment, especially if it is based on a sufficient number of individual IOA assessments with a small range (e.g., 73 to 80%).

The degree of behavior change revealed by the data should also be considered when determining an acceptable level of interobserver agreement. When behavior change from one condition to another is small, the variability in the data might represent inconsistent observation more than actual change in the behavior. Therefore, the smaller the change in behavior across conditions, the higher the criterion should be for an acceptable IOA percentage (Kennedy, 2005).

How Should IOA Be Reported?

IOA scores can be reported in narrative, table, and graphic form. Whichever format is chosen, it is important to note how, when, and how often interobserver agreement was assessed.

Narrative Description. The most common approach for reporting IOA is a simple narrative description of the mean and range of agreement percentages. For example, Craft, Alber, and Heward (1998) described the methods and results of IOA assessments in a study in which four dependent variables were measured as follows:

> *Student recruiting and teacher praise.* A second observer was present for 12 (30%) of the study's 40

sessions. The two observers independently and simultaneously observed the 4 students, recording the number of recruiting responses they emitted and teacher praise they received. Descriptive narrative notes recorded by the observers enabled each recruiting episode to be identified for agreement purposes. Interobserver agreement was calculated on an episode-by-episode basis by dividing the total number of agreements by the total number of agreements plus disagreements and multiplying by 100%. Agreement for frequency of student recruiting ranged across students from 88.2% to 100%; agreement for frequency of recruited teacher praise was 100% for all 4 students; agreement for frequency of nonrecruited teacher praise ranged from 93.3% to 100%.

Academic work completion and accuracy. A second observer independently recorded each student's work completion and accuracy for 10 (25%) sessions. Interobserver agreement for both completion and accuracy on the spelling worksheets was 100% for all 4 students.

Table. An example of reporting interobserver agreement outcomes in table format is shown in Table 5.1. Krantz and McClannahan (1998) reported the range and mean IOA computed for three types of so-cial interactions by three children across each experimental condition.

Graphic Display. Interobserver agreement can be represented visually by plotting the measures obtained by the secondary observer on a graph of the primary observer's data as shown in Figure 5.6. Looking at both observers' data on the same graph reveals the extent of agreement between the observers and the existence of observer drift or bias. The absence of observer drift is suggested in the hypothetical study shown in Figure 5.6 because the secondary observer's measures changed in concert with the primary observer's measures. Although the two observers obtained the same measure on only 2 of the 10 sessions in which IOA was assessed (Sessions 3 and 8), the fact that neither observer consistently reported measures that were higher or lower than the other suggests the absence of observer bias. An absence of bias is usually indicated by a random pattern of overestimation and underestimation. In addition to revealing observer drift and bias, a third way that graphically displaying IOA assessments can enhance the believability of measurement is illustrated by the

Table 5.1 Interobserver Agreement Results for Each Dependent Variable by Participant and Experimental Condition

Range and Mean Percentage Interobserver Agreement on Scripted Interaction, Elaborations, and Unscripted Interaction by Child and Condition

Type of interaction	Condition									
	Baseline		Teaching		New recipient		Script fading		New activities	
	Range	M	Range	M	Range	M	Range	M	Range	M
Scripted										
David			88–100	94		100		100		
Jeremiah			89–100	98		100		—[a]		
Ben			80–100	98		90		—[a]		
Elaborations										
David			75–100	95	87–88	88	90–100	95		
Jeremiah			83–100	95	92–100	96		—[a]		
Ben			75–100	95		95		—[a]		
Unscripted										
David		100		100	87–88	88	97–100	98	98–100	99
Jeremiah		100		100	88–100	94	93–100	96		98
Ben		100		100		100	92–93	92	98–100	99

[a]No data are available for scripted responses and elaborations in the script-fading condition, because interobserver agreement was obtained after scripts were removed (i.e., because scripts were absent, there could be only unscripted responses).

From "Social Interaction Skills for Children with Autism: A Script-Fading Procedure for Beginning Readers," by P. J. Krantz and L. E. McClannahan, 1998, *Journal of Applied Behavior Analysis, 31,* p. 196. Copyright 1998 by the Society for the Experimental Analysis of Behavior, Inc. Reprinted by permission.

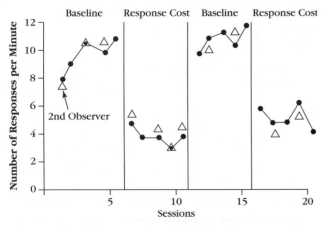

Figure 5.6 Plotting measures obtained by a second observer on a graph of the primary observer's data provide a visual representation of the extent and nature of interobserver agreement.

data in Figure 5.6. When the data reported by the primary observer show clear change in the behavior between conditions or phases and all of the measures reported by the secondary observer within each phase fall within the range of observed values obtained by the primary observer, confidence increases that the data represent actual changes in the behavior measured rather than changes in the primary observer's behavior due to drift or extra-experimental contingencies.

Although published research reports in applied behavior analysis seldom include graphic displays of IOA measures, creating and using such displays during a study is a simple and direct way for researchers to detect patterns in the consistency (or inconsistency) with which observers are measuring behavior that might be not be as evident in comparing a series of percentages.

Which Approach Should Be Used for Assessing the Quality of Measurement: Accuracy, Reliability, or Interobserver Agreement?

Assessments of the accuracy of measurement, the reliability of measurement, and the extent to which different observers obtain the same measures each provide different indications of data quality. Ultimately, the reason for conducting any type of assessment of measurement quality is to obtain quantitative evidence that can be used for the dual purposes of improving measurement during the course of an investigation and judging and convincing others of the trustworthiness of the data.

After ensuring the validity of what they are measuring and how they are measuring it, applied behavior analysts should choose to assess the accuracy of measurement whenever possible rather than reliability or

interobserver agreement. If it can be determined that all measurements in a data set meet an acceptable accuracy criterion, questions regarding the reliability of measurement and interobserver agreement are moot. For data confirmed to be accurate, conducting additional assessments of reliability or IOA is unnecessary.

When assessing the accuracy of measurement is not possible because true values are unavailable, an assessment of reliability provides the next best quality indicator. If natural or contrived permanent products can be archived, applied behavior analysts can assess the reliability of measurement, allowing consumers to know that observers have measured behavior consistently from session to session, condition to condition, and phase to phase.

When true values and permanent product archives are unavailable, interobserver agreement provides a level of believability for the data. Although IOA is not a direct indicator of the validity, accuracy, or reliability of measurement, it has proven to be a valuable and useful research tool in applied behavior analysis. Reporting interobserver agreement has been an expected and required component of published research in applied behavior analysis for several decades. In spite of its limitations, "the homely measures of observer agreement so widely used in the field are exactly relevant" (Baer, 1977, p. 119) to efforts to develop a robust technology of behavior change.

> Percentage of agreement, in the interval-recording paradigm, does have a direct and useful meaning: how often do two observers watching one subject, and equipped with the same definitions of behavior, see it occurring or not occurring at the same standard times? The two answers, "They agree about its occurrence X% of the relevant intervals, and about its nonoccurrence Y% of the relevant intervals," are superbly useful. (Baer, 1977, p. 118)

There are no reasons to prevent researchers from using multiple assessment procedures to evaluate the same data set. When time and resources permit, it may even be desirable to include combinations of assessments. Applied behavior analysts can use any possible combination of the assessment (e.g., accuracy plus IOA, reliability plus IOA). In addition, some aspects of the data set could be assessed for accuracy or reliability while other aspects are assessed with IOA. The previous example of accuracy assessment reported by Brown and colleagues (1996) included assessments for accuracy and IOA. Independent observers recorded correct and incorrect student-delayed retells. When IOA was less than 100%, data for that student and session were assessed for accuracy. IOA was used as an assessment to enhance believability, and also as a procedure for selecting data to be assessed for accuracy.

Summary

Indicators of Trustworthy Measurement

1. To be most useful for science, measurement must be valid, accurate, and reliable.

2. Valid measurement in ABA encompasses three equally important elements: (a) measuring directly a socially significant target behavior, (b) measuring a dimension of the target behavior relevant to the question or concern about the behavior, and (c) ensuring that the data are representative of the behavior under conditions and during times most relevant to the reason(s) for measuring it.

3. Measurement is accurate when observed values, the data produced by measuring an event, match the true state, or true values, of the event.

4. Measurement is reliable when it yields the same values across repeated measurement of the same event.

Threats to Measurement Validity

5. Indirect measurement—measuring a behavior different from the behavior of interest—threatens validity because it requires that the researcher or practitioner make inferences about the relationship between the measures obtained and the actual behavior of interest.

6. A researcher who employs indirect measurement must provide evidence that the behavior measured directly reflects, in some reliable and meaningful way, something about the behavior for which the researcher wishes to draw conclusions.

7. Measuring a dimension of the behavior that is ill suited for, or irrelevant to, the reason for measuring the behavior compromises validity.

8. Measurement artifacts are data that give an unwarranted or misleading picture of the behavior because of the way measurement was conducted. Discontinuous measurement, poorly scheduled observations, and insensitive or limiting measurement scales are common causes of measurement artifacts.

Threats to Measurement Accuracy and Reliability

9. Most investigations in applied behavior analysis use human observers to measure behavior, and human error is the biggest threat to the accuracy and reliability of data.

10. Factors that contribute to measurement error include poorly designed measurement systems, inadequate observer training, and expectations about what the data should look like.

11. Observers should receive systematic training and practice with the measurement system and meet predetermined accuracy and reliability criteria before collecting data.

12. Observer drift—unintended changes in the way an observer uses a measurement system over the course of an investigation—can be minimized by booster training sessions and feedback on the accuracy and reliability of measurement.

13. An observer's expectations or knowledge about predicted or desired results can impair the accuracy and reliability of data.

14. Observers should not receive feedback about the extent to which their data confirm or run counter to hypothesized results or treatment goals.

15. Measurement bias caused by observer expectations can be avoided by using naive observers.

16. Observer reactivity is measurement error caused by an observer's awareness that others are evaluating the data he reports.

Assessing the Accuracy and Reliability of Behavioral Measurement

17. Researchers and practitioners who assess the accuracy of their data can (a) determine early in an analysis whether the data are usable for making experimental or treatment decisions, (b) discover and correct measurement errors, (c) detect consistent patterns of measurement error that can lead to the overall improvement or calibration of the measurement system, and (d) communicate to others the relative trustworthiness of the data.

18. Assessing the accuracy of measurement is a straightforward process of calculating the correspondence of each measure, or datum, assessed to its true value.

19. True values for many behaviors of interest to applied behavior analysts are evident and universally accepted or can be established conditionally by local context. True values for some behaviors (e.g., cooperative play) are difficult because the process for determining a true value must be different from the measurement procedures used to obtain the data one wishes to compare to the true value.

20. Assessing the extent to which observers are reliably applying a valid and accurate measurement system provides a useful indicator of the overall trustworthiness of the data.

21. Assessing the reliability of measurement requires a natural or contrived permanent product so the observer can remeasure the same behavioral events.

22. Although high reliability does not confirm high accuracy, discovering a low level of reliability signals that the data are suspect enough to be disregarded until problems in the measurement system can be determined and repaired.

Using Interobserver Agreement to Assess Behavioral Measurement

23. The most commonly used indicator of measurement quality in ABA is interobserver agreement (IOA), the degree

to which two or more independent observers report the same observed values after measuring the same events.

24. Researchers and practitioners use measures of IOA to (a) determine the competence of new observers, (b) detect observer drift, (c) judge whether the definition of the target behavior is clear and the system not too difficult to use, and (d) convince others of the relative believability of the data.

25. Measuring IOA requires that two or more observers (a) use the same observation code and measurement system, (b) observe and measure the same participant(s) and events, and (c) observe and record the behavior independent of influence by other observers.

26. There are numerous techniques for calculating IOA, each of which provides a somewhat different view of the extent and nature of agreement and disagreement between observers.

27. Percentage of agreement between observers is the most common convention for reporting IOA in ABA.

28. IOA for data obtained by event recording can be calculated by comparing (a) the total count recorded by each observer per measurement period, (b) the counts tallied by each observer during each of a series of smaller intervals of time within the measurement period, or (c) each observer's count of 1 or 0 on a trial-by-trial basis.

29. Total count IOA is the simplest and crudest indicator of IOA for event recording data, and exact count-per-interval IOA is the most stringent for most data sets obtained by event recording.

30. IOA for data obtained by timing duration, response latency, or interresponse time (IRT) is calculated in essentially the same ways as for event recording data.

31. Total duration IOA is computed by dividing the shorter of the two durations reported by the observers by the longer duration. Mean duration-per-occurrence IOA is a more conservative and usually more meaningful assessment of IOA for total duration data and should always be calculated for duration-per-occurrence data.

32. Three techniques commonly used to calculate IOA for interval data are interval-by-interval IOA, scored-interval IOA, and unscored-interval IOA.

33. Because it is subject to random or accidental agreement between observers, interval-by-interval IOA is likely to overestimate the degree of agreement between observers measuring behaviors that occur at very low or very high rates.

34. Scored-interval IOA is recommended for behaviors that occur at relatively low frequencies; unscored-interval IOA is recommended for behaviors that occur at relatively high frequencies.

35. IOA assessments should occur during each condition and phase of a study and be distributed across days of the week, times of day, settings, and observers.

36. Researchers should obtain and report IOA at the same levels at which they report and discuss the results of their study.

37. More stringent and conservative IOA methods should be used over methods that may overestimate agreement as a result of chance.

38. The convention for acceptable IOA has been a minimum of 80%, but there can be no set criterion. The nature of the behavior being measured and the degree of behavior change revealed by the data must be considered when determining an acceptable level of IOA.

39. IOA scores can be reported in narrative, table, and graphic form.

40. Researchers can use multiple indices to assess the quality of their data (e.g., accuracy plus IOA, reliability plus IOA).

PART 3

Evaluating and Analyzing Behavior Change

In Part Two we described considerations and procedures for selecting and defining target behaviors and discussed detailed methods for measuring behavior; we also examined techniques for improving, assessing, and reporting the veracity of measurement. The product of these measurements, called *data*, is the medium with which the behavior analyst works. But what does the behavior analyst do with the data? The five chapters in Part Three are devoted to the presentation and interpretation of behavioral data and to the design, conduct, and evaluation of experiments analyzing the effects of interventions.

In Chapter 6 we describe the graphic displays used by researchers, practitioners, and consumers to make sense of behavioral data. We discuss considerations for selecting, constructing, and interpreting the major types of graphs most often used by behavior analysts. Although measurement and graphic displays can reveal whether, when, and to what extent behavior has changed, they alone cannot reveal what brought about the behavior change. Chapters 7 through 10 are devoted to the *analysis* in applied behavior analysis. Chapter 7 describes the requisite components of any experiment in behavior analysis and explains how researchers and practitioners apply steady-state strategy and the three elements of basic logic—prediction, verification, and replication—-to seek and verify functional relations between behavior and its controlling variables. In Chapters 8 and 9 we describe the logic and operation of the reversal, alternating treatments, multiple baseline, and changing criterion designs—the most commonly used experimental designs in applied behavior analysis. Chapter 10 covers a wide range of topics necessary for developing a more complete understanding of behavioral research. Beginning with the assumption that the research methods of any science should reflect the characteristics of its subject matter, we examine the importance of analyzing behavior at the level of individual client or research participant, discuss the value of flexibility in experimental design, identify some common confounds to the internal validity of experiments, present methods for assessing the social validity of an applied behavior analysis, and describe how replication is used to determine the external validity of research. We conclude Chapter 10 and Part Three with a series of issues and questions that should be considered in evaluating the "goodness" of a published study in applied behavior analysis.

CHAPTER 6

Constructing and Interpreting Graphic Displays of Behavioral Data

Key Terms

bar graph	independent variable	split-middle line of progress
cumulative record	level	Standard Celeration Chart
cumulative recorder	line graph	trend
data	local response rate	variability
data path	overall response rate	visual analysis
dependent variable	scatterplot	
graph	semilogarithmic chart	

Behavior Analyst Certification Board® BCBA® & BCABA® Behavior Analyst Task List©, Third Edition

	Content Area 7: Displaying and Interpreting Behavioral Data
7-1	Select a data display that effectively communicates quantitative relations.
7-2	Use equal-interval graphs.
7-3	Use Standard Celeration Charts (for BCBA only—excluded for BCABA).
7-4	Use a cumulative record to display data.
7-5	Use data displays that highlight patterns of behavior (e.g., scatterplot).
7-6	Interpret and base decision making on data displayed in various formats.

Applied behavior analysts document and quantify behavior change by direct and repeated measurement of behavior. The product of these measurements, called **data,** is the medium with which behavior analysts work. In everyday usage the word *data* refers to a wide variety of often imprecise and subjective information offered as facts. In scientific usage the word *data* means "the results of measurement, usually in quantified form" (Johnston & Pennypacker, 1993a, p. 365).[1]

Because behavior change is a dynamic and ongoing process, the behavior analyst—the practitioner and the researcher—must maintain direct and continuous contact with the behavior under investigation. The data obtained throughout a behavior change program or a research study are the means for that contact; they form the empirical basis for every important decision: to continue with the present procedure, to try a different intervention, or to reinstitute a previous condition. But making valid and reliable decisions from the raw data themselves (a series of numbers) is difficult, if not impossible, and inefficient. Inspecting a long row of numbers will reveal only very large changes in performance, or no change at all, and important features of behavior change can easily be overlooked.

Consider the three sets of data that follow; each consists of a series of numbers representing consecutive measures of some target behavior. The first data set shows the results of successive measures of the number of responses emitted under two different conditions (A and B):

Condition A

120, 125, 115, 130,
126, 130, 123, 120,
120, 127

Condition B

114, 110, 115, 121,
110, 116, 107, 120,
115, 112

Here are some data showing consecutive measures of the percentage of correct responses:

80, 82, 78, 85, 80, 90, 85, 85, 90, 92

The third data set consists of measures of responses per minute of a target behavior obtained on successive school days:

65, 72, 63, 60, 55, 68, 71, 65, 65, 62, 70, 75, 79, 63, 60

What do these numbers tell you? What conclusions can you draw from each data set? How long did it take you to reach your conclusions? How sure of them are you? What if the data sets contained many more measures to interpret? How likely is it that others interested

in the behavior change program or research study would reach the same conclusions? How could these data be directly and effectively communicated to others?

Graphs—relatively simple formats for visually displaying relationships among and between a series of measurements and relevant variables—help people "make sense" of quantitative information. Graphs are the major device with which applied behavior analysts organize, store, interpret, and communicate the results of their work. Figure 6.1 includes a graph for each of the three data sets presented previously. The top graph reveals a lower level of responding during Condition B than during Condition A. The middle graph clearly shows an upward trend

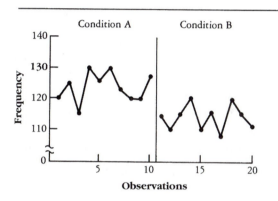

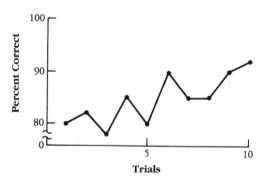

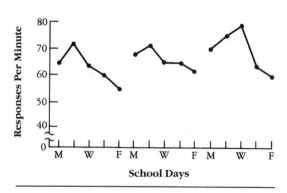

Figure 6.1   Graphic displays of three sets of hypothetical data illustrating changes in the level of responding across conditions (top), trend (middle), and cyclical variability (bottom).

---

[1]Although often used as a singular construction (e.g., "The data *shows* that . . ."), *data* is a plural noun of Latin origin and is correctly used with plural verbs (e.g., "These data *are* . . .").

over time in the response measure. A variable pattern of responding, characterized by an increasing trend during the first part of each week and a decreasing trend toward the end of each week, is evident in the bottom graph. The graphs in Figure 6.1 illustrate three fundamental properties of behavior change over time—level, trend, and variability—each of which will be discussed in detail later in the chapter. The graphic display of behavioral data has proven an effective means of detecting, analyzing, and communicating these aspects of behavior change.

Purpose and Benefits of Graphic Displays of Behavioral Data

Numerous authors have discussed the benefits of using graphs as the primary vehicle for interpreting and communicating the results of behavioral treatments and research (e.g., Baer, 1977; Johnston & Pennypacker, 1993a; Michael, 1974; Parsonson, 2003; Parsonson & Baer, 1986, 1992; Sidman, 1960). Parsonson and Baer (1978) said it best:

> In essence, the function of the graph is to communicate, in a readily assimilable and attractive manner, descriptions and summaries of data that enable rapid and accurate analysis of the facts. (p. 134)

There are at least six benefits of graphic display and visual analysis of behavioral data. First, plotting each measure of behavior on a graph right after the observational period provides the practitioner or researcher with immediate access to an ongoing visual record of the participant's behavior. Instead of waiting until the investigation or teaching program is completed, behavior change is evaluated continually, allowing treatment and experimental decisions to be responsive to the participant's performance. Graphs provide the "close, continual contact with relevant outcome data" that can lead to "measurably superior instruction" (Bushell & Baer, 1994, p. 9).

Second, direct and continual contact with the data in a readily analyzable format enables the researcher as well as the practitioner to explore interesting variations in behavior as they occur. Some of the most important research findings about behavior have been made because scientists followed the leads suggested by their data instead of following predetermined experimental plans (Sidman, 1960, 1994; Skinner, 1956).

Third, graphs, like statistical analyses of behavior change, are judgmental aids: devices that help the practitioner or experimenter interpret the results of a study or treatment (Michael, 1974). In contrast to the statistical tests of inference used in group comparison research, however, visual analysis of graphed data takes less time, is relatively easy to learn, imposes no predetermined or

arbitrary level for determining the significance of behavior change, and does not require the data to conform to certain mathematical properties or statistical assumptions to be analyzed.

Fourth, visual analysis is a conservative method for determining the significance of behavior change. A behavior change deemed statistically significant according to a test of mathematical probabilities may not look very impressive when the data are plotted on a graph that reveals the range, variability, trends, and overlaps in the data within and across experimental or treatment conditions. Interventions that produce only weak or unstable effects are not likely to be reported as important findings in applied behavior analysis. Rather, weak or unstable effects are likely to lead to further experimentation in an effort to discover controlling variables that produce meaningful behavior change in a reliable and sustained manner. This screening out of weak variables in favor of robust interventions has enabled applied behavior analysts to develop a useful technology of behavior change (Baer, 1977).[2]

Fifth, graphs enable and encourage independent judgments and interpretations of the meaning and significance of behavior change. Instead of having to rely on conclusions based on statistical manipulations of the data or on an author's interpretations, readers of published reports of applied behavior analysis can (and should) conduct their own visual analysis of the data to form independent conclusions.[3]

Sixth, in addition to their primary purpose of displaying relationships between behavior change (or lack thereof) and variables manipulated by the practitioner or researcher, graphs can also be effective sources of feedback to the people whose behavior they represent (e.g., DeVries, Burnettte, & Redmon, 1991; Stack & Milan, 1993). Graphing one's own performance has also been demonstrated to be an effective intervention for a variety of academic and behavior change objectives (e.g., Fink & Carnine, 1975; Winette, Neale, & Grier, 1979).

Types of Graphs Used in Applied Behavior Analysis

Visual formats for the graphic display of data most often used in applied behavior analysis are line graphs, bar graphs, cumulative records, semilogarithmic charts, and scatterplots.

---

[2]A comparison of the visual analysis of graphed data and inferences based on statistical tests of significance is presented in Chapter 10.

[3]Graphs, like statistics, can also be manipulated to make certain interpretations of the data more or less likely. Unlike statistics, however, most forms of graphic displays used in behavior analysis provide direct access to the original data, which allows the inquisitive or doubtful reader to re-graph (i.e., manipulate) the data.

Line Graphs

The simple **line graph,** or frequency polygon, is the most common graphic format for displaying data in applied behavior analysis. The line graph is based on a Cartesian plane, a two-dimensional area formed by the intersection of two perpendicular lines. Any point within the plane represents a specific relationship between the two dimensions described by the intersecting lines. In applied behavior analysis, each point on a line graph shows the level of some quantifiable dimension of the target behavior (i.e., the **dependent variable**) in relation to a specified point in time and/or environmental condition (i.e., the **independent variable**) in effect when the measure was taken. Comparing points on the graph reveals the presence and extent of changes in level, trend, and/or variability within and across conditions.

Parts of a Basic Line Graph

Although graphs vary considerably in their final appearance, all properly constructed line graphs share certain elements. The basic parts of a simple line graph are shown in Figure 6.2 and described in the following sections.

1. Horizontal Axis. The *horizontal axis,* also called the x *axis,* or *abcissa,* is a straight horizontal line that most often represents the passage of time and the presence, absence, and/or value of the independent variable. A defining characteristic of applied behavior analysis is the repeated measurement of behavior across time. Time is also the unavoidable dimension in which all manipulations of the independent variable occur. On most line graphs the passage of time is marked in equal intervals on the horizontal axis. In Figure 6.2 successive 10-minute sessions during which the number of property destruction responses (including attempts) was measured are marked on the horizontal axis. In this study, 8 to 10 sessions were conducted per day (Fisher, Lindauer, Alterson, & Thompson, 1998).

The horizontal axis on some graphs represents different values of the independent variable instead of time. For example, Lalli, Mace, Livezey, and Kates (1998) scaled the horizontal axis on one graph in their study from less than 0.5 meters to 9.0 meters to show how the occurrence of self-injurious behavior by a girl with severe mental retardation decreased as the distance between the therapist and the girl increased.

2. Vertical Axis. The *vertical axis,* also called the y *axis,* or *ordinate,* is a vertical line drawn upward from the left-hand end of the horizontal axis. The vertical axis most often represents a range of values of the dependent variable, which in applied behavior analysis is always some quantifiable dimension of behavior. The intersection of the horizontal and vertical axes is called the *origin* and usually, though not necessarily, represents the zero value of the dependent variable. Each successive point upward on the vertical axis represents a greater value of the dependent variable. The most common practice is to mark the vertical axis with an equal-interval scale. On an *equal-interval vertical axis* equal distances on the axis represent equal amounts of behavior. The vertical axis in Figure 6.2 represents the number of property destruction responses (and attempts) per minute with a range of 0 to 4 responses per minute.

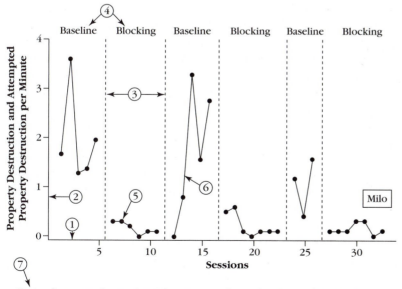

Figure 6.2 The major parts of a simple line graph: (1) horizontal axis, (2) vertical axis, (3) condition change lines, (4) condition labels, (5) data points, (6) data path, and (7) figure caption.

From "Assessment and Treatment of Destructive Behavior Maintained by Stereotypic Object Manipulation" by W. W. Fisher, S. E. Lindauer, C. J. Alterson, and R. H. Thompson, 1998, *Journal of Applied Behavior Analysis, 31,* p. 522. Copyright 1998 by the Society for the Experimental Analysis of Behavior, Inc. Used by permission.

Rates of property destruction (plus attempts) during baseline and the blocking condition for Milo.

3. Condition Change Lines.   *Condition change lines* are vertical lines drawn upward from the horizontal axis to show points in time at which changes in the independent variable occurred. The condition change lines in Figure 6.2 coincide with the introduction or withdrawal of an intervention the researchers called blocking. Condition change lines can be drawn as solid or dashed lines. When relatively minor changes occur within an overall condition, dashed vertical lines should be used to distinguish minor changes from major changes in conditions, which are shown by solid lines (see Figure 6.18).

4. Condition Labels.   *Condition labels,* in the form of single words or brief descriptive phrases, are printed along the top of the graph and parallel to the horizontal axis. These labels identify the experimental conditions (i.e., the presence, absence, or some value of the independent variable) that are in effect during each phase of the study.[4]

5. Data Points.   Each *data point* on a graph represents two facts: (a) a quantifiable measure of the target behavior recorded during a given observation period and (b) the time and/or experimental conditions under which that particular measurement was conducted. Using two data points from Figure 6.2 as examples, we can see that during Session 5, the last session of the first baseline phase, property destruction and attempted property destruction responses occurred at a rate of approximately 2 responses per minute; and in Session 9, the fourth session of the first blocking phase, 0 instances of the target behavior were recorded.

6. Data Path.   Connecting successive data points within a given condition with a straight line creates a data path. The **data path** represents the level and trend of behavior between successive data points, and it is a primary focus of attention in the interpretation and analysis of graphed data. Because behavior is rarely observed and recorded continuously in applied behavior analysis, the data path represents an estimate of the actual course taken by the behavior during the time elapsed between the two measures. The more measurements and resultant data points per unit of time (given an accurate observation and recording system),

the more confidence one can place in the story told by the data path.

7. Figure Caption.   The *figure caption* is a concise statement that, in combination with the axis and condition labels, provides the reader with sufficient information to identify the independent and dependent variables. The figure caption should explain any symbols or observed but unplanned events that may have affected the dependent variable (see Figure 6.6) and point out and clarify any potentially confusing features of the graph (see Figure 6.7).

Variations of the Simple Line Graph: Multiple Data Paths

The line graph is a remarkably versatile vehicle for displaying behavior change. Whereas Figure 6.2 is an example of the line graph in its simplest form (one data path showing a series of successive measures of behavior across time and experimental conditions) by the addition of multiple data paths, the line graph can display more complex behavior–environment relations. Graphs with multiple data paths are used frequently in applied behavior analysis to show (a) two or more dimensions of the same behavior, (b) two or more different behaviors, (c) the same behavior under different and alternating experimental conditions, (d) changes in target behavior relative to the changing values of an independent variable, and (e) the behavior of two or more participants.

Two or More Dimensions of the Same Behavior. Showing multiple dimensions of the dependent variable on the same graph enables visual analysis of the absolute and relative effects of the independent variable on those dimensions. Figure 6.3 shows the results of a study of the effects of training three members of a women's college basketball team proper foul shooting form (Kladopoulos & McComas, 2001). The data path created by connecting the open triangle data points shows changes in the percentage of foul shots executed with the proper form, whereas the data path connecting the solid data points reveals the percentage of foul shots made. Had the experimenters recorded and graphed only the players' foul shooting form, they would not have known whether any improvements in the target behavior on which training was focused (correct foul shooting form) coincided with improvements in the behavior by which the social significance of the study would ultimately be judged—foul shooting accuracy. By measuring and plotting both form and outcome on the same graph, the experimenters were able to analyze the effects of their treatment procedures on two critical dimensions of the dependent variable.

---

[4]The terms *condition* and *phase* are related but not synonymous. Properly used, *condition* indicates the environmental arrangements in effect at any given time; *phase* refers to a period of time within a study or behavior-change program. For example, the study shown in Figure 6.2 consisted of two conditions (baseline and blocking) and six phases.

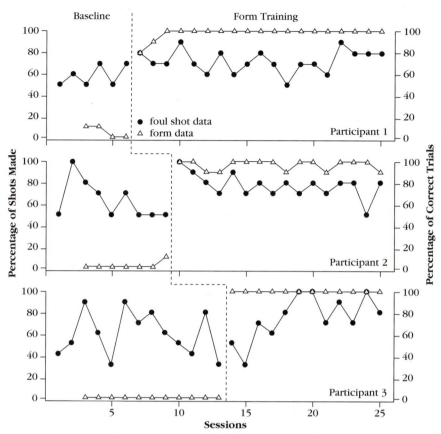

Figure 6.3 Graph using multiple data paths to show the effects of the independent variable (Form Training) on two dimensions (accuracy and topography) of the target behavior.

From "The Effects of Form Training on Foul-Shooting Performance in Members of a Women's College Basketball Team" by C. N. Kladopoulos and J. J. McComas, 2001, *Journal of Applied Behavior Analysis, 34,* p. 331. Copyright 2001 by the Society for the Experimental Analysis of Behavior, Inc. Used by permission.

Figure 1. Percentage of shots made (filled circles) and percentage of shots taken with correct form (open triangles) across sessions for each participant.

Two or More Different Behaviors. Multiple data paths are also used to facilitate the simultaneous comparison of the effects of experimental manipulations on two or more different behaviors. Determining the co-variation of two behaviors as a function of changes in the independent variable is accomplished more easily if both can be displayed on the same set of axes. Figure 6.4 shows the percentage of intervals in which a boy with autism exhibited stereotypy (e.g., repetitive body movements, rocking) across three conditions and the number of times that he raised his hand for attention (in the attention condition), signed for a break (in the demand condition), and signed for access to preferred tangible stimuli (in the no-attention condition) in a study investigating a strategy called functional communication training (Kennedy, Meyer, Knowles, & Shukla, 2000).[5] By recording and graphing both stereotypic responding and appropriate behavior, the investigators were able to determine whether increases in alternative communication responses (raising his hand and signing) were accompanied by reductions in stereotypy. Note that a second vertical axis is used on Figure 6.4 to

show the proper dimensional units and scaling for signing frequency. Because of the differences in scale, readers of dual-vertical axis graphs must view them with care, particularly when assessing the magnitude of behavior change.

Measures of the Same Behavior under Different Conditions. Multiple data paths are also used to represent measures of the same behavior taken under different experimental conditions that alternate throughout an experimental phase. Figure 6.5 shows the number of self-injurious response per minute by a 6-year-old girl with developmental disabilities under four different conditions (Moore, Mueller, Dubard, Roberts, & Sterling-Turner, 2002). Graphing an individual's behavior under multiple conditions on the same set of axes allows direct visual comparisons of differences in absolute levels of responding at any given time as well as relative changes in performance over time.

Changing Values of an Independent Variable. Multiple data path graphs are also used to show changes in the target behavior (shown on one data path) relative to changing values of the independent variable (represented by a second data path). In each of the two graphs

---

[5]Functional communication training is described in Chapter 23.

Figure 6.4 Graph with multiple data paths showing two different behaviors by one participant during baseline and training across three different conditions. Note the different dimensions and scaling of the dual vertical axes.

From "Analyzing the Multiple Functions of Stereotypical Behavior for Students with Autism: Implications for Assessment and Treatment" by C. H. Kennedy, K. A. Meyer, T. Knowles, and S. Shukla, 2000, *Journal of Applied Behavior Analysis, 33,* p. 565. Copyright 2000 by the Society for the Experimental Analysis of Behavior, Inc. Used by permission.

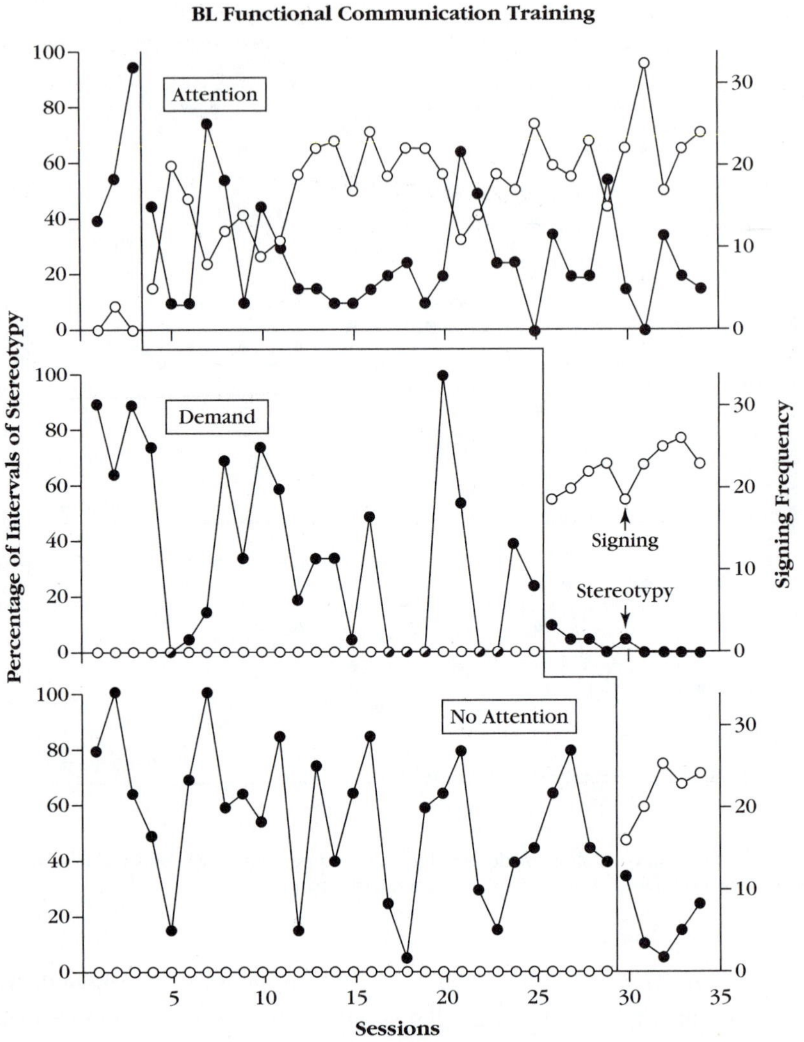

BL Functional Communication Training

Figure 2. Occurrence of stereotypy for James across attention, demand, and no-attention conditions. Data are arrayed as the percentage of intervals of stereotypy on the left *y* axis and number of signs per sessions on the right *y* axis.

in Figure 6.6 one data path shows the duration of problem behavior (plotted against the left-hand *y* axis scaled in seconds) relative to changes in noise level, which are depicted by the second data path (plotted against the right-hand *y* axis scaled in decibels) (McCord, Iwata, Galensky, Ellingson, & Thomson, 2001).

The Same Behavior of Two or More Participants. Multiple data paths are sometimes used to show the behavior of two or more participants on the same graph.

Depending on the levels and variability of the data encompassed by each data path, a maximum of four different data paths can be displayed effectively on one set of axes. However, there is no rule; Didden, Prinsen, and Sigafoos displayed five data paths in a single display (2000, p. 319). If too many data paths are displayed on the same graph, the benefits of making additional comparisons may be outweighed by the distraction of too much visual "noise." When more than four data paths must be

included on the same graph, other methods of display can be incorporated.[6] For example, Gutowski and Stromer (2003) effectively used striped and shaded bars in combination with conventional data paths to display the number of names spoken and the percentage of correct matching-to-sample responses by individuals with mental retardation (see Figure 6.7).

Bar Graphs

The **bar graph,** or histogram, is a simple and versatile format for graphically summarizing behavioral data. Like the line graph, the bar graph is based on the Cartesian

---

[6]A superb example of combining visual display techniques is Charles Minard's use of space-time-story graphics to illustrate the interrelations of six variables during Napoleon's ill-fated Russian campaign of 1812–1813 (see Tufte, 1983, p. 41). Tufte called Minard's graph perhaps "the best statistical graphic ever drawn" (p. 40).

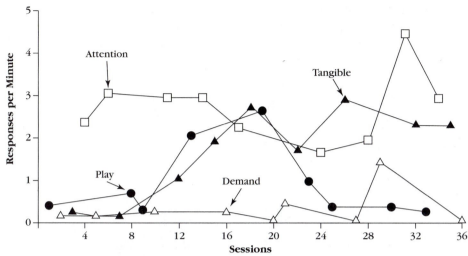

Figure 6.5 Graph with multiple data paths showing the same behavior measured under four different conditions.

From "The Influence of Therapist Attention on Self-Injury during a Tangible Condition" by J. W. Moore, M. M. Mueller, M. Dubard, D. S. Roberts, and H. E. Sterling-Turner, 2002, *Journal of Applied Behavior Analysis, 35,* p. 285. Copyright 2002 by the Society for the Experimental Analysis of Behavior, Inc. Used by permission.

Figure 1. Rate of self-injurious behavior during the initial functional analysis.

plane and shares most of the line graph's features with one primary difference: The bar graph does not have distinct data points representing successive response measures through time. Bar graphs can take a wide variety of forms to allow quick and easy comparisons of performance across participants and/or conditions.

Bar graphs serve two major functions in applied behavior analysis. First, bar graphs are used for displaying and comparing discrete sets of data that are not related to one another by a common underlying dimension by which the horizontal axis can be scaled. For example, Gottschalk, Libby, and Graff (2000), in a study analyzing

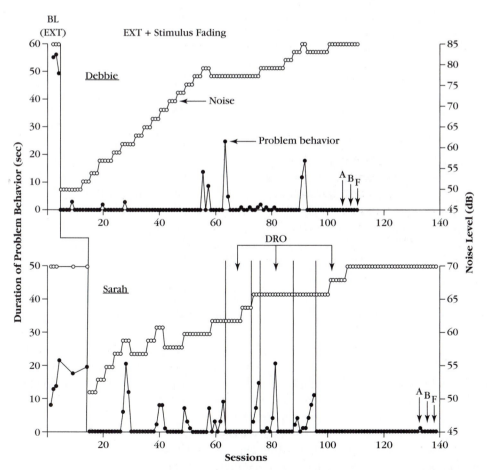

Figure 6.6 Graph using two data paths to show the duration of problem behavior (dependent variable) by two adults with severe or profound mental retardation as noise level was increased gradually (independent variable).

From "Functional Analysis and Treatment of Problem Behavior Evoked by Noise" by B. E. McCord, B. A. Iwata, T. L. Gelensky, S. A. Ellingson, and R. J. Thomson, 2001, *Journal of Applied Behavior Analysis, 34,* p. 457. Copyright 2001 by the Society for the Experimental Analysis of Behavior, Inc. Used by permission.

Figure 4. Results of Debbie's and Sarah's treatment evaluation. Sessions marked A and B near the end of treatment indicate two generalization probes in the natural environment; F indicates a follow-up probe.

Figure 6.7 Graph using a combination of bars and data points to display changes in two response classes to two types of matching stimuli under different prompting conditions.

From "Delayed Matching to Two-Picture Samples by Individuals With and Without Disabilities: An Analysis of the Role of Naming" by S. J. Gutowski and Robert Stromer, 2003, *Journal of Applied Behavior Analysis, 36*, p. 498. Copyright 2003 by the Society for the Experimental Analysis of Behavior, Inc. Reprinted by permission.

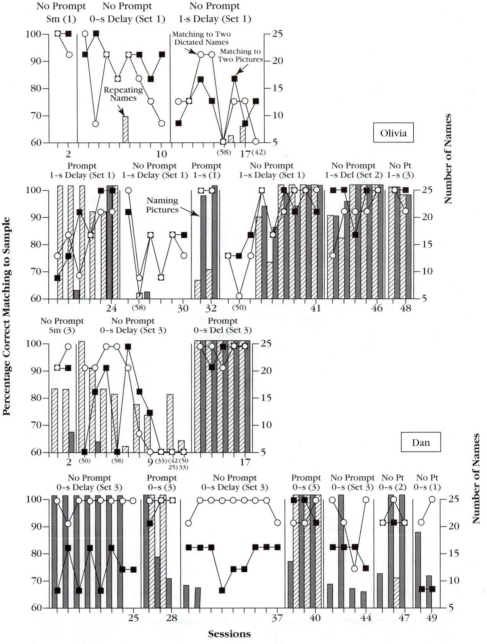

Figure 4. Results for Olivia and Dan across simultaneous, delay, prompt, and no-prompt conditions: open circles and solid squares reflect percentages of correct matching. Striped bars and shaded bars reflect the number of names spoken on trials with two-name and two-picture samples, respectively. Bars with extended tic marks on the abscissa indicate that the number of names exceeded 25.

the effects of establishing operations on preference assessments, used bar graphs to show the percentage of trials in which four children reached toward and picked up different items (see Figure 6.8).

Another common use of bar graphs is to give a visual summary of the performance of a participant or group of participants during the different conditions of an experiment. For example, Figure 6.9 shows the mean percentage of spelling worksheet items completed and the mean percentage of completed items that were done correctly by four students during baseline and combined generalization programming and maintenance conditions

that followed training each child how to recruit teacher attention while they were working (Craft, Alber, & Heward, 1998).

Bar graphs sacrifice the presentation of the variability and trends in behavior (which are apparent in a line graph) in exchange for the efficiency of summarizing and comparing large amounts of data in a simple, easy-to-interpret format. They should be viewed with the understanding that they may mask important variability in the data. Although bar graphs are typically used to present a measure of central tendency, such as the mean or median score for each condition, the range of measures repre-

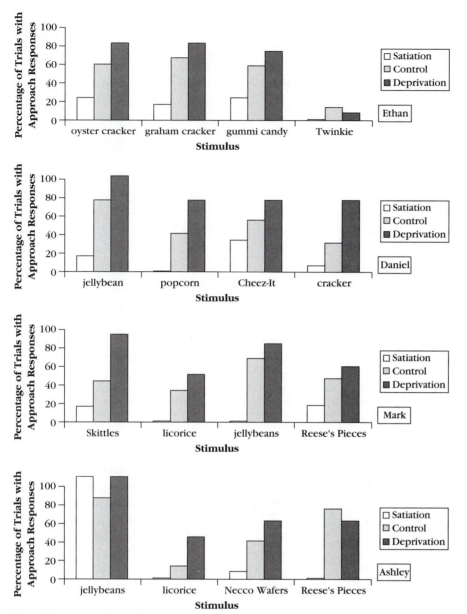

Figure 6.8   Bar graph used to summarize and display results of measurements taken under discrete conditions lacking an underlying dimension by which the horizontal axis could be scaled (e.g., time, duration of stimulus presentations).

From "The Effects of Establishing Operations on Preference Assessment Outcomes" by J. M. Gottschalk, M. E. Libby, and R. B Graff, 2000, *Journal of Applied Behavior Analysis, 33,* p. 87. Copyright 2000 by the Society for the Experimental Analysis of Behavior, Inc. Reprinted by permission.

Figure 1. Percentage of approach responses across conditions for Ethan, Daniel, Mark, and Ashley.

sented by the mean can also be incorporated into the display (e.g., see Figure 5 in Lerman, Kelley, Vorndran, Kuhn, & LaRue, 2002).

Cumulative Records

The **cumulative record** (or graph) was developed by Skinner as the primary means of data collection in the experimental analysis of behavior. A device called the **cumulative recorder** enables a subject to actually draw its own graph (see Figure 6.10). In a book cataloging 6 years of experimental research on schedules of reinforcement, Ferster and Skinner (1957) described cumulative records in the following manner:

A graph showing the number of responses on the ordinate against time on the abscissa has proved to be the most convenient representation of the behavior observed in this research. Fortunately, such a "cumulative" record may be made directly at the time of the experiment. The record is raw data, but it also permits a direct inspection of rate and changes in rate not possible when the behavior is observed directly. . . . Each time the bird responds, the pen moves one step across the paper. At the same time, the paper feeds continuously. If the bird does not respond at all, a horizontal line is drawn in the direction of the paper feed. The faster the bird pecks, the steeper the line. (p. 23)

When cumulative records are plotted by hand or created with a computer graphing program, which is most

Figure 6.9 Bar graph comparing mean levels for two dimensions of participants' performance between experimental conditions.

From "Teaching Elementary Students with Developmental Disabilities to Recruit Teacher Attention in a General Education Classroom: Effects on Teacher Praise and Academic Productivity" by M. A. Craft, S. R. Alber, and W. L. Heward, 1998, *Journal of Applied Behavior Analysis, 31,* p. 410. Copyright 1998 by the Society for the Experimental Analysis of Behavior, Inc. Reprinted by permission.

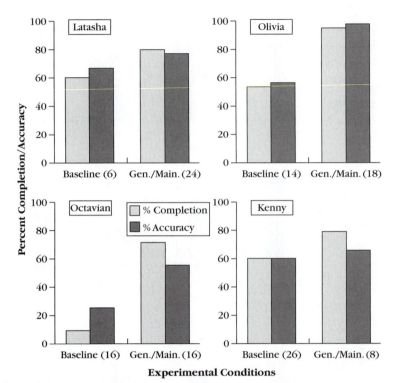

Figure 4. Mean percentage of spelling worksheet items completed and mean percentage of accuracy by each student during baseline and combined generalization programming and maintenance conditions. Numbers in parentheses show total number of sessions per condition.

often the case in applied behavior analysis, the number of responses recorded during each observation period is added (thus the term *cumulative*) to the total number of responses recorded during all previous observation periods. In a cumulative record the *y* axis value of any data point represents the total number of responses recorded since the beginning of data collection. The exception occurs when the total number of responses has exceeded the upper limit of the *y* axis scale, in which case the data path on a cumulative curve resets to the 0 value of the

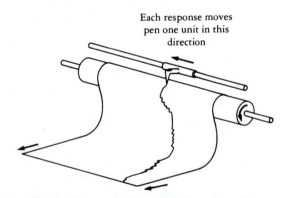

Figure 6.10 Diagram of a cumulative recorder.

From *Schedules of Reinforcement,* pp. 24–25, by C. B. Ferster and B. F. Skinner, 1957, Upper Saddle River, NJ: Prentice Hall. Copyright 1957 by Prentice Hall. Used by permission.

y axis and begins its ascent again. Cumulative records are almost always used with frequency data, although other dimensions of behavior, such as duration and latency, can be displayed cumulatively.

Figure 6.11 is an example of a cumulative record from the applied behavior analysis literature (Neef, Iwata, & Page, 1980). It shows the cumulative number of spelling words mastered by a person with mental retardation during baseline and two training conditions. The graph shows that the individual mastered a total of 1 word during the 12 sessions of baseline (social praise for correct spelling responses and rewriting incorrectly spelled words three times), a total of 22 words under the interspersal condition (baseline procedures plus the presentation of a previously learned word after each unknown word), and a total of 11 words under the high-density reinforcement condition (baseline procedures plus social praise given after each trial for task-related behaviors such as paying attention and writing neatly).

In addition to the total number of responses recorded at any given point in time, cumulative records show the overall and local response rates. Rate is the number of responses emitted per unit of time, usually reported as responses per minute in applied behavior analysis. An **overall response rate** is the average rate of response over a given time period, such as during a specific session, phase, or condition of an experiment. Overall rates are

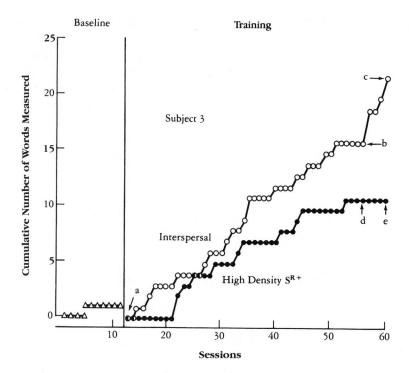

Figure 6.11 Cumulative graph of number of spelling words learned by a man with mental retardation during baseline, interspersal training, and high-density reinforcement training. Points a–e have been added to illustrate the differences between overall and local response rates.

From "The Effects of Interspersal Training Versus High Density Reinforcement on Spelling Acquisition and Retention" by N. A. Neef, B. A. Iwata, and T. J. Page, 1980, *Journal of Applied Behavior Analysis, 13*, p. 156. Copyright 1980 by the Society for the Experimental Analysis of Behavior, Inc. Adapted by permission.

calculated by dividing the total number of responses recorded during the period by the number of observation periods indicated on the horizontal axis. In Figure 6.11 the overall response rates are 0.46 and 0.23 words mastered per session for the interspersal and high-density reinforcement conditions, respectively.[7]

On a cumulative record, the steeper the slope, the higher the response rate. To produce a visual representation of an overall rate on a cumulative graph, the first and last data points of a given series of observations should be connected with a straight line. A straight line connecting Points a and c in Figure 6.11 would represent the learner's overall rate of mastering spelling words during the interspersal condition. A straight line connecting Points a and e represents the overall rate during the high-density reinforcement condition. Relative rates of response can be determined by visually comparing one slope to another; the steeper the slope, the higher the rate of response. A visual comparison of Slopes a–c and a–e shows that the interspersal condition produced the higher overall response rate.

Response rates often fluctuate within a given period. The term **local response rate** refers to the rate of response during periods of time smaller than that for which an overall rate has been given. Over the last four sessions of the study shown in Figure 6.11, the learner exhibited a local rate of responding during interspersal

training (Slope b–c) that was considerably higher than his overall rate for that condition. At the same time his performance during the final four sessions of the high-density reinforcement condition (Slope d–e) shows a lower local response rate than his overall rate for that condition.

A legend giving the slopes of some representative rates can aid considerably in the determination and comparison of relative response rates both within and across cumulative curves plotted on the same set of axes (e.g., see Kennedy & Souza, 1995, Figure 2). However, very high rates of responding are difficult to compare visually with one another on cumulative records.

> Although the rate of responding is directly proportional to the slope of the curve, at slopes above 80 degrees small differences in angle represent very large differences in rate; and although these can be measured accurately, they cannot be evaluated easily by [visual] inspection. (Ferster & Skinner, 1957, pp. 24–25)

Even though cumulative records derived from continuous recording are the most directly descriptive displays of behavioral data available, two other features of behavior, in addition to the comparison of very high rates, can be difficult to determine on some cumulative graphs. One, although the total number of responses since data collection began can be easily seen on a cumulative graph, the number of responses recorded for any given session can be hard to ascertain, given the number of data points and the scaling of the vertical axis. Two, gradual changes in slope from one rate to another can be hard to detect on cumulative graphs.

---

[7]Technically, Figure 6.11 does not represent true rates of response because the number of words spelled correctly was measured and not the rate, or speed, at which they were spelled. However, the slope of each data path represents the different "rates" of mastering the spelling words in each session within the context of a total of 10 new words presented per session.

Four situations in which a cumulative graph may be preferable to a noncumulative line graph are as follows. First, cumulative records are desirable when the total number of responses made over time is important or when progress toward a specific goal can be measured in cumulative units of behavior. The number of new words learned, dollars saved, or miles trained for an upcoming marathon are examples. One look at the most recent data point on the graph reveals the total amount of behavior up to that point in time.

Second, a cumulative graph might also be more effective than noncumulative graphs when the graph is used as a source of feedback for the participant. This is because both total progress and relative rate of performance are easily detected by visual inspection (Weber, 2002).

Third, a cumulative record should be used when the target behavior is one that can occur or not occur only once per observation session. In these instances the effects of any intervention are easier to detect on a cumulative graph than on a noncumulative graph. Figure 6.12 shows the same data plotted on a noncumulative graph and a cumulative graph. The cumulative graph clearly shows a relation between behavior and intervention, whereas the noncumulative graph gives the visual impression of greater variability in the data than really exists.

Fourth, cumulative records can "reveal the intricate relations between behavior and environmental variables" (Johnston & Pennypacker, 1993a, p. 317) Figure 6.13 is

an excellent example of how a cumulative graph enables a detailed analysis of behavior change (Hanley, Iwata, & Thompson, 2001). By plotting the data from single sessions cumulatively by 10-second intervals, the researchers revealed patterns of responding not shown by a graph of session-by-session data. Comparing the data paths for the three sessions for which the results were graphed cumulatively (Mult #106, Mixed #107, and Mixed #112) revealed two undesirable patterns of responding (in this case, pushing a switch that operated a voice output device that said "talk to me, please" as an alternative to self-injurious behavior and aggression) that are likely to occur during mixed schedules, and the benefits of including schedule-correlated stimuli (Mult #106).

Semilogarithmic Charts

All of the graphs discussed so far have been equal-interval graphs on which the distance between any two consecutive points on each axis is always the same. On the *x* axis the distance between Session 1 and Session 2 is equal to the distance between Session 11 and Session 12; on the *y* axis, the distance between 10 and 20 responses per minute is equal to the distance between 35 and 45 responses per minute. On an equal-interval graph equal absolute changes in behavior, whether an increase or decrease in performance, are expressed by equal distances on the *y* axis.

Figure 6.12 Same set of hypothetical data plotted on noncumulative and cumulative graphs. Cumulative graphs more clearly reveal patterns of and changes in responding for behaviors that can occur only once during each period of measurement.

From *Working with Parents of Handicapped Children*, p. 100, by W. L. Heward, J. C. Dardig, and A. Rossett, 1979, Columbus, OH: Charles E. Merrill. Copyright 1979 by Charles E. Merrill. Used by permission.

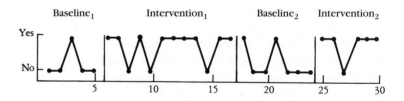

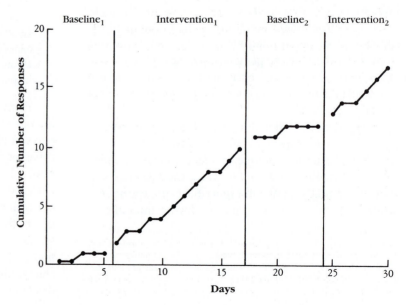

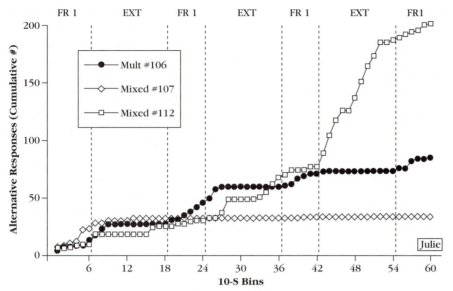

Figure 6.13   Cumulative record used to make a detailed analysis and comparison of behavior across components of multiple- and mixed-reinforcement schedules within specific sessions of a study.

From "Reinforcement Schedule Thinning Following Treatment with Functional Communication Training" by G. P. Hanley, B. A. Iwata, and R. H. Thompson, 2001, *Journal of Applied Behavior Analysis, 34,* p. 33. Copyright 2001 by the Society for the Experimental Analysis of Behavior, Inc. Used by permission.

Figure 4. Cumulative number of alternative responses across schedule components for three sessions from Julie's assessment of schedule-correlated stimuli. Open symbols represent two mixed-schedule sessions; filled symbols represent a single multiple-schedule session.

Another way of looking at behavior change is to examine proportional or relative change. Logarithmic scales are well suited to display and communicate proportional change. On a logarithmic scale equal relative changes in the variable being measured are represented by equal distances. Because behavior is measured and charted over time, which progresses in equal intervals, the *x* axis is marked off in equal intervals and only the *y* axis is scaled logarithmically. Hence, the term **semilogarithmic chart** refers to graphs in which only one axis is scaled proportionally.

On semilog charts all behavior changes of equal proportion are shown by equal vertical distances on the vertical axis, regardless of the absolute values of those changes. For example, a doubling of response rate from 4 to 8 per minute would appear on a semilogarithmic chart as the same amount of change as a doubling of 50 to 100 responses per minute. Likewise, a decrease in responding from 75 to 50 responses per minute (a decrease

of one third) would occupy the same distance on the vertical axis as a change from 12 to 8 responses per minute (a decrease of one third).

Figure 6.14 shows the same data graphed on an equal-interval chart (sometimes called arithmetic or add-subtract charts) and on a semilogarithmic chart (sometimes called ratio or multiply-divide charts). The behavior change that appears as an exponential curve on the arithmetic chart is a straight line when plotted on the semilog chart. The vertical axis in the semilog chart in Figure 6.14 is scaled by log-base-2 or X2 cycles, which means that each cycle going up on the *y* axis represents a times-2 increase (i.e., a doubling) of the cycle below it.

Standard Celeration Charts

In the 1960s, Ogden Lindsley developed the **Standard Celeration Chart** to provide a standardized means of charting and analyzing how frequency of behavior

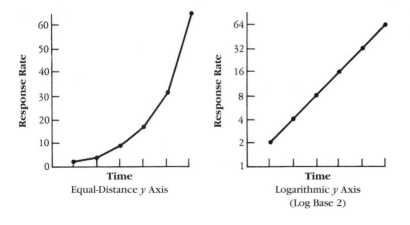

Figure 6.14   Same set of data plotted on equal-interval arithmetic scale (left) and on equal-proportion ratio scale (right).

changes over time (Lindsley, 1971; Pennypacker, Gutierrez & Lindsley, 2003). The Standard Celeration Chart is a semilogarithmic chart with six X10 cycles on the vertical axis that can accommodate response rates as low as 1 per 24 hours (0.000695 per minute) or as high as 1,000 per minute.

There are four standard charts, differentiated from one another by the scaling on the horizontal axis: a daily chart with 140 calendar days, a weekly chart, a monthly chart, and a yearly chart. The daily chart shown in Figure 6.15 is used most often. Table 6.1 describes major parts of the Standard Celeration Chart and basic charting conventions.

The size of the chart and the consistent scaling of the *y* axis and *x* axis do not make the Standard Celeration Chart *standard*, as is commonly believed. What makes the Standard Celeration Chart standard is its consistent display of *celeration*, a linear measure of frequency change across time, a factor by which frequency multiplies or divides per unit of time. The terms *acceleration* and *deceleration* are used to describe accelerating performances or decelerating performances.

A line drawn from the bottom left corner to the top right corner has a slope of 34° on all Standard Celeration Charts. This slope has a celeration value of X2 (read as "times-2"; celerations are expressed with multiples or divisors). A X2 celeration is a doubling in frequency per celeration period. The celeration period for the daily chart is per week; it is per month for the weekly chart, per 6 months for the monthly chart, and per 5 years for the yearly chart.

Figure 6.15 Standard Celeration Chart showing basic charting conventions. See Table 6.1 for explanation.

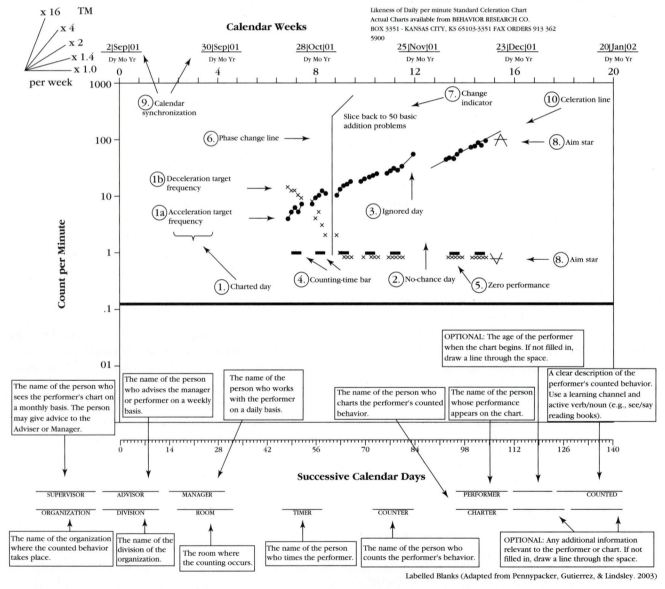

From the *Journal of Precision Teaching and Celeration, 19*(1), p. 51. Copyright 2003 by The Standard Celeration Society. Used by permission.

Table 6.1   Basic Charting Conventions for the Daily Standard Celeration Chart (See also Figure 6.15)

Term	Definition	Convention
1. Charted day	A day on which the behavior is recorded and charted.	1. Chart the behavior frequency on the chart on the appropriate day line. 2. Connect charted days except across *phase change lines, no chance days,* and *ignored days.*
a) Acceleration target frequency	Responses of the performer intended to accelerate.	Chart a dot (•) on the appropriate day line.
b) Deceleration target frequency	Responses of the performer intended to decelerate.	Chart an (x) on the appropriate day line.
2. No chance day	A day on which the behavior had *no chance* to occur.	Skip day on daily chart.
3. Ignored day	A day on which the behavior could have occurred but no one recorded it.	Skip day on daily chart. (Connect data across ignored days.)
4. Counting-time bar (aka record floor)	Designates on the chart the performer's lowest possible performance (other than zero) in a counting time. Always designated as "once per counting time."	Draw solid horizontal line from the Tuesday to Thursday day lines on the chart at the "counting-time bar."
5. Zero performance	No performance recorded during the recording period.	Chart on the line directly below the "counting-time bar."
6. Phase change line	A line drawn in the space between the last charted day of one intervention phase and the first charted day of a new intervention phase.	Draw a vertical line between the intervention phases. Draw the line from the top of the data to the "counting-time bar."
7. Change indicator	Words, symbols, or phrases written on the chart in the appropriate phase to indicate changes during that phase.	Write word, symbol, and/or phrase. An arrow (→) may be used to indicate the continuance of a change into a new phase.
8. Aim star	A symbol used to represent (a) the desired frequency, and (b) the desired date to achieve the frequency.	Place the point of the caret . . . ∧ for acceleration data ∨ for deceleration data . . . on the desired aim date. Place the horizontal bar on the desired frequency. The caret and horizontal line will create a "star."
9. Calendar synchronize	A standard time for starting all charts.	It requires three charts to cover a full year. The Sunday before Labor Day begins the first week of the first chart. The twenty-first week after Labor Day begins the second chart. The forty-first week after Labor Day begins the third chart.
10. Celeration line	A straight line drawn through 7–9 or more charted days. This line indicates the amount of improvement that has taken place in a given period of time. A new line is drawn for each phase for both acceleration and deceleration targets. (Note: For nonresearch projects it is acceptable to draw freehand celeration lines.)	 Acceleration target Deceleration target

Figure 6.16   Standard Celeration Chart showing advanced charting conventions. See Table 6.2 for explanation.

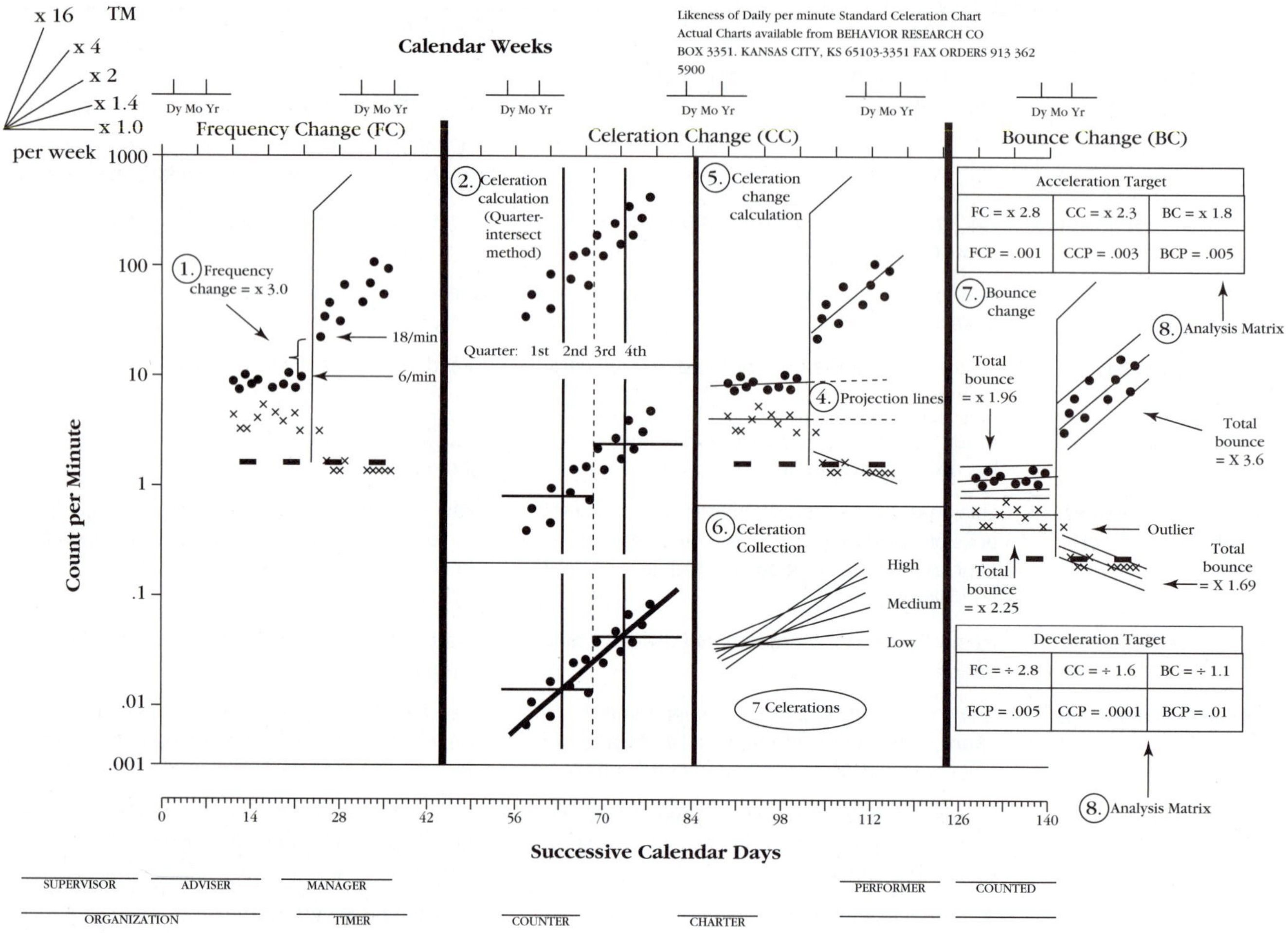

From the *Journal of Precision Teaching and Celeration, 19*(1), p. 54. Copyright 2002 by The Standard Celeration Society. Used by permission.

An instructional decision-making system, called *precision teaching,* has been developed for use with the Standard Celeration Chart.[8] Precision teaching is predicated on the position that (a) learning is best measured as a change in response rate, (b) learning most often occurs through proportional changes in behavior, and (c) past changes in performance can project future learning.

Precision teaching focuses on celeration, not on the specific frequency of correct and incorrect responses as many believe. That frequency is not an emphasis on the Chart is clear because the Chart uses estimations for most frequency values. A practitioner or researcher might say, "I don't use the chart because I can't tell by looking at the chart if the student emitted 24, 25, 26, or 27 responses."

However, the purpose of the Chart makes such a fine discrimination irrelevant because celeration, not specific frequency, is the issue. A frequency of 24 or 27 will not change the line of progress—the celeration course.

Advanced charting conventions used by precision teachers are illustrated in Figure 6.16 and described in Table 6.2. Detailed explanations of the Standard Celeration Chart and its uses can be found in Cooper, Kubina, and Malanga (1998); Graf and Lindsley (2002); and Pennypacker, Gutierrez, and Lindsley (2003).

Scatterplots

A **scatterplot** is a graphic display that shows the relative distribution of individual measures in a data set with respect to the variables depicted by the *x* and *y* axes. Data points on a scatterplot are unconnected. Scatterplots show how much changes in the value of the variable depicted by one axis correlate with changes in the value of the variable represented by the other axis. Patterns of data

---

[8]Detailed descriptions and examples of precision teaching are provided by the *Journal of Precision Teaching and Celeration;* the Standard Celeration Society's Web site (http://celeration.org/); Binder (1996); Kubina and Cooper (2001); Lindsley (1990, 1992, 1996); Potts, Eshleman, and Cooper (1993); West, Young, and Spooner (1990); and White and Haring (1980).

Table 6.2   Advanced Charting Conventions for the Daily Standard Celeration Chart (See also Figure 6.16)

Term	Definition	Convention
Frequency:		
1. Frequency change (FC) (aka frequency jump up or jump down)	The multiply "×" or divide "÷" value that compares the final frequency of one phase to the beginning frequency in the next phase. Compute this by comparing (1) the frequency where the celeration line crosses the *last* day of one phase to (2) the frequency where the celeration line crosses the *first* day of the next phase (e.g., a frequency jump from 6/minute to 18/minute. FC = × 3.0).	Place an "FC =" in the upper left cell of the analysis matrix. Indicate the value with a "×" or "÷" sign (e.g., FC = × 3.0).
Celeration:		
2. Celeration calculation (quarter-intersect method)	The process for *graphically* determining a celeration line (aka "the line of best fit"). (1) Divide the frequencies for each phase into four equal quarters (include ignored and no chance days), (2) locate the median frequency for each half, and (3) draw a celeration line connecting the quarter intersect points.	See advanced charting conventions sample chart.
3. Celeration finder	A piece of mylar with standard celeration lines that can be used to compute celeration line values.	Buy commercially or copy and cut out part of the vertical axis on the Standard Celeration Chart.
4. Projection line	A dashed line extending to the future from the celeration line. The projection offers a forecast that enables the calculation of the celeration change value.	See advanced charting conventions sample chart.
5. Celeration change (CC) (aka celeration turn up or turn down)	The multiply "×" or divide "÷" value that compares the celeration of one phase to the celeration in the next phase (e.g., a celeration turn down from × 1.3 to ÷ 1.3. CC = ÷ 1.7).	Place a "CC =" in the upper middle cell of the analysis matrix with the value indicated with a "×" or "÷" sign (e.g., CC = ÷ 1.7).
6. Celeration collection	A group of three or more celerations for different performers relating to the same behavior over approximately the same time period.	Numerically identify the high, middle, and low celeration in the celeration collection and indicate the total number of celerations in the collection.
7. Bounce change (BC)	The multiply "×" or divide "÷" value that compares the bounce in one phase to the bounce in the next phase. Computed by comparing (1) the total bounce of one phase to (2) the total bounce of the next phase (e.g., a bounce change from 5.0 to × 1.4, BC = ÷ 3.6).	Place a "BC =" in the upper right cell of the analysis matrix with the value indicated with a multiply "×" or divide "÷" symbol (e.g., BC = ÷ 3.6).
8. Analysis matrix	The analysis matrix provides the numeric change information regarding the effects of the independent variable(s) on frequency, celeration, and bounce between two phases.	Place the analysis matrix between the two phases being compared. For acceleration targets place the matrix above the data. For deceleration targets place the matrix below the data.
Optional:		
9. Frequency change p-value (FCP)	The frequency change p-value is the probability that the noted change in frequency would have occurred by chance. (Use the Fisher exact probability formula to compute the p-value.)	Use "FCP =" and indicate the p-value in the lower left cell on the analysis matrix (e.g., FCP = .0001).
10. Celeration change p-value (CCP)	The celeration change p-value is the probability that the change noted in celeration would have occurred by chance. (Use the Fisher exact probability formula to compute the p-value.)	Use "CCP =" and indicate the p-value in the lower middle cell of the matrix (e.g., CCP = .0001).
11. Bounce change p-value (BCP)	The bounce change p-value is the probability that the change noted in bounce would have occurred by chance. (Use the Fisher exact probability formula to compute the p-value.)	Use "BCP =" and indicate the p-value in the lower right cell of the analysis matrix (e.g., BCP = .0001).

Figure 6.17 Scatterplot showing how the behavior of individuals from different demographic groups relates to a standard measure of safe driving.

From "A Technology to Measure Multiple Driving Behaviors without Self-Report or Participant Reactivity" by T. E. Boyce and E. S. Geller, 2001, *Journal of Applied Behavior Analysis, 34,* p. 49. Copyright 2001 by the Society for the Experimental Analysis of Behavior, Inc. Used by permission.

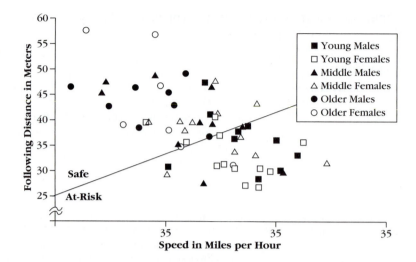

points falling along lines on the plane or clusters suggest certain relationships.

Scatterplots can reveal relationships among different subsets of data. For example, Boyce and Geller (2001) created the scatterplot shown in Figure 6.17 to see how the behavior of individuals from different demographic groups related to a ratio of driving speed and following distance that represents one element of safe driving (e.g., the proportion of data points for young males falling in the at-risk area of the graph compared to the proportion of drivers from other groups). Each data point shows a single driver's behavior in terms of speed and following distance and whether the speed and following distance combination is considered safe or at risk for accidents. Such data could be used to target interventions for certain demographic groups.

Applied behavior analysts sometimes use scatterplots to discover the temporal distribution of a target behavior (e.g., Kahng et al., 1998; Symons, McDonald, & Wehby, 1998; Touchette, MacDonald, & Langer, 1985). Touchette and colleagues described a procedure for observing and recording behavior that produces a scatterplot that graphically shows whether the behavior's occurrence is typically associated with certain time periods. The use of scatterplot recording is described further in Chapter 24.

Constructing Line Graphs

The skills required to construct effective, distortion-free graphic displays are as important as any in the behavior analyst's repertoire. As applied behavior analysis has developed, so have certain stylistic conventions and expectations regarding the construction of graphs. An effective graph presents the data accurately, completely, and clearly, and makes the viewer's task of understanding the data as easy as possible. The graph maker must strive to fulfill each of these requirements while remaining alert to

features in the graph's design or construction that might create distortion and bias—either the graph maker's or that of a future viewer when interpreting the extent and nature of the behavior change depicted by the graph.

Despite the graph's prominent role in applied behavior analysis, relatively few detailed treatments of how to construct behavioral graphs have been published. Notable exceptions have been chapters by Parsonson and Baer (1978, 1986) and a discussion of graphic display tactics by Johnston and Pennypacker (1980, 1993a). Recommendations from these excellent sources and others (*Journal of Applied Behavior Analysis,* 2000; American Psychological Association, 2001; Tufte, 1983, 1990) contributed to the preparation of this section. Additionally, hundreds of graphs published in the applied behavior analysis literature were examined in an effort to discover those features that communicate necessary information most clearly.

Although there are few hard-and-fast rules for constructing graphs, adhering to the following conventions will result in clear, well-designed graphic displays consistent in format and appearance with current practice. Although most of the recommendations are illustrated by graphs presented throughout this text, Figures 6.18 and 6.19 have been designed to serve as models for most of the practices suggested here. The recommendations given here generally apply to all behavioral graphs. However, each data set and the conditions under which the data were obtained present their own challenges to the graph maker.

Drawing, Scaling, and Labeling Axes
Ratio of the Vertical and Horizontal Axes

The relative length of the vertical axis to the horizontal axis, in combination with the scaling of the axes, determines the degree to which a graph will accentuate or min-

Figure 6.18   Graph of hypothetical data illustrating a variety of conventions and guidelines for graphic display.

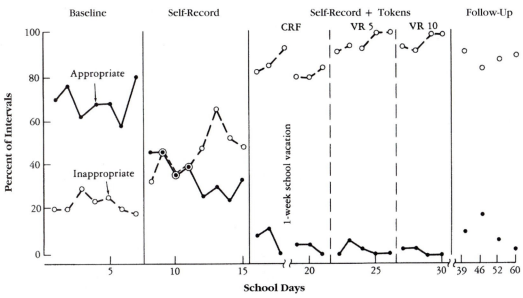

Figure 1.   Percent of 10-second intervals in which an 8-year-old boy emitted appropriate and inappropriate study behaviors. Each interval was scored as appropriate, inappropriate, or neither, so the two behaviors do not always total 100%.

imize the variability in a given data set. The legibility of a graph is enhanced by a balanced ratio between the height and width so that data are neither too close together nor too spread apart. Recommendations in the behavioral literature for the ratio, or relative length, of the vertical axis to the horizontal axis range from 5:8 (Johnston & Pennypacker, 1980) to 3:4 (Katzenberg, 1975). Tufte (1983), whose book *The Visual Display of Quantitative Information* is a wonderful storehouse of guidelines and examples of effective graphing techniques, recommends a 1:1.6 ratio of vertical axis to horizontal axis.

A vertical axis that is approximately two-thirds the length of the horizontal axis works well for most behavioral graphs. When multiple sets of axes will be presented atop one another in a single figure and/or when the number of data points to be plotted on the horizontal axis is very large, the length of the vertical axis relative to the horizontal axis can be reduced (as shown in Figures 6.3 and 6.7).

Scaling the Horizontal Axis

The horizontal axis should be marked in equal intervals, with each unit representing from left to right the chronological succession of equal time periods or response opportunities in which the behavior was (or will be) measured and from which an interpretation of behavior change is to be made (e.g., days, sessions, trials). When many data points are to be plotted, it is not necessary to

mark each point along the *x* axis. Instead, to avoid unnecessary clutter, regularly spaced points on the horizontal axis are indicated with *tic marks* numbered by 5s, 10s, or 20s.

When two or more sets of axes are stacked vertically and each horizontal axis represents the same time frame, it is not necessary to number the tic marks on the horizontal axes of the upper tiers. However, the hatch marks corresponding to those numbered on the bottom tier should be placed on each horizontal axis to facilitate comparison of performance across tiers at any given point in time (see Figure 6.4).

Representing Discontinuities of Time on the Horizontal Axis

Behavior change, its measurement, and all manipulations of treatment or experimental variables occur within and across time. Therefore, time is a fundamental variable in all experiments that should not be distorted or arbitrarily represented in a graphic display. Each equally spaced unit on the horizontal axis should represent an equal passage of time. Discontinuities in the progression of time on the horizontal axis should be indicated by a *scale break:* an open spot in the axis with a squiggly line at each end. Scale breaks on the *x* axis can also be used to signal periods of time when data were not collected or when regularly spaced data points represent consecutive measurements made at unequal intervals (see the

Figure 6.19   Graph of hypothetical data illustrating a variety of conventions and guidelines for graphic display.

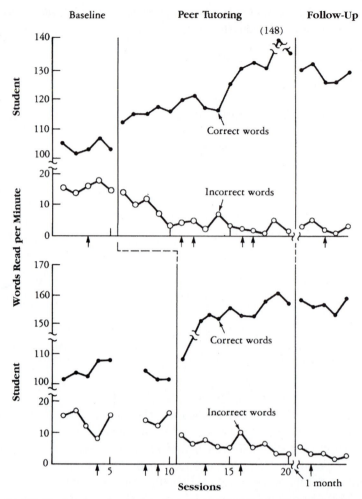

Figure 1. Number of words read correctly and incorrectly during 1-minute probes following each session. Arrows under horizontal axes indicate sessions in which student used reading material brought from home. Break in data path for Student 2 was caused by 2 days' absence.

numbering of school days for the follow-up condition in Figure 6.18).

When measurement occurs across consecutive observations (e.g., stories read, meals, interactions) rather than standard units of time, the horizontal axis still serves as a visual representation of the progression of time because the data plotted against it have been recorded one after the other. The text accompanying such a figure should indicate the real time in which the consecutive measurements were made (e.g., "Two or three peer tutoring sessions were conducted each school week"), and discontinuities in that time context should be clearly marked with scale breaks (see Figure 6.19).

Labeling the Horizontal Axis

The dimension by which the horizontal axis is scaled should be identified in a brief label printed and centered below and parallel to the axis.

Scaling the Vertical Axis

On an equal-interval graph the scaling of the vertical axis is the most significant feature of the graph in terms of its portrayal of changes in level and variability in the data. Common practice is to mark the origin at 0 (on cumulative graphs the bottom on the vertical axis must be 0) and then to mark off the vertical axis so that the full range of values represented in the data set are accommodated. Increasing the distance on the vertical axis between each unit of measurement magnifies the variability in the data, whereas contracting the units of measurement on the vertical axis minimizes the portrayal of variability in the data set. The graph maker should plot the data set against several different vertical axis scales, watching for distortion of the graphic display that might lead to inappropriate interpretations.

The social significance of various levels of behavior change for the behavior being graphed should be considered in scaling the vertical axis. If relatively small numerical changes in performance are socially significant, the y-axis scale should reflect a smaller range of values. For example, to display data most effectively from a training program in which an industrial employee's percentage of correctly executed steps in a safety checklist increased from an unsafe preintervention range of 80% to 90% to an accident-free postintervention level of 100%, the vertical axis should focus on the 80% to 100% range. On the other hand, the scaling of the vertical axis should be contracted when small numerical changes in behavior are not socially important and the degree of variability obscured by the compressed scale is of little interest.

Horizontal numbering of regularly spaced tic marks on the vertical axis facilitates use of the scale. The vertical axis should not be extended beyond the hatch mark indicating the highest value on the axis scale.

When the data set includes several measures of 0, starting the vertical axis at a point slightly above the horizontal axis keeps data points from falling directly on the axis. This produces a neater graph and helps the viewer discriminate 0-value data points from those representing measures close to 0 (see Figure 6.18).

In most instances, scale breaks should not be used on the vertical axis, especially if a data path would cross the break. However, when two sets of data with widely different and nonoverlapping ranges are displayed against the same y axis, a scale break can be used to separate the range of measures encompassed by each data set (see Figure 6.19).

In multiple-tier graphs, equal distances on each vertical axis should represent equal changes in behavior to aid the comparison of data across tiers. Also, whenever possible, similar positions on each vertical axis of multiple-tier graphs should represent similar absolute values of the dependent variable. When the differences in behavioral measures from one tier to another would result in an overly long vertical axis, a scale break can be used to highlight the difference in absolute values, again aiding a point-to-point comparison of y axis positions.

Labeling the Vertical Axis

A brief label, printed and centered to the left and parallel to the vertical axis, should identify the dimension by which the axis is scaled. On multiple-tiered graphs, one label identifying the dimension portrayed on all of the vertical axes can be centered along the axes as a group. Additional labels identifying the different behaviors (or some other relevant aspect) graphed within each set of axes are sometimes printed to the left and parallel to each vertical axis. These individual tier labels should be printed to the right of and in smaller-sized font than the label identifying the dimension by which all of the vertical axes are scaled.

Identifying Experimental Conditions

Condition Change Lines

Vertical lines extending upward from the horizontal axis indicate changes in treatment or experimental procedures. Condition change lines should be placed after (to the right of) the data point representing the last measure prior to the change in conditions signified by the line and before (to the left of) the data point representing the first measure obtained after the change in procedure. In this way data points fall clearly on either side of change lines and never on the lines themselves. Drawing condition change lines to a height equal to the height of the vertical axis helps the viewer estimate the value of data points near the top of the vertical axis range.

Condition change lines can be drawn with either solid or dashed lines. However, when an experiment or a treatment program includes relatively minor changes within an ongoing condition, a combination of solid and dashed lines should be used to distinguish the major and minor changes in conditions. For example, the solid lines in Figure 6.18 change from baseline, to self-record, to self-record + tokens, to follow-up conditions, and dashed lines indicate changes in the schedule of reinforcement from CRF, to VR 5, to VR 10 within the self-record + tokens condition.

When the same manipulation of an independent variable occurs at different points along the horizontal axes of multiple-tiered graphs, a dog-leg connecting the condition change lines from one tier to the next makes it easy to follow the sequence and timing of events in the experiment (see Figure 6.19).

Unplanned events that occur during an experiment or treatment program, as well as minor changes in procedure that do not warrant a condition change line, can be indicated by placing small arrows, asterisks, or other symbols next to the relevant data points (see Figure 6.6) or just under the x axis (see Figure 6.19). The figure caption should explain any special symbols.

Condition Labels

Labels identifying the conditions in effect during each period of an experiment are centered above the space delineated by the condition change lines. Whenever space permits, condition labels should be parallel to the horizontal axis. Labels should be brief but descriptive (e.g., *Contingent Praise* is preferable to *Treatment*), and the labels should use the same terms or phrases used in the accompanying text describing the condition. Abbreviations may be used when space or design limitations prohibit printing the complete label. A single condition label should be placed above and span across labels identifying minor changes within that condition (see Figure 6.18). Numbers are sometimes added to condition labels to indicate the number of times the condition has been in effect during the study (e.g., Baseline 1, Baseline 2).

Plotting Data Points and Drawing Data Paths

Data Points

When graphing data by hand, behavior analysts must take great care to ensure that they plot each data point exactly on the coordinate of the horizontal and vertical axis values of the measurement it represents. The inaccurate placement of data points is an unnecessary source of error in graphic displays, which can lead to mistakes in clinical judgment and/or experimental method. Accurate placement is aided by careful selection of graph paper with grid lines sized and spaced appropriately for the data to be plotted. When many different values must be plotted within a small distance on the vertical axis, a graph paper with many grid lines per inch should be used.[9]

Should a data point fall beyond the range of values described by the vertical axis scale, it is plotted just above the scale it transcends with the actual value of the measurement printed in parentheses next to the data point. Breaks in the data path leading to and from the off-the-scale data point also help to highlight its discrepancy (see Figure 6.19, Session 19).

Data points should be marked with bold symbols that are easily discriminated from the data path. When only one set of data is displayed on a graph, solid dots are most often used. When multiple data sets are plotted on the same set of axes, a different geometric symbol should be used for each set of data. The symbols for each data set should be selected so that the value of each data point can be determined when data points fall near or on the same coordinates on the graph (see Figure 6.18, Sessions 9–11).

Data Paths

Data paths are created by drawing a straight line from the center of each data point in a given data set to the center of the next data point in the same set. All data points in a given data set are connected in this manner with the following exceptions:

- Data points falling on either side of a condition change line are not connected.

- Data points should not be connected across a significant span of time in which behavior was not measured. To do so implies that the resultant data path represents the level and trend of the behavior during the span of time in which no measurement was conducted.

- Data points should not be connected across discontinuities of time in the horizontal axis (see Figure 6.18, 1-week school vacation).

- Data points on either side of a regularly scheduled measurement period in which data were not collected or were lost, destroyed, or otherwise not available (e.g., participant's absence, recording equipment failure) should not be joined together (see Figure 6.18, baseline condition of bottom graph).

- Follow-up or postcheck data points should not be connected with one another (see Figure 6.18) unless they represent successive measures spaced in time in the same manner as measures obtained during the rest of the experiment (see Figure 6.19).

- If a data point falls beyond the values described by the vertical axis scale, breaks should be made in the data path connecting that data point with those that fall within the described range (Figure 6.19, top graph, Session 19 data point).

When multiple data paths are displayed on the same graph, different styles of lines, in addition to different symbols for the data points, may be used to help distinguish one data path from another (see Figure 6.19). The behavior represented by each data path should be clearly identified, either by printed labels with arrows drawn to the data path (see Figures 6.18 and 6.19) or by a legend showing models of the symbols and line styles (see Figure 6.13). When two data sets travel the same path, their lines should be drawn close to and parallel with one another to help clarify the situation (see Figure 6.18, Sessions 9–11).

Writing the Figure Caption

Printed below the graph, the figure caption should give a concise but complete description of the figure. The caption should also direct the viewer's attention to any fea-

---

[9]Although most graphs published in behavior analysis journals since the mid-1990s were constructed with computer software programs that ensure precise placement of data points, knowing how to draw graphs by hand is still an important skill for applied behavior analysts, who often use hand-drawn graphs to make treatment decisions on a session-by-session basis.

tures of the graph that might be overlooked (e.g., scale changes) and should explain the meaning of any added symbols representing special events.

Printing Graphs

Graphs should be printed in only one color—black. Although the use of color can enhance the attractiveness of a visual display and can effectively highlight certain features, it is discouraged in the scientific presentation of data. Every effort must be made to let the data stand on their own. The use of color can encourage perceptions of performance or experimental effects that differ from perceptions of the same data displayed in black. The fact that graphs and charts may be reproduced in journals and books is another reason for using black only.

Constructing Graphs with Computer Software

Software programs for producing computer-generated graphs have been available and are becoming both increasingly sophisticated and easier to use. Most of the graphs displayed throughout this book were constructed with computer software. Even though computer graphics programs offer a tremendous time savings over hand-plotted graphs, careful examination should be made of the range of scales available and the printer's capability for both accurate data point placement and precise printing of data paths.

Carr and Burkholder (1998) provided an introduction to creating single-subject design graphs with Microsoft Excel. Silvestri (2005) wrote detailed, step-by-step instructions for creating behavioral graphs using Microsoft Excel. Her tutorial can be found on the companion Web site that accompanies this text, www.prenhall.com/cooper.

Interpreting Graphically Displayed Behavioral Data

The effects of an intervention that produces dramatic, replicable changes in behavior that last over time are readily seen in a well-designed graphic display. People with little or no formal training in behavior analysis can read the graph correctly in such cases. Many times, however, behavior changes are not so large, consistent, or durable. Behavior sometimes changes in sporadic, temporary, delayed, or seemingly uncontrolled ways; and sometimes behavior may hardly change at all. Graphs displaying these kinds of data patterns often reveal equally important and interesting subtleties about behavior and its controlling variables.

Behavior analysts employ a systematic form of examination known as **visual analysis** to interpret graphically displayed data. Visual analysis of data from an applied behavior analysis study is conducted to answer two questions: (a) Did behavior change in a meaningful way, and (b) if so, to what extent can that change in behavior be attributed to the independent variable? Although there are no formalized rules for visual analysis, the dynamic nature of behavior, the scientific and technological necessity of discovering effective interventions, and the applied requirement of producing socially meaningful levels of performance all combine to focus the behavior analyst's interpretive attention on certain fundamental properties common to all behavioral data: (a) the extent and type of variability in the data, (b) the level of the data, and (c) trends in the data. Visual analysis entails an examination of each of these characteristics both within and across the different conditions and phases of an experiment.

As Johnston and Pennypacker (1993b) so aptly noted, "It is impossible to interpret graphic data without being influenced by various characteristics of the graph itself" (p. 320). Therefore, before attempting to interpret the meaning of the data displayed in a graph, the viewer should carefully examine the graph's overall construction. First, the figure legend, axis labels, and all condition labels should be read to determine a basic understanding of what the graph is about. The viewer should then look at the scaling of each axis, taking note of the location, numerical value, and relative significance of any scale breaks.

Next, a visual tracking of each data path should be made to determine whether data points are properly connected. Does each data point represent a single measurement or observation, or are the data "blocked" such that each data point represents an average or some other summary of multiple measurements? Do the data show the performance of an individual subject or the average performance of a group of subjects? If blocked or group data are displayed, is a visual representation of the range or variation of scores provided (e.g., Armendariz & Umbreit, 1999; Epstein et al., 1981); or do the data themselves allow determination of the amount of variability that was collapsed in the graph? For example, if the horizontal axis is scaled in weeks and each data point represents a student's average score for a week of daily five-word spelling tests, data points falling near 0 or at the top end of the closed scale, such as 4.8, pose little problem because they can be the result of only minimal variability in the daily scores for that week. However, data points near the center of the scale, such as 2 to 3, can result from either stable or highly variable performance.

If the viewer suspects distortion produced by a graph's construction, interpretive judgments of the data should be withheld until the data are replotted on a new set of axes. Distortion due to a loss of important data features in summarizing is not so easily remedied. The viewer must consider the report incomplete and forestall any interpretive conclusions until he has access to the raw data.

Only when the viewer is satisfied that the graph is properly constructed and does not visually distort the behavioral and environmental events it represents, should the data themselves be examined. The data are then inspected to find what they reveal about the behavior measured during each condition of the study.

Visual Analysis within Conditions

Data within a given condition are examined to determine (a) the number of data points, (b) the nature and extent of variability in the data, (c) the absolute and relative level of the behavioral measure, and (d) the direction and degree of any trend(s) in the data.

Number of Data Points

First, the viewer should determine the quantity of data reported during each condition. This entails a simple counting of data points. As a general rule, the more measurements of the dependent variable per unit of time and the longer the period of time in which measurement occurred, the more confidence one can have in the data path's estimation of the true course of behavior change (given, of course, a valid and accurate observation and measurement system).

The number of data points needed to provide a believable record of behavior during a given condition also depends on how many times the same condition has been repeated during the study. As a rule, fewer data points are needed in subsequent replications of an experimental condition if the data depict the same level and trend in performance that were noted in earlier applications of the condition.

The published literature of applied behavior analysis also plays a part in determining how many data points are sufficient. In general, less lengthy phases are required of experiments investigating relations between previously studied and well-established variables if the results are also similar to those of the previous studies. More data are needed to demonstrate new findings, whether or not new variables are under investigation.

There are other exceptions to the rule of the-more-data-the-better. Ethical concerns do not permit the repeated measurement of certain behaviors (e.g.,

self-injurious behavior) under an experimental condition in which there is little or no expectation for improvement (e.g., during a no-treatment baseline condition or a condition intended to reveal variables that exacerbate problem behavior). Also, there is little purpose in repeated measurement in situations in which the subject cannot logically perform the behavior (e.g., measuring the number of correct answers to long division problems when concurrent observations indicate that the student has not learned the necessary component skills of multiplication and subtraction). Nor are many data points required to demonstrate that behavior did not occur when in fact it had no opportunity to occur.

Familiarity with the response class measured and the conditions under which it was measured may be the graph viewer's biggest aid in determining how many data points constitute believability. The quantity of data needed in a given condition is also partly determined by the analytic tactics employed in a given study. Experimental design tactics are described in Chapters 7 through 10.

Variability

How often and the extent to which multiple measures of behavior yield different outcomes is called **variability.** A high degree of variability within a given condition usually indicates that the researcher or practitioner has achieved little control over the factors influencing the behavior. (An important exception to this statement is when the purpose of an intervention is to produce a high degree of variability.) In general, the greater the variability within a given condition, the greater the number of data points that are necessary to establish a predictable pattern of performance. By contrast, fewer data points are required to present a predictable pattern of performance when those data reveal relatively little variability.

Level

The value on the vertical axis scale around which a set of behavioral measures converge is called **level.** In the visual analysis of behavioral data, level is examined within a condition in terms of its absolute value (mean, median, and/or range) on the *y*-axis scale, the degree of stability or variability, and the extent of change from one level to another. The graphs in Figure 6.20 illustrate four different combinations of level and variability.

The mean level of a series of behavioral measures within a condition can be graphically illustrated by the addition of a *mean level line:* a horizontal line drawn through a series of data points within a condition at that point on the vertical axis equaling the average value of the

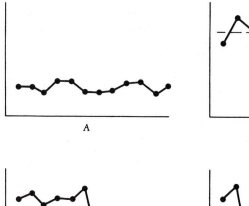

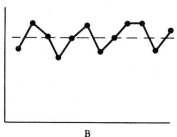

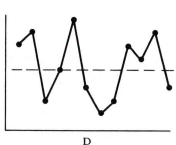

Figure 6.20   Four data paths illustrating (A) a low, stable level of responding; (B) a high, variable level of responding; (C) an initially high, stable level of responding followed by a lower, more variable level of responding; and (D) an extremely variable pattern of responding not indicative of any overall level of responding. Dashed horizontal lines on graphs B, C, and D represent the mean levels of responding.

series of measures (e.g., Gilbert, Williams, & McLaughlin, 1996). Although mean level lines provide an easy-to-see summary of average performance within a given condition or phase, they should be used and interpreted with caution. With highly stable data paths, mean level lines pose no serious drawbacks. However, the less variability there is within a series of data points, the less need there is for a mean level line. For instance, a mean level line would serve little purpose in Graph A in Figure 6.20. And although mean level lines have been added to Graphs B, C, and D in Figure 6.20, Graph B is the only one of the three for which a mean level line provides an appropriate visual summary of level. The mean level line in Graph C is not representative of any measure of behavior taken during the phase. The data points in Graph C show a behavior best characterized as occurring at two distinct levels during the condition and beg for an investigation of the factor(s) responsible for the clear change in levels. The mean level line in Graph D is also inappropriate because the variability in the data is so great that only 4 of the 12 data points fall close to the mean level line.

A *median level line* is another method for visually summarizing the overall level of behavior in a condition. Because a median level line represents the most typical performance within a condition, it is not so influenced by one or two measures that fall far outside the range of the remaining measures. Therefore, one should use a median level line instead of a mean level line to graphically represent the central tendency of a series of data points that include several outliers, either high or low.

Change in level within a condition is determined by calculating the difference in absolute values on the *y* axis

between the first and last data points within the condition. Another method, somewhat less influenced by variability in the data, is to compare the difference between the median value of the first three data points in the condition with the median value of the final three data points in the condition (Koenig & Kunzelmann, 1980).

Trend

The overall direction taken by a data path is its **trend.** Trends are described in terms of their direction (increasing, decreasing, or zero trend), degree or magnitude, and extent of variability of data points around the trend. The graphs in Figure 6.21 illustrate a variety of trends. The direction and degree of trend in a series of graphed data points can be visually represented by a straight line drawn through the data called a *trend line* or *line of progress.* Several methods for calculating and fitting trends lines to a series of data have been developed. One can simply inspect the graphed data and draw a straight line that visually provides the best fit through the data. For this freehand method, Lindsley (1985) suggested ignoring one or two data points that fall well beyond the range of the remaining values in a data series and fitting the trend line to the remaining scores. Although the freehand method is the fastest way of drawing trend lines and can be useful for the viewer of a published graph, hand-drawn trend lines may not always result in an accurate representation of trend and are typically not found in graphs of published studies.

Trend lines can also be calculated using a mathematical formula called the ordinary least-squares linear

Figure 6.21 Data patterns indicating various combinations of trend direction, degree, and variability: (A) zero trend, high stability; (B) zero trend, high variability; (C) gradually increasing stable trend; (D) rapidly increasing variable trend; (E) rapidly decreasing stable trend; (F) gradually decreasing variable trend; (G) rapidly increasing trend followed by rapidly decreasing trend; (H) no meaningful trend, too much variability and missing data. Split-middle lines of progress have been added to Graphs C–F.

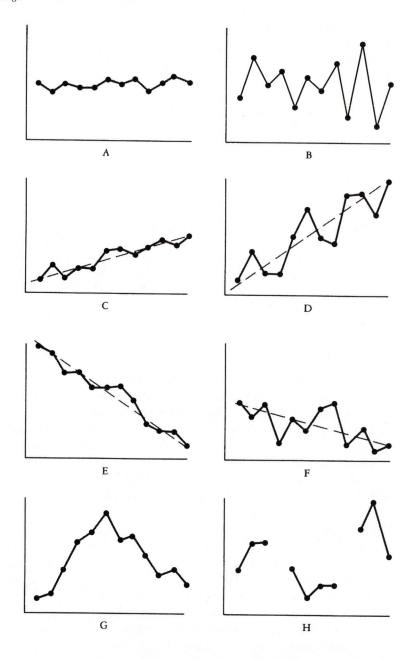

regression equation (McCain & McCleary, 1979; Parsonson & Baer, 1978). Trend lines determined in this fashion have the advantage of complete reliability: The same trend line will always result from the same data set. The disadvantage of this method is the many mathematical operations that must be performed to calculate the trend line. A computer program that can perform the equation can eliminate the time concern in calculating a least-squares trend line.

A method of calculating and drawing lines of progress that is more reliable than the freehand method and much less time-consuming than linear regression methods is the **split-middle line of progress.** The split-middle technique was developed by White (1971, 2005) for use with rate data plotted on semilogarithmic charts,

and it has proven a useful technique for predicting future behavior from such data. Split-middle lines of progress can also be drawn for data plotted against an equal-interval vertical axis, but it must be remembered that such a line is only an estimate that summarizes the overall trend (Bailey, 1984). Figure 6.22 provides a step-by-step illustration of how to draw split-middle lines of progress. A trend line cannot be drawn by any method through a series of data points spanning a scale break in the vertical axis and generally should not be drawn across scale breaks in the horizontal axis.

The specific degree of acceleration or deceleration of trends in data plotted on semilogarithmic charts can be quantified in numerical terms. For example, on the daily Standard Celeration Chart a "times-2" celeration means

Figure 6.22   How to draw a split-middle line of progress through a series of graphically displayed data points.

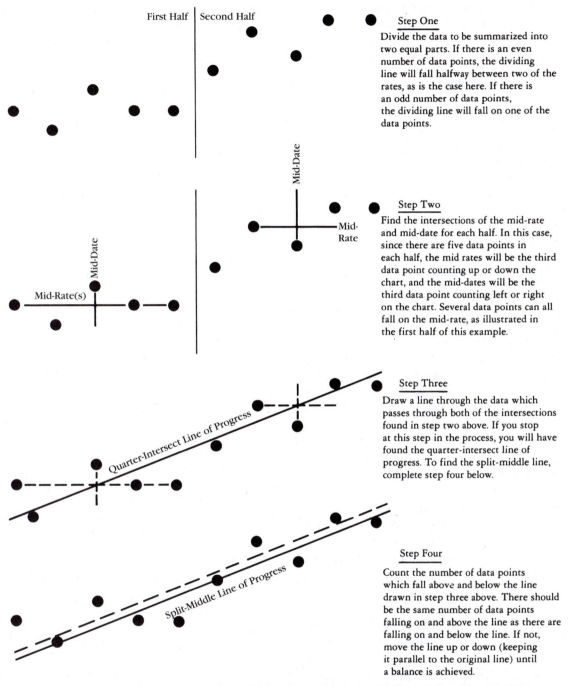

First Half | Second Half

Step One

Divide the data to be summarized into two equal parts. If there is an even number of data points, the dividing line will fall halfway between two of the rates, as is the case here. If there is an odd number of data points, the dividing line will fall on one of the data points.

Mid-Date

Mid-Rate

Step Two

Find the intersections of the mid-rate and mid-date for each half. In this case, since there are five data points in each half, the mid rates will be the third data point counting up or down the chart, and the mid-dates will be the third data point counting left or right on the chart. Several data points can all fall on the mid-rate, as illustrated in the first half of this example.

Mid-Date

Mid-Rate(s)

Quarter-Intersect Line of Progress

Step Three

Draw a line through the data which passes through both of the intersections found in step two above. If you stop at this step in the process, you will have found the quarter-intersect line of progress. To find the split-middle line, complete step four below.

Split-Middle Line of Progress

Step Four

Count the number of data points which fall above and below the line drawn in step three above. There should be the same number of data points falling on and above the line as there are falling on and below the line. If not, move the line up or down (keeping it parallel to the original line) until a balance is achieved.

Adapted from *Exceptional Teaching*, p. 118, by O. R. White and N. G. Haring, 1980, Columbus, OH: Charles E. Merrill. Copyright 1980 by Charles E. Merrill. Used by permission.

that the response rate is doubling each week, and a "times-1.25" means that the response rate is accelerating by a factor of one fourth each week. A "divide-by-2" celeration means that each week the response rate will be one half of what it was the week before, and a "divide-by-1.5" means that the frequency is decelerating by one third each week.

There is no direct way to determine visually from data plotted on equal-interval charts the specific rates at which trends are increasing or decreasing. But visual comparison of trend lines drawn through data on equal-interval charts can provide important information about the relative rates of behavior change.

A trend may be highly stable with all of the data points falling on or near the trend line (see Figure 6.21, Graphs C and E). Data paths can also follow a trend even though a high degree of variability exists among the data points (see Figure 6.21, Graphs D and F).

Visual Analysis between Conditions

After inspection of the data within each condition or phase of a study, visual analysis proceeds with a comparison of data between conditions. Drawing proper conclusions entails comparing the previously discussed properties of behavioral data—level, trend, and stability/variability—between different conditions and among similar conditions.

A condition change line indicates that an independent variable was manipulated at a given point in time. To determine whether an immediate change in behavior occurred at that point in time, one needs to examine the difference between the last data point before the condition change line and the first data point in the new condition.

The data are also examined in terms of the overall level of performance between conditions. In general, when all data points in one condition fall outside the range of values for all data points in an adjacent condition (that is, there is no overlap of data points between the highest values obtained in one condition and the lowest values obtained in the other condition), there is little doubt that behavior changed from one condition to the next. When many data points in adjacent conditions overlap one another on the vertical axis, less confidence can be placed in the effect of the independent variable associated with the change in conditions.[10]

Mean or median level lines can be helpful in examining the overall level between conditions. However, using mean or median level lines to summarize and compare the overall central tendency of data across conditions poses two serious problems. First, the viewer of such a visual display must guard against letting "apparently large differences among measures of central tendency visually overwhelm the presence of equally large amounts of uncontrolled variability" (Johnston & Pennypacker, 1980, p. 351). Emphasis on mean changes in performance in a graphic display can lead the viewer to believe that a greater degree of experimental control was obtained than is warranted by the data. In the top graph of Figure 6.23 half of the data points in Condition B fall within the range of values of the measures taken during Condition A, but the mean level lines suggest a clear change in behavior. Second, measures of central tendency can obscure important trends in the data that warrant interpretations other than those suggested by the central tendency indicators. Although a mean or median line accurately represents the average or typical performance, neither provides any indication of increasing or decreasing performance. In the bottom graph of Figure 6.23, for example, the mean line suggests a higher level of performance in Condition B than in Condition A, but an examination of trend yields a very different picture of behavior change within and between Conditions A and B.

Those analyzing behavioral data should also note any changes in level that occur after a new condition has been in place for some time and any changes in level that occur early in a new condition but are later lost. Such delayed or temporary effects can indicate that the independent variable must be in place for some time before behavior changes, or that the temporary level change was the result of an uncontrolled variable. Either case calls for further investigation in an effort to isolate and control relevant variables.

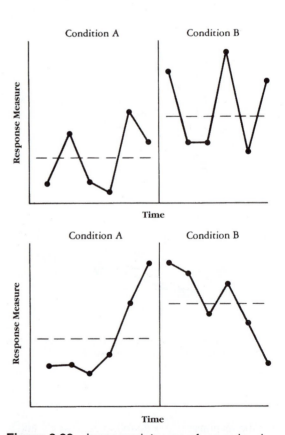

Figure 6.23   Inappropriate use of mean level lines, encouraging interpretation of a higher overall level of responding in Condition B when extreme variability (top graph) and trends (bottom graph) warrant different conclusions.

---

[10]Whether a documented change in behavior should be interpreted as a function of the independent variable depends on the experimental design used in the study. Strategies and tactics for designing experiments are presented in Chapters 7 through 10.

Visual analysis of data between adjacent conditions includes an examination of the trends exhibited by the data in each condition to determine whether the trend found in the first condition changed in direction or slope during the subsequent condition. In practice, because each data point in a series contributes to level and trend, the two characteristics are viewed in conjunction with one another. Figure 6.24 presents stylized data paths illustrating four basic combinations of change or lack of change in level and trend between adjacent conditions. Of course, many other data patterns could display the same characteristics. Idealized, straight-line data paths that eliminate the variability found in most repeated measures of behavior have been used to highlight level and trend.

Visual analysis includes not only an examination and comparison of changes in level and trend between adjacent conditions, but also an examination of performance across similar conditions. Interpreting what the data from an applied behavior *analysis* mean requires more than visual analysis and the identification and description of level, trend, and variability. When behavior change is demonstrated over the course of a treatment program or research study, the next question to be asked is, Was the change in behavior a function of the treatment or experimental variables? The remaining chapters of Part Three describe strategies and tactics of experimental design used by applied behavior analysts in an effort to provide a meaningful answer.

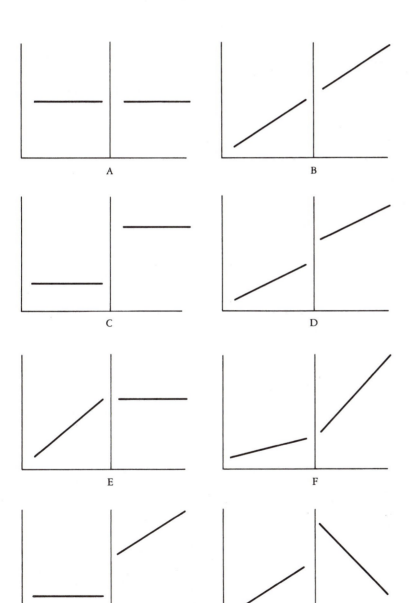

Figure 6.24 Stylized data paths illustrating the different combinations of change or lack of change in level and trend between two adjacent conditions: Graphs A and B show no change in either level or trend between the two conditions, Graphs C and D show changes in level and no change in trend, Graphs E and F depict no immediate change in level and a change in trend, and Graphs G and H reveal change in both level and trend.

From "Time-Series Analysis in Operant Research" by R. R. Jones, R. S. Vaught, and M. R. Weinrott, 1977, *Journal of Applied Behavior Analysis*, 10, p. 157. Copyright 1977 by the Society for the Experimental Analysis of Behavior, Inc. Adapted by permission.

Summary

1. Applied behavior analysts document and quantify behavior change by direct and repeated measurement of behavior, and the product of those measurements called *data.*

2. Graphs are relatively simple formats for visually displaying relationships among and between a series of measurements and relevant variables.

Purpose and Benefits of Graphic Display of Behavioral Data

3. Graphing each measure of behavior as it is collected provides the practitioner or researcher with an immediate and ongoing visual record of the participant's behavior, allowing treatment and experimental decisions to be responsive to the participant's performance.

4. Direct and continual contact with the data in a readily analyzable format enables the practitioner or researcher to identify and investigate interesting variations in behavior as they occur.

5. As a judgmental aid for interpreting experimental results, graphic display is a fast, relatively easy-to-learn method that imposes no arbitrary levels of significance for evaluating behavior change.

6. Visual analysis of graphed data is a conservative method for determining the significance of behavior change; only variables able to produce meaningful effects repeatedly are considered significant, and weak and unstable variables are screened out.

7. Graphs enable and encourage independent judgments of the meaning and significance of behavior change by others.

8. Graphs can serve as effective sources of feedback to the people whose behavior they represent.

Types of Graphs Used in Applied Behavior Analysis

9. Line graphs, the most commonly used format for the graphic display of behavioral data, are based on the Cartesian plane, a two-dimensional area formed by the intersection of two perpendicular lines.

10. Major parts of the simple line graph are the horizontal axis (also called the *x* axis), the vertical axis (also called the *y* axis), condition change lines, condition labels, data points, the data path, and the figure caption.

11. Graphs with multiple data paths on the same set of axes are used in applied behavior analysis to show (a) two or more dimensions of the same behavior, (b) two or more different behaviors, (c) the same behavior under different and alternating experimental conditions, (d) changes in target behavior relative to the changing values of an independent variable, and (e) the behavior of two or more participants.

12. A second vertical axis, which is drawn on the right-hand side of the horizontal axis, is sometimes used to show different scales for multiple data paths.

13. Bar graphs are used for two primary purposes: (a) to display discrete data not related by an underlying dimension that can be used to scale the horizontal axis and (b) to summarize and enable easy comparison of the performance of a participant or group of participants during the different conditions of an experiment.

14. Each data point on a cumulative record represents the total number of responses emitted by the subject since measurement began. The steeper the slope of the data path on a cumulative graph, the higher the response rate.

15. Overall response rate refers to the average rate of response over a given time period; a local response rate refers to the rate of response during a smaller period of time within a larger period for which an overall response rate has been given.

16. Cumulative records are especially effective for displaying data when (a) the total number of responses made over time is important, (b) the graph is used as a source of feedback to the subject, (c) the target behavior can occur only once per measurement period, and (d) a fine analysis of a single instance or portions of data from an experiment is desired.

17. Semilogarithmic charts use a logarithmic-scaled *y* axis so that changes in behavior that are of equal proportion (e.g., doublings of the response measure) are represented by equal distances on the vertical axis.

18. The Standard Celeration Chart is a six-cycle multiply-divide graph that enables the standardized charting of celeration, a linear measure of frequency change across time, a factor by which frequency multiplies or divides per unit of time.

19. A scatterplot shows the relative distribution of individual measures in a data set with respect to the variables depicted by the *x* and *y* axes.

Constructing Line Graphs

20. The vertical axis is drawn to a length approximately two thirds that of the horizontal axis.

21. The horizontal axis is marked off in equal intervals, each representing from left to right the chronological succession of equal time periods within which behavior was measured.

22. Discontinuities of time are indicated on the horizontal axis by scale breaks.

23. The vertical axis is scaled relative to the dimension of behavior measured, the range of values of the measures obtained, and the social significance of various levels of change in the target behavior.

24. Condition change lines indicate changes in the treatment program or manipulations of an independent variable and are drawn to the same height as the vertical axis.

25. A brief, descriptive label identifies each condition of an experiment or behavior change program.

26. Data points should be accurately placed with bold, solid dots. When multiple data paths are used, different geometric symbols are used to distinguish each data set.

27. Data paths are created by connecting successive data points with a straight line.

28. Successive data points should not be connected when (a) they fall on either side of a condition change line; (b) they span a significant period of time in which behavior was not measured; (c) they span discontinuities of time on the horizontal axis; (d) they fall on either side of a regularly scheduled measurement period in which data were not collected or were lost, destroyed, or otherwise not available; (e) they fall in a follow-up or postcheck period that is not regularly spaced in time in the same manner as the rest of the study; or (f) one member of the pair falls outside the range of values described by the vertical axis.

29. The figure caption provides a concise but complete description of the graph, giving all of the information needed to interpret the display.

30. Graphs should be printed in black ink only.

Interpreting Graphically Displayed Behavioral Data

31. Visual analysis of graphed data attempts to answer two questions: (a) did a socially meaningful change in behavior take place, and (b) if so, can the behavior change be attributed to the independent variable?

32. Before beginning to evaluate the data displayed in a graph, a careful examination of the graph's construction should be undertaken. If distortion is suspected from the features of the graph's construction, the data should be replotted on a new set of axes before interpretation is attempted.

33. Blocked data and data representing the average performance of a group of subjects should be viewed with the understanding that significant variability may have been lost in the display.

34. Visual analysis of data within a given condition focuses on the number of data points, the variability of performance, the level of performance, and the direction and degree of any trends in the data.

35. As a general rule, the more data in a condition and the greater the stability of those data, the more confidence one can place in the data path's estimate of behavior during that time. The more variability in the behavioral measures during a condition, the greater the need for additional data.

36. *Variability* refers to the frequency and degree to which multiple measures of behavior yield different outcomes. A high degree of variability within a given condition usually indicates that little or no control has been achieved over the factors influencing the behavior.

37. *Level* refers to the value on the vertical axis around which a series of data points converges. When the data in a given condition all fall at or near a specific level, the behavior is considered stable with respect to level; to the extent that the behavioral measures vary considerably from one to another, the data are described as showing variability with respect to level. In cases of extreme variability, no particular level of performance is evidenced.

38. Mean or median level lines are sometimes added to graphic displays to represent the overall average or typical performance during a condition. Mean and median level lines should be used and interpreted with care because they can obscure important variability and trends in the data.

39. *Trend* refers to the overall direction taken by a data path; trends are described in terms of their direction (increasing, decreasing, or zero trend), degree (gradual or steep), and the extent of variability of data points around the trend.

40. Trend direction and degree can be visually represented by drawing a trend line, or line of progress, through a series of data points. Trend lines can be drawn freehand, using the least-squares regression equation, or using a method called the split-middle line of progress. Split-middle lines of progress can be drawn quickly and reliably and have proven useful in analyzing behavior change.

41. Visual analysis of data across conditions determines whether change in level, variability, and/or trend occurred and to what extent any changes were significant.

CHAPTER 7

Analyzing Behavior Change: Basic Assumptions and Strategies

Key Terms

A-B design
affirmation of the consequent
ascending baseline
baseline
baseline logic
confounding variable
dependent variable
descending baseline
experimental control

experimental design
experimental question
external validity
extraneous variable
independent variable
internal validity
parametric analysis
practice effects

prediction
replication
single-subject designs
stable baseline
steady state responding
steady state strategy
variable baseline
verification

Behavior Analyst Certification Board® BCBA® & BCABA® Behavior Analyst Task List©, Third Edition

	Content Area 3: Principles, Processes, and Concepts
3–10	Define and provide examples of functional relations.
	Content Area 5: Experimental Evaluation of Interventions
5–1	Systematically manipulate independent variables to analyze their effects on treatment.
5–2	Identify and address practical and ethical considerations in using various experimental designs.
5–4	Conduct a parametric analysis (i.e., determining effective parametric values of consequences, such as duration or magnitude).

Measurement can show whether, when, and how much behavior has changed, but measurement alone cannot reveal why, or more accurately *how*, behavior change occurred. A useful technology of behavior change requires an understanding of the specific arrangements of environmental variables that will produce desired behavior change. Without this knowledge, efforts to change behavior could only be considered one-shot affairs consisting of procedures selected randomly from a bag of tricks with little or no generality from one situation to the next.

The search for and demonstration of functional and reliable relations between socially important behavior and its controlling variables is a defining characteristic of applied behavior analysis. A major strength of applied behavior analysis is its insistence on experimentation as its method of proof, which enables and demands an on-going, self-correcting search for effectiveness.

> Our technology of behavior change is also a technology of behavior measurement and of experimental design; it developed as that package, and as long as it stays in that package, it is a self-evaluating enterprise. Its successes are successes of known magnitude; its failures are almost immediately detected as failures; and whatever its outcomes, they are attributable to known inputs and procedures rather than to chance events or coincidences. (D. M. Baer, personal communication, October 21, 1982)

An experimental analysis must be accomplished to determine if and how a given behavior functions in relation to specific changes in the environment. This chapter introduces the basic concepts and strategies that underlie the *analysis* in applied behavior analysis.[1] The chapter begins with a brief review of some general conceptions of science, followed by a discussion of two defining features and two assumptions about the nature of behavior that dictate the experimental methods most conducive to the subject matter. The chapter then describes the necessary components of any experiment in applied behavior analysis and concludes by explaining the basic logic that guides the experimental methods used by applied behavior analysts.

Concepts and Assumptions Underlying the Analysis of Behavior

As was discussed in Chapter 1, scientists share a set of common perspectives that include assumptions about the nature of the phenomena they study (determinism), the kind of information that should be gathered on the phenomena of interest (empiricism), the way questions about the workings of nature are most effectively examined (experimentation), and how the results of experiments should be judged (with parsimony and philosophic doubt). These attitudes apply to all scientific disciplines, including the scientific study of behavior. "The basic characteristics of science are not restricted to any particular subject matter" (Skinner, 1953, p. 11).

The overall goal of science is to achieve an understanding of the phenomena under study—socially significant behavior, in the case of applied behavior analysis. Science enables various degrees of understanding at three levels: description, prediction, and control. First, systematic observation enhances the understanding of natural phenomena by enabling scientists to describe them accurately. Descriptive knowledge of this type yields a collection of facts about the observed events—facts that can be quantified and classified, a necessary and important element of any scientific discipline.

A second level of scientific understanding occurs when repeated observation discovers that two events consistently covary. That is, the occurrence of one event (e.g., marriage) is associated with the occurrence of another event at some reliable degree of probability (e.g., longer life expectancy). The systematic covariation between two events—termed a *correlation*—can be used to predict the probability that one event will occur based on the presence of the other event.

The ability to predict successfully is a useful result of science; prediction allows preparation. However, the greatest potential benefits of science are derived from the third, and highest, level of scientific understanding, which comes from establishing experimental control. "The experimental method is a method for isolating the relevant variables within a pattern of events. Methods that depend merely on observed correlations, without experimental intervention, are inherently ambiguous" (Dinsmoor, 2003, p. 152).

Experimental Control: The Path to and Goal of Behavior Analysis

Behavior is the interaction between an organism and its environment and is best analyzed by measuring changes in behavior that result from imposed variations on the

---

[1]The analysis of behavior has benefited immensely from two particularly noteworthy contributions to the literature on experimental method: Sidman's *Tactics of Scientific Research* (1960/1988) and Johnston and Pennypacker's *Strategies and Tactics of Human Behavioral Research* (1980, 1993a). Both books are essential reading and working references for any serious student or practitioner of behavior analysis, and we acknowledge the significant part each has played in the preparation of this chapter.

environment. This statement embodies the general strategy and the goal of behavioral research: to demonstrate that measured changes in the target behavior occur because of experimentally manipulated changes in the environment.

Experimental control is achieved when a predictable change in behavior (the dependent variable) can be reliably produced by the systematic manipulation of some aspect of the person's environment (the independent variable). Experimentally determining the effects of environmental manipulation on behavior and demonstrating that those effects can be reliably produced constitute the *analysis* in applied behavior analysis. An analysis of a behavior has been achieved when a reliable functional relation between the behavior and some specified aspect of the environment has been demonstrated convincingly. Knowledge of functional relations enables the behavior analyst to reliably alter behavior in meaningful ways.

An analysis of behavior "requires a believable demonstration of the events that can be responsible for the occurrence or nonoccurrence of that behavior. An experimenter has achieved an analysis of a behavior when he can exercise control over it" (Baer, Wolf, & Risley, 1968, p. 94).[2] Baer and colleague's original definition of analysis highlights an important point. Behavior analysis' seeking and valuing of the experimental isolation of a given environmental variable of which a behavior is shown to be a function has often been misinterpreted as support for a simplistic conception of the causes of behavior. The fact that a behavior varies as a function of a given variable does not preclude its varying as a function of other variables. Thus, Baer and colleagues described an experimental analysis as a convincing demonstration that a variable *can* be responsible for the observed behavior change. Even though a complete analysis (i.e., understanding) of a behavior has not been achieved until all of its multiple causes have been accounted for, an *applied* (i.e., technologically useful) analysis has been accomplished when the investigator has isolated an environmental variable (or group of variables that operate together as a treatment package) that reliably produces socially significant behavior change. An *applied* analysis of behavior also requires that the target behavior be a function of an environmental event that can be practically and ethically manipulated.

Experiments that show convincingly that changes in behavior are a function of the independent variable and are not the result of uncontrolled or unknown variables are said to have a high degree of **internal validity.** A study without internal validity can yield no meaningful statements regarding functional relations between the variables examined in the experiment, nor can it be used as the basis for any statements regarding the generality of the findings to other persons, settings, and/or behaviors.[3]

When initially planning an experiment and later when examining the actual data from an ongoing study, the investigator must always be on the lookout for threats to internal validity. Uncontrolled variables known or suspected to exert an influence on the dependent variable are called **confounding variables.** For example, suppose a researcher wants to analyze the effects of guided lecture notes on high school biology students' learning as measured by their scores on next-day quizzes. One potential confounding variable that the researcher would need to take into account would be each student's changing level of interest in and background knowledge about the specific curriculum content (e.g., a student's high score on a quiz following a lecture on sea life may be due to his prior knowledge about fishing, not the guided notes provided during that lecture).

A primary factor in evaluating the internal validity of an experiment is the extent to which it eliminates or controls the effects of confounding variables while still investigating the research questions of interest. It is impossible to eliminate all sources of uncontrolled variability in an experiment, although the researcher always strives for that ideal. In reality, the goal of experimental design is to eliminate as many uncontrolled variables as possible and to hold constant the influence of all other variables except the independent variable, which is purposefully manipulated to determine its effects.

Behavior: Defining Features and Assumptions that Guide Its Analysis

> Behavior is a difficult subject matter, not because it is inaccessible, but because it is extremely complex. Since it is a process, rather than a thing, it cannot easily be held still for observation. It is changing, fluid, evanescent, and for this reason it makes great technical demands upon the ingenuity and energy of the scientist.
> —B. F. Skinner (1953, p. 15)

How a science defines its subject matter exerts profound influence and imposes certain constraints on the experimental strategies that will be most effective in an understanding of it. "In order for the scientific study of behavior to be as effective as possible, it is necessary for the methods of the science to accommodate the characteristics of its subject matter" (Johnston & Pennypacker, 1993a,

---

[2]The researcher's audience ultimately determines whether a claimed functional relation is believable, or convincing. We will explore the believability of research findings further in Chapter 10.

[3]**External validity** commonly refers to the degree to which a study's results are generalizable to other subjects, settings, and/or behaviors. Strategies for assessing and extending the external validity of experimentally demonstrated functional relations are discussed in Chapter 10.

p. 117). The experimental methods of behavior analysis are guided by two defining features of behavior: (a) the fact that behavior is an individual phenomenon and (b) the fact that behavior is a continuous phenomenon; and by two assumptions about its nature: (a) that behavior is determined and (b) that behavioral variability is extrinsic to the organism.

Behavior Is an Individual Phenomenon

If behavior is defined as a person's interaction with the environment, it follows that a science seeking to discover general principles or laws that govern behavior must study the behavior of individuals. Groups of people do not behave; individual people do. Thus, the experimental strategy of behavior analysis is based on within-subject (or single-subject) methods of analysis.

The average performance of a group of individuals is often interesting and useful information and may, depending on the methods by which individuals were selected to be in the group, enable probability statements about the average performance within the larger population represented by the group. However, "group data" provide no information about the behavior of any individual or how any individual might perform in the future. For example, although administrators and taxpayers may be justifiably interested in the average increase in students' reading comprehension from grade level to grade level, such information is of little use to the classroom teacher who must decide how to improve a given student's comprehension skills.

Nonetheless, learning how behavior–environment relations work with many individuals is vital. A science of behavior contributes to a useful technology of behavior change only to the extent that it discovers functional relations with generality across individuals. The issue is how to achieve that generality. Behavior analysts have found that discovery of behavioral principles with generality across persons is best accomplished by replicating the already demonstrated functional relations with additional subjects.

Behavior Is a Dynamic, Continuous Phenomenon

Just as behavior cannot take place in an environmental void (it must happen somewhere), so must behavior occur at particular points in time. Behavior is not a static event; it takes place in and changes over time. Therefore, single measures, or even multiple measures sporadically dispersed over time, cannot provide an adequate description of behavior. Only continuous measurement over time yields a complete record of behavior as it occurs in context with its environmental influences. Because true con-

tinuous measurement is seldom feasible in applied settings, the systematic repeated measurement of behavior (as described in Chapters 4 and 5) has become the hallmark of applied behavior analysis.

Behavior Is Determined

As discussed in Chapter 1, all scientists hold the assumption that the universe is a lawful and orderly place and that natural phenomena occur in relation to other natural events.

> The touchstone of all scientific research is order. In the experimental analysis of behavior, the orderliness of relations between environmental variables and the subject's behavior is at once the operating assumption upon which the experimenter proceeds, the observed fact that permits doing so, and the goal that continuously focuses experimental decisions. That is, the experimenter begins with the assumption that the subject's behavior is the result of variables in the environment (as opposed to having no causes at all). (Johnston & Pennypacker, 1993a, p. 238)

In other words, the occurrence of any event is determined by the functional relations it holds with other events. Behavior analysts consider behavior to be a natural phenomenon that, like all natural phenomena, is determined. Although determinism must always remain an assumption—it cannot be proven—it is an assumption with strong empirical support.

> Data gathered from all scientific fields indicate that *determinism* holds throughout nature. It has become clear that the *law of determinism,* that is, that all things are determined, holds for the behavioral area also. . . . When looking at actual behavior we've found that in situation 1, behavior is caused; in situation 2, behavior is caused; in situation 3, behavior is caused; . . . and in situation 1001, behavior is caused. Every time an experimenter introduces an independent variable that produces some behavior or some change in behavior, we have further *empirical* evidence that behavior is caused or deterministic. (Malott, General, & Snapper, 1973, pp. 170, 175)

Behavioral Variability Is Extrinsic to the Organism

When all conditions during a given phase of an experiment are held constant and repeated measures of the behavior result in a great deal of "bounce" in the data (i.e., the subject is not responding in a consistent fashion), the behavior is said to display variability.

The experimental approach most commonly used in psychology and other social and behavioral sciences (e.g., education, sociology, political science) makes two assumptions about such variability: (a) Behavioral variability is an intrinsic characteristic of the organism, and

(b) behavioral variability is distributed randomly among individuals in any given population. These two assumptions have critical methodological implications: (a) Attempting to experimentally control or investigate variability is a waste of time—it simply exists, it's a given; and (b) by averaging the performance of individual subjects within large groups, the random nature of variability can be statistically controlled or canceled out. Both of these assumptions about variability are likely false (empirical evidence points in the opposite direction), and the methods they encourage are detrimental to a science of behavior. "Variables are not canceled statistically. They are simply buried so their effects are not seen" (Sidman, 1960/1988, p. 162).[4]

Behavior analysts approach variability in their data quite differently. A fundamental assumption underlying the design and guiding the conduct of experiments in behavior analysis is that, rather than being an intrinsic characteristic of the organism, behavioral variability is the result of environmental influence: the independent variable with which the investigator seeks to produce change, some uncontrolled aspect of the experiment itself, and/or an uncontrolled or unknown factor outside of the experiment.

The assumption of extrinsic variability yields the following methodological implication: Instead of averaging the performance of many subjects in an attempt to mask variability (and as a result forfeiting the opportunity to understand and control it), the behavior analyst experimentally manipulates factors suspected of causing the variability. Searching for the causal factors contributes to the understanding of behavior, because experimental demonstration of a source of variability implies experimental control and thus another functional relation. In fact, "tracking down these answers may even turn out to be more rewarding than answering the original experimental question" (Johnston & Pennypacker, 1980 p. 226).

From a purely scientific viewpoint, experimentally tracking down sources of variability is always the preferred approach. However, the applied behavior analyst, with a problem to solve, must often take variability as it presents itself (Sidman, 1960/1988). Sometimes the applied researcher has neither the time nor the resources to experimentally manipulate even suspected and likely sources of variability (e.g., a teacher who interacts with a student for only part of the day has no hope of controlling the many variables outside the classroom). In most settings the applied behavior analyst seeks a treatment variable robust enough to overcome the variability in-

duced by uncontrolled variables and produce the desired effects on the target behavior (Baer, 1977b).

Components of Experiments in Applied Behavior Analysis

> Nature to be commanded must be obeyed. . . . But, that coin has another face. Once obeyed, nature can be commanded.
> —*B. F. Skinner (1956, p. 232)*

Experimentation is the scientist's way of discovering nature's rules. Discoveries that prove valid and reliable can contribute to a technology of effective behavior change. All experiments in applied behavior analysis include these essential components:

- At least one participant (subject)
- At least one behavior (dependent variable)
- At least one setting
- A system for measuring the behavior and ongoing visual analysis of the data
- At least one treatment or intervention condition (independent variable)
- Manipulations of the independent variable so that its effects on the dependent variable, if any, can be detected (experimental design)

Because the reason for conducting any experiment is to learn something from nature, a well-planned experiment begins with a specific question for nature.

Experimental Question

> We conduct experiments to find out something we do not know.
> —*Murray Sidman (1960/1988, p. 214)*

For the applied behavior analyst, Sidman's "something we do not know" is cast in the form of a question about the existence and/or specific nature of a functional relation between meaningful improvement in socially significant behavior and one or more of its controlling variables. An **experimental question** is "a brief but specific statement of what the researcher wants to learn from conducting the experiment" (Johnston & Pennypacker (1993b, p. 366). In published reports of applied behavior analysis studies, the experimental (or research) question is sometimes stated explicitly in the form of a question, as in these examples:

- Which method of self-correction, after attempting each of 10 words or after attempting a list of 10

---

[4]Some investigators use group comparison designs not just to cancel randomly distributed variability but also to produce results that they believe will have more external validity. Group comparison and within subject experimental methods are compared in Chapter 10.

words, will produce better effects on (a) the acquisition of new spelling words as measured by end-of-the-week tests, and (b) the maintenance of practiced spelling words as measured by 1-week maintenance tests by elementary school students with learning disabilities? (Morton, Heward, & Alber, 1998)

- What are the effects of training middle school students with learning disabilities to recruit teacher attention in the special education classroom on (a) the number of recruiting responses they emit in the general education classroom, (b) the number of teacher praise statements received by the students in the general education classroom, (c) the number of instructional feedback statements received by the students in the general education classroom, and (d) the students' academic productivity and accuracy in the general education classroom? (Alber, Heward, & Hippler, 1999, p. 255)

More often, however, the research question examined by the experiment is implicit within a statement of the study's purpose. For example:

- The purpose of the present study was to compare the relative effectiveness of nonremoval of the spoon and physical guidance as treatments for food refusal and to assess the occurrence of corollary behaviors produced by each procedure. (Ahearn, Kerwin, Eicher, Shantz, & Swearingin, 1996, p. 322)

- The present study was conducted to determine if habit reversal is effective in treating verbal tics in children with Tourette syndrome. (Woods, Twohig, Flessner, & Roloff, 2003, p. 109)

- The purpose of this study was to determine if observed SIB during the tangible condition was confounded by the simultaneous delivery of therapist attention. (Moore, Mueller, Dubard, Roberts, & Sterling-Turner, 2002, p. 283)

- The purpose of this study was to determine whether naturally occurring meals would affect performance adversely during postmeal sessions in which highly preferred food was used as reinforcement. (Zhou, Iwata, & Shore, 2002, pp. 411–412)

Whether an experimental question is stated explicitly in the form of a question or implicit within a statement of purpose, all aspects of an experiment's design and conduct should follow from it.

A good design is one that answers the question convincingly, and as such needs to be constructed in reaction to the question and then tested through arguments in that context (sometimes called, "thinking through"), rather than imitated from a textbook. (Baer, Wolf, & Risley, 1987, p. 319)

Subject

Experiments in applied behavior analysis are most often referred to as **single-subject** (or *single-case*) **designs.** This is not because behavior analysis studies are necessarily conducted with only one subject (though some are), but because the experimental logic or reasoning for analyzing behavior changes often employs the subject as her own control.[5] In other words, repeated measures of each subject's behavior are obtained as she is exposed to each condition of the study (e.g., the presence and absence of the independent variable). A subject is often exposed to each condition several times over the course of an experiment. Measures of the subject's behavior during each phase of the study provide the basis for comparing the effects of experimental variables as they are presented or withdrawn in subsequent conditions.

Although most applied behavior analysis studies involve more than one subject (four to eight is common), each subject's data are graphed and analyzed separately.[6] Instead of using *single-subject design* to refer to the experiments in which each subject serves as his or her own control, some authors use more aptly descriptive terms such as *within-subject design* or *intra-subject design.*

Sometimes the behavior analyst is interested in assessing the total effect of a treatment variable within a group of subjects—for example, the number of homework assignments completed by members of a class of

---

[5]It has become commonplace in the behavior analysis literature to refer to the person(s) whose behavior is the dependent variable in an experiment as a *participant,* instead of the more traditional term, *subject.* We use both terms in this text and urge readers to consider Sidman's (2002) perspective on the issue: "[W]e are no longer permitted to call our subjects 'subjects.' The term is supposed to be dehumanizing, and so we are supposed to call them 'participants.' I think this is completely misguided. Experimenters, too, are participants in their experiments. What does making them nonparticipants do to our perception of science and of scientists? Are experimenters merely robots who follow prescribed and unbreakable scientific rules? Are they supposed just to manipulate variables and coldly record the results of their manipulations? Separating them as nonparticipating manipulators and recorders of the behavior of participants really dehumanizes not only experimenters but, along with them, the whole scientific process." (p. 9)

[6]An experiment by Rindfuss, Al-Attrash, Morrison, and Heward (1998) provides a good example of the extent to which the term *single-subject research* can be a misnomer. A within-subject reversal design was used to evaluate the effects of response cards on the quiz and exam scores of 85 students in five eighth-grade American history classes. Although a large group of subjects participated in this study, it actually consisted of 85 individual experiments; or 1 experiment and 84 replications!

fifth-grade students. In such cases the total number of assignments completed may be measured, graphed, and analyzed as a dependent variable within a "single-subject" design. However, it must be remembered that unless each student's data are individually graphed and interpreted, no individual student's behavior has been analyzed, and the data for the group may not be representative of any individual subject.

Use of a single participant, or a small number of participants, each of whom is considered an intact experiment, stands in sharp contrast to the group comparison designs traditionally used in psychology and the other social sciences that employ large numbers of subjects.[7] Proponents of group comparison designs believe that large numbers of subjects control for the variability discussed earlier and increase the generality (or external validity) of any findings to the population from which the subjects were selected. The advantages and disadvantages of an experimental approach based on within-subject comparisons of the behavior of individual subjects versus comparisons of the average performance of different groups of subjects will be discussed in Chapter 10. For now, we will leave this issue with Johnston and Pennypacker's (1993b) astute observation:

> When well done, the procedures of within-subject designs preserve the pure characteristics of behavior, uncontaminated by intersubject variability. In contrast, the best between groups design practices obfuscate the representation of behavior in various ways, particularly by mixing intersubject variability with treatment-induced variability. (p. 188)

Behavior: Dependent Variable

The target behavior in an applied behavior analysis experiment, or more precisely a measurable dimensional quantity of that behavior (e.g., rate, duration), is called the **dependent variable.** It is so labeled because the experiment is designed precisely to determine whether the behavior is, in fact, *dependent on* (i.e., a function of) the independent variable(s) manipulated by the investigator. (The criteria and procedures for selecting and defining response classes that meet the *applied* requirements for an applied behavior analysis were described in Chapter 3.)

In some studies more than one behavior is measured. One reason for measuring multiple behaviors is to provide data patterns that can serve as controls for evaluating and replicating the effects of an independent variable as it is

sequentially applied to each of the behaviors.[8] A second reason for multiple dependent measures is to assess the presence and extent of the independent variable's effects on behaviors other than the response class to which it was applied directly. This strategy is used to determine whether the independent variable had any collateral effects—either desired or undesired—on other behaviors of interest. Such behaviors are referred to as secondary dependent variables. The experimenter obtains regular measures of their rate of occurrence, though perhaps not with the same frequency with which measures of the primary dependent variable are recorded.

Still another reason for measuring multiple behaviors is to determine whether changes in the behavior of a person other than the subject occur during the course of an experiment and whether such changes might in turn explain observed changes in the subject's behavior. This strategy is implemented primarily as a control strategy in assessing the effects of a suspected confounding variable: The extra behavior(s) measured are not true dependent variables in the sense of undergoing analysis. For example, in a classic study analyzing the effects of the self-recording by a junior high school girl on her classroom study behavior, Broden, Hall, and Mitts (1971) observed and recorded the number of times the girl's teacher paid attention to her throughout the experiment. If teacher attention had been found to covary with changes in study behavior, a functional relation between self-recording and study behavior would not have been demonstrated. In that case, teacher attention would likely have been identified as a potential confounding variable, and the focus of the investigation would likely have shifted to include efforts to experimentally control it (i.e., to hold teacher attention constant) or to systematically manipulate and analyze its effects. However, the data revealed no functional relation between teacher attention and study behavior during the first four phases of the experiment, when concern was highest that teacher attention may have been a confounding variable.

Setting

> Control the environment and you will see order in behavior.
> —*B. F. Skinner (1967, p. 399)*

Functional relations are demonstrated when observed variations in behavior can be attributed to specific operations imposed on the environment. **Experimental control** is

---

[7]For a history of single-case research, see Kennedy (2005).

[8]This is the distinguishing feature of the *multiple baseline across behaviors design,* an experimental tactic used widely in applied behavior analysis. Multiple baseline designs are presented in Chapter 9.

achieved when a predictable change in behavior (the dependent variable) can be reliably and repeatedly produced by the systematic manipulation of some aspect of the subject's environment (the independent variable). To make such attributions properly, the investigator must, among other things, control two sets of environmental variables. First, the investigator must control the independent variable by presenting it, withdrawing it, and/or varying its value. Second, the investigator must control, by holding constant, all other aspects of the experimental setting—**extraneous variables**—to prevent unplanned environmental variation. These two operations—precisely manipulating the independent variable and maintaining the constancy of every other relevant aspect of the experimental setting—define the second meaning of *experimental control.*

In basic laboratory research, experimental space is designed and furnished to maximize experimental control. Lighting, temperature, and sound, for example, are all held constant, and programmed apparatus virtually guarantee the presentation of antecedent stimuli and the delivery of consequences as planned. Applied behavior analysts, however, conduct their studies in the settings where socially important behaviors naturally occur—the classroom, home, and workplace. It is impossible to control every feature of an applied environment; and to add to the difficulty, subjects are typically in the experimental setting for only part of each day, bringing with them the influences of events and contingencies operating in other settings.

In spite of the complexity and ever-changing nature of applied settings, the behavior analyst must make every effort to hold constant all seemingly relevant aspects of the environment. When unplanned variations take place, the investigator must either wait out their effects or try to incorporate them into the design of the experiment. In any event, repeated measures of the subject's behavior are the barometer for assessing whether unplanned environmental changes are of concern.

Applied studies are often conducted in more than one setting. Researchers sometimes use concurrent measures of the same behavior obtained in multiple settings as controls for analyzing the effects of an independent variable that is sequentially applied to the behavior in each setting.[9] In addition, data are often collected in multiple settings to assess the extent to which behavior changes observed in the primary setting have also occurred in the other setting(s). (Strategies for promoting the generalization of behavior change across settings are described in Chapter 28.)

Measurement System and Ongoing Visual Analysis

Beginning students of behavior analysis sometimes believe that the discipline is preoccupied with issues and procedures related to the observation and measurement of behavior. They want to get on with the analysis. However, the results of any experiment can be presented and interpreted only in terms of what was measured, and the observation and recording procedures used in the study determine not only what was measured, but also how well it was measured (i.e., how representative of the subject's actual behavior is the estimate provided by the experimental data—all measurements of behavior, no matter how frequent and technically precise, are estimates of true values). It is critical that observation and recording procedures be conducted in a completely standardized manner throughout each session of an experiment. Standardization involves every aspect of the measurement system, from the definition of the target behavior (dependent variable) to the scheduling of observations to the manner in which the raw data are transposed from recording sheets to session summary sheets to the way the data are graphed. As detailed in Chapter 5, an adventitious change in measurement tactics can result in unwanted variability or confounded treatment effects.

The previous chapter outlined the advantages that accrue to the behavioral researcher who maintains direct contact with the experimental data by ongoing visual inspection of graphic displays. The behavior analyst must become skilled at recognizing changes in level, trend, and degree of variability as these changes develop in the data. Because behavior is a continuous, dynamic phenomenon, experiments designed to discover its controlling variables must enable the investigator to inspect and respond to the data continuously as the study progresses. Only in this way can the behavior analyst be ready to manipulate features of the environment at the time and in the manner that will best reveal functional relations and minimize the effects of confounding variables.

Intervention or Treatment: Independent Variable

Behavior analysts seek reliable relations between behavior and the environmental variables of which it is a function. The particular aspect of the environment that the experimenter manipulates to find out whether it affects the subject's behavior is called the **independent variable.** Sometimes called the *intervention, treatment,* or *experimental variable,* this component of an experiment is called the independent variable because the researcher

---

[9]This analytic tactic is known as a *multiple-baseline across settings design.* Multiple-baseline designs are presented in Chapter 9.

can control or manipulate it independent of the subject's behavior or any other event. (Though, as we will soon see, manipulating the independent variable without regard to what is happening with the dependent variable is unwise.) Whereas any changes that must be made in the experimental setting to conduct the study (e.g., the addition of observers to measure behavior) are made with the goal of minimizing their effects on the dependent variable, "changes in the independent variable are arranged by the experimenter in order to maximize . . . its influence on responding" (Johnston & Pennypacker, 1980, p. 260).

Manipulations of the Independent Variable: Experimental Design

Experimental design refers to the particular arrangement of conditions in a study so that meaningful comparisons of the effects of the presence, absence, or different values of the independent variable can be made. Independent variables can be introduced, withdrawn, increased or decreased in value, or combined across behaviors, settings, and/or subjects in an infinite number of ways.[10] However, there are only two basic kinds of independent variable changes that can be made with respect to the behavior of a given subject in a given setting.

> A new condition can be introduced or an old condition can be reintroduced. . . . Experimental designs are merely temporal arrangements of various new and old conditions across behaviors and settings in ways that produce data that are convincing to the investigator and the audience. (Johnston & Pennypacker, 1980, p. 270)

In the simplest case—from an analytic perspective, but not necessarily a practical point of view—an independent variable can be manipulated so that it is either present or absent during each time period or phase of the study. When the independent variable is in either of these conditions during a study, the experiment is termed a nonparametric study. In contrast, a **parametric analysis** seeks to discover the differential effects of a range of values of the independent variable. For example, Lerman, Kelley, Vorndran, Kuhn, and LaRue (2002) conducted a parametric study when they assessed the effects of different reinforcer magnitudes (i.e., 20 seconds, 60 seconds, or 300 seconds of access to toys or escape from demands) on the duration of postreinforcement pause and resistance to extinction. Parametric experiments are sometimes used because a functional relation may have

more generality if it is based on several values of the independent variable.

Sometimes the investigator is interested in comparing the effects of several treatment alternatives. In this case multiple independent variables become part of the experiment. For example, perhaps two separate treatments are evaluated as well as the effects of a third treatment, which represents a combination of both variables. However, even in experiments with multiple independent variables, the researcher must heed a simple but fundamental rule of experimentation: *Change only one variable at a time.* Only in this manner can the behavior analyst attribute any measured changes in behavior to a specific independent variable. If two or more variables are altered simultaneously and changes in the dependent variable are noted, no conclusions can be made with regard to the contribution of any one of the altered variables to the behavior change. If two variables changed together, both could have contributed equally to the resultant behavior change; one variable could have been solely, or mostly, responsible for the change; or one variable may have had a negative or counterproductive effect, but the other independent variable was sufficiently strong enough to overcome this effect, resulting in a net gain. Any of these explanations or combinations may have accounted for the change.

As stated previously, applied behavior analysts often conduct their experiments in "noisy" environments where effective treatments are required for reasons related to personal safety or exigent circumstances. In such cases, applied behavior analysts sometimes "package" multiple and well-documented and effective treatments, knowing that multiple independent variables are being introduced. As implied earlier, a package intervention is one in which multiple independent variables are being combined or bundled into one program (e.g., token reinforcement + praise, + self-recording + time out). However, from the perspective of experimental analysis, the rule still holds. When manipulating a treatment package, the experimenter must ensure that the entire package is presented or withdrawn each time a manipulation occurs. In this situation, it is important to understand that the entire package is being evaluated, not the discrete components that make up the package. If at a later time, the analyst wishes to determine the relative contributions of each part of the package, a component analysis would need to be carried out. Chapters 8 and 9 describe experimental tactics for component analyses.

There are no off-the-shelf experimental designs available for a given research problem (Baer et al., 1987; Johnston & Pennypacker, 1980, 1993a; Sidman, 1960/1988; Skinner, 1956, 1966). The investigator must not get locked into textbook "designs" that (a) require a priori assumptions about the nature of the functional relations

---

[10]How many different experimental designs are there? Because an experiment's design includes careful selection and consideration of all of the components discussed here (i.e., subject, setting, behavior, etc.), not counting the direct replication of experiments, one could say that there are as many experimental designs as there are experiments.

one seeks to investigate and (b) may be insensitive to unanticipated changes in behavior. Instead, the behavior analyst should select and combine experimental tactics that best fit the research question, while standing ever ready to "explore relevant variables by manipulating them in an improvised and rapidly changing design" (Skinner, 1966, p. 21).

Simultaneous with, and to a large degree responsible for, the growth and success of applied behavior analysis have been the development and refinement of a powerful group of extremely flexible experimental tactics for analyzing behavior-environment relations. The most widely used of these tactics will be described in detail in Chapters 8 and 9. However, to most effectively select, modify, and combine these tactics into convincing experiments, the behavior analyst must first fully understand the experimental reasoning, or logic, that provides the foundation for within-subject experimental comparisons.

Steady State Strategy and Baseline Logic

Steady or **stable state responding**—which "may be defined as a pattern of responding that exhibits relatively little variation in its measured dimensional quantities over a period of time" (Johnston & Pennypacker, 1993a, p. 199)—provides the basis for a powerful form of experimental reasoning commonly used in behavior analysis, called baseline logic. **Baseline logic** entails three elements—prediction, verification, and replication—each of which depends on an overall experimental approach called steady state strategy. **Steady state strategy** entails repeatedly exposing a subject to a given condition while trying to eliminate or control any extraneous influences on the behavior and obtaining a stable pattern of responding before introducing the next condition.

Nature and Function of Baseline Data

Behavior analysts discover behavior–environment relations by comparing data generated by repeated measures of a subject's behavior under the different environmental conditions of the experiment. The most common method of evaluating the effects of a given variable is to impose it on an ongoing measure of behavior obtained in its absence. These original data serve as the **baseline** against which any observed changes in behavior when the independent variable is applied can be compared. A baseline serves as a control condition and does not necessarily mean the absence of instruction or treatment as such, only the absence of a specific independent variable of experimental interest.

Why Establish a Baseline?

From a purely scientific or analytic perspective, the primary purpose for establishing a baseline level of responding is to use the subject's performance in the absence of the independent variable as an objective basis for detecting the effects of the independent variable when it is introduced in the future. However, obtaining baseline data can yield a number of applied benefits. For one, systematic observation of the target behavior before a treatment variable is introduced provides the opportunity to look for and note environmental events that occur just before and just after the behavior. Such empirically obtained descriptions of antecedent-behavior-consequent correlations are often invaluable in planning an effective intervention (see Chapter 24). For example, baseline observations revealing that a child's disruptive outbursts are consistently followed by parent or teacher attention can be used in designing an intervention of ignoring outbursts and contingent attention following desired behavior.

Second, baseline data can provide valuable guidance in setting initial criteria for reinforcement, a particularly important step when a contingency is first put into effect (see Chapter 11). If the criteria are too high, the subject never comes into contact with the contingency; if they are too low, little or no improvement can be expected.

From a practical perspective, a third reason for collecting baseline data concerns the merits of objective measurement versus subjective opinion. Sometimes the results of systematic baseline measurement convince the behavior analyst or significant others to alter their perspectives on the necessity and value of attempting to change the behavior. For example, a behavior being considered for intervention because of several recent and extreme instances is no longer targeted because baseline data show it is decreasing. Or, perhaps a behavior's topography attracted undue attention from teachers or parents, but objective baseline measurement over several days reveals that the behavior is not occurring at a frequency that warrants an intervention.

Types of Baseline Data Patterns

Examples of four data patterns sometimes generated by baseline measurement are shown in Figure 7.1. It must be stressed that these hypothetical baselines represent only four examples of the wide variety of baseline data patterns an experimenter or practitioner will encounter. The potential combinations of different levels, trends, and degrees of variability are, of course, infinite. Nevertheless, in an effort to provide guidance to the beginning behavior analyst, some general statements will be given about the experimental decisions that might be warranted by the data patterns shown in Figure 7.1.

Figure 7.1 Data patterns illustrating stable (A), ascending (B), descending (C), and variable (D) baselines.

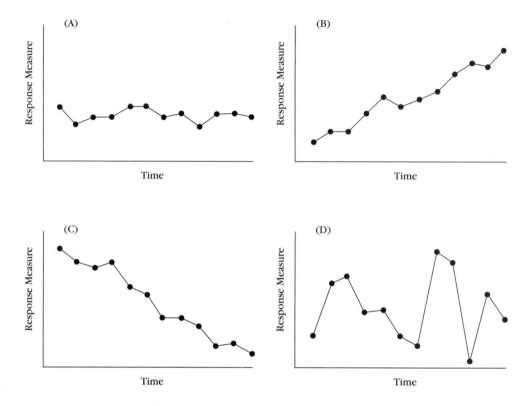

Graph A shows a relatively **stable baseline.** The data show no evidence of an upward or downward trend, and all of the measures fall within a small range of values. A stable baseline provides the most desirable basis, or context, against which to look for effects of an independent variable. If changes in level, trend, and/or variability coincide with the introduction of an independent variable on a baseline as stable as that shown in Graph A, one can reasonably suspect that those changes may be related to the independent variable.

The data in Graphs B and C represent an **ascending baseline** and a **descending baseline,** respectively. The data path in Graph B shows an increasing trend in the behavior over time, whereas the data path in Graph C shows a decreasing trend. The applied behavior analyst must treat ascending and descending baseline data cautiously. By definition, dependent variables in applied behavior analysis are selected because they represent target behaviors that need to be changed. But ascending and descending baselines reveal behaviors currently in the process of changing. The effects of an independent variable introduced at this point are likely to be obscured or confounded by the variables responsible for the already-occurring change. But what if the applied investigator needs to change the behavior immediately? The applied perspective can help solve the dilemma.

Whether a treatment variable should be introduced depends on whether the trending baseline data represent improving or deteriorating performance. When an ascending or descending baseline represents behavior change in the therapeutically desired direction, the investigator should withhold treatment and continue to monitor the dependent variable under baseline conditions. When the behavior ceases to improve (as evidenced by stable responding) or begins to deteriorate, the independent variable can be applied. If the trend does not level off and the behavior continues to improve, the original problem may no longer be present, leaving no reason for introducing the treatment as planned (although the investigator might be motivated to isolate and analyze the variables responsible for the "spontaneous" improvement). Introducing an independent variable to an already-improving behavior makes it difficult, and often impossible, to claim any continued improvement as a function of the independent variable.

An ascending or descending baseline that represents significantly deteriorating performance signals an immediate application of the independent variable. From an applied perspective the decision to intervene is obvious: The subject's behavior is deteriorating, and a treatment designed to improve it should be introduced. An independent variable capable of affecting desired behavior change in spite of other variables "pushing" the behavior in the opposite direction is most likely a robust variable, one that will be a welcome addition to the behavior analyst's list of effective treatments. The decision to introduce a treatment variable on a deteriorating baseline is also a sound one from an analytic perspective, which will be discussed in the next section.

Graph D in Figure 7.1 shows a highly unstable or **variable baseline.** The data in Graph D show just one of many possible patterns of unstable responding. The data points do not consistently fall within a narrow range of values, nor do they suggest any clear trend. Introducing the independent variable in the presence of such variability is unwise from an experimental standpoint. Variability is assumed to be the result of environmental variables, which in the case shown by Graph D, seem to be operating in an uncontrolled fashion. Before the researcher can analyze the effects of an independent variable effectively, these uncontrolled sources of variability must be isolated and controlled.

Stable baseline responding provides an index of the degree of experimental control the researcher has established. Johnston and Pennypacker stressed this point in both editions of *Strategies and Tactics of Human Behavioral Research:*

> If unacceptably variable responding occurs under baseline conditions, this is a statement that the researcher is probably not ready to introduce the treatment conditions, which involves adding an independent variable whose effects are in question. (1993a, p. 201)

These authors were more direct and blunt in the first edition of their text:

> If sufficiently stable responding cannot be obtained, the experimenter is in no position to add an independent variable of suspected but unknown influence. To do so would be to compound confusion and lead to further ignorance. (1980, p. 229)

Again, however, applied considerations must be balanced against purely scientific pursuits. The applied problem may be one that cannot wait to be solved (e.g., severe self-injurious behavior). Or, confounding variables in the subject's environment and the setting(s) of the investigation may simply be beyond the experimenter's control.[11] In such situations the independent variable is introduced with the hope of producing stable responding in its presence. Sidman (1960/1988) agreed that "the behavioral engineer must ordinarily take variability as he finds it, and deal with it as an unavoidable fact of life" (p. 192).

Prediction

Prediction can be defined as "the anticipated outcome of a presently unknown or future measurement. It is the most elegant use of quantification upon which validation of all scientific and technological activity rests" (Johnston & Pennypacker, 1980, p. 120). Figure 7.2 shows a series of hypothetical measures representing a stable pattern of baseline responding. The consistency of the first five data points in the series encourage the prediction that—if no changes occur in the subject's environment—subsequent measures will fall within the range of values obtained thus far. Indeed, a sixth measure is taken that gives credence to this prediction. The same prediction is made again, this time with more confidence, and another measure of behavior shows it to be correct. Throughout a baseline (or any other experimental condition), an ongoing prediction is made and confirmed until the investigator has every reason to believe that the response measure will not change appreciably under the present conditions. The data within the shaded portion of Figure 7.2 represent unobtained but predicted measures of future responding under "relatively constant environmental conditions."[12] Given the stability of the obtained measures, few experienced scientists would quarrel with the prediction.

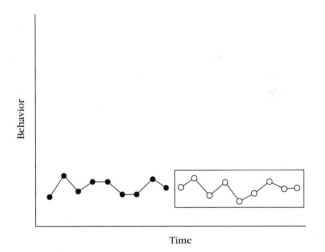

Figure 7.2 Solid data points represent actual measures of behavior that might be generated in a stable baseline; open data points within the box represent the level of responding that would be predicted on the basis of the obtained measures, should the environment remain constant.

---

[11]The applied researcher must guard very carefully against assuming automatically that unwanted variability is a function of variables beyond his capability or resources to isolate and control, and thus fail to pursue the investigation of potentially important functional relations.

[12]"The above reference to 'relatively constant environmental conditions' means only that the experimenter is not knowingly producing uncontrolled variations in functionally related environmental events" (Johnston & Pennypacker, 1980, p. 228).

How many measures must be taken before an experimenter can use a series of data points to predict future behavior with confidence? Baer and colleagues (1968) recommended continuing baseline measurement until "its stability is clear." Even though there are no set answers, some general statements can be made about the predictive power of steady states. All things being equal, many measurements are better than a few; and the longer the period of time in which stable responding is obtained, the better the predictive power of those measures. Also, if the experimenter is not sure whether measurement has produced stable responding, in all likelihood it has not, and more data should be collected before the independent variable is introduced. Finally, the investigator's knowledge of the characteristics of the behavior being studied under constant conditions is invaluable in deciding when to terminate baseline measurement and introduce the independent variable. That knowledge can be drawn from personal experience in obtaining stable baselines on similar response classes and from familiarity with patterns of baseline responding found in the published literature.

It should be clear that guidelines such as "collect baseline data for at least five sessions" or "obtain baseline measures over two consecutive weeks" are misguided or naive. Depending on the situation, five data points obtained over one or two weeks of baseline conditions may or may not provide a convincing picture of steady state responding. The question that must be addressed is: Are the data sufficiently stable to serve as the basis for experimental comparison? This question can be answered only by ongoing prediction and confirmation using repeated measures in an environment in which all relevant conditions are held constant.

Behavior analysts are often interested in analyzing functional relations between an instructional variable and the acquisition of new skills. In such situations it is sometimes assumed that baseline measures are zero. For example, one would expect repeated observations of a child who has never tied her shoes to yield a perfectly stable baseline of zero correct responses. However, casual observations that have never shown a child to use a particular skill do not constitute a scientifically valid baseline and should not be used to justify any claims about the effects of instruction. It could be that if given repeated opportunities to respond, the child would begin to emit the target behavior at a nonzero rate. The term **practice effects** refers to improvements in performance resulting from repeated opportunities to emit the behavior so that baseline measurements can be obtained. For example, attempting to obtain stable baseline data for students performing arithmetic problems can result in improved levels of responding simply because of the repeated

practice inherent in the measurement process. Practice effects confound a study, making it impossible to separate and account for the effects of practice and instruction on the student's final performance. Repeated baseline measures should be used either to reveal the existence or to demonstrate the nonexistence of practice effects. When practice effects are suspected or found, baseline data collection should be continued until steady state responding is attained.

The necessity to demonstrate a stable baseline and to control for practice effects empirically does not require applied behavior analysts to withhold needed treatment or intervention. Nothing is gained by collecting unduly long baselines of behaviors that cannot reasonably be expected to be in the subject's repertoire. For example, many behaviors cannot be emitted unless the subject is competent in certain prerequisite behaviors; there is no legitimate possibility of a child's tying his shoes if he currently does not pick up the laces, or of a student's solving division problems if she cannot subtract and multiply. Obtaining extended baseline data in such cases is unnecessary pro forma measurement. Such measures would "not so much represent zero behavior as zero opportunity for behavior to occur, and there is no need to document at the level of well-measured data that behavior does not occur when it cannot" (Horner & Baer, 1978, p. 190).

Fortunately, applied behavior analysts need neither abandon the use of steady state strategy nor repeatedly measure nonexistent behavior at the expense of beginning treatment. The multiple probe design, described in Chapter 9, is an experimental tactic that enables the use of steady state logic to analyze functional relations between instruction and the acquisition of behaviors shown to be nonexistent in the subject's repertoire prior to the introduction of the independent variable.

Affirmation of the Consequent

The predictive power of steady state responding enables the behavior analyst to employ a kind of inductive logic known as **affirmation of the consequent** (Johnston & Pennypacker, 1980). When an experimenter introduces an independent variable on a stable baseline, an explicit assumption has been made: If the independent variable were not applied, the behavior, as indicated by the baseline data path, would not change. The experimenter is also predicting that (or more precisely, questioning whether) the independent variable will result in a change in the behavior.

The logical reasoning behind affirmation of the consequent begins with a true antecedent–consequent (if-A-then-B) statement and proceeds as follows:

1. If A is true, then B is true.

2. B is found to be true.

3. Therefore, A is true.

The behavior analyst's version goes like this:

1. If the independent variable is a controlling factor for the behavior (A), then the data obtained in the presence of the independent variable will show that the behavior has changed (B).

2. When the independent variable is present, the data show that the behavior has changed (B is true).

3. Therefore, the independent variable is a controlling variable for the behavior (therefore, A is true).

The logic, of course, is flawed; other factors could be responsible for the truthfulness of A. But, as will be shown, a successful (i.e., convincing) experiment affirms several if-A-then-B possibilities, each one reducing the likelihood of factors other than the independent variable being responsible for the observed changes in behavior.

Data shown in Figures 7.3 to 7.5 illustrate how prediction, verification, and replication are employed in a hypothetical experiment using the reversal design, one of the most common and powerful analytic tactics used by behavior analysts (see Chapter 8). Figure 7.3 shows a successful affirmation of the consequent. Steady state responding during baseline enabled the prediction that, if no changes were made in the environment, continued measurement would yield data similar to those in the shaded portion of the graph. The independent variable was then introduced, and repeated measures of the dependent variable during this treatment condition showed that the behavior did indeed change. This enables two comparisons, one real and one hypothetical. First, the real difference between the obtained measures in the presence of the independent variable and the baseline level of responding represents the extent of a possible effect of the independent variable and supports the prediction that treatment would change the behavior.

The second, hypothetical, comparison is between the data obtained in the treatment condition with the predicted measures had the treatment variable not been introduced (i.e., the open data points within the boxed area of Figure 7.3). This comparison represents the behavior analyst's hypothetical approximation of the ideal but impossible-to-achieve experimental design: the simultaneous measurement and comparison of the behavior of an individual subject in both the presence and absence of the treatment variable (Risley, 1969).

Although the data in Figure 7.3 affirm the initial antecedent–consequent statement—a change in the behavior was observed in the presence of the independent

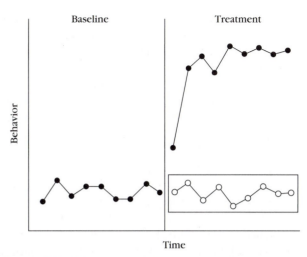

Figure 7.3 Affirmation of the consequent supporting the possibility of a functional relation between the behavior and treatment variable. The measures obtained in the presence of the treatment variable differ from the predicted level of responding in the absence of the treatment variable (open data points within boxed area).

variable—asserting a functional relation between the independent and dependent variables at this point is unwarranted. The experiment has not yet ruled out the possibility of other variables being responsible for the change in behavior. For example, perhaps some other event that is responsible for the change in behavior occurred at the same time that the independent variable was introduced.[13]

A firmer statement about the relation between the treatment and the behavior can be made at this point, however, if changes in the dependent variable are *not* observed in the presence of the independent variable. Assuming accurate measures of the behavior and a measurement system sensitive to changes in the behavior, then no behavior change in the presence of the independent variable constitutes a disconfirmation of the consequent (B was shown not to be true), and the independent variable is eliminated as a controlling variable. However, eliminating a treatment from the ranks of controlling variables on the basis of no observed effects presupposes experimental control of the highest order (Johnston & Pennypacker, 1993a).

---

[13]Although two-phase experiments consisting of a pretreatment baseline condition followed by a treatment condition (called *A–B design*) enable neither verification of the prediction of continued responding at baseline levels nor replication of the effects of the independent variable, studies using A–B designs can nevertheless contribute important and useful findings (e.g., Azrin & Wesolowski, 1974; Reid, Parsons, Phillips, & Green, 1993).

However, in the situation illustrated in Figure 7.3, a change in behavior was observed in the presence of the independent variable, revealing a correlation between the independent variable and the behavior change. To what extent was the observed behavior change a function of the independent variable? To pursue this question, the behavior analyst employs the next component of baseline logic: verification.

Verification

The experimenter can increase the probability that an observed change in behavior was functionally related to the introduction of the independent variable by verifying the original prediction of unchanging baseline measures. **Verification** can be accomplished by demonstrating that the prior level of baseline responding would have remained unchanged had the independent variable not been introduced (Risley, 1969). If that can be demonstrated, this operation verifies the accuracy of the original prediction of continued stable baseline responding and reduces the probability that some uncontrolled (confounding) variable was responsible for the observed change in behavior. Again, the reasoning behind affirmation of the consequent is the logic that underlies the experimental strategy.

Figure 7.4 illustrates the verification of effect in our hypothetical experiment. When steady state responding has been established in the presence of the independent variable, the investigator removes the treatment variable, thereby returning to the previous baseline conditions. This tactic allows the possibility of affirming two different antecedent–consequent statements. The first statement and its affirmation follows this pattern:

1. If the independent variable is a controlling factor for the behavior (A), then its removal will coincide with changes in the response measure (B).

2. Removal of the independent variable is accompanied by changes in the behavior (B is true).

3. Therefore, the independent variable controls responding (therefore, A is true).

The second statement and affirmation follows this pattern:

1. If the original baseline condition controlled the behavior (A), then a return to baseline conditions will result in similar levels of responding (B).

2. The baseline condition is reinstated and levels of responding similar to those obtained during the original baseline phase are observed (B is true).

3. Therefore, the baseline condition controlled the behavior both then and now (therefore, A is true).

The six measures within the shaded area obtained during Baseline 2 of our hypothetical experiment in Figure 7.4 verify the prediction made for Baseline 1. The open data points in the shaded area in Baseline 2 represent the predicted level of responding if the independent variable had not been removed. (The prediction component of baseline logic applies to steady state responding obtained during any phase of an experiment, baseline and treatment conditions alike.) The difference between the data actually obtained during Treatment (solid data points) and the data obtained during Base-line 2 (solid data points) affirms the first if-A-then-B statement: If the treatment is a controlling variable, then its removal will result in changes in behavior. The similarity between measures obtained during Baseline 2 and those obtained during Baseline 1 confirms the second if-A-then-B statement: If baseline conditions controlled the behavior before, reinstating baseline conditions will result in similar levels of responding.

Again, of course, the observed changes in behavior associated with the application and withdrawal of the independent variable are subject to interpretations other

Figure 7.4 Verification of a previously predicted level of baseline responding by termination or withdrawal of the treatment variable. The measures obtained during Baseline 2 (solid data points within shaded area) show a successful verification and a second affirmation of the consequent based on a comparison with the predicted level of responding (open dots in Baseline 2) in the continued presence of the treatment variable.

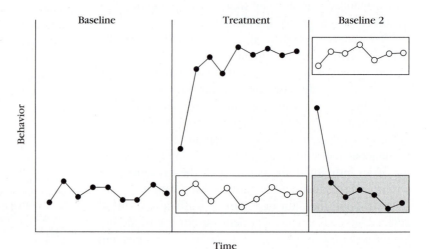

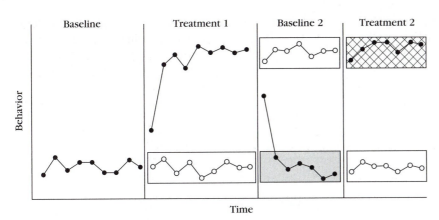

Figure 7.5 Replication of experimental effect accomplished by reintroducing the treatment variable. The measures obtained during Treatment 2 (data points within area shaded with cross hatching) enhance the case for a functional relation between the treatment variable and the target behavior.

than a claim of a functional relation between the two events. However, the case for the existence of a functional relation is becoming stronger. When the independent variable was applied, behavior change was observed; when the independent variable was withdrawn, behavior again changed and responding returned to baseline levels. To the extent that the experimenter effectively controls the presence and absence of the independent variable and holds constant all other variables in the experimental setting that might influence the behavior, a functional relation appears likely: An important behavior change has been produced and reversed by the introduction and withdrawal of the independent variable. The process of verification reduces the likelihood that a variable other than the independent variable was responsible for the observed behavior changes.

Does this two-step strategy of prediction and verification constitute sufficient demonstration of a functional relation? What if some uncontrolled variable covaried with the independent variable as it was presented and withdrawn and this uncontrolled variable was actually responsible for the observed changes in behavior? If such was the case, claiming a functional relation between the target behavior and the independent variable would at best be inaccurate and at the worst perhaps end a search for the actual controlling variables whose identification and control would contribute to an effective and reliable technology of behavior change.

The appropriately skeptical investigator (and research consumer) will also question the reliability of the obtained effect. How reliable is this verified behavior change? Was the apparent functional relation a fleeting, one-time-only phenomenon, or will repeated application of the independent variable reliably (i.e., consistently) produce a similar pattern of behavior change? An effective (i.e., convincing) experimental design yields data that are responsive to these important questions. To investigate uncertain reliability, the behavior analyst employs the final, and perhaps the most important, component of baseline logic and experimental design: replication.

Replication

> Replication is the essence of believability.
> —*Baer, Wolf, and Risley (1968, p. 95)*

Within the context of any given experiment, **replication** means repeating independent variable manipulations conducted previously in the study and obtaining similar outcomes.[14] Replication within an experiment has two important purposes. First, replicating a previously observed behavior change reduces the probability that a variable other than the independent variable was responsible for the now twice-observed behavior change. Second, replication demonstrates the reliability of the behavior change; it can be made to happen again.

Figure 7.5 adds the component of replication to our hypothetical experiment. After steady state responding was obtained during Baseline 2, the independent variable is reintroduced; this is the Treatment 2 phase. To the extent that the data obtained during the second application of the treatment (data points within area shaded with cross-hatched lines) resemble the level of responding observed during Treatment 1, replication has occurred. Our hypothetical experiment has now produced powerful evidence of a functional relation exists between the independent and the dependent variable. The extent to which one has confidence in the assertion of a functional relation rests on numerous factors, some of the most important of which are the accuracy and sensitivity of the measurement system, the degree of control the experimenter maintained over all relevant variables, the duration of experimental phases, the stability of responding within each phase, and the speed, magnitude, and consistency of behavior change between conditions. If each of these

---

[14]Replication also refers to the repeating of experiments to determine the reliability of functional relations found in previous experiments and the extent to which those findings can be extended to other subjects, settings, and/or behaviors (i.e., generality or external validity). The replication of experiments is examined in Chapter 10.

considerations is satisfied by the experimental design and is supported by the data as displayed within the design, then replication of effect becomes perhaps the most critical factor in claiming a functional relation.

An independent variable can be manipulated in an effort to replicate an effect many times within an experiment. The number of replications required to demonstrate a functional relation convincingly is related to many considerations, including all of those just enumerated, and to the existence of other similar experiments that have produced the same effects.

 Summary

Introduction

1. Measurement can show whether and when behavior changes, but measurement alone cannot reveal how the change has come about.

2. Knowledge of specific functional relations between behavior and environment is necessary if a systematic and useful technology of behavior change is to develop.

3. An experimental analysis must be performed to determine how a given behavior functions in relation to specific environmental events.

Concepts and Assumptions Underlying the Analysis of Behavior

4. The overall goal of science is to achieve an understanding of the phenomena under study—socially important behaviors, in the case of applied behavior analysis.

5. Science produces understanding at three levels: description, prediction, and control.

6. Descriptive research yields a collection of facts about the observed events—facts that can be quantified and classified.

7. A correlation exists when two events systematically covary with one another. Predictions can be made about the probability that one event will occur based on the occurrence of the other event.

8. The greatest potential benefits of science are derived from the third, and highest, level of scientific understanding, which comes from establishing experimental control.

9. Experimental control is achieved when a predictable change in behavior (the dependent variable) can be reliably produced by the systematic manipulation of some aspect of the person's environment (the independent variable).

10. A functional analysis does not eliminate the possibility that the behavior under investigation is also a function of other variables.

11. An experiment that shows convincingly that changes in behavior are a function of the independent variable and not the result of uncontrolled or unknown variables has internal validity.

12. External validity refers to the degree to which a study's results are generalizable to other subjects, settings, and/or behaviors.

13. Confounding variables exert unknown or uncontrolled influences on the dependent variable.

14. Because behavior is an individual phenomenon, the experimental strategy of behavior analysis is based on within-subject (or single-subject) methods of analysis.

15. Because behavior is a continuous phenomenon that occurs in and changes through time, the repeated measurement of behavior is a hallmark of applied behavior analysis.

16. The assumption of determinism guides the methodology of behavior analysis.

17. Experimental methods in behavior analysis are based on the assumption that variability is extrinsic to the organism; that is, variability is imposed by environmental variables and is not an inherent trait of the organism.

18. Instead of masking variability by averaging the performance of many subjects, behavior analysts attempt to isolate and experimentally manipulate the environmental factors responsible for the variability.

Components of Experiments in Applied Behavior Analysis

19. The experimental question is a statement of what the researcher seeks to learn by conducting the experiment and should guide and be reflected in all aspects of the experiment's design.

20. Experiments in applied behavior analysis are most often referred to as *single-subject* (or *single-case*) research designs because the experimental logic or reasoning for analyzing behavior change often employs the subject as her own control.

21. The dependent variable in an applied behavior analysis experiment is a measurable dimensional quantity of the target behavior.

22. Three major reasons behavior analysts use multiple-response measures (dependent variables) in some studies are (a) to provide additional data paths that serve as controls for evaluating and replicating the effects of an independent variable that is sequentially applied to each behavior, (b) to assess the generality of treatment effects to behaviors other than the response class to which the independent variable was applied, and (c) to determine whether changes in the behavior of a person other than the subject occur during the course of an experiment and

whether such changes might in turn explain observed changes in the subject's behavior.

23. In addition to precise manipulation of the independent variable, the behavior analyst must hold constant all other aspects of the experimental setting—extraneous variables—to prevent unplanned environmental variation.

24. When unplanned events or variations occur in the experimental setting, the behavior analyst must either wait out their effects or incorporate them into the design of the experiment.

25. Observation and measurement procedures must be conducted in a standardized manner throughout an experiment.

26. Because behavior is a continuous and dynamic phenomenon, ongoing visual inspection of the data during the course of an experiment is necessary to identify changes in level, trend, and/or variability as they develop.

27. Changes in the independent variable are made in an effort to maximize its effect on the target behavior.

28. The term *experimental design* refers to the way the independent variable is manipulated in a study.

29. Although an infinite number of experimental designs are possible as a result of the many ways independent variables can be manipulated and combined, there are only two basic kinds of changes in independent variables: introducing a new condition or reintroducing an old condition.

30. A parametric study compares the differential effects of a range of different values of the independent variable.

31. The fundamental rule of experimental design is to change only one variable at a time.

32. Rather than follow rigid, pro forma experimental designs, the behavior analyst should select experimental tactics suited to the original research questions, while standing ready to "explore relevant variables by manipulating them in an improvised and rapidly changing design" (Skinner, 1966, p. 21).

Steady State Strategy and Baseline Logic

33. Stable, or steady state, responding enables the behavior analyst to employ a powerful form of inductive reasoning, sometimes called baseline logic. Baseline logic entails three elements: prediction, verification, and replication.

34. The most common method for evaluating the effects of a given variable is to impose it on an ongoing measure of behavior obtained in its absence. These preintervention data serve as the baseline by which to determine and evaluate any subsequent changes in behavior.

35. A baseline condition does not necessarily mean the absence of instruction or treatment per se, only the absence of the specific independent variable of experimental interest.

36. In addition to the primary purpose of establishing a baseline as an objective basis for evaluating the effects of the independent variable, three other reasons for baseline data collection are as follows: (a) Systematic observation of the target behavior prior to intervention sometimes yields information about antecedent-behavior-consequent correlations that may be useful in planning an effective intervention; (b) baseline data can provide valuable guidance in setting initial criteria for reinforcement; and (c) sometimes baseline data reveal that the behavior targeted for change does not warrant intervention.

37. Four types of baseline data patterns are stable, ascending, descending, and variable.

38. The independent variable should be introduced when stable baseline responding has been achieved.

39. The independent variable should not be introduced if either an ascending or descending baseline indicates improving performance.

40. The independent variable should be introduced if either an ascending or descending baseline indicates deteriorating performance.

41. The independent variable should not be imposed on a highly variable, unstable baseline.

42. Prediction of future behavior under relatively constant environmental conditions can be made on the basis of repeated measures of behavior showing little or no variation.

43. In general, given stable responding, the more data points there are and the longer the time period in which they were obtained, the more accurate the prediction will likely be.

44. Practice effects refer to improvements in performance resulting from opportunities to emit the behavior that must be provided to obtain repeated measures.

45. Extended baseline measurement is not necessary for behaviors that have no logical opportunity to occur.

46. The inductive reasoning called affirmation of the consequent lies at the heart of baseline logic.

47. Although the logic of affirming the consequent is not completely sound (some other event may have caused the change in behavior), an effective experimental design confirms several if-A-then-B possibilities, thereby eliminating certain other factors as responsible for the observed changes in behavior.

48. Verification of prediction is accomplished by demonstrating that the prior level of baseline responding would have remained unchanged if the independent variable had not been introduced.

49. Replication within an experiment means reproducing a previously observed behavior change by reintroducing the independent variable. Replication within an experiment reduces the probability that a variable other than the independent variable was responsible for the behavior change and demonstrates the reliability of the behavior change.

CHAPTER 8

Reversal and Alternating Treatments Designs

Key Terms

A-B-A design
A-B-A-B design
alternating treatments design
B-A-B design
DRI/DRA reversal technique

DRO reversal technique
irreversibility
multielement design
multiple treatment interference
multiple treatment reversal design

(NCR) reversal technique
reversal design
sequence effects
withdrawal design

Behavior Analyst Certification Board® BCBA® & BCABA® Behavior Analyst Task List©, Third Edition

Content Area 5: Experimental Evaluation of Interventions	
5-1	Systematically manipulate independent variables to analyze their effects on treatment.
(a)	Use withdrawal designs.
(b)	Use reversal designs.
(c)	Use alternating treatments (i.e., multielement, simultaneous treatment, multiple or concurrent schedule) designs.
5-2	Identify and address practical and ethical considerations in using various experimental designs.

This chapter describes the reversal and alternating treatments designs, two types of experimental analysis tactics widely used by applied behavior analysts. In a reversal design, the effects of introducing, withdrawing (or "reversing" the focus of), and reintroducing an independent variable are observed on the target behavior. In an alternating treatments analysis, two or more experimental conditions are rapidly alternated, and the differential effects on behavior are noted. We explain how each design incorporates the three elements of steady state strategy—prediction, verification, and replication—and present representative examples illustrating the major variations of each. Considerations for selecting and using reversal and alternating treatments designs are also presented.

Reversal Design

An experiment using a **reversal design** entails repeated measures of behavior in a given setting that requires at least three consecutive phases: (a) an initial baseline phase in which the independent variable is absent, (b) an intervention phase during which the independent variable is introduced and remains in contact with the behavior, and (c) a return to baseline conditions accomplished by withdrawal of the independent variable. In the widely used notation system for describing experimental designs in applied behavior analysis, the capital letters *A* and *B* denote the first and second conditions, respectively, that are introduced in a study. Typically baseline (A) data are collected until steady state responding is achieved. Next, an intervention (B) condition is applied that signifies the presence of a treatment—the independent variable. An experiment entailing one reversal is described as an **A-B-A design.** Although studies using an A-B-A design are reported in the literature (e.g., Christle & Schuster, 2003; Geller, Paterson, & Talbott, 1982; Jacobson, Bushell, & Risley, 1969; Stitzer, Bigelow, Liebson, & Hawthorne, 1982), an **A-B-A-B design** is preferred because reintroducing the B condition enables the replication of treatment effects, which strengthens the demonstration of experimental control (see Figure 8.1).[1]

The A-B-A-B reversal is the most straightforward and generally most powerful within-subject design for demonstrating a functional relation between an environmental manipulation and a behavior. When a functional relation is revealed with a reversal design, the data show how the behavior works.

> As explanations go, the one offered by the reversal design was not at all a bad one. In answer to the question, "How does this response work?" we could point out demonstrably that it worked like so [e.g., see Figure 8.1]. Of course, it might also work in other ways; but, we would wait until we had seen the appropriate graphs before agreeing to any other way. (Baer, 1975, p. 19)

Baer's point must not be overlooked: Showing that a behavior works in a predictable and reliable way in the presence and absence of a given variable provides only one answer to the question, How does this behavior work? There may be (and quite likely are) other controlling variables for the targeted response class. Whether additional experimentation is needed to explore those other possibilities depends on the social and scientific importance of obtaining a more complete analysis.

Operation and Logic of the Reversal Design

Risley (2005) described the rationale and operation of the reversal design as follows:

> The reversal or ABAB design that Wolf reinvented from Claude Bernard's early examples in experimental medicine entailed establishing a baseline of repeated quantified observations sufficient to see a trend and forecast that trend into the near future (A); to then alter conditions and see if the repeated observations become different than they were forecast to be (B); to then change back and see if the repeated observations return to confirm the original forecast (A); and finally, to reintroduce the altered conditions and see if the repeated observations again become different than forecast (B). (pp. 280–281)[2]

Because the reversal design was used in Chapter 7 to illustrate baseline logic, a brief review here of the roles of prediction, verification, and replication in the reversal design will suffice. Figure 8.2 shows the same data from Figure 8.1 with the addition of the open data points representing predicted measures of behavior if conditions in the previous phase had remained unchanged. After a stable pattern of responding, or a countertherapeutic trend, is obtained during Baseline 1, the independent variable is

---

[1] Some authors use the term ***withdrawal design*** to describe experiments based on an A-B-A-B analysis and reserve the term *reversal design* for studies in which the behavioral focus of the treatment variable is reversed (or switched to another behavior), as in the DRO and DRI/DRA reversal techniques described later in this chapter (e.g., Leitenberg, 1973; Poling, Method, & LeSage, 1995). However, *reversal design,* as the term is used most often in the behavior analysis literature, encompasses both withdrawals and reversals of the independent variable, signifying the researcher's attempt to demonstrate "behavioral reversibility" (Baer, Wolf, & Risley, 1968; Thompson & Iwata, 2005). Also, *withdrawal design* is sometimes used to describe an experiment in which the treatment variable(s) are sequentially or partially withdrawn after their effects have been analyzed in an effort to promote maintenance of the target behavior (Rusch & Kazdin, 1981).

[2] Risley (1997, 2005) credits Montrose Wolf with designing the first experiments using the reversal and multiple baseline designs. "The research methods that Wolf pioneered in these studies were groundbreaking. That methodology came to define applied behavior analysis" (pp. 280–281).

Figure 8.1 Graphic prototype of the A-B-A-B reversal design.

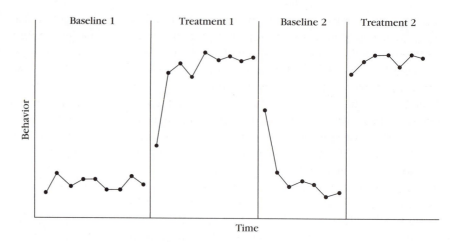

introduced. In our hypothetical experiment the measures obtained during Treatment 1, when compared with those from Baseline 1 and with the measures *predicted* by Baseline 1, show that behavior change occurred and that the change in behavior coincided with the intervention. After steady state responding is attained in Treatment 1, the independent variable is withdrawn and baseline conditions are reestablished. If the level of responding in Baseline 2 is the same as or closely approximates the measures obtained during Baseline 1, *verification* of the prediction made for Baseline 1 data is obtained. Stated otherwise, had the intervention not been introduced and had the initial baseline condition remained in effect, the predicted data path would have appeared as shown in Baseline 2. When withdrawal of the independent variable results in a reversal of the behavior change associated with its introduction, a strong case builds that the intervention is responsible for the observed behavior change. If reintroduction of the independent variable in Treatment 2 reproduces the behavior change observed during Treatment 1, *replication* of effect has been achieved, and a functional relation has been demonstrated. Again stated in other terms, had the intervention continued and had the second baseline condition not been

introduced, the predicted data path of the treatment would have appeared as shown in Treatment 2.

Romaniuk and colleagues (2002) provided an excellent example of the A-B-A-B design. Three students with developmental disabilities who frequently displayed problem behaviors (e.g., hitting, biting, whining, crying, getting out of seat, inappropriate gestures, noises, and comments) when given academic tasks participated in the study. Prior to the experiment a functional analysis (see Chapter 24) had shown that each student's problem behaviors were maintained by escape from working on the task (i.e., problem behavior occurred most often when followed by being allowed to take a break from the task). The researchers wanted to determine whether providing students with a choice of which task to work on would reduce the frequency of their problem behavior, even though problem behavior, when it occurred, would still result in a break. The experiment consisted of two conditions: no choice (A) and choice (B). The same set of teacher-nominated tasks was used in both conditions.

Each session during the no-choice condition began with the experimenter providing the student with a task and saying, "This is the assignment you will be working on today" or "It's time to work on _____" (p. 353). Dur-

Figure 8.2 Illustration of A-B-A-B reversal design. Open data points represent data predicted if conditions from previous phase remained in effect. Data collected during Baseline 2 (within shaded box) verify the prediction from Baseline 1. Treatment 2 data (cross-hatched shading) replicate the experimental effect.

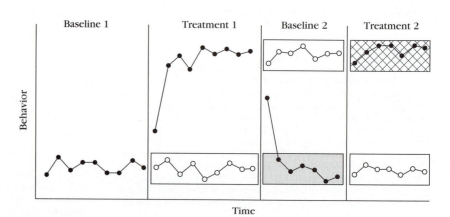

ing the choice condition (B), the experimenter placed the materials for four to six tasks on the table before the student and said, "Which assignment would you like to work on today?" (p. 353). The student was also told that he or she could switch tasks at any time during the session by requesting to do so. Occurrences of problem behavior in both conditions resulted in the experimenter stating, "You can take a break now" and giving a 10-second break.

Figure 8.3 shows the results of the experiment. The data reveal a clear functional relation between the opportunity to choose which tasks to work on and reduced occurrence of problem behavior by all three students. The percentage of session time in which each student exhibited problem behavior (reported as a total duration measure obtained by recording the second of onset and offset as shown by the VCR timer) decreased sharply from the no-choice (baseline) levels when the choice condition was implemented, returned (reversed) to baseline levels when choice was withdrawn, and decreased again when choice was reinstated. The A-B-A-B design enabled Romaniuk and colleagues to conduct a straightforward, un-

ambiguous demonstration that significant reductions in problem behavior exhibited by each student were a function of being given a choice of tasks.

In the 1960s and early 1970s applied behavior analysts relied almost exclusively on the A-B-A-B reversal design. The straightforward A-B-A-B design played such a dominant role in the early years of applied behavior analysis that it came to symbolize the field (Baer, 1975). This was no doubt due, at least in part, to the reversal design's ability to expose variables for what they are—strong and reliable or weak and unstable. Another reason for the reversal design's dominance may have been that few alternative analytic tactics were available at that time that effectively combined the intrasubject experimental elements of prediction, verification, and replication. Although the reversal design is just one of many experimental designs available to applied behavior analysts today, the simple, unadorned A-B-A-B design continues to play a major role in the behavior analysis literature (e.g., Anderson & Long, 2002 [see Figure 21.2]; Ashbaugh & Peck, 1998 [see Figure 15.7]; Cowdery, Iwata, & Pace, 1990 [see

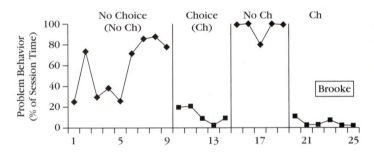

Figure 8.3   An A-B-A-B reversal design.

From "The Influence of Activity Choice on Problems Behaviors Maintained by Escape versus Attention" by C. Romaniuk, R. Miltenberger, C. Conyers, N. Jenner, M. Jurgens, and C. Ringenberg, 2002, *Journal of Applied Behavior Analysis, 35*, p. 357. Copyright 2002 by the Society for the Experimental Analysis of Behavior, Inc. Reprinted by permission.

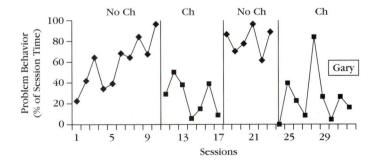

Figure 22.7]; Deaver, Miltenberger, & Stricker, 2001 [see Figure 21.3]; Gardner, Heward, & Grossi, 1994; Levondoski & Cartledge, 2000; Lindberg, Iwata, Kahng, & DeLeon, 1999 [see Figure 22.7]; Mazaleski, Iwata, Rodgers, Vollmer, & Zarcone, 1994; Taylor & Alber, 2003; Umbreit, Lane, & Dejud, 2004).

Variations of the A-B-A-B Design

Many applied behavior analysis studies use variations or extensions of the A-B-A-B design.

Repeated Reversals

Perhaps the most obvious variation of the A-B-A-B reversal design is a simple extension in which the independent variable is withdrawn and reintroduced a second time; A-B-A-B-A-B (see the graph for Maggie in Figure 8.3). Each additional presentation and withdrawal that reproduces the previously observed effects on behavior increases the likelihood that the behavior changes are the result of manipulating the independent variable. All other things being equal, an experiment that incorporates multiple reversals presents a more convincing and compelling demonstration of a functional relation than does an experiment with one reversal (e.g., Fisher, Lindauer, Alterson, & Thompson, 1998 [Figure 6.2]; Steege et al., 1990). That said, it is also possible to reach a point of redundancy beyond which the findings of a given analysis are no longer enhanced significantly by additional reversals.

B-A-B Design

The **B-A-B design** begins with the application of the independent variable: the treatment. After stable responding has been achieved during the initial treatment phase (B), the independent variable is withdrawn. If the behavior worsens in the absence of the independent variable (the A condition), the treatment variable is reintroduced in an attempt to recapture the level of responding obtained during the first treatment phase, which would verify the prediction based on the data path obtained during the initial treatment phase.

Compared to the A-B-A design, the B-A-B design is preferable from an applied sense in that the study ends with the treatment variable in effect. However, in terms of demonstrating a functional relation between the independent variable and dependent variable, the B-A-B design is the weaker of the two because it does not enable an assessment of the effects of the independent variable on the preintervention level of responding. The nonintervention (A) condition in a B-A-B design cannot verify a prediction of a previous nonexistent baseline. This weakness can be remedied by withdrawing and then reintroducing the independent variable, as in a B-A-B-A-B design (e.g., Dixon, Benedict, & Larson, 2001 [see Figure 22.1]).

Because the B-A-B design provides no data to determine whether the measures of behavior taken during the A condition represent preintervention performance, sequence effects cannot be ruled out: The level of behavior observed during the A condition may have been influenced by the fact that the treatment condition preceded it. Nevertheless, there are exigent situations in which initial baseline data cannot be collected. For instance, the B-A-B design may be appropriate with target behaviors that result in physical harm or danger to the participant or to others. In such instances, withholding a possibly effective treatment until a stable pattern of baseline responding can be obtained may present ethical problems. For example, Murphy, Ruprecht, Baggio, and Nunes (1979) used a B-A-B design to evaluate the effectiveness of mild punishment combined with reinforcement on the number of self-choking responses by a 24-year-old man with profound mental retardation. After the treatment was in effect for 24 sessions, it was withdrawn for three sessions, during which an immediate and large increase in self-choking was recorded (see Figure 8.4). Reintroduction of the treatment package reproduced behavior levels noted during the first treatment phase. The average number of self-chokes during each phase of the B-A-B study was 22, 265, and 24, respectively.

Despite the impressive reduction of behavior, the results of Murphy and colleagues' study using a B-A-B design may have been enhanced by gathering and reporting objectively measured data on the level of behavior prior to the first intervention. Presumably, Murphy and colleagues chose not to collect an initial baseline for ethical and practical reasons. They reported anecdotally that self-chokes averaged 434 per day immediately prior to their intervention when school staff had used a different procedure to reduce the self-injurious behavior. This anecdotal information increased the believability of the functional relation suggested by the experimental data from the B-A-B design.

At least two other situations exist in which a B-A-B design might be warranted instead of the more conventional A-B-A-B design. These include (a) when a treatment is already in place (e.g., Marholin, Touchette, & Stuart, 1979; Pace & Troyer, 2000) and (b) when the behavior analyst has limited time in which to demonstrate practical and socially significant results. For instance, Robinson, Newby, and Ganzell (1981) were asked to develop a behavior management system for a class of 18 hyperactive boys with the stipulation that the program's effectiveness be demonstrated within 4 weeks. Given "the stipulation of success in 4 weeks, a B-A-B design was used" (pp. 310–311).

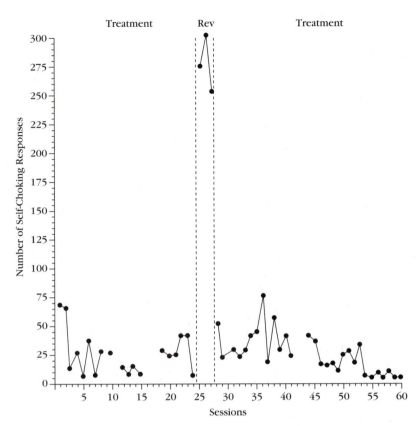

Figure 8.4 A B-A-B reversal design.

From "The Use of Mild Punishment in Combination with Reinforcement of Alternate Behaviors to Reduce the Self-Injurious Behavior of a Profoundly Retarded Individual" by R. J. Murphy, M. J. Ruprecht, P. Baggio, and D. L. Nunes, 1979, *AAESPH Review, 4,* p. 191. Copyright 1979 by the *AAESPH Review.* Reprinted by permission.

Multiple Treatment Reversal Designs

Experiments that use the reversal design to compare the effects of two or more experimental conditions to baseline and/or to one another are said to use a **multiple treatment reversal design.** The letters *C, D,* and so on, denote additional conditions, as in the A-B-C-A-C-B-C design used by Falcomata, Roane, Hovanetz, Kettering, and Keeney (2004); the A-B-A-B-C-B-C design used by Freeland and Noell (1999); the A-B-C-B-C-B-C design used by Lerman, Kelley, Vorndran, Kuhn, and LaRue (2002); the A-B-A-C-A-D-A-C-A-D design used by Weeks and Gaylord-Ross (1981); and the A-B-A-B-B+C-B-B+C design of Jason and Liotta (1982). As a whole, these designs are considered variations of the reversal design because they embody the experimental method and logic of the reversal tactic: Responding in each phase provides baseline (or control condition) data for the subsequent phase (prediction), independent variables are withdrawn in an attempt to reproduce levels of behavior observed in a previous condition (verification), and each independent variable that contributes fully to the analysis is introduced at least twice (replication). Independent variables can be introduced, withdrawn, changed in value, combined, and otherwise manipulated to produce an endless variety of experimental designs.

For example, Kennedy and Souza (1995) used an A-B-C-B-C-A-C-A-C design to analyze and compare the

effects of two kinds of competing sources of stimulation on eye poking by a 19-year-old student with profound disabilities. Geoff had a 12-year history of poking his forefinger into his eyes during periods of inactivity, such as after lunch or while waiting for the bus. The two treatment conditions were music (B) and a video game (C). During the music condition, Geoff was given a Sony Walkman radio with headphones. The radio was tuned to a station that his teacher and family thought he preferred. Geoff had continuous access to the music during this condition, and he could remove the headphones at any time. During the video game condition, Geoff was given a small handheld video game on which he could observe a variety of visual patterns and images on the screen with no sound. As with the music condition, Geoff had continuous access to the video game and could discontinue using it at any time.

Figure 8.5 shows the results of the study. Following an initial baseline phase (A) in which Geoff averaged 4 eye pokes per hour, the music condition (B) was introduced and eye pokes decreased to a mean of 2.8 per hour. The video game (C) was implemented next, and eye pokes decreased further to 1.1 per hour. Measures obtained during the next two phases—a reintroduction of music (B) followed by a second phase of the video game (C)—replicated previous levels of responding under each condition. This B-C-B-C portion of the experiment

Figure 8.5 Example of multiple-treatment reversal design (A-B-C-B-C-A-C-A-C).

From "Functional Analysis and Treatment of Eye Poking" by C. H. Kennedy and G. Souza, 1995, *Journal of Applied Behavior Analysis, 28,* p. 33. Copyright 1995 by the Society for the Experimental Analysis of Behavior, Inc. Reprinted by permission.

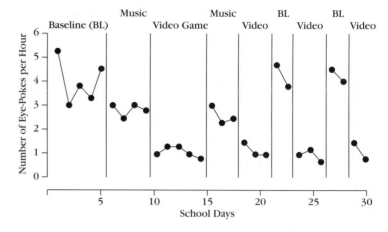

revealed a functional relation between video game condition and lower frequency of eye pokes compared to music. The final five phases of the experiment (C-A-C-A-C) provided an experimental comparison of the video game and baseline (no-treatment) condition.

In most instances, extended designs involving multiple independent variables are not preplanned. Instead of following a predetermined, rigid structure that dictates when and how experimental manipulations must be made, the applied behavior analyst makes design decisions based on ongoing assessments of the data.

> In this sense, a single experiment may be viewed as a number of successive designs that are collectively necessary to clarify relations between independent and dependent variables. Thus, some design decisions might be made in response to the data unfolding as the investigation progresses. This sense of design encourages the experimenter to pursue in more dynamic fashion the solutions to problems of experimental control immediately upon their emergence. (Johnston & Pennypacker, 1980, pp. 250–251)

Students of applied behavior analysis should not interpret this description of experimental design as a recommendation for a completely free-form approach to the manipulation of independent variables. The researcher must always pay close attention to the rule of changing only one variable at a time and must understand the opportunities for legitimate comparisons and the limitations that a given sequence of manipulations places on the conclusions that can be drawn from the results.

Experiments that use the reversal design to compare two or more treatments are vulnerable to confounding by sequence effects. **Sequence effects** are the effects on a subject's behavior in a given condition that are the result of the subject's experience with a prior condition. For example, caution must be used in interpreting the results from the A-B-C-B-C design that results from the following fairly common sequence of events in practice: After baseline (A), an initial treatment (B) is implemented

and little or no behavioral improvements are noted. A second treatment (C) is then tried, and the behavior improves. A reversal is then conducted by reintroducing the first treatment (B), followed by reinstatement of the second treatment (C) (e.g., Foxx & Shapiro, 1978 [Figure 15.3]). In this case, we can only speak knowingly about the effects of C when it follows B. Recapturing the original baseline levels of responding before introducing the second treatment condition (i.e., an A-B-A-C-A-C sequence) reduces the threat of sequence effects (or helps to expose them for what they are).

An A-B-A-B-C-B-C design, for instance, enables direct comparisons of B to A and C to B, but not of C to A. An experimental design consisting of A-B-A-B-B+C-B-B+C (e.g., Jason & Liotta, 1982) permits an evaluation of the additive or interactive effects of B+C, but does not reveal the independent contribution of C. And in both of these examples, it impossible to determine what effects, if any, C may have had on the behavior if it had been implemented prior to B. Manipulating each condition so that it precedes and follows every other condition in the experiment (e.g., A-B-A-B-C-B-C-A-C-A-C) is the only way to know for sure. However, manipulating multiple conditions requires a large amount of time and resources, and such extended designs become more susceptible to confounding by maturation and other historical variables not controlled by the experimenter.

NCR Reversal Technique

With interventions based on positive reinforcement, it can be hypothesized that observed changes in behavior are the result of the participant's feeling better about himself because of the improved environment created by the reinforcement, not because a specific response class has been immediately followed by contingent reinforcement. This hypothesis is most often advanced when interventions consisting of social reinforcement are involved. For example, a person may claim that it doesn't matter *how* the teacher's praise and attention were given; the student's behavior improved because the praise and attention created a warm and supporting environment. If, however, the behavioral improvements observed during a contingent reinforcement condition are lost during a condition when equal amounts of the same consequence are delivered independent of the occurrence of the target behavior, a functional relation between the reinforcement contingency and behavior change is demonstrated. In other words, such an experimental control technique can show that behavior change is the result of *contingent* reinforcement, not simply the presentation of or contact with the stimulus event (Thompson & Iwata, 2005).

A study by Baer and Wolf (1970a) on the effects of teachers' social reinforcement on the cooperative play of a preschool child provides an excellent example of the **NCR reversal technique** (Figure 8.6). The authors described the use and purpose of the design as follows:

> [The teachers first collected] baselines of cooperative and other related behaviors of the child, and of their own interaction with the child. Ten days of observation indicated that the child spent about 50% of each day in proximity with other children (meaning within 3 feet of them indoors, or 6 feet outdoors). Despite this frequent proximity, however, the child spent only about 2% of her day in cooperative play with these children. The teachers, it was found, interacted with this girl about 20% of the

day, not all of it pleasant. The teachers, therefore, set up a period of intense social reinforcement, offered not for cooperative play but free of any response requirement at all: the teachers took turns standing near the girl, attending closely to her activities, offering her materials, and smiling and laughing with her in a happy and admiring manner. The results of 7 days of this noncontingent extravagance of social reinforcement were straightforward: the child's cooperative play changed not at all, despite the fact that the other children of the group were greatly attracted to the scene, offering the child nearly double the chance to interact with them cooperatively. These 7 days having produced no useful change, the teachers then began their planned reinforcement of cooperative behavior. . . . Contingent social reinforcement, used in amounts less than half that given during the noncontingent period, increased the child's cooperative play from its usual 2% to a high of 40% in the course of 12 days of reinforcement. At that point, in the interests of certainty, the teachers discontinued contingent reinforcement in favor of noncontingent. In the course of 4 days, they lost virtually all of the cooperative behavior they had gained during the reinforcement period of the study, the child showing about a 5% average of cooperative play over that period of time. Naturally, the study concluded with a return to the contingent use of social reinforcement, a recovery of desirable levels of cooperative play, and a gradual reduction of the teacher's role in maintaining that behavior. (pp. 14–15)

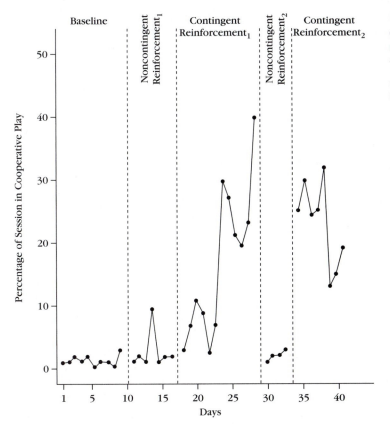

Figure 8.6   Reversal design using noncontingent reinforcement (NCR) as a control technique.

From "Recent Examples of Behavior Modification in Pre-School Settings" by D. M. Baer and M. M. Wolf in *Behavior Modification in Clinical Psychology,* pp. 14–15, edited by C. Neuringer and J. L. Michael, 1970, Upper Saddle River, NJ: Prentice Hall. Copyright 1970 by Prentice Hall. Adapted by permission.

Using NCR as a control conditions to demonstrate a functional relation is advantageous when it is not possible or appropriate to eliminate completely the event or activity used as a contingent reinforcement. For example, Lattal (1969) employed NCR as a control condition to "reverse" the effects of swimming as reinforcement for tooth brushing by children in a summer camp. In the contingent reinforcement condition, the campers could go swimming only if they had brushed their teeth; in the NCR condition, swimming was available whether or not tooth brushing occurred. The campers brushed their teeth more often in the contingent reinforcement condition.

The usual procedure is to deliver NCR on a fixed or variable time schedule independent of the subject's behavior. A potential weakness of the NCR control procedure becomes apparent when a high rate of the desired behavior has been produced during the preceding contingent reinforcement phase. It is probable in such situations that at least some instances of NCR, delivered according to a predetermined time schedule, will follow occurrences of the target behavior closely in time, and thereby function as adventitious, or "accidental reinforcement" (Thompson & Iwata, 2005). In fact, an intermittent schedule of reinforcement might be created inadvertently that results in even higher levels of performance than those obtained under contingent reinforcement. (Intermittent schedules of reinforcement and their effects are described in Chapter 13). In such cases the investigator might consider using one of the two control techniques described next, both of which involve "reversing" the behavioral focus of the contingency.[3]

DRO Reversal Technique

One way to ensure that reinforcement will not immediately follow the target behavior is to deliver reinforcement immediately following the subject's performance of *any behavior other than the target behavior*. With a **DRO reversal technique**, the control condition consists of delivering the event suspected of functioning as reinforcement following the emission of any behavior other than the target behavior (e.g., Baer, Peterson, & Sherman, 1967; Osbourne, 1969; Poulson, 1983). For example, Reynolds and Risley (1968) used contingent teacher attention to increase the frequency of talking in a 4-year-old girl enrolled in a preschool program for disadvan-

taged children. After a period of teacher attention contingent on verbalization, in which the girl's talking increased from a baseline average of 11% of the intervals observed to 75%, a DRO condition was implemented during which the teachers attended to the girl for any behavior except talking. During the 6 days of DRO, the girl's verbalization dropped to 6%. Teacher attention was then delivered contingent on talking, and the girl's verbalization "immediately increased to an average of 51%" (p. 259).

DRI/DRA Reversal Technique

During the control condition in a **DRI/DRA reversal technique**, occurrences of a specified behavior that is either incompatible with the target behavior (i.e., the two behaviors cannot possibly be emitted at the same time) or an alternative to the target behavior are immediately followed by the same consequence previously delivered as contingent reinforcement for the target behavior. Goetz and Baer's (1973) investigation of the effects of teacher praise on preschool children's creative play with building blocks illustrates the use of a DRI control condition. Figure 8.7 shows the number of different block forms (e.g., arch, tower, roof, ramp) constructed by the three children who participated in the study. During baseline (data points indicated by the letter *N*), "the teacher sat by the child as she built with the blocks, watching closely but quietly, displaying neither criticism nor enthusiasm about any particular use of the blocks" (p. 212). During the next phase (the *D* data points), "the teacher remarked with interest, enthusiasm, and delight every time that the child placed and/or rearranged the blocks so as to create a form that had not appeared previously in that session's construction(s). . . . 'Oh, that's very nice—that's different!'" (p. 212). Then, after increasing form diversity was clearly established, instead of merely withdrawing verbal praise and returning to the initial baseline condition, the teacher provided descriptive praise only when the children had constructed the same forms (the *S* data points). "Thus, for the next two to four sessions, the teacher continued to display interest, enthusiasm, and delight, but only at those times when the child placed and/or rearranged a block so as to create a repetition of a form already apparent in that session's construction(s). . . . Thus, no first usage of a form in a session was reinforced, but every second usage of that form and every usage thereafter within the session was. . . . 'How nice—another arch!'" (p. 212). The final phase of the experiment entailed a return to descriptive praise for different forms. Results show that the form diversity of children's block building was a function of teacher praise and comments. The DRI reversal tactic allowed Goetz and Baer to determine that it was not just the delivery of teacher praise and comment that

---

[3]Strictly speaking, using NCR as an experimental control technique to demonstrate that the contingent application of reinforcement is requisite to its effectiveness is not a separate variation of the A-B-A reversal design. Technically, the NCR reversal technique, as well as the DRO and DRI/DRA reversal techniques described next, is a multiple treatment design. For example, the Baer and Wolf (1970a) study of social reinforcement shown in Figure 8.6 used an A-B-C-B-C design, with B representing the NCR conditions and C representing the contingent reinforcement conditions.

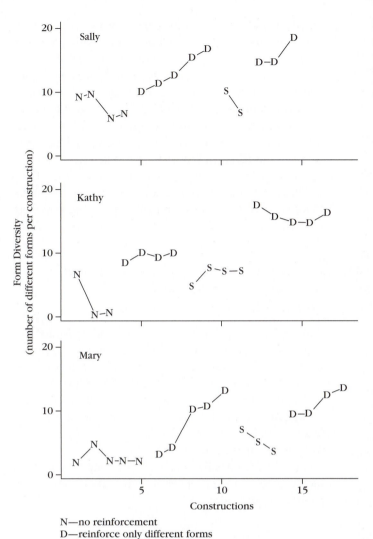

Figure 8.7   Reversal design using a DRI control technique.

From "Social Control of Form Diversity and the Emergence of New Forms in Children's Blockbuilding" by E. M. Goetz and D. M. Baer, 1973, *Journal of Applied Behavior Analysis, 6*, p. 213. Copyright 1973 by the Society for the Experimental Analysis of Behavior, Inc. Reprinted by permission.

N—no reinforcement
D—reinforce only different forms
S—reinforce only same forms

resulted in more creative block building by the children; the praise and attention had to be contingent on different forms to produce increasing form diversity.[4]

Considering the Appropriateness of the Reversal Design

The primary advantage of the reversal design is its ability to provide a clear demonstration of the existence (or absence) of a functional relation between the independent and dependent variables. An investigator who reliably turns the target behavior on and off by presenting and withdrawing a specific variable makes a clear and convincing demonstration of experimental control. In addition, the reversal design enables quantification of the amount of behavior change over the preintervention level of responding. And the return to baseline provides information on the need to program for maintenance. Furthermore, a complete A-B-A-B design ends with the treatment condition in place.[5]

In spite of its strengths as a tool for analysis, the reversal design entails some potential scientific and social disadvantages that should be considered prior to its use. The considerations are of two types: irreversibility, which affects the scientific utility of the design; and the social, educational, and ethical concerns related to withdrawing a seemingly effective intervention.

---

[4]The extent to which the increased diversity of the children's block building can be attributed to the attention and praise ("That's nice") or the descriptive feedback (". . . that's different") in the teacher's comments cannot be determined from this study because social attention and descriptive feedback were delivered as a package.

[5]Additional manipulations in the form of the partial or sequential withdrawal of intervention components are made when it is necessary or desirable for the behavior to continue at its improved level in the absence of the complete intervention (cf., Rusch & Kazdin, 1981).

Irreversibility: A Scientific Consideration

A reversal design is not appropriate in evaluating the effects of a treatment variable that, by its very nature, cannot be withdrawn once it has been presented. Although independent variables involving reinforcement and punishment contingencies can be manipulated with some certainty—the experimenter either presents or withholds the contingency—an independent variable such as providing information or modeling, once presented, cannot simply be removed. For example, a reversal design would not be an effective element of an experiment investigating the effects of attending an in-service training workshop for teachers during which participants observed a master teacher use contingent praise and attention with students. After the participants have listened to the rationale for using contingent praise and attention and observed the master teacher model it, the exposure provided by that experience could not be withdrawn. Such interventions are said to be irreversible.

Irreversibility of the dependent variable must also be considered in determining whether a reversal would be an effective analytic tactic. Behavioral **irreversibility** means that a level of behavior observed in an earlier phase cannot be reproduced even though the experimental conditions are the same as they were during the earlier phase (Sidman, 1960). Once improved, many target behaviors of interest to the applied behavior analyst remain at their newly enhanced level even when the intervention responsible for the behavior change is removed. From a clinical or educational standpoint, such a state of affairs is desirable: The behavior change is shown to be durable, persisting even in the absence of continued treatment. However, irreversibility is a problem if demonstration of the independent variable's role in the behavior change depends on verification by recapturing baseline levels of responding.

For example, baseline observations might reveal very low, almost nonexistent, rates of talking and social interaction for a young child. An intervention consisting of teacher-delivered social reinforcement for talking and interacting could be implemented, and after some time the girl might talk to and interact with her peers at a frequency and in a manner similar to that of her classmates. The independent variable, teacher-delivered reinforcement, could be terminated in an effort to recapture baseline rates of talking and interacting. But the girl might continue to talk to and interact with her classmates even though the intervention, which may have been responsible for the initial change in her behavior, is withdrawn. In this case a source of reinforcement uncontrolled by the experimenter—the girl's classmates talking to and playing with her as a consequence of her increased talking and interacting with them—could maintain high rates of behavior after the teacher-delivered reinforcement is no longer pro-

vided. In such instances of irreversibility, an A-B-A-B design would fail to reveal a functional relation between the independent variable and the target behavior.

Nonetheless, one of the major objectives of applied behavior analysis is establishing socially important behavior through experimental treatments so that the behavior will contact natural "communities of reinforcement" to maintain behavioral improvements in the absence of treatment (Baer & Wolf, 1970b). When irreversibility is suspected or apparent, in addition to considering DRO or DRI/DRA conditions as control techniques, investigators can consider other experimental tactics, most notably the multiple baseline designs described in Chapter 9.

Withdrawing an Effective Intervention: A Social, Educational, and Ethical Consideration

Although it can yield an unambiguous demonstration of experimental control, withdrawing a seemingly effective intervention to evaluate its role in behavior change presents a legitimate cause for concern. One must question the appropriateness of any procedure that allows (indeed, seeks) an improved behavior to deteriorate to baseline levels of responding. Various concerns have been voiced over this fundamental feature of the reversal design. Although there is considerable overlap among the concerns, they can be classified as having primarily a social, educational, or ethical basis.

Social Concerns. Applied behavior analysis is, by definition, a social enterprise. Behaviors are selected, defined, observed, measured, and modified by and for people. Sometimes the people involved in an applied behavior analysis—administrators, teachers, parents, and participants—object to the withdrawal of an intervention they associate with desirable behavior change. Even though a reversal may provide the most unqualified picture of the behavior–environment relation under study, it may not be the analytic tactic of choice because key participants do not want the intervention to be withdrawn. When a reversal design offers the best experimental approach scientifically and poses no ethical problems, the behavior analyst may choose to explain the operation and purpose of the tactic to those who do not favor it. But it is unwise to attempt a reversal without the full support of the people involved, especially those who will be responsible for withdrawing the intervention (Tawney & Gast, 1984). Without their cooperation the procedural integrity of the experiment could easily be compromised. For example, people who are against the withdrawal of treatment might sabotage the return to baseline conditions by implementing the

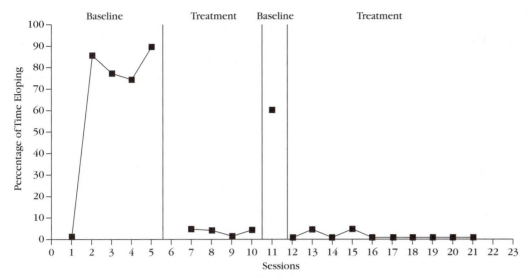

Figure 8.8   Reversal design with a single-session return-to-baseline probe to evaluate and verify effects of treatment for a potentially dangerous behavior.

From "Functional Analysis and Treatment of Elopement for a Child with Attention Deficit Hyperactivity Disorder" by T. Kodak, L. Grow, and J. Northrup, 2004, *Journal of Applied Behavior Analysis, 37,* p. 231. Copyright 2004 by the Society for the Experimental Analysis of Behavior, Inc. Reprinted by permission.

intervention, or at least those parts of it that they consider the most important.

Educational and Clinical Issues.   Educational or clinical issues concerning the reversal design are often raised in terms of instructional time lost during the reversal phases, as well as the possibility that the behavioral improvements observed during intervention may not be recaptured when treatment is resumed after a return to baseline conditions. We agree with Stolz (1978) that "extended reversals are indefensible." If preintervention levels of responding are reached quickly, reversal phases can be quite short in duration. Sometimes only three or four sessions are needed to show that initial baseline rates have been reproduced (e.g., Ashbaugh & Peck, 1998 [Figure 15.7]; Cowdery Iwata, & Pace, 1990 [Figure 22.6]). Two or three brief reversals can provide an extremely convincing demonstration of experimental control. Concern that the improved levels of behavior will not return when the treatment variable is reintroduced, while understandable, has not been supported by empirical evidence. Hundreds of published studies have shown that behavior acquired under a given set of environmental conditions can be reacquired rapidly during subsequent reapplication of those conditions.

Ethical Concerns.   A serious ethical concern must be addressed when the use of a reversal design is considered for evaluating a treatment for self-injurious or dangerous behaviors. With mild self-injurious or aggressive behaviors, short reversal phases consisting of one or two baseline probes can sometimes provide the empirical evidence needed to reveal a functional relation (e.g., Kelley, Jarvie, Middlebrook, McNeer, & Drabman, 1984; Luce, Delquadri, & Hall, 1980; Murphy et al., 1979 [Figure 8.4]). For example, in their study evaluating a treatment for elopement (i.e., running away from supervision) by a child with attention-deficit/hyperactivity disorder, Kodak, Grow, and Northrup (2004) returned to baseline conditions for a single session (see Figure 8.8).

Nonetheless, with some behaviors it may be determined that withdrawing an intervention associated with improvement for even a few one-session probes would be inappropriate for ethical reasons. In such cases experimental designs that do not rely on the reversal tactic must be used.

Alternating Treatments Design

An important and frequently asked question by teachers, therapists, and others who are responsible for changing behavior is, Which of these treatments will be most effective with this student or client? In many situations, the research literature, the analyst's experience, and/or logical extensions of the principles of behavior point to several possible interventions. Determining which of several possible treatments or combination of treatments will produce the greatest improvement in behavior is a primary task for applied behavior analysts. As described earlier, although a multiple treatment reversal design (e.g., A-B-C-B-C) can be used to compare the effects of two or more treatments, such designs have some inherent limitations. Because the different treatments in a multiple treatment reversal design are implemented during separate phases that occur in a particular order, the design is particularly vulnerable to confounding because of sequence effects (e.g., Treatment C may have produced its effect only because it followed Treatment B, not because it was more robust in its own right). A second disadvantage of comparing multiple treatments with the reversal tactic is the extended time required to demonstrate differential effects. Most behaviors targeted for change by teachers and therapists are selected because they need immediate improvement. An experimental design that will quickly reveal the most effective treatment among several possible approaches is important for the applied behavior analyst.

The alternating treatments design provides an experimentally sound and efficient method for comparing the effects of two or more treatments. The term *alternating treatments design,* proposed by Barlow and Hayes (1979), accurately communicates the operation of the design. Other terms used in the applied behavior analysis literature to refer to this analytic tactic include **multielement design** (Ulman & Sulzer-Azaroff, 1975), *multiple schedule design* (Hersen & Barlow, 1976), *concurrent schedule design* (Hersen & Barlow, 1976), and *simultaneous treatment design* (Kazdin & Hartmann, 1978).[6]

Operation and Logic of the Alternating Treatments Design

The **alternating treatments design** is characterized by the rapid alternation of two or more distinct treatments (i.e., independent variables) while their effects on the target behavior (i.e., dependent variable) are measured. In contrast to the reversal design in which experimental manipulations are made after steady state responding is achieved in a given phase of an experiment, the different

interventions in an alternating treatments design are manipulated independent of the level of responding. The design is predicated on the behavioral principle of stimulus discrimination (see Chapter 17). To aid the subject's discrimination of which treatment condition is in effect during a given session, a distinct stimulus (e.g., a sign, verbal instructions, different colored worksheets) is often associated with each treatment.

> The data are plotted separately for each intervention to provide a ready visual representation of the effects of each treatment. Because confounding factors such as time of administration have been neutralized (presumably) by counterbalancing, and because the two treatments are readily discriminable by subjects through instructions or other discriminative stimuli, differences in the individual plots of behavior change corresponding with each treatment should be attributable to the treatment itself, allowing a direct comparison between two (or more) treatments. (Barlow & Hayes, 1979, p. 200)

Figure 8.9 shows a graphic prototype of an alternating treatments design comparing the effects of two treatments, A and B, on some response measure. In an alternating treatments design, the different treatments can be alternated in a variety of ways. For example, the treatments might be (a) alternated across daily sessions, one treatment in effect each day; (b) administered in separate sessions occurring within the same day; or (c) implemented each during a portion of the same session. Counterbalancing the days of the week, times of day, sequence in which the different treatments occur (e.g., first or second each day), persons delivering the different treatments, and so forth, reduces the probability that any observed differences in behavior are the result of variables other than the treatments themselves. For example, assume that Treatments A and B in Figure 8.9 were each administered

---

[6]A design in which two or more treatments are concurrently or simultaneously presented, and in which the subject chooses between treatments, is correctly termed a concurrent schedule or simultaneous treatment design. Some published studies described by their authors as using a simultaneous treatment design have, in fact, employed an alternating treatments design. Barlow and Hayes (1979) could find only one true example of a simultaneous treatment design in the applied literature: a study by Browning (1967) in which three techniques for reducing the bragging of a 10-year-old boy were compared.

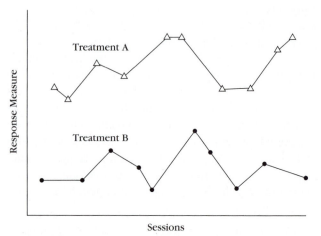

Figure 8.9   Graphic prototype of an alternating treatments design comparing the differential effects of two treatments (A and B).

for a single 30-minute session each day, with the daily sequence of the two treatments determined by a coin flip.

The data points in Figure 8.9 are plotted on the horizontal axis to reflect the actual sequence of treatments each day. Thus, the horizontal axis is labeled *Sessions,* and each consecutive pair of sessions occurred on a single day. Some published reports of experiments using an alternating treatments design in which two or more treatments were presented each day (or session) plot the measures obtained during each treatment above the same point on the horizontal axis, thus implying that the treatments were administered simultaneously. This practice masks the temporal order of events and has the unfortunate consequence of making it difficult for the researcher or reader to discover potential sequence effects.

The three components of steady state strategy—prediction, verification, and replication—are found in the alternating treatments design. However, each component is not readily identified with a separate phase of the design. In an alternating treatments design, each successive data point for a specific treatment plays all three roles: It provides (a) a basis for the *prediction* of future levels of responding under that treatment, (b) potential *verification* of the previous prediction of performance under that treatment, and (c) the opportunity for *replication* of previous effects produced by that treatment.

To see this logic unfold, the reader should place a piece of paper over all the data points in Figure 8.9 except those for the first five sessions of each treatment. The visible portions of the data paths provide the basis for predicting future performance under each respective treatment. Moving the paper to the right reveals the two data points for the next day, each of which provides a degree of verification of the previous predictions. As more data are recorded, the predictions of given levels of responding within each treatment are further strengthened by continued verification (if those additional data conform to the same level and/or trend as their predecessors). Replication occurs each time Treatment A is reinstated and measurement reveals responding similar to previous Treatment A measures and different from those obtained when Treatment B is in effect. Likewise, another mini-replication is achieved each time a reintroduction of Treatment B results in measures similar to previous Treatment B measures and different from Treatment A levels of responding. A consistent sequence of verification and replication is evidence of experimental control and strengthens the investigator's confidence of a functional relation between the two treatments and different levels of responding.

The presence and degree of experimental control in an alternating treatments design is determined by visual inspection of the differences between (or among) the data paths representing the different treatments. Experimental control is defined in this instance as objective, believable evidence that different levels of responding are predictably and reliably produced by the presence of the different treatments. When the data paths for two treatments show no overlap with each other and either stable levels or opposing trends, a clear demonstration of experimental control has been made. Such is the case in Figure 8.9, in which there is no overlap of data paths and the picture of differential effects is clear. When some overlap of data paths occurs, a degree of experimental control over the target behavior can still be demonstrated if the majority of data points for a given treatment fall outside the range of values of the majority of data points for the contrasting treatment.

The extent of any differential effects produced by two treatments is determined by the vertical distance—or fractionation—between their respective data paths and quantified by the vertical axis scale. The greater the vertical distance, the greater the differential effect of the two treatments on the response measure. It is possible for experimental control to be shown between two treatments but for the amount of behavior change to be socially insignificant. For instance, experimental control may be demonstrated for a treatment that reduces a person's severe self-injurious behavior from 10 occurrences per hour to 2 per hour, but the participant is still engaged in self-mutilation. However, if the vertical axis is scaled meaningfully, the greater the separation of data paths on the vertical axis, the higher the likelihood that the difference represents a socially significant effect.

Data from an experiment that compared the effects of two types of group-contingent rewards on the spelling accuracy of fourth-grade underachievers (Morgan, 1978) illustrate how the alternating treatments design reveals experimental control and the quantification of differential effects. The six children in the study were divided into two equally skilled teams of three on the basis of pretest scores. Each day during the study the students took a five-word spelling test. The students received a list of the words the day before, and a 5-minute study period was provided just prior to the test. Three different conditions were used in the alternating treatments design: (a) *no game,* in which the spelling tests were graded immediately and returned to the students, and the next scheduled activity in the school day was begun; (b) *game,* in which test papers were graded immediately, and each member of the team who had attained the highest total score received a mimeographed Certificate of Achievement and was allowed to stand up and cheer; and (c) *game plus,* consisting of the same procedure as the game condition, plus each student on the winning team also received a small trinket (e.g., a sticker or pencil).

The results for Student 3 (see Figure 8.10) show that experimental control over spelling accuracy was obtained

Figure 8.10   Alternating treatments design comparing the effects of three different treatments on the spelling accuracy of a fourth-grade student.

From *Comparison of Two "Good Behavior Game" Group Contingencies on the Spelling Accuracy of Fourth-Grade Students* by Q. E. Morgan, 1978, unpublished master's thesis, The Ohio State University. Reprinted by permission.

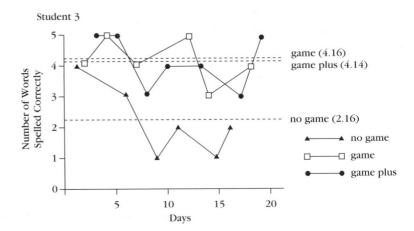

between the no-game condition and both the game and the game-plus conditions. Only the first two no-game data points overlap the lower range of scores obtained during the game or the game-plus conditions. However, the data paths for the game and game-plus conditions overlap completely and continuously throughout the study, revealing no difference in spelling accuracy between the two treatments. The vertical distance between the data paths represents the amount of improvement in spelling accuracy between the no-game condition and the game and the game-plus conditions. The mean difference between the two game conditions and the no-game condition was two words per test. Whether such a difference represents a significant improvement is an educational question, not a mathematical or statistical one, but most educators and parents would agree that an increase of two words spelled correctly out of five is socially significant, especially if that gain can be sustained from week to week. The cumulative effect over a 180-day school year would be impressive. There was virtually no difference in Student 3's spelling performance between the game and game-plus conditions. However, even a larger mean difference would not have contributed to the conclusions of the study because of the lack of experimental control between the game and the game-plus treatments.

Student 6 earned consistently higher spelling scores in the game-plus condition than he did in the game or no-game conditions (see Figure 8.11). Experimental control was demonstrated between the game-plus and the other two treatments for Student 6, but not between the no-game and game conditions. Again, the difference in responding between treatments is quantified by the vertical distance between the data paths. In this case there was a mean difference of 1.55 correctly spelled words per test between the game-plus and no-game conditions.

Figures 8.10 and 8.11 illustrate two other important points about the alternating treatments design. First, the two graphs show how an alternating treatments design enables a quick comparison of interventions. Although the study would have been strengthened by the collection of additional data, after 20 sessions the teacher had sufficient empirical evidence for selecting the most effective consequences for each student. If only two conditions had been compared, even fewer sessions may have been required to identify the most effective intervention. Second, these data underscore the importance of evaluating treatment effects at the level of the individual subject. All six

Figure 8.11   Alternating treatments design comparing the effects of three different treatments on the spelling accuracy of a fourth-grade student.

From *Comparison of Two "Good Behavior Game" Group Contingencies on the Spelling Accuracy of Fourth-Grade Students* by Q. E. Morgan, 1978, unpublished master's thesis, The Ohio State University. Reprinted by permission.

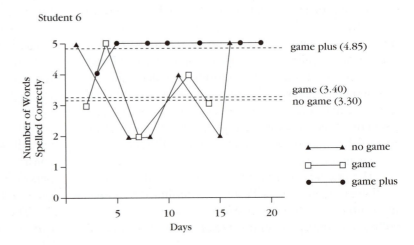

children spelled more words correctly under one or both of the game conditions than they did under the no-game condition. However, Student 3's spelling accuracy was equally enhanced by either the game or the game-plus contingency, whereas Student 6's spelling scores improved only when a tangible reward was available.

Variations of the Alternating Treatments Design

The alternating treatments design can be used to compare one or more treatments to a no-treatment or baseline condition, assess the relative contributions of individual components of a package intervention, and perform parametric investigations in which different values of an independent variable are alternated to determine differential effects on behavior change. Among the most common variations of the alternating treatments design are the following:

- Single-phase alternating treatments design without a no-treatment control condition

- Single-phase design in which two or more conditions, one of which is a no-treatment control condition, are alternated

- Two-phase design consisting of an initial baseline phase followed by a phase in which two or more conditions (one of which may be a no-treatment control condition) are alternated

- Three-phase design consisting of an initial baseline, a second phase in which two or more conditions (one of which may be a no-treatment control condition) are alternated, and a final phase in which only the treatment that proved most effective is implemented

Alternating Treatments Design without a No-Treatment Control Condition

One application of the alternating treatments design consists of a single-phase experiment in which the effects of two or more treatment conditions are compared (e.g., Barbetta, Heron, & Heward, 1993; McNeish, Heron, & Okyere, 1992; Morton, Heward, & Alber, 1998). A study by Belfiore, Skinner, and Ferkis (1995) provides an excellent example of this design. They compared the effects of two instructional procedures—trial-repetition and response-repetition—on the acquisition of sight words by three elementary students with learning disabilities in reading. An initial training list of five words for each condition was created by random selection from a pool of unknown words (determined by pretesting each student). Each session began with a noninstructional assessment of

unknown and training words, followed by both conditions. The order of instructional conditions was counterbalanced across sessions. Words spoken correctly on three consecutive noninstructional assessments were considered mastered and replaced as training words with unknown words.

The trial-repetition condition consisted of one response opportunity within each of five interspersed practice trials per word. The experimenter placed a word card on the table and said, "Look at the word, and say the word." If the student made a correct response within 3 seconds, the experimenter said, "Yes, the word is _____." (p. 347). If the student's initial response was incorrect, or the student made no response within 3 seconds, the experimenter said, "No, the word is _____," and the student repeated the word. The experimenter then presented the next word card and the procedure repeated until five practice trials (antecedent-response-feedback) were provided with each word.

The response-repetition condition also consisted of five response opportunities per word, but all five responses occurred within a single practice trial for each word. The experimenter placed a word card on the table and said, "Look at the word, and say the word." If the student made a correct response within 3 seconds, the experimenter said, "Yes, the word is _____, please repeat the word four more times" (p. 347). If the student made an incorrect response or no response within 3 seconds, the experimenter said, "No, the word is _____." The student then repeated the word and was instructed to repeat it four more times.

Figure 8.12 shows the cumulative number of words mastered by each student under both conditions. Even though the number of correct responses per word during instruction was identical in both conditions, all three students had higher rates of learning new words in the trial-repetition condition than in the response-repetition condition. These results obtained within the simple alternating treatments design enabled Belfiore and colleagues (1995) to conclude that, "Response repetition outside the context of the learning trial (i.e., of the three-term contingency) was not as effective as repetition that included antecedent and consequent stimuli in relation to the accurate response" (p. 348).

Alternating Treatments Design with No-Treatment Control Condition

Although not a requirement of the design, a no-treatment condition is often incorporated into the alternating treatments design as one of the treatments to be compared. For example, the no-game condition in the Morgan (1978) study served as a no-treatment control condition against which the students' spelling scores in the game

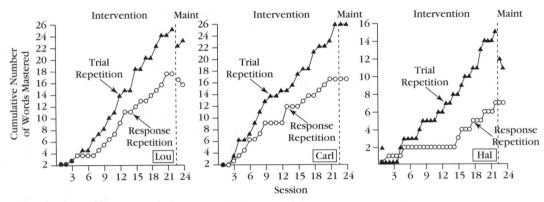

Figure 8.12   Single-phase alternating treatments design without a no-treatment control condition.

From "Effects of Response and Trial Repetition on Sight-Word Training for Students with Learning Disabilities" by P. J. Belfiore, C. H. Skinner, and M. A. Ferkis, 1995, *Journal of Applied Behavior Analysis, 28,* p. 348. Copyright 1995 by the Society for the Experimental Analysis of Behavior, Inc. Reprinted by permission.

and game-plus conditions were compared (see Figures 8.10 and 8.11).

Including a no-treatment control condition as one of the experimental conditions in an alternating treatments design provides valuable information on any differences in responding under the intervention treatment(s) and no treatment. However, the measures obtained during the no-treatment control condition should not be considered representative of an unknown preintervention level of responding. It may be that the measures obtained in the no-treatment condition represent only the level of behavior under a no-treatment condition when it is interspersed within an ongoing series of treatment condition(s), and do not represent the level of behavior that existed before the alternating treatments design was begun.

Alternating Treatments Design with Initial Baseline

Investigators using the alternating treatments tactic often use a two-phase experimental design in which baseline measures are collected until a stable level of responding or countertherapeutic trend is obtained prior to the alternating treatments phase (e.g., Martens, Lochner, & Kelly, 1992 [see Figure 13.6]). Sometimes the baseline condition is continued during the alternating treatments phase as a no-treatment control condition.

A study by J. Singh and N. Singh (1985) provides an excellent example of an alternating treatments design incorporating an initial baseline phase. The experiment evaluated the relative effectiveness of two procedures for reducing the number of oral reading errors by students with mental retardation. The first phase of the study consisted of a 10-day baseline condition in which each student was given a new 100-word passage three times each day and told, "Here is the story for this session. I want you to read it. Try your best not to make any errors"

(p. 66). The experimenter sat nearby but did not assist the student, correct any errors, or attend to self-corrections. If a student requested help with new or difficult words, he was prompted to continue reading.

During the alternating treatments phase of the study, three different conditions were presented each day in separate sessions of about 5 minutes each: control (the same procedures as during baseline), word supply, and word analysis. To minimize any sequence or carryover effects from one condition to another, the three conditions were presented in random order each day, each condition was preceded with specific instructions identifying the procedure to be implemented, and an interval of at least 5 minutes separated consecutive sessions. During the word-supply condition, each student was instructed, "Here is the story for this session. I want you to read it. I will help you if you make a mistake. I will tell you the correct word while you listen and point to the word in the book. After that, I want you to repeat the word. Try your best not to make any errors" (p. 67). The experimenter supplied the correct word when an oral reading error was made, had the child repeat the correct word once, and instructed the child to continue reading. During the word-analysis condition, each student was instructed, "Here is the story for this session. I want you to read it. I will help you if you make a mistake. I will help you sound out the word and then you can read the word correctly before you carry on reading the rest of the story. Try your best not to make any errors" (p. 67). When errors were made in this condition, the experimenter directed the child's attention to the phonetic elements of the word and coaxed the child to sound out correctly each part of the word. Then the experimenter had the student read the entire word at the normal speed and instructed him or her to continue reading the passage.

The results for the four students who participated in the study are shown in Figure 8.13. Each baseline data

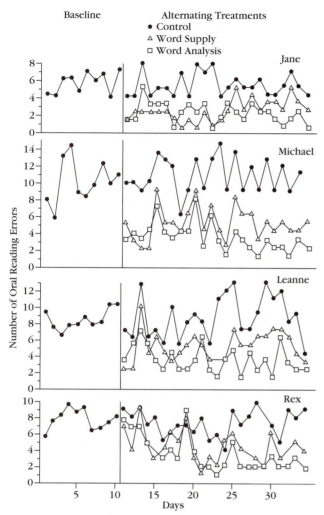

Figure 8.13 Alternating treatments design with an initial baseline.

From "Comparison of Word-Supply and Word-Analysis Error-Correction Procedures on Oral Reading by Mentally Retarded Children" by J. Singh and N. Singh, 1985, *American Journal of Mental Deficiency, 90,* p. 67. Copyright 1985 by the *American Journal of Mental Deficiency.* Reprinted by permission.

point is the mean number of errors for the three daily sessions. Although the data in each condition are highly variable (perhaps because of the varied difficulty of the different passages used), experimental control is evident. All four students committed fewer errors during the word-supply and the word-analysis conditions than they did during the control condition. Experimental control of oral reading errors, although not complete because of some overlap of the data paths, is also demonstrated between the word-supply and word-analysis conditions, with all four students making fewer errors during the word-analysis condition.

By beginning the study with a baseline phase, J. Singh and N. Singh (1985) were able to compare the level of responding obtained during each of the treatments to the natural level of performance uncontaminated by the introduction of either error-correction

intervention. In addition, the initial baseline served as the basis for predicting and assessing the measures obtained during the control sessions of the alternating treatments phase of the study. The measures obtained in the alternating control condition matched the relatively high frequency of errors observed during the initial baseline phase, providing evidence that (a) the vertical distance between the data paths for the word-supply and word-analysis conditions and the data path for the control condition represents the true amount of improvement produced by each treatment and (b) the frequency of errors during the control condition was not influenced by reduced errors during the other two treatments (i.e., no generalized reduction in oral reading errors from the treated passages to untreated passages occurred).

Alternating Treatments Design with Initial Baseline and Final Best Treatment Phase

A widely used variation of the alternating treatments design consists of three sequential phases: an initial baseline phase, a second phase comparing alternating treatments, and a final phase in which only the most effective treatment is administered (e.g., Heckaman, Alber, Hooper, & Heward, 1998; Kennedy & Souza, 1995, Study 4; Ollendick, Matson, Esvelt-Dawson, & Shapiro, 1980; N. Singh, 1990; N. Singh & J. Singh, 1984; N. Singh & Winton, 1985). Tincani (2004) used an alternating treatments design with an initial baseline and final best treatment phase to investigate the relative effectiveness of sign language and picture exchange training on the acquisition of mands (requests for preferred items) by two children with autism.[7] A related research question was whether a relation existed between students' preexisting motor imitation skills and their abilities to learn mands through sign language or by picture exchange. Two assessments were conducted for each student prior to baseline. A stimulus preference assessment (Pace, Ivancic, Edwards, Iwata, & Page, 1985) was conducted to identify a list of 10 to 12 preferred items (e.g., drinks, edibles, toys), and each student's ability to imitate 27 hand, arm, and finger movements similar to those required for sign language was assessed.[8]

The purpose of baseline was to ensure that the participants were not able to request preferred items with picture exchange, sign language, or speech prior to training. Baseline trials consisted of giving the student 10 to 20 seconds of noncontingent access to a preferred item, removing the item briefly, and then placing it out of the

---

[7]The mand is one of six types of elementary verbal operants identified by Skinner (1957). Chapter 25 describes Skinner's analysis of verbal behavior and its importance to applied behavior analysis.

[8]Stimulus preference assessment procedures are described in Chapter 11.

student's reach. A laminated 2-inch-by-2-inch picture of the item was placed in front of the student. If the student placed the picture symbol in the experimenter's hand, signed the name of the item, or spoke the name of the item within 10 seconds, the experimenter provided access to the item. If not, the item was removed and the next item on the list was presented. Following a three-session baseline, during which neither participant emitted an independent mand in any modality, the alternating treatments phase was begun.

The sign language training procedures were adapted from Sundberg and Partington's (1998) *Teaching Language to Children with Autism or Other Developmental Disabilities.* The simplest sign from American Sign Language for each item was taught. Procedures used in the PECS training condition were adapted from Bondy and Frost's (2002) *The Picture Exchange Communication*

System Training Manual. In both conditions, training on each preferred item continued for five to seven trials per session, or until the participant showed no interest in the item. At that time training then began on the next item and continued until all 10 or 12 items on the participant's list of preferred items had been presented. During the study's final phase, each participant received either sign language or PECS training only, depending on which method had been most successful during the alternating treatments phase.

The percentage of independent mands by the two students throughout the study is shown in Figures 8.14 (Jennifer) and 8.15 (Carl). Picture exchange training was clearly more effective than sign language for Jennifer. Jennifer demonstrated weak motor imitation skills in the prebaseline assessment, correctly imitating 20% of the motor movements attempted in the prebaseline imitation

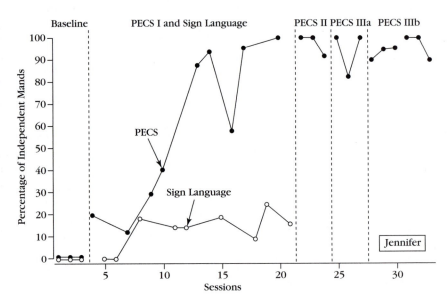

Figure 8.14 Alternating treatments design with an initial baseline and a final best-treatment-only condition.

From "Comparing the Picture Exchange Communication System and Sign Language Training for Children with Autism" by M. Tincani, 2004, *Focus on Autism and Other Developmental Disabilities, 19,* p. 160. Copyright 2004 by Pro-Ed. Used by permission.

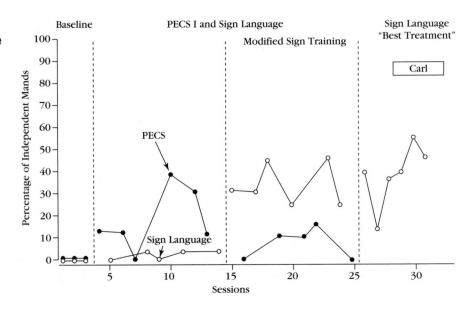

Figure 8.15 Alternating treatments design with an initial baseline and a final best-treatment-only condition.

From "Comparing the Picture Exchange Communication System and Sign Language Training for Children with Autism" by M. Tincani, 2004, *Focus on Autism and Other Developmental Disabilities, 19,* p. 159. Copyright 2004 by Pro-Ed. Used by permission.

assessment. After a slight modification in sign language training procedures was implemented to eliminate Carl's prompt dependency, he emitted independent mands more often during sign language training than with picture exchange training. Carl's preexisting motor imitation skills were better than Jennifer's. He imitated correctly 43% of the attempted motor movements in the prebaseline imitation assessment.

This study highlights the importance of individual analyses and exploring the possible influence of variables not manipulated during the study. In discussing the study's results, Tincani (2004) noted that

> For learners without hand-motor imitation skills, including many children with autism, PECS training may be more appropriate, at least in terms of initial mand acquisition. Jennifer had weak hand-motor imitation skills prior to intervention and learned picture exchange more rapidly than sign language. For learners who have moderate hand-motor imitation skills, sign language training may be equally, if not more, appropriate. Carl had moderate hand-motor imitation skills prior to intervention and learned sign language more rapidly than picture exchange. (p. 160)

Advantages of the Alternating Treatments Design

The alternating treatments design offers numerous advantages for evaluating and comparing two or more independent variables. Most of the benefits cited here were described by Ulman and Sulzer-Azaroff (1975), who are credited with first bringing the rationale and possibilities of the alternating treatments design to the attention of the applied behavior analysis community.

Does Not Require Treatment Withdrawal

A major advantage of the alternating treatments design is that it does not require the investigator to withdraw a seemingly effective treatment to demonstrate a functional relation. Reversing behavioral improvements raises ethical issues that can be avoided with the alternating treatments design. Regardless of ethical concerns, however, administrators and teachers may be more likely to accept an alternating treatments design over a reversal design even when one of the alternating treatments is a no-treatment control condition. "It would appear that a return to baseline conditions every other day or every third day is not as disagreeable to a teacher as is first establishing a high level of desirable behavior for a prolonged period, and then reinstating the baseline behaviors" (Ulman & Sulzer-Azaroff, 1975, p. 385).

Speed of Comparison

The experimental comparison of two or more treatments can often be made quickly with the alternating treatments design. In one study an alternating treatments design enabled the superiority of one treatment over another in increasing the cooperative behavior of a 6-year-old boy to be determined after only 4 days (McCullough, Cornell, McDaniel, & Mueller, 1974). The alternating treatments design's ability to produce useful results quickly is a major reason that it is the basic experimental tactic used in functional behavior analysis (see Chapter 24 and Figures 24.4, 24.5, 24.6, and 24.9).

When the effects of different treatments become apparent early in an alternating treatments design, the investigator can then switch to programming only the most effective treatment. The efficiency of the alternating treatments design can leave a researcher with meaningful data even when an experiment must be terminated early (Ulman & Sulzer-Azaroff, 1975). A reversal or multiple baseline design, on the other hand, must be carried through to completion to show a functional relation.

Minimizes Irreversibility Problem

Some behaviors, even though they have been brought about or modified by the application of the intervention, do not return to baseline levels when the intervention is withdrawn and thereby resist analysis with an A-B-A-B design. However, rapidly alternating treatment and no-treatment (baseline) conditions may reveal differences in responding between the two conditions, especially early in an experiment before responding in the no-treatment condition begins to approximate the level of responding in the treatment condition.

Minimizes Sequence Effects

An alternating treatments design, when properly conducted, minimizes the extent to which an experiment's results are confounded by sequence effects. Sequence effects pose a threat to the internal validity of any experiment, but especially to those involving multiple treatments. The concern over sequence effects can be summed up by this simple question: Would the results have been the same if the sequence of treatments had been different? Sequence effects can be extremely difficult to control in experiments using reversal or multiple tactics (see Chapter 9) to compare two or more independent variables because each experimental condition must remain in effect for a fairly long period of time, thereby producing a specific sequence of events. However, in an alternating treatments design, the independent variables are rapidly alternated with one another in a random fashion that produces no particular sequence. Also, each treatment is in effect for short periods of time, reducing the likelihood of carryover effects (O'Brien, 1968). The ability to minimize sequence effects makes the alternating treatments design a powerful tool for achieving complex behavior analyses.

Can Be Used with Unstable Data

Determining functional behavior–environment relations in the presence of unstable data presents a serious problem for the applied behavior analyst. Using steady state responding to predict, verify, and replicate behavioral changes is the foundation of experimental reasoning in behavior analysis (Sidman, 1960). Obtaining stable baseline responding, however, is extremely difficult with many socially important behaviors of interest to applied behavior analysts. Merely providing a subject with repeated opportunities to emit a target response can result in gradually improved performance. Although practice effects are worthy of empirical investigation because of their applied and scientific importance (Greenwood, Delquadri, & Hall, 1984; Johnston & Pennypacker, 1993a), the unstable baselines they create pose problems for the analysis of intervention variables. The changing levels of task difficulty inherent in moving through a curriculum of progressively more complex material also make obtaining steady state responding for many academic behaviors difficult.

Because the different treatment conditions are alternated rapidly in an alternating treatments design, because each treatment is presented many times throughout each time period encompassed by the study, and because no single condition is present for any considerable length of time, it can be presumed that any effects of practice, change in task difficulty, maturation, or other historical variables will be equally represented in each treatment condition and therefore will not differentially affect any one condition more or less than the others. For example, even though each of two data paths representing a student's reading performance under two different teaching procedures shows variable and ascending trends that might be due to practice effects and uneven curriculum materials, any consistent separation and vertical distance between the data paths can be attributed to differences in the teaching procedures.

Can Be Used to Assess Generalization of Effects

By alternating various conditions of interest, an experimenter can continually assess the degree of generalization of behavior change from an effective treatment to other conditions of interest. For example, by alternating different therapists in the final phase of their study of pica behavior, N. Singh and Winton (1985) were able to determine the extent to which the overcorrection treatment was effective when presented by different persons.

Intervention Can Begin Immediately

Although determining the preintervention level of responding is generally preferred, the clinical necessity of immediately attempting to change some behaviors precludes repeated measurement in the absence of intervention. When necessary, an alternating treatments design can be used without an initial baseline phase.

Considering the Appropriateness of the Alternating Treatments Design

The advantages of the alternating treatments design are significant. As with any experimental tactic, however, the alternating treatments design presents certain disadvantages and leaves unanswered certain questions that can be addressed only by additional experimentation.

Multiple Treatment Interference

The fundamental feature of the alternating treatments design is the rapid alternation of two or more independent variables irrespective of the behavioral measures obtained under each treatment. Although the rapid alternation minimizes sequence effects and reduces the time required to compare treatments, it raises the important question of whether the effects observed under any of the alternated treatments would be the same if each treatment were implemented alone. **Multiple treatment interference** refers to the confounding effects of one treatment on a subject's behavior being influenced by the effects of another treatment administered in the same study.

Multiple treatment interference must always be suspected in the alternating treatments design (Barlow & Hayes, 1979; McGonigle, Rojahn, Dixon, & Strain, 1987). However, by following the alternating treatments phase with a phase in which only the most effective treatment condition is in effect, the experimenter can assess the effects of that treatment when administered in isolation.

Unnatural Nature of Rapidly Alternating Treatments

The rapid back-and-forth switching of treatments does not reflect the typical manner in which clinical and educational interventions are applied. From an instructional perspective, rapid switching of treatments can be viewed as artificial and undesirable. In most instances, however, the quick comparison of treatments offered by the alternating treatments design compensates for concerns about its contrived nature. The concern of whether participants might suffer detrimental effects from the rapid alternation of conditions is an empirical question that can be determined only by experimentation. Also, it is helpful for practitioners to remember that one purpose of the alternating treatments design is to identify an effective intervention as quickly as possible so that the participant does not have to endure ineffective instructional approaches or treatments that would delay progress toward educational goals. On balance, the advantages of rapidly switching treatments to identify an efficacious intervention outweigh any undesirable effects that such manipulation may cause.

Limited Capacity

Although the alternating treatments design enables an elegant, scientifically sound method for comparing the differential effects of two or more treatments, it is not an open-ended design in which an unlimited number of treatments can be compared. Although alternating treatments designs with up to five conditions have been reported (e.g., Didden, Prinson, & Sigafoos, 2000), in most situations a maximum of four different conditions (one of which may be a no-treatment control condition) can be compared effectively within a single phase of an alternating treatments design, and in many instances only two different treatments can be accommodated. To separate the effects of each treatment condition from any effects that may be caused by aspects of the alternating treatments design, each treatment must be carefully counterbalanced across all potentially relevant aspects of its administration (e.g., time of day, order of presentation, settings, therapists). In many applied settings the logistics of counterbalancing and delivering more than two or three treatments would be cumbersome and would cause the experiment to require too many sessions to complete. Also, too many competing treatments can decrease the subject's ability to discriminate between treatments, thereby reducing the design's effectiveness.

Selection of Treatments

Theoretically, although an alternating treatments design can be used to compare the effects of any two discrete treatments, in reality the design is more limited. To enhance the probability of discrimination between conditions (i.e., obtaining reliable, measurable differences in

behavior), the treatments should embody significant differences from one to the other. For example, an investigator using an alternating treatments design to study the effects of group size on students' academic performance during instruction might include conditions of 4, 10, and 20 students. Alternating conditions of 6, 7, and 8 students, however, is less likely to reveal a functional relation between group size and performance. However, a treatment condition should not be selected for inclusion in an alternating treatments design only because it might yield a data path that is easily differentiated from that of another condition. The *applied* in applied behavior analysis encompasses the nature of treatment conditions as well as the nature of behaviors investigated (Wolf, 1978). An important consideration in selecting treatment conditions should be the extent to which they are representative of current practices or practices that could conceivably be implemented. For example, although an experiment comparing the effects of 5 minutes, 10 minutes, and 30 minutes of math homework per school night on math achievement might be useful, a study comparing the effects of 5 minutes, 10 minutes, and 3 hours of math homework per night probably would not be. Even if such a study found 3 hours of nightly math homework extremely effective in raising students' achievement in math, few teachers, parents, administrators, or students would carry out a program of 3 hours of nightly homework for a single content area.

Another consideration is that some interventions may not produce important behavior change unless and until they have been implemented consistently over a continuous period of time.

> When a multielement baseline design is employed, overlapping data do not necessarily rule out the possible efficacy of an experimental procedure. The session-by-session alternation of conditions might obscure effects that could be observed if the same condition was presented during several consecutive sessions. It is therefore possible that a given treatment may prove to be effective with a reversal or multiple baseline design, but not with a multielement baseline design. (Ulman & Sulzer-Azaroff, 1975, p. 382)

The suspicion that a given treatment may be effective if it is presented in isolation for an extended period is an empirical question that can be explored properly only through experimentation. At one level, if extended application of a single treatment results in behavioral improvement, the practitioner might be satisfied, and no further action would be needed. However, the practitioner-researcher who is interested in determining experimental control might return to an alternating treatments design and compare the performance of the single treatment with that of another intervention.

Summary

Reversal Design

1. The reversal tactic (A-B-A) entails repeated measurement of behavior in a given setting during three consecutive phases: (a) a baseline phase (absence of the independent variable), (b) a treatment phase (introduction of the independent variable), and (c) a return to baseline conditions (withdrawal of the independent variable).

2. The reversal design is strengthened tremendously by reintroducing the independent variable in the form of an A-B-A-B design. The A-B-A-B design is the most straightforward and generally most powerful intrasubject design for demonstrating functional relations.

Variations of the A-B-A-B Design

3. Extending the A-B-A-B design with repeated reversals may provide a more convincing demonstration of a functional relation than a design with one reversal.

4. The B-A-B reversal design can be used with target behaviors for which an initial baseline phase is inappropriate or not possible for ethical or practical reasons.

5. Multiple treatment reversal designs use the reversal tactic to compare the effects of two or more experimental conditions to baseline and/or to one another.

6. Multiple treatment reversal designs are particularly susceptible to confounding by sequence effects.

7. The NCR reversal technique enables the isolation and analysis of the contingent aspect of reinforcement.

8. Reversal techniques incorporating DRO and DRI/DRA control conditions can also be used to demonstrate the effects of contingent reinforcement.

Considering the Appropriateness of the Reversal Design

9. An experimental design based on the reversal tactic is ineffective in evaluating the effects of a treatment variable that, by its very nature, cannot be withdrawn once it has been presented (e.g., instruction, modeling).

10. Once improved, some behaviors will not reverse to baseline levels even though the independent variable has been withdrawn. Such behavioral irreversibility precludes effective use of the reversal design.

11. Legitimate social, educational, and ethical concerns are often raised over withdrawing a seemingly effective treatment variable to provide scientific verification of its function in changing behavior.

12. Sometimes very brief reversal phases, or even one-session baseline probes, can demonstrate believable experimental control.

Alternating Treatments Design

13. The alternating treatments design compares two or more distinct treatments (i.e., independent variables) while their effects on the target behavior (i.e., dependent variable) are measured.

14. In an alternating treatments design, each successive data point for a specific treatment plays three roles: it provides (a) a basis for the *prediction* of future levels of responding under that treatment, (b) potential *verification* of the previous prediction of performance under that treatment, and (c) the opportunity for *replication* of previous effects produced by that treatment.

15. Experimental control is demonstrated in the alternating treatments design when the data paths for two different treatments show little or no overlap.

16. The extent of any differential effects produced by two treatments is determined by the vertical distance between their respective data paths and quantified by the vertical axis scale.

Variations of the Alternating Treatments Design

17. Common variations of the alternating treatments design include the following:
   - Single-phase alternating treatments design without a no-treatment control condition
   - Single-phase design with a no-treatment control condition
   - Two-phase design: initial baseline phase followed by the alternating treatments phase
   - Three-phase design: initial baseline phase followed by the alternating treatments phase and a final best treatment phase

Advantages of the Alternating Treatments Design

18. Advantages of the alternating treatments design include the following:
   - Does not require treatment withdrawal.
   - Quickly compares the relative effectiveness of treatments.
   - Minimizes the problem of irreversibility.
   - Minimizes sequence effects.
   - Can be used with unstable data patterns.
   - Can be used to assess generalization of effects.
   - Intervention can begin immediately.

Considering the Appropriateness of the Alternating Treatments Design

19. The alternating treatments design is susceptible to multiple treatment interference. However, by following the alternating treatments phase with a phase in which only one

treatment is administered, the experimenter can assess the effects of that treatment in isolation.

20. The rapid back-and-forth switching of treatments does not reflect the typical manner in which interventions are applied and may be viewed as artificial and undesirable.

21. An alternating treatments phase is usually limited to a maximum of four different treatment conditions.

22. The alternating treatments design is most effective in revealing the differential effects of treatment conditions that differ significantly from one another.

23. The alternating treatments design is not effective for assessing the effects of an independent variable that produces important changes in behavior only when it is consistently administered over a continuous period of time.

CHAPTER 9

Multiple Baseline and Changing Criterion Designs

Key Terms

changing criterion design
delayed multiple baseline design
multiple baseline across
   behaviors design

multiple baseline across settings
   design
multiple baseline across subjects
   design

multiple baseline design
multiple probe design

Behavior Analyst Certification Board® BCBA® & BCABA® Behavior Analyst Task List©, Third Edition

Content Area 5: Experimental Evaluation of Interventions	
5-1	Systematically manipulate independent variables to analyze their effects on treatment.
(d)	Use changing criterion design.
(e)	Use multiple baseline designs.
5-2	Identify and address practical and ethical considerations in using various experimental designs.

This chapter describes two additional experimental tactics for analyzing behavior–environment relations—the multiple baseline design and the changing criterion design. In a multiple baseline design, after collecting initial baseline data simultaneously across two or more behaviors, settings, or people, the behavior analyst then applies the treatment variable sequentially across these behaviors, settings, or people and notes the effects. The changing criterion design is used to analyze improvements in behavior as a function of stepwise, incremental criterion changes in the level of responding required for reinforcement. In both designs, experimental control and a functional relation are demonstrated when the behaviors change from a steady state baseline to a new steady state after the introduction of the independent variable is applied, or a new criterion established.

Multiple Baseline Design

The multiple baseline design is the most widely used experimental design for evaluating treatment effects in applied behavior analysis. It is a highly flexible tactic that enables researchers and practitioners to analyze the effects of an independent variable across multiple behaviors, settings, and/or subjects without having to withdraw the treatment variable to verify that the improvements in behavior were a direct result of the application of the treatment. As you recall from Chapter 8, the reversal design by its very nature requires that the independent variable be withdrawn to verify the prediction established in baseline. This is not so with the multiple baseline design.

Operation and Logic of the Multiple Baseline Design

Baer, Wolf, and Risley (1968) first described the **multiple baseline design** in the applied behavior analysis literature. They presented the multiple baseline design as an alternative to the reversal design for two situations: (a) when the target behavior is likely to be irreversible or (b) when it is undesirable, impractical, or unethical to reverse conditions. Figure 9.1 illustrates Baer and colleagues' explanation of the basic operation of the multiple baseline design.

> In the multiple baseline technique, a number of responses are identified and measured over time to provide baselines against which changes can be evaluated. With these baselines established, the experimenter then applies an experimental variable to one of the behaviors, produces a change in it, and perhaps notes little or no change in the other baselines. If so, rather than reversing the just-produced change, he instead applies the experimental variable to one of the other, as yet unchanged, responses. If it changes at that point, evidence is accruing

that the experimental variable is indeed effective, and that the prior change was not simply a matter of coincidence. The variable then may be applied to still another response, and so on. The experimenter is attempting to show that he has a reliable experimental variable, in that each behavior changes maximally only when the experimental variable is applied to it. (p. 94)

The multiple baseline design takes three basic forms:

- The multiple baseline across behaviors design, consisting of two or more different behaviors of the same subject
- The multiple baseline across settings design, consisting of the same behavior of the same subject in two or more different settings, situations, or time periods
- The multiple baseline across subjects design, consisting of the same behavior of two or more different participants (or groups)

Although only one of the multiple baseline design's basic forms is called an "across behaviors" design, all multiple baseline designs involve the time-lagged application of a treatment variable across technically different (meaning independent) behaviors. That is, in the multiple baseline across settings design, even though the subject's performance of the same target behavior is measured in two or more settings, each behavior–setting combination is conceptualized and treated as a different behavior for analysis. Similarly, in a multiple baseline across subjects design, each subject–behavior combination functions as a different behavior in the operation of the design.

Figure 9.2 shows the same data set displayed in Figure 9.1 with the addition of data points representing predicted measures if baseline conditions were not changed and shaded areas illustrating how the three elements of baseline logic—prediction, verification, and replication—are operationalized in the multiple baseline design.[1] When stable baseline responding has been achieved for Behavior 1, a *prediction* is made that if the environment were held constant, continued measurement

---

[1] Although most of the graphic displays created or selected for this text as examples of experimental design tactics show data plotted on noncumulative vertical axes, the reader is reminded that repeated measurement data collected within any type of experimental design can be plotted on both noncumulative and cumulative graphs. For example, Lalli, Zanolli, and Wohn (1994) and Mueller, Moore, Doggett, and Tingstrom (2000) used cumulative graphs to display the data they collected in multiple baseline design experiments; and Kennedy and Souza (1995) and Sundberg, Endicott, and Eigenheer (2000) displayed the data they obtained in reversal designs on cumulative graphs. Students of applied behavior analysis should be careful not to confuse the different techniques for graphically displaying data with tactics for experimental analysis.

Figure 9.1 Graphic prototype of a multiple baseline design.

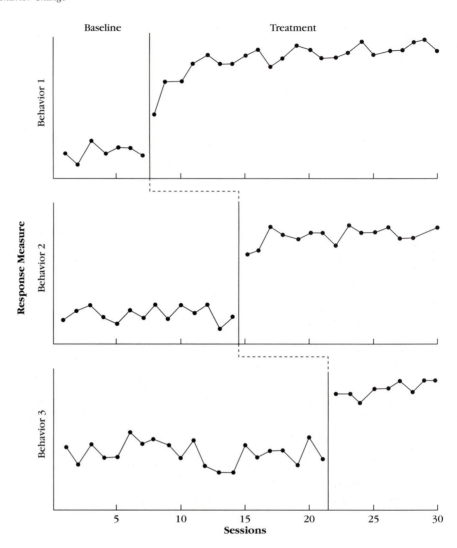

would reveal similar levels of responding. When the researcher's confidence in such a prediction is justifiably high, the independent variable is applied to Behavior 1. The open data points in the treatment phase for Behavior 1 represent the predicted level of responding. The solid data points show the actual measures obtained for Behavior 1 during the treatment condition. These data show a discrepancy with the predicted level of responding if no changes had been made in the environment, thereby suggesting that the treatment may be responsible for the change in behavior. The data collected for Behavior 1 in a multiple baseline design serve the same functions as the data collected during the first two phases of an A-B-A-B reversal design.

Continued baseline measures of the other behaviors in the experiment offer the possibility of verifying the prediction made for Behavior 1. In a multiple baseline design, *verification* of a predicted level of responding for one behavior (or tier) is obtained if little or no change is observed in the data paths of the behaviors (tiers) that are

still exposed to the conditions under which the prediction was made. In Figure 9.2 those portions of the baseline condition data paths for Behaviors 2 and 3 within the shaded boxes verify the prediction for Behavior 1. At this point in the experiment, two inferences can be made: (a) The prediction that Behavior 1 would not change in a constant environment is valid because the environment was held constant for Behaviors 2 and 3 and their levels of responding remained unchanged; and (b) the observed changes in Behavior 1 were brought about by the independent variable because only Behavior 1 was exposed to the independent variable and only Behavior 1 changed.

In a multiple baseline design, the independent variable's function in changing a given behavior is inferred by the lack of change in untreated behaviors. However, verification of function is not demonstrated directly as it is with the reversal design, thereby making the multiple baseline design an inherently weaker tactic (i.e., less convincing from the perspective of experimental control) for revealing a functional relation between the independent

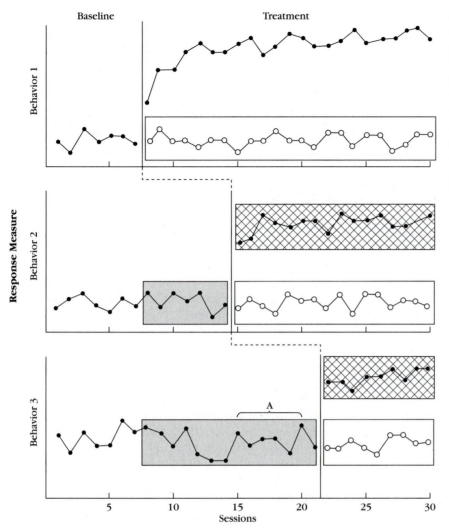

Figure 9.2 Graphic prototype of a multiple baseline design with shading added to show elements of baseline logic. Open data points represent predicted measures if baseline conditions were unchanged. Baseline data points for Behaviors 2 and 3 within shaded areas verify of the prediction made for Behavior 1. Behavior 3 baseline data within Bracket A verify the prediction made for Behavior 2. Data obtained during the treatment condition for Behaviors 2 and 3 (cross-hatched shading) provide replications of the experimental effect.

variable and a target behavior. However, the multiple baseline design compensates somewhat for this weakness by providing the opportunity to verify or refute a series of similar predictions. Not only is the prediction for Behavior 1 in Figure 9.2 verified by continued stable baselines for Behavior 2 and 3, but the bracketed portion of the baseline data for Behavior 3 also serves as verification of the prediction made for Behavior 2.

When the level of responding for Behavior 1 under the treatment condition has stabilized or reached a predetermined performance criterion, the independent variable is then applied to Behavior 2. If Behavior 2 changes in a manner similar to the changes observed for Behavior 1, *replication* of the independent variable's effect has been achieved (shown by the data path shaded with cross-hatching). After Behavior 2 has stabilized or reached a predetermined performance criterion, the independent variable is applied to Behavior 3 to see whether the effect will be replicated. The independent variable may be applied to additional behaviors in a similar manner until a convinc-

ing demonstration of the functional relation has been established (or rejected) and all of the behaviors targeted for improvement have received treatment.

As with verification, replication of the independent variable's specific effect on each behavior in a multiple baseline design is not manipulated directly. Instead, the generality of the independent variable's effect across the behaviors comprising the experiment is demonstrated by applying it to a series of behaviors. Assuming accurate measurement and proper experimental control of relevant variables (i.e., the only environmental factor that changes during the course of the experiment should be the presence—or absence—of the independent variable), each time a behavior changes when, and only when, the independent variable is introduced, confidence in the existence of a functional relation increases.

How many different behaviors, settings, or subjects must a multiple baseline design include to provide a believable demonstration of a functional relation? Baer, Wolf, and Risley (1968) suggested that the number of replications needed in any design is ultimately a matter to be decided by the consumers of the research. In this sense, an experiment using a multiple baseline design must contain the minimum number of replications necessary to convince those who will be asked to respond to the experiment and to the researcher's claims (e.g., teachers, administrators, parents, funding sources, journal editors). A two-tier multiple baseline design is a complete experiment and can provide strong support for the effectiveness of the independent variable (e.g., Lindberg, Iwata, Roscoe, Worsdell, & Hanley, 2003 [see Figure 23.2]; McCord, Iwata, Galensky, Ellingson, & Thomson, 2001 [see Figure 6.6]; Newstrom, McLaughlin, & Sweeney, 1999 [see Figure 26.2]; Test, Spooner, Keul, & Grossi, 1990 [see Figure 20.7]). McClannahan, McGee, MacDuff, and Krantz (1990) conducted a multiple baseline design study in which the independent variable was sequentially implemented in an eight-tier design across 12 participants. Multiple baseline designs of three to five tiers are most common. When the effects of the independent variable are substantial and reliably replicated, a three- or four-tier multiple baseline design provides a convincing demonstration of experimental effect. Suffice it to say that the more replications one conducts, the more convincing the demonstration will be.

Some of the earliest examples of the multiple baseline design in the applied behavior analysis literature were studies by Risley and Hart (1968); Barrish, Saunders, and Wolf (1969); Barton, Guess, Garcia, and Baer (1970); Panyan, Boozer, and Morris (1970); and Schwarz and Hawkins (1970). Some of the pioneering applications of the multiple baseline technique are not readily apparent with casual examination: The authors may not have identified the experimental design as a multiple baseline design (e.g., Schwarz & Hawkins, 1970), and/or the now-common practice of stacking the tiers of a multiple baseline design one on the other so that all of the data can be displayed graphically in the same figure was not always used (e.g., Maloney & Hopkins, 1973; McAllister, Stachowiak, Baer, & Conderman, 1969; Schwarz & Hawkins, 1970).

In 1970, Vance Hall, Connie Cristler, Sharon Cranston, and Bonnie Tucker published a paper that described three experiments, each an example of one of the three basic forms of the multiple baseline design: across behaviors, across settings, and across subjects. Hall and colleagues' paper was important not only because it provided excellent illustrations that today still serve as models of the multiple baseline design, but also because the studies were carried out by teachers and parents, indicating that practitioners "can carry out important and significant studies in natural settings using resources available to them" (p. 255).

Multiple Baseline across Behaviors Design

The **multiple baseline across behaviors design** begins with the concurrent measurement of two or more behaviors of a single participant. After steady state responding has been obtained under baseline conditions, the investigator applies the independent variable to one of the behaviors while maintaining baseline conditions for the other behavior(s). When steady state or criterion-level performance has been reached for the first behavior, the independent variable is applied to the next behavior, and so on (e.g., Bell, Young, Salzberg, & West, 1991; Gena, Krantz, McClannahan, & Poulson, 1996; Higgins, Williams, & McLaughlin, 2001 [see Figure 26.8]).

Ward and Carnes (2002) used a multiple baseline across behaviors design to evaluate the effects of self-set goals and public posting on the execution of three skills by five linebackers on a college football team: (a) *reads,* in which the linebacker positions himself to cover a specified area on the field on a pass play or from the line of scrimmage on a run; (b) *drops,* in which the linebacker moves to the correct position depending on the offensive team's alignment; and (c) *tackles.* A video camera recorded the players' movements during all practice sessions and games. Data were collected for the first 10 opportunities each player had with each skill. Reads and drops were recorded as correct if the player moved to the zone identified in the coaches' playbook; tackles were scored as correct if the offensive ball carrier was stopped.

Following baseline, each player met with one of the researchers, who described the player's mean baseline performance for a given skill. Players were asked to set a goal for their performances during practice sessions; no goals were set for games. The correct performances during baseline for all five players ranged from 60 to 80%, and all players set goals of 90% correct performance. The players were informed that their performance in each day's practice would be posted on a chart prior to the next practice session. A *Y* (yes) or an *N* (no) was placed next to each player's name to indicate whether he had met his goal. A player's performance was posted on the chart only for the skill(s) in intervention. The chart was mounted on a wall in the locker room where all players on the team could see it. The head coach explained the purpose of the chart to other players on the team. Players' performances during games were not posted on the chart.

The results for one of the players, John, are shown in Figure 9.3. John met or exceeded his goal of 90% correct performance during all practices for each of the three skills. Additionally, his improved performance generalized to games. The same pattern of results was obtained for each of the other four players in the study, illustrating

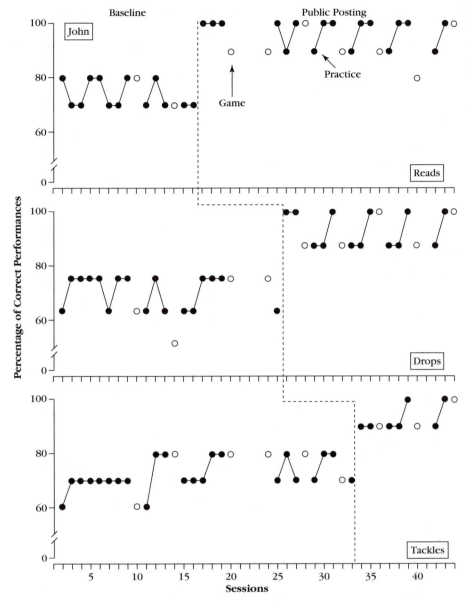

Figure 9.3 A multiple baseline across behaviors design showing percentage of correct read, drops, and tackles by a college football player during practices and games.

From "Effects of Posting Self-Set Goals on Collegiate Football Players' Skill Execution During Practice and Games" by P. Ward and M. Carnes, 2002, *Journal of Applied Behavior Analysis, 35,* p. 5. Copyright 2002 by the Society for the Experimental Analysis of Behavior, Inc. Reprinted by permission.

that the multiple baseline across behaviors design is a single-subject experimental strategy in which each subject serves as his own control. Each player constituted a complete experiment, replicated in this case with four other participants.

Multiple Baseline across Settings Design

In the **multiple baseline across settings design,** a single behavior of a person (or group) is targeted in two or more different settings or conditions (e.g., locations, times of day). After stable responding has been demonstrated under baseline conditions, the independent variable is introduced in one of the settings while baseline conditions

remain in effect in the other settings. When maximum behavior change or criterion-level performance has been achieved in the first setting, the independent variable is applied in the second setting, and so on.

Roane, Kelly, and Fisher (2003) employed a multiple baseline across settings design to evaluate the effects of a treatment designed to reduce the rate at which an 8-year-old boy put inedible objects in his mouth. Jason, who had been diagnosed with autism, cerebral palsy, and moderate mental retardation, had a history of putting objects such as toys, cloth, paper, tree bark, plants, and dirt into his mouth.

Data on Jason's mouthing were obtained concurrently in a classroom, a playroom, and outdoors—three settings that contained a variety of inedible objects and

Figure 9.4 A multiple baseline across settings design showing the number of object mouthing responses per minute during baseline and treatment conditions.

From "The Effects of Noncontingent Access to Food on the Rate of Object Mouthing across Three Settings" by H. S. Roane, M. L. Kelly, and W. W. Fisher, 2003, *Journal of Applied Behavior Analysis, 36,* p. 581. Copyright 2003 by the Society for the Experimental Analysis of Behavior, Inc. Reprinted by permission.

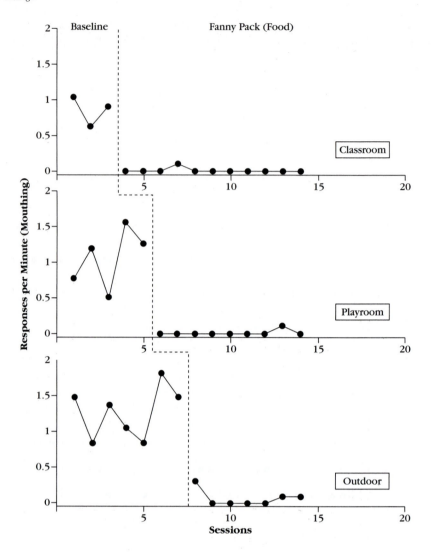

where caretakers had reported Jason's mouthing to be problematic. Observers in each setting unobtrusively tallied the number of times Jason inserted an inedible object past the plane of his lips during 10-minute sessions. The researchers reported that Jason's object mouthing usually consisted of a series of discrete episodes, rather than an extended, continuous event, and that he often placed multiple objects (inedible objects and food) in his mouth simultaneously.

Roane and colleagues (2003) described the baseline and treatment conditions for Jason as follows:

> The baseline condition was developed based on the functional analysis results, which showed that mouthing was maintained by automatic reinforcement and occurred independent of social consequences. During baseline, a therapist was present (approximately 1.5 to 3 m from Jason), but all occurrences of mouthing were ignored (i.e., no social consequences were arranged for mouthing, and Jason was allowed to place items in his mouth). No food items were available during baseline. The treatment condition was identical to baseline except that Jason had continuous access to foods that had been

previously identified to complete with the occurrence of object mouthing: chewing gum, marshmallows, and hard candy. Jason wore a fanny pack containing these items around his waist. (pp. 580–581)[2]

The staggered sequence in which the treatment was implemented in each setting and the results are shown in Figure 9.4. During baseline, Jason's mouthed objects at mean rates of 0.9, 1.1, and 1.2 responses per minute in the classroom, a playroom, and outdoor settings, respectively. Introduction of the fanny pack with food in each setting produced an immediate drop to a zero or near zero rate of mouthing. During treatment, Jason put items of food from the fanny pack into his mouth at mean rates of 0.01, 0.01, and 0.07 responses per minute in the classroom, a playroom, and outdoor settings, respectively. The multiple baseline across settings design revealed a clear functional relation between the treatment and the frequency of Jason's object mouthing. No measures obtained during the treatment condition were as

---

[2]Functional analysis and automatic reinforcement are described in Chapters 24 and 11, respectively.

high as the lowest measures in baseline. During 22 of 27 treatment sessions across the three settings, Jason put no inedible objects in his mouth.

As was done in the study by Roane and colleagues (2003), the data paths that comprise the different tiers in a multiple baseline across settings design are typically obtained in different physical environments (e.g., Cushing & Kennedy, 1997; Dalton, Martella, & Marchand-Martella, 1999). However, the different "settings" in a multiple baseline across settings design may exist in the same physical location and be differentiated from one another by different contingencies in effect, the presence or absence of certain people, and/or the different times of the day. For example, in a study by Parker and colleagues (1984), the presence or absence of other people in the training room constituted the different settings (environments) in which the effects of the independent variable were evaluated. The attention, demand, and no-attention conditions (i.e., contingencies in effect) defined the different settings in a multiple baseline design study by Kennedy, Meyer, Knowles, and Shukla (2000, see Figure 6.4). The afternoon and the morning portions of the school day functioned as different settings in the multiple baseline across settings design used by Dunlap, Kern-Dunlap, Clarke, and Robbins (1991) to analyze the effects of curricular revisions on a student's disruptive and off-task behaviors.

In some studies using a multiple baseline across settings design, the participants are varied, changing, and perhaps even unknown to the researchers. For example, Van Houten and Malenfant (2004) used a multiple baseline design across two crosswalks on busy streets to evaluate the effects of an intensive driver enforcement program on the percentage of drivers yielding to pedestrians and the number of motor vehicle–pedestrian conflicts. Watson (1996) used a multiple baseline design across men's rest rooms on a college campus to assess the effectiveness of posting signs in reducing bathroom graffiti.

Multiple Baseline across Subjects Design

In the **multiple baseline across subjects design,** one target behavior is selected for two or more subjects (or groups) in the same setting. After steady state responding has been achieved under baseline conditions, the independent variable is applied to one of the subjects while baseline conditions remain in effect for the other subjects. When criterion-level or stable responding has been attained for the first subject, the independent variable is applied to another subject, and so on. The multiple baseline across subjects design is the most widely used of all three forms of the design, in part because teachers, clinicians, and other practitioners are commonly confronted by more than one student or client needing to learn the

same skill or eliminate the same problem behavior (e.g., Craft, Alber, & Heward, 1998; Kahng, Iwata, DeLeon, & Wallace, 2000 [see Figure 23.1]; Killu, Sainato, Davis, Ospelt, & Paul, 1998 [see Figure 23.3]; Kladopoulos & McComas, 2001 [see Figure 6.3]). Sometimes a multiple baseline design is conducted across "groups" of participants (e.g., Dixon & Holcomb, 2000 [see Figure 13.7]; Lewis, Powers, Kelk, & Newcomer, 2002 [see Figure 26.12]; White & Bailey, 1990 [see Figure 15.2]).

Krantz and McClannahan (1993) used a multiple baseline across subjects design to investigate the effects of introducing and fading scripts to teach children with autism to interact with their peers. The four participants, ages 9 to 12, had severe communication deficits and minimal or absent academic, social, leisure skills. Prior to the study each of the children had learned to follow first photographic activity schedules (Wacker & Berg, 1983) and later written activity schedules that prompted them through chains of academic, self-care, and leisure activities. Although their teachers modeled social interactions, verbally prompted the children to interact, and provided contingent praise and preferred snacks and activities for doing so, the children consistently failed to initiate interactions without adult prompts.

Each session consisted of a continuous 10-minute interval in which observers recorded the number of times each child initiated and responded to peers while engaged in three art activities—drawing, coloring, and painting—that were rotated across sessions throughout the study. Krantz and McClannahan (1993) described the dependent variables as follows:

> *Initiation to peers* was defined as understandable statements or questions that were unprompted by an adult, that were directed to another child by using his or her name or by facing him or her, and that were separated from the speaker's previous vocalizations by a change in topic or a change in recipient of interaction. . . . *Scripted interactions* were those that matched the written script, . . . e.g., "Ross, I like your picture." *Unscripted interactions* differed from the script by more than changes in conjunctions, articles, prepositions, pronouns, or changes in verb tense; the question, "Would you like some more paper?" was scored as an unscripted initiation because the noun "paper" did not occur in the script. A *response* was defined as any contextual utterance (word, phrase, or sentence) that was not prompted by the teacher and that occurred within 5 s of a statement or question directed to the target child. . . . Examples of responses were "what?" "okay," and "yes, I do." (p. 124)

During baseline, each child found art materials at his or her place and a sheet of paper with the written instructions, "Do your art" and "Talk a lot." The teacher prompted each child to read the written instructions, then moved away. During the script condition, the two written instructions in baseline were supplemented by scripts consisting of 10 statements and questions such as, "{Name}, did you like to {swing/rollerskate/ride the bike} outside today?" "{Name}, do you want to use one of my pencils/crayons/brushes}?" (p. 124). Immediately before each session, the teacher completed blank portions of the scripts so that they reflected activities the children had completed or were planning and objects in the classroom environment. Each child's script included the three other children's names, and the order of the questions or statements varied across sessions and children.

The script condition was implemented with one child at a time, in staggered fashion (see Figure 9.5). Initially the teacher manually guided the child through the script, prompting him or her to read the statement to another child and to pencil a check mark next to it after doing so.

Krantz and McClannahan (1993) described the prompting and script-fading procedures as follows:

> Standing behind a participant, the teacher manually guided him or her to pick up a pencil, point to an instruction or a scripted statement or question, and move the pencil along below the text. If necessary, the teacher also manually guided the child's head to face another child to whom a statement or question was addressed. If the child did not verbalize the statement or questions within 5 s, the manual guidance procedure was repeated. If the child read or said a statement or read or asked a question, the teacher used the same type of manual guidance to ensure that the child placed a check mark to the left of that portion of the script.

Manual prompts were faded as quickly as possible; no prompts were delivered to Kate, Mike, Walt, and

Figure 9.5 A multiple baseline across subjects design showing the number of scripted and unscripted initiations to peers and responses by four children with autism during baseline, script, and follow-up sessions. Arrows indicate when fading steps occurred.

From "Teaching Children with Autism to Initiate to Peers: Effects of a Script-Fading Procedure" by P. J. Krantz and L. E. McClannahan, 1993, *Journal of Applied Behavior Analysis, 26,* p. 129. Copyright 1993 by the Society for the Experimental Analysis of Behavior, Inc. Reprinted by permission.

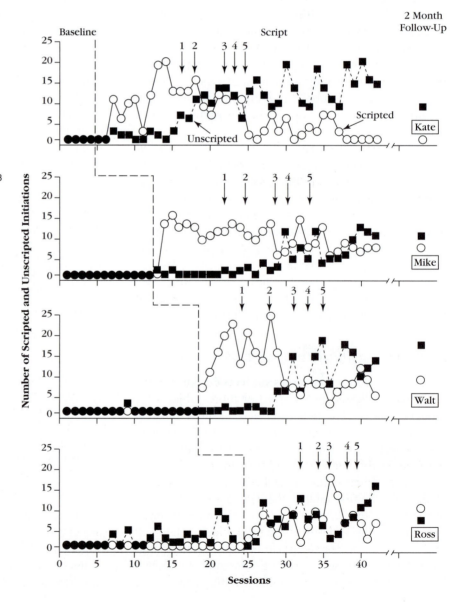

Ross after Sessions 15, 18, 23, and 27, respectively, and the teacher remained at the periphery of the classroom throughout subsequent sessions. After manual guidance had been faded for a target child, fading of the script began. Scripts were faded from end to beginning in five phases. For example, the fading steps for the question "Mike, what do you like to do best on Fun Friday?" were (a) "Mike, what do you like to do best," (b) "Mike, what do you," (c) "Mike, what," (d) "M," and (e) "." (p. 125)

Kate and Mike, who never initiated during baseline, had mean initiations per session of 15 and 13, respectively, during the script condition. Walt's initiations increased from a baseline mean of 0.1 to 17 during the script condition, and Ross averaged 14 initiations per session during script compared to 2 during baseline. As the scripts were faded, each child's frequency of unscripted initiations increased. After the scripts were faded, the four participants' frequency of initiations were within the same range as that of a sample of three typically developing children. The researchers implemented the script-fading steps with each participant in response to his or her performance, not according to a predetermined schedule, thereby retaining the flexibility needed to pursue the behavior–environment relations that are the focus of the science of behavior.

However, because each subject did not serve as his or her own control, this study illustrates that the multiple baseline across subjects design is not a true single-subject design. Instead, verification of predictions based on the baseline data for each subject must be inferred from the relatively unchanging measures of the behavior of other subjects who are still in baseline, and replication of effects must be inferred from changes in the behavior of other subjects when they come into contact with the independent variable. This is both a weakness and a potential advantage of the multiple baseline across subjects design (Johnston & Pennypacker, 1993a), discussed later in the chapter.

Variations of the Multiple Baseline Design

Two variations of the multiple baseline design are the multiple probe design and the delayed multiple baseline design. The multiple probe design enables the behavior analyst to extend the operation and logic of the multiple baseline tactic to behaviors or situations in which concurrent measurement of all behaviors comprising the design is unnecessary, potentially reactive, impractical, or too costly. The delayed multiple baseline technique can be used when a planned reversal design is no longer possible or proves ineffective; it can also add additional tiers to an already operational multiple baseline design, as would be the case if new subjects were added to an ongoing study.

Multiple Probe Design

The **multiple probe design,** first described by Horner and Baer (1978), is a method of analyzing the relation between the independent variable and the acquisition of a successive approximation or task sequence. In contrast to the multiple baseline design—in which data are collected simultaneously throughout the baseline phase for each behavior, setting, or subject in the experiment—in the multiple probe design intermittent measures, or probes, provide the basis for determining whether behavior change has occurred prior to intervention. According to Horner and Baer, when applied to a chain or sequence of related behaviors to be learned, the multiple probe design provides answers to four questions: (a) What is the initial level of performance on each step (behavior) in the sequence? (b) What happens when sequential opportunities to perform each step in the sequence are provided prior to training on that step? (c) What happens to each step as training is applied? and (d) What happens to the performance of untrained steps in the sequence as criterion-level performance is reached on the preceding steps?

Figure 9.6 shows a graphic prototype of the multiple probe design. Although researchers have developed many variations of the multiple probe technique, the basic design has three key features: (a) An initial probe is taken to determine the subject's level of performance on each behavior in the sequence; (b) a series of baseline measures is obtained on each step prior to training on that step; and (c) after criterion-level performance is reached on any training step, a probe of each step in the sequence is obtained to determine whether performance changes have occurred in any other steps.

Thompson, Braam, and Fuqua (1982) used a multiple probe design to analyze the effects of an instructional procedure composed of prompts and token reinforcement on the acquisition of a complex chain of laundry skills by three students with developmental disabilities. Observations of people doing laundry resulted in a detailed task analysis of 74 discrete responses that were organized into seven major components (e.g., sorting, loading washer). Each student's performance was assessed via probe and baseline sessions that preceded training on each component. Probe and baseline sessions began with instructions to the student to do the laundry. When an incorrect response was emitted or when no response occurred within 5 seconds of a prompt to continue, the student was seated away from the laundry area. The trainer then performed the correct response and called the student back to the area so that assessment of the rest of the laundry sequence could continue.

Probe sessions differed from baseline sessions in two ways. First, a probe measured each response in the entire

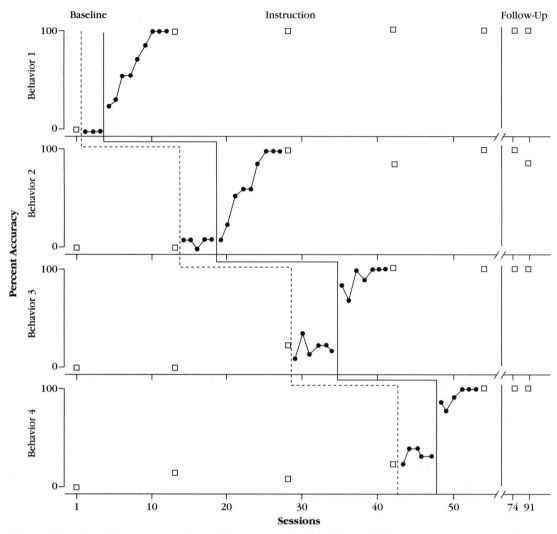

Figure 9.6 Graphic prototype of a multiple probe design. Square data points represent results of probe sessions in which the entire sequence or set of behaviors (1–4) are tested.

chain and occurred immediately prior to baseline and training for every component. Baseline sessions occurred following the probe and measured only previously trained components plus the component about to be trained. Baseline data were gathered on a variable number of consecutive sessions immediately prior to training sessions. Second, no tokens or descriptive praise were delivered during probes. During baseline, tokens were delivered for previously trained responses only. . . . Following baseline, each component was trained using a graduated 3-prompt procedure (Horner & Keilitz, 1975), consisting of verbal instruction, modeling, and graduated guidance. If one prompt level failed to produce a correct response within 5 sec, the next level was introduced. . . . When the student performed a component at 100% accuracy for two consecutive trials, he was required to perform the entire laundry chain from the beginning through the component most recently mastered. The entire chain of previously mastered components was

trained (chain training condition) until it was performed without errors or prompts for two consecutive trials. (Thompson, Braam, & Fuqua, 1982, p. 179)

Figure 9.7 shows the results for Chester, one of the students. Chester performed a low percentage of correct responses during the probe and baseline sessions, but performed with 100% accuracy after training was applied to each component. During a generalization probe conducted at a community laundromat after training, Chester performed correctly 82% of the 74 total responses in the chain. Five additional training sessions were needed to retrain responses performed incorrectly during the generalization probe and to train "additional responses necessitated by the presence of coin slots and minor differences between the training and laundromat equipment" (p. 179). On two follow-up sessions conducted 10 months after training, Chester performed at 90% accu-

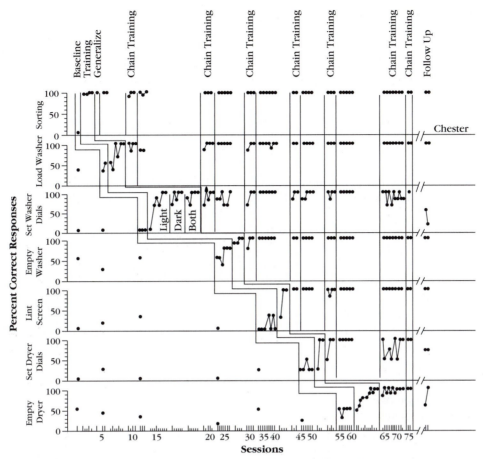

Figure 9.7   A multiple probe design showing the percentage of correct responses for each trial on each component of a laundry task by a young adult male with mental retardation. Heavy vertical lines on the horizontal axis represent successive training sessions; lighter and shorter vertical lines indicate trials within a session.

From "Training and Generalization of Laundry Skills: A Multiple-Probe Evaluation with Handicapped Persons" by T. J. Thompson, S. J. Braam, and R. W. Fuqua, 1982, *Journal of Applied Behavior Analysis, 15*, p. 180. Copyright 1982 by the Society for the Experimental Analysis of Behavior, Inc. Reprinted by permission.

racy even though he had not performed the laundry task for the past 2 months. Similar results were obtained for the other two students who participated in the study.

Thompson and colleagues (1982) added the chain training condition to their study because they believed that components trained as independent skills were unlikely to be emitted in correct sequence without such practice. It should be noted that the experimenters did not begin training a new component until stable responding had been achieved during baseline observations (see the baseline data for the bottom four tiers in Figure 9.7). Delaying the training in this manner enabled a clear demonstration of a functional relation between training and skill acquisition.

The multiple probe design is particularly appropriate for evaluating the effects of instruction on skill sequences in which it is highly unlikely that the subject can improve performance on later steps in the sequence with-

out acquiring the prior steps. For example, the repeated measurement of the accuracy in solving division problems of a student who possesses no skills in addition, subtraction, and multiplication would add little to an analysis. Horner and Baer (1978) made this point exceedingly well:

> The inevitable zero scores on the division baseline have no real meaning: division could be nothing else than zero (or chance, depending on the test format), and there is no real point in measuring it. Such measures are *pro forma:* they fill out the picture of a multiple baseline, true, but in an illusory way. They do not so much represent zero behavior as zero opportunity for the behavior to occur, and there is no need to document at the level of well-measured data that behavior does not occur when it cannot. (p. 190)

Thus, the multiple probe design avoids the necessity of collecting ritualistic baseline data when the performance of any component of a chain or sequence is impossible or unlikely before acquisition of its preceding components. In addition to the two uses already mentioned—analysis of the effects of instruction on complex skill sequences and reduction in the amount of baseline measurement for behaviors that have no plausible opportunity to occur—the multiple probe technique is also an effective experimental strategy for situations in which extended baseline measurement may prove reactive, impractical, or costly. The repeated measurement of a skill under nontreatment conditions can prove aversive to some students; and extinction, boredom, or other undesirable responses can occur. In his discussion of multiple baseline designs, Cuvo (1979) suggested that researchers should recognize that "there is a trade-off between repeatedly administering the dependent measure to establish a stable baseline on one hand and risking impaired performance by subjecting participants to a potentially punishing experience on the other hand" (pp. 222–223). Furthermore, complete assessment of all skills in a sequence may require too much time that could otherwise be spent on instruction.

Other examples of the multiple probe design can be found in Arntzen, Halstadtr, and Halstadtr (2003); Coleman-Martin & Wolff Heller (2004); O'Reilly, Green, and Braunling-McMorrow, (1990); and Werts, Caldwell and Wolery (1996, see Figure 20.6).

Delayed Multiple Baseline Design

The **delayed multiple baseline design** is an experimental tactic in which an initial baseline and intervention are begun, and subsequent baselines are added in a staggered or delayed fashion (Heward, 1978). Figure 9.8 shows a graphic prototype of the delayed multiple baseline design. The design employs the same experimental reasoning as a full-scale multiple baseline design with the exception that data from baselines begun after the independent variable has been applied to previous behaviors, settings, or subjects cannot be used to verify predictions based on earlier tiers of the design. In Figure 9.8 baseline measurement of Behaviors 2 and 3 was begun early

Figure 9.8 Graphic prototype of a delayed multiple baseline design.

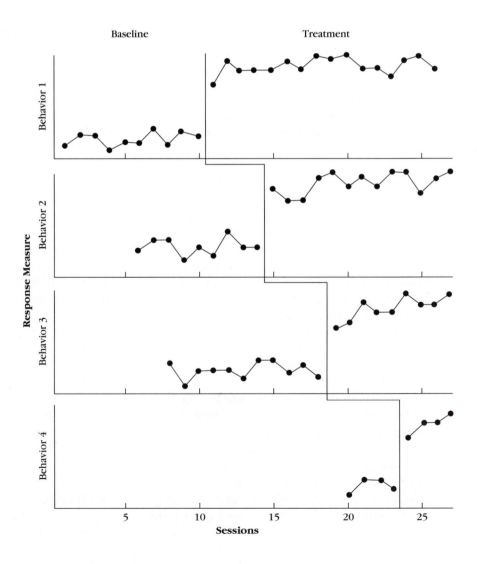

enough for those data to be used to verify the prediction made for Behavior 1. The final four baseline data points for Behavior 3 also verify the prediction for Behavior 2. However, baseline measurement of Behavior 4 began after the independent variable had been applied to each of the previous behaviors, thus limiting its role in the design to an additional demonstration of replication.

A delayed multiple baseline design may allow the behavior analyst to conduct research in certain environments in which other experimental tactics cannot be implemented. Heward (1978) suggested three such situations.

- *A reversal design is no longer desirable or possible.* In applied settings the research environment may shift, negating the use of a previously planned reversal design. Such shifts may involve changes in the subject's environment that make the target behavior no longer likely to reverse to baseline levels, or changes in the behavior of parents, teachers, administrators, the subject/client, or the behavior analyst that, for any number of reasons, make a previously planned reversal design no longer desirable or possible. . . . If there are other behaviors, settings, or subjects appropriate for application of the independent variable, the behavior analyst could use a delayed multiple baseline technique and still pursue evidence of a functional relation.
- *Limited resources, ethical concerns, or practical difficulties preclude a full-scale multiple baseline design.* This situation occurs when the behavior analyst only controls resources sufficient to initially record and intervene with one behavior, setting, or subject, and another research strategy is inappropriate. It may be that as a result of the first intervention, more resources become available for gathering additional baselines. This might occur following the improvement of certain behaviors whose pretreatment topography and/or rate required an inordinate expenditure of staff resources. Or, it could be that a reluctant administrator, after seeing the successful results of the first intervention, provides the resources necessary for additional analysis. Ethical concerns may preclude extended baseline measurement of some behaviors (e.g., Linscheid, Iwata, Ricketts, Williams, & Griffin, 1990). Also under this heading would fall the "practical difficulties" cited by Hobbs and Holt (1976) as a reason for delaying baseline measurement in one of three settings.
- *A "new" behavior, setting, or subject becomes available.* A delayed multiple baseline technique might be employed when another research design was originally planned but a multiple baseline analysis becomes the preferred approach due to changes in the environment (e.g., the subject begins to emit another behavior appropriate for intervention with the experimental variable, the subject begins to emit the original target behavior in another setting, or additional subjects displaying the same target behavior become available.) (adapted from pp. 5–6)

Researchers have used the delayed multiple baseline technique to evaluate the effects of a wide variety of interventions (e.g., Baer, Williams, Osnes, & Stokes, 1984; Copeland, Brown, & Hall, 1974; Hobbs & Holt, 1976; Jones, Fremouw, & Carples, 1977; Linscheid et al., 1990; Risley & Hart, 1968; Schepis, Reid, Behrmann, & Sutton, 1998; White & Bailey, 1990 [Figure 15.1]). Poche, Brouwer, and Swearingen (1981) used a delayed multiple baseline design to evaluate the effects of a training program designed to prevent children from being abducted by adults. Three typically developing preschool children were selected as subjects because, during a screening test, each readily agreed to leave with an adult stranger. The dependent variable was the level of appropriateness of self-protective responses emitted by each child when an adult suspect approached the child and attempted to lure her away with a simple lure ("Would you like to go for a walk?"), an authoritative lure ("Your teacher said it was all right for you to come with me"), or an incentive lure ("I've got a nice surprise in my car. Would you like to come with me and see it?").

Each session began with the child's teacher bringing the child outdoors, then pretending to have to return to the building for some reason. The adult suspect (a confederate of the experimenters but unknown to the child) then approached the child and offered one of the lures. The confederate also served as observer, scoring the child's response on a 0 to 6 scale, with a score of 6 representing the desired response (saying, "No, I have to go ask my teacher" and moving at least 20 feet away from the suspect within 3 seconds) and a score of 0 indicating that the child moved some distance away from the school building with the suspect. Training consisted of modeling, behavioral rehearsal, and social reinforcement for correct responses.

Figure 9.9 shows the results of the training program. During baseline, all three children responded to the lures with safety ratings of 0 or 1. All three children mastered correct responses to the incentive lure in one to three training sessions, with one or two more sessions required for each child to master correct responses to the other two lures. Overall, training took approximately 90 minutes per child distributed over five or six sessions. All three children responded correctly when the lures were administered in generalization probes on sidewalk locations 150 to 400 feet from the school.

Although each baseline in this study was of equal length (i.e., had an equal number of data points), contradicting the general rule that the baselines in a multiple baseline design should vary significantly in length, there are two good reasons that Poche and colleagues began training when they did with each subject. First, the nearly total stability of the baseline performance of each child provided an ample basis for evaluating the training program

Figure 9.9 A delayed multiple baseline design showing the level of appropriateness of self-protective responses during baseline, training, and generality probes in school and community settings. Closed symbols indicate data gathered near the school; open symbols, in a location away from the school.

From "Teaching Self-Protection to Young Children" by C. Poche, R. Brouwer, and M. Swearingen, 1981, *Journal of Applied Behavior Analysis, 14*, p. 174. Copyright 1981 by the Society for the Experimental Analysis of Behavior, Inc. Reprinted by permission.

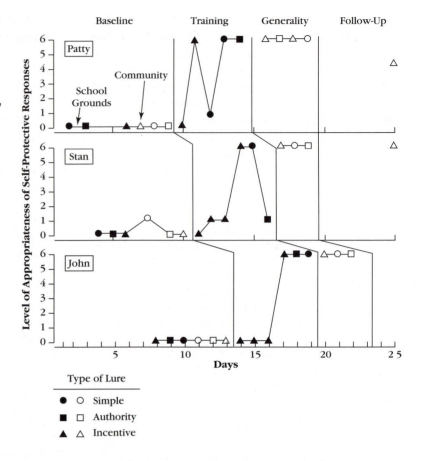

(the only exception to complete susceptibility to the adult suspect's lures occurred when Stan stayed near the suspect instead of actually going away with him on his fourth baseline observation). Second, and more important, the nature of the target behavior required that it be taught to each child as soon as possible. Although continuing baseline measurement for varying lengths across the different tiers of any multiple baseline design is good practice from a purely experimental viewpoint, the ethics of such a practice in this instance would be highly questionable, given the potential danger of exposing the children to adult lures repeatedly while withholding training.

The delayed multiple baseline design presents several limitations (Heward, 1978). First, from an applied standpoint the design is not a good one if it requires the behavior analyst to wait too long to modify important behaviors, although this problem is inherent in all multiple baseline designs. Second, in a delayed multiple baseline design there is a tendency for the delayed baseline phases to contain fewer data points than are found in a standard multiple baseline design, in which all baselines are begun simultaneously, resulting in baseline phases of considerable and varying length. Long baselines, if stable, provide the predictive power that permits convincing demonstrations of experimental control. Behavior analysts using any type of multiple baseline design must be

sure that all baselines, regardless of when they are begun, are of sufficient and varied length to provide a believable basis for comparing experimental effects. A third limitation of the delayed multiple baseline design is that it can mask the interdependence of dependent variables.

> The strength of any multiple baseline design is that little or no change is noticed in the other, as yet untreated, behaviors until, and only until, the experimenter applies the independent variable. In a delayed multiple baseline design, the "delayed baseline" data gathered for subsequent behaviors may represent changed performance due to the experimental manipulation of other behaviors in the design and, therefore, may not be representative of the true, preexperimental operant level. . . . In such instances, the delayed multiple baseline might result in a "false negative," and the researcher may erroneously conclude that the intervention was not effective on the subsequent behavior(s), when in reality the lack of simultaneous baseline data did not permit the discovery that the behaviors covaried. This is a major weakness of the delayed multiple baseline design and makes it a research tactic of second choice whenever a full-scale multiple baseline can be employed. However, this limitation can and should be combated whenever possible by beginning subsequent baselines at least several sessions prior to intervention on previous baselines. (Heward, 1978, pp. 8–9)

Both the multiple probe design and the delayed multiple baseline design offer the applied behavior analyst alternative tactics for pursuing a multiple baseline analysis when extended baseline measurement is unnecessary, impractical, too costly, or unavailable. Perhaps the most useful application of the delayed multiple baseline technique is in adding tiers to an already operational multiple baseline design. Whenever a delayed baseline can be supplemented by probes taken earlier in the course of the study, experimental control is strengthened. As a general rule, the more baseline data, the better.

Assumptions and Guidelines for Using Multiple Baseline Designs

Like all experimental tactics, the multiple baseline design requires the researcher to make certain assumptions about how the behavior–environment relations under investigation function, even though discovering the existence and operation of those relations is the very reason for conducting the research. In this sense, the design of behavioral experiments resembles an empirical guessing game—the experimenter guesses; the data answer. The investigator makes assumptions, hypotheses in the informal sense, about behavior and its relation to controlling variables and then constructs experiments designed to produce data capable of verifying or refuting those conjectures.[3]

Because verification and replication in the multiple baseline design depends on what happens, or does not happen, to other behaviors as a result of the sequential application of the independent variable, the experimenter must be particularly careful to plan and carry out the design in a manner that will afford the greatest degree of confidence in any relations suggested by the data. Although the multiple baseline design appears deceptively simple, its successful application entails much more than selecting two or more behaviors, settings, or subjects, collecting some baseline data, and then introducing a treatment condition to one behavior after the other. We

suggest the following guidelines for designing and conducting experiments using multiple baseline designs.

Select Independent, yet Functionally Similar, Baselines

Demonstration of a functional relation in a multiple baseline design depends on two occurrences: (a) the behavior(s) still in baseline showing no change in level, variability, or trend while the behavior(s) in contact with the independent variable changes; and (b) each behavior changes when, and only when, the independent variable has been applied to it. Thus, the experimenter must make two, at times seemingly contradictory, assumptions about the behaviors targeted for analysis in a multiple baseline design. The assumptions are that the behaviors are functionally independent of one another (the behaviors will not covary with one another), and yet the behaviors share enough similarity that each will change when the same independent variable is applied to it (Tawney & Gast, 1984). An error in either assumption can result in a failure to demonstrate a functional relation.

For example, let us suppose that the independent variable is introduced with the first behavior, and changes in level and/or trend are noted, but the other behaviors still in baseline also change. Do the changes in the still-in-baseline behaviors mean that an uncontrolled variable is responsible for the changes in all of the behaviors and that the independent variable is an effective treatment? Or do the simultaneous changes in the untreated behaviors mean that the changes in the first behavior were affected by the independent variable and have generalized to the other behaviors? Or, let us suppose instead that the first behavior changes when the independent variable is introduced, but subsequent behaviors do not change when the independent variable is applied. Does this failure to replicate mean that a factor other than the independent variable was responsible for the change observed in the first behavior? Or does it mean only that the subsequent behaviors do not operate as a function of the experimental variable, leaving open the possibility that the change noted in the first behavior was affected by the independent variable?

Answers to these questions can be pursued only by further experimental manipulations. In both kinds of failure to demonstrate experimental control, the multiple baseline design does not rule out the possibility of a functional relation between the independent variable and the behavior(s) that did change when the variable was applied. In the first instance, the failure to demonstrate experimental control with the originally planned design is offset by the opportunity to investigate and possibly isolate the variable robust enough to change multiple behaviors simultaneously. Discovery of variables that reliably produce

---

[3]*Hypothesis,* as we are using the term here, should not be confused with the formal hypothesis testing models that use inferential statistics to confirm or reject a hypothesis deduced from a theory. As Johnston and Pennypacker (1993a) pointed out, "Researchers do not need to state hypotheses if they are asking a question about nature. When the experimental question simply asks about the relation between independent and dependent variables, there is no scientific reason to make a prediction about what will be learned from the data" (p. 48). However, Johnston and Pennypacker (1980) also recognized that "more modest hypotheses are constantly being subjected to experimental tests, if only to establish greater confidence in the details of the suspected controlling relations. Whenever an experimenter arranges to affirm the consequent of a particular proposition, he or she is testing a hypothesis, although it is rare to encounter the actual use of such language [in behavior analysis]. Hypothesis testing in this relatively informal sense guides the construction of experiments without blinding the researcher to the importance of unexpected results" (pp. 38–39).

generalized changes across behaviors, settings, and/or subjects is a major goal of applied behavior analysis; and if the experimenter is confident that all other relevant variables were held constant before, during, and after the observed behavior changes, the original independent variable is the first candidate for further investigation.

In the second situation, with its failure to replicate changes from one behavior to another, the experimenter can pursue the possibility of a functional relation between the independent variable and the first behavior, perhaps using a reversal technique, and seek to discover later an effective intervention for the behavior(s) that did not change. Another possibility is to drop the original independent variable altogether and search for another treatment that might be effective with all of the targeted behaviors.

Select Concurrent and Plausibly Related Multiple Baselines

In an effort to ensure the functional independence of behaviors in a multiple baseline design, experimenters should not select response classes or settings so unrelated to one another as to offer no plausible means of comparison. For the ongoing baseline measurement of one behavior to provide the strongest basis for verifying the prediction of another behavior that has been exposed to an independent variable, two conditions must be met: (a) The two behaviors must be measured concurrently, and (b) all of the relevant variables that influence one behavior must have an opportunity to influence the other behavior. Studies that employ a multiple baseline approach across subjects and settings often stretch the logic of the design beyond its capabilities. For example, using the stable baseline measures of one child's compliance with parental requests as the basis for verifying the effect of intervention on the compliance behavior of another child living with another family is questionable practice. The sets of variables influencing the two children are surely differentiated by more than the presence or absence of the experimental variable.

> There are some important limits to designating multiple behavior/setting combinations that are intended to function as part of the same experiment. In order for the use of multiple behaviors and settings to be part of the same design and thus augment experimental reasoning, the general experimental conditions under which the two responses (whether two from one subject or one from each of two subjects) are emitted and measured must be ongoing concurrently. . . . Exposure [to the independent variable] does not have to be simultaneous for the different behavior/setting combinations, [but] it must be the identical treatment conditions along with the associated extraneous variables that impinge on the two responses and/or settings. This is because the conditions imposed

on one behavior/setting combination must have the *opportunity* of influencing the other behavior/setting combination at the same time, regardless of the condition that actually prevails for the second. . . . It follows that using responses of two subjects each responding in different settings would not meet the requirement that there be a coincident opportunity for detecting the treatment effect. A treatment condition [as well as the myriad other variables possibly responsible for changes in the behavior of one subject] could not then come into contact with the responding of the other subject, because the second subject's responding would be occurring in an entirely different location. . . . Generally, the greater the plausibility that the two responses would be affected by the single treatment [and all other relevant variables], the more powerful is the demonstration of experimental control evidenced by data showing a change in only one behavior. (Johnston and Pennypacker, 1980, pp. 276–278)

The requirements of concurrency and plausible influence must be met for the verification element of baseline logic to operate in a multiple baseline design. However, replication of effect is demonstrated each time a baseline steady state is changed by the introduction of the independent variable, more or less regardless of where or when the variable is applied. Such nonconcurrent and/or unrelated baselines can provide valuable data on the generality of a treatment's effectiveness.[4]

This discussion should not be interpreted to mean that a valid (i.e., logically complete) multiple baseline design cannot be conducted across different subjects, each responding in different settings. Numerous studies using mixed multiple baselines across subjects, responses classes, and/or settings have contributed to the development of an effective technology of behavior change (e.g., Dixon et al., 1998; Durand, 1999 [see Figure 23.4]; Ryan, Ormond, Imwold, & Rotunda, 2002).

Let us consider an experiment designed to analyze the effects of a particular teacher training intervention, perhaps a workshop on using tactics to increase each student's opportunity to respond during group instruction. Concurrent measurement is begun on the frequency of student response opportunities in the classrooms of the teachers who are participating in the study. After stable

---

[4]A related series of A-B designs across different behaviors, settings, and/or participants in which each A-B sequence is conducted at a different point in time is sometimes called a *nonconcurrent multiple baseline design* (Watson & Workman, 1981). The absence of concurrent measurement, however, violates and effectively neuters the experimental logic of the multiple baseline design. Putting the graphs of three A-B designs on the same page and tying them together with a dogleg dashed line might produce something that "looks like" a multiple baseline design, but doing so is of questionable value and is likely to mislead readers by suggesting a greater degree of experimental control than is warranted. We recommend describing such a study as a series or collection of A-B designs and graphing the results in a manner that clearly depicts the actual time frame in which each A-B sequence occurred with respect to the others (e.g., Harvey, May, & Kennedy, 2004, Figure 2).

baselines have been established, the workshop is presented first to one teacher (or group of teachers) and eventually, in staggered multiple baseline fashion, to all of the teachers.

In this example, even though the different subjects (teachers) are all behaving in different environments (different classrooms), comparison of their baseline conditions is experimentally sound because the variables likely to influence their teaching styles operate in the larger, shared environment in which they all behave (the school and teaching community). Nevertheless, whenever experiments are proposed or published that involve different subjects responding in different settings, researchers and consumers should view the baseline comparisons with a critical eye toward their logical relation to one other.

Do Not Apply the Independent Variable to the Next Behavior Too Soon

To reiterate, for verification to occur in a multiple baseline design, it must be established clearly that as the independent variable is applied to one behavior and change is noted, little or no change is observed in the other, as-yet-untreated behaviors. The potential for a powerful demonstration of experimental control has been destroyed in many studies because the independent variable was applied to subsequent behaviors too soon. Although the operational requirement of sequential application in the multiple baseline tactic is met by introduction of the independent variable even in adjacent time intervals, the experimental reasoning afforded by such closely spaced manipulations is minimal.

> The influence of unknown, concomitant, extraneous variables that might be present could still be substantial, even a day or two later. This problem can be avoided by demonstrating continued stability in responding for the second behavior/setting combination during and after the introduction of the treatment for the first combination until a sufficient period of time has elapsed to detect any effect on the second combination that might appear. (Johnston & Pennypacker, 1980, p. 283)

Vary Significantly the Lengths of Multiple Baselines

Generally, the more the baseline phases in a multiple baseline design differ in length from one another, the stronger the design will be. Baselines of significantly different lengths allow the unambiguous conclusion (assuming an effective treatment variable) that each behavior not only changes when the independent variable is applied, but also that each behavior does not change until the independent variable has been applied. If the different baselines are of the same or similar length, the possibility

exists that changes noted when the independent variable is introduced are the result of a confounding variable, such as practice or reactivity to observation and measurement, and not a function of the experimental variable.

> Those effects . . . called practice, adaptation, warm-up, self-analysis, etc.; whatever they may be and whatever they may be called, the multiple baseline design controls for them by systematically varying the length of time (sessions, days, weeks) in which they occur prior to the introduction of the training package. . . . Such control is essential, and when the design consists of only two baselines, then the number of data points in each prior to experimental intervention should differ as radically as possible, at least by a factor of 2. I cannot see not systematically varying lengths of baselines prior to intervention, and varying them as much as possible/practical. Failure to do that . . . weakens the design too much for credibility. (D. M. Baer, personal communication, June 2, 1978)

Intervene on the Most Stable Baseline First

In the ideal multiple baseline design, the independent variable is not applied to any of the behaviors until steady state responding has been achieved for each. However, the applied behavior analyst is sometimes denied the option of delaying treatment just to increase the strength of an experimental analysis. When intervention must begin before stability is evident across each tier of the design, the independent variable should be applied to the behavior, setting, or subject that shows the most stable level of baseline responding. For example, if a study is designed to evaluate the effects of a teaching procedure on the rate of math computation of four students and there is no a priori reason to teach the students in any particular sequence, instruction should begin with the student showing the most stable baseline. However, this recommendation should be followed only when the majority of the baselines in the design show reasonable stability.

Sequential application of the independent variable should be made in the order of greatest stability at the time of each subsequent application. Again, however, the realities of the applied world must be heeded. The social significance of changing a particular behavior must sometimes take precedence over the desire to meet the requirements of experimental design.

Considering the Appropriateness of Multiple Baseline Designs

The multiple baseline design offers significant advantages, which no doubt have accounted for its widespread use by researchers and practitioners. Those advantages, however, must be weighed against the limitations and weaknesses of the design to determine its appropriateness in any given situation.

Advantages of the Multiple Baseline Design

Probably the most important advantage of the multiple baseline design is that it does not require withdrawing a seemingly effective treatment to demonstrate experimental control. This is a critical consideration for target behaviors that are self-injurious or dangerous to others. This feature of the multiple baseline design also makes it an appropriate method for evaluating the effects of independent variables that cannot, by their nature, be withdrawn and for investigating target behaviors that are likely or that prove to be irreversible (e.g., Duker & van Lent, 1991). Additionally, because the multiple baseline design does not necessitate a reversal of treatment gains to baseline levels, parents, teachers, or administrators may accept it more readily as a method of demonstrating the effects of an intervention.

The requirement of the multiple baseline design to sequentially apply the independent variable across multiple behaviors, settings, or subjects complements the usual practice of many practitioners whose goal is to develop multiple behavior changes. Teachers are charged with helping multiple students learn multiple skills to be used in multiple settings. Likewise, clinicians typically need to help their clients improve more than one response class and emit more adaptive behavior in several settings. The multiple baseline design is ideally suited to the evaluation of the progressive, multiple behavior changes sought by many practitioners in applied settings.

Because the multiple baseline design entails concurrent measurement of two or more behaviors, settings, or subjects, it is useful in assessing the occurrence of generalization of behavior change. The simultaneous monitoring of several behaviors gives the behavior analyst the opportunity to determine their covariation as a result of manipulations of the independent variable (Hersen & Barlow, 1976). Although changes in behaviors still under baseline conditions eliminate the ability of the multiple baseline design to demonstrate experimental control, such changes reveal the possibility that the independent variable is capable of producing behavioral improvements with desirable generality, thereby suggesting an additional set of research questions and analytic tactics (e.g., Odom, Hoyson, Jamieson, & Strain, 1985).

Finally, the multiple baseline design has the advantage of being relatively easy to conceptualize, thereby offering an effective experimental tactic for teachers and parents who are not trained formally in research methodology (Hall et al., 1970).

Limitations of the Multiple Baseline Design

The multiple baseline design presents at least three scientific limitations or considerations. First, a multiple baseline design may not allow a demonstration of experimental control even though a functional relation exists between the independent variable and the behaviors to which it is applied. Changes in behaviors still under baseline conditions and similar to concurrent changes in a behavior in the treatment condition preclude the demonstration of a functional relation within the original design. Second, from one perspective, the multiple baseline design is a weaker method for showing experimental control than the reversal design. This is because verification of the baseline prediction made for each behavior within a multiple baseline design is not directly demonstrated with that behavior, but must be inferred from the lack of change in other behaviors. This weakness of the multiple baseline design, however, should be weighed against the design's advantage of providing multiple replications across different behaviors, settings, or subjects. Third, the multiple baseline design provides more information about the effectiveness of the treatment variable than it does about the function of any particular target behavior.

> Consistently [the] multiple baseline is less an experimental analysis of the response than of the technique used to alter the response. In the reversal design, the response is made to work again and again; in the multiple-baseline designs, it is primarily the technique that works again and again, and the responses either work once each [if different responses are used] or else a single response works once each per setting or once each per subject. Repetitive working of the same response in the same subject or the same setting is not displayed. But, while repetitive working of the response is foregone, repetitive and diverse working of the experimental technique is maximized, as it would not be in the reversal design. (Baer, 1975, p. 22)

Two important applied considerations that must be evaluated in determining the appropriateness of the multiple baseline design are the time and resources required for its implementation. Because the treatment variable cannot be applied to subsequent behaviors, settings, or subjects until its effects have been observed on previous behaviors, settings, or subjects, the multiple baseline design requires that intervention be withheld for some behaviors, settings, or subjects, perhaps for a long time. This delay raises practical and ethical concerns. Treatment cannot be delayed for some behaviors; their importance makes delaying treatment impractical. And as Stolz (1978) pointed out, "If the intervention is generally acknowledged to be effective, denying it simply to achieve a multiple-baseline design might be unethical" (p. 33). Second, the resources needed for the concurrent measurement of multiple behaviors must be considered. Use of a multiple baseline design can be particularly costly when behavior must be observed and measured in several settings. However, when the use of intermittent probes during baseline can be justified in lieu of continuous measurement (Horner & Baer, 1978), the cost of concurrently measuring multiple behaviors can be reduced.

Changing Criterion Design

The changing criterion design can be used to evaluate the effects of a treatment that is applied in a graduated or stepwise fashion to a single target behavior. The changing criterion design was first described in the applied behavior analysis literature in two papers coauthored by Vance Hall (Hall & Fox, 1977; Hartmann & Hall, 1976).

Operation and Logic of the Changing Criterion Design

The reader can refer to Figure 9.10 before and after reading Hartmann and Hall's (1976) description of the **changing criterion design.**

> The design requires initial baseline observations on a single target behavior. This baseline phase is followed by implementation of a treatment program in each of a series of treatment phases. Each treatment phase is associated with a step-wise change in criterion rate for the target behavior. Thus, each phase of the design provides a baseline for the following phase. When the rate of the target behavior changes with each stepwise change in the criterion, therapeutic change is replicated and experimental control is demonstrated. (p. 527)

The operation of two elements of baseline logic—prediction and replication—is clear in the changing cri-

terion design. When stable responding is attained within each phase of the design, a prediction of future responding is made. Replication occurs each time the level of behavior changes in a systematic way when the criterion is changed. Verification of the predictions based on each phase is not so obvious in this design but can be approached in two ways. First, varying the lengths of phases systematically enables a form of self-evident verification. The prediction is made that the level of responding will not change if the criterion is not changed. When the criterion is not changed and stable responding continues, the prediction is verified. When it can be shown within the design that levels of responding do not change unless the criterion is changed, regardless of the varied lengths of phases, experimental control is evident. Hall and Fox (1977) suggested another possibility for verification: "The experimenter may return to a former criterion and if the behavior conforms to this criterion level there is also a cogent argument for a high degree of behavioral control" (p. 154). Such a reversed criterion is shown in the next-to-last phase of Figure 9.10. Although returning to an earlier criterion level requires a brief interruption of the steady improvement in behavior, the reversal tactic strengthens the analysis considerably and should be included in the changing criterion design unless other factors indicate its inappropriateness.

One way to conceptualize the changing criterion design is as a variation of the multiple baseline design. Both Hartmann and Hall (1976, p. 530) and Hall and Fox (1977, p. 164) replotted data from changing criterion design experiments in a multiple baseline format with each tier of the multiple baseline showing the occurrence or nonoccurrence of the target behavior at one of the criterion levels used in the experiment. A vertical condition change line doglegs through the tiers indicating when the criterion for reinforcement was raised to the level

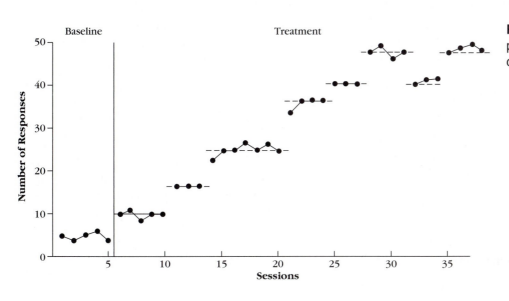

Figure 9.10 Graphic prototype of a changing criterion design.

represented by each tier. By graphing whether the target behavior was emitted during each session at or above the level represented on each tier both before and after the change in criterion to that level, a kind of multiple baseline analysis is revealed. However, the strength of the multiple baseline argument is not quite so convincing because the "different" behaviors represented by each tier are not independent of one another. For example, if a target behavior is emitted 10 times in a given session, all of the tiers representing criteria below 10 responses would have to show that the behavior occurred, and all of the tiers representing criteria of 11 or more would have to show no occurrence of the behavior, or zero responding. The majority of the tiers that would appear to show verification and replication of effect, in fact, could only show these results because of the events plotted on another tier. A multiple baseline design provides its convincing demonstration of experimental control because the measures obtained for each behavior in the design are a function of the controlling variables for that behavior, not artifacts of the measurement of another behavior. Thus, recasting the data from a changing criterion design into a many-tiered multiple baseline format will often result in a biased picture in favor of experimental control.

Even though the multiple baseline design is not completely analogous, the changing criterion design can be conceptualized as a method of analyzing the development of new behaviors. As Sidman (1960) pointed out, "It is possible to make reinforcement contingent upon a specified value of some aspect of behavior, and to treat that value as a response class in its own right" (p. 391). The changing criterion design can be an effective tactic for showing the repeated production of new rates of behavior as a function of manipulations of the independent variable (i.e., criterion changes).

Other than the experiments included in the Hartmann and Hall (1976) and Hall and Fox (1977) papers, there have been relatively few examples of pure changing criterion designs published in the applied behavior analysis literature (e.g., DeLuca & Holborn, 1992 [see Figure 13.2]; Foxx & Rubinoff, 1979; Johnston & McLaughlin, 1982). Some researchers have employed a changing criterion tactic as an analytic element within a larger design (e.g., Martella, Leonard, Marchand-Martella, & Agran, 1993; Schleien, Wehman, & Kiernan, 1981).

Allen and Evans (2001) used a changing criterion design to evaluate the effects of an intervention to reduce the excessive checking of blood sugar levels by Amy, a 15-year-old girl diagnosed with insulin-dependent diabetes about 2 years prior to the study. Persons with this form of diabetes must guard against hypoglycemia (i.e., low blood sugar), a condition that produces a cluster of symptoms such as headaches, dizziness, shaking, impaired vision, and increased heart rate, and can lead to

seizures and loss of consciousness. Because hypoglycemic episodes are physically unpleasant and can be a source of social embarrassment, some patients become hypervigilent in avoiding them, checking for low blood sugar more often than is necessary and deliberately maintaining high blood glucose levels. This leads to poor metabolic control and increased risk of complications such as blindness, renal failure, and heart disease.

At home Amy's parents helped her monitor her blood sugar levels and insulin injections; at school Amy checked her blood glucose levels independently. Her physician recommended that Amy keep her blood sugar levels between 75 and 150 mg/dl, which required her to check her blood sugar 6 to 12 times per day. Soon after she had been diagnosed with diabetes, Amy experienced a single hypoglycemic episode in which her blood sugar fell to 40 mg/dl, and she experienced physical symptoms but no loss of consciousness. After that episode Amy began checking her glucose levels more and more often, until at the time of her referral she was conducting 80 to 90 checks per day, which cost her parent approximately $600 per week in reagent test strips. Amy was also maintaining her blood sugar level between 275 to 300 mg/dl, far above the recommended levels for good metabolic control.

Following a 5-day baseline condition, a treatment was begun in which Amy and her parents were exposed to a gradually decreasing amount of information about her blood glucose level. Over a 9-month period Amy's parents gradually reduced the number of test strips she was given each day, beginning with 60 strips during the first phase of the treatment. Allen and Evans (2001) explained the treatment condition and method for changing criteria as follows:

> The parents expressed fears, however, that regardless of the criterion level, Amy might encounter a situation in which additional checking would be necessary. Concerns about adherence to the exposure protocol by the parents resulted in a graduated protocol in which Amy could earn a small number of additional test strips above and beyond the limit set by the parents. One additional test strip could be earned for each half hour of engagement in household chores. Amy was allowed to earn a maximum of five additional tests above the criterion when the criterion was set at 20 test strips or higher. Amy was allowed two additional test strips when the criterion was set below 20. Access to test strips was reduced in graduated increments, with the parents setting criteria to levels at which they were willing to adhere. Criteria changes were contingent upon Amy successfully reducing total test strip use to below the criterion on 3 successive days. (p. 498)

Figure 9.11 shows the criterion changes and the number of times Amy monitored her blood glucose level during the last 10 days of each criterion level. The results

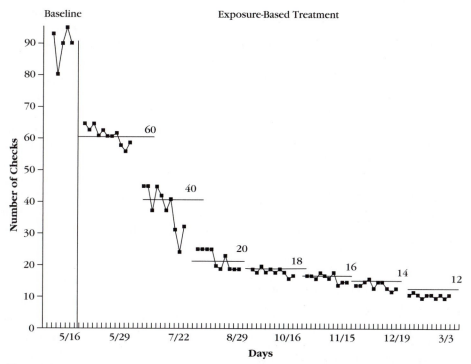

Figure 9.11 A changing criterion design showing the number of blood glucose monitoring checks conducted during the last 10 days of each criterion level. Dashed lines and corresponding numbers indicate the maximum number of test strips allotted at each level. Checks above the criterion levels were conducted with additional test strips earned by Amy.

From "Exposure-Based Treatment to Control Excessive Blood Glucose Monitoring" by K. D. Allen and J. H. Evans, 2001, *Journal of Applied Behavior Analysis, 12,* p. 499. Copyright 2001 by the Society for the Experimental Analysis of Behavior, Inc. Reprinted by permission.

clearly show that Amy responded well to the treatment and rarely exceeded the criterion. Over the course of the 9-month treatment program, Amy reduced the number of times she monitored her blood sugar from 80 to 95 times per day during baseline to fewer than 12 tests per day, a level that she maintained at a 3-month follow-up. Amy's parents indicated that they did not plan to decrease the criterion any further. A concern was that Amy might maintain high blood sugar levels during treatment. The authors reported that her blood sugar levels increased initially during treatment, but gradually decreased over the treatment program to a range of 125 to 175 mg/dl, within or near the recommended level.

Although the figure shows data only for the final 10 days of each criterion level, it is likely that the phases varied in length.[5] The study consisted of seven criterion changes of two magnitudes, 20 and 2. Although greater variation in the magnitude of criterion changes and a return to a previously attained higher criterion level may

have provided a more convincing demonstration of experimental control, the practical and ethical considerations of doing so would be questionable. As always, the applied behavior analyst must balance experimental concerns with the need to improve behavior in the most effective, efficient, ethical manner.

This study illustrates very well the changing criterion design's flexibility and is a good example of behavior analysts and clients working together. "Because the parents were permitted to regulate the extent of each criterion change, the intervention was quite lengthy. However, by allowing the parents to adjust their own exposure to acceptable levels, adherence to the overall procedure may have been improved." (Allen & Evans, 2001, p. 500)

Guidelines for Using the Changing Criterion Design

Proper implementation of the changing criterion design requires the careful manipulation of three design factors: length of phases, magnitude of criterion changes, and number of criterion changes.

---

[5]Data on the number of checks by Amy throughout the intervention are available from Allen and Evans (2001).

Length of Phases

Because each phase in the changing criterion design serves as a baseline for comparing changes in responding measured in the next phase, each phase must be long enough to achieve stable responding. "Each treatment phase must be long enough to allow the rate of the target behavior to restabilize at a new and changed rate; it is stability after change has been achieved, and before introduction of the next change in criterion, that is crucial to producing a convincing demonstration of control" (Hartmann & Hall, 1976, p. 531). Target behaviors that are slower to change therefore require longer phases.

The length of phases in a changing criterion design should vary considerably to increase the design's validity. For experimental control to be evident in a changing criterion design, the target behavior not only must change to the level required by each new criterion in a predictable (preferably immediate) fashion, but also must conform to the new criterion for as long as it is in effect. When the target behavior closely follows successively more demanding criteria that are held in place for varied periods of time, the likelihood is reduced that the observed changes in behavior are a function of factors other than the independent variable (e.g., maturation, practice effects). In most situations, the investigator should not set a predetermined number of sessions for which each criterion level will remain in effect. It is best to let the data guide ongoing decisions whether to extend the length of a current criterion phase or introduce a new criterion.

Magnitude of Criterion Changes

Varying the size of the criterion changes enables a more convincing demonstration of experimental control. When changes in the target behavior occur not only at the time a new criterion is implemented but also to the level specified by the new criterion, the probability of a functional relation is strengthened. In general, a target behavior's immediate change to meet a large criterion change is more impressive than a behavior change in response to a small criterion change. However, two problems arise if criterion changes are too large. First, setting aside practical considerations, and speaking from a design standpoint only, large criterion changes may not permit inclusion of a sufficient number of changes in the design (the third design factor) because the terminal level of performance is reached sooner. The second problem is from an applied view: Criterion changes cannot be so large that they conflict with good instructional practice. Criterion changes must be large enough to be detectable, but not so large as to be unachievable. Therefore, the variability of the data in each phase must be considered in determining the size of criterion changes. Smaller criterion changes can be employed with very stable levels of responding, whereas larger criterion changes are required to demonstrate behavior change in the presence of variability (Hartmann & Hall, 1976).

When using a changing criterion design, behavior analysts must guard against imposing artificial ceilings (or floors) on the levels of responding that are possible in each phase. An obvious mistake of this sort would be to give a student only five math problems to complete when the criterion for reinforcement is five. Although the student could complete fewer than five problems, the possibility of exceeding the criterion has been eliminated, resulting perhaps in an impressive-looking graph, but one that is badly affected by poor experimental procedure.

Number of Criterion Changes

In general, the more times the target behavior changes to meet new criteria, the more convincing the demonstration of experimental control is. For example, eight criterion changes, one of which was a reversal to a previous level, were implemented in the changing design illustrated in Figure 9.10, and Allen and Evans (2001) conducted seven criterion changes (Figure 9.11). In both of these cases, a sufficient number of criterion changes occurred to demonstrate experimental control. The experimenter cannot, however, simply add any desired number of criterion changes to the design. The number of criterion changes that are possible within a changing criterion design is interrelated with the length of phases and the magnitude of criterion changes. Longer phases mean that the time necessary to complete the analysis increases; with a limited time to complete the study, the greater the number of phases, the shorter each phase can be.

Considering the Appropriateness of the Changing Criterion Design

The changing criterion design is a useful addition to the behavior analyst's set of tactics for evaluating systematic behavior change. Like the multiple baseline design, the changing criterion design does not require that improvement in behavior be reversed. However, partial reversals to earlier levels of performance enhance the design's capability to demonstrate experimental control. Unlike the multiple baseline design, only one target behavior is required.

Several characteristics of the changing criterion design limit its effective range of applications. The design can be used only with target behaviors that are already in the subject's repertoire and that lend themselves to stepwise modification. However, this is not as severe a limitation as it might seem. For example, students perform many academic skills to some degree, but not at a useful rate. Many of these skills (e.g., solving math problems, reading) are appropriate for analysis with a changing criterion design. Allowing students to progress as efficiently as possible while meeting the design requirements of changing criterion analysis can be especially difficult. Tawney and Gast (1984) noted that "the challenge of identifying criterion levels that will permit the demonstration of experimental control without impeding optimal learning rates" is problematic with all changing criterion designs (p. 298).

Although the changing criterion design is sometimes suggested as an experimental tactic for analyzing the effects of shaping programs, it is not appropriate for this purpose. In shaping, a new behavior that initially is not in the person's repertoire is developed by reinforcing responses that meet a gradually changing criterion, called successive approximations, toward the terminal behavior (see Chapter 19). However, the changing response criteria employed in shaping are topographical in nature, requiring different forms of behavior at each new level. The multiple probe design (Horner & Baer, 1978), however, is an appropriate design for analyzing a shaping program because each new response criterion (successive approximation) represents a different response class whose frequency of occurrence is not wholly dependent on the frequency of behaviors meeting other criteria in the shaping program. Conversely, the changing criterion design is best suited for evaluating the effects of instructional techniques on stepwise changes in the rate, frequency, accuracy, duration, or latency of a single target behavior.

 ## Summary

Multiple Baseline Design

1. In a multiple baseline design, simultaneous baseline measurement is begun on two or more behaviors. After stable baseline responding has been achieved, the independent variable is applied to one of the behaviors while baseline conditions remain in effect for the other behavior(s). After maximum change has been noted in the first behavior, the independent variable is then applied in sequential fashion to the other behaviors in the design.

2. Experimental control is demonstrated in a multiple baseline design by each behavior changing when, and only when, the independent variable is applied.

3. The multiple baseline design takes three basic forms: (a) a multiple baseline across behaviors design consisting of two or more different behaviors of the same subject; (b) a multiple baseline across settings design consisting of the same behavior of the same subject in two or more different settings; and (c) a multiple baseline across subjects design consisting of the same behavior of two or more different participants.

Variations of the Multiple Baseline Design

4. The multiple probe design is effective for evaluating the effects of instruction on skill sequences in which it is highly unlikely that the subject's performance on later steps in the sequence can improve without instruction or mastery of the earlier steps in the chain. The multiple probe design is also appropriate for situations in which prolonged baseline measurement may prove reactive, impractical, or too costly.

5. In a multiple probe design, intermittent measurements, or probes, are taken on all of the behaviors in the design at the outset of the experiment. Thereafter, probes are taken each time the subject has achieved mastery of one of the behaviors or skills in the sequence. Just prior to instruction on each behavior, a series of true baseline measures are taken until stability is achieved.

6. The delayed multiple baseline design provides an analytic tactic in situations in which (a) a planned reversal design is no longer desirable or possible; (b) limited resources preclude a full-scale multiple baseline design; or (c) a new behavior, setting, or subject appropriate for a multiple baseline analysis becomes available.

7. In a delayed multiple baseline design, baseline measurement of subsequent behaviors is begun sometime after baseline measurement was begun on earlier behaviors in the design. Only baselines begun while earlier behaviors in the design are still under baseline conditions can be used to verify predictions made for the earlier behaviors.

8. Limitations of the delayed multiple baseline design include (a) having to wait too long to modify certain behaviors, (b) a tendency for baseline phases to contain too few data points, and (c) the fact that baselines begun after the independent variable has been applied to earlier behaviors in the design can mask the interdependence (covariation) of behaviors.

Assumptions and Guidelines for Using Multiple Baseline Designs

9. Behaviors comprising multiple baseline designs should be functionally independent of one another (i.e., they do not covary) and should share a reasonable likelihood that each will change when the independent variable is applied to it.

10. Behaviors selected for a multiple baseline design must be measured concurrently and must have an equal opportunity of being influenced by the same set of relevant variables.

11. In a multiple baseline design, the independent variable should not be applied to the next behavior until the previous behavior has changed maximally and a sufficient period of time has elapsed to detect any effects on behaviors still in baseline conditions.

12. The length of the baseline phases for the different behaviors comprising a multiple baseline design should vary significantly.

13. All other things being equal, the independent variable should be applied first to the behavior showing the most stable level of baseline responding.

14. Conducting a reversal phase in one or more tiers of a multiple baseline design can strengthen the demonstration of a functional relation.

Considering the Appropriateness of Multiple Baseline Designs

15. Advantages of the multiple baseline design include the fact that (a) it does not require withdrawing a seemingly effective treatment, (b) sequential implementation of the independent variable parallels the practice of many teachers and clinicians whose task is to change multiple behaviors in different settings and/or subjects, (c) the concurrent measurement of multiple behaviors allows direct monitoring of generalization of behavior change, and (d) the design is relatively easy to conceptualize and implement.

16. Limitations of the multiple baseline design include the fact that (a) if two or more behaviors in the design covary, the multiple baseline design may not demonstrate a functional relation even though one exists; (b) because verification must be inferred from the lack of change in other behaviors, the multiple baseline design is inherently weaker than the reversal design in showing experimental control between the independent variable and a given behavior; (c) the multiple baseline design is more an evaluation of the independent variable's general effectiveness than an analysis of the behaviors involved in the design; and (d) conducting a multiple baseline design experiment requires considerable time and resources.

Changing Criterion Design

17. The changing criterion design can be used to evaluate the effects of a treatment on the gradual or stepwise improvement of a behavior already in the subject's repertoire.

18. After stable baseline responding has been achieved, the first treatment phase is begun, in which reinforcement (or punishment) is usually contingent on the subject's performing at a specified level (criterion). The design entails a series of treatment phases, each requiring an improved level of performance over the previous phase. Experimental control is demonstrated in the changing criterion design when the subject's behavior closely conforms to the gradually changing criteria.

19. Three features combine to determine the potential of a changing criterion design to demonstrate experimental control: (a) the length of phases, (b) the magnitude of criterion changes, and (c) the number of criterion changes. The believability of the changing criterion design is enhanced if a previous criterion is reinstated and the subject's behavior reverses to the level previously observed under that criterion.

Considering the Appropriateness of the Changing Criterion Design

20. The primary advantages of the changing criterion design are that (a) it does not require a withdrawal or reversal of a seemingly effective treatment, and (b) it enables an experimental analysis within the context of a gradually improving behavior, thus complementing the practice of many teachers.

21. Limitations of the changing criterion design are that the target behavior must already be in the subject's repertoire, and that incorporating the necessary features of the design may impede optimal learning rates.

CHAPTER 10

Planning and Evaluating Applied Behavior Analysis Research

Key Terms

component analysis
direct replication
double-blind control
placebo control

procedural fidelity
replication
systematic replication
treatment drift

treatment integrity
Type I error
Type II error

Behavior Analyst Certification Board® BCBA® & BCABA® Behavior Analyst Task List©, Third Edition

	Content Area 1: Ethical Considerations
1-12	Give preference to assessment and intervention methods that have been scientifically validated, and use scientific methods to evaluate those that have not yet been scientifically validated.

	Content Area 5: Experimental Evaluation of Interventions
5-1	Systematically manipulate independent variables to analyze their effects on treatment.
5-3	Conduct a component analysis (i.e., determining effective component(s) of an intervention package).

	Content Area 10: Systems Support
10-3	Design and use systems for monitoring procedural integrity.

Previous chapters outlined considerations and procedures for selecting target behaviors, detailed strategies for designing measurement systems, presented guidelines for displaying and interpreting behavioral data, and described experimental tactics for revealing whether observed changes in a target behavior can be attributed to an intervention. This chapter supplements the information described thus far by examining questions and considerations that should be addressed when designing, replicating, and evaluating behavioral research. We begin by reviewing the central role of the individual subject in behavioral research, and follow with a discussion of the value of flexibility in experimental design.

Importance of the Individual Subject in Behavioral Research

To achieve maximum effectiveness, the research methods of any science must respect the defining characteristics of that science's subject matter. Behavior analysis—a science devoted to discovering and understanding the controlling variables of *behavior*—defines its subject matter as the activity of living organisms, a dynamic phenomenon that occurs at the level of the individual organism. It follows that the research methods most often used by behavior analysts feature repeated measures of behavior of individual organisms (the only place, by definition, where behavior can be found). This focus on the behavior of individual subjects has enabled applied behavior analysts to discover and refine effective interventions for a wide range of socially significant behavior.

To further explain the importance that this focus on the individual subject or client holds for applied behavior analysis, we will now contrast it with a research model that revolves around comparisons of data representing the aggregate measures of different groups of subjects. This groups-comparison approach to designing and evaluating experiments has predominated "behavioral research" in psychology, education, and other social sciences for decades.

Brief Outline of a Groups-Comparison Experiment

The basic format for a groups-comparison experiment can be described as follows.[1] A pool of subjects (e.g., 60 first-grade nonreaders) is selected randomly from the population (e.g., all first-grade nonreaders in a school district) relevant to the research question (e.g., Will the XYZ intensive phonics program improve first-grade nonreaders' ability to decode unpredictable text?). The subjects are divided randomly into two groups: the experimental group and the control group. An initial measure (pretest) of the dependent variable (e.g., score on a test of decoding skills) is obtained for all subjects in the study, the individual pretest scores for the subjects in each group are combined, and the mean and standard deviation are calculated for each group's performance on the pretest. Subjects in the experimental group are then exposed to the independent variable (e.g., 6 weeks of the XYZ program), which is not provided to subjects in the control group. After the treatment program has been completed, a posttest measure of the dependent variable is obtained for all subjects, and the mean and standard deviation posttest scores for each group are computed.[2] The researcher then compares any changes in each group's scores from pretest to posttest, applying various statistical tests to the data that enable inferences regarding the likelihood that any differences between the two groups' performances can be attributed to the independent variable. For example, assuming that the mean pretest scores for the experimental and control groups were similar, and the posttest measure revealed an improved mean score for the experimental group but not for the control group, statistical analyses would indicate the mathematical probability that the difference was due to chance. When a statistical test rules out chance as a likely factor, the researcher infers that that independent variable was responsible for effects on the dependent variable (e.g., the experimental group's improvement from pretest to posttest).

Researchers who combine and compare measures of groups of subjects in this way do so for two primary reasons, each of which was introduced in Chapter 7. First, advocates of group designs assume that averaging the measures of many subjects' performance controls for intersubject variability; thus, they assume that any changes in performance are the work of the independent variable. The second rationale for using large groups of subjects is the assumption that increasing the number of subjects in a study increases the external validity of the findings. That is, a treatment variable found effective with the subjects in the experimental group will also be effective with other subjects in the population from which the sample subjects were selected. The assumption of increased generality of findings is discussed later in this chapter in the section on replication. In the next section we comment on

---

[1]This brief sketch of the simplest form of a groups-comparison design study omits many important details and controls. Readers interested in a thorough explication and examples of group research methods should consult an authoritative text such as Campbell and Stanley (1966).

[2]Perhaps in part because the researcher must attend to "the purely logistical demands forced by the management of a battalion of subjects" (Johnston & Pennypacker, 1980, p. 256), group designs are characterized by few measures of the dependent variable (often just two measures: pretest and posttest).

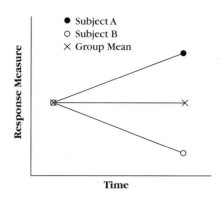

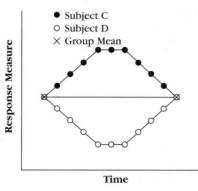

Figure 10.1 Hypothetical data showing that the mean performance of a group of subjects may not represent an individual subject's behavior.

the first reason for the use of groups of subjects—that doing so controls for intersubject variability. Our discussion identifies three fundamental concerns with typical groups-comparison designs that bear heavily on experimental reasoning.[3]

Group Data May Not Represent the Performance of Individual Subjects

By definition, applied behavior analysis is concerned with improving the behavior of the individual. Knowing that the average performance of a group of subjects changed may not reveal anything about the performance of individual subjects. It is quite possible for the average performance of subjects in the experimental group to have improved, while the performance of some subjects stayed the same, and the performance of others even deteriorated. It is even possible for the majority of subjects to show no improvement, for some subjects to get worse, and for a few subjects to improve sufficiently to yield an overall average improvement of statistical significance.

In defense of the groups-comparison approach, it might be said that it can show that a treatment is generally effective, that no treatment works with everyone, that people respond differently, and so on. But the fact that a group's average performance improves with a treatment is insufficient reason to adopt it, particularly for people in dire need of help with academic, social, or other behavioral challenges. General effectiveness is insufficient; the factors responsible for one subject's improvement with the treatment and another's lack of improvement must be discovered. To be most useful, a treatment must be understood at the level at which people come into contact with it and are affected by it: the individual level.

The two graphs in Figure 10.1 suggest some of the many faulty conclusions that are possible when an in-

vestigator's interpretation of a study is based on group mean scores. Each graph presents hypothetical data for the individual and average performances of two groups, each group consisting of two subjects. The data show no change in the mean response measure from pretest to posttest for either group. The pre- and posttest group data in both graphs in Figure 10.1 would suggest that the independent variable had no effect on the subjects' behavior. However, the left-hand graph in Figure 10.1 shows that Subject A's performance improved from pretest to posttest, and Subject B's behavior deteriorated over the same period of time.[4] The right-hand graph shows that although the pre- and posttest measures for Subjects C and D were identical, if repeated measures of Subject C's and Subject D's behavior between the pretest and posttest had been conducted, significant variability within and between the two subjects would have been revealed.

Group Data Masks Variability in the Data

A second problem associated with the mean performance of a group of subjects is that it hides variability in the data. Even if repeated measures of Subject C's and Subject D's behavior between the pre- and posttest had been conducted as shown in Figure 10.1, a researcher who relied on the group's mean performance as the primary indicator of behavior change would be ignorant of the variability that occurred within and between subjects.

When repeated measurement reveals significant levels of variability, an experimental search with the goal of identifying and controlling the factors responsible for the variability is in order. The widespread belief that the effects of uncontrolled variables in a study can be somehow controlled by statistical manipulations of the dependent variable is faulty.

---

[3]A complete discussion of the many problems posed by commingling data from multiple subjects is beyond the scope of this text. Students wishing to obtain a more complete understanding of this important issue are encouraged to read Johnston and Pennypacker (1980, 1993b) and Sidman (1960).

[4]The posttest data point in the left-hand graph of Figure 10.1 is reminiscent of the man whose bare feet were in a bucket of ice while his head was on fire. When asked how he was feeling, the man replied, "On the average, I feel fine."

Statistical control is never a substitute for experimental control. . . . The only way to determine whether or not uncontrolled variables are influencing the data is to inspect the data at the finest available level of decomposition, usually point-by-point for each individual subject. No purpose is served by combining the data statistically to obscure such effects. (Johnston & Pennypacker, 1980, p. 371)

Instead of controlling its sources before the fact, the between groups approach emphasizes controlling variability statistically after the fact. These two tactics do not have the same effects on the database. Whereas efforts to control actual variability lead to improved control over responding and, thus, a clearer picture of the effects of each condition, statistical manipulation of variable data cannot remove the influences already represented in the data. (Johnston & Pennypacker, 1993b, p. 184)

Attempting to "cancel out" variability through statistical manipulation neither eliminates it from the data nor controls the variables responsible for it. And the researcher who attributes the effects of unknown or uncontrolled variables to chance removes himself or herself even further from the identification and analysis of important variables. In his monumental work, *Tactics of Scientific Research,* Sidman (1960) dealt repeatedly and forcefully with this critical issue.

> To some experimenters, chance is simply a name for the combined effects of uncontrolled variables. If such variables are, in fact, controllable, then chance in this sense is simply an excuse for sloppy experimentation, and no further comment is required. If the uncontrolled variables are actually unknown, then chance is, as Boring (1941) has pointed out, a synonym for ignorance. . . . One of the most discouraging and at the same time challenging aspects of behavioral science is the sensitivity of behavior to a tremendous array of variables. . . . But variables are not canceled statistically. They are simply buried so that their effects cannot be seen. The rationale for statistical immobilization of unwanted variables is based on the assumed random nature of such variables. . . . Not only is the assumption of randomness with respect to the uncontrolled variables an untested one but it is also highly improbable. There are few, if any, random phenomena in the behavioral world. (pp. 45, 162–163)

Sidman (1960) also commented on an experimenter's use of statistics in an attempt to deal with troublesome sequence effects.

> He has a neat trick up his sleeve. By averaging together the data for both subjects under Condition A, and again under Condition B, he "cancels out" the order effect, and completely bypasses the problem of irreversibility. By a simple arithmetical operation, two subjects have become one, and a variable has been eliminated.
>
> It has not, in fact, gone anywhere. Numbers may be made to disappear by adding and subtracting them from

each other. Five apples minus three apples are two apples. The numbers are easily changed by a few strokes of the pen, but some eating has to be done before the apples themselves will vanish. (p. 250)

The "eating" that must be done to control the effects of any variable can be accomplished in only two ways: (a) holding the variable constant throughout the experiment, or (b) isolating the suspected factor as an independent variable and manipulating its presence, absence, and/or value during the experiment.

Intrasubject Replication Is Absent from Group Designs

A third weakness of the groups-comparison statistical inference research model is that the power of replicating effects with individual subjects is lost. One of the great strengths of within-subject experimental designs is the convincing demonstration of a functional relation made possible by replication within the design itself. Even though multiple subjects are typically involved in applied behavior analysis research, each subject is always treated as a separate experiment. Although behavior analysts often display and describe the data for all subjects as a group, data from individual subjects are used as the basis for determining and interpreting experimental effects. Applied behavior analysts are wise to heed Johnston and Pennypacker's (1980) admonition, "An effect that emerges *only* after individual data have been combined is probably artifactual and not representative of any real behavioral processes" (p. 257).

This discussion should not be interpreted to mean that the overall performance of groups of subjects cannot, or should not, be studied with the strategies and tactics of applied behavior analysis. There are many applied situations in which the overall performance of a group is socially significant. For example, Brothers, Krantz, and McClannahan (1994) evaluated an intervention to increase the number of pounds of recyclable office paper recycled by 25 staff members at a school. Still, it is important to remember that group data may not represent the performance of individual participants, and vice versa. For example, Lloyd, Eberhardt, and Drake (1996) compared the effects of group versus individual reinforcement contingencies within the context of collaborative group study conditions on quiz scores by students in a Spanish language class. The results showed that the group contingencies resulted in higher mean quiz scores for the class as a whole compared to the individual contingencies condition. However, overall benefits at the class level were mitigated by differential results for individual students. When group results do not represent individual performances, researchers should supplement group data with individual results, ideally in the form of graphic displays (e.g., Lloyd et al., 1996; Ryan & Hemmes, 2005).

In some instances, however, the behavior analyst may not be able to control the access of subjects to the experimental setting and contingencies or even be able to identify who the subjects are (e.g., Van Houten & Malenfant, 2004; Watson, 1996). The dependent variable must then consist of all of the responses made by individuals who enter the experimental setting. This approach is used frequently in community-based behavior analysis research. For example, group data have been collected and analyzed on such dependent variables as litter control on a university campus (Bacon-Prue, Blount, Pickering, & Drabman, 1980), car pooling by university students (Jacobs, Fairbanks, Poche, & Bailey, 1982), drivers' compliance and caution at stop signs (Van Houten & Malenfant, 2004), the use of child safety belts in shopping carts (Barker, Bailey, & Lee, 2004), and reducing graffiti on restroom walls (Watson, 1996).

Importance of Flexibility in Experimental Design

On one level, an effective experimental design is any arrangement of type and sequence of independent variable manipulations that produces data that are interesting and convincing to the researcher and the audience. In this context the word *design* is particularly appropriate as a verb as well as a noun; the effective behavioral researcher must actively *design* each experiment so that each achieves its own unique *design*. There are no ready-made experimental designs awaiting selection. The prototype designs presented in the previous two chapters are examples of analytic tactics that afford a form of experimental reasoning and control that has proven effective in advancing our understanding of a wide range of phenomena of interest to applied behavior analysts. Johnston and Pennypacker (1980, 1993a) have been clear and consistent in stating that the "suspicion some may hold that generic categories of design types exist and should be botanized" (1980, p. 293) is counterproductive to the practice of the science of behavior.

> In order to explain how to design and interpret within subject comparisons, it is tempting to develop categories of similar arrangements or designs. This almost requires giving each category a label, and the labeled categories then imply that there is something importantly different that distinguishes each from the others. (1993a, p. 267)
>
> The requirements for creating useful comparisons cannot be reduced to a cookbook of simple rules or formulas. . . . It misleads students by suggesting that particular types of arrangements have specific functions and

by failing to encourage them to understand the underlying considerations that open up unlimited experimental options. (1993a, p. 285)

Sidman (1960) was even more adamant in his warning regarding the undesirable effects of researchers' believing in the existence of a given set of rules for experimental design.

> The examples may be accepted as constituting a set of rules that must be followed in the design of experiments. I cannot emphasize too strongly that this would be disastrous. I could make the trite statement that every rule has its exception, but this is not strong enough. Nor is the more relaxed statement that the rules of experimental design are flexible, to be employed only where appropriate. The fact is that *there are no rules of experimental design.* (p. 214)

We agree with Sidman. The student of applied behavior analysis should not be led to believe that any of the analytic tactics described in Chapters 8 and 9 constitute experimental designs per se.[5] Still, we believe that it is useful to present the most commonly used analytic tactics in design form, as we have in Chapters 8 and 9, for two reasons. First, the vast majority of studies that have advanced the field of applied behavior analysis have used experimental designs that incorporated one or more of the analytic tactics described in Chapters 8 and 9. Second, we believe that the beginning student of behavior analysis benefits from an examination of specific examples of isolated experimental tactics and their application; it is one step in learning the assumptions and strategic principles that guide the selection and arrangement of analytic tactics into an experimental design that effectively and convincingly addresses the research question(s) at hand.

Experimental Designs That Combine Analytic Tactics

Combining multiple baseline and reversal tactics may allow a more convincing demonstration of experimental control than either tactic alone. For example, by withdrawing the treatment variable (a return to baseline) and then reapplying it within one or more tiers in a multiple baseline design, researchers are able to determine the existence of a functional relation between the independent variable and each behavior, setting, or subject of the multiple baseline element and also to analyze the effectiveness of the independent variable across the tiers

---

[5]The analytic tactics presented in Chapters 8 and 9 should not be considered soley as experimental designs for another reason: All experiments incorporate design elements in addition to the type and sequence of independent variable manipulations (e.g., subjects, setting, dependent variable, measurement system).

(e.g., Alexander, 1985; Ahearn, 2003; Barker, Bailey, & Lee, 2004; Blew, Schwartz, & Luce, 1985; Bowers, Woods, Carlyon, & Friman, 2000; Heward & Eachus, 1979; Miller & Kelley, 1994 [see Figure 26.3]; Zhou, Goff, & Iwata, 2000).

To investigate the research questions of interest, investigators often build experimental designs that entail a combination of analytic tactics. For example, it is not uncommon for experimenters to evaluate multiple treatments by sequentially applying each in a multiple baseline fashion (e.g., Bay-Hinitz, Peterson, & Quilitch, 1994; Iwata, Pace, Cowdery, & Miltenberger, 1994; Van Houten, Malenfant, & Rolider, 1985; Wahler & Fox, 1980; Yeaton & Bailey, 1983). Experimental designs that combine multiple baseline, reversal, and/or alternating treatments tactics can also provide the basis for comparing the effects of two or more independent variables or conducting a **component analysis** of elements of a treatment package. For example, the experimental designs used by L. J. Cooper and colleagues' (1995) used alternating treatments comparisons within a sequence of multiple treatment reversals to identify the active variables in treatment packages for children with feeding disorders.

Haring and Kennedy (1990) used multiple baseline across settings and reversal tactics in their experimental design that compared the effectiveness of time-out and differential reinforcement of other behavior (DRO) on the frequency of problem behaviors by two secondary students with severe disabilities (see Figure 10.2).[6] Sandra and Raff each frequently engaged in repetitive, stereotypic problem behaviors (e.g., body rocking, loud vocalizations, hand flapping, spitting) that interfered with classroom and community activities. In addition to assessing the effects of the time-out and DRO interventions against a no-treatment baseline condition, the design also enabled the researchers to conduct two comparisons of the relative effects of each treatment during an instructional task and leisure context. The design enabled Haring and Kennedy to discover that the time-out and DRO interventions produced different outcomes depending on the activity context in which they were applied. For both students, DRO was more effective than time-out in suppressing problem behavior in the task context; the opposite results were obtained in the leisure context, where time-out suppressed problem behavior and DRO proved ineffective.

Experimenters have also incorporated alternating treatments into experimental designs containing multiple baseline elements. For example, Ahearn, Kerwin,

Eicher, Shantz, and Swearingin (1996) evaluated the relative effects of two treatments for food refusal in an alternating treatments design implemented in a multiple baseline across subjects format. Likewise, McGee, Krantz, and McClannahan (1985) evaluated the effects of several procedures for teaching language to autistic children with an experimental design that incorporated alternating treatments within a multiple baseline across behaviors component that was, in turn, nested within an overall multiple baseline across subjects format. Zanolli and Daggett (1998) investigated the effects of reinforcement rate on the spontaneous social initiations of socially withdrawn preschoolers with an experimental design consisting of multiple baseline, alternating treatments, and reversal tactics.

Figure 10.3 shows how Sisson and Barrett (1984) incorporated a multiple probe across behaviors component, an alternating treatments analysis, and a multiple baseline across behaviors element in a design comparing the effects of two language-training procedures. The design enabled the investigators to discover the superiority of the total communication method for these two children, as well as the fact that direct application of the treatment was required for learning to occur on specific sentences. Results for a third subject revealed a functional relation of the same form and direction as that found for the two children whose results are shown in Figure 10.3, but one not so strongly in favor of the total communication procedure.

Our intent in describing several experiments that combined analytic tactics is not to offer any of these examples as model designs. They are presented instead as illustrations of the infinite number of experimental designs that are possible by arranging different combinations and sequences of independent variable manipulations. In every instance the most effective (i.e., convincing) experimental designs are those that use an ongoing evaluation of data from individual subjects as the basis for employing the three elements of baseline logic—prediction, verification, and replication.

Internal Validity: Controlling Potential Sources of Confounding in Experimental Design

An experiment is interesting and convincing, and yields the most useful information for application, when it provides an unambiguous demonstration that the independent variable was solely responsible for the observed behavior change. Experiments that demonstrate a clear functional relation are said to have a high degree of internal validity. The strength of an experimental design is

---

[6]Time-out and differential reinforcement of other behavior (DRO) are explained in Chapters 15 and 22, respectively.

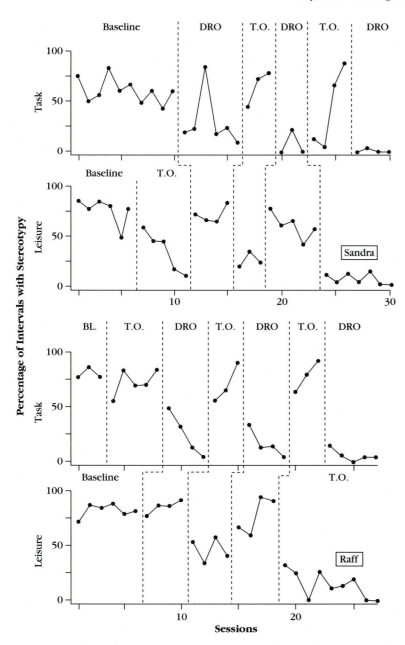

Figure 10.2 Experimental design employing multiple baselines across settings and reversal tactics counterbalanced across two subjects to analyze the effects of time-out (TO) and differential reinforcement of other behavior (DRO) treatment conditions.

From "Contextual Control of Problem Behavior" by T. G. Haring and C. H. Kennedy, 1990, *Journal of Applied Behavior Analysis, 23,* pp. 239–240. Copyright 1990 by the Society for the Experimental Analysis of Behavior, Inc. Reprinted by permission.

determined by the extent to which it (a) demonstrates a reliable effect (i.e., repeated manipulation of the independent variable produces a consistent pattern of behavior change) and (b) eliminates or reduces the possibility that factors other than the independent variable produced the behavior change (i.e., controls for confounding variables).

Implicit in the term *experimental control,* which is often used to signify a researcher's ability to reliably produce a specified behavior change by manipulating an independent variable, is the idea that the researcher controls the subject's behavior. However, "control of *behavior*" is inaccurate because the experimenter can control only some aspect of the subject's *environment.* Therefore, the level of experimental control obtained by a researcher

refers to the extent to which she controls all relevant variables in a given experiment. The researcher exerts this control within the context of an experimental design that, even though carefully planned at the outset, takes its ultimate form from the researcher's ongoing examination and response to the data.

As we noted in Chapter 7, an effective experimental design simultaneously reveals a reliable functional relation between independent and dependent variables (if one exists) and minimizes the likelihood that the observed behavior changes are the result of unknown or uncontrolled variables. An experiment has high internal validity when changes in the dependent variable are demonstrated to be a function only of the independent variable. When

Figure 10.3   Experimental design employing an alternating treatments tactic, a multiple probe, and a multiple baseline across behaviors analysis.

From "Alternating Treatments Comparison of Oral and Total Communication Training with Minimally Verbal Retarded Children" by L. A. Sisson and R. P. Barrett, 1984, *Journal of Applied Behavior Analysis, 17,* p. 562. Copyright 1984 by the Society for the Experimental Analysis of Behavior, Inc. Reprinted by permission.

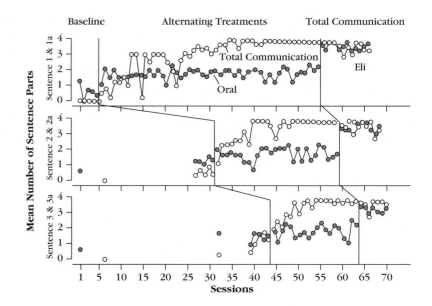

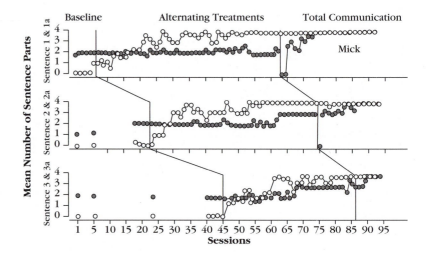

planning an experiment and later when examining the actual data from an ongoing study, the investigator must always be on the lookout for threats to internal validity. Uncontrolled factors known or suspected to have exerted influence on the dependent variable are called *confounding variables.* Much of a researcher's efforts during the course of a study are aimed at eliminating or controlling confounding variables.

The attainment of steady state responding is the primary means by which applied behavior analysts assess the degree of experimental control. Separating the effects of the independent variable from the effects of a potentially confounding variable requires clear, empirical evidence that the potentially confounding variable is no longer present, has been held constant across experimental conditions, or has been isolated for manipulation as an independent variable. Any experiment can be af-

fected by a virtually unlimited number of potential confounds; and as with every aspect of experimental design, there are no set rules for identifying and controlling confounding variables to which researchers can turn. However, some common and likely sources of confounding can be identified as well as tactics that can be considered to control them. Confounding variables can be viewed as related primarily to one of four elements of an experiment: subject(s), setting, measurement of the dependent variable, and independent variable.

Subject Confounds

A variety of subject variables can confound the results of a study. *Maturation,* which refers to changes that take place in a subject over the course of an experiment, is a potential confounding variable. For example, a subject's improved performance during the later phases of a study may be the result of physical growth or the acquisition of academic, social, or other behaviors and be unrelated to manipulations of the independent variable. Experimental designs that incorporate rapidly changing conditions or multiple introductions and withdrawals of the independent variable over time usually control for maturation effectively.

In most applied behavior analysis research, a subject is in the experimental setting and contacting the contingencies implemented by the investigator for only a portion of the day. As it is in any study, the assumption is made that each subject's behavior during each session will be primarily a function of the experimental conditions in effect. In reality, however, each subject's behavior may also be influenced by events that have occurred outside of the experiment. For example, suppose that the frequency of contributions to a class discussion is the dependent variable in a study. Now suppose that just prior to a session a student who has been contributing to discussions at a high rate was involved in a fight in the lunchroom and emits substantially fewer contributions compared to his level of responding in previous sessions. This change in the student's behavior may, or may not, be a result of the lunchroom fight. If the lunchroom fight coincided with a change in the independent variable, it would be especially difficult to detect or separate any effects of the experimental conditions from those of the extra-experimental event.

Although the researcher may be aware of some events that are likely causes of variability during a study, many other potential confounds go undetected. Repeated measurement is both the control for and the means to detect the presence and effects of such variables. The uncontrolled variables responsible for a subject's having a "bad day" or an unusually "good day" are particularly troublesome in research designs with few and/or widely spaced measurements of the dependent variable. This is one of the major weaknesses of using pretest-posttest comparisons to evaluate the effects of a treatment program.

Because groups-comparison experiments are predicated on subjects' similarity in relevant characteristics (e.g., gender, age, ethnicity, cultural and linguistic background, current skills), they are vulnerable to confounding by differences among subjects. Concern that the characteristics of one or more subjects may confound an experiment's results is generally not an issue in the single-subject experiments of applied behavior analysis. First, a person should participate in a study because she will benefit if the target behavior is changed successfully. Second, a subject's idiosyncratic characteristics cannot confound a study using a true within-single experimental design. With the exception of a multiple baseline across

subjects analysis, each participant in a behavioral study serves as her own control, which guarantees identically matched subjects in all experimental conditions because those subjects are the same person. Third, the external validity of results from a single-subject analysis is not dependent on the extent to which the subject(s) shares certain characteristics with others. The extent to which a functional relation applies to other subjects is established by replicating the experiment with different subjects.

Setting Confounds

Most applied behavior analysts conduct studies in natural settings where a host of variables are beyond their control. Studies in natural settings are more prone to confounding by uncontrolled events than are studies conducted in laboratories where extraneous variables can be more tightly managed. Even so, the applied experimenter is not without resources to mitigate the detrimental effects of setting confounds. For instance, when the applied researcher observes that an uncontrolled event has coincided with changes in the data, he should hold all possible aspects of the experiment constant until repeated measurement again reveals stable responding. If the unplanned event appears to have a robust effect on the target behavior, or is otherwise of interest to the investigator, and is amenable to experimental manipulation, the investigator should treat it as an independent variable and explore its possible effects experimentally.

Applied researchers concerned about setting confounds must also be on the lookout for the availability of "bootleg" reinforcement within and outside the experimental situation. A good example of how a setting confound operates occurs when, unbeknownst to the experimenter, subjects have ready access to potential reinforcers. In such a case, the effectiveness of those consequences as reinforcers diminishes.

Measurement Confounds

Chapters 4 and 5 discussed many factors that should be considered in designing an accurate and nonreactive measurement system. Still, numerous sources of confounding may exist within a well-planned measurement system. For instance, data might be confounded by observer drift, the influence of the experimenter's behavior on observers, and/or observer bias. Although admittedly difficult to accomplish in applied settings where observers often see the independent variable being implemented, keeping observers naive to the conditions and expected outcomes of an experiment reduces the potential of confounding by observer bias. On a related note, when observers score permanent products, the products should not contain identifying marks that indicate who produced each product and under what experimental conditions it was produced. Having observers score papers from baseline and treatment conditions in randomized order reduces the likelihood that observer drift or bias will confound the data within one treatment condition phase. (This procedure is more suitable to controlling for drift or bias by observers conducting postexperiment accuracy or IOA assessments.)

Unless a completely unobtrusive measurement system is devised (e.g., a covert system using one-way mirrors, or observations conducted at some distance from the subject), reactivity to the measurement procedure must always be considered as a possible confound. To offset this possible confound, the experimenter must maintain baseline conditions long enough for any reactive effects to run their course and for stable responding to be obtained. If reactivity to measurement produces undesirable effects (e.g., aggressive behavior, cessation of productivity) and a more unobtrusive measurement procedure cannot be devised, intermittent probes should be considered. Measures can also be confounded by practice, adaptation, and warm-up effects, especially during the initial stages of baseline. Again, the proper procedure is to continue baseline conditions until stable responding is obtained or variability is reduced to minimal levels. Intermittent probes should not be used for baseline measurement of behaviors for which practice effects would be expected. This is because, if the target behavior is susceptible to practice effects, those effects will occur during the intervention condition when more frequent measures are conducted, thereby confounding any effects of the independent variable.

Independent Variable Confounds

Most independent variables are multifaceted; that is, there is usually more to a treatment condition than the specific variable of interest to the investigator. For example, the effects of a token economy on students' academic productivity may be confounded by variables such as the personal relationship between the students and the teacher who delivers the tokens, social interactions associated with delivering and exchanging tokens, the expectation of teacher and students that performance will improve when the token system is implemented, and so on. If the intent is to analyze the effects of token reinforcement per se, these potentially confounding variables must be controlled.

Schwarz and Hawkins (1970) provided a good example of a control procedure for ruling out an aspect associated with a treatment as responsible for behavior change. The researchers evaluated the effects of token reinforcement on three maladaptive behaviors of an elementary student who was described as severely withdrawn. During treatment, the therapist and the girl met each day after school and viewed a videotape that had been made earlier that day of the student's classroom behavior. The therapist also administered tokens contingent on the girl's videotaped behavior displaying progressively fewer occurrences of maladaptive behaviors.

Schwarz and Hawkins recognized an independent confound potentially lurking in the design of their study. They reasoned that if improvement occurred as a function of the treatment, the question would remain whether the student's behavior had improved because the therapist-delivered positive attention and rewards improved her self-concept, which in turn changed her maladaptive behaviors in the classroom, which were symptomatic of her poor self-concept. In that case, Schwarz and Hawkins could not be certain that the contingent tokens played an important role in changing the behavior. Schwarz and Hawkins, anticipating this possible confound, controlled for it in a simple and direct way. Following baseline, they implemented a condition in which the therapist met with the girl each day after school and provided her with social attention and token reinforcement contingent on improvements in handwriting. During this control phase, the three target behaviors—face touching, slouching, and low voice volume—showed no change, thereby increasing their confidence in a conclusion that the girl's ultimate behavioral improvements during the subsequent intervention phases were due to the token reinforcement.

When medical researchers design experiments to test the effects of a drug, they use a technique called a **placebo control** to separate effects that may be produced by a subject's perceived expectations of improvement because of taking the drug apart from the effects actually produced by the drug. In the typical groups-comparison design, the subjects in the experimental group receive the real drug, and subjects in the control group receive placebo pills. Placebo pills contain an inert substance, but they look, feel, and taste exactly like the pills containing the real drug being tested.

Applied behavior analysts have also employed placebo controls in single-subject experiments. For example, in their study evaluating a pharmacological treatment of the impulsivity by students with attention-deficit/hyperactivity disorder (ADHD), Neef, Bicard, Endo, Coury, and Aman (2005) had a pharmacist prepare placebos and medications in identical gelatin capsules in 1-week supplies for each child. Neither the students nor the observers knew if a child had taken the medication or had taken the placebos. When neither the subject(s) nor the observers know whether the independent variable is present or absent from session to session, this type of control procedure is called a **double-blind control**. A double-blind control procedure eliminates confounding by subject expectations, parent and teacher expectations, differential treatment by others, and observer bias.

Treatment Integrity

The results of many experiments have been confounded by the inconsistent application of the independent variable. The researcher must make a concerted effort to ensure that the independent variable is applied exactly as planned and that no other unplanned variables are administered inadvertently along with the planned treatment. The terms **treatment integrity** and **procedural fidelity** refer to the extent to which the independent variable is implemented or carried out as planned.

Low treatment integrity invites a major source of confounding into an experiment, making it difficult, if not impossible, to interpret the results with confidence. Data from an experiment in which the independent variable was administered improperly, applied inconsistently, conducted piecemeal, and/or delivered in overdose or underdose form often lead to conclusions that—depending on the results obtained—represent either a false positive (claiming a functional relation when no such relation exists) or a false negative (failing to detect a functional relation when one actually does exist). If a functional relation is apparent from the analysis of the data, one cannot be sure whether the treatment variable as described by the experimenter was responsible or whether the effects were a function of extraneous, uncontrolled elements of the intervention as it was actually applied. On the other hand, it may be equally erroneous to interpret the failure to produce significant behavior change as evidence that the independent variable is ineffective. In other words, had the independent variable been implemented as planned, it might have been effective.

Numerous threats to treatment integrity exist in applied settings (Billingsley, White, & Munson, 1980; Gresham, Gansle, & Noell, 1993; Peterson, Homer, & Wonderlich, 1982). Experimenter bias can cause the researcher to administer the independent variable in such a way that it enjoys an unfair advantage over the baseline or comparative conditions. **Treatment drift** occurs when the application of the independent variable during later phases of an experiment differs from the way it was applied at the outset of the study. Treatment drift can result from the complexity of the independent variable, which can make it difficult for practitioners to implement all of the elements consistently over the course of an experiment. Contingencies influencing the behavior of those responsible for implementing the independent variable can also result in treatment drift. For example, a teacher

might implement only those aspects of a procedure that she favors and might implement the full intervention only when the experimenter is present.

Precise Operational Definition.   Achieving a high level of treatment integrity begins with developing a complete and precise operational definition of the treatment procedures. Besides providing the basis for training the persons who will implement an intervention and judging the level of treatment integrity attained, operational definitions of treatment conditions are a requisite for meeting the technological dimension of applied behavior analysis (Baer et al., 1968). An investigator's failure to provide explicit operational definitions of the treatment variable hampers the dissemination and proper use of the intervention by practitioners, and makes it difficult for other researchers to replicate and ultimately validate the findings.

Gresham and colleagues (1993) recommended that descriptions of the independent variable be judged by the same standards of explicitness that are used in assessing the quality of definitions of dependent variable. That is, they should be clear, concise, unambiguous, and objective. More specifically, Gresham and colleagues also suggested that treatments be operationally defined in each of four dimensions: verbal, physical, spatial, and temporal. They used Mace, Page, Ivancic, and O'Brien's (1986) definition of a time-out procedure as an example of an operational definition of an independent variable.

> (a) Immediately following the occurrence of a target behavior (temporal dimension), (b) the therapist said "No, go to time-out" (verbal dimension), (c) led the child by the arm to a prepositioned time-out chair (physical dimension), (d) seated the child facing the corner (spatial dimension). If the child's buttocks were raised from the time-out chair or if the child's head was turned more than 45° (spatial dimension), the therapist used the least amount of force necessary to guide compliance with the time-out procedure (physical dimension). (f) At the end of 2 min (temporal dimension), the therapist turned the time-out chair 45° from the corner (physical and spatial dimensions) and walked away (physical dimension). (pp. 261–262)

Simplify, Standardize, and Automate.   When planning an experiment, placing a high priority on simplifying and standardizing the independent variable and providing criterion-based training and practice for the people who will be responsible for implementing it enhances treatment integrity. Treatments that are simple, precise, and brief, and that require relatively little effort, are more likely to be delivered with consistency than those that are not. Simple, easy-to-implement techniques also have a higher probability of being accepted and used by practitioners than those that are not, and thus possess a certain degree of self-evident social validity. Simplicity is, of course, a relative concern, not a mandate; effecting change in some socially important behaviors may require the application of intense, complex interventions over a long period of time and may involve many people. Baer (1987) made this point succinctly when he stated:

> Long problems are simply those in which the task analysis requires a series of many behavior changes, perhaps in many people, and although each of them is relatively easy and quick, the series of them requires not so much effort as time, and so it is not arduous but merely tedious. (pp. 336–337)

Practitioners need not be thwarted or dismayed by complex interventions; they simply need to realize the treatment integrity implications. All things being equal, however, a simple and brief treatment will probably be applied more accurately and consistently than will a complex and extended one.

To ensure the consistent implementation of the independent variable, experimenters should standardize as many of its aspects as cost and practicality allow. Standardization of treatment can be accomplished in a variety of ways. When a treatment requires a complex and/or extended sequence of behaviors, a script for the person administering it may improve the accuracy and consistency with which the independent variable is applied. For example, Heron, Heward, Cooke, and Hill (1983) used a scripted lesson plan with overhead transparencies to ensure that a classwide peer tutor training program was implemented consistently across groups of children.

If automating the intervention will not compromise it in any way, researchers might consider "canning" the independent variable so that an automated device can be used for its delivery. Although a videotaped tutor training presentation in Heron and colleagues' (1983) study would have eliminated any potential confounding caused by the teacher's slightly different presentations of the lesson from group to group and across sets of tutoring skills, using a canned presentation would also have eliminated the desired interactive and personal aspects of the training program. Some treatment variables are well suited to automated presentation in that automation neither limits the desirability of the treatment nor seriously reduces its social validity in terms of acceptability or practicability (e.g., use of videotaped programs to model residential energy conservation).

Training and Practice. Training and practice in properly implementing the independent variable provides the person(s) who will be responsible for conducting the treatment or experimental sessions with the necessary

skills and knowledge to carry out the treatment. It would be a mistake for the researcher to assume that a person's general competence and experience in the experimental setting (e.g., a classroom) guarantees correct and consistent application of an independent variable in that setting (e.g., implementing a peer-mediated tutoring program).

As stated earlier, scripts detailing treatment procedures and cue cards or other devices that remind and prompt people through steps of an intervention can be helpful. Researchers should not, however, assume that merely providing the intervention agent with a detailed script will ensure a high degree of treatment integrity. Mueller and colleagues (2003) found that a combination of verbal instructions, modeling, and/or rehearsal was required for parents to implement pediatric feeding protocols with a high level of treatment integrity. Performance feedback has also been shown to improve the integrity with which parents and practitioners implement behavior support plans and explicit teaching techniques (e.g., Codding, Feinberg, Dunn, & Pace, 2005; Sarakoff & Strumey, 2004; Witt, Noell, LaFleur, & Mortenson, 1997).

Assessing Treatment Integrity. Although simplification, standardization, and training help increase the degree of treatment integrity, they do not guarantee it. If there is any doubt about the correct and consistent application of the independent variable, investigators should provide data on the accuracy and reliability of the independent variable (Peterson et al., 1982; Wolery, 1994). Treatment integrity (or procedural fidelity) data reveal the extent to which the actual implementation of all of the experimental conditions over the course of a study matches their descriptions in the method section of a research report.[7]

Even though the effective control of the presence and absence of the independent variable is a requisite to an internally valid experiment, applied behavior analysts have not always made sufficient efforts to assure the integrity of the independent variable. Two reviews of articles published in the *Journal of Applied Behavior Analysis* from 1968 to 1990 found that the majority of authors did not report data assessing the degree to which the independent variable was properly and consistently applied (Gresham et al., 1993; Peterson et al., 1982). Peterson and colleagues noted that a "curious double standard" had developed in applied behavior analysis in which data on the interobserver agreement of dependent variable mea-

---

[7]Different levels or degrees of treatment integrity can be manipulated as an independent variable to analyze the effects of full versus partial implementations of an intervention, or various kinds of treatment "mistakes" (e.g., Holcombe, Wolery, & Snyder, 1994; Vollmer, Roane, Ringdahl, & Marcus, 1999).

sures were required for publication, but such data were seldom provided or required for the independent variable.

Peterson and colleagues (1982) suggested that the technology developed for assessing and increasing the accuracy and believability of measures of the dependent variable (see Chapter 5) is fully applicable to the collection of procedural fidelity data. Importantly, observation and recording of the independent variable provides the experimenter with data indicating whether calibration of the treatment agent is necessary (i.e., bringing the intervention agent's behavior into agreement with the true value of the independent variable). Observation and calibration give the researcher an ongoing ability to use retraining and practice to ensure a high level of treatment integrity over the course of an experiment.

Figure 10.4 shows the data collection form used by trained observers to collect treatment integrity data in a study evaluating the effects of different qualities and durations of reinforcement for problem behavior, compliance, and communication within a treatment package for escape-maintained problem behavior (Van Norman, 2005). The observers viewed videotapes of randomly selected sessions representing approximately one third to one half of all sessions in each condition and phase of the study. The percentage of treatment integrity for each condition was calculated by dividing the number of steps the experimenter completed correctly during a session by the total number of steps completed.

This overview of sources of potential confounding variables is, of necessity, incomplete. A complete inventory of all possible threats to the internal validity of experimental research would be well beyond the scope of this text. And presenting such a list might suggest that a researcher need only control for the variables listed and not worry about anything else. In truth, the list of potential confounds is unique to every experiment. The effective researcher is the one who questions and probes the influence of as many relevant variables as possible. No experimental design can control all potential confounds; the challenge is to reduce, eliminate, or identify the influence of as many potentially confounding variables as possible.

Social Validity: Assessing the Applied Value of Behavior Changes and the Treatments That Accomplish Them

In his landmark article, "Social Validity: The Case for Subjective Measurement or How Applied Behavior Analysis Is Finding Its Heart," Montrose Wolf (1978) proposed the then "radical concept that clients (including parents and guardians of dependent people, and even those whose taxes support social programs) must understand and admire the goals, outcomes, and methods of an intervention" (Risley, 2005, p. 284). Wolf recommended that the social validity of a study in applied behavior analysis

---

Video Clip # ___1-1AL___   Rater Initials: ___E. B.___   Date: ___7/6/05___

Phase 1/A (SD)

Procedural Steps	Opportunities	Correct	% Correct	Yes	No	N/A
1. The instructor delivers a task prompt <u>at the beginning</u> of the session, e.g., "it's time to work" or similar.				Ⓨ	N	N/A
2. If the participant does not respond, the instructor represents the choice by replacing materials or restating the contingencies.	—	—	—	Y	N	Ⓝ/Ⓐ
3. The break card (or similar) is presented simultaneously (within 3 seconds) with work task materials.	⫫⫫ ⫫⫫ ⫫⫫ |	⫫⫫ ⫫⫫ ⫫|	16/16	Ⓨ	N	N/A

4. Following <u>work choice (touching materials associated with work)</u>
  a. Removes the task materials
  b. Presents a timer with green colored cue card
  c. Provides access to high preference items
  d. Engages in play with the participant for 1 minute
	⫫⫫ ||	⫫⫫ ||	7/7	Ⓨ	N	N/A

5. Following <u>break requests</u>
  a. Removes the task materials
  b. Presents timer with yellow cue card
  c. Provides access to moderately preferred tangible items and neutral commenting for 30 seconds
	⫫⫫ ||||	⫫⫫ ||||	8/8	Ⓨ	N	N/A

6. Following <u>problem behavior</u> within 10 s the instructor
  a. Removes the task/play materials
  b. Presents a timer with red cue card
  c. Provides no attentiion or tangible items for 10 seconds
				Y	N	Ⓝ/Ⓐ

7. Which side was the break card (or similar) presented (<u>*the participant's*</u> R = right or L = left) for each choice presentation.	R R L L L R L R R L R L R L L R					

Figure 10.4   Example of a form used to record treatment integrity data.

Adapted from "The Effects of Functional Communication Training, Choice Making, and an Adjusting Work Schedule on Problem Behavior Maintained by Negative Reinforcement" by R. K. Van Norman, 2005, p. 204. Unpublished doctoral dissertation. Columbus, OH: The Ohio State University. Used by permission.

should be assessed in three ways: the social significance of the target behavior, the appropriateness of the procedures, and the social importance of the results.

Although social validity assessments may increase the likelihood that a study will be published and can be helpful in the marketing and public relations of behavioral programs (Hawkins, 1991; Winett, Moore, & Anderson, 1991), the ultimate purpose of social validity assessments is "to help choose and guide [behavior change] program developments and applications" (Baer & Schwartz, 1991, p. 231). Social validity assessments are most often accomplished by asking the direct consumers of a behavior change program (the learners, clients, research subjects) and/or a group of indirect consumers (e.g., family members, teachers, therapists, community people) questions about how satisfied they are with the relevance and importance of the goals of the program, the acceptability of the procedures, and the value of the behavior change outcomes achieved.[8]

Verbal statements by practitioners and consumers that they find a treatment or program acceptable and effective should not be viewed as either evidence that the program was effective, or if it was, that consumers will continue to use the methods. Noting Baer, Wolf, and Risley's (1968) admonition that "a subject's verbal description of his own nonverbal behavior usually would not be accepted as a measure of his actual behavior" (p. 93), Hawkins (1991) recommended that the term *consumer satisfaction* be used instead of *social validity* because it acknowledges that what is typically obtained in social validity assessments "is essentially a collection of consumer opinions" (p. 205), the validity of which has not been determined.

> In measuring consumers' verbal judgments, we are only hoping that these verbal behaviors are substantially controlled by variables directly relevant to the habilitation task at hand, and thus that they predict habilitative outcomes to some degree. The validity of such consumer judgments has yet to be established; they should not be viewed as a validity criterion but rather as a second opinion from a lay person who may or may not be better informed and less biased than the professional is. (p. 212)

Validating the Social Importance of Behavior Change Goals

The social validity of behavior change goals begins with a clear description of those goals.

To assess the social importance of goals, the researcher must be precise about the goals of the behavior change effort at the levels of (a) the broad social goal (e.g., improved parenting, enhanced social skills, improved cardiovascular health, increased independence), (b) the categories of behavior hypothesized to be related to the broad goal (e.g., parenting—providing instructional feedback, using time-out, etc.), and/or (c) the responses that comprise the behavioral category of interest (e.g., using time-out—directing the child to a location away from other people, instructing the child to "sit out" for a specified duration, etc.). Social validation may be conducted for any of these levels of goals. (Fawcett, 1991, pp. 235–236)

Van Houten (1979) suggested two basic approaches to determining socially valid goals: (a) Assess the performance of persons considered competent, and (b) experimentally manipulate different levels of performance to determine empirically which produces optimal results. Observations of the performance of typical performers can be used to identify and validate behavior change goals and target levels of performance. To arrive at a socially valid performance criterion for a social skills training program for two adults with disabilities who worked in a restaurant, Grossi, Kimball, and Heward (1994) observed four restaurant employees without disabilities over a period of 2 weeks to determine the frequency with which they acknowledged verbal initiations from coworkers. Results from these observations revealed that the employees without disabilities acknowledged an average of 90% of initiations directed toward them. This level of performance was selected as the goal for the two target employees in the study.

A study by Warren, Rogers-Warren, and Baer (1976) provided a good example of testing the effects of different levels of performance to determine socially valid outcomes. The researchers assessed the effect of different frequencies of children's offers to share play materials with their peers on the peers' reactions to those offers. They found that peers accepted offers to share most consistently when those offers were made at a middle frequency; that is, not too frequently, not too seldom.

Validating the Social Acceptance of Interventions

Several scales and questionnaires for obtaining consumers' opinions of the acceptability of behavioral interventions have been developed. For example, the *Intervention Rating Profile* is a 15-item Likert-type scale for assessing the acceptability of classroom interventions (Martens, Witt, Elliott, & Darveaux, 1985). The *Treatment Acceptability Rating Form* (TARF) consists of 20 questions with which parents rate the acceptability of behavioral treat-

---

[8]Detailed discussions of social validity and procedures for assessing it can be found in Fuqua and Schwade (1986), Van Houten (1979), Wolf (1978), and the special section on social validity in the summer 1991 issue of the *Journal of Applied Behavior Analysis.*

ments used in outpatient clinic (Reimers & Wacker, 1988). Figure 10.5 shows the experimenter-modified version of the TARF used by Van Norman (2005) to obtain treatment acceptability information from each participant's parents, teachers, therapists, and behavior support staff. Although some of the people whose opinions were being sought had witnessed, or had watched a video of, the intervention being used with the student, the following description of the intervention was read to each consumer before he or she was asked to answer each of the questions:

> First we conducted an assessment to find out what motivated Zachary to engage in challenging behavior(s) such as throwing materials, hitting people, and dropping to the floor. We found that Zachary engaged in challenging behavior(s), at least in part, in order to escape or avoid task demands.
>
> Next, we taught Zachary to ask for a break as a replacement behavior for challenging behavior by using physical prompting and attaching the response of asking for a break to access to a highly preferred item, lots of attention, and a long duration break (3 min).
>
> Then we gave Zachary the choice to ask for work by simply touching the work materials (essentially engaging in the first step of the task) and getting access to highly preferred items, attention, and long duration break (1 min) or asking for a break and getting access to moderately preferred items for a shorter duration break (30 sec). At any time during this procedure if Zachary engaged in problem behavior he was given a 10 s break with no attention and no activities/items.
>
> Finally, we continued to give Zachary the choice to ask for work, a break or engage in problem behavior, however now we required Zachary to comply with a greater number of task-related instructions before he was given access to the highly preferred activities, attention, and a 1 min break. Each session we increased the number of task-related instructions that were given and needed to be complied with before access to the highly preferred break.
>
> Physical prompting was only used during the initial phase to teach Zachary new responses, specifically how to ask for a break and how to ask for work. Otherwise Zachary was making all independent choices as they were presented. (p. 247)

Validating the Social Importance of Behavior Changes

Methods for assessing the social validity of outcomes include (a) comparing participants' performance to the performance of a normative sample, (b) asking consumers to rate the social validity of participants' performance, (c) asking experts to evaluate participants' performance, (d) using a standardized assessment instrument, and (e) testing participants' newly learned level of performance in the natural environment.

Normative Sample

Van den Pol and colleagues (1981) used the performance of a normative sample of typical fast-food restaurant customers to assess the social validity of the posttraining performance of the young adults with disabilities whom they had taught to order or pay for a meal without assistance. The researchers simply observed 10 randomly selected, typical customers who ordered and ate a meal in fast-food restaurants. They recorded the accuracy with which these customers performed each step of a 22-step task analysis. The students' performance at the follow-up probe equaled or exceeded that of the customers in the normative sample in all but 4 of 22 specific skills.

Using normative samples to assess the social validity of behavior change is not limited to posttreatment comparisons. Comparing subjects' behavior to ongoing probes of the behavior of a normative sample provides a formative assessment measure of how much improvement has been made and how much is still needed. An excellent sample of ongoing social validity assessment is a study by Rhode, Morgan, and Young (1983), in which token reinforcement and self-evaluation procedures were used to improve the classroom behavior of six students with behavior disorders. The overall goal of the study was to help the six students improve their appropriate classroom behavior (e.g., following classroom rules, completing teacher-assigned tasks, volunteering relevant responses) and decrease inappropriate behavior (e.g., talking out, noncompliance, aggression) so that they would be accepted and successful in regular (general education) classrooms. At least once per day throughout the course of the 17-week study, the researchers randomly selected classmates in the regular classrooms for observation. The same observation codes and procedures that were used to measure the six target students' behavior were used to obtain the normative sample data.

Figure 10.6 shows the mean and range of the six students' appropriate behavior during each condition and phase of the study compared to the normative sample. (Individual graphs showing the percentage of appropriate behavior in the resource and regular classroom of all six subjects in each of nearly 90 sessions were also included in Rhode and colleagues' article.) During baseline, the six boys' levels of appropriate behavior were well below those of their nondisabled peers. During Phase I of the study, in which the subjects learned to self-evaluate, their behavior in the resource room improved to a level matching that of their regular classroom peers. However, when the subjects were in the regular classroom during Phase I, their behavior compared poorly with that of the other

Figure 10.5   Examples of questions adapted from the Treatment Acceptability Rating Form—Revised (Reimers and Wacker, 1988) to obtain consumers' opinions of the acceptability of intervention procedures used to treat challenging behaviors of secondary students with severe disabilities.

Treatment Acceptability Rating Form—Revised (TARF-R)

1. How clear is your understanding of the suggested procedures?

Not at   Neutral   Very
all clear   clear

2. How acceptable do you find the strategies to be regarding your concerns about the identified learner?

Not at all   Neutral   Very
acceptable   acceptable

3. How willing are you to implement the suggested procedures as you heard them described?

Not at   Neutral   Very
all willing   willing

4. Given the learner's behavior issues, how reasonable do you find the suggested procedures?

Not at all   Neutral   Very
reasonable   reasonable

5. How costly will it be to implement these strategies?

Not at   Neutral   Very
all costly   costly

11. How disruptive will it be to your classroom to implement the suggested procedures?

Not at all   Neutral   Very
disruptive   disruptive

13. How affordable are these procedures?

Not at all   Neutral   Very
affordable   affordable

14. How much do you like the proposed procedures?

Do not like   Neutral   Like them
them at all   very much

17. How much *discomfort* is your learner likely to experience as a result of these procedures?

No discomfort   Neutral   Very much
at all   discomfort

19. How willing would you be to change your classroom routine to implement these procedures?

Not at   Neutral   Very
all willing   willing

20. How well will carrying out these procedures fit into your classroom routine?

Not at   Neutral   Very
all well   well

From "The Effects of Functional Communication Training, Choice Making, and an Adjusting Work Schedule on Problem Behavior Maintained by Negative Reinforcement" by R. K. Van Norman, 2005, pp. 248–256. Unpublished doctoral dissertation. Columbus, OH: The Ohio State University. Used by permission.

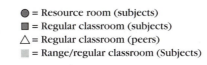

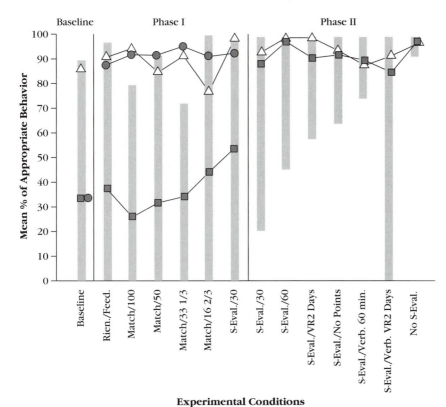

Experimental Conditions

Figure 10.6   Example of using measures of the behavior of a normative sample standard for assessing the social validity of outcomes of a behavior change program.

From "Generalization and Maintenance of Treatment Gains of Behaviorally Handicapped Students from Resource Rooms to Regular Classrooms Using Self-Evaluation Procedures" by G. Rhode, D. P. Morgan, and K. R. Young, 1983, *Journal of Applied Behavior Analysis, 16,* p. 184. Copyright 1984 by the Society for the Experimental Analysis of Behavior, Inc. Reprinted by permission.

students in the normative sample. As Phase II progressed, which involved various strategies for generalization and maintenance of the treatment gains, the mean level of appropriate behavior by the six students matched that of their nondisabled peers, and variability among the six students decreased (except for one subject who exhibited no appropriate behavior on one session in the next-to-last condition).

Consumer Opinion

The most frequently used method for assessing social validity is to ask consumers, including subjects or clients whenever possible, if they thought behavior changes occurred during the study or program, and if so, if they thought those behavior changes were important and valuable. Figure 10.7 shows the questionnaire Van Norman (2005) used to obtain opinions of consumers (i.e., the subjects' parents, teachers, and instructional aides; school administrators; behavior support staff; an occupational therapist; a school psychologist; and a psychology aide) on the social validity of results of an intervention designed to reduce challenging behavior maintained by escape. Van Norman created a series of 5-minute video clips

from randomly selected before-intervention and after-intervention sessions and placed the clips in random order on a CD. The social validity evaluators did not know whether each clip represented a before- or after-intervention session. After viewing each clip, the consumer completed the questionnaire shown in Figure 10.7.

Expert Evaluation

Experts can be called on to judge the social validity of some behavior changes. For example, as one measure of the social validity of changes in the unaided notetaking skills of high school students with learning disabilities in social studies lectures as a result of having been exposed to teacher-prepared guided notes, White (1991) asked 16 secondary social studies teachers to rate the students' baseline and post-intervention lecture notes on three dimensions: (1) accuracy and completeness compared to lecture content; (2) usefulness for study for tests over the lecture content; and (3) how the notes compared to those taken by typical general education students. (The teachers did not know whether each set of notes they were rating was from baseline or post-intervention condition.)

Figure 10.7   Form for obtaining consumer opinions of social validity of results of an intervention used to treat challenging behavior of secondary students with severe disabilities.

Social Validity of Results Questionnaire

Directions: Video Clip # _____

Please view the video and then circle one of the five choices that best describes the extent to which you agree or disagree with each of the three statements below.

1. The student is engaged in academic or vocational work tasks, sitting appropriately (bottom in seat), and attending to the teacher or materials.

1	2	3	4	5
Strongly Disagree	Disagree	Undecided	Agree	Strongly Agree

2. The student is engaged in challenging behavior and not attending to the teacher or materials.

1	2	3	4	5
Strongly Disagree	Disagree	Undecided	Agree	Strongly Agree

3. The student appears to have a positive affect (e.g., smiling, laughing).

1	2	3	4	5
Strongly Disagree	Disagree	Undecided	Agree	Strongly Agree

Comments about the student's behavior in the video clip: _____

_____

_____

General comments about this student's behavior: _____

_____

_____

Name (optional): _____

Relation to the learner in video (optional): _____

Adapted from "The Effects of Functional Communication Training, Choice Making, and an Adjusting Work Schedule on Problem Behavior Maintained by Negative Reinforcement" by R. K. Van Norman, 2005, p. 252. Unpublished doctoral dissertation. Columbus, OH: The Ohio State University. Used by permission.

Fawcett (1991) observed that, "If expert ratings are not sufficiently high, [the researcher should] consider what else might be done to program for social validity. Despite the best efforts, assessments may show that research goals are regarded by consumer judges as insignificant, interventions procedures as unacceptable, or results as unimportant" (p. 238).

Standardized Tests

Standardized tests can be used to assess the social validity of some behavior change program outcomes. Iwata, Pace, Kissel, Nau, and Farber (1990) developed the *Self-Injury Trauma Scale (SITS)* to enable researchers and therapists to measure the number, type, severity, and location of injuries produced by self-injurious behavior.

The *SITS* yields a Number Index and Severity Index with scores of 0 to 5, and an estimate of current risk. Although the data collected in a treatment program may show significant decreases in the behaviors that produce self-injury (e.g., eye poking, face slapping, head banging), the social significance of the treatment must be validated by evidence of reduced injury. Iwata and colleagues wrote:

> . . . the social relevance of the behavior lies in its traumatic outcome. The measurement of physical injuries prior to treatment can establish the fact that a client or subject actually displays behavior warranting serious attention. . . . Conversely, injury measurement following treatment can corroborate observed changes in behavior because reduction of an injury-producing response below a certain level should be reflected in the eventual disappearance of observable trauma. In both of these in-

stances, data on injuries provide a means of assessing social validity. (Wolf, 1978, pp. 99–100)

Twohig and Woods (2001) used the *SITS* to validate the outcomes of a habit-reversal treatment for the chronic skin picking of two typically developing adult males. Both men reported that they had engaged in skin picking since childhood, digging the fingernails into the ends of a finger and pulling or scrapping the skin, which sometimes caused bleeding, scarring, and infections. Two observers independently rated pretreatment, posttreatment, and follow-up photographs of the two men's hands with the *SITS*. The Number Index (NI) and Severity Index (SI) *SITS* scores on the pretreatment photographs for both men were 1 and 2, respectively, indicating one to four injuries on either hand and distinct but superficial breaks in the skin. NI and SI scores of 0 on the posttreatment photos for both men indicated no apparent injuries. On the follow-up photos taken 4 months after treatment had ended, both men had SITS NI and SI scores of 1, indicating red or irritated skin.

Real-World Test

Perhaps the most socially valid way to assess the social validity of a learner's newly acquired behavior is to put it to an authentic test in the natural environment. For instance, the validity of what three adolescents with learning disabilities had learned about road signs and traffic laws was validated when they passed the Ohio Department of Motor Vehicles test and earned their temporary driver's permits (Test & Heward, 1983).

In a similar way, the social validity of the cooking skills being learned by three secondary students with developmental disabilities and visual impairments was tested frequently when their friends arrived at the end of probe sessions to share the food they had just prepared (Trask-Tyler, Grossi, & Heward, 1994). In addition to providing a direct and authentic assessment of social validity, real-world tests put the learner's repertoire in contact with naturally occurring contingencies of reinforcement, which may promote maintenance and generalization of the newly acquired behaviors.

External Validity: Replicating Experiments to Determine the Generality of Research Findings

External validity refers to the degree to which a functional relation found reliable and socially valid in a given experiment holds under different conditions. An intervention that works only within a circumscribed set of conditions and proves ineffective when any aspect in the original experiment is altered makes a limited contribution to the development of a reliable and useful technology of behavior change. When a carefully controlled experiment has shown that a particular treatment produces consistent and socially significant improvements in the target behavior of a given subject, a series of important questions should then be asked: Will this same treatment be as effective if it is applied to other behaviors? Will the procedure continue to work if it is changed in some way (e.g., if implemented at a different time of the day, by another person, on a different schedule)? Will it work in a setting different from the original experiment? Will it work with participants of different ages, backgrounds, and repertoires? Questions about external validity are not abstract or rhetorical; they are empirical questions that can be addressed only by empirical methods.

A functional relation with external validity, or generality, will continue to operate under a variety of conditions. External validity is a matter of degree, not an all-or-nothing property. A functional relation that cannot be reproduced under any conditions other than the exact set of original variables (including the original subject) possesses no external validity. At the other end of the continuum, a procedure that is effective at any time, under any conditions, in any setting, with any behavior, and for any subject has complete generality (an improbable situation). Most functional relations fall somewhere between the two ends of this continuum, and those found to have higher degrees of generality make the greater contribution to applied behavior analysis. Investigators who use groups-comparison research methods approach the issue of external validity quite differently than do investigators who use within-subjects research methods.

External Validity and Groups Design Research

As stated previously, practitioners of group-comparison experimental designs claim two advantages for the use of large groups of subjects. In addition to the assumption that aggregating the data of a group of subjects will control for intersubject variability, researchers who employ group designs assume that including many subjects in an experiment increases the external validity of a study's results. On the surface this assumption is perfectly logical, and when viewed at the proper level of extrapolation, it is also true. The more subjects with which a functional relation has been demonstrated, the more likely it is that that functional relation will also be effective with other subjects who share similar characteristics. And in fact, demonstrating a functional relation with various subjects in different settings is exactly how applied behavior analysts document external validity.

However, the investigator who claims that the findings of a groups-comparison study possess generality to other *individuals* in the population from which the experimental subjects were chosen violates a fundamental premise of the groups-comparison method and ignores a defining characteristic of behavior. The proper inferences about the results of a groups-design study are from the sample to the *population,* not from the sample to the individual (Fisher, 1956). The careful methods of random sampling used in groups-design research are followed to ensure that the participants in the study represent a heterogeneous sample of all the relevant characteristics found in the population from which they were selected. Indeed, the better the sample represents the population from which it is drawn, the less meaningful are the results for any individual subject. "The only statement that can be made concerns the average response of a group with that particular makeup which, unfortunately, is unlikely to be duplicated" (Hersen & Barlow, 1976, p. 56).

A second problem inherent in attempting to extend the results of a groups-comparison study to other people (and unless care is taken, sometimes even to a subject who participated in the study, as was illustrated in Figure 10.1) is that the groups-design experiment does not demonstrate a functional relation between the behavior of any subject and some aspect of his or her environment. In other words, from the perspective of behavior analysis, there is nothing in the results of a groups-design experiment that can have external validity; there is nothing to generalize. Johnston and Pennypacker (1993a) made this point repeatedly and well.

> Between groups designs tend to put the cart before the horse. The tactic of exposing different levels of the independent variable to different groups composed of a large number of subjects and treating their responses collectively by asking if they represent the untested portion of the population provides comparisons that describe no member of any group. By failing to focus on individuals with careful attention to experiment control, these traditional methods greatly decrease the chances of discovering orderly relationships in the first place, thereby making the questions of subject generality moot. (1993a, p. 352)

> The researcher's first objective is to obtain data that truly represent the relationship between the experimental conditions and the dependent variable for each subject. If this is not accomplished, nothing else matters. Only when the findings are "true" does the question of the meaningfulness or universality of these results become relevant. (1993a, p. 250)

Groups-comparison designs and statistical inference have long dominated research in psychology, education, and the other social sciences. Despite its long-standing dominance, the extent to which this research tradition has contributed to an effective technology of behavior change is highly questionable (Baer, 1977b; Birnbrauer, 1981; Michael, 1974). The field of education is perhaps the most telling example of the inability of groups-design research to provide data that lead to improved practice (Greer, 1983; Heward & Cooper, 1992). Instructional methods in the classroom are often influenced more by fad, the personal style of individual teachers, and ideology than by the cumulative knowledge and understanding provided by rigorous and sustained experimental analysis of the variables of which learning is a function (Heron, Tincani, Peterson, & Miller, 2005; Kozloff, 2005; Zane, 2005).

The methods of groups-comparison experimentation are simply inappropriate for answering the questions of primary interest to the applied behavior analyst—empirical questions that can be pursued only by analysis of repeated measures of individual behavior under all relevant conditions. We agree with Johnston and Pennypacker (1993b):

> We find the reasoning underlying all such procedures alien to both the subject matter and the goals of a natural science of behavior and regard the utility of group comparisons as extremely limited, no matter how elegant the mathematical treatment of data they afford. . . . [group comparison experimentation constitutes] a process of scientific inquiry that is almost totally inverted; instead of using questions about natural phenomena to guide decisions about experimental design, models of design are allowed to dictate both the form and content of the questions asked. Not only is this antithetical to the established role of experimentation in science, the types of questions allowed by groups comparison designs are largely inappropriate or irrelevant to gaining an understanding of the determinants of behavior. (pp. 94–95)

Our discussion of the inherent limitations of groups-comparison designs for behavior analysis should not be confused with a position that group designs and statistical inference have no value as research methods for seeking empirical knowledge about the world. On the contrary, group-comparison designs and statistical inference are highly effective tools for seeking answers to the kinds of questions for which they were devised. Properly designed and well-executed groups-comparison experiments can provide answers with a specific degree of confidence (i.e., probability) to questions involved in many large-scale evaluations. For example, a government body is less interested in the effects of a new regulation on any individual person (and even less interested in whether a functional relation exists between the regulation and that person's behavior) than it is in the probability that the behavior of a predictable percentage of the population will be affected by the regulation. The former concern is a behavioral one, and the experimental methods of behavior analysis provide the means to address it. The latter concern is an actuarial one, and it is best pursued with the methods of random sampling, groups comparison, and statistical inference.

External Validity and Applied Behavior Analysis

The external validity (generality) of research findings in applied behavior analysis is assessed, established, and specified through the replication of experiments.

> In order to know whether a particular result will be obtained for a subject in another study or under applied circumstances, what we really need to know is what variables are necessary to make the effect occur, what variables will prevent it from occurring, and what variables will modulate it. . . . This information cannot be learned by increasing the size of the control and experimental groups. It requires conducting a series of experiments that identify and study variables that might fall into one of these three categories. (Johnson & Pennypacker, 1993a, p. 251)

Replication in this context means repeating a previous experiment.[9] Sidman (1960) described two major types of scientific replication—direct and systematic.

Direct Replication

In a **direct replication**, the researcher makes every effort to duplicate exactly the conditions of an earlier experiment. If the same subject is used in a direct replication, the study is an *intrasubject direct replication*. Intrasubject replication within experiments is a defining characteristic of applied behavior analysis research and the primary tactic for establishing the existence and reliability of a functional relation. An *intersubject direct replication* maintains every aspect of the earlier experiment except that different, although similar, subjects are involved (i.e., same age, similar repertoires). Intersubject replication is the primary method for determining the extent to which research findings have generality across subjects.

The many uncontrolled variables in natural settings make the direct replication of experiments outside of the laboratory extremely difficult. Nevertheless, intersubject replication is the rule rather than the exception in applied behavior analysis. Although numerous single-subject studies involve just one subject (e.g., Ahearn, 2003; Dixon & Falcomata, 2004; Kodak, Grow, & Northrup, 2004; Tarbox, Williams, & Friman, 2004), the vast majority of published studies in applied behavior analysis include direct intersubject replications. This is because each subject is usually considered an intact experiment. For example, a behavior analysis study in which the independent variable is manipulated in exactly the same way for six subjects in the same setting yields five intersubject replications.

Systematic Replication

The direct replication of experiments demonstrates the reliability of a functional relation, but the generality of that finding to other conditions can be established only through repeated experimentation in which the conditions of interest are purposefully and systematically varied. In a **systematic replication** the researcher purposefully varies one or more aspects of an earlier experiment. When a systematic replication successfully reproduces the results of previous research, it not only demonstrates the reliability of the earlier findings but also adds to the external validity of the earlier findings by showing that the same effect can be obtained under different conditions. In a systematic replication, any aspect of a previous experiment can be altered: subjects, setting, administration of the independent variable, target behaviors.

Although systematic replication offers greater potential rewards than direct replication does because it can provide new knowledge about the variables under investigation, it entails some risk. Sidman (1960) described systematic replication as a gamble, but one well worth taking.

> If systematic replication fails, the original experiment will still have to be redone, else there is no way of determining whether the failure to replicate stemmed from the introduction of new variables in the second experiment, or whether the control of relevant factors was inadequate in the first experiment.
>
> On the other hand, if systematic replication succeeds, the pay-off is handsome. Not only is the reliability of the original finding increased, but also its generality with respect to other organisms *and* to other experimental procedures is greatly enhanced. Furthermore, additional data are now available which could not have been obtained by a simple repetition of the first experiment. (pp. 111–112)

Sidman went on to explain that economic husbandry of limited resources must also play an important role in

---

[9]Johnston and Pennypacker (1980) pointed out a distinction between replicating an experiment and reproducing its results. They stated that the quality of the replication should be judged only by "the extent to which equivalent environmental manipulations associated with [the original experiment] are duplicated. . . . Thus, one replicates procedures in an effort to reproduce effects" (pp. 303–304). However, when most researchers report a "failure to replicate," they mean that the results of the replication did not match those obtained in the earlier research (e.g., Ecott, Foate, Taylor, & Critchfield, 1999; Friedling & O'Leary, 1979).

the scientist's determination of how a research program should proceed. Direct replication of a long and costly experiment can provide data on only the reliability of a functional relation, whereas systematic replication can provide information on the reliability and generality of the phenomena under investigation, as well as new information for additional experimentation.

The external validity of results of groups-comparison research is viewed as an inherent characteristic of a given experiment, as something that can be directly assessed by examining the methods used to conduct the study (e.g., sampling procedures). If that logic is extended to single-subject experiments, then the findings of single-subject experiments cannot be said to have any external validity. But as Birnbrauer (1981) pointed out, external validity is not something a single study *has,* but rather the product of many studies. External validity can be pursued only through the active process of systematic replication.

> Generality is established, or more likely limited, by accumulating studies which are internally valid *and* by placing the results into a systematic context, i.e., seeking out the principles and parameters that particular procedures appear to be enunciating. The most informative studies ask *how* can an earlier positive result be repeated in the present circumstances, with the present problem? (p. 122)

Much of the applied behavior analysis literature consists of systematic replications. Indeed, one could argue quite persuasively that almost any applied behavior analysis study is a systematic replication of at least some aspect of an earlier experiment. Even when the authors have not pointed it out, virtually every published experiment reveals significant procedural similarity with previous experiments. However, as we are using the term here, systematic replication refers to concerted and directed efforts to establish and specify the generality of a functional relation. For example, Hamlet, Axelrod, and Kuerschner (1984) found a functional relation between demanded eye contact (e.g., "[Name], turn around") and compliance with adult instructions in two 11-year-old school children. Included in the same published report were the results of six replications conducted by the same researchers over a period of one year with nine students aged 2 to 21 years. Similar results were reproduced in eight of the nine replication subjects. Although some might consider this an example of direct intersubject replication, Hamlet and colleagues' replications were conducted in various settings (i.e., classrooms, homes, institutions) and therefore should be viewed as a series of systematic replications that demonstrated not only the reliability of the results but also considerable generality across subjects of different ages in different settings.

Systematic replications across subjects sometimes reveal different patterns of effects, which the researcher might then study as a function of specific subject characteristics or contextual variables. For example, Hagopian, Fisher, Sullivan, Acquisto, and LeBlanc (1998) reported the results of a series of systematic replications with 21 inpatient cases of functional communication training with and without extinction and punishment.[10] Lerman, Iwata, Shore, and DeLeon (1997) found that thinning FR 1 schedules of punishment to intermittent punishment produced different effects on the self-injurious behavior of five adults with profound mental retardation.

Some systematic replications are attempts to reproduce the results reported by another researcher in a slightly different situation or context. For example, Saigh and Umar (1983) successfully reproduced in a Sudanese classroom the positive results originally reported with the Good Behavior Game in an American classroom (Barrish, Saunders & Wolf, 1969; see Figure 26.13). Saigh and Umar reported that a "considerable degree of support for the cross-cultural utility of the game was established" (p. 343).

Researchers sometimes report multiple experiments, with each experiment serving as a systematic replication investigating the variables influencing a given functional relation. For example, Fisher, and colleagues (1993) conducted four studies designed to explore the effectiveness of functional communication training (FCT) with and without extinction and punishment.

Systematic replication is evident when a research team pursues a consistent line of related studies over time. Examples of this approach to replication can be found in Van Houten and colleagues' studies investigating variables affecting driver behavior and pedestrian safety (e.g., Huybers, Van Houten, & Malenfant, 2004; Van Houten & Nau, 1981, 1983; Van Houten, Nau, & Marini, 1980; Van Houten & Malenfant, 2004; Van Houten, Malenfant, & Rolider, 1985; Van Houten & Retting, 2001); Neef, Markel, and colleagues' experiments on the impulsivity of students with attention-deficit/hyperactivity disorder (ADHD) (e.g., Bicard & Neef, 2002; Ferreri, Neef, & Wait, 2006; Neef, Bicard, & Endo, 2001; Neef, Bicard, Endo, Coury, & Aman, 2005; Neef, Markel et al., 2005); and Miltenberger and colleagues' line of research on teaching safety skills to children (e.g., Himle, Miltenberger, Flessner, & Gatheridge, 2004; Himle, Miltenberger, Gatheridge, & Flessner, & 2004; Johnson, Miltenberger et al., 2005; Johnson, Miltenberger et al., 2006; Miltenberger et al., 2004; Miltenberger et al., 2005).

---

[10]Functional communication training (FCT) is described in Chapter 24.

In many instances, the systematic replications necessary to explore and extend a significant line of research require the independent efforts of investigators at different sites who are aware of, and build on, one another's work. When independent teams of researchers at different geographical locations report similar findings, the net result is a body of knowledge with significant scientific integrity and technological value. This collective effort speeds and enhances the refinement and rigorous testing of interventions that is necessary to the development and refinement of evidence-based practices (Horner et al., 2005; Peters & Heron, 1993). One such example of independent research teams at various sites reporting systematic replications is a growing body of studies exploring the effects of response cards on students' academic engagement, learning, and deportment during group instruction. Investigators have reported a similar pattern of results—increased participation during instruction, improved retention of lesson content, and/or reductions in off-task and disruptive behaviors—with response cards in a wide range of students (general education students, special education students, and ESL learners), curriculum content (e.g., math, science, social studies, spelling), and instructional settings (e.g., elementary, middle, secondary, and college classrooms) (e.g., Armendariz & Umbreit, 1999; Cavanaugh, Heward, & Donelson, 1996; Christle & Schuster, 2003; Davis & O'Neill, 2004; Gardner, Heward, & Grossi, 1994; Kellum, Carr, & Dozier, 2001; Lambert, Cartledge, Lo, & Heward, 2006; Marmolejo, Wilder, & Bradley, 2004).

Evaluating Applied Behavior Analysis Research

A list of all the expectations and characteristics of exemplary research in applied behavior analysis would be very long. Thus far we have identified a considerable number of requirements for good applied behavior analysis. Our purpose now is to summarize those requirements in a sequence of questions one might ask in evaluating the quality of research in applied behavior analysis. Those questions can be organized under four major headings: internal validity, social validity, external validity, and scientific and theoretical significance.

Internal Validity

To determine whether an analysis of behavior has been made, the reader of an applied behavior analysis study must decide whether a functional relation has been demonstrated. This decision requires a close examination of the measurement system, the experimental design,

and the degree to which the researcher controlled potential confounds, as well as a careful visual analysis and interpretation of the data.

Definition and Measurement of the Dependent Variable

The initial step in evaluating internal validity is to decide whether to accept the data as valid and accurate measures of the target behavior over the course of the experiment. Some of the important issues to be considered in this decision are captured by the questions shown in Figure 10.8.

Graphic Display

If the data are accepted as a valid and accurate representation of the dependent variable over the course of the experiment, the reader should next assess the extent of stability of the target behavior during each phase of the study. Before evaluating the stability of the data paths, however, the reader should examine the graphic display for any sources of distortion (e.g., scaling of axes, distortions of time on the horizontal axis; see Chapter 6). The researcher or consumer who suspects that any element of the graph may encourage interpretations unwarranted by the data should replot the data using a new set of appropriately scaled axes. In an assessment of the stability of the dependent variable within the different phases of an experiment, the length of the phase or condition must be considered as well as the presence of trends in the data path. The reader should ask whether the conditions in effect during each phase were conducive to practice effects. If so, were these effects allowed to play themselves out before experimental variables were manipulated?

Meaningfulness of Baseline Conditions

The representativeness or fairness of the baseline conditions as the basis for evaluating subsequent performance in the presence of the independent variable should be assessed. In other words, were the baseline conditions meaningful in relation to the target behavior, setting, and research questions addressed by the experiment? For example, consider two experiments by Miller, Hall, and Heward (1995) that evaluated the effects of two procedures for conducting 1-minute time trials during a daily 10-minute practice session on the rate and accuracy with which students answered math problems. Throughout all conditions and phases of both experiments, the students were instructed to answer as many problems as they could

Figure 10.8   Questions that should be asked when evaluating the definition and measurement of the dependent variable in an applied behavior analysis study.

- Was the dependent variable precisely, completely, and unambiguously defined?
- Were examples and nonexamples of the target behavior provided, if doing so would enhance clarity?
- Were the most relevant, measurable dimensions of the target behavior specified (e.g., rate, duration)?
- Were important concomitant behaviors also measured?
- Were the observation and recording procedures appropriate for the target behavior?
- Did the measurement provide valid (i.e., meaningful) data for the problem or research question addressed?
- Was the measurement scale broad and sensitive enough to capture the socially significant changes in the behavior?
- Have the authors provided sufficient information on the training and calibration of observers?
- What procedures were used to assess and ensure the accuracy of measurement?
- Were interobserver agreement (IOA) assessments reported at the levels at which the study's results are presented (e.g., by subject and experimental condition)?
- Were observation sessions scheduled during the times, activities, and places most relevant to the problem or research question?
- Did observations occur often enough and closely enough in time to provide a convincing estimate of behavior change over time?
- Were any contingencies operating in the study that may have influenced the observers' behavior?
- Was there any expectation or indication that the dependent variable may have been reactive to the measurement system? If so, were procedures taken to assess and/or control reactivity?
- Were appropriate accuracy and/or reliability assessments of the data reported?

and they received feedback on their performance. Throughout both experiments, students' worksheets were marked and scored as follows:

> Experimenters marked each student's worksheets by putting an 'X' next to incorrect answers. The number of correct answers over the total number of problems attempted was marked at the top of the first worksheet along with a positive comment to encourage the students to keep trying. If a student's score was lower than his or her highest previous score, comments such as "Keep trying, Sally!" "Work faster!" or "Keep working on it!" were written. Whenever a student achieved his or her highest score to date, comments such as "Great job, Jimmy! This is your best ever!" were written on the packet. In the event a student equaled her highest previous score, "You tied your best score!" was written on the packet.

At the beginning of each session, scored and marked worksheets from the prior day's session were returned to the students. Each session during the 10-minute continuous work period condition that functioned as the baseline condition began with the classroom teachers saying to the students: "I want you to work hard and try to do your best. Answer as many problems as you can. Don't

worry if you do not answer all of the problems. There are more problems in the packet than anyone can do. Just try your best" (p. 326).

The initial baseline (A) phase was followed by the two time-trial conditions (B and C) in an A-B-A-B-C-B-C design. Results for students in both classrooms showed a clear functional relation between both of the time-trial conditions and increased correct rate and accuracy over the baseline condition. However, if the classroom teachers had not instructed and reminded the students to do their best and to answer as many problems as they could prior to each baseline session, and if the students had not received feedback on their worksheets, the improved performance during the time-trial conditions would have been suspect. Even if a clear functional relation had been demonstrated against such baseline conditions, applied researchers and consumers could, and should, question the importance of such results. Maybe the children simply did not know they were expected to work fast. Perhaps the students would have solved problems in the baseline condition at the same high rates that they did in the time-trial conditions if they had been told to "go fast" and received feedback on their performance, praise for their improvements, and encouragement to answer more problems. By including the daily instruction to work hard and answer as many problems as they could and returning the worksheets to the students as components of the baseline condition, Miller and colleagues obtained meaningful data paths during baseline against which to test and compare the effects of the two time-trial conditions.

Experimental Design

The experimental design should be examined to determine the type of experimental reasoning it affords. What elements of the design enable prediction, verification, and replication? Is the design appropriate for the research questions addressed by the study? Does the design effectively control for confounding variables? Does the design provide the basis for component and/or parametric analyses if such questions are warranted?

Visual Analysis and Interpretation

Although various statistical methods for evaluating behavioral data and determining the existence of functional relations in single-subject designs have been recommended (e.g., Gentile, Rhoden, & Klein, 1972; Hartmann, 1974; Hartmann et al., 1980; Jones, Vaught, & Weinrott, 1977; Pfadt & Wheeler, 1995; Sideridis & Greenwood, 1996), visual inspection remains the most commonly used, and we believe the most appropriate, method for interpreting data in applied behavior analysis. We will briefly present four factors that favor visual analysis over tests of statistical significance in applied behavior analysis.

First, applied behavior analysts have little interest in knowing that a behavior change is a statistically significant outcome of an intervention. Applied behavior analysts are concerned with producing socially significant behavior changes: "If a problem has been solved, you

can *see* that; if you must test for statistical significance, you do not have a solution" (Baer, 1977a, p. 171).

Second, visual analysis is well suited for identifying variables that produce strong, large, and reliable effects, which contribute to an effective, robust technology of behavior change. On the other hand, powerful tests of statistical analysis can detect the slightest possible correlation between the independent and dependent variables, which may lead to the inclusion of weak, unreliable variables in the technology.

Two types of errors are possible when determining experimental effect (see Figure 10.9). A **Type I error** (also called a *false positive*) is made when the researcher concludes that the independent variable had an effect on the dependent variable, when in truth no such relation exists in nature. A **Type II error** (also called a *false negative*) is the opposite of a Type I error. In this case, the researcher concludes that an independent variable did not have an effect on the dependent variable, when in truth it did. Ideally, a researcher using well-reasoned experimental tactics coupled with a sound experimental design and buttressed by appropriate methods of data analysis will conclude correctly that a functional relation between the independent and dependent variables exists (or does not exist).

Baer (1977b) pointed out that the behavior analyst's reliance on visual inspection to determine experimental effects results in a low incidence of Type I errors but increases the commission of Type II errors. The researcher who relies on tests of statistical significance to determine experimental effects makes many more Type I errors than the behavior analyst, but misses few, if any, variables that might produce some effect.

> Scientists who commit relatively many Type 1 errors are bound to memorize very long lists of variables that are supposed to affect diverse behaviors, some predictable portion of which are not variables at all. By contrast,

Functional Relations Exist in Nature

		Yes	No
Researcher Concludes Functional Relations Exists	**Yes**	Correct Conclusion	Type I Error (false positive)
	No	Type II Error (false negative)	Correct Conclusion

Figure 10.9 Ideally, an experimental design and methods of data analysis help a researcher conclude correctly that a functional relation between the independent and dependent variables exists (or does not exist) when in fact such a relation does (or does not) exist in nature. Concluding that the results of an experiment reveal a functional relation when no such relation exists in nature is a Type I error. Conversely, concluding that that independent variable did not have an effect on the dependent variable when such a relation did occur is a Type II error.

scientists who commit very few Type 1 errors have relatively short lists of variables to remember. Furthermore, and much more important, it is usually only the very robust, uniformly effective variables that will make their list. Those who will risk Type 1 errors more often will uncover a host of weak variables. Unquestionably, they will know more, although some of that more is wrong, and much of it is tricky. . . . Those who keep their probability of Type 2 errors low do not often reject an actually functional variable, relative to those whose Type 2 error probability is higher. Again, unquestionably, the practitioner with the lower probability of Type 2 errors will know more; but again, the nature of that more is seen often in its weakness, inconsistency of function, or its tight specialization. . . . Individual-subject-design practitioners . . . necessarily fall into very low probabilities of Type 1 errors and very high probabilities of Type 2 errors, relative to their group-paradigm colleagues. As a result, they learn about fewer variables, but these variables are typically more powerful, general, dependable, and—very important—sometimes actionable. These are exactly the variables on which a technology of behavior might be built. (Baer, 1977b, pp. 170–171)

A third problem with using statistical methods to determine the existence of functional relations in behavioral data occurs with borderline data sets containing significant amounts of variability. Such data sets should motivate a researcher to engage in additional experimentation in an effort to achieve more consistent experimental control and to discover the factors causing the variability. The researcher who forgoes the additional experimentation in favor of accepting the results of a test of statistical significance as evidence of a functional relation risks leaving important findings in the realm of the unknown.

> The situation where a significance test might seem helpful is typically one involving sufficient uncontrolled variability in the dependent variable that neither the experimenter nor his readers can be sure that there is an interpretable relationship. This is evidence that the relevant behavior is not under good experimental control, a situation calling for more effective experimentation, not a more complex judgmental aid. (Michael, 1974, p. 650)

Fourth, statistical tests of significance can be applied only to data sets that conform to predetermined criteria. If statistical methods for determining experimental effects were to become highly valued in applied behavior analysis, researchers might begin to design experiments so that such tests could be computed. The resultant loss of flexibility in experimental design would be counterproductive to the continued development of behavior analysis (Johnston & Pennypacker, 1993b; Michael, 1974).

Social Validity

The reader of a published study in applied behavior analysis should judge the social significance of the target behavior, the appropriateness of the procedures, and the social importance of the outcomes (Wolf, 1978).

Chapter 3 detailed many considerations that should guide the applied behavior analyst's selection of target behaviors. The social validity of the dependent variable should be assessed in light of those factors. Ultimately, all of the issues and considerations relative to target behavior selection point to one question: Will an increase (or decrease) in the measured dimension of this behavior improve the person's life directly or indirectly?

The independent variable should be evaluated not only in terms of its effects on the dependent variable, but also in terms of its social acceptability, complexity, practicality, and cost. Regardless of their effectiveness, treatments that are perceived by practitioners, parents, and/or clients as unacceptable or undesirable for whatever reason are unlikely to be used. Consequently, such treatments will never have the chance to contribute to a technology of behavior change. The same can be said of independent variables that are extremely complex and thus difficult to learn, teach, and apply. Similarly, treatment procedures that require large amounts of time and/or money to implement have less social validity than do procedures that can be applied quickly and/or inexpensively.

Even though behavior change is clearly visible on a graphic display, it may not represent a socially valid improvement for the participant and/or significant others in his environment. In evaluating the results of an applied behavior analysis study, the reader should ask questions such as these: Is the participant (or significant others in the participant's life) better off now that the behavior has changed? Will this new level of performance result in increased reinforcement (or decreased punishment) for the subject now or in the future? (Hawkins, 1984). In some instances it is relevant to ask whether the subject (or significant others) believes that her behavior has improved (Wolf, 1978).

Maintenance and Generalization of Behavior Change

Improvements in behavior are most beneficial when they are long-lasting, appear in other appropriate environments, and spill over to other related behaviors. Producing these kinds of effects is a major goal of applied behavior analysis. (Chapter 28 examines strategies and tactics to facilitate the maintenance and generalization of behavior change.) When evaluating applied behavior analysis research, consumers should consider the maintenance and generalization of behavior change in their evaluation of a study. An impressive behavior change that does not last or is limited to a specialized training setting may not be socially significant. Did the researchers report the results of assessment of maintenance and generalization through follow-up observations and measurement in nontraining environments? Better yet, if maintenance and/or generalization were not evident in such follow-up observations, did the experimenters modify their design and implement procedures in an attempt to produce and analyze the occurrence of maintenance and/or generalization? Additionally, the reader should ask whether response generalization—changes in functionally similar but untreated behaviors concomitant with changes in the target behavior(s)—is an appropriate concern in a given study. If so, did the experimenters attempt to assess, analyze, or discuss this phenomenon?

External Validity

As discussed earlier in this chapter, the generality of the findings of a given experiment to other subjects, settings, and behaviors cannot be assessed solely on inherent aspects of the study itself. The generality of a behavior–environment relation can be established only through the active process of systematic replication. Therefore, the reader of an applied behavior analysis study should compare the study's results with those of other published research with which it shares relevant features. The authors of a published report identify in the paper's introduction the experiments that they believe are most relevant. To make an effective judgment of the external validity of the data from a given study, the reader must often locate previous studies in the literature and compare the results of those studies with those of the current experiment.

Even though external validity should not be considered a characteristic of a study per se (Birnbrauer, 1981), various features of an experiment suggest to the reader an expected, or likely, level of generality for the results. For example, an experiment that demonstrated a functional relation of similar form and degree in six subjects of different ages, backgrounds, and current repertoires would indicate a higher probability of generality to other subjects than would an identical study demonstrating the same results across six subjects of the same age, background, and current repertoire. Similarly, if the experiment was conducted in various settings and a number of different people administered the independent variable, additional confidence in the external validity of the results may be warranted.

Theoretical Significance and Conceptual Sense

A published experiment should also be evaluated in terms of its scientific merit. It is possible for a study to clearly demonstrate a functional relation between the independent variable and a socially important target behavior—and thus be judged significant from an applied perspective—yet contribute little to the advancement of the field.[11] It is possible to reliably reproduce an important behavior change while at the same time not fully understand which variables are responsible for the observed functional relation. Sidman (1960) differentiated this kind of simple reliability from "knowledgeable reproducibility," a more complete level of analysis in which all of the important factors have been identified and are controlled.

The Need for More Thorough Analyses of Socially Important Behavior

Even though no behavior analyst would argue the necessity of systematic replication and the central role it plays in the development of an effective technology of behavior change, and even though the literature provides evidence that at least a loose form of systematic replication is commonly practiced, a more critical examination of the literature suggests the need for more thorough analyses of the functional relations under study. Numerous authors have discussed the importance of focusing on the analytic side of applied behavior analysis as much as the applied side (e.g., Baer, 1991; Birnbrauer, 1979, 1981; Deitz, 1982; Hayes, 1991; Iwata, 1991; Michael, 1980; Morris, 1991; Johnston, 1991; Pennypacker, 1981). After examining the majority of the experimental articles published in the first 10 volumes of the *Journal of Applied Behavior Analysis* (1968 to 1977), Hayes, Rincover, and Solnick (1980) concluded that a technical drift had occurred in the field away from conceptual analyses and toward an emphasis on client cure. They warned of a likely loss of scientific understanding as a result of focusing purely on the technical aspects of improving behavior in applied settings, and they recommended an increased effort to perform more thorough analyses of behavior.

---

[11]It is important to remember that although some research in applied behavior analysis can rightfully be criticized as superficial because it adds little to our conceptual understanding of behavior, studies in which meaningful target behaviors are improved to a socially valid level by the application of a socially valid treatment variable (whether a package or not) are never superficial to the participants and the significant others who share their environment.

The importance of component analyses, parametric analyses, and other more sophisticated analytic attempts are often to be found less in "control" (in an immediately applied sense) and more in "understanding" (in a scientific sense). One may easily control, say, aggressive behavior through the use of punishment without having contributed significantly to an understanding of aggression. . . . For example, if one has a package program that is effective, there may be little obvious value in doing a component analysis. But these more complicated analyses may increase our knowledge of the actual functional variables and subsequently increase our ability to generate more efficient and general behavioral programs. Perhaps, we have gone too far in our attempt to be *immediately* applied at the expense of being *ultimately* more effective, in failing to encourage more analogue and analytical studies that have treatment implications. (Hayes, Rincover, & Solnick, 1980, pp. 282–283)

Baer, Wolf, and Risley (1987), writing in the 20th anniversary issue of the *Journal of Applied Behavior Analysis,* emphasized the need to shift from demonstrations of behavior changes—as convincing as they might be—to a more complete analysis and conceptual understanding of the principles that underlie the successful demonstrations.

Twenty years ago, *analytic* meant a convincing experimental design, and *conceptual* meant relevance to a comprehensive theory about behavior. Now, applied behavior analysis is considered an analytic discipline only when it demonstrated convincingly how to make specified behavior changes *and* when its behavior-change methods make systematic, conceptual sense. In the past 20 years, we have sometimes demonstrated convincingly that we had changed behavior as specified, but by methods that did not make systematic, conceptual sense—it was not clear *why* those methods had worked. Such cases let us see that we were sometimes convincingly applied and behavioral, yet even so, not sufficiently analytic. (p. 318)

We agree with the need for more sophisticated, thorough analyses of the variables controlling socially important behavior. Fortunately, examination of the recent literature reveals numerous examples of the component and parametric analyses that are necessary steps to a more complete understanding of behavior—an understanding that is prerequisite to the development of a thoroughly effective technology of behavior change. Several of the studies cited earlier in this chapter as examples of systematic replication incorporated component and parametric analyses.

The extent of a phenomenon's generality is known only when all of the necessary and sufficient conditions for its reproducibility have been specified. Only when all of the variables influencing a functional relation have been identified and accounted for can an analysis be considered complete. Even then, the notion of a complete analysis is misleading: "Further dissection or elaboration of either variable in a functional relation inevitably reveals fresh variability, and analysis proceeds anew. . . . the analysis of behavior can never be complete" (Pennypacker, 1981, p. 159).

Evaluation of scientific significance takes into consideration such things as the authors' technological description of the experiment as well as their interpretation and discussion of the results. Are the procedures described in sufficient detail so that at least the unique aspects of the study can be replicated?[12]

Readers should consider the level of conceptual integrity displayed in an experimental report. Does the literature review reveal a careful integration of the study with previous research? Does the literature review provide sufficient justification for the study's research questions? Are the authors' conclusions based on the data obtained in the study? Have the authors respected the difference between basic principles of behavior and behavior change tactics? Do the authors speculate beyond the data without making it clear that they are doing so? Do the authors suggest directions for additional research to further analyze the problem studied? Is the study important for reasons other than the results actually obtained? For example, an experiment that demonstrates a new measurement technique, investigates a new dependent or independent variable, or incorporates a novel tactic for controlling a confounding variable can contribute to the scientific advancement of behavior analysis, even though the study failed to achieve experimental control or produce socially significant behavior change.

Numerous criteria and considerations are involved in evaluating the "goodness" of a published study in applied behavior analysis. Although each criterion is important on one level or another, it is unlikely that any experiment will meet all of the criteria. And, in fact, it is unnecessary for an experiment to do so to be considered good. Nevertheless, incorporating as many of these considerations as possible into a study enhances its social significance and scientific value as an applied behavior analysis.

---

[12]Ideally, published procedural descriptions should include sufficient detail to allow an experienced investigator to replicate the experiment. However, space limitations of most journals often prohibit such detail. The common and recommended practice in replicating published studies is to request complete experimental protocols from the original investigator(s).

Summary

Importance of the Individual Subject in Behavioral Research

1. The focus on the behavior of individual subjects has enabled applied behavior analysts to discover and refine effective interventions for a wide range of socially significant behavior.

2. Knowing that the average performance of a group of subjects changed may not reveal anything about the performance of individual subjects.

3. To be most useful, a treatment must be understood at the level at which people come into contact with it and are affected by it: the individual level.

4. When repeated measurement reveals significant variability, the researcher should seek to identify and control the factors responsible for it.

5. Attempting to cancel out variability through statistical manipulation neither eliminates its presence in the data nor controls the variables responsible for it.

6. The researcher who attributes the effects of unknown or uncontrolled variables to chance is unlikely to identify and analyze important variables.

7. To control the effects of any variable, a researcher must either hold it constant throughout the experiment or manipulate it as an independent variable.

8. A great strength of within-subject experimental designs is the convincing demonstration of a functional relation made possible by replication within the design itself.

9. The overall performance of a group is socially significant in many situations.

10. When group results do not represent individual performances, researchers should supplement group data with individual results.

11. When the behavior analyst cannot control access to the experimental setting or identify individual subjects, the dependent variable must consist of the responses made by individuals who enter the experimental setting.

Importance of Flexibility in Experimental Design

12. A good experimental design is any sequence and type of independent variable manipulations that produces data that effectively and convincingly address the research question(s).

13. To investigate the research question(s) of interest, an experimenter must often build an experimental design that employs a combination of analytic tactics.

14. The most effective experimental designs use ongoing evaluation of data from individual subjects as the basis for employing the three elements of baseline logic—prediction, verification, and replication.

Internal Validity: Controlling Potential Sources of Confounding in Experimental Design

15. Experiments that demonstrate a clear functional relation between the independent variable and the target behavior are said to have a high degree of internal validity.

16. The strength of an experimental design is determined by the extent to which it (a) demonstrates a reliable effect and (b) eliminates or reduces the possibility that factors other than the independent variable produced the behavior change.

17. The phrase *control of behavior* is technically inaccurate because the experimenter controls only some aspect of the subject's environment.

18. A confounding variable is an uncontrolled factor known or suspected to have exerted influence on the dependent variable.

19. Steady state responding is the primary means by which applied behavior analysts assess the degree of experimental control.

20. Confounding variables can be viewed as related primarily to one of four elements of an experiment: subject, setting, measurement of the dependent variable, and independent variable.

21. A placebo control is designed to separate any effects that may be produced by a subject's expectations of improvement as a result of receiving treatment from the effects actually produced by the treatment.

22. With a double-blind control procedure neither the subject(s) nor the observers know when the independent variable is present or absent.

23. Treatment integrity and procedural fidelity refer to the extent to which the independent variable is implemented or carried out as planned.

24. Low treatment integrity invites a major source of confounding into an experiment, making it difficult, if not impossible, to interpret the results with confidence.

25. One threat to treatment integrity, treatment drift, occurs when application of the independent variable during later phases of an experiment differs from the way the treatment was applied at the outset of the study.

26. Achieving a high level of treatment integrity begins with an operational definition of treatment procedures.

27. Treatments that are simple, precise, and brief, and that require relatively little effort, are more likely to be delivered with consistency than those that are not.

28. Researchers should not assume that a person's general competence or experience in the experimental setting, or that providing the intervention agent with detailed written instructions or a script, will ensure a high degree of treatment integrity.

29. Treatment integrity (or procedural fidelity) data measure the extent to which the actual implementation of experimental procedures matches their descriptions in the method section of a research report.

Social Validity: Assessing the Applied Value of Behavior Changes and the Treatments That Accomplish Them

30. The social validity of an applied behavior analysis can be assessed in three ways: the social significance of the target behavior, the appropriateness of the procedures, and the social importance of the results.

31. Social validity assessments are most often accomplished by seeking consumer opinions.

32. Socially valid goals can be determined empirically by assessing the performance of individuals judged to be highly competent, and experimentally manipulating different levels of performance to determine socially valid outcomes.

33. Several scales and questionnaires for obtaining consumers' opinions of the acceptability of behavioral interventions have been developed.

34. Methods for assessing the social validity of outcomes include (a) comparing participants' performance to the performance of a normative sample, (b) using a standardized assessment instrument, (c) asking consumers to rate the social validity of participants' performance, (d) asking experts to evaluate participants' performance, and (e) testing participants' newly learned level of performance in the natural environment.

External Validity: Replicating Experiments to Determine the Generality of Research Findings

35. External validity refers to the degree to which a functional relation found reliable and socially valid in a given experiment will hold under different conditions.

36. The proper inferences about the results of a groups-design study are from the sample to the population, not from the sample to the individual.

37. Because a groups-design experiment does not demonstrate a functional relation between the behavior of any subject and some aspect of his or her environment, the external validity of the results is moot.

38. Although groups-comparison designs and tests of statistical significance are necessary and effective tools for cer-

tain types of research questions, they have contributed little to an effective technology of behavior change.

39. The generality of research findings in applied behavior analysis is assessed, established, and specified by the replication of experiments.

40. In a direct replication the researcher makes every effort to duplicate exactly the conditions of an earlier experiment.

41. In a systematic replication the researcher purposefully varies one or more aspects of an earlier experiment.

42. When a systematic replication successfully reproduces the results of previous research, it not only demonstrates the reliability of the earlier findings but also adds to the external validity of the earlier findings by showing that the same effect can be obtained under different conditions.

43. Systematic replications occur in both planned and unplanned ways through the work of many experimenters in a given area, and they result in a body of knowledge with significant scientific integrity and technological value.

Evaluating Applied Behavior Analysis Research

44. The quality and value of an applied behavior analysis study may be evaluated by seeking answers to a sequence of questions related to the internal validity, social validity, external validity, and the scientific and theoretical significance of the study.

45. A Type I error occurs when a researcher concludes that the independent variable had an effect on the dependent variable when it did not. A Type II error occurs when a researcher concludes that the independent variable did not have an effect on the dependent variable when it did.

46. Visual analysis effectively identifies variables that produce strong, large, and reliable effects, which contribute to an effective and robust technology of behavior change. Statistical analysis detects the slightest possible correlations between the independent and dependent variables, which may lead to the identification and inclusion of weak and unreliable variables in the technology.

47. A study can demonstrate a functional relation between the independent variable and a socially important target behavior—and thus be significant from an applied perspective—yet contribute little to the advancement of the field.

48. Only when all of the variables influencing a functional relation have been identified and accounted for can an analysis be considered complete.

49. When evaluating the scientific significance of a research report, readers should consider the technological description of the experiment, the interpretation and discussion of the results, and the level of conceptual sense and integrity.

PART 4

Reinforcement

The three chapters in Part Four are devoted to reinforcement, the most important and widely applied principle of behavior analysis. Reinforcement, a deceptively simple behavior-consequence relation, is the fundamental building block for the selection of operant behavior. In Chapter 11, Positive Reinforcement, we examine the operation and defining effect of reinforcement, describe briefly how antecedent stimulus conditions modulate the effects of reinforcement, discuss factors that influence the effectiveness of reinforcement, identify how a stimulus change acquires a reinforcing function and the types of events that often serve as reinforcers, detail methods for identifying potential reinforcers and assessing their effects, outline experimental control techniques for verifying whether a positive reinforcement contingency is responsible for increased responding, and offer several guidelines for using reinforcement effectively.

In Chapter 12, Brian Iwata and Richard Smith describe one of the most consistently misunderstood principles of behavior, negative reinforcement: an operant contingency in which responding increases as a result of the termination, reduction, or postponement of a stimulus as a consequence of responding. Iwata and Smith define negative reinforcement, compare and contrast it with positive reinforcement and punishment, distinguish between escape and avoidance contingencies, describe events that may serve as negative reinforcers, illustrate ways in which negative reinforcement may be used to strengthen desired behavior, and discuss ethical issues that arise when using negative reinforcement.

One of Skinner's most important discoveries was that reinforcement does not have to follow every response. In fact, responding under many intermittent schedules of reinforcement—in which reinforcement follows some, but not all, occurrences of the target behavior—occurs at higher, more consistent rates than under a continuous schedule of reinforcement in which each response is reinforced. In Chapter 13, Schedules of Reinforcement, we describe some of the ways that reinforcement can be scheduled based on various combinations of response and/or temporal requirements, and we identify the characteristic patterns of responding associated with each schedule. The practitioner who understands the influence of schedules of reinforcement of behavior is able to program reinforcement for effective and efficient acquisition of new skills, for improved performance and endurance of established skills, and for the maintenance of important behavior changes in the learner's post-intervention environment.

CHAPTER 11

Positive Reinforcement

Key Terms

automatic reinforcement
conditioned reinforcer
generalized conditioned reinforcer
positive reinforcement

positive reinforcer
Premack principle
reinforcer assessment

response-deprivation hypothesis
stimulus preference assessment
unconditioned reinforcer

Behavior Analyst Certification Board® BCBA® & BCABA® Behavior Analyst Task List©, Third Edition

	Content Area 3: Principles, Processes, and Concepts
3-3	Define and provide examples of positive (and negative) reinforcement.
3-4	Define and provide examples of conditioned and unconditioned reinforcement.
3-14	Describe and provide examples of the operant conditioning paradigm.
3-19	Define and provide examples of contingency-shaped and rule-governed behavior and distinguish between them by providing examples.

	Content Area 9: Behavior Change Procedures
9-2	Use positive (and negative) reinforcement:
(a)	Identify and use reinforcers.
(b)	Use appropriate parameters and schedules of reinforcement.
(c)	Use response-deprivation procedures (e.g., the Premack principle).

In looking back, it seems to me that the most important thing I learned in graduate school was from another student, Burrhus Frederic Skinner (I called him Burrhus, others called him Fred). This man had a box, within which was a smaller box, within which he would place a hungry laboratory rat. When the animal, in its explorations, would depress a lever that projected from one wall, a pellet of food would be discharged into a tray beneath the lever. Under such conditions, the rat would learn, in a matter of minutes, sometimes seconds, how to get its meal by depression of the lever. It would even keep on pressing, sometimes at a rapid rate, when pellets were delivered only now and then; and if the food supply was cut off entirely, the animal would still keep working for awhile.

—Fred Keller (1982, p. 7)

 Although some people still believe that findings from laboratory research on animal learning are not applicable to human behavior, by the mid-1960s applied researchers had established the significance of positive reinforcement in education and treatment. "It is safe to say that without Skinner's detailed laboratory analyses of reinforcement (Skinner, 1938), there would be no field of 'applied behavior analysis' today, least not as we know it" (Vollmer & Hackenberg, 2001, p. 241). Positive reinforcement is the most important and most widely applied principle of behavior analysis.

Fittingly, the lead article in the first issue of the *Journal of Applied Behavior Analysis* reported several experiments showing the effects of positive reinforcement on student behavior (Hall, Lund, & Jackson, 1968). Six elementary students who were disruptive or dawdled frequently participated in this classic study. The dependent variable, study behavior, was defined individually for each student depending on the subject matter being

taught, but it generally consisted of the student being seated and oriented toward the appropriate object or person (e.g., looking at course materials or the lecturing teacher) and class participation (e.g., writing the assignment, answering the teacher's question). The independent variable was teacher attention, cued by an observer who held up a small square of colored paper not likely to be noticed by the target student. On this signal, the teacher attended to the child by moving to his desk, making a verbal comment, giving him a pat on the shoulder, or the like.

The effects of contingent teacher attention on the behavior of all six students were striking. Figure 11.1 shows the results for Robbie, a third-grader chosen to participate because he was "a particularly disruptive student who studied very little" (p. 3). During baseline, Robbie engaged in study behavior for an average of 25% of the observed intervals. The remainder of the time he snapped rubber bands, played with objects in his pocket, talked and laughed with classmates, and played with an empty milk carton from this earlier-served drink. The majority of attention Robbie received during baseline followed these nonstudy behaviors. During baseline, Robbie's teacher often urged him to work, told him to put his milk carton away, and told him to stop bothering his classmates.

Following baseline, the experimenters showed the teacher a graph of Robbie's study behavior, presented the results of previous studies in which contingent adult attention had improved child behavior, and discussed the fundamentals of providing social reinforcement. Hall and colleagues (1968) described the procedure implemented during the two reinforcement phases as follows:

> Whenever Robbie had engaged in 1 min of continuous study the observer signaled his teacher. On this cue, the

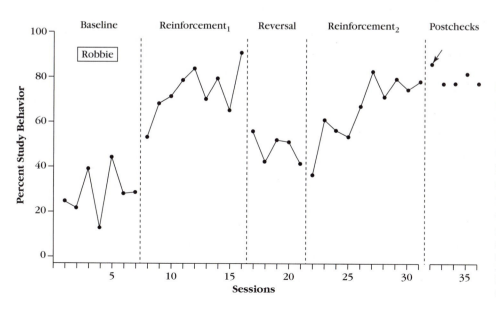

Figure 11.1 Percentage of intervals of study behavior by a third-grade student during baseline and reinforcement conditions. The arrow to the first postcheck data point shows when cueing the teacher to provide attention was discontinued.

teacher approached Robbie, saying, "Very good work Robbie," "I see you are studying," or some similar remark. She discontinued giving attention for nonstudy behaviors including those which were disruptive to the class. (p. 4)

During Reinforcement 1, Robbie's study behavior increased to a mean of 71%. When a reversal to baseline conditions was introduced, his study behavior decreased to a mean of 50%; but when Robbie's teacher again provided attention for study behavior (Reinforcement 2), his study behavior recovered and stabilized at a level ranging between 70 and 80% of the observed intervals. Results of follow-up observations over a 14-week period after signaling the teacher had been discontinued showed that Robbie's study behavior had maintained at 79%. The teacher reported positive behavior changes associated with Robbie's increased study behavior. By the final week of Reinforcement 2, Robbie completed his spelling assignments more consistently, his disruptive behavior had diminished, and he continued to study while drinking his milk and did not play with the carton afterwards.

The intervention used by Robbie's teacher to help him be more successful in the classroom was based on the principle of positive reinforcement. In this chapter we examine the definition and nature of positive reinforcement, describe methods for identifying potential reinforcers and assessing their effects, outline experimental control techniques for verifying whether a positive reinforcement contingency is responsible for increased responding, and offer guidelines for using positive reinforcement effectively.

Definition and Nature of Positive Reinforcement

The principle of reinforcement is deceptively simple. "The basic operant functional relation for reinforcement is the following: When a type of behavior (R) is followed by reinforcement (S^R) there will be an increased future frequency of that type of behavior" (Michael, 2004, p. 30).[1] However, as Michael and other authors have pointed out, three qualifications must be considered regarding the conditions under which the effects reinforcement will occur. These qualifications are (a) the delay between the response and onset of the consequence, (b) the stimulus conditions in effect when the response was emitted, and

(c) the strength of the current motivation with respect to the consequence. In this section we examine these qualifications and several other concepts requisite to acquiring a full understanding of how reinforcement "works."

Operation and Defining Effect of Positive Reinforcement

Positive reinforcement has occurred when a response is followed immediately by the *presentation* of a stimulus and, as a result, similar responses occur more frequently in the future. Figure 11.2 illustrates the two-term contingency—a response followed closely in time by the presentation of a stimulus—and the effect on future responding that define positive reinforcement. This two-term contingency is the fundamental building block for the selection of all operant behavior (Glenn, Ellis, & Greenspoon, 1992).

The stimulus presented as a consequence and responsible for the subsequent increase in responding is called a **positive reinforcer,** or, more simply, a reinforcer. Teacher attention in the form of positive comments was the reinforcer that increased Robbie's study behavior. Cold water flowing into a cup and the sight of a colorful bird are the reinforcers for the two behaviors shown in Figure 11.2.

It is important to remember that a reinforcer does not (and cannot) affect the response that it follows. Reinforcement only increases the frequency with which similar responses are emitted in the future.

> It is not correct to say the operant reinforcement "strengthens the response which precedes it." The response has already occurred and cannot be changed. What is changed is the future probability of responses in the same class. It is the operant as a class of behavior, rather than the response as a particular instance, which is conditioned. (Skinner, 1953, p. 87)

Skinner (1966) used rate of responding as the fundamental datum for his research on reinforcement. To strengthen an operant is to make it occur more frequently.[2] However, rate (or frequency) is not the only dimension of behavior selected, shaped, and maintained by reinforcement. Reinforcement can also strengthen the duration, latency, magnitude, and/or topography of behavior. For example, if reinforcement only follows those responses that fall within a range of magnitude—that is, above a minimum force but below a maximum force—and responses

---

[1]Various terms, such as *strengthening the behavior* or *increasing the likelihood of future responding,* are sometimes used by behavior analysts to describe the basic effect of reinforcement. Although such terms appear occasionally in this book, recognizing Michael's (1995) concern that use of such terms "encourages a language of intervening variables, or an implied reference to something other than an observable aspect of behavior" (p. 274), we most often use *increased future frequency* to refer to the primary effect of reinforcement.

[2]When the consequence that produced the increase in responding is best described as the *termination* or *withdrawal* of an already present stimulus, *negative reinforcement* has occurred. The fundamental nature and qualifying conditions for positive reinforcement and negative reinforcement are the same. Negative reinforcement is examined in detail in Chapter 12.

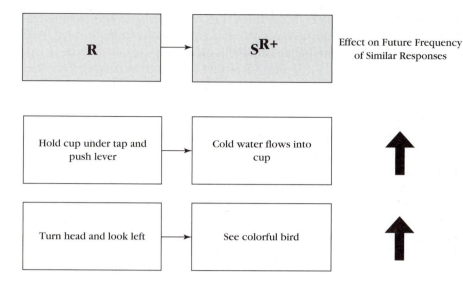

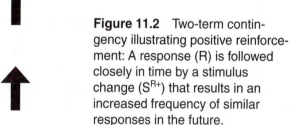

Figure 11.2   Two-term contingency illustrating positive reinforcement: A response (R) is followed closely in time by a stimulus change (S^{R+}) that results in an increased frequency of similar responses in the future.

outside of that range of magnitudes are not followed by reinforcement, the effect will be a higher frequency of responses within that range. Reinforcement contingent on responses meeting multiple criteria will strengthen a subset of responses meeting those criteria (e.g., responses by a golfer practicing 10-foot putts must fall within a narrow range of force and form to be successful).

Importance of Immediacy of Reinforcement

Emphasizing the importance of the immediacy of reinforcement is essential. The direct effects of reinforcement involve "temporal relations between behavior and its consequences that are on the order of a few seconds" (Michael, 2004, p. 161). Research with nonhumans suggests that at one end of the continuum as much as 30 seconds can elapse without critical loss of effect (e.g., Byrne, LeSage, & Poling, 1997; Critchfield & Lattal, 1993; Wilkenfeld, Nickel, Blakely, & Poling, 1992). However, a response-to-reinforcement delay of 1 second will be less effective than a 0-second delay. This is because behaviors other than the target behavior occur during the delay; the behavior temporally closest to the presentation of the reinforcer will be strengthened by its presentation. As Sidman (1960) described, "If the reinforcer does not immediately follow the response that was required for its production, then it will follow some other behavior. Its major effect will then be upon the behavior that bears, adventitiously to be sure, the closest prior temporal relationship to the reinforcement" (p. 371).

Malott and Trojan Suarez (2004) discussed the importance of immediacy as follows:

> If the reinforcer is to reinforce a particular response, it must immediately follow that response. But how immediate is immediate? We don't have any experimental

data on this one for human beings, but the research on nonverbal animals suggests that a minute or two pushes the limit (even 30 seconds is hard). And if you talk to most behavior analysts working with nonverbal children, they'd agree. They'd quit their jobs if they had to wait 60 seconds before delivering each reinforcer to their children. Such a delay is a good way to ensure that no learning would occur, even with people—at least no desirable learning.

> So, if you're trying to reinforce a response, don't push that 60-second limit. Push the other end—the 0-second end. The direct effect of reinforcement drops off quickly as you increase the delay, even to 3 or 4 seconds. And even a 1-second delay may reinforce the wrong behavior. If you ask a young child to look at you and deliver the reinforcer 1 second after the response, you're liable to reinforce looking in the wrong direction. So one problem with delayed reinforcement is that it reinforces the wrong response—the one that occurred just before the delivery of the reinforcer. (p. 6)

A common misconception is that delayed consequences can reinforce behavior, even if the consequences occur days, weeks, or even years after the responses occurred. "When human behavior is apparently affected by long-delayed consequences, the change is accomplished by virtue of the human's complex social and verbal history, and should not be thought of as an instance of the simple strengthening of behavior by reinforcement" (Michael, 2004, p. 36).

For example, suppose that a piano student practiced dutifully every day for several months in preparation for a statewide competition, at which she received a first-place award for her solo piano performance. Although some might believe that the award reinforced her persistent daily practice, they would be mistaken. Delayed consequences do not reinforce behavior directly. Delayed consequences can, when combined with language, *influence* future behavior through instructional control and rule following. A *rule* is a verbal description of a behavioral contingency (e.g., "Turnip seeds planted by August 15 will yield a crop before a killing freeze"). Learning to follow rules is one way that a person's behavior can come under the control of consequences that are too delayed to influence behavior directly. A statement by the piano teacher such as "If you practice your assignments every day for one hour between now and the competition, you could win first place" could have functioned as a rule that influenced the piano student's daily practice. The student's daily practice was *rule governed* if daily practice occurred because of her teacher's rule.[3] The following conditions provide strong indicators that behavior is the result of instructional control or rule following rather than a direct effect of reinforcement (Malott, 1988, Michael, 2004).

- No immediate consequence for the behavior is apparent.

- The response–consequence delay is greater than 30 seconds.

- Behavior changes without reinforcement.

- A large increase in the frequency of the behavior occurs following one instance of reinforcement.

- No consequence for the behavior exists, including no automatic reinforcement, but the rule exists.

Reinforcement Is Not a Circular Concept

A commonly held misconception is that reinforcement is the product of circular reasoning and therefore contributes nothing to our understanding of behavior. Circular reasoning is a form of faulty logic in which the name used to describe an observed effect is mistaken as the cause for the phenomenon. This confusion of cause and effect is circular because the observed effect is the sole basis for identifying the presumed cause. In circular reasoning, the suspected cause is not independent of its effect—they are one and the same.

Here is an example of circular reasoning that occurs often in education. A student's persistent difficulties in learning to read (effect) leads to a diagnosis of a learning disability, which is then offered as an explanation for the reading problem: "Paul's reading problem is due to his learning disability." How do you know Paul has a learning disability? Because he hasn't learned to read. Why

hasn't Paul learned to read? Because his learning disability has prevented him from learning to read. And around and around it goes.

Similarly, it would be circular reasoning if we said that teacher attention increased Robbie's study behavior *because* it is a reinforcer. However, the correct use is to say that because Robbie's study behavior increased when (and only when) it was followed immediately by teacher attention, teacher attention is a reinforcer. The difference is more than the direction of the relation, or a semantic sleight-of-hand. In circular reasoning the suspected cause is not manipulated as an independent variable to see whether it affects the behavior. In circular reasoning such experimental manipulation is impossible because the cause and effect are the same. Paul's learning disability cannot be manipulated as an independent variable because, as we used the concept in this example, it is nothing more than another name for the dependent variable (effect).

Reinforcement is not a circular concept because the two components of the response–consequence relation can be separated, allowing the delivery of a consequence to be manipulated to determine whether it increases the frequency of the behavior it follows. Epstein (1982) described it as follows:

> If we can show that a response increases in frequency because (and only because) it is followed by a particular stimulus, we call that stimulus a *reinforcer* and its presentation, *reinforcement*. Note the lack of circularity. *Reinforcement* is a term we invoke when we observe certain relations between events in the world. . . . [However,] If we say, for example, that a particular stimulus strengthens a response behavior *because* it is a reinforcer, we are using the term *reinforcer* in a circular fashion. It is *because* it strengthens behavior that we call the stimulus a *reinforcer.* (p. 4)

Epstein (1982) went on to explain the difference between using an empirically demonstrated principle such as reinforcement in a theoretical account of behavior and using a circular argument.

> In some of his writings, Skinner speculates that certain behavior (for example, verbal behavior) has come about through reinforcement. He may suggest, for example, that certain behavior is strong *because* it was reinforced. This use of the concept is not circular, only speculative or interpretive. Using the language of reinforcement in this way is reasonable when you have accumulated a large data base. . . . When Skinner attributes some everyday behavior to past reinforcers, he is making a plausible guess based on a large data base and principles of behavior established under controlled conditions. (p. 4)

Used properly, *reinforcement* describes an empirically demonstrated (or speculative, in a theoretical or conceptual analysis) functional relation between a stimulus

---

[3]Excellent discussions of rule-governed behavior can be found in Baum (1994); Chase and Danforth (1991); Hayes (1989); Hayes, Zettle, and Rosenfarb (1989); Malott and Garcia (1991); Malott and Trojan Suarez (2004); Reitman and Gross (1996); and Vaughan (1989).

Table 11.1 The Vocabulary of Reinforcement*

Term	Restrictions	Examples
reinforcer (noun)	A stimulus	Food pellets were used as reinforcers for the rat's lever presses.
reinforcing (adjective)	A property of a stimulus	The reinforcing stimulus was produced more often than the other, nonreinforcing stimuli.
reinforcement (noun)	As an operation, the delivery of consequences when a response occurs	The fixed-ratio schedule of reinforcement delivered food after every tenth key peck.
	As a process, the increase in responding that results from the reinforcement	The experiment with monkeys demonstrated reinforcement produced by social consequences.
to reinforce (verb)	As on operation, to deliver consequences when a response occurs; responses are reinforced and not organisms	When a period of free play was used to reinforce the child's completion of school work, the child's grades improved.
	As a process, to increase responding through the reinforcement operation	The experiment was designed to find out whether gold stars would reinforce cooperative play among first-graders.

*This vocabulary is appropriate if and only if three conditions exist: (1) A response produces consequences; (2) that type of response occurs more often when it produces those consequences than when it does not produce them; and (3) the increased responding occurs *because* the response has those consequences. A parallel vocabulary is appropriate to punishment (including *punisher* as a stimulus and *punish* as a verb), with the difference being that a punishing consequence makes responding occur less rather than more often.
From *Learning* (4th ed.) by A. C. Catania, 1998, p. 69. Upper Saddle River, NJ: Prentice Hall. Copyright 1998 by Prentice Hall. Used by permission.

change (consequence) immediately following a response and an increase in the future frequency of similar responses. Table 11.1 shows restrictions and examples of appropriate use of the terms *reinforcer, reinforcing, reinforcement,* and *to reinforce* suggested by Catania (1998). Box 11.1 describes four mistakes commonly made when speaking and writing about reinforcement.

Reinforcement Makes Antecedent Stimulus Conditions Relevant

Reinforcement does more than increase the future frequency of behavior it follows; it also changes the function of stimuli that immediately precede the reinforced behavior. By virtue of being temporally paired with the response-reinforcer contingency, certain antecedent events acquire the ability to evoke (make more likely) instances of the reinforced response class. As introduced in Chapter 2, a *discriminative stimulus* (S^D, pronounced "ess-dee") is an antecedent stimulus correlated with the availability of reinforcement for a particular response class. Responding in the presence of the S^D produces reinforcement, and responding in the S^D's absence (a condition called *stimulus delta* [S^Δ, pronounced "ess-delta"]) does not. As a result of this history of reinforcement, a person learns to make more responses in the presence of the S^D than in its absence. The behavior is then considered to be under *stimulus control* (see Chapter 17).

With the addition of the S^D, the two-term contingency for reinforcement is transformed to the three-term contingency of the *discriminated operant*. Figure 11.3 shows examples of three-term contingencies for positive reinforcement. Assuming that cold water is currently reinforcing and the person has a history of receiving cold water only under blue taps, he is more likely to hold his cup under the blue tap on the cooler (than, say, a red tap). Similarly, assuming that seeing a colorful bird is currently reinforcing and a person has a history of seeing birds more often when looking toward chirping sounds (than, say, other sounds or silence), turning one's head and looking to the left will occur at a higher frequency when the chirping sound is heard.

Reinforcement Depends on Motivation

The phrase *assuming that cold water is currently reinforcing* in the previous paragraph holds another key to understanding reinforcement. Although reinforcement is commonly thought of as a way of motivating people—and it can be—the momentary effectiveness of any stimulus change as reinforcement depends on an existing level of motivation with respect to the stimulus change in question. As introduced in Chapter 2, *motivating operations* alter the current value of stimulus changes as reinforcement (Michael 2004).

Motivating operations (MOs) are environmental variables that have two effects on behavior: (1) They alter the operant reinforcing effectiveness of some specific stimuli, objects, or events (the value-altering effect);

Box 11.1
Common Mistakes in Talking and Writing about Reinforcement

A standard set of technical terms is prerequisite to the meaningful description of any scientific activity. Effectively communicating the design, implementation, and outcomes of an applied behavior analysis depends on the accurate use of the discipline's technical language. The language of reinforcement includes some of the most important elements of the behavior analyst's vocabulary.

In this box we identify four mistakes made frequently by students of applied behavior analysis when describing reinforcement-based interventions. Perhaps the most common mistake—confusing negative reinforcement with punishment—is not discussed here. That terminology error was introduced in Chapter 2 and receives additional attention in Chapter 12.

Reinforcing the Person

Although it is proper to speak of presenting a *reinforcer* to a learner (e.g., "The teacher gave a token to Bobby each time he asked a question"), statements such as, "The teacher reinforced Bobby when he asked a question" and "Chloe was reinforced with praise each time she spelled a word correctly" are incorrect. *Behaviors* are reinforced, not people. Bobby's teacher reinforced question asking, not Bobby. Of course, reinforcement acts on and affects the overall person, in that it strengthens behaviors within the person's repertoire. However, the procedural focus and the primary effect of reinforcement are on the behaviors that it follows.

Practice As Reinforcement for a Skill

Educators will sometimes say that students should practice a skill because "practicing reinforces the skill." The phrase poses no problem if the speaker is describing a common outcome of practice with the everyday language connotation of *reinforce,* as in "to make something stronger" (e.g., to reinforce concrete by embedding steel rods in it). Well-designed drill and practice on a skill usually yields stronger performance in the form of better retention, reduced latency, higher response rates, and/or increased endurance (e.g., Johnson & Layng, 1994; Swanson & Sachse-Lee, 2000). Unfortunately, a phrase such as "practicing reinforces the skill" is often misused and misinterpreted as technical usage of the language of operant conditioning.

Although a skill that has been practiced is often stronger as a result of the practice, the practice itself could not be a *reinforcer* for the behavior practiced.

Practice refers to the form and manner in which the target skill is emitted (e.g., answering as many math problems as you can in 1 minute). Practicing is a behavior that could be reinforced with various consequences such as a preferred activity (e.g., "Practice solving these math problems; then you can have 10 minutes of free time"). Depending on a learner's history and preferences, the opportunity to practice a certain skill may function as a reinforcer for practicing another skill (e.g., "Finish your math problems; then you'll get to do 10 minutes of repeated reading practice").

Artificial Reinforcement

A distinction between natural and artificial reinforcers is made sometimes, as in this statement, "As the students' success rates improved, we gradually stopped using artificial reinforcers, such as stickers and trinkets, and increased the use of natural reinforcers." Some authors have suggested that applications of the principles of behavior result in "artificial control" (e.g., Smith, 1992). A behavior–consequence contingency may be effective or ineffective as reinforcement, but none of its elements (the behavior, the consequence, or the resultant behavior change) is, or can be, artificial.

The reinforcement contingencies and stimuli used as reinforcers in any behavior change program are always contrived—otherwise there would be no need for the program—but they are never artificial (Skinner, 1982). The meaningful distinction when talking about reinforcement contingencies is not between the natural and the artificial, but between contingencies that already exist in a given setting prior to a behavior change program and contingencies that are contrived as part of the program (Kimball & Heward, 1993). Although the ultimate effectiveness of a behavior change program may depend on shifting control from contrived to naturally occurring contingencies, there is no such thing as artificial reinforcement.

Reinforcement and Feedback As Synonyms

Some speakers and writers mistakenly use *reinforcement* and *feedback* interchangeably. The two terms refer to different operations and outcomes, though some of each term encompasses parts of the other term's meaning. *Feedback* is information a person receives about a particular aspect of his or her behavior following its completion (e.g., "Very good, Kathy. Two quarters equal 50 cents."). Feedback is most often provided in the form of verbal descriptions of performance, but it can also be provided by other means such as vibration or lights (e.g., Greene, Bailey, & Barber, 1981). Because feedback is a consequence that often results in the increased future frequency of behavior, it sometimes leads to the faulty assumption that reinforcement must involve feedback or that reinforcement is just a behaviorist's term for feedback.

Reinforcement always increases the future frequency of responding. Feedback may result in (a) an increase in the future frequency of the student's performance as a reinforcement effect and/or as a prompt or instruction on how to respond next time (e.g. "You're handwriting is improving, Jason, but don't forget to cross your Ts"), and/or (b) a reduction in the frequency of some aspect of the learner's performance as a function of punishment or instruction (e.g., "You dropped your elbow on that pitch. Don't do that."). Feedback may have multiple effects, increasing one aspect of performance and decreasing another. Feedback may also have no effect on future responding whatsoever.

Reinforcement is defined functionally by its effect on future responding; feedback is defined by its formal characteristics (information about some aspect of performance). The operation of either concept is neither necessary nor sufficient for the other. That is, reinforcement may occur in the absence of feedback, and feedback may occur without a reinforcement effect.

Sometimes Commonsense Language Is Better

The technical language of behavior analysis is complex, and mastering it is no simple matter. Beginning students of behavior analysis are not the only ones who commit terminology errors. Well-trained practitioners, established researchers, and experienced authors also make mistakes now and then when speaking and writing about behavior analysis. Using behavioral concepts and principles—such as positive reinforcement—to confidently explain complex situations involving multiple processes and uncontrolled and unknown variables is a mistake that catches the most attentive and conscientious of behavior analysts at times.

Instead of invoking the terminology and concepts of reinforcement to explain the influence of temporally distant consequences on behavior, it is probably wiser to follow Jack Michael's (2004) advice and simply use everyday descriptive language and commonsense relations.

Incorrectly used technical language is worse than common sense language because it suggests that the situation is well understood, and it may displace serious attempts at further analysis. Until we are able to provide an accurate analysis of the various processes relevant to indirect effects [of reinforcement], we are better off using ordinary descriptive language. Thus, say "the successful grant application is *likely to encourage* future efforts in the same direct," but don't say it as though you had the science of behavior behind you. Stop referring to successful settlements of a labor dispute as reinforcement for striking, and successful election of a political candidate as reinforcement for political activity. . . . Don't talk about good grades as reinforcement for effective study behavior, although they are no doubt responsible for maintaining it in some cases. Just say that they're responsible for maintaining it. Restraint of this sort will deprive some of us of an opportunity to (incorrectly) display our technical knowledge, but so much the better. (p. 165, emphasis in original)

and (2) They alter the momentary frequency of all behavior that has been reinforced by those stimuli, objects, or events (the behavior-altering effect). The value-altering effect, like response-reinforcement delay, is relevant to the effectiveness of the reinforcer at the time of conditioning, and stating that the consequence is a form of reinforcement implies that a relevant MO is in effect and at sufficient strength. (p. 31)

In other words, for a stimulus change to "work" as reinforcement at any given time, the learner must already *want* it. This is a critical qualification in terms of the environmental conditions under which the effects of reinforcement will be seen. Michael (2004) explained this qualification as follows:

The behavior-altering effect is relevant to the increased future frequency of the reinforced behavior, and must be added as a third qualification to the operant reinforcement relation: In a given stimulus situation (S) when a type of behavior (R) is followed immediately by reinforcement (S^R) there will be an increase in the future frequency of that type of behavior in the same or similar stimulus conditions, *but the increased frequency will only be seen when the MO relevant to the reinforcement that was used is again in effect.* (p. 31, emphasis in original)

Motivating operations take two forms. An MO that increases the current effectiveness of a reinforcer is called an *establishing operation (EO)* (e.g., food deprivation makes food more effective as a reinforcer); an MO that decreases the current effectiveness of a reinforcer is an *abolishing operation (AO)* (e.g., food ingestion reduces the effectiveness of food as a reinforcer).[4]

---

[4]Motivating operations are described in detail in Chapter 16.

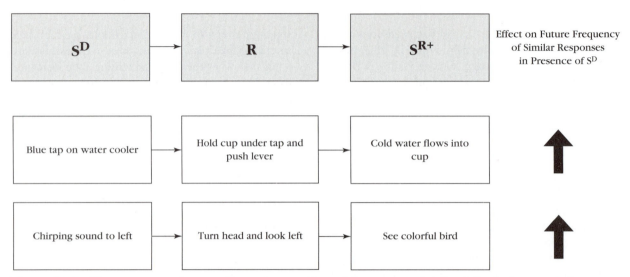

Figure 11.3 Three-term contingency illustrating positive reinforcement of a discriminated operant: A response (R) emitted in the presence of a discriminative stimulus (S^D) is followed closely in time by a stimulus change (S^{R+}) and results in an increased frequency of similar responses in the future when the S^D is present. A discriminated operant is the product of a conditioning history in which responses in the presence of the S^D produced reinforcement while similar responses in the absence of the S^D (a condition called stimulus delta [S^Δ]) have not been reinforced (or resulted in a reduced amount or quality of reinforcement than in the S^D condition).

Adding the *establishing operation (EO)* to a discriminated operant results in a four-term contingency as shown in Figure 11.4. Spending several hours in a hot and stuffy room without water is an EO that (a) makes water more effective as a reinforcer and (b) increases the momentary frequency of all behaviors that have produced water in the past. Similarly, a park ranger stating prior to a hike that any hiker who describes the coloring of the bird that makes a certain chirping sound will receive a $5 token for the gift shop is an EO that will (a) make seeing a bird that makes the chirping sound effective as reinforcement and (b) increase the frequency of all behaviors (e.g., turning one's head and looking around) that have produced similar consequences (in this case, seeing the source of sounds) in the past.

In plain English, establishing operations (EOs) determine what an individual *wants* at any particular moment. EOs are dynamic, always changing. The reinforcer value (the want) goes up with increasing levels of deprivation and goes down with levels of satiation. Vollmer and Iwata (1991) demonstrated how the reinforcing effectiveness of three classes of stimuli—food, music, and social attention—varied under conditions of deprivation and satiation. Participants were five adults with developmental disabilities, and the dependent variable was the number of responses per minute on two motor tasks—pressing a switch or picking up small blocks from a container and putting them through the

hole in the top of another container. All sessions lasted 10 minutes and began with the experimenter saying, "Do this, [participant's name]," and modeling the response. During baseline, participants' responses received no programmed consequences. During the deprivation and satiation conditions, responses were followed by presentation of either food, music, or social attention. Initially each response was followed by the programmed consequence; this gradually shifted to every third, fifth, or tenth response being followed by the consequence.

Different procedures were used to create deprivation and satiation conditions for each stimulus class. With food, for example, baseline and deprivation condition sessions were conducted 30 minutes prior to a participant's scheduled lunchtime; sessions during the satiation condition were conducted within 15 minutes after the participant had eaten lunch. For social attention, baseline and deprivation condition sessions were conducted immediately following a 15-minute period in which the participant had either been alone or had been observed to have had no social interaction with another person. Immediately prior to each session in the satiation condition, the experimenter provided continuous social interaction (e.g., played a simple game, conversation) with the participant for 15 minutes.

All five participants responded at higher rates under the deprivation condition than during the satiation

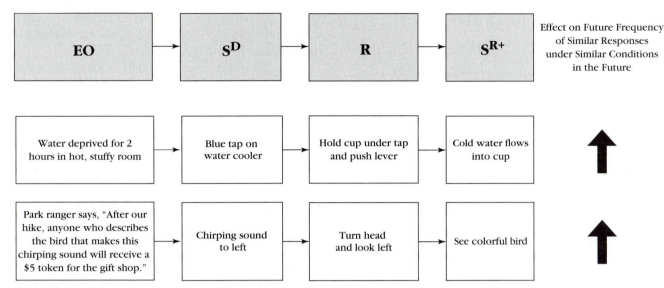

Figure 11.4 Four-term contingency illustrating positive reinforcement of a discriminated operant made current by a motivating operation: An establishing operation (EO) increases the momentary effectiveness of a stimulus change as a reinforcer, which in turn makes the S^D more likely to evoke behavior that has been reinforced by that stimulus change in the past.

condition. Figure 11.5 shows the effects of deprivation and satiation of social attention on the effectiveness of social attention as a reinforcer for two of the study's participants, Donny and Sam. Other researchers have reported similar findings concerning the effects of depri-

vation and satiation of various stimuli and events as motivating operations that affect the relative effectiveness of reinforcement (e.g., Gewirtz & Baer, 1958; Klatt, Sherman, & Sheldon, 2000; North & Iwata, 2005; Zhou, Iwata, & Shore, 2002).

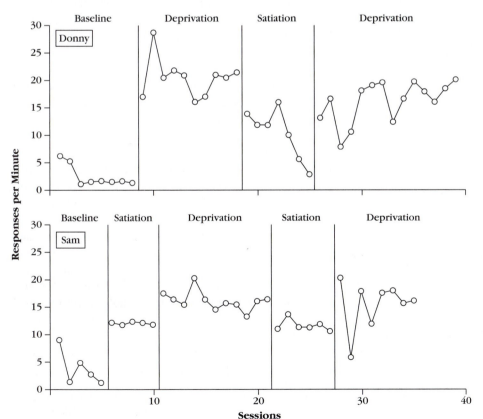

Figure 11.5 Responses per minute by two students during baseline and when social attention was used as reinforcement under deprivation and satiation conditions for social attention.

From "Establishing Operations and Reinforcement Effects" by T. R. Vollmer and B. A. Iwata, 1997, *Journal of Applied Behavior Analysis, 24,* p. 288. Copyright 1991 by the Society for the Experimental Analysis of Behavior, Inc. Reprinted by permission.

Automaticity of Reinforcement

> A reinforcing connection need not be obvious to the individual reinforced.
>
> —B. F. Skinner (1953, p. 75)

The fact that a person does not have to understand or verbalize the relation between his actions and a reinforcing consequence, or for that matter even be aware that a consequence has occurred, for reinforcement to occur is known as the *automaticity of reinforcement*. Skinner (1983) provided an interesting example of automaticity in the third and final volume of his autobiography, *A Matter of Consequences*. He described an incident that took place at a meeting of distinguished scholars who had been invited to discuss the role of intention in political activity. At one point during the meeting, the psychologist Erich Fromm began to argue that "people were not pigeons," perhaps implying that an operant analysis based on positive reinforcement could not explain human behavior, which is the product of thought and free will. Skinner recounted what happened next:

> I decided that something had to be done. On a scrap of paper I wrote, "Watch Fromm's left hand. I am going to shape [reinforce by successive approximations] a chopping motion" and passed it down the table to Halleck [a member of the group]. Fromm was sitting directly across the table and speaking mainly to me. I turned my chair slightly so that I could see him out of the corner of my eye. He gesticulated a great deal as he talked, and whenever his left hand came up, I looked straight at him. If he brought the hand down, I nodded and smiled. Within five minutes he was chopping the air so vigorously that his wristwatch kept slipping out over his hand. (p. 150–151, words in brackets added)

Arbitrariness of the Behavior Selected

> So far as the organism is concerned, the only important property of the contingency is temporal.
>
> —B. F. Skinner (1953, p. 85)

No logical or adaptive connection between behavior and a reinforcing consequence is necessary for reinforcement to occur. In other words, reinforcement will strengthen any behavior that immediately precedes it. This arbitrary nature of the behavior selected is critical to understanding reinforcement. All other relations (e.g., what's logical, desirable, useful, appropriate) must compete with the critical temporal relation between behavior and consequence. "To say that reinforcement is contingent upon a response may mean nothing more than that it followed the response . . . conditioning takes place presumably be-

cause of the temporal relation only, expressed in terms of the order and proximity of response and reinforcement" (Skinner, 1948, p. 168).

Skinner (1948) demonstrated the arbitrary nature of the behaviors selected by reinforcement in one of his most famous experimental papers, "'Superstition' in the Pigeon." He gave pigeons a small amount of food every 15 seconds, "with no reference whatsoever to the bird's behavior" (p. 168). The fact that reinforcement will strengthen whatever behavior it immediately follows was soon evident. Six of the eight birds developed idiosyncratic behaviors "so clearly defined, that two observers could agree perfectly in counting instances" (p. 168). One bird walked counterclockwise around the cage; another repeatedly thrust its head into one of the upper corners of the cage. Two birds acquired a "pendulum motion of the head and body, in which the head was extended forward and swung from right to left with a sharp movement followed by a somewhat slower return" (p. 169). The pigeons had exhibited none of those behaviors at "any noticeable strength" during adaptation to the cage or before the food was periodically presented.

Whatever behavior the pigeons happened to be executing when the food hopper appeared tended to be repeated, which made it more likely to be occurring when food appeared the next time. That is, reinforcement was not contingent (in the sense of, dependent) on the behavior; it was only a coincidence that reinforcement sometimes followed the behavior. Such accidentally reinforced behavior is called "superstitious" because it has no influence on whether reinforcement follows. Humans engage in many superstitious behaviors. Sports provide countless examples: A basketball player tugs on his shorts before shooting a foul shot, a golfer carries his lucky ball marker, a batter goes through the same sequence of adjusting his wristbands before each pitch, a college football fan wears a goofy-looking necklace made of inedible nuts to bring good luck to his team.[5]

The importance of understanding the arbitrariness of reinforcement goes far beyond providing a possible explanation for the development of harmless superstitious and idiosyncratic behaviors. The arbitrary nature of selection by reinforcement may explain the acquisition and maintenance of many maladaptive and challenging behaviors. For example, a caregiver's well-meaning social attention provided in an attempt to console or divert a person who is hurting himself may help shape and maintain the very behavior the caregiver is trying to prevent or

---

[5]It is a mistake to assume that all superstitious behavior is the direct result of adventitious reinforcement. Many superstitious behaviors are probably the result of following cultural practices. For example, high school baseball players may wear their caps inside out and backwards when a late-inning rally is needed because they have seen major leaguers don such "rally caps" in the same situation.

eliminate. Kahng, Iwata, Thompson, and Hanley (2000) documented with a functional analysis that social reinforcement maintained the self-injurious behavior (SIB) and aggression of three adults with developmental disabilities. Kahng and colleagues' data support the hypothesis that aberrant behaviors may have been selected and maintained by social attention because of the arbitrariness of reinforcement.

Automatic Reinforcement

Some behaviors produce their own reinforcement independent of the mediation of others. For example, scratching an insect bite relieves the itch. Behavior analysts use the term **automatic reinforcement** to identify a behavior–reinforcement relation that occurs without the presentation of consequences by other people (Vaughan & Michael, 1982; Vollmer, 1994, 2006). Automatic reinforcement occurs independent of social mediation by others. Response products that function as automatic reinforcement are often in the form of a naturally produced sensory consequence that "sounds good, looks good, tastes good, smells good, feels good to the touch, or the movement itself is good" (Rincover, 1981, p. 1).

Persistent, nonpurposeful, repetitive self-stimulatory behaviors (e.g., flipping fingers, head rolling, body rocking, toe walking, hair pulling, fondling body parts) may produce sensory stimuli that function as automatic reinforcement. Such "self-stimulation" is thought to be a factor in the maintenance of self-injurious behavior (Iwata, Dorsey, Slifer, Bauman, & Richman, 1994), stereotypic repetitive movements, and "nervous habits" such as hair pulling (Rapp, Miltenberger, Galensky, Ellingson, & Long, 1999), nail biting, chewing on the mouth or lips, and object manipulation such as continually twirling a pencil or fondling jewelry (Miltenberger, Fuqua, & Woods, 1998).

The response product that functions as automatic reinforcement may be an unconditioned reinforcer or a once neutral stimulus that, because it has been paired with other forms of reinforcement, has become a conditioned reinforcer. Sundberg, Michael, Partington, and Sundberg (1996) described a two-stage conditioning history that may account for this type of conditioned automatic reinforcement.

> For example, a person may persist in singing or humming a song while coming home for a movie despite no obvious direct reinforcement for singing. In order for this behavior to occur as automatically reinforced behavior, a special two-stage conditioning history is necessary. In stage one, some stimulus (e.g., a song) must be paired with an existing form of conditioned or unconditioned reinforcement (e.g., an enjoyable movie, popcorn,

relaxation). As a result, the new stimulus can become a form of conditioned reinforcement (e.g., hearing the song may now be a new form of conditioned reinforcement). In stage two, the emission of a response (for whatever reason) produces a response product (i.e., the auditory stimuli produced by singing the song) that has topographical similarity to that previously neutral stimulus (e.g., the song), and may now have self-strengthening properties. (pp. 22–23)

Several theorists have suggested that automatic reinforcement may help to explain the extensive babbling of infants and how babbling shifts naturally, without apparent intervention from others, from undifferentiated vocalizations to the speech sounds of their native language (e.g., Bijou & Baer, 1965; Mowrer, 1950; Skinner, 1957; Staats & Staats, 1963; Vaughan & Michael, 1982). Caregivers frequently talk and sing while holding, feeding, and bathing a baby. As a result of repeated pairing with various reinforcers (e.g., food, warmth), the sounds of a caregiver's voice may become conditioned reinforcers for the baby. The baby's babbling is automatically reinforced when it produces sounds that match or closely approximate the caregiver's. At that point, "The young child alone in the nursery may automatically reinforce his own exploratory vocal behavior when he produces sounds that he has heard in the speech of others" (Skinner, 1957, p. 58).

Although the idea that automatic reinforcement is a factor in early language acquisition has been proposed for many years, experimental analyses of the phenomenon have appeared in the literature only recently (e.g., Miguel, Carr, & Michael, 2002; Sundberg et al., 1996; Yoon & Bennett, 2000). Sundberg and colleagues (1996) reported the first study showing the effects of a stimulus–stimulus pairing procedure on the frequency with which children emitted new vocal sounds without direct reinforcement or prompts to respond. Five children, ages 2 to 4 and representing a broad range of language abilities, served as subjects. During the prepairing (baseline) condition, the parents and in-home trainers sat a few feet away from the child and recorded each word or vocal sound emitted by the child as he played with a train set and several toys. Data were collected in consecutive 1-minute intervals. The adults did not interact with the subject during the prepairing baseline. The stimulus–stimulus pairing procedure consisted of a familiar adult approaching the child, emitting a target vocal sound, word, or phrase, and then immediately delivering a stimulus that had been established previously as a form of reinforcement for the child (e.g., tickles, praise, bouncing in a parachute held by adults). This stimulus–stimulus pairing procedure was repeated 15 times per minute for 1 or 2 minutes. The adult used a variety of pitches and intonations when voicing the target sound, word, or phrase.

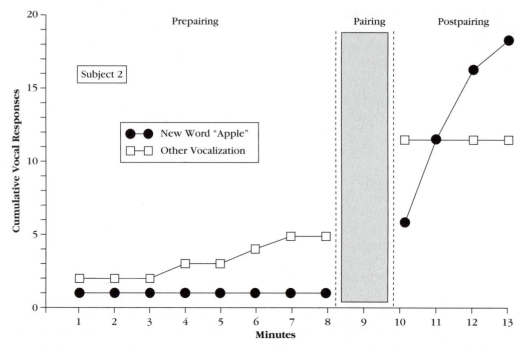

Figure 11.6   Cumulative number of times a 4-year-old child with autism vocalized "apple" before and after "apple" had been paired repeatedly with an established form of reinforcement. Automatic reinforcement may explain the increased frequency of the child's vocalizing "apple" after pairing.

From "Automatic Reinforcement" by M. L. Sundberg, J. Michael, J. W. Partington, and C. A. Sundberg, 1996, "Repertoire-Altering Effects of Remote Contingencies" *The Analysis of Verbal Behavior, 13,* p. 27. Copyright 1996 by the Association for Behavior Analysis, Inc. Used by permission.

During the postpairing condition, which began immediately after the stimulus–stimulus pairings, the adult moved away from the child and conditions were the same as during the prepairing condition.

The stimulus–stimulus pairing of a vocal sound, word, or phrase with an established reinforcer was followed by an increased frequency of the targeted word during the postpairing condition for all five children. Figure 11.6 shows the results of a representative sample of one of three pairings conducted with Subject 2, a 4-year-old boy with autism. Subject 2 had a verbal repertoire of more than 200 mands, tacts, and intraverbals, but rarely emitted spontaneous vocalizations or engaged in vocal play.[6] During the prepairing condition, the child did not say the target word and emitted four other vocalizations at a mean rate of 0.5 per minute. The stimulus–stimulus pairing procedure consisted of pairing the word *apple* with tickles approximately 15 times in 60 seconds. Immediately after the pairing, the subject said "apple" 17 times in 4 minutes, a rate of 4.25 responses per minute. In addition, the child said "tickle" four times within the

first minute of the postpairing condition. Sundberg and colleagues' results provide evidence that the children's vocal response products may have functioned as automatic conditioned reinforcement after being paired with other forms of reinforcement.

Kennedy (1994) noted that applied behavior analysts use two meanings of the term *automatic reinforcement*. In the first instance, automatic reinforcement is determined by the absence of social mediation (Vollmer, 1994; 2006). In the second instance, when functional behavior assessments do not identify a reinforcer for a persistent behavior, some behavior analysts hypothesize that automatic reinforcement is the controlling variable (see Chapter 24 for functional behavior assessment). When SIB occurs in the absence of social attention or any other known form of reinforcement, automatic reinforcement is often assumed to be involved (e.g., Fisher, Lindauer, Alterson, & Thompson, 1998; Ringdahl, Vollmer, Marcus, & Roane, 1997; Roscoe, Iwata, & Goh, 1998). Determining that a behavior may be maintained by automatic reinforcement, and when possible isolating or substituting the source of that reinforcement (e.g., Kennedy & Souza, 1995, see Figure 8.5; Shore, Iwata, DeLeon, Kahng, & Smith, 1997), has important implications for designing interventions to either capitalize on

---

[6]Mands, tacts, and intraverbals—three elementary verbal operants first described by Skinner (1957)—are explained in Chapter 25.

the automatic reinforcing nature of the behavior or counteract it (see Chapters 21, 22, and 23).

In summing up the uses and limitations of automatic reinforcement as a concept, Vollmer (2006) suggested that:

- Practitioners should recognize that not all reinforcement is planned or socially mediated.

- Some behaviors maintained by automatic reinforcement (e.g., self-stimulation, stereotypy) may not be reduced or eliminated with certain procedures (e.g., timeout, planned ignoring, or extinction).

- Affixing the label *automatic reinforcement* to an observed phenomenon too quickly may limit our analysis and effectiveness by precluding further efforts to identify the actual reinforcer-maintaining behavior.

- When socially mediated contingencies are difficult to arrange or simply not available, practitioners might consider automatic reinforcement as a potential aim.

Classifying Reinforcers

In this section we review the technical classification of reinforcers by their origin as well as several practical categories by which practitioners and researchers often describe and classify reinforcers by their formal characteristics. The reader should recognize, however, that all reinforcers, regardless of type or classification, are the same in their most important (i.e., defining) characteristic: All reinforcers increase the future frequency of behavior that immediately precedes them.

Classification of Reinforcers by Origin

As introduced in Chapter 2, there are two basic types of reinforcers by origin—that is, whether a reinforcer is the product of the evolution of the species (an unconditioned reinforcer) or the result of the learning history of the individual (a conditioned reinforcer).

Unconditioned Reinforcers

A stimulus change that functions as reinforcement even though the learner has had no particular learning history with it is called an ***unconditioned reinforcer.*** (Some authors use the terms *primary reinforcer* and *unlearned reinforcer* as synonyms for unconditioned reinforcers.) Because unconditioned reinforcers are the product of the evolutionary history of a species (phylogeny), all biologically intact members of a species are more or less susceptible to reinforcement by the same unconditioned

reinforcers. For example, food, water, oxygen, warmth, and sexual stimulation are examples of stimuli that do not have to undergo a learning history to function as reinforcers. Food will function as an unconditioned reinforcer for a human deprived of sustenance; water will function as an unconditioned reinforcer for a person deprived of liquid, and so forth.

Human touch may also be an unconditioned reinforcer (Gewirtz & Pelaez-Nogueras, 2000). Pelaez-Nogueras and colleagues (1996) found that infants preferred face-to-face interactions that included touch stimulation. Two conditioning treatments were implemented in alternated counterbalanced order. Under the touch condition, infants' eye-contact responses were followed immediately by adult attention (eye contact), smiling, cooing, and rubbing the infants' legs and feet. Eye-contact responses during the no-touch condition were followed by eye contact, smiles, and coos from the adult, but no touching. All of the babies in the study emitted eye contact for longer durations, smiled and vocalized at higher rates, and spent less time crying and protesting in the contingent condition that included touch. From these results and several related studies, Pelaez-Nogueras and colleagues concluded that "these results suggest that . . . touch stimulation can function as a primary reinforcer for infant behavior" (p. 199).

Conditioned Reinforcers

A **conditioned reinforcer** (sometimes called a *secondary reinforcer* or *learned reinforcer*) is a previously neutral stimulus change that has acquired the capability to function as a reinforcer through stimulus–stimulus pairing with one or more unconditioned reinforcers or conditioned reinforcers. Through repeated pairings, the previously neutral stimulus acquires the reinforcement capability of the reinforcer(s) with which it has been paired.[7] For example, after a tone has been paired repeatedly with food, when food is delivered as a reinforcer, the tone will function as a reinforcer when an EO has made food a currently effective reinforcer.

Neutral stimuli can also become conditioned reinforcers for humans without direct physical pairing with another reinforcer through a pairing process Alessi (1992) called *verbal analog conditioning.*

> For example, a class of preschool children who have been receiving M&M candies for good school work might be shown pieces of cut up yellow construction

---

[7]Remember, it is the environment, not the learner, that does the pairing. The learner does not have to "associate" the two stimuli.

paper and told, "These pieces of yellow paper are what big kids work for" (Engelmann, 1975, pp. 98–100). Many children in the group immediately refuse M&Ms, and work extra hard, but accept only pieces of yellow paper as their rewards.

We might say that the pieces of yellow paper act as "learned reinforcers." Laboratory research tells us that neutral stimuli become reinforcers only through direct pairing with primary reinforcers (or other "learned reinforcers"). Yellow paper was not paired with any reinforcer and certainly not with the primary (M&Ms) reinforcers. Yellow paper acquired reinforcing properties even more powerful than the primary M&Ms reinforcers, as demonstrated by the children's refusal to accept M&Ms, demanding instead pieces of yellow paper. (For the sake of this example, assume that the children had not been satiated with M&Ms just before the session.) (p. 1368)

It is sometimes thought that the "power" of a conditioned reinforcer is determined by the number of times it has been paired with other reinforcers. However, a statement such as, "The more often the tone is paired with food, the more reinforcing the tone will become" is not completely accurate. Although numerous pairings will increase the likelihood that the tone will function as a conditioned reinforcer in the first place (though a single pairing is sometimes sufficient), the momentary effectiveness of the tone as a reinforcer will be a function of the relevant EO for the reinforcer(s) with which the conditioned reinforcer has been paired. A tone that has been paired only with food will function as an effective reinforcer for a food-deprived learner, but the tone will have little effect as a reinforcer if the learner has just consumed a lot of food, regardless of the number of times it has been paired with food.

A **generalized conditioned reinforcer** is a conditioned reinforcer that as a result of having been paired with many unconditioned and conditioned reinforcers does not depend on a current EO for any particular form of reinforcement for its effectiveness. For example social attention (proximity, eye contact, praise) is a generalized conditioned reinforcer for many people because it occurs simultaneously with many reinforcers. The more reinforcers with which a generalized conditioned reinforcer has been paired, the greater is the likelihood that it will be effective at any given time. Because it can be exchanged for a nearly limitless variety of backup reinforcers, money is a generalized conditioned reinforcer whose effectiveness is usually independent of current establishing operations.

It is sometimes thought that a conditioned reinforcer is called a generalized conditioned reinforcer because it can function as reinforcement across a wide range of behaviors. But this is not so—any reinforcer is capable of strengthening any behavior that immediately precedes its

occurrence. A conditioned reinforcer is called a generalized conditioned reinforcer because it is effective as reinforcement across a wide range of EO conditions. Because of their versatility across EO conditions, generalized conditioned reinforcers offer great advantages for practitioners, who often have limited control of the EOs for particular reinforcers.

Generalized conditioned reinforcers provide the basis for implementing a *token economy,* a reinforcement-based system capable of improving multiple behaviors of multiple participants (e.g., Higgins, Williams, & McLaughlin, 2001; Phillips, Phillips, Fixen, & Wolf, 1971). In a token economy, participants receive tokens (e.g., points, check marks, poker chips) contingent on a variety of target behaviors. Participants accumulate the tokens and exchange them at specific times for their choices from a menu of backup reinforcers (e.g., free time, computer time, snacks). Examples of token economy systems and guidelines for designing and implementing them are provided in Chapter 26.

Classification of Reinforcers by Formal Properties

When applied behavior analysts describe reinforcers by their physical properties—a practice that can enhance communication among researchers, practitioners, and the agencies and people they serve—reinforcers are typically classified as edible, sensory, tangible, activity, or social.

Edible Reinforcers

Researchers and practitioners have used bites of preferred foods, snacks, or candy, and sips of drinks, as reinforcers. One interesting and important use of edibles as reinforcers is in the treatment of chronic food refusal in children. For example, Riordan, Iwata, Finney, Wohl, and Stanley (1984) used "highly preferred food items" as reinforcers to increase the food intake of four children at a hospital treatment facility. The treatment program consisted of dispensing the high-preference food items (e.g., cereal, yogurt, canned fruit, ice cream) contingent on the consumption of a target food item (e.g., vegetables, bread, eggs).

Edible reinforcers were also used by Kelley, Piazza, Fisher, and Oberdorff (2003) to increase cup drinking by Al, a 3-year-old boy who had been admitted to a day treatment program for food refusal and bottle dependency. The researchers measured the percentage of trials in which Al consumed 7.5 ml of three different liquids from the cup. During baseline, when Al was praised if he consumed the drink, his consumption averaged 0%, 44.6% and 12.5% of trials for orange juice, water, and a chocolate drink, respectively. During the positive reinforcement component of the cup-drinking intervention, each time Al consumed the drink the therapist praised him (as was done in baseline) and delivered a level spoon of peaches (a preferred food) to his mouth. Al consumed all three beverages on 100% of the trials during the positive reinforcement condition.

Sensory Reinforcers

Various forms of sensory stimulation such as vibration (e.g., massager), tactile stimulation (e.g., tickles, strokes with a feather boa), flashing or sparkling lights, and music have been used effectively as reinforcers (e.g., Bailey & Meyerson, 1969; Ferrari & Harris, 1981; Gast et al., 2000; Hume & Crossman, 1992; Rincover & Newsom, 1985; Vollmer & Iwata, 1991).

Tangible Reinforcers

Items such as stickers, trinkets, school materials, trading cards, and small toys often serve as tangible reinforcers. An object's intrinsic worth is irrelevant to its ultimate effectiveness as a positive reinforcer. Virtually any tangible item can serve as a reinforcer. Remember Engelmann's (1975) kindergarten students who worked for yellow slips of paper!

Activity Reinforcers

When the opportunity to engage in a certain behavior serves as reinforcement, that behavior may be called an activity reinforcer. Activity reinforcers may be everyday activities (e.g., playing a board game, leisure reading, listening to music), privileges (e.g., lunch with the teacher, shooting baskets in the gym, first in line), or special events (e.g., a trip to the zoo).

McEvoy and Brady (1988) evaluated the effects of contingent access to play materials on the completion of math worksheets by three students with autism and behavior disorders. During baseline, the teacher told the students to complete the problems as best that they could, and that they should either complete other unfinished assignments or "find something else to do" if they finished the worksheets before a 6-minute timing elapsed. No other prompts or instructions were given for completing the worksheets. The teacher praised the completion of the worksheets.

On the first day of intervention for each student, he was taken to another room and shown a variety of toys and play materials. The teacher told the student he would have approximately 6 minutes to play with the materials

if he met a daily criterion for completing math problems. Figure 11.7 shows the results. During baseline, the rate at which all three students correctly completed problems was either low (Dicky) or highly variable (Ken and Jimmy). When contingent access to the play activities was introduced, each student's completion rate increased and eventually exceeded criterion levels.

Premack (1959) hypothesized that activity reinforcers can be identified by looking at the relative distribution of behaviors in a free operant situation. Premack believed that behaviors themselves could be used as reinforcers and that the relative frequency of behavior was an important factor in determining how effective a given behavior might be as a reinforcer if the opportunity to engage in the behavior is contingent on another behavior. The **Premack principle** states that making the opportunity to engage in a behavior that occurs at a relatively high free operant (or baseline) rate contingent on the occurrence of low-frequency behavior will function as reinforcement for the low-frequency behavior. For a student who typically spends much more time watching TV than doing homework, a contingency based on the Premack principle (informally known as "Grandma's Law") might be, "When you have finished your homework, you can watch TV."

Building on Premack's concept, Timberlake and Allison (1974) proposed the **response-deprivation hypothesis** as a model for predicting whether access to one behavior (the contingent behavior) will function as reinforcement for another behavior (the instrumental response) based on the relative baseline rates at which each behavior occurs and whether access to the contingent behavior represents a restriction compared to the baseline level of engagement. Restricting access to a behavior presumably acts as a form of deprivation that serves as an EO, thus making the opportunity to engage in the restricted behavior an effective form of reinforcement (Allison, 1993; Iwata & Michael, 1994).

Iwata and Michael (1994) cited a series of three studies by Konarski and colleagues as demonstrating the veracity and applied implications of the response-deprivation hypothesis. In the first study, when students were given access to coloring (a high-probability behavior contingent on completing math problems (a low-probability behavior), they spent more time doing math, but only if the reinforcement schedule represented a restriction of the amount of time spent coloring compared to baseline (Konarski, Johnson, Crowell, & Whitman, 1980). The researchers found that a contingency in which students could earn *more time* coloring than they did in baseline for completing math problems was ineffective. These basic findings were reproduced in a subsequent study in which access to reading (or math, depending on the subject) was contingent on math (or reading)

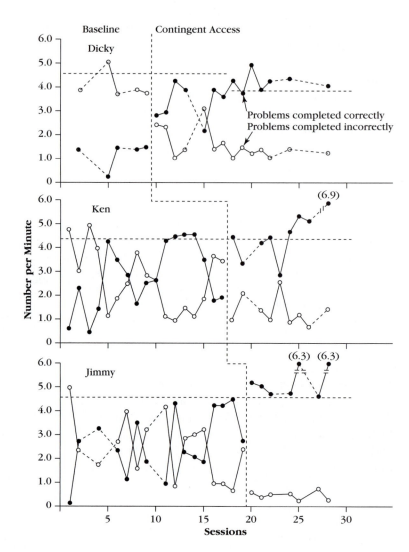

Figure 11.7 Number of math problems completed correctly and incorrectly per minute by three special education students during baseline and contingent access to play materials. Dashed horizontal lines indicate criteria.

From "Contingent Access to Play Materials as an Academic Motivator for Autistic and Behavior Disordered Children" by M. A. McEvoy and M. P. Brady, 1988, *Education and Treatment of Children, 11,* p. 15. Copyright 1998 by the Editorial Review Board of *Education and Treatment of Children.* Used by permission.

(Konarski, Crowell, Johnson, & Whitman (1982). In the third study, Konarski, Crowell, and Duggan (1985) took the response-deprivation hypothesis a step further by examining the "reversibility of reinforcement" within subjects; that is, engaging in either of two activities—reading or math—could serve as reinforcement for increased performance in the other activity, in a response-deprivation condition for the contingent activity. Response deprivation for writing as the contingent response resulted in increases in math (instrumental response); conversely, response deprivation for math as the contingent response produced increases in reading. In all three studies, response restriction was the key factor in determining whether access to the contingent response would be reinforcing.

Iwata and Michael (1994) concluded that the collective results of Konarski and colleagues' studies illustrate each of three predictions based on the response-deprivation hypothesis (assume the ratio of baseline rates of doing homework to watching TV is 1:2 in the following examples):

- Reinforcement of a low-rate target behavior when access to a high-rate contingent behavior is restricted below baseline levels (e.g., 30 minutes of homework gets access to 30 minutes of TV)

- Nonreinforcement of a low-rate behavior when access to a high-rate contingent behavior is not restricted below baseline levels (e.g., 30 minutes of homework gets access to 90 minutes of TV)

- Reinforcement of a high-rate target behavior when access to the low-rate behavior is restricted below baseline levels (e.g., 30 minutes of TV yields 5 minutes of homework)

Although recognizing that practitioners seldom design reinforcement programs to increase the rate of behaviors such as TV watching that already occur at high rates, Iwata and Michael (1994) noted that:

There are a number of instances in which one may wish to produce highly accelerated performance (e.g., as in superlative academic or athletic performance that is good to begin with). In such cases, one need not find another activity that occurs at a higher rate to serve as reinforcement if one could arrange a suitable deprivation schedule with an activity that occurs at a relatively low rate. (p. 186)

As with all other descriptive categories of reinforcers, there is no a priori list that reveals what activities will or will not function as reinforcers. An activity that serves as effective reinforcement for one learner might have quite another effect on the behavior of another learner. For example, in Konarski, Crowell, and colleagues' (1982) study, access to math functioned as reinforcement for doing more reading for three students, whereas getting to read was the reinforcer for completing math problems for a fourth student. Many years ago, a classic cartoon brought home this crucial point very well. The cartoon showed two students dutifully cleaning the chalkboard and erasers after school. One student said to the other, "You're cleaning erasers for punishment!? I get to clean erasers as a reward for completing my homework."

Social Reinforcers

Physical contact (e.g., hugs, pats on the back), proximity (e.g., approaching, standing, or sitting near a person), attention, and praise are examples of events that often serve as social reinforcers. Adult attention is one of the most powerful and generally effective forms of reinforcement for children. The nearly universal effects of contingent social attention as reinforcement has led some behavior analysts to speculate that some aspects of social attention may entail unconditioned reinforcement (e.g., Gewirtz & Pelaez-Nogueras, 2000; Vollmer & Hackenberg, 2001).

The original experimental demonstrations and discovery of the power of adults' social attention as reinforcement for children's behavior took place in a series of four studies designed by Montrose Wolf and carried out by the preschool teachers at the Institute of Child Development at the University of Washington in the early 1960s (Allen, Hart, Buell, Harris, & Wolf, 1964; Harris, Johnston, Kelly, & Wolf, 1964; Hart, Allen, Buell, Harris, & Wolf, 1964; Johnston, Kelly, Harris, & Wolf, 1966). Describing those early studies, Risley (2005) wrote:

We had never seen such power! The speed and magnitude of the effects on children's behavior in the real world of simple adjustments of something so ubiquitous as adult attention was astounding. Forty years later, social reinforcement (positive attention, praise, "catching them being good") has become the core of most American advice and training for parents and teachers—making this arguably the most influential discovery of modern psychology. (p. 280)

Because of the profound importance of this long-known but underused phenomenon, we describe a second study showing the effects of contingent attention as reinforcement for children's behavior. The first volume of the *Journal of Applied Behavior Analysis* included no fewer than seven studies building on and extending Wolf and colleagues' pioneering research on social reinforcement.[8] R. Vance Hall and colleagues conducted two of those studies. Like the Hall, Lund, and Jackson (1968) study, from which we selected the example of a teacher's use of positive reinforcement with Robbie that introduced this chapter, the three experiments reported by Hall, Panyan, Rabon, and Broden (1968) continue to serve as powerful demonstrations of the effects of teacher attention as social reinforcement.

A first-year teacher whose class of 30 sixth-graders exhibited such high rates of disruptive and off-task behaviors that the school principal described the class as "completely out of control" participated in one of the experiments. Throughout the study, Hall, Panyan, and colleagues (1968) measured teacher attention and students behavior during a continuous 30-minute observation period in the first hour of the school day. The researchers used a 10-second partial-interval observation and recording procedure to measure study behavior (e.g., writing the assignment, looking in the book, answering the teacher's question) and nonstudy behavior (e.g., talking out, being out of seat, looking out the window, fighting or poking a classmate). The observers also recorded the occurrence of teacher attention in each interval. Each instance of teacher verbal attention, defined as a comment directed to a student or group of students, was recorded with a "+" if it followed appropriate study behavior, and with a "−" if it followed nonstudy behavior.

During baseline the class had a mean percentage of intervals of study behavior of 44%, and the teacher made an average of 1.4 comments following study behavior per session (see Figure 11.8). "Almost without exception those [comments] that followed study behavior were approving and those that followed nonstudy behavior were in the form of a verbal reprimand" (Hall, Panyan et al., 1968, p. 316). The level of study behavior by the class was 90% on one day when the helping teacher presented a demonstration lesson (see data points marked by solid arrow). On three occasions during baseline (data points marked by open arrows), the principal met with the teacher to discuss his organizational procedures in an effort to improve the students' behavior. These counseling

---

[8]The first volume of the *Journal of Applied Behavior Analysis* (1968) is a treasure trove of classic studies in which simple and elegant experimental designs revealed the powerful effects of operant conditioning and contingency management. We strongly encourage any serious student of applied behavior analysis to read it from cover to cover.

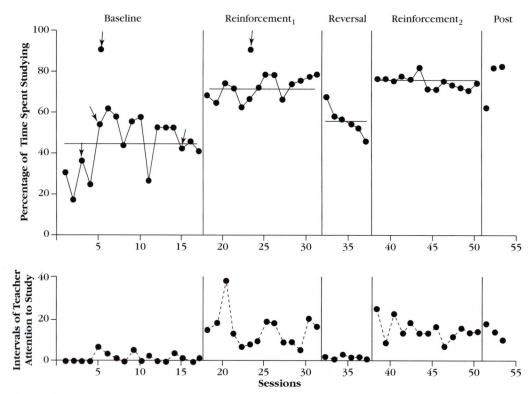

Figure 11.8 A record of class study behavior and teacher attention for study behavior during reading period in a sixth-grade classroom. Baseline = before experimental procedures; reinforcement 1 = increased teacher attention for study; reversal = removal of teacher attention for study; reinforcement 2 = return to increased teacher attention for study. Post-follow-up checks occurred up to 20 weeks after termination of the experimental procedures.

From "Instructing Beginning Teachers in Reinforcement Procedures Which Improve Classroom Control" by R. V. Hall, M. Panyan, D. Rabon, and M. Broden, 1968, *Journal of Applied Behavior Analysis, 1,* p. 317. Copyright by the Society for the Experimental Analysis of Behavior, Inc. Reprinted by permission.

sessions resulted in the teacher writing all assignments on the board (after the first meeting) and changing the seating chart (after the third meeting). Those changes had no apparent effect on the students' behavior.

Prior to the first day of the reinforcement condition, the teacher was shown baseline data on the class study behavior and the frequency of teacher attention following study behavior. The teacher was instructed to increase the frequency of positive comments to students when they were engaged in study behavior. After each session during this condition the teacher was shown data on the level of class study behavior and the frequency of his comments that followed study behavior. During the first reinforcement phase, teacher comments following study behavior increased to a mean frequency of 14.6, and the mean level of study behavior was 72%. The teacher, principal, and data collectors reported that the class was under better control and that noise had decreased significantly.

During a brief return of baseline conditions, the teacher provided "almost no reinforcement for study behavior," and a sharp downward trend in class study behavior was observed. The teacher, principal, and data collectors all reported that disruptive behavior and high noise levels had returned. The reinforcement conditions were then reinstated, which resulted in a mean frequency of 14 teacher comments following study behavior, and a mean level of 76% of intervals of study behavior.

Identifying Potential Reinforcers

In the laboratory, we had learned to use a simple test: Place a candy in the palm of our hand, show it to the child, close our fist fairly tightly around the candy, and see if the child will try to pull away our fingers to get at the candy. If he or she will do that, even against increasingly tightly held fingers, the candy is obviously a reinforcer.

—Murray Sidman (2000, p. 18)

The success of many behavior change programs requires an effective reinforcer that the practitioner or researcher can control. Fortunately, identifying effective and accessible reinforcers for most learners is relatively easy. Sidman (2000) described a quick and simple method for determining whether candy would likely function as a reinforcer. However, every stimulus, event, or activity that might function as a reinforcer cannot be held in the palm of the hand.

Identifying robust and reliable reinforcers for many learners with severe and multiple disabilities poses a major challenge. Although many common events serve as effective reinforcers for most people (e.g., praise, music, free time, tokens), these stimuli may not serve as reinforcers for all learners. Time, energy, and resources would be lost if planned interventions were to fail because a practitioner used a presumed, instead of an actual, reinforcer.

Also, reinforcer preferences shift, and the transitory nature of preference has been reported repeatedly in the literature (Carr, Nicholson, & Higbee, 2000; DeLeon et al., 2001; Kennedy & Haring, 1993; Logan & Gast, 2001; Ortiz & Carr, 2000; Roane, Vollmer, Ringdahl, & Marcus, 1998). Preference assessments may change with the person's age, interest level, time of day, social interactions with peers, and the presence of certain establishing operations (EOs) (Gottschalk, Libby, & Graff, 2000, see Figure 6.8). What a teacher asks in September to determine preferences may have to be repeated a month later (or sooner). Likewise, a therapist who asks a client what is reinforcing during a morning session may find that this stimulus is not stated as a preferred item in an afternoon session.

After reviewing 13 published studies that evaluated preferences and reinforcers for people with profound multiple disabilities, Logan and Gast (2001) concluded that preferred stimuli do not always function as reinforcers, and preferred stimuli at one point in time changed later. Additionally, people with severe-to-profound developmental disabilities may engage in activities for such a limited time that it is difficult to clearly determine whether a stimulus change is a reinforcer.

To meet the challenge of identifying effective reinforcers, researchers and practitioners have developed a variety of procedures that fall under the twin headings of stimulus preference assessment and reinforcer assessment. Stimulus preference assessment and reinforcer assessment are often conducted in tandem, as described by Piazza, Fisher, Hagopian, Bowman, and Toole (1996):

> During preference assessments, a relatively large number of stimuli are evaluated to identify preferred stimuli. The reinforcing effects of a small subset of stimuli (i.e., the highly preferred stimuli) are then evaluated during reinforcer assessment. Although the preference assessment is an efficient procedure identifying potential reinforcers from a large number of stimuli, it does not evaluate the reinforcing effects of the stimuli. (pp. 1–2)

Stimulus preference assessment identifies stimuli that are likely to serve as reinforcers, and reinforcer assessment puts the potential reinforcers to a direct test by presenting them contingent on occurrences of a behavior and measuring any effects on response rate. In this section we describe a variety of techniques developed by researchers and practitioners for conducting stimulus preference assessments and reinforcer assessment (see Figure 11.9). Together these methods form a continuum of approaches ranging from simple and quick to more complex and time-consuming.

Stimulus Preference Assessment

Stimulus preference assessment refers to a variety of procedures used to determine (a) the stimuli that the person prefers, (b) the relative preference values of those stimuli (high preference versus low preference), and (c) the conditions under which those preference values

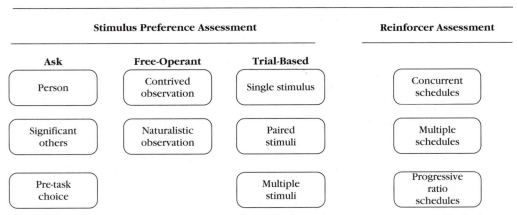

Figure 11.9 Stimulus preference assessment and reinforcer assessment methods for identifying potential reinforcers.

change when task demands, deprivation states, or schedules of reinforcement are modified. Generally speaking, stimulus preference assessment is usually conducted using a two-step process: (1) A large pool of stimuli that might be used as reinforcers is gathered, and (2) those stimuli are presented to the target person systematically to identify preference. It is essential for practitioners to narrow the field of possible stimuli to those that have good odds of functioning as reinforcers.

In more specific terms, stimulus preference assessments can be conducted using three basic methods: asking the person (or his or her significant others) to identify preferred stimuli; observing the person interacting or engaging with various stimuli in a free operant situation; and measuring the person's responses to trial-based tests of paired or multiply presented stimuli. In choosing which method to use, practitioners must balance two competing perspectives: (a) gaining the maximum amount of preference assessment data within the least amount of time, but without false positives (i.e., believing a stimulus is preferred when it is not), versus (b) conducting a more time- and labor-intensive assessment that will delay intervention, but may yield more conclusive results.

Asking about Stimulus Preferences

A person's preference for various stimuli might be determined by merely asking what she likes. Asking can greatly reduce the time needed for stimulus preference assessment, and it often yields information that can be integrated in an intervention program. Several variations of asking exist: asking the target person, asking significant others in the person's life, or offering a pretask choice assessment.

Asking the Target Person. A straightforward method for determining stimulus preference is to ask the target person what he likes. Typical variations include asking open-ended questions, providing the person with a list of choices or asking him to rank-order a list of choices.

- *Open-ended questions.* Depending on the learner's language abilities, an open-ended assessment of stimulus preference can be done orally or in writing. The person may be asked to name preferences among general categories of reinforcers—for example, What do you like to do in your free time? What are your favorite foods and drinks? Are there any types of music or performers whose music you like? An open-ended assessment can be accomplished simply by asking the learner to list as many favorite activities or items as possible. She should list not only everyday favorite things and

activities, but also special items and activities. Figure 26.6 is simply a sheet with numbered lines on which family members identify potential rewards they would like to earn by completing tasks on contingency contracts.

- *Choice format.* This format could include asking questions such as the following: "Which would you do a lot of hard work to get? Would you rather get things to eat, like chips, cookies, popcorn, or get to do things, like art projects, play computer games, or go to the library?" (Northup, George, Jones, Broussard, & Vollmer, 1996, p. 204)

- *Rank-ordering.* The learner can be given a list of items or stimuli and instructed to rank-order them from most to least preferred.

For learners with limited language skills, pictures of items, icons, or, preferably, the actual stimuli can be presented. For example, a teacher, while pointing to an icon, might ask a student, "Do you like to drink juice, use the computer, ride the bus, or watch TV?" Students simply nod yes or no.

Surveys have been developed to assess students' preferences. For example, elementary school teachers might use the *Child Reinforcement Survey,* which includes 36 rewards in four categories: edible items (e.g., fruit, popcorn), tangible items (e.g., stickers), activities (e.g., art projects, computer games), and social attention (e.g., a teacher or friend saying, "I like that") (Fantuzzo, Rohrbeck, Hightower, & Work, 1991). Other surveys are the *School Reinforcement Survey Schedule* for students in grades 4 through 12 (Holmes, Cautela, Simpson, Motes, & Gold, 1998) and the *Reinforcement Assessment for Individuals with Severe Disabilities* (Fisher, Piazza, Bowman, & Almari, 1996).

Although asking for personal preferences is relatively uncomplicated, the procedure is not foolproof with respect to confirming that a preferred choice will later serve as a reinforcer. "Poor correspondence between verbal self-reports and subsequent behavior has been long noted and often demonstrated" (Northup, 2000, p. 335). Although a child might identify watching cartoons as a preferred event, watching cartoons may function as a reinforcer only when the child is at home on Saturday mornings, but not at Grandma's house on Sunday night.

Further, surveys may not differentiate accurately between what children claim to be high-preference and low-preference items for reinforcers. Northup (2000) found that preferences of children with attention-deficit/hyperactivity disorder (ADHD) did not rise beyond chance levels when survey results were later compared to reinforcer functions. "The relatively high number of false positives and low number of false negatives again suggest that surveys may more accurately identify stimuli that are not reinforcers than those that are" (p. 337). Merely asking children their preferences once might lead to false positives (i.e., children may choose an event or stimulus as a reinforcer, but it may not be reinforcing).

Asking Significant Others. A pool of potential reinforcers can be obtained by asking parents, siblings, friends, or caregivers to identify the activities, items, foods, hobbies, or toys that they believe the learner prefers. For example, the *Reinforcer Assessment for Individuals with Severe Disabilities (RAISD)* is an interview protocol that asks caregivers to identify preferred stimuli across visual, auditory, olfactory, edible, tactile, and social domains (Fisher et al., 1996). Significant others then rank-order the selected preferences based on likely high- versus low-preference items. Finally, significant others are asked to identify the conditions under which they predict that specific items might function as reinforcers (e.g., cookies with milk versus just cookies alone). Again, although stimuli that are identified as highly preferred by significant others are not always effective as reinforcers, they often are.

Offering a Pretask Choice. In this method the practitioner asks the participant to choose what he wants to earn for doing a task. The participant then chooses one item from two or three options presented (Piazza et al., 1996). All of the stimuli presented as pretask choices will have been identified as preferred stimuli by other assessment procedures. For instance, a teacher might make the following statement: "Robyn, when you finish your math problems, you may have 10 minutes to play Battleship with Martin, read quietly, or help Ms. Obutu prepare the social studies poster. Which activity do you want to work for?" A learner's choice of a consequence will not necessarily be a more effective reinforcer than one selected by the researcher or practitioner (Smith, Iwata, & Shore, 1995).

Free Operant Observation

The activities that a person engages in most often when able to choose freely from among behaviors will often serve as effective reinforcers when made contingent on engaging in low-probability behaviors. Observing and recording what activities the target person engages in when she can choose during a period of unrestricted access to numerous activities is called *free operant observation.* A total duration measure of the time the person engages with each stimulus item or activity is recorded. The longer the person engages with an item, the stronger the inference that the item is preferred.

Procedurally, the person has unconstrained and simultaneous access to a predetermined set of items or activities or to the materials and activities that are naturally available in the environment. There are no response requirements, and all stimulus items are available and within the person's sight and reach. An item is never removed after engagement or selection. According to Ortiz and Carr (2000), free operant responding is less likely to produce aberrant behavior that might otherwise be observed if a stimulus is removed. Free operant observations can be contrived or conducted in naturalistic settings.

Contrived Free Operant Observation. Practitioners use contrived observation to determine whether, when, how, and the extent to which the person engages with each of a predetermined set of activities and materials. The observation is contrived because the researcher or practitioner "salts" the environment with a variety of items that may be of interest to the learner.

Free operant assessment presupposes that the person has had sufficient time to move about and explore the environment and has had the chance to experience each of the stimuli, materials, or activities. Just prior to the free operant observation period, the learner is provided brief noncontingent exposure to each item. All of the items are then placed within view and easy access to the learner, who then has the opportunity to sample and choose among them freely. Observers record the total duration of time that the learner engages with each stimulus item or activity.

Naturalistic Free Operant Observation. Naturalistic observations of free operant responding are conducted in the learner's everyday environment (e.g., playground, classroom, home). As unobtrusively as possible, the observer notes how the learner allocates his time and records the number of minutes the learner devotes to each activity. For instance, Figure 11.10 shows how a teenager, Mike, distributed his time during 2 hours of free time each day after school. Mike's parents collected these data by keeping a chart of the total number of minutes their son was engaged in each activity. The summary chart for the week shows that Mike played computer video games, watched television, and talked on the phone to his friends every day. On two different days Mike spent 10 minutes reading a library book, and he played with a new construction toy for a brief time on Wednesday. Two activities—watching television and playing video games—occurred the most often and for the longest duration. If Mike's parents wanted to apply the Premack principle introduced earlier in this chapter to increase the amount of time he spends reading for pleasure or playing with the construction toy (i.e., low-probability behaviors), they

Figure 11.10   Number of minutes Mike spent engaged in activities during 2 hours of free time after school.

Activity	Mon	Tue	Wed	Thu	Fri	Total
Leisure reading	—	10	—	10	—	20
Watch TV	35	50	60	30	30	205
Phone with friends	15	15	10	20	10	70
Play video games	70	45	40	60	80	295
Play with construction toy	—	—	10	—	—	10
Minutes observed	**120**	**120**	**120**	**120**	**120**	**600**

might make watching television or playing video games (i.e., high-probability behaviors) contingent on a certain amount of time spent leisure reading or playing with the construction toy.

Trial-Based Methods

In trial-based methods of stimulus preference assessment, stimuli are presented to the learner in a series of trials and the learner's responses to the stimuli are measured as an index of preference. One or more of three measures of the learner's behavior are recorded in trial-based stimulus preference assessment: approach, contact (DeLeon & Iwata, 1996), and engagement with the stimulus (DeLeon, Iwata, Conners, & Wallace, 1999; Hagopian, Rush, Lewin, & Long, 2001; Roane et al., 1998). *Approach* responses typically include any detectable movement by the person toward the stimulus (e.g., eye gaze, head turn, body lean, hand reach), a *contact* is tallied each time the person touches or holds the stimulus, and *engagement* is a measure of the total time or percentage of observed intervals in which the person interacts with the stimulus (e.g., in which the person held a massager against her leg). An assumption is made that the more frequently the person approaches, touches or holds, or engages with a stimulus, the more likely it is that the stimulus is preferred. As DeLeon and colleagues (1999) stated, "duration of item contact is a valid index of reinforcer value" (p. 114).

Preferred stimuli are sometimes labeled as high-preference (HP), medium-preference (MP), or low-preference (LP) stimuli based on predetermined criteria (e.g., stimuli chosen 75% or more of the time are HP) (Carr, Nicolson, & Higbee, 2000; Northup, 2000; Pace, Ivancic, Edwards, Iwata, & Page, 1985; Piazza et al., 1996). An implicit, but testable, assumption is that a highly preferred stimulus will serve as a reinforcer. Although this assumption does not always hold (Higbee, Carr, & Harrison, 2000), it has proven to be an efficient assumption with which to begin.

The many variations of trial-based stimulus preference assessment can be grouped by presentation method as single stimulus (successive choice), paired stimuli (forced choice), and multiple stimuli.

Single Stimulus.   A single-stimulus presentation method, also called a "successive choice" method, represents the most basic assessment available for determining preference. Simply stated, a stimulus is presented and the person's reaction to it is noted. Presenting one stimulus at a time "may be well suited for individuals who have difficulty selecting among two or more stimuli" (Hagopian et al., 2001, p. 477).

Target stimuli across all sensory systems (i.e., visual, auditory, vestibular, tactile, olfactory, gustatory, and multisensory) are presented one at a time in random order, and the person's reaction to each stimulus is recorded (Logan, Jacobs et al., 2001; Pace et al., 1985). Approach or rejection responses are recorded in terms of occurrence (yes or no), frequency (e.g., number of touches per minute), or duration (i.e., time spent engaged with an item). After recording, the next item in the sequence is presented. For example, a mirror might be presented to determine the duration of time the person gazes into it, touches it, or rejects the mirror (i.e., pushes it away). Each item should be presented several times, and the order of presentation should be varied.

Paired Stimuli.   Each trial in the paired-stimuli presentation method, also sometimes called the "forced choice" method, consists of the simultaneous presentation of two stimuli. The observer records which of the two stimuli the learner chooses. During the course of the assessment, each stimulus is matched randomly with all other stimuli in the set (Fisher et al., 1992). Data from a paired-stimuli assessment show how many times each stimulus is chosen. The stimuli are then rank-ordered in terms of high, medium, or low preference. Piazza and colleagues (1996) used 66 to 120 paired-stimuli trials to determine high, middle, and low preferences. Pace and colleagues (1985) found that paired-stimuli presentations yielded more accurate distinctions between high- and low-preference items than did single-stimulus presentations. Paired-stimuli sometimes outperform single-stimulus presentation formats with respect to ultimately identifying reinforcers (Paclawskyj & Vollmer, 1995).

Because every possible pair of stimuli must be presented, paired-stimuli assessing may take more time than the simultaneous presentation of an array of multiple stimuli (described in the next section). However, DeLeon and Iwata (1996) argued that ultimately the paired-stimuli method may be more time efficient because "the more consistent results produced by the PS method may indicate that stable preferences can be determined in fewer, or even single, sessions" (p. 520).

Multiple Stimuli. The multiple-stimuli presentation method is an extension of the paired-stimuli procedure developed by Fisher and colleagues (1992). The person chooses a preferred stimulus from an array of three or more stimuli (Windsor, Piche, & Locke, 1994). By presenting multiple stimuli together, assessment time is reduced. For example, instead of presenting a series of trials consisting of all possible pairs of stimuli from a group of six stimuli and continuing until all pairs have been presented, all six stimuli are presented simultaneously.

The two major variations of the multiple-stimuli preference assessment are multiple stimuli with replacement and multiple stimuli without replacement. The difference between the two is which stimuli are removed or replaced after the person indicates a preference among the displayed items in preparation for the next trial. In the multiple stimuli with replacement procedure, the item chosen by the learner remains in the array and items that were not selected are replaced with new items. In the multiple stimuli without replacement procedure, the chosen item is removed from the array, the order or placement of the remaining items is rearranged, and the next trial begins with a reduced number of items in the array.

In any case, each trial begins by asking the person, "Which one do you want the most?" (Higbee et al., 2000) "Choose one" (Ciccone, Graff, & Ahearn, 2005) and then continuing until all items from the original array, or the gradually reducing array, have been selected. The entire sequence is usually repeated several times, although a single round of trials may identify stimuli that function as reinforcers (Carr et al., 2000).

The stimuli presented in each trial might be tangible objects themselves, pictures of the items, or verbal descriptions. Higbee, Carr, and Harrison (1999) provided a variation of the multiple-stimuli procedure that included stimulus preference selection based on a tangible object versus a picture of the object. The tangible objects pro-

duced greater variation and distribution of preferences than the picture objects did. Cohen-Almeida, Graff, and Ahearn (2000) found that the tangible object assessment was about as effective as a verbal preference assessment, but the clients completed the verbal preference assessment in less time.

DeLeon and Iwata (1996) used an adaptation of the multiple-stimuli and paired-stimuli presentations they described as a *brief stimulus assessment* to reduce the time needed to determine stimulus preference. Basically, in the brief stimulus assessment, once a particular stimulus item is chosen, that item is *not* returned to the array. Subsequent trials present a reduced number of items from which to choose (Carr et al., 2000; DeLeon et al., 2001; Roane et al., 1998). DeLeon and Iwata (1996) found that multiple stimuli without replacement identified preferred items in approximately half the time that the multiple stimuli with replacement procedure did. According to Higbee and colleagues (2000), "With a brief stimulus preference procedure, practitioners have a method for reinforcer identification that is both efficient and accurate" (pp. 72–73).

Guidelines for Selecting and Using Stimulus Preference Assessments

Practitioners can combine assessment procedures to compare single versus paired, paired versus multiple, or free operant versus trial-based methods (Ortiz & Carr, 2000). In day-to-day practice, brief stimulus presentations using comparative approaches might facilitate reinforcer identification, thereby speeding up possible interventions using those reinforcers. In summary, the goal of stimulus preference assessments is to identify stimuli that are most likely to function as reinforcers. Each method for assessing preference has advantages and limitations with respect to identifying preferences (Roane et al., 1998). Practitioners may find the following guidelines helpful when conducting stimulus preference assessments (DeLeon & Iwata, 1996; Gottschalk et al., 2000; Higbee et al., 2000; Ortiz & Carr, 2000; Roane et al., 1998; Roscoe, Iwata, & Kahng, 1999):

- Monitor the learner's activities during the time period before the stimulus preference assessment session to be aware of EOs that may affect the results.

- Use stimulus preference assessment options that balance the cost-benefit of brief assessments (but possible false positives) with more prolonged assessments that may delay reinforcer identification.

- Balance using a stimulus preference method that may yield a ranking of preferred stimuli against an assessment method that occurs without rankings, but occurs more frequently, to counteract shifts in preference.

- When time is limited, conduct a brief stimulus preference assessment with fewer items in an array.
- When possible, combine data from multiple assessment methods and sources of stimulus preference (e.g., asking the learner and significant others, free operant observation, pretask choice, and trial-based methods).

Reinforcer Assessment

The only way to tell whether or not a given event is reinforcing to a given organism under given conditions is to make a direct test.
—B. F. Skinner (1953, pp. 72–73)

Highly preferred stimuli may not always function as reinforcers (Higbee et al., 2000); even the candy that a child pried out of Sidman's hand may not have functioned as reinforcement under certain conditions. Conversely, least preferred stimuli might serve as reinforcers under some conditions (Gottschalk et al., 2000). The only way to know for sure whether a given stimulus serves as a reinforcer is to present it immediately following the occurrence of a behavior and note its effects on responding.

Reinforcer assessment refers to a variety of direct, data-based methods used to present one or more stimuli contingent on a target response and then measuring the future effects on the rate of responding. Researchers and practitioners have developed reinforcer assessment methods to determine the relative effects of a given stimulus as reinforcement under different and changing conditions and to assess the comparative effectiveness of multiple stimuli as reinforcers for a given behavior under specific conditions. Reinforcer assessment is often accomplished by presenting stimuli suspected of being reinforcers contingent on responding within concurrent, multiple, or progressive-ratio reinforcement schedules.[9]

Concurrent Schedule Reinforcer Assessment

When two or more contingencies of reinforcement operate independently and simultaneously for two or more behaviors a *concurrent schedule of reinforcement* is in effect. When used as a vehicle for reinforcer assessment, a concurrent schedule arrangement essentially pits two

stimuli against each other to see which will produce the larger increase in responding when presented as a consequence for responding. If a learner allocates a greater proportion of responses to one component of the concurrent schedule over the other, the stimulus used as a contingent consequence for that component is the more effective reinforcer. For example, using a concurrent schedule in this way shows the relative effectiveness of high-preference (HP) and low-preference (LP) stimuli as reinforcers (Koehler, Iwata, Roscoe, Rolider, & O'Steen, 2005; Piazza et al., 1996).

Concurrent schedules may also be used to determine differences between *relative* and *absolute* reinforcement effects of stimuli. That is, will an LP stimulus now presented contingently in the absence of the HP stimulus serve as a reinforcer? Roscoe and colleagues (1999) used concurrent schedules to compare the effects of HP and LP stimuli as reinforcers for eight adults with developmental disabilities. Following the preference assessments, a concurrent schedule of reinforcement was established using the high-preference and low-preference stimuli. The target response was pressing either of two micro switch panels. Each panel was a different color. Pressing a panel would illuminate a small light in the center of the panel. A training condition took place prior to baseline to establish panel pressing in the subjects' repertoires and to expose them to the consequences of responding. During baseline, pressing either panel resulted in no programmed consequences. During the reinforcement phase, an HP stimulus was placed on a plate behind one of the panels and an LP stimulus was placed on a plate behind another panel. All responses to either panel resulted in the participant immediately receiving the item on the plate behind the respective panel (i.e., an FR 1 schedule of reinforcement).

Under the concurrent schedule of reinforcement that enabled participants to choose reinforcers on the same FR 1 schedule, the majority of participants allocated most of their responding to the panel that produced the HP stimulus as reinforcement (e.g., see results for Sean, Peter, and Matt on Figure 11.11). However, these same participants, when later presented with the opportunity to obtain LP stimuli as reinforcers on a single-schedule contingency (i.e., only one panel to push), showed increased levels of responding over baseline similar to those obtained with the HP stimuli in the concurrent schedule. The study by Roscoe and colleagues (1999) demonstrated how concurrent schedules may be used to identify the relative effects of stimuli as reinforcers. The study also showed that the potential effects of a stimulus as a reinforcer may be masked or overshadowed when that stimulus is pitted against another stimulus on a concurrent schedule. In such cases, a potentially reinforcing stimulus might be abandoned prematurely.

---

[9]These and other types of schedules of reinforcement and their effects on behavior are described in Chapter 13.

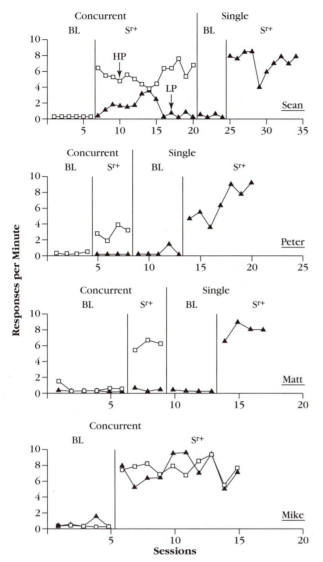

Figure 11.11   Responses per minute during concurrent-schedule and single-schedule baseline and reinforcement conditions for four adults with mental retardation.

From "Relative versus Absolute Reinforcement Effects: Implications for Preference Assessments" by E. M. Roscoe, B. A. Iwata, and S. Kahng, 1999, *Journal of Applied Behavior Analysis, 32,* p. 489. Copyright 1999 by the Society for the Experimental Analysis of Behavior, Inc. Used by permission.

Multiple Schedule Reinforcer Assessment

A *multiple schedule of reinforcement* consists of two or more component schedules of reinforcement for a single response with only one component schedule in effect at any given time. A discriminative stimulus (S^D) signals the presence of each component schedule, and that stimulus is present as long as the schedule is in effect. One way that a multiple schedule could be used for reinforcer assessment would be to present the same stimulus event contingent (i.e., response dependent) on each occurrence of the target behavior in one component of the multiple

schedule and on a fixed-time schedule (i.e., response independent) in the other component. For example, if a practitioner wanted to use a multiple schedule to assess whether social attention functioned as a reinforcer, she would provide social attention contingent on occurrences of cooperative play when one component of the multiple schedule is in effect, and during the other component the practitioner would present the same amount and kind of social attention except on a fixed-time schedule, independent of cooperative play (i.e., noncontingent reinforcement). The teacher could apply the response-dependent schedule during the morning play period, and the response-independent schedule during the afternoon play period. If social attention functioned as reinforcement, cooperative play would likely increase over its baseline rate in the morning periods, and because of no relationship with cooperative play, attention would likely have no effect in the afternoon period. This situation follows a multiple schedule because there is one class of behavior (i.e., cooperative play), a discriminative stimulus for each contingency in effect (i.e., morning and afternoon play periods), and different conditions for reinforcement (i.e., response dependent and response independent).

Progressive-Ratio Schedule Reinforcer Assessment

Stimulus preference assessments with low response requirements (e.g., FR 1) may not predict the effectiveness of the stimulus as a reinforcer when presented with higher response requirements (e.g., on an FR 10 schedule, a student must complete 10 problems to obtain reinforcement). As DeLeon, Iwata, Goh, and Worsdell (1997) stated:

> Current assessment methods may make inaccurate predictions about reinforcer efficacy when the task used in training regimens requires either more responses or more effort before the delivery of reinforcement. . . . for some classes of reinforcers, simultaneous increases in schedule requirements may magnify small differences in preferences that are undetected when requirements are low. In such cases, a stimulus preference assessment involving low response requirements (FR1) schedules does not accurately predict the relative potency of reinforcers under increased response requirements. (pp. 440, 446)

Progressive-ratio schedules provide a framework for assessing the relative effectiveness of a stimulus as reinforcement as response requirements increase. In a *progressive-ratio schedule of reinforcement* the response requirements for reinforcement are increased systematically over time independent of the participant's behavior. In a progressive-ratio schedule, the practitioner gradually requires more responses per presentation of the preferred stimulus until a breaking point is reached and the response rate declines (Roane, Lerman, & Vorndran, 2001). For example, initially each response produces reinforcement (FR 1), then reinforcement is delivered after every second response (FR 2), then perhaps after every fifth, tenth, and twentieth response (FR 5, FR 10, and FR 20). At some point, a preferred stimulus may no longer function as reinforcement (Tustin, 1994).

DeLeon and colleagues (1997) used a progressive ratio within a concurrent schedule to test the relative effectiveness of two similarly preferred stimuli (e.g., cookie and cracker) and two dissimilar stimuli (e.g., drink and balloon) as reinforcers for micro switch panel pressing for Elaine and Rick, two adults with mental retardation. One panel was blue and one was yellow. The experimenters placed two reinforcers on separate plates, and put one plate behind each of the panels. Each trial (24 per session for Rick; 14 per session for Elaine) consisted of the subject pushing either one of the panels and immediately

receiving the item on the plate behind that panel. During the first phase, an FR 1 schedule was used (i.e., each response produced the item on the plate). Later, the response requirement for obtaining the items was gradually increased (FR 2, FR 5, FR 10, and FR 20).

Elaine and Rick made responses that produced the two dissimilar items at roughly the same rates during the FR 1 phase (see the top two graphs in Figure 11.12). As response requirements for receiving the dissimilar stimuli increased, Elaine and Rick continued to evenly allocate responding between the two panels. However, when initially equivalent and similar reinforcers (food in FR 1) were compared under increasing schedule requirements, the differences in responses rates on the two panels revealed clear and consistent preferences (see the bottom two graphs in Figure 11.12). For example, when Elaine needed to work more to receive food, she allocated the majority of her responses to the panel that produced chips rather than the one that produced pretzels. In

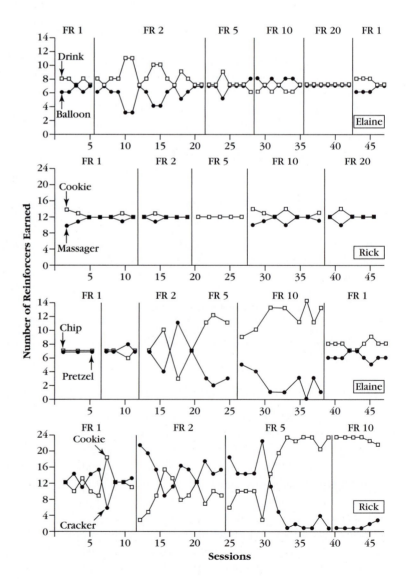

Figure 11.12 Responses per minute during concurrent-schedule and single-schedule baseline and reinforcement conditions for four adults with mental retardation.

From "Emergence of Reinforcer Preference as a Function of Schedule Requirements and Stimulus Similarity" by I. G. DeLeon, B. A. Iwata, H. Goh, and A. S. Worsdell, 1997, *Journal of Applied Behavior Analysis, 30,* p. 444. Copyright 1997 by the Society for the Experimental Analysis of Behavior, Inc. Used by permission.

the same way, as the number of responses required to receive reinforcement increased, Rick showed a clear preference for cookies over crackers. These results suggest that "for some classes of reinforcers, simultaneous increases in schedule requirements may magnify small differences in preference that are undetected when requirements are low" (DeLeon et al., 1997, p. 446).

Increasing response requirements within a concurrent schedule may reflect the effects of increasing response requirements on the choice between reinforcers and also reveal whether and under what conditions two reinforcers are substitutable for each other. If two reinforcers serve the same function (i.e., are made effective by the same establishing operation), an increase in the price (i.e., response requirement) for one of the reinforcers will lead to a decreased consumption of that item if a substitutable reinforcer is available (Green & Freed, 1993). DeLeon and colleagues (1997) used a hypothetical person with a slight preference for Coke over Pepsi as an analogy to explain the results shown in Figure 11.12.

> Assuming that Coke and Pepsi are both available for $1.00 per serving and that a person has only a slight preference for Coke, the individual may allocate choices rather evenly, perhaps as a function of periodic satiation for the preferred item, but with slightly more overall selections of Coke. Now assume that the cost of each is increased to $5.00 per serving. At this price, the preference for Coke is likely to be expressed. By contrast, a similar arrangement involving Coke and bus tokens may produce different results. Again, at $1.00 per item, roughly equal selection between the two options would not be surprising, assuming that the establishing operation for each dictates that both are momentarily equally valuable. However, these items serve distinctly different functions and are not substitutable; that is, the person is not free to trade one for the other and to continue to receive functionally similar reinforcement at the same rate. The person is more likely to continue choosing equally, even when the price for both reinforcers increases substantially.
>
> The same might be said for the results obtained in the present study. When choices involved two substitutable items, such as a cookie and a cracker, concurrent increases in the cost of each may have "forced" the expression of slight preference for one of the items. However, when reinforcers that were unlikely to be substitutes, such as a cookie and a massager, were concurrently available and equally preferred, increases in cost had little effect on preference. (pp. 446–447)

Although Stimulus X and Stimulus Y may each function as reinforcers when task demands are low, or when the reinforcement schedule is dense, when the task demands increase or when the schedule becomes leaner (i.e., more responses required per reinforcement), participants may choose only Stimulus Y. DeLeon and colleagues (1997) pointed out that practitioners who are alert to these relationships might be more skeptical in believing that original preferences will be sustained under changing environmental conditions, and judicious in how they plan reinforcement delivery relative to task assignment once intervention is underway. That is, it might be better to save some types of preferred stimuli for when task demands are high rather than substituting them for other equally preferred stimuli when task demands are low.

Control Procedures for Positive Reinforcement

Positive reinforcement control procedures are used to manipulate the contingent presentation of a potential reinforcer and observe any effects on the future frequency of behavior. *Control,* as the term is used here, requires an experimental demonstration that the presentation of a stimulus contingent on the occurrence of a target response functions as positive reinforcement. Control is demonstrated by comparing response rates in the absence and presence of a contingency, and then showing that with the absence and presence of the contingency the behavior can be turned on and off, or up and down (Baer, Wolf, & Risley, 1968). Historically, researchers and practitioners have used the reversal technique as the major control technique for positive reinforcement. Briefly, the reversal technique includes two conditions and a minimum of four phases (i.e., *ABAB*). In the *A* condition, the behavior is measured over time until it achieves stability in the absence of the reinforcement contingency. The absence of the contingency is the *control* condition. In the *B* condition, the reinforcement contingency is presented; the same target behavior continues to be measured to assess the effects of the stimulus change. The presence of the reinforcement contingency is the *experimental* condition. If the rate of responding increases in the presence of the contingency, the analyst then withdraws the reinforcement contingency and returns to the *A* and *B* conditions to learn whether the absence and presence of the contingency will turn the target behavior down and up.

However, using extinction as the control condition during the reversal phase presents practical and conceptual problems. First, withdrawing reinforcement may result in extinction-produced side effects (e.g., an initial increase in response rate, emotional responses, aggression—see Chapter 21) that affect the demonstration of control. Second, in some situations it may be impossible to withdraw the reinforcement contingency completely (Thompson & Iwata, 2005). For example, it is unlikely that a teacher could completely remove teacher attention during the *A* condition. In addition to these problems, Thompson and Iwata (2005) noted that, although

> extinction has often been successful in reversing the behavioral effects of positive reinforcement, its use as a control procedure presents interpretive difficulties. Essentially, extinction does not adequately isolate the reinforcement *contingency* as the variable controlling the target response, because mere stimulus presentation cannot be ruled out as an equally viable explanation. (p. 261, emphasis added)

According to Thompson and Iwata (2005), "the ideal control procedure for positive reinforcement eliminates the contingent relation between the occurrence of the target response and the presentation of the stimulus while controlling for the effects of stimulus presentation alone" (p. 259). They reviewed the effectiveness of three variations of the reversal technique as control procedures for determining reinforcement: noncontingent reinforcement (NCR), differential reinforcement of other behavior (DRO), and differential reinforcement of alternative behavior (DRA).[10]

Noncontingent Reinforcement

Noncontingent reinforcement (NCR) is the presentation of a potential reinforcer on a fixed-time (FT) or variable-time (VT) schedule independent of the occurrence of the target behavior. The response-independent presentation of the potential reinforcer eliminates the contingent relation between the target behavior and the stimulus presentation while allowing any effects of the stimulus presentation alone to be detected. Thus, NCR meets Thompson and Iwata's (2005) criteria for an ideal control procedure for positive reinforcement.

The NCR reversal technique should entail a minimum of five phases (*ABCBC*): *A* is a baseline condition; *B* is an NCR condition, where the potential reinforcer is presented on a fixed- or variable-interval schedule independent of the target behavior; and *C* is a condition in which the potential reinforcer is presented contingent on the occurrence of the target behavior. The *B* and *C* conditions are then repeated to learn whether the level of responding decreases and increases as a function of the absence and presence of the response-consequence contingency. The quality, amount, and rate of reinforcement should be approximately the same during the contingent and noncontingent *B* and *C* conditions of the analysis.

NCR often produces persistent responding, perhaps because of accidental reinforcement that sometimes occurs with a response-independent schedule, or because similar EOs and antecedent stimulus conditions evoke the persistent responding. Whatever the cause, persistent

responding is a limitation of the NCR control procedure because it makes achieving a reversal effect (reduced responding) more time-consuming than the reversal technique with extinction. Achieving the effect may require lengthy contact with the NCR schedule.

Differential Reinforcement of Other Behavior

A practitioner using *differential reinforcement of other behavior (DRO)* delivers a potential reinforcer whenever the target behavior has not occurred during a set time interval. The DRO reversal technique includes a minimum of five phases (i.e., *ABCBC*): *A* is a baseline condition; *B* is a reinforcement condition, in which the potential reinforcer is presented contingent on the occurrence of the target behavior; and *C* is the DRO control condition in which the potential reinforcer is presented contingent on the absence of the target behavior. The analyst then repeats the *B* and *C* conditions to determine whether the level of responding decreases and increases as a function of the absence and presence of the response-consequence contingency.

The DRO schedule allows for the continued presentation of the reinforcement contingency during the reversal phases of the control procedure. In one condition, the contingency is active with occurrences of the target behavior. In another condition, the contingency is active for the omission of the target behavior. The DRO control procedure may produce the reversal effect in less time than the NCR schedule, perhaps because of the elimination of accidental reinforcement of the target behaviors.

Differential Reinforcement of Alternative Behavior

When *differential reinforcement of an alternative behavior (DRA)* is used as a control condition, the potential reinforcer is presented contingent on occurrences of a desirable alternative to the target behavior.[11] The DRA reversal technique includes a minimum of five phases (i.e., *ABCBC*): *A* is a baseline condition; *B* is a reinforcement condition, in which the potential reinforcer is presented contingent on the occurrence of the target behavior; and *C* is a condition in which the potential reinforcer is presented contingent on the occurrence of an alternative behavior (i.e., DRA). The analyst will then repeat phases *B* and *C* to ascertain whether the level of responding decreases and increases as a function of the absence and presence of the response–consequence contingency.

Thompson and Iwata (2005) summarized the limitations of using DRO and DRA as control conditions procedures to test for positive reinforcement:

---

[10]Chapter 8 presents the ABAB, NCR, DRO, and DRA control techniques in the context of single-case experimental designs.

[11]Chapter 22 describes the use of DRO and DRA as behavior change tactics for decreasing the frequency of undesirable behavior.

[DRO and DRA] introduce a new contingency that was not present in the original experimental arrangement. As a result, reductions in the target response under a contingency reversal might be attributed to either (a) termination of the contingency between the target response and the reinforcer or (b) introduction of reinforcement for the absence of the target response or for the occurrence of a competing response. In addition, given that reinforcement is provided contingent on some characteristic of responding during the contingency reversal, it may be difficult to control for the rate of stimulus presentation across experimental and control conditions. If responding is not quickly reduced (DRO) or reallocated toward responses that produce reinforcement (DRA), the rate of reinforcement in the control condition may be low relative to the rate of reinforcement in the experimental conditions. When this occurs, the contingency-reversal strategy is functionally similar to the conventional extinction procedure. (p. 267)

Given the considerations for the reversal technique with extinction, and its three variations, Thompson and Iwata (2005) concluded that NCR offers the most thorough and unconfounded demonstration of the effects of positive reinforcement.

Using Reinforcement Effectively

We offer practitioners nine guidelines for applying positive reinforcement effectively. These guidelines come from three main sources: the research literatures of the experimental analysis of behavior, applied behavior analysis and our personal experiences.

Set an Easily Achieved Initial Criterion for Reinforcement

A common mistake in applications of reinforcement is setting the initial criterion for reinforcement too high, which prohibits the learner's behavior from contacting the contingency. To use reinforcement effectively, practitioners should establish an initial criterion so that the participant's first responses produce reinforcement, and then increase the criterion for reinforcement gradually as performance improves. Heward (1980) suggested the following method for establishing initial criteria for reinforcement based on the learner's level of responding during baseline (see Figure 11.13).

Figure 11.13   Examples of using data from a learner's baseline performance to set an initial criterion for reinforcement.

The criterion-setting formulas are

For increasing behaviors:
    baseline average < initial criterion ≤ highest performance during baseline

For decreasing behaviors:
    baseline average > initial criterion ≥ lowest performance during baseline

Examples

Target Behavior	Performance Goal	Lowest	Highest	Baseline Average	Range for Initial Criterion
Playing alone	Increase	2 min.	14 min.	6 min.	7–14 min.
Identifying letters of the alphabet	Increase	4 letters	9 letters	5 letters	6–9 letters
Number of leg exercises completed	Increase	0	22	8	9–22
Percentage of math problems correctly solved	Increase	25%	60%	34%	40–60%
Number of typing errors in one letter	Decrease	16	28	22	16–21
Number of calories consumed per day	Decrease	2,260	3,980	2,950	2,260–2,900

From "A Formula for Individualizing Initial Criteria for Reinforcement" by W. L. Heward, 1980, *Exceptional Teacher, 1* (9), p. 8. Copyright 1980 by the *Exceptional Teacher*. Used by permission.

For a behavior you wish to increase, set the initial criterion higher than the child's average baseline performance and lower than or equal to his best performance during baseline. For a behavior you want to decrease in frequency, the initial criterion for reinforcement should be set below the child's average performance during baseline and greater than or equal to his lowest (or best) baseline performance. (p. 7)

Use High Quality Reinforcers of Sufficient Magnitude

Reinforcers that maintain responding on simple tasks may not have the potency to produce similar levels of responding on more difficult or longer tasks. Practitioners will likely need to use a reinforcer of higher quality for behaviors that require more effort or endurance. A highly preferred stimulus chosen during preference assessments sometimes functions as a high-quality reinforcer. Neef and colleagues (1992), for example, found that behaviors that received a lower reinforcer rate but a higher quality reinforcer increased in frequency, whereas behaviors that received a higher reinforcer rate with a lower quality reinforcer decreased in frequency. Reinforcer quality is relative also to other consequences for responding currently available to the learner.

Applied behavior analysts define the magnitude (or amount) of a reinforcer as (a) the duration of time for access to the reinforcer, (b) the number of reinforcers per unit of time (i.e., *reinforcer rate*), or (c) the intensity of the reinforcer. Increases in reinforcer magnitude may correlate with an increased effectiveness of the behavior-reinforcer relation. However, the effects of reinforcer magnitude are not well understood because "few applied studies have examined the effects of magnitude on responding in a single-operant arrangement" (Lerman, Kelly, Vorndran, Kuhn, & LaRue, 2002, p. 30). Consideration of how much reinforcement to use should follow the maxim, "Reinforce abundantly, but don't give away the store." We suggest that the amount of reinforcement be proportional to the quality of the reinforcer and the effort required to emit the target response.

Use Varied Reinforcers to Maintain Potent Establishing Operations

Reinforcers often decrease in potency with frequent use. Presenting an overabundance of a specific reinforcer is likely to diminish the momentary effectiveness of the reinforcer due to satiation. Practitioners can minimize satiation effects by using a variety of reinforcers. If reading a specific book on sports functions as a reinforcer and the teacher relies solely on this reinforcer, ultimately reading that book may no longer produce reinforcement. Con-

versely, known reinforcers that are not always available may have increased effectiveness when they are reintroduced. If a teacher has demonstrated that "being first in line" is a reinforcer, but uses this reinforcer only once per week, the reinforcement effect will be greater than if "being first in line" is used frequently.

Varying reinforcers may enable less preferred stimuli to function as reinforcers. For example, Bowman et al. (1997) found that some learners responded better to a variety of less preferred stimuli as compared to a continuous access to a single, more highly preferred stimulus. Also, using a variety of reinforcers may keep the potency of any one particular reinforcer higher. For example, Egel (1981) found that students' correct responding and on-task behavior were higher when they had access to one of three randomly selected reinforcers across trials versus a constant reinforcement condition in which one of the stimuli was presented following each successful trial. Even within a session, teachers could let students select a variety of consequences from a menu. Similarly, varying a property of a reinforcer may keep its reinforcing potency for a longer time. If comic books are used as reinforcers, having several different genres of comic books available is likely to maintain their potency.

Use Direct Rather than Indirect Reinforcement Contingencies When Possible

With a direct reinforcement contingency, emitting the target response produces direct access to the reinforcer; the contingency does not require any intervening steps. With an indirect reinforcement contingency, the response does not produce reinforcement directly. The practitioner presents the reinforcer. Some research suggests that direct reinforcement contingencies may enhance performance (Koegel & Williams, 1980; Williams, Koegel, & Egel, 1981). Thompson and Iwata (2000), for example, linked the definitions of direct and indirect contingencies to the difference between automatic reinforcement (i.e., direct) and socially mediated reinforcement (i.e., indirect) and summarized their research on response acquisition under direct and indirect contingencies of reinforcement this way:

> Under both contingencies, completion of identical tasks (opening one of several types of containers) produced access to identical reinforcers. Under the direct contingency, the reinforcer was placed inside the container to be opened; under the indirect contingency, the therapist held the reinforcer and delivered it to the participant upon task completion. One participant immediately performed the task at 100% accuracy under both contingencies. Three participants showed either more immediate or larger improvements in performance

under the direct contingency. The remaining two participants showed improved performance only under the direct reinforcement contingency. Data taken on the occurrence of "irrelevant" behaviors under the indirect contingency (e.g., reaching for the reinforcer instead of performing the task) provided some evidence that these behaviors may have interfered with task performance and that their occurrence was a function of differential stimulus control. (p. 1)

Whenever possible, practitioners should use direct reinforcement contingency, especially with learners with limited behavioral repertoires.

Combine Response Prompts and Reinforcement

Response prompts are supplementary antecedent stimuli used to occasion a correct response in the presence of an S^D that will eventually control the behavior. Applied behavior analysts give response prompts before or during the performance of a target behavior. The three major forms of response prompts are verbal instructions, modeling, and physical guidance.

Concerning verbal instructions, sometimes describing the contingency (i.e., the verbal instructions) may function as a motivating operation for learners with verbal skills, thereby, making it more likely that the learner will more quickly contact the reinforcer. For example, Mayfield and Chase (2002) explained their reinforcement contingency to college students who were learning five basic algebra rules.

> The reinforcement procedures were described to the participants in the general instructions administered at the beginning of the study. Participants earned money for correct answers on all the tests and were not penalized for incorrect answers. During the session following a test, participants were presented with a record of their total earnings on the test. This was the only feedback provided concerning their performance on the tests. (p. 111)

Bourret, Vollmer, and Rapp (2004) used verbal response prompts during an assessment of the vocal verbal mand repertoires of three participants with autism.

> Each vocalization assessment session consisted of 10 trials, each 1 min in duration. A nonspecific prompt [describing the contingency] was delivered (e.g., "If you want this, ask me for it") 10 s after the onset of the trial. A prompt including a model of the complete targeted utterance (e.g., "If you want this, say 'chip' ") was delivered 20 s into the trial. The participant was prompted to say just the first phoneme of the targeted response (e.g., "If you want this, say 'ch' ") 30 s after the initiation of the trial.

Chapter 17 provides further discussion of response prompts, including specific procedures for combining re-

sponse prompts with reinforcement, and additional examples of using verbal instruction, modeling, and physical guidance response prompts.

Reinforce Each Occurrence of the Behavior Initially

Provide reinforcement for each occurrence of the target behavior (i.e., continuous reinforcement) to strengthen behavior, primarily during the initial stages of learning a new behavior. After the behavior is established, gradually thin the rate of reinforcement so that some but not all occurrences of the behavior are reinforced (i.e., intermittent reinforcement). For example, a teacher might initially reinforce each correct response to sight words printed on flash cards and then use a ratio schedule to thin reinforcement. To firm the responses after the initial learning, provide reinforcement following two correct responses for a few trials, then following each set of four correct responses, and so on. Hanley and colleagues (2001) gradually moved from a very dense fixed interval (FI) 1-second schedule of reinforcement (on an FI schedule, the first target response following the end of the interval produced reinforcement) to thinner schedule with the following increments of intervals: 2 s, 4 s, 8 s, 16 s, 25 s, 35 s, 46 s, and finally to an FI-58 seconds. For example, target responses that occurred before the end of the FI 58 seconds were not reinforced, but the first response after 58 seconds was reinforced. Chapter 13 provides more information on using continuous and intermittent reinforcement.

Use Contingent Attention and Descriptive Praise

As discussed earlier in this chapter, social attention and praise are powerful reinforcers for many people. However, behavioral improvements following praise often involve something more, or altogether different from, the direct effects of reinforcement. Michael (2004) discussed the common conceptual mistake of assuming that increased responding following praise and attention are a function of reinforcement.

> Consider the common use of *descriptive praise,* providing some general sign of social approval (a smile plus some comment such as "Good work!") *and, in addition,* a brief description of the behavior that is responsible for the approval ("I like the way you're . . .!"). When such praise is provided to a normally verbal person over 5 or 6 years of age, it probably functions as a form of instruction or as a rule, much as if the praiser had said, "If you want my continued approval you have to . . ." For example, a factory supervisor walks up to an employee who is cleaning up an oil spill on the factory floor,

smiles broadly, and says, "George, I really like the way you're cleaning up that spill before anyone steps in it. That's very considerate of you." Now suppose that George cleans up spills from that time forward—a rather larger change in behavior considering that it was followed by only a single instance of reinforcement. We might suspect that the praise functioned not simply as reinforcement but rather as a form of rule or instruction, and that George, for various reasons, provided himself with similar instruction every time another spill occurred. (pp. 164–165, emphasis in original)

A study by Goetz and Baer (1973) investigating the effects of teacher praise on preschool children's creative play with building blocks used descriptive praise in one condition of the study. "The teacher remarked with interest, enthusiasm, and delight every time that the child placed and/or rearranged the blocks so as to create a form that had not appeared previously in that session's construction(s). . . . 'Oh, that's very nice—that's different'!)" (p. 212). The three 4-year-old girls increased the construction of block form diversity during each phase of contingent descriptive praise. Goetz and Baer did not conduct a component analysis to determine how much of the girls' improved performance could be attributed to reinforcement in the form of positive attention ("That's very nice!") or to the feedback they received ("That's different!"), which enabled them to create a rule to follow ("Building *different things* with the blocks gets the teacher's attention."). The authors surmised that

> for some children, either [reinforcing attention and descriptive praise] will be sufficient without the other, but that for other children, the mix of the two will be more effective than either alone. If so, then for applied purposes a package of positive attention and descriptive praise is probably the best technique to apply to children in general. (p. 216, words in brackets added)

We recommend that, in the absence of data showing that attention and praise have produced counter therapeutic effects for a given learner, practitioners incorporate contingent praise and attention into any intervention entailing positive reinforcement.

Gradually Increase the Response-to-Reinforcement Delay

We recommended in the previous guideline that practitioners reinforce each occurrence of a target behavior during the initial stages of learning, and then thin the delivery of reinforcers by switching to an intermittent schedule of reinforcement. Because the consequences that maintain responding in natural environments are often delayed, Stromer, McComas, and Rehfeldt (2000) reminded us that using continuous and intermittent sched-

ules of reinforcement might be just the first steps of programming consequences for everyday situations. "Establishing the initial instances of a behavioral repertoire typically requires the use of programmed consequences that occur immediately after the target response occurs. However, the job of the applied behavior analyst also involves the strategic use of delayed reinforcement. Behaviors that yield delayed reinforcement are highly adaptive in everyday life, but they may be difficult to establish and maintain" (p. 359).[12]

Examples of the tactics that applied behavior analysts have used to help people learn to respond effectively for delayed consequences include: (a) a delay-to-reinforcement time interval that begins with a short delay and is then gradually increased the extent of the delay (Dixon, Rehfeldt, & Randich, 2003; Schweitzer & Sulzer-Azaroff, 1988); (b) a gradual increase in work requirements during the delay (Dixon & Holcomb, 2000); (c) an activity during the delay to "bridge the gap" between the behavior and reinforcer (Mischel, Ebbesen, & Zeiss, 1972); and, importantly, (d) verbal instruction in the form of an assurance that the reinforcer will be available following a delay (e.g., "The calculator will show the amount of money to be placed in a savings account for you. You will be given all the nickels in your savings account on [day]" (Neef, Mace, & Shade, 1993, p. 39). We present more on using delayed consequences to promote generalization and maintenance of behavior changes in Chapter 28.

Gradually Shift from Contrived to Naturally Occurring Reinforcers

We end this chapter with an extract from Murray Sidman's (2000) insightful and thought-provoking account of what he learned in the "early days" of applying behavioral principles to human behavior. In describing a project from 1965 to 1975 that emphasized the use of positive reinforcement with boys between the ages of 6 and 20 years who were diagnosed with mental retardation and living in a state institution, Sidman recollected how introducing tokens as generalized conditioned reinforcers eventually led to praise from the project staff,

---

[12]Moving from continuous reinforcement to an intermittent schedule of reinforcement is sometimes described as a means of increasing reinforcer delay (e.g., Alberto & Troutman, 2006; Kazdin, 2001). However, an intermittent schedule of reinforcement does not entail "delayed reinforcement" unless specified. Although only some occurrences of the target behavior are reinforced on an intermittent schedule of reinforcement (see Chapter 13), reinforcement is delivered immediately following the response that meets the contingency. For example, on a fixed ratio 10 schedule of reinforcement, every tenth response produces immediate reinforcement. *Delay-to-reinforcement* or *reinforcement delay* describes the time lapse between the response and delivery of the reinforcer after the contingency has been met (e.g., the reinforcer was delivered 45 seconds after every tenth response).

and later to learning itself, becoming powerful reinforcers for the boys.

> We began with tokens, which had the advantage of being visible and easily handled. Later, after the boys had learned to save tokens and to understand numbers, we were able to introduce points. For some, points led eventually to money. As the boys saw how pleased we were when they earned the tokens and points that brought them other reinforcers, our pleasure also became important to them, and we became able to use praise as a reinforcer. As they learned more and more, many of the boys found that what they learned permitted them to deal more effectively with their gradually enlarging world. For them, learning itself became reinforcing. (p. 19)

Success in manipulating the environment may be the ultimate naturally occurring reinforcer. As Skinner (1989) pointed out, this powerful reinforcer "does not need to be contrived for instructional purposes; it is unrelated to any particular kind of behavior and hence always available. We call it *success*." (p. 91)

 ## Summary

Definition and Nature of Positive Reinforcement

1. Positive reinforcement is a functional relation defined by a two-term contingency: A response is followed immediately by the presentation of a stimulus, and, as a result, similar responses occur more frequently in the future.

2. The stimulus change responsible for the increase in responding is called a reinforcer.

3. The importance of the immediacy of reinforcement must be emphasized; a response-to-reinforcement delay of just 1 second can diminish intended effects because the behavior temporally closest to the presentation of the reinforcer will be strengthened by its presentation.

4. The effects of long-delayed consequences on human behavior should not be attributed to the direct effect of reinforcement.

5. A misconception held by some is that reinforcement is a circular concept. Circular reasoning is a form of faulty logic in which cause and effect are confused and not independent of each other. Reinforcement is not a circular concept because the two components of the response–consequence relation can be separated and the consequence manipulated to determine whether it increases the frequency of the behavior it follows.

6. In addition to increasing the future frequency of the behavior it follows, reinforcement changes the function of antecedent stimuli. An antecedent stimulus that evokes behavior because it has been correlated with the availability of reinforcement is called a discriminative stimulus (S^D).

7. A discriminated operant is defined by a three-term contingency of $S^D \rightarrow R \rightarrow S^{R+}$.

8. The momentary effectiveness of any stimulus change as reinforcement depends on an existing level of motivation with respect to that stimulus change. An establishing operation (EO) (e.g., deprivation) increases the current effectiveness of a reinforcer; an abolishing operation (AO) (e.g., satiation) decreases the current effectiveness of a reinforcer.

9. A complete description of reinforcement of a discriminated operant entails a four-term contingency: EO $\rightarrow$ $S^D \rightarrow R \rightarrow S^{R+}$

10. Automaticity of reinforcement refers to the fact that a person does not have to understand or be aware of the relation between his behavior and a reinforcing consequence for reinforcement to occur.

11. Reinforcement strengthens any behavior that immediately precedes it; no logical or adaptive connection between behavior and the reinforcing consequence is necessary.

12. The development of superstitious behaviors that often appear when reinforcement is presented on a fixed-time schedule irrespective of the subject's behavior demonstrates the arbitrary nature of the behaviors selected by reinforcement.

13. Automatic reinforcement occurs when behaviors produce their own reinforcement independent of the mediation of others.

Classifying Reinforcers

14. Unconditioned reinforcers are stimuli that function as reinforcement without requiring a learning history. These stimuli are the product of phylogenic development, meaning that all members of a species are susceptible to the same properties of stimuli.

15. Conditioned reinforcers are previously neutral stimuli that function as reinforcers as a result of prior pairing with one or more other reinforcers.

16. A generalized conditioned reinforcer is a conditioned reinforcer that as a result of having been paired with many unconditioned and conditioned reinforcers does not depend on a current EO for any particular form of reinforcement for its effectiveness.

17. When reinforcers are described by their physical properties, they are typically classified as edible, sensory, tangible, activity, or social reinforcers.

18. The Premack principle states that making the opportunity to engage in a high-probability behavior contingent on the

occurrence of low-frequency behavior will function as reinforcement for the low-frequency behavior.

19. The response-deprivation hypothesis is a model for predicting whether contingent access to one behavior will function as reinforcement for engaging in another behavior based on whether access to the contingent behavior represents a restriction of the activity compared to the baseline level of engagement.

Identifying Potential Reinforcers

20. Stimulus preference assessment refers to a variety of procedures used to determine (a) the stimuli that a person prefers, (b) the relative preference values (high versus low) of those stimuli, and (c) the conditions under which those preferences values remain in effect.

21. Stimulus preference assessments can be performed by asking the target person and/or significant others what the target person prefers, conducting free operant observations, and conducting trial-based assessments (i.e., single-, paired-, or multiple-stimulus presentations).

22. Preferred stimuli do not always function as reinforcers, and stimulus preferences often change over time.

23. Reinforcer assessment refers to a variety of direct, data-based methods for determining the relative effects of a given stimulus as reinforcement under different and changing conditions or the comparative effectives of multiple stimuli as reinforcers for a given behavior under specific conditions. Reinforcer assessment is often conducted with concurrent schedules of reinforcement, multiple schedules of reinforcement, and progressive reinforcement schedules.

Control Procedures for Positive Reinforcement

24. Positive reinforcement control procedures are used to manipulate the presentation of a potential reinforcer and ob-

serve any effects on the future frequency of behavior. Positive reinforcement control procedures require a believable demonstration that the contingent presentation following the occurrence of a target response functions as positive reinforcement. Control is demonstrated by comparing rates of responding in the absence and presence of a contingency, and then showing that with the absence and presence of the contingency the behavior can be turned on and off, or up and down.

25. In addition to a reversal design using the withdrawal of the reinforcement contingency (i.e., extinction) as the control condition, noncontingent reinforcement (NCR), differential reinforcement of other behavior (DRO), and differential reinforcement of alternative behavior (DRA) can be used as control conditions for reinforcement.

Using Reinforcement Effectively

26. Guidelines for increasing the effectiveness of positive reinforcement interventions include:
    - Set an easily achieved initial criterion for reinforcement
    - Use high quality reinforcers of sufficient magnitude
    - Use varied reinforcers
    - Use a direct rather than indirect reinforcement contingency whenever possible
    - Combine response prompts and reinforcement
    - Reinforce each occurrence of the behavior initially, then gradually thin reinforcement schedule
    - Use contingent praise and attention
    - Gradually increase the response-to-reinforcement delay
    - Gradually shift from contrived to naturally occurring reinforcers

CHAPTER 12

Negative Reinforcement

Key Terms

avoidance contingency
conditioned negative reinforcer
discriminated avoidance

escape contingency
free-operant avoidance

negative reinforcement
unconditioned negative reinforcer

Behavior Analyst Certification Board® BCBA® & BCABA® Behavior Analyst Task List©, Third Edition

Content Area 3: Principles, Processes, and Concepts	
3-3	Define and provide examples of (positive and) negative reinforcement.

Content Area 9: Behavior Change Procedures	
9-2	Use (positive and) negative reinforcement:
(a)	Identify and use (negative) reinforcers.
(b)	Use appropriate parameters and schedules of (negative) reinforcement.
(d)	State and plan for the possible unwanted effects of the use of (negative) reinforcement.

This chapter was written by Brian A. Iwata and Richard G. Smith.

Chapter 11 described the most fundamental principle of learning—positive reinforcement. The use of positive reinforcement in educational and therapeutic programs is so commonplace that the terms *positive reinforcement* and *reinforcement* have become almost synonymous; in fact, the usual lay term for reinforcement is simply *reward*. As noted in Chapter 11, positive reinforcement involves an increase in responding as a function of stimulus *presentation*. In a complementary way, responding can lead to the *termination* of a stimulus, as in turning off an alarm clock in the morning, which results in the cessation of noise. When responding increases as a result of stimulus termination, learning has occurred through *negative reinforcement*. This chapter expands the discussion of operant contingencies to include negative reinforcement. We define negative reinforcement, distinguish between escape and avoidance contingencies, describe events that may serve as the basis for negative reinforcement, illustrate ways negative reinforcement may be used to strengthen behavior, and discuss ethical issues that arise when using negative reinforcement. Readers interested in more in-depth discussions of basic and applied research on negative reinforcement are referred to reviews by Hineline (1977) and Iwata (1987).

Definition of Negative Reinforcement

A **negative reinforcement** contingency is one in which the occurrence of a response produces the removal, termination, reduction, or postponement of a stimulus, which leads to an increase in the future occurrence of that response. A full description of negative reinforcement requires specification of its four-term contingency (see Figure 12.1): (a) The establishing operation (EO) for behavior maintained by negative reinforcement is an antecedent event in whose presence escape (termination of the event) is reinforcing, (b) the discriminative stimulus (S^D) is another antecedent event in whose presence a response is more likely to be reinforced, (c) the response is the act that produces reinforcement, and (d) the reinforcer is the termination of the event that served as the EO.

Positive versus Negative Reinforcement

Positive and negative reinforcement have a similar effect on behavior in that both produce an increase in responding. They differ, however, with respect to the type of stimulus change that follows behavior, as illustrated in Figure 12.2. In both examples, a stimulus change (consequence) strengthens the behavior that preceded it: Asking the sibling to make a sandwich is strengthened by obtaining food; carrying rain protection is strengthened by blocking the rain. However, behavior maintained by positive reinforcement produces a stimulus that was absent prior to responding, whereas behavior maintained by negative reinforcement terminates a stimulus that was present prior to responding: Food was unavailable prior to asking for it but available after (positive reinforcement); rain was landing on one's clothing before raising the newspaper but not after (negative reinforcement).

Thus, the key distinction between positive and negative reinforcement is based on the type of stimulus change that occurs following a response. Many stimulus changes have discrete onsets and offsets and involve an "all-or-none" operation. For example, one can readily see the effect of turning on a television (positive reinforcement) or turning off the light in a bedroom (negative reinforcement). Other stimulus changes exist on a continuum from less to more, such as turning up the volume of a stereo to hear it better (positive reinforcement) or turning it down when it is too loud (negative reinforcement). Sometimes, however, it is difficult to determine whether an increase in responding resulted from positive or negative reinforcement because the stimulus change is ambiguous. For example, although a change in temperature can be measured quantitatively so we know that it either increased or decreased following behavior, it is unclear whether turning on a heater when the temperature is 40° F is an example of positive reinforcement because the response "produced heat" or negative reinforcement because the response "removed cold." Another example can be found in a classic study by Osborne (1969) on the use of free time as a reinforcer in the classroom. During baseline, students were observed to get out of their seats frequently during long

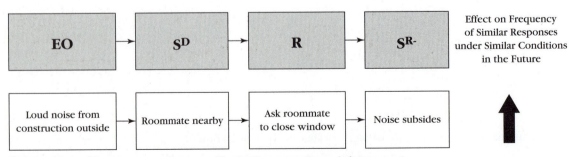

Figure 12.1   Four-term contingency illustrating negative reinforcement.

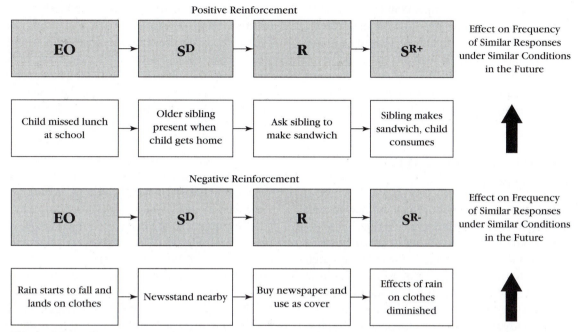

Figure 12.2 Four-term contingency illustrating similarities and difference between positive and negative reinforcement.

work periods. During treatment, the students were given 5 minutes of free time if they remained in their seats during 10-minute work periods, and in-seat behavior increased. At first glance, the free-time contingency appears to involve negative reinforcement (termination of the in-seat requirement contingent on appropriate behavior). As Osborne noted, however, activities (games, social interaction, etc.) to which the students had access during free time may have functioned as positive reinforcement.

Given the ambiguous nature of some stimulus changes, Michael (1975) suggested that the distinction between positive and negative reinforcement, based on whether a stimulus is presented or removed, may be unnecessary. Instead, he emphasized the importance of specifying the type of environmental change produced by a response in terms of key stimulus features that comprised both the "prechange" and "postchange" conditions. This practice, he proposed, would eliminate the necessity of describing the transition between prechange and postchange conditions as one involving the presentation or removal of stimuli and would facilitate a more complete understanding of functional relations between environment and behavior.

Little has changed since the publication of Michael's (1975) article; the distinction between positive and negative reinforcement continues to be emphasized in every text on learning principles, and citations to the term *negative reinforcement* have even increased in applied research (Iwata, 2006). In an attempt to renew the discussion, Baron and Galizio (2005) reiterated Michael's position and included some additional points of emphasis.

This terminological issue is a complex one that can be considered from several perspectives—conceptual, procedural, and historical—and is unresolved at the current time. Readers interested in the topic are referred to a series of reactions to Baron and Galizio (Chase, 2006; Iwata, 2006; Lattal & Lattal, 2006; Marr, 2006; Michael, 2006; Sidman, 2006) and their rejoinder (Baron & Galizio, 2006).

Negative Reinforcement versus Punishment

Negative reinforcement is sometimes confused with punishment for two reasons. First, because the lay term for positive reinforcement is *reward,* people mistakenly consider negative reinforcement as the technical term for the opposite of reinforcement (punishment). The terms *positive* and *negative,* however, do not refer to "good" and "bad" but to the type of stimulus change (presentation versus termination) that follows behavior (Catania, 1998). A second source of confusion stems from the fact that the stimuli involved in both negative reinforcement and punishment are considered "aversive" to most people.[1] Although it is true that the same stimulus may serve as a negative reinforcer in one context and as a punisher in a different context, both the nature of the stimulus change and its effect on behavior differ. In a negative reinforcement contingency, a stimulus that was present is terminated by a response, which leads to an

---

[1]The term *aversive* is not meant to describe an inherent characteristic of a stimulus but, rather, a stimulus whose presentation functions as punishment or whose removal functions as negative reinforcement.

increase in responding; in a punishment contingency, a stimulus that was absent is presented following a response, which leads to a decrease in responding. Thus, a response that terminates loud noise would increase as a function of negative reinforcement, but one that produces loud noise would decrease as a function of punishment (see Chapter 14 for a more extensive discussion of punishment).

Escape and Avoidance Contingencies

In its simplest form, negative reinforcement involves an **escape contingency,** in which a response terminates (produces escape from) an ongoing stimulus. An early study by Keller (1941) illustrates typical laboratory research on escape. When a rat was placed in an experimental chamber, and a bright light was turned on, the rat quickly learned to a press lever, which turned off the light. Osborne's (1969) study on free-time contingencies may also serve as an example of escape learning in an applied context. To the extent that the important feature of the contingency was the termination of work requirements, in-seat behavior during 10-minute work periods produced 5 minutes of escape.

Although situations involving escape are commonly encountered in everyday life (e.g., we turn off loud noises, shield our eyes from the sun, flee from an aggressor), most behavior maintained by negative reinforcement is characterized by an **avoidance contingency,** in which a response prevents or postpones the presentation of a stimulus. Returning to the previous laboratory example, an experimenter can add to the escape contingency an arrangement in which another stimulus such as a tone precedes the presentation of the bright light, and a response in the presence of the tone eliminates the presentation of the light or postpones it until the tone is next presented. This type of arrangement has been called **discriminated avoidance,** in which responding in the presence of a signal prevents the onset of a stimulus from which escape is a reinforcer. Because responses in the presence of the tone are reinforced, whereas those in the absence of the tone have no effect, the tone is a discriminative stimulus (S^D) in whose presence there is an increased likelihood of reinforcement for responding. (See Chapter 17 for more on stimulus control.)

Avoidance behavior also can be acquired in the absence of a signal. Suppose the experimenter arranges a schedule in which the bright light turns on for 5 seconds every 30 seconds, and a response (or some number of responses) at any time during the interval resets the clock to zero. This type of arrangement is known as **free-operant avoidance** because the avoidance behavior is "free to occur" at any time and will delay the presentation of the bright light.

Each of the three types of contingencies described earlier was illustrated in an ingenious study by Azrin, Rubin, O'Brien, Ayllon, and Roll (1968) on postural slouching (see Figure 12.3). Participants wore an apparatus that closed an electrical circuit when slouching occurred. Closure of the switch produced an audible click, which was followed 3 seconds later by a 55-db tone. Postural correction in the presence of the tone turned off the tone (escape) but prevented the tone if correction occurred during the 3 seconds following the click (discriminated avoidance). Furthermore, maintenance of correct posture prevented the click (free-operant avoidance). A hypothetical example involving homework management also illustrates these contingencies. A parent who sends a child to his or her room immediately following school and allows the child to leave the room only after completing homework has arranged an escape contingency: Homework completion produces escape from the bedroom. A parent who first delivers a warning (e.g., "If you don't

Figure 12.3 Three types of negative reinforcement contingencies used by Azrin and colleagues (1968) to maintain correct posture.

Free-Operant Avoidance

Correct posture maintained → Avoid click and tone

Discriminated Avoidance

Slouching (incorrect posture) → Audible click

Correct posture within 3 seconds of click → Avoid tone

Escape

Slouching (incorrect posture) → Audible click

Posture not corrected within 3 seconds → 55-db tone

Posture corrected → Tone turns off

---

start your homework in 10 minutes, you'll have to do it in your bedroom") has arranged a discriminated avoidance contingency: Starting homework following the warning avoids having to do it in the bedroom. Finally, the parent who waits until later in the evening to impose the in-room requirement has arranged a free-operant avoidance contingency: Homework completion at any time after school avoids having to do it in the bedroom later.

Characteristics of Negative Reinforcement

Responses Acquired and Maintained by Negative Reinforcement

It a well-known fact that aversive stimulation produces a variety of responses (Hutchinson, 1977). Some of these may be respondent behaviors (as in reflexive actions to intense stimuli), but the focus in this chapter is on operant behaviors. Recall that the presentation of an aversive stimulus serves as an EO for escape and occasions behavior that has produced escape from similar stimulation in the past. Any response that successfully terminates the stimulation will be strengthened; as a result, a wide range of behaviors may be acquired and maintained by negative reinforcement. All of these behaviors are adaptive because they enable one to interact effectively with the environment; some behaviors, however, are more socially appropriate than others. As will be seen later in the chapter, negative reinforcement may play an important role in the development of academic skills, but it also can account for the development of disruptive or dangerous behavior.

Events That Serve as Negative Reinforcers

In discussing the types of stimuli that can strengthen behavior through negative reinforcement, a problem arises when attempting to use the same terminology as that applied to the description of positive reinforcers. It is quite common to refer to positive reinforcers by listing things such as food, money, praise, and so on. It is, however, the presentation of the stimulus that strengthens behavior: Food presentation, and not food per se, is a positive reinforcer. Nevertheless, we often simply list the stimulus and assume that "presentation" is understood. In a similar way, to say that negative reinforcers include shock, noise, parental nagging, and so on, is an incomplete description. It is important to remember that a stimulus described as a negative reinforcer refers to its removal because, as noted previously, the same stimulus serves as an EO when presented prior to behavior and as punishment when presented following behavior.

Learning History

As is the case with positive reinforcers, negative reinforcers influence behavior because (a) we have the inherited capacity to respond to them or (b) their effects have been established through a history of learning. Stimuli whose removal strengthens behavior in the absence of prior learning are **unconditioned negative reinforcers.** These stimuli are typically noxious events such as shock, loud noise, intense light, extremely high or low temperature, or strong pressure against the body. In fact, any source of pain or discomfort (e.g., a headache) will occasion behavior, and any response that successfully eliminates the discomfort will be reinforced. Other stimuli are **conditioned negative reinforcers,** which are previously neutral events that acquire their effects through pairing with an existing (unconditioned or conditioned) negative reinforcer. A bicyclist, for example, usually heads for home when seeing a heavily overcast sky because dark clouds have been highly correlated with bad weather. Various forms of social coercion, such as parental nagging, are perhaps the most commonly encountered conditioned negative reinforcers. For example, reminding a child to clean his bedroom may have little effect on the child's behavior unless failure to respond is followed by another consequence such as having to stay in the room until it is clean. To the extent that the nagging is reliably "backed up" by sending the child to his room, the child will eventually respond simply to stop or prevent the nagging. It is interesting to note that, in the case of negative reinforcement, neutral events (dark sky, nagging) function as both (a) discriminative stimuli because responding in their presence constitutes avoidance of another consequence and (b) conditioned negative reinforcers because, due to their pairing with another consequence, they become stimuli to avoid or escape.

The Source of Negative Reinforcement

Another way to classify negative reinforcers is based on how they are removed (i.e., their source). In Chapter 11, a distinction was made between socially mediated reinforcement, in which the consequence results from the action of another person, and automatic reinforcement, in which the consequence is produced directly by a response independent of the actions of another. This distinction also applies to negative reinforcement. Returning to the example in Figure 12.1, we can see that termination of the construction noise was an instance of *social negative reinforcement* (the roommate's action closed the window). The person "being bothered" by the noise, however, could simply have walked across the room and closed the window (*automatic negative reinforcement*). This example illustrates the fact that many reinforcers can be administered either way: One can consult a physician when experiencing a headache (social) or take a pain medication (automatic), ask the teacher for help with a difficult problem (social) or persist until it is solved (automatic), and so on.

Consideration of the source of negative reinforcement may facilitate the design of behavior change interventions by determining the focus of intervention. For example, when faced with a perplexing work task, an employee may finish it incorrectly just to get it out of the way (automatic reinforcement) or ask for help (social reinforcement). Aside from reassigning the employee, the quickest solution would be to reinforce the employee's seeking help by offering assistance. Ultimately, however, the supervisor would want to teach the employee the necessary skills to complete the work tasks independently.

Identifying the Context of Negative Reinforcement

Chapter 11 outlined several ways to identify positive reinforcers; the difference with negative reinforcers is that equal emphasis must be placed on the antecedent event (EO) as well as on the reinforcing consequence because, once the behavior occurs, the negative reinforcer may be gone and cannot be observed. The identification of EOs may be difficult with people who have limited verbal ability and cannot tell someone they are experiencing aversive stimulation. These people may engage in other behaviors, such as tantrums, attempts to leave the situation, destructive behavior, aggression, or even self-injury. Weeks and Gaylord-Ross (1981), for example, observed students with severe disabilities when no task, an easy task, and a difficult task were presented. Little or no problem behavior occurred during the no-task condition, and problem behavior occurred somewhat more often in the difficult-task condition than in the easy-task condition. These results suggested that the students' problem behavior was maintained by escape from task demands and that difficult tasks were more "aversive" than were easy tasks. However, because the consequences that followed problem behavior were unknown, it is possible that the behaviors were maintained by some other consequence, such as attention, which would be a positive reinforcer.

Iwata, Dorsey, Slifer, Bauman, and Richman (1994) developed a method for identifying the types of contingencies that maintain problem behavior by observing people under a series of conditions that differed with respect to both antecedent and consequent events. One condition involved the presentation of task demands (EO) and the removal of demands (escape) if problem behavior occurred; higher rates of problem behavior under this condition relative to others indicated that problem behavior was maintained by negative reinforcement (see Chapter 24 for further discussion of this approach to assessment).

Smith, Iwata, Goh, and Shore (1995) extended the findings of Weeks and Gaylord-Ross (1981) and Iwata et al. (1994) by identifying some characteristics of task demands that make them aversive. After first determining that their participants' (people with severe disabilities) problem behavior was maintained by escape from task demands, Smith and colleagues examined several dimensions along which tasks might differ: task novelty, duration of the work session, and rate of demand presentation. Results of one of these analyses are shown in Figure 12.4, which depicts frequency distributions and cumulative records of problem behavior from the beginning to the end of sessions. These data illustrate the importance of individualized assessments in identifying the basis for negative reinforcement because two participants (Evelyn and Landon) showed increasing rates of problem behavior as work sessions progressed, whereas two other participants (Milt and Stan) showed the opposite trend.

Factors That Influence the Effectiveness of Negative Reinforcement

The factors that determine whether a negative reinforcement contingency will be effective in changing behavior are similar to those that influence positive reinforcement (see Chapter 11) and are related to (a) the strength of the contingency and (b) the presence of competing contingencies. In general, negative reinforcement for a given response will be more effective under the following conditions:

1. The stimulus change *immediately* follows the occurrence of the target response.

2. The *magnitude* of reinforcement is large, referring to the difference in stimulation present before and after the response occurs.

3. Occurrence of the target response *consistently* produces escape from or postponement of the EO.

4. Reinforcement is *unavailable* for competing (nontarget) responses.

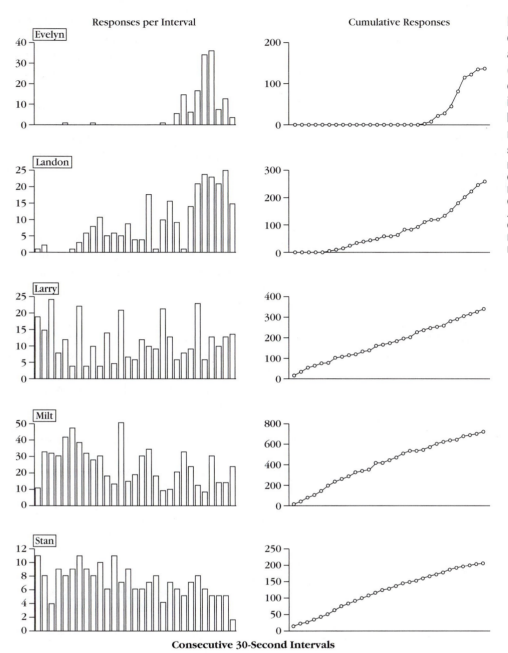

Figure 12.4 Frequency distributions (left column) and cumulative records (right column) summed over sessions of self-injurious behavior (SIB) by five adults with developmental disabilities as work sessions progressed.

From "Analysis of Establishing Operations for Self-Injury Maintained by Escape" by R. G. Smith, B. A. Iwata, H. Goh, and B. A. Shore, 1995, *Journal of Applied Behavior Analysis, 28,* p. 526. Copyright 1995 by the Society for the Experimental Analysis of Behavior, Inc. Reprinted by permission.

Applications of Negative Reinforcement

Negative reinforcement is a fundamental principle of learning that has been studied extensively in basic research (Hineline, 1977). Although many examples of escape and avoidance learning can be found in everyday life, research in applied behavior analysis has heavily emphasized the use of positive reinforcement over negative reinforcement, mostly for ethical reasons, which are noted in the final section of this chapter. Still, negative reinforcement has been used as one means of establishing a variety of behaviors. This section illustrates several therapeutic uses of negative reinforcement, as well as the un-intended role it may play in strengthening problem behavior.

Acquisition and Maintenance of Appropriate Behavior

Chronic Food Refusal

Pediatric feeding problems are common and are especially prevalent among children with developmental disabilities. These disorders may take a variety of forms, including selective eating, failure to consume solid foods, and complete food refusal, and may be serious enough to require tube feeding or other artificial means to ensure adequate nutritional intake. A large proportion of feeding problems cannot be attributed to a medical cause but, instead, appear to be learned responses most likely maintained by escape or avoidance.

Results from a number of studies have shown that operant learning-based interventions can be highly effective in treating many childhood feeding disorders, and a study by Ahearn, Kerwin, Eicher, Shantz, and Swearingin (1996) illustrated the use of negative reinforcement as a form of intervention. Three children admitted to a hospital who had histories of chronic food refusal were first observed under a baseline (positive reinforcement) condition in which food was presented and access to toys was available contingent on accepting food. Food refusal, however, produced escape in that it terminated a trial. Subsequently, the experimenters compared the effects of two interventions. One treatment condition (nonremoval of the spoon) involved presenting food and keeping the spoon positioned at the child's lower lip until the bite was accepted. The other treatment (physical guidance) involved presenting food and, if the child did not accept, opening the child's mouth so that the food could be delivered. Both treatments involved a negative reinforcement contingency because food acceptance terminated the trial by producing removal of the spoon or avoidance of the physical guidance.

Figure 12.5 shows the results obtained for the three children. All children exhibited low rates of acceptance during baseline in spite of the availability of positive re-

inforcement. The two interventions were implemented in a multiple baseline across subjects design and were compared in a multielement design. As can be seen in the second phase of the study, both interventions produced immediate and large increases in food acceptance. These results showed that positive reinforcement for appropriate behavior may have limited effects if other behaviors (refusal) produce negative reinforcement, and that negative reinforcement that maintains problem behavior can be used to establish alternative behavior.

Error-Correction Strategies

As noted in Chapter 11, positive reinforcement is a basic motivational component of effective instruction. Teachers commonly deliver praise, privileges, and other forms of reward contingent on correct performance. Another common procedure, but one that has received less attention than positive reinforcement, involves the correction of student errors by repeating a learning trial, having the student practice correct performance, or giving the student additional work. To the extent that correct performance avoids these remedial procedures, improvements may be just as much a function of negative reinforcement as positive reinforcement.

Worsdell and colleagues (2005) examined the relative contributions of these contingencies during behavioral acquisition. The learning task involved reading words presented on flash cards, and the intervention of interest

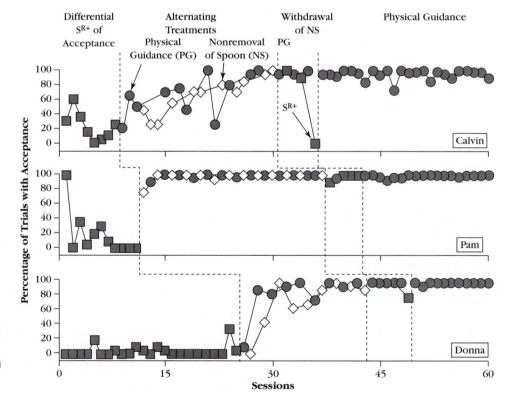

Figure 12.5 Percentage of trials in which three children with histories of chronic food refusal accepted bites during a baseline condition of positive reinforcement and two treatment conditions, nonremoval of the spoon and physical guidance, both of which involved a negative reinforcement contingency.

From "An Alternating Treatments Comparison of Two Intensive Interventions for Food Refusal" by W. H. Ahearn, M .E. Kerwin, P. S. Eicher, J. Shantz, and W. Swearingin, 1996, *Journal of Applied Behavior Analysis, 29,* p. 326. Copyright 1996 by the Society for the Experimental Analysis of Behavior, Inc. Reprinted by permission.

was the correct repetition of misread words. As noted by the authors, the procedure provided additional practice of correct responses but also represented an avoidance contingency. To separate these effects (in Study 3), the authors implemented two error correction conditions. In the "relevant" condition, which combined the effects of practice and negative reinforcement, students were prompted to pronounce the misread word correctly five times contingent on an error. In the "irrelevant" condition, students were prompted to repeat an unrelated, nontarget word five times contingent on an error. The irrelevant condition contained only the negative reinforcement contingency because repetition of irrelevant words provided no practice in correctly reading misread words.

Figure 12.6 shows the results of Study 3, expressed as the cumulative number of words mastered by the 9 participants. All participants' performance improved during both error-correction conditions relative to baseline, when no error-correction procedure was in effect. Performance by 3 participants (Tess, Ariel, and Ernie) was better during relevant error correction. However, Mark's performance was clearly superior during irrelevant error correction, and performance of the remaining 5 participants (Hayley, Becky, Kara, Maisy, and Seth) was similar in both conditions. Thus, all participants showed improvement in reading performance even when they practiced irrelevant words, and most participants (6 of 9) did just as well or better practicing irrelevant rather than relevant words. These results suggest that the

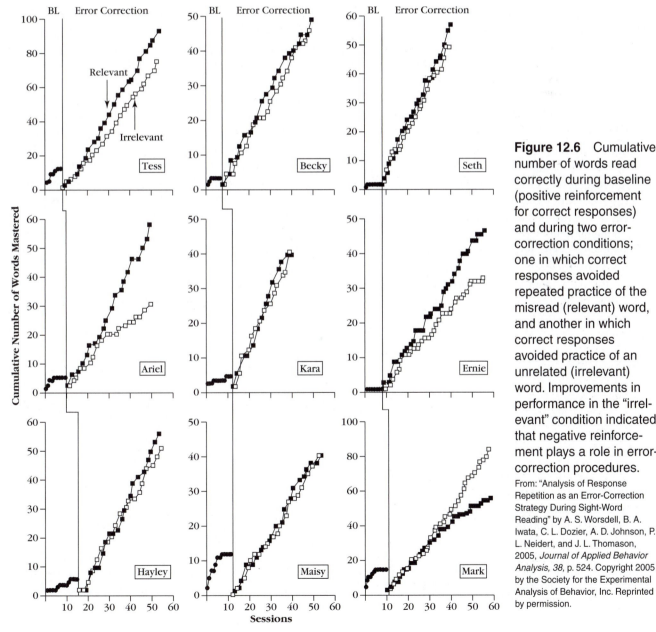

Figure 12.6 Cumulative number of words read correctly during baseline (positive reinforcement for correct responses) and during two error-correction conditions; one in which correct responses avoided repeated practice of the misread (relevant) word, and another in which correct responses avoided practice of an unrelated (irrelevant) word. Improvements in performance in the "irrelevant" condition indicated that negative reinforcement plays a role in error-correction procedures.

From: "Analysis of Response Repetition as an Error-Correction Strategy During Sight-Word Reading" by A. S. Worsdell, B. A. Iwata, C. L. Dozier, A. D. Johnson, P. L. Neidert, and J. L. Thomason, 2005, *Journal of Applied Behavior Analysis, 38,* p. 524. Copyright 2005 by the Society for the Experimental Analysis of Behavior, Inc. Reprinted by permission.

success of many remedial (error-correction) procedures may be due at least in part to negative reinforcement.

Acquisition and Maintenance of Problem Behavior

Well-designed instructional procedures maintain a high degree of on-task behavior and lead to improved learning. Occasionally, however, the presentation of task demands may function as an EO for escape behavior due to the difficult or repetitive nature of the work requirements. Initial forms of escape may include lack of attention or mild forms of disruption. To the extent that positive reinforcement for compliance is less than optimal, attempts to escape may persist and may even escalate to more severe forms of problem behavior. In fact, research on the assessment and treatment of problem behaviors has shown that escape from task demands is a common source of negative reinforcement for property destruction, aggression, and even self-injury. This topic is covered more extensively in Chapter 24 and is included here as well because of its special relevance to negative reinforcement.

O'Reilly (1995) conducted an assessment of a person's episodic aggressive behavior. The participant was an adult with severe mental retardation who attended a vocational day program. To determine whether aggressive behavior was maintained by positive versus negative reinforcement, O'Reilly observed the participant under two conditions, which were alternated in a multielement design. In one condition (attention), a therapist ignored the participant (EO) except to deliver reprimands following aggression (positive reinforcement). In the second condition (demand), a therapist presented difficult tasks to the participant (EO) and briefly terminated the trial following aggression (negative reinforcement).

As Figure 12.7 shows, aggressive behavior occurred more often in the demand condition, indicating that it was maintained by negative reinforcement. Because anecdotal reports suggested that the participant also was more likely to be aggressive following nights when he had not slept well, the data for both conditions were further divided based on whether the participant slept for more or less than 5 hours the previous night. The highest rates of aggression occurred following sleep deprivation. These data are particularly interesting in that they illustrate the influence of two antecedent events on behavior maintained by negative reinforcement: Work tasks functioned as EOs for escape but even more so in the absence of sleep.

Behavioral Replacement Strategies

Problem behaviors maintained by negative reinforcement can be treated in a number of ways. One strategy is to strengthen a more socially appropriate replacement behavior using negative reinforcement, as illustrated in a study by Durand and Carr (1987). After determining that the "stereotypic" behaviors of four special education students were maintained by escape from task demands, the authors taught the students an alternative response ("Help me"), which was followed by assistance with the task at hand. As can be seen in Figure 12.8, all students engaged in moderate-to-high levels of stereotypy during baseline. After being taught to use the phrase "Help me," the students began to exhibit that behavior, and their stereotypy decreased.

Results of the Durand and Carr (1987) study showed that an undesirable behavior could be replaced with a desirable one; however, the replacement behavior might be considered less than ideal because it did not necessarily facilitate better task performance. This was shown

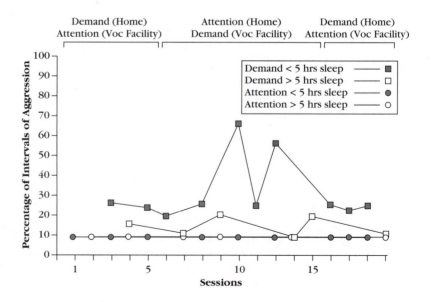

Figure 12.7 Data showing that the effects of work tasks as EOs for escape-maintained aggression by an adult male with severe mental retardation were exacerbated by sleep deprivation.

From "Functional Analysis and Treatment of Escape-Maintained Aggression Correlated with Sleep Deprivation" by M. F. O'Reilly, 1995, *Journal of Applied Behavior Analysis, 28,* p. 226. Copyright 1995 by the Society for the Experimental Analysis of Behavior, Inc. Reprinted by permission.

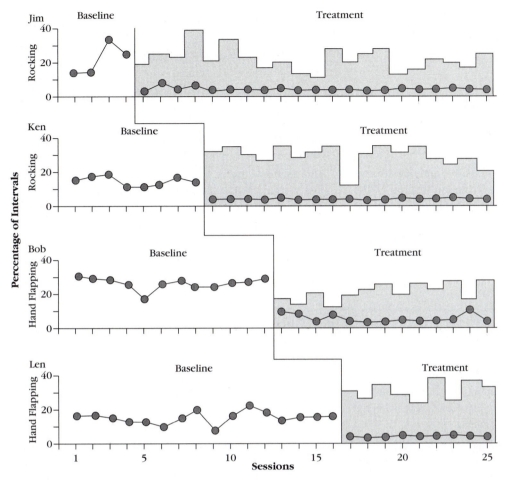

Figure 12.8 Percentage of intervals of stereotypic behaviors maintained by escape from task demands of four special education students during baseline and treatment in which the students were taught an alternative response ("Help me") to attain assistance with the task at hand. Shaded bars show students' use of the "Help me" response.

From "Social Influences on 'Self-Stimulatory' Behavior: Analysis and Treatment Application" by V. M. Durand and E. G. Carr, E. G., 1987, *Journal of Applied Behavior Analysis, 20,* 128. Copyright 1987 by the Society for the Experimental Analysis of Behavior, Inc. Reprinted by permission.

in a subsequent study by Marcus and Vollmer (1995). After collecting baseline data on a young girl's compliant and disruptive behavior, the authors compared the effects of two treatments in a reversal design. In one condition, which was called DNR (differential negative reinforcement) communication, the girl was given a brief break from the task when she said "Finished." In the second condition, called DNR compliance, the girl was given a break after complying with an instruction (the criterion for a break was later increased to compliance with three instructions). The results of this comparison (see Figure 12.9) showed that both treatments produced

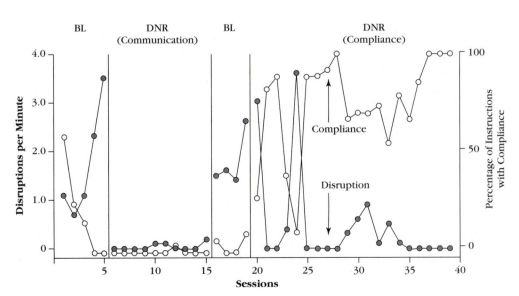

Figure 12.9 Disruptions and compliance by a 5-year-old girl during baseline and two differential negative reinforcement conditions.

From "Effects of Differential Negative Reinforcement on Disruption and Compliance" by B. A. Marcus and T. R. Vollmer, 1995, *Journal of Applied Behavior Analysis, 28,* p. 230. Copyright 1995 by the Society for the Experimental Analysis of Behavior, Inc. Reprinted by permission.

marked reductions in disruptive behavior. However, only the DNR compliance condition produced an increase in task performance.

Ethical Considerations in the Use of Negative Reinforcement

Ethical concerns about the use of positive and negative reinforcement are similar and arise from the severity of the antecedent event (EO) that occasions behavior. Most EOs for behavior maintained by positive reinforcement can be characterized as deprivation states, which, if severe, can constitute undue restriction of rights. By contrast, most EOs for behavior maintained by negative reinforcement can be viewed as aversive events. Extremely noxious events, when presented as antecedent stimuli, cannot be justified as part of a typical behavior change program.

Another concern with negative reinforcement is that the presence of aversive stimuli can itself generate behaviors that compete with the acquisition of desired behavior (Hutchinson, 1977; Myer, 1971). For example, a socially withdrawn child, when placed in the midst of others, may simply scream and run away instead of playing with the peers, and running away is incompatible with social interaction. Finally, undesirable side effects typically associated with punishment (see Chapter 14) might also be observed when implementing behavior change programs based on negative reinforcement.

 Summary

Definition of Negative Reinforcement

1. Negative reinforcement involves the termination, reduction, or postponement of a stimulus contingent on the occurrence of a response, which leads to an increase in the future occurrence of that response.

2. A negative reinforcement contingency involves (a) an establishing operation (EO) in whose presence escape is reinforcing, (b) a discriminative stimulus (S^D) in whose presence a response is more likely to be reinforced, (c) the response that produces reinforcement, and (d) termination of the event that served as the EO.

3. Positive and negative reinforcement are similar in that both lead to an increase in responding; they differ in that positive reinforcement involves contingent stimulus presentation, whereas negative reinforcement involves contingent stimulus termination.

4. Negative reinforcement and punishment differ in that (a) negative reinforcement involves contingent stimulus termination, whereas punishment involves contingent stimulation, and (b) negative reinforcement leads to an increase in responding, whereas punishment leads to a decrease in responding.

Escape and Avoidance Contingencies

5. An escape contingency is one in which responding terminates an ongoing stimulus. An avoidance contingency is one in which responding delays or prevents the presentation of a stimulus.

6. In discriminated avoidance, responding in the presence of a signal prevents stimulus presentation; in free-operant avoidance, responding at any time prevents stimulus presentation.

Characteristics of Negative Reinforcement

7. Any response that successfully terminates aversive stimulation will be strengthened; as a result, a wide range of behaviors may be acquired and maintained by negative reinforcement.

8. Negative reinforcement may play an important role in the development of academic skills, but it also can account for the development of disruptive or dangerous behavior.

9. Unconditioned negative reinforcers are stimuli whose removal strengthens behavior in the absence of prior learning. Conditioned negative reinforcers are stimuli whose removal strengthens behavior as a result of previous pairing with other negative reinforcers.

10. Social negative reinforcement involves stimulus termination through the action of another person. Automatic negative reinforcement involves stimulus termination as a direct result of a response.

11. Identification of negative reinforcers requires the specification of the stimulus conditions in effect prior to and following responding.

12. In general, negative reinforcement for a given response will be more effective when (a) the stimulus change immediately follows the occurrence of the target response, (b) the magnitude of reinforcement is large, (c) the target response consistently produces escape from or postponement of the EO, and (d) reinforcement is unavailable for competing responses.

Applications of Negative Reinforcement

13. Although negative reinforcement is a fundamental principle of learning that has been studied extensively in basic research, applied behavior analysis has heavily

emphasized the use of positive reinforcement over negative reinforcement.

14. Applied researchers have explored the therapeutic uses of negative reinforcement in treating pediatric feeding problems.

15. Improvements in student performance as a result of error correction that involve repeating a learning trial, having the student practice correct performance, or giving the student additional work may be a function of negative reinforcement.

16. The presentation of task demands during instruction may function as an EO for escape; initial forms of escape may include lack of attention or mild forms of disruption. To the extent that positive reinforcement for compliance is less than optimal, escape behaviors may persist and may even escalate.

17. One strategy for treating problem behaviors maintained by negative reinforcement is to strengthen a more socially appropriate replacement behavior through negative reinforcement.

Ethical Considerations in the Use of Negative Reinforcement

18. Ethical concerns about the use of positive and negative reinforcement are similar and arise from the severity of the antecedent event (EO) that occasions behavior. Most EOs for behavior maintained by negative reinforcement can be viewed as aversive events. Extremely noxious events, when presented as antecedent stimuli, cannot be justified as part of a typical behavior change program.

19. Another concern with negative reinforcement is that the presence of aversive stimuli can itself generate behaviors that compete with the acquisition of desired behavior.

CHAPTER 13

Schedules of Reinforcement

Key Terms

adjunctive behaviors
alternative schedule (alt)
chained schedule of
 reinforcement (chain)
compound schedule of
 reinforcement
concurrent schedule (conc)
conjunctive schedule (conj)
continuous reinforcement (CRF)
differential reinforcement of
 diminishing rates (DRD)

differential reinforcement of high
 rates (DRH)
differential reinforcement of low
 rates (DRL)
fixed interval (FI)
fixed ratio (FR)
intermittent schedule of
 reinforcement (INT)
limited hold
matching law
mixed schedule (mix)

multiple schedule (mult)
postreinforcement pause
progressive schedule of
 reinforcement
ratio strain
schedule of reinforcement
schedule thinning
tandem schedule (tand)
variable interval (VI)
variable ratio (VR)

Behavior Analyst Certification Board® BCBA® & BCABA® Behavior Analyst Task List©, Third Edition

Content Area 9: Behavior Change Procedures	
9-2 (b)	Use appropriate parameters and schedules of reinforcement.
9-6	Use differential reinforcement.
9-24	Use the matching law and recognize factors influencing choice.

A **schedule of reinforcement** is a rule that describes a contingency of reinforcement, those environmental arrangements that determine conditions by which behaviors will produce reinforcement. Continuous reinforcement and extinction provide the boundaries for all other schedules of reinforcement. A schedule of **continuous reinforcement (CRF)** provides reinforcement for each occurrence of behavior. For example, a teacher using a continuous schedule of reinforcement would praise a student each time she identified a sight word correctly. Examples of behaviors that tend to produce continuous reinforcement include turning on a water faucet (water comes out), answering a telephone after it rings (a voice is heard), and putting money into a vending machine (a product is obtained). During extinction (EXT), no occurrence of the behavior produces reinforcement. (For a detailed description of extinction, see Chapter 21.)

Intermittent Reinforcement

Between continuous reinforcement and extinction many **intermittent schedules of reinforcement (INT)** are possible in which some, but not all, occurrences of the behavior are reinforced. Only selected occurrences of behavior produce reinforcement with an intermittent schedule of reinforcement. CRF is used to strengthen behavior, primarily during the initial stages of learning new behaviors. Applied behavior analysts use intermittent reinforcement to maintain established behaviors.

Maintenance of Behavior

Maintenance of behavior refers to a lasting change in behavior. Regardless of the type of behavior change technique employed or the degree of success during treatment, applied behavior analysts must be concerned with sustaining gains after terminating a treatment program. For example, Mary is in the seventh grade and taking French, her first foreign language class. After a few weeks, the teacher informs Mary's parents that she is failing the course. The teacher believes that Mary's problems in French have resulted from lack of daily language practice and study. The parents and teacher decide that Mary will record a tally on a chart kept on the family bulletin board each evening that she studies French for 30 minutes. Mary's parents praise her practice and study accomplishments and offer encouragement. During a follow-up meeting 3 weeks later, the parents and teacher decide that Mary has done so well that the tally procedure can be stopped. Unfortunately, a few days later Mary is once again falling behind in French.

A successful program was developed to establish daily French language practice. However, gains did not maintain after removing the tally procedure. The parents and the teacher did not establish intermittent reinforcement procedures. Let us review what happened and what could have happened. Continuous reinforcement was used correctly to develop daily study behavior. However, after the study behavior was established and the tally procedure removed, the parents should have continued to praise and encourage daily practice and gradually offer fewer encouragements. The parents could have praised Mary's accomplishments after every second day of daily practice, then every fourth day, then once per week, and so on. With the intermittent praise, Mary might have continued daily practice after removing the tally procedure.

Progression to Naturally Occurring Reinforcement

A major goal of most behavior change programs is the development of naturally occurring activities, stimuli, or events to function as reinforcement. It is more desirable for people to read because they like to read, rather than to obtain contrived reinforcement from a teacher or parent; to engage in athletics for the enjoyment of the activity, rather than for a grade or because of a physician's directive; to help around the house for the personal satisfaction it brings, rather than to earn an allowance. Intermittent reinforcement is usually necessary for the progression to naturally occurring reinforcement. Even though some individuals spend hours each day practicing a musical instrument because they enjoy the activity, chances are good that this persistent behavior developed gradually. At first the beginning music student needs a great deal of reinforcement to continue the activity: "You really practiced well today," "I can't believe how well you played," "Your mother told me you received a first place in the contest—that's super!" These social consequences are paired with other consequences from teachers, family members, and peers. As the student develops more proficiency in music, the outside consequences occur less frequently, intermittently. Eventually, the student spends long periods making music without receiving reinforcement from others because making music has itself become a reinforcer for doing that activity.

Some might explain the transition of our music student from an "externally reinforced person" to a "self-reinforced musician" as the development of intrinsic motivation, which seems to imply that something inside the person is responsible for maintaining the behavior. This view is incorrect from a behavioral standpoint. Applied behavior analysts describe intrinsic motivation as reinforcement that is received by manipulating the physical environment. Some individuals ride bicycles, go backpacking, read, write, or help others because manipulations of the environment provide reinforcement for engaging in those activities.

Defining Basic Intermittent Schedules of Reinforcement

Ratio and Interval Schedules

Applied behavior analysts directly or indirectly embed ratio and interval intermittent schedules of reinforcement in most treatment programs, especially ratio schedules (Lattal & Neef, 1996). Ratio schedules require a number of responses before one response produces reinforcement. If the ratio requirement for a behavior is 10 correct responses, only the 10th correct response produces reinforcement. Interval schedules require an elapse of time before a response produces reinforcement. If the interval requirement is 5 minutes, reinforcement is provided contingent on the first correct response that occurs after 5 minutes has elapsed since the last reinforced response.

Ratio schedules require a number of responses to be emitted for reinforcement; an elapse of time does not change the number contingency. The participant's response rate, however, determines the rate of reinforcement. The more quickly the person completes the ratio requirement, the sooner reinforcement will occur. Conversely, interval schedules require an elapse of time before a single response produces reinforcement. The total number of responses emitted on an interval schedule is irrelevant to when and how often the reinforcer will be delivered. Emitting a high rate of response during an interval schedule does not increase the rate of reinforcement. Reinforcement is contingent only on the occurrence of one response after the required time has elapsed. The availability of reinforcement is time-controlled with interval schedules, and rate of reinforcement is "self-controlled" with ratio schedules, meaning that the more quickly the individual completes the ratio requirement, the sooner reinforcement will occur.

Fixed and Variable Schedules

Applied behavior analysts can arrange ratio and interval schedules to deliver reinforcement as a fixed or a variable contingency. With a fixed schedule, the response ratio or the time requirement remains constant. With a variable schedule, the response ratio or the time requirement can change from one reinforced response to another. The combinations of ratio or interval and fixed or variable contingencies define the four basic schedules of intermittent reinforcement: fixed ratio, variable ratio, fixed interval, and variable interval.

The following sections define the four basic schedules of intermittent reinforcement, provide examples of each schedule, and present some well-established schedule effects derived from basic research.

Fixed Ratio Defined

A **fixed ratio (FR)** schedule of reinforcement requires the completion of a number of responses to produce a reinforcer. For example, every fourth correct (or target) response produces reinforcement on an FR 4 schedule. An FR 15 schedule means that 15 responses are required to produce reinforcement. Skinner (1938) conceptualized each ratio requirement as a response unit. Accordingly, the response unit produces the reinforcer, not just the last response of the ratio.

Some business and industrial tasks are paid on an FR schedule (e.g., piecework). A worker might receive a pay credit after completing a specified number of tasks (e.g., assembling 15 pieces of equipment or picking a box of oranges). A student might receive either a happy face after learning 5 new sight words or a certain number of points after completing 10 math problems.

De Luca and Holborn (1990) reported a comparison of obese and nonobese children's rate of pedaling an exercise bicycle under baseline and FR schedules of reinforcement. The baseline and FR conditions used the same duration of exercise. After establishing a stable rate of pedaling during baseline, De Luca and Holborn introduced an FR schedule that matched the rate of reinforcement produced during baseline. All participants increased their rate of pedaling with the introduction of the FR schedule.

Fixed Ratio Schedule Effects

Consistency of Performance

FR schedules produce a typical pattern of responding: (a) After the first response of the ratio requirement, the participant completes the required responses with little hesitation between responses; and (b) a **postreinforcement pause** follows reinforcement (i.e., the participant does not respond for a period of time following reinforcement). The size of the ratio influences the duration of the postreinforcement pause: Large ratio requirements produce long pauses; small ratios produce short pauses.

Rate of Response

FR schedules often produce high rates of response. Quick responding on FR schedules maximizes the delivery of reinforcement because the quicker the rate of response, the greater the rate of reinforcement. People work rapidly with a fixed ratio because they receive reinforcement with the completion of the ratio requirements. Computer keyboarders (typists) who contract their services usually work on an FR schedule. They receive a specified amount for the work contracted. A typist with a 25-page manuscript to complete is likely to type at the maximum rate. The sooner the manuscript is typed, the sooner payment is received, and the more work the typist can complete in a day.

The size of the ratio can influence the rate of response on FR schedules. To a degree, the larger the ratio requirement, the higher the rate of response. A teacher could reinforce every third correct answer to arithmetic facts. With this ratio requirement, the student might complete 12 problems within the specified time, producing reinforcement four times. The student might complete more problems in less time if the teacher arranged reinforcement contingent on 12 correct answers rather than 3. The higher ratio is likely to produce a higher rate of response. The rate of response decreases, however, if the ratio requirements are too large. The maximum ratio is determined in part by the participant's past FR history of reinforcement, motivating operations, the quality of the reinforcer, and the procedures that change the ratio requirements. For example, if ratio requirements are raised gradually over an extended period of time, extremely high ratio requirements can be reached.

Figure 13.1 summarizes the schedule effects typically produced by FR schedules of reinforcement.

Variable Ratio Defined

A **variable ratio (VR)** schedule of reinforcement requires the completion of a variable number of responses to produce a reinforcer. A number representing the average (e.g., mean) number of responses required for reinforcement identifies the VR schedule. For example, with a VR 10 schedule every tenth correct response on the average produces reinforcement. Reinforcement can come after 1 response, 20 responses, 3 responses, 13 responses, or n responses, but the average number of responses required for reinforcement is 10 (e.g., $1 + 20 + 3 + 13 + 18 = 55$; $55/5 = 10$).

The operation of a slot machine, the one-armed bandit, provides a good example of a VR schedule. These machines are programmed to pay off only a certain proportion of the times they are played. A player cannot predict when the next operation of the machine will pay off. The player might win 2 or 3 times in succession and then not win again for 20 or more plays.

De Luca and Holborn (1992) examined the effects of a VR schedule on three obese and three nonobese children's rate of pedaling an exercise bicycle. The children could use the exercise bicycle Monday to Friday during each week of the analysis, but received no encouragement to do so. The participants received the instruction to "exercise as long as you like" to initiate the baseline condition. De Luca and Holborn introduced the VR schedule of reinforcement after establishing a stable baseline rate of pedaling. They calculated the baseline mean number of pedal revolutions per minute and programmed the first VR contingency at approximately 15% faster pedaling than the baseline mean. The children received points on

---

Definition: Reinforcement delivered contingent on emission of a specified number of responses.

Schedule Effects:
After reinforcement a postreinforcement pause occurs. After the pause the ratio requirement is completed with a high rate of response and very little hesitation between responses. The size of the ratio influences both the pause and the rate.

Stylized Graphic Curve of Cumulative Responses:

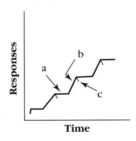

a = postreinforcement pause
b = high rate of response "run"
c = reinforcer delivered upon emission of nth response

Figure 13.1 Summary of FR schedule effects during ongoing reinforcement.

the VR schedule to exchange for backup reinforcers. De Luca and Holborn increased the VR schedule in two additional increments by approximately 15% per increment. All participants had systematic increases in their rate of pedaling with each VR value, meaning that the larger the variable ratio, the higher the rate of response. De Luca and Holborn reported that the VR schedule produced higher rates of response than did the FR schedule in their previous study (De Luca & Holborn, 1990).

Figure 13.2 presents the participants' performances under baseline and VR (i.e., VR ranges 70 to 85, 90 to 115, 100 to 130) conditions.

Student behaviors usually produce reinforcement following the completion of variable ratios. Usually a student cannot predict when the teacher will call on him to give an answer, and receive reinforcement. Good grades, awards, promotions—all may come after an unpredictable number of responses. And in checking

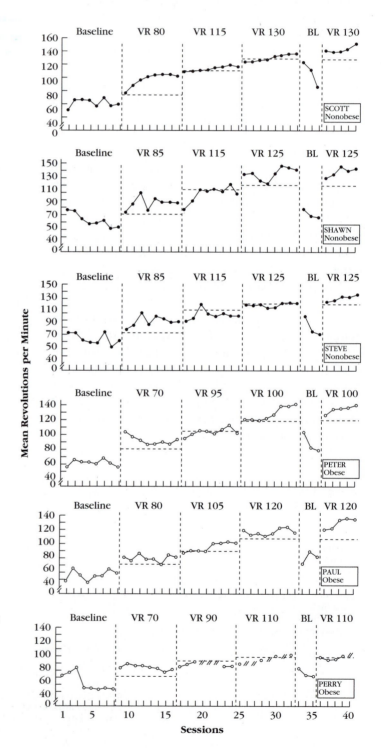

Figure 13.2 Mean revolutions per minute during baseline, VR 1 (VR range, 70 to 85), VR 2 (VR range 90 to 115), VR 3 (VR range 100 to 130), return to baseline, and return to VR 3 phases for obese and nonobese subjects.

From "Effects of a Variable-Ratio Reinforcement Schedule with Changing Criteria on Exercise in Obese and Nonobese Boys" by R. V. De Luca and S. W. Holborn, 1992, *Journal of Applied Behavior Analysis, 25* p. 674. Copyright 1992 by the Society for the Experimental Analysis of Behavior, Inc. Reprinted by permission.

seatwork, the teacher might reinforce a student's work after the completion of 10 tasks, another student's work after 3 tasks, and so on.

Variable Ratio Schedule Effects

Consistency of Performance

VR schedules produce consistent, steady rates of response. They typically do not produce a postreinforcement pause, as do FR schedules. Perhaps the absence of pauses in responding is due to the absence of information about when the next response will produce reinforcement. Responding remains steady because the next response may produce reinforcement.

Rate of Response

Like the FR schedule, the VR schedule tends to produce a quick rate of response. Also similar to the FR schedule, the size of the ratio influences the rate of response. To a degree, the larger the ratio requirement, the higher the rate of response. Again like FR schedules, when variable ratio requirements are thinned gradually over an extended period of time, participants will respond to extremely high ratio requirements. Figure 13.3 summarizes the schedule effects typically produced by VR schedules of reinforcement.

Variable Ratio Schedules in Applied Settings

Basic researchers use computers to select and program VR schedules of reinforcement. VR schedules used in applied settings are seldom implemented with a planned and systematic approach. In other words, the reinforcer is delivered by chance, hit or miss in most interventions. This nonsystematic delivery of reinforcement is not an effective use of VR schedules. Teachers can select and preplan VR schedules that approximate the VR schedules used in basic research. For example, teachers can plan variable ratios by (a) selecting a maximum ratio for a given activity (e.g., 15 responses) and (b) using a table of random numbers to produce the specific variable ratios for the schedule of reinforcement. A table of random numbers might produce the following sequence of ratios: 8, 1, 1, 14, 3, 10, 14, 15, and 6, producing a VR 8 schedule of reinforcement (on the average each 8th response produces the reinforcer) with the ratios ranging from 1 to 15 responses.

Teachers can apply the following VR procedures as individual or group contingencies of reinforcement for academic or social behavior:

Tic-Tac-Toe VR Procedure

1. The teacher establishes a maximum number for the individual student or group. The larger the maximum number selected, the greater the odds against meeting the contingency. For example, 1 chance out of 100 has less chance of being selected than 1 chance out of 20.

2. The teacher gives the individual or group a tic-tac-toe grid.

3. Students fill in each square of the grid with a number no greater than the maximum number. For example, if the maximum number is 30, the score sheet might look like this:

1	20	13
3	5	30
7	11	6

Definition: Reinforcer is delivered after the emission of a variable number of responses.

Schedule Effects: Ratio requirements are completed with a very high rate of response and little hesitation between responses. Postreinforcement pauses are not a characteristic of the VR schedule. Rate of response is influenced by the size of the ratio requirements.

Stylized Graphic Curve of Cumulative Responses:

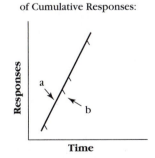

a = high, steady rate of responding
b = reinforcement delivered after a varying number of required responses are emitted

Figure 13.3   Summary of VR schedule effects during ongoing reinforcement.

4. The teacher fills a box or some other type of container with numbered slips of paper (with numbers no higher than the maximum number). Each number should be included several times; for example, five 1s, five 2s, five 3s.

5. Contingent on the occurrence of the target behavior, students withdraw one slip of paper from the box. If the number on the paper corresponds with a number on the tic-tac-toe sheet, the students mark out that number on the grid.

6. The reinforcer is delivered when students have marked out three numbers in a row—horizontally, vertically, or diagonally.

For example, a student might withdraw one slip of paper for each homework assignment completed. Selecting an activity from the class job board (e.g., teacher's helper, collecting milk money, running the projector) could serve as the consequence for marking out three numbers in a row.

Classroom Lottery VR Procedure

1. Students write their names on index cards after successfully completing assigned tasks.

2. Students put signature cards into a box located on the teacher's desk.

3. After an established interval of time (e.g., 1 week), the teacher draws a signature card from the box and declares that student the winner. The lottery can have first, second, and third place, or any number of winners. The more cards students earn, the greater is the chance that one of their cards will be picked.

Teachers have used classroom lotteries with a variety of student accomplishments, such as nonassigned book reading. For example, for each book read, students write their names and the titles of the book they have read on a card. Every 2 weeks the teacher picks one card from the box and gives the winning student a new book. To make the book an especially desirable consequence, the teacher lets students earn the privilege of returning the book to the school, inscribed with the student's name, class, and date (e.g., *Brian Lee, fifth grade, donated this book to the High Street Elementary School Library on May 22, 2007*).

Desk Calendar VR Procedure

1. Students receive desk calendars with loose-leaf date pages secured to the calendar base.

2. The teacher removes the loose-leaf date pages from the calendar base.

3. The teacher establishes a maximum ratio for the students.

4. The teacher numbers index cards consecutively from 1 to the maximum ratio. Multiple cards are included for each number (e.g., five 1s, five 2s). If a large average ratio is desired, the teacher includes more large numbers; for small average ratios, the teacher uses smaller numbers.

5. The teacher uses a paper punch to punch holes in the index cards for attaching the cards to the calendar base.

6. The teacher or student shuffles the index cards to quasi-randomize the order and attaches the index cards to a calendar base face down.

7. Students produce their own VR schedules by turning over one index card at a time. After meeting that ratio requirement, students flip the second card to produce the next ratio, and so on.

Students can use the desk calendar base to program VR schedules for most curriculum area (e.g., arithmetic facts). For example, after receiving an arithmetic worksheet, the student flips the first card. It has a 5 written on it. After completing five problems, she holds up her hand to signal her teacher that she has completed the ratio requirement. The teacher checks the student's answers, provides feedback, and presents the consequence for correct problems. The student flips the second card; the ratio requirement is 1. After completing that single problem, she receives another consequence and flips the third card. This time the ratio is 14. The cycle continues until all of the cards in the stack are used. New cards can then be added or old cards reshuffled to create a new sequence of numbers. The average of the numbers does not change in the reshuffling.

Fixed Interval Schedules

A **fixed interval (FI)** schedule of reinforcement provides reinforcement for the first response following a fixed duration of time. With an FI 3-minute schedule, the first response following the elapse of 3 minutes produces the reinforcer. A common procedural misunderstanding with the FI schedule is to assume that the elapse of time alone is sufficient for the delivery of a reinforcer, assuming that the reinforcer is delivered at the end of each fixed interval of time. However, more time than the fixed interval can elapse between reinforced responses. The reinforcer is available after the fixed time interval has elapsed, and it remains available until the first response. When the first response occurs sometime after the elapse of a fixed interval, that response is immediately reinforced, and the timing of another fixed interval is usually started with the delivery of the reinforcer. This FI cycle is repeated until the end of the session.

Actual examples of FI schedules in everyday life are difficult to find. However, some situations do approximate and in reality function as FI schedules. For example, mail is often delivered close to a fixed time each day. An individual can make many trips to the mailbox to look for mail, but only the first trip to the mailbox following the mail delivery will produce reinforcement. Many textbook examples of FI schedules, such as the mail example, do not meet the definition of an FI schedule; but the examples do appear similar to an FI schedule. For example, receiving a paycheck as wages for work by the hour, day, week, or month is contingent on the first response on payday that produces the paycheck. Of course, receiving the paycheck requires many responses during the interval that eventually lead to receiving the paycheck. In a true FI schedule, responses during the interval do not influence reinforcement.

FI schedules are relatively easy to use in applied settings. A teacher could make reinforcement available on an FI 2-minute schedule for correct answers on an arithmetic worksheet. The teacher or student could use an electronic timer with a countdown function to signal the elapse of the 2-minute interval. The student's first correct answer following the interval produces reinforcement, and then the teacher resets the timer for another 2-minute interval. Similarly, the teacher could use small timing instruments such as the Gentle Reminder (dan@gentlereminder.com) and MotivAiders (www.habitchange.com) that vibrate to signal the elapse of an interval.

Fixed Interval Schedule Effects

Consistency of Performance

FI schedules typically produce a postreinforcement pause in responding during the early part of the interval. An initially slow but accelerating rate of response is evident toward the end of the interval, usually reaching a maximum rate just before delivery of the reinforcer. This gradually accelerating rate of response toward the end of the interval is called an *FI scallop* because of the rounded curves that are shown on a cumulative graph (see Figure 13.4).

FI postreinforcement pause and scallop effects can be seen in many everyday situations. When college students are assigned a term paper, they typically do not rush to the library and start to work on the paper immediately. More often they wait a few days or weeks before starting to work. However, as the due date approaches, their work on the assignment increases in an accelerating fashion, and many are typing the final draft just before class. Cramming for a midterm or final examination is another example of the FI scallop effect.

These examples with the reinforcement pause and scallop effects appear to be produced by FI schedules of reinforcement. They are not, however, because like the paycheck example, college students must complete many responses during the interval to produce the term paper or a good grade on the examinations, and the term paper and examinations have deadlines. With FI schedules, responses during the interval are irrelevant, and FI schedules have no deadlines for the response.

Why does an FI schedule produce a characteristic pause and scallop effect? After adjustment to an FI schedule, participants learn (a) to discriminate the elapse of time and (b) that responses emitted right after a reinforced response are never reinforced. Therefore, extinction during the early part of the interval might account for the postreinforcement pause. The effects of FI and FR schedules of reinforcement are similar in that both schedules produce postreinforcement pauses. However, it is important to recognize the different characteristics of behavior that emerge under each schedule. Responses under

Definition: The first correct response after a designated and constant amount of time produces the reinforcer.

Schedule Effects: FI schedules generate slow to moderate rates of responding with a pause in responding following reinforcement. Responding begins to accelerate toward the end of the interval.

Stylized Graphic Curve of Cumulative Responses:

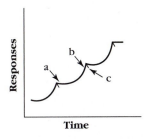

a = postreinforcement pause
b = increase in response rates as interval progresses and reinforcer becomes available
c = reinforcer delivered contingent on first correct response after interval

Figure 13.4   Summary of FI schedule effects during ongoing reinforcement.

an FR schedule are emitted at a consistent rate until completing the ratio requirement, whereas responses under an FI schedule begin at a slow rate and accelerate toward the end of each interval.

Rate of Responding

Overall, FI schedules tend to produce a slow to moderate rates of response. The duration of the time interval influences the postreinforcement pause and the rate of response; to a degree, the larger the fixed interval requirement, the longer the postreinforcement pause and the lower the overall rate of response.

Variable Interval Schedules

A **variable interval (VI)** schedule of reinforcement provides reinforcement for the first correct response following the elapse of variable durations of time. The distinguishing feature of VI schedules is that "the intervals between reinforcement vary in a random or nearly random order" (Ferster & Skinner, 1957, p. 326). Behavior analysts use the average (i.e., mean) interval of time before the opportunity for reinforcement to describe VI schedules. For example, in a VI 5-minute schedule the average duration of the time intervals between reinforcement and the opportunity for subsequent reinforcement is 5 minutes. The actual time intervals in a VI 5-minute schedule might be 2 minutes, 5 minutes, 3 minutes, 10 minutes, or *n* minutes (or seconds).

An example of VI reinforcement in everyday situations occurs when one person telephones another person whose line is busy. This is a VI schedule because a variable interval of time is necessary for the second person to conclude the telephone conversation and hang up so that another call can be connected. After that interval the first dialing of the second person's number will probably produce an answer (the reinforcer). The number of responses (attempts) does not influence the availability of reinforcement in a VI schedule; no matter how many times the busy number is dialed, the call will not be completed until the line is free. And the time interval is unpredictable in a VI schedule: The busy signal may last for a short or long time.

Variable Interval Schedule Effects

Consistency of Performance

A VI schedule of reinforcement tends to produce a constant, stable rate of response. The slope of the VI schedule on a cumulative graph appears uniform with few pauses in responding (see Figure 13.5). A VI schedule typically produces few hesitations between responses. For example, pop quizzes at unpredictable times tend to occasion more consistent study behavior from students than do quizzes scheduled at fixed intervals of time. Furthermore, students are less apt to engage in competing off-task behaviors during instructional and study periods when a pop quiz is likely. The pop quiz is used often as an example of a VI schedule because the performance effect is similar to a VI performance. The pop quiz does not represent a true VI schedule, however, because of the required responses during the interval, and the deadline for receiving reinforcement.

Rate of Responding

VI schedules of reinforcement tend to produce low to moderate rates of response. Like the FI schedule, the average duration of the time intervals on VI schedules influences the rate of response; to a degree, the larger the average interval, the lower the overall rate of response. Figure 13.5 summarizes the schedule effects typically produced by VI schedules during ongoing reinforcement.

Definition: The first correct response following varying intervals of time produces the reinforcer.

Schedule Effects: A VI schedule generates a slow to moderate response rate that is constant and stable. There are few, if any, post-reinforcement pauses with VI schedules.

Stylized Graphic Curve of Cumulative Responses:

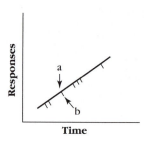

a = steady response rate; few, if any, postreinforcement pauses
b = reinforcer delivered

Figure 13.5   Summary of VI schedule effects during ongoing reinforcement.

Variable Interval Schedules in Applied Settings

Basic researchers use computers to select and program VI schedules of reinforcement, as they do with VR schedules. Teachers seldom apply VI schedules in a planned and systematic way. For example, a teacher might set an electronic countdown timer with varied intervals of time ranging from 1 minute to 10 minutes without any prior plan as to which intervals or which order will be used. This set-them-as-you-go selection of intervals approximates the basic requirements for a VI schedule; however, it is not the most effective way of delivering reinforcement on a VI schedule. A planned, systematic application of varied intervals of time should increase the effectiveness of a VI schedule.

For example, applied behavior analysts can select the maximum time interval, whether in seconds or minutes, that will maintain performance and still be appropriate for the situation. Preferably, applied behavior analysts will use data from a direct assessment to guide the selection of the maximum VI interval, or at the least clinical judgment based on direct observation. Analysts can use a table of random numbers to select the varied intervals between 1 and the maximum interval, and then identify the VI schedule by calculating an average value for the VI schedule. The VI schedule may need adjustments following the selection of time intervals. For example, if a larger average interval of time appears reasonable, the teacher can replace some of the smaller intervals with larger ones. Conversely, if the average appears too large, the teachers can replace some of the higher intervals with smaller ones.

Interval Schedules with a Limited Hold

When a **limited hold** is added to an interval schedule, reinforcement remains available for a finite time following the elapse of the FI or VI interval. The participant will miss the opportunity to receive reinforcement if a targeted response does not occur within the time limit. For example, on an FI 5-minute schedule with a limited hold of 30 seconds, the first correct response following the elapse of 5 minutes is reinforced, but only if the response occurs within 30 seconds after the end of the 5-minute interval. If no response occurs within 30 seconds, the opportunity for reinforcement has been lost and a new interval begins. The abbreviation LH identifies interval schedules using a limited hold (e.g., FI 5-minute LH 30-second, VI 3-minute LH 1-minute). Limited holds with interval schedules typically do not change the overall response characteristics of FI and VI schedules beyond a possible increase in rate of response.

Martens, Lochner, and Kelly (1992) used a VI schedule of social reinforcement to increase the academic engagement of two 8-year-old boys in a third-grade classroom. The classroom teacher reported that the boys had serious off-task behaviors. The experimenter wore an earphone connected to a microcassette recorder containing a 20-second fixed-time cueing tape. The cueing tape was programmed for a VI schedule of reinforcement in which only some of the 20-second intervals provided the opportunity for reinforcement in the form of verbal praise for academic engagement. If the boys were not academically engaged when the VI interval timed out, they lost that opportunity for reinforcement until the next cue. Thus, this VI schedule entailed a very short limited hold for the availability of reinforcement. Following baseline, the experimenter delivered contingent praise on a VI 5-minute or VI 2-minute schedule that alternated daily on a quasi-random basis. Both boys' academic engagement on the VI 5-minute schedule resembled their baseline engagement. Both students had a higher percentage of academic engagement on the VI 2-minute schedule than they had during baseline and VI 5-minute conditions. Figure 13.6 presents percentages of academic engagement across baseline and VI conditions.

Thinning Intermittent Reinforcement

Applied behavior analysts often use one of two procedures for **schedule thinning**. First, they thin an existing schedule by gradually increasing the response ratio or the duration of the time interval. If a student has answered addition facts effectively and responded well to a CRF schedule for two or three sessions, the teacher might thin the reinforcement contingency slowly from one correct addition fact (CRF) to a VR 2 or VR 3 schedule. The student's performance should guide the progression from a dense schedule (i.e., responses produce frequent reinforcement) to a thin schedule (i.e., responses produce less frequent reinforcement). Applied behavior analysts should use small increments of schedule changes during thinning and ongoing evaluation of the learner's performance to adjust the thinning process and avoid the loss of previous improvements.

Second, teachers often use instructions to clearly communicate the schedule of reinforcement, facilitating a smooth transition during the thinning process. Instructions include rules, directions, and signs. Participants do not require an awareness of environmental contingencies for effective intermittent reinforcement, but instructions may enhance the effectiveness of interventions when participants are told what performances produce reinforcement.

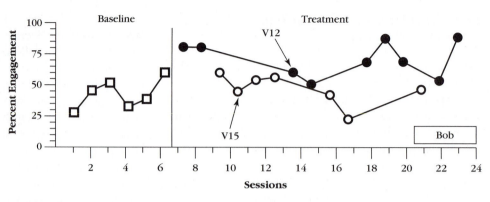

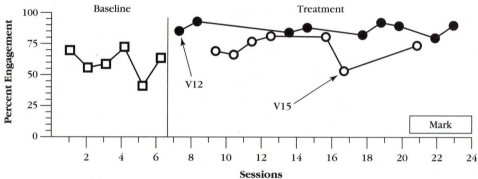

Figure 13.6 Percentage of academic engagement for each child across all conditions in Experiment 2.

From "The Effects of Variable-Interval Reinforcement on Academic Engagement: A Demonstration of Matching Theory" by B. K. Martens, D. G. Lochner, and S. Q. Kelly, 1992, *Journal of Applied Behavior Analysis, 25*, p. 149. Copyright 1992 by the Society for the Experimental Analysis of Behavior, Inc. Reprinted by permission.

Ratio strain can result from abrupt increases in ratio requirements when moving from denser to thinner reinforcement schedules. Common behavioral characteristics associated with ratio strain include avoidance, aggression, and unpredictable pauses in responding. Applied behavior analysts should reduce the ratio requirement when ratio strain is evident. The analyst can again gradually thin ratio requirements after recovering the behavior. Small and gradual increases in ratio requirements help to avoid the development of ratio strain. Ratio strain will occur also when the ratio becomes so large that the reinforcement cannot maintain the response level or the response requirement exceeds the participant's physiological capabilities.

Variations on Basic Intermittent Schedules of Reinforcement

Schedules of Differential Reinforcement of Rates of Responding

Applied behavior analysts frequently encounter behavior problems that result from the rate that people perform certain behaviors. Responding too infrequently, or too often, may be detrimental to social interactions or academic learning. Differential reinforcement provides an intervention for behavior problems associated with rate of response. Differential reinforcement of particular rates of behavior is a variation of ratio schedules. Delivery of the reinforcer is contingent on responses occurring at a rate either higher than or lower than some predetermined criterion. The reinforcement of responses higher than a predetermined criterion is called **differential reinforcement of high rates (DRH).** When responses are reinforced only when they are lower than the criterion, the schedule provides **differential reinforcement of low rates (DRL).** DRH schedules produce a higher rate of responding. DRL schedules produce a lower rate of responding.

Applied behavior analysts use three definitions of DRH and DRL schedules. The first definition states that reinforcement is available only for responses that are separated by a given duration of time. This first definition is sometimes called spaced-responding DRH or spaced-responding DRL. An interresponse time (IRT) identifies the duration of time that occurs between two responses. IRT and rate of response are functionally related. Long IRTs produce low rates of responding; short IRTs produce high rates of responding. Responding on a DRH schedule produces reinforcement whenever a response occurs before a time criterion has elapsed. If the time criterion is 30 seconds, the participant's response produces reinforcement only when the IRT is 30 seconds or less.

Under the DRL schedule, a response produces reinforcement when it occurs after a time criterion has elapsed. If the stated DRL time criterion is again 30 seconds, a response produces reinforcement only when the IRT is 30 seconds or greater.

This first definition of DRH and DRL as IRT schedules of reinforcement has been used almost exclusively in laboratory settings. There are two apparent reasons for its lack of application in applied settings: (a) Most applied settings do not have sufficient automated equipment to measure IRT and to deliver reinforcement using an IRT criterion; and (b) reinforcement is delivered usually, but not necessarily, following each response that meets the IRT criterion. Such frequent reinforcement would disrupt student activity in most instructional settings. However, with increased use of computers for tutorial and academic response practice, opportunities increasingly should become available for using IRT-based schedules of reinforcement to accelerate or decelerate academic responding. Computers can monitor the pauses between academic responses and provide consequences for each response meeting the IRT criterion, with little disruption in instructional activity.

Based on the laboratory procedures for programming DRL schedules presented previously, Deitz (1977) labeled and described two additional procedures for using differential reinforcement of rates of responding in applied settings: full-session DRH or DRL and interval DRH or DRL. Deitz initially used the full-session and interval procedures as a DRL intervention for problem behaviors. The full-session and interval procedures, however, apply also for DRH.

A DRH full-session schedule provides reinforcement if the total number of responses during the session meets or exceeds a number criterion. If the participant emits fewer than the specified number of responses during the session, the behavior is not reinforced. The DRL full-session schedule is procedurally the same as the DRH schedule, except reinforcement is provided for responding at or below the criterion limit. If the participant emits more than the specified number of responses during the session, reinforcement is not delivered.

The interval definition for DRH and DRL schedules states that reinforcement is available only for responses that occur at a minimum or better rate of response over short durations of time during the session. To apply an interval DRH schedule, the applied behavior analyst organizes the instructional session into equal intervals of time and dispenses a reinforcer at the end of each interval when the student emits a number of responses equal to, or greater than, a number criterion. The interval DRL schedule is procedurally like the DRH interval schedule, except that reinforcement is provided for responding at or below the criterion limit.

The **differential reinforcement of diminishing rates (DRD)** schedule provides reinforcement at the end of a predetermined time interval when the number of responses is less than a criterion that is gradually decreased across time intervals based on the individual's performance (e.g., fewer than five responses per 5 minutes, fewer than four responses per 5 minutes, fewer than three responses per 5 minutes, etc.). Deitz and Repp (1973) used a group DRD contingency to reduce off-task talking of 15 high school senior girls. They set the first DRD criterion limit at five or fewer occurrences of off-task talking during each 50-minute class session. The DRL criterion limits were then gradually reduced to three or fewer, one or fewer, and finally no responses. The students earned a free Friday class when they kept off-task talking at or below the DRD limit Monday through Thursday.

The previous example of a DRD schedule used an identical procedure as described for the full-session DRL. DRD is also a procedural variation on interval DRL schedules described by Deitz (1977) and Deitz and Repp (1983). The typical procedure for using an interval DRL as an intervention for problem behavior provided reinforcement contingent on emitting one or no responses per brief interval. After the problem behavior stabilizes at the initial criterion, the applied behavior analyst maintains the maximum criterion of one or no response per interval, but increases the duration of the session intervals to further diminish the behavior. Increasing the duration of session intervals continues gradually until the problem behavior achieves a terminal low rate of responding.

Later Deitz and Repp (1983) programmed the interval DRL with a criterion greater than one response per interval, then gradually diminished the maximum number of responses per interval while the duration of the interval remained constant (e.g., fewer than five responses per 5 minutes, fewer than four responses per 5 minutes, fewer than three responses per 5 minutes, etc.). The DRD schedule and the interval DRL schedule that use a maximum number criterion greater than one per interval are different terms for the same procedure. Full-session and interval DRL has a long history of application in applied behavior analysis. (For a detailed description of differential reinforcement of rates of response, see Chapter 22.) DRD offers applied behavior analysts a new, and perhaps improved, label for the interval DRL procedure.

Progressive Schedules of Reinforcement

A **progressive schedule of reinforcement** systematically thins each successive reinforcement opportunity independent of the participant's behavior. Progressive ratio

(PR) and progressive interval (PI) schedules of reinforcement change schedule requirements using (a) arithmetic progressions to add a constant amount to each successive ratio or interval or (b) geometric progressions to add successively a constant proportion of the preceding ratio or interval (Lattal & Neef, 1996). Progressive schedules of reinforcement are often used for reinforcer assessment and behavioral intervention as described in the following sections. (See also Chapter 14.)

Using Progressive Schedules for Reinforcer Assessment

Applied behavior analysts typically use a dense schedule of reinforcement (e.g., CRF) during reinforcer assessment while presenting preferred stimuli to increase or maintain existing behavior. However, Roane, Lerman, and Vorndran (2001) cautioned that "reinforcement effects obtained during typical reinforcer assessments may have limited generality to treatment efficacy when schedule thinning and other complex reinforcement arrangements are used" (p. 146). They made an important clinical point by showing that two reinforcers could be equally effective for dense schedules of reinforcement, but differentially effective when the schedule of reinforcement requires more responses per reinforcement. Progressive schedules of reinforcement provide an assessment procedure for identifying reinforcers that will maintain treatment effects across increasing schedule requirements. During the session, progressive schedules are typically thinned to the "breaking point," when the participant stops responding. Comparing the breaking points and corresponding number of responses associated with each reinforcer can identify relative reinforcement effects.

Using Progressive Schedules for Intervention

Applied behavior analysts have used progressive schedules to develop self-control (e.g., Binder, Dixon, & Ghezzi, 2000; Dixon & Cummins, 2001). For example, Dixon and Holcomb (2000) used a progressive schedule to develop cooperative work behaviors and self-control of six adults dually diagnosed with mental retardation and psychiatric disorders. The adults participated in two groups comprised of three men in Group 1 and three women in Group 2. During a natural baseline condition, the groups received instruction to exchange or share cards to complete a cooperative task of sorting playing cards into piles by categories (i.e., hearts with hearts, etc.). Dixon and Holcomb terminated a natural baseline session for the group when one of the adults quit sorting cards.

The groups received points for working on the card-sorting task during the choice baseline condition and the self-control training condition. Groups exchanged their points earned for items such as soda pop or cassette players, ranging in values from 3 points to 100 points.

During the choice baseline conditions, the group's participants could choose an immediate 3 points before doing the card sorting or a delayed 6 points after sorting the cards. Both groups chose the immediate smaller number of points rather than the larger amount following a delay in reinforcement.

During self-control training, the participants were asked while working on a cooperative task, "Do you want 3 points now, or would you like 6 points after sorting the cards for Z minutes and seconds?" (pp. 612–613). The delay was initially 0 seconds for both groups. The progressive delay to reinforcement ranged from an increase of 60 seconds to 90 seconds following each session that the group performance met the exact criterion for number of seconds of task engagement. The terminal goals for the delay to reinforcement were 490 seconds for Group 1 and 772 seconds for Group 2. Both groups achieved these delay-to-reinforcement goals. Following the introduction of the progressive delay procedure, both groups improved their cooperative work engagement and the self-control necessary to select progressively larger delays to reinforcement that resulted in more points earned. Figure 13.7 shows the performance of both groups of adults during natural baselines, choice baselines, and self-control training conditions.

Compound Schedules of Reinforcement

Applied behavior analysts combine the elements of continuous reinforcement (CRF), the four intermittent schedules of reinforcement (FR, VR, FI, VI), differential reinforcement of various rates of responding (DRH, DRL), and extinction (EXT) to form **compound schedules** of reinforcement. Elements from these basic schedules can occur

- successively or simultaneously;
- with or without discriminative stimuli; and
- as a reinforcement contingency for each element independently, or a contingency formed by the combination of all elements (Ferster & Skinner, 1957).

Concurrent Schedules

A **concurrent schedule (conc)** of reinforcement occurs when (a) two or more contingencies of reinforcement (b) operate independently and simultaneously (c) for two

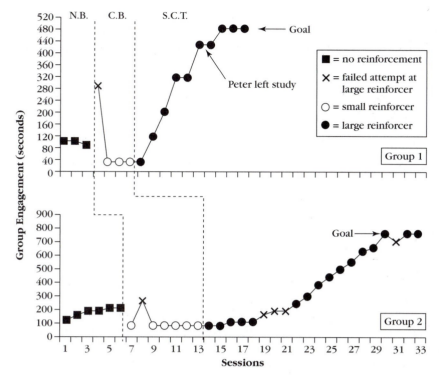

Figure 13.7 Number of seconds of engagement in the concurrent delay activity of cooperative card sorting during natural baseline (N.B.), choice baseline (C.B.), and self-control training (S.C.T.) for each group of participants. Filled circles represent performance at exactly the criterion level, and X data points represent the number of seconds of engagement below the criterion.

From "Teaching Self-Control to Small Groups of Dually Diagnosed Adults" by M. R. Dixon and S. Holcomb, 2000, *Journal of Applied Behavior Analysis, 33*, p. 613. Copyright 1992 by the Society for the Experimental Analysis of Behavior Inc. Reprinted by permission.

or more behaviors. People in the natural environment have opportunities for making choices among concurrently available events. For example, Sharon receives a weekly allowance from her parents contingent on doing daily homework and cello practice. After school she can choose when to do homework and when to practice the cello, and she can distribute her responses between these two simultaneously available schedules of reinforcement. Applied behavior analysts use concurrent schedules for reinforcer assessment and for behavioral interventions.

Using Concurrent Schedules for Reinforcer Assessment

Applied behavior analysts have used concurrent schedules extensively to provide choices during the assessment of consequence preferences and the assessment of response quantities (e.g., force, amplitude) and reinforcer quantities (e.g., rate, duration, immediacy, amount). Responding to concurrent schedules provides a desirable assessment procedure because (a) the participant makes choices, (b) making choices during assessment approximates the natural environment, (c) the schedule is effective in producing hypotheses about potential reinforcers operating in the participant's environment, and (d) these assessments require the participant to choose between stimuli rather than indicating a preference for a given stimulus (Adelinis, Piazza, & Goh, 2001; Neef, Bicard, & Endo, 2001; Piazza et al., 1999).

Roane, Vollmer, Ringdahl, and Marcus (1998) presented 10 items to a participant, 2 items at a time. The participant had 5 seconds to select 1 item by using a reaching response to touch the selected item. As a consequence for the selection, the participant received the item for 20 seconds. The analyst verbally prompted a response if the participant did not respond within 5 seconds, waiting another 5 seconds for the occurrence of a prompted response. Items were eliminated from the assessment (a) if they were not chosen during the first five presentations or (b) if they were chosen two or fewer times during the first seven presentations. The participant made a total of 10 choices among the remaining items. The number of selections out of the 10 opportunities served as a preference index.

Using Concurrent Schedules for Intervention

Applied behavior analysts have used concurrent schedules extensively for improving vocational, academic, and social skills in applied settings (e.g., Cuvo, Lerch, Leurquin, Gaffaney, & Poppen, 1998; Reid, Parsons, Green, & Browning, 2001; Romaniuk et al., 2002). For example, Hoch, McComas, Johnson, Faranda, and Guenther (2002) arranged two concurrent response alternatives for three boys with autism. The boys could play in one setting with a peer or sibling, or play alone in another area. Hoch and colleagues manipulated the duration of access to toys (i.e., reinforcer magnitude) and preference (i.e., reinforcer quality). In one condition, the magnitude and quality of the reinforcer was equal in both settings. In the other condition, the magnitude and quality of the reinforcer was greater for play in the setting with a peer or sibling than in the play-alone setting. With the introduction of the condition with greater magnitude and quality of the reinforcer, the boys allocated more play responses to the setting with the peer or sibling, rather than playing alone. The magnitude and quality of the reinforcer influenced choices made by the three boys. Figure 13.8 reports the percentage of responses allocated to the concurrent play areas.

Concurrent Performances: Formalizing the Matching Law

Cuvo and colleagues (1998) reported that concurrent schedules typically produce two response patterns. With concurrent interval schedules (conc VI VI, conc FI FI), participants "typically do not allocate all of their responses exclusively to the richer schedule [i.e., the schedule producing the higher rate of reinforcement]; rather, they distribute their responding between the two schedules to match or approximate the proportion of reinforcement that is actually obtained on each independent schedule" (p. 43). Conversely, with concurrent ratio

schedules (conc VR VR, conc FR FR), participants are sensitive to the ratio schedules and tend to maximize reinforcement by responding primarily to the ratio that produces the higher rate of reinforcement.

Williams (1973) identified three types of interactions found with concurrent schedules. First, when similar reinforcement is scheduled for each of the concurrent responses, the response receiving the higher frequency of reinforcement will increase in rate whereas a corresponding decrease will occur in the response rate of the other behavior. Second, when one response produces reinforcement and the other produces punishment, responses associated with punishment will decrease in occurrence. That decrease may produce a higher rate of response for the behavior producing reinforcement. Third, with a concurrent schedule programmed for one response to produce reinforcement and the other response to produce avoidance of an aversive stimulus, the rate of avoidance responding will accelerate with an increase in the intensity or the frequency of the aversive stimulus. As avoidance responding accelerates, typically responding on the reinforcement schedule will then decrease.

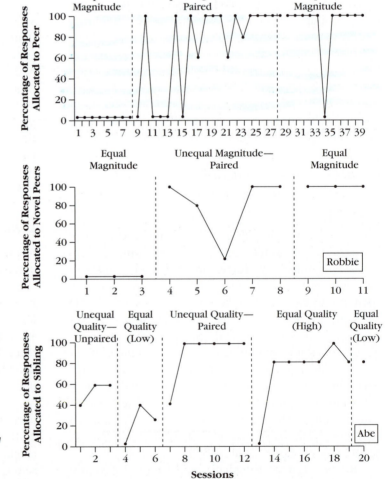

Figure 13.8 Percentage of responses allocated to the play area with the peer across experimental sessions (top panel) and in natural-setting probes with different peers in the classroom (middle panel) for the analysis of magnitude of reinforcement with Robbie, and the percentage of responses allocated to the play area with the sibling across experimental sessions for the analysis of quality of reinforcement with Abe (bottom panel).

From "The Effects of Magnitude and Quality of Reinforcement on Choice Responding During Play Activities" by H. Hoch, J. J. McComas, L. Johnson, N. Faranda, and S. L. Guenther, 2002, *Journal of Applied Behavior Analysis, 35*, p. 177. Copyright 1992 by the Society for the Experimental Analysis of Behavior Inc. Reprinted by permission.

The characteristics of performance on concurrent schedules as detailed previously by Cuvo and colleagues and Williams are consistent with the relationships formalized by Herrnstein (1961, 1970) as the **matching law.** The matching law addresses response allocation to choices available with concurrent schedules of reinforcement. Basically, the rate of responding typically is proportional to the rate of reinforcement received from each choice alternative.

Discriminative Schedules of Reinforcement

Multiple Schedules

A **multiple schedule (mult)** presents two or more basic schedules of reinforcement in an alternating, usually random, sequence. The basic schedules within the multiple schedule occur successively and independently. A discriminative stimulus is correlated with each basic schedule, and that stimulus is present as long as the schedule is in effect.

Academic behaviors can become sensitive to the control of multiple schedules of reinforcement. A student might respond to basic arithmetic facts with her teacher, and also with her tutor. With the teacher, the student responds to arithmetic facts during small-group instruction. The tutor then provides individual instruction and practice on the facts. This situation follows a multiple schedule because there is one class of behavior (i.e., math facts), a discriminative stimulus for each contingency in effect (i.e., teacher/tutor, small group/individual), and different conditions for reinforcement (i.e., reinforcement is less frequent in group instruction). In another everyday example of the multiple schedule, Jim helps his mother and father clean house on Friday afternoons and Saturday mornings. Jim cleans his grandmother's bedroom and bathroom on Friday afternoons and the family room and downstairs bathroom on Saturday mornings. Jim receives $5 per week for cleaning his grandmother's rooms but does not receive money for cleaning the family room or downstairs bathroom. Again, there is one class of behaviors of interest (i.e., cleaning the house), a cue for each contingency in effect (i.e., grandmother's rooms on Fridays or other rooms on Saturdays), and different schedules of reinforcement associated with the different cues (i.e., $5 for grandmother's rooms and no money for the other rooms).

Chained Schedules

A **chained schedule (chain)** is similar to a multiple schedule. The multiple and chained schedules have two or more basic schedule requirements that occur successively, and have a discriminative stimulus correlated with each independent schedule. A chained schedule differs from a multiple schedule in three ways. First, the basic schedules in a chain schedule always occur in a specific order, never in the random or unpredictable order of multiple schedules. Second, the behavior may be the same for all elements of the chain, or different behaviors may be required for different elements in the chain. Third, conditioned reinforcement for responding in the first element in a chain is the presentation of the second element; conditioned reinforcement for responding in the second element is presentation of the third element, and so on until all elements in the chain have been completed in a specific sequence. The last element normally produces unconditioned reinforcement in a laboratory setting, or unconditioned or conditioned reinforcement in applied settings.

The following example shows an elaborate sequence of different behaviors that must occur in a specific order. To service a bicycle headset, the mechanic will complete a chain with 13 components: (1) Disconnect the front brake cable; (2) remove handlebar and stem; (3) remove front wheel; (4) remove locknut; (5) unscrew adjusting race; (6) take fork out of frame; (7) inspect races; (8) grease and replace bearing balls for lower stack; (9) grease and replace bearing balls for upper race; (10) grease threads of steering column; (11) put fork into frame and thread the screwed race; (12) return lock washer; (13) adjust and lock the headset. The final outcome (i.e., a clean, greased, and adjusted bicycle headset) is contingent on the completion of all 13 components. (For a detailed description of behavior chains and how applied behavior analysts help individuals learn new and more complex chains of behavior, see Chapter 20.)

Nondiscriminative Schedules of Reinforcement

Mixed Schedules

The **mixed schedule (mix)** uses a procedure identical to the multiple schedules, except the mixed schedule has no discriminative stimuli correlated with the independent schedules. For example, with a mix FR 10 FI 1 schedule, reinforcement sometimes occurs after the completion of 10 responses and sometimes occurs with the first correct response after a 1-minute interval from the preceding reinforcement.

Tandem Schedules

The **tandem schedule (tand)** uses a procedure identical to the chained schedule, except, like the mix schedule, the tandem schedule does not use discriminative stimuli with the elements in the chain. After a participant makes 15 responses on a tand FR 15 FI 2, then the first correct response following an elapse of 2 minutes produces reinforcement.

Antecedent stimuli appear to relate functionally to most occurrences of behaviors in natural environments. Perhaps, therefore, the mixed and tandem schedules have little applied application at this time. However, basic research has produced considerable data concerning the effects of mixed and tandem schedules on behavior. It may become more apparent how applied behavior analysts can effectively apply mixed and tandem schedules in assessment, intervention, and analysis as the knowledge base of applied behavior analysis continues to develop.

Schedules Combining the Number of Responses and Time

Alternative Schedules

An **alternative schedule (alt)** provides reinforcement whenever the requirement of either a ratio schedule or an interval schedule—the basic schedules that comprise the alt—is met, regardless of which of the component schedule's requirements is met first. With an alt FR 50 FI 5-minute schedule, reinforcement is delivered whenever either of these two conditions have been met: (a) 50 correct responses, provided the 5-minute interval of time has not elapsed; or (b) the first response after the elapse of 5 minutes, provided that fewer than 50 responses have been emitted.

For instance, a teacher using an alt FR 25 FI 3-minute schedule of reinforcement assigns 25 math problems and assesses the student's correct and incorrect answers following the elapse of 3 minutes. If the student completes the 25 problems before the elapse of 3 minutes, the teacher checks the student's answers and provides a consequence consistent with the FR 25 schedule. However, if the ratio requirement of 25 math problems has not been completed after an elapse of 3 minutes, the first correct answer following the 3 minutes produces reinforcement. The alternative schedule offers the advantage of a second chance for reinforcement if the student has not met the FR requirement in a reasonable amount of time. The FI provides reinforcement for one response, and that one reinforced response might encourage continued responding with the new start of the FR requirement.

Conjunctive Schedules

A **conjunctive schedule (conj)** of reinforcement is in effect whenever reinforcement follows the completion of response requirements for both a ratio schedule and an interval schedule of reinforcement. For example, a student behavior produces reinforcement when at least 2 minutes have elapsed and 50 responses have been made. This arrangement is a conj FI 2 FR 50 schedule of reinforcement. With the conjunctive schedule of reinforcement, the first response following the conclusion of the time interval produces reinforcement if the criterion number of responses have been completed.

A 14-year-old boy with autism had higher rates of aggression with two of his four therapists during instruction. The higher rates of aggression were directed toward the two therapists who previously worked with the boy at a different treatment facility. Progar and colleagues (2001) intervened to reduce the levels of aggression with the therapists from the different facility to the levels that occurred with the other two therapists in the current setting. The boy's aggression occurred in demand situations (e.g., making his bed) and was escape maintained. The initial intervention used three consequences: (1) a 10-minute chair time-out for attempts to choke, (2) escape extinction (see Chapter 21), and (3) differential-reinforcement-other-behavior (DRO, see Chapter 22) for the omission of aggression during the 10-minute sessions. This intervention was identical to the treatment used with the boy at the other facility. It was ineffective in reducing the boy's aggression in the current setting.

Because of the ineffectiveness of the initial intervention, Progar and colleagues added a conj FR VI-DRO schedule of reinforcement to their initial intervention. They delivered edible reinforcers contingent on completing a three-component task such as dusting or straightening objects (i.e., an FR 3 schedule) and the omission of aggression for an average of every 2.5 minutes (i.e., the VI-DRO 150-second). An occurrence of aggression reset the conj schedule. (*Note:* Resetting this conj schedule used a standard procedure because any occurrence of the problem behavior during a DRO interval immediately resets the time to the beginning of the interval.) Progar and colleagues demonstrated that the conj FR VI-DRO schedule produced a substantial reduction in aggression directed toward the two therapists previously from the other treatment facility.

Duvinsky and Poppen (1982) found that human performance on a conjunctive schedule is influenced by the ratio and interval requirements. When task requirements are high in relationship to the interval requirements, people are likely to work steadily on the task throughout the time available. However, people are likely to engage in behaviors other than the task requirements when there is a large time interval and a low ratio requirement.

Table 13.1 provides a summary of the characteristics of compound schedules of reinforcement.

Table 13.1 Summary and Comparison of Basic Dimensions Defining Compound Schedules of Reinforcement

	Compound Schedule Name						
Dimension	Concurrent	Multiple	Chained	Mixed	Tandem	Alternative	Conjunctive
Number of basic schedules of reinforcement in effect	2 or more	2 or more	2 or more	2 or more	2 or more	2 or more	2 or more
Number of response classes involved	2 or more	1	1 or more	1	1 or more	1	1
Discriminative stimuli or cues associated with each component schedule	Possible	Yes	Yes	No	No	Possible	Possible
Successive presentation of basic schedules	No	Yes	Yes	Yes	Yes	No	No
Simultaneous presentation of basic schedules	Yes	No	No	No	No	Yes	Yes
Reinforcement limited to final component of basic schedule	No	No	Yes	No	Yes	No	Yes
Reinforcement for independent components of basic schedule	Yes	Yes	No	Yes	No	Yes	No

Perspectives on Applying Schedules of Reinforcement in Applied Settings

Applied Research with Intermittent Schedules

Basic researchers have systematically analyzed the effects of intermittent schedules of reinforcement on the performance of organisms (e.g., Ferster & Skinner, 1957). Their results have produced well-established schedule effects. These schedule effects have strong generality across many species, response classes, and laboratories. However, a review of the applied literature on schedule effects (e.g., *Journal of Applied Behavior Analysis,* 1968 to 2006) will show that applied behavior analysts have not embraced the analysis of schedule effects with enthusiasm, as have basic researchers. Consequently, schedule effects have not been documented clearly in applied settings. Uncontrolled variables in applied settings, such as the following, influence a partic-

ipant's sensitivity and insensitivity to the schedule of reinforcement:

1. Instructions given by the applied behavior analyst, self-instructions, and environmental aids (e.g., calendars, clocks) make human participants resistant to temporal schedule control.

2. Past histories of responding to intermittent schedules of reinforcement can affect current schedule sensitivity or insensitivity.

3. Immediate histories from schedules of reinforcement may affect current schedule performances more than remote past histories.

4. Sequential responses required in many applied applications of intermittent schedules of reinforcement (e.g., work leading to the paycheck, studying for a pop quiz) are uncommon applications of schedules of reinforcement, particularly with interval schedules.

5. Uncontrolled establishing operations in conjunction with schedules of reinforcement in applied settings will confound schedule effects.

Some well-established schedule effects found in basic research were presented earlier in this chapter. Applied behavior analysts, however, should use caution in extrapolating these effects to applied settings, for the following reasons:

1. Most applied applications of schedules of reinforcement only approximate true laboratory schedules of reinforcement, especially the interval schedules that may occur rarely in natural environments (Nevin, 1998).

2. Many uncontrolled variables in applied settings will influence a participant's sensitivity and insensitivity to the schedule of reinforcement (Madden, Chase, & Joyce, 1998).

Applied Research with Compound Schedules

Applied researchers have seldom analyzed the effects of compound reinforcement schedules, with the notable exceptions of concurrent schedules and, to a lesser degree, chained schedules. Applied researchers should include the analysis of compound schedules in their research agendas. A better understanding of the effects of compound schedules on behavior will advance the development of applied behavior analysis and its applications. This perspective is important because compound schedules of reinforcement act directly on human behavior, and they influence behavior also by interacting with other environmental variables (e.g., antecedent stimuli, motivating operations) (Lattal & Neef, 1996).

Applied Research with Adjunctive Behavior

This chapter has stressed the effects of schedules of reinforcement on the specific behaviors that produce reinforcement. Other behaviors can occur when an individual responds to a given contingency of reinforcement. These other behaviors occur independently of schedule control. Typical examples of such behaviors include normal time fillers, such as doodling, smoking, idle talking, drinking. Such behaviors are called **adjunctive behaviors,** or schedule-induced behaviors, when the frequency of these time-filling behaviors increases as a side effect of other behaviors maintained by a schedule of reinforcement (Falk, 1961, 1971).

A substantial body of experimental literature has developed on many types of adjunctive behaviors with nonhuman subjects (see reviews, Staddon, 1977; Wetherington, 1982) and some basic research with human subjects (e.g., Kachanoff, Leveille, McLelland, & Wayner 1973; Lasiter, 1979). Common diverse examples of adjunctive behaviors observed in laboratory experiments include aggression, defecation, pica, and wheel running. Some common excessive human problem behaviors might develop as adjunctive behaviors (e.g., the use of drugs, tobacco, caffeine, and alcohol; overeating; nail biting; self-stimulation; and self-abuse). These potentially excessive adjunctive behaviors are socially significant, but the possibility that such excesses are developed and maintained as adjunctive behaviors has been essentially ignored in applied behavior analysis.

Foster (1978), in an extended communication to the readership of the *Journal of Applied Behavior Analysis,* reported that applied behavior analysts have neglected the potentially important area of adjunctive behavior. He stated that applied behavior analysis does not have a data or knowledge base for adjunctive phenomena. Similarly, Epling and Pierce (1983) called for applied behavior analysts to extend the laboratory-based findings in adjunctive behavior to the understanding and control of socially significant human behavior. To our knowledge, Lerman, Iwata, Zarcone, and Ringdahl's (1994) article provides the only research on adjunctive behavior published in the *Journal of Applied Behavior Analysis* from 1968 through 2006. Lerman and colleagues provided an assessment of stereotypic and self-injurious behavior as adjunctive responses. Data from this preliminary study suggest that intermittent reinforcement did not induce self-injury, but with some individuals, stereotypic behavior showed characteristics of adjunctive behavior.

Foster (1978) and Epling and Pierce (1983) cautioned that many teachers and therapists may apply interventions directly to adjunctive behaviors rather than to the variables functionally related to their occurrence. These direct interventions may be futile and costly in terms of money, time, and effort because adjunctive behaviors appear resistant to interventions using operant contingencies.

The condition under which adjunctive behaviors are developed and maintained is a major area for future research in applied behavior analysis. Applied research directed to adjunctive behaviors will advance the science of applied behavior analysis and will provide an important foundation for improved practices in therapy and instruction.

 **Summary**

Intermittent Reinforcement

1. A schedule of reinforcement is a rule that establishes the probability that a specific occurrence of a behavior will produce reinforcement.

2. Only selected occurrences of behavior produce reinforcement with an intermittent schedule of reinforcement.

3. Applied behavior analysts use continuous reinforcement during the initial stages of learning and for strengthening behavior.

4. Applied behavior analysts use intermittent reinforcement to maintain behavior.

Defining Basic Intermittent Schedules of Reinforcement

5. A fixed ratio schedule requires a specified number of responses before a response produces reinforcement.

6. A variable ratio requires a variable number of responses before reinforcement is delivered.

7. A fixed interval schedule provides reinforcement for the first response following the elapse of a specific, constant duration of time since the last reinforced response.

8. A variable interval schedule provides reinforcement for the first response following the elapse of variable duration of time since the last reinforced response.

9. When a limited hold is added to an interval schedule, reinforcement remains available for a finite time following the elapse of the FI or VI interval.

10. Each basic schedule of reinforcement has unique response characteristics that determine the consistency of responding, the rate of responding, and performance during extinction.

Thinning Intermittent Reinforcement

11. Applied behavior analysts often use one of two procedures to thin schedules of reinforcement. An existing schedule is thinned by gradually increasing the response ratio or by gradually increasing the duration of the time interval.

12. Applied behavior analysts should use small increments of schedule changes during thinning and ongoing evaluation of the learner's performance to adjust the thinning process and avoid the loss of previous improvements.

13. Ratio strain can result from abrupt increases in ratio requirements when moving from denser to thinner reinforcement schedules.

Variations on Basic Intermittent Schedules of Reinforcement

14. DRH and DRL are variations of ratio schedules and specify that reinforcement will be delivered contingent on responses occurring above or below criterion response rates.

15. The differential reinforcement of diminishing rates schedule provides reinforcement at the end of a predetermined time interval when the number of responses is below a criterion. The criterion for the number of responses is gradually decreased across time intervals based on the individual's performance.

16. Progressive schedules of reinforcement systematically thin each successive reinforcement opportunity independent of the participant's behavior.

Compound Schedules of Reinforcement

17. Continuous reinforcement, the four simple intermittent schedules of reinforcement, differential reinforcement of rates of responding, and extinction, when combined, produce compound schedules of reinforcement.

18. Compound schedules of reinforcement include concurrent, multiple, chained, mixed, tandem, alternative, and conjunctive schedules.

Perspectives on Applying Schedules of Reinforcement in Applied Settings

19. Some well-established schedule effects found in basic research were presented in this chapter. Applied behavior analysts, however, should use caution in extrapolating these effects to applied settings.

20. Applied researchers should include an analysis of the basic intermittent schedules and the compound schedules in their research agendas. A better understanding of the schedule effects in applied settings will advance the development of applied behavior analysis and its applications.

21. The conditions under which adjunctive behaviors are developed and maintained is an important area for future research in applied behavior analysis.

PART 5

Punishment

Punishment teaches us not to repeat responses that cause us harm. Although punishment is often considered bad—an unfortunate counterpart to reinforcement—it is as important to learning as reinforcement. Learning from consequences that produce pain, discomfort, or the loss of reinforcers has survival value for the individual organism and for the species.

As with reinforcement, a stimulus change that serves as the consequence in a punishment contingency can often be described as either of two types of operations: a new stimulus is presented or an existing stimulus is removed. In Chapter 14, Punishment by Stimulus Presentation, we define the basic principle of punishment and distinguish positive punishment and negative punishment based on the operational nature of the response-suppressing consequence. The remainder of the chapter focuses on positive punishment; we discuss side effects and limitations of punishment, identify factors that influence the effectiveness of punishment, describe several examples of interventions involving positive punishment, present guidelines for using punishment effectively, and discuss ethical considerations regarding the use of punishment. In Chapter 15, Punishment by Removal of a Stimulus, we describe two behavior change tactics based on negative punishment: time-out from positive reinforcement and response cost. We provide examples of how applied behavior analysts have used time out and response cost to reduce or eliminate undesired behavior, and we offer guidelines for effectively implementing these two tactics.

CHAPTER 14

Punishment
by Stimulus Presentation

Key Terms

behavioral contrast
conditioned punisher
discriminative stimulus for
    punishment
generalized conditioned punisher

negative punishment
overcorrection
positive practice overcorrection
positive punishment
punisher

punishment
response blocking
restitutional overcorrection
unconditioned punisher

Behavior Analyst Certification Board® BCBA® & BCABA®
Behavior Analyst Task List©, Third Edition

Content Area 3: Principles, Processes, and Concepts	
3-5	Define and provide examples of positive and negative punishment.
3-6	Define and provide examples of conditioned and unconditioned punishment.
Content Area 9: Behavior Change Procedures	
9-3	Use positive (and negative) punishment.
(a)	Identify and use punishers.
(b)	Use appropriate parameters and schedules of punishment.
(c)	State and plan for the possible unwanted effects of the use of punishment.

Have you ever stubbed your toe while walking too fast in a darkened room and then walked slowly the rest of the way to the light switch? Have you ever left a sandwich unattended at a beach party, watched a seagull fly away with it, and then refrained from turning your back on the next treat you pulled from the picnic basket? If you have had these or similar experiences, you have been the beneficiary of punishment.

It may strike you as strange that we would refer to someone who stubbed his toe or lost his sandwich as benefiting from the experience, as opposed to referring to that person as a "victim" of punishment. Although many people consider punishment a bad thing—reinforcement's evil counterpart—punishment is as important to learning as reinforcement. Learning from the consequences that produce pain or discomfort, or the loss of reinforcers, has survival value for the individual organism and for the species. Punishment teaches us not to repeat responses that cause us harm. Fortunately, it usually does not take too many stubbed toes or lost picnic treats to reduce the frequency of the behaviors that produced those outcomes.

Although punishment is a natural phenomenon that "occurs like the wind and the rain" (Vollmer, 2002, p. 469) and is one of the basic principles of operant conditioning, it is poorly understood, frequently misapplied, and its application can be controversial. At least some of the misunderstanding and controversy surrounding the use of punishment in behavior change programs derives from confusing punishment as an empirically derived principle of behavior with the variety of everyday and legal connotations of the concept. One common meaning of punishment is the application of aversive consequences—such as physical pain, psychological hurt, and the loss of privileges, or fines—for the purpose of teaching a lesson to a person who has misbehaved so she will not repeat the misdeed. Punishment is sometimes used as an act of retribution on the part of the person or agency administering the punishment, or to provide "a lesson for others" on how to behave. Punishments meted out by the legal system, such as jail time and fines, are often considered a process by which convicted lawbreakers must repay their debt to society.

These everyday and legal notions of punishment, although having various degrees of validity within their own contexts, have little, if anything, to do with punishment as a principle of behavior. In the everyday connotation of punishment, most people would agree that a teacher who sends a student to the principal's office for fooling around in class, or a police officer who issues a ticket to a speeding motorist, has punished the offender. However, as a principle of behavior, punishment is not about *punishing the person;* punishment is a response →

consequence contingency that suppresses the future frequency of similar responses. From the perspective of both the science and the practice of behavior analysis, the trip to the principal's office did not punish fooling around in class unless the future frequency at which the student fools around in class decreases as a function of his trip to the principal's office, and the police officer's ticket did not punish speeding unless the motorist drives above the speed limit less often than she did before receiving the ticket.

In this chapter we define the principle of punishment, discuss its side effects and limitations, identify factors that influence the effectiveness of punishment, describe examples of several behavior change tactics that incorporate punishment, discuss ethical considerations in the use of punishment, and present guidelines for using punishment effectively. In the chapter's concluding section, we underscore the need for more basic and applied research on punishment and reiterate Iwata's (1988) recommendation that behavior analysts view punishment by contingent stimulation as a default technology to be implemented when other interventions have failed.

Definition and Nature of Punishment

This section presents the basic functional relation that defines punishment, the two operations by which punishment can be implemented, discrimination effects of punishment, recovery from punishment, unconditioned and conditioned punishers, factors that influence the effectiveness of punishment, and possible side effects of and problems with punishment.

Operation and Defining Effect of Punishment

Like reinforcement, punishment is a two-term, behavior → consequence functional relation defined by it effects on the future frequency of behavior. **Punishment** has occurred when a response is followed immediately by a stimulus change that decreases the future frequency of similar responses (Azrin & Holz, 1966).

An early study by Hall and colleagues (1971) provides a straightforward example of punishment. Andrea, a 7-year-old girl with hearing impairments, "pinched and bit herself, her peers, the teacher, and visitors to the classroom at every opportunity and was so disruptive the teacher reported that academic instruction was impossible" (p. 24). During an initial 6-day baseline period, Andrea bit or pinched an average of 71.8 times per day. Whenever Andrea bit or pinched anyone during the

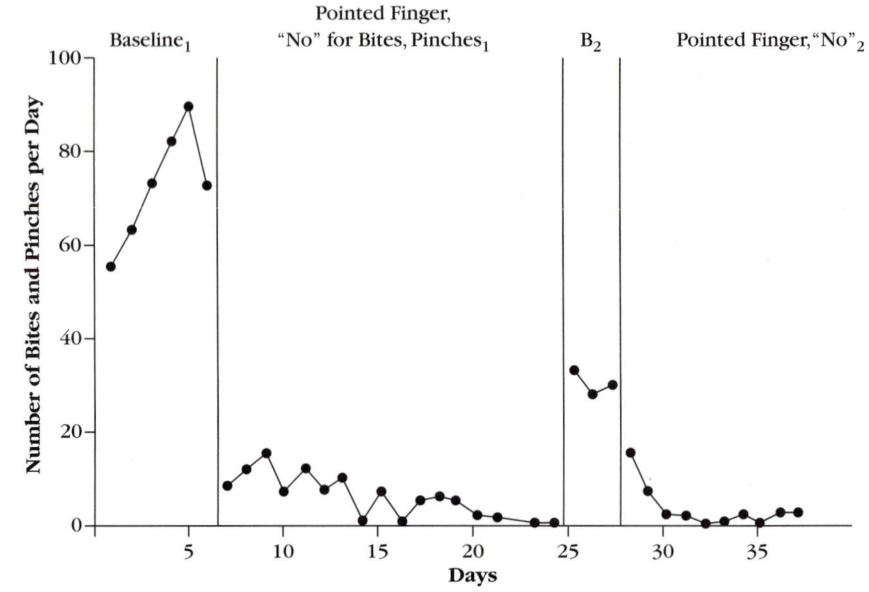

Pointed Finger,
Baseline₁   "No" for Bites, Pinches₁   B₂   Pointed Finger, "No"₂

Figure 14.1 Number of bites and pinches by a 7-year-old girl during baseline and punishment ("No" plus pointing) conditions.

From "The Effective Use of Punishment to Modify Behavior in the Classroom" by R. V. Hall, S. Axelrod, M. Foundopoulos, J. Shellman, R. A. Campbell, and S. S. Cranston, 1971, *Educational Technology, 11*(4), p. 25. Copyright 1971 by Educational Technology. Used by permission.

intervention condition, her teacher immediately pointed at her with an outstretched arm and shouted "No!" On the first day of intervention, the frequency of Andrea's biting and pinching decreased substantially (see Figure 14.1). Her aggressive behavior followed a downward trend during the initial intervention phase, ending in an average of 5.4 incidents per day. A 3-day return to baseline conditions resulted in Andrea's biting and pinching at a mean rate of 30 times per day. When the teacher reinstated the intervention, pointing her finger and stating "No!" each time Andrea pinched or bit, Andrea's problem behavior dropped to 3.1 incidents per day. During the second intervention phase, the teacher reported that Andrea's classmates were no longer avoiding her, perhaps because their behavior of being near Andrea was punished less often by bites and pinches.

It is important to point out that punishment is defined neither by the actions of the person delivering the consequences (in the case of socially mediated punishment) nor by the nature of those consequences.[1] A decrease in the future frequency of the occurrence of the behavior must be observed before a consequence-based intervention qualifies as punishment. The intervention that proved successful in reducing the frequency of Andrea's biting and pinching—her teacher's pointed finger and "No!"—is classified as a punishment-based treatment only because of its suppressive effects. If Andrea had continued to bite and pinch at the baseline level of re-

sponding when the intervention was applied, her teacher's pointing and "No!" would not have been punishment.

Because the presentation of punishers often evokes behavior incompatible with the behavior being punished, the immediate suppressive effects of punishment can easily be overestimated. Michael (2004) explained and provided a good example:

> The decreased frequency of the punished response that is due to its having been followed by punishment will not be seen until after behavior evoked by the punishing stimulus changes has ceased. Because the evocative effect of the punishment stimulus change (as a respondent unconditioned or conditioned elicitor or as operant S^D or MO) is in the same direction as the future change due to punishment as a response consequence (weakening of the punished behavior), the former can be easily misinterpreted as the latter. For example, when a small child's misbehavior is followed by a severe reprimand, the misbehavior will cease immediately, but primarily because the reprimand controls behavior incompatible with the misbehavior—attending to the adult who is doing the reprimanding, denying responsibility for the misbehavior, emotional behavior such as crying, etc. This sudden and total cessation of the misbehaver does not imply, however, that the future frequency of its occurrence has been reduced, which would be the true effect of punishment. (pp. 36–37)

Another factor that contributes to the difficulty of determining the true effectiveness of punishment is that the reduction in response rate is often confounded by extinction effects caused by withholding reinforcement for the problem behavior (something that should be part of a punishment-based intervention whenever possible) (Iwata, Pace, Cowdery, & Miltenberger, 1994).

---

[1]Although the term *automatic punishment* is used infrequently in the behavior analysis literature, it is similar to *automatic reinforcement*. Automatic punishment occurs when a punishing consequence (e.g., burned finger) is a socially unmediated, unavoidable outcome of a response (e.g., touching a hot stove).

Positive Punishment and Negative Punishment

Like reinforcement, punishment can be accomplished by either of two types of stimulus change operations. Positive punishment occurs when the presentation of a stimulus (or an increase in the intensity of an already present stimulus) immediately following a behavior results in a decrease in the frequency of the behavior. Stubbing one's toe on a chair leg is a form of positive punishment—if it suppresses the frequency of the behavior that preceded the toe stub—because the painful stimulation is best described as the presence of a new stimulus. Behavior change tactics based on positive punishment involve the contingent presentation of a stimulus immediately following occurrences of the target behavior. The intervention used by Andrea's teacher constituted positive punishment; the teacher's pointed finger and "No!" were stimuli presented or added to Andrea's environment.

Negative punishment involves the termination of an already present stimulus (or a decrease in the intensity of an already present stimulus) immediately following a behavior that results in a decrease in the future frequency of the behavior. The beach party attendee's behavior of turning his back on his food was negatively punished when the seagull flew off with his sandwich. For a stimulus change to function as negative punishment, which amounts to the removal of a positive reinforcer, a "motivating operation for the reinforcer must be in effect, otherwise removing it will not constitute punishment" (Michael, 2004, p. 36). A seagull's flying off with a hungry person's sandwich would function as punishment for his inattentiveness but perhaps have little effect on the behavior of a person who has eaten his fill and set the sandwich down.

Behavior change tactics based on negative punishment involve the contingent loss of available reinforcers immediately following a behavior (i.e., response cost, a procedure akin to a fine) or the removal of the opportunity to acquire additional reinforcers for a period of time (i.e., timeout from reinforcement, a procedure akin to being sidelined during a game). Negative punishment in the form of response cost and time-out is the focus of Chapter 15.

As was noted in Chapter 2, a wide variety of terms are used in the behavioral literature to refer to the two types of consequence operations for punishment. Positive punishment and negative punishment are sometimes identified as *Type I punishment* and *Type II punishment,* respectively (Foxx, 1982). Malott and Trojan Suarez (2004) use the term *penalty principle* to refer to negative punishment. The Behavior Analyst Certification Board (BACB, 2001) and some textbook authors (e.g., Baum,

1994; Catania, 1998; Michael, 2004; Miltenberger, 2001) use the terms *positive punishment* and *negative punishment,* paralleling the terms *positive reinforcement* and *negative reinforcement.* As with reinforcement, the modifiers *positive* and *negative* used with *punishment* connote neither the intention nor the desirability of the behavior change produced; they specify only how the stimulus change that served as the punishing consequence was affected—whether it is best described as the presentation of a new stimulus (positive punishment) or the termination (or reduction in intensity or amount) of an already present stimulus (negative punishment).[2]

Positive punishment and negative reinforcement are frequently confused. Because aversive events are associated with positive punishment and with negative reinforcement, the umbrella term *aversive control* is often used to describe interventions involving either or both of these two principles. Distinguishing between the two principles is difficult when the same aversive event is involved in concurrent positive punishment and negative reinforcement contingencies. For example, Baum (1994) described how the application and threat of physical beatings might condition the behavior of people living in a police state.

> If speaking out results in a beating, then speaking out is positively punished. If lying avoids a beating, then lying is negatively reinforced. The two tend to go hand-in-hand; if one action is punished, there is usually some alternative that avoids punishment. (p. 153)

The keys to identifying and distinguishing concurrent positive punishment and negative reinforcement contingencies involving the same aversive stimulus event are (a) recognizing the opposite effects the two contingencies have on the future frequency of behavior, and (b) realizing that two different behaviors must be involved because the same consequence (i.e., stimulus change) cannot serve as positive punishment and negative reinforcement for the same behavior. In a positive punishment contingency, the stimulus is absent prior to a response and is presented as a consequence; in a negative reinforcement contingency, the stimulus is present prior to a response and is removed as a consequence. For example, positive punishment and negative reinforcement contingencies operated concurrently in a study by Azrin, Rubin, O'Brien, Ayllon, and Roll (1968) in which adults wore an apparatus throughout the normal working day that automatically produced a

---

[2]As with reinforcement, the terms *positive punishment* and *negative punishment* are, as Michael (2004) noted, "quite susceptible to misunderstanding. Assuming that you must receive either positive or negative punishment, which would you prefer? As with reinforcement, you should certainly not decide until you know specifically what each consists of. Would you prefer negative reinforcement or positive punishment? Of course, negative reinforcement" (p. 37).

55 dB tone contingent on slouching (sustained rounding of the shoulders or upper back for 3 seconds) and immediately terminated the tone when they straightened their shoulders. Slouching produced a tone (positive punishment), straightening the shoulders escaped the tone (negative reinforcement), and nonslouching avoided a tone (negative reinforcement).

Threatening a person with punishment if she engages in a behavior should not be confused with punishment. Punishment is a behavior → consequence relation, and a threat of what might happen if a person subsequently behaves in a certain way is an antecedent event to the behavior. When the threat of punishment suppresses behavior, it may be due to the threat functioning as an establishing operation that evokes alternative behaviors that avoid the threatened punishment.

Discriminative Effects of Punishment

Punishment does not operate in a contextual vacuum. The antecedent stimulus situation in which punishment occurs plays an important role in determining the environmental conditions in which the suppressive effects of punishment will be observed. The three-term contingency for "the operant functional relation involving punishment can be stated much like that involving reinforcement: (1) In a particular stimulus situation (S), (2) some kinds of behavior (R), when followed immediately by (3) certain stimulus changes (S^P), show a decreased future frequency of occurrence in the same or in similar situations" (Michael, 2004, p. 36).

If punishment occurs only in some stimulus conditions and not in others (e.g., a child gets scolded for reaching into the cookie jar before dinner only when an adult is in the room), the suppressive effects of punishment will be most prevalent under those conditions (Azrin & Holz, 1966; Dinsmoor, 1952). A discriminated operant for punishment is the product of a conditioning history in which responses in the presence of a certain stimulus have been punished and similar responses in the absence of that stimulus have not been punished (or have resulted in a reduced frequency or magnitude of punishment). Highway speeding is a discriminated operant in the repertoire of many motorists who drive within the speed limit in and around locations where they have been pulled over by the police for speeding but continue to drive above the speed limit on roads where they have never seen a police cruiser.

There is no standard term or symbol in the behavior analysis literature for an antecedent stimulus that acquires stimulus control related to punishment. Some authors have modified the shorthand symbol for a discriminative stimulus for reinforcement (S^D) to indicate the antecedent stimulus in a three-term punishment contingency, such as the S^{D-} used by Sulzer-Azaroff and Mayer (1971). Other authors simply refer to an antecedent stimulus correlated with the presence of a punishment contingency as a *punishment-based* S^D (e.g., Malott & Trojan Suarez, 2004; Michael, 2004). We have adopted S^{Dp} as the symbol for the **discriminative stimulus for punishment** as proposed by O'Donnell (2001). "An S^{Dp} can be defined as a stimulus condition in the presence of which a response has a lower probability of occurrence than it does in its absence as a result of response-contingent punishment delivery in the presence of the stimulus" (p. 262). Figure 14.2 shows three-term contingency diagrams for discriminated operants for positive punishment and negative punishment.

Recovery from Punishment

When punishment is discontinued, its suppressive effects on responding are usually not permanent, a phenomenon often called *recovery from punishment,* which is analogous to extinction. Sometimes the rate of responding after punishment is discontinued will not only recover but also briefly exceed the level at which it was occurring prior to punishment (Azrin, 1960; Holz & Azrin, 1962). Recovery of responding to prepunished levels is more likely to occur when the punishment was mild or when the person can discriminate that the punishment contingency is no longer active. Although the response-weakening effects of punishment often wane when punishment is discontinued, so too are the response strengthening effects of reinforcement often fleeting when previously reinforced behavior is placed on extinction (Vollmer, 2002). Michael (2004) noted that

> Recovery from punishment is sometimes given as an argument against the use of punishment to cause a decrease in behavior. "Don't use punishment because the effect is only temporary." But of course the same argument could be made for reinforcement. The strengthening effect of reinforcement decreases when the behavior occurs without the reinforcement. The weakening effect of punishment decreases when the behavior occurs without the punishment. (p. 38)

Virtually permanent response suppression may occur when complete suppression of behavior to a zero rate of responding has been achieved with intense punishment. In their review of basic research on punishment, Azrin and Holz (1966) noted that:

> Intense punishment did not merely reduce responses to the unconditioned or operant level, but reduced them to an absolute level of zero. Since punishment is delivered only after a response occurs, there is no opportunity for the subject to detect the absence of punishment unless he responds. If punishment is severe as to completely eliminate the responses then the opportunity for detecting the absence of punishment no longer exists. (p. 410)

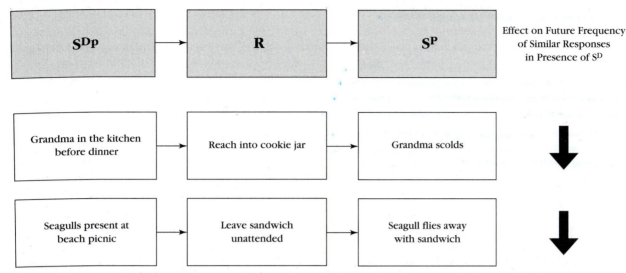

Figure 14.2 Three-term contingencies illustrating positive and negative punishment of discriminated operants: A response (R) emitted in the presence of a discriminative stimulus (S^{Dp}) is followed closely in time by a stimulus change (S^P) and results in a decreased frequency of similar responses in the future when the S^{Dp} is present. A discriminated operant for punishment is the product of a conditioning history in which responses in the presence of the S^{Dp} have been punished and similar responses in the absence of the S^{Dp} have not been punished (or have resulted in a reduced frequency or magnitude of punishment than in the presence of the S^{Dp}).

Unconditioned and Conditioned Punishers

A **punisher** is a stimulus change that immediately follows the occurrence of a behavior and reduces the future frequency of that type of behavior. The stimulus change in a positive punishment contingency may be referred to as a *positive punisher,* or more simply as a *punisher.* Likewise the term *negative punisher* can be applied to a stimulus change involved in negative punishment. However, this usage is clumsy because it refers to a positive reinforcer that is removed contingent on occurrences of the target behavior. Therefore, when most behavior analysts use the term *punisher,* they are referring to a stimulus whose presentation functions as punishment (i.e., a positive punisher). As with reinforcers, punishers can be classified as unconditioned or conditioned.

Unconditioned Punishers

An **unconditioned punisher** is a stimulus whose presentation functions as punishment without having been paired with any other punishers. (Some authors use *primary punisher* or *unlearned punisher* as synonyms for an unconditioned punisher.) Because unconditioned punishers are the product of the evolutionary history of a species (phylogeny), all biologically intact members of a species are more or less susceptible to punishment by the same unconditioned punishers. Painful stimulation such as that caused by physical trauma to the body, certain odors and tastes, physical restraint, loss of bodily support, and extreme muscular effort are examples of stimulus changes that typically serve as unconditioned punishers for humans (Michael, 2004). Like unconditioned reinforcers, unconditioned punishers are "phylogenically important events that bear directly on fitness" of the organism (Baum, 1994, p. 59).

However, virtually any stimulus to which an organism's receptors are sensitive—light, sound, and temperature, to name a few—can be intensified to the point that its delivery will suppress behavior even though the stimulus is below levels that actually cause tissue damage (Bijou & Baer, 1965). Unlike unconditioned reinforcers, such as food and water, whose effectiveness depends on a relevant establishing operation, under most conditions many unconditioned punishers will suppress any behavior that precedes their onset. For example, an organism does not have to be "deprived of electric stimulation" for the onset of electric shock to function as punishment. (However, the behavior of an organism that has just received many shocks in a short period of time, particularly shocks of mild intensity, may be relatively unaffected by another shock.)

Conditioned Punishers

A **conditioned punisher** is a stimulus change that functions as punishment as a result of a person's conditioning history. (Some authors use *secondary punisher* or *learned* *punisher* as synonyms for a conditioned punisher.) A conditioned punisher acquires the capability to function as a punisher through stimulus–stimulus pairing with one or more unconditioned or conditioned punishers. For example, as a result of its onset at or very near the same time as an electric shock, a previously neutral stimulus change, such as an audible tone, will become a conditioned punisher capable of suppressing behavior that immediately precedes the tone when it occurs later in the absence of the shock (Hake & Azrin, 1965).[3] If a conditioned punisher is repeatedly presented without the punisher(s) with which it was initially paired, its effectiveness as punishment will wane until it is no longer a punisher.

Previously neutral stimuli can also become conditioned punishers for humans without direct physical pairing with another punisher through a pairing process Alessi (1992) called *verbal analog conditioning*. This is similar to the example of verbal pairing described in Chapter 11 for the conditioning of a conditioned reinforcer in which Engelmann (1975) showed cut up pieces of yellow construction paper to a group of preschool children and told them, "These pieces of yellow paper are what big kids work for" (pp. 98–100). From that point on, many children began working extra hard for yellow pieces of paper. Miltenberger (2001) gave the example of a carpenter telling his apprentice that if the electric saw starts to make smoke, the saw motor may become damaged or the blade may break. The carpenter's statement establishes smoke from the saw as a conditioned punisher capable of decreasing the frequency of any behaviors that immediately precede the smoke (e.g., pushing too forcefully on the saw, holding the saw at an inappropriate angle).

A stimulus change that has been paired with numerous forms of unconditioned and conditioned punishers becomes a **generalized conditioned punisher.** For example, reprimands ("No!" "Don't do that!") and social disapproval (e.g., scowl, head shake, frowns) are generalized conditioned punishers for many people because they have been paired repeatedly with a wide range of unconditioned and conditioned punishers (e.g., burned finger, loss of privileges). As with generalized conditioned reinforcers, generalized conditioned punishers are free from the control of specific motivating conditions and will function as punishment under most conditions.

At the risk of redundancy, we will again stress the critical point that punishers, like reinforcers, are not defined by their physical properties, but by their functions

(Morse & Kelleher, 1977). Even stimuli whose presentation under most conditions would function as unconditioned reinforcers or punishers can have the opposite effect under certain conditions. For example, a bite of food will function as a punisher for a person who has eaten too much, and an electric shock may function as a conditioned reinforcer if it signals the availability of food for a food-deprived organism (e.g., Holz & Azrin, 1961). If a student receives smiley face stickers and praise for his academic work and his productivity decreases as a result, smiley face stickers and praise are punishers for that student. What might serve as a punisher at home might not be a punisher at school. What might be a punisher under one set of circumstances might not be a punisher under a different set of circumstances. Although common experiences mean that many of the same stimulus events function as conditioned punishers for most people, a punisher for one person may be a reinforcer for another. (Remember the cartoon described in Chapter 11 of two students cleaning erasers after school: The activity was punishment for one and reinforcement for the other.)

Factors That Influence the Effectiveness of Punishment

Reviews of basic and applied research on punishment consistently identify the following variables as keys to the effectiveness of punishment: the immediacy of punishment, the intensity of the punisher, the schedule or frequency of punishment, the availability of reinforcement for the target behavior, and the availability of reinforcement for an alternative behavior (e.g., Axelrod, 1990; Azrin & Holz, 1966; Lerman & Vorndran, 2002; Matson & Taras, 1989).

Immediacy

Maximum suppressive effects are obtained when the onset of the punisher occurs as soon as possible after the occurrence of a target response.

> The longer the time delay between the occurrence of the response and the occurrence of the stimulus change, the less effective the punishment will be in changing the relevant response frequency, but not much is known about upper limits. (Michael, 2004, p. 36)

Intensity/Magnitude

Basic researchers examining the effects of the punishers of varying intensity or magnitude (in terms of amount or duration) have reported three reliable findings: (1) a positive correlation between the intensity of the punishing

---

[3]A stimulus that becomes a conditioned punisher by being paired with another punisher does not have to be a neutral stimulus prior to the pairing. The stimulus could already function as a reinforcer under other conditions. For example, a blue light that has been paired repeatedly with reinforcement in one setting and with punishment in another setting is a conditioned reinforcer or a conditioned punisher depending on the setting.

stimulus and response suppression: the greater the magnitude of the punishing stimulus, the more immediately and thoroughly it suppresses the occurrence of the behavior (e.g., Azrin & Holtz, 1966); (2) recovery from punishment is negatively correlated with intensity of the punishing stimulus: the more intense the punisher, the less likely that responding will reoccur when punishment is terminated (e.g., Hake, Azrin, & Oxford, 1967); and (3) a high-intensity stimulus may be ineffective as punishment if the stimulus used as punishment was initially of low intensity and gradually increased (e.g., Terris & Barnes, 1969). However, as Lerman and Vorndran (2002) pointed out, relatively few applied studies have examined the relation between punishment magnitude and treatment efficacy, and that research has yielded inconsistent results sometimes contradictory with basic research findings (e.g., Cole, Montgomery, Wilson, & Milan, 2000; Singh, Dawson, & Manning, 1981; Williams, Kirkpatrick-Sanchez, & Iwata, 1993). When selecting the magnitude of a punishing stimulus, the practitioner should ask: Will this amount of the punishing stimulus suppress occurrences of the problem behavior? Lerman and Vorndran (2002) recommended:

> While the punishing stimulus needs to be intensive enough for an effective application, it should not be more intense than necessary. Until further applied research on magnitude is conducted, practitioners should select magnitudes that have been shown to be safe and effective in clinical studies, as long as the magnitude is considered acceptable and practical by those who will be implementing treatment. (p. 443)

Schedule

The suppressive effects of a punisher are maximized by a continuous schedule of punishment (FR 1) in which each occurrence of the behavior is followed by the punishing consequence. In general, the greater the proportion of responses that are followed by the punisher, the greater the response reduction will be (Azrin, Holz, & Hake, 1963; Zimmerman & Ferster, 1962). Azrin and Holz (1966) summarized the comparative effects of punishment on continuous and intermittent schedules as follows:

> Continuous punishment produces more suppression than does intermittent punishment for as long as the punishment contingency is maintained. However, after the punishment contingency has been discontinued, continuous punishment allows more rapid recovery of the responses, possibly because the absence of punishment can be more rapidly discriminated. (p. 415)

Intermittent punishment may be somewhat effective under some conditions (e.g., Clark, Rowbury, Baer, & Baer, 1973; Cipani, Brendlinger, McDowell, & Usher,

1991; Romanczyk, 1977). Results of a study by Lerman, Iwata, Shore, and DeLeon (1997) demonstrated that a gradual thinning of the punishment schedule might maintain the suppressive effects of punishment that was initially delivered on a continuous schedule (FR 1). Participants were five adults with profound mental retardation and histories of chronic self-injurious behavior (SIB) in the form of hand mouthing or head hitting. Treatment by punishment (timeout from reinforcement for one participant and contingent restraint for the other four) delivered on a continuous (FR 1) schedule produced marked reductions in SIB from baseline levels for all five participants. (Figure 14.3 shows the results for three of the five participants.) The participants were then exposed to intermittent schedules of punishment (either fixed-interval [FI] 120 seconds or FI 300 seconds). On the FI 120-second schedule, the therapist delivered punishment contingent on the first SIB response after 120 seconds had elapsed since the previous application of punishment or the start of the session. The frequency of SIB under the intermittent schedule of punishment for all but one participant (Wayne, not shown in Figure 14.3) increased to baseline levels.

After reestablishing low levels of SIB for each participant with FR 1 punishment, the researchers gradually thinned the punishment schedules. For example, schedule thinning for Paul consisted of increasing the duration of the fixed-interval duration by 30-second increments to FI 300 seconds (i.e., FR 30 seconds, FR 60 seconds, FR 90 seconds, etc.). With the exception of a few sessions, Paul's SIB remained at low levels as the punishment schedule was progressively thinned over 57 sessions. During the final 11 sessions in which punishment was delivered on an FI 300-second schedule, his SIB occurred at a mean of 2.4% of observed intervals (compared to 33% in baseline). A similar pattern of success with a gradually thinning punishment schedule was obtained for another subject, Wendy (not shown in Figure 14.3).

The effectiveness of punishment on an FI 300-second schedule for three of the five participants—Paul, Wendy, and Wayne (whose SIB remained low even though punishment was abruptly changed from FR 1 to FI 120 seconds and then FI 300 seconds)—enabled an infrequent application of punishment. In practice, this would free therapists or staff from continuous monitoring of behavior.

For Melissa and Candace, however, repeated attempts to gradually thin the punishment schedule proved unsuccessful in maintaining the frequency of their SIB at levels attained by FR 1 punishment. Lerman and colleagues (1997) speculated that one explanation for the ineffectiveness of punishment on a fixed-interval schedule was that after a person has experienced an FI schedule for some time, the delivery of punishment could

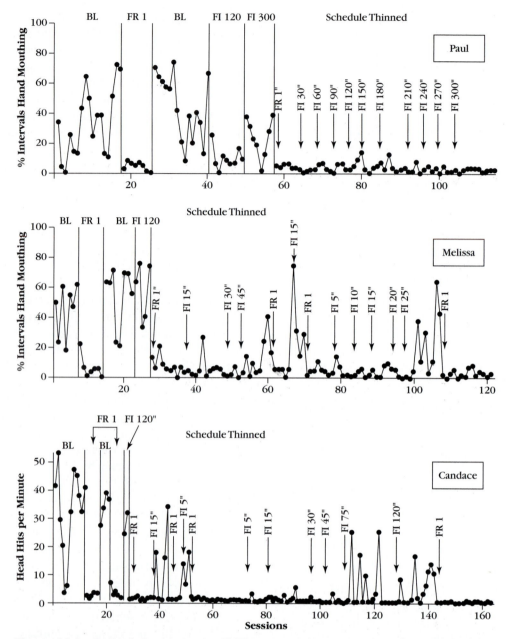

Figure 14.3 Self-injurious behavior (SIB) by three adults with profound mental retardation during baseline and punishment delivered on continuous (FR 1) and various fixed-interval schedules.

From "Effects of Intermittent Punishment on Self-Injurious Behavior: An Evaluation of Schedule Thinning" by D. C. Lerman, B. A. Iwata, B. A. Shore, and I. G. DeLeon, 1997, *Journal of Applied Behavior Analysis, 30*, p. 194. Copyright 1997 by the Society for the Experimental Analysis of Behavior, Inc. Used by permission.

function "as a discriminative stimulus for punishment-free periods, leading to a gradual overall increase in responding under FI punishment" (p. 198).

Reinforcement for the Target Behavior

The effectiveness of punishment is modulated by the reinforcement contingencies maintaining the problem behavior. If a problem behavior is occurring at a frequency sufficient to cause concern, it is presumably producing reinforcement. If the target response was never reinforced, then "punishment would scarcely be possible since the response would rarely occur" (Azrin & Holz, 1966, p. 433).

To the extent that the reinforcement maintaining the problem behavior can be reduced or eliminated, punishment will be more effective. Of course, if all reinforcement for the problem behavior was withheld, the resulting extinction schedule would result in the reduction of the behavior independent of the presence of a punishment contingency. However, as Azrin and Holz (1966) pointed out:

> The physical world often provides reinforcement contingences that cannot be eliminated easily. The faster we move through space, the quicker we get to where we are going, whether the movement be walking or driving an auto. Hence, running and speeding will inevitably be reinforced. Extinction of running and speeding could be accomplished only by the impossible procedure of eliminating all reinforcing events that result from movement through space. Some other reductive method, such as punishment must be used. (p. 433)

Reinforcement for Alternative Behaviors

Holz, Azrin, and Ayllon (1963) found that punishment was ineffective in reducing psychotic behavior when that behavior was the only means by which patients could attain reinforcement. However, when patients could emit an alternative response that resulted in reinforcement, punishment was effective in reducing their inappropriate behavior. Summing up laboratory and applied studies that have reported the same finding, Millenson (1967) stated:

> If punishment is employed in an attempt to eliminate certain behavior, then whatever reinforcement the undesirable behavior had led to must be made available via a more desirable behavior. Merely punishing school children for "misbehavior" in class may have little permanent effect. . . . The reinforcers for "misbehavior" must be analyzed and the attainment of these reinforcers perhaps permitted by means of different responses, or in other situations. . . . But for this to happen, it appears important to provide a rewarded alternative to the punished response. (p. 429)

A study by Thompson, Iwata, Conners, and Roscoe (1999) is an excellent illustration of how the suppressive effects of punishment can be enhanced by reinforcement for an alternative response. Four adults with developmental disabilities who had been referred to a day treatment program for self-injurious behavior (SIB) participated in the study. Twenty-eight-year-old Shelly, for example, expelled saliva and then rubbed it onto her hands and other surfaces (e.g., tables, windows), which led to frequent infections; and Ricky, a 34-year-old man with deaf-blindness, frequently hit his head and body resulting in bruises or contusions. Previous interventions such as differential reinforcement of appropriate behavior, response blocking, and protective equipment had been ineffective in reducing the SIB of all four participants.

The results of a functional behavior analysis (see Chapter 24) with each participant suggested that SIB was maintained by automatic reinforcement. Reinforcer assessments were conducted to identify materials that produced the highest levels of contact or manipulation and the lowest levels of SIB (e.g., wooden stringing beads, a mirrored microswitch that produced vibration and music, a balloon). The researchers then conducted a punisher assessment to determine the least intrusive consequences that produced at least a 75% reduction in SIB for each participant.

Thompson and colleagues (1999) analyzed the effects of punishment with and without reinforcement of alternative behavior with an experimental design that combined alternating treatments, reversal, and multiple baseline across subjects' elements. During the no-punishment condition, the therapist was present in the room but did not interact with the participant or provide any consequences for SIB. Immediately following each occurrence of SIB during the punishment condition, the therapist delivered the consequence that had previously been identified as a punisher for the participant. For example:

> Each time Shelly expelled saliva, the therapist delivered a reprimand ("no spitting") and briefly dried each of her hands (and any other wet surfaces) with a cloth. Ricky's hands were held in his lap for 15 s each time he engaged in SIB. Donna and Lynn both received a verbal reprimand and had their hands held across their chests for 15 s following SIB. (p. 321)

Within each no-punishment and punishment phase, sessions of reinforcement and no-reinforcement conditions were alternated. During reinforcement sessions, participants had continual access to leisure materials or activities previously identified as highly preferred; during no-reinforcement sessions, participants had no access to leisure materials. Because Ricky never independently manipulated any of the leisure materials during the reinforcer assessment but approached M&M candies on the highest percentage of assessment trials, during the reinforcement sessions he received edible reinforcement for each 2 seconds that he manipulated any of several items attached to a vest (e.g., Koosh ball, beads, fur).

Figure 14.4 shows the results of the study. During the no-punishment baseline phase, only Shelly's SIB was consistently lower during the reinforcement sessions than during the no-reinforcement sessions. Although the introduction of punishment reduced SIB from baseline levels for all four participants, punishment was more effective during those sessions in which reinforcement for alternative behaviors was available. Also of interest to practitioners should be the finding that fewer punishers were delivered during the punishment condition sessions when reinforcement was available. (Ricky began to resist the hands-down restraint procedure during the punishment with no reinforcement condition, and several

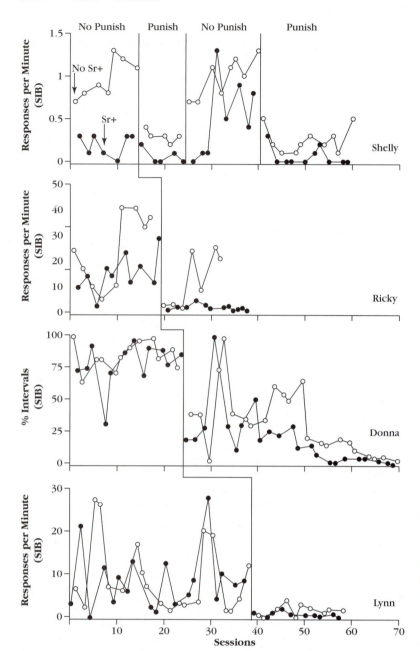

Figure 14.4 Self-injurious behavior by four adults with developmental disabilities during alternating reinforcement and no reinforcement conditions across no-punishment and punishment phases.

From "Effects of Reinforcement for Alternative Behavior during Punishment for Self-Injury," by R. H. Thompson, B. A. Iwata, J. Conners, and E. M. Roscoe, 1999, *Journal of Applied Behavior Analysis, 32*, p. 323. Copyright 1999 by the Society for the Experimental Analysis of Behavior, Inc. Used by permission.

sessions were terminated early because the therapist could not implement the procedure safely. Therefore, the punishment with no reinforcement condition was terminated after seven sessions and the punishment with reinforcement continued for six additional sessions.)

Thompson and colleagues (1999) summarized the main findings of their study with these conclusions:

> Consistent with the recommendation made by Azrin and Holz (1966), results of this study indicate that the effects of punishment can be enhanced when reinforcement is provided for an alternative response. Furthermore, these results suggest a method for increasing the effectiveness of punishment through means other than increasing the

aversiveness of the punishing stimulus, thereby resulting in the development of more effective yet less restrictive interventions. (p. 326)

Possible Side Effects and Problems with Punishment

A variety of side effects and problems are often correlated with the applications of punishment, including the elicitation of undesirable emotional responses and aggression, escape and avoidance, and an increased rate of the problem behavior under nonpunishment conditions (e.g., Azrin & Holz, 1966; Hutchinson, 1977; Linscheid

& Meinhold, 1990). Other problems noted include modeling undesirable behavior and overusing punishment because of the negative reinforcement it provides for the punishing agent's behavior.

Emotional and Aggressive Reactions

Punishment sometimes evokes emotional and aggressive reactions that can involve a combination of respondent and conditioned operant behaviors. Punishment, especially positive punishment in the form of aversive stimulation, may evoke aggressive behavior with respondent and operant components (Azrin & Holz, 1966). For example, electric shock elicited reflexive forms of aggression and fighting in laboratory animals (Azrin, Hutchinson, & Hake, 1963; Ulrich & Azrin, 1962; Ulrich, Wolff, & Azrin, 1962). Such pain-elicited, or *respondent aggression,* is directed toward any nearby person or object. For example, a student who is punished severely may begin to throw and destroy materials within her reach. Alternatively, the student may try to attack the person delivering the punishment. Aggressive behavior following punishment that occurs because it has enabled the person to escape the aversive stimulation in the past is referred to as *operant aggression* (Azrin & Holz, 1966).

Although basic laboratory researchers, using intense and unavoidable punishers, have reliably produced respondent and operant aggression with nonhuman animals, many applied studies of punishment report no evidence of aggression (e.g., Linscheid & Reichenbach, 2002; Risley, 1968).

Escape and Avoidance

Escape and avoidance are natural reactions to aversive stimulation. Escape and avoidance behaviors take a wide variety of forms, some of which may be a greater problem than the target behavior being punished. For example, a student who is admonished repeatedly for sloppy work or coming to class unprepared may stop coming to class altogether. A person may lie, cheat, hide, or exhibit other undesirable behaviors to avoid punishment. Mayer, Sulzer, and Cody (1968) indicated that avoidance and escape need not always take form in the literal sense of those terms. People sometimes escape punishing environments by taking drugs or alcohol, or by simply "tuning out."

As the intensity of a punisher increases, so does the likelihood of escape and avoidance. For example, in a study evaluating the effectiveness of a specially designed cigarette holder that delivered an electric shock to the user when it was opened as an intervention for reducing cigarette smoking, Powell and Azrin (1968) found that

"As the punishment intensity increased, the duration decreased for which the subjects would remain in contact with the contingency; ultimately, an intensity was reached at which they refused to experience it altogether" (p. 69).

Escape and avoidance as side effects to punishment, like emotional and aggressive reactions, can be minimized or precluded altogether by providing the person with desirable alternative responses to the problem behavior that both avoid the delivery of punishment and provide reinforcement.

Behavioral Contrast

Reynolds (1961) introduced the term **behavioral contrast** to refer to the phenomenon in which a change in one component of a multiple schedule that increases or decreases the rate of responding on that component is accompanied by a change in the response rate in the opposite direction on the other, unaltered component of the schedule.[4] Behavioral contrast can occur as a function of a change in reinforcement or punishment density on one component of a multiple schedule (Brethower & Reynolds, 1962; Lattal & Griffin, 1972). For example, behavioral contrast for punishment takes the following general form: (a) Responses are occurring at similar rates on two components of a multiple schedule (e.g., a pigeon pecks a backlit key, which alternates between blue and green, reinforcement is delivered on the same schedule on both keys, and the bird pecks at roughly the same rate regardless of the key's color); (b) responses on one component of the schedule are punished, whereas responses on the other component continue to go unpunished (e.g., pecks on the blue key are punished, and pecks on the green key continue to produce reinforcement at the prior rate); (c) rate of responding decreases on the punished component and increases on the unpunished component (e.g., pecks on the blue key are suppressed and pecks on the green key increase even though pecks on the green key produce no more reinforcement than before).

Here is a hypothetical applied example of a contrast effect of punishment. A child is eating cookies before dinner from the kitchen cookie jar at equal rates in the presence and absence of his grandmother. One day, Grandma scolds the child for eating a cookie before dinner, which suppresses his rate of predinner cookie eating when she is in the kitchen (see Figure 14.2); but when Grandma's not in the kitchen, the boy eats cookies from the jar at a higher rate than he did when unsupervised prior to punishment. Contrast effects of punishment can be minimized, or prevented altogether, by consistently

---

[4]Multiple schedules of reinforcement are described in Chapter 13.

punishing occurrences of the target behavior in all relevant settings and stimulus conditions, withholding or at least minimizing the person's access to reinforcement for the target behavior, and providing alternative desirable behaviors. (With respect to our hypothetical case of the child eating cookies before dinner, we recommend simply removing the cookie jar!)

Punishment May Involve Undesirable Modeling

Most readers are familiar with the example of the parent who, while spanking a child, says, "This will teach you not to hit your playmates!" Unfortunately, the child may be more likely to imitate the parent's actions, not the parent's words. More than two decades of research have found a strong correlation between young children's exposure to harsh and excessive punishment and antisocial behavior and conduct disorders as adolescents and adults (Patterson, 1982; Patterson, Reid, & Dishion, 1992; Sprague & Walker, 2000). Although the proper use of behavior change tactics based on the principle of punishment does not involve harsh treatment or negative personal interactions, practitioners should heed Bandura's (1969) valuable counsel in this regard:

> Anyone attempting to control specific troublesome responses should avoid modeling punitive forms of behavior that not only counteract the effects of direct training but also increase the probability that on future occasions the individual may respond to interpersonal thwarting in an imitative manner. (p. 313)

Negative Reinforcement of the Punishing Agent's Behavior

Negative reinforcement may be a reason for the widespread use of (too often ineffective and unnecessary) and reliance on (mostly misguided) punishment in child rearing, education, and society. When Person A delivers a reprimand or other aversive consequence to Person B for misbehaving, the immediate effect is often the cessation of the troubling behavior, which serves as negative reinforcement for Person A's behavior. Or, as Ellen Reese (1966) said so succinctly, "Punishment reinforces the punisher" (p. 37). Alber and Heward (2000) described how the natural contingencies at work in a typical classroom could strengthen a teacher's use of reprimands for disruptive behavior while undermining her use of contingent praise and attention for appropriate behavior.

> Paying attention to students when they are behaving inappropriately (e.g., "Carlos, you need to sit down right now!") is negatively reinforced by the immediate cessation of the inappropriate behavior (e.g., Carlos stops running around and returns to his seat). As a result, the teacher is more likely to attend to student disruptions in

the future. . . . Although few teachers must be taught to reprimand students for misbehavior, many teachers need help increasing the frequency with which they praise student accomplishments. Teacher-praising behavior is usually not reinforced as effectively as teacher-reprimanding behavior. Praising a student for appropriate behavior usually produces no immediate effects—the child continues to do his work when praised. Although praising a student for working productively on an assignment may increase the future likelihood of that behavior, there are no immediate consequences for the teacher. By contrast, reprimanding a student often produces an immediate improvement in the teacher's world (if only temporary)—that functions as effective negative reinforcement for reprimanding. (pp. 178–179)

Even though the reprimands may be ineffective in suppressing future frequency of misbehavior, the immediate effect of stopping the annoying behavior is powerful reinforcement that increases the frequency with which the teacher will issue reprimands when confronted with misbehavior.

Examples of Positive Punishment Interventions

Interventions based on positive punishment take a wide variety of forms. We describe five in this section: reprimands, response blocking, contingent exercise, overcorrection, and contingent electric stimulation.

Reprimands

It may seem strange that immediately following a discussion of teachers' overreliance on and misuse of reprimands our first example of a positive punishment intervention is reprimands. The delivery of verbal reprimands following the occurrence of misbehavior is without doubt the most common form of *attempted* positive punishment. However, a number of studies have shown that a firm reprimand such as "No!" or "Stop! Don't do that!" delivered immediately on the occurrence of a behavior can suppress future responding (e.g., Hall et al., 1971, see Figure 14.1; Jones & Miller, 1974; Sajwaj, Culver, Hall, & Lehr, 1972; Thompson et al., 1999).

In spite of the widespread use of reprimands in an effort to suppress undesired behavior, surprisingly few studies have examined the effectiveness of reprimands as punishers. Results of a series of experiments by Van Houten, Nau, Mackenzie-Keating, Sameoto, and Colavecchia (1982) designed to identify variables that increased the effectiveness of reprimands as punishers for disruptive behavior in the classroom found that (a) reprimands delivered with eye contact and "a firm grasp of the student's shoulders" were more effective than reprimands without those nonverbal components, and (b) reprimands delivered in close proximity to the student were more effective than reprimands delivered from across the room.

The teacher who repeatedly admonishes her students in a mild fashion to "sit down" would be advised instead to state once strongly, "SIT DOWN!" When the command is issued once, students are more likely to follow the direction. If the command is given repeatedly, students may habituate to the increased frequency, and the reprimand will gradually lose its effect as a punisher. A loud reprimand, however, is not necessarily more effective than a reprimand stated in a normal voice. An interesting study by O'Leary, Kaufman, Kass, and Drabman (1970) found that quiet reprimands that were audible only to the child being reprimanded were more effective in reducing disruptive behavior than loud reprimands that could be heard by many children in the classroom.

If the only way a child receives adult attention is in the form of reprimands, it should not be surprising that reprimands function as reinforcement for that child rather than as punishment. Indeed, Madsen, Becker, Thomas, Koser, and Plager (1968) found that the repeated use of a reprimand while students were out of seat served to increase, rather than reduce, the behavior. Consistent with research on other punishing stimuli, reprimands are more effective as punishers when motivation for the problem behavior has been minimized and the availability of an alternative behavior has been maximized (Van Houten & Doleys, 1983).

A parent or teacher does not want to be in a pattern of constantly reprimanding. Reprimands should be used thoughtfully and sparingly in combination with frequent praise and attention contingent on appropriate behavior. O'Leary and colleagues (1970) recommended that

> An ideal combination would probably be frequent praise, some soft reprimands, and very occasional loud reprimands. . . . Combined with praise, soft reprimands might be very helpful in reducing disruptive behaviors. In contrast, it appears that loud reprimands lead one into a vicious cycle of more and more reprimands resulting in even more disruptive behavior. (p. 155)

Response Blocking

Response blocking—physically intervening as soon as the person begins to emit the problem behavior to prevent or "block" the completion of the response—has been shown to be effective in reducing the frequency of some problem behaviors such as chronic hand mouthing, eye poking, and pica (e.g., Lalli, Livezy, & Kates, 1996; Lerman & Iwata, 1996; Reid, Parsons, Phillips, & Green,

1993). In addition to preventing the response from occurring by using the least amount of physical contact and restraint possible, the therapist might issue a verbal reprimand or prompt to stop engaging in the behavior (e.g., Hagopian & Adelinis, 2001).

Lerman and Iwata (1996) used response blocking in treating the chronic hand mouthing (contact between any part of the hand and the lips or mouth) of Paul, a 32-year-old man with profound mental retardation. Following a baseline condition, in which Paul was seated in a chair with no one interacting with him and no leisure materials were available, response blocking on an FR 1 schedule was implemented. A therapist sat behind Paul and blocked his attempts to put his hand in his mouth. "Paul was not prevented from bringing his hand to his mouth; however, the therapist blocked the hand from entering the mouth by placing the palm of her hand about 2 cm in front of Paul's mouth" (p. 232). Response blocking produced an immediate and rapid decrease in hand mouthing attempts to near-zero levels (see Figure 14.5).

Response blocking is often implemented as a treatment for SIB or self-stimulatory behavior when functional analysis reveals consistent responding in the absence of socially mediated consequences, which suggests the possibility that the behavior is maintained by automatic reinforcement by sensory stimuli produced by the response. Because response blocking prevents the learner from contacting the sensory stimuli that are normally produced by the response, subsequent decreases in responding could be due to extinction. Lerman and Iwata (1996) presented their study as a potential method for distinguishing whether the suppressive effects of response blocking are due to punishment or extinction mechanisms. They explained their reasoning as follows:

> Depending on the mechanism through which behavior is reduced (extinction vs. punishment), different schedules of reinforcement or punishment are in effect when a given proportion of responses is blocked. For example when every fourth response is blocked (.25), the behavior is exposed to either a fixed-ratio (FR) 1.3 schedule of reinforcement (if blocking functions as extinction) or an FR 4 schedule of punishment (if blocking functions as punishment); when three out of four responses are blocked (.75), the behavior is exposed to either an FR 4 schedule of reinforcement or an FR 1.3 schedule of punishment. Thus, as larger proportions of responses are blocked, the reinforcement schedule becomes leaner and the punishment schedule becomes richer. If response blocking produces extinction, response rates should increase or be maintained as more responses are blocked (i.e., as the reinforcement schedule is thinned), until [the effects of] extinction [i.e., reduced response rate] occurs at some point along the progression. Conversely, if the

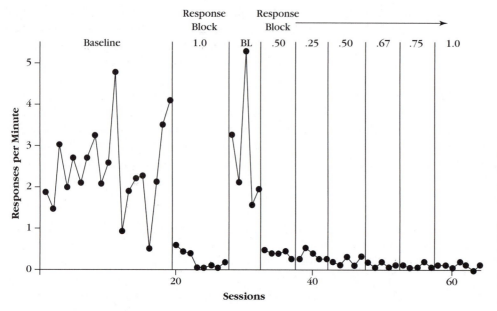

Figure 14.5 Rates of hand mouthing during baseline and varying schedules of response blocking.

From "A Methodology for Distinguishing between Extinction and Punishment Effects Associated with Response Blocking," by D. C. Lerman and B. A. Iwata, 1996, *Journal of Applied Behavior Analysis, 29,* p. 232. Copyright 1996 by the Society for the Experimental Analysis of Behavior, Inc. Used by permission.

procedure functions as punishment, response rates should decrease as more responses are blocked (i.e., as the punishment schedule becomes richer). (pp. 231–232, words in brackets added)

A condition in which all responses are blocked might function as an extinction schedule (i.e., reinforcement in the form of sensory stimuli is withheld for all responses) or as a continuous (FR 1) schedule of punishment (i.e., all responses are followed by physical contact). As Lerman and Iwata (1996) explained, if only some responses are blocked, the situation may function as an intermittent schedule of reinforcement or as an intermittent schedule of punishment. Therefore, comparing response rates among conditions in which different proportions of responses are blocked should indicate whether the effects are due to extinction or to punishment.

If response blocking functioned as extinction for Paul's hand mouthing, an initial increase in response rate would be expected when the blocking procedure was implemented for every response; however, no such increase was observed.[5] If response blocking functioned as punishment, blocking every response would constitute a continuous schedule of punishment and a rapid decrease in responding would be expected; and that is exactly what the results showed (see data for the first response block [1.0] phase in Figure 14.5).

On the other hand, if response blocking functioned as extinction for Paul's hand mouthing, then blocking some but not all responses would place the hand

mouthing on an intermittent schedule of reinforcement and responding would be expected to increase from baseline levels. And blocking an ever-larger proportion of responses thins the reinforcement schedule further causing the response rate to rise even higher. Instead, as a greater proportion of responses were blocked, the suppressive effects on Paul's SIB became more pronounced, a result expected as a punishment schedule becomes denser. Overall, therefore, the results of the experiment indicated that response blocking functioned as punishment for Paul's hand mouthing.

On the other hand, a systematic replication of Lerman and Iwata's (1996) experiment, conducted by Smith, Russo, and Le (1999), found that the frequency of eye-poking by a 41-year-old woman treated with response blocking decreased gradually—a response pattern indicative of extinction. The authors concluded that, "whereas blocking may reduce one participant's behavior via punishment, it may extinguish another participant's behavior" (p. 369).[6]

Although response blocking may be viewed as a less restrictive and more humane intervention than delivering aversive stimulation after a response has occurred, it must

---

[5]When an extinction procedure is first implemented, an increase in responding, called an *extinction burst,* is sometimes observed before the response rate begins to decline. The principle, procedure, and effects of extinction are detailed in Chapter 21.

[6]It might be argued that the suppressive effects of response blocking cannot be due to punishment or to extinction on the grounds that response blocking occurs *before* the response has been emitted and punishment and extinction are both response → consequence relations (in the case of extinction, the consequence is absence of the reinforcement that followed the behavior in the past). As Lalli, Livezy, and Kates (1996) noted, response blocking prevents the response → consequence cycle from occurring. However, if the problem behavior response class is conceptualized to include the occurrence of any portion of a relevant response, then blocking a person's hand *after* it begins to move toward contact with his head is a consequence whose suppressive effects can be analyzed in terms of extinction, punishment, or both.

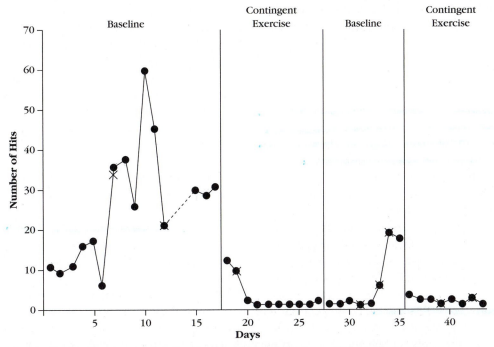

Figure 14.6   Number of times a 7-year-old boy hit other children during 6-hour school days during baseline and contingent exercise. *X*s represent response measures recorded by a second observer.

From "Contingent Exercise: A Mild but Powerful Procedure for Suppressing Inappropriate Verbal and Aggressive Behavior," by S. C. Luce, J. Delquadri, and R. V. Hall, 1980, *Journal of Applied Behavior Analysis, 13*, p. 587. Copyright 1980 by the Society for the Experimental Analysis of Behavior, Inc. Used by permission.

be approached with great care. Side effects such as aggression and resistance to the response blocking procedure have occurred in some studies (Hagopian & Adelinis, 2001; Lerman, Kelley, Vorndran, & Van Camp, 2003). Providing prompts and reinforcement for an alternative response can minimize resistance and aggression. For example, the aggressive behavior by 26-year-old man with moderate mental retardation and bipolar disorder during treatment with response blocking for pica (ingesting paper, pencils, paint chips, and human feces) was reduced by supplementing response blocking with a prompt and redirection to engage in an alternative behavior, in this case moving to an area of the room where popcorn was available (Hagopian & Adelinis, 2001).

Contingent Exercise

Contingent exercise is an intervention in which the person is required to perform a response that is not topographically related to the problem behavior. Contingent exercise has been found effective as punishment for various self-stimulatory, stereotypic, disruptive, aggressive, and self-injurious behaviors (e.g., DeCatanzaro & Baldwin, 1978; Kern, Koegel, & Dunlap, 1984; Luce & Hall,

1981; Luiselli, 1984).[7] In perhaps the most frequently cited example of contingent exercise as a punisher, Luce, Delquadri, and Hall (1980) found that the repetition of mild exercise contingent on aggressive behavior by two boys with severe disabilities reduced it to near-zero levels. Figure 14.6 shows the results for Ben, a 7-year-old who frequently hit other children at school. Each time Ben hit someone, he was required to stand up and sit down 10 times. Initially, Ben had to be physically prompted to stand; an assistant held the child's hand while pulling his upper body forward. Physical prompts were accompanied by verbal prompts of "stand up" and "sit down." Soon, whenever hitting occurred, the nearest adult simply said, "Ben, no hitting. Stand up and sit down 10 times" and the verbal prompts alone were sufficient

---

[7]Increasing the effort or force required to perform a behavior can be an effective tactic for reducing responding (Friman & Poling, 1995). There is no consensus as to whether punishment accounts for the reduced responding. As with response blocking, one perspective from which increased response effort can be conceptualized as a punishment procedure is to consider the movement necessary to come into contact with the increased effort requirement as a member of the target behavior response class. In that case, the increased effort required to continue the response to completion is (a) a consequence for the response that brought the learner into contact with it, and (b) aversive stimulation that functions as punishment as the frequency of future responding decreases.

for Ben to complete the exercise. If a hitting episode occurred during the contingent exercise, the procedure was reinstated.

Overcorrection

Overcorrection is a behavior reduction tactic in which, contingent on each occurrence of the problem behavior, the learner is required to engage in effortful behavior that is directly or logically related to the problem. Originally developed by Foxx and Azrin (1972, 1973; Foxx & Bechtel, 1983) as a method for decreasing disruptive and maladaptive behaviors of adults with mental retardation in institutional settings, overcorrection combines the suppressive effects of punishment and the educative effects of positive practice. Overcorrection includes either or both of two components: restitution and positive practice.

In **restitutional overcorrection,** contingent on the problem behavior, the learner is required to repair the damage caused by the problem behavior by returning the environment to its original state and then to engage in additional behavior that brings the environment to a condition vastly better than it was prior to the misbehavior. A parent applying restitutional overcorrection with a child who repeatedly tracks mud onto the kitchen floor might require the child to first wipe up the mud and clean his shoes and then to *over*correct the effects of his misbehavior by mopping and waxing a portion of the floor and polishing his shoes.

Azrin and Foxx (1971) used restitutional overcorrection in their toilet training program by requiring a person who had an accident to undress, wash her clothes, hang them up to dry, shower, dress in clean clothing, and then clean up a portion of the lavatory. Azrin and Wesolowki (1975) eliminated stealing of food by hospitalized adults with mental retardation by requiring residents to return not only the stolen food, or the portion that remained uneaten, but also to purchase an additional item of that food at the commissary and give it to the victim.

Azrin and Besalel (1999) differentiated a procedure they called *simple correction* from overcorrection. With simple correction, the learner is required, subsequent to the occurrence of an inappropriate behavior, to restore the environment to its previous state. For example, a simple correction procedure is in effect when requiring a student who cuts to the head of the lunch line to go to the back of the line. Requiring the student to wait until all others get in line and are served before reentering the line would constitute a form of overcorrection in this instance. Azrin and Besalel recommended that simple correction be used to reduce behaviors that are not severe, occur infrequently, are not deliberate, and do not severely interfere with or annoy other people.

Correction is not possible if the problem behavior produces an irreversible effect (e.g., a one-of-a-kind dish is broken) or if the corrective behavior is beyond the person's means or skills. In such instances, Azrin and Besalel (1999) recommended that the person be required to correct as much of the damage his behavior caused as possible, be present at all points in the correction, and assist with any parts of the correction that he is able to perform. For example, a child who broke a neighbor's expensive window should clean up the pieces of glass, measure the window, contact the store for a replacement pane, be present while the new window pane is installed, and assist with every step.

In **positive practice overcorrection,** contingent on an occurrence of the problem behavior, the learner is required to repeatedly perform a correct form of the behavior, or a behavior incompatible with the problem behavior, for a specified duration of time or number of responses. Positive practice overcorrection entails an educative component in that it requires the person to engage in an appropriate alternative behavior. The parent whose son tracks mud into the house could add a positive practice component by requiring him to practice wiping his feet on the outside door mat and entering the house for 2 minutes or 5 consecutive times. Overcorrection that includes restitution and positive practice helps teach what to do in addition to what not to do. The child who breaks an irreplaceable dish could be required to gently and slowly wash a number dishes, perhaps with an exaggerated carefulness.

Researchers and practitioners have used positive practice overcorrection to reduce the frequency of problem behaviors such as toilet training (Azrin & Foxx, 1971), self-stimulation and stereotypic behavior (Azrin, Kaplan, & Foxx, 1973; Foxx & Azrin, 1973), pica (Singh & Winton, 1985), bruxism (Steuart, 1993), sibling aggression (Adams & Kelley, 1992), and classroom disruptions (Azrin & Powers, 1975). Positive practice overcorrection has been used for academic behaviors (Lenz, Singh, & Hewett, 1991), most often to decrease oral reading and spelling errors (e.g., Ollendick, Matson, Esveldt-Dawson, & Shapiro, 1980; Singh & Singh, 1986; Singh, Singh, & Winton, 1984; Stewart & Singh, 1986).

Positive practice overcorrection can also be applied to reduce or eliminate behaviors that do not create permanent response products that can be repaired or restored to their original state. For example, Heward, Dardig, and Rossett (1979) described how parents used positive practice overcorrection to help their teenage daughter stop making a grammatical error in her speech. Eunice frequently used the contraction "don't" instead of "doesn't" with the third person singular (e.g., "He don't want to go."). A positive reinforcement program in which Eunice earned points she could redeem for preferred activities each time she used "doesn't" correctly had little effect on her speech. Eunice agreed with her parents that she should speak correctly but claimed the behavior was a habit. Eunice and her parents then decided to supplement the reinforcement program with a mild punishment procedure. Each time Eunice or her parents caught her using "don't" incorrectly in her speech, she was required to say the complete sentence she had just spoken 10 times in a row using correct grammar. Eunice wore a wrist counter that reminded her to listen to her speech and to keep track of the number of times she employed the positive practice procedure.

When positive practice effectively suppresses the problem behavior, it is not clear what behavioral mechanisms are responsible for the behavior change. Punishment may result in decreased frequency of responding, because the person engages in effortful behavior as a consequence of the problem behavior. A reduction in the frequency of the problem behavior as an outcome of positive practice may also be a function of an increased frequency of an incompatible behavior, the correct behavior that is strengthened in the person's repertoire as the result of the intensive, repeated practice. Azrin and Besalel (1999) suggested that the reason why positive practice is effective varies depending upon the whether the problem behavior is "deliberate" or the result of a skill deficit:

> Positive practice may be effective because of the inconvenience and effort involved, or because it provides additional learning. If the child's errors are caused by a deliberate action, the extra effort involved in positive practice will discourage future misbehaviors. But if the misbehavior is the result of insufficient learning, the child will stop the misbehavior—or error—because of the intensive practice of the correct behavior. (p. 5)

Although specific procedures for implementing overcorrection vary greatly depending upon the problem behavior and its effects on the environment, the setting, the desired alternative behavior, and the learner's current skills, some general guidelines can be suggested (Azrin & Besalel, 1999; Foxx & Bechtel, 1983; Kazdin, 2001; Miltenberger & Fuqua, 1981):

1. Immediately upon the occurrence of the problem behavior (or the discovery of its effects), in a calm, unemotional tone of voice, tell the learner that he has misbehaved and provide a brief explanation for why the behavior must be corrected. Do not criticize or scold. Overcorrection entails a logically related consequence to reduce future occurrences of the problem behavior; criticism and scolding do not enhance the tactic's effectiveness and may harm the relationship between the learner and practitioner.

2. Provide explicit verbal instructions describing the overcorrection sequence the learner must perform.

3. Implement the overcorrection sequence as soon as possible after the problem behavior has occurred. When circumstances prevent immediately commencing the overcorrection sequence, tell the learner when the overcorrection process will be conducted. Several studies have found that overcorrection conducted at a later time can be effective (Azrin, & Powers, 1975; Barton & Osborne, 1978).

4. Monitor the learner throughout the overcorrection activity. Provide the minimal number of response prompts, including gentle physical guidance, needed to ensure that the learner performs the entire overcorrection sequence.

5. Provide the learner with minimal feedback for correct responses. Do not give too much praise and attention to the learner during the overcorrection sequence.

6. Provide praise, attention, and perhaps other forms of reinforcement to the learner each time he "spontaneously" performs the appropriate behavior during typical activities. (Although technically not part of the overcorrection procedure, reinforcing an alternative behavior is a recommended complement to all punishment-based interventions.)

Although "the results of a few minutes of corrective training after the undesired behavior have often led to rapid and long-lasting therapeutic effects" (Kazdin, 2001, p. 220), practitioners should be aware of several potential problems and limitations associated with overcorrection. First, overcorrection is a labor intensive, time-consuming procedure that requires full attention of the practitioner implementing it. Implementing overcorrection usually requires the practitioner to monitor the learner directly throughout the overcorrection process. Second, for overcorrection to be effective as punishment, the time that the learner spends with the person monitoring the overcorrection sequence must not be reinforcing. "If it is, it just might be worth waxing the entire kitchen floor if Mom chats with you and provides a milk and cookies break" (Heward et al., 1979, p. 63).

Third, a child who misbehaves frequently may not execute a long list of "cleanup" behaviors just because he was told to do so. Azrin and Besalel (1999) recommended three strategies to minimize the likelihood of refusal to perform the overcorrection sequence: (1) remind the learner what the more severe disciplinary action will be and, if the refusal persists, then impose that discipline; (2) discuss the need for correction before the problem behavior occurs; and (3) establish correction as an expectation and routine habit for any disruptive behavior. If the child resists too strongly or becomes aggressive, over-correction may not be a viable treatment. Adult learners must voluntarily make the decision to perform the over-correction routine.

Contingent Electric Stimulation

Contingent electric stimulation as punishment involves the presentation of a brief electrical stimulus immediately following an occurrence of the problem behavior. Although the use of electric stimulation as treatment is controversial and evokes strong opinions, Duker and Seys (1996) reported that 46 studies have demonstrated that contingent electric stimulation can be a safe and highly effective method for suppressing chronic and life-threatening self-injurious behavior (SIB). One of the most rigorously researched and carefully applied procedures for implementing punishment by electric stimulation for self-inflicted blows to the head or face is the Self-Injurious Behavior Inhibiting System (SIBIS) (Linscheid, Iwata, Ricketts, Williams, & Griffin, 1990; Linscheid, Pejeau, Cohen, & Footo-Lenz, 1994; Linscheid & Reichenbach, 2002). The SIBIS apparatus consists of a sensor module (worn on the head) and a stimulus module (worn on the leg or arm) that contains a radio receiver, a 9 V battery, and circuitry for the generation and timing of the electric stimulus. Above–threshold blows to the face or to the head trip an impact detector in the sensor module that transmits a radio signal to a receiver in the stimulus module that in turn produces an audible tone followed by electric stimulation (84 V, 3.5 mA) for 0.08 seconds. "Subjectively, the experience has been described at its extremes as imperceptible (low) and similar to having a rubber band snapped on the arm (high)" (Linscheid et al., 1990, p. 56).

Linscheid and colleagues (1990) evaluated SIBIS as treatment for five people with "longstanding, severe, and previously unmanageable" self-injurious behavior. One of the participants was Donna, a 17-year-old girl with profound mental retardation, no language, and no independent feeding or toileting skills. Donna's parents reported that she began hitting herself with sufficient force to produce lesions on her face and head more than 10 years prior to the study. Numerous treatments to stop Donna from hurting herself had been tried without success, including differential reinforcement of other behaviors (DRO), "gentle teaching," redirection, and response prevention. "For example, in order to prevent head hitting in bed, her parents had to hold her arms each night until she fell asleep. This sometimes required 3 to 4 hours of undivided attention, which the parents felt they were unable to continue" (pp. 66–67). Although Donna was ambulatory, when the study began she was spending most of the day with her wrists restrained to the arms of a wheelchair to prevent her SIB.

The effects of SIBIS on Donna's SIB were evaluated with a reversal design that included SIBIS-active and SIBIS-inactive conditions. All sessions lasted for 10 minutes or until Donna hit her head 25 times. During SIBIS-inactive sessions, Donna wore the sensor and stimulus modules but the stimulus module was inoperative. During six sessions each of initial baseline and SIBIS-inactive phases, Donna hit her head at a mean rate of at least once per minute (68.1 and 70.2 responses per minute, respectively) (see Figure 14.7). In the first session in which SIBIS was applied, Donna's SIB decreased to 2.4 head hits per minute. The mean rate of head hitting during all SIBIS-active sessions was 0.5 responses per minute (a range of 0 to 5.6), compared to rates of 50.2 (1.7 to 78.9) and 32.5 (0 to 48.0) responses per minute for all baseline and SIBIS-inactive sessions combined, respectively. SIBIS reduced Donna's head hitting 98.9% from baseline levels. Across all of the SIBIS-active sessions combined, Donna received 32 electric stimulations lasting a combined 2.6 seconds. No sessions during the SIBIS-active condition had to be terminated early because of risk, whereas 100% of the baseline sessions and 64% of the SIBIS-inactive sessions were terminated because Donna hit her head 25 times.

Similar results were obtained for all five participants: SIBIS treatment produced an immediate and almost complete cessation of SIB. Although legal, ethical, and moral issues and concerns surround the use of electric aversive stimulation, Linscheid and Reichenbach (2002) offered the following perspective: "While the decision to use an aversive treatment must be made in consideration of numerous factors, it is suggested that the speed and degree of suppression of SIB must be among these considerations" (p. 176). Formal data and anecdotal reports indicated an absence of negative side effects and the occurrence of some positive side effects. For example, Donna's parents reported a general improvement in her overall adaptive functioning and that she no longer had to be restrained in bed at night. Donna's teacher reported that:

> Since the introduction of SIBIS, it is like we have a totally new girl in the classroom. Donna no longer has to have her hands restrained. She is walking around the classroom without the wrestling helmet or cervical collar. She smiles more frequently and fusses a lot less. She pays more attention to what is going on in the classroom. She reaches out for objects and people more than she did. (p. 68)

Although the maintenance of suppressive effects has not been universally demonstrated (Ricketts, Goza, &

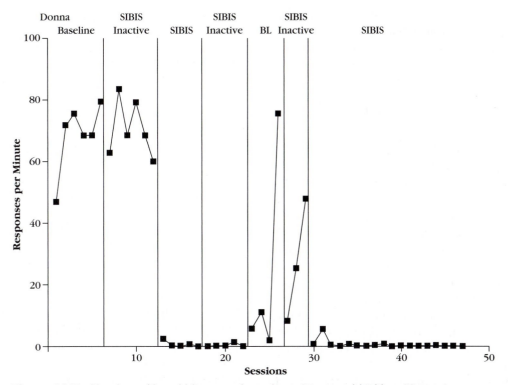

Figure 14.7   Number of head hits per minute by a 17-year-old with a 10-year history of self-injurious behavior during baseline and SIBIS-inactive and SIBIS-active conditions.

From "Clinical Evaluation of SIBIS: The Self-Injurious Behavior Inhibiting System" by T. R. Linscheid, B. A. Iwata, R. W. Ricketts, D. E. Williams, and J. C. Griffin, 1990, *Journal of Applied Behavior Analysis, 23,* p. 67. Copyright 1990 by the Society for the Experimental Analysis of Behavior, Inc. Used by permission.

Matese, 1993), some have reported the long-term effectiveness of SIBIS (Linscheid & Reichenbach, 2002). For example, Salvy, Mulick, Butter, Bartlett, and Linscheid (2004) reported that the SIB of a 3-year-old female with an 18-month history of chronic and repetitive head banging remained at virtually zero levels at a 1-year post-SIBIS follow-up.

Guidelines for Using Punishment Effectively

Research and clinical applications have demonstrated that punishment can yield rapid, long-lasting suppression of problem behavior. Increasingly, agency policies, human subject review procedures, and historic practices have limited the use of punishment for research and treatment in clinic-based settings (Grace, Kahng, & Fisher, 1994). Punishment, however, may be a treatment of choice when: (a) the problem behavior produces serious physical harm and must be suppressed quickly, (b) reinforcement-based treatments have not reduced the problem behavior to socially acceptable levels, or (c) the reinforcer maintaining

the problem behavior cannot be identified or withheld (Lerman & Vorndran, 2002).

If the decision is made to use a punishment-based treatment, steps should be taken to ensure that the punishing stimulus is as effective as possible. The guidelines that follow will help practitioners apply punishment with optimal effectiveness while minimizing undesirable side effects and problems. We based these guidelines on the assumption that the analyst has conducted a functional behavior assessment to identify the variables that maintain the problem behavior (see Chapter 24), that the problem behavior has been defined in a manner that minimizes ambiguity concerning its parameters (see Chapter 3), and that the participant cannot avoid or escape the punisher.

Select Effective and Appropriate Punishers

Conduct Punisher Assessments

As with the reinforcer assessment methods presented in Chapter 11, a parallel process can be applied to identify stimuli that are likely to function as punishers. Fisher and colleagues (1994), who differentially applied a combination of empirically derived punishers and reinforcers to reduce the pica behavior of three children referred to an inpatient treatment facility, identified two advantages of conducting punisher assessments. First, the sooner an effective punisher can be identified, the sooner it can be applied to treat the problem behavior. Second, data from punisher assessments might reveal the magnitude or intensity of the punisher necessary for behavioral suppression, enabling the practitioner to deliver the lowest intensity punisher that is still effective.

Punisher assessment mirrors stimulus preference and/or reinforcement assessment, except that instead of measuring engagement or duration of contact with each stimulus, the behavior analyst measures negative verbalizations, avoidance movements, and escape attempts associated with each stimulus. Data from the punisher assessments are then used to develop a hypothesis on the relative effectiveness of each stimulus change as a punisher.

The decision of which among several potentially effective punishers to choose should be based on the relative degree of intrusiveness the punisher creates and the ease with which it can be consistently and safely delivered by the therapists, teachers, or parents who will implement the punishment procedure in the clinic, classroom, or home. Subsequent observation might reveal that a consequence that is less intrusive, time-consuming, or difficult to apply might be used, as in the following experience reported by Thompson and colleagues (1999):

> We conducted brief evaluations to identify an effective punishment procedure for each participant. Procedures were chosen for evaluation based on topographies of SIB, an apparent degree of minimal intrusiveness, and the ability of the experimenter to safely and efficiently implement the procedure. During this phase, we used brief AB designs to evaluate several procedures and chose the least restrictive procedure that resulted in a 75% or greater decrease in SIB. For example, we initially evaluated a 15-s manual restraint with Shelly. During this procedure, the therapist delivered a verbal reprimand, held Shelly's hands in her lap for 15 s, and then dried her hands with a cloth. This procedure reduced SIB to the criterion level. Subsequently, however, we observed a comparable decrease in SIB when the therapist simply delivered a reprimand (e.g., "no spitting") and dried Shelly's hands (without holding her hands in her lap). Therefore, we chose to implement the reprimand and hand-drying procedure. (p. 321)

Use Punishers of Sufficient Quality and Magnitude

The quality (or effectiveness) of a punisher is relative to a number of past and current variables that affect the participant. For example, Thompson and colleagues found that 15 seconds of physical restraint was a high-quality punisher for Ricky, Donna, and Lynn, but the physical restraint was not influential for Shelly. Although stimuli that reliably evoke escape and avoidance behaviors often function as high-quality punishers, practitioners should recognize that a stimulus change that effectively suppresses some behaviors may not affect other behaviors and that highly motivated problem behaviors may only be suppressed by a particularly high-quality punisher.

Generally, basic and applied researchers have found that the greater the intensity (magnitude, or amount) of a punishing stimulus, the greater the suppression of behavior. This finding is conditional on delivering the punishing stimulus at its optimum level of magnitude initially, rather than gradually increasing the level over time (Azrin & Holtz, 1966). For example, Thompson and colleagues (1999) used the previously described punisher assessment procedure to determine an optimum level of magnitude for the punishing stimulus: a magnitude that produced a 75%, or greater, decrease in self-injurious behaviors (SIB) from baseline occurrences of four adult participants. The punishing stimuli meeting their criterion included: "Ricky's hands were held in his lap for 15 s each time he engaged in SIB. Donna and Lynn both received a verbal reprimand and had their hands held across their chests for 15 s following SIB" (p. 321).

Beginning with a punishing stimulus of sufficient magnitude is important, because participants may adapt to the punishing stimulus when levels of magnitude are increased gradually. For example, it is possible that 15 seconds of movement restriction would have been ineffective as punishment for Ricky, Donna, and Lynn's SIB if Thompson and colleagues had begun with a punishing stimulus of 3 seconds and gradually increased its magnitude in 3-second intervals.

Use Varied Punishers

The effectiveness of a punishing stimulus can decrease with repeated presentations of that stimulus. Using a variety of punishers may help to reduce habituation effects. In addition, using various punishers may increase the effectiveness of less intrusive punishers. For example, Charlop, Burgio, Iwata, and Ivancic (1988) compared various punishers to a single presentation of one the punishers (i.e., a stern "No!" overcorrection, time-out with physical restraint, a loud noise). Three-, 5-, and 6-year-old children with developmental disabilities served as participants. Their problem behaviors included aggression (Child 1), self-stimulation and destructive behavior (Child 2), and aggression and out-of-seat (Child 3). The varied-punisher condition was slightly more effective than the single-presentation condition and enhanced the sensitivity of the behavior to less intrusive punishing stimuli. Charlop and colleagues concluded, "It appears that by presenting a varied format of commonly used punishers, inappropriate behaviors may further decrease without the use of more intrusive punishment procedures" (p. 94; see Figure 14.8).

Deliver the Punisher at the Beginning of a Behavioral Sequence

Punishing an inappropriate behavior as soon as it begins is more effective than waiting until the chain of behavior has been completed (Solomon, 1964). Once the sequence of responses that make up the problem behavior is initiated, powerful secondary reinforcers associated with completing each step of the chain may prompt its continuation, thereby counteracting the inhibiting or suppressing effects of the punishment that occurs at the end of the sequence. Therefore, whenever practical, the punishing stimulus should be presented early in the behavioral sequence

rather than later. For example, if violent arm swinging is a reliable precursor to self-injurious eye poking, then punishment (e.g., response blocking, restraint) should be delivered as soon as arm swinging starts.

Punish Each Instance of the Behavior Initially

Punishment is most effective when the punisher follows each response. This is especially important when a punishment intervention is first implemented.

Gradually Shift to an Intermittent Schedule of Punishment

Although punishment is most effective when the punisher immediately follows each occurrence of the problem behavior, practitioners may find a continuous schedule of punishment unacceptable because they lack the resources and time to attend to each occurrence of the behavior (O'Brien & Karsh, 1990). Several studies have found that, after responding has been reduced by a continuous schedule of punishment, an intermittent schedule of punishment may be sufficient to maintain the behavior at a

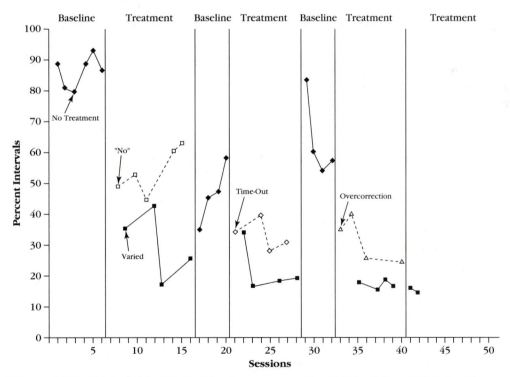

Figure 14.8   Percentage of intervals of occurrence of self-stimulation and destructive behavior for a 6-year-old girl with autism.

From "Stimulus Variation as a Means of Enhancing Punishment Effects," by M. H. Charlop, L. D. Burgio, B. A. Iwata, and M. T. Ivancic, 1988, *Journal of Applied Behavior Analysis, 21*, p. 92. Copyright 1988 by the Society for the Experimental Analysis of Behavior, Inc. Used by permission.

socially acceptable frequency (e.g. Clark, Rowbury, Baer, & Baer, 1973; Lerman et al., 1997; Romanczyk, 1977).

We recommend two guidelines for using intermittent punishment. First—and this is especially important—a continuous (FR 1) schedule of punishment should be used to diminish the problem behavior to a clinically acceptable level before gradually thinning to an intermittent schedule of punishment. Second, combine intermittent punishment with extinction. It is unlikely that reduced responding will continue under intermittent punishment if the reinforcer that maintains the problem behavior cannot be identified and withheld. If these two guidelines for intermittent punishment are met and the frequency of the problem behavior increases to an unacceptable level, return to a continuous schedule of punishment and then, after recovery of acceptably low rates of responding, gradually shift to an intermittent schedule of punishment that is denser than used previously (e.g., VR 2 rather than a VR 4).

Use Mediation with a Response-to-Punishment Delay

As with reinforcers, punishers that occur immediately following a response are more effective than are punishers presented after a period of time has elapsed since the response occurred. In the context of reinforcement, Stromer, McComas, and Rehfeldt (2000) reminded us that using continuous and intermittent schedules of reinforcement might be just the first steps of programming consequences for everyday situations, because the consequences that maintain responding in natural environments are often delayed:

> Establishing the initial instances of a behavioral repertoire typically requires the use of programmed consequences that occur immediately after the target response occurs. However, the job of the applied behavior analyst also involves the strategic use of delayed reinforcement. (p. 359)

The job of the applied behavior analyst could also involve the strategic programming of contingencies involving a delay-to-punishment interval. As Lerman and Vorndran, (2002) noted:

> Consequences for problem behavior are frequently delayed in the natural environment. Caregivers and teachers often are unable to monitor behavior closely or to deliver lengthy punishers (e.g., 15-min contingent work) immediately following instances of problem behavior. Punishment also may be delayed when the individual actively resists application of the programmed consequences by struggling with the punishing agent or running away. In some cases, problem behavior occurs primarily in the absence of the punishing agent, necessarily delaying programmed consequences until the behavior is detected. (pp. 443-444)

Generally, applied behavior analysts have avoided programming a delay-to-punishment interval. In their review of the basic and applied punishment literature, Lerman and Vorndran (2002) found just two applied studies that addressed the variables related to the effective use of a delay-to-punishment (Rolider & Van Houten, 1985; Van Houten & Rolider, 1988), and noted that these applied behavior analysts used a variety of techniques to mediate the delay between the occurrence of the problem behavior and the punishing consequences.

> [They] demonstrated the efficacy of delayed punishment using various mediated consequences with children with emotional and developmental disabilities. One form of mediation involved playing audiotape recordings of the child's disruptive behavior that were collected earlier in the day. The punishing consequence (physical restraint, verbal reprimands) then was delivered. In some cases, the tape recorder was clearly visible to the child while the recordings were being collected, and a verbal explanation of its role in the delivery of delayed punishment was provided. These factors may have served to bridge the temporal gap between inappropriate behavior and its consequence (e.g., by functioning as discriminative stimuli for punishment). (p. 444)

Supplement Punishment with Complementary Interventions

Applied behavior analysts typically do not use punishment as a single intervention: they supplement punishment with other interventions, primarily, differential reinforcement, extinction, and a variety of antecedent interventions. Basic and applied researchers consistently find that the effectiveness of punishment is enhanced when the learner can make other responses for reinforcement. In most circumstances applied behavior analysts should incorporate differential reinforcement of alternative behavior (DRA), differential reinforcement of incompatible behavior (DRI), or differential reinforcement of other behaviors (DRO) (see Chapter 22) into a treatment program to supplement a punishment. When used as a reductive procedure for problem behavior, differential reinforcement consists of two components: (1) providing reinforcement contingent on the occurrence of a behavior other than the problem behavior, and (2) withholding reinforcement for the problem behavior (i.e., extinction, see Chapter 21). The study by Thompson and colleagues (1999) presented previously in this chapter (see Figure 14.4) provides an excellent example of how reinforcement of an alternative behavior can enhance the suppressive effects of punishment and enable "relatively benign punishment procedures" to be effective even for chronic problem behaviors that have been resistant to change.

We recommend that practitioners reinforce alternative behaviors copiously. Additionally, the more reinforcement the learner obtains by emitting appropriate behaviors, the less motivated he will be to emit the problem behavior. In other words, heavy and consistent doses of reinforcement for alternative behaviors function as an abolishing operation that weakens (abates) the frequency of the problem behavior.

There is still another important reason for recommending the reinforcement of alternative behaviors. Applied behavior analysts are in the business of building repertoires by teaching the clients and students they serve new skills and more effective ways of controlling their environments and achieving success. Punishment (with the exception of some overcorrection procedures) eliminates behaviors from a person's repertoire. Although the person will be better off without those behaviors in her repertoire, punishment only teaches her what *not* to do, it does not teach her what to do instead.

The effectiveness of antecedent interventions such as functional communication training (FCT), high-probability (high-p) request sequence, and noncontingent reinforcement (NCR), which diminish the frequency of problem behaviors by decreasing the effectiveness of the reinforcers that maintain the problem behaviors (see Chapter 23), can be made more effective when combined with punishment. For instance, Fisher and colleagues (1993) found that, although functional communication training (FCT) did not reduce to clinically significant levels the destructive behaviors of four participants with severe retardation and communication deficits, a combination of FCT and punishment produced the largest and most consistent reductions in problem behaviors.

Be Prepared for Negative Side Effects

It is difficult to predict the side effects that may result from punishment (Reese, 1966). The suppression of one problem behavior by punishment may lead to an increase in other undesirable behaviors. For example, punishment of self-injurious behavior may produce increased levels of noncompliance or aggression. Punishing one problem behavior may lead to a parallel decrease in desirable behaviors. For example, requiring that a student rewrite an ill-conceived paragraph may result in his ceasing to produce any academic work. Although punishment may produce no undesirable side effects, practitioners should be alert to problems such as escape and avoidance, emotional outbursts, and behavioral contrast, and should have a plan for dealing with such events should they occur.

Record, Graph, and Evaluate Data Daily

Data collection in the initial sessions of a punishment-based intervention is especially critical. Unlike some behavior reduction procedures, such as extinction and differential reinforcement of alternative behavior, whose suppressive effects are often gradual, the suppressive effects of punishment are abrupt. In their classic review of the basic research on punishment, Azrin and Holz (1966) wrote:

> Virtually all studies of punishment have been in complete agreement that the reduction of responses by punishment is immediate if the punishment is at all effective. When the data have been presented in terms of the number or responses per day, the responses have been drastically reduced or eliminated on the very first day in which punishment was administered. When the data have been presented in terms of moment-to-moment changes, the reduction of responses has results with the first few deliveries of punishment or within a few minutes. (p. 411)

The first data points from the punishment conditions in all of the graphs presented in this chapter provide additional empirical evidence for Azrin and Holz's statement of the immediate effects of punishment. Because of the abrupt effect of punishment, the practitioner should pay particular attention to the data from the first session or two of intervention. If a noticeable reduction of the problem behavior has not occurred within two sessions of a punishment-based intervention, we recommend that the practitioner make adjustments to the intervention.

Frequent inspection of the data from a punishment perspective reminds those involved of the purpose of the intervention and reveals whether the problem behavior is being reduced or eliminated as intended. When the data indicate that a clinically or socially significant change has occurred and has been maintained, punishment can be shifted to an intermittent schedule or perhaps terminated altogether.

Ethical Considerations Regarding the Use of Punishment

Ethical considerations regarding the use of punishment revolve around three major issues: the client's right to safe and humane treatment, the professional's responsibility to use least restrictive procedures, and the client's right to effective treatment.[8]

---

[8]Chapter 29 provides a detailed discussion of ethical issues and practices for applied behavior analysts.

Right to Safe and Humane Treatment

Dating from the Hippocratic Oath (Hippocrates, 460 BC–377 BC), the first ethical canon and responsibility for any human services provider is to do no harm. Accordingly, any behavior change program, be it a punishment-based intervention to reduce life-threatening self-injurious behavior or an application of positive reinforcement to teach a new academic skill, must be physically safe for all involved and contain no elements that are degrading or disrespectful to participants.

Treatments are deemed safe when they put neither the caregiver nor the target individual at physical, psychological, or social risk (Favell & McGimsey, 1993). Although there exists no universally accepted definition of what constitutes humane treatment, a reasonable case could be made that humane treatments are (a) designed for therapeutic effectiveness, (b) delivered in a compassionate and caring manner, (c) assessed formatively to determine effectiveness and terminated if effectiveness is not demonstrated, and (d) sensitive and responsive to the overall physical, psychological, and social needs of the person.

Least Restrictive Alternative

A second canon of ethics for human services professionals is to intrude on a client's life only as necessary to provide effective intervention. The *doctrine of the least restrictive alternative* holds that less intrusive procedures should be tried and found to be ineffective before more intrusive procedures are implemented. Interventions can be viewed as falling along a continuum of restrictiveness from least to most. The more a treatment procedure affects a person's life or independence, such as his ability to go about daily activities in his normal environment, the greater its restrictiveness. A completely unrestrictive intervention is a logical fallacy. Any treatment must affect the person's life in some way to qualify as an intervention. At the other end of the continuum, absolute restrictiveness exists during solitary confinement, where personal independence is unavailable. All behavior change interventions developed and implemented by applied behavior analysts fall within these extremes.

Selecting any punishment-based intervention essentially rules out as ineffective all positive or positive reductive approaches based on their demonstrated inability to improve the behavior. For example, Gaylord-Ross (1980) proposed a decision-making model for reducing aberrant behavior that suggested that practitioners rule out assessment considerations, inappropriate or ineffective schedules of reinforcement, ecological variables, and curriculum modifications *before* punishment is implemented.

Some authors and professional organizations have advanced the position that all punishment-based procedures are inherently intrusive and should never be used (e.g., Association for Persons with Severe Handicaps, 1987; LaVigna & Donnellen, 1986; Mudford, 1995). Others have advanced the counter position that punishment-based procedures, because of their inherent level of intrusiveness, should be used only as a last resort (Gaylord-Ross, 1980).

Most people would rate interventions based on positive reinforcement as less restrictive than interventions based on negative reinforcement; reinforcement interventions as less restrictive than punishment interventions; and interventions using negative punishment as less restrictive than those using positive punishment. However, the intrusiveness or restrictiveness of an intervention cannot be determined by the principles of behavior on which it is based. Restrictiveness is a relative concept that depends on the procedural details and ultimately rests at the level of the person with whom it is applied. A positive reinforcement intervention that requires deprivation may be more restrictive than a positive punishment procedure in which a buzzer sounds each time an incorrect response is made, and what one person considers intrusive may pose no discomfort for another person. Horner (1990) suggested that most people accept punishment interventions to reduce challenging behavior as long as those interventions: "(a) do not involve the delivery of physical pain, (b) do not produce effects that require medical attention, and (c) are subjectively judged to be within the typical norm of how people in our society should treat each other" (pp. 166-167).

In their review of response-reduction interventions based on the principle of punishment, Friman and Poling (1995) pointed out that punishment-based tactics, such as those that require that the person make an effortful response contingent on the occurrence of target behavior, meet Horner's (1990) criteria for acceptable response-reduction interventions. They stated: "None of the procedures caused pain or required medical attention, nor did they contrast with societal norms. For example, coaches often require disobedient players to run laps, and drill instructors make misbehaving recruits do push-ups" (p. 585).

Although least restrictive alternative practices assume that the less intrusive procedures are tried and found ineffective before a more restrictive intervention is introduced, practitioners must balance that approach against an effectiveness standard. Gast and Wolery (1987) suggested that, if a choice must be made between a less intrusive but ineffective procedure and a more intrusive but effective procedure, the latter should be chosen. A Task Force on the Right to Effective Treatment appointed by the Association for Behavior Analysis provided the following perspective on the importance of judging the ultimate restrictiveness of treatment options on the basis of their degree of proven effectiveness:

> Consistent with the philosophy of least restrictive yet effective treatment, exposure of an individual to restrictive procedures is unacceptable unless it can be shown that such procedures are necessary to produce safe and clinically significant behavior change. It is equally unacceptable to expose an individual to a nonrestrictive intervention (or a series of such interventions) if assessment results or available research indicate that other procedures would be more effective. Indeed, a slow-acting but nonrestrictive procedure could be considered highly restrictive if prolonged treatment increases risk, significantly inhibits or prevents participation in needed training programs, delays entry into a more optimal social or living environment, or leads to adaptation and the eventual use of a more restrictive procedure. Thus, in some cases, a client's right to effective treatment may dictate the immediate use of quicker-acting, but temporarily more restrictive, procedures.
>
> A procedure's overall level of restrictiveness is a combined function of its absolute level of restrictiveness, the amount of time required to produce a clinically acceptable outcome, and the consequences associated with delayed intervention. Furthermore, selection of a specific treatment technique is not based on personal conviction. Techniques are not considered either "good" or "bad" according to whether they involve the use of antecedent rather than consequent stimuli or reinforcement rather than punishment. For example, positive reinforcement, as well as punishment, can produce a number of indirect effects, some of which are undesirable.
>
> In summary, decisions related to treatment selection are based on information obtained during assessment about the behavior, the risk it poses, and its controlling variables; on a careful consideration of the available treatment options, including their relative effectiveness, risks, restrictiveness, and potential side effects; and on examination of the overall context in which treatment will be applied. (Van Houten et al., 1988, pp. 113, 114)

Right to Effective Treatment

Ethical discussions regarding the use of punishment revolve most often around its possible side effects and how experiencing the punisher may cause unnecessary pain and possible psychological harm for the person. Although each of these concerns deserves careful consideration, the right to effective treatment raises an equally important ethical issue, especially for persons

who experience chronic, life-threatening problem behaviors. Some maintain that failing to use a punishment procedure that research has shown to be effective in suppressing self-destructive behavior similar to their client's is unethical because doing so withholds a potentially effective treatment and risks maintaining a dangerous or uncomfortable state for the person. For example, Baer (1971) stated that, "[Punishment] is a legitimate therapeutic technique that is justifiable and commendable when it relieves persons of the even greater punishments that result from their own habitual behavior" (p. 111).

For some clients, punishment-based intervention may be the only means of reducing the frequency, duration, or magnitude of chronic and dangerous behaviors that have proven resistant to change using positive reinforcement, extinction, or positive reductive approaches such as differential reinforcement of alternative behavior. Such circumstances "may justify, if not necessitate, the use of punishment" (Thompson et al., 1999, p. 317). As Iwata (1988) explained, if all other less-intrusive treatments with a sufficient research base to promise a legitimate chance of success have failed, the use of punishment procedures is the only ethical option:

> In the ideal world, treatment failures do not occur. But in the actual world failures do occur, in spite of our best efforts, leaving us with these options: continued occurrence of the behavior problem toward some devastating endpoint, restraint, sedating drugs, or aversive contingencies. I predict that if we apply our skills to maximize the effectiveness of positive reinforcement programs, we will succeed often. After following such a course, my further prediction is that if we reach the point of having to decide among these ultimate default options, the client's advocate, the parent, or, if necessary, the courts will select or use the option of aversive contingencies. Why? Because under such circumstances it is the only ethical action. (pp. 152-153)

Punishment Policy and Procedural Safeguards

Armed with knowledge from the experimental literature, real-world variables and contingencies with which to contend (i.e., chronic, life-threatening problems), and practices and procedures rooted in ethical codes of conduct, practitioners can consider punishment approaches, when necessary, to provide meaningful programs for the persons in their care. One mechanism for ensuring that best practice approaches are used (Peters & Heron, 1993) is to adopt and use dynamic policies and procedures that provide clear guidelines and safeguards to practitioners.

Figure 14.9   Suggested components in an agency's policy and procedures guidelines to help ensure the ethical, safe, and effective use of punishment.

Policy Requirements
- Intervention must conform to all local, state, and federal statutes.
- Intervention must conform to the policies and codes of ethical conduct of relevant professional organizations.
- Intervention should include procedures for strengthening and teaching alternative behaviors.
- Intervention must include plans for generalization and maintenance of behavior change and criteria for eventual termination or reduction of punishment.
- Informed consent must be obtained from the client or a parent or legal advocate before intervention begins.

Procedural Safeguards
- Before intervention begins, all relevant staff must be trained in (a) the technical details of properly administering the punishment procedure, (b) procedures for ensuring the physical safety of the client and staff and the humane treatment of the client, and (c) what to do in the event of negative side effects such as emotional outbursts, escape and avoidance aggression, and noncompliance.
- Supervision and feedback of staff administering the punishment intervention must be provided and, if necessary, booster training sessions provided.

Evaluation Requirements
- Each occurrence of the problem behavior must be observed and recorded.
- Each delivery of the punisher must be recorded and client's reactions noted.
- Periodic review of the data (e.g., daily, weekly) by a team of parent/advocates, staff, and technical consultants must be conducted to ensure that ineffective treatment is not prolonged or effective treatment terminated.
- Social validity data must be obtained from client, significant others, and staff on (a) treatment acceptability and (b) the real and likely impact of any behavior change on the client's current circumstances and future prospects.

Agencies can help protect and ensure their clients' rights to safe, humane, least-restrictive, and effective treatment by developing policy and procedural guidelines that must be followed when any punishment-based intervention is implemented (Favell & McGimsey, 1993; Griffith, 1983; Wood & Braaten, 1983). Figure 14.9 provides an outline and examples of the kinds of components that might be included in such a document.

Practitioners should also consult their local, state, or national professional association policy statements regarding the use of punishment. For example, the Association for the Advancement of Behavior Therapy (AABT) provides guidelines that address treatment selection, including punishment (Favell et al., 1982). The Association for Behavior Analysis adheres to the American Psychological Association's Ethics Code (2004), which, in turn, addresses treatment issues. Collectively, policy statements address implementation requirements, procedural guidelines and precautions, and evaluation methods that an agency should use when implementing any punishment-based intervention. Chapter 29 provides ad-

ditional information on ethical standards for applied behavior analysts and procedures for securing informed consent, protecting client's rights, and ensuring safe and humane interventions.

Concluding Perspectives

We conclude this chapter with brief comments on three complementary perspectives regarding the principle of punishment and the development and application of interventions involving punishment by contingent aversive stimulation. We believe that applied behavior analysis would be a stronger, more competent discipline, and its practitioners would be more effective if (a) punishment's natural role and contributions to survival and learning are recognized and appreciated, (b) more basic and applied research on punishment is conducted, and (c) treatments featuring positive punishment are viewed as default technologies to be used only when all other methods have failed.

Punishment's Natural and Necessary Role in Learning Should Be Recognized

Behavior analysts should not shy away from punishment. Positive and negative punishment contingencies occur naturally in everyday life as part of a complex mix of concurrent reinforcement and punishment contingencies, as Baum (1994) illustrated so well in this example:

> Life is full of choices between alternatives that offer different mixes of reinforcement and punishment. Going to work entails both getting paid (positive reinforcement) and suffering hassles (positive punishment), whereas calling in sick may forfeit some pay (negative punishment), avoid the hassles (negative reinforcement), allow a vacation (positive reinforcement), and incur some workplace disapproval (positive punishment). Which set of relations wins out depends on which relations are strong enough to dominate, and that depends on both the present circumstances and the person's history of reinforcement and punishment. (p. 60)

Punishment is a natural part of life. Vollmer (2002) suggested that the scientific study of punishment should continue because unplanned and planned punishment occur frequently and that planned, sophisticated applications of punishment are within the scope of inquiry for applied behavior analysts. Whether punishment is socially mediated, planned or unplanned, or conducted by sophisticated practitioners, we agree with Vollmer that a science of behavior should study punishment.

> Scientists interested in the nature of human behavior cannot ignore or otherwise obviate the study of punishment. There should be no controversy. Scientists and practitioners are obligated to understand the nature of punishment if for no other reason than because punishment happens. (p. 469)

More Research on Punishment Is Needed

Although many of the inappropriate and ineffective applications of punishment are the result of misunderstanding, other misapplications no doubt reflect our incomplete knowledge of the principle as a result of inadequate basic and applied research (Lerman & Vorndran, 2002).

Most of our knowledge about and recommendations for applying punishment are derived from basic research conducted more than 40 years ago. Although sound scientific data that describe still-relevant questions have an unlimited shelf life, much more basic research on the mechanisms and variables that produce effective punishment is needed.

Basic laboratory research allows for the control of variables that is difficult or impossible to attain in applied settings. Once mechanisms are revealed in basic research, however, applications to real-world challenges can be devised and adapted with more confidence regarding the degree of potential effectiveness and limitations. Practitioners must recognize when, how, why, and under what conditions punishment techniques produce behavioral suppression for the people with whom they work.

We support Horner's (2002) call for practical applications of punishment research in field settings. It is important to determine how punishment works in situations in which environmental variables may not be as well controlled and in which the practitioner delivering the punisher might not be a trained professional. Educational and clinical applications of punishment also demand that behavior analysts understand the individual, contextual, and environmental variables that produce effective application. Without a clear and refined knowledge base about these variables and conditions, applied behavior analysis as a science of behavior cannot make a legitimate claim to have achieved a comprehensive analysis of its own basic concepts (Lerman & Vorndran, 2002; Vollmer, 2002).

Interventions Featuring Positive Punishment Should Be Treated as Default Technologies

Iwata (1988) recommended that punishment-based interventions involving the contingent application of aversive stimulation be treated as default technologies. A default technology is one that a practitioner turns to when all other methods have failed. Iwata recommended that behavior analysts not advocate for the use of aversive technologies (because advocacy is not effective, not necessary, and not in the best interests of the field), but that they be involved in research and the development of effective aversive technologies.

> We must do the work because, whether or not we like it, default technologies will evolve whenever there is failure and, in the case of aversive stimulation, we are in a unique position to make several contributions. First, we can modify the technology so that it is effective and safe. Second, we can improve it by incorporating contingencies of positive reinforcement. Third, we can regulate it so that application will proceed in a judicious and ethical manner. Last, and surely most important, by studying the conditions under which default technologies arise, as well as the technologies themselves, we might eventually do away with both. Can you think of a better fate for the field of applied behavior analysis? (p. 156)

Summary

Definition and Nature of Punishment

1. Punishment has occurred when a stimulus change immediately follows a response and decreases the future frequency of that type of behavior in similar conditions.

2. Punishment is defined neither by the actions of the person delivering the consequences nor by the nature of those consequences. A decrease in the future frequency of the occurrence of the behavior must be observed before a consequence-based intervention qualifies as punishment.

3. Positive punishment has occurred when the frequency of responding has been decreased by the presentation of a stimulus (or an increase in stimulus intensity) immediately following a behavior.

4. Negative punishment has occurred when the frequency of responding has been decreased by the removal of a stimulus (or a decrease in the stimulus intensity) immediately following a behavior.

5. Because aversive events are associated with positive punishment and with negative reinforcement, the term *aversive control* is often used to describe interventions involving either or both of these two principles.

6. A discriminative stimulus for punishment, or S^{Dp}, is a stimulus condition in the presence of which a response class occurs at a lower frequency than it does in the absence of the S^{Dp} as a result of a conditioning history in which responses in the presence of the S^{Dp} have been punished and similar responses in the absence of that stimulus have not been punished (or have resulted in a reduced frequency or magnitude of punishment).

7. A punisher is a stimulus change that immediately follows the occurrence of a behavior and reduces the future frequency of that type of behavior.

8. An unconditioned punisher is a stimulus whose presentation functions as punishment without having been paired with any other punishers.

9. A conditioned punisher is a stimulus that has acquired its punishing capabilities by being paired with unconditioned or conditioned punishers.

10. A generalized conditioned punisher will function as punishment under a wide range of motivating operations because of its previous pairing with numerous unconditioned and conditioned punishers.

11. In general, the results of basic and applied research show that punishment is more effective when
    - the onset of the punisher occurs as soon as possible after the occurrence of a target response,
    - the intensity of the punisher is high,
    - each occurrence of the behavior is followed by the punishing consequence,

    - reinforcement for the target behavior is reduced, and
    - reinforcement is available for alternative behaviors.

12. Punishment sometimes causes undesirable side effects and problems, such as the following:
    - Emotional and aggressive reactions to aversive stimulation
    - Escape and avoidance behaviors
    - Behavioral contrast: reduced responding from punishment in one situation may be accompanied by increased responding in situations in which responses go unpunished
    - The modeling of undesirable behavior
    - Overuse of punishment caused by the negative reinforcement of the punishing agent's behavior (i.e., the immediate cessation of problem behavior)

Examples of Positive Punishment Interventions

13. Reprimands: Used sparingly, a firm reprimand such as "No!" can suppress future responding.

14. Response blocking: When the learner begins to emit the problem behavior, the therapist physically intervenes to prevent or "block" the completion of the response.

15. Overcorrection is a punishment-based tactic in which, contingent on each occurrence of the problem behavior, the learner is required to engage in effortful behavior that is directly or logically related to the problem.

16. In restitutional overcorrection, the learner must repair the damage caused by the problem behavior and then bring the environment to a condition vastly better than it was prior to the misbehavior.

17. In positive practice overcorrection, the learner repeatedly performs a correct form of the behavior, or a behavior incompatible with the problem behavior, for a specified time or number of responses.

18. Contingent electric stimulation can be a safe and effective method for suppressing chronic and life-threatening self-injurious behavior.

Guidelines for Using Punishment Effectively

19. To apply punishment with optimal effectiveness while minimizing undesirable side effects, a practitioners should:
    - Select effective and appropriate punishers: (a) conduct punisher assessments to identify the least intrusive punisher that can be applied consistently and safely; (b) use punishers of sufficient quality and magnitude; (c) use a variety of punishers to combat habituation and increase the effectiveness of less intrusive punishers.
    - If problem behavior consists of a response chain, deliver the punisher as early in the response sequence as possible.
    - Punish each occurrence of the behavior.

- Gradually shift to an intermittent schedule of punishment if possible.
- Use mediation with a response-to-punishment delay.
- Supplement punishment with complementary interventions, in particular, differential reinforcement, extinction, and antecedent interventions
- Watch and be prepared for unwanted side effects.
- Record, graph, and evaluate data daily.

Ethical Considerations Regarding the Use of Punishment

20. The first ethical responsibility for any human services professional or agency is to do no harm. Any intervention must be physically safe for all involved and contain no elements that are degrading or disrespectful to the client.

21. The doctrine of the least restrictive alternative holds that less intrusive procedures (e.g., positive reductive approaches) must be tried first and found to be ineffective before more intrusive procedures are implemented (e.g., a punishment-based intervention).

22. A client's right to effective treatment raises an important ethical issue. Some maintain that the failure to use a punishment procedure that research has shown to suppress self-destructive behavior similar to the client's is unethical because it withholds a potentially effective treatment and may maintain a dangerous or uncomfortable state for the person.

23. Agencies and individuals providing applied behavior analysis services can help ensure that applications of punishment-based interventions are safe, humane, ethical, and effective by creating and following a set of policy standards, procedural safeguards, and evaluation requirements.

Concluding Perspectives on Punishment

24. Applied behavior analysts should recognize and appreciate the natural role of punishment and the importance of punishment to learning.

25. Many misapplications of punishment reflect the field's incomplete knowledge of the principle. More basic and applied research on punishment is needed.

26. Iwata (1988) recommended that punishment-based interventions involving the contingent application of aversive stimulation be treated as default technologies; that is, as interventions to be used only when other methods have failed. He argued that applied behavior analysts should not advocate for the use of aversive technologies, but instead must be involved in conducting research on such interventions to (a) make them effective and safe, (b) improve them by incorporating contingencies of positive reinforcement, (c) regulate their judicious and ethical application, and (d) study the conditions under which default technologies are used so as to eventually make them unnecessary.

CHAPTER 15

Punishment by Removal of a Stimulus

Key Terms

bonus response cost
contingent observation
exclusion time-out
hallway time-out

nonexclusion time-out
partition time-out
planned ignoring
response cost

time-out from positive
reinforcement
time-out ribbon

Behavior Analyst Certificiation Board® BCBA® & BCABA® Behavior Analyst Task List©, Third Edition

Content Area 3: Principles, Processes and Concepts	
3-5	Define and provide examples of (positive and) negative punishment.
3-6	Define and provide examples of conditioned and unconditioned punishment.
Content Area 9: Behavior Change Procedures	
9-3	Use (positive and) negative punishment:
(a)	Identify and use punishers.
(b)	Use appropriate parameters and schedules of punishment.
(c)	State and plan for the possible unwanted effects of the use of punishment.

Punishment by the contingent removal of a stimulus is referred to as negative punishment. In negative punishment, an environmental change occurs such that a stimulus is *removed* subsequent to the performance of a behavior, and the corresponding future frequency of the preceding behavior is reduced. By contrast, in positive punishment, a stimulus is *presented,* and the corresponding future frequency of that behavior is reduced. Table 15.1 shows the distinction between positive and negative punishment with respect to an environmental stimulus change.

Negative punishment occurs in two principal ways: time-out from positive reinforcement and response cost (see the shaded area of Table 15.1). This chapter defines and operationalizes time-out from positive reinforcement and response cost, provides examples of how these punishment procedures are used in applied settings, and offers guidelines to help practitioners implement time-out and response cost effectively.

Definition of Time-Out

Time-out from positive reinforcement, or simply time-out, is defined as the withdrawal of the opportunity to earn positive reinforcement or the loss of access to positive reinforcers for a specified time, contingent on the occurrence of a behavior. The effect of either of these procedures is the same: The future frequency of the target behavior is reduced. Implicit in the definition of time-out are three important aspects: (a) the discrepancy between the "time-in" and the time-out environment, (b) the response-contingent loss of access to reinforcement, and (c) a resultant decrease in the future frequency of the behavior. Contrary to popular thinking, time-out is not exclusively defined, nor does it require only removing an individual to an isolated or secluded setting. Although such a removal procedure may accurately describe isolation time-out (Costenbader & Reading-Brown, 1995), it is by no means the only way by which time-out can be used. Technically, time-out as a nega-

tive punishment procedure removes a reinforcing stimulus for a specified time contingent on the occurrence of a behavior, the effect of which is to decrease the future frequency of the behavior.

Time-out can be viewed from procedural, conceptual, and functional perspectives. Procedurally, it is that period of time when the person is either removed from a reinforcing environment (e.g., a student is removed from the classroom for 5 minutes) or loses access to reinforcers within an environment (e.g., a student is ineligible to earn reinforcers for 5 minutes). Conceptually, the distinction between the time-in and the time-out environment is of paramount importance. The more reinforcing the time-in setting is, the more effective time-out is likely to be as a punisher. Stated otherwise, the greater the difference between the reinforcing value of time-in and absence of that reinforcing value in the time-out setting, the more effective time-out will be. From a functional perspective, time-out involves the reduced frequency of the future occurrence of the behavior. Without a reduction in frequency of future behavior, time-out is not in effect, even if the person is procedurally removed from the setting or loses access to reinforcers. For instance, if a teacher removes a student from the classroom (presumably the time-in setting), but upon the student's return, the problem behavior continues, effective time-out cannot be claimed.

Time-Out Procedures for Applied Settings

There are two basic types of time-out: nonexclusion and exclusion. Within each type, several variations allow the practitioner flexibility in deciding a course of action for reducing behavior. As a rule, nonexclusion time-out is the recommended method of first choice because practitioners are ethically bound to employ the most powerful, but least restrictive, alternative when deciding on eligible variations.

Table 15.1 Distinction Between Positive and Negative Punishment

Future frequency	Stimulus change	
	Stimulus presented	*Stimulus removed*
Behavior is reduced	Positive punishment (e.g., "No!," overcorrection)	Negative punishment (e.g., time-out, response cost)

Nonexclusion Time-Out

Nonexclusion time-out means that the participant is not completely removed physically from the time-in setting. Although the person's position relative to that setting shifts, he or she remains within the environment. Nonexclusion time-out occurs in any one of four ways: planned ignoring, withdrawal of a specific reinforcer, contingent observation, and the time-out ribbon. Each variation has a common element: Access to reinforcement is lost, but the person remains within the time-in setting. For instance, if a student misbehaves during outdoor recess, he would be required to stand next to the adult playground monitor for a period of time.

Planned Ignoring

Planned ignoring occurs when social reinforcers—usually attention, physical contact, or verbal interaction—are removed for a brief period, contingent on the occurrence of an inappropriate behavior. Planned ignoring assumes that the time-in setting is reinforcing and that *all* extraneous sources of positive reinforcement can be eliminated.

Operationally, planned ignoring can involve systematically looking away from the individual, remaining quiet, or refraining from any interaction whatsoever for a specific time (Kee, Hill, & Weist, 1999). Planned ignoring has the advantage of being a nonintrusive time-out procedure that can be applied quickly and conveniently.

For example, let us suppose that during a group therapy session for drug rehabilitation a client begins to express her fascination with stealing money to buy narcotics. If at that point the other members of the group break eye contact and do not respond to her verbalizations in any way until her comments are more consistent with the group's discussion, then planned ignoring is in effect. In this case, because the members of the group participated in the reductive procedure, it would be termed *peer-mediated time-out* (Kerr & Nelson, 2002).

Withdrawal of a Specific Positive Reinforcer

Bishop and Stumphauzer (1973) demonstrated that the withdrawal of a specific positive reinforcer contingent on an inappropriate behavior decreased the level of that behavior. In their study, the contingent termination of television cartoons successfully reduced the frequency of thumb sucking in three young children. Unknown to the children, a remote on/off switch was attached to the television. Baseline data indicated that each child emitted a high rate of thumb sucking while viewing the cartoons. During this variation of time-out, the television was immediately turned off when thumb sucking occurred and was turned back on when thumb sucking

stopped. The procedure was effective in reducing thumb sucking not only in the treatment location (an office), but also during a story period at school.

West and Smith (2002) reported on a novel group application of this time-out variation. They mounted a facsimile traffic signal light to a cafeteria wall and rigged the light with a sensor to detect noise at various threshold levels. For instance, if an acceptable level of conversation was evident, a green light registered on the traffic signal and prerecorded music played (i.e., the time-in condition was in effect). The music remained available as long as the students engaged in an appropriate level of conversation. As the conversational level increased, the traffic light changed from green to yellow, visibly warning the students that any further increase in noise would lead to red light onset and music loss (i.e., time-out). The music was switched off automatically for 10 seconds after the sensor registered the noise above a certain decibel threshold shown by the red light. Under this group procedure, the inappropriate behavior was reduced.

A group time-out contingency has several advantages. First, it can be used in an existing environment; special provisions for removing students are not needed. Second, using an electronic device automatically signals when time-in and time-out are in effect. In the West and Smith study, students soon discriminated that continued inappropriate loud conversation resulted in the loss of the reinforcer (e.g., music).

Contingent Observation

In **contingent observation,** the person is repositioned within an existing setting such that observation of ongoing activities remains, but access to reinforcement is lost. A teacher uses contingent observation when upon the occurrence of an undesirable behavior the teacher redirects the offending student to sit away from the group, and reinforcement for a specific time is withheld (Twyman, Johnson, Buie, & Nelson, 1994). In short, the student is told to "sit and watch" (White & Bailey, 1990). When the contingent observation period ends, the student rejoins the group and is able to earn reinforcement for appropriate behavior. Figure 15.1 shows the effects of White and Bailey's (1990) use of contingent observation in reducing the number of disruptive behaviors in two inclusive physical education classes. When contingent observation was in effect, the number of disruptive behaviors across two classrooms decreased and remained near zero levels.

Time-Out Ribbon

The **time-out ribbon** is defined as a colored band that is placed on a child's wrist and becomes discriminative for receiving reinforcement (Alberto, Heflin, & Andrews,

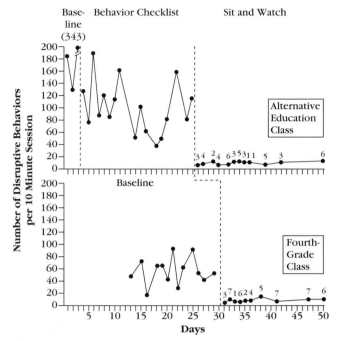

Figure 15.1 Number of disruptive behaviors per 10-minute observation period. The numbers above the data points represent the number of times "sit and watch" was implemented during the class.

From "Reducing Disruptive Behaviors of Elementary Physical Education Students with Sit and Watch" by A. G. White and J. S. Bailey, 1990, *Journal of Applied Behavior Analysis, 23*, p. 357. Copyright 1990 by the Society for the Experimental Analysis of Behavior, Inc. Reprinted by permission.

2002). When the ribbon is on the child's wrist, she is eligible to earn reinforcers. If the child misbehaves, the ribbon is removed, and all forms of social interaction with the child are terminated for a specific period (e.g., 2 minutes).

Foxx and Shapiro (1978) used the time-out ribbon to reduce the disruptive behavior of four elementary students. Contingent on an inappropriate behavior, the rib-

bon was removed from the student, and all forms of social interaction with the offender were terminated for 3 minutes. The student was permitted to remain in the room, however. If inappropriate behavior still occurred after 3 minutes, the time-out was extended until the misbehavior was finished. Figure 15.2 shows that when the time-out ribbon plus reinforcement was in effect, the mean percentage of disruptive behavior was markedly reduced for the four students.

Laraway, Snycerski, Michael, and Poling (2003) discussed the removal of the time-out ribbon in the context of motivating operations (MOs). In their view, removing the time-out ribbon functioned as a punisher because of its relationship to the existing establishing operation (EO). In a retrospective analysis of Foxx and Shapiro's (1978) study, Laraway and colleagues stated, "Thus, the EOs for the programmed reinforcers in time-in also established the punishing effect of the ribbon loss (i.e., functioned as EOs for ribbon loss as a punishing event) and abated misbehaviors that resulted in ribbon loss" (p. 410). With respect to the role of MOs as they relate to the time-out ribbon, Laraway and colleagues went on to state:

> In commonsense terms, losing the opportunity to earn a consequence is only important if you currently "want" that consequence. Therefore, MOs that increase the reinforcing effectiveness of particular objects or events also increase the punishing effectiveness of making those objects or events unavailable (i.e., time-out). . . . a single environmental event can have multiple and simultaneous motivating effects. (p. 410)

Exclusion Time-Out

The distinguishing feature of **exclusion time-out** is that the person is removed from the environment for a specified period, contingent on the occurrence of the targeted

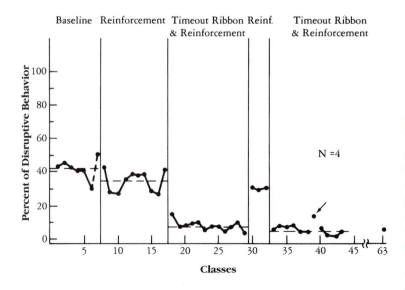

Figure 15.2 The mean percentage of time spent in disruptive classroom behavior by four subjects. The horizontal broken lines indicate the mean for each condition. The arrow marks a 1 day probe (Day 39) during which the time-out contingency was suspended. A follow-up observation occurred on Day 63.

From "The Timeout Ribbon: A Nonexclusionary Timeout Procedure" by R. M. Foxx and S. T. Shapiro, 1978, *Journal of Applied Behavior Analysis, 11*, p. 131. Copyright 1978 by the Society for the Experimental Analysis of Behavior, Inc. Reprinted by permission.

inappropriate behavior. Exclusion time-out can be conducted in classroom settings in three ways: (a) The student can be removed to a time-out room, (b) the student can be separated from the rest of the group by a partition, or (c) the student can be placed in the hallway.

Time-Out Room

A time-out room is any confined space outside the participat's normal educational or treatment environment that is devoid of positive reinforcers and in which the person can be safely placed for a temporary period. The time-out room should preferably be located near the time-in setting and should have minimal furnishing (e.g., a chair and a table). It should have adequate light, heat, and ventilation but should not have other potentially reinforcing features available (e.g., pictures on the wall, telephone, breakable objects). The room should be secure, but not locked.

A time-out room has several advantages that make it attractive to practitioners. First, the opportunity to acquire reinforcement during time-out is eliminated or reduced substantially because the time-out environment is physically constructed to minimize such an occurrence. Second, after a few exposures to the time-out room, students learn to discriminate this room from other rooms in the building. The room assumes conditioned aversive properties, thus increasing the probability that the time-in setting will be viewed as more desirable. Finally, the risk of a student hurting other students in the time-in setting is reduced when the offending student is removed to this space.

However, the practitioner must also weigh several disadvantages of using a time-out room. Foremost is the necessity of escorting the student to the time-out room. From the time the individual is informed that time-out is in effect until the time she is actually placed in the setting, resistance can be encountered. Practitioners should anticipate and be fully prepared to deal with emotional outbursts when using this exclusion time-out variation. In addition, unlike the nonexclusion options mentioned previously, removing an individual from the time-in environment prohibits that individual from access to ongoing academic or social instruction. Missed instructional time should be minimized, and in instances in which time-out has been used excessively and in which it has been shown to serve as a negative reinforcer for the teacher, it should be reconsidered altogether (Skiba & Raison, 1990). Further, in the time-out room the person may engage in behaviors that should be stopped but that go undetected (e.g., self-destructive or self-stimulatory behaviors). Finally, practitioners must be sensitive to the public's perception of the time-out room. Even the most benign time-out room can be viewed with dread by persons who might be misinformed about its purpose or place in an overall behavior management program.

Partition Time-Out

In **partition time-out,** the person remains within the time-in setting, but his view within the setting is restricted by a partition, wall, cubicle, or similar structure. A teacher would use partition time-out by directing a student, contingent on a misbehavior, to move from his assigned seat to a location behind an in-class cubicle for a specified time period. Although partition time-out has the advantage of keeping the student within the time-in setting—presumably to hear academic content and the teacher praising other students for appropriate behavior—it also can be disadvantageous. That is, the person may still be able to obtain covert reinforcement from other students. If he does receive reinforcement from students, it is unlikely that the disruptive behavior will decrease. Also, public perceptions must be taken into account with this form of exclusion. Even though the student remains in the room, and the partition time-out area might be called by an innocuous name (e.g., quiet space, office, personal space), some parents may view any type of separation from other members of the class as discriminatory.

Hallway Time-Out

Hallway time-out is a particularly popular method with teachers—and perhaps parents—when dealing with disruptive behavior. In this method, the student is directed to leave the classroom and sit in the hallway. Although it shares the advantages of the variations just mentioned, this approach is not highly recommended for two reasons: (a) The student can obtain reinforcement from a multitude of sources (e.g., students in other rooms, individuals walking in the hallway), and (b) there is increased likelihood of escape if the student is combative on the way to time-out. Even with the door of the classroom open, teachers are often too busy with activities in the time-in setting to monitor the student closely in the hallway. This approach might be more beneficial for younger children who follow directions, but it is clearly inappropriate for any student who lacks basic compliance skills.

Desirable Aspects of Time-Out

Ease of Application

Time-out, especially the nonexclusion variations, is relatively easy to apply. Even physically removing a student from the environment can be accomplished with comparative ease if the teacher acts in a businesslike fashion and does not attempt to embarrass the student. Issuing a direction privately (e.g., "Deion, you have disrupted Monique twice; time-out is now in effect") can help the teacher handle a student who has misbehaved but who does not want to leave the room. If the behavior warrants time-out, the teacher must insist that the student leave; however, that insistence should be communicated at close range so that the student is not placed in a position of challenging the teacher openly to save face with a peer group. Teachers should consult district policy on whether an administrator should be called to remove the student.

Acceptability

Time-out, especially nonexclusion variations, meets an acceptability standard because practitioners regard it as appropriate, fair, and effective. Even so, prior to implementation, practitioners should always check with the appropriate administering body to ensure compliance with agency policy before applying time-out for major or minor infractions.

Rapid Suppression of Behavior

When effectively implemented, time-out usually suppresses the target behavior in a moderate-to-rapid fashion. Sometimes only a few applications are needed to achieve an acceptable reduction levels. Other reductive procedures (e.g., extinction, differential reinforcement of low rates) also produce decreases in behavior, but they can be time-consuming. Many times the practitioner does not have the luxury of waiting several days or a week for a behavior to decrease. In such instances, time-out merits strong consideration.

Combined Applications

Time-out can be combined with other procedures, extending its usability in applied settings. When it is combined with differential reinforcement, desirable behavior can be increased and undesirable behavior can be decreased (Byrd, Richards, Hove, & Friman, 2002).

Using Time-Out Effectively

Effective implementation of time-out requires that the practitioner make several decisions prior to, during, and after time-out implementation. Figure 15.3 shows Powell and Powell's (1982) time-out implementation checklist, which can aid in the decision-making process. The following sections expand on the major points underlying many of these decisions.

Figure 15.3 Implementation checklist for time-out.

Step	Task	Date Completed	Teacher's Initials
1.	Try less aversive techniques and document results.	_____	_____
2.	Operationally define disruptive behaviors.	_____	_____
3.	Record baseline on target behaviors.	_____	_____
4.	Consider present levels of reinforcement (strengthen if necessary).	_____	_____
5.	Decide on time-out procedure to be used.	_____	_____
6.	Decide on time-out area.	_____	_____
7.	Decide on length of time-out.	_____	_____
8.	Decide on command to be used to place child in time-out.	_____	_____
9.	Set specific criteria that will signal discontinuance of time-out.	_____	_____
10.	Set dates for formal review of the time-out procedure.	_____	_____
11.	Specify back-up procedures for typical time-out problems.	_____	_____
12.	Write up the entire procedure.	_____	_____
13.	Have the procedure reviewed by peers and supervisors.	_____	_____
14.	Secure parental/guardian approval and include the written program in the child's IEP.	_____	_____
15.	Explain procedure to the student and class (if appropriate).	_____	_____
16.	Implement the procedure, take data, and review progress daily.	_____	_____
17.	Formally review procedure as indicated.	_____	_____
18.	Modify the procedure as needed.	_____	_____
19.	Record results for future teachers/programs.	_____	_____

Reinforcing and Enriching the Time-In Environment

The time-in environment must be reinforcing if time-out is to be effective. In making the time-in environment reinforcing, the practitioner should seek ways to reinforce behaviors that are alternative or incompatible with behaviors that lead to time-out (e.g., using differential reinforcement of alternative behavior, differential reinforcement of incompatible behavior). Differential reinforcement will facilitate the development of appropriate behaviors. Additionally, upon return from time-out, reinforcement for appropriate behavior must be delivered as quickly as possible.

Defining Behaviors Leading to Time-Out

Before time-out is implemented, all of the appropriate parties must be informed of the behaviors that will lead to time-out. If a teacher decides to use time-out, she should describe in explicit, observable terms those behaviors that will result in time-out. For instance, merely informing students that disruptive behavior will result in time-out is not sufficient. Providing specific examples and nonexamples of what is meant by disruptive behavior is a better course to follow. Readdick and Chapman (2000) discovered in post-time-out interviews that children are not always aware of the reasons time-out was implemented. Providing explicit examples and nonexamples addresses this problem.

Defining Procedures for the Duration of Time-Out

In most applied settings such as schools and residential and day treatment centers, the initial duration of time-out should be short. A period of 2 to 10 minutes is sufficient, although a short duration may be ineffective initially if an individual has had a history of longer time-out periods. As a rule, time-out periods exceeding 15 minutes are not likely to be effective. Further, longer time-out periods are counterproductive for several reasons. First, the person may develop a tolerance for the longer duration and find ways to obtain reinforcement during time-out. This situation is likely to occur with people with a history of self-stimulatory behavior. The longer the duration of time-out, the more opportunity there is to engage in reinforcing activities (e.g., self-stimulation) and the less effective time-out becomes. Also, longer time-out periods remove the person from the educational, therapeutic, or family time-in environment in which the opportunity to learn and earn reinforcers is available. Third, given the undesirable

practical, legal, and ethical aspects of longer time-out periods, a prudent initial course of action is for the practitioner to use relatively short, but consistent, time-out periods. When time-out periods are short, student academic achievement is not affected adversely (Skiba & Raison, 1990).

Defining Exit Criteria

If a person is misbehaving when time-out ends, it should be continued until the inappropriate behavior ceases (Brantner & Doherty, 1983). Thus, the decision to terminate time-out should not be based exclusively on the passage of time; an improved behavioral condition should also be used as the ultimate criterion for ending time-out. Under no conditions should time-out be terminated if any inappropriate behavior is occurring.

If the practitioner anticipates that the inappropriate behavior that led to time-out may occur at the point of scheduled termination, two strategies can be tried. First, the practitioner can inform the person that the scheduled time-out period (e.g., 5 minutes) will not begin until the inappropriate behavior ceases. The second alternative is to simply extend the time until the disruptive behavior stops.

Deciding on Nonexclusion or Exclusion Time-Out

School board policy or institutional constraints may be established that set the parameters for time-out variations that can be used in applied settings. In addition, physical factors within the building (e.g., a lack of available space) may prohibit exclusionary forms of time-out. In the main, nonexclusion time-out is the preferred method.

Explaining the Time-Out Rules

In addition to posting the behaviors that will lead to time-out, the teacher should also state the rules. Minimally, these rules should focus on the initial duration of time-out and the exit criteria (i.e., rules that determine when time-out is over and what happens if ongoing inappropriate behavior occurs when time-out is over).

Obtaining Permission

One of the most important tasks a practitioner must perform prior to using time-out, especially the exclusionary variations, is to obtain permission. Because of the potential to misuse time-out (e.g., leaving the person in time-out too long, continuing to use time-out when it is not effective), practitioners must obtain administrative approval before employing it. However, interactions happen so fast in most applied settings that obtaining permission on an instance-by-instance basis would be unduly cumbersome. A preferred method is for the practitioner, in cooperation with administrators, to decide beforehand the type of time-out that will be implemented for certain offenses (e.g., nonexclusion versus exclusion), the duration of time-out (e.g., 5 minutes), and the behaviors that will demonstrate reinstatement to the time-in environment. Communicating these procedures and/or policies to parents is advisable.

Applying Time-Out Consistently

Each occurrence of the undesirable behavior should lead to time-out. If a teacher, parent, or therapist is not in a position to deliver the time-out consequence after each occurrence of the target behavior, it may be better to use an alternative reductive technique. Using time-out occasionally may lead to student or client confusion about which behaviors are acceptable and which are not.

Evaluating Effectiveness

Universally, educators and researchers call for the regular evaluation of the use of time-out in applied settings (Reitman & Drabman, 1999). At the very least, data need to be obtained on the inappropriate behavior that initially led to time-out. If time-out was effective, the level of that behavior should be reduced substantially, and that reduction should be noticed by other persons in the environment. For legal and ethical reasons, additional records should be kept documenting the use of time-out; the duration of each time-out episode; and the individual's behavior before, during, and after time-out (Yell, 1994).

In addition to collecting data on the target behavior, it is sometimes beneficial to collect data on collateral behaviors, unexpected side effects, and the target behavior in other settings. For instance, time-out may produce emotional behavior (e.g., crying, aggressiveness, withdrawal) that might overshadow positive gains and spill over into other settings. Keeping a record of these episodes is helpful. Also, Reitman and Drabman (1999) suggested that for home-based applications of time-out, parents keep a record of the date, time, and duration of time-out as well as a brief anecdotal description of the effects of time-out. When reviewed with skilled professionals, these anecdotal logs provide a session-by-session profile of performance, making adjustments to the time-out procedure more informed. In their view,

> The timeout record and discussions centered around it yielded a wealth of information including the type, frequency, context, and rate of misbehavior. . . . Graphing

these data provided visual feedback to both the therapists and the clients regarding the extent to which behavior change had occurred and facilitated the setting of new goals (p. 143).

Considering Other Options

Although time-out has been shown to be effective in reducing behavior, it should not be the method of first choice. Practitioners faced with the task of reducing behavior should initially consider extinction or positive reductive procedures (e.g., differential reinforcement of other behavior, differential reinforcement of incompatible).[1] Only when these less intrusive procedures have failed should time-out be considered.

Legal and Ethical Time-Out Issues

The use of time-out in applied settings has been much discussed. Although litigation surrounding the use of this procedure has focused primarily on institutionalized populations (e.g., *Morales v. Turman,* 1973; *Wyatt v. Stickney,* 1974), the rulings in these cases have had a profound effect on the use of time-out in other settings. The issues before the courts focus on the protection of client rights, whether time-out represents cruel and unusual punishment, and the degree of public acceptability of the time-out procedure.

The upshot of major court rulings has been that a person's right to treatment includes the right to be free from unnecessary and restrictive isolation. However, rulings also include language that permits the use of time-out in a behavior change program as long as the program is closely monitored and supervised and is designed to protect the individual or others from bodily harm.

At least two conclusions have been drawn from the court rulings. First, removing a person to a locked room is considered illegal unless it can be demonstrated that the seclusion is part of an overall treatment plan and unless the program is carefully and closely monitored. Second, the duration of time-out is intended to be brief (i.e., less than 10 minutes). Extensions can be obtained but only from a duly constituted review committee.

Definition of Response Cost

Teachers who need to reduce inappropriate behavior may find response cost a functional alternative to time-out from positive reinforcement because it is quick, avoids

---

[1] We additionally recommend consideration of the Gaylord-Ross decision-making model as an option for when to use punishment procedures, including time-out (see Gaylord-Ross, 1980).

confrontations with students, and offers a treatment option that may be shorter than other reductive procedures (e.g., extinction).

Response cost is a form of punishment in which the loss of a specific amount of reinforcement occurs, contingent on an inappropriate behavior, and results in the decreased probability of the future occurrence of the behavior. As negative punishment, response cost can be classified and is defined by function. Specifically, if the future frequency of the punished behavior is reduced by the response-contingent withdrawal of a positive reinforcer, then response cost has occurred. However, if the removal of the reinforcer increases the level of the behavior or has no effect on it, response cost has not occurred. This distinction between application and effect is the key aspect in the definition of response cost.

Response cost occurs any time a teacher reduces the number of minutes of recess, reclaims previously earned or awarded stickers, or otherwise "fines" the student for an infraction, with the results being a decrease in the future frequency of the targeted behavior. Each occurrence of the inappropriate behavior results in the loss of a specific amount of positive reinforcement already held by the individual. Response cost usually involves the loss of generalized conditioned reinforcers (e.g., money, tokens), tangibles (e.g., stickers), or activities (e.g., minutes of listening to music) (Keeney, Fisher, Adelinis, & Wilder, 2000; Musser, Bray, Kehle, & Jenson, 2001).

Desirable Aspects of Response Cost

Response cost has several features that make it desirable to use in applied settings: its moderate-to-rapid effects on decreasing behavior, its convenience, and its ability to be combined with other procedures.

Moderate-to-Rapid Decrease in Behavior

Like other forms of punishment, response cost usually produces a moderate-to-rapid decrease in behavior. The practitioner does not have to wait long to determine the suppressive effects of response cost. If the procedure is going to be effective in reducing behavior, a two- to three-session trial period is usually sufficient to note the effect.

Convenience

Response cost is convenient to implement and can be used in a variety of school- and home-based settings (Ashbaugh & Peck, 1998; Musser et al., 2001). For example, if students are expected to follow classroom pro-

cedures, rules, or contracts, then any rule infraction will produce a fine. Each occurrence of a misbehavior means that an explicit fine will be levied and that a positive reinforcer will be lost. The fine further signals that future occurrences of the misbehavior will result in the same consequence.

Hall and colleagues (1970) found that the response-contingent removal of slips of paper bearing the student's name had a reductive effect on the number of complaints an emotionally disturbed boy emitted. Prior to a reading and math session, the teacher placed five slips of paper bearing the boy's name on his desk. Each time the boy cried, whined, or complained during reading or math, a slip was removed. Figure 15.4 shows that when response cost was in effect, disruptive behaviors decreased markedly; when response cost was not in effect, these behaviors increased.

Keeney and colleagues (2000) compared response cost with baseline conditions and noncontingent reinforcement after conducting a functional analysis of the destructive behavior of a 33-year-old woman with severe developmental disabilities. The purpose of the functional analysis was to determine the conditions that maintained the behavior. Figure 15.5 (top panel) shows that a functional analysis revealed that the demand (escape) and attention condition produced the highest levels of destructive behavior. The bottom panel shows a baseline condition during which compliance to requests was praised, and episodes of destructive behavior resulted in a 30-second break from the task at hand (escape). During noncontingent reinforcement, caretaker proximity, positive statements, or music was available to the woman. During response cost, the music or attention was available at the beginning of a session. However, any episode of destructive behavior produced an immediate 30-second loss of music or attention.

Overall, the data show an ascending baseline, with mean percentages averaging approximately 30%. Noncontingent music did not result in a reduction in destructive behavior. However, response cost (withdrawal of music for 30 seconds) produced an immediate and replicable change in destructive behavior. An important key to this study was that the functional analysis provided the evidence of the controlling variable (demand), and a prior reinforcer assessment had identified music as a preferred reinforcer. In effect, the reinforcer preference assessment served as a mechanism to develop the response cost program as a treatment for the escape-maintained destructive behavior.

At home, response cost is convenient to the extent that it can be incorporated into an existing allowance program. For instance, if a child earns an allowance of $7 per week ($1 per day) for cleaning his room and placing his dishes in the sink after eating, noncompliance with one

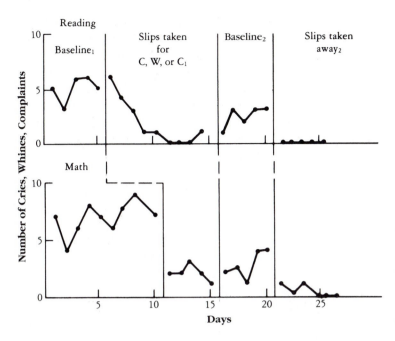

Figure 15.4 The number of cries, whines, and complaints by Billy during the 30-minute reading and arithmetic periods.

From "Modification of Disrupting and Talking-Out Behavior with the Teacher as Observer and Experimenter" by R. V. Hall, R. Fox, D. Williard, L. Goldsmith, M. Emerson, M. Owen, E. Porcia, and R. Davis, 1970, paper presented at the American Educational Research Association Convention, Minneapolis. Reprinted with permission.

or both of these behaviors would lead to a monetary loss (e.g., 50¢ per infraction). In both home and school settings a response cost chart would provide the child feedback on his status, while making the visual notation of progress convenient for teachers and parents (Bender & Mathes, 1995).

Figure 15.6 shows a sample response cost chart as it might be used in a classroom or tutorial setting. To implement the response cost procedure, the teacher writes a column of decreasing numbers on the board. Whenever a disruptive behavior occurs, the teacher crosses off the highest remaining number. If the teacher places the

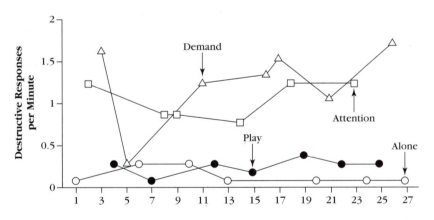

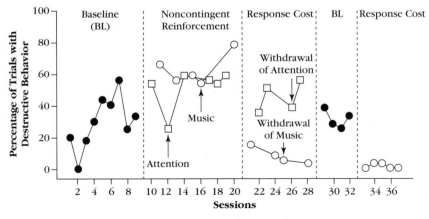

Figure 15.5 Rates of destructive behavior during functional analysis (top panel) and treatment analysis (bottom panel) of noncontingent reinforcement (NCR) and response cost.

From "The Effects of Response Cost in the Treatment of Aberrant Behavior Maintained by Negative Reinforcement" by K. M. Keeney, W. W. Fisher, J. D. Adelinis, and D. A. Wilder, 2000, *Journal of Applied Behavior Analysis, 33*, p. 257. Copyright 2000 by the Society for the Experimental Analysis of Behavior, Inc. Reprinted by permission.

Figure 15.6 A sample response cost chart showing the total number of minutes of free time remaining after three rule infractions.

numbers 15 through 0 on the board and three disruptive behaviors happened, the students had 12 minutes of free time left that day.

Combining with Other Approaches

Response cost can be combined with other behavior change procedures (Long, Miltenberger, Ellingson, & Ott, 1999). For instance, response cost was combined

with a faded bedtime procedure to treat sleep problems (Ashbaugh & Peck, 1998; Piazza & Fisher, 1991). In the Ashbaugh and Peck (1998) study, a systematic replication of Piazza and Fisher (1991), two principal phases were examined: baseline and faded bedtime plus response cost. During baseline, the typical family ritual of placing the child in bed was followed. That is, she was placed in bed when she appeared tired, and no attempts were made to awaken her if she slept during the day when she was supposed to be awake or if she was awake at times when she was supposed to be asleep (e.g., the middle of the night). If the child awoke during the night, she typically went to her parents' room and slept with them.

During faded bedtime plus response cost, an average "fall-asleep" time was calculated based on the baseline data; this time was adjusted each night as a function on the previous night's fall-asleep time. For instance, an average sleep time during baseline may have been 10:30 P.M., adjusted to 10 P.M., if she fell asleep within 15 minutes of the 10:30 P.M. time from the night before. Response cost consisted of having the child get out of her bed for 30 minutes if she was not asleep within 15 minutes of being placed in bed. She was kept awake for the 30 minutes thereafter by playing with toys or talking to her parents. Also, if the child awoke during the night and attempted to sleep in her parents' bed, she was escorted back to her own bed.

Figure 15.7 shows that during baseline 15-minute intervals of disruptive sleep averaged 24 intervals. However, when faded bedtime plus response cost was implemented, the number of 15-minute intervals of disruptive sleep fell to approximately 3 intervals. The child's parents reported a better night's sleep of their own, and gains were maintained a year later.

Figure 15.7 Number of 15-minute intervals of disturbed sleep per 24-hour period during baseline and faded bedtime with response cost.

From "Treatment of Sleep Problems in a Toddler" by R. Ashbaugh and S. Peck, 1998, *Journal of Applied Behavior Analysis, 31*, p. 129. Copyright 1998 by the Society for the Experimental Analysis of Behavior, Inc. Reprinted by permission.

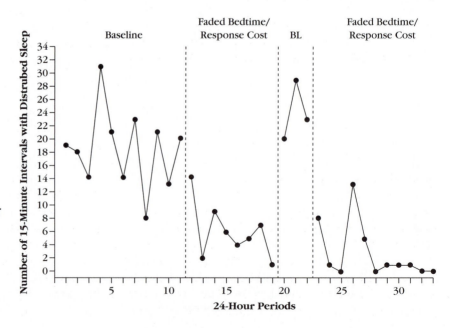

Response cost has been combined with differential reinforcement of alternative behavior (DRA) to treat the food refusal behavior of a 5-year-old child with developmental delay. Kahng, Tarbox, and Wilke (2001) replicated the Keeney and colleagues (2000) study, except that response cost was combined with DRA. During a baseline condition, trials across various food groups were presented every 30 seconds. If food was accepted, praise was delivered. If food was refused, the behavior was ignored. Based on reinforcer assessments, during DRA and response cost, books and audiotapes were made available at the meal. If food was accepted, praise was delivered. If food was refused, the books and audiotapes were removed for 30 seconds. The books and audiotapes were replaced during the next trial contingent on accepting food (i.e., DRA). Parents and grandparents were also trained in the DRA plus response cost procedures. Results showed a substantial increase in the percentage of intervals of food acceptance and a dramatic decrease in the percentage of intervals of food refusal and disruption.

In sum, the findings of studies directly combining response cost with other procedures have been positive. In any case, whether response cost is used alone or in combination with other procedures, practitioners who provide ample reinforcement during time-in occasions are more likely to be successful. Stated differently, response cost should not be used as the sole approach to modifying behavior because response cost, like any punishment procedure, does not teach new behavior. Combining response cost procedures with behavior-building approaches (e.g., DRA) is a good plan.

Response Cost Methods

Four methods for implementing response cost are as a direct fine, as bonus response cost, combined with positive reinforcement, and within a group arrangement.

Fines

Response cost can be implemented by directly fining the person a specific amount of positive reinforcers. A student who loses 5 minutes of free time for each occurrence of noncompliant behavior is an example. In this case, response cost is applied to stimuli known to be reinforcing and available to the person. In some situations, however, removing unconditioned and conditioned reinforcers (e.g., food, free time) from a person would be considered legally and ethically inappropriate or undesirable. For instance, it would be inadvisable to take structured leisure or free time from a person with developmental disabilities. To avoid any potential prob-

lems, practitioners must obtain permission from the local human rights review committee or modify the response cost contingency.

Bonus Response Cost

Practitioners can make additional reinforcers available noncontingently to the participant, specifically for removal with a response cost contingency. For example, if the school district normally allocates 15 minutes of recess each morning for students at the elementary level, in a **bonus response cost** method, students would have an additional 15 minutes of recess available, subject to removal in prespecified amounts if classroom rules are violated. The students retain the regularly scheduled recess, but each infraction or misbehavior reduces their *bonus* minutes by a certain number (e.g., 3 minutes). So, if a student emitted three misbehaviors, his recess that day would consist of his regularly scheduled time (i.e., 15 minutes) plus 6 additional bonus minutes. As students improve, gradually reduce the number of bonus minutes available.

Combining with Positive Reinforcement

Response cost can be combined with positive reinforcement. For example, a student might earn tokens for improved academic performance and simultaneously lose tokens for instances of inappropriate behavior. In another instance, a student could receive a point, a star, or a sticker for each of 10 academic assignments completed during the morning but lose a point, a star, or a sticker for each of 6 occurrences of calling out. In this scenario, the student would net a total of 4 points for that day (i.e., 10 points earned for academic performance minus 6 points for calling out equals a net of 4 points).

Musser and colleagues (2001) combined response cost and positive reinforcement to improve the compliant behavior of three students with emotional disturbance and oppositional defiant behavior. Briefly, the procedures involved the teacher making a normal request for compliance (e.g., "Take out your book please"). If the student complied within 5 seconds, praise was delivered. If a 30-minute period expired and no episodes of noncompliance were recorded, a sticker was delivered to the student. If the student failed to comply with a request within 5 seconds, the teacher waited 5 seconds and issued another directive (e.g., "Take out your book"). The teacher then waited an additional 5 seconds for compliance. If the student complied, praise was issued. If not, one sticker was deducted for noncompliance. Stickers were later exchanged for a "mystery motivator" (e.g., a backup reinforcer from a grab bag). Results for all three students showed marked decreases in noncompliant behavior. Thus, a dual system, which was user friendly and convenient, proved to be effective insofar as the students earned stickers for intervals of compliant behavior, but lost stickers for noncompliant behavior (response cost).

This third method of response cost has at least two advantages: (a) If all of the tokens or points are not lost via response cost, the remaining ones can be traded for backup reinforcers, thus adding a reinforcement component that is incorporated into many programs; and (b) reinforcers can be resupplied by performing appropriate behavior, thereby reducing legal and ethical concerns. The following vignette illustrates how a father might implement a bonus response cost procedure with his two sons to reduce their fighting at dinnertime.

Father: Boys, I'd like to talk to you.

Tom and Pete: OK.

Father: We have to find a way to stop the fighting and squabbling at dinnertime. The way you two go at each other upsets everyone in the family, and I can't eat my dinner in peace.

Tom: Well, Pete usually starts it.

Pete: I do not!

Tom: You do, too . . .

Father: (Interrupting) That's enough! This is just what I mean, nit-picking at each other. It's ridiculous and it needs to stop. I've given it some thought, and here's what we're going to do. Since each of you earns an allowance of $5 per week for doing household chores, I was tempted to take it away from you the next time either of you got into a fight. But I've decided against doing that. Instead, I'm going to make an additional $5 available to each of you, but for each sarcastic comment or squabble you get into at the dinner table, you'll lose $1 of that extra money. So if you act properly, you'll get an additional $5. If you have two fights, you'll lose $2 and get only $3 Do you understand?

Pete: How about if Tom starts something and I don't?

Father: Whoever does any fighting or squabbling loses $1. If Tom starts something and you ignore him, only he loses. Tom, the same thing holds true for you. If Pete starts something and you ignore him, only Pete loses. One more thing. Dinnertime starts when you are called to the table; it ends when you are excused from the table. Any other questions?

Tom: When do we begin?

Father: We'll begin tonight.

It is important to note that the father described the contingencies completely to his sons. He told them what would happen if no fights occurred, and he told them what would happen if one sibling attempted to start a fight but the other ignored him. In addition, he clearly defined when dinnertime would begin and end. Each of these explanations was necessary for a complete description of the contingencies. Presumably, the father praised his sons for their appropriate mealtime behaviors so that they were reinforced and strengthened.

Combining with Group Consequences

The final way that response cost can be implemented involves group consequences. That is, contingent on the inappropriate behavior of any member of a group, the whole group loses a specific amount of reinforcement. The Good Behavior Game, discussed in Chapter 26, serves as an illustration of how response cost can be applied to groups and presents this method of response cost in more depth.

Using Response Cost Effectively

To use response cost effectively, the behavior targeted for response cost and the amount of the fine need to be explicitly stated. Further, any rules that would apply for refusal to comply with the response cost procedure need to be explained. Included in the definition of target behaviors should be the corresponding point loss for each behavior. However, in situations in which multiple behaviors are subject to the response cost contingency or in which the degree of severity of the behavior determines the response cost, correspondingly greater fines should be associated with more severe behaviors. In effect, the magnitude of the punishment (response cost) should fit the offense.

According to Weiner (1962)—the originator of the term *response cost*—the magnitude of the response cost fine is important. It is likely that as the magnitude of the fine increases, larger reductions in the rate of the undesirable behavior may occur. However, if the loss of reinforcers is too great and too rapid, the rate of the reduction of the inappropriate target behavior may be affected adversely. The person will soon be exhausted of his or her supply of reinforcers, and a deficit situation will exist. As a general rule, the fine should be large enough to suppress the future occurrence of the behavior, but not so large as to bankrupt the person or cause the system to lose its effectiveness. In short, if a client loses tokens or other reinforcers at too high a rate, he may give up and become passive or aggressive, and the procedure will become ineffective. Furthermore, fines should not be changed arbitrarily. If a 5-minute loss of recess is imposed on each noncompliant behavior in the morning, the teacher should not impose a 15-minute fine on the same noncompliant behavior in the afternoon.

Determining the Immediacy of the Fines

Ideally, the fine should be imposed immediately after the occurrence of each undesirable behavior. The more quickly response cost is applied subsequent to the occurrence of the behavior, the more effective the procedure becomes. For example, Ashbaugh and Peck (1998) applied a response cost contingency successfully with a young toddler with sleep disruptive behavior immediately after a failure-to-sleep interval passed without sleep onset.

Response Cost or Bonus Response Cost?

Deciding which variation of response cost would be the most effective to reduce behavior is usually an empirical question. However, three considerations can help practitioners. First, the least aversive procedure should be attempted initially. Consistent with the principle of the least restrictive alternative, an effort should be made to ensure that the minimum loss of reinforcers occurs for the minimum amount of time. Bonus response cost may be the less aversive of the two variations because the reinforcers are not deducted directly from the person; instead they are lost from a pool of potentially available (i.e., bonus) reinforcers.

The second consideration is similar to the first and can be stated in the form of a question: What is the potential for aggressive, emotional outbursts? From a social validity perspective, students (and their parents) would probably find it more agreeable to lose reinforcers from an available reserve than from their earnings. Consequently, a bonus response cost procedure might be less likely to spark aggressive or emotional outbursts, or be offensive to students or their parents.

A third consideration is the need to reduce the behavior quickly. Combative or noncompliant behavior may be more appropriately suppressed with response cost because the contingency directly reduces the student's available reinforcers. The response-contingent withdrawal of reinforcers serves to reduce the behavior swiftly and markedly.

Ensuring Reinforcement Reserve

Positive reinforcers cannot be removed from a person who does not have any. Prior to using response cost, the practitioner must ensure a sufficient reinforcer reserve. Without such a reserve, the procedure is unlikely to be successful. For example, if a teacher used response-contingent withdrawal of free time for each occurrence of inappropriate behavior in a highly disruptive class, the students could exhaust all of their available free time before the end of the first hour, leaving the teacher wondering what to do for the remainder of the day. Deducting free time for succeeding days would hardly be beneficial.

Two suggestions apply to reduce the likelihood of having no reinforcers available. First, the ratio of points earned to points lost can be managed. If baseline data indicate that the inappropriate behavior occurs at a high rate, more reinforcers can be programmed for removal. Also, determining the magnitude of the fine, and stating it explicitly beforehand, is helpful. Minor infractions may warrant relatively small fines, whereas major infractions may warrant substantially higher fines. Second, if all reinforcers are lost and another inappropriate behavior occurs, time-out might be applied. After that, when reinforcers have again been earned for appropriate behavior, response cost can be reinstituted.

To establish the initial number of available reinforcers, practitioners collect baseline data on the occurrence of inappropriate behavior during the day or session. The mean baseline figure can be increased for the number of reinforcers to ensure that all reinforcers are not lost when response cost is in effect. Although no empirically verifiable guidelines are available, a prudent approach is to increase the number of reinforcers 25% above the mean number of occurrences during baseline. For example, if baseline data indicate that the mean number of disruptions per day is 20, the practitioner might establish 25 minutes of free time (the positive reinforcer) as the initial level (i.e., 20×1.25). If the practitioner calculates points instead of percentages, she could add an additional 10 to 20 points to ensure an adequate buffer.

Recognizing the Potential for Unplanned or Unexpected Outcomes

Two situations may require the implementation of a contingency plan. One occurs when the repeated imposition of response cost serves to reinforce, rather than punish, the undesirable behavior. When this situation arises, the practitioner should stop using response cost and switch to another reductive procedure (e.g., time-out or DRA). The second situation occurs when the person refuses to give up her positive reinforcers. To reduce the likelihood of this event, the practitioner should clarify the consequences of such refusal beforehand and (a) make sure that an adequate supply of backup reinforcers is available, (b) impose an additional penalty fine for not giving up the reinforcer (e.g., the sticker) (Musser et al., 2001), and/or (c) reimburse the person with some fractional portion of the fine for complying with immediate payment.

Avoiding the Overuse of Response Cost

Response cost should be saved for those major undesirable behaviors that call attention to themselves and need to be suppressed quickly. The teacher's or parent's primary attention should always be focused on positive behavior to reinforce; response cost should be a last resort and should be combined with other procedures to build adaptive behavior.

Keeping Records

Each occurrence of response cost and the behavior that occasioned it should be recorded. Minimally, the analyst should record the number of times fines are imposed, the persons to whom fines are issued, and the effects of the fines. Daily data collection helps to determine the efficacy of the response cost procedure. By graphing the effects of the program, the behavior analyst can determine the suppressive effect of the procedure.

Response Cost Considerations

Increased Aggression

Response-contingent withdrawal of positive reinforcers may increase student verbal and physical aggressiveness. The student who loses several tokens, especially within a short time, may verbally or physically assault the teacher. Emotional behaviors should be ignored whenever possible if they accompany the implementation of response cost (Walker 1983). Still, teachers should anticipate this possibility and (a) preempt a decision to use response cost if they suspect that a worse condition will result in the aftermath of an emotional episode, or (b) be prepared to "ride out the storm."

Avoidance

The setting in which response cost occurs or the person who administers it can become a conditioned aversive stimulus. If this situation occurs in school, the student may avoid the school, the classroom, or the teacher by being absent or tardy. A teacher can reduce the likelihood of becoming a conditioned aversive stimulus by contingently delivering positive reinforcement for appropriate behavior.

Collateral Reductions of Desired Behavior

The response-contingent withdrawal of positive reinforcers for one behavior can affect the frequency of other behaviors as well. If the teacher fines Shashona 1 minute of recess each time she calls out during math class, the response cost procedure may reduce not only her call-outs but also her math productivity. Shashona may say to the teacher, "Since I lost my recess time for calling out, I am not going to do my math." She could also just become passive-aggressive by just sitting in her seat with arms folded and not work. Teachers and other practitioners should anticipate such collateral behaviors and clearly explain the response cost rules, reinforce other classmates as models of appropriate behavior, and avoid face-to-face confrontations.

Calling Attention to the Punished Behavior

Response cost calls attention to the undesirable behavior. That is, upon the occurrence of an inappropriate behavior, the student is informed of reinforcer loss. The teacher's attention—even in the form of notification of reinforcer loss—could serve as a reinforcing consequence. In effect, her attention may increase the frequency of future misbehavior. For instance, a teacher may have difficulty with some students because every mark that the teacher places on the chalkboard indicates that a positive reinforcer has been lost (e.g., minutes of free time). Further, it calls attention to the undesirable behavior and may inadvertently reinforce it. In such a situation, the teacher should change his tactic, perhaps combining response cost with time-out. Also, to counteract the possibility of calling attention to inappropriate behavior, practitioners should ensure that the ratio of reinforcement to response cost contingencies favors reinforcement.

Unpredictability

As with other forms of punishment, side effects of response cost can be unpredictable. The effects of response cost seem to be related to a number of variables that are not fully understood and have not been well investigated across participants, settings, or behaviors. These variables include the magnitude of the fine, the previous punish-ment and reinforcement history of the individual, the frequency with which behaviors are fined, and the availability of alternative responses that are eligible for reinforcement.

 # Summary

Definition of Time-Out

1. Time-out from positive reinforcement, or simply time-out, is defined as the withdrawal of the opportunity to earn positive reinforcement or the loss of access to positive reinforcers for a specified time, contingent on the occurrence of a behavior.

2. Time-out is a negative punisher, and it has the effect of reducing the future frequency of the behavior that preceded it.

Time-Out Procedures for Applied Settings

3. There are two basic types of time-out: nonexclusion and exclusion.

4. Within the nonexclusion type, planned ignoring, withdrawal of a specific positive reinforcer, contingent observation, and time-out ribbons are the main methods.

5. Within exclusion time-out, the time-out room, partition time-out, and hallway time-out serve as the principal methods.

6. Time-out is a desirable alternative for reducing behavior because of its ease of application, acceptability, rapid suppression of behavior effects, and ability to be combined with other approaches.

Using Time-Out Effectively

7. The time-in environment must be reinforcing if time-out is to be effective.

8. Effective use of time-out requires that the behaviors leading to, the duration of, and exit criteria for time-out be explicitly stated. Further, practitioners must decide whether to use nonexclusion or exclusion time-out.

9. In most applications, permission is required before time-out can be implemented.

10. Practitioners should be aware of legal and ethical considerations before implementing time-out. As a punishment procedure, it should be used only after positive reductive procedures have failed, and with planned monitoring, supervision, and evaluation considerations in place.

Definition of Response Cost

11. Response cost is a form of punishment in which the loss of a specific amount of reinforcement occurs, contingent on the performance of an inappropriate behavior, and results in the decreased probability of the future occurrence of the behavior.

12. Four methods for implementing response cost are: attractive procedure for practitioners, including moderate-to-rapid suppression of behavior, convenience, and its ability to be combined with other procedures.

Response Cost Methods

13. Four methods for implementing response cost are: as a direct fine, as a bonus response cost, combined with positive reinforcement, and within a group arrangement.

Using Response Cost Effectively

14. To use response cost effectively, practitioners should determine the immediacy of the fine, decide whether bonus response cost is a preferred option, ensure reinforcer reserve, recognize the potential for unplanned or unexpected outcomes, avoid overusing response cost, and keep good records on its effects.

Response Cost Considerations

15. Implementing response cost may increase student aggressiveness, produce avoidance responses, affect collateral reductions of desired behaviors, and call attention to the punished behavior. The effects of response cost can also be unpredictable.

PART 6

Antecedent Variables

Parts 4 and 5 detailed the effects of various types of stimulus changes immediately following behavior. The two chapters in Part 6 address the effects of stimulus conditions and changes that occur prior to behavior. Behavior does not occur in an environmental void or vacuum. Every response is emitted in the context of a particular set of antecedent conditions, and these antecedent events play a critical part in motivation and learning.

What people do at any particular moment is at least partly a function of what they want at that moment. In Chapter 16, Jack Michael provides a thorough description of motivating operations, environmental variables that (a) alter the momentary effectiveness of some stimulus, object, or event as a reinforcer (or punisher); and (b) alter the current frequency of all behaviors that has been followed by that form of reinforcement. Enhanced understanding of motivating operations represents one of the major advances in behavior analysis in recent years.

Although the defining feature of reinforcement is an increase in the future frequency of behavior, reinforcement produces a second important effect. Chapter 17, Stimulus Control, details how stimuli immediately preceding the response or present during reinforcement acquire an evocative function over future occurrence of the behavior. The chapter describes how behavior analysts use differential reinforcement under changing antecedent stimulus conditions to achieve the desired degrees of stimulus discrimination and to develop stimulus classes with equivalent functions.

CHAPTER 16

Motivating Operations

Key Terms

abative effect
abolishing operation (AO)
behavior-altering effect
conditioned motivating operation (CMO)
discriminative stimulus (S^D) related to punishment
establishing operation (EO)
evocative effect

function-altering effect
motivating operation (MO)
recovery from punishment procedure
reflexive conditioned motivating operation (CMO-R)
repertoire-altering effect
reinforcer-abolishing effect
reinforcer-establishing effect

surrogate conditioned motivating operation (CMO-S)
transitive conditioned motivating operation (CMO-T)
unconditioned motivating operation (UMO)
unpairing
value-altering effect

Behavior Analyst Certification Board® BCBA® & BCABA® Behavior Analyst Task List,© Third Edition

Content Area 3: Principles, Processes, and Concepts	
3-8	Define and provide examples of establishing operations.

This chapter was written by Jack Michael.

In commonsense psychology what people do at any particular moment is at least partly a function of what they want at that moment. From a behavioral perspective based on Skinner's analysis of drive (1938, 1953), wanting something may be interpreted to mean that (a) the occurrence of what is wanted would function as a reinforcer at that moment, and (b) the current frequency of any behavior that has previously been so reinforced will increase. This chapter surveys and classifies variables that have these two motivating effects.

Definition and Characteristics of Motivating Operations

Basic Features

In their treatment of motivation, Keller and Schoenfeld (1950) identified the drive concept in terms of a relation between certain environmental variables, which they called *establishing operations,* and certain changes in behavior. Although not conforming exactly to their usage, **establishing operation (EO)** was reintroduced in 1982 (Michael, 1982, 1993) as a term for any environmental variable that (a) alters the effectiveness of some stimulus, object, or event as a reinforcer; and (b) alters the current frequency of all behavior that has been reinforced by that stimulus, object, or event. The term *establishing operation (EO)* is now commonly used in applied behavior analysis (e.g., Iwata, Smith, & Michael, 2000; McGill, 1999; Michael, 2000; Smith & Iwata, 1997; Vollmer & Iwata, 1991).

The term **motivating operation (MO)** has recently been suggested as a replacement for the term *establishing operation* (Laraway, Snycerski, Michael, & Poling, 2003), along with the terms *value altering* and *behavior altering* for the two defining effects described previously. This more recent arrangement will be presented in this chapter.[1]

The **value-altering effect** is either (a) an increase in the reinforcing effectiveness of some stimulus, object, or event, in which case the MO is an establishing operation (EO); or (b) a decrease in reinforcing effectiveness, in which case the MO is an **abolishing operation (AO).** The **behavior-altering effect** is either (a) an increase in the current frequency of behavior that has been reinforced

by some stimulus, object, or event, called an **evocative effect;** or (b) a decrease in the current frequency of behavior that has been reinforced by some stimulus, object, or event, called an **abative effect.**[2] These relations are shown in Figure 16.1.

For example, food deprivation is an EO that *increases* the effectiveness of food as a reinforcer and evokes all behavior that has been reinforced with food. Food ingestion (consuming food) is an AO that *decreases* the effectiveness of food as a reinforcer, and *abates* all behavior that has been followed by food reinforcement. These relations are shown in Figure 16.2.

An increase in painful stimulation is an EO that *increases* the effectiveness of pain reduction as a reinforcer and *evokes* all behavior that has been reinforced by pain reduction. A decrease in painful stimulation is an AO that *decreases* the effectiveness of pain reduction as a reinforcer and *abates* all behavior that has been followed by pain reduction. These relations are shown in Figure 16.3.

Most of the statements in this chapter about value-altering and behavior-altering effects refer to relations involving reinforcement rather than punishment. It is reasonable to assume that MOs also alter the effectiveness of stimuli, objects, and events as *punishers,* with either establishing or abolishing effects; and also alter the current frequency of all behavior that has been *punished* by those stimuli, objects, or events, either abating or evoking such behavior. At the present time, however, motivation with respect to punishment is just beginning to be dealt with in applied behavior analysis. Later in the chapter a small section considers the role of UMOs for punishment, but it is likely that most of what is said about MOs and reinforcement will be extended to punishment in future treatments of motivation.

Additional Considerations

Direct and Indirect Effects

Behavior-altering effects are actually more complex than has been implied so far. The alteration in frequency can be the result of (a) a direct evocative or abative effect of the MO on response frequency and (b) an indirect effect on the evocative or abative strength of relevant discriminative stimuli (S^Ds). One would also expect an MO to have a value-altering effect on any relevant conditioned reinforcers, which, in turn, would have a behavior-altering effect on the type of behavior that has been reinforced by those conditioned reinforcers. This relation will be considered later in connection with conditioned motivating operations.

---

[1]J. R. Kantor's *setting factor* (1959d, p. 14) included motivating operations as described, but also includes some events that do not fit the specific definition in terms of the two effects. See Smith and Iwata (1997, pp 346–348) for a treatment of the setting factor as an antecedent influence on behavior.

[2]The usefulness of the new term, *abative,* is described in detail in Laraway, Snycerski, Michael, and Poling (2001).

Figure 16.1   Motivating operations (MOs) and their two defining effects.

Establishing Operation (EO)

- Value-altering effect: An increase in the current effectiveness of some stimulus, object, or event as reinforcement.
- Behavior-altering effect: An increase in the current frequency of all behavior that has been reinforced by that stimulus, object, or event (i.e., an evocative effect).

Abolishing Operation (AO)

- Value-altering effect: A decrease in the current effectiveness of some stimulus, object, or event as reinforcement.
- Behavior-altering effect: A decrease in the current frequency of all behavior that has been reinforced by that stimulus, object, or event (i.e., an abative effect).

Figure 16.2   Motivating operations related to food.

Food Deprivation as an Establishing Operation (EO)

- Value-altering effect: An increase in the reinforcing effectiveness of food.
- Behavior-altering evocative effect: An increase in the current frequency of all behavior that has been reinforced by food.

Food Ingestion as an Abolishing Operation (AO)

- Value-altering effect: A decrease in the reinforcing effectiveness of food.
- Behavior-altering abative effect: A decrease in the current frequency of all behavior that has been reinforced by food.

Figure 16.3   Motivating operations related to painful stimulation.

Increase in Painful Stimulation as an Establishing Operation (EO)

- Value-altering effect: An increase in the reinforcing effectiveness of pain reduction.
- Behavior-altering evocative effect: An increase in the current frequency of all behavior that has been reinforced by pain reduction.

Decrease in Painful Stimulation as an Abolishing Operation (AO)

- Value-altering effect: A decrease in the reinforcing effectiveness of pain reduction.
- Behavior-altering abative effect: A decrease in the current frequency of all behavior that has been reinforced by pain reduction.

Not Just Frequency

In addition to frequency, other aspects of behavior can result from a change in an MO, such as response magnitude (a more or less forceful response), response latency (a shorter or longer time from MO or S^D occurrence until the first response), relative frequency (a larger or smaller proportion of responses to the total number of response opportunities), and others. However, because frequency is the best known measure of operant relations, it will be the behavioral alteration referred to in the remainder of this chapter.

A Common Misunderstanding

Sometimes the behavior-altering effect is interpreted as an alteration in frequency due to the organism's encountering a more or less effective form of reinforcement. This implies that the increase or decrease occurs only *after* the reinforcer has been obtained. The critical observation contradicting this notion is that a strong relation exists between MO level and responding *in extinction*—when no reinforcers are being received (see Keller & Schoenfeld, 1950, pp. 266–267 and Figure 60). In terms of an organism's general effectiveness, an MO should evoke the relevant behavior even if it is not at first successful. At present, the two effects (value-altering and behavior-altering) will be considered independent in the sense that one does not derive from the other, although they are probably related at the neurological level.

Current versus Future Effects: Behavior-Altering versus Function-Altering Effects

As a result of an environmental history, an organism has an operant repertoire of MO (motivating operation), S^D (discriminative stimulus), and R (response) relations. (Also present is a respondent repertoire of stimuli capable of eliciting responses, as described in Chapter 2.) MOs and S^Ds are components of the existing repertoire; they are antecedent variables that have behavior-altering effects. Antecedent events can evoke or abate responses, but their simple occurrence does not alter the organism's operant repertoire of functional relations. These antecedent variables are in contrast to consequence variables, whose main effect *is* to change the organism's repertoire of functional relations so that the organism behaves differently in the future. Consequence variables include reinforcers, punishers, and the occurrence of a response without its reinforcer (extinction procedure) or without its punisher (**recovery from punishment procedure**). This is what is meant when MOs and S^Ds are said to alter the *current* frequency of all behavior relevant to that MO; but reinforcers, punishers, and response occurrence without consequence alter the *future* frequency of whatever behavior immediately preceded those consequences.

It is useful to have a different name for these two quite different effects of a behaviorally relevant event; thus **repertoire-altering effect** (Schlinger & Blakely, 1987) is contrasted with behavior-altering *effect* in this chapter. In this chapter the distinction between the two will usually be implied by referring to *current* frequency or to *future* frequency.

A Critical Distinction: Motivative versus Discriminative Relations

MOs and S^Ds are both antecedent variables that alter the current frequency of some particular type of behavior. They are also both operant (rather than respondent) variables in that they control response frequency because of their relation to reinforcing or punishing consequences (rather than to a respondent unconditioned stimulus). At this point, therefore, it may be useful to review the contrasting definitions of these two types of antecedent variables.

An S^D is a stimulus that controls a type of behavior because that stimulus has been related to the *differential*

availability of an effective reinforcer for that type of behavior. Differential availability means that the relevant consequence has been available in the presence of, and unavailable in the absence of, the stimulus. Considering food deprivation and pain increase as putative S^Ds requires that food and pain removal be available in the presence of those conditions. This is somewhat problematic in that both can and often do occur under conditions when the reinforcers are not available. A true S^D constitutes at least a probabilistic guarantee that the relevant consequence will follow the response. Organisms may be food deprived or subjected to painful stimulation for considerable periods during which the condition cannot be alleviated.

More serious for the interpretation as an S^D is that the unavailability of a reinforcer in the absence of the stimulus implies that the unavailable event would have been effective as a reinforcer if it had been obtained. It is with respect to this requirement that most motivative variables fail to qualify as discriminative stimuli. It is true that food reinforcement is, in a sense, unavailable in the absence of food deprivation, and pain-reduction reinforcement is unavailable in the absence of pain, but this is not the kind of unavailability that occurs in discrimination training and that develops the evocative effect of a true S^D (Michael, 1982). In the absence of food deprivation or painful stimulation, no MO is making food or pain removal effective as a reinforcer; therefore, there is no reinforcer unavailability in the sense that is relevant to the discriminative relation.

However, food deprivation and painful stimulation easily qualify as MOs, as conditions that alter the effectiveness of some stimuli, objects, or events as reinforcers, and that simultaneously alter the frequency of the behavior that has been reinforced by those stimuli, objects, or events.

To summarize, a useful contrast can usually be made as follows: Discriminative stimuli are related to the differential availability of a currently effective form of reinforcement for a particular type of behavior; motivative variables (MOs) are related to the differential reinforcing effectiveness of a particular type of environmental event.

Unconditioned Motivating Operations (UMOs)

For all organisms there are events, operations, and stimulus conditions with *value-altering* motivating effects that are unlearned. Humans are born with the capacity to be more affected by food reinforcement as a result of food deprivation, or more affected by pain reduction reinforcement as a result of pain onset or increase. Thus, food deprivation and painful stimulation are called **unconditioned**

motivating operations (UMOs)[3]. By contrast, needing to enter a room through a locked door establishes the key to the door as an effective reinforcer, but this value-altering effect is clearly a function of a learning history involving doors and keys. MOs of this kind are called conditioned motivating operations (CMOs) and will be considered in detail later in this chapter.

Note that it is the unlearned aspect of the value-altering effect that results in an MO being classified as unconditioned. The behavior-altering effect of an MO is usually learned. Said another way, we are born with the capacity to be more affected by food reinforcement as a result of food deprivation, but we have to learn most of the behavior that obtains food—asking for some, going to where it is kept, and so forth.

Nine Main UMOs for Humans

Deprivation and Satiation UMOs

Deprivation with respect to food, water, oxygen, activity, and sleep all have resultant **reinforcer-establishing** and evocative **effects.** By contrast, food and water ingestion, oxygen intake, engaging in activity, and sleeping have **reinforcer-abolishing** and abative **effects.**

UMOs Relevant to Sexual Reinforcement

For many nonhuman mammals, hormonal changes in the female are related to time passage, ambient light conditions, daily average temperature, or other features of the environment that are related phylogenically to successful reproduction. These environmental features, or hormonal changes, or both, can be considered UMOs that cause contact with a male to be an effective reinforcer for the female. They may produce visual changes in some aspect of the female's body and elicit chemical (olfactory) attractants that function as UMOs for the male, establishing contact with a female as a reinforcer and evoking any behavior that has produced such contact. The various hormonal changes may also evoke certain behaviors by the female (e.g., the assumption of a sexually receptive posture) that as stimuli function as UMOs for sexual behavior by the male. Superimposed on this collection of UMOs and unconditioned elicitors is a deprivation effect that may also function as a UMO.

---

[3]The terms *unconditioned* and *conditioned* are used to modify MOs in the same way they modify respondent-eliciting stimuli and operant reinforcers and punishers. Unconditioned motivating operations, like unconditioned eliciting stimuli for respondent behavior and unconditioned reinforcers and punishers, have effects that are not dependent on a learning history. The effects of conditioned motivating operations, like the effects of conditioned eliciting stimuli and conditioned reinforcers and punishers, *are* dependent on a learning history.

In the human, learning plays such a strong role in the determination of sexual behavior that the role of unlearned environment–behavior relations has been difficult to determine. The effect of hormonal changes in the female on the female's behavior is unclear, as is the role of chemical attractants on the male's behavior. Other things being equal, both male and female seem to be affected by the passage of time since last sexual activity (deprivation), functioning as a UMO that establishes the effectiveness of sexual stimulation as a reinforcer and that evokes the behavior that has achieved that kind of reinforcement. Working in the opposite direction, sexual orgasm functions as a UMO that abolishes the effectiveness of sexual stimulation as a reinforcer and abates (decreases the frequency of) behavior that has achieved that kind of reinforcement. In addition, tactile stimulation of erogenous regions of the body seems to function as a UMO in making further similar stimulation even more effective as reinforcement and in evoking all behavior that in the past has achieved such further stimulation.

Temperature Changes

Becoming uncomfortably cold is a UMO that establishes becoming warmer as a reinforcer, and evokes any behavior that has had that effect. A return to a normal temperature condition is a UMO that abolishes an increase in warmth as a reinforcer and abates behavior that has had a warming effect. Becoming uncomfortably warm is a UMO that establishes a decrease in the temperature condition as an effective reinforcer and evokes any behavior that has resulted in a body-cooling effect. A return to a normal temperature condition abolishes being cooler as a reinforcer and abates body-cooling behavior.

These temperature-related UMOs could be combined by specifying becoming uncomfortable with respect to temperature as a UMO that establishes a change for the better as a reinforcer, and that evokes any behavior that has achieved such an effect. Returning to a normal condition would then have appropriate UMO abolishing and abative effects. Still, it seems better at this point to conceptualize the situation as involving different UMOs. Also, these UMOs could be grouped with the pain UMO and included under the broad category of aversive stimulation, but it will be clearer at this point to consider them separately.

Painful Stimulation

An increase in painful stimulation establishes pain reduction as a reinforcer and evokes the behavior (called *escape behavior*) that has achieved such reduction. A decrease in painful stimulation abolishes the effectiveness of pain reduction as a reinforcer and abates the behavior that has been reinforced by pain reduction.

Table 16.1 Nine Unconditioned Motivating Operations (UMOs) and Their Reinforcer-Establishing and Evocative Effects

Unconditioned Motivating Operation (UMO)	Reinforcer-Establishing Effect	Evocative Effect
Food deprivation	Increases effectiveness of food ingestion as a reinforcer	Increases current frequency of all behavior previously reinforced with food
Water deprivation	Increases effectiveness of water ingestion as a reinforcer	Increases current frequency of all behavior previously reinforced with water
Sleep deprivation	Increases effectiveness of sleep as a reinforcer	Increases current frequency of all behavior previously reinforced with being able to sleep
Activity deprivation	Increases effectiveness of activity as a reinforcer	Increases current frequency of all behavior previously reinforced with activity
Oxygen deprivation*	Increases effectiveness of breathing as a reinforcer	Increases current frequency of all behavior previously reinforced with being able to breathe
Sex deprivation	Increases effectiveness of sex stimulation as a reinforcer	Increases current frequency of all behavior previously reinforced with sexual stimulation
Becoming too warm	Increases effectiveness of temperature decrease as a reinforcer	Increases current frequency of all behavior previously reinforced with becoming cooler
Becoming too cold	Increases effectiveness of temperature increase as a reinforcer	Increases current frequency of all behavior previously reinforced with becoming warmer
Increase in painful stimulus	Increases effectiveness of a decrease in pain as a reinforcer	Increases current frequency of all behavior previously reinforced with a decrease in painful stimulation

*It is not actually oxygen deprivation that functions as a UMO, but rather the buildup of carbon dioxide in the blood as a result of not being able to excrete carbon dioxide because of not being able to breathe or because of breathing in air that is as rich in carbon dioxide as the exhaled air.

In addition to establishing pain reduction as a reinforcer and evoking the behavior that has produced pain reduction, painful stimulation in the presence of another organism evokes aggressive behavior toward that organism. In some organisms, including humans, some of this aggression may be the elicitative result of the pain functioning as a respondent unconditioned stimulus (US) (Ulrich & Azrin, 1962). However, a case can be made for the painful stimulation also functioning as a UMO that makes events such as signs of damage to another organism effective as reinforcers and evokes the behavior that has been reinforced by the production of such signs. Skinner made such a case (1953, pp. 162–170) in his analysis of anger, and extended the analysis to the emotions of love and fear.[4]

Review of UMO Effects

Table 16.1 summarizes the reinforcer-establishing and evocative effects of the nine UMOs for humans. Similarly, Table 16.2 shows the reinforcer-abolishing and abative effects.

---

[4]For a discussion of Skinner's approach to emotional predispositions in the general context of MOs, see Michael (1993, p. 197).

The Cognitive Misinterpretation

The behavior-altering effects of UMOs on human behavior are generally understood to some degree. Increased current frequency of behavior that has made us warmer as a result of becoming too cold is a part of our everyday experience, as is the cessation of this behavior when normal temperature returns. That water deprivation should evoke behavior that has obtained water, and that this behavior should cease when water has been obtained, seems only reasonable. However, the variables responsible for these effects are often misconstrued.

The cognitive interpretation of the behavior-altering effects of UMOs on the behavior of a verbally sophisticated individual are in terms of that individual's understanding (being able to verbally describe) the situation and then behaving appropriately as a result of that understanding. On the contrary, the behavioral interpretation that reinforcement *automatically* adds the reinforced behavior to the repertoire that will be evoked and abated by the relevant UMO is not always well appreciated. From the behavioral perspective, the person, verbally sophisticated or not, does not have to "understand" anything for an MO to have value-altering and behavior-altering effects.

Table 16.2 UMOs that Decrease Reinforcer Effectiveness and Abate Relevant Behavior

Unconditioned Motivating Operation (UMO)	Reinforcer-Abolishing Effect	Abative Effect
Food ingestion (after food deprivation)	Decreases effectiveness of food as a reinforcer	Decreases current frequency of all behavior previously reinforced with food
Water ingestion (after water deprivation)	Decreases effectiveness of water as a reinforcer	Decreases current frequency of all behavior previously reinforced with water
Sleeping (after sleep deprivation)	Decreases effectiveness of sleep as a reinforcer	Decreases current frequency of all behavior previously reinforced with sleep
Being active (after activity deprivation)	Decreases effectiveness of activity as a reinforcer	Decreases current frequency of all behavior previously reinforced with activity
Breathing (after not being able to breathe)	Decreases effectiveness of breathing as a reinforcer	Decreases current frequency of all behavior previously reinforced with being able to breathe
Orgasm or sex stimulation (after sex deprivation)	Decreases effectiveness of sexual stimulation as a reinforcer	Decreases current frequency of all behavior previously reinforced with sexual stimulation
Becoming cooler (after being too warm)	Decreases effectiveness of temperature decrease as a reinforcer	Decreases current frequency of all behavior previously reinforced with becoming cooler
Becoming warmer (after being too cold)	Decreases effectiveness of temperature increase as a reinforcer	Decreases current frequency of all behavior previously reinforced with becoming warmer
Painful stimulation decrease (while in pain)	Decreases effectiveness of pain decrease as a reinforcer	Decreases current frequency of all behavior previously reinforced with a decrease in pain

The cognitive misinterpretation of the behavior-altering effect encourages two forms of practical ineffectiveness. First, insufficient effort may be made to teach appropriate behavior to individuals with limited verbal repertoires, on the grounds that they will not be able to understand the relevant environment–behavior relations. Second, there may be insufficient preparation for an increase in whatever behavior preceded the relevant reinforcement (often some form of inappropriate behavior such as yelling and crying), again because it is not thought that the individual would understand the relation between his behavior and any consequence.

Relevance of the MO to a Generality of Effects

In the applied area, the reinforcer-establishing effect of MOs seems to be increasingly understood and used. Edibles may be temporarily withheld so that they will be more effective as reinforcers for behavior that is being taught; similarly with music, toys, and attention from an adult. However, it is not so widely recognized that the behavior being taught with these reinforcers will *not* occur in future circumstances, even if it was well learned and is a part of the learner's repertoire, *unless the relevant MO is in effect.* This issue is considered in the case of punishment (see the section "UMOs for Punishment" on p. 381), where the role of the MO in the occurrence of behavior in future circumstances is more complex and even more likely to be overlooked.

The importance of making the stimulus conditions during instruction similar to those present in the settings and situations in which generalization of the learned behavior is desired is generally understood. However, the fact that the relevant MO must *also* be in effect for responding to be generalized and maintained seems more easily overlooked.

Weakening the Effects of UMOs

For practical reasons it may be necessary to weaken the effects of an MO. Both reinforcer-establishing and evocative effects of UMOs can be *temporarily* weakened by the relevant reinforcer-abolishing and abative operations. For example, food ingestion will have an abative effect on undesirable behavior being evoked by food deprivation, such as food stealing, but the behavior will return when deprivation is again in effect. In general it is not possible to permanently weaken the value-altering effects of UMOs. Water deprivation will always make water more effective as a reinforcer, and pain increase will always make pain decrease more effective as a reinforcer. But the behavior-altering effects are clearly based on a history of reinforcement, and such histories can be reversed by an extinction procedure—let the evoked response occur without its reinforcement. (And the abative effects of a punishment history can be reversed by allowing the response to occur without punishment—the recovery from punishment procedure.) With respect to the UMOs, however, the relevant reinforcer must be obtainable in some acceptable way as the undesirable behavior is being extinguished. People cannot be expected to do without the various unconditioned reinforcers controlled by UMOs.

UMOs for Punishment

An environmental variable that alters the punishing effectiveness of a stimulus, object, or event, and alters the frequency of the behavior that has been so punished, is an MO for punishment. If the value-altering effect does not depend on a learning history, then such a variable would qualify as a UMO.

Value-Altering Effect

An increase in painful stimulation functions as punishment as long as the current level of painful stimulation is not so high that an increase cannot occur. So the UMO must consist of a current pain level that is still capable of increase, or a change to such a level from one that is so high that further increase is not possible. This means that in general a pain increase will almost always function as an unconditioned punisher.[5] This is also true for other kinds of stimulation that function as unconditioned punishers—some sounds, odors, tastes, and so on.

Most of the punishers that affect humans, however, are effective because of a learning history; that is, they are *conditioned* rather than *unconditioned* punishers. If the learning history consisted of pairing conditioned punishers with unconditioned punishers, then the UMOs for those unconditioned punishers are CMOs for the conditioned punishers. (This UMO–CMO relation is described in more detail in the following section on CMOs.) If they are punishers because of a historical relation to a reduced availability of reinforcers, then the MOs for those reinforcers are the MOs for the conditioned punishers. Removing food as a punisher, or more commonly a change to a stimulus in the presence of which food has been less available, will only function as a punisher if food is currently effective as a reinforcer. Thus, the MO for food removal as a punisher is food deprivation.

Social disapproval (expressed by a frown, a head shake, or a specific vocal response such as "No" or "Bad") constitutes a stimulus condition in the presence

of which the typical reinforcers provided by the disapproving person have been withheld. However, such a stimulus condition will function as punishment only if the MOs for those withheld reinforcers are currently in effect. The punishment procedure called *time-out from reinforcement* is similar and will only function as punishment if the reinforcers that are made unavailable—from which the person is *timed out*—are truly effective reinforcers at the time the person is being punished. *Response cost*—taking away objects such as tokens that can be exchanged for various reinforcers or imposing a monetary fine or a fine with respect to some kind of point or score bank—is a more complex type of procedure involving a time delay between when the punishment operation occurs and when the decrease in reinforcers takes effect. Still, unless the events that have been subjected to delayed removal (the things that the tokens, points, or money can be exchanged for) are effective as reinforcers at the time the response cost procedure occurs, punishment will not have occurred. Punishment is covered in more detail in Chapters 14 and 15.

Behavior-Altering Effect

In general, observing a punishment effect is more complex than observing a reinforcement effect because one must also consider the status of the variable responsible for the occurrence of the punished behavior. This applies to the effects of MOs as well. The behavior-altering evocative effect of an MO for reinforcement consists of an increase in the current frequency of any behavior that had been so reinforced. For example, food deprivation evokes (increases the current frequency of) all behavior that had been reinforced with food. The behavior-altering effect of an MO for punishment is a decrease in the current frequency of all behavior that had been so punished. The onset of the MO will have an abative effect with respect to the type of behavior that had been punished. However, the observation of such an abative effect would not be possible unless the previously punished behavior was already occurring at a frequency sufficient that its decrease could be observed when the MO for punishment occurred. That is, the observation of the abative effect of an MO for punishment requires the evocative effect of an MO for reinforcement with respect to the punished behavior. In the absence of the MO for reinforcement, there would be no behavior to be abated by the MO for punishment, even though it had such an abative effect.

Suppose that a time-out procedure had been used to punish some behavior that was disruptive to the therapy situation. Only if the MOs relevant to the reinforcers available in the situation were in effect would one expect the time-out to function as punishment. And then only if those MOs were in effect would one expect to see the

[5]Painful stimulation can be a *conditioned* punisher if it had been historically associated with some other punisher, such as when pain has been evidence that something more serious is wrong. On the other hand, painful stimulation can be a conditioned *reinforcer* if historically associated with some reinforcer in addition to its own termination, such as when muscle pain is related to having had an effective exercise workout, or when painful stimulation has been paired with some form of sexual reinforcement.

abative effect of the punishment procedure on the disruptive behavior. But only if the MO for the disruptive behavior were also in effect would there be any disruptive behavior to be abated. These complex behavioral relations have not received much attention in the conceptual, experimental, or applied literatures, but seem to follow naturally from existing knowledge of reinforcement, punishment, and motivating operations. Behavior analysts should be aware of the possible participation of these behavioral relations in any situation involving punishment.[6]

A Complication: Multiple Effects of the Same Variable

Any behaviorally important event typically has more than one effect, and it is important both conceptually and practically that the various effects all be recognized and not confused with each other (Skinner, 1953, pp. 204–224). Multiple effects are apparent in the animal laboratory demonstration of a simple operant chain. A food-deprived rat is taught to pull a cord hanging from the ceiling of the chamber that turns on an auditory stimulus such as a buzzer. In the presence of the buzzer sound the rat is then taught to make a lever press that delivers a food pellet. The onset of the buzzer will now have two obvious operant effects: (a) It is an S^D that evokes the lever-press response, and (b) it is a conditioned reinforcer that increases the future frequency of the cord-pulling response. The first is a behavior-altering evocative effect, and the second is a function-altering reinforcement effect. These effects are in the same direction, an increase in current frequency and an increase in future frequency, although not necessarily for the same type of response.[7]

Similarly, a stimulus that functions as a *discriminative stimulus (S^D) related to punishment,* will have abative effects on the current frequency of some type of response, and will function as a conditioned punisher that decreases the future frequency of the type of response that preceded its onset. Again, the effects are in the same direction, but in this case both are decreases.

Environmental events that function as UMOs, like those that function as S^Ds, will (in their function as UMOs) typically have behavior-altering effects on the current frequency of a type of behavior, and (as consequences) have repertoire-altering effects on the future frequency of whatever behavior immediately preceded the onset of the event. An increase in painful stimulation will, as an MO, *increase* the *current* frequency of all behavior that has alleviated pain, and as a behavioral consequence *decrease* the *future* frequency of whatever behavior preceded that instance of pain increase. In this case of multiple control, however, the effects will be in opposite directions.

In general, events that have a UMO evocative effect will also function as punishment for the response immediately preceding the onset of the event. This statement must be qualified somewhat for events that have such gradual onsets (like food deprivation) that they cannot easily function as response consequences. Table 16.3 shows these multiple effects for the UMOs that establish the effectiveness of certain events as reinforcers. Events that have a UMO abative effect with respect to current frequency generally do have onsets sufficiently sudden to function as behavioral consequences (e.g., food ingestion) and will be reinforcers for the immediately preceding behavior.

Applied Implications

Many behavioral interventions involve a manipulation chosen because of (a) its MO value-altering or behavior-altering effect, or (b) its function-altering effect as a reinforcer or a punisher. But irrespective of the purpose of the manipulation, it is important to be aware that an effect in the opposite direction will also occur, which may or may not be a problem. The fact that reinforcement is also a form of satiation will not be a problem if the reinforcer magnitude can be quite small. The fact that a satiation operation will also reinforce the behavior preceding it will not be a problem if that behavior is not undesirable. The fact that a deprivation operation with respect to an event that will be used productively as a reinforcer could also function as a punisher for the behavior that preceded the deprivation operation will not be a problem if the deprivation onset is very slow, or if the behavior that is punished is not a valuable part of the person's repertoire.

Table 16.3 shows that any UMO used to make some event more effective as, reinforcement or to evoke the type of behavior that has been reinforced by that event will also function as a punisher for whatever behavior immediately preceded the manipulation. Restricting breathing ability, making the environment too cold or too warm, or increasing painful stimulation are not likely to

---

[6]As an aside, it is sometimes argued that behavioral principles are too simple for the analysis of the complexities of human behavior, and therefore some nonbehavioral—usually cognitive—approach is required. It may well be true that the behavioral repertoire of the people who make this argument is too simple for the task. However, the principles themselves are not so simple, as can be seen from the preceding effort to understand the effects of punishment MOs, or from footnote 5 with respect to the learned functions of painful stimulation.

[7]The buzzer sound will also function as a respondent conditioned eliciting stimulus for smooth muscle and gland responses typically elicited by food in the mouth, and will condition such responses to any other stimulus that is present at that time—an instance of higher order conditioning—but this chapter focuses on operant relations.

Table 16.3 Contrasting the Behavior-Altering and Function-Altering Effects of Environmental Events as UMOs and as Punishers

Environmental Event	Evocative Effect on Current Behavior as a UMO	Function-Altering Effect on Future Behavior as Punishment
Deprivation of food, water, sleep, activity, or sex	Increases the current frequency of all behavior that has been reinforced with food, water, sleep, activity, or sex	Should be punishment, but onset is too gradual to function as a behavioral consequence
Oxygen deprivation	Increases the current frequency of all behavior that has been reinforced with being able to breathe	The sudden inability to breathe decreases the future frequency of the type of behavior that preceded that instance of being unable to breathe
Becoming too cold	Increases the current frequency of all behavior that has been reinforced by becoming warmer	Decreases the future frequency of the type of behavior that preceded that instance of becoming too cold
Becoming too warm	Increases the current frequency of all behavior that has been reinforced by becoming cooler	Decreases the future frequency of the type of behavior that preceded that instance of becoming too warm
Increase in painful stimulation	Increases the current frequency of all behavior that has been reinforced with pain reduction	Decreases the future frequency of the type of behavior that preceded that instance of pain increase

be used deliberately to control behavior in applied settings, but such changes could occur for other reasons (not under the behavior analyst's control). For this reason it is important to be aware of the two different kinds of effects they could have.

Similar opposite effects can be expected from manipulations that worsen[8] the person's situation in any way, even though the worsening is related to a learning history. Such worsening will establish improvement as a reinforcer and will evoke any behavior that has been so reinforced. The nature of social attention as a reinforcer is unclear as to provenance (Michael, 2000, p. 404), but it would be safe to assume that any manipulation designed to increase the effectiveness of attention as a reinforcer (attention deprivation, for example) would also function as a punisher for the behavior that preceded the manipulation.

Conversely, any operation (e.g., a time-out procedure) designed as punishment to decrease the *future* frequency of the behavior preceding the manipulation will also function as an MO in evoking any behavior that has escaped the condition produced by the manipulation.

The behavior analyst should also recognize that any reinforcer-abolishing operation designed to make some event less effective as reinforcement (e.g., a satiation procedure) or to abate the type of behavior that has achieved that type of reinforcement will also function as reinforcement for the behavior immediately preceding the operation. Food ingestion is an abolishing operation for food as reinforcement and abates any food-reinforced behavior, but food ingestion also functions as reinforcement for the behavior immediately preceding the food ingestion. Presenting a high level of noncontingent attention will have a reinforcer-abolishing and an abative effect, but will function as a reinforcer for whatever behavior precedes the operation. Obversely, any operation designed to function as reinforcement will also have MO reinforcer-abolishing and behavior-abating effects.

Aversive Stimuli

Environmental events with combined MO evocative effects, function-altering punishment effects, and respondent evocative effects with respect to certain smooth muscle and gland responses (heart rate increase, adrenal secretion, etc.) are often referred to as *aversive stimuli*, where the specific behavioral function [MO, unconditioned stimulus (S^P), unconditioned stimulus (US)] is not specified.

---

[8]*Worsening* here refers to any stimulus change that *would* function as punishment for behavior that preceded it. The term *punishment* is not quite appropriate in describing this CMO because reference is not being made to a decrease in future frequency of any behavior. Similarly *improvement* is used to refer to a change that would function as reinforcement for behavior that preceded it, but when no reference is being made to an increase in the future frequency of any behavior. Although *worsening* and *improving* are useful terms in this context, they are not presented here as technical terms.

It is not clear at present just how close the correlation among these several functions is, nor is it clear that the advantages of an omnibus term of this sort outweigh the disadvantage of its lack of specificity. It *is* clear that some use of the term *aversive stimulus* is simply a behavioral translation of commonsense expressions for "unpleasant feelings," "unpleasant states of mind," and so on—a form of usage that is possibly fostered by the term's lack of specificity. For these reasons, *aversive stimulus* has not been used in this chapter to refer to MO or to function-altering variables.

Conditioned Motivating Operations (CMOs)

Motivating variables that alter the reinforcing effectiveness of other stimuli, objects, or events, but only as a result of the organism's learning history, are called **conditioned motivating operations (CMOs).** As with UMOs, CMOs also alter the momentary frequency of all behavior that has been reinforced by those other events. In commonsense terms, some environmental variables, as a result of our experiences, make us want something different from what we wanted prior to encountering those variables, and induce us to try to obtain what we now want.

There seem to be at least three kinds of CMOs, all of which were motivationally neutral stimuli prior to their relation to another MO or to a form of reinforcement or punishment. Depending on their relation to the behaviorally significant event or condition, the three kinds of conditioned motivating operations are classified as *surrogate, reflexive,* or *transitive.* The **surrogate CMO (CMO-S)** accomplishes what the MO it was paired with accomplishes (is a surrogate for that MO), the **reflexive CMO (CMO-R)** alters a relation to itself (makes its own removal effective as reinforcement), and the **transitive CMO (CMO-T)** makes something else effective as reinforcement (rather than altering itself).

Surrogate CMO (CMO-S): A Stimulus That Has Been Paired with Another MO

CMO-S Description

The respondent conditioned stimulus (CS), operant conditioned reinforcer (S^r), and operant conditioned punisher (S^p) are each stimuli that acquired a form of behavioral effectiveness by being paired with a behaviorally effective stimulus. It is possible that stimuli that are paired with a UMO[9] will become capable of the same value-altering and behavior-altering effects as that UMO. With respect to its MO characteristics, such a stimulus will be called a surrogate CMO, or a CMO-S.

This relation would be illustrated if stimuli that had been temporally related to decreases in temperature would have MO effects similar to the temperature decreases themselves. That is, in the presence of such stimuli, a temperature increase would be a more effective reinforcer, and behavior that had produced such an increase would occur at a higher frequency than would be appropriate for the actual temperature. Research in this area is discussed at length in Michael, 1993 (pp. 199–202), but will not be reviewed here. Suffice it to say that the evidence for such an effect is not strong. Also, the existence of this type of learned motivating operation is somewhat problematic from an evolutionary perspective (Mineka, 1975). Behaving as though an MO were in effect when it was not would seem to be opposed to the organism's best interest for survival. Trying to get warmer than is necessary for the existing temperature condition would not seem healthy, and such behavior might displace more important behavior. However, evolution does not always work perfectly.

With sexual motivation, MOs for aggressive behavior, and the other emotional MOs, the issue has not been addressed in terms specific to the CMO because its distinction from CS, S^r, and S^p has not been previously emphasized. The surrogate CMO is only just beginning to be considered within applied behavior analysis (see McGill, 1999, p. 396), but its effects could be quite prevalent. From a practical perspective, it may be helpful to consider the possibility of this type of CMO when trying to understand the origin of some puzzling or especially irrational behavior.

Weakening the Effects of Surrogate CMOs

Any relationship developed by a pairing procedure can generally be weakened by two kinds of **unpairing,** presenting the previously neutral stimulus without the previously effective stimulus, or presenting the effective stimulus as often in the absence as in the presence of the previously neutral one. For example, if the CMO-S, let's say a visual stimulus, that had often been paired with extreme cold now occurs frequently in normal temperature, its value-altering and behavior-altering effects would be weakened. Similarly, if extreme cold now occurred just as often in the absence of the CMO-S as in its presence, the effectiveness of the CMO-S would be reduced.

---

[9]The neutral stimulus could be correlated with a CMO rather than a UMO, with the same transfer of effects.

As mentioned earlier, the CMO-S is just beginning to be dealt with in applied behavior analysis (e.g., see McGill, 1999, p. 396), but its possible relation to problem behavior means that the behavior analyst should know how to weaken such CMOs.

Reflexive CMO (CMO-R): A Stimulus That Has Systematically Preceded Some Form of Worsening or Improvement

CMO-R Description

In the traditional "discriminated avoidance procedure,"[10] an intertrial interval is followed by the onset of an initially neutral warning stimulus, which is in turn followed by the onset of painful stimulation—usually electric shock. Some arbitrary response (one that is not part of the animal's phylogenic pain–escape repertoire), such as lever pressing, terminates the painful stimulation (the animal *escapes* the pain) and restarts the intertrial interval. The same response, if it occurs during the warning stimulus, terminates that stimulus and the shock does not occur on that trial. The response at this phase of the procedure is said to have avoided the pain and is called an *avoidance response*. As a result of exposure to this procedure, many organisms learn to emit the relevant response during most of the warning stimulus occurrences, and thus receive very few of the shocks.

Recall the analysis of the role of the shock as an MO for the escape response, the reinforcement for which is shock termination. The warning stimulus has a similar function, except that its capacity to establish its own termination as an effective form of reinforcement is of ontogenic provenance—as a result of the individual's own history involving the relation of the warning stimulus to the onset of the painful stimulus. In other words, the warning stimulus evokes the so-called avoidance response as a CMO, just as the painful stimulation evokes the escape response as a UMO. In neither case is the relevant stimulus related to the *availability* of the response consequence, but rather to its *reinforcing effectiveness.*

In more general terms, any stimulus that systematically precedes the onset of painful stimulation becomes a CMO-R, in that its own offset will function as a reinforcer, and its occurrence will evoke any behavior that has been followed by such reinforcement. This set of functional relations is not limited to painful stimulation as a form of worsening (or even to worsening in general,

as will be seen later). It is well known that organisms can learn to terminate stimuli that warn of stimulus changes other than the onset of pain—stimuli that warn of a lowered frequency of food presentation, increased effort, a higher response ratio requirement, longer delays to food, and so forth. Such events have in common some form of worsening, and stimuli related to such events are often called conditioned aversive stimuli without specifying any particular behavioral function.

It may be useful to repeat the argument against such stimuli being considered discriminative stimuli (S^Ds). A discriminative stimulus is related to the current availability of a type of consequence for a given type of behavior. Availability has two components: (a) An effective consequence (one whose MO is currently in effect) must have followed the response in the presence of the stimulus; and (b) the response must have occurred without the consequence (which would have been effective as a reinforcer if it had been obtained) in the absence of the stimulus. The relation between the warning stimulus and consequence availability does not meet the second component. In the absence of the warning stimulus, there is no effective consequence that could have failed to follow the response in an analog to the extinction responding that occurs in the absence of an S^D. The fact that the avoidance response does not turn off the absent warning stimulus is in no sense extinction responding, but rather is behaviorally neutral, like the unavailability of food reinforcement for a food-satiated organism.

Now consider a stimulus that is positively correlated with some form of improvement. Its CMO-R effects occur if the stimulus establishes its own offset as an effective punisher and abates any behavior that has been so punished. The relation is quite plausible, although there seems to have been little directly relevant research.

Human Examples of the CMO-R

The CMO-R plays an important role in identifying a negative aspect of many everyday interactions that might seem free from any deliberate aversiveness by one person toward another. Typically such interactions are interpreted as a sequence of discriminative stimuli, a sequence of opportunities for each participant to provide some form of positive reinforcement to the other person.

Reactions to Mands.   Imagine that a stranger asks you where a particular building on campus is located, or asks for the time. (Questions are usually mands for verbal action; see Chapter 25.) The appropriate response is to give the information quickly or to say that you don't know. Typically the person who asked will smile and thank you for the information. Also your question may be reinforced by the knowledge that a

---

[10]The term *discriminated* arose so that this type of procedure could be distinguished from an avoidance procedure with no programmed exteroceptive stimulus except for the shock itself (also sometimes called avoidance without a warning stimulus).

fellow human being has been helped. In a sense the question is an opportunity to obtain these reinforcers that were not available before the question. However, the question also begins a brief period that can be considered a warning stimulus, and if a response is not made soon, a form of social worsening will occur. The asker may repeat the question, stating it more clearly or more loudly, and will certainly think you are strange if you do not respond quickly. You too would consider it socially inappropriate for you to provide no answer. Even when no clear threat for nonresponding is implied by the person who asked, our social history under such conditions implies a form of worsening for continued inappropriate behavior. Many such situations probably involve a mixture of the positive and negative components, but in those cases in which answering the question is an inconvenience (e.g., the listener is in a hurry), the asker's thanks is not a strong reinforcer, nor is helping one's fellow human being. The reflexive CMO is probably the main controlling variable.

Complication with Respect to Stimulus Termination

In the typical laboratory avoidance procedure, the response terminates the warning stimulus. In extending this type of analysis to the human situation, it must be recognized that the warning stimulus is not simply the event that initiated the interaction. In the previous example, the reflexive CMO is not the vocal request itself, which is too brief to be actually terminated. It is, instead, the more complex stimulus situation consisting of having been asked and not having made a response during the time when such a response would be appropriate. The termination of that stimulus situation is the reinforcement for the response. Some social interactions with a stimulus—a facial expression, an aggressive posture—are more like the warning stimulus of the animal laboratory that can be terminated by the avoidance response, but most involve the more complex stimulus condition consisting of the request and the following brief period described earlier.

Thanks and You're Welcome. When a person does something for another person that is a kindness of some sort, it is customary to thank the person. What evokes the thanking response, and what is its reinforcement? It is clearly evoked by the person's performing the favor or the kindness. Should performing the favor be considered purely an S^D, in the presence of which one can say "thanks" and receive the reinforcement consisting of the other person saying "you're welcome"? In many cases, ordinary courteous remarks may involve a CMO-R component. Consider the following scenario. Person A has his arms full carrying something out of the build-

ing to his car. As he approaches the outer door, Person B opens the door and holds it open while Person A goes out. Person A then usually smiles and says "Thanks". The CMO-R component can be illustrated by supposing that Person A just walks out without acknowledging the favor. In such circumstances it would not be unusual for Person B to call out sarcastically, "You're welcome!" Someone's doing a favor for someone else is a warning stimulus (a CMO-R) that has systematically preceded some form of disapproval if the favor is not acknowledged in some way.

In applied behavior analysis, the CMO-R is often part of procedures for training or teaching individuals with defective social and verbal repertoires. In language training programs, for example, learners are typically asked questions or given verbal instructions that clearly function as reflexive CMOs, which will be followed by further intense social interaction if they do not respond to them appropriately. Such questions and instructions may well be functioning primarily as reflexive CMOs, rather than S^Ds related to the possibility of receiving praise or other positive reinforcers. Although it may not be possible to completely eliminate this type of aversiveness, it is important to understand its nature and origin.

Weakening the Effects of Reflexive CMOs

Extinction and two forms of unpairing can weaken the effects of CMO-Rs. Extinction consists of the occurrence of a response without its reinforcement. The reinforcement for the response evoked by the CMO-R is the termination of the warning stimulus. When the response occurs repeatedly without terminating the warning stimulus, and the ultimate worsening occurs when the relevant time period elapses, the response will be weakened as with any extinction procedure.

Two forms of unpairing will also weaken the reflexive CMO relation. One involves the nonoccurrence of the ultimate form of worsening when the warning stimulus is not terminated.[11] This type of unpairing weakens the CMO relation by weakening the reinforcement that consists of warning-stimulus termination. Warning-stimulus termination is only reinforcing to the extent that the warning-stimulus-off condition is an improvement over the warning-stimulus-on condition. When warning-stimulus-on is not followed by the ultimate worsening, it becomes no worse than warning-stimulus-off, and the reinforcement for the avoidance response decreases.

The other type of unpairing occurs when the response continues to terminate the warning stimulus, but

---

[11]This procedure is often incorrectly referred to as extinguishing the avoidance response, but a true avoidance extinction procedure requires response occurrence without termination of the warning stimulus.

the ultimate worsening occurs anyway when it would have occurred if the warning stimulus had not been terminated. In this case the warning-stimulus-off condition becomes just as bad as the warning-stimulus-on condition, and again the reinforcement for the avoidance response decreases.

In the usual academic demand situation with some developmentally disabled individuals, typical problem behavior (e.g., tantrumming, self-injury, aggressive behavior) is sometimes evoked by the early phases of the demand sequence and reinforced by terminating the early phase and not progressing to the later and possibly more demanding phases. Assuming that the ultimate phases of the demand sequence *must* occur because of the importance of the relevant repertoire being taught, and assuming that they cannot be made less aversive, then extinction of the problem behavior is the only procedure that is of practical value. This would consist of continuing the demand sequence irrespective of the occurrence of problem behavior. Neither of the unpairing procedures would be effective. The first would not result in any training, and the other would result in the problem behavior occurring as soon as the later phases of training began.

But of course, one should not assume that the ultimate phases of the demand cannot be made less aversive. Increasing instructional effectiveness will result in less failure, more frequent reinforcement, and other general improvements in the demand situation to the point at which it may function as an opportunity for praise, edibles, and so forth, rather than a demand.

Transitive CMO (CMO-T): A Stimulus That Alters the Value of Another Stimulus

CMO-T Description

When an environmental variable is related to the relation between another stimulus and some form of improvement, the presence of that variable functions as a transitive CMO, or CMO-T, to establish the second condition's reinforcing effectiveness and to evoke the behavior that has been followed by that reinforcer. All variables that function as UMOs also function as transitive CMOs for the stimuli that are conditioned reinforcers because of their relation to the relevant unconditioned reinforcer. Consider the simple operant chain described earlier: A food-deprived rat pulls a cord that turns on a buzzer sound. In the presence of the buzzer sound the rat emits some other response that causes the delivery of a food pellet. Food deprivation makes food effective as an unconditioned reinforcer, a relation that requires no learning history. Food deprivation also makes the buzzer sound effective as a conditioned reinforcer, which clearly does

require a learning history. Thus, food deprivation is a UMO with respect to the reinforcing effectiveness of food, but a CMO-T with respect to the reinforcing effectiveness of the buzzer sound. In the human situation food deprivation establishes not only food as a reinforcer, but also all of the stimuli that have been related to obtaining food—an attentive server in a restaurant, a menu, the utensils with which one transports the food to the mouth, and so forth.

Understanding transitive CMOs that result from UMOs in this way requires no special knowledge beyond what is needed to understand the effects of UMOs. Also, the evocative effect of such transitive CMOs is not easily confused with the evocative effect of an S^D. If one can see food deprivation as an MO (rather than an S^D) with respect to the behavior that has been reinforced with food, then its function as an MO (rather than an S^D) with respect to behavior that has been reinforced with the various food-related conditioned reinforcers is an easy extension.

The reinforcing effectiveness of many (probably most) conditioned reinforcers is not only altered by relevant UMOs as described previously, but also dependent on other stimulus conditions because of an additional learning history. This notion underlies the fact that conditioned reinforcing effectiveness is often said to be dependent on a "context." When the context is not appropriate, the stimuli may be available but are not accessed because they are not effective as reinforcers in that context. A change to an appropriate context will evoke behavior that has been followed by those stimuli, which are now effective as conditioned reinforcers. The occurrence of the behavior is not related to the availability, but rather to the value, of its consequence. For example, flashlights are usually available in home settings, but are not accessed until a power failure makes them valuable. In this sense the power failure (the sudden darkness) *evokes* the behavior that has obtained the flashlight in the past (rummaging around in a particular drawer). The motivative nature of this CMO-T relation is not widely recognized, and the evocative variable (the sudden darkness) is usually interpreted as an S^D.

Human CMO-T Examples

Consider a workman disassembling a piece of equipment, with his assistant handing him tools as he requests them.[12] The workman encounters a slotted screw that must be removed and requests a screwdriver. The sight of the screw evoked the request, the reinforcement for which is receiving the tool. Prior to an analysis in terms of the CMO-T, the sight of the screw would have been considered an

---

[12]This scenario was first described in Michael, 1982. At that time CMO-T was called an *establishing stimulus*, or S^E.

S^D for the request, but such screws have *not* been differentially related to the availability of reinforcement for requests for tools. In the typical workman's history, assistants have generally provided requested tools irrespective of the stimulus conditions in which the request occurred. The sight of the screw is more accurately interpreted as a CMO-T for the request, not as an S^D.

The fact that several S^Ds are involved in this complex situation makes the analysis more difficult. The screw *is* an S^D for unscrewing movements (with a screwdriver in hand). The verbal request, although evoked by the sight of the slotted screw as a CMO-T, *is* dependent on the presence of the assistant as an S^D. The offered screwdriver *is* an S^D for reaching movements. The critical issue, however, is the role of the screw in evoking the request, and this is a motivating rather than a discriminative relation.

Another common human example involves a stimulus related to some form of danger that evokes some relevant protective behavior. A night security guard is patrolling an area and hears a suspicious sound. He pushes a button on his phone that signals another security guard, who then activates his own phone and asks if help is needed (which reinforces the first guard's call). The suspicious sound is not an S^D in the presence of which the second security guard's response is more available, but rather a CMO-T in the presence of which it is more valuable. S^Ds are involved, however. A phone's ringing *is* an S^D in the presence of which one has activated the phone, said something into the receiver, and been reinforced by hearing a response from another person. Answering phones that are not ringing has typically not been so reinforced. (Note, incidentally, that the effect of the danger signal is not to evoke behavior that produces its own termination as with the CMO-R, but rather behavior that produces some other event, in this case, the sound of the security guard's colleague offering to help.)

For an animal analog of the CMO-T[13] consider a food-deprived monkey in a chamber with a retractable lever and a chain hanging from the ceiling. Pulling the chain causes the lever to come into the chamber for 5 seconds. If a light (on the wall of the chamber) is on, a lever press delivers a food pellet, but if the light is off, the lever press has no effect. The light comes on and goes off on a random time basis, unrelated to the monkey's behavior. Note that the chain pull will cause the lever to come into the chamber for 5 seconds irrespective of the condition of the light. A well-trained monkey's chain-pulling behavior would be infrequent when the light is off, but evoked by the light onset. The light onset would be the CMO-T in this situation, like the slotted screw or the suspicious sound in the previous examples.

Until recently most behavior analysts interpreted transitive CMOs as S^Ds. The distinction hinges on the relation between reinforcer availability and the presence or absence of the stimulus. If the reinforcer is more available in the presence than in the absence of the stimulus, the stimulus is an S^D; if it is just as available in the absence as in the presence of the stimulus, the stimulus is a CMO-T. Screwdrivers have typically been just as available in the absence as in the presence of screws. The response by the security guard's colleague has been just as available in the absence as in the presence of a suspicious noise. The retractable lever was just as available to the monkey (for pulling the chain) in the absence as in the presence of the light.

Weakening the Effects of Transitive CMOs

The evocative effect of the CMO-T can be temporarily weakened by weakening the MO related to the ultimate outcome of the sequence of behaviors. Consider the example of the workman requesting a screwdriver and also the example of the monkey pulling the chain to cause the lever to come into the chamber. Temporary weakening of the CMO relation could be accomplished by eliminating the reason for doing the work—the workman is told that the equipment does not have to be disassembled, and the monkey is fed a large amount of food prior to being placed in the experimental chamber. Of course, the next time the workman saw a screw that had to be unscrewed, he would again ask his assistant for a screwdriver. When the monkey was again food deprived in the chamber and the light came on, the chain-pulling response would occur.

More permanent weakening can be accomplished by an extinction procedure and by two kinds of unpairing. To extinguish the request that is evoked by the slotted screw, something in the environment would have to change so that such requests are no longer honored (e.g., assistants now believe that workmen should get their tools themselves). In the monkey example, the chain pull would no longer cause the lever to come into the chamber. One type of unpairing would be illustrated if screwdrivers no longer worked to unscrew slotted screws if, say, all such screws were now welded. The workman can still obtain a screwdriver by asking, but the value of the screwdriver is ultimately lost because such a tool wouldn't work anymore. In the monkey scenario, the monkey can still cause the lever to come into the chamber by pulling the chain, but pressing the lever does not deliver food. A second kind of

---

[13]This animal example was first described in Michael, 1982. The language has been changed to be more in line with current terminology.

unpairing would be illustrated if construction practices changed so that slotted screws could now be easily unscrewed by hand as well as with a screwdriver, or if the lever press delivers food when the light is off as well as when it is on.

Importance of the CMO-T for Language Training

It is increasingly being recognized that mand training is an essential aspect of language programs for individuals with severely defective verbal repertoires (see Chapter 25). For such individuals, manding does not spontaneously arise from tact and receptive language training. The learner has to want something, make an appropriate verbal response, and be reinforced by receiving what was wanted. With this procedure the response comes under the control of the relevant MO. UMOs can be taken advantage of to teach mands for unconditioned reinforcers, but this is a relatively small repertoire. Use of a CMO-T, however, is a way to make the learner want anything that can be a means to another end. Any stimulus, object, or event can be a basis for a mand simply by arranging an environment in which that stimulus can function as a conditioned reinforcer. Thus, if a pencil mark on a piece of paper is required for an opportunity to play with a favored toy, a mand for a pencil and for a piece of paper can be taught. The rationale for this kind of training and the various necessary procedures are described in more detail in Chapter 25.

Practical Implications of the CMO-T in General

A CMO-T is a stimulus onset that evokes behavior because of its relation to the *value* of a consequence rather than to the *availability* of a consequence. This distinction must be relevant in subtle ways to the effective understanding and manipulation of behavioral variables for a variety of practical purposes. Two forms of behavioral control, the S^D and the CMO-T, which are so different in origin, would be expected to differ in other important ways. This issue is an example of terminological refinement, not a discovery of any new empirical relations. The value of this refinement, should it have value, will be found in the improved theoretical and practical effectiveness of those whose verbal behavior has been affected by it.

General Implications of Motivating Operations for Behavior Analysis

Behavior analysis makes extensive use of the three-term contingency relation involving stimulus, response, and consequence. However, the reinforcing or punishing effectiveness of the consequence in developing control by the stimulus depends on an MO, and the future effectiveness of the stimulus in evoking the response depends on the presence of the same MO in that future condition. In other words, the three-term contingency cannot be fully understood, or most effectively used for practical purposes, without a thorough understanding of motivating operations.

 Summary

Definition and Characteristics of Motivating Operations

1. A motivating operation (MO) (a) alters the effectiveness of some stimulus as a reinforcer, the value-altering effect; and (b) alters the current frequency of all behavior that has been reinforced by that stimulus, the behavior-altering effect.

2. The value-altering effect is either (a) an increase in the reinforcing effectiveness of some stimulus, in which case the MO is an establishing operation (EO); or (b) a decrease in reinforcing effectiveness, in which case the MO is an abolishing operation (AO).

3. The behavior-altering effect is either (a) an increase in the current frequency of behavior that has been reinforced by some stimulus, called an evocative effect; or (b) a decrease in the current frequency of behavior that has been reinforced by some stimulus, called an abative effect.

4. The alteration in frequency can be (a) the direct evocative or abative effect of the MO on response frequency and/or (b) the indirect effect on the evocative or abative strength of relevant discriminative stimuli (S^Ds).

5. In addition to frequency, other aspects of behavior such as response magnitude, latency, and relative frequency can be altered by an MO.

6. It is not correct to interpret the behavior-altering effect of an MO as due to the organism's encountering a more or less effective form of reinforcement; a strong relation exists between MO level and responding when no reinforcers are being received.

7. Behavior-altering versus function-altering effects: MOs and S^Ds are antecedent variables that have behavior-altering effects. Reinforcers, punishers, or the occurrence of a response without its reinforcer (extinction procedure)

or without its punisher (recovery from punishment procedure) are consequences that change the organism's repertoire so that it behaves differently in the future. S^Ds and MOs alter the current frequency of behavior, but reinforcers, punishers, and response occurrence without consequence alter the future frequency of behavior.

A Critical Distinction: Motivative versus Discriminative Relations

8. An S^D controls a type of behavior because it has been related to the *differential availability* of an effective reinforcer for that type of behavior. This means that the relevant consequence has been available in the presence of, and unavailable in the absence of, the stimulus. Most variables that qualify as motivating operations fail to meet this second S^D requirement because in the absence of the variable, there is no MO for the relevant reinforcer, and thus no reinforcer unavailability.

9. A useful contrast: S^Ds are related to the differential availability of a currently effective form of reinforcement for a particular type of behavior; MOs are related to the differential reinforcing effectiveness of a particular type of environmental event.

Unconditioned Motivating Operations (UMOs)

10. The main UMOs for humans are those related to deprivation and satiation with respect to food, water, oxygen, activity, and sleep; and those related to sexual reinforcement, comfortable temperature conditions, and painful stimulation. For each variable, there are two MOs, one with an establishing operation (EO), and one with an abolishing operation (AO). Also, each variable has an evocative effect and an abative effect. Thus food deprivation is an EO and has evocative effects on relevant behavior, and food ingestion is an AO and has abative effects on relevant behavior.

11. The cognitive interpretation of behavior-altering effects is that the person understands (i.e., can verbally describe) the situation and then behaves appropriately as a result of that understanding. But in fact, reinforcement automatically adds the reinforced behavior to the repertoire that will be evoked and abated by the relevant UMO; the person does not have to "understand" anything for an MO to have its effects. Two different kinds of ineffectiveness can result from this misinterpretation. There may be insufficient effort to train individuals who have very limited verbal repertoires, and inadequate preparation for an increase in problem behavior that preceded reinforcement.

12. The role of stimulus conditions in the generality of training effects is well known, but unless the MO for the reinforcers that were used in training is also in effect, the trained behavior will not occur in the new conditions.

13. Temporary weakening of EO effects can be accomplished by the relevant AO and abative operations. For example, undesirable behavior based on food deprivation can be abated by food ingestion, but the behavior will come back when deprivation is again in effect. More permanent weakening of behavior-altering effects can be accomplished by an extinction procedure (i.e., letting undesired behavior evoked by the MO occur without reinforcement).

14. A variable that alters the punishing effectiveness of a stimulus, object, or event, and alters the frequency of the behavior that has been so punished, is an MO for punishment. If the value-altering effect does not depend on a learning history, then the variable is a UMO. An increase in pain will function as punishment as long as the current level is not so high that an increase cannot occur. If a stimulus is a punisher because of its relation to a reduced availability of a reinforcer, then the MO for that reinforcer is the MO for the punisher. Thus the MO for food removal as a punisher is food deprivation.

15. Social disapproval, time-out from reinforcement, and response cost are stimulus conditions that usually function as punishment because they are related to a reduction in the availability of some kinds of reinforcers. The MOs for those forms of punishment are the MOs for the reinforcers that are being made less available.

16. Multiple effects: Environmental events that function as UMOs will typically have behavior-altering effects on the current frequency of a type of behavior, and (as consequences) function-altering effects with respect to the future frequency of whatever behavior immediately preceded the onset of the event.

17. A behavioral intervention is often chosen because of (a) its MO behavior-altering effect, or (b) its repertoire-altering effect (as a reinforcer or a punisher). But irrespective of the purpose of the intervention, an effect in the opposite direction from the targeted one will also occur, and should be planned for.

Conditioned Motivating Operations (CMOs)

18. Motivating variables that alter the reinforcing effectiveness of other stimuli, objects, or events, but only as a result of the organism's learning history, are called conditioned motivating operations (CMOs). As with the UMOs, they also alter the momentary frequency of all behavior that has been reinforced (or punished) by those other events.

19. The surrogate CMO (CMO-S) is a stimulus that acquires its MO effectiveness by being paired with another MO, and has the same value-altering and behavior-altering effects as the MO with which it was paired.

20. A stimulus that acquires MO effectiveness by preceding some form of worsening or improvement is called a reflexive CMO (CMO-R). It is exemplified by the warning stimulus in a typical escape–avoidance procedure, which establishes its own offset as reinforcement and evokes all behavior that has accomplished that offset.

21. In evoking the avoidance response, the CMO-R has usually been interpreted as an S^D. The CMO-R fails to qualify as

an S^D, however, because in its absence there is no MO for a reinforcer that could be unavailable and thus no reinforcer unavailability. It clearly qualifies as an MO and, because its MO characteristics depend on its learning history, as a CMO.

22. The CMO-R identifies a negative aspect of many everyday interactions that otherwise would be interpreted as a sequence of opportunities for positive reinforcement. One example is a request for information, which initiates a brief period during which a response must be made to terminate a period of increasing social awkwardness.

23. The CMO-R is often an unrecognized component of procedures used in teaching effective social and verbal behavior. Learners are asked questions or given instructions, which are followed by further intense social interaction if they do not respond to them appropriately. The question or instruction may be functioning more as a warning stimulus, as a CMO-R, than as an S^D related to an opportunity for receiving praise or other positive reinforcers.

24. The CMO-R can be weakened by extinction if the response occurs without terminating the warning stimulus (e.g., continuing the demand sequence irrespective of the occurrence of problem behavior), or by two kinds of unpairing (the ultimate worsening fails to occur or occurs irrespective of the avoidance response).

25. An environmental variable that establishes (or abolishes) the reinforcing effectiveness of another stimulus and evokes (or abates) the behavior that has been reinforced by that other stimulus is a transitive CMO, or CMO-T.

26. Variables that function as UMOs also function as transitive CMOs for the stimuli that are conditioned reinforcers because of their relation to the unconditioned reinforcer. Food deprivation (as a UMO) establishes as a reinforcer not only food but also (as a CMO-T) all of the stimuli that have been related to obtaining food (e.g., the utensils with which one transports food to the mouth).

27. The reinforcing effectiveness of many conditioned reinforcers is not only altered by relevant UMOs, but also may be dependent on other stimulus conditions because of an additional learning history. Those stimulus conditions, as CMO-Ts, then also evoke behavior that has obtained the conditioned reinforcers. The occurrence of the behavior is not related to the availability, but rather to the value, of its consequence.

28. A model for the CMO-T is a feature of the environment that must be manipulated with a tool—evoking behavior that obtains that tool—for example, requesting it of another person. Another human example is a stimulus related to some form of danger evoking the relevant protective behavior.

29. The evocative effect of the CMO-T can be temporarily weakened by weakening the MO related to the ultimate outcome of the sequence of behaviors (e.g., the job related to the request for a tool is no longer necessary). More permanent weakening can be accomplished by an extinction procedure (e.g., requests for tools are no longer honored) and by two kinds of unpairing (e.g., the tool no longer accomplishes the task, or the task can be accomplished without the tool).

30. The CMO-T is especially valuable in language programs for teaching mands. It is a way to make the learner want anything that can be a means to another end, and then to reinforce an appropriate mand with the object that is wanted.

General Implications of Motivating Operations for Behavior Analysis

31. The three-term contingency of stimulus, response, and consequence is an essential component of behavior analysis, but this relation cannot be fully understood, or most effectively used, without a thorough understanding of motivating operations.

CHAPTER 17

Stimulus Control

Key Terms

antecedent stimulus class
arbitrary stimulus class
concept formation
discriminative stimulus (S^D)
feature stimulus class

matching-to-sample
reflexivity
stimulus control
stimulus delta (S^Δ)
stimulus discrimination training

stimulus equivalence
stimulus generalization
stimulus generalization gradient
symmetry
transitivity

Behavior Analyst Certification Board® BCBA® & BCABA® Behavior Analyst Task List,© Third Edition

	Content Area 3: Principles, Processes and Concepts
3-2	Define and provide examples of stimulus and stimulus class.
3-7	Define and provide examples of stimulus control.
3-8	Define and provide examples of establishing operations.
3-12	Define and provide examples of generalization and discrimination.
	Content Area 9: Behavior Change Procedures
9-7	Use discrimination training procedures.
9-8	Use prompt and prompt fading.
9-21	Use stimulus equivalence procedures.

Reinforcement of an operant response increases the frequency of future responding and influences the stimuli that immediately precede the response. The stimuli preceding the response (i.e., antecedent stimuli) acquire an evocative effect on the relevant behavior. In a typical laboratory demonstration of operant conditioning, a rat is placed in an experimental chamber and given the opportunity to press a lever. Contingent on a lever press the rat receives a food pellet. Reinforcement of the lever press increases the frequency of lever pressing.

Researchers can make this simple demonstration more complex by manipulating other variables. For example, occasionally a buzzer might sound, and the rat receives a food pellet only when the lever is pressed in the presence of the buzzer. The buzzer sound preceding the lever press is called a **discriminative stimulus** (S^D, pronounced "ess-dee"). With some experience, the rat will make more lever presses in the presence of the buzzer sound (S^D) than in its absence, a condition called **stimulus delta** (S$^\Delta$, pronounced "ess-delta"). Behavior that occurs more often in the presence of an S^D than in its absence is under stimulus control. Technically, **stimulus control** occurs when the rate, latency, duration, or amplitude of a response is altered in the presence of an antecedent stimulus (Dinsmoor, 1995a, b). A stimulus acquires control only when responses emitted in the presence of that stimulus produce reinforcement more often than responses in the absence of stimulus.

Stimulus control should not be viewed as just an interesting procedure for laboratory demonstrations. Stimulus control plays a fundamental role in everyday complex behaviors (e.g., language systems, conceptual behavior, problem solving), education, and treatment (Shahan & Chase, 2002; Stromer, 2000). People do not answer the telephone in the absence of a ring. A person driving a car stops the car more often in the presence of a red traffic light than in its absence. People who use both Spanish and English languages will likely use Spanish, not English, to communicate with a Spanish-speaking audience.

Behaviors considered inappropriate in one context are accepted as appropriate when emitted in another context. For example, teachers will accept loud talking as appropriate on the playground, but not in the classroom. Arriving 15 to 20 minutes late is appropriate for a party, but not for a job interview. Some behaviors that parents, teachers, and society in general may call inappropriate are not behavior problems per se. The problem is emitting behaviors at a time or in a place or circumstance that is deemed inappropriate by others. This represents a problem of stimulus control, and it is a major concern for applied behavior analysts. This chapter addresses the factors related to the development of stimulus control.

Antecedent Stimuli

Stimulus control of an operant response appears similar to the control of respondent behavior by a conditioned stimulus. The S^D and the conditioned stimulus are antecedent stimuli that evoke the occurrence of behavior. Applied behavior analysts, however, need to distinguish between the function of an S^D for operant behavior and a conditioned stimulus for respondent conditioning; this is a crucial distinction for understanding environmental control of operant behavior. In a typical laboratory demonstration of respondent conditioning, the experimenter presents food to a dog. The food functions as an unconditioned stimulus to elicit the unconditioned response—salivation. The experimenter then introduces a buzzer sound (a neutral stimulus). The buzzer sound does not elicit salivation. Then after several occurrences of pairing the buzzer sound with food delivery, the buzzer sound becomes a conditioned stimulus that will elicit salivation (a conditioned response) in the absence of food (an unconditioned stimulus).

Laboratory experiments on operant and respondent conditioning have demonstrated consistently that antecedent stimuli can acquire control over a behavior. A buzzer sounds, and a rat presses a bar. A buzzer sounds, and a dog salivates. Despite the similarities, the bar press is an operant behavior, salivation is a respondent behavior, and the manner in which the S^D and the conditioned stimulus acquire their controlling functions is very different. An S^D acquires its controlling function through association with stimulus changes that occur immediately following behavior. Conversely, a conditioned stimulus acquires its controlling function through association with other antecedent stimuli that elicit the behavior (i.e., an unconditioned stimulus or conditioned stimulus).

The environment contains many forms of energy that a person can perceive. Evolutionary adaptation to the environment has provided organisms with anatomical structures (i.e., organ receptors) that detect these forms of energy. For example, the eye detects electromagnetic radiation; the ear, air-pressure vibrations; the tongue and nose, chemical energies; skin receptors, mechanical pressure and thermal changes (Michael, 1993).

Applied behavior analysts use the physical properties of a stimulus to investigate its effect on behavior. The physical energy, however, must relate to the sensory capabilities of the organism. For instance, ultraviolet radiation is physical energy, but ultraviolet radiation does not function as a stimulus for humans because that energy does not result in any relationship with operant behavior. Ultraviolet radiation would function as a stimulus for humans in the presence of a special device that detects the radiation. A dog whistle functions as a stimulus for dogs but not for humans. Dogs can hear the air pressure vibrations of the whistle, but humans cannot. Any form of physical energy capable of detection by the organism can function as a discriminative stimulus.

Discriminative and Motivational Functions of Stimuli

Discriminative stimuli and motivating operations share two important similarities: (a) both events occur before the behavior of interest, and (b) both events have evocative functions. To evoke behavior means to occasion behavior by calling it up or producing it. Distinguishing the nature of the antecedent control is often difficult. Was the behavior evoked by an S^D, an establishing operation (EO), or both?

In some situations, an antecedent stimulus change alters the frequency of a response and appears to have an S^D effect. For example, in a typical shock–escape procedure an animal is placed in an experimental chamber. Shock is administered until a response removes the shock for a designated period of time. Then the shock is reintroduced until it is again terminated with a response, and so on. An experienced animal removes the shock immediately. In such a situation some would say that the shock serves as an S^D. The shock, an antecedent stimulus, evokes a response that is negatively reinforced (the shock is removed). In this situation, however, shock does not function as an S^D. A response in the presence of an S^D must produce more frequent reinforcement than it does in its absence. Even though the animal receives reinforcement by removing the shock, the absence of shock does not constitute a state of lower frequency reinforcement. Before the response can be reinforced, the shock must be on. Shock in this example is functioning as an EO because it changes what *functions* as reinforcement rather than the availability of reinforcement (Michael, 2000). Often the apparent S^D effect does not have a history of effective differential reinforcement correlated with the altered frequency of response. These situations are probably related to motivating operations (MOs) rather than stimulus control.

The following scenario puts Michael's laboratory example into an applied context: A teacher requests a response from a student. The student emits aggressive behaviors immediately following the request. The aggressive behaviors remove the request. Later, the teacher again requests a response, and the cycle of aggressive behaviors and removal of the request continues. As in the laboratory example, some would say that the requests serve as an S^D. The request, an antecedent stimulus, evokes aggression that is negatively reinforced (the request is removed). In this applied example, the request

is an EO that evokes the aggressive behaviors rather than an S^D. It makes no sense to talk about an S^D evoking the aggressive behavior in the absence of the request (McGill, 1999), just as it makes no sense to talk about an S^D evoking a response in the absence of the shock. The organism does not "want" to escape in the absence of the shock/demand (EO) situation. An antecedent stimulus functions as an S^D only when in its presence a specific response or set of responses produces reinforcement, and the same response does not produce reinforcement in the absence of that stimulus (Michael, 2000).

The laboratory and applied examples can be changed to show the difference between the evocative functions of MOs and stimulus control. The experimental conditions could change so that a buzzer sounds at different periods of time throughout the session, the shock would be removed only when a response is made while the buzzer is sounding, and a response would not produce reinforcement in the absence of the buzzer (i.e., the shock would not be removed). Under these conditions the buzzer would function as an S^D, and stimulus control would be demonstrated. The applied conditions could change so that two teachers work with the student. One teacher allows the student's aggressive behavior to remove requests. The other teacher does not remove the requests. The different procedures produce effective negative reinforcement in the presence of one teacher but not in the presence of the other. The teacher who allows the removal of the request would become an S^D that evokes aggressive behaviors from the student. In these modified examples, the characteristics of the antecedent control would be different in the presence and absence of the buzzer and the other teacher, and the buzzer and the other teacher would be correlated with an increased frequency of reinforcement.

An understanding of the S^D and MO evocative functions will improve the technological descriptions of antecedent control and the understanding of behavior change (Laraway, Snycerski, Michael, & Poling, 2003). Ultimately, these understandings will produce greater effectiveness in education and treatment.

Stimulus Generalization

When an antecedent stimulus has a history of evoking a response that has been reinforced in its presence, there is a general tendency for similar stimuli to also evoke that response. This evocative function occurs with stimuli that share similar physical properties with the controlling antecedent stimulus. This tendency is called **stimulus generalization.** Conversely, *stimulus discrimination* occurs when different stimuli do not evoke the response. Different degrees of stimulus control produce the defining characteristics of stimulus generalization and discrimination. Stimulus generalization and discrimination are relative relations. Stimulus generalization reflects a loose degree of stimulus control, whereas discrimination has a relatively tight degree of control. In a simple everyday situation, stimulus generalization can be observed when a young child who has learned to say "daddy" in the presence of her father says "daddy" in the presence of a neighbor, a clerk in a store, or Uncle Joe. Further conditioning will sharpen the degree of stimulus control to one specific stimulus, the child's father.

Stimulus generalization occurs with new stimuli that share similar physical dimensions with the controlling antecedent stimulus. For instance, if the response has a history of producing reinforcement in the presence of a blue stimulus, stimulus generalization is more likely with a lighter or darker color of blue than with a red or yellow stimulus. Also, stimulus generalization is likely when the new stimuli have other elements (e.g., size, shape) in common with the controlling stimulus. A student whose behavior has produced reinforcement for making a response to a circle is more likely to make the same response to an oval shape than to a triangular shape.

A **stimulus generalization gradient** graphically depicts the degree of stimulus generalization and discrimination by showing the extent to which responses reinforced in one stimulus condition are emitted in the presence of untrained stimuli. When the slope of the gradient is relatively flat, little stimulus control is evident. However, an increasing slope of the gradient shows more stimulus control.

Behavior analysts have used several procedures to produce stimulus generalization gradients. The classic technique of Guttman and Kalish (1956) provides a representative example. Their technique is important because many prior researchers had obtained stimulus generalization gradients by conditioning groups of subjects on the same stimulus value and then testing them individually, each with a different stimulus value. Obviously, this type of technique cannot demonstrate the degree of stimulus control for individual subjects. Guttman and Kalish provided a method of acquiring gradients for each subject and laid the foundation for greater understanding of the principles governing stimulus control.

Guttman and Kalish reinforced pigeons on a VI 1-minute schedule for pecking a disk illuminated with a light source appearing yellow-green to humans (i.e., a wavelength of 550 mμ). After the disk peck had stabilized, the pigeons were tested under extinction conditions on the original stimulus and a randomized series of 11 different wavelengths never presented during training as the test for stimulus generalization.

Stimulus generalization occurs with responses to a new stimulus after a response has been conditioned in

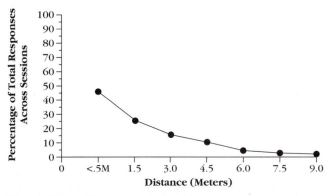

Stimulus Generalization Gradient of Self-Injurious Behavior

Figure 17.1 The percentage of total responses across sessions at a given distance during generalization tests. <0.5, 1.5, 3.0, 4.5, 6.0, 7.5, and 9.0 refer to the distance (in meters) between the therapist and the participant.

From "Assessment of Stimulus Generalization Gradients in the Treatment of Self-Injurious Behavior" by J. S. Lalli, F.C Mace, K. Livezey, and K. Kates (1998). *Journal of Applied Behavior Analysis, 31,* p. 481. Copyright 1988 by the Society for the Experimental Analysis of Behavior, Inc. Used by permission.

the presence of another similar stimulus. If responding produces reinforcement during testing for stimulus generalization, it cannot be clear whether any responses to a new stimulus after the first response represent generalization or if the responses are a function of the reinforcement schedule. Guttman and Kalish avoided this problem of confounding their results by testing for generalization during extinction.

Lalli, Mace, Livezey, and Kates (1998) reported an excellent applied example of assessing and displaying a stimulus generalization gradient. They used a stimulus generalization gradient in an assessment of the relation between the physical proximity of an adult and the self-injurious behavior (SIB) of a 10-year-old girl with severe mental retardation. The results presented in Figure 17.1 show that the percentage of total SIB across sessions became progressively lower as the distance between the therapist and the girl increased.

Development of Stimulus Control

Stimulus Discrimination Training

The conventional procedure for **stimulus discrimination training** requires one behavior and two antecedent stimulus conditions. Responses are reinforced in the presence of one stimulus condition, the S^D, but responses are not reinforced in the presence of the other stimulus, the

S^Δ. When a teacher applies this training procedure appropriately and consistently, responding in the presence of the S^D will come to exceed responding in the presence of the S^Δ. Often, over time, the participant will learn not to respond in the presence of the S^Δ.

Applied behavior analysts often describe the conventional procedures for discrimination training with differential reinforcement as alternating conditions of reinforcement and extinction, meaning that a response produces reinforcement in the S^D condition but not in the S^Δ condition. To clarify and stress an important point, however, the S^Δ is used not only to show a condition of zero reinforcement (extinction) but also to denote a condition that provides a lesser amount or quality of reinforcement than the S^D condition (Michael, 1993).

Maglieri, DeLeon, Rodriguez-Catter, and Sevin (2000) used discrimination training as part of an intervention to decrease the food stealing of a 14-year-old girl with Prader-Willi syndrome, a serious medical condition usually correlated with obesity and food stealing. During discrimination training, a teacher showed the girl two containers of cookies. One container contained a warning label, the S^Δ, and the other container had no warning label, the S^D. The teacher told the girl that she could eat cookies only from the container without the warning label. The teacher asked the girl in the presence of the two containers, "Which cookies can you eat?" If the girl answered that she could eat the cookies from the container without the warning, the teacher let her eat one cookie from the container. This discrimination training procedure decreased stealing food from the containers marked with the warning label.

Concept Formation

The preceding section on discrimination training describes how an antecedent stimulus can acquire control over a response, meaning that the behavior occurs more frequently in the presence of the stimulus than in its absence. A discrimination training procedure might be used to teach a preschool student to name the primary colors. For instance, to teach the color red, the teacher could use a red object such as a red ball as the S^D condition and a nonred object such as a yellow ball as the S^Δ condition. The teacher could position both balls randomly in front of the student, direct the student to name and point to the red ball, and reinforce correct responses, but not incorrect responses. After a few trials the red ball would acquire stimulus control over the student's response, and the student would reliably differentiate the red ball from the yellow ball. This simple discrimination training, however, may not sufficiently meet the instructional objective of identifying the color red. The teacher may want the student to learn not only to discriminate between red

balls and balls of different color, but also the concept of redness.

Terms such as *concept formation* or *concept acquisition* imply for many people some hypothetical construct of a mental process. Yet acquiring a concept is clearly dependent on responses in the presence of antecedent stimuli and the consequences following those responses. Concept formation is a behavioral outcome of stimulus generalization and discrimination (Keller & Schoenfeld, 1950/1995). **Concept formation** is a complex example of stimulus control that requires both stimulus generalization within a class of stimuli and discrimination between classes of stimuli. An **antecedent stimulus class** is a set of stimuli that share a common relationship. All of the stimuli in an antecedent stimulus class will evoke the same operant response class, or elicit the same respondent behavior. This evocative or eliciting function is the only common property among the stimuli in the class (Cuvo, 2000). For example, consider a stimulus class for the concept *red*. A red object is called red because of a particular conditioning history. This conditioning history of differential reinforcement will evoke the response *red* to light waves of different wavelengths, from light red to dark red. These different shades of the color red that will evoke the response *red* share a conditioning history and are included in the same stimulus class. The different shades of red (e.g., light red) that do not evoke the response *red* are not members of that stimulus class. Therefore the concept of redness requires stimulus generalization from the trained stimuli to many other stimuli within the stimulus class. If the preschool student described earlier had acquired the concept of redness, he would be able to identify the red ball and, without specific training or reinforcement, choose a red balloon, a red toy car, a red pencil, and so on.

In addition to stimulus generalization, a concept requires discrimination between members and nonmembers of the stimulus class. For example, the concept of redness requires discriminating between red and other colors and irrelevant stimulus dimensions such as shape or size. The concept begins with discrimination between the red ball and the yellow ball but results in discriminating a red dress from a blue dress, a red toy car from a white toy car, and a red pencil from a black pencil.

Discrimination training is fundamental to teaching conceptual behavior. Antecedent stimuli representative of a group of stimuli sharing a common relationship (i.e., the stimulus class) and antecedent stimuli from other stimulus classes must be presented. Before a concept can be acquired, the teacher must present exemplars of what the concept is (i.e., the S^D condition) and what the concept is not (i.e., the S^Δ condition). This approach holds true for all conceptual development, even for highly abstract concepts (e.g., honesty, patriotism, justice, freedom, sharing). It is also possible to acquire a concept through vicarious discrimination training and differential reinforcement. A verbal definition of a concept, with examples and nonexamples of the concept, may be sufficient for concept formation without additional direct training.

Authors of children's literature often teach concepts vicariously, such as good and bad, honest and dishonest, courageous and cowardly. For example, consider the story of an owner of a mom-and-pop grocery store who wanted to hire a young person to work in the store. The job included sweeping the floor, bagging groceries, and keeping the shelves neat. The owner wanted an honest person to work for him, so he decided to test all applicants to see whether they were honest. The first young person who applied was given the opportunity to try the job before the owner made the commitment to hire him. But before the applicant came to work, the owner hid a dollar bill where he knew the young person would find it. At the end of the test period the owner asked the applicant how he had liked working in the store, whether he wanted the job, and whether anything surprising or unusual had happened to him. The applicant replied that he wanted the job and that nothing surprising had happened to him. The grocer told the first applicant that he wanted to consider others who had applied also. The second applicant worked a test period with the same results as the first person. He did not get the job. The third young person to work for the grocer was sweeping the floor, found the dollar bill, and took it immediately to the grocer. The third applicant said she turned in the dollar bill in case one of the customers or the grocer had dropped it. The grocer asked the applicant whether she liked the job and wanted to work for him. The young person replied that she did. The grocer told the applicant that she had the job because she was an honest person. The grocer also let her keep the dollar bill.

The previous children's story presents exemplars of honest and dishonest behavior. The honest behavior was rewarded (i.e., the honest person obtained the job), and the dishonest behavior was not rewarded (i.e., the first two applicants did not get the job). This story might vicariously teach a certain concept of honesty.

Stimuli comprising a class may function within feature stimulus classes and arbitrary stimulus classes (McIlvane, Dube, Green, & Serna, 1993). Stimuli in a **feature stimulus class** share common physical forms (i.e., topographical structures) or common relative relations (i.e., spatial arrangements). Feature stimulus classes include an infinite number of stimuli and comprise a large portion of our conceptual behavior. For instance, a concept of *dog* is based on a feature stimulus class. The common physical forms of all dogs will be members of that stimulus class. A young child, through differential reinforcement, will learn to differentiate dogs from horses, cats, cows, and so on. Physical forms provide common relations for many feature stimulus classes, such as stimulus classes that evoke the responses *book, table, house, tree, cup, cat, rug, onion,* and *car.* A relational, or a relative relation, exists among stimuli in other feature classes. Examples of these feature stimulus classes based on relative relations are found with concepts such as *bigger than, hotter than, higher than, on top of,* and *to the left of.*

Stimuli comprising an **arbitrary stimulus class** evoke the same response, but they do not share a common stimulus feature (i.e., they do not resemble each other in physical form, nor do they share a relational relationship). Arbitrary stimulus classes are comprised of a limited number of stimuli. For example, a teacher could form an arbitrary stimulus class using the stimuli *50%, 1/2, divided evenly,* and *.5* (see Figure 17.2). Following training, each of these stimuli of different physical forms will evoke the same response, *a half. Green bean, asparagus, potato,* and *corn* could be developed into an arbitrary stimulus class to evoke the response *vegetable.* Students learn to associate vowels with the arbitrary class of the letters *A, E, I, O, U* and sometimes *Y.*

The development of concepts and complex verbal relations plays an important role in parenting, caregiving, education, and treatment. Applied behavior analysts need to consider different instructional procedures when teaching concepts and complex verbal relations that produce feature stimulus classes and arbitrary stimulus classes. A common instructional procedure used with feature stimulus classes is to differentially reinforce responses to *is* (S^D) and *is not* (S$^\Delta$) examples of the concept.

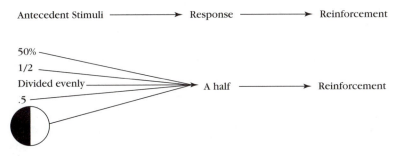

Figure 17.2 Antecedent stimuli with different physical forms that evoke the same response, *a half.* An example of an arbitrary stimulus class.

Broad generalization is common with feature stimulus classes; depending on the functioning level of the participants, a few trained examples may be sufficient to develop the concept. Stimulus generalization, however, is not a characteristic of arbitrary stimulus classes. Applied behavior analysts have developed arbitrary stimulus classes by using **matching-to-sample** procedures to create stimulus equivalance among arbitrary stimuli.

Stimulus Equivalence

In a historically influential experiment, Sidman (1971) demonstrated the development of an equivalence stimulus class among arbitrary stimuli. A boy with severe retardation served as the participant. Before the experiment, the boy could

1. match pictures to their spoken names and

2. name the pictures.

Also before the experiment, the boy could not

3. match written words to the spoken names,

4. match written words to the pictures,

5. match pictures to the written words, or

6. say the written words.

Sidman discovered that after the boy was taught to match written names to spoken names (#3), he could, without additional instruction, match written names to the pictures (#4), match pictures to the written names (#5), and say the written words (#6). In other words, as a result of learning one new stimulus–stimulus relation (#3), the other three stimulus–stimulus relations (#4, #5, and #6) emerged without additional training or reinforcement. When Sidman linked two or more sets of stimulus–stimulus relations, these other noninstructed or unreinforced stimulus–stimulus relations emerged. Without instruction, the boy's receptive and expressive language expanded beyond what existed before the start of the experiment. This is the big prize—something to shoot for in curriculum design and training programs.

Following Sidman's research (see Sidman, 1994), stimulus equivalence has become a major area of basic and applied research in many areas of complex verbal relations, such as reading (Kennedy, Itkonen, & Lindquist, 1994), language arts (Lane & Critchfield, 1998), and mathematics (Lynch & Cuvo, 1995). For example, Rose, De Souza, and Hanna (1996) taught seven nonreading children to read 51 training words. The children matched written words to spoken words, and copied words and named the words. All of the children learned to read the 51 training words, and five of the seven children read

generalization words. Data from Rose and colleagues demonstrate the potential power of stimulus equivalence as a process for teaching reading.

Research on stimulus equivalence has contributed to the understanding of stimulus–stimulus relations among complex human behaviors. Sidman (1971) and others who researched stimulus equivalence during the 1970s (e.g., Sidman & Cresson, 1973; Spradlin, Cotter, & Baxley, 1973) gave future applied behavior analysts a powerful method for teaching stimulus–stimulus relations (i.e., conditional stimulus control).

Defining Stimulus Equivalence

Equivalence describes the emergence of accurate responding to untrained and nonreinforced stimulus–stimulus relations following the reinforcement of responses to some stimulus–stimulus relations. Behavior analysts define **stimulus equivalence** by testing for reflexivity, symmetry, and transitivity among stimulus–stimulus relations. A positive demonstration of all three behavioral tests (i.e., reflexivity, symmetry, and transitivity) is necessary to meet the definition of an equivalence relation among a set of arbitrary stimuli. Sidman and Tailby (1982) based this definition on the mathematical statement:

a. If A = B, and

b. B = C, then

c. A = C

Reflexivity occurs when in the absence of training and reinforcement a response will select a stimulus that is matched to itself (e.g., A = A). For example, a participant is shown a picture of a bicycle and three choice pictures of a car, an airplane, and a bicycle. Reflexivity, also called *generalized identity matching,* has occurred if the participant without instruction selects the bicycle from the three choice pictures.

Lane and Critchfield (1998) taught generalized identity matching of printed letters and a spoken word (vowel or consonant) to two adolescent females with moderate mental retardation. The comparison stimuli of A and D, and O and V accompanied the sample spoken word vowel. Generalized identity matching occurred when participants presented with the sample spoken word vowel selected comparison O from the O and V stimuli and rejected the nonmatching sample V stimulus; and selected the comparison A from the A and D stimuli and rejected the nonmatching sample D stimulus.

Symmetry occurs with the reversibility of the sample stimulus and comparison stimulus (e.g., if A = B, then B = A). For example, the learner is taught, when presented with the spoken word *car* (sample stimulus A), to select

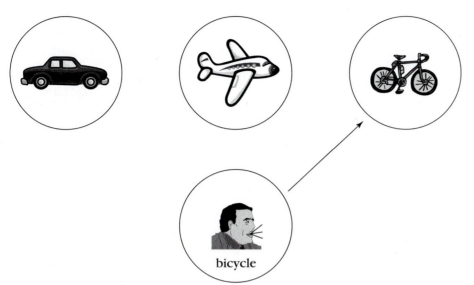

Figure 17.3 Example of an A = B relation (spoken name and picture).

a comparison picture of a car (comparison B). When presented with the picture of a car (sample stimulus B), without additional training or reinforcement, the learner selects the comparison spoken word *car* (comparison A).

Transitivity, the final and critical test for stimulus equivalance, is a derived (i.e., untrained) stimulus–stimulus relation (e.g., A = C, C = A) that emerges as a product of training two other stimulus–stimulus relations (e.g., A = B and B = C). For example, transitivity would be demonstrated if, after training the two stimulus–stimulus realtions shown in 1 and 2 below, the relation shown in 3 emerges without additional instruction or reinforcement:

1. If A (e.g., spoken word *bicycle*) = B (e.g., the picture of a bicycle) (see Figure 17.3), and

2. B (the picture of a bicycle) = C (e.g., the written word *bicycle*) (see Figure 17.4), then

3. C (the written word *bicycle*) = A (the spoken name, *bicycle*) (see Figure 17.5).

Matching-to-Sample

Basic and applied researchers have used the matching-to-sample procedure to develop and test for stimulus equivalence. Dinsmoor (1995b) reported that Skinner introduced the experimental procedure called matching-to-sample, and he described Skinner's procedure in the following way. A pigeon was presented with three horizontal keys to peck. The middle key was illuminated with a color to start the trial. A peck on the illuminated key turned it off and lighted two side keys. One of the side keys was the same color as the sample color illuminated on the middle key. A peck on the side key with the same color as the sample key produced reinforcement. An error response was not reinforced.

The three-term contingency is the basic unit of analysis in the development of complex stimulus-control

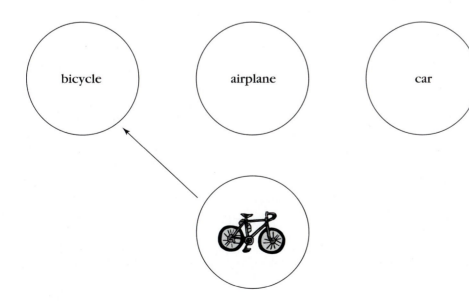

Figure 17.4 Example of a B = C relation (picture and written word).

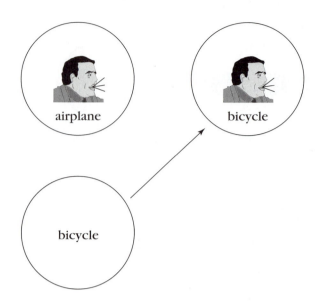

Figure 17.5 Example of a transitive relation, C = A (written word and spoken name), that emerges as a result of training A = B (spoken name and picture) and B = C (picture and written word) relations.

repertoires. Skinner's matching-to-sample procedure included the three-term contingency:

S^D ------------→ Response ------------→ Reinforcement
Side key with   Key peck   Grain
color

This basic contingency, however, is incomplete because of constraints from the environmental context. The contextual events operating on the three-term contingency become conditional discriminations (Sidman, 1994). The sample stimulus in Skinner's procedure is the conditional stimulus. The three-term contingency is effective only when it matches the sample stimulus. Other three-term contingencies (nonmatches) are ineffective. Reinforcement is conditional on the context of discriminative stimuli other than the S^D; that is, the effectiveness of the three-term contingency comes under contextual control. Conditional discriminations operate at the level of a four-term contingency:

Contextual stimulus ---→ S^D ------→ Response → Reinforcement

Conditional sample   Side key   Key peck   Grain
                     with color
Key color

                        S^Δ
                        Color not
                        matching sample

     To start a matching-to-sample trial, the participant will make a response (called the observing response) to present the sample stimulus (i.e., the conditional sample). The comparison stimuli (i.e., the discriminative events) are presented usually after removing the sample stimulus, but not always, and provide for an effective three-term contingency and other noneffective three-term contingencies. A certain comparison will match the conditional sample. A response that selects the matched comparison and rejects

the nonmatched comparisons will produce reinforcement. Figure 17.6 presents an example of the observing response, the conditional sample, the discriminative events, and the comparison match. Responses that select the nonmatching comparison stimuli are not reinforced. During conditional discrimination training, the same selection must be correct with one conditional stimulus, but incorrect with one or more other sample stimuli. Most matching-to-sample applications use a correction procedure with error responses. One correction procedure has the learner respond to the same sample and comparison stimuli until a correct response has been reinforced. Error correction procedures and the random positioning of the comparison stimuli control for position responding.

Factors Affecting the Development of Stimulus Control

Applied behavior analysts establish stimulus control with frequent differential reinforcement of behavior in the presence and in the absence of the S^D condition. Effective differential reinforcement requires the consistent use of consequences that function as reinforcers. Additional factors such as preattending skills, stimulus salience, masking, and overshadowing also will affect the development of stimulus control.

Preattending Skills

The development of stimulus control requires certain prerequisite skills. For academic or social skills the student should engage in orienting behaviors appropriate to the S^Ds in the instructional setting. Such preattending skills include looking at the instructional materials, looking at

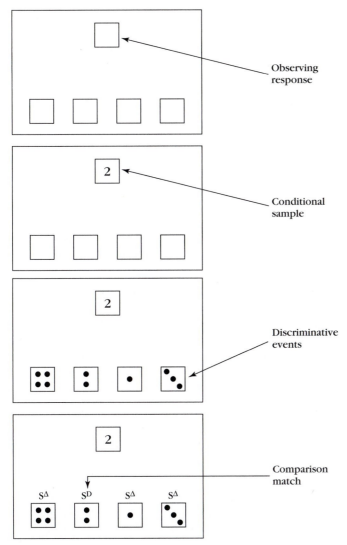

Figure 17.6 An example of the observing response, the conditional sample, the discriminative events, and the comparison match during a matching-to-sample trial.

the teacher whenever a response is modeled, listening to oral instructions, and sitting quietly for short periods of time. Teachers should use direct behavioral interventions to specifically teach preattending skills to learners who have not developed these skills. Learners must emit behaviors that orient the sensory receptors to the appropriate S^D for the development of stimulus control.

Stimulus Salience

The salience of the stimulus influences attention to the stimulus and ultimately the development of stimulus control (Dinsmoor, 1995b). Salience refers to the prominence of the stimulus in the person's environment. For example, Conners and colleagues (2000) included salient cues (e.g., specific room color, specific therapist) into the context of multielement functional analyses. Their results sug-

gested that salient cues facilitated the efficiency of functional analyses by producing faster and clearer outcomes in the presence of the salient cues than in the absence of the salient cues.

Some stimuli have more salience than others depending on the sensory capabilities of the individual, the past history of reinforcement, and the context of the environment. For instance, a student may not attend to words written on the blackboard because of poor vision, or to the teacher's oral directions because of poor hearing, or to the curriculum materials because of past failures to learn, or to teacher directions because of focusing attention on a toy in the student's desk.

Masking and Overshadowing

Masking and overshadowing are methods for increasing or decreasing the salience of stimuli (Dinsmoor, 1995b). In masking, even though one stimulus has acquired stimulus control over behavior, a competing stimulus can block the evocative function of that stimulus. For example, a student may know the answers to a teacher's questions, but will not respond in the presence of the peer group, which in this example is competition of different contingencies of reinforcement, not just an antecedent stimulus that makes it harder to "attend to" the relevant S^D. With overshadowing, the presence of one stimulus condition interferes with the acquisition of stimulus control by another stimulus. Some stimuli are more salient than others. For example, looking out of the window to watch the cheerleaders' practice may distract some students from attending to the instructional stimuli presented during the algebra lesson.

Applied behavior analysts need to recognize that masking and overshadowing can hinder the development of stimulus control, and apply procedures that reduce these effects. Examples of reducing the influence of masking and overshadowing include (a) rearranging the physical environment (e.g., lowering the window shade, removing distractions, changing seating assignments), (b) making instructional stimuli appropriately intense (e.g., providing a rapid pace of instruction, many opportunities to respond, an appropriate level of difficulty, and opportunities to set goals), and (c) consistently reinforcing behavior in the presence of the instructionally relevant stimuli.

Using Prompts to Develop Stimulus Control

Prompts are supplementary antecedent stimuli used to occasion a correct response in the presence of an S^D that will eventually control the behavior. Applied behavior analysts give response and stimulus prompts before or during the performance of a behavior. Response prompts operate directly on the response. Stimulus prompts operate directly on the antecedent task stimuli to cue a correct response in conjunction with the critical S^D.

Response Prompts

The three major forms of response prompts are verbal instructions, modeling, and physical guidance.

Verbal Instructions

Applied behavior analysts use functionally appropriate verbal instructions as supplementary response prompts. Verbal response prompts occur frequently in almost all training contexts in the forms of vocal verbal instruction (e.g., oral, telling) and nonvocal verbal instruction (e.g., written words, manual signs, pictures)

Teachers often use vocal verbal instructional prompts. Suppose a teacher asked a student to read the sentence, "Plants need soil, air, and water to grow." The student reads, "Plants need . . . Plants need . . . Plants need . . ." The teacher could use any number of verbal prompts to occasion the next word. She might say, "The next word is *soil.* Point to *soil* and say *soil.*" Or she might use a rhyming word for *soil.* For another example, Adkins and Mathews (1997) taught in-home caregivers to use vocal verbal response prompts to improve voiding procedures for two adults with urinary incontinence and cognitive impairments. The in-home caregiver checked for dryness each hour or every 2 hours between 6:00 A.M. and 9:00 P.M. The caregiver praised dryness, asked the adult to use the toilet, and provided assistance as needed when the adult was dry at the regularly scheduled check. This simple response prompt procedure, which was introduced following a baseline condition, produced in one of the adults a mean 22% reduction of grams of urine collected per day in wet diapers during the 2-hour prompted voiding condition, and a mean 69% reduction during the 1-hour prompt condition. The second adult received only the 1-hour prompted voiding condition, which resulted in a mean 55% reduction of urine collected per day.

Krantz and McClannahan (1998) and Sarokoff, Taylor, and Poulson (2001) used nonvocal verbal instructional response prompts in the form of embedded scripts to improve the spontaneous social exchanges of children with autism. Examples of the embedded scripts in the children's photographic activity schedules included *look, watch,* and *let's eat our snack.* In another example of nonvocal verbal instructional response prompts, Wong, Seroka, and Ogisi (2000) developed a checklist with 54 steps to prompt self-assessment of blood glucose level by a diabetic woman with memory impairments. This participant followed the checklist sequence and checked off each step as she completed it.

Modeling

Applied behavior analysts can demonstrate or model the desired behavior as a response prompt. Modeling can effectively prompt behaviors especially for learners who have already learned some of the component behaviors required for the imitation. Modeling is an easy, practical, and successful way for a coach to show a player an appropriate form for shooting a basketball through a hoop when the player already can hold the ball, raise it over his head, and push the ball away from his body. Few teachers would use modeling to teach a child with severe disabilities to tie her shoes if she could not hold the laces in her hands. In addition, attending skills are important. The learner must observe the model to enable the imitation of the performance. Finally, modeling as a response prompt should be used only with students who have already developed imitative skills. The use of models to assist in the development of appropriate academic and social behavior has been demonstrated repeatedly. Chapter 18 provides a detailed discussion of modeling and imitation.

Physical Guidance

Physical guidance is a response prompt applied most often with young children, learners with severe disabilities, and older adults experiencing physical limitations. Using physical guidance, the teacher partially physically guides the student's movements, or physically guides the student throughout the entire movement of the response.

Hanley, Iwata, Thompson, and Lindberg (2000) reported the use of physical guidance to help participants with profound mental retardation manipulate leisure items. Conaghan, Singh, Moe, Landrum, and Ellis (1992) used physical guidance to prompt adults with mental retardation and hearing impairments to use manual signs. When a participant made an error in sign production, the teacher physically guided the person's hands to prompt a correct response. In another example, a personal trainer worked with three older adults with severe disabilities, osteoporosis, and arthritis. The trainer physically guided the participants' arm movements whenever they did not begin independent pushes with a dumbbell or stopped the pushes before reaching their exercise criterion (K. Cooper & Browder, 1997).

Physical guidance is an effective response prompt, but it is more intrusive than verbal instruction and modeling. It requires direct physical involvement between the teacher and the student, making precise assessment of student progress difficult. Physical response prompts provide little opportunity for the student to emit the behavior without the direct assistance of the teacher. Another possible problem is some learners' resistance to physical touch. Some learners, however, will require the use of physical guidance.

Stimulus Prompts

Applied behavior analysts have frequently used movement, position, and redundancy of antecedent stimuli as stimulus prompts. For example, movement cues can help a learner discriminate between a penny and a dime by pointing to, tapping, touching, or looking at the coin to be identified. In the coin discrimination task, the teacher could use a position cue and place the correct coin closer to the student. Redundancy cues occur when one or more stimulus or response dimensions (e.g., color, size, shape) are paired with the correct choice. For instance, a teacher might use a color mediation procedure of associating a numeral with a color, then link the name of a color to an answer for an arithmetic fact (Van Houten & Rolider, 1990).

Transfer of Stimulus Control

Applied behavior analysts should provide response and stimulus prompts as *supplementary* antecedent stimuli only during the acquisition phase of instruction. With the reliable occurrence of behavior, applied behavior analysts need to transfer stimulus control from the response and stimulus prompts to the naturally existing stimulus. Applied behavior analysts transfer stimulus control by gradually fading stimuli in or out, gradually presenting or removing antecedent stimuli. Eventually, the natural stimulus, a partially changed stimulus, or a new stimulus will evoke the response. Fading response prompts and stimulus prompts is the procedure used to transfer stimulus control from the prompts to the natural stimulus, and also to minimize the number of error responses occurring in the presence of the natural stimulus.

Terrace's (1963a, b) influential research on the transfer of stimulus control using fading and superimposition of stimuli provides a classic example of transferring stimulus control. In these studies Terrace taught pigeons to make red–green and vertical–horizontal discriminations with a minimum of errors. His use of techniques for gradually transferring stimulus control was called *errorless learning*. To teach a red–green discrimination, Terrace presented the S^Δ (red light) at the beginning of discrimination training, before the S^D (green light) had stimulus control over the pigeon's responses. The initial introduction of the red light was with low illumination and for

brief time intervals. During successive presentations of the stimuli, Terrace gradually increased the intensity of the red light and the duration of time it was illuminated until it differed from the green light only in hue. With this procedure Terrace taught pigeons to discriminate red from green with only a minimum number of errors (responses to the S^Δ).

Terrace further demonstrated that stimulus control acquired with red and green lights could be transferred to vertical and horizontal lines with a minimum number of errors (i.e., responses in the presence of the S^Δ). His procedure consisted of first superimposing a white vertical line on the green light (S^D) and a white horizontal line on the red light (S^Δ). Then the pigeons were given several presentations of the two compound stimuli. Finally, the amplitude of the red and green lights was reduced gradually until only the vertical and horizontal lines remained as stimulus conditions. The pigeons showed almost perfect transfer of stimulus control from the red–green lights to the vertical–horizontal lines. That is, they emitted responses in the presence of the vertical line (S^D) and seldom responded in the presence of the horizontal line (S^Δ).

Following Terrace's work, other pioneer researchers (e.g., Moore & Goldiamond, 1964) produced landmark studies showing that the transfer of stimulus control with few incorrect responses was possible with human learners, which provided the foundations for developing effective procedures to transfer stimulus control from response prompts to natural stimuli in the applied context.

Transferring Stimulus Control from Response Prompts to Naturally Existing Stimuli

Wolery and Gast (1984) described four procedures for transferring stimulus control from response prompts to natural stimuli. They describe these procedures as most-to-least prompts, graduated guidance, least-to-most prompts, and time delay.

Most-to-Least Prompts

The applied behavior analyst can use most-to-least response prompts to transfer stimulus control from response prompts to the natural stimulus whenever the participant does not respond to the natural stimulus or makes an incorrect response. To apply most-to-least response prompts, the analyst physically guides the participant through the entire performance sequence, then gradually reduces the amount of physical assistance provided as training progresses from trial to trial and session to session. Customarily, most-to-least prompting moves from physical guidance to visual prompts to verbal instructions, and finally to the natural stimulus with prompts.

Graduated Guidance

The applied behavior analyst provides physical guidance as needed, but using graduated guidance she will immediately start to fade out the physical prompts to transfer stimulus control. Graduated guidance begins with the applied behavior analyst following the participant's movements closely with her hands, but not touching the participant. The analyst then increases the distance of her hands from the participant by gradually changing the location of the physical prompt. For example, if the applied behavior analyst used physical guidance for a participant's hand movement in zippering a coat, she might move the prompt from the hand to the wrist, to the elbow, to the shoulder, and then to no physical contact. Graduated guidance provides the opportunity for an immediate physical prompt as needed.

Least-to-Most Prompts

When transferring stimulus control from response prompts using least-to-most prompts, the applied behavior analyst gives the participant an opportunity to perform the response with the least amount of assistance on each trial. The participant receives greater degrees of assistance with each successive trial without a correct response. The procedure for least-to-most prompting requires the participant to make a correct response within a set time limit (e.g., 3 seconds) from the presentation of the natural S^D. If the response does not occur within the specified time, the applied behavior analyst will again present the natural S^D and a response prompt of least assistance, such as a verbal response prompt. If after the same specified time limit (e.g., another 3 seconds), the participant does not make a correct response, the analyst gives the natural S^D and another response prompt, such as a gesture. The participant receives partial or full physical guidance if the lesser prompting does not evoke a correct response. Applied behavior analysts using the least-to-most response prompt procedure present the natural S^D and the same time limit during each training trial. For example, Heckaman, Alber, Hooper, and Heward (1998) used instructions, nonspecific verbal prompts, modeling, and physical prompting in a least-to-most 5-second response prompt hierarchy to improve the disruptive behavior of four students with autism.

Time Delay

To produce a transfer of stimulus control, most-to-least prompts, graduated guidance, and least-to-most prompts occur as consequences to gradual changes in the form, position, or intensity of a response evoked by the natural stimulus. Conversely, as an antecedent response prompt,

the time delay procedures use only variations in the time intervals between presentation of the natural stimulus and the presentation of the response prompt. Constant time delay and progressive time delay transfer stimulus control from a prompt to the natural stimulus by delaying the presentation of the prompt following the presentation of the natural stimulus.

The constant time delay procedure first presents several trials using a 0-second delay—that is, the simultaneous presentation of the natural stimulus and the response prompt. Usually, but not always (Schuster, Griffen, & Wolery, 1992), the trials that follow the simultaneous prompt condition apply a fixed time delay (e.g., 3 seconds) between the presentation of the natural stimulus and the presentation of the response prompt (Caldwell, Wolery, Werts, & Caldwell, 1996).

The progressive time delay procedure, like the progressive time delay, starts with a 0-second delay between the presentation of the natural stimulus and the response prompt. Usually, a teacher will use several 0-second trials before extending the time delay. The number of 0-second trials will depend on the task difficulty and the functioning level of the participant. Following the simultaneous presentations, the teacher will gradually and systematically extend the time delay, often in 1-second intervals. The time delay can be extended after a specific number of presentations, after each session, after a specific number of sessions, or after meeting a performance criterion.

Heckaman and colleagues (1998) used the following progressive time delay procedure: They began with 0-second trials, simultaneously presenting the controlling response prompt (e.g., physical prompt, model) and the task instruction. The simultaneous presentations continued until the participant met the criteria of nine correct responses. The first time delay was set at 0.5 seconds. After meeting the 0.5-second criterion, the researchers increased the delay by 1-second increments up to 5 seconds. Correct responses occurring before the response prompt or within 3 seconds after the prompt received a positive feedback statement (e.g., "That's right"). Error responses received a negative feedback statement (e.g., "No, that's not right") and the controlling prompt. Also, the next trial following an error response moved back to the previous delay level. The controlling prompt was also presented with disruptive behavior.

Transfer of Stimulus Control Using Stimulus Control Shaping

The preceding sections focused on response prompts that do not change the task stimuli or materials. The stimulus control shaping procedures presented here modify the task stimuli or materials gradually and systematically to prompt a response. Supplementary stimulus conditions are faded in or faded out to transfer stimulus control from the stimulus prompt to the natural stimulus. Stimulus control shaping can be accomplished with stimulus fading and stimulus shape transformations (McIlvane & Dube, 1992; Sidman & Stoddard, 1967).

Stimulus Fading

Stimulus fading involves highlighting a physical dimension (e.g., color, size, position) of a stimulus to increase the likelihood of a correct response. The highlighted or exaggerated dimension is faded gradually in or out. The following examples of (a) handwriting the uppercase letter *A,* and (b) giving the answer 9 to an arithmetic problem are illustrations of systematically fading out stimuli.

$$ \textbf{A A A A A A} $$

$$ 4 + 5 = 9, 4 + 5 = \textbf{9}, 4 + 5 = \textbf{9}, 4 + 5 = \textbf{9}. $$

Krantz and McClannahan (1998) faded out scripts (i.e., the words *Look* and *Watch me*) embedded in photographic activity schedules. The embedded scripts prompted the social exchanges of children with autism. The words *Look* and *Watch me* were printed with 72-point font and bold letters on white 9-cm note cards. Krantz and McClannahan began fading out the words by removing one third of the script card, then another third. Sometimes, during the script fading, portions of letters were still shown on the card such as a part of an *o* in *Look.* Finally, the scripts and cards were removed.

The treatment of a feeding disorder reported by Patel, Piazza, Kelly, Ochsner, and Santana (2001) provides an example of fading stimuli in and out. Severe food selectivity is a common problem for children with feeding disorders. For example, some children find highly textured foods aversive and dangerous because of gagging. Patel and colleagues faded in Carnation Instant Breakfast (CIB) and then milk to water in treating a 6-year-old boy with pervasive developmental feeding disorder. The boy would drink small amounts of water. The researchers began the fading in procedure by adding 20% of the CIB packet to 240 ml of water. Following three sessions of drinking the 20% mixture, more CIB was gradually added to the water, initially by 5% and later 10% increments. The researchers

then faded in milk to the CIB and water mixture after the boy would drink one CIB packet with 240 ml of water. Milk was gradually added to CIB/water mixture in 10% increments as the water was faded out (e.g., 10% milk and 90% water, plus one packet of CIB; then 20% milk and 80% water).

Applied behavior analysts have used the superimposition of stimuli with stimulus fading. In one instance, the transfer of stimulus control occurs when one stimulus is faded out; in another application, one stimulus is faded in as the other stimulus is faded out. The research by Terrace (1963a, b) demonstrating the transfer of stimulus control from a red–green discrimination to a vertical–horizontal discrimination shows the superimposition of two specific classes of stimuli and the fading out of one stimulus class. The lines were superimposed on the colored lights; then the lights were gradually faded out, leaving only the vertical and horizontal lines as the discriminative stimuli. Figure 17.7 provides an applied example of the superimposition and stimulus fading procedures used by Terrace. The figure shows a series of steps from an arithmetic program to teach $7 - 2 = \underline{\quad}$.

The other frequently used procedure fades in the natural stimulus and fades out the stimulus prompt. Figure 17.8 illustrates this superimposition procedure, in which the prompt is faded out and the natural stimulus $8 + 5 = \underline{\quad}$ is faded in.

Stimulus Shape Transformations

The procedure for stimulus shape transformations uses an initial stimulus shape that will prompt a correct response. That initial shape is then gradually changed to form the natural stimulus, while maintaining correct responding. For example, a program to transform the shape of stimuli to teach number recognition could include the following steps (Johnston, 1973):

$$ \underline{\circ}\, \underline{2}\, 2\, \underline{2}\, 2 $$

The shape of the stimulus prompt must change gradually so that the student continues to respond correctly. In teaching word identification, using stimulus shape transformations could include the following steps (Johnston, 1973):

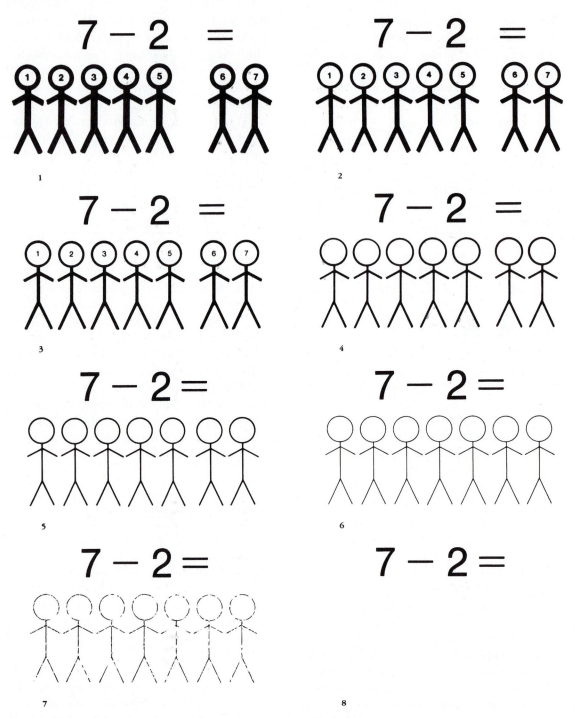

Figure 17.7 Illustration of two classes of superimposed stimuli with one class then faded out.

From *Addition and Subtraction Math Program with Stimulus Shaping and Stimulus Fading* by T. Johnson, 1973, unpublished project, Ohio Department of Education. Reprinted by permission.

Figure 17.9 shows how superimposition of stimuli can be used with stimulus shaping in arithmetic instruction. The + and = signs are superimposed on the stimulus shaping program and are gradually faded in.

In summary, a variety of procedures exist for transferring stimulus control from response and stimulus prompts to natural stimuli. Currently, procedures for transferring stimulus control of response prompts are more practical in teaching situations than stimulus shape transformations because of the greater skill and time required for material preparation with stimulus change procedures.

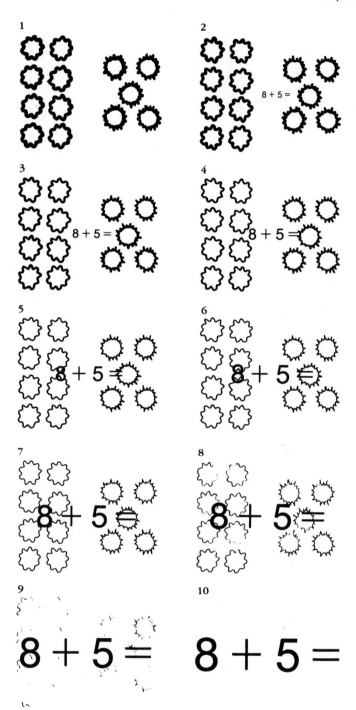

Figure 17.8   Illustration of superimposition and stimulus fading to fade in the natural stimulus and fade out the stimulus prompt.

From *Addition and Subtraction Math Program with Stimulus Shaping and Stimulus Fading* by T. Johnson, 1973, unpublished project, Ohio Department of Education. Reprinted by permission.

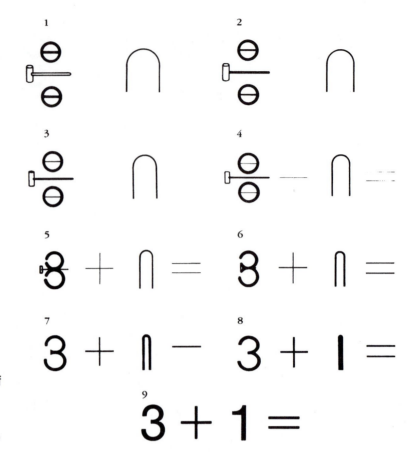

Figure 17.9   Illustration of superimposition of stimuli and stimulus shaping.

(From *Addition and Subtraction Math Program with Stimulus Shaping and Stimulus Fading* by T. Johnson, 1973, unpublished project, Ohio Department of Education. Reprinted by permission.)

⚡ Summary

Antecedent Stimuli

1. Reinforcement of an operant response increases the frequency of future responding and influences the stimuli that immediately precede the response. The stimuli preceding the response (i.e., antecedent stimuli) will acquire an evocative effect on the relevant behavior.

2. Stimulus control occurs when the rate, latency, duration, or amplitude of a response is altered in the presence of an antecedent stimulus (Dinsmoor, 1995a, b). A stimulus acquires control only when responses emitted in the presence of that stimulus produce reinforcement.

3. Discriminative stimuli and motivating operations share two important similarities: (a) Both events occur before the behavior of interest, and (b) both events have evocative functions.

4. Often an evocative effect that appears to be the function of an S^D is not the product of a history of differential reinforcement correlated with the altered frequency of response. These situations are probably related to motivational operations (MOs) rather than stimulus control.

Stimulus Generalization

5. When an antecedent stimulus has a history of evoking a behavior that has been reinforced in its presence, there is a general tendency for other antecedent stimuli to also evoke that behavior. This evocative function occurs with stimuli that share similar physical properties with the controlling antecedent stimulus. This tendency is called stimulus generalization. Conversely, stimulus discrimination occurs when the new stimuli do not evoke the response.

6. Stimulus generalization reflects a loose degree of stimulus control, whereas discrimination indicates a relatively tight degree of stimulus control.

7. A stimulus generalization gradient graphically depicts the degree of stimulus generalization and discrimination by showing the extent to which responses reinforced in one stimulus condition are emitted in the presence of untrained stimuli.

Development of Stimulus Control

8. The conventional procedure for stimulus discrimination training requires one behavior and two antecedent stimulus conditions. Responses are reinforced in the presence of one stimulus condition, the S^D, but responses are not reinforced in the presence of the other stimulus, the S^Δ.

9. Concept formation is a complex example of stimulus control that requires both stimulus generalization within a class of stimuli and discrimination between stimulus classes.

10. An antecedent stimulus class is a set of stimuli that share a common relationship. All of the stimuli in the class will evoke the same operant response class, or elicit the same response in the case of respondent behavior.

11. Stimuli comprising a class may function within feature stimulus classes and arbitrary stimulus classes.

Stimulus Equivalence

12. Equivalence describes the emergence of accurate responding to untrained and nonreinforced stimulus–stimulus relations following the reinforcement of responses to some other stimulus–stimulus relations.

13. Behavior analysts define stimulus equivalence by testing for reflexivity, symmetry, and transitivity among stimulus–stimulus relations. A positive demonstration of all three tests (i.e., reflexivity, symmetry, and transitivity) is necessary to meet the definition of an equivalence relation among a set of arbitrary stimuli.

14. Basic and applied researchers have used the matching-to-sample procedure to develop and test for stimulus equivalence.

Factors Affecting the Development of Stimulus Control

15. Applied behavior analysts establish stimulus control with frequent differential reinforcement of behavior in the presence and in the absence of the S^D condition. Effective differential reinforcement requires the consistent use of consequences that function as reinforcers. Additional factors such as preattending skills, stimulus salience, masking, and overshadowing will also affect the development of stimulus control.

Using Prompts to Develop Stimulus Control

16. Prompts are supplementary antecedent stimuli (e.g., instructions, modeling, physical guidance) used to occasion a correct response in the presence of an S^D that will eventually control the behavior. Applied behavior analysts provide response and stimulus prompts before or during the performance of a behavior.

17. Response prompts operate directly on the response. Stimulus prompts operate directly on antecedent task stimuli to cue a correct response in conjunction with the critical S^D.

Transfer of Stimulus Control

18. Applied behavior analysts should provide response and stimulus prompts as *supplementary* antecedent stimuli only during the acquisition phase of instruction.

19. Fading response prompts and stimulus prompts is the procedure used to transfer stimulus control from the prompts to the natural stimulus, and also to minimize the number of error responses occurring in the presence of the natural stimulus.

20. Procedures for transferring stimulus control from response prompts to natural stimuli include (a) most-to-least prompts, (b) graduated guidance, (c) least-to-most prompts, and (d) time delay.

21. Stimulus fading involves exaggerating a dimension of a stimulus to increase the likelihood of a correct response. The exaggerated dimension is faded gradually in or out.

22. The procedure for stimulus shape transformations uses an initial stimulus shape that will prompt a correct response. That initial shape is then gradually changed to form the natural stimulus, while maintaining correct responding.

PART 7

Developing New Behavior

The three chapters in Part 7 describe methods for developing new behavioral repertoires. Chapter 18, Imitation, discusses different types of models, the characteristics of imitative behavior, procedures for developing an imitative repertoire, and imitation training techniques. Chapter 19, Shaping, describes how to shape new behavior within and across response topographies by reinforcing successive approximations to a terminal behavior. The chapter also includes procedures for increasing the efficiency of behavior shaping and guidelines for using shaping in applied settings. Chapter 20, Chaining, explains how discrete responses can be linked to form behavior chains of more complex behaviors. Procedures for a task analysis are provided. The chapter addresses the varied uses of chaining and factors affecting the performance of behavior chains.

CHAPTER 18

Imitation

Key Terms

imitation

Behavior Analyst Certification Board® BCBA® & BCABA® Behavior Analyst Task List,© Third Edition

Content Area 3: Principles, Processes and Concepts	
3-15	Define and provide examples of echoics and imitation.

An imitative repertoire promotes the relatively quick acquisition of behaviors such as a young child's development of social and communication skills. With an understanding of the imitation process, applied behavior analysts can use imitation as an intervention to evoke *new* behaviors. Without an imitative repertoire, a person has little chance for the agile acquisition of behaviors.

Imitation has received considerable experimental and theoretical attention spanning several decades (e.g., Baer & Sherman, 1964; Carr & Kologinsky, 1983; Garcia & Batista-Wallace, 1977; Garfinkle & Schwartz, 2002; Wolery & Schuster, 1997). The experimental literature shows that individuals can acquire and maintain imitative and echoic behavior in the same fashion as they acquire and maintain other operant behaviors.[1] That is, (a) reinforcement increases the frequency of imitation; (b) when some imitative behaviors receive reinforcement, other imitative behaviors occur without specific training and reinforcement; and (c) some children who do not imitate may be taught to do so. This chapter defines imitation and suggests a protocol for imitation training with learners who do not imitate.

Definition of Imitation

Four behavior–environment relations functionally define **imitation:** (a) Any physical movement may function as a *model* for imitation. A model is an antecedent stimulus that evokes the imitative behavior. (b) An imitative behavior must immediately follow the presentation of the model (e.g., within 3 to 5 seconds). (c) The model and the behavior must have formal similarity. (d) The model must be the controlling variable for an imitative behavior (Holth, 2003).

Models

Planned Models

Planned models are prearranged antecedent stimuli that help learners acquire new skills or refine the topography of certain elements of existing skills. A planned model shows the learner exactly what to do. A videotape of a person emitting specific behaviors can serve as a planned model. LaBlanc and colleagues (2003), for example, used video models to teach three children with autism perspective-taking skills. The children learned to imitate a video model touching or pointing to an object such as a bowl or box. (The children also echoed vocal-verbal behaviors such as saying "under the bowl," or saying "one" to identify a box marked *1*.)

Unplanned Models

All antecedent stimuli with the capacity to evoke imitation are potentially unplanned models. Unplanned models occasion many new forms of behavior because imitating the behavior of others in everyday social interactions (e.g., school, work, play) frequently produces new and helpful adaptive behaviors. For example, a young person during her first outing on a city bus may learn how to pay the fare by imitating the fare-paying of other boarders.

Formal Similarity

Formal similarity occurs when the model and the behavior physically resemble each other and are in the same sense mode (i.e., they look alike, sound alike) (Michael, 2004). For example, when a student observes a teacher finger-spell the word *house* (i.e., the model), and then duplicates the finger spelling (i.e., the imitation), the imitative finger spelling has formal similarity with the model. A baby sitting in a high chair immediately taps the tray with his hand after seeing his mother tap the tray with her hand. The baby's imitative tap has formal similarity to the mother's tap.

Immediacy

The temporal relation of the *immediacy* between the model and the imitative behavior is an important feature of imitation. However, a form (topography) of an imitation may occur at a later time in the context of everyday life situations. For example, the young person on her first bus ride who used imitation to learn how to pay the fare may use her newly learned behavior to pay the bus fare for her return trip when no other boarders have paid fares before her. The parent of the student who imitated the finger spelling of *house* might ask, "What did you learn at school today?" and in response, the student may produce the finger spelling for *house*.

When the topography of a previous imitation occurs in the absence of the model (e.g., paying the bus fare, finger spelling), that delayed behavior is *not* an imitative behavior. The delayed behaviors of paying the bus fare and the finger spelling in the contexts previously presented have similar topographies as the imitated behaviors but occur as the result of different controlling variables. The relation between discriminative stimuli (e.g., the device for collecting the bus fare) or motivating

---

[1]Chapter 25 defines the echoic operant and functionally separates it from imitation. Basically, *echoic* is the technical term used in the context of vocal verbal behavior, and *imitation* applies to nonvocal verbal and nonverbal behaviors.

operations (e.g., the parent's question) and delayed behaviors are functionally different from the relation between a model and an imitative behavior. Therefore, delayed behaviors using the topography of a prior imitative model, by definition, are not imitative.[2]

A Controlled Relation

We often view imitative behavior as *doing the same*. Although the formal similarity of *doing the same* is a necessary condition for imitation, it is not sufficient. Formal similarity can exist without the model functionally controlling the similar behavior. The controlling relation between a model and a similar behavior is the most important property that defines imitation. A controlling relation between the behavior of a model and the behavior of the imitator is inferred when a novel model evokes a similar behavior in the absence of a history of reinforcement for that behavior. An imitative behavior is a new behavior that follows a *novel* antecedent event (i.e., the model). After the model evokes an imitation, that behavior comes into contact with contingencies of reinforcement. These new contingencies of reinforcement then become the controlling variable for the discriminated operant (i.e., $MO/S^D \rightarrow R \rightarrow S^R$).

Holth (2003) explained the discriminated operant in the context of imitation training this way:

> Let us imagine that a dog is trained to sit whenever the owner sits down in a chair, and to turn around in a circle whenever the owner turns around. Does the dog imitate the owner's behavior? Almost certainly not. The dog could have as easily been taught to sit whenever the owner turns around in a circle and to turn around in a circle when the owner sits down. Thus, what may look like imitation may be nothing more than a series of directly taught *discriminated operants*. The source of control can be determined only by introducing novel exemplars. In the absence of a demonstration that the dog responds to novel performances by "doing the same," there is no evidence that a similarity to the owner's behavior is important in determining the form of the dog's response. Hence, there is no true demonstration that the dog imitates the behavior of the owner unless it also responds to new instances of the owner's behavior by "doing the same." (p. 157)

Is *and* Is-Not *Examples of Controlled Relations and Imitation*

Consider two guitarists performing in a contemporary rock band. One guitarist improvises a short riff (i.e., a novel model). The other guitarist hears the riff and then immediately reproduces the riff cord-for-cord and note-for-note (i.e., imitative behavior—a new behavior). This *is* example meets all of the conditions for imitation; immediacy, formal similarity, and the model (i.e., the improvised riff) produced the controlling relation.

Continuing with the two guitarists in the contemporary rock band, suppose one musician says to the other, "I have a great idea for our opening song. Let me play it for you. If you like it, I will teach it to you." The other guitarist likes what she hears. They practice the riff together until the second guitarist learns it. The guitarists add the riff to the opening number. On stage, one guitarist plays the riff, and then the other guitarist immediately reproduces the riff. This is not an example of imitation because the riff played by the first guitarist was not a novel model and the similar behavior of the second guitarist was a trained similar response with a history of reinforcement. It is an example of a discriminated operant.

As another *is-not* example of imitative behavior, let's now consider two classical musicians playing a fugue using a musical score. A fugue is a form of music based on a short melody that is played at the beginning by one player or one section of an ensemble, and then another player or section repeats the short melody. The performance of a fugue appears similar to imitation in that one player or section presents a melody, then another player or section immediately repeats the melody, and the two melodies have formal similarity. A fugue is not an example of imitation, however, because the first introduction of the short melody does not control the similar behavior. The printed notes on the music manuscript provide the controlling variables. Playing a fugue using a musical score is an example of a discriminated operant rather than of imitation.

As a final *is-not* example, Tim throws a baseball to Bill (a person with some baseball experience). Bill catches the ball, and then immediately throws it back to Tim. Did Bill imitate Tim's throw? It gives an appearance of imitation. Tim's throw was an antecedent event (a model); Bill's throw immediately followed and had formal similarity to the model. This *is not* an example of imitation because Bill's throw to Tim was not a new behavioral instance of throwing under the control of Tim's throw. Again, the controlling variable was the history of reinforcement that produced a discriminated operant.

Imitation Training

Typically developing children acquire many skills by imitating unplanned models. Parents and other caregivers do not usually have to apply specific interventions to facilitate the development of imitative skills. However,

---

[2]*Delayed imitation* is, however, a commonly used term in the imitation literature (e.g., Garcia, 1976).

some infants and children with developmental disabilities do not imitate. Without an imitative repertoire, these children will have great difficulty developing beyond the most basic of skills. Still, it is possible to teach imitation to some children who do not imitate.

Applied behavior analysts have validated repeatedly the procedures used by Baer and colleagues as an effective method for teaching imitation to children who do not imitate (e.g., Baer, Peterson, & Sherman, 1967; Baer & Sherman, 1964). For example, three children with severe to profound mental retardation served as participants in one of their studies (Baer, Peterson, & Sherman, 1967). During imitation training, the children were taught to emit simple discriminated (i.e., similar to the model) responses (e.g., raising an arm) when the teacher presented the verbal response cue "do this," and then provided the model (e.g., raised his arm). Baer and colleagues selected appropriate skill levels for their participants (e.g., gross motor movements, fine motor movements) Also, the teacher initially used physical guidance to prompt the similar response, and then gradually reduced the guidance over several trials; shaped the discriminated response by using bits of food to reinforce closer and closer similarity to the model; and reinforced responses with formal similarity.

The imitation training protocol developed by Baer and colleagues taught some nonimitative learners to imitate, meaning that a novel model controlled imitative behaviors in the absence of specific training and reinforcement of those behaviors. One participant imitated a novel model only after receiving imitation training for similarity on 130 different models. The second participant showed similar results to those of the first. The third participant learned to imitate with less training than the other participants had. This participant imitated the ninth training model, a novel model without a history of training and reinforcement.

To summarize the results from Baer and colleagues: (a) Children who did not have an imitative repertoire learned to imitate with training that used response cues and prompts, shaping, and reinforcement; (b) when some imitative behaviors produced reinforcement, the participants imitated novel models without reinforcement; and (c) the participants demonstrated an effect sometimes known as *learning set* (Harlow, 1959), or a learning-to-learn phenomenon. As the participants progressed through imitation training, they required fewer and fewer training trials to learn a new discriminated response with similarity to the models.

The major objective of imitation training is to teach learners to do what the person providing the model does regardless of the behavior modeled. A learner who learns to do what the model does is likely to imitate models that have not been associated with specific training, and

those imitations are likely to occur in many situations and settings, frequently in the absence of planned reinforcement.[3] Imitation, however, may depend on the parameters of the response class used during training. For example, Young, Krantz, McClannahan, and Poulson (1994) found that children with autism imitated novel models within the vocal, toy-play, and pantomime response types used for training, but the imitations did not generalize across response types. Even so, imitation provides for the relatively quick acquisition of new, complex behaviors that are characteristic of many human endeavors. Imitation produces those new behaviors without undue reliance on physical help or previous reinforcement considerations.

Building on the experimental methods of Baer and colleagues, Striefel (1974) developed an imitation training program for practitioners. The components of Striefel's protocol are as follows: (a) assessing, and teaching if necessary, prerequisite skills for imitation training, (b) selecting models for training, (c) pretesting, (d) sequencing models for training, and (e) performing imitation training.

Assessing, and Teaching If Necessary, Prerequisite Skills for Imitation Training

Learners cannot imitate if they do not attend to the presentation of the model. Therefore, attending to the model is a prerequisite for imitation training. Striefel (1974) defined *attending* as staying seated during instruction, keeping one's hands in one's lap, looking at the trainer whenever one's name is called, and looking at objects identified by the trainer. Also, practitioners often need to decrease problem behaviors that interfere with training (e.g., aggression, screaming, odd hand movements).

Suggested procedures for assessing attending skills include the following:

1. *Staying seated.* Seat the learner and record the duration of time the learner remains seated.

2. *Looking at the teacher.* Say the learner's name in a commanding voice and record whether the student makes eye contact.

3. *Keeping hands in lap.* Prompt the student to put his hands in his lap and record the duration of time the student's hands remain in that position.

4. *Looking at objects.* Place several objects on a table and say, "Look at this." Immediately following the

---

[3]*Generalized imitation* is a term used frequently in the imitation literature to label a participant's unprompted, untrained, nonreinforced responses with formal similarity to the actions of a model. We label such responses to novel models as, simply, *imitation.*

command, move a finger from in front of the learner's eye to one of the objects and record whether the student looked at the object.

Teachers often assess attending skills for a minimum of three sessions. The teacher can begin imitation training if the assessment data show adequate attending skills. The teacher will need to teach these skills before beginning imitation training if attending skills need to be developed.

Selecting Models for Imitation Training

Practitioners may need to select and use about 25 behaviors as models during initial imitation training. Including gross motor movements (e.g., raising a hand) and fine motor movements (e.g., manual sign language) as models provides learners with opportunities to develop more refined differentiations with their imitative skills.

Practitioners usually use one model at a time during the initial training trials rather than a sequence of movements. Practitioners may choose to use more complex models such as sequences of behavior after the learner can imitate one model per occasion successfully. Also, the initial training usually includes models of (a) the movement of body parts (e.g., touching nose, hopping on one foot, bringing hand to mouth) and (b) the manipulation of physical objects (e.g., passing a basketball, picking up a glass, zipping a coat).

Pretesting

The learner's responses to the selected models should be pretested. The pretest may show that the learner will imitate some models without training. The pretesting procedures advocated by Striefel (1974) are as follows:

1. Prepare the learner's attending behaviors for the pretest (e.g., seated, hands in lap) and often assume the same ready position as the learner.

2. If you are using an object model, place one object in front of the learner and one object in front of yourself.

3. Say the learner's name to start the pretest, and when the learner makes eye contact, say, "Do this" (i.e., child's name, pause, "Do this").

4. Present the model. For example, if the selected behavior is to pick up a ball, pick up the ball yourself and hold it for a few seconds.

5. Immediately praise each response that has formal similarity to the model, and deliver the reinforcer (e.g., a hug, an edible) as quickly as possible.

6. Record the learner's response as correct or incorrect (or no response), or as an approximation of the model (e.g., touches the ball, but does not pick it up).

7. Continue pretesting with the remaining models.

Practitioners can use the pretest procedure with all motor and vocal verbal models (e.g., name, pause, "Do this," "Say ball"). Striefel recommended pretesting for several sessions until all models have been pretested at least three times. If the learner correctly responds during pretesting to a selected model at a set criterion level (e.g., three of three correct), then the practitioner should advance to other models. If the learner does not meet the criterion, the practitioner should select that model for imitation training.

Sequencing the Selected Models for Training

Practitioners use the pretest results to arrange the presentation sequence for the selected models, arranging the sequence from the easiest to the most difficult models to imitate. The first models selected for imitation training are those that the learner imitated correctly on some, but not all, of the pretest trials. The models that the learner responded to incorrectly, but approximated the model, are selected next. Finally, the models that the learner failed to perform, or performed incorrectly, are the last to be selected for training.

Conducting Imitation Training

Striefel (1974) suggested using four conditions for imitation training: preassessment, training, postassessment, and probing for imitative behaviors. The procedures used in imitation training are the same as those in the pretest with the exception of when and how often the practitioner presents the selected models.

Preassessment

The preassessment is a short pretest given before each training session. Practitioners use the first three models currently selected for training for the preassessment. These three models are presented three times each in random order during the preassessment. If the learner's behavior has similarity to the model on all three presentations, that model is removed from the training. The preassessment procedure allows practitioners to evaluate the learner's current performance on the models selected for training that session, and to determine the learner's progress in learning to respond to the model.

Training

During training, practitioners use repeated presentations of one of the three models used in the preassessment. The model selected first for training is the one most often responded to during the preassessment (i.e., the behavior was similar to the model on some, but not all, of the preassessment presentations). If, however, the learner made approximations only, the behavior with the closest similarity to the model is selected first for training. Training continues until the learner responds to the model correctly on five consecutive trials.

Imitation training will likely include physical guidance to prompt the response if the learner fails to respond. For example, the practitioner may physically guide the learner's behavior through the complete response. Physical guidance allows the learner to experience the response and the reinforcer for that specific movement. After physically assisting the complete response, the practitioner will gradually withdraw the physical guidance, letting go of the student's body just before the entire movement is completed, and then continue to fade the physical guidance by withdrawing the physical support earlier on each subsequent trial. Eventually, the learner may complete the movement without assistance. When the learner responds to the model without prompting for five consecutive trials, that model is included in the postassessment.

Postassessment

During the postassessment, the practitioner presents, three times each, five previously learned models and five models that are still included in imitation training. The practitioner will remove a most recently learned behavior from imitation training following three consecutive postassessments in which the learner responds correctly without physical guidance to the model 14 out of the 15 opportunities. Physical guidance, however, is appropriate to use during the postassessment. If the learner does not reach this criterion (14 out of 15 postassessment opportunities), Striefel (1974) recommended continuing imitation training with that model. The postassessment procedure allows the practitioner to evaluate how well a learner performs the previously and most recently learned behaviors.

Probes for Imitative Behaviors

Practitioners will use approximately five nontrained, novel models to probe for occurrences of imitation at the end of each imitation training session, or they will intermix the probes with the training trials. The probe procedure uses the same procedures as the preassessment activities, but without using the antecedent verbal response prompt (i.e.,

child's name, pause, "Do this") or other forms of response prompts (e.g., physical guidance). Probing for nontrained imitations provides data on the learner's progress in developing an imitation repertoire—in other words, learning to do what the model does.

Guidelines for Imitation Training

Keep Training Sessions Active and Brief

Most practitioners use short training sessions during imitation training, typically 10 to 15 minutes, but often schedule more than one session per day. Two or three brief sessions can be more effective than one long session. To maintain quick and active training, practitioners should allow no more than a few seconds between trials.

Reinforce Both Prompted and Imitative Responses

In the early stages of imitation training, practitioners should reinforce each occurrence of either prompted responses or true imitation. If the learner's participation requires a reinforcer other than praise, it should be presented immediately in small amounts that the learner can consume quickly (e.g., cereal bits, 5 seconds music). Practitioners should reinforce only matching responses or imitative behaviors that occur within 3 to 5 seconds of the model. Learners who consistently emit correct matching responses but not immediately following the model should be reinforced for shorter response latencies (e.g., a decreasing contingency from 7 seconds to 6 seconds to 5 seconds to 4 seconds).

Pair Verbal Praise and Attention with Tangible Reinforcers

During imitation training, many learners, particularly children with severe to profound developmental disabilities, need tangible consequences such as edibles or liquids. As training progresses, practitioners try to use social attention and verbal praise to maintain the matching responses or imitative behaviors. They do this by pairing the delivery of other consequences with social and verbal praise. Social attention (e.g., patting the student's arm affectionately) and/or descriptive verbal praise should immediately follow each correct response or approximation, simultaneously with the other consequence. A learner's willingness to participate in imitation training may increase when the practitioner schedules a preferred activity to follow each session.

If Progress Breaks Down, Back Up and Move Ahead Slowly

There may be identifiable reasons for worsening performance, such as reinforcer satiation or context distractions; or perhaps the practitioner presented models that were too complex for the learner. Regardless of whether a clear reason exists for the worsening performance, the practitioner should return to an earlier level of successful performance. Once successful imitative responses are reestablished, training can advance.

Keep a Record

As with all behavior change programs, applied behavior analysts should directly measure and record the learner's performance and review the data after each session. With the use of frequent and direct measurement, the practitioner can make objective, informed, data-based decisions concerning the effects of the training program.

Fade Out Verbal Response Prompts and Physical Guidance

Parents and caregivers in the everyday environments of young children almost always teach imitation skills using verbal response prompts and physical guidance. For ex-

ample, a caregiver may tell a child to "Wave bye-bye," model waving, and then physically guide the wave of the child. Or, a parent may ask a child, *What does the cow say?* The parent then presents a model ("The cow says moo"), tells the child to *say "moo,"* and then provides praise and attention if the child says *"moo."* This natural instructional process is the same process advocated in this chapter for teaching imitative skills to learners who do not imitate: A verbal response prompt is given (*"Do this"*), a model is presented, and physical guidance is used when needed. However, imitation training is not complete until all response prompts have been withdrawn. Children need to learn to do what the model does without the supports of response prompting. Therefore, to promote the effective use of imitation, practitioners should fade out the response prompts used during the acquisition of trained matching responses.

Ending Imitation Training

Decisions to stop imitation training depend on the learner's behavior and program goals. For example, the practitioner could stop motor imitation training when the student imitates the first presentations of novel models, or when the student imitates a sequence of behaviors (e.g., washing hands, brushing teeth, finger spelling).

 # Summary

Definition of Imitation

1. Four behavior–environment relations define imitation: (a) Any physical movements may function as a *model* for imitation. A model is an antecedent stimulus that evokes the imitative behavior. (b) An imitative behavior must be emitted within 3 seconds of the presentation of the model. (c) The model and the behavior must have formal similarity. (d) The model must be the controlling variable for an imitative behavior.

Formal Similarity

2. *Formal similarity* occurs when the model and the behavior physically resemble each other and are in the same sense mode (i.e., they look alike, sound alike).

Immediacy

3. The temporal relation of the *immediacy* between the model and the imitative behavior is an important feature of imitation. However, a form (topography) of imitation may occur in the context of everyday life situations, and at any time. When the form of a previous imitation occurs in the absence of the model, that delayed behavior is *not* an imitative behavior.

A Controlled Relation

4. We often view imitative behavior as *doing the same.* Although the formal similarity of *doing the same* is a necessary condition for imitation, it is not sufficient. Formal similarity can exist without the model functionally controlling the similar behavior.

5. A controlling relation between the behavior of a model and the behavior of the imitator is inferred when a novel model evokes a similar behavior in the absence of a history of reinforcement.

6. An imitative behavior is a new behavior emitted following a novel antecedent event (i.e., the model). After the model evokes the imitation, that behavior comes into contact with contingencies of reinforcement. These new contingencies of reinforcement then provides the controlling variables for the discriminated operant (i.e., $MO/S^D \rightarrow R \rightarrow S^R$).

Imitation Training for Learners Who Do Not Imitate

7. Applied behavior analysts have validated repeatedly the instructional method used by Baer and colleagues as an effective method for teaching imitation to children who do not imitate.

8. Building on the experimental methods of Baer and colleagues, Striefel (1974) developed an imitation training program for practitioners.

9. The components of Striefel's protocol are as follows: (a) assessing, and teaching if necessary, prerequisite skills for imitation training, (b) selecting models for training, (c) pretesting, (d) sequencing models for training, and (e) conducting imitation training.

Guidelines for Imitation Training

10. Keep training sessions active and brief.

11. If the learner's participation requires a reinforcer other than praise, it should be presented immediately in small amounts that the learner can consume quickly.

12. Pair verbal praise and attention with tangible reinforcers.

13. If progress breaks down, back up and move ahead slowly.

14. Measure and record the learner's performance and review the data after each session.

15. Fade out verbal response prompts and physical guidance.

16. Stop motor imitation training when the student consistently imitates novel models, or when the student imitates a sequence of behaviors (e.g., washing hands, brushing teeth, finger spelling).

CHAPTER 19

Shaping

Key Terms

clicker training

differential reinforcement

response differentiation

shaping

successive approximation

Behavior Analyst Certification Board® BCBA® & BCABA® Behavior Analyst Task List,© Third Edition

Content Area 9: Behavior Change Procedures	
9-6	Use differential reinforcement.
9-11	Use shaping.

Shaping is the process of systematically and differentially reinforcing successive approximations to a terminal behavior. Shaping is used in many everyday situations to help learners acquire new behaviors. For example, language therapists use shaping when they develop speech with a client by first reinforcing lip movements, then sound production, and finally word and sentence expression. Teachers working with students with severe disabilities shape social interactions when they differentially reinforce eye contact, one-word greetings, and conversational speech. A basketball coach shapes the foul-shooting behavior of her players when she differentially reinforces accurate shooting from positions a few feet in front of the basket to positions closer to the 15-foot regulation foul line. Further, trainers use shaping to teach desirable behavior to animals for function (e.g., loading horses into a trailer without injury to the horse or the attendant), or for appeal or utility duty (e.g., teaching porpoises to execute show routines).

Depending on the complexity of a given behavior and the learner's prerequisite skills, shaping may require many successive approximations before the terminal behavior is achieved. Achievement of the terminal behavior with respect to time, trials, or direction is seldom predictable, immediate, or linear. If the learner emits a closer approximation to the terminal behavior, and the practitioner fails to detect and reinforce it, achievement of the terminal behavior will be delayed. However, if a systematic approach is used—that is, if each instance of closer approximations to the terminal behavior is detected and reinforced—progress can usually be attained more quickly. Although shaping can be time-consuming, it represents an important approach to teaching new behaviors, especially those behaviors that cannot easily be learned by instructions, incidental experience or exposure, imitation, physical cues, or verbal prompts.

This chapter defines shaping, presents examples of how to shape behavior across and within different response topographies, and suggests ways to improve the efficiency of shaping. Clicker training is illustrated as one method that trainers use to shape new behaviors in animals. Next, guidelines for implementing shaping are presented. The chapter concludes with a look at future applications of shaping.

Definition of Shaping

In *Science and Human Behavior,* Skinner (1953) presented the concept of shaping with an analogy:

> Operant conditioning shapes behavior as a sculptor shapes a lump of clay. ... The final product seems to have a special unity or integrity of design, but we cannot find a point at which this suddenly appears. In the same sense, an operant is not something which appears full grown in the behavior of the organism. It is the result of a continuous shaping process. (p. 91)

Through careful and skillful manipulation of the original, undifferentiated lump of clay, the artisan keeps some aspects of the clay in its primary location, cuts other pieces away, and reforms and molds still other sections so that the form is slowly transfigured into the final sculpted design. Similarly, the skillful practitioner can shape novel forms of behavior from responses that initially bear little resemblance to the final product. A practitioner using behavioral **shaping** differentially reinforces successive approximations toward a terminal behavior. The end product of shaping—*a terminal behavior*—can be claimed when the topography, frequency, latency, duration, or amplitude/magnitude of the target behavior reaches a predetermined criterion level. The two key procedural components of shaping, differential reinforcement and successive approximations, are described next.

Differential Reinforcement

> When a heavy ball is thrown beyond a certain mark, when a horizontal bar is cleared in vaulting or in jumping, when a ball is batted over the fence (and when, as a result, a record is broken or a match or game won), differential reinforcement is at work.
> – B. F. Skinner (1953, p. 97)

Differential reinforcement is a procedure in which reinforcement is provided for responses that share a predetermined dimension or quality, and in which reinforcement is withheld for responses that do not demonstrate that quality. For example, differential reinforcement is used by a parent who complies with his child's requests for an item at the dinner table when those requests include polite words such as "please" or "may I," and who does not pass the requested item following requests in which polite words are missing. Differential reinforcement has two effects: responses similar to those that have been reinforced occur with greater frequency, and responses resembling the unreinforced members are emitted less frequently (i.e., they undergo extinction).

When differential reinforcement is applied consistently within a response class, its dual effects result in a new response class composed primarily of responses sharing the characteristics of the previously reinforced subclass. This emergence of a new response class is called **response differentiation.** Response differentiation as a result of the parent's differential reinforcement at the dinner table would be evident if all of the child's requests contained polite words.

Successive Approximations

The practitioner using shaping differentially reinforces responses that resemble the terminal behavior in some way. The shaping process begins with reinforcement of responses in the learner's current repertoire that share an important topographical feature with the terminal behavior or are a prerequisite behavior for the final terminal behavior. When the initially reinforced responses become more frequent, the practitioner shifts the criterion for reinforcement to responses that are a closer approximation of the terminal behavior. The gradually changing criterion for reinforcement during shaping results in a succession of new response classes, or **successive approximations,** each one closer in form to the terminal behavior than the response class it replaces. Skinner (1953) discussed the critical nature of successive approximations as follows:

> The original probability of the response in its final form is very low; in some cases it may even be zero. In this way we build complicated operants that would never appear in the repertoire of the organism otherwise. By reinforcing a series of successive approximations, we bring a rare response to a very high probability in a short time. This is an effective procedure because it recognizes and utilizes the continuous nature of a complex act. (p. 92)

Figure 19.1 illustrates the progression of successive approximations used by Wolf, Risley, and Mees (1964) in

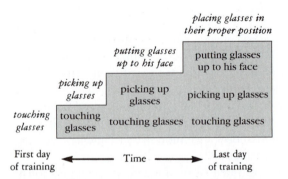

Figure 19.1 Approximations in differentially reinforcing the wearing of eyeglasses. Shaded portion includes behaviors no longer reinforced.

From *How to Use Shaping* by M. Panyan, 1980, p. 4, Austin, TX: PRO-ED. Copyright 1980 by PRO-ED. Reprinted by permission.

shaping the wearing of eyeglasses in a preschooler who was in danger of losing his eyesight if he did not wear corrective glasses regularly. Touching glasses was the first behavior that was reinforced. When touching glasses was established, picking up glasses was reinforced, and touching glasses was placed on extinction (see shaded portion of figure). Next, putting glasses up to his face was reinforced, and the two previously reinforced behaviors were placed on extinction. Training continued until the terminal behavior, placing the glasses on his face, was emitted, and all previous behaviors were placed on extinction.

Shaping Different Dimensions of Performance

Behavior can be shaped in terms of topography, frequency, latency, duration, and amplitude/magnitude (see Table 19.1). Differential reinforcement could also be used to teach a child to talk within a conversational decibel range. Let us suppose a behavior analyst is working with a student who usually talks at such a low volume (e.g., below 45 decibels) that his teacher and peers have difficulty hearing him. Successive approximations to 65 decibels (dB)—the amplitude of normal conversational speech—might be 45, 55, and ultimately 65 dB. Differential reinforcement of speaking at a minimum volume of 45 dB would place responses below that amplitude on extinction. When the student is speaking consistently at or above 45 dB, the criterion would be raised to 55 db. Likewise, when 55 dB and finally 65 dB are achieved, previous lower amplitude levels are not reinforced (i.e., they are placed on extinction).

Fleece and colleagues (1981) used shaping to increase the voice volume of two children enrolled in a private preschool for students with physical and developmental disabilities. Baseline data were collected on voice volume in the regular classroom. Voice volume was measured on a 0- to 20-point scale with 0 indicating that the child's voice level was usually inaudible, 10 indicating normal voice volume, and 20 indicating screaming. The shaping procedure consisted of having the children recite a nursery rhyme in the presence of a voice-activated relay device, whereby voice volume activated a light display. The intensity of the light corresponded to increased levels of voice volume: Higher voice volume produced brighter light, and lower voice volume produced a dimmer light. The teacher shaped voice volume by increasing the sensitivity threshold of the relay device. That is, whereas a low voice was sufficient to activate the dim light in the beginning stages of training, a much higher volume was needed to produce the same effect in later stages. Each raising of the volume

Table 19.1   Examples of Performance Improvements that Could Be Shaped in Various Dimensions of Behavior

Dimension	Example
Topography (form of the behavior)	• Refining motor movements associated with a golf swing, throwing motion, or vaulting behavior. • Improving cursive or manuscript letter formation during handwriting exercises.
Frequency (number of responses per unit of time)	• Increasing the number of problems completed during each minute of a math seatwork assignment. • Increasing the number of correctly spelled and appropriately used words written per minute.
Latency (time between the onset of the antecedent stimulus and the occurrence of the behavior)	• Decreasing compliance time between a parental directive to "clean your room" and the onset of room-cleaning behavior. • Increasing the delay between the onset of an aggressive remark and retaliation by a student with severe emotional disabilities.
Duration (total elapsed time for occurrence of the behavior)	• Increasing the length of time that a student stays on task. • Increasing the number of minutes of engaged study behavior.
Amplitude/Magnitude (response strength or force)	• Increasing the projected voice volume of a speaker from 45 dB to 65 dB. • Increasing the height of the high jump bar for students enrolled in a physical education class.

level required to activate the light represented a successive approximation to the terminal volume.

Analysis of the children's performance using a multiple-baseline across students design indicated that the voice volume increased in the classroom setting as a function of treatment (see Figure 19.2). Also, the children's voice volume remained high after a 4-month period. Finally, according to anecdotal reports by school staff, the

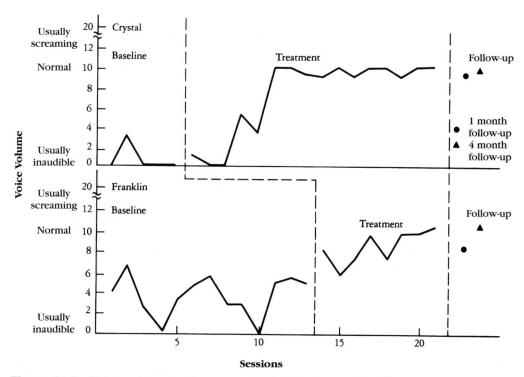

Figure 19.2   Voice-volume levels per session in the classroom setting.

From "Elevation of Voice Volume in Young Developmentally Delayed Children via an Operant Shaping Procedure" by L. Fleece, A. Gross, T. O'Brien, J. Kistner, E. Rothblum, and R. Drabman, 1981, *Journal of Applied Behavioral Analysis, 14*, p. 354. Copyright by the Society for the Experimental Analysis of Behavior, Inc. Reprinted by permission.

children's higher voice volume generalized to other settings beyond the classroom.

From a practical standpoint, measures of increased decibels could be obtained with a voice-sensitive tape recorder or an audiometric recording device that emits a signal (light or sound) only when a specific threshold level is achieved (Fleece et al., 1981). Productions below the criterion level would not activate the recording device.

Shaping across and within Response Topographies

Shaping behavior across different response topographies means that select members of a response class are differentially reinforced, whereas members of other response classes are not reinforced. As stated previously, lip movements, speech sounds, one-word utterances, and phrase or sentence productions represent the different topographies of the layer response class of speaking behaviors; they are the prerequisite behaviors of speaking. When shaping behavior across different response topographies, the practitioner gradually increases the criterion of performance before delivering reinforcement.

Isaacs, Thomas, and Goldiamond (1960) reported a classic study showing how behaviors can be shaped across and within response topographies. They successfully shaped the vocal behavior of Andrew, a man diagnosed with catatonic schizophrenia, who had not spoken for 19 years despite many efforts to encourage speech production. Essentially, the shaping procedure was initiated when an astute psychologist noticed that Andrew's usually passive expression changed slightly when a package of chewing gum inadvertently dropped on the floor. Realizing that gum might be an effective reinforcer for building behaviors in the response class of talking, the psychologist selected speech production as the terminal behavior.

The next step in the shaping process was to select an initial behavior to reinforce. Lip movement was chosen because the psychologist noted that slight lip movements had occurred in the presence of the pack of gum, and more important, lip movement was in the response class of speech. As soon as lip movement was established by differential reinforcement, the psychologist waited for the next approximation of the terminal behavior. During this phase, lip movement alone was no longer reinforced; only lip movements with sound produced the reinforcement. When Andrew began making guttural sounds, vocalizations were differentially reinforced. Then the

guttural sound itself was shaped (differential reinforcement within a response topography) until Andrew said the word *gum.* After the 6th week of shaping, the psychologist asked Andrew to say *gum,* to which Andrew responded, "Gum, please." During that session and afterwards, Andrew went on to converse with the psychologist and others at the institution about his identity and background. In this powerful demonstration of shaping, after selection of the terminal behavior and the initial starting point, each member of the response class was shaped by differential reinforcement of successive approximations to the terminal behavior.

Shaping a behavior within a response topography means that the form of the behavior remains constant, but differential reinforcement is applied to another measurable dimension of the behavior. To illustrate, let us suppose that in a college-level physical education class, the teacher is instructing the students on water safety. Specifically, she is teaching them how to throw a life preserver a given distance to a person struggling in the water. Since the important skill in this activity is to throw the life preserver near the person, the physical education teacher might shape accurate tossing by reinforcing successive approximations to a toss of a given distance. In other words, each toss that is near the person (e.g., within 2 meters) will be praised, whereas tosses outside that range will not be. As students become more accurate, the area can be reduced so that the terminal behavior is a toss within arm's length of the person. In this case, the magnitude of the behavior is being shaped; the form of the toss remains the same.

Another example of shaping within a response topography is a parent who attempts to increase the duration of her child's piano practice. The criterion for success—the terminal behavior—in this particular program might be to have the child practice for 30 minutes three times per week (e.g., Monday, Wednesday, and Friday). To accomplish her objective, the parent could reinforce progressively longer periods of practice, perhaps beginning with a few minutes one night per week. Next, the parent might reinforce increasing durations of practice: 10, 12, 15, 20, 25, and ultimately 30 minutes of practice only on Mondays. No contingency would be in effect for the other two days. As soon as an intermediate criterion level is reached (e.g., 20 minutes), reinforcement is no longer delivered for less than 20 minutes of practice unless performance stalls at a higher level and progress is impeded.

During the next phase of shaping, the process is repeated for Wednesday nights. Now the child must meet the criterion on both days before reinforcement is delivered. Finally, the sequence is repeated for all three nights. It is important to remember that the behavior being shaped in this example is not piano playing. The child can already play the piano; the topography of that response class has been learned. What is being shaped by differential reinforcement is a dimension of behavior within the response class, namely, the duration of piano practice.

Positive Aspects of Shaping

Shaping teaches new behaviors. Because shaping is implemented systematically and gradually, the terminal behavior is always in sight. Also, shaping uses a positive approach to teach new behavior. Reinforcement is delivered consistently upon the occurrence of successive approximations to the terminal behavior, whereas nonapproximations are placed on extinction. Punishment or other aversive procedures are typically not involved in a shaping program. Finally, shaping can be combined with other established behavior change or behavior-building procedures (e.g., chaining). For example, suppose that a behavior analyst designed a seven-step task analysis to teach a child to tie his shoes. However, the child was unable to complete Step 5 in the task analysis. Shaping can be used in isolation to teach a closer approximation to that step. Once Step 5 was learned through shaping, chaining would continue with the rest of the steps in the task analysis.

Limitations of Shaping

At least five limitations of shaping can be identified. Practitioners should be aware of these limitations and be prepared to deal with them as they arise. First, shaping new behavior can be time-consuming because many approximations may be necessary before the terminal behavior is achieved (Cipani & Spooner, 1994).

Second, progress toward the terminal behavior is not always linear. That is, the learner does not always proceed from one approximation to the next in a continuous, logical sequence. Progress may be erratic. If the behavior is too erratic (i.e., not resembling a closer approximation to the terminal behavior), an approximation may need to be further reduced, allowing for more reinforcement and progress. The skill of the practitioner in noting and reinforcing the next smallest approximation to the terminal behavior is critical to the success of shaping. If the practitioner fails to reinforce responses at the next approximation—because of neglect, inexperience, or preoccupation with other tasks—the occurrence of similar responses may be few and far between. If reinforcement for performance at a given approximation continues longer than necessary, progress toward the terminal behavior will be impeded.

Third, shaping requires the practitioner to consistently monitor the learner to detect subtle indications that the next approximation that is closer to the terminal behavior has been performed. Many practitioners—for example, teachers in busy or demanding classrooms—are not able to monitor behavior closely to note small changes. Consequently, shaping may be conducted inappropriately or at least inefficiently.

Fourth, shaping can be misapplied. Consider the child trying to obtain her father's attention by emitting low-volume demands (e.g., "Dad, I want some ice cream"). The father does not attend to the initial calls. As the child's attempts become increasingly unsuccessful, she may become more determined to gain her father's attention. In doing so, the frequency and amplitude of the calls may increase (e.g., "DAD, I want ice cream!"). After listening to the crescendo of vocal demands, the father eventually provides the ice cream. The next time, the child states what she wants in an even louder voice before getting her father's attention. In this scenario, the father has differentially reinforced an ever-rising level of attention-getting behavior and shaped higher levels of call-outs for ice cream. Using this example as a backdrop, Skinner (1953) pointed out: "Differential reinforcement applied by a preoccupied or negligent parent is very close to the procedure we should adopt if we were given the task of conditioning a child to be annoying" (p. 98).

Finally, harmful behavior can be shaped. For example, Rasey and Iversen (1993) showed that differential reinforcement could be used to shape a rat's behavior to the point that the rat fell from the edge of a platform. By differentially reinforcing the rat for sticking its nose farther over the edge for food, the rat eventually fell off the ledge.[1] It is not difficult to speculate that adolescent games such as Dare and Double Dare, which have evolved and become popularized in thrill- and fear-seeking television shows, capitalize on persons receiving differential reinforcement for increasingly higher levels of risk-taking that can lead to dangerous—and sometimes tragic—behavior.

Shaping versus Stimulus Fading

Shaping and fading both change behavior gradually, albeit in much different ways. In shaping, the antecedent stimulus stays the same, while the response progressively becomes more differentiated. In stimulus fading, the

---

[1]The researcher provided a safety net so that the rat was not injured.

opposite occurs: The antecedent stimulus changes gradually, while the response stays essentially the same.

Increasing the Efficiency of Shaping

In addition to showing how behaviors are shaped across and within response topographies, the Isaacs and colleagues (1960) study illustrates another aspect of shaping—efficiency. During the early stages of the program, the psychologist waited for the next approximation of the behavior to appear before delivering the reinforcer. Waiting can be time-consuming and wasteful, so Isaacs and colleagues improved efficiency by using a verbal response prompt, "Say *gum,*" after the sixth training session. Presumably, if the psychologist had not used a verbal prompt, several additional sessions would have been necessary before a successful outcome was achieved.

Shaping can be enhanced in three ways. First, a discriminative stimulus (S^D) may be combined with shaping. For example, when attempting to shape hand shaking as a greeting skill for an adult with developmental disabilities, the teacher might say, "Frank, hold out your arm." Scott, Scott, and Goldwater (1997) used a vocal prompt ("Reach!") as a university-level pole-vaulter ran a path to plant his pole in the vault box. The prompt was designed to focus the vaulter's attention on extending his arms prior to take-off in the vault. Kazdin (2001) suggested that priming a response using any variety of prompting mechanisms can be helpful, especially if the individual's repertoire is weak and the likelihood of distinguishable successive approximations is low. "Even if the responses are not in the client's repertoire of responses, the priming procedure can initiate early response components and facilitate shaping" (p. 277). The second way to enhance shaping is through physical guidance. In the Frank example cited earlier, the teacher might manually assist Frank in holding out his arm. Using the third shaping-enhancing technique, the teacher might use an imitative prompt to demonstrate arm extension (e.g., "Frank, hold out your arm like this"). Any contrived prompt that is used to speed shaping should later be faded.

Clicker Training

Pryor (1999) described **clicker training** as a science-based system for shaping behavior using positive reinforcement. The clicker is a handheld device that produces a click sound when a metal tab is pressed. Reinforcement is paired with the sound of the clicker so that the sound becomes a conditioned reinforcer. Initially used to shape dolphin behavior without physical guidance (Pryor & Norris, 1991), clicker training was later used with other animals (e.g., cats and horses) and ultimately humans to shape complex behaviors such as airplane pilot skills (Pryor, 2005).

> Clicker trainers focus on building behavior, not stopping behavior. Instead of yelling at the dog for jumping up, you click it for sitting. Instead of kicking the horse to make it go, you click it for walking. Then, click by click, you "shape" longer sits, or more walking, until you have the final results you want. Once the behavior is learned, you keep it going with praise and approval and save the clicker and treats for the next new thing you want to train. (Pryor, 2003, p. 1)

Figure 19.3 provides 15 tips for getting started with clicker training (Pryor, 2003).

Guidelines for Implementing Shaping

The practitioner should consider many factors before deciding to use shaping. First, the nature of the terminal behavior to be learned and the resources available should be assessed. For example, a fifth-grade teacher might be interested in increasing the number of math problems performed by a student with learning disabilities. Perhaps the student currently completes 5 problems per math period, with a range of 0 to 10 problems. If the student is able to finish and check her performance independently at the end of the period, shaping could be implemented in which the number of completed math problems would be differentially reinforced. Reinforcement might be presented for 5, 7, 9, and then 11 or more problems completed correctly per period. In this case, solving the math problem is within a specific response topography, and the student can monitor her own performance.

In addition, because shaping requires multiple approximations and linear progression cannot be predicted, the practitioner is advised to estimate the total amount of time required to achieve the terminal behavior. Such estimates can be determined by asking colleagues how many sessions it took them to shape similar behaviors, or by differentially reinforcing a few behaviors that approximate the terminal behavior and then extrapolating from that experience the total amount of time that might be needed to shape the terminal behavior. These two procedures are likely to yield only rough estimates because any number of unforeseen factors can accelerate or

Figure 19.3 Pryor's 15 tips for getting started with the clicker.

1. Push and release the springy end of the clicker, making a two-toned click. Then treat. Keep the treats small. Use a delicious treat at first: for a dog or cat, little cubes of roast chicken, not a lump of kibble.
2. Click DURING the desired behavior, not after it is completed. The timing of the click is crucial. Don't be dismayed if your pet stops the behavior when it hears the click. The click ends the behavior. Give the treat after that; the timing of the treat is not important.
3. Click when your dog or other pet does something you like. Begin with something easy that the pet is likely to do on its own (ideas: sit, come toward you, touch your hand with its nose, lift a foot, touch and follow a target object such as a pencil or a spoon).
4. Click once (in-out). If you want to express special enthusiasm, increase the number of treats, not the number of clicks.
5. Keep practice sessions short. Much more is learned in three sessions of five minutes each than in an hour of boring repetition. You can get dramatic results, and teach your pet many new things, by fitting a few clicks a day here and there in your normal routine.
6. Fix bad behavior by clicking good behavior. Click the puppy for relieving itself in the proper spot. Click for paws on the ground, not on the visitors. Instead of scolding for making noise, click for silence. Cure leash-pulling by clicking and treating those moments when the leash happens to go slack.
7. Click for voluntary (or accidental) movements toward your goal. You may coax or lure the animal into a movement or position, but don't push, pull, or hold it. Let the animal discover how to do the behavior on its own. If you need a leash for safety's sake, loop it over your shoulder or tie it to your belt.
8. Don't wait for the "whole picture" or the perfect behavior. Click and treat for small movements in the right direction. You want the dog to sit, and it starts to crouch in back: click. You want it to come when called, and it takes a few steps your way: click.
9. Keep raising your goal. As soon as you have a good response—when a dog, for example, is voluntarily lying down, coming toward you, or sitting repeatedly—start asking for more. Wait a few beats, until the dog stays down a little longer, comes a little further, sits a little faster. Then click. This is called "shaping" a behavior.
10. When your animal has learned to do something for clicks, it will begin showing you the behavior spontaneously, trying to get you to click. Now is the time to begin offering a cue, such as a word or a hand signal. Start clicking for that behavior if it happens during or after the cue. Start ignoring that behavior when the cue wasn't given.
11. Don't order the animal around; clicker training is not command-based. If your pet does not respond to a cue, it is not disobeying; it just hasn't learned the cue completely. Find more ways to cue it and click it for the desired behavior. Try working in a quieter, less distracting place for a while. If you have more than one pet, separate them for training, and let them take turns.
12. Carry a clicker and "catch" cute behaviors like cocking the head, chasing the tail, or holding up one foot. You can click for many different behaviors, whenever you happen to notice them, without confusing your pet.
13. If you get mad, put the clicker away. Don't mix scoldings, leash-jerking, and correction training with clicker training; you will lose the animal's confidence in the clicker and perhaps in you.
14. If you are not making progress with a particular behavior, you are probably clicking too late. Accurate timing is important. Get someone else to watch you, and perhaps to click for you, a few times.
15. Above all, have fun. Clicker-training is a wonderful way to enrich your relationship with any learner.

From *Click to Win!* by Karen Pryor, 2002. Sunshine Books, Waltham, MA.

Figure 19.4   Pryor's ten laws of shaping.

1. Raise criteria in increments small enough so that the subject always has a realistic chance of reinforcement.
2. Train one aspect of any particular behavior at a time. Don't try to shape for two criteria simultaneously.
3. During shaping, put the current level of response on a variable ratio schedule of reinforcement before adding or raising the criteria.
4. When introducing a new criterion, or aspect of the behavioral skill, temporarily relax the old ones.
5. Stay ahead of your subject: Plan your shaping program completely so that if the subject makes sudden progress, you are aware of what to reinforce next.
6. Don't change trainers in midstream. You can have several trainers per trainee, but stick to one shaper per behavior.
7. If one shaping procedure is not eliciting progress, find another. There are as many ways to get behavior as there are trainers to think them up.
8. Don't interrupt a training session gratuitously; that constitutes a punishment.
9. If behavior deteriorates, "Go back to kindergarten." Quickly review the whole shaping process with a series of easily earned reinforcers.
10. End each session on a high note, if possible, but in any case quit while you're ahead.

Reprinted with the permission of Simon & Schuster Adult Publishing Group from *Don't Shoot the Dog! The New Art of Teaching and Training* (revised edition) by K. Pryor, 1999, pp. 38–39. Copyright © 1984 by Karen Pryor.

decelerate progress. If it appears that more time is needed than can be arranged, the practitioner might consider another strategy. Some behaviors seem to preclude the use of shaping as a behavior-building technique. For instance, if a high school English teacher is interested in increasing the public-speaking repertoires of his students, prompting, modeling, or peer tutoring might be more efficient than shaping. That is, telling or showing the students how to use gestures, inflection, or metaphors would be much faster than attempting to shape each of these distinct response classes alone.

After the decision has been made to use shaping, Pryor's Ten Laws of Shaping can assist the practitioner in implementing this process in applied settings (see Figure 19.4).

Select the Terminal Behavior

Practitioners often work with learners who have to change multiple behaviors. Consequently, they must identify the highest priority behavior quickly. The ultimate criterion in this decision is the individual's expected independence after the behavior change; that is, the likelihood of her attaining additional reinforcers from the environment (Snell & Brown, 2006). For example, if a student frequently roams the classroom poking other students, taking their papers, and verbally harassing them, a shaping procedure might best begin with a behavior that is incompatible with roaming the room because of the utility it would have for the individual and the other students. In addition, if in-seat behavior is developed, the staff with whom the student interacts will likely notice and reinforce it. In this case, shaping should differentially reinforce longer durations of in-seat behavior.

It is also important to define the terminal behavior precisely. For example, a behavior analyst might want to shape the appropriate sitting behavior of an individual with severe retardation. To do so, sitting might be defined as being located upright in the chair, facing the front of the room with buttocks against the bottom of the chair and back against the chair rest during a 15-minute morning activity. Using this definition, the analyst can determine when the behavior is achieved, as well as what does not constitute the behavior—an important discrimination if shaping is to be conducted efficiently (e.g., the student might be half in and half out of the seat, or the student might be in the seat but turned toward the back of the room).

Determine the Criterion for Success

After identifying the terminal behavior, the practitioner should specify the criterion for success. Here, the practitioner decides how accurate, fast, intense, or durable the behavior must be before it can be considered shaped. Several measures can be applied to establish a criterion of success. Some of the more common include frequency, magnitude, and duration. Depending on the terminal behavior, any or all of these dimensions can be used to assess achievement. For instance, a special education teacher might shape frequency performance in solving mathematics calculations problems that would proceed from the student's current level of performance (say, half a problem per minute) to a higher rate (e.g., four problems per minute).

Norms for success can be determined by measuring the behavior in a similar peer group or consulting established norms in the literature. For instance, norms and guidelines for reading rate by grade level (Kame´enui, 2002), physical education skills for children by age group (President's Council on Physical Fitness, 2005), and homework guidelines per grade level (Heron, Hippler, & Tincani, 2003) can be referenced to validate progress toward the terminal behavior.

In the earlier illustration, the criterion for success could be the student's sitting in her seat appropriately 90% of the time during the morning activity for 5 consecutive days. In this example, two criteria are specified: the percentage of acceptable sitting behavior per session (i.e., 90%) and the number of days that the criterion must be met to establish the behavior (i.e., 5 consecutive days).

Analyze the Response Class

The purpose of analyzing the response class is to attempt to identify the approximations that might be emitted in the shaping sequence. When approximation behaviors are known—and anticipated—the practitioner is in a better position to observe and reinforce an approximation when it is emitted. However, the practitioner must recognize the projected approximations are guesstimates of behaviors that might be emitted. In actuality, the learner may emit behaviors that are merely approximations of these projections. The practitioner must be able to make the professional judgment that the previously emitted behavior either is or is not a closer approximation to the terminal behavior than the behaviors that occurred and were reinforced in the past. According to Galbicka (1994):

> The successful shaper must carefully ascertain characteristics of an individual's present response repertoire, explicitly define characteristics the final behavior will have at the end of training, and plot a course between reinforcement and extinction that will bring the right responses along at the right time, fostering the final behavioral sequence while never losing responding altogether. (p. 739)

The relevant approximations across or within a response class can be analyzed in several ways. First, practitioners can consult experts in the field to determine their views on the proper sequence of approximations for a given behavior (Snell & Brown, 2006). For example, teachers who have taught three-digit multiplication for several years can be consulted to learn their experiences with prerequisite behaviors for performing this type of calculation task. Second, as stated earlier, normative data from published studies may be used to provide an estimate of the approximations involved. Third, a videotape can be used to analyze the component behaviors. The videotape would help the practitioner to see motion that might be undetectable in an initial live performance, but become detectable as the practitioner becomes skilled with observing it. Finally, the practitioner can perform the target behavior himself, carefully noting the discrete behavioral components as he produces them.

The ultimate determination of the approximations, the approximation order, the duration of time that reinforcement should be delivered at a given approximation, and the criteria for skipping or repeating approximations rests with the skill and the judgment of the practitioner. Ultimately, the learner's performance should dictate when approximation size should be increased, maintained, or decreased, making consistent and vigilant monitoring by the practitioner essential.

Identify the First Behavior to Reinforce

Two criteria are suggested for identifying the initial behavior for reinforcement:(a) The behavior should already occur at some minimum frequency, and (b) the behavior should be a member of the targeted response class. The first condition reduces the need to wait for the occurrence of the initial behavior. Waiting for a behavior to be emitted can be therapeutically counterproductive and is usually unnecessary. The second criterion sets the occasion for reinforcing an existing behavioral component that has one dimension in common with the terminal behavior. For example, if the terminal behavior is expressive speech, as was the case with Andrew, lip movement would be a good first choice.

Eliminate Interfering or Extraneous Stimuli

Eliminating sources of distraction during shaping enhances the effectiveness of the process. For example, if

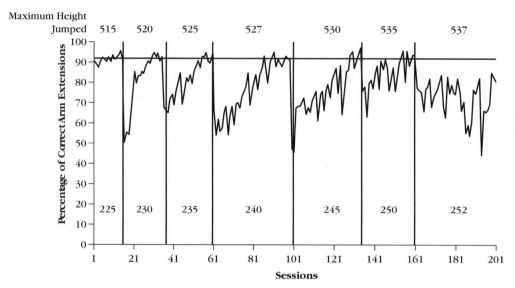

Figure 19.5   Percentage of correct arm extensions at seven different heights. The numbers contained within each criterion condition refer to the height of the photoelectric beam.

From "A Performance Improvement Program for an International-Level Track and Field Athlete" by D. Scott, L. M. Scott, & B. Goldwater, 1997, *Journal of Applied Behavior Analysis, 30* (3), p. 575. Copyright by the Society for the Experimental Analysis of Behavior, Inc. Reprinted by permission.

a parent is interested in shaping one dimension of her daughter's dressing behavior at the local gymnasium (e.g., the rate of dressing) and decides to begin the shaping procedure in a room where cartoons are shown on the television, the shaping program may not be successful because the cartoons will be competing for the daughter's attention. It would be more efficient to choose a time when and a location where sources of distraction can be reduced or eliminated.

Proceed in Gradual Stages

The importance of proceeding toward the terminal goal in gradual stages cannot be overemphasized. The practitioner should anticipate changes in the rate of progress and be prepared to go from approximation to approximation as the learner's behavior dictates. Each new occurrence of a successive approximation to the terminal behavior must be detected and reinforced. If not, shaping will be, at worst, unsuccessful or, at best, haphazard, requiring much more time. Furthermore, the occurrence of a behavior at a given approximation does not mean that the next response that approximates the terminal behavior will be immediately or accurately produced. Figure 19.5 shows the results of a study by Scott and colleagues (1997), who found that the percentage of correct arm extensions by the pole-vaulter decreased initially as the

height of the bar was raised. Whereas a 90% correct arm extension was noted at the initial height, the vaulter's correct performance typically dropped to approximately 70% each time the bar was raised. After successive attempts at the new height, the 90% correct criterion was reestablished.

The practitioner must also be aware that many trials may be required at a given approximation before the subject can advance to the next approximation. Figure 19.5 illustrates this point as well. On the other hand, only a few trials may be required. The practitioner must watch carefully and be prepared to reinforce many trials at a given approximation or to move rapidly toward the terminal objective.

Limit the Number of Approximations at Each Level

Just as it is important to proceed gradually from approximation to approximation, it is equally important to ensure that progress is not impeded by offering too many trials at a given approximation. This may cause the behavior to become firmly established, and because that approximation has to be extinguished before progress can begin again (Catania, 1998), the more frequently reinforcement is delivered at a given approximation, the longer the process can take. In general, if the learner is progressing steadily, reinforcement is probably being delivered at the correct pace. If too many mistakes are being made or behavior ceases altogether, the criterion for reinforcement has probably being raised too quickly. Finally, if the performance stabilizes at a certain level, shaping is probably going too slowly. Practitioners may experience all three of these conditions over the course of successive approximations that ultimately lead to the behavior being shaped. Therefore, they must be vigilant and adjust the procedure, if necessary.

Continue to Reinforce When the Terminal Behavior Is Achieved

When the terminal behavior is demonstrated and reinforced, it is necessary to continue to reinforce it. Otherwise the behavior will be lost, and performance will return to a lower level. Reinforcement must continue until the criterion for success is achieved and a maintenance schedule of reinforcement is established.

Future Applications of Shaping

New applications of shaping are being reported in the literature that extend its utility, promote its efficiency, and ultimately benefit the individual with respect to shorter training time and/or skill development (Shimoff & Catania, 1995). At least three future applications of shaping can be considered: using percentile schedules, using computers to teach shaping skills, and combining shaping procedures with robotics engineering.

Percentile Schedules

Galbicka (1994) argued against the often-heard notion that shaping is more art than science and that practitioners can learn to use shaping only by hard-earned direct experience. Building on more than two decades of laboratory research on percentile reinforcement schedules, Galbicka's conceptualization of shaping specifies the criteria for responses and reinforcement in mathematical terms, thereby standardizing the shaping process regardless of the person doing the shaping. He stated:

> Percentile schedules disassemble the process of shaping into its constituent components, translate those components into simple, mathematical statements, and then use these equations, with parameters specified by the experimenter or trainer, to determine what presently consti-

tutes a criterional response and should therefore be reinforced. (p. 740)

Galbicka (1994) conceded that for percentile schedules to be used effectively in applied settings, behaviors must be (a) measured constantly and (b) rank-ordered using a system of comparisons to previous responses. If a response exceeds a criterion value, reinforcement is delivered. If not, reinforcement is withheld. Galbicka projected that understanding how percentile schedules work may

> increase our understanding of the complex social and non-social dynamics that shape behavior . . . allow[ing] unprecedented control over experimentally relevant stimuli in operant conditioning and differential procedures and provide a seemingly endless horizon against which to cast our sights for extensions and applications. (p. 759)

Using Computers to Teach Shaping

Several options are currently available to teach shaping skills using computers or a combination of specialized software with computer-based applications. For example, Sniffy, the Virtual Rat, is a computer-based, digitized animation of a white rat within a Skinner box. Students can practice basic shaping on their own personal computers using this virtual simulation.

Acknowledging the practical limitations of teaching behavior analysis principles (e.g., shaping) interactively to a large student body, Shimoff and Catania (1995) developed and refined computer simulations to teach the concepts of shaping.[2] In their simulation, The Shaping Game, four levels of difficulty (easy, medium, hard, and very hard) were programmed over a series of refinements. Beginning with easier tasks and advancing to the very hard level, students are taught to detect successive approximations to bar-pressing behaviors that should be reinforced, and those that should not. In still later versions, students are expected to shape the movement of the animated rat from one side of a Skinner box to another. Shimoff and Catania provided a case for computer simulations when they stated, "Computers can be important and effective tools for establishing sophisticated behavior that appears to be contingency shaped even in classes that do not provide real (unsimulated) laboratory experience" (pp. 315–316).

Martin and Pear (2003) contended that computers might be used to shape some dimensions of behavior (e.g., topography) more quickly than humans because a

---

[2]They also developed simulations for reinforcement schedules.

computer can be calibrated and programmed with specific decision rules for delivering reinforcement. They further suggested that in medical application cases (e.g., amputees, stroke victims), in which minute muscle movements may go undetected by a human observer, a microprocessor could detect shapeable responses. In their view, "Computers . . . are both accurate and fast and may therefore be useful in answering fundamental questions concerning which shaping procedures are most effective . . . computers may be able to shape at least some kinds of behavior as effectively as humans" (p. 133).

Combining Shaping with Robotics Engineering

Some researchers have begun to explore how shaping can be applied to robot training (e.g., Dorigo & Colombetti, 1998; Saksida, Raymond, & Touretzky, 1997). Essentially, shaping is being considered as one method of programming robots to progress from a start state through a series of intermediate and end-goal states to achieve more complicated sets of commands. According to Savage (1998):

> Given that shaping is a significant determinant of how a wide variety of organisms adapt to the changing circumstances of the real world, then shaping may, indeed, have potential as a model for real-world robotic interactions. However, the success of this strategy depends on a clear understanding of the principles of biological shaping on the part of the roboticists, and the effective robotic implementation of these principles. (p. 321)

Although Dorigo and Colombetti (1998) and Saksida and colleagues (1997) concede the difficulty in applying behavioral principles of successive approximations to robots, this line of inquiry, combined with emerging knowledge on artificial intelligence, offers exciting prospects for the future.

 Summary

Definition of Shaping

1. Shaping is the differential reinforcement of successive approximations to a desired behavior. In shaping, differential reinforcement is applied to produce a series of slightly different response classes, with each successive response class becoming a closer approximation to the terminal behavior than the previous one.

2. A terminal behavior—the end product of shaping—can be claimed when the topography, frequency, latency, duration, or amplitude/magnitude of the target behavior reaches a predetermined criterion level.

3. Differential reinforcement is a procedure in which reinforcement is provided for responses that share a predetermined dimension or quality, and in which reinforcement is withheld for responses that do not demonstrate that quality.

4. Differential reinforcement has two effects: responses similar to those that have been reinforced occur with greater frequency, and responses resembling the unreinforced members are emitted less frequently (i.e., undergo extinction).

5. The dual effects of differential reinforcement result in response differentiation, the emergence of a new response class composed primarily of responses sharing the characteristics of the previously reinforced subclass.

6. The gradually changing criterion for reinforcement during shaping results in a succession of new response classes, or successive approximations, each one closer in form to the terminal behavior than the response class it replaces.

Shaping across and within Response Topographies

7. Shaping behavior across different response topographies means that select members of a response class are differentially reinforced, while members of other response classes are not reinforced.

8. When shaping a behavior within a response topography, the form of the behavior remains constant, but differential reinforcement is applied to a dimension of the behavior (e.g., frequency, duration).

9. Shaping entails several limitations that practitioners should consider before applying it.

10. In shaping, the antecedent stimulus stays the same, while the response progressively becomes more differentiated. In stimulus fading, the response remains the same, while the antecedent stimulus changes gradually.

Increasing the Efficiency of Shaping

11. The efficiency of shaping may be improved in several ways, including using a discriminative stimulus, a vocal prompt, physical guidance, an imitative prompt, or priming. Any prompt that is introduced is later faded.

Clicker Training

12. Clicker training is a science-based system for shaping behavior using positive reinforcement.

13. The clicker, a handheld device that produces a click sound when a metal tab is pressed, provides the signal that when a behavior is being performed in the presence of the click, reinforcement follows.

Guidelines for Implementing Shaping

14. Before deciding to use shaping, the nature of the behaviors to be learned and the resources available must be assessed.

15. After the decision has been made to use a shaping procedure, the practitioner performs the following steps: select the terminal behavior, decide the criterion for success, analyze the response class, identify the first behavior to reinforce, eliminate interfering or extraneous stimuli, proceed in gradual stages, limit the number of approximations at each level, and continue reinforcement when the terminal behavior is achieved.

Future Applications of Shaping

16. Future applications of shaping include applying percentile schedules, integrating computer technology to teach behavior analysis using shaping procedures, and combining shaping procedures with emerging robotics technology.

CHAPTER 20

Chaining

Key Terms

backward chaining
backward chaining with leaps ahead
behavior chain

behavior chain interruption strategy
behavior chain with a limited hold
  chaining

forward chaining
task analysis
total-task chaining

Behavior Analyst Certification Board® BCBA® & BCABA®
Behavior Analyst Task List,© Third Edition

	Content Area 8: Selecting Intervention Outcomes and Strategies
8-1	Conduct a task analysis.
	Content Area 9: Behavior Change Procedures
9-12	Use chaining.

This chapter defines a behavior chain, provides a rationale for establishing behavior chains in applied settings, and discusses the importance of task analysis in behavior chain training. The chapter presents a procedure for constructing and validating a task analysis, along with procedures for assessing individual mastery levels. Forward chaining, total-task chaining, backward chaining, and backward chaining with leap aheads are addressed, followed by guidelines for deciding which behavior chain procedure to use in applied settings and a description of behavior chains with limited holds. Techniques for breaking inappropriate chains are also addressed. The chapter concludes with an examination of factors affecting the performance of a behavior chain.

Definition of a Behavior Chain

A **behavior chain** is a specific sequence of discrete responses, each associated with a particular stimulus condition. Each discrete response and the associated stimulus condition serve as an individual component of the chain. When individual components are linked together, the result is a behavior chain that produces a terminal outcome. Each response in a chain produces a stimulus change that simultaneously serves as a conditioned reinforcer for the response that produced it and as a discriminative stimulus (S^D) for the next response in the chain. Each stimulus that links the two response components together serves a dual function: It is both a conditioned reinforcer and an S^D (Reynolds, 1975; Skinner, 1953). Reinforcement produced by the final response in the chain maintains the effectiveness of the stimulus changes that serve as conditioned reinforcers and S^Ds

for each response in the chain. The notable exception to the dual function of the components occurs with the first and last stimulus in the chain. In these instances, the stimulus serves only one function: either as the S^D or as the conditioned reinforcer.

Reynolds (1975) provided this laboratory example of a behavioral chain (illustrated in Figure 20.1):

> An experimental example of a chain may begin when a pigeon is presented with a blue key. When the pigeon pecks the key, it changes to red. After the key turns red, the pigeon presses a pedal that turns the key yellow. During yellow, displacing a bar changes the key to green. Finally, during green, pecks are reinforced with the operation of a grain-delivery mechanism and its associated stimuli, in the presence of which the bird approaches the grain magazine and eats. (pp. 59–60)

In Reynolds' example, the links are arranged in the following sequence: blue-key-peck-red; red-peddle-press-yellow; yellow-bar-press-green; green-key-peck-grain magazine; grain magazine-eat-food intake. "Because each stimulus has a dual function, as discriminative stimulus and conditioner reinforcer, the links overlap. In fact, it is this dual function of the stimuli that holds the chain together" (Reynolds, 1975, p. 60).

As Figure 20.1 shows, this chain includes four responses (R_1, R_2, R_3, and R_4), with a specific stimulus condition (S_1, S_2, S_3, and S_4) associated with each response. The blue light (S_1) is an S^D to occasion the first response (R_1), a key peck that terminates the blue light and produces the onset of the red light (S_2). The red light serves as conditioned reinforcement for R_1 and as an S^D for R_2 (a pedal press). The pedal press (R_2) terminates the red light and produces the onset of the yellow light (S_3), and so on. The last response produces food, thus completing and maintaining the chain.

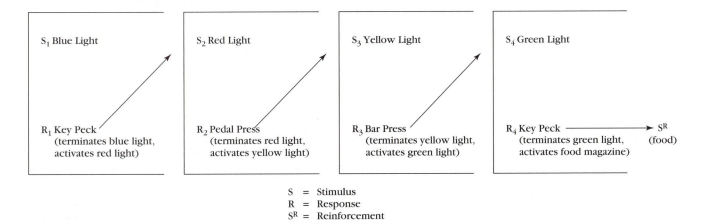

Figure 20.1 Illustration of a behavior chain consisting of four components.
Based on a chain described by Reynolds (1975, pp. 59–60).

Table 20.1 Delineation of the Relationship between Each Discriminative Stimulus, Response, and Reinforcement in a Sample Behavior Chain

Discriminative stimulus	Response	Conditioned reinforcement
S_1 "Put on your coat."	R_1 Obtain coat from closet	Coat in hands
S_2 Coat in hands	R_2 Place one arm in sleeve	One arm in sleeve
S_3 One arm in sleeve/one arm out	R_3 Place second arm in sleeve	Coat on
S_4 Coat on	R_4 Zip up the coat	Teacher praise

Table 20.1 shows the links of a behavior chain using a classroom example. In preparing a class of preschool students for recess, the teacher might say to one student, "Please put on your coat." The teacher's statement would serve as the S^D (S_1) evoking the first response (R_1) in the chain, obtaining the coat from the closet. That response in the presence of the teacher's statement terminates the teacher's statement and produces the onset of the coat in the student's hands (S_2). The coat in the student's hands serves as conditioned reinforcement for obtaining the coat from the closet (R_1) and as an S^D (S_2) for putting one arm through a sleeve (R_2). That response, putting one arm through the sleeve in the presence of the coat in both hands, terminates the stimulus condition of the coat in the student's hands and produces the onset of one arm in a sleeve and one arm out (S_3), a stimulus change that serves as conditioned reinforcement for putting one arm through a sleeve and as an S^D (S_3) for placing the second arm through the other sleeve (R_3). That response terminates the condition of one arm in a sleeve and one arm out, and produces the S^D (S_4) of the coat being completely on. The coat being fully on serves as a conditioned reinforcer for putting the second arm through the other sleeve and as an S^D for zipping it (R_4). Finally, zipping up the coat completes the chain and produces teacher praise.

A behavior chain has the following three important characteristics: (a) A behavior chain involves the performance of a specific series of discrete responses; (b) the performance of each behavior in the sequence changes the environment in such a way that it produces conditioned reinforcement for the preceding response and serves as an S^D for the next response; and (c) the responses within the chain must be performed in a specific sequence, usually in close temporal succession.

Behavior Chains with a Limited Hold

A **behavior chain with a limited hold** is a sequence of behaviors that must be performed correctly and within a specified time to produce reinforcement. Thus, behavior chains with limited holds are characterized by perfor-

mance that is accurate and proficient. An assembly task on a production line exemplifies a chain with a limited hold. To meet the production requirements of the job, an employee might have to assemble 30 couplers onto 30 shafts within 30 minutes (one per minute). If the coupler is placed on the shaft, the retaining clip applied, and the unit forwarded to the next person in line within the prescribed period of time, reinforcement is delivered. In a behavior chain with a limited hold, the person must not only have the prerequisite behaviors in his repertoire, but must also emit those behaviors in close temporal succession to obtain reinforcement.

The behavior analyst must recognize that accuracy and rate are essential dimensions of chains with limited holds. For example, if a person is able to complete a chain in the correct sequence but the speed with which he performs one or more responses in the chain is slow, changing the focus to increase the rate of performance is warranted. One way to do this is to set a time criterion for completion of each response within the chain; another is to set a designated time criterion for completion of the total chain.

Rationale for Using Chaining

Whereas *behavior chain* connotes a particular sequence of responses ending in reinforcement, the term **chaining** refers to various methods for linking specific sequences of stimuli and responses to form new performances. In forward chaining, behaviors are linked together beginning with the *first* behavior in the sequence. In backward chaining, the behaviors are linked together beginning with the *last* behavior in the sequence. Both of these procedures and their variations are discussed in detail later in this chapter.

There are several reasons for teaching new behavior chains to people. First, an important aspect of the education of students with development disabilities is to increase independent living skills (e.g., using public utilities, taking care of personal needs, executing travel skills, socializing appropriately). As these skills develop, the student is more likely to function effectively in least restrictive environments or participate in activities without adult supervision. Complex behaviors developed with chaining procedures allow individuals to function more on their own.

Second, chaining provides the means by which a series of discrete behaviors can be combined to form a series of responses that occasion the delivery of positive reinforcement. That is, essentially, chaining can be used to add behaviors to an existing behavioral repertoire. For example, a person with a developmental disability might consistently seek assistance from a coworker or job coach while completing an assembly task. A chaining procedure could be used to increase the number of tasks that must be performed before reinforcement is delivered. To that end, the teacher might give the individual a written or pictorial list of the parts that must be assembled to complete the job. When the first portion of the task is finished, the individual crosses off the first word or picture on the list and proceeds to the second task. In behavioral terms, the first word or picture on the list serves as the S^D to occasion the response of completing the first task. That response, in the presence of the word or picture on the list, terminates the initial stimulus and produces the next stimulus, the second word or picture on the list. The completion of the second task serves as conditioned reinforcement for completing the task and produces the onset of the third S^D. In this way the chaining procedure enables simple behaviors to be combined into a longer series of complex responses.

Finally, chaining can be combined with other behavior change prompting, instructing, and reinforcing procedures to build more complex and adaptive repertoires (McWilliams, Nietupski, & Hamre-Nietupski, 1990).

Task Analysis

Before individual components of a chain can be linked together, the behavior analyst must construct and validate a task analysis of the components of the behavioral sequence, and assess the mastery level of the learner with respect to each behavior in the task analysis. **Task analysis** involves breaking a complex skill into smaller, teachable units, the product of which is a series of sequentially ordered steps or tasks.

Constructing and Validating a Task Analysis

The purpose of constructing and validating a task analysis is to determine the sequence of behaviors that are necessary and sufficient to complete a given task efficiently.

The sequence of behaviors that one person might have to perform may not be identical to what another person needs to achieve the same outcome. A task analysis should be individualized according to the age, skill level, and prior experience of the person in question. Further, some task analyses are comprised of a limited number of major steps, with each major step containing four to five subtasks. Figure 20.2 illustrates a task analysis for making a bed developed by McWilliams and colleagues (1990).

At least three methods can be used to identify and validate the components of a task analysis. In the first method the behavioral components of the sequence are developed after observing competent individuals perform the desired sequence of behaviors. For example, Test, Spooner, Keul, and Grossi (1990) produced a task analysis for using a public telephone by observing two adults perform the task, and then validating that sequence by training a person with developmental disabilities to use the task analysis. Based on the training, the researchers made subsequent modifications to the original sequence of tasks. Table 20.2 shows the final task analysis containing 17 steps.

Some of the steps in the task analysis of using a public telephone might appear in a different order or be combined differently. For instance, Step 3, choose the correct change, could be interchanged with Step 2, find the telephone number; or an 18th step could be added, "Place change back in your pocket." There are no absolute rules for determining the number or sequence of steps. However, practitioners are advised to consider the learner's physical, sensory, or motoric skill levels when determining the scope and sequence of the steps, and be prepared to adjust if necessary.

A second method of validating a task analysis is to consult with experts or persons skilled in performing the task (Snell & Brown, 2006). For instance, when teaching mending skills to young adults with developmental disabilities, consultation with a seamstress or a secondary-level home economics teacher is advisable. Based on such expert evaluation, a task analysis could be constructed that would serve as the basis for assessment and training.

A third method of determining and validating the sequence of behaviors in a task analysis is to perform the behaviors oneself (Snell & Brown, 2006). For example, a practitioner interested in teaching shoe tying could repeatedly tie her own shoes, noting the discrete, observable steps necessary to achieve a correctly tied shoe. The advantage of self-performing the task is the opportunity to come into contact with the task demands of the sequence prior to training a learner, getting a clearer idea of the behaviors to be taught and the associated S^Ds necessary to occasion each behavior. Self-performing the task repeatedly would refine the response topography necessary for

Figure 20.2 Task analysis of bedmaking skills.

Given an unmade bed that included a messed-up bedspread, blanket, pillow, and flat sheet and a fitted sheet, the student will:

Section 1: bed preparation
1. remove pillow from bed
2. pull bedspread to foot of bed
3. pull blanket to foot of bed
4. pull flat sheet to foot of bed
5. smooth wrinkles of fitted sheet

Section 2: flat sheet
6. pull top of flat sheet to headboard
7. straighten right corner of flat sheet at foot of bed
8. repeat #7 for the left corner
9. make sheet even across top end of mattress
10. smooth wrinkles

Section 3: blanket
11. pull top of blanket to headboard
12. straighten right corner of blanket at foot of bed
13. repeat #12 for the left corner
14. make blanket even with sheet across top end of mattress
15. smooth wrinkles

Section 4: bedspread
16. pull top of bedspread to headboard
17. pull right corner of bedspread at foot to floor
18. repeat #17 for left side
19. make bedspread even with floor on both sides
20. smooth wrinkles

Section 5: pillow
21. fold top of spread to within 4 inches of the pillow width
22. place pillow on folded portion
23. cover pillow with the folded portion
24. smooth bedspread wrinkles on and around the pillow

From "Teaching Complex Activities to Students with Moderate Handicaps Through the Forward Chaining of Shorter Total Cycle Response Sequences," by R. McWilliams, J. Nietupski, & S. Hamre-Nietupski, 1990, *Education and Training in Mental Retardation, 25,* p. 296. Copyright 1990 by the Council for Exceptional Children. Reprinted by permission.

the learner to use the sequence most efficiently. Table 20.3 shows how an initial 7-step sequence for tying a shoe might be expanded to 14 steps after self-performing the behavior (cf. Bailey & Wolery, 1992).

A systematic trial-and-error procedure can assist the behavior analyst in developing a task analysis. Using a systematic trial-and-error method, an initial task analysis is generated and then refined and revised as it is being tested. With revisions and refinements obtained through field tests, a more functional and appropriate task analysis can be achieved. For instance, as mentioned earlier, Test and colleagues (1990) generated their initial task analysis for using a public telephone by watching two adults complete the task. They subsequently carried the process a step further by asking a person with developmental disabilities to perform the same task and modified the task analysis accordingly.

Regardless of the method used to put the steps in sequence, the S^Ds and corresponding responses must be identified. But being able to perform a response is not sufficient; the individual must be able to discriminate the conditions under which a given response should be performed. Listing the discriminative stimuli and associated responses helps the trainer determine whether naturally occurring S^Ds will evoke different or multiple responses. This topic will be discussed in detail later in the chapter.

Assessing Mastery Level

Mastery level is assessed to determine which components of the task analysis a person can perform independently. There are two principal ways to assess a person's mastery level of task analysis behaviors prior to

Table 20.2 Task Analysis and Time Limits for Performing Each Task for Using a Public Telephone

	Step	Time Limit
1.	Locate the telephone in the environment	2 minutes
2.	Find the telephone number	1 minute
3.	Choose the correct change	30 seconds
4.	Pick up receiver using left hand	10 seconds
5.	Put receiver to left ear and listen for dial tone	10 seconds
6.	Insert first coin	20 seconds
7.	Insert second coin	20 seconds
8-14.	Dial seven-digit number	10 seconds per
15.	Wait for telephone to ring a minimum of five times	25 seconds
16.	If someone answers, initiate conversation	5 seconds
17.	If telephone is busy, hang up phone and collect money	15 seconds

From "Teaching Adolescents with Severe Disabilities to Use the Public Telephone," by D. W. Test, F. Spooner, P. K. Keul, & T. A. Grossi, 1990, *Behavior Modification,* 3rd ed., p. 161. Copyright 1990 by Sage Publications. Reprinted by permission.

Table 20.3 Initial and Expanded Steps for Teaching Shoe Tying

Shorter sequence[a]	Longer sequence[b]
1. Partially tighten shoe laces.	1. Pinch lace.
2. Pull shoe laces tight—vertical pull.	2. Pull lace.
3. Cross shoe laces.	3. Hang lace ends from corresponding sides of shoe.
4. Tighten laces—horizontal pull.	4. Pick up laces in corresponding hands.
5. Tie laces into a knot.	5. Lift laces above shoe.
6. Make a bow.	6. Cross right lace over the left to form a tepee.
7. Tighten bow.	7. Bring left lace toward student.
	8. Pull left lace through tepee.
	9. Pull laces away from each other.
	10. Bend left lace to form a loop.
	11. Pinch loop with left hand.
	12. Bring right lace over the fingers—around loop.
	13. Push right lace through hole.
	14. Pull loops away from each other.

Sources: (a) Santa Cruz County Office of Education, Behavioral Characteristics Progression. Palo Alto, California, VORT Corporation, 1973. (b) Smith, D. D., Smith, J. O., & Edgar, E. "Research and Application of Instructional Materials Development." In N. G. Haring & L. Brown (Eds.), *Teaching the Severely Handicapped* (Vol. 1). New York: Grune & Stratton, 1976. From *Teaching Infants and Preschoolers with Handicaps,* p. 47, by D. B. Bailey & M. Wolery, 1984, Columbus, OH: Charles E. Merrill. Used by permission.

training—the single-opportunity method and the multiple-opportunity method (Snell & Brown, 2006).

Single-Opportunity Method

The single-opportunity method is designed to assess a learner's ability to perform each behavior in the task analysis in correct sequence. Figure 20.3 is an example of a form used to record a learner's performance. Specifically, a plus sign (+) or minus sign (–) is marked for each behavior that is correctly or incorrectly emitted.

Assessment in this example began when the teacher said, "Tom, put on your hearing aid." Tom's responses to the steps in the task analysis were then recorded. The figure shows Tom's data for the first four days of assessment. On Day 1 Tom opened the hearing aid container and removed the harness; each of these steps was performed correctly, independently, sequentially, and within a 6-second time limit. However, Tom then attempted to put the hearing aid harness over his head (Step 5) without first doing Steps 3 and 4. Because he continued to perform this behavior for more than 10 seconds, the teacher stopped the assessment and scored Steps 3 and 4 and all remaining steps as incorrect. On Day 2 Tom was stopped after Step 1 because he performed a subsequent step out of order. On Days 3 and 4 the assessment was discontinued after Step 4 because Tom took more than 6 seconds to perform Step 5. Given a criterion for mastery of 100% accuracy within 6 seconds over three consecutive probes, the data indicate that Tom only met the criterion for Step 1 (the three +'s for Step 2 were not recorded consecutively).

Multiple-Opportunity Method

The multiple-opportunity method of task analysis assessment evaluates the person's level of mastery across all the behaviors in the task analysis. If a step is performed incorrectly, out of sequence, or the time limit for completing the step is exceeded, the behavior analyst completes that step for the learner and then positions her for the next step. Each step performed correctly is scored as correct response, even if the learner erred on the previous steps.

Figure 20.3 Task analysis data sheet for single-opportunity assessment of inserting a hearing aid.

Task Analysis Assessment of Inserting a Hearing Aid
Instructional cue: "Put on your hearing aid"
Teacher: Christine
Assessment method: Single opportunity
Student: Tom

Step Behavior	Date 10/1	10/2	10/3	10/4
1 Open container	+	+	+	+
2 Remove harness	+	–	+	+
3 Arm 1/Strap 1	–	–	+	+
4 Arm 2/Strap 2	–	–	+	+
5 Harness over head	–	–	–	–
6 Fasten harness	–	–	–	–
7 Unsnap pocket	–	–	–	–
8 Remove aid from container	–	–	–	–
9 Insert aid into pocket	–	–	–	–
10 Snap pocket	–	–	–	–
11 Pick up earmold	–	–	–	–
12 Insert earmold into ear	–	–	–	–
13 Turn on aid	–	–	–	–
14 Set the control	–	–	–	–
Percentage of Steps Correct	14%	7%	28%	28%

Materials: Hearing aid container, harness, earmold
Response latency: 6 seconds
Recording key: + (correct) – (incorrect)
Criterion: 100% correct performance for 3 consecutive days

From "Teaching Severely Multihandicapped Students to Put on Their Own Hearing Aids," by D. J. Tucker & G. W. Berry, 1980, *Journal of Applied Behavior Analysis, 13,* p. 69. Copyright 1980 by the Society for the Experimental Analysis of Behavior, Inc. Adapted by permission.

Figure 20.4 Task analysis data sheet for multiple-opportunity assessment of inserting a hearing aid.

Task Analysis Assessment of Inserting a Hearing Aid
Instructional cue: "Put on your hearing aid"
Teacher: Marge
Assessment method: Multiple opportunity
Student: Kathy

| *Step Behavior* | *Date* | | | |
	10/1	10/2	10/3	10/4
1 Open container	−	+	+	+
2 Remove harness	+	−	+	+
3 Arm 1/Strap 1	+	−	+	+
4 Arm 2/Strap 2	−	−	+	+
5 Harness over head	+	−	+	−
6 Fasten harness	−	+	−	+
7 Unsnap pocket	+	−	+	+
8 Remove aid from container	+	−	−	+
9 Insert aid into pocket	+	+	−	+
10 Snap pocket	+	−	+	−
11 Pick up earmold	+	−	+	−
12 Insert earmold into ear	−	−	−	+
13 Turn on aid	−	−	−	−
14 Set the control	−	−	−	−
Percentage of Steps Correct	57%	21%	57%	64%

Materials: Hearing aid container, harness, earmold
Response latency: 6 seconds
Recording key: + (correct) − (incorrect)
Criterion: 100% correct performance for 3 consecutive days

From "Teaching Severely Multihandicapped Students to Put on Their Own Hearing Aids," by D. J. Tucker and G. W. Berry, 1980, *Journal of Applied Behavior Analysis, 13,* p. 69. Copyright 1980 by the Society for the Experimental Analysis of Behavior, Inc. Adapted by permission.

Figure 20.4 shows that Kathy, after receiving the instructional cue, did not perform the first step in the sequence (opening the container), so a minus was recorded. The teacher then opened the container and positioned Kathy in front of it. Kathy then removed the harness (Step 2) and placed her arm through the strap (Step 3), so a plus was recorded for each of these steps. Because 6 seconds passed before Step 4 was completed, the teacher performed the step for Kathy, scored a minus, and positioned her to do Step 5. Kathy then performed Step 5, and the rest of the assessment continued in this fashion.

The key to using the multiple-opportunity method for a task analysis assessment is to ensure that teaching is not commingled with assessment. That is, if the teacher physically guides or models the step, an accurate assessment cannot be obtained. Therefore, it is important that the teacher does not help the student do any step.

Single-opportunity and multiple-opportunity methods can both be effective ways to determine mastery of initial skills in a behavior chain. Of the two, the single-opportunity method is the more conservative measure because the assessment terminates at the first step at which performance breaks down. It also provides less information to the teacher once instruction is initiated; but it is probably quicker to conduct, especially if the task analysis is long, and it reduces the likelihood of learning taking place during assessment (Snell & Brown, 2006). The multiple-opportunity method takes more time to complete, but it provides the behavior analyst with more information. That is, the teacher could learn which steps in the task analysis the learner has already mastered, thus eliminating the need to instruct steps already in the learner's repertoire.

We have looked at two of the prerequisites for linking components of a chain: (a) conducting and validating a task analysis of the components of the behavioral sequence and (b) assessing the learner's pre-existing skill with each component in the chain. In the following section, we will address the third component: teaching the individual to perform each step of the chain in close temporal succession.

Behavior Chaining Methods

After the task analysis has been constructed and validated and the criterion for success and the data collection procedures have been determined, the next step is to decide which chaining procedure to use to teach the new sequence of behavior. The behavior analyst has four options: forward chaining, total-task chaining, backward chaining, and backward chaining with leap aheads.

Forward Chaining

In **forward chaining** the behaviors identified in the task analysis are taught in their naturally occurring order. Specifically, reinforcement is delivered when the predetermined criterion for the first behavior in the sequence is achieved. Thereafter, reinforcement is delivered for criterion completion of Steps 1 and 2. Each succeeding step requires the cumulative performance of all previous steps in the correct order.

For example, a child learning to tie her shoes according to the 14-step task analysis shown in Table 20.3 would be reinforced when the first step, "Pinch lace," is performed accurately three consecutive times. Next, reinforcement would be delivered when that step and the next one, "Pull lace," are performed to the same criterion. Then, "Hang lace ends from corresponding sides of shoe" would be added, and all three steps would have to be performed correctly before reinforcement is delivered. Ultimately, all 14 steps in the task analysis should be performed in a similar manner. However, at any given training step a variety of response prompting and other strategies may be employed to occasion the response.

Longer chains of behaviors can be broken down into smaller chains or skill clusters, each of which can be taught in a manner similar to that used with a single-response unit. When one skill cluster is mastered, it is linked to the next. The final response in the first skill cluster sets the occasion for the first response in the second skill cluster. Essentially, in this variation skill clusters become the analogue for units of behaviors, and these clusters are linked.

McWilliams and colleagues (1990) combined skill clusters in forward chaining to teach bedmaking skills to three students with developmental disabilities. Based on a task analysis of bedmaking responses (see Figure 20.2), five skill clusters were identified, each containing four to five subtasks. Once baseline was collected showing minimal accuracy with completing the entire chain in the presence of the cue, "Show me how to make the bed," an instructional procedure was chosen that involved teaching the clusters one at a time by breaking the complex behaviors into smaller chains (see Figure 20.5).

Initial training began with the teacher demonstrating the chain of tasks for Sections 1 and 2. Subsequent training involved teaching the prior section, the current section targeted for instruction, and the next section in the sequence. For example, if training was to be conducted on Section 2, Sections 1, 2, and 3 were demonstrated. Next, the students practiced the targeted sequences two to five times. When the sequence was performed correctly, praise was delivered. When an error occurred, a three-part correction procedure involving verbal redirection, redirection plus modeling, and/or physical guidance was initiated until the trial ended on a correct response. When the first skill cluster was mastered (S_1), the second skill cluster (S_2) was introduced, followed by the third (S_3), the fourth (S_4), and so forth.

The results indicated that the forward chaining procedure was effective in teaching the students bedmaking skills. That is, all the students were able to make their beds independently, or with only minimal assistance, when the teacher directed them to do so. Furthermore, all of them were able to make their beds in the generalization setting (i.e., the home).

The McWilliams and colleagues study (1990) illustrates two main advantages of forward chaining: (a) It can be used to link smaller chains into larger ones, and (b) it is relatively easy, so teachers are likely to use it in the classroom.

Our discussion thus far has focused on teaching behavior chains through direct teacher instruction. However, some evidence suggests that chained responses can also be learned through observation (Wolery, Ault, Gast, Doyle, & Griffen, 1991). Griffen, Wolery, and Schuster (1992) used a constant time delay (CTD) procedure to teach students with mental retardation a series of chains tasks food preparation behavior. During CTD with one student where the chained response was taught, two other students watched. Results showed that the two observing students learned at least 85% of the correct steps in the chain even though direct instruction on those steps had not occurred.

Total-Task Chaining

Total-task chaining (sometimes called *total-task presentation* or *whole-task presentation*) is a variation of forward chaining in which the learner receives training on each step in the task analysis during every session. Trainer assistance is provided with any step the person is unable to perform independently, and the chain is trained until the learner is able to perform all the behaviors in the sequence to the predetermined criterion. Depending on the complexity of the chain, the learner's repertoire, and available resources, physical assistance and/or graduated guidance may be incorporated.

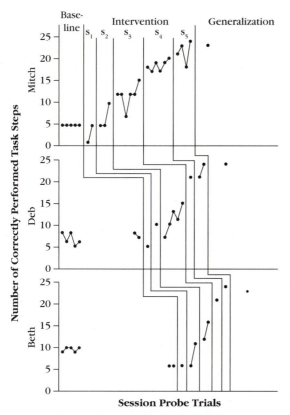

Figure 20.5 Number of correctly performed task steps across baseline, intervention, and generalization probe trials.

From "Teaching Complex Activities to Students with Moderate Handicaps Through the Forward Chaining of Shorter Total Cycle Response Sequences," by R. McWilliams, J. Nietupski, & S. Hamre-Nietupski, 1990, *Education and Training in Mental Retardation, 25,* p. 296. Copyright 1990 by the Council for Exceptional Children. Reprinted by permission.

Werts, Caldwell, and Wolery (1996) used peer models and total-task chaining to teach skills such as operating an audiotape, sharpening a pencil, and using a calculator to three elementary-level students with disabilities who were enrolled in general education classrooms. Response chains were individualized for each student based on teacher-recommended sequences that the students had to learn. Each session was divided into three parts: (a) The students with disabilities were probed on their ability to perform the total task response chain; (b) a peer model competent with the chain demonstrated the chain in its entirety while simultaneously describing each step; and (c) the student partner was probed again to determine performance of the chain. During the probes before and after peer modeling, the students with disabilities were directed to complete the chain. If a student was successful, a correct response was noted, but no feedback was delivered. If a student was unsuccessful, the student's view was blocked temporarily while the teacher completed that step in the chain, and then the student was

redirected to complete the remaining steps. Each behavior in the response chain was scored.

All three students learned to complete the response chain after peer modeling, and reached criterion on the response chain (100% correct for 2 out of 3 days) over the course of the study. The results for Charlie, one of the three students in the study, are shown in Figure 20.6.

Test and colleagues (1990) used total-task chaining with a least-to-most prompting procedure to teach two adolescents with severe mental retardation to use a public telephone. After identifying and validating a 17-step task analysis (see Table 20.2), baseline data were obtained by giving the students a 3 × 5 index card with their home phone number and two dimes, and directing them to "phone home." During training, a least-to-most prompting procedure consisting of three levels of prompts (verbal, verbal plus gesture, and verbal plus guidance) was implemented when errors occurred on any of the 17 steps that comprised the task analysis. Each instructional session consisted of two training trials followed by a probe to measure the number of independent steps completed. In addition, generalization probes were conducted in two other settings at least once per week.

Results showed that the combination of total-task chaining plus prompts increased the number of steps in the task analysis performed correctly by each student and that the skills generalized to two community-based settings (see Figure 20.7). Test and colleagues (1990) concluded that total-task chaining, especially as used within the context of a two-per-week training regimen, offered benefits to practitioners working with learners in community-based settings.

Backward Chaining

When a **backward chaining** procedure is used, all the behaviors identified in the task analysis are initially completed by the trainer, except for the final behavior in the chain. When the learner performs the final behavior in the sequence at the predetermined criterion level, reinforcement is delivered. Next, reinforcement is delivered when the last and the next-to-last behaviors in the sequence are performed to criterion. Subsequently, reinforcement is delivered when the last three behaviors are performed to criterion. This sequence proceeds backward through the chain until all the steps in the task analysis have been introduced in reverse order and practiced cumulatively.

Pierrel and Sherman (1963) conducted a classic demonstration of backward chaining at Brown University with a white rat named Barnabus. Pierrel and Sherman taught Barnabus to climb a spiral staircase, push down and cross a drawbridge, climb a ladder, pull a toy

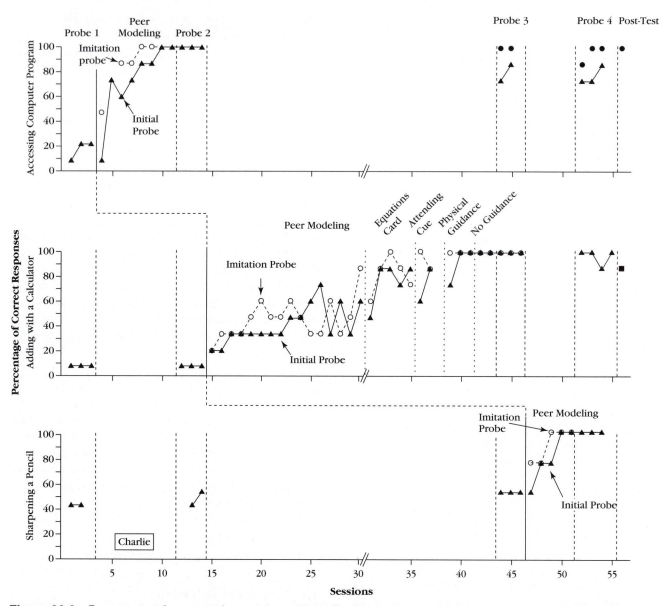

Figure 20.6 Percentage of steps performed correctly by Charlie for the three response chains. Triangles represent percentage of steps correct in initial probes; open circles represent percentage of steps correct in imitation probes.

From "Peer Modeling of Response Chains: Observational Learning by Students with Disabilities," by M. G. Werts, N. K. Caldwell, & M. Wolery, 1996, *Journal of Applied Behavior Analysis, 29*, p. 60. Copyright 1996 by the Society for the Experimental Analysis of Behavior, Inc. Reprinted by permission.

car by a chain, enter the car and pedal through a tunnel, climb a flight of stairs, run through an enclosed tube, enter an elevator, raise a miniature replica of the Brown University flag, exit the elevator, and finally press a bar for which he received a pellet of food. Barnabus became so famous for his performance of this elaborate sequence that he acquired the reputation of being "the rat with a college education." This chain of 11 responses was trained by initially conditioning the last response in the sequence (the bar press) in the presence of a buzzer sound, which was established as the S^D for the bar press. Then the next-to-last response in the sequence (exiting the elevator) was conditioned in

the presence of the elevator at the bottom of the shaft. Each response in the chain was added in turn so that a discrete stimulus served as the S^D for the next response and as the conditioned reinforcer for the preceding response.

To illustrate backward chaining with a classroom example, let us suppose that a preschool teacher wants to teach a student to tie his shoes. First, the teacher conducts a task analysis of shoe tying and puts the component behaviors in logical sequence.

1. Cross over laces on the shoe.

2. Tie a knot.

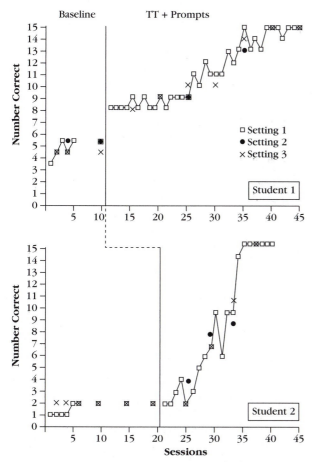

Figure 20.7 Number of correctly performed steps in the public-telephone task analysis by two students during baseline and total-task chaining (TT) plus response prompts. Data points for settings 2 and 3 show performance on generalization probes.

From "Teaching Adolescents with Severe Disabilities to Use the Public Telephone," by D. W. Test, F. Spooner, P. K. Keul, and T. A. Grossi, 1990, *Behavior Modification*, p. 165. Copyright 1990 by Sage Publications. Reprinted by permission.

3. Make a loop with the lace on the right side of the shoe, and hold it in the right hand.

4. With the left hand, wrap the other lace around the loop.

5. Use index or middle finger of the left hand to push the left lace through the opening between the laces.

6. Grasp both loops, one in each hand.

7. Draw the loops snug.

The teacher begins by training with the last step in the sequence, Step 7, until the student is able to complete it without mistakes for three consecutive trials. After each correct trial at Step 7, reinforcement is delivered. The teacher then introduces the next-to-last step, Step 6, and begins training the student to perform that step in conjunction with the student's performance of the final

step in the chain. Reinforcement is contingent on the successful performance of Steps 6 and 7. The teacher then introduces Step 5, making sure that the training step and all previously learned steps (i.e., Steps 5, 6, and 7) are executed in the proper sequence prior to reinforcement. The teacher can use supplemental response prompts to evoke correct responding on behavior at any step. However, any supplemental response prompts—verbal, pictorial, demonstration, or physical—introduced during training must be faded later in the program so that the student's behavior comes under stimulus control of the naturally occurring S^Ds. In brief, when using a backward chaining procedure, the system of task analysis is arranged in reverse order and the last step is trained first.

With backward chaining, the first behavior the learner performs independently produces the terminal reinforcement: The shoe is tied. The next-to-last response produces the onset of a stimulus condition that reinforces that step and serves as an S^D for the last behavior, which is now established in the learner's behavioral repertoire. This reinforcing sequence is repeated for the remainder of the steps.

Hagopian, Farrell, and Amari (1996) combined backward chaining with fading to reduce the life-threatening behavior of Josh, a 12-year-old male with autism and mental retardation. Because of medical complications associated with a variety of gastrointestinal factors, frequent vomiting, and constipation during the 6 months prior to the study, Josh refused to ingest any food or liquids by mouth. Indeed, when he did ingest food by mouth previously, he expelled it.

Over the 70-day course of Josh's treatment program, data were collected on liquid acceptance, expulsions, swallows, and avoidance of the target behavior: drinking water from a cup. After baseline was collected on Josh's ability to swallow 10 cc of water, a swallow condition without water was implemented. Basically, an empty syringe was placed and depressed in his mouth, and he was directed to swallow. Next, the syringe was filled with a small volume of water, and reinforcement delivered when Josh swallowed the water. In subsequent phases, the volume of water in the syringe was gradually increased from 0.2 cc to 0.5 cc to 1 cc, and ultimately to 3 cc. To earn reinforcement in subsequent conditions, Josh had to emit the target chain using at first 3 cc of water from a cup to ultimately 30 cc of water. At the end of the study, a successful generalization probe was implemented with 90 cc of a mixture of water and juice. The results showed that the chaining procedure improved Josh's ability to emit the target chain (see Figure 20.8). Hagopian and colleagues explained their procedure this way:

> We began by targeting a preexisting response (swallowing), which was the third and final response in the chain of behaviors that constitute drinking from a cup. Next,

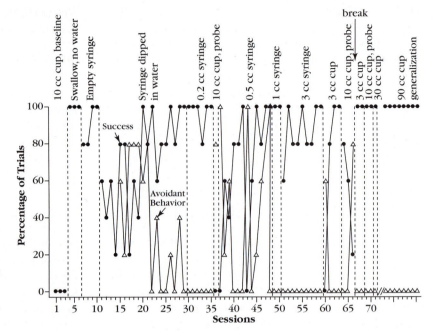

Figure 20.8 Percentage of trials with successful drinking and trials with avoidance behaviors.

From "Treating Total Liquid Refusal with Backward Chaining and Fading," by L. P. Hagopian, D. A. Farrell, & A. Amari, 1996, *Journal of Applied Behavior Analysis, 29,* p. 575. Copyright 1996 by the Society for the Experimental Analysis of Behavior, Inc. Used with permission.

reinforcement was delivered for the last two responses in the chain (accepting and swallowing). Finally, reinforcement was delivered only when all three responses in the chain occurred. (p. 575)

A primary advantage of backward chaining is that on every instructional the learner comes into contact with the terminal reinforcer for the chain. As a direct outcome of reinforcement, the stimulus that is present at the time of reinforcement increases its discriminative properties. Further, the repeated reinforcement of all behaviors in the chain increases the discriminative capability of all the stimuli associated with these behaviors and with the reinforcer. The main disadvantage of backward chaining is that the potential passive participation of the learner in earlier steps in the chain may limit the total number of responses made during any given training session.

Backward Chaining with Leap Aheads

Spooner, Spooner, and Ulicny (1986) reported the use of a variation of backward chaining they called backward chaining with leap aheads. **Backward chaining with leap aheads** follows essentially the same procedures as backward chaining, except that not every step in the task analysis is trained. Some steps are simply probed. The purpose of the leap-aheads modification is to decrease total training time needed to learn the chain. With conventional backward chaining, the stepwise repetition of the behaviors in the sequence may slow down the learning process, especially when the learner has thoroughly mastered some of the steps in the chain. For instance, in the previous shoe-tying illustration, the child

might perform Step 7, the last behavior in the sequence, and then leap ahead to Step 4 because Steps 5 and 6 are in her repertoire. It is important to remember, however, that the learner must still perform Steps 5 and 6 correctly and in sequence with the other steps to receive reinforcement.

Forward, Total-Task, or Backward Chaining: Which to Use?

Forward chaining, total-task chaining, and backward chaining have each been shown to be effective with a wide range of self-care, vocational, and independent-living behaviors. Which chaining procedure should be the method of first choice? Research conducted to date does not suggest a clear answer. After examining evidence reported between 1980 and 2001, Kazdin (2001) concluded: "Direct comparisons have not established that one [forward chaining, backward chaining, or total-task chaining] is consistently more effective than the other" (p. 49).

Although overwhelming conclusive data do not favor one chaining method over another, anecdotal evidence and logical analysis suggest that total-task chaining may be appropriate when the student (a) can perform many of the tasks in the chain, but needs to learn them in sequence; (b) has an imitative repertoire; (c) has moderate to severe disabilities (Test et al., 1990); and/or (d) when the task sequence or cycle is not very long or complex (Miltenberger, 2001).

The uncertainty about which approach to follow may be minimized by conducting a personalized task analysis for the learner, systematically applying the single- or multiple-opportunity method to determine the starting point for instruction, relying on empirically sound data-based studies in the literature, and collecting evaluation data on the approach to determine its efficacy for that person.

Interrupting and Breaking Behavior Chains

Our discussion thus far has focused on procedures for building behavior chains. As we have seen, chaining has been used successfully to increase and improve the repertoires of a wide range of people and across a variety of tasks. Still, simply knowing how to link behavior to behavior is not always sufficient for practitioners. In some situations, knowing how a behavior chain works can be used to interrupt the execution of an existing chain (e.g., making toast) to advance a different response class of skills (e.g., a speech skill). Further, because some chains are inappropriate (e.g., excessive consumption of food), knowing how to break an inappropriate behavior chain can achieve positive results (e.g., the person eats an appropriate amount of food and stops eating at that point).

Behavior Chain Interruption Strategy

The **behavior chain interruption strategy (BCIS)** relies on the participant's skill to perform the critical elements of a chain independently, but the chain is interrupted at a predetermined step so that another behavior can be emitted. Initially developed to increase speech and oral responding (Goetz, Gee, & Sailor, 1985; Hunt & Goetz, 1988), the BCIS has been extended into pictorial communication systems (Roberts-Pennell & Sigafoos, 1999), manual signing (Romer, Cullinan, & Schoenberg, 1994), and switch activation (Gee, Graham, Goetz, Oshima, & Yoshioka, 1991).

The BCIS works as follows. First, an assessment is conducted to determine if the person can independently complete a chain of three or more components. Figure 20.9 shows an example of how a toast-making chain, divided into five steps, was assessed across degrees of distress and attempts to complete when specific steps were blocked or interrupted by an observer. Degree of distress was ranked on a 3-point scale, and attempts were registered using a dichotomous scale (i.e., yes or no). The assessment yielded a mean distress ranking of 2.3 and a total percentage of attempts (66%).

With respect to using BCIS in applied settings to increase behavior, a chain is selected for training based on

Figure 20.9 Sample score sheet used to evaluate chains.

Chain Pretesting

Student's Name: Chuck — Chain: making toast

Date: 5/2 — *interrupt at start of step

Sequence of steps	Degree of distress	Attempts to complete	Comments
1. Pull bread from bag*	1 (low) (2) 3 (high)	yes (no)	
2. Put in toaster	1 2 3	yes no	
3. Push down*	1 (2) 3	(yes) no	tries to touch knob
4. Take toast out	1 2 3	yes no	
5. Put on plate*	1 2 (3)	(yes) no	very upset; self-abusive

$\bar{x}$ distress: $\frac{7}{3} = 2.3$ — Total 2/3 = 66%

From "Using a Chain Interruption Strategy to Teach Communication Skills to Students with Severe Disabilities," by L. Goetz, K. Gee, & W. Sailor, *Journal of the Association of Persons with Severe Handicaps, 13* (1), p. 24. Copyright by the Association for Persons with Severe Handicaps. Used by permission.

it being moderately distressful for the individual when she is interrupted while performing the chain, but not so distressful that the person's behavior becomes episodic or self-injurious. After collecting baseline on a target behavior (e.g., vocalizations), the person is directed to start the chain (e.g., "Make toast"). At a predetermined step in the chain—say, Step 3 (push down)—the individual's ability to complete the chain is restricted. For example, the practitioner might momentarily and passively block access to the toaster. The person would then be prompted, "What do you want?" A vocalization would be required for the chain to be completed. That is, the person would have to make a response such as saying, "Push down."

Although the exact behavioral mechanisms responsible for improved performance as a result of using BCIS have not been pinpointed, field-based research efforts, including those examining generalized outcomes (Grunsell & Carter, 2002), have established it as an efficacious approach, especially for persons with severe disabilities. For example, Carter and Grunsell's (2001) review of the literature on the efficacy of BCIS shows that it is positive and beneficial. In their view,

> The BCIS may be seen as empirically supported and complementary to other naturalistic techniques. . . . A small, but growing body of research literature has demonstrated that individuals with severe disabilities have acquired requesting with the BCIS. In addition, research demonstrates that implementation of the BCIS may increase the rate of requesting. (p. 48)

The assumption underlying BCIS assessment is that "persistence in task completion and emotional response to the interruption would serve as operational definitions of high motivation for task completion" (Goetz et al., 1985, p. 23). It could also be claimed that the interruption, because it momentarily detains the learner from obtaining the reinforcer for completing the task, and serves as a blocked establishing operation, a condition that exists when a reinforcer cannot be obtained without some other additional action or behavior occurring (see Chapter 16). Further, the role that negative reinforcement plays in BCIS and the systematic environmental change that occurs at the point of the interruption have not been fully analyzed to determine their relative contributions.

According to Carter and Grunell (2001), the BCIS consists of several components and features that make it useful as a behavior change tactic in natural settings. Figure 20.10 provides a review of these key features.

Breaking an Inappropriate Chain

An inappropriate behavior chain (e.g., nail biting, smoking, excessive food consumption) can be broken by determining the initial S^D and substituting an S^D for an alternative behavior, or by extending the chain and building in time delays. Given that the first S^D in a chain evokes for the first response, which in turn terminates that S^D and produces the second S^D, and so on throughout the chain. If the first S^D appears less frequently, the entire chain occurs less often. Martin and Pear (2003) suggested that a behavior chain that reinforces excessive food consumption, for example, might be broken by introducing links that require the individual to place the eating utensil on the table between bites or introducing a 3- to 5-second time delay before the next bite can be initiated. In their view, "In the undesirable chain, the person gets ready to consume the next mouthful before even finishing the present one. A more desirable chain separates these components and introduces brief delays" (p. 143).

Figure 20.10 Key components and features of the BCIS.

- Instruction begins in the middle of the chain sequence, not the start, differing from forward and backward chaining procedures. Because the instruction begins in the middle of the sequence, interrupting the sequence might function as a transitive conditioned motivating operation or negative reinforcer, the removal of which increases behavior.
- Procedurally, the BCIS is predicated on an assessment that verifies that the person is able to complete the chain independently, but experiences moderate distress when the chain is interrupted in the middle of the sequence.
- Verbal prompts are used at the point of interruption (e.g., "What do you want?"), but a full range of response prompts—modeling and physical guidance—has also been employed.
- Interruption training occurs in the natural setting (e.g., a water basin for washing hair; the microwave oven for making cookies).
- Maintenance, generalization, and social validity data, although not overwhelmingly evident in every study, are sufficiently robust to suggest that the BCIS be included with other interventions (e.g., mand-model, time delay, and incidental teaching).

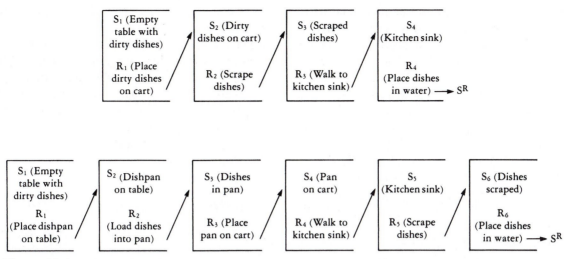

Figure 20.11 Illustration of an original behavior chain (upper panel) and its revision (lower panel) to break an inappropriate response sequence.

With respect to separating chain components, let us consider the case of a restaurant trainee with moderate mental retardation who has been taught to bus tables. Upon completion of the training program, the trainee was able to perform each of the necessary behaviors in the table-bussing chain accurately and proficiently (see Figure 20.11, upper panel). However, on the job site, the new employee started to emit an inappropriate sequence of behaviors. Specifically, in the presence of the dirty dishes on the empty table, the individual scraped excess food scraps onto the table itself, instead of placing the dirty items on the food cart. In other words, the initial S^D for the table-bussing chain, the empty table with the dirty plates, was setting the occasion for a response (dish scraping) that should have occurred later in the chain. To break this inappropriate chain, the behavior analyst should consider several possible sources of difficulty, including (a) reexamining the S^Ds and responses, (b) determining whether similar S^Ds cue different responses, (c) analyzing the job setting to identify relevant and irrelevant S^Ds, (d) determining whether S^Ds in the job setting differ from training S^Ds, and (e) identifying the presence of novel stimuli in the environment.

Reexamine the S^Ds and Responses

The purpose of reexamining the list of S^Ds and responses in the task analysis is to determine whether the original chain of associated responses they evoke is arbitrary, based primarily on expert opinion, time and motion studies, and practical efficiency. In our example, the trainer wants the presence of the dirty dishes on the empty table to evoke the response of placing those dishes in the bus cart. Consequently, a rearranged chain of S^Ds and responses was trained (see Figure 20.11, lower panel).

Determine Whether Similar S^Ds Cue Different Responses

Figure 20.11 (upper panel) shows two similar S^Ds—dirty dishes on the empty table and dirty dishes on the cart—which might have contributed to the scraping of food onto the table. In other words, R_2 (scrape dishes) might have come under the control of S_1 (dirty dishes on table). Figure 20.11 (lower panel) shows how the behavior analyst corrected the sequence by rearranging the S^Ds and their associated responses. Scraping the dishes is now the fifth response in the chain and occurs at the kitchen sink, an area away from the restaurant tables and diners. Thus, any potential confusion would be reduced or eliminated.

Analyze the Natural Setting to Identify Relevant and Irrelevant S^Ds

The training program should be designed so that the learner is trained to discriminate the relevant (i.e., critical) components of a stimulus from the irrelevant variations. Figure 20.11 (lower panel) shows at least two relevant characteristics of S_1: an empty table and the presence of dirty dishes on that table. An irrelevant stimulus might be the location of the table in the restaurant, the number of place settings on the table, or the arrangement of the place settings. A relevant characteristic of S_5, presence of the kitchen sink, would be water faucets, the sink configuration, or dirty dishes. Finally, irrelevant stimuli might be the size of the kitchen sink and the type or style of faucets.

Determine Whether S^Ds in the Natural Setting Differ from Training S^Ds

It is possible that some variations of the S^Ds cannot be taught during training phases. For this reason many authors recommend conducting the final training sessions in the natural setting where the behavior chain is expected to be performed. This allows any differences that exist to be recognized by the trainer, and subsequent discrimination training to be further refined on site.

Identify the Presence of Novel Stimuli in the Environment

The presence of a novel stimulus unexpected in the original training situation can also prompt the occurrence of an inappropriate chain. In the restaurant example, the presence of a crowd of customers might set the occasion for the chain to be performed out of sequence. Likewise, distracting stimuli (e.g., customers coming and going, tips left on the table) might set the occasion for an inappropriate chain. Also, a coworker might unwittingly give contradictory instructions to the trainee. In any of these situations, the novel stimuli should be identified and the learner taught to discriminate them along with other S^Ds in the environment.

Factors Affecting the Performance of a Behavior Chain

Several factors affect the performance of a behavior chain. The following sections outline these factors and provide recommendations for addressing them.

Completeness of the Task Analysis

The more complete and accurate the task analysis is, the more likely a person will be to progress through the sequence efficaciously. If the elements making up the chain are not sequenced appropriately, or if the corresponding S^Ds are not identified for each response, learning the chain will be more difficult.

The behavior analyst should remember two key points when attempting to develop an accurate task analysis. First, planning must occur before training. The time

devoted to constructing and validating the task analysis is well spent. Second, after the task analysis is constructed, training should begin with the expectation that adjustments in the task analysis, or the use of more intrusive prompts may be needed at various steps in the task analysis. For example, McWilliams and colleagues (1990) noted that one of their students required extensive trials and more intrusive prompts with some steps in the task analysis before improved performance was obtained.

Length or Complexity of the Chain

Longer or more complex behavior chains take more time to learn than shorter or less complex behavior chains. Likewise, the behavior analyst might expect training time to be longer if two or more chains are linked.

Schedule of Reinforcement

When a reinforcer is presented subsequent to the performance of a behavior in a chain, it affects each of the responses making up the chain. However, the effect on each response is not identical. For example, in backward chaining, responses performed at the end of the chain are strengthened faster than responses made earlier in the chain because they are reinforced more frequently. The behavior analyst is advised to remember two points: (a) A chain can be maintained if an appropriate schedule of reinforcement is used (see Chapter 13), and (b) the number of responses in a chain may need to be considered when defining the schedule of reinforcement.

Stimulus Variation

Bellamy, Horner, and Inman (1979) provided an excellent pictorial representation of how stimulus variation affects the performance of a chain. The upper photograph in Figure 20.12 shows a cam switch bearing before and after its placement on a cam switch axle. The lower photograph shows the four different types of bearings that can be used in the assembly process. The response of placing the bearing on the axle must be under the control of the presence of the bearing (S^D); however, variation among bearings requires that the response be under the control of several S^Ds, each sharing a critical feature. In the illustration each bearing has a 1.12-cm hole in the center and one or more hex nut slots on a face of the bearing. Any bearing with these stimulus features should evoke the response of placing the bearing on the axle, even if other irrelevant dimensions

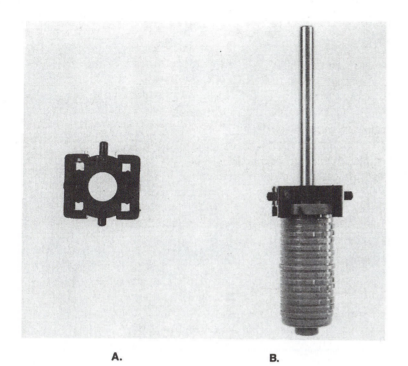

A.   B.

A cam switch bearing before and after placement on a cam switch axle.

Figure 20.12   Upper panel: A cam switch bearing before and after placement on a cam switch axle. Lower panel: Four different types of bearings used in cam switch assembly.

From Vocational Habilitation of Severely Retarded Adults, pp. 40 & 42, by G. T. Bellamy, R. H. Horner, and D. P. Inman, 1979, Austin, TX: PRO-ED. Copyright 1979 by PRO-ED. Reprinted by permission.

are present (e.g., color, material composition, weight). Stimuli without these features should not occasion the response.

If possible, the behavior analyst should introduce all possible variations of the S^D that the learner will encounter. Regardless of the behavior chain, presentation of stimulus variations increases the probability that the correct response will occur in their presence. This includes, for example, in an assembly task, various canisters, and shafts; with dressing skills, different fasteners, zippers, and buttons; and with tooth brushing, assorted tubes and pumps.

Response Variation

Often when stimulus variations occur, response variation also must occur to produce the same effect. Again,

Bellamy and colleagues (1979) provided an illustration with the cam shaft assembly. In the upper-left photograph of Figure 20.13, the bearing has been placed on the cam shaft, and the retaining clip is being positioned for placement with a pair of nose pliers. The upper-right photograph shows the clip in position. The lower-left photograph shows a different bearing configuration (i.e., the S^D is different) requiring a different response. Instead of the retaining clip being lifted over the bearing cap with pliers, it must be pushed over the cap with a wrench-type tool. The response of lifting or pushing has changed, as has the response of selecting the appropriate tool. Thus, the behavior analyst should be aware that when stimulus variation is introduced, training or retraining of responses within the chain might also be required.

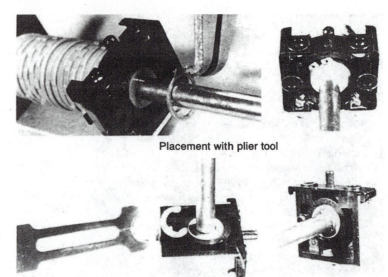

Placement with plier tool

Placement with push tool

Figure 20.13   Two ways that retaining rings are applied to affix bearings to cam axles.

From *Vocational Habilitation of Severely Retarded Adults,* p. 44, by G. T. Bellamy, R. H. Horner, and D. P. Inman, 1979, Austin, TX: PRO-ED. Copyright 1979 by PRO-ED. Reprinted by permission.

 **Summary**

Definition of a Behavior Chain

1. A behavior chain is a specific sequence of discrete responses, each associated with a particular stimulus condition. Each discrete response and the associated stimulus condition serve as an individual component of the chain. When individual components are linked together, the result is a behavior chain that produces a terminal outcome.

2. Each stimulus that links two sequential responses in a chain serves dual functions: It is a conditioned reinforcer for the response that produced it and an S[D] for the next response in the chain.

3. In a behavior chain with a limited hold, a sequence of behaviors must be performed correctly and within a specific time for reinforcement to be delivered. Proficient responding is a distinguishing features of chains with limited holds.

Rationale for Using Chaining

4. Three reasons a behavior analyst should be skilled in building behavior chains: (a) chains can be used to improve independent-living skills; (b) chains can provide the means by which other behaviors are combined into more complex sequences; and (c) chains can be combined with other procedures to build behavioral repertoires in generalized settings.

5. Chaining refers to the way these specific sequences of stimuli and responses are linked to form new performances. In forward chaining, behaviors are linked together beginning with the *first* behavior in the sequence. In backward chaining, the behaviors are linked together beginning with the *last* behavior in the sequence.

Task Analysis

6. Task analysis involves breaking a complex skill into smaller, teachable units, the product of which is a series of sequentially ordered steps or tasks.

7. The purpose of constructing and validating a task analysis is to determine the sequence of stepwise critical behaviors that comprise the complete task and that would lead to it being performed efficiently. Task analyses can be constructed by observing a competent person perform the task, consulting experts, and self-performing the sequence.

8. The purpose of assessing mastery level is to determine which components of the task analysis can already be performed independently. Assessment can be conducted with the single-opportunity or multiple-opportunity method.

Behavior Chaining Methods

9. In forward chaining, the behaviors identified in the task analysis are taught in their natural sequence. Specifically, reinforcement is delivered when the predetermined criterion for the first behavior in the sequence is achieved. Thereafter, reinforcement is delivered for criterion completion of Steps 1 and 2. With each successive step, reinforcement is delivered contingent on the correct performance of all steps trained thus far.

10. Total-task chaining is a variation of forward chaining in which the learner receives training on each step in the task analysis during every session. Trainer assistance is provided using response prompts with any step that the individual is not able to perform. The chain is trained until the learner performs all the behaviors in the sequence to criterion.

11. In backward chaining, all the steps identified in the task analysis are completed by the trainer, except the last one. When the final step in the sequence is performed to criterion, reinforcement is delivered. Next, reinforcement is delivered when the next-to-last step and the last step are performed. Subsequently, the individual must perform the last three steps before reinforcement is delivered, and so on. The primary advantage of backward chaining is that the learner comes into contact with the contingencies of reinforcement immediately, and the functional relationship begins to develop.

12. Backward chaining with leap aheads follows essentially the same procedures as in backward chaining, except that not every step in the task analysis is trained. The leap-aheads modification provides for probing or assessing untrained behaviors in the sequence. Its purpose is to speed up training of the behavior chain.

13. The decision to use forward chaining, total-task chaining, or backward chaining should be based on the results of a task analysis assessment, empirically sound data-based studies, and a functional evaluation, taking into consideration the cognitive, physical, and motoric abilities and needs of the individual.

Interrupting and Breaking Behavior Chains

14. The behavior chain interruption strategy (BCIS) is an intervention that relies on the participant's skill in performing the critical elements of a chain independently, but the chain is interrupted at a predetermined step so that another behavior can be emitted.

15. An inappropriate chain can be broken if the initial S^D that sets the occasion for the first behavior in the chain is recognized and an alternative S^D is substituted. Alternative S^Ds can be determined by reexamining the list of S^Ds and responses in the task analysis, determining whether similar S^Ds cue different responses, analyzing the natural setting to identify relevant and irrelevant S^Ds, determining whether the S^Ds in the natural setting differ from training S^Ds, and/or identifying the presence of novel S^Ds in the environment.

Factors Affecting the Performance of a Behavior Chain

16. Factors affecting the performance of a behavior chain include: (a) completeness of the task analysis, (b) length or complexity of the chain, (c) schedule of reinforcement, (d) stimulus variation, and (e) response variation.

PART 8

Decreasing Behavior
with Nonpunishment Procedures

Part 8 describes nonpunishment interventions to decrease or eliminate problem behaviors. In Chapter 21, Extinction, we provide extinction procedures for problem behaviors linked to behavior maintained by positive reinforcement, negative reinforcement, and automatic reinforcement. This chapter includes sections on extinction effects, variables affecting resistance to extinction, and guidelines for using extinction effectively. Chapter 22, Differential Reinforcement, introduces the four most frequently researched variations of differential reinforcement for decreasing problem behavior: differential reinforcement of (a) incompatible behavior, (b) alternative behavior, (c) other behavior, and (d) low rates of responding. Examples of applications and guidelines for the effective use of each of these differential reinforcement procedures are provided. Chapter 23, Antecedent Interventions, defines, gives examples of, and offers guidelines for using three antecedent interventions for problem behavior: noncontingent reinforcement, high-probability request sequence, and functional communication training.

CHAPTER 21

Extinction

Key Terms

escape extinction
extinction (operant)

extinction burst
resistance to extinction

sensory extinction
spontaneous recovery

Behavior Analyst Certification Board® BCBA® & BCABA®
Behavior Analyst Task List,© Third Edition

Content Area 3: Principles, Processes and Concepts	
3-11	Define and provide examples of extinction.
Content Area 9: Behavior Change Procedures	
9-4	Use extinction:
(a)	Identify possible reinforcers maintaining behavior and use extinction.
(b)	State and plan for the possible unwanted effects of the use of extinction.

This chapter describes how to reduce the frequency of a previously reinforced behavior by withholding reinforcement, a principle known as *extinction.* Extinction as a procedure provides zero probability of reinforcement. It is also a behavioral process of a diminishing rate of response. Practitioners have applied this principle of behavior effectively in a wide variety of settings, such as homes, schools, and institutions, and with diverse problem behaviors ranging from severe self-destruction to mild disruptions. However, the effectiveness of extinction in an applied setting depends primarily on the identification of reinforcing consequences and consistent application of the procedure. Extinction does not require the application of aversive stimuli to decrease behavior; it does not provide verbal or physical models of punishers directed toward others. Extinction simply requires the withholding of reinforcers. This chapter defines extinction and describes procedures for applying extinction. Additionally, it discusses extinction behavior and resistance to extinction. Although extinction appears to be a simple process, its application in applied settings can be difficult.

Definition of Extinction

Extinction as a procedure occurs when reinforcement of a previously reinforced behavior is discontinued; as a result, the frequency of that behavior decreases in the future.[1] To restate this principle: Keller and Schoenfeld (1950/1995) defined extinction this way; "Conditioned operants are extinguished by severing the relation between the act and the effect. . . . The principle of Type R [operant] extinction may be put as follows: The strength of a conditioned operant may be diminished by withholding its reinforcement" (pp. 70–71). Similarly, Skinner (1953) wrote, "When reinforcement is no longer forthcoming, a response becomes less and less frequent in what is called 'operant extinction'" (p. 69).

DeShawna, a third-grade student, frequently interrupted her teacher when he instructed other students. It appeared that DeShawna tried to direct the teacher's attention from the other students to herself. The teacher always responded to DeShawna's interruptions by answering her questions, asking her to return to her seat, telling her not to interrupt him while he worked with the other students, or explaining that she needed to wait for her turn. DeShawna usually agreed that she would not interrupt her teacher, but her annoying interruptions did not

stop. The teacher knew that DeShawna interrupted his instruction to get his attention. Since telling DeShawna not to interrupt him at certain times did not work, the teacher decided to try ignoring her interruptions. DeShawna stopped interrupting her teacher after 4 days during which her interruptions produced no teacher attention.

In this example, student interruptions (i.e., the problem behavior) were maintained by teacher attention (i.e., the reinforcer). The teacher applied the extinction procedure by ignoring DeShawna's interruptions, and the procedure produced a decrease in the frequency of the interruptions. Note that the extinction procedure does not prevent occurrences of a problem behavior (e.g., the interruptions). Rather, the environment is changed so that the problem behavior no longer produces reinforcement (e.g., teacher attention).

Procedural and Functional Forms of Extinction

The use of functional behavior assessments (see Chapter 24) have enabled applied behavior analysts to distinguish clearly between the procedural variations of extinction (ignoring) and the functional variations of extinction (withholding maintaining reinforcers). This clarification between procedural and functional variations of extinction has led to more effective treatments (Lerman & Iwata, 1996a).

Historically, some applied behavior analysts have emphasized the procedural form of extinction (e.g., just ignore the problem behavior and it will go away) rather than the functional form (i.e., withholding the maintaining reinforcers). Applications of the procedural form of extinction are often ineffective. Functional behavior assessments enabled applied behavior analysts to distinguish clearly between the procedural (ignoring) and the functional forms of extinction (withholding maintaining reinforcers), and as an outcome, may have increased research in using basic extinction procedures in applied settings. When the extinction procedure is matched to the behavioral function, the intervention is usually effective.

Extinction: Misuses of a Technical Term

With the possible exception of *negative reinforcement, extinction* is perhaps the most misunderstood and misused technical term in applied behavior analysis. *Extinction* is a technical term that applied behavior analysts should use only to identify the procedure of withholding reinforcers that maintain behavior. Four common misuses of the technical term are presented in the following sections.

---

[1] The term *extinction* is also used with respondent conditioned reflexes (see Chapter 2). Presenting a conditioned stimulus (CS) again and again without the unconditioned stimulus until the CS no longer elicits the conditioned response is called *respondent extinction.*

Using Extinction to Refer to Any Decrease in Behavior

Some use the term *extinction* when referring to any decrease in responding, regardless of what produced the behavior change. For example, if a person's responding decreased as a result of punishment such as time-out from reinforcement or a physical restriction of the behavior, a statement such as "the behavior is extinguishing" is misleading and incorrect in a technical sense. Labeling any reduction in behavior that reaches a zero rate of occurrence as extinction is another common misuse of this technical term.

Confusing Forgetting and Extinction

A misuse of the term *extinction* occurs when the speaker confuses extinction with forgetting. In forgetting, a behavior is weakened by the passage of time during which the person does not have an opportunity to emit the behavior. In extinction, behavior is weakened because it does not produce reinforcement.

Confusing Response Blocking and Sensory Extinction

Applied behavior analysts have used goggles, gloves, helmets, and wrist weights to *block* the occurrence of responses maintained by automatic reinforcement, rather than masking the sensory stimulation. The applications of response blocking to reduce problem behaviors appear similar to sensory extinction. Response blocking, however, is not an extinction procedure. With all extinction procedures, including sensory consequences, the persons can emit the problem behavior, but that behavior will not produce reinforcement. By contrast, response blocking prevents the occurrence of the target behavior (Lerman & Iwata, 1996).

Confusing Noncontingent Reinforcement and Extinction

Two definitions of extinction now appear in the applied behavior analysis literature. Each definition uses a different procedure to diminish behavior. We use one definition for extinction throughout this chapter (i.e., Keller & Schoenfeld, 1950/1995; Skinner 1953). It is the definition most associated with the principle of behavior called extinction. This definition of extinction has served the experimental analysis of behavior and applied behavior analysis well for many years.

The procedure for the second definition does not withhold the reinforcers that maintain the problem behavior. It presents those reinforcers noncontingently

(NCR), meaning that the applied behavior analyst delivers stimuli with known reinforcing properties to an individual on a fixed-time or variable-time schedule completely independent of responding (see Chapter 23).

NCR provides an important and effective intervention for diminishing problem behaviors, but NCR operates on behavior in a different way than does the principle of extinction. Extinction diminishes behavior by changing consequence stimuli; NCR diminishes behavior by changing antecedent stimuli. Although both procedures produce a decrease in behavior, the behavioral effects result from different controlling variables. Using an established technical term to describe effects produced by two different procedures is confusing.

Extinction Procedures

Specifically, procedures for extinction take three distinct forms that are linked to behavior maintained by positive reinforcement,[2] negative reinforcement, and automatic reinforcement.

Extinction of Behavior Maintained by Positive Reinforcement

Behaviors maintained by positive reinforcement are placed on extinction when those behaviors do not produce the reinforcer. Williams (1959) in a classic study described the effects of the removal of positive reinforcement (extinction) on the tyrant-like behavior of a 21-month-old boy. The child had been seriously ill for the first 18 months of his life but had completely recovered when the study began. The boy demanded special attention from his parents, especially at bedtime, and responded with temper tantrums (e.g., screaming, fussing, crying) when his parents did not provide the attention. A parent spent ½ to 2 hours each bedtime waiting in the bedroom until the boy went to sleep.

Although Williams did not speculate about how the tantrums developed, a likely explanation is not difficult to imagine. Because the child had been seriously ill for much of his first 18 months, crying had been his signal that he was experiencing discomfort or pain or needed help. In effect, his crying may have been reinforced by his parents' attention. Crying became a high-frequency behavior during the extended illness and continued after the child's health improved. The parents probably realized

---

[2]Extinction linked to behaviors maintained by positive reinforcement is often called *attention extinction* in the applied behavior analysis literature, especially in the functional behavior assessment (FBA) literature in which reinforcement by social attention is one of the conditions or hypotheses explored by FBA.

eventually that their child cried at bedtime to gain their attention and tried to ignore the crying. The crying increased in intensity and emotion when they did not stay in the room. As the days and weeks went by, the child's demand for absolute attention at bedtime grew worse. The parents probably decided again not to stay with the child at bedtime; but the intensity of the crying increased, and some new tantrum behaviors occurred. The parents returned to the room and, by giving in to the tantrums, taught their child to behave like a tyrant.

After 3 months of the tyrant-like behavior, the parents decided that they must do something about their child's tantrums. It appeared that parental attention maintained the tantrums; therefore, they planned to apply the principle of extinction. The parents, in a leisurely and relaxed manner, put the child to bed, left the bedroom, and closed the door. The parents recorded the duration of screaming and crying from the moment the door was closed.

Figure 21.1 shows the duration of the tantrums during extinction. The child had a tantrum for 45 minutes the first time he was put to bed without his parents staying in the room. The tantrums gradually decreased until the 10th session, when the child "no longer whimpered, fussed, or cried when the parents left the room. Rather, he smiled as they left. The parents reported that their child made happy sounds until he dropped off to sleep" (Williams, 1959, p. 269).

No tantrums occurred for approximately 1 week, but they resumed after his aunt put him to bed. When the

child started to tantrum, the aunt returned to the bedroom and stayed with the child until he went to sleep. Tantrums then returned to the previous high level and had to be decreased a second time.

Figure 21.1 also shows the duration of tantrums for the 10 days following the aunt's intervention. The data curve is similar to that of the first removal of parent attention. The duration of the tantrums was somewhat greater during the second removal, but reached zero by the ninth session. Williams reported that the child had no further bedtime tantrums during 2 years of follow-up.

Extinction of Behavior Maintained by Negative Reinforcement

Behaviors maintained by negative reinforcement are placed on extinction (a.k.a., **escape extinction**) when those behaviors do not produce a removal of the aversive stimulus, meaning that the person cannot escape from the aversive situation. Anderson and Long (2002) and Dawson and colleagues (2003) provided excellent examples of using escape extinction as a behavioral intervention.

Anderson and Long (2002) provided treatment to reduce the problem behaviors of Drew, an 8-year-old boy with autism and moderate to severe retardation. Drew's problem behaviors consisted of self-injurious behavior (SIB), aggression, and disruptions. Anderson and Long completed a functional behavior assessment, and then hypothesized that escape from task situations maintained the problem behaviors. Based on this hypothesis, the speech therapist used escape extinction to diminish the problem behaviors that occurred while Drew worked on match-to-sample and receptive language tasks. These tasks evoked the highest rates of problem behavior. The speech therapist provided instructional prompts during the tasks. When Drew emitted problem behaviors following the instructional prompt, the speech therapist physically guided him to task completion. Escape extinction produced a significant reduction in problem behaviors during the match-to-sample and receptive language tasks. Figure 21.2 shows the number of problem behaviors emitted per minute during baseline (i.e., escape) and escape extinction conditions.

Dawson and colleagues (2003) reported the use of escape extinction to diminish food refusal by Mary, a 3-year-old who was admitted to a day program for the treatment of total food refusal. Her medical history included gastroesophageal reflex, delayed gastric emptying, and gastrostomy tube dependence among other medical issues. Her food refusal included head turning when presented with a bite of food, putting her hand on the spoon or therapist's hand or arm, and using her hands or bib to cover her face.

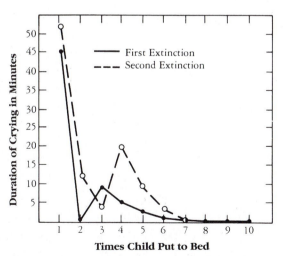

Figure 21.1 Two extinction series showing duration of crying as a function of being put to bed.

From "The Elimination of Tantrum Behavior by Extinction Procedures" by C. D. Williams, 1959, *Journal of Abnormal and Social Psychology, 59,* p. 269. Copyright 1959 by the American Psychological Association. Reprinted by permission of the publisher and author.

Figure 21.2   The number of problem behaviors per minute by Drew during baseline and escape extinction conditions.

From "Use of a Structured Descriptive Assessment Methodology to Identify Variables Affecting Problem Behavior" by C. M. Anderson & E. S. Long, 2002, *Journal of Applied Behavior Analysis, 35* (2), p. 152. Copyright 2002 by Society for the Experimental Analysis of Behavior, Inc. Adapted by permission.

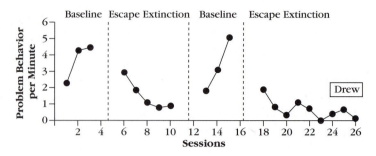

The escape extinction procedure followed 12 sessions of food refusal. If Mary refused the bite of food, the therapist held the spoon to Mary's mouth until she took the bite. When Mary expelled the bite, the food was re-presented until swallowed. With this procedure, Mary's refusals did not produce an escape from the food. The therapist terminated the session after Mary had swallowed 12 bites of food. Mary accepted no food during the 12 baseline sessions; but after two sessions of escape extinction, Mary's food acceptance increased to 100% compliance.

Extinction of Behavior Maintained by Automatic Reinforcement

Behaviors maintained by automatic reinforcement are placed on extinction (a.k.a. **sensory extinction;**) by masking or removing the sensory consequence (Rincover, 1978). Some behaviors produce natural sensory consequences that maintain the behavior. Rincover (1981) described a naturally occurring sensory consequence as a stimulus that "sounds good, looks good, tastes good, smells good, feels good to the touch, or the movement itself is good" (p. 1).

Extinction linked to automatic reinforcement is not a recommended treatment option for problem behaviors, even self-stimulatory behaviors that are maintained by social consequences or negative reinforcement. Automatic reinforcement, however, can maintain self-injurious behaviors (SIB) and persistent, nonpurposeful, repetitive self-stimulatory behaviors (e.g., flipping fingers, head rocking, toe walking, hair pulling, fondling body parts). For example, Kennedy and Sousa (1995) reported that a 19-year-old man with profound disabilities had poked his eyes for 12 years, which resulted in visual impairment in both eyes. Eye poking was thought to serve a sensory stimulation function because it occurred most frequently when he was alone. When Kennedy and Sousa used goggles to mask contact with his eyes, eye-poking behavior decreased markedly (see Figure 8.5).

Social consequences frequently maintain aggression, but not always. Automatic reinforcement can maintain

aggression also, as it can with SIB and self-stimulatory behaviors (Thompson, Fisher, Piazza, & Kuhn, 1998). Deaver, Miltenberger, and Stricker (2001) used extinction to decrease hair twirling. Hair twirling is a frequent precursor to hair pulling, a serious self-injury. Tina, at 2 years and 5 months of age, received treatment for hair twirling and pulling. A functional analysis documented that Tina did not twirl or pull hair to obtain attention, and that hair twirling most often occurred when Tina was alone at bedtime. The sensory extinction procedure consisted of Tina wearing thin cotton mittens on both hands at naptime during day care and during bedtime at home. Figure 21.3 shows that sensory extinction diminished hair twirling to near-zero levels at home and at day care.

Rincover, Cook, Peoples, and Packard (1979) and Rincover (1981) provided the following examples of applying extinction with automatic reinforcement:

1. A child persisted in flipping a light switch on and off. The visual sensory consequence was removed by disconnecting the switch.

2. A child persistently scratched his body until it bled. The tactile (touch) sensory consequence was removed by putting a thin rubber glove on his hand so that he could not feel his skin. Later, the glove was faded by gradually cutting off portions of it.

3. A child would throw up, and then eat the vomit. The gustatory (taste) extinction procedure consisted of adding lima beans to the vomit. The child did not like lima beans; therefore, the vomit did not taste as good, and the positive sensory consequence was masked.

4. A child received kinesthetic stimulation (i.e., stimulation of muscles, tendons, and joints) by holding his arms out to his side and incessantly flapping his fingers, wrists, and arms. The extinction procedure consisted of taping a small vibratory mechanism on the back of his hand to mask the kinesthetic stimulation.

5. A child produced auditory stimulation by persistently twirling an object, such as a plate, on a table.

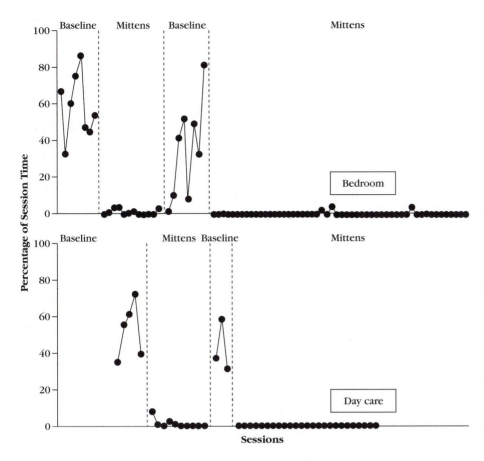

Figure 21.3   The percentage of session time of hair twirling during baseline and treatment conditions in the home and day care settings.

From "Functional Analysis and Treatment of Hair Twirling in a Young Child" by C. M. Deaver, R. G. Miltenberger, and J. M. Stricker, 2001, *Journal of Applied Behavior Analysis, 34* p. 537. Copyright 2001 by Society for Experimental Analysis of Behavior, Inc. Used by permission.

Carpeting the surface of the table he used for spinning objects masked the auditory stimulation from his plate spinning.

Extinction Effects

When a previously reinforced behavior is emitted but is not followed by the usual reinforcing consequences, the occurrence of that behavior should either gradually decrease to its prereinforcement level or stop entirely. Behaviors undergoing extinction are usually associated with predictable characteristics in rate and topography of response. These extinction effects have strong generality across species, response classes, and settings (Lerman & Iwata, 1995, 1996a; Spradlin, 1996). Applied behavior analysts, however, have not devoted much research effort to the basic extinction procedure beyond using extinction as a component in treatment packages for problem behaviors (Lerman & Iwata, 1996a). Consequently, extinction effects have not been documented clearly in applied settings.

Lerman and Iwata (1996) cautioned applied behavior analysts that these clearly documented extinction effects may have limited generality in applied behavior analysis. Applied researchers and practitioners should

view all of the following comments on the extinction effects tentatively when they relate to behavioral interventions or applied research rather than basic research. Applied behavior analysts almost always apply extinction as an element of a treatment package, thereby confounding the understanding of extinction behavior in applied settings.

Gradual Decrease in Frequency and Amplitude

Extinction produces a gradual reduction in behavior. However, when reinforcement is removed abruptly, numerous unreinforced responses can follow. This gradual decrease in response frequency will tend to be sporadic with a gradual increase in pauses between responses (Keller & Schoenfeld, 1950/1995). The extinction procedure is often difficult for teachers and parents to apply because of the initial increase in frequency and magnitude and the gradual decrease in behavior. For example, parents may be unwilling to ignore tantrum behavior for a sufficient amount of time because tantrums are so aversive to parents. Rolider and Van Houten (1984) presented a tactic for this practical problem. They suggested teaching parents to ignore gradually increasing durations of bedtime crying. They used baseline data to assess how long the parents could ignore bedtime crying comfortably before attending to their child. Then, the parents gradually increased their duration of ignoring. Every 2 days they waited an additional 5 minutes before attending to the child until a sufficient total duration of time was achieved.

Extinction Burst

A general effect of the extinction procedure is an immediate increase in the frequency of the response after the removal of the positive, negative, or automatic reinforcement. The behavioral literature uses the term **extinction burst** to identify this initial increase in response frequency. Figure 21.4 presents an illustration of an extinction burst. Operationally, Lerman, Iwata, and Wallace (1999) defined extinction burst as "an increase in responding during any of the first three treatment sessions above that observed during all of the last five baseline sessions or all of baseline" (p. 3). The extinction burst is well documented in basic research, but not well documented in applied research (Lerman & Iwata, 1995, 1996a). When reported, the bursts have occurred for only a few sessions without notable problems.

Goh and Iwata (1994) provided data showing an extinction burst. Steve was a 40-year-old man with profound mental retardation. He had been referred for evaluation for self-injury (head banging, head hitting). A functional analysis showed that self-injury was reinforced by escape from instructions. Goh and Iwata used extinction for the treatment of Steve's self-injury. The top panel in Figure 21.5 shows extinction bursts occurring with the onset of each of the two extinction phases.

Even though applied researchers have rarely reported on extinction bursts, they do occur in applied settings (e.g., Richman, Wacker, Asmus, Casey, & Anderson, 1999; Vollmer et al., 1998). Problem behaviors can worsen during extinction before they show improvement. For example, teachers should anticipate an initial increase in disruption during extinction. Thereafter, problem behaviors should begin to decrease and should return to their prereinforcement level. Applied behavior analysts need to anticipate extinction bursts and be prepared to consistently withhold the reinforcing consequence. Extinction bursts usually suggest that the reinforcer(s) maintaining the problem behavior was successfully identified, indicating that there is a good chance of an effective intervention.

Initial Increase in Response Amplitude

In addition to the extinction burst, which is an increase in the frequency of the response, an initial increase in the amplitude or force of the response also may occur during extinction. Parents who begin to ignore a child's bedtime tantrums might experience an increase in the loudness (i.e., amplitude) of screaming and the force of kicking before the tantrums begin to diminish.

Spontaneous Recovery

During extinction a behavior will typically continue a decreasing trend until it reaches a prereinforced level or ultimately ceases. However, a phenomenon commonly associated with the extinction process is the reappearance of the behavior after it has diminished to its prereinforcement level or stopped entirely. Basic researchers

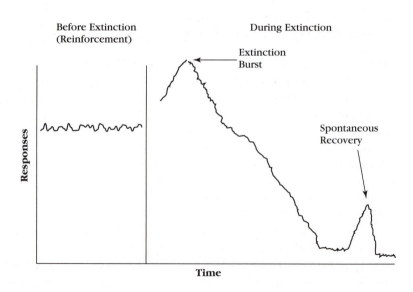

Figure 21.4   Illustration of an extinction burst and spontaneous recovery.

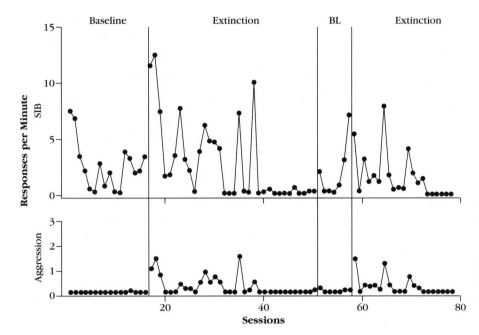

Figure 21.5   Number of responses per minute of self-injurious behavior (SIB) (top panel) and aggression (bottom panel) for Steve during baseline and extinction.

From "Behavioral Persistence and Variability during Extinction of Self-Injury Maintained by Escape" by H-L. Goh and B. A. Iwata, 1994, *Journal of Applied Behavior Analysis, 27,* p. 174. Copyright 1994 by Society for the Experimental Analysis of Behavior, Inc. Used by permission.

commonly report this extinction effect and call it **spontaneous recovery.** With spontaneous recovery, the behavior that diminished during the extinction process recurs even though the behavior does not produce reinforcement. Spontaneous recovery is short-lived and limited if the extinction procedure remains in effect (see Figure 21.4).

Applied behavior analysts have not researched the characteristics and prevalence of spontaneous recovery (Lerman & Iwata, 1996a). Therapists and teachers need to know about spontaneous recovery, however, or they might conclude erroneously that the extinction procedure is no longer effective.

Variables Affecting Resistance to Extinction

Behavior analysts refer to continued responding during the extinction procedure as **resistance to extinction.** Behavior that continues to occur during extinction is said to have greater resistance to extinction than behavior that diminishes quickly. Resistance to extinction is a relative concept. Three methods are commonly used to measure resistance to extinction. Reynolds (1968) described two measurement procedures: the rate of decline in response frequency, and the total number of responses emitted before responding either attains some final low level or ceases. Lerman, Iwata, Shore, and Kahng (1996) reported measuring resistance to extinction as the duration of time required for a behavior to reach a predetermined criterion.

Continuous and Intermittent Reinforcement

Chapter 13 described the effects of continuous (CRF) and intermittent (FR, VR, FI, VI) schedules of reinforcement. Three tentative statements describe resistance to extinction as it relates to continuous and intermittent reinforcement. (a) Intermittent reinforcement may produce behavior with greater resistance to extinction than the resistance produced by continuous reinforcement. For example, behavior maintained on a continuous schedule of reinforcement may diminish more quickly than behavior maintained on intermittent schedules of reinforcement (Keller & Schoenfeld, 1950/1995). (b) Some intermittent schedules may produce more resistant than others (Ferster & Skinner, 1957). The two variable schedules (VR, VI) may have more resistance to extinction than the fixed schedules (FR, FI). (c) To a degree, the thinner the intermittent schedule of reinforcement is, the greater the resistance to extinction will be.

An undergraduate student in an introductory class in applied behavior analysis gave an interesting example of the effects of intermittent reinforcement on persistence. About 2 months after a lecture on resistance to extinction, the student shared this experience:

> You know, intermittent reinforcement really does affect persistence. This guy I know was always calling me for a date. I didn't like him and didn't enjoy being with him. Most of the time when he asked for a date I would not go out with him. Occasionally, because of his persistence, I would give in and accept a date. After your lecture I realized that I was maintaining his calling on an

intermittent schedule of reinforcement, which could account for his persistence. I decided to change this situation and put him on a continuous schedule of reinforcement. Every time he called for a date, I agreed to go out with him. We spent about four evenings a week together for 3 weeks. Then without giving any reason, I abruptly stopped accepting dates with him. Since then he's called only three times, and I have not heard from him in 4 weeks.

Establishing Operation

All stimuli that function as reinforcers require a minimum level of an establishing operation (i.e., motivation must be present). The strength of the establishing operation (EO) above the minimum level will influence resistance to extinction. Basic research has shown that "[R]esistance to extinction is greater when extinction is carried out under high motivation than under low" (Keller & Schoenfeld, 1950/1995, p. 75). We assume that the functional relation between an establishing operation and resistance to extinction exists in applied settings as well as laboratory settings. For example, the fellow might persist in calling the woman for a date if he had made a sizable bet with his buddies that the woman would date him again.

Number, Magnitude, and Quality of Reinforcement

The number of times a behavior has produced reinforcement may influence resistance to extinction. A behavior with a long history of reinforcement may have more resistance to extinction than a behavior with a shorter history of reinforcement. If bedtime tantrums have produced reinforcement for 1 year, they might have more resistance to extinction than tantrums that have produced reinforcement for only 1 week.

Lerman, Kelley, Vorndran, Duhn, and LaRue (2002) reported that applied behavior analysts have not established what effects the magnitude of a reinforcer has on the resistance to extinction. However, the magnitude and quality of a reinforcer will likely influence resistance to extinction. A reinforcer of greater magnitude and quality might produce more resistance to extinction than a reinforcer with less magnitude and quality.

Number of Previous Extinction Trials

Successive applications of conditioning and extinction may influence the resistance to extinction. Sometimes problem behaviors diminish during extinction, and then are accidentally strengthened with reinforcement. When this happens, applied behavior analysts can reapply the extinction procedure. Typically, behavior may diminish quickly with fewer total responses during a reapplication of extinction. This effect is additive when the participant can discriminate the onset of extinction. With each successive application of extinction, decreases in behavior become increasingly rapid until only a single response occurs following the withdrawal of reinforcement.

Response Effort

Even though limited, applied researchers have produced some data on response effort and its effect on resistance to extinction (Lerman & Iwata, 1996a). The effort required for a response apparently influences its resistance to extinction. A response requiring greater effort diminishes more quickly during extinction than a response requiring less effort.

Using Extinction Effectively

Numerous guidelines for using extinction effectively have been published, with most authors providing similar recommendations. Presented below are 10 guidelines to follow before and during the application of extinction. They are: withholding all reinforcers maintaining the problem behavior, withholding reinforcement consistently, combining extinction with other procedures, using instructions, planning for extinction-produced aggression, increasing the number of extinction trials, including significant others in extinction, guarding against unintentional extinction, maintaining extinction-decreased behavior, and circumstances under which extinction should not be used.

Withholding All Reinforcers Maintaining the Problem Behavior

A first step in using extinction effectively is to identify and withhold all possible sources of reinforcement that maintain the target behavior. The effectiveness of extinction is dependent on the correct identification of the consequences that maintain the problem behavior (Iwata, Pace, Cowdery, & Miltenberger, 1994). Functional behavior assessments have improved greatly the application and effectiveness of using extinction in applied settings (Lerman, Iwata, & Wallace, 1999; Richman, Wacker, Asmus, Casey, & Anderson, 1999).

Applied behavior analysts collect data on antecedent and consequent stimuli that are temporally related to the problem behavior and provide answers to questions such as the following:

1. Does the problem behavior occur more frequently when something happens in the environment to occasion the behavior (e.g., a demand or request)?

2. Is the frequency of the problem behavior unrelated to antecedent stimuli and social consequences?

3. Does the problem behavior occur more frequently when it produces attention from other persons?

If the answer to the first question is yes, the problem behavior may be maintained with negative reinforcement. If the answer to the second question is yes, the applied behavior analyst will need to consider withholding tactile, auditory, visual, gustatory, olfactory, and kinesthetic consequences alone or in combination. If the answer to the third question is yes, the behavior may be maintained by positive reinforcement in the form of social attention.

The consequence that maintains the problem behavior appears obvious in some applied settings. In the Williams (1959) study, for instance, parental attention appeared to be the only source of reinforcement maintaining the tyrant-like behavior at bedtime. However, behaviors are frequently maintained by multiple sources of reinforcement. The class clown's behavior might be maintained by the teacher's reaction to the disruptive behavior, by the attention received from peers, or a combination of both. Johnny might cry when his parent brings him to preschool to escape from preschool, to keep his parents with him, to occasion his teacher's concern and attention, or to achieve some combination of all three. When multiple sources of reinforcement maintain problem behavior, identifying and withholding one source of reinforcement may have minimal or no affect on behavior. If teacher and peer attention maintain clownish classroom behavior, then withholding only teacher attention may produce little change in the problem behavior. The teacher must withhold her attention and also teach the other students to ignore the clownish behavior to effectively apply the extinction procedure.

Withholding Reinforcement Consistently

When the reinforcing consequences have been identified, teachers must withhold them consistently. All behavior change procedures require consistent application, but consistency is essential for extinction. Teachers, parents, therapists, and applied behavior analysts often report that consistency is the single most difficult aspect in using extinction. The error of not withholding reinforcement consistently negates the effectiveness of the extinction procedure, and this point cannot be overemphasized.

Combining Extinction with Other Procedures

Extinction is an effective singular intervention. However, teachers and therapists, applied researchers, and writers of textbooks have rarely recommended it as such (Vollmer et al., 1998). We also recommend that applied behavior analysts always consider combining extinction with other treatments, especially the reinforcement of alternative behaviors. Two reasons support this recommendation. First, the effectiveness of extinction may increase when it is combined with other procedures, especially positive reinforcement. By combining extinction with differential reinforcement of appropriate behaviors, for example, the applied behavior analyst alters the environment by reinforcing appropriate alternative behaviors and placing problem behaviors on extinction. During intervention, the extinction procedure should not reduce the overall amount of positive consequences received by a participant. Second, differential reinforcement and antecedent procedures hold promise for reducing extinction effects such as bursting and aggression (Lerman, Iwata, & Wallace, 1999).

Rehfeldt and Chambers (2003) combined extinction with differential reinforcement for the treatment of verbal perseverance maintained by positive reinforcement in the form of social attention. The participant was an adult with autism. Rehfeldt and Chambers presented social attention contingent on appropriate and nonperseveration speech, and applied attention extinction by not responding to the participant's inappropriate verbal behavior. This combined treatment produced an increase in appropriate verbal responses and a decrease in perseverance. These data suggest that contingencies of reinforcement might maintain the unusual speech of some individuals with autism.

Using Instructions

The contingencies of reinforcement affect the future frequency of behavior automatically. It is not necessary for people to know, to describe, or even to perceive that contingencies are affecting their behavior. However, behaviors sometime diminish more quickly during extinction when teachers describe the extinction procedure to students. For example, teachers frequently provide small-group instruction while other students do independent seatwork. When seatwork students ask questions, they interrupt instruction. Many teachers correct this problem by placing question asking on extinction. They simply ignore student questions until after the end of small-group instruction. This tactic is often effective. The extinction procedure, however, tends to be more effective when teachers tell students that they will ignore all their questions until after the end of small-group instruction.

Planning for Extinction-Produced Aggression

Behaviors that occurred infrequently in the past will sometime become prominent during extinction by replacing the problem behaviors. Frequently, these side effect replacement behaviors are aggressive (Lerman et al., 1999). Skinner (1953) interpreted the change in response topographies (e.g., side effects) as emotional behaviors, including aggression that sometimes accompanies extinction.

Goh and Iwata (1994) provided a convincing demonstration showing how aggression-induced behaviors occurred when a target behavior was placed on extinction. Steve was a 40-year-old man with profound mental retardation. He had been referred for evaluation for self-injury (head banging, head hitting). A functional analysis showed that self-injury was reinforced by escape from instructions. Goh and Iwata used extinction for the treatment of Steve's self-injury. Steve rarely slapped or kicked other persons (i.e., aggression) during the two baseline phases, but aggression increased with the onset of the two extinction phases (see Figure 21.5, bottom panel). Aggression essentially stopped by the end of each extinction phase when self-injury was stable and low, even though Steve's aggression remained untreated during the baseline and extinction conditions.

Applied behavior analysts need to plan on managing aggressive behaviors when they occur as side effects of extinction. It is critical that extinction-produced aggression not produce reinforcement. Frequently, parents, teachers, and therapists react to the aggression with attention that may function as reinforcement of the extinction-produced aggression. For instance, a teacher decides to ignore DeShawna's questions while providing small-group instruction. When DeShawna interrupts the teacher with a question, the teacher does not respond. DeShawna then starts disrupting other seatwork students. To quiet DeShawna down, the teacher responds, "Oh, all right, DeShawna, what did you want to know?" In effect, the teacher's behavior may have reinforced DeShawna interruptions during small-group instruction and the accompanying inappropriate disruptions of the other seatwork students.

Many times extinction-produced aggression takes the form of verbal abuse. Often, teachers and parents do not need to react to it. If extinction-produced aggression produces reinforcement, individuals simply use other inappropriate behavior such as verbal abuse to produce reinforcement. Teachers and parents cannot and should not ignore some forms of aggression and self-injurious behavior. Teachers and parents need to know (a) that they can ignore some aggression, (b) when they need to intervene on the aggression, and (c) what they will do for the intervention.

Increasing the Number of Extinction Trials

An extinction trial occurs each time the behavior does not produce reinforcement. Whenever possible, applied behavior analysts should increase the number of extinction trials for the problem behaviors. Increasing extinction trials improves the efficiency of extinction by accelerating the extinction process. Applied behavior analysts can increase extinction trials when applied settings will accommodate frequent occurrences of the problem behavior. For example, Billy's parents employed an extinction procedure to reduce his tantrums. His parents noticed that Billy had tantrums most often when he did not get his way about staying up late, eating a snack, and going outside. For the purpose of the program, they decided to set up several additional situations each day in which Billy did not get his way. Billy was then more likely to emit the inappropriate behavior at a higher rate, thereby giving his parents more occasions to ignore it. As a result, his tantrums decreased in a shorter period of time than they would have if left at their usual rate.

Including Significant Others in Extinction

It is important that other persons in the environment not reinforce undesirable behavior. A teacher, for example, needs to share extinction plans with other people who might help in the classroom—parent volunteers, grandparents, music teachers, speech therapists, industrial arts specialists—to avoid their reinforcing inappropriate behaviors. All people in contact with the learner must apply the same extinction procedure for effective treatment.

Guarding against Unintentional Extinction

Desirable behaviors are often unintentionally placed on extinction. A beginning teacher confronted with one student who is on task and many other students who are not will probably direct most of his attention to the majority and will provide little or no attention to the student who is working. It is common practice to give the most attention to problems (the squeaky wheel gets the grease) and to ignore situations that are going smoothly. However, behaviors must continue to be reinforced if they are to be maintained. All teachers must give attention to students who are on-task.

Maintaining Extinction-Decreased Behavior

Applied behavior analysts leave the extinction procedure in effect permanently for maintaining the extinction-diminished behavior. A permanent application of escape extinction and attention extinction is a preferred procedure. Applied behavior analysts can use a permanent application also with some sensory extinction procedures. For example, the carpeting on a table used for spinning objects could remain in place indefinitely. Some applications of sensory extinction appear inappropriate and inconvenient if kept permanently in effect. For example, requiring Tina to permanently wear thin cotton mittens on both hands at naptime during day care and during bedtime at home appears inappropriate and inconvenient (see Figure 21.3). In such a case, the applied behavior analysts can maintain treatment gains by gradually fading out the sensory extinction procedure—for example, cutting off 1 inch of the glove palm every 3 to 4 days until the glove palm is removed. The analyst may then remove the fingers and thumb one at a time to gradually remove the mittens.

When Not to Use Extinction

Imitation

Extinction can be inappropriate if the behaviors placed on extinction are likely to be imitated by others. Some behaviors can be tolerated if only one person emits them, but become intolerable if several persons emit them.

Extreme Behaviors

With few exceptions, most applications of extinction as a singular intervention have focused on important but relatively minor behavior problems (e.g., disruptive classroom behavior, tantrums, excessive noise, mild forms of aggression). However, some behaviors are so harmful to self or others or so destructive to property that they must be controlled with the most rapid and humane procedure available. Extinction as a singular intervention is not recommended in such situations.

The use of extinction as a singular intervention to decrease severe aggression toward self, others, or property raises ethical concerns. Addressing the issue of ethics, Pinkston, Reese, LeBlanc, and Baer (1973) analyzed the effects of an extinction technique that did not allow a person to harm himself or his victim. In their approach the aggressor was ignored, but the victim was sheltered from attack. Pinkston and colleagues demonstrated the effectiveness of a safe extinction technique with an extremely aggressive preschool boy, whose aggressive behaviors included choking, biting, pinching, hitting, and kicking classmates. During the baseline condition the teachers responded to the child's aggression as they had in the past. "Typically, this took the form of verbal admonitions or reproofs such as: 'Cain, we do not do that here,' or 'Cain, you can't play here until you are ready to be a good boy'" (p. 118). The teachers did not attend to the boy's aggressive behaviors during extinction. When he attacked a peer, the teachers immediately attended to the peer. The victim was consoled and provided with an opportunity to play with a toy. In addition, the teachers attended to the boy's positive behaviors. This extinction procedure was effective in greatly reducing aggression. The application of extinction requires sound, mature, humane, and ethical professional judgment.

 Summary

Definition of Extinction

1. Extinction as a procedure provides zero probability of reinforcement. It is also a behavioral process of a diminishing rate of response.

2. Functional behavior assessments have enabled applied behavior analysts to distinguish clearly between the procedural variations of extinction (ignoring) and the functional variations of extinction (withholding maintaining reinforcers).

3. *Extinction* is a technical term that applied behavior analysts should use only to identify the procedure of withholding reinforcers that maintain behavior.

Extinction Procedures

4. Procedures for extinction take three distinct forms that are linked to behavior maintained by positive reinforcement, negative reinforcement, and automatic reinforcement.

5. Behaviors maintained by positive reinforcement are placed on extinction when those behaviors do not produce the reinforcer.

6. Behaviors maintained by negative reinforcement are placed on extinction (a.k.a., escape extinction) when those behaviors do not produce a removal of the aversive stimulus, meaning that the individual cannot escape from the aversive situation.

7. Behaviors maintained by automatic reinforcement are placed on extinction (a.k.a., sensory extinction) by masking or removing the sensory consequence.

Extinction Effects

8. Behaviors undergoing extinction are usually associated with predictable characteristics in rate and topography of response.

9. Extinction produces a gradual reduction in behavior.

10. A general effect of the extinction procedure is an immediate increase in the frequency of the response after the removal of the positive, negative, or automatic reinforcement. The behavioral literature uses the term *extinction burst* to identify this initial increase in response frequency.

11. With spontaneous recovery, the behavior that diminished during the extinction process recurs even though the behavior does not produce reinforcement.

Variables Affecting Resistance to Extinction

12. Behavior that continues to occur during extinction is said to have greater resistance to extinction than behavior that diminishes quickly. Resistance to extinction is a relative concept.

13. Intermittent schedules of reinforcement may produce behavior with greater resistance to extinction than the resistance produced by a continuous reinforcement schedule.

14. Variables schedules of reinforcement (e.g., VR, VI) may have more resistance to extinction than fixed schedules (e.g., FR, FI).

15. To a degree, the thinner the intermittent schedule of reinforcement is, the greater the resistance to extinction will be.

16. Resistance to extinction is likely to increase with the strength of the establishing operation (EO) for the reinforcer being withheld.

17. The number, magnitude, and quality of the reinforcer may affect resistance to extinction.

18. Successive applications of conditioning and extinction may influence the resistance to extinction.

19. The effort required for a response apparently influences its resistance to extinction.

Using Extinction Effectively

20. A first step in using extinction effectively is to withhold all reinforcers that are maintaining the problem behavior.

21. When the reinforcing consequences have been identified, teachers must withhold them consistently.

22. Applied behavior analysts should always consider combining extinction with other procedures.

23. Behaviors often decrease more quickly during extinction when the person is informed of the procedure being applied.

24. When using extinction, applied behavior analysts should plan for extinction-produced aggression.

25. Increasing the number of extinction trials improves the efficiency of extinction by accelerating the extinction process.

26. All people in contact with the learner must apply the same extinction procedure for effective treatment.

27. Extinction should not be used for behaviors that are likely to be imitated by others or for behaviors that are harmful to self or others.

CHAPTER 22

Differential Reinforcement

Key Terms

differential reinforcement of alternative behavior (DRA)

differential reinforcement of incompatible behavior (DRI)

differential reinforcement of low rates (DRL)

differential reinforcement of other behavior (DRO)

fixed-interval DRO (FI-DRO)

fixed-momentary DRO (FM-DRO)

full-session DRL

interval DRL

spaced-responding DRL

variable-interval DRO (VI-DRO)

variable-momentary DRO (VM-DRO)

Behavior Analyst Certification Board® BCBA® & BCABA® Behavior Analyst Task List,© Third Edition

Content Area 9: Behavior Change Procedures	
9-6	Use differential reinforcement.

Practitioners can choose from among a wide range of effective procedures for decreasing or eliminating problem behaviors. Although often effective in reducing targeted problem behaviors, interventions based primarily on extinction or punishment may produce unwanted side effects. Maladaptive emotional behavior and a higher-than-usual rate of responding are commonly observed when a behavior with a long and consistent history of reinforcement is placed on extinction. Punishment may evoke escape, avoidance, aggression, and other forms of undesirable countercontrol. In addition to unwanted side effects, another limitation of extinction and punishment as primary methods for reducing problem behaviors is that neither approach strengthens or teaches adaptive behaviors with which individuals can attain the reinforcers previously achieved by the undesirable behaviors. Finally, beyond the possibility of unwanted side effects and their lack of educative value, interventions that rely on extinction alone or punishment in any of its varied forms raise important ethical and legal concerns (Repp & Singh, 1990).

Because of all these concerns, applied behavior analysts have developed effective reinforcement-based procedures for reducing problem behaviors (e.g., Kazdin, 1980; Lerman & Vorndran, 2002; Singh & Katz, 1985). These positive reductive procedures are based on differential reinforcement to diminish or eliminate problem behaviors.

Basic Description of Differential Reinforcement

All applications of *differential reinforcement* entail reinforcing one response class and withholding reinforcement for another response class.[1] When used as a reductive procedure for problem behavior, differential reinforcement consists of two components: (a) providing reinforcement contingent on either the occurrence of a behavior other than the problem behavior or the problem behavior occurring at a reduced rate, and (b) withholding reinforcement as much as possible for the problem behavior. Although implementing differential reinforcement involves extinction, as Cowdery, Iwata, and Pace (1990) pointed out,

> differential reinforcement does not involve extended interruptions of ongoing activities (e.g., time out), contingent removal of positive reinforcers (e.g., response cost),

or presentation of aversive stimuli (e.g., punishment). These characteristics make differential reinforcement the least intrusive of all behavior interventions and probably account for its widespread popularity. (p. 497)

Differential reinforcement in its various forms is one of the most effective, widely known, and commonly used techniques to reduce problem behavior. The four most researched variations of differential reinforcement for decreasing inappropriate behavior are differential reinforcement of incompatible behavior (DRI), differential reinforcement of alternative behavior (DRA), differential reinforcement of other behavior (DRO), and differential reinforcement of low rates (DRL). This chapter defines, gives examples of applications of, and suggests guidelines for the effective use of each of these differential reinforcement procedures for decreasing problem behavior.

Differential Reinforcement of Incompatible Behavior and Differential Reinforcement of Alternative Behavior

DRI and DRA have the dual effects of weakening the problem behavior while simultaneously strengthening acceptable behaviors that are either incompatible with or an alternative to the targeted problem behaviors. When properly implemented as a treatment for problem behavior, differential reinforcement of an incompatible or alternative behavior can be conceptualized as a schedule of reinforcement in which two concurrent operants—the inappropriate behavior targeted for reduction and the appropriate behavior selected—receive reinforcement at different rates (Fisher & Mazur, 1997). Because the differential reinforcement schedule favors the appropriate behavior, the client allocates more responding to the appropriate behavior and less responding to the problem behavior (which is placed on extinction) (Vollmer, Roane, Ringdahl, & Marcus, 1999). For example, when Friman (1990) reinforced the in-seat behavior of a preschool student with hyperactivity, out-of-seat behavior decreased markedly.

With the proper selection of behaviors, these two interventions may promote educational, social, and personal skill development. With DRI/DRA, the practitioner controls the development of appropriate behaviors and concurrently measures both the problem behavior and the desired replacement behavior. Teachers, therapists, and parents have a long history of using DRI/DRA interventions in education, treatment, and everyday social

---

[1] Differential reinforcement is not only for reducing problem behaviors. As described elsewhere in this text, differential reinforcement is a defining feature of shaping new behaviors (see Chapter 19). Various forms of differential reinforcement contingencies are also used as experimental control procedures (see Chapter 8 and Thompson & Iwata, 2005).

interactions. Practitioners usually find DRI/DRA the easiest of the four differential reinforcement procedures to apply.

Differential Reinforcement of Incompatible Behavior

A practitioner applying **differential reinforcement of incompatible behavior (DRI)** reinforces a behavior that cannot occur simultaneously with the problem behavior and withholds reinforcement following instances of the problem behavior. The behavior that gets reinforced (e.g., a student seated at his seat) and the problem behavior that is placed on extinction (e.g., student is out of seat) are mutually exclusive response classes whose different topographies make it impossible to emit both behaviors at the same time.

Dixon, Benedict, and Larson (2001) used DRI to treat the inappropriate verbal behavior of Fernando, a 25-year-old man with moderate mental retardation and a psychotic disorder. Inappropriate vocalizations included utterances not related to the context, sexually inappropriate remarks, illogical placement of words within a sentence, and "psychotic" statements (e.g., "There's a purple moose on my head named Chuckles," p. 362). The researchers defined appropriate verbal behavior as any vocal utterance that did not meet the defining characteristics of inappropriate vocalization. A functional analysis revealed that the inappropriate verbal statements were maintained by social attention.

The researchers implemented DRI by ignoring Fernando's inappropriate verbal behavior and attending to his appropriate statements with 10 seconds of comments that were relevant to Fernando's statements. For example, if Fernando said something about an activity he liked to do, the experimenter told him it was interesting and hoped he could do it again soon. During a comparison baseline condition, inappropriate behavior resulted in attention and appropriate verbal behavior was ignored. The DRI intervention effectively reduced Fernando's inappropriate verbal behavior and increased appropriate utterances (Figure 22.1).

Differential Reinforcement of Alternative Behavior

Differential reinforcement of alternative behavior (DRA) and DRI are similar procedures. A practitioner using **differential reinforcement of alternative behavior (DRA)** reinforces occurrences of a behavior that provides a desirable alternative to the problem behavior but is not necessarily incompatible with it. Behavior analysts can use an alternative behavior to occupy the time that the problem behavior would ordinarily use. The al-

ternative behavior and the problem behavior, however, are not topographically incompatible. For example, a classroom teacher could assign two students who frequently argue with each other to work on a class project together, thus reinforcing cooperative behaviors associated with project development. Working together on a class project is not incompatible with arguing; the two response classes could occur together. However, the two students might argue less when engaged in cooperative behaviors.[2]

Roane, Lerman, and Vorndran (2001) selected placing a plastic block in a bucket as an alternative behavior to screaming (i.e., a brief vocal sound above conversational levels). Lerman, Kelley, Vorndran, Kuhn, and LaRue (2002) shaped and maintained touching a communication card as an alternative behavior to disruptions such as throwing task materials and aggression.

When escape from a task or demand situation is used as the reinforcer in a differential reinforcement procedure for reducing inappropriate behavior, the intervention is sometimes called *differential negative reinforcement of alternative* (or *incompatible*) *behavior* (DNRA or DNRI) (Vollmer & Iwata, 1992). DRI/DRA interventions can use negative reinforcers also (Marcus & Vollmer, 1995; Piazza, Moses, & Fisher, 1996). Applying DNRA/DNRI to reduce the occurrence of a problem behavior maintained by escape from a task or demand context consists of providing negative reinforcement of the alternative behavior in the form of brief periods of escape from the task and escape extinction for the problem behavior. Positive reinforcement for the alternative/incompatible behavior is often provided as well.

Lalli, Casey, and Kates (1995) allowed participants to escape from a task for 30 seconds contingent on using an alternative response (e.g., giving the therapist a card with "BREAK" printed on it, or saying "no") as an alternative to their aberrant behavior. The researchers also provided praise for using the alternative responses. As training progressed, the participants' escape from a task was contingent on using the trained verbal responses and completing a gradually increasing number of required

---

[2]Any behavior selected for reinforcement with DRI provides the learner with an "alternative" to the problem behavior, but not all behaviors selected for reinforcement in a DRA are incompatible with the problem behavior. Sometimes the difference between DRI and DRA is a fine one and provokes legitimate debate. For example, the interventions used in studies by Dixon and colleagues (2001) and Wilder, Masuda, O'Conner, and Baham (2001) were described as applications of DRA. However, because appropriate verbal behavior was defined in each study as vocal utterances that did not meet the defining characteristics of inappropriate vocalizations, the response classes they reinforced were *incompatible* with the problem behavior. If the "alternative" behavior selected for reinforcement cannot occur simultaneously with the problem behavior, we believe the procedure is properly labeled DRI.

Figure 22.1 Number of appropriate and inappropriate verbal utterances by an adult male during DRI and baseline conditions.

Adapted from "Functional Analysis and Treatment of Inappropriate Verbal Behavior" by M. R. Dixon, H. Benedict, & T. Larson (2001), *Journal of Applied Behavior Analysis, 34,* p. 362. Copyright 2001 by the Society for the Experimental Analysis of Behavior, Inc. Used by permission.

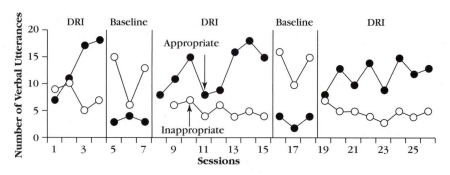

steps of the task. The DNRA intervention increased the use of the trained verbal response and decreased the problem behavior.[3]

Guidelines for Using DRI/DRA

Practitioners often use DRI and DRA as interventions for a wide range of problem behaviors. Many researchers and practitioners have discovered that the following guidelines improve the effectiveness of DRI and DRA.

Select Incompatible/Alternative Behavior

Ideally, the behavior selected to be incompatible with or alternative to the inappropriate behavior (a) already exists in the learner's current repertoire; (b) requires equal, or preferably less, effort than the problem behavior; (c) is being emitted at a rate prior to the DRI/DRA intervention that will provide sufficient opportunities for reinforcement; and (d) is likely to be reinforced in the learner's natural environment after intervention is terminated. Behaviors meeting these criteria will increase the initial effectiveness of DRI/DRA and facilitate the maintenance and generalization of behavior changes after intervention is terminated.

When possible, the practitioner should differentially reinforce incompatible/alternative behaviors that will lead to or increase the opportunities for the learner to acquire new or other useful skills. When no behaviors meeting those criteria can be identified, the practitioner can select an alternative behavior that can be easily taught or consider using a DRO procedure. Figure 22.2 shows some examples of incompatible or alternative behaviors (Webber & Scheuermann, 1991).

Select Reinforcers That Are Powerful and Can Be Delivered Consistently

Perhaps the greatest threat to the effectiveness of any reinforcement-based intervention is the use of stimulus changes following behaviors that the practitioner only assumes function as reinforcement. Providing as consequences for the incompatible/alternative behavior stimulus changes identified by stimulus preference assessment and reinforcer assessment (see Chapter 11) or functional behavior assessments (see Chapter 24) will increase the effectiveness of DRI/DRA. In addition, reinforcers should be selected that are relevant to the establishing operations that naturally exist in the treatment setting or that can be created (e.g., by deprivation prior to treatment sessions).

The same consequence that is maintaining the problem behavior prior to intervention is often the most effective reinforcer for the alternative or incompatible behavior (Dixon et al., 2001; Wilder et al., 2001). After discovering that the problem behaviors emitted by different students in a classroom were maintained by different reinforcers, Durand, Crimmins, Caufield, and Taylor (1989) effectively used individually selected reinforcers to differentially reinforce appropriate alternative behaviors for each student, and the inappropriate behaviors decreased in frequency.

The effectiveness of any intervention involving differential reinforcement depends on the practitioner's ability to deliver and withhold consistently stimulus changes that currently function as reinforcement. Therefore, in addition to their potential effectiveness as reinforcers, the stimulus changes that the practitioner selects must be ones he can deliver immediately and consistently when the alternative/incompatible behavior occurs and withhold following instances of the problem behavior.

The magnitude of the reinforcer used in a differential reinforcement intervention is probably less important than its consistent delivery and control. Lerman, Kelley, Vorndran, Kuhn, and LaRue (2002) provided positive reinforcement (access to toys) and negative reinforcement (escape from demands) in magnitudes ranging from 20 seconds to 300 seconds. They found that reinforcement magnitude only affected responding minimally

---

[3]DRA is a primary component of *functional communication training (FCT),* an intervention in which an alternative behavior is selected to serve the same communicative function as the problem behavior (e.g., saying "Break please" results in the same reinforcement as aggression or tantrumming did previously). FCT is described in detail in Chapter 23.

Figure 22.2   Examples of behaviors selected as incompatible/alternative behaviors when implementing DRI/DRA for common classroom behavior problems.

Problem Behavior	Positive Incompatible Alternative
Talking back	Positive response such as "Yes, sir" or "OK" or "I understand"; or acceptable questions such as "May I ask you a question about that?" or "May I tell you my side?"
Cursing	Acceptable exclamations such as "darn," "shucks."
Being off-task	Any on-task behavior: looking at book, writing, looking at teacher, etc.
Being out of seat	Sitting in seat (bottom on chair, with body in upright position).
Noncompliance	Following directions within _____ seconds (time limit will depend upon age of student); following directions by second time direction is given.
Talking out	Raising hand and waiting quietly to be called on.
Turning in messy papers	No marks other than answers.
Hitting, pinching, kicking, pushing/shoving	Using verbal expression of anger; pounding fist into hand; sitting or standing next to other students without touching them.
Tardiness	Being in seat when bell rings (or by desired time).
Self-injurious or self-stimulatory behaviors	Sitting with hands on desk or in lap; hands not touching any part of body; head up and not touching anything (desk, shoulder, etc.).
Inappropriate use of materials	Holding/using materials appropriately (e.g., writing *only* on appropriate paper, etc.).

Adapted from "Accentuate the Positive . . . Eliminate the Negative" by J. Webber and B. Scheuermann, 1991, *Teaching Exceptional Children, 24(*1), p. 15. Copyright 1991 by Council for Exceptional Children. Used by permission.

during treatment and had little effect on maintenance after treatment was discontinued.

Reinforcing Incompatible/Alternative Behavior Immediately and Consistently

Initially, a practitioner should use a continuous (CRF) schedule of reinforcement for the incompatible or alternative behavior, and then transition to an intermittent schedule. The reinforcer should be presented consistently and immediately following each occurrence of the incompatible or alternative behavior. After firmly establishing the incompatible or alternative behavior, the practitioner should gradually thin the reinforcement schedule.

Withhold Reinforcement for the Problem Behavior

The effectiveness of differential reinforcement as an intervention for problem behavior depends on the incompatible or alternative behavior yielding a higher rate of reinforcement than the problem behavior. Maximizing the

difference between rates of reinforcement obtained by the two response classes entails withholding all reinforcement for the problem behavior (i.e., extinction schedule).

Ideally, the alternative behavior would always be reinforced (at least initially) and the problem behavior would never be reinforced. As Vollmer and colleagues (1999) noted, "Perfect implementation of differential reinforcement entails providing reinforcers as immediately as possible after an appropriate behavior occurs (e.g., within 5 s). Treatment effects may degrade as the delay to reinforcement increases, especially if inappropriate behavior is occasionally reinforced" (p. 21). However, practitioners must often implement DRI/DRA procedures in less than optimal conditions, in which some occurrences of the alternative/incompatible behavior are not followed by a reinforcer and the problem behavior sometimes inadvertently produces reinforcement.

Results from a study by Vollmer and colleagues (1999) suggest that even when such treatment "mistakes" occur, differential reinforcement may still be effective. These researchers compared a "full implementation" of DRA, in which 100% of instances of alternative behavior were reinforced (CRF) and 0% of instances of aberrant behavior were reinforced (extinction), with various levels of "partial implementation." For example, with a 25/75 implementation schedule, only one in every four instances of appropriate behavior was reinforced, whereas a reinforcer followed three of every four instances of inappropriate behavior. As expected, full implementation of differential reinforcement produced the greatest effects with inappropriate behavior being "virtually replaced by appropriate behavior, and lower levels of implementation eventually reducing treatment efficacy if the schedule of reinforcement favored inappropriate behavior" (p. 20). Figure 22.3 shows the results for Rachel, a 17-year-old girl with profound mental retardation who engaged in self-injurious behavior (e.g., head hitting and hand biting) and aggression toward others (e.g., scratching, hitting, hair pulling).

An important and perhaps surprising finding of the Vollmer and colleagues (1999) study was that partial implementation was effective under certain conditions. During partial implementation, the participants' behavior showed a "disproportional tendency toward appropriate behavior" (p. 20) if they had prior exposure to full implementation. The researchers concluded that this finding suggests the possibility of intentionally thinning implementation levels prior to extending differential reinforcement interventions to settings in which maintaining treatment fidelity will be difficult. Recognizing that treatment effects might erode over time, they recommended that full implementation booster sessions be conducted periodically to reestablish the predominance of appropriate behavior.

Combine DRI/DRA with Other Procedures

Considering that the DRI/DRA interventions do not specifically provide consequences for the problem behavior, a practitioner will seldom apply DRI/DRA (or DRL) as a single intervention if the problem behavior is destructive, dangerous to the learner or to others, or if it interferes with health and safety. In these situations, the practitioner might combine DRI/DRA with other reductive procedures (e.g., response blocking, time-out, stimulus fading) to produce a more potent intervention (e.g., Patel, Piazza, Kelly, Oschsher, & Santana, 2001).

For example, Ringdahl and colleagues (2002) compared the effects of DRA with and without instructional fading on the frequency of problem behaviors of an 8-year-old girl, Kristina, who had been diagnosed with autism and functioned in the moderate range of mental retardation. Kristina's problem behaviors during academic tasks (destruction: throwing, tearing, or breaking work materials; aggression: hitting, kicking, biting; and self-injurious behavior: biting herself) had become so severe that she had been admitted to a hospital day treatment program for help. Because a previous functional analysis

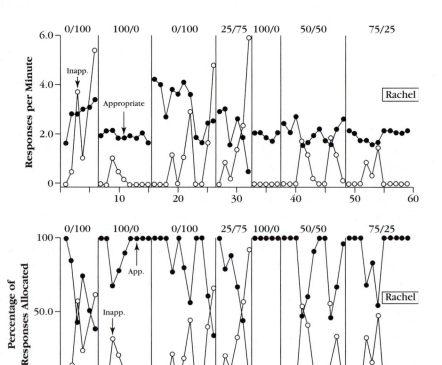

Figure 22.3 Number of appropriate and inappropriate responses per minute (upper panel) and allocation of appropriate and inappropriate behavior (lower panel) by 17-year-old student with disabilities during full (100/0) and partial levels of implementation of DRA.

Adapted from "Evaluating Treatment Challenges with Differential Reinforcement of Alternative Behavior" by T. R. Vollmer, H. S. Roane, J. E. Ringdahl, and B. A. Marcus, 1999, *Journal of Applied Behavior Analysis, 32,* p. 17. Copyright 1999 by the Society for the Experimental Analysis of Behavior, Inc. Used by permission.

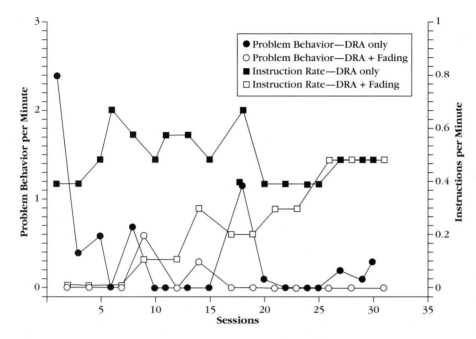

Figure 22.4 Problem behavior by an 8-year-old student with autism and developmental disabilities (left *y* axis) and instructions given per minute (right *y* axis) under DRA only and DRA implemented with instructional fading.

From "Differential Reinforcement with and without Instructional Fading" by J. E. Ringdahl, K. Kitsukawa, M. S. Andelman, N. Call, L. C. Winborn, A. Barretto, & G. K. Reed (2002), *Journal of Applied Behavior Analysis, 35,* p. 293. Copyright 2002 by the Society for the Experimental Analysis of Behavior, Inc. Used by permission.

revealed that Kristina's problem behavior was maintained by escape from instructions to complete tasks, the DRA procedure in both conditions consisted of giving Kristina a 1-minute break from the task and access to leisure materials contingent on independent completion of the task (e.g., counting items, matching cards with the same colors or shapes) without exhibiting problem behavior. In the DRA without instructional fading condition, Kristina was given an instruction to complete a work task at a rate of approximately one instruction every other minute. In the DRA with instructional fading, Kristina was given no instructions during the first three sessions, then one instruction every 15 minutes. The rate of instructions was gradually increased until it equaled the rate in the DRA without the fading condition. Problem behavior was high at the outset of the DRA without the instructional fading condition but decreased across sessions to a mean of 0.2 responses per minute over the final three sessions (see Figure 22.4). During DRA with instructional fading, problem behavior was low from the outset and occurred during only two sessions (Sessions 9 and 14). Over the final three sessions of DRA with instructional fading, Kristina exhibited no problem behavior and the instruction rate was equal to the DRA without instructional fading (0.5 instructions per minute).

Differential Reinforcement of Other Behavior

A practitioner using **differential reinforcement of other behavior (DRO)** delivers a reinforcer whenever the problem behavior has not occurred during or at specific times (see momentary DRO later in chapter). As de-

scribed by Reynolds (1961), DRO provides "reinforcement for not responding" (p. 59). Because reinforcement is contingent on the absence or omission of target behavior, DRO is sometimes called *differential reinforcement of zero responding* or *omission training* (e.g., Weiher & Harman, 1975).[4]

The delivery of reinforcement with DRO is determined by a combination of how the omission requirement is implemented and scheduled. The omission requirement can make reinforcement contingent on the problem behavior not occurring either (a) throughout an entire interval of time (*interval DRO*), or (b) at specific moments of time (*momentary DRO*). With an interval DRO, reinforcement is delivered if no occurrences of the problem behavior were observed throughout the entire interval. Any instance of the target behavior resets the interval, thereby postponing reinforcement. With a momentary DRO procedure, reinforcement is contingent on the absence of the problem behavior at specific points in time.

The researcher or practitioner can determine whether the omission requirement has been met (i.e., at the ends of intervals or at specific moments in time) according to a fixed or variable schedule. The combinations of these two factors—an interval or momentary omission requirement implemented on either a fixed or a variable schedule—yield the four basic DRO arrangements shown in Figure 22.5 (Lindberg, Iwata, Kahng, & DeLeon, 1999).

---

[4]Because instances of target problem behavior in DRO and DRL (to be discussed later in this chapter) often postpone reinforcement, some behavior analysts have suggested that DRO and DRL be conceptualized as negative punishment procedures rather than reinforcement techniques. For example, Van Houten and Rolider (1990) consider DRO and DRL variations of a procedure they called *contingent reinforcement postponement (CRP)*.

Figure 22.5 Four basic variations of DRO that can be created by altering the schedule (fixed or variable) and omission requirement (interval or momentary).

Adapted from "DRO Contingencies: An Analysis of Variable-Momentary Schedules" by J. S. Lindberg, B. A. Iwata, S. W. Kahng, & I. G. DeLeon, 1999. *Journal of Applied Behavior Analysis, 32*, p. 125. Copyright 1999 by the Society for the Experimental Analysis of Behavior, Inc. Used by permission.

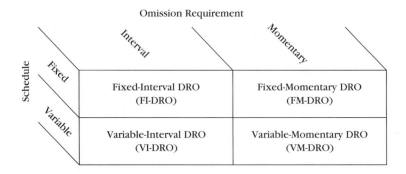

Interval DRO

The following sections introduce procedures for applying the fixed-interval DRO, variable-interval DRO, fixed-momentary DRO, and variable-momentary DRO schedules. Most researchers and practitioners use the fixed-interval DRO as an intervention for problem behaviors. However, a growing number of researchers and practitioners are exploring applications of variable-interval DRO and momentary DRO schedules.

Fixed-Interval DRO (FI-DRO)

Most applications of interval DRO apply the omission requirement at the end of successive time intervals of equal duration. To apply a **fixed-interval DRO (FI-DRO)** procedure, a practitioner (a) establishes an interval of time; (b) delivers reinforcement at the end of that interval if the problem did not occur during the interval; and (c) upon any occurrence of the problem behavior, immediately resets the timer to begin a new interval.[5] For example, Allen, Gottselig, and Boylan (1982) applied an FI-DRO procedure as a group contingency to decrease the disruptive classroom behaviors of third-grade students.[6] A kitchen timer was set to 5-minute intervals and continued to run as long as no disruptive behaviors occurred. If any student engaged in disruptive behavior at any time during the 5-minute interval, the timer was reset and a new 5-minute interval began. When the timer signaled the end of a 5-minute interval without disruptive behavior, the class was awarded 1 minute of free time, which they accumulated and used at the end of the class period.

The DRO interval and treatment session length can be increased gradually as the person's behavior improves. Cowdery, Iwata, and Pace (1990) used FI-DRO to help

Jerry, a 9-year-old who had never attended school and spent most of his time hospitalized because he scratched and rubbed his skin so often and hard that he had open lesions all over his body. During treatment, the experimenter left the room and watched Jerry through an observation window. Cowdery and colleagues initially made praise and token reinforcement contingent on 2-minute "scratch-free" intervals, which were determined by baseline assessment. If Jerry scratched during the interval, the experimenter entered the room and told him she regretted he had not earned a penny and asked him to try again. Jerry's SIB immediately decreased to zero when DRO was first implemented and remained low as the DRO interval and session length were gradually increased (from three 2-minute intervals to three 4-minute intervals). Following a brief return to baseline conditions in which Jerry's scratching quickly increased, DRO was reinstated with five intervals per session and session length was increased in 1-minute increments. Jerry could now earn a total of 10 tokens per session, a token for each interval in which he did not scratch plus a 5-token bonus if he refrained from scratching for all five intervals. Jerry's SIB gradually reduced to zero as session length and DRO intervals were extended (see Figure 22.6). Session 61 consisted of a single 15-minute DRO interval, which was followed by 25- and 30-minute intervals.

Variable-Interval DRO (VI-DRO)

When reinforcement is delivered contingent on the absence of the targeted problem behavior during intervals of varying and unpredictable durations, a **variable-interval DRO (VI-DRO)** schedule is in effect. For example, on a VI-DRO 10-second schedule, reinforcement would be delivered contingent on the omission of the behavior throughout intervals of varying duration that average 10 seconds (e.g., a random sequence of 2-second, 5-second, 8-second, 15-second, and 20-second intervals).

Chiang, Iwata, and Dorsey (1979) used a VI-DRO intervention to decrease the inappropriate behaviors during bus rides to and from school of a 10-year-old student

---

[5]A DRO contingency can also be applied using data from permanent product measurement. For example, Alberto and Troutman (2006) described a procedure in which a teacher provided reinforcement each time a student submitted a paper that contained no doodles. If the papers were basically of the same length or type, the procedure would be a variation of the fixed-interval DRO.

[6]Group contingencies are described in Chapter 26.

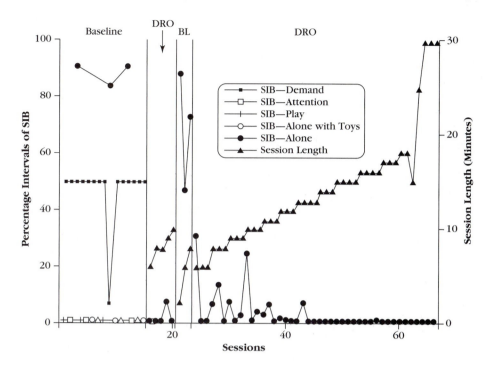

Figure 22.6   Percentage intervals of SIB by Jerry during baseline and DRO and duration of DRO sessions (right *y* axis). Other data points during first baseline phase show results of functional analysis confirming that Jerry's SIB occurred most often when he was left alone.

From Cowdery, G., Iwata, B. A., & Pace, G. M. (1990). Effects and Side Effects of DRO as Treatment for Self-injurious Behavior. *Journal of Applied Behavior Analysis, 23,* 497–506. Copyright 1990 by the Society for the Experimental Analysis of Behavior, Inc. Used by permission.

with developmental disabilities. The boy's disruptive behaviors included aggression (e.g., slapping, poking, hitting, kicking), being out of seat, stereotypic behaviors, and inappropriate vocalizations (e.g., screaming, yelling). Instead of basing the DRO intervals on elapsed time, the researchers used an interesting procedure they described as a "distance-based" DRO schedule. The driver divided the bus route into sections designated by landmarks such as stop signs and traffic lights and mounted a four-digit hand counter on the dashboard of the bus. The counter was within reach of the driver and within view of the student. At each predetermined landmark the bus driver praised the student's behavior and added one point to the hand counter if no disruptive behaviors had been emitted during the DRO interval. Upon arrival at home or school the driver recorded the number of points earned on a card and gave the card to the boy's foster father or teacher. The student exchanged the points earned for rewards (e.g., access to toys, home and school privileges, small snacks).

Chiang and colleagues used a two-tier multiple baseline across settings design to evaluate the VI-DRO intervention. During baseline, disruptive behavior ranged from 20 to 100% with an average of 66.2% for the afternoon rides and 0 to 92% with an average of 48.5% in the mornings. When the VI-DRO procedure was implemented on the afternoon rides only, disruptive behavior decreased immediately to an average of 5.1% (range of 0 to 40%) on the afternoon rides but remained unchanged during the morning rides. When the intervention was applied also in the mornings, all disruptive behavior was eliminated.

Progar and Colleagues (2001) implemented VI-DRO as one component of a conjunctive schedule of reinforcement to reduce the aggressive behaviors of Milty, a 14-year-old boy with autism. Reinforcement is delivered on a conjunctive schedule when the requirements of both schedule components had been met; in this case a fixed-ratio 3 schedule for task completion and a variable-interval 148-second schedule for the absence of aggression. Milty received an edible reinforcer each time he completed three components of a task (e.g., making his bed, vacuuming, straightening objects in his room) in the absence of aggression for the duration of the variable interval. An occurrence of aggression prior to completing the FR 3-second requirement reset both components of the conjunctive schedule. This intervention produced a substantial reduction of aggressive behavior.

Momentary DRO

Fixed-momentary DRO (FM-DRO) and **variable-momentary DRO (VM-DRO)** schedules use the same procedures as interval DRO (FI-DRO, VI-DRO) except that reinforcement is contingent on the absence of the problem behavior only when each interval ends, rather than throughout the entire interval as with the whole-interval DRO.

Lindberg, Iwata, Kahng, and DeLeon (1999) used a VM-DRO intervention to help Bridget, a 50-year-old woman with severe developmental disabilities who often banged her head and hit herself on the head and body. A functional analysis indicated that Bridget's self-injurious behaviors (SIB) were maintained by social-positive reinforcement. During the VM-DRO intervention, her SIB was placed on extinction, and Bridget received 3 to 5 seconds of attention from the therapist if she was not banging her head or hitting herself when each interval ended. Bridget did not have to refrain from SIB throughout the interval, only at the end of the interval. As shown in Figure 22.7, when a VM-DRO 15-second schedule was implemented for five sessions following baseline, Bridget's SIB decreased abruptly from baseline levels to almost zero. Following a return to baseline in which Bridget's SIB increased, the researchers returned to a VM-DRO treatment condition of 11 seconds, which was later thinned to 22 seconds, and then to the maximum target interval of 300 seconds.

Guidelines for Using DRO

Interval DRO has been used more widely than momentary DRO. Some researchers have found that interval DRO is more effective than momentary DRO for suppressing problem behavior, and that momentary DRO might be most useful in maintaining reduced levels of problem behavior produced by interval DRO (Barton, Brulle, & Repp, 1986; Repp, Barton, & Brulle, 1983). Lindberg and colleagues (1999) noted two potential advantages of VM-DRO schedules over FI-DRO schedules. First, the VM-DRO schedule appears more practical because the practitioner does not need to monitor the participant's behavior at all times. Second, data obtained by these researchers showed that participants obtained higher overall rates of reinforcement with VM-DRO than they did with FI-DRO.

In addition to the importance of selecting potent reinforcers, we recommend the following guidelines for the effective use of DRO.

Recognize the Limitations of DRO

Although DRO is often positive and highly effective for reducing problem behaviors, it is not without shortcomings. With interval DRO, reinforcement is delivered contingent only on the absence of problem behavior during the interval, even though another inappropriate behavior might have occurred during that time. For instance, let us assume that a 20-second interval DRO is to be implemented to reduce the facial tics of an adolescent with Tourette's syndrome. Reinforcement will be delivered at the end of each 20-second interval containing no facial tics. However, if the adolescent engages in cursing behavior at any time during the interval or at the end of the interval, reinforcement will still be delivered. It is possible that reinforcement delivered contingent on the absence of facial tics will occur in close temporal proximity to cursing, thereby inadvertently strengthening another inappropriate behavior. In such cases, the length of the DRO interval should be shortened and/or the definition of the problem behavior expanded to include the other undesirable behaviors (e.g., reinforcement contingent on the absence of facial tics *and* cursing).

With momentary DRO, reinforcement is delivered contingent on the problem behavior not occurring at the end of each interval, even though the inappropriate behavior might have occurred throughout most of an interval. Continuing the previous example, on an FM-DRO 20-second schedule, reinforcement will be delivered at

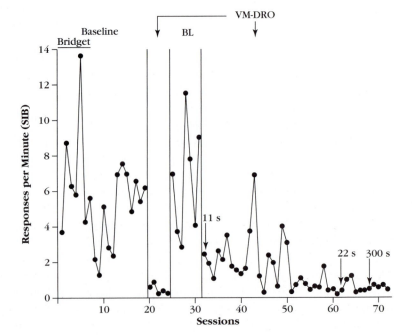

Figure 22.7   Responses per minute of self-injurious behavior (SIB) during baseline and treatment conditions.

From "DRO Contingencies: An Analysis of Variable-momentary Schedules" by J. S. Lindberg, B. A. Iwata, S. W. Kahng, & I. G. DeLeon, 1999. *Journal of Applied Behavior Analysis, 32,* p. 131. Copyright 1999 by the Society for the Experimental Analysis of Behavior, Inc. Reprinted by permission.

each successive 20th second if facial tics are not occurring at those precise moments, even if tics occurred for 50%, 75%, or even 95% of the interval. In such circumstances, the practitioner should use interval DRO and reduce the length of the DRO interval.

DRO may not always be successful, and practitioners must be alert to their data to make informed decisions. For instance, Linscheid, Iwata, Ricketts, Williams, and Griffin (1990) found that the systematic application of neither DRO nor DRI eliminated the chronic self-injurious behavior of five people with developmental disabilities. A more intrusive punishment procedure eventually had to be instituted to eliminate the behavior.

Set Initial DRO Intervals That Assure Frequent Reinforcement

Practitioners should establish an initial DRO time interval that ensures that the learner's current level of behavior will contact reinforcement when the DRO contingency is applied. For example, Cowdery and colleagues (1990) initially made praise and token reinforcement contingent on 2-minute "scratch-free" intervals because that was "the longest we had previously seen Jerry refrain from scratching while left alone" (p. 501). Beginning with an interval that is equal to or slightly less than the mean baseline interresponse time (IRT) usually will make an effective initial DRO interval. To calculate a mean IRT, the practitioner divides the total duration of all baseline measurements by the total number of responses recorded during baseline. For example, if a total of 90 responses were recorded during 30 minutes of baseline measurement, the mean IRT would be 30 seconds (i.e., 1,800 seconds ÷ 90 responses). Using these baseline data as a guide, the practitioner could set the initial DRO interval at 30 seconds or less.

Do Not Inadvertently Reinforce Other Undesirable Behaviors

Reinforcement on a "pure" DRO schedule is contingent on a very general response class that is defined only by the absence of the targeted problem behavior. Consequently, a "pure" DRO is typically used as a treatment of choice for serious behavior problems that occur at very high rates by people whose current repertoires provide few, if any, other behaviors that might function as alternative or incompatible behaviors and for whom just about anything else they might do is less of a problem than the target behavior.

Because DRO does not require that any certain behaviors be emitted for reinforcement, whatever the person is doing when reinforcement is delivered is likely to

occur more often in the future. Therefore, practitioners using DRO must be careful not to strengthen inadvertently other undesirable behaviors. When using DRO, the practitioner should deliver reinforcement at the intervals or moments in time specified by the schedule contingent on the absence of the problem behavior *and* the absence of any other significant inappropriate behaviors.

Gradually Increase the DRO Interval

The practitioner can increase the DRO interval after the initial DRO interval effectively controls the problem behavior (i.e., thinning the reinforcement schedule). The DRO schedule should be thinned by increasing the interval through a series of initially small and gradually increasing increments.

Poling and Ryan (1982) suggested three procedures for increasing the duration of the DRO interval.

1. Increase the DRO interval by a *constant duration* of time. For example, a practitioner could, at each opportunity for an interval increase, increase the DRO interval by 15 seconds.

2. Increase intervals *proportionately*. For example, a practitioner, at each opportunity to change the interval, could increase the DRO interval by 10%.

3. Change the DRO interval each session based on the *learner's performance*. For example, a practitioner could set the DRO interval for each session equal to the mean IRT from the preceding session.

If problem behavior worsens when a larger DRO interval is introduced, the practitioner can decrease the duration of the interval to a level that again controls the problem behavior. The DRO interval can then be extended with smaller, more gradual durations after previously obtained reductions in problem behavior have been reestablished.

Extend the Application of DRO to Other Settings and Times of Day

When the frequency of the problem behavior is reduced substantially in the treatment setting, the DRO intervention can be introduced during other activities and times in the person's natural environment. Having teachers, parents, or other caregivers begin to deliver reinforcement on the DRO schedule will help extend the effects. For example, after Jerry's SIB was under good control during treatment sessions (see Figure 22.6), Cowdery and Colleagues (1990) began to implement the DRO intervention at other times and places during the day. At first, various staff members would praise Jerry and give him tokens for refraining from scratching during single 30-minute DRO intervals during leisure activities, instructional sessions, or free time. Then they began added additional 30-minute DRO intervals until the DRO contingency was extended to all of Jerry's waking hours. Jerry's SIB decreased sufficiently to allow him to be discharged to his home for the first time in two years. Jerry's parents were taught how to implement the DRO procedure at home.

Combine DRO with Other Procedures

DRO can be used as a single intervention. However, as with DRI/DRA, including DRO in a treatment package with other behavior-reduction procedures often yields more efficient and effective behavior change. De Zubicaray and Clair (1998) used a combination of DRO, DRI, and a restitution (punishment) procedure to reduce the physical and verbal abuse and physical aggression of a 46-year-old woman with mental retardation living in a residential facility for people with chronic psychiatric disorders. Further, the results of three experiments by Rolider and Van Houten (1984) showed that an intervention consisting of DRO plus reprimands was more effective than DRO alone in decreasing a variety of problem behaviors by children (e.g., physical abuse by a 4-year-old girl toward her baby sister, thumb sucking by a 12-year-old boy, and bedtime tantrums).

DRO can also be added as a supplement to an intervention that has produced insufficient results. McCord, Iwata, Galensky, Ellingson, and Thomson (2001) added DRO to a stimulus fading intervention that was "having limited success" in decreasing the problem behaviors of Sarah, a 41-year-old woman with severe mental retardation and visual impairment. Her problem behaviors included severe self-injurious behavior, property destruction, and aggression evoked by noise. Gradually increasing the noise volume by 2 dB when DRO was in effect, "a therapist delivered a preferred edible item (half a cheese puff) to Sarah following each 6-s interval in which problem behavior was not observed. If problem behavior occurred, the food was withheld and the DRO interval was reset" (p. 455). Each time Sarah completed three consecutive 1-minute sessions with no occurrences of the problem behavior, the researchers increased the DRO interval by 2 seconds. This schedule thinning continued until Sarah could complete the session with no occurrences of the problem behavior. The therapist then delivered the edible item only at the end of the session. The addition of DRO to the intervention produced an immediate decrease in Sarah's problem behavior, which remained at or near zero in the treatment setting for more than 40 sessions (see Chapter 6, the bottom graph of Figure 6.6). Probes conducted in noisy conditions after treatment ended showed that the treatment effects had maintained and generalized to Sarah's home.

Differential Reinforcement of Low Rates of Responding

In laboratory research, Ferster and Skinner (1957) found that delivering a reinforcer following a response that had been preceded by increasingly longer intervals of time without a response reduced the overall rate of responding. When reinforcement is applied in this manner as an intervention to reduce the occurrences of a target behavior, the procedure is called **differential reinforcement of low rates (DRL).** Because reinforcement with a DRL schedule is delivered following an *occurrence* of the target behavior, as contrasted with DRO in which reinforcement is contingent on the complete *absence* of the behavior, behavior analysts use DRL to decrease the rate of a behavior that occurs too frequently, but not to eliminate the behavior entirely. For example, a practitioner may identify a certain behavior as a problem behavior not because of the form of that behavior, but because the behavior occurs too often. For example, a student raising his hand or coming to the teacher's desk to ask for help during independent seatwork is a good thing, but becomes a problem behavior if it occurs excessively.

Some learners may emit a behavior less frequently when told to do the behavior less often, or when given rules stating an appropriate rate of response. When instruction alone does not diminish occurrences of the problem behavior, the practitioner may need to use a consequence-based intervention. DRL offers practitioners an intervention for diminishing problem behaviors that is stronger than instruction alone, but still falls short of more restrictive consequences (e.g., punishment). Deitz (1977) named and described three DRL procedures: full-session DRL, interval DRL, and spaced-responding DRL.

Full-Session DRL

In a **full-session DRL** procedure, reinforcement is delivered at the end of an instructional or treatment session if during the entire session the target behavior occurred at a number equal to or below a predetermined criterion. If the number of responses exceeds the specified limit during the session, reinforcement is withheld. For example, a teacher applying a full-session DRL with a criterion limit of four disruptive acts per class period would provide reinforcement at the end of the class period contingent on four or fewer disruptive acts. Full-session DRL is an effective, efficient, and easy-to-apply intervention for problem behaviors in education and treatment settings.

Deitz and Repp (1973) demonstrated the efficacy and manageability of full-session DRL for diminishing classroom misbehavior. They decreased the talk-outs of an 11-year-old boy with developmental disabilities. During 10 days of baseline, the student averaged 5.7 talk-outs per 50-minute session. With the introduction of full-session DRL, the student was allowed 5 minutes for play at the end of the day contingent on 3 or fewer talk-outs during a 50-minute session. Talk-outs during the DRL condition decreased to an average of 0.93 talk-outs per 50 minutes. A return to baseline slightly increased the talk-outs to an average of 1.5 per session (see Figure 22.8)

Interval DRL

To apply an **interval DRL** schedule of reinforcement, the practitioner divides a total session into a series of equal intervals of time and provides reinforcement at the end of each interval in which the number of occurrences of the problem behavior during that interval is equal to or below a criterion limit. The practitioner removes the opportunity for reinforcement and begins a new interval if the learner exceeds the criterion number of responses during the time interval. For example, if a DRL criterion limit is four problem behaviors per hour, the practitioner delivers a reinforcer at the end of each 15 minutes contingent on the occurrence of no more than one problem behavior. If the participant emits a second problem behavior during the interval, the practitioner immediately begins a new 15-minute interval. Beginning a new interval postpones the opportunity for reinforcement.

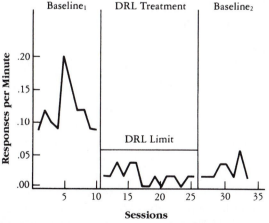

Figure 22.8 Rate of talk-outs during baseline and treatment phases for a student with developmental disabilities.

Deitz (1977) initially defined the interval DRL schedule of reinforcement using a criterion of one response or no responses per interval. However, Deitz and Repp (1983) reported programming an interval DRL schedule with a criterion above one per interval. "A response which occurs an average of 14 times per hour could be limited to three occurrences per 15-minute interval. The response limit of three could then be lowered to two responses per interval, and then to one response per interval" (p. 37).

Deitz and colleagues (1978) used an interval DRL schedule of reinforcement to reduce the disruptive behaviors of a student with learning disabilities. The 7-year-old student had several difficult classroom misbehaviors (e.g., running, shoving, pushing, hitting, throwing objects). The student received a sheet of paper ruled into 15 blocks, with each block representing a 2-minute interval. A star was placed in a block each time the student completed 2 minutes with 1 or no misbehaviors. Each star permitted the student to spend 1 minute on the playground with the teacher. If the student emitted 2 misbehaviors during the interval, the teacher immediately started a new 2-minute interval.

Effective application of interval DRL (as well as the spaced-responding DRL procedure described in the following section) requires continuous monitoring of problem behavior, careful timing, and frequent reinforcement. Without the help of an assistant, many practitioners may have difficulty applying the interval DRL procedure in group settings. Interval and spaced-responding DRL procedures are quite reasonable for one-on-one instruction or when competent assistance is available.

Spaced-Responding DRL

Using a **spaced-responding DRL** schedule of reinforcement, the practitioner delivers a reinforcer following an occurrence of a response that is separated by at least a minimum amount of time from the previous response.[7] As you will recall from Chapter 4, *interresponse time (IRT)* is the technical term for the duration of time between two responses. IRT and rate of responding are directly correlated: the longer the IRT, the lower the overall rate of responding; shorter IRTs correlate with higher response rates. When reinforcement is contingent on increasingly longer IRTs, response rate will decrease.

Favell, McGimsey, and Jones (1980) used a spaced-responding DRL schedule of reinforcement and response prompts to decrease the rapid eating of four persons with

---

[7]Because reinforcement in a spaced-responding DRL immediately follows an instance of the target behavior, it is the applied variation of DRL that most closely resembles the DRL schedules of reinforcement described by Ferster and Skinner (1957).

profound developmental disabilities. At the start of treatment, reinforcement was contingent on short independent pauses (IRTs) between bites of food, and then gradually required longer and longer pauses between bites. The researchers also manually prompted a separation between bites of food and faded out those response prompts when a minimum of 5-second pauses occurred independently between approximately 75% of all bites. Finally, Favell and colleagues gradually thinned food reinforcement and praise. The frequency of eating was decreased from a pretreatment baseline average of 10 to 12 bites per 30 seconds to 3 to 4 bites per 30 seconds during the spaced-responding DRL condition.

Most behavior-reduction procedures that manipulate consequences have the potential to reduce behavior to zero occurrences. Spaced-responding DRL is unlikely to do that. For that reason, spaced-responding DRL becomes an important intervention for diminishing behavior: A spaced-responding DRL contingency tells learners that their behavior is acceptable, but they should do it less often. For example, a teacher could use a spaced-responding DRL schedule to diminish a student's problem behavior of asking too many questions. The questions occurred so frequently that they interfered with the classroom learning and teaching. To intervene, the teacher could respond to the student's question if the student had not asked a question during a preceding minimum of 5 minutes. This spaced-responding DRL intervention could decrease, yet not eliminate, asking questions.

Singh, Dawson, and Manning (1981) used a spaced-responding DRL intervention to reduce the stereotypic responding (e.g., repetitive body movements, rocking) of three teenage girls with profound mental retardation. During the first phase of spaced-responding DRL intervention, the therapist praised each girl whenever she emitted a stereotypic response at least 12 seconds after the last response. One of the experimenters timed the intervals and used a system of automated lights to signal the therapist when reinforcement was available. After the DRL 12-second IRT resulted in an abrupt decrease in stereotypic behavior by all three girls (see Figure 22.9), Singh and colleagues systematically increased the IRT criterion to 30, 60, and then 180 seconds. The spaced-responding DRL procedure not only produced substantial reductions in stereotypic responding in all three subjects but also had the concomitant effect of increasing appropriate behavior (e.g., smiling, talking, playing).

Guidelines for Using DRL

Several factors influence the effectiveness of the three DRL schedules in diminishing problem behaviors. The following guidelines address those factors.

Recognize the Limitations of DRL

If a practitioner needs to reduce an inappropriate behavior quickly, DRL would not be the method of first choice. DRL is slow. Reducing the inappropriate behavior to appropriate levels may take more time than the practitioner can afford. Further, DRL would not be advisable for use with self-injurious, violent, or potentially dangerous behaviors. Finally, from a practical standpoint, using DRL means that the practitioner must focus on the inappropriate behavior. If a teacher, for example, is not cautious, he may inadvertently give too much attention to the inappropriate behavior, inadvertently reinforcing it.

Choose the Most Appropriate DRL Procedure

Full-session, interval, and spaced-responding DRL schedules provide different levels of reinforcement for learners. Of the three DRL procedures, only spaced-responding DRL delivers reinforcement immediately following the occurrence of specific response; a response must be emitted following a minimum IRT before reinforcement. Practitioners use spaced-responding DRL to reduce the occurrences of a behavior while maintaining those behaviors at lower rates.

With full-session and interval DRL, a response does not need to occur for the participant to receive the reinforcer. Practitioners may apply full-session or interval DRL when it is acceptable that the rate of the problem behavior reaches zero or as an initial step toward the goal of eliminating the behavior.

Spaced-responding and interval DRL usually produce reinforcement at a higher rate than full-session DRL does. Arranging frequent contact with the reinforcement contingency is especially appropriate, and most often necessary, for learners with severe problem behaviors.

Use Baseline Data to Guide the Selection of the Initial Response or IRT Limits

Practitioners can use the mean number of responses emitted during baseline sessions, or slightly lower than that average, as the initial full-session DRL criterion. For example, 8, 13, 10, 7, and 12 responses recorded per session over five baseline sessions produce a mean of 10 responses. Therefore, 8 to 10 responses per session makes an appropriate initial full-session DRL criterion.

Interval DRL and spaced-responding DRL initial time criteria can be set at the baseline mean or slightly lower. For example, 1 response per 15 minutes makes an acceptable initial interval DRL criterion as calculated from a baseline mean of 4 responses per 60-minute session. With the same baseline data (i.e., 4 responses per 60-minute session), it appears reasonable to use 15 minutes

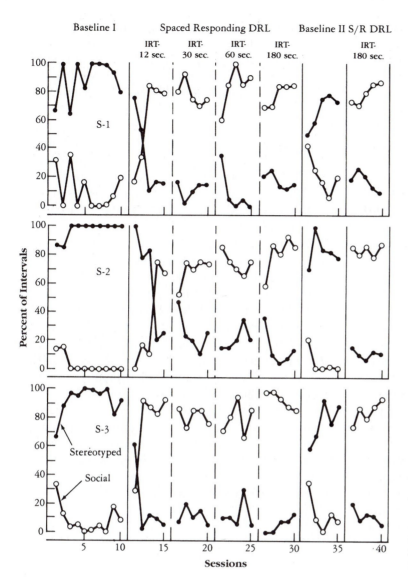

Figure 22.9 Effects of spaced-responding DRL on stereotypic responding of three teenage girls with profound mental retardation.

From "Effects of Spaced Responding DRL on the Stereotyped Behavior of Profoundly Retarded Persons" by N. N. Singh, M. J. Dawson, and P. Manning, 1981. *Journal of Applied Behavior Analysis, 38,* p. 524. Copyright 1981 by the Society for the Experimental Analysis of Behavior, Inc. Reprinted by permission.

as the initial IRT criterion for a spaced-responding DRL schedule. That is, a response will produce reinforcement only if it is separated from the prior response by a minimum of 15 minutes.

Gradually Thin the DRL Schedule

Practitioners should gradually thin the DRL schedule to achieve the desired final rate of responding. Practitioners commonly use three procedures for thinning the initial DRL time criterion.

1. *With full-session DRL,* the practitioner can set a new DRL criterion using the participant's current DRL performances. Another option is to set a new DRL criterion at slightly less than the mean num-ber of responses emitted during recent DRL sessions.

2. *With interval DRL,* the practitioner can gradually decrease the number of responses per interval if the current criterion is more than one response per interval; or, gradually increase the duration of the criterion interval if the current criterion is one response per interval.

3. *With spaced-responding DRL,* the practitioner can adjust the IRT criterion based on the mean IRT of recent sessions, or slightly less than that average. For example, Wright and Vollmer (2002) set the IRT for the DRL component of a treatment package that successfully reduced the rapid eating of a 17-year-old girl at the mean IRT of the previous five sessions. The researchers did not exceed an

IRT of 15 seconds because it was not necessary to reduce the girl's eating below a rate of four bites per minute.

Practitioners who successfully thin DRL schedules of reinforcement make only gradual, but systematic, changes in time and response criteria associated with full, interval, and space-responding DRL variations.

Two possible decision rules for thinning the DRL schedule are:

Rule 1: Practitioners may want to change the DRL criterion whenever the learner meets or exceeds the criterion during three consecutive sessions.

Rule 2: Practitioners may want to change the DRL criterion whenever the learner receives reinforcement for at least 90% of the opportunities during three consecutive sessions.

Provide Feedback to the Learner

The effectiveness of a DRL procedure can be enhanced by feedback to help the learner monitor her rate of responding. Full-session, interval, and spaced-responding DRL procedures provide different levels of feedback for participants. The most accurate feedback comes with spaced-responding DRL because reinforcement follows each response that meets the IRT criterion. When a response occurs that does not meet the IRT criterion, reinforcement is withheld, the time interval is immediately reset,

and a new interval begins. This process provides learners with immediate feedback on responding per interval.

Interval DRL also provides a high level of feedback, although it is less than that of spaced-responding DRL. Interval DRL provides the learner with two types of feedback. The first problem behavior does not provide feedback. The second response, however, resets the time interval, providing a consequence for the problem behavior. Reinforcement occurs at the end of the interval when one or no problem behaviors occurred during the interval. These two types of feedback improve the effectiveness of the interval DRL intervention (Deitz et al., 1978).

Applied behavior analysts can arrange full-session DRL with or without feedback. The usual arrangement does not provide feedback concerning moment-to-moment accumulation of responses. Deitz (1977) stated that with full-session DRL, learners would respond only to the DRL criterion: If learners exceeded the criterion they lose the opportunity for reinforcement. Once the learner loses the opportunity for reinforcement, he could then emit high rates of misbehavior without consequence. When the schedule is arranged without moment-to-moment feedback, learners usually stay well below the DRL limit. Full-session DRL, without moment-to-moment feedback, may not be as effective for learners with severe problem behaviors as spaced-responding and interval DRL. The effectiveness of full-session DRL relies heavily on an initial verbal description of the contingencies of reinforcement (Deitz, 1977).

 Summary

Basic Description of Differential Reinforcement

1. When used as a reductive procedure for problem behavior, differential reinforcement consists of two components: (a) providing reinforcement contingent on either the occurrence of a behavior other than the problem behavior or the problem behavior occurring at a reduced rate, and (b) withholding reinforcement as much as possible for the problem behavior.

Differential Reinforcement of Incompatible Behavior and Differential Reinforcement of Alternative Behavior

2. Differential reinforcement of an incompatible or alternative behavior can be conceptualized as a schedule of reinforcement in which two concurrent operants—the inappropriate behavior targeted for reduction and the appropriate behavior selected—receive reinforcement at different rates.

3. DRI and DRA have the dual effect of weakening the problem behavior while simultaneously strengthening acceptable behaviors that are either incompatible with or an alternative to the targeted problem behaviors.

4. With DRI, reinforcement is delivered for a behavior topographically incompatible with the target problem behavior and withheld following instances of the problem behavior.

5. With DRA, reinforcement is delivered for a behavior that serves as a desirable alternative to the target problem behavior and withheld following instances of the problem behavior.

6. When using DRI/DRA, practitioners should do the following:

   - Select incompatible or alternative behaviors that are present in the learner's repertoire, require equal or less effort than the problem behavior, are being emitted prior to intervention with sufficient frequency to provide opportunities for reinforcement, and are likely to produce reinforcement when the intervention ends.

   - Select potent reinforcers that can be delivered when the alternative/incompatible behavior occurs and withheld following instances of the problem behavior. The same consequence that has been maintaining the problem behavior prior to intervention is often the most effective reinforcer for DRI/DRA.

- Reinforce the alternative/incompatible behavior on a continuous reinforcement schedule initially and then gradually thin the schedule of reinforcement.

- Maximize the difference between rates of reinforcement for the alternative/incompatible behavior and the problem behavior by putting the problem behavior on an extinction schedule.

- Combine DRI/DRA with other reductive procedures to produce a more potent intervention.

Differential Reinforcement of Other Behavior

7. With DRO, reinforcement is contingent on the absence of the problem behavior during or at specific times (i.e., momentary DRO).

8. On an interval DRO schedule, reinforcement is delivered at the end of specific intervals of time if the problem did not occur during the interval.

9. On a momentary DRO schedule, reinforcement is delivered at specific moments in time if the problem is not occurring at those times.

10. Availability of reinforcement with interval and momentary DRO procedures can occur on fixed- or variable-time schedules.

11. When using DRO, practitioners should do the following:
    - Establish an initial DRO time interval that ensures that the learner's current level of behavior will produce frequent reinforcement when the DRO contingency is applied.
    - Be careful not to reinforce inadvertently other inappropriate behaviors.
    - Deliver reinforcement at the intervals or moments in time specified by the DRO schedule contingent on the absence of the problem behavior *and* the absence of any other significant inappropriate behaviors.
    - Gradually increase the DRO interval based on decreases in the problem behavior.

- Extend DRO in other settings and times of day after the problem behavior is substantially reduced in the treatment setting.

- Combine DRO with other reductive procedures.

Differential Reinforcement of Low Rates of Responding

12. DRL schedules produce low, consistent rates of responding.

13. Reinforcement on a full-session DRL schedule is delivered when responding during an entire instructional or treatment session is equal to or below a criterion limit.

14. On an interval DRL schedule, the total session is divided into equal intervals and reinforcement is provided at the end of each interval in which the number of responses during the interval is equal to or below a criterion limit.

15. Reinforcement on a spaced-responding DRL schedule follows each occurrence of the target behavior that is separated from the previous response by a minimum inter-response time (IRT).

16. When using DRL, practitioners should do the following:
    - Not use DRL if a problem behavior needs to be reduced quickly.
    - Not use DRL with self-injurious or other violent behaviors.
    - Select the most appropriate DRL schedules: full-session or interval DRL when it is acceptable that the rate of the problem behavior reaches zero or as an initial step toward the goal of eliminating the behavior; spaced-responding DRL for reducing the rate of a behavior to be maintained in the learner's repertoire.
    - Use baseline data to guide the selection of the initial response or IRT limits.
    - Gradually thin the DRL schedule to achieve the desired final rate of responding.
    - Provide feedback to help the learner monitor the rate of responding.

CHAPTER 23

Antecedent Interventions

Key Terms

antecedent intervention
behavioral momentum
fixed-time schedule (FT)
functional communication
   training (FCT)

high-probability (high-*p*) request
   sequence

noncontinent reinforcement (NCR)
variable-time schedule (VT)

Behavior Analyst Certification Board® BCBA® & BCABA® Behavior Analyst Task List,© Third Edition

Content Area 9: Behavior Change Procedures	
9-1	Use antecedent-based interventions, such as: contextual or ecological variables, establishing operations, and discriminative stimuli.
9-5	Use response-independent (time-based) schedules of reinforcement.
9-23	Use behavioral momentum.
9-26	Use language acquisition/communication training procedures.

Applied behavior analysts traditionally emphasized the three-term contingency: how consequences affect behavior, and how differential consequences produce stimulus discrimination (S^D) and stimulus control. Rarely did applied behavior analysts address how an antecedent event itself affected behavior. However, this situation changed following the publication of two greatly influential articles: one on establishing operations (Michael, 1982) and the other on functional analysis (Iwata, Dorsey, Slifer, Bauman, & Richman, 1982/1994). The convergence of motivating operations (MOs) and functional behavior assessments allowed applied behavior analysts to conceptually align applied research on the effects of antecedent conditions other than stimulus control (e.g., S^Ds) to basic principles of behavior. This convergence advanced our understanding of how antecedents affect behavior, a historically underemphasized area of applied behavior analysis.

Practitioners have long used antecedents effectively to develop desirable behaviors, to diminish problem behaviors, and to design environments that select adaptive behaviors in social, academic, leisure, and work environments. Arguably, teachers may use antecedent interventions more frequently than consequence arrangements (e.g., reinforcement, punishment, extinction) to change behavior. The long-established practice of arranging antecedent conditions for behavior change adds support to an increasing experimental database of desirable behavioral outcomes that are functionally related to changing antecedent conditions (e.g., Wilder & Carr, 1998). Table 23.1 shows common behavior challenges and the antecedent interventions that practitioners have used to address them.

Defining Antecedent Interventions

Conceptual Understanding of Antecedent Interventions

Some textbooks and journal articles classify all antecedent-based behavior change strategies under a single term such as *antecedent procedures, antecedent control, antecedent manipulations,* or *antecedent interventions.* Although economical, using the same term to identify interventions based on stimulus control (S^Ds) and interventions involving motivating operations (MOs) can lead to confusion about, or failure to recognize, the different functions of these antecedent events. S^Ds evoke behavior because they have been correlated with increased availability of reinforcement. The evocative function of MOs, however, is independent of the differential availability of effective reinforcement. MOs (e.g., an establishing operation) increase the current frequency of certain types of behavior even when an effective reinforcer is not available. Applied behavior analysts should be cognizant of the different factors underlying the evocative functions of S^Ds and MOs.

In addition to improved conceptual clarity and consistency, understanding the different reasons for the evocative functions of S^Ds and MOs has important applied implications. Antecedent treatments involving stimulus control must include manipulating consequent

Table 23.1 Examples of Behavior Challenges and Antecedent Interventions That Might Address Them

Challenging behavior situation	Antecedent intervention
Disruptive or noncompliant behaviors associated with doing homework or taking a bath.	Provide a choice: "Do you want to do your homework first, or take a bath first?"
Poor socialization and communication skills among persons with developmental disabilities eating at a cafeteria-style-arranged dinner table.	Switch the seating arrangement to a family-style configuration.
A student misbehaves by disrupting other students.	Move the misbehaving student's desk closer to the teacher and away from the peers bothered by the student's misbehavior.
Infant during the creeping and crawling stage can encounter many potentially dangerous events.	Attach gates to stairways, plug electrical outlets, put locks on cabinet doors, remove table lamps.
Student causes disruptions when requested to complete a math worksheet with 25 problems.	Present five sets of five problems each.
Some students misbehave when entering the resource room. Long transition times are clearly correlated with the misbehavior and lead to many difficult problem behaviors.	The teacher pins an index card for each student on the bulletin board. The card contained a personalized question. When entering the resource room, students take their cards from the bulletin board, go to their desks, and write a response to the question on the card.

events, changing the differential availability of reinforcement in the presence and absence of the S^D. Behavior change strategies based on motivating operations must change antecedent events. Understanding these differences may improve the development of more effective and efficient behavior change efforts involving antecedent events.

Classifying Functions of Antecedent Stimuli

Contingency Dependent

A *contingency-dependent* antecedent event is dependent on the consequences of behavior for developing evocative and abative effects. All stimulus control functions are contingency dependent. For example, in the presence of $2 + 2 = ?$, a student responds 4, not because of the stimulus $2 + 2 = ?$, but because of a past reinforcement history for saying 4, including perhaps a history of non-reinforcement for making any other response except 4. This chapter uses the term *antecedent control* to identify contingency-dependent antecedent events.

Contingency Independent

A *contingency-independent* antecedent event is not dependent on the consequences of behavior for developing evocative and abative effects. The antecedent event itself affects behavior–consequence relations. The effects of motivating operations are contingency independent. For example, sleep deprivation can influence the occurrences of problem behaviors in the absence of a history of pair-

ing sleep deprivation with reinforcement or punishment of those behaviors. This chapter uses the term **antecedent intervention** to identify behavior change tactics based on contingency-independent antecedent events.[1]

Antecedent Intervention

Abolishing Operations

Applied behavior analysts have used several antecedent interventions, singularly or in treatment packages, to decrease the effectiveness of reinforcers that maintain problem behaviors (i.e., abolishing operations). Table 23.2 provides examples of antecedent interventions that used abolishing operations to decrease the effectiveness of reinforcers maintaining the problem behaviors and a corresponding reduction of those behaviors.

Temporary Effects

Smith and Iwata (1997) reminded us that the effects of MOs are temporary. Antecedent interventions by themselves will not produce permanent improvements in behavior. However, while using an antecedent intervention to diminish a problem behavior, a teacher or therapist can simultaneously apply procedures such as extinction to reduce the problem behavior and differential reinforcement of alternative behaviors to compete with the problem behavior. Because of the temporary effects of MOs, antecedent interventions most often serve as one component

---

[1]Because Chapter 17 addressed contingency-dependent antecedent events (i.e., stimulus control), this chapter focuses on contingency-independent antecedent events (i.e., MOs).

Table 23.2   Examples of Antecedent Interventions Using Abolishing Operations

Abolishing operation	Example
Provide corrective prompts as an antecedent event.	Antecedent corrective academic prompts reduced destructive behavior to zero (Ebanks & Fisher, 2003).
Provide presession exposure to stimuli that function as reinforcers.	A father–son playtime preceding compliance sessions improved son's compliance to father's requests (Ducharme & Rushford, 2001).
Provide free access to leisure activities.	Manipulation of leisure items effectively competed with SIB maintained by automatic reinforcement (Lindberg et al., 2003).
Reduce noise levels.	Reducing noise levels decreased stereotypical covering ears with hands (Tang et al., 2002).
Change levels of social proximity.	Low levels of distant-proximity reduced aggressive behaviors (Oliver et al., 2001).
Offer choices.	Escape-maintained problem behaviors were decreased when students had opportunities to choose among tasks (Romaniuk et al., 2002).
Increasing response effort.	Increasing response effort for pica produced reductions in pica (Piazza et al., 2002).

of a treatment package (e.g., combining an antecedent intervention with extinction, differential reinforcement of alternative behavior, or other procedures). These kinds of treatments may produce maintaining effects.

Three antecedent interventions with established experimental results are noncontingent reinforcement, high-probability request sequence, and functional communication training. The remainder of this chapter will elaborate on these three antecedent interventions and present definitions and guidelines for their effective use.

Noncontingent Reinforcement

Noncontingent reinforcement (NCR) is an antecedent intervention in which stimuli with known reinforcing properties are delivered on a fixed-time (FT) or variable-time (VT) schedule independent of the learner's behavior (Vollmer, Iwata, Zarcone, Smith, & Mazaleski, 1993).[2] Noncontingent reinforcement may effectively diminish problem behaviors because the reinforcers that maintain

---

[2]This chapter uses the phrase *presenting stimuli with known reinforcing properties* to describe the delivery of noncontinent reinforcers. Interpreting the NCR procedure as presenting a reinforcer, or presenting a reinforcer noncontingent, on a fixed-time or variable-time schedule is technically inconsistent with the functional definition of reinforcement (Poling & Normand, 1999). Reinforcement requires a response–reinforcer relation. We use the term *NCR* in this chapter to describe the time-based procedures for reducing problem behaviors because the discipline of applied behavior analysis has continued its use, and the term *NCR* serves a useful descriptive purpose.

the problem behavior are available freely and frequently. This enriched environment with positive stimuli may function as an abolishing operation (AO), reducing the motivation to engage in the problem behavior.

NCR uses three distinct procedures that identify and deliver stimuli with known reinforcing properties: (a) positive reinforcement (i.e., social mediation), (b) negative reinforcement (i.e., escape), and (c) automatic reinforcement (i.e., without social mediation). NCR provides an important and effective intervention for problem behaviors. It is a common treatment for persons with developmental disabilities.

NCR with Positive Reinforcement

Kahng, Iwata, Thompson, and Hanley (2000) provided an excellent example of applying NCR with positive reinforcement. A functional analysis showed that social-positive reinforcement maintained self-injurious behavior (SIB) or aggression in three adults with developmental disabilities. During baseline, each occurrence of SIB or aggression produced attention for two of the adults, and a small bit of food for the third adult. During the initial sessions of NCR, the adults received attention or small bits of food on an initial fixed-time (FT) schedule (e.g., 5 seconds). Later, the schedule was thinned to a terminal criterion of 300 seconds. Figure 23.1 presents the baseline and NCR performances of the three adults and shows that the NCR procedure effectively decreased occurrences of SIB and aggression.

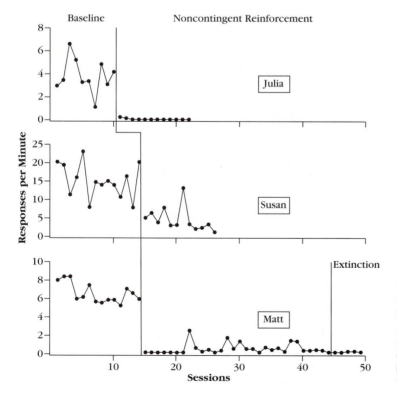

Figure 23.1 Number of SIB or aggressive responses per minute during baseline and NCR by three adults with developmental disabilities.

From "A Comparison of Procedures for Programming Noncontingent Reinforcement Schedules" by S. W. Kahng, B. A. Iwata, I. G. DeLeon, & M. D. Wallace 2000, *Journal of Applied Behavior Analysis, 33,* p. 426. Used by permission. Copyright 2000 by the Society for the Experimental Analysis of Behavior. Reproduced by permission.

NCR with Negative Reinforcement

Kodak, Miltenberger, and Romaniuk (2003) analyzed the effects of NCR escape on the instructional task compliance and problem behaviors of Andy and John, 4-year-old boys with autism. Andy's task was to point to cards with teacher-specified pictures, words, or letters on them. John used a marker to trace each letter of written words. Problem behaviors included resisting prompts, throwing materials, and hitting. During baseline, the therapist gave an instruction for task engagement, and contingent on problem behavior following the instruction, removed the task materials and turned away from the child for 10 seconds. During the NCR escape condition, the therapist used an initial FT 10-second schedule for escape, meaning that the student had a break from the instructional requests every 10 seconds of the session. The initial 10-second FT schedule was thinned each time the boy achieved a criterion for two consecutive sessions: 10 seconds to 20 seconds, to 30 seconds, to 1 minute, to 1.5 minutes, and finally to a terminal criterion of 2 minutes. The NCR escape procedure increased compliance and decreased problem behaviors.

NCR with Automatic Reinforcement

Lindberg, Iwata, Roscoe, Worsdell, and Hanley (2003) used NCR as a treatment to decrease the self-injurious behavior (SIB) of two women with profound mental retardation. A functional analysis documented that automatic reinforcement maintained their SIB. The NCR procedure provided Julie and Laura with free access to a variety of home-based, highly preferred leisure items (e.g., beads, string) that they could manipulate throughout the day. Figure 23.2 shows that NCR object manipulation of preferred leisure items effectively diminished SIB, and the effects were maintained up to a year later. This experiment is important because it showed that NCR object manipulation could compete with automatic reinforcement to reduce the occurrence of SIB.

Using NCR Effectively

Enhancing Effectiveness

The following procedural recommendations identify three key elements for enhancing the effectiveness of NCR. (a) The amount and quality of stimuli with known reinforcing properties influence the effectiveness of NCR. (b) Most treatments include extinction with NCR interventions. (c) Reinforcer preferences can change during intervention. That is, the NCR stimuli may not continue competing with the reinforcers that maintain the problem behavior. DeLeon, Anders, Rodriguez-Catter, and Neider (2000) recommended periodically using a variety of available stimuli with the NCR intervention to reduce problems of changing preferences.

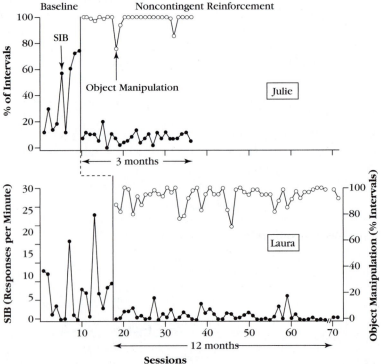

Figure 23.2 Levels of SIB and object manipulation exhibited by Julie and Laura during observations at home while NCR was implemented daily.

From "Treatment Efficacy of Noncontingent Reinforcement during Brief and Extended Application" by J. S. Lindberg, B. A. Iwata, E. M. Roscoe, A. S. Worsdell, & G. P. Hanley, 2003, *Journal of Applied Behavior Analysis, 36,* p. 14. Copyright 2003 by the Society for Experimental Analysis of Behavior. Reproduced by permission.

Functional Behavior Assessment

The effectiveness of using NCR is dependent on the correct identification of the positive, negative, or automatic reinforcers maintaining the problem behavior. Advances in functional behavior assessments have greatly improved the effectiveness of NCR by facilitating the identification of maintaining contingences of reinforcement (Iwata et al., 1982/1994).[3]

Emphasizing NCR

Applied behavior analysts can enhance the effectiveness of an NCR intervention by presenting a greater amount of stimuli with known reinforcing properties than the rate of reinforcement in the non-NCR condition. For example, Ringdahl, Vollmer, Borrero, and Connell (2001) found that NCR was ineffective when the baseline condition and the NCR condition contained a similar amount of reinforcer delivery. NCR was effective, however, when the NCR schedule was denser (i.e., continuous reinforcement) than the baseline schedule. Applied behavior analysts can use the rates of reinforcement during baseline to establish an initial NCR schedule to ensure a discrepancy between baseline and NCR conditions.

Ringdahl and colleagues (2001) suggested three procedures for emphasizing reinforcement during the NCR intervention: (a) Increase the delivery of stimuli with known reinforcing properties, (b) use an obviously different schedule of reinforcement at treatment onset (e.g., continuous reinforcement), and (c) combine differential reinforcement of other behavior (DRO) with the NCR treatment package. DRO will decrease the adventitious reinforcement of the problem behavior from the time-based NCR schedule.

Time-Based NCR Schedules

Most applications of NCR use a **fixed-time schedule (FT)** for the delivery of stimuli with known reinforcing properties. The interval of time for the presentation of these stimuli remains the same from delivery to delivery. When applied behavior analysts program the NCR time interval to vary from delivery to delivery, it is called a **variable-time schedule (VT).** For example, an NCR VT schedule of 10 seconds means that, on the average, stimuli with known reinforcing properties are presented every 10 seconds. This VT schedule could use time intervals such as 5, 7, 10, 12 and 15 seconds, arranged to occur in random sequence. Even though most applications of the NCR procedures have used FT schedules, VT schedules can be effective also (Carr, Kellum, & Chong, 2001).

Setting the initial NCR time schedule is an important aspect of the NCR procedure. The initial schedule can have an have an impact on the effectiveness of the intervention (Kahng, Iwata, DeLeon, & Wallace, 2000). Applied behavior analysts consistently recommend an initial dense FT or VT schedule (e.g., Van Camp, Lerman, Kelley, Contrucci, & Vorndran, 2000). The therapist can set a dense time value (e.g., 4 seconds) arbitrarily. Usually, however, it is more effective to set the initial time value based on the number of occurrences of the problem behavior, which will ensure frequent contact with the NCR stimuli.

The following procedure can be used to determine an initial NCR schedule: Divide the total duration of all baseline sessions by the total number of occurrences of the problem behavior recorded during baseline, and set the initial interval at or slightly below the quotient. For example, if the participant emitted 300 aggressive acts during 5 days of the baseline, and each baseline session was 10 minutes in duration, then 3,000 seconds divided by 300 responses produces a quotient of 10 seconds. Accordingly, these baseline data suggest an initial FT interval of 7 to 10 seconds.

Thinning Time-Based Schedules

Applied behavior analysts use a dense FT or VT schedule to begin the NCR procedure. They thin the schedule by adding small time increments to the NCR interval. However, thinning a time-based schedule is best begun only after the initial NCR interval has produced a reduction in the problem behavior.

Applied behavior analysts have used three procedures to thin NCR schedules: (a) constant time increase, (b) proportional time increase, and (c) session-to-session time increase or decrease (Hanley, Iwata, & Thompson, 2001; Van Camp et al., 2000).

Constant Time Increase. A therapist can increase the FT or VT schedule intervals by using a constant duration of time, and decrease the amount of time that the learner has access to the NCR stimuli by a constant amount of time. For example, a therapist can increase the schedule interval by 7 seconds at each opportunity, and each time decrease access to the stimuli by 3 seconds.

Proportional Time Increase. A therapist can increase the FT or VT schedule intervals proportionately,

---

[3]Chapter 24 provides a detailed description of functional behavior assessment.

meaning that each time, the schedule interval is increased by the same proportion of time. For example, each time interval is increased by 5% (e.g., 60 seconds = initial FT schedule; first schedule increase = 90 seconds [5% of 60 = 30]; second increase = 135 seconds [5% of 90 = 45]).

Session-to-Session Time Increase or Decrease. A therapist can use the learner's performance to change the schedule interval on a session-to-session basis. For example, at the end of a session, the therapist establishes a new NCR time interval for the next session by dividing the number of problem behaviors that occurred in that session by the duration of the session and using that quotient as the next session's FT interval.

A therapist will decrease the interval if the problem behavior starts to worsen during schedule thinning. The duration of the NCR interval can be increased again after control of the problem behavior has been reestablished, but in more gradual increments.

Setting Terminal Criteria

Applied behavior analysts usually select an arbitrary terminal criterion for NCR schedule thinning. Kahng and colleagues (2000) reported that the terminal criterion of a 5-minute FT schedule has been used commonly in applied research, and that it seems to be a practical and effective criterion. In addition, they reported that research has not established an advantage for a terminal criterion of a 5-minute FT schedule over denser schedules (e.g., 3 minutes) or thinner schedules (e.g., 10 minutes).

Considerations for Using NCR

NCR makes an effective intervention. It has advantages in addition to effectiveness, and some disadvantages. Table 23.3 lists the advantages and disadvantages of using NCR.

High-Probability Request Sequence

When using a **high-probability (high-*p*) request sequence,** the teacher presents a series of easy-to-follow requests for which the participant has a history of compliance (i.e., high-*p* requests); when the learner complies with several such high-*p* requests in sequence, the teacher immediately gives the target request (i.e., low-*p*). The behavioral effects of the high-probability request sequence suggests the abative effects of an abolishing operation (AO) by (a) reducing the value of reinforcement for noncompliance to the low-probability requests (i.e., reducing the value of escape from requests), and (b) reducing the aggression and self-injury often associated with low-*p* requests.

To apply the high-*p* request sequence, the teacher or therapist selects two to five short tasks with which the learner has a history of compliance. These short tasks provide the responses for the high-*p* requests. The teacher or therapist presents the high-*p* request sequence immediately before requesting the target task, the low-*p* request. Sprague and Horner (1990) used the following dressing anecdote to explain the high-*p* procedure:

Typical Instruction

Teacher: "Put on the shirt." (low-*p* request)

Student: Avoids the hard task by throwing a tantrum

Typical Instruction with High-*p* Request Sequence

Teacher: "Give me five." (high-*p* request)

Student: Slaps teacher's outstretched hand

Teacher: "All right, nice job! Now, take this ball and put it in your pocket." (high-*p* request)

Student: Puts the ball in pocket

Table 23.3 Possible Advantages and Disadvantages of NCR

Advantages
NCR is easier to apply than other positive reductive techniques, which require monitoring student behavior for the contingent delivery of the reinforcer (Kahng, Iwata, DeLeon, & Wallace, 2000).
NCR helps create a positive learning environment, which is always desirable during treatment.
A package treatment that includes NCR with extinction may reduce extinction-induced response bursts (Van Camp et al., 2000).
Chance pairings of appropriate behavior and NCR delivery of stimuli with known reinforcing properties could strengthen and maintain those desirable behaviors (Roscoe, Iwata, & Goh, 1998).

Disadvantages
Free access to NCR stimuli may reduce motivation to engage in adaptive behavior.
Chance pairings of problem behavior and NCR delivery of stimuli with known reinforcing properties could strengthen the problem behavior (Van Camp et al., 2000).
NCR escape (i.e., negative reinforcement) can disrupt the instructional process.

Teacher: "Great! That is right! Now, put on the shirt."
(low-*p* request)

Student: Puts on shirt with assistance

Student compliance provides opportunities for the development of many important behaviors. Noncompliance, however, is a prevalent problem with persons with developmental disabilities and behavior disorders. The high-*p* request sequence provides a nonaversive procedure for improving compliance by diminishing escape-maintained problem behaviors. The high-*p* request sequence may decrease excessive slowness in responding to requests and in the time used for completing tasks (Mace et al., 1988).

Engelmann and Colvin (1983) provided one of the first formal descriptions of the high-*p* request sequence in their compliance training procedure for managing severe behavior problems. They used the term *hard task* to identify the procedure of giving three to five easy requests immediately before requesting compliance with a difficult task. Applied behavior analysts have used several labels to identify this intervention, including *interspersed requests* (Horner, Day, Sprague, O'Brien,

& Heathfield, 1991), *pretask requests* (Singer, Singer, & Horner, 1987), and **behavioral momentum** (Mace, & Belfiore, 1990). Currently, most applied behavior analysts identify this antecedent intervention with the label *high-*p *request sequence.*

Killu, Sainato, Davis, Ospelt, and Paul (1998) evaluated the effects of the high-*p* request sequence on compliant responding to low-*p* requests and occurrences of problem behaviors by three preschool children with developmental delays. They used a compliance criterion of 80% or higher for selecting high-*p* requests for two children, and a 60% criterion for the third child. Compliance of less than 40% was used to select the low-*p* requests.

The request sequence began with the experimenter or a trainer presenting three to five high-*p* requests. When a child complied to at least three consecutive high-*p* requests, a low-*p* request was immediately presented. Praise was provided immediately following each compliant response. Figure 23.3 shows the children's performances before, during, and after the high-*p* sequence. The sequence delivered by two different trainers increased compliant responding to the low-*p* requests of the three

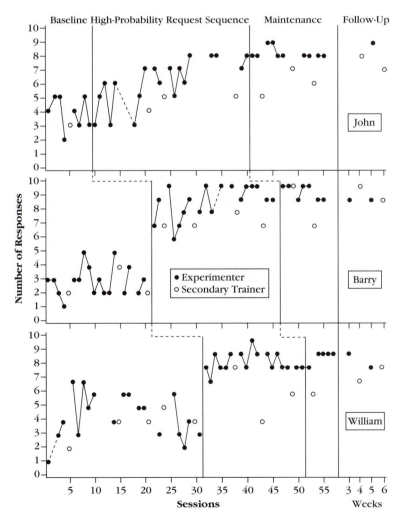

Figure 23.3 Number of compliant responses to low-probability requests delivered by the investigator and second trainer across sessions and conditions. Participants were given 10 low-*p* requests each session. Dashed lines indicate student absences.

From "Effects of High-Probability Request Sequences on Preschoolers' Compliance and Disruptive Behavior" by K. Killu, D. M. Sainato, C. A. Davis, H. Ospelt, & J. N. Paul, 1998, *Journal of Behavioral Education, 8,* p. 358. Used by permission.

children. Compliant responding maintained across time and settings.

Using the High-p Request Sequence Effectively

Selecting from Current Repertoire

The tasks selected for the high-*p* request sequence should be in the learner's current repertoire, occur with regularity of compliance, and have a very short duration of occurrence. Ardoin, Martens, and Wolfe (1999) selected high-*p* requests by (a) creating a list of requests that corresponded to student compliance, (b) presenting each request on the list for five separate sessions, and (c) selecting as high-*p* requests only those tasks that the student complied with 100% of the time.

Mace (1996) reported that the effectiveness of the high-*p* sequence increases, apparently, as the number of high-*p* requests increases. A high-*p* request sequence with five requests may be more effective than a sequence with two requests; but the increase in effectiveness may have a trade-off in efficiency. For example, if the same, or nearly the same, effectiveness can be obtained with two or three high-*p* requests as can be obtained with five or six, a teacher might select the shorter sequence because it is more efficient. When participants consistently comply with the low-*p* requests, the trainer should gradually reduce the number of high-*p* requests.

Presenting Requests Rapidly

The high-*p* requests should be presented in rapid succession, with short interrequest intervals. The first low-*p* request should immediately follow the reinforcer for high-*p* compliance (Davis & Reichle, 1996).

Acknowledging Compliance

The learner's compliance should be acknowledged immediately. Notice how the teacher in the previous dressing example acknowledged and praised the student's compliance before presenting the next request ("All right, nice job!").

Using Potent Reinforcers

Individuals may emit aggression and self-injurious behaviors to escape from the demands of the low-*p* requests. Mace and Belfiore (1990) cautioned that social praise may not increase compliance if motivation for escape behavior is high. Therefore, high-quality positive stimuli immediately following compliance will increase the effectiveness of the high-*p* intervention (Mace, 1996). Figure 23.4 lists consideration for the application of the high-*p* request sequence.

Functional Communication Training

Functional communication training (FCT) establishes an appropriate communicative behavior to compete with problem behaviors evoked by an establishing operation (EO). Rather than changing EOs, functional communication training develops alternative behaviors that are sensitive to the EOs. This is in contrast to the noncontingent reinforcement and high-probability request sequence interventions that alter the effects of EOs.

Functional communication training is an application of differential reinforcement of alternative behavior (DRA) because the intervention develops an alternative communicative response as an antecedent to diminish the problem behavior (Fisher, Kuhn, & Thompson, 1998). The alternative communicative response produces the reinforcer that has maintained the problem behavior, making the communicative response functionally equivalent to the problem behavior (Durand & Carr, 1992). The alternative communicative responses can take many forms, such as vocalizations, signs, communication boards, word or picture cards, vocal output systems, or gestures (Brown et al., 2000; Shirley, Iwata, Kahng, Mazaleski, & Lerman, 1997).

Figure 23.4 Considerations for using the high-*p* request sequence.

1. Do not use the high-*p* request sequence just after an occurrence of the problem behavior. The student might learn that responding to a low-*p* request with the problem behavior will produce a series of easier requests.
2. Present the high-*p* request sequence at the beginning and throughout the instructional period to reduce the possibility of problem behaviors producing reinforcement (Horner et al., 1991).
3. Teachers might knowingly or unknowingly let instruction drift from low-*p* requests to only high-*p* requests, and select easy tasks to avoid student escape-motivated behavior, a possible outcome from escape-motivated aggression and self-injury associated with low-*p* requests (Horner et al., 1991).

Carr and Durand (1985) defined functional communication training as a two-step process: (a) completing a functional behavior assessment to identify the stimuli with known reinforcing properties that maintain the problem behavior, and (b) using those stimuli as reinforcers to develop an alternative behavior to replace the problem behavior. FCT provides an effective treatment for many problem behaviors maintained by social attention.

FCT-based interventions typically involve several behavior change tactics in addition to teaching the alternative communicative response. For example, applied behavior analysts often use a combination of response prompting, time-out, physical restraint, response blocking, redirection, and extinction with the problem behavior.

Durand (1999) used FCT in school and community settings to reduce the problem behaviors of five students with severe disabilities. Durand first completed functional behavior assessments to identify the objects and activities maintaining the problem behaviors. Following the functional assessments, the students learned to use a communication device that produced digitized speech with which they could request the objects and activities identified during the functional behavior assessments. The five students reduced the occurrences of their problem behaviors in a school and in a community setting in which they used digitized speech to communicate with persons in the community. Figure 23.5 presents data on the percentage of intervals of problem behaviors occurring in community settings for each student. These data are socially significant because they show the importance of teaching skills that recruit reinforcement in natural settings, thereby promoting generalization and maintenance of intervention effects.

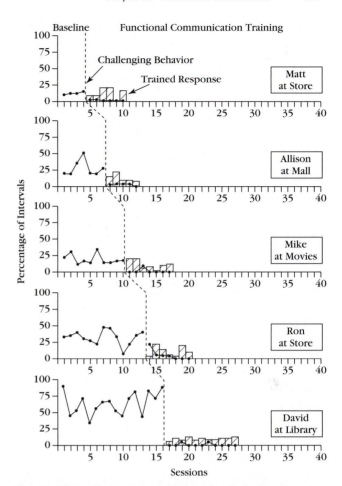

Figure 23.5 Percentage of intervals of challenging behavior by each of the five participants in baseline and FCT in community settings. The hatched bars show the percentage of intervals of unprompted communication by each student.

From "Functional Communication Training Using Assistive Devices: Recruiting Natural Communities of Reinforcement" by V. M. Durand, 1999, *Journal of Applied Behavior Analysis, 32,* p. 260. Copyright 1999 by the Society for Experimental Analysis of Behavior. Reproduced by permission.

Effective Use of FCT

Dense Schedule of Reinforcement

The alternative communicative response should produce the reinforcers that maintain the problem behavior on a continuous schedule of reinforcement during the early stages of communication training.

Decreased Use of Verbal Prompts

While teaching the alternative communicative response, verbal prompts such as *look* or *watch me,* are used often. After the communicative response is established firmly, the trainer should gradually reduce the verbal prompts and if possible eliminate them altogether to remove any prompt dependence associated with the intervention (Miltenberger, Fuqua, & Woods, 1998).

Behavior Reduction Procedures

The effectiveness of FCT is likely to be enhanced if the treatment package includes extinction for the problem behavior and other behavior-reduction procedures such as time-out (Shirley et al., 1997).

Schedule Thinning

Thinning the reinforcement schedule for a firmly established communicative response is an important part of the FCT treatment package. The time-based procedures described earlier for thinning NCR schedules—constant time increase, proportional time increase, and session-to-session time increase or decrease—are not appropriate for schedule thinning with the alternative communicative response. They are incompatible with the methods used to differentially reinforce the alternative communicative behavior because the FCT intervention does not alter the EO that evokes the problem behavior. The alternative communicative behavior must remain sensitive to the evocative function of the EO to compete with the problem behavior. For example, consider a child with developmental disabilities who has a history of engaging in self-stimulatory behavior when presented with difficult tasks. A therapist teaches the child to ask for assistance with the difficult tasks (i.e., the alternative communicative behavior), which reduces the self-stimulatory behavior. After firmly establishing *asking for assistance,* therapists and caregivers would not want to decrease giving assistance with the tasks when asked (thinning the reinforcement schedule). A decrease in giving assistance has the potential to produce the recovery of the self-stimulatory behavior by breaking the alternative communicative behavior-reinforcer contingency.

Hanley and colleagues (2001) recommended a procedure for schedule thinning that used a dense fixed-interval schedule of reinforcement (e.g., FI 2 seconds, FI 3 seconds) during the initial teaching of the alternative commutation response. Once the communicative response was established, they suggested gradually thinning the FI schedule. This procedure, in contrast to time-based procedures, maintained the contingency between responding and reinforcement. They cautioned that thinning the FI schedule during FCT interventions could produce undesirable high rates of the alternative communicative response that could disrupt the home or classroom settings. Hanley and colleagues further suggested the use of picture cues and external "clocks" to announce when reinforcement is available as a possible way to control the undesirably high rate of the communicative response. Table 23.4 summarizes the advantages and disadvantages of using FCT.

Table 23.4 Possible Advantages and Disadvantages of Functional Communication Training

Advantages

Excellent chance for generalization and maintenance of the alternative communicative response because the communicative response often functions to recruit reinforcement from significant others (Fisher et al., 1998).

May have high social validity. Participants report preferences for FCT over other procedures to diminish behavior (Hanley, Piazza, Fisher, Contrucci, & Maglieri, 1997).

When the alternative communicative behavior and the problem behavior have the same schedule of reinforcement (e.g., FR 1), an FCT intervention may be effective without using extinction (Worsdell, Iwata, Hanley, Thompson, & Kahng, 2000).

Disadvantages

The FCT treatment package usually includes extinction. May produce undesirable effects (see the discussion of extinction effects in Chapter 19).

The extinction procedure is very difficult to use consistently, allowing for intermittent reinforcement of problem behaviors.

Participants may emit inappropriately high rates of the alternative communicative response to recruit reinforcement (Fisher et al., 1998).

Recruitment of reinforcement can occur at inconvenient or impossible times for the caregiver (Fisher et al., 1998).

The fact that FCT leaves intact the environment that evoked the problem behavior, may limit its overall effectiveness (McGill, 1999).

 Summary

Defining Antecedent Interventions

1. The term *antecedent* refers to the temporal relation of stimuli or events coming before an occurrence of behavior.

2. The convergence of research on motivating operations (MOs) and functional behavior assessments has allowed applied behavior analysts to conceptually align applied research on the effects of antecedent conditions other than stimulus control (e.g., S^Ds) to basic principles of behavior.

3. Functions of antecedent stimuli or events can be classified as contingency dependent (stimulus control) or contingency independent (MO).

4. Conceptually, this chapter uses the term *antecedent intervention* to identify behavior-change tactics based on contingency-independent antecedent stimuli.

5. Applied behavior analysts have used several antecedent interventions, singularly or in treatment packages, to decrease the effectiveness of reinforcers that maintain problem behaviors (i.e., abolishing operations).

Antecedent Intervention

6. Because of the temporary effects of MOs, antecedent interventions most often serve as one component of a multicomponent treatment package (i.e., in which antecedent interventions are paired with extinction, differential reinforcement, or other procedures).

Noncontingent Reinforcement

7. Noncontingent reinforcement (NCR) consists of presenting of stimuli with known reinforcing properties on a fixed-time (FT) or variable-time (VT) schedule independent of the participant's behavior.

8. NCR uses three distinct procedures that identify and deliver stimuli with known reinforcing properties: (a) positive reinforcement (i.e., social mediation), (b) negative reinforcement (i.e., escape), and (c) automatic reinforcement (i.e., without social mediation).

9. An NCR-enriched environment may function as an abolishing operation (AO), reducing the motivation to engage in the problem behavior.

High-Probability Request Sequence

10. The behavioral effects of the high-probability (high-*p*) request sequence suggests the abative effects of an AO by (a) reducing the potency of reinforcement for noncompliance to the low-probability requests (i.e., reducing the value of escape from requests), and (b) reducing the aggression and self-injury often associated with low-*p* requests.

11. To apply the high-*p* request sequence, the teacher or therapist selects two to five short tasks with which the learner has a history of compliance. These short tasks provide the responses for the high-*p* requests. The teacher or therapist presents the high-*p* request sequence immediately before requesting the target task, the low-*p* request.

12. Applied behavior analysts have used several labels to identify this intervention, including *interspersed requests, pretask requests,* and *behavioral momentum.*

Functional Communication Training

13. Functional communication training (FCT) is a form of differential reinforcement of alternative behavior (DRA) because the intervention develops an alternative communicative response as an antecedent to diminish the problem behavior.

14. Functional communication training is an antecedent intervention package for establishing an appropriate communicative behavior to compete with problem behaviors evoked by an establishing operation (EO). Rather than altering the value of EOs as does NCR and the high-*p* request sequence, functional communication training develops alternative behaviors that are sensitive to the EOs that maintain the problem behavior.

15. The alternative communicative response produces the reinforcer that has maintained the problem behavior, making the communicative response functionally equivalent to the problem behavior.

PART 9

Functional Analysis

As noted in the Preface, changing behavior is often challenging, perplexing, and frustrating. The behavior analyst's task of determining what to do and how to do it can be particularly difficult when helping people with chronic problem behaviors. In Chapter 24, Functional Behavior Assessment, Nancy Neef and Stephanie Peterson describe an assessment process that provides information about the function (or purpose) that a behavior serves for a person. In plain English, functional behavior assessments enable behavior analysts to make empirically based hypotheses for why problem behaviors occur, which can point to the design of effective interventions. Neef and Peterson describe the basis for functional behavior assessments and their role in treating and preventing problem behavior; they present numerous examples of functional behavior assessments and detail methods and procedures for conducting them.

CHAPTER 24

Functional Behavior Assessment

Key Terms

conditional probability
contingency reversal
descriptive functional behavior
  assessment

functional analysis
functional behavior assessment
  (FBA)
functionally equivalent

indirect functional assessment

Behavior Analyst Certification Board® BCBA® & BCABA®
Behavior Analyst Task List,© Third Edition

	Content Area 4: Behavioral Assessment
4-1	State the primary characteristics of and rationale for conducting a descriptive assessment.
4-2	Gather descriptive data.
(a)	Select various methods.
(b)	Use various methods.
4-3	Organize and interpret descriptive data.
(a)	Select various methods.
(b)	Use various methods.
4-4	State the primary characteristics of and rationale for conducting a functional analysis as a form of assessment.
4-5	Conduct functional analyses.
(a)	Select various methods.
(b)	Use various methods.
4-6	Organize and interpret functional analysis data.
(a)	Select various methods.
(b)	Use various methods.

This chapter was written by Nancy A. Neef and Stephanie M. Peterson.

When it is time to wash hands before lunch, one child turns the handles of the faucet and places her hands under the running water, but another child screams and tantrums. Why? Consistent with the scientific precept of determinism described in Chapter 1, those behaviors are lawfully related to other events in the environment. **Functional behavior assessment (FBA)** enables hypotheses about the relations among specific types of environmental events and behaviors. Specifically, FBA is designed to obtain information about the purposes (functions) a behavior serves for a person. This chapter describes the basis for FBA, its role in the intervention and prevention of behavior difficulties, and alternative approaches to functional assessment.

Functions of Behavior

Evidence from decades of research indicates that both desirable and undesirable behaviors, whether washing hands or screaming and tantrumming, are learned and maintained through interaction with the social and physical environment. As explained in Chapters 11 and 12, these behavior–environment interactions are described as positive or negative reinforcement contingencies. Behaviors can be strengthened by either "getting something" or "getting out of something."

FBA is used to identify the type and source of reinforcement for challenging behaviors as the basis for intervention efforts designed to decrease the occurrence of those behaviors. FBA can be thought of as a reinforcer assessment of sorts. It identifies the reinforcers currently maintaining problem behavior. Those reinforcers might be positive or negative social reinforcers provided by someone who interacts with the person, or automatic reinforcers produced directly by the behavior itself. The idea behind FBA is that if these reinforcement contingencies can be identified and interventions can be designed to decrease problem behavior and increase adaptive behavior by altering these contingencies. FBA fosters proactive, positive interventions for problem behavior. Although reinforcement contingencies are discussed in other chapters, a brief review of their role in FBA is warranted.

Positive Reinforcement

Social Positive Reinforcement (Attention)

Problem behavior often results in immediate attention from others, such as head turns; surprised facial expressions; reprimands; attempts to soothe, counsel, or distract; and so on. These reactions can serve to positively reinforce problem behavior (even if inadvertently), and the problem behavior is then more likely to occur in similar circumstances. Problem behavior maintained by positive reinforcement in the form of reactions from others can often occur in situations in which attention is otherwise infrequent, whether because the person does not have a repertoire to gain attention in desirable ways, or because others in the environment are typically otherwise occupied.

Tangible Reinforcement

Many behaviors result in access to reinforcing materials or other stimuli. Just as pressing a button on the television remote changes the channel to a desired television show, problem behaviors can produce reinforcing outcomes. A child may cry and tantrum until a favorite television show is turned on; stealing another child's candy produces access to the item taken. Problem behaviors may develop when they consistently produce a desired item or event. This often occurs because providing the item temporarily stops the problem behavior (e.g., tantrum), although it can have the inadvertent effect of making the problem behavior more probable in the future under similar circumstances.

Automatic Positive Reinforcement

Some behaviors do not depend on the action of others to provide an outcome; some behaviors directly produce their own reinforcement. For example, thumb sucking might be reinforced by physical stimulation of either the hand or the mouth. A behavior is assumed to be maintained by automatic reinforcement only after social reinforcers have been ruled out (e.g., when the behavior occurs even when the individual is alone).

Negative Reinforcement

Social Negative Reinforcement (Escape)

Many behaviors are learned as a result of their effectiveness in terminating or postponing aversive events. Hanging up the phone terminates interactions with a telemarketer; completing a task or chore terminates requests from others to complete it or the demands associated with the task itself. Problem behaviors can be maintained in the same way. Behaviors such as aggression, self-injurious behavior (SIB), and bizarre speech may terminate or avoid unwanted interactions with others. For example, noncompliance postpones engagement in a nonpreferred activity, and disruptive classroom behavior often results in the student being sent out of the classroom, thereby allowing escape from instructional tasks or teacher demands. All of these behaviors can be strengthened by negative reinforcement to the extent that they serve to allow the individual to escape or avoid difficult or unpleasant tasks, activities, or interactions.

Automatic Negative Reinforcement

Aversive stimulation, such as a physically painful or uncomfortable condition, is a motivating operation that makes its termination reinforcing. Behaviors that directly terminate aversive stimulation are therefore maintained by negative reinforcement that is an automatic outcome of the response. Automatic negative reinforcement can account for behaviors that are either appropriate or harmful. For example, putting calamine lotion on a poison ivy rash can be negatively reinforced by alleviation of itching, but intense or prolonged scratching that breaks the skin can be negatively reinforced in the same manner. Some forms of SIB may serve to distract from other sources of pain, which may account for their correlation with specific medical conditions (e.g., DeLissovoy, 1963).

Function versus Topography

Several points can be made from the previous discussion of the sources of reinforcement for behavior. It is important to recognize that environmental influences do not make distinctions between desirable and undesirable topographies of behavior; the same reinforcement contingencies that account for desirable behavior can also account for undesirable behavior. For example, the child who washes and dries her hands before lunch has probably received praise for doing so. A child who frequently engages in tantrums in the same situation may have received attention (in the form of reprimands). Both forms of attention have the potential to reinforce the respective behaviors.

Likewise, the same topography of behavior can serve different functions for different individuals. For example, tantrums may be maintained by positive reinforcement in the form of attention for one child, and by negative reinforcement in the form of escape for another child (e.g., Kennedy, Meyer, Knowles, & Shukla, 2000).

Because different behaviors that look quite different can serve the same function, and behavior of the same form can serve different functions under different conditions, the *topography,* or form, of a behavior often reveals little useful information about the conditions that account for it. Identifying the *conditions* that account for a behavior (its function), on the other hand, suggests what conditions need to be altered to change the behavior. Assessment of the function of a behavior can therefore yield useful information with respect to intervention strategies that are likely to be effective.

Role of Functional Behavior Assessment in Intervention and Prevention

FBA and Intervention

If the cause-and-effect relation between environmental events and a behavior can be determined, that relation can be altered, thereby diminishing subsequent occurrences of a problem behavior. FBA interventions can consist of at least three strategic approaches: altering antecedent variables, altering consequent variables, and teaching alternative behaviors.

Altering Antecedent Variables

FBA can identify antecedents that might be altered so the problem behavior is less likely to occur. Altering the antecedents for problem behavior can change and/or eliminate either (a) the motivating operation for problem behavior or (b) the discriminative stimuli that trigger problem behavior. For example, the motivating operation for tantrums when a child is asked to wash her hands before lunch could be modified by changing the characteristics associated with lunch so that the avoidance of particular events is no longer reinforcing (e.g., initially reducing table-setting demands, altering seating arrangements to minimize taunts from a sibling or peer, reducing snacks before lunch and offering more preferred foods during lunch). Alternatively, if the FBA shows that running water is the discriminative stimulus that triggers problem behavior when a child is asked to wash her hands, the child might be given waterless antibacterial hand gel instead. In this case, the discriminative stimulus for problem behavior has been removed, thereby decreasing problem behavior.

Altering Consequence Variables

FBA can also identify a source of reinforcement to be eliminated for the problem behavior. For example, an FBA that indicates tantrums are maintained by social negative reinforcement (avoidance or escape) suggests a variety of treatment options, which, by altering that relation, are likely to be effective, such as the following:

1. The problem behavior can be placed on extinction by ensuring that the reinforcer (e.g., avoidance of lunch) is no longer delivered following problem behavior (tantrums).

2. The schedule might be modified so that hand washing follows (and thereby provides escape from) an event that is less preferred.

Teaching Alternative Behaviors

FBA can also identify the source of reinforcement to be provided for appropriate replacement behaviors. Alternative appropriate behaviors that serve the same function (i.e., produce the same reinforcer) as tantrums could be taught. For example, the student might be taught to touch a card communicating "later" after washing his hands to produce a delay in being seated at the lunch table.

FBA and Default Technologies

Interventions based on an FBA are more likely to be effective than those selected arbitrarily (e.g., Ervin et al., 2001; Iwata et al., 1994b). Understanding *why* a behavior occurs (its function) often suggests *how* it can be changed for the better. On the other hand, premature efforts to treat problem behavior before seeking an understanding of the purposes it serves for a person can be inefficient, ineffective, and even harmful. For example, suppose that a time-out procedure is implemented in an attempt to attenuate the problem of the child who consistently tantrums when she is asked to wash her hands before lunch. The child is removed from the hand-washing activity to a chair in the corner of the room. It may be, however, that the events that typically follow washing hands (those associated with lunch time, such as the demands of setting the table or interactions with others) are aversive for the child; tantrums have effectively served to allow the child to avoid those events. In this case, the intervention would be ineffective because it has done nothing to alter the relation between tantrums and the consequence of postponing the aversive events associated with lunch. In fact, the intervention may exacerbate the problem if it produces a desired outcome for the child. If stopping the hand-washing activity and having the child sit on a chair as "time-out" for tantrumming enables the child to avoid the aversive lunchtime events—or to escape them altogether—tantrums may be more likely under similar circumstances in the future. When the time-out intervention proves unsuccessful, other interventions might be attempted. Without understanding the function that the problem behavior serves, however, the effectiveness of those interventions cannot be predicted.

At best, a trial-and-error process of evaluating arbitrarily selected interventions can be lengthy and inefficient. At worst, such an approach may cause the problem behavior to become more frequent or severe. As a result, caregivers might resort to increasingly intrusive, coercive, or punishment-based interventions, which are often referred to as *default technologies*.

FBA can decrease reliance on default technologies and contribute to more effective interventions in several ways. When FBAs are conducted, reinforcement-based interventions are more likely to be implemented than are interventions that include a punishment component (Pelios, Morren, Tesch, & Axelrod, 1999). In addition, the effects of interventions based on FBAs are likely to be more durable than those that do not take the function of problem behavior into account. If contrived contingencies are superimposed on unknown contingencies that are maintaining the behavior, their continuation is often necessary to maintain improvements in the behavior. If those superimposed contingencies are discontinued, the behavior will continue to be influenced by the unchanged operative contingencies.

FBA and Prevention

By furthering understanding of the conditions under which certain behaviors occur, FBA can also contribute to the prevention of difficulties. Although problem behavior may be suppressed without regard to its function by using punishment procedures, additional behaviors not subject to the punishment contingencies may emerge because the motivating operations for problem behavior remain. For example, contingent loss of privileges might eliminate tantrums that occur whenever a child is asked to wash her hands, but it will not eliminate avoidance as a reinforcer or the conditions that establish it as a reinforcer. Thus, other behaviors that result in avoidance may develop, such as aggression, property destruction, or running away. These unintended effects are less likely to occur with interventions that address (rather than override or compete with) the reinforcing functions of problem behavior.

On a broader scale, the accumulation of FBA data may further assist in prevention efforts by identifying the conditions that pose risks for the future development of problem behaviors. Preventive efforts can then focus on those conditions. For example, based on data from 152 analyses of the reinforcing functions of self-injurious behavior (SIB), Iwata and colleagues (1994b) found that escape from task demands or other aversive stimuli accounted for the behavior in the largest proportion of cases. The authors speculated that this outcome might have been an unintended result of a move toward providing more aggressive treatment. For example, if a child tantrums when she is required to wash her hands, the teacher might assume that she does not know how to wash her hands. The teacher might decide to replace playtime with a period of intensive instruction on hygiene. Rather than decreasing problem behavior, such interventions may exacerbate it. The data reported by Iwata and colleagues (1994b) suggest that preventive efforts should be directed toward modifying instructional environments (such as providing more frequent reinforcement for desirable behavior, opportunities for breaks, or means to request and obtain help with difficult tasks) so that they are less likely to serve as sources of aversive stimulation (motivating operations) for escape.

Overview of FBA Methods

FBA methods can be classified into three types: (a) functional (experimental) analysis, (b) descriptive assessment, and (c) indirect assessment. The methods can be ordered on a continuum with respect to considerations such as ease of use and the type and precision of information they yield. Selecting the method or combination of methods that will best suit a particular situation requires consideration of each method's advantages and limitations. We discuss functional analysis first because descriptive and indirect methods of functional assessment developed as an outgrowth of functional analysis. As noted later, functional analysis is the only FBA method that allows practitioners to confirm hypotheses regarding functional relations between problem behavior and environmental events.

Functional (Experimental) Analysis

Basic Procedure

In a **functional analysis,** antecedents and consequences representing those in the person's natural environment are arranged so that their separate effects on problem behavior can be observed and measured. This type of assessment is often referred to as an *analog* because antecedents and consequences similar to those occurring in the natural routines are presented in a systematic manner, but the analysis is not conducted in the context of naturally oc-

curring routines. Analog conditions are often used because they allow the behavior analyst to better control the environmental variables that may be related to the problem behavior than can be accomplished in naturally occurring situations. Analogs refer to the arrangement of variables rather than the setting in which assessment occurs. Research has found that functional analyses conducted in natural environments (e.g., classroom settings) often yield the same (and, in some cases, clearer) results compared to those conducted in simulated settings (Noell, Van-Dertteyden, Gatti, & Whitmarsh, 2001).

Functional analyses typically are comprised of four conditions: three test conditions—contingent attention, contingent escape, and alone—and a control condition, in which problem behavior is expected to be low because reinforcement is freely available and no demands are placed on the individual (see Table 24.1). Each test condition contains a motivating operation (MO) and a potential source of reinforcement for problem behavior. The conditions are presented systematically one at a time and in an alternating sequence to identify which conditions predictably result in problem behavior. Occurrences of problem behavior are recorded during each session. Sessions are repeated to determine the extent to which problem behavior consistently occurs more often under one or more conditions relative to another.

Interpreting Functional Analyses

The function that problem behavior serves for a person can be determined by visually inspecting a graph of the results of the analysis to identify the condition(s) under which high rates of the behavior occurred. A graph for each potential behavioral function is shown in Figure 24.1. Problem behavior is expected to be low in the play condition because no motivating operations for problem

Table 24.1 Motivating Operations and Reinforcement Contingencies for Typical Control and Test Conditions of a Functional Analysis

Condition	Antecedent conditions (motivating operation)	Consequences for problem behavior
Play (control)	Preferred activities continuously available, social attention provided, and no demands are placed on the person.	Problem behavior is ignored or neutrally redirected.
Contingent attention	Attention is diverted or withheld from the person.	Attention in the form of mild reprimands or soothing statements (e.g., "Don't do that. You'll hurt someone.").
Contingent escape	Task demands are delivered continuously using a three-step prompting procedure (e.g., [1] "You need to fold the towel." [2] Model folding the towel. [3] Provide hand-over-hand assistance to fold the towel.)	Break from the task provided by removing task materials and stopping prompts to complete the task.
Alone	Low level of environmental stimulation (i.e., therapist, task materials, and play materials are absent).	Problem behavior is ignored or neutrally redirected.

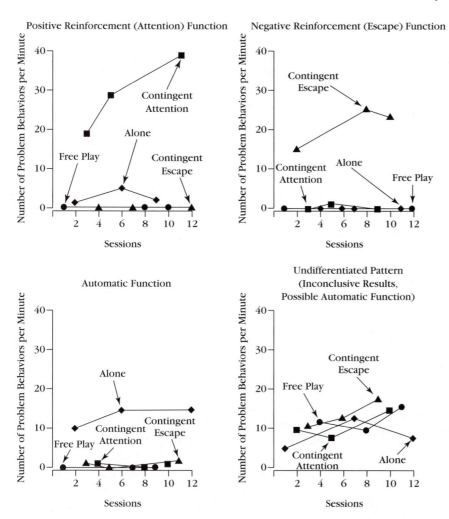

Figure 24.1 Data patterns typical of each behavioral function during a functional analysis.

behavior are present. Elevated problem behavior in the contingent attention condition suggests that problem behavior is maintained by social positive reinforcement (see graph in top left of Figure 24.1). Elevated problem behavior in the contingent escape condition suggests that problem behavior is maintained by negative reinforcement (graph in top right of Figure 24.1). Elevated problem behavior in the alone condition suggests that problem behavior is maintained by automatic reinforcement (graph in bottom left of Figure 24.1). Further analysis is needed to determine if the source of the automatic reinforcement is positive or negative. Problem behavior may be maintained by multiple sources of reinforcement. For example, if problem behavior is elevated in the contingent attention and contingent escape conditions, it is most likely maintained by both positive and negative reinforcement.

If problem behavior occurs frequently in all conditions (including the play condition), or is variable across conditions, responding is considered *undifferentiated* (see graph in bottom right of Figure 24.1). Such results are inconclusive, but can also occur with behavior that is maintained by automatic reinforcement.

Functional analysis has been replicated and extended in hundreds of studies, thereby demonstrating its generality as an approach to the assessment and treatment of a wide range of behavior difficulties. (See the 1994 special issue of the *Journal of Applied Behavior Analysis* for a sample of such applications.)

Advantages of Functional Analysis

The primary advantage of functional analysis is its ability to yield a clear demonstration of the variable(s) that relate to the occurrence of a problem behavior. In fact, functional (experimental) analyses serve as the standard of scientific evidence by which other assessment alternatives are evaluated, and represent the method most often used in research on the assessment and treatment of problem behavior (Arndorfer & Miltenberger, 1993). Because functional analyses allow valid conclusions concerning the variables that maintain problem behavior, they have enabled the development of effective reinforcement-based treatments and less reliance on punishment procedures (Ervin et al., 2001; Iwata et al., 1994b; Pelios et al., 1999).

Limitations of Functional Analysis

A risk of functional analysis, however, is that the assessment process may temporarily strengthen or increase the undesirable behavior to unacceptable levels, or possibly result in the behavior acquiring new functions. Second, although little is known about the acceptability of functional analysis procedures to practitioners (Ervin et al., 2001), the deliberate arrangement of conditions that set the occasion for, or potentially reinforce, problem behavior can be counterintuitive to persons who do not understand its purpose (or that such conditions are analogs for what occurs in the natural routine). Third, some behaviors (e.g., those that, albeit serious, occur infrequently) may not be amenable to functional analyses. Fourth, functional analyses that are conducted in contrived settings might not detect the variable that accounts for the occurrence of the problem behavior in the natural environment, particularly if the behavior is controlled by idiosyncratic variables that are not represented in the functional analysis conditions (e.g., Noell et al., 2001). Finally, the time, effort, and professional expertise required to conduct and interpret functional analyses have been frequently cited as obstacles to its widespread use in practice (e.g., Spreat & Connelly, 1996; 2001, Volume 2 issue of *School Psychology Review*).

Of course, untreated or ineffectively treated problem behaviors also consume a great deal of time and effort (without a constructive long-term outcome), and implementation of effective treatments (based on an understanding of the variables that maintain them) is likely to require skills similar to those involved in conducting functional analyses. These concerns have led to research on ways to enhance the practical use of functional analyses, such as methods of practitioner training (Iwata et al., 2000; Pindiprolu, Peterson, Rule, & Lignugaris/Kraft, 2003), abbreviated assessments (Northup et al., 1991), and the development of alternative methods of FBA described in the following sections.

Descriptive Functional Behavior Assessment

As with functional analyses, **descriptive functional behavior assessment** encompasses direct observation of behavior; unlike functional analyses, however, observations are made under naturally occurring conditions. Thus, descriptive assessments involve observation of the problem behavior in relation to events that are not arranged in a systematic manner. Descriptive assessments have roots in the early stages of applied behavior analysis; Bijou, Peterson, and Ault (1968) initially described a method for objectively defining, observing, and coding behavior and contiguous environmental events. This method has been used subsequently to identify events that may be correlated with the target behavior. Events that are shown to have a high degree of correlation with the target behavior may suggest hypotheses about behavioral function. We describe three variations of descriptive analysis: ABC (antecedent-behavior-consequence) continuous recording, ABC narrative recording, and scatterplots.

ABC Continuous Recording

With ABC continuous recording, an observer records occurrences of the targeted problem behaviors and selected environmental events in the natural routine during a period of time. Codes for recording specific antecedents, problem behaviors, and consequences can be developed based on information obtained from a functional assessment interview or ABC narrative recording (described later). For example, following an interview and observations using narrative recording, Lalli, Browder, Mace, and Brown (1993) developed stimulus and response codes to record the occurrence or nonoccurrence of antecedent (e.g., one-to-one instruction, group instruction) and subsequent events (attention, tangible reinforcement, escape) for problem behavior during classroom activities.

With ABC continuous recording, the occurrence of a specified event is marked on the data sheet (using partial interval, momentary time sampling, or frequency recording) (see Figure 24.2). The targeted environmental events (antecedents and consequences) are recorded whenever they occur, regardless of whether problem behavior occurred with it. Recording data in this manner may reveal events that occur in close temporal relations with the target behavior. For example, descriptive data may show that tantrums (behavior) often occur when a student is given an instruction to wash her hands (antecedent); the data may also show that tantrums are typically followed by the removal of task demands. A possible hypothesis in this situation is that disruptions are motivated by academic demands and are maintained by escape from those demands (negative reinforcement).

Advantages of ABC Continuous Recording. Descriptive assessments based on continuous recording use precise measures (similar to functional analyses), and in some cases the correlations may reflect causal

Figure 24.2   Sample data collection form for ABC continuous recording.

ABC Recording Form
Observer: R. Van Norman
Time begin: 9:30 A.M.   Time end: 10:15 A.M.
Date: January 25, 2006

Antecedent	Behavior	Consequence
☐ Task prompt /instruction ☒ Attention diverted ☐ Social interaction ☐ Engaged in preferred activity ☐ Preferred activity removed ☐ Alone (no attention/no activities)	☒ Tantrum ☐ Aggression	☐ Social attention ☒ Reprimand ☐ Task demand ☐ Access to preferred item ☐ Task removed ☐ Attention diverted
☒ Task prompt /instruction ☐ Attention diverted ☐ Social interaction ☐ Engaged in preferred activity ☐ Preferred activity removed ☐ Alone (no attention/no activities)	☒ Tantrum ☐ Aggression	☐ Social attention ☐ Reprimand ☐ Task demand ☐ Access to preferred item ☒ Task removed ☐ Attention diverted
☒ Task prompt /instruction ☐ Attention diverted ☐ Social interaction ☐ Engaged in preferred activity ☐ Preferred activity removed ☐ Alone (no attention/no activities)	☒ Tantrum ☐ Aggression	☐ Social attention ☐ Reprimand ☐ Task demand ☐ Access to preferred item ☒ Task removed ☐ Attention diverted
☐ Task prompt /instruction ☒ Attention diverted ☐ Social interaction ☐ Engaged in preferred activity ☐ Preferred activity removed ☐ Alone (no attention/no activities)	☒ Tantrum ☐ Aggression	☐ Social attention ☐ Reprimand ☐ Task demand ☐ Access to preferred item ☐ Task removed ☒ Attention diverted
☒ Task prompt /instruction ☐ Attention diverted ☐ Social interaction ☐ Engaged in preferred activity ☐ Preferred activity removed ☐ Alone (no attention/no activities)	☐ Tantrum ☐ Aggression	☐ Social attention ☐ Reprimand ☐ Task demand ☐ Access to preferred item ☐ Task removed ☐ Attention diverted
☒ Task prompt /instruction ☐ Attention diverted ☐ Social interaction ☐ Engaged in preferred activity ☐ Preferred activity removed ☐ Alone (no attention/no activities)	☒ Tantrum ☐ Aggression	☐ Social attention ☐ Reprimand ☐ Task demand ☐ Access to preferred item ☒ Task removed ☐ Attention diverted
☐ Task prompt /instruction ☒ Attention diverted ☐ Social interaction ☐ Engaged in preferred activity ☐ Preferred activity removed ☐ Alone (no attention/no activities)	☐ Tantrum ☐ Aggression	☐ Social attention ☐ Reprimand ☐ Task demand ☐ Access to preferred item ☐ Task removed ☐ Attention diverted

(continued)

Figure 24.2 (*continued*)

Antecedent	Behavior	Consequence
☒ Task prompt /instruction ❑ Attention diverted ❑ Social interaction ❑ Engaged in preferred activity ❑ Preferred activity removed ❑ Alone (no attention/no activities)	☒ Tantrum ❑ Aggression	❑ Social attention ❑ Reprimand ❑ Task demand ❑ Access to preferred item ☒ Task removed ❑ Attention diverted
❑ Task prompt /instruction ❑ Attention diverted ☒ Social interaction ❑ Engaged in preferred activity ❑ Preferred activity removed ❑ Alone (no attention/no activities)	☒ Tantrum ❑ Aggression	❑ Social attention ☒ Reprimand ❑ Task demand ❑ Access to preferred item ❑ Task removed ❑ Attention diverted
☒ Task prompt /instruction ❑ Attention diverted ❑ Social interaction ❑ Engaged in preferred activity ❑ Preferred activity removed ❑ Alone (no attention/no activities)	☒ Tantrum ❑ Aggression	❑ Social attention ❑ Reprimand ❑ Task demand ❑ Access to preferred item ☒ Task removed ❑ Attention diverted
❑ Task prompt /instruction ❑ Attention diverted ☒ Social interaction ❑ Engaged in preferred activity ❑ Preferred activity removed ❑ Alone (no attention/no activities)	☒ Tantrum ❑ Aggression	❑ Social attention ❑ Reprimand ❑ Task demand ❑ Access to preferred item ❑ Task removed ☒ Attention diverted

Source Recording form developed by Renée Van Norman. Used by permission.

relations (e.g., Sasso et al., 1992). Because the assessments are conducted in the context in which the problem behaviors occur, they are likely to provide useful information for designing a subsequent functional analysis if that proves necessary. In addition, they do not require disruption to the person's routine.

Limitations of ABC Continuous Recording. Although descriptive analyses of this type may show a correlation between particular events and the problem behavior, such correlations can be difficult to detect in many situations. This is especially likely if the influential antecedents and consequences do not reliably precede and follow the behavior. In such cases, it may be necessary to analyze descriptive data by calculating conditional probabilities. A **conditional probability** is the likelihood that a target problem behavior will occur in a given circumstance. Given the example provided in Figure 24.2, the conditional probability of tantrums is computed by calculating (a) the proportion of occurrences of tantrums that were preceded by the antecedent of an instruction and (b) the proportion of occurrences of tantrums for which task removal was

the consequence. In this example, 9 instances of tantrums were recorded, and 6 of those occurrences were followed by task removal. Thus, the conditional probability that tantrums occur in the presence of task demands and are followed by escape is .66. The closer the conditional probability is to 1.0, the stronger the hypothesis is that escape is a variable maintaining problem behavior.

However, conditional probabilities can be misleading. If a behavior is maintained by intermittent reinforcement, the behavior might occur often even though it is not followed consistently by a particular consequence. For example, the teacher might send the student to time-out only when tantrums are so frequent or severe that they are intolerable. In this case, only a small proportion of tantrums would be followed by that consequence, and the conditional probability would be low. One possibility, therefore, is that a functional relation that exists (e.g., tantrums negatively reinforced by escape) will not be detected. Furthermore, the child's current behavior intervention plan might require three repetitions of the instruction and an attempt to provide physical assistance before time-out is implemented. In that situation, the conditional probability of tantrums being followed by attention would be high. A descriptive analysis might, therefore, suggest a functional relation (e.g., tantrums positively reinforced by attention) that does *not* exist. Perhaps for these reasons, studies that have used conditional probability calculations to examine the extent to which descriptive methods lead to the same hypotheses as functional analyses have generally found low agreement (e.g., Lerman & Iwata, 1993; Noell et al., 2001).

ABC Narrative Recording

ABC narrative recording is a form of descriptive assessment that differs from continuous recording in that (a) data are collected only when behaviors of interest are observed, and (b) the recording is open-ended (any events that immediately precede and follow the target behavior are noted) (see Figure 3.3 on page 54). Because data are recorded only when the target behavior occurs, narrative recording may be less time-consuming than continuous recording. On the other hand, narrative recording has several disadvantages in addition to those described earlier.

Limitations of Narrative Recording. Because narrative recording data are seldom reported in published research, their utility in identifying behavioral function has not been established. However, ABC narrative recording might identify functional relations that do not exist because antecedent and consequent events are recorded only in relation to the target behavior; it would not be evident from ABC data if particular events occurred just as often in the absence of the target behavior. For example, ABC data might erroneously indicate a correlation between peer attention and disruption even though peer attention also occurred frequently when the student was not disruptive.

Another potential limitation of ABC narrative recording concerns its accuracy. Unless observers receive adequate training, they may report inferred states or subjective impressions (e.g., "felt embarrassed," "was frustrated") instead of describing observable events in objective terms. In addition, given the likelihood that a number of environmental events occur in close temporal proximity to one another, discriminating the events that occasion a behavior can be difficult. ABC narrative recording may be best suited as a means of gathering preliminary information to inform continuous recording or functional analyses.

Scatterplots

Scatterplot recording is a procedure for recording the extent to which a target behavior occurs more often at particular times than others (Symons, McDonald, & Wehby, 1998; Touchette, MacDonald, & Langer, 1985). Specifically, scatterplots involve dividing the day into blocks of time (e.g., a series of 30-minute segments). For every time segment, an observer uses different symbols on an observation form to indicate whether the target problem behavior occurred a lot, some, or not at all. After data have been collected over a series of days, they are analyzed for patterns (specific time periods that are typically associated with problem behavior). If a recurring response pattern is identified, the temporal distributions in the behavior can be examined for a relation to particular environmental events. For example, a time period in which the behavior occurs often might be correlated with increased demands, low attention, certain activities, or the presence of a particular person. If so, changes can be made on that basis.

Advantages of Scatterplots. The primary advantage of scatterplots is that they identify time periods during which the problem behavior occurs. Such information can be useful in pinpointing periods of the day when more focused ABC assessments might be conducted to obtain additional information regarding the function of the problem behavior.

Limitations of Scatterplots. Although scatterplots are often used in practice, little is known about their utility. It is unclear whether temporal patterns are routinely evident (Kahng et al., 1998). Another problem is that obtaining accurate data with scatterplots may be difficult (Kahng et al., 1998). In addition, the subjective nature of the ratings of how often the behavior occurs (e.g., "a lot" versus "some") can contribute to difficulties with interpretation (standards for these values might differ across teachers or raters).

Indirect Functional Behavior Assessment

Indirect functional assessment methods use structured interviews, checklists, rating scales, or questionnaires to obtain information from persons who are familiar with the person exhibiting the problem behavior (e.g., teachers, parents, caregivers, and/or the individual him- or herself) to identify possible conditions or events in the natural environment that correlate with the problem behavior. Such procedures are referred to as "indirect" because they do not involve direct observation of the behavior, but rather solicit information based on others' recollections of the behavior.

Behavioral Interviews

Interviews are used routinely in assessment. The goal of a behavioral interview is to obtain clear and objective information about the problem behaviors, antecedents, and consequences. This might include clarifying descriptions of the behavior (consequences); when (times), where (settings, activities, events), with whom, and how often it occurs; what typically precedes the behavior (antecedents); what the child and others typically do immediately following the behavior (consequences); and what steps have previously been taken to address the problem, and with what result. Similar information might be solicited about desirable behavior (or the conditions under which undesirable behavior does not occur) to identify patterns or conditions that predict appropriate versus problem behavior. Information can also be obtained about the child's apparent preferences (e.g., favorite items or activities), skills, and means of communicating. A skillful interviewer poses questions in a way that evokes specific, complete, and factual responses about events, with minimal interpretation or inferences.

Lists of interview questions have been published, and they provide a consistent, structured format for obtaining information through either an interview or questionnaire format. For example, the Functional Assessment Interview (O'Neill et al., 1997) has 11 sections, which include description of the form (topography) of the behavior, general factors that might affect the behavior (medications, staffing patterns, daily schedule), antecedents and outcomes of the behavior, functional behavior repertoires, communication skills, potential reinforcers, and treatment history.

A form of the Functional Assessment Interview for students who can serve as their own informants is also available (Kern, Dunlap, Clarke, & Childs, 1995; O'Neill et al., 1997). Questions include the behavior(s) that cause trouble for the students at school, a description of the student's class schedule and its relation to problem behavior, rating of intensity of behaviors on a scale of 1 to 6 across class periods and times of day, aspects of the situation related to the behavior (e.g., difficult, boring, or unclear material; peer teasing; teacher reprimands), other events that might affect the behavior (e.g., lack of sleep, conflicts), consequences (what occurs when the individual engages in the behavior), possible behavior alternatives, and potential strategies for a support plan.

Two other questionnaires are the Behavioral Diagnosis and Treatment Information Form (Bailey & Pyles, 1989) and the Stimulus Control Checklist (Rolider & Van Houten, 1993), which also address questions about the conditions under which the behavior occurs or doesn't occur, and how often. In addition, they include questions about physiological factors that might affect the behavior.

Behavior Rating Scales

Behavior rating scales designed for functional assessment ask informants to estimate the extent to which behavior occurs under specified conditions, using a Likert scale (e.g., *never, seldom, usually, always*). Hypotheses about the function of a behavior are based on the scores associated with each condition. Those conditions that are assigned the highest cumulative or average rating are hypothesized to be related to the problem behavior. For example, if an informant states that problem behavior always occurs when demands are placed on a child, a negative reinforcement hypothesis might be made. Features of several behavior rating scales are summarized in Table 24.2.

Advantages of Indirect FBA

Some indirect assessment methods can provide a useful source of information in guiding subsequent, more objective assessments, and contribute to the development of hypotheses about variables that might occasion or maintain the behaviors of concern. Because indirect forms of FBA do not require direct observation of problem behavior, many people view them as convenient.

Limitations of Indirect FBA

A major limitation of indirect FBA is that informants may not have accurate and unbiased recall of behavior and the conditions under which it occurred, or be able to report such recollections in a way that conforms to the requirements of the question. Perhaps for these reasons, little research exists to support the reliability of the information obtained from indirect assessment methods. The Motivation Assessment Scale (MAS) is one of the few behavior rating scales that has been evaluated for its technical adequacy. Several studies have evaluated the interrater agreement of the MAS, and almost all of them have found it to be low (Arndorfer, Miltenberger, Woster, Rotvedt, & Gaffaney, 1994; Barton-Arwood, Wehby, Gunter, & Lane, 2003; Conroy, Fox, Bucklin, & Good, 1996; Crawford, Brockel, Schauss, & Miltenberger, 1992; Newton & Sturmey, 1991; Sigafoos, Kerr, & Roberts, 1994; Zarcone, Rodgers, & Iwata, 1991). Barton-Arwood and colleagues (2003) also evaluated the technical adequacy of the Problem Behavior Questionnaire (PBQ). They reported variable intrarater agreement and questionable stability of the identified behavioral function with both the PBQ and MAS as applied to students with emotional or behavioral disorders. Because of the lack of empirical data to support their validity and interrater agreement, indirect methods of FBA are not recommended as the principal means of identifying the functions of behaviors. These scales can, however, provide information useful for forming initial hypotheses, which can later be tested.

Table 24.2 Overview of Behavior Rating Scales Used to As

Behavior rating scale	Functions assessed	Forma
Motivation Assessment Scale (MAS) (Durand & Crimmins, 1992)	Sensory reinforcement, escape, attention, and tangible reinforcement	16 ques functions *always* to
Motivation Analysis Rating Scale (MARS) (Wieseler, Hanson, Chamberlain, & Thompson, 1985)	Sensory reinforcement, escape, and attention	6 statemen functions), 4 *always* to nev
Problem Behavior Questionnaire (PBQ) (Lewis, Scott, & Sugai, 1994)	Peer attention, teacher attention, escape/avoid peer attention, escape/avoid teacher attention, and assessment of setting events	Questions, 7-p
Functional Analysis Screening Tool (FAST) (Iwata & DeLeon, 1996)	Social reinforcement (attention, preferred items), social reinforcement (escape), automatic reinforcement by sensory stimulation, automatic reinforcement by pain attenuation	Yes or no as to whe ments are descriptiv ...on the behavior occurs, do you usually try to calm the person down or distract the person with preferred activities (leisure items, snacks, etc.)? (social reinforcement, attention, preferred items)
Questions About Behavioral Function (QABF) (Paclawskyj, Matson, Rush, Smalls, & Vollmer, 2000)	Attention, escape, nonsocial, physical, tangible	Statements, 4-point range Participant engages in the behavior to try to get a reaction from you. (attention)

Conducting a Functional Behavior Assessment

Given the strengths and limitations of the different FBA procedures, FBA can best be viewed as a four-step process as follows:

1. Gather information via indirect and descriptive assessment.

2. Interpret information from indirect and descriptive assessment and formulate hypotheses about the purpose of problem behavior.

3. Test hypotheses using functional analysis.

4. Develop intervention options based on the function of problem behavior.

Gathering Information

It is often helpful to begin the FBA process by conducting functional assessment interviews with the person's teacher, parent, caregiver, and/or others who work closely with the person. The interview can be helpful in preparing the evaluator to conduct direct observations by identifying and defining the target problem be-

haviors, identifying and defining potential antecedents and consequences that may be observed, and gaining an overall picture of the problem behavior as well as the strengths of the person. The interview can also help determine if other assessments are warranted before a more extensive FBA is conducted. For example, if the interview reveals that the person has chronic ear infections that are currently untreated, a medical evaluation should be conducted before further behavioral assessment takes place.

In many cases conducting an interview with the person who has problem behavior can be helpful if he has the language skills to understand and respond to interview questions. Sometimes the person has useful insights regarding why he displays problem behavior in specific contexts (Kern et al., 1995).

At this point, conducting direct observations of the problem behavior within the natural routine is useful. Such observations help confirm or disconfirm the information obtained through the interviews. If it is not clear when the problem behavior occurs most often, a scatterplot analysis may be useful to determine when further behavioral observations should be conducted. When the problematic time periods have been determined, the behavior analyst

on obtained from
the ABC assessment
ready have clear defini-
(s), antecedents, and conse-
behavior analyst must also be
nal, unexpected antecedents and con-
ight present themselves in the natural en-
eachers or caregivers sometimes overlook or
ware of specific stimuli triggering or following
blem behavior.

Interpreting Information and Formulating Hypotheses

Results from indirect assessments should be analyzed for patterns of behavior and environmental events so that hypotheses regarding the function of the problem behavior can be made. If problem behavior occurs most frequently when low levels of attention are available and problem behavior frequently produces attention, a hypothesis that attention maintains the problem behavior is appropriate. If the problem behavior occurs most frequently in high-demand situations and often produces a reprieve from the task (e.g., through time-out, suspension, or another form of task delay), then a hypothesis that escape maintains the problem behavior is appropriate. If problem behavior occurs in an unpredictable pattern or at high rates across the school day, a hypothesis that the behavior is maintained by automatic reinforcement may be appropriate. In reviewing assessment results and considering possible hypotheses, behavior analysts should remember that behaviors may serve multiple functions and different topographies of problem behavior may serve different functions.

Hypothesis statements should be written in ABC format. Specifically, the hypothesis statement should state the antecedent(s) hypothesized to trigger the problem behavior, the topography of problem behavior, and the maintaining consequence. For example:

Hypothesized function	Antecedent	Behavior	Consequence
Escape from hand washing and/or lunch.	When Tonisha is prompted to wash her hands in preparation for lunch, . . .	she screams and tantrums, which is followed by . . .	termination of hand washing and lunch by being sent to time-out.

Writing hypothesis statements in this manner is useful because it requires the behavior analyst to focus on potential avenues for intervention: modifying the antecedent and/or modifying the reinforcement contingencies (which may involve teaching a new behavior and altering what behaviors are reinforced or placed on extinction).

Testing Hypotheses

After hypotheses have been developed, a functional analysis can be conducted to test them. The functional analysis should always contain a control condition that serves to promote the lowest frequency of problem behavior. For most individuals, this is the play condition, which consists of (a) continuous availability of preferred toys and/or activities, (b) no demands, and (c) continuously available attention. Then, conditions are selected to test specific hypotheses. For example, if the primary hypothesis is that the problem behavior is maintained by escape, then a contingent escape condition should be implemented. Other test conditions may not need to be implemented.

Being selective about the test conditions implemented will help keep the functional analysis as brief as possible; however, no conclusions can be made regarding additional functions of problem behavior if additional test conditions are not implemented. For example, if play and contingent escape are the only conditions tested, and problem behavior occurs most frequently in the contingent escape condition and seldom or never occurs in the play condition, the conclusion that the problem behavior is maintained by escape is supported. However, because a contingent attention condition was not implemented, one could not rule out the possibility that the problem behavior is also maintained by attention.

One way to test all possible hypotheses within a short period of time is to use a brief functional analysis procedure (e.g., Boyagian, DuPaul, Wartel, Handler, Eckert, & McGoey, 2001; Cooper et al., 1992; Derby et al., 1992; Kahng & Iwata, 1999; Northup et al., 1991; Wacker et al., 1990). This technique involves implementing one session each of the control condition and each of the test conditions. If an increase in problem behavior is observed in one of the test conditions, a **contingency reversal** is implemented to confirm the hypothesis rather than conducting many repetitions of all of the conditions. For example, after conducting one of each of the control and test conditions, assume that Tonisha's tantrums were elevated in the contingent escape condition (see Figure 24.3). To confirm this hypothesis, the behavior analyst could reinstate the contingent escape condition, followed by a contingency reversal in which problem behavior no longer produces escape. Rather, another behavior (often a request) is substituted for problem behavior. For example, in Tonisha's case, she could be prompted to form the manual sign "break," and contingent on signing "break," a task break is provided. The contingency reversal is then followed by reinstatement of the contingent escape condition, in which the sign "break" is placed on extinction and the tantrums again produces escape. This process could be repeated for any and all conditions in which the problem behavior was elevated during the initial analysis.

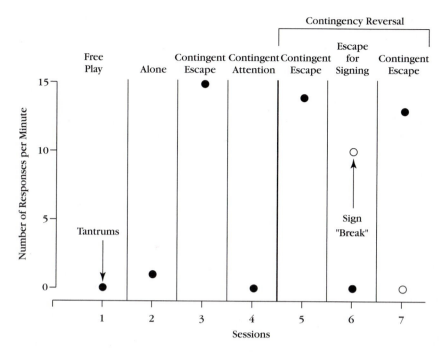

Figure 24.3 Hypothetical data from brief functional analysis of Tonisha's tantrums. The closed data points represent tantrums, and the open data points represent manual signs for breaks. The first four sessions represent the brief functional analysis, while Sessions 5 through 7 represent the contingency reversal.

Kahng and Iwata (1999) found that brief functional analysis identified the function of problem behavior accurately (i.e., it yielded results similar to extended functional analyses) in 66% of the cases. Brief functional analyses are useful when time is very limited. However, given that brief functional analyses do not match the results of extended functional analyses at least a third of the time, it is probably wise to conduct an extended functional analysis whenever circumstances permit. In addition, when brief functional analyses are inconclusive, it is recommended that a more extended functional analysis be conducted (Vollmer, Marcus, Ringdahl, & Roane, 1995).

Developing Interventions

When an FBA has been completed, an intervention that matches the function of problem behavior can be developed. Interventions can take many forms. Although FBA does not identify which interventions will be effective in treating problem behavior, it does identify antecedents that may trigger problem behavior, potential behavioral deficits that should be remedied, and reinforcement contingencies that can be altered, as described earlier in this chapter. However, FBA *does* identify powerful reinforcers that can be used as part of the intervention package. The intervention should be **functionally equivalent** to problem behavior. That is, if problem behavior serves an escape function, then the intervention should provide escape (e.g., in the form of breaks from task demands) for a more appropriate response or involve altering task demands in a fashion that makes escape less reinforcing.

One effective way to design interventions is to review confirmed hypotheses to determine how the ABC contingency can be altered to promote more positive behavior. For example, consider the hypothesis developed for Tonisha:

Hypothesized function	Antecedent	Behavior	Consequence
Escape from hand washing and/or lunch.	When Tonisha is prompted to wash her hands in preparation for lunch, . . .	she screams and tantrums, which is followed by . . .	termination of hand washing and lunch by being sent to time-out.

The antecedent could be altered by changing the time of day when Tonisha is asked to wash her hands (so that it does not precede lunch, thereby decreasing the motivation for escape-motivated tantrums).

Hypothesized function	Antecedent	Behavior	Consequence
Escape from hand washing and/or lunch.	~~When Tonisha is prompted to wash her hands in preparation for lunch, . . .~~ Tonisha is prompted to wash her hands before recess.	N/A (Problem behavior is avoided.)	N/A (The consequence is irrelevant because problem behavior did not occur.)

The behavior could be altered by teaching Tonisha a new behavior (e.g., signing "break") that results in the same outcome (escape from lunch).

Hypothesized function	Antecedent	Behavior	Consequence
Escape from hand washing and/or lunch.	When Tonisha is prompted to wash her hands in preparation for lunch, . . .	~~she screams and tantrums~~ Tonisha is prompted to sign "break," which is followed by . . .	termination of hand washing and lunch.

Or, the consequences could be altered. For example, the reinforcer for problem behavior could be withheld so that problem behavior is extinguished.

Hypothesized function	Antecedent	Behavior	Hypothesized function (consequence)
Escape from hand washing and/or lunch.	When Tonisha is prompted to wash her hands in preparation for lunch, . . .	she screams and tantrums, which is followed by . . .	~~termination of hand washing and lunch by being sent to timeout.~~ continued presentation of hand-washing and lunch activities.

An intervention can also consist of several different components. For example, Tonisha could be taught a replacement behavior (signing "break"), which results in breaks from lunch, while tantrums are simultaneously placed on escape extinction.

FBA can also help identify interventions that are likely to be ineffective or that may worsen the problem behavior. Interventions involving time-out, in- or out-of-school suspension, or planned ignoring are contraindicated for problem behaviors maintained by escape. Interventions involving reprimands, discussion, or counseling are contraindicated for problem behaviors maintained by attention.

A final word about intervention: When an intervention has been developed, FBA is not "done." Assessment is an ongoing practice that continues when intervention is implemented. It is important for continued monitoring of intervention effectiveness. The functions of behavior are not static. Rather, they are dynamic and change over time. Intervention may lose its effectiveness over time because the function of problem behavior may change over time (Lerman, Iwata, Smith, Zarcone, & Vollmer, 1994). In such cases, additional functional analyses may need to be conducted to revise the intervention.

Case Examples Illustrating the FBA Process

FBA is a highly idiosyncratic process. It is unusual for any two FBAs to be exactly the same because each person presents with a unique set of skills and behaviors, as well as a unique history of reinforcement. FBA requires a thorough understanding of behavioral principles to parcel out the relevant information from interviews and ABC assessments, to form relevant hypotheses, and to test those hypotheses. Beyond these skills, a solid understanding of behavioral interventions (e.g., differential reinforcement procedures, schedules of reinforcement, and tactics for promoting maintenance and generalization) is needed to match effective treatments to the function of challenging behavior. This can seem like a daunting process. In an attempt to demonstrate the application of FBA across the idiosyncratic differences in people, we present four case examples.

Brian—Multiple Functions of Problem Behavior

Gathering Information

Brian was 13 years old and diagnosed with pervasive developmental delay, oppositional defiant disorder, and attention-deficit/hyperactivity disorder. He had moderate delays in cognitive and adaptive skills. Brian displayed several problem behaviors, including aggression, property destruction, and tantrums. Brian's aggression had resulted in several of his teachers having bruises, and his property destruction and tantrums frequently disrupted the daily activities of the classroom.

A Functional Assessment Interview (O'Neill et al., 1997) was conducted with Brian's teacher, Ms. Baker, who reported that Brian's problem behavior occurred most frequently when he was asked to perform a task that required any kind of physical labor (e.g., shredding papers) and occurred least during leisure activities. However, Ms. Baker reported that Brian often engaged in problem behavior when he was asked to leave a preferred activity. She noted that Brian used complex speech (sentences), although he often used verbal threats (e.g., curse words) and/or aggression, property destruction, and tantrums to communicate his wants and needs.

Because Brian was verbal, a Student-Assisted Functional Assessment Interview (Kern et al., 1995) was also conducted. In this interview, Brian reported that he found his math work too difficult but that writing and using a calculator were too easy. He reported that he sometimes received help from his teachers when he asked for it, that sometimes teachers and staff noticed when he was doing a good job, and that he sometimes received rewards for

Table 24.3   Results of ABC Assessments for Brian's Aggression, Property Destruction, and Tantrums

Antecedent	Behavior	Consequence
Adult attention diverted to another student; denied access to Nintendo by teacher (i.e., told no when he asked if he could play it)	Yelled at teacher, "That's not fair! Why do you hate me?!"	Told to "calm down"
Teacher attending to another student	Hit sofa, attempted to leave classroom	Given choice of activity and verbal warning to stay in classroom
Teacher attention diverted to another student	Yelled, "Stop!" at another student	Reprimand from teacher: "Don't worry, Brian. I will take care of it."
Story time, teacher attending to other students	Laughed loudly	Reprimand from teacher: "Stop it!"
Story time, teacher listening to other students	Interrupted other students while they were talking: "Hey, it's my turn. I know what happens next!"	Reprimand from teacher: "You need to listen."

doing good work. Brian indicated that his work periods were always too long, especially those that consisted of shredding papers. Brian reported that he had the fewest problems in school when he was allowed to answer the phone (his classroom job), when he was completing math problems, and when he was playing with his Gameboy. He stated that he felt he had the most problems at school when he was outside playing with the other students because they often teased him, called him names, and cursed at him.

An ABC assessment was conducted on two separate occasions. The results of the ABC assessment are shown in Table 24.3.

Interpreting Information and Formulating Hypotheses

Based on the interviews and ABC assessments, the function of Brian's problem behavior was unclear. It was hypothesized that some of Brian's problem behaviors were maintained by access to adult attention and preferred items. This hypothesis was a result of the ABC assessment, which indicated that many of Brian's problem behaviors occurred when adult attention was low or when access to preferred items was restricted. Brian's problem behavior often resulted in access to adult attention or preferred activities. It was also hypothesized that Brian's problem behavior was maintained by escape because his teacher reported that Brian frequently engaged in problem behavior in the presence of task demands and because Brian reported that some of his work was too hard and work periods lasted too long. Thus, a functional analysis was conducted to test these hypotheses. The hypothesis statements for Brian are summarized in Table 24.4.

Testing hypotheses

Next, a functional analysis was completed for Brian. The functional analysis consisted of the same conditions as described previously, with two exceptions. First, an alone condition was not conducted because there was no reason

Table 24.4   Hypothesis Statements for Brian

Hypothesized function	Antecedent	Behavior	Consequence
Gain attention from adults and peers	When adult or peer attention is diverted from Brian, . . .	he engages in a variety of problem behaviors, which result in . . .	attention from adults and peers.
Gain access to preferred toys and activities	When Brian's access to preferred toys and activities is restricted, . . .	he engages in a variety of problem behaviors, which result in . . .	gaining access to preferred toys and activities.
Escape from difficult and/or nonpreferred tasks	When Brian is required to perform difficult or undesirable tasks, . . .	he engages in a variety of problem behaviors, which result in . . .	the tasks being removed.

to believe that Brian's problem behavior served an automatic function. Second, a contingent tangible condition was added because there was reason to believe Brian engaged in problem behavior to gain access to preferred tangibles and activities. This condition was just like the play condition (i.e., Brian had access to adult attention and preferred toys at the beginning of the session), except that intermittently throughout the session, he was told it was time to give his toy to the teacher and to play with something else (which was less desirable). If Brian complied with the request to give the toy to the teacher, he was given a less preferred toy. If he engaged in problem behavior, he was allowed to continue playing with his preferred toys for a brief period of time.

The results of the functional analysis are shown in Figure 24.4. Notice that problem behavior never occurred in the play condition, but it occurred at high rates in all three of the test conditions (contingent attention, escape, and tangible). These results indicated that Brian's problem behavior was maintained by escape, attention, and access to preferred items. During the play condition, however, when continuous attention and preferred items were available and no demands were placed on Brian, problem behavior never occurred.

Developing an Intervention

Based on the results of the functional analysis, a multi-component intervention was implemented. The intervention components changed at different points in time depending on the context. These components, as they relate to the functions of problem behavior, are summarized in Table 24.5. For example, when Brian was engaged in a work task, it was recommended that he be given frequent opportunities to request breaks. In addition, the time-out intervention that the teacher had been using was discontinued in the work context. During

leisure times, when Brian had previously been expected to play alone, the classroom schedule was rearranged so that Brian could play and interact with peers. Brian was also taught to request toys appropriately while playing with peers. In addition, several interventions aimed at increasing teacher attention for appropriate behavior were implemented. Brian was taught how to request teacher attention appropriately, and teachers began to respond to these requests rather than ignore them (as they had previously done). In addition, a self-monitoring plan was established, in which Brian was taught to monitor his own behavior and match his self-recordings to his teachers'. Accurate self-recording resulted in teacher praise and access to preferred activities with the teacher. Brian's teachers also implemented their own plan to increase attention and praise to Brian every 5 minutes as long as he was not engaged in problem behavior during independent work.

Kaitlyn—Attention Function for Problem Behavior

Gathering Information

Kaitlyn was 12 years old and diagnosed with attention-deficit/hyperactivity disorder. She also displayed some fine and gross motor deficits. Kaitlyn attended classes in both her general education sixth-grade classroom and a special education classroom. She frequently displayed off-task behavior, which consisted of being out of her seat, touching others (e.g., playing "footsie" under the desk with peers), making noises, and talking out of turn. A Functional Assessment Interview (O'Neill et al., 1997) was conducted with Kaitlyn's teacher, who stated that, typically, Kaitlyn asked questions constantly when she was given a difficult task. The teacher also stated that Kaitlyn often became confused when her routines were changed, and that she therefore needed a lot of assistance.

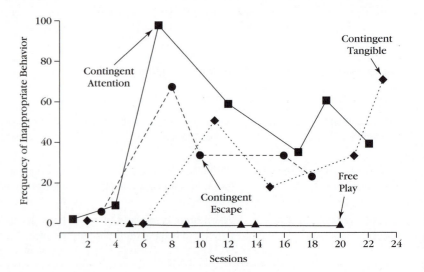

Figure 24.4 Results of Brian's functional analysis. Inappropriate behavior consists of aggression, property destruction, and tantrums.

Functional analysis conducted by Renée Van Norman and Amanda Flaute.

Table 24.5   Summary of Brian's Intervention Components

Intervention Options for Attention Function			
Intervention	*Antecedent*	*Behavior*	*Consequence*
Teach a new behavior (social attention)	When adult or peer attention is diverted from Brian, . . .	he will raise his hand and say, "Excuse me . . ."	and adults and peers will provide attention to Brian.
Teach a new behavior	When adult or peer attention is diverted from Brian, . . .	he will self-monitor his appropriate independent work and match teacher recordings . . .	and the teachers will provide him with one-on-one time if he meets a specific criterion.
Change the antecedent	During independent work times, adults will provide attention to Brian every 5 minutes . . .	to increase the probability that Brian will appropriately work independently, . . .	which will increase adult opportunities to praise and attend to appropriate behavior.
Change the antecedent	Allow Brian to play with peers during leisure times . . .	to increase the probability that Brian will play appropriately, . . .	which will increase adult opportunities to praise appropriate behavior and for peers to respond positively.
Intervention Options for Tangible Function			
Intervention	*Antecedent*	*Behavior*	*Consequence*
Teach a new behavior	When Brian's access to preferred toys and activities is restricted, . . .	he will say, "Can I have that back, please?" . . .	and the teacher will provide access to preferred toys and activities.
Intervention Options for Escape Function			
Intervention	*Antecedent*	*Behavior*	*Consequence*
Teach a new behavior	When Brian is required to perform a difficult or undesirable task, . . .	he will say, "May I take a break now?" . . .	and the teacher will allow Brian to take a break from the task.
Change the reinforcement contingency	When Brian is required to perform difficult or undesirable tasks . . .	and he engages in a variety of problem behaviors, . . .	he will be required to continue working on the task and the time-out intervention will be discontinued.

Because there was only one teacher in the classroom and 25 other students, Kaitlyn received little additional attention, and her teacher hypothesized that she engaged in off-task behavior to gain attention.

The results of an ABC assessment showed that Kaitlyn often received little adult attention in the classroom, except when she displayed off-task behavior. Although off-task behavior occurred when attention was diverted, Kaitlyn was often engaged in demanding tasks simultaneously. Thus, it was unclear which antecedent—the low attention or the high-demand activity—was related to her problem behavior.

Interpreting Information and Formulating Hypotheses

Based on the information obtained from interviews and ABC assessments, it was hypothesized that Kaitlyn's off-task behavior served an attention function. The hypotheses developed for Kaitlyn are summarized in Table 24.6.

Table 24.6   Hypotheses Regarding the Function of Kaitlyn's Off-Task Behavior

Hypothesized function	*Antecedent*	*Behavior*	*Consequence*
Primary hypothesis—Gain attention from adults	When teacher attention is diverted from Kaitlyn, . . .	she engages in off-task behavior, which results in . . .	teacher attention (reprimands, task prompts).
Alternative hypothesis— Escape from difficult academic tasks	When Kaitlyn is required to work on academic tasks, . . .	she engages in off-task behavior, which results in . . .	those tasks being removed.

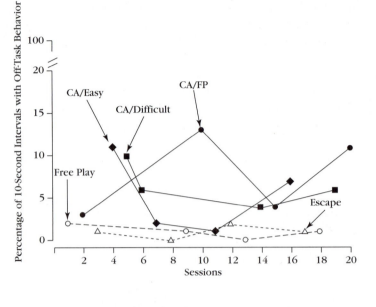

Figure 24.5 Results of the functional analysis for Kaitlyn's off-task behavior. FP = free play; CA/FP = contingent attention during free play activities; CA/Easy = contingent attention during easy academic activities; CA/Difficult = contingent attention during difficult academic activities.

Functional analysis conducted by Jessica Frieder, Jill Grunkemeyer, and Jill Hollway.

However, because Kaitlyn was typically observed in academic activities that were paired with low attention situations, it was unclear what role task difficulty played in her off-task behavior. It was unclear whether she engaged in problem behavior to gain attention or because the academic tasks were too difficult. Would Kaitlyn engage in similar levels of problem behavior when play materials were present as compared to easy or difficult academic materials while attention was diverted? It was important to design a functional analysis that would address these questions.

Testing Hypotheses

Kaitlyn's functional analysis demonstrates how functional analysis conditions can be constructed to test many kinds of hypotheses. Her functional analysis consisted of the standard play and escape conditions described previously. However, several different contingent attention conditions were implemented to determine whether demands interacted with low attention conditions to evoke problem behavior.

Three contingent attention conditions were conducted: contingent attention during free play activities (CA/FP), contingent attention during easy academic activities (CA/Easy), and contingent attention during difficult academic activities (CA/Difficult). In all three conditions, attention was diverted from Kaitlyn until she engaged in off-task behavior. Contingent on off-task behavior, a teacher approached her and delivered a mild reprimand (e.g., "Kaitlyn, what are you doing? You're supposed to be doing this activity. I need you to get back to your activity now".). The conditions differed in the type of activity Kaitlyn was asked to work on. During CA/FP,

Kaitlyn was allowed to play with a game of her choice. During CA/Easy, Kaitlyn was required to solve single-digit addition problems. During CA/Difficult, Kaitlyn was required to solve multidigit subtraction problems that required regrouping.

The results of the functional analysis are shown in Figure 24.5. Little off-task behavior occurred in the free play and escape conditions. Thus, the hypothesis that Kaitlyn engaged in off-task behavior to escape tasks was not supported. Increased off-task behavior was observed in all three of the contingent attention conditions. These data suggested that Kaitlyn's off-task behavior served an attention function regardless of the type of activity in which she was involved.

Developing an Intervention

Kaitlyn was verbal and often requested attention appropriately. Therefore, Kaitlyn was taught to monitor her on- and off-task behavior when she was required to work or play independently. Initially, Kaitlyn was taught to monitor her behavior every 10 seconds. (This was the longest she was able to stay on task without prompting during baseline.) Both she and a classroom assistant wore a vibrating timer (a MotivAider)[1] that would not distract the other students. When the timer vibrated, Kaitlyn marked on a self-monitoring sheet if she was on or off task. She then looked up at the assistant. If Kaitlyn was on task, the assistant gave Kaitlyn a thumbs-up signal and a smile.

---

[1]The MotivAider is a device that can be set to vibrate at specific intervals of time. The MotivAider can be obtained at www.habitchange.com.

Occasionally, the assistant also approached Kaitlyn, gave her a pat on the back, and said, "Way to stay on task!" If she was not on task, the assistant looked away from her. At the end of 10 minutes, the assistant and Kaitlyn compared marks. If Kaitlyn was on task on 50 of 60 checks and she matched the teacher on 57 of 60 checks, she was allowed to engage in a special activity with the assistant for 5 minutes. Over time, the interval length and duration of the observation period were increased until Kaitlyn worked appropriately for the entire period.

DeShawn—Automatic Function of Problem Behavior

Gathering Information

DeShawn was 10 years old and diagnosed with autism. He had severe developmental delays and was blind. He took Resperidol for behavioral control. DeShawn frequently threw objects across the room, dropped objects and task materials off the table, and knocked objects from tables with a sweeping motion of his arm, which interfered with work on academic tasks. A Functional Assessment Interview (O'Neill et al., 1997) yielded little useful information because the teacher stated that DeShawn's throwing, dropping, and sweeping were unpredictable. She could not identify any antecedents that typically preceded the problem behavior. The intervention in place at the time was to limit DeShawn's access or proximity to objects that he might throw. ABC observations conducted within the natural routine also produced little useful information because the teachers prevented

and blocked all occurrences of the problem behavior. Thus, very few occurrences of the problem behavior were observed. However, it was noted that DeShawn was rarely actively involved in lessons. For example, when the teacher read a book to the class, DeShawn was unable to participate because he could not see the pictures. At other times, DeShawn was engaged in individual work tasks, but these tasks did not appear to be meaningful or appropriate for his skill level.

Interpreting Information and Formulating Hypotheses

It was difficult to formulate a hypothesis based on the limited information from the teacher and direct observations. Because DeShawn did not seem actively involved or interested in the classroom activities, it was hypothesized that throwing, dropping, and sweeping were automatically reinforcing. However, other hypotheses, such as attention, escape, or multiple functions, could not be ruled out.

Testing Hypotheses

The functional analysis consisted of play, contingent attention, and contingent escape conditions. An alone condition was not conducted because there was not a room that allowed DeShawn to be observed and supervised covertly. The results of the functional analysis are shown in Figure 24.6. Throwing, dropping, and sweeping occurred at high and variable rates across all three conditions,

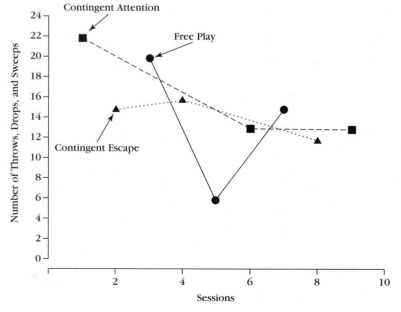

Figure 24.6 Results of DeShawn's functional analysis.

Functional analysis conducted by Susan M. Silvestri, Laura Lacy Rismiller, and Jennie E. Valk.

demonstrating an undifferentiated pattern. These results were inconclusive, but suggested an automatic reinforcement function for throwing, dropping, and sweeping.

Further analysis might have identified more precisely the source of reinforcement (e.g., sweeping motion, sound of objects falling, a clear table surface). Instead, we sought to identify alternative reinforcers that might compete with automatically maintained problem behavior.

We conducted a forced-choice preference assessment (Fisher et al., 1992) to identify highly preferred stimuli. (See Chapter 11 for a detailed discussion of these procedures.) The results of this assessment are shown in Figure 24.7. DeShawn most frequently chose potato chips. Data were also collected on the number of seconds DeShawn played with each item before he threw it. (He was allowed to have access to each item for 30 seconds, so a data point at 30 seconds indicates that he played with the item the entire time and never threw it.) No data were collected on how long DeShawn "played" with potato chips because he did not play with them; he consumed them. However, it should be noted that DeShawn never threw the potato chips, nor did he throw any other objects in the area when he had access to potato chips. He immediately put them in his mouth and ate them. These two pieces of information indicated that potato chips were highly preferred and might function as a reinforcer that could compete with throwing, dropping, and sweeping. Although the tube that made noise was chosen second most frequently, DeShawn typically threw it after playing with it for only 12 seconds.

The next assessment evaluated whether potato chips served as a reinforcer for pressing a microswitch that said "Chip, please" and whether the use of potato chips would compete with throwing (based on the microswitch assessment procedures of Wacker, Berg, Wiggins, Muldoon, & Cavanaugh, 1985). First, baseline data were collected on the number of appropriate switch presses (pressing the switch once to activate the voice); the number of inappropriate switch presses (repeatedly pressing or banging the switch); the number of attempts to throw the switch; and the number of throws, drops, and sweeps of other objects. During baseline, DeShawn was provided with access to the microswitch; however, neither chips nor the Slinky was delivered for pressing the switch. Next, the voice on the switch said "Chip, please," and a potato chip was provided contingent on appropriate switch pressing. In the next condition, the voice on the switch said "Slinky, please," and the Slinky (a nonpreferred toy) was provided contingent on appropriate switch pressing. Finally, the voice on the switch said "Chip, please" again, and a potato chip was provided contingent on appropriate switch pressing to form an ABCB reversal design.

The results of the microswitch assessment are shown in Figure 24.8. Appropriate microswitch presses increased when potato chips were provided contingently. Interestingly, no throwing, dropping, or sweeping occurred when the potato chip was available. Some inappropriate switch presses also occurred, but appropriate switch presses were more frequent. When microswitch pressing resulted in a nonpreferred toy, appropriate switch pressing decreased and throwing, dropping, and sweeping increased. This suggested that potato chips competed effectively with throwing, dropping, and sweeping.

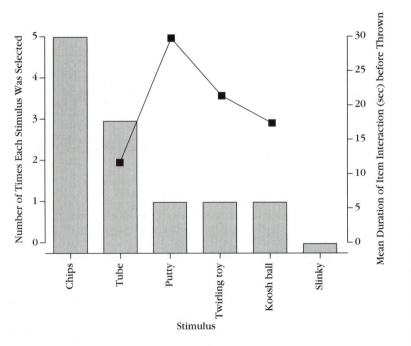

Figure 24.7 Results of DeShawn's preference assessment. The bars indicate the number of times each stimulus was selected. The line graph represents the mean number of seconds DeShawn played with each item stimulus before throwing it.

Preference assessment conducted by Susan M. Silvestri, Laura Lacy Rismiller, and Jennie E. Valk.

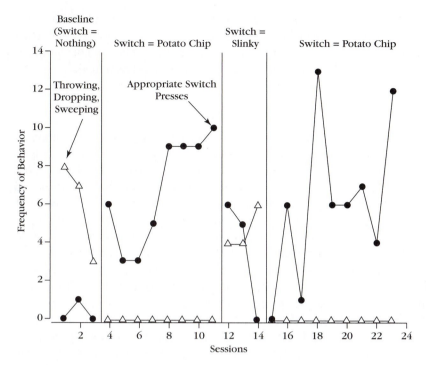

Figure 24.8 Results of DeShawn's microswitch assessment. During Baseline, touching the switch did not result in any tangible stimuli. During Switch = Chip, touching the switch resulted in a bite of potato chip. During Switch = Slinky, touching the switch resulted in access to the Slinky for 30 seconds.

Reinforcer assessment conducted by Renée Van Norman, Amanda Flaute, Susan M. Silvestri, Laura Lacy Rismiller, and Jennie E. Valk.

Developing an Intervention

Based on these assessments, an intervention was developed that involved giving DeShawn small bites of potato chips for participating in classroom activities appropriately. In addition, classroom activities and routines were modified to increase DeShawn's participation, and his curriculum was modified to include instruction on more functional activities.

Lorraine—Multiple Topographies That Serve Multiple Functions

Lorraine was 32 years old and functioned in the moderate range of mental retardation. She had a diagnosis of Down syndrome and bipolar disorder with psychotic symptoms, for which Zoloft and Resperidol were prescribed. She also took Tegretol for seizure control. She was verbal, but her verbal skills were low and her articulation was poor. She communicated through some signs, a simple communication device, gestures, and some words.

Lorraine had resided in a group home for 9 years and attended a sheltered workshop during the day. Lorraine displayed noncompliance, aggression, and SIB in both settings, but the FBA focused on her problem behavior in the group home, where it was more severe and frequent. Noncompliance consisted of Lorraine putting her head down on the table, pulling away from people, or leaving the room when requests were made of her; aggression consisted of kicking others, throwing objects at others, biting others, and squeezing others' arms very hard; SIB consisted of biting her arm, pulling her hair, or pinching her skin.

Gathering Information

Interviews were conducted with Lorraine, her parents, and workshop and group home staff. Lorraine's parents noted that some of her behavior problems had increased when changes in her medication had been made. Workshop staff noted that Lorraine was more likely to have problem behavior at work if many people were around her. Workshop staff had also noted that noncompliance had increased shortly after a dosage change in medication 2 months previously. The group home staff noted that they were most concerned about Lorraine's leaving the group home when she was asked to perform daily chores. Lorraine would often leave the group home and not return until the police had picked her up. Many neighbors had complained because Lorraine would sit on their porches for hours until the police came and removed her.

An ABC assessment was conducted at the workshop and group home to determine whether environmental variables differed across the two settings (e.g., the manner in which tasks were presented, the overall level of attention). At the workshop, Lorraine was engaged in a jewelry assembly task (one she reportedly enjoyed), and she worked well for 2 1/2 hours. She appeared to work better when others paid attention to her and often became off task when she was ignored; however, no problem behavior was observed at work. At the group home, aggression was observed when staff ignored Lorraine. No other problem behavior occurred. No demands were placed on Lorraine in the group home during the ABC observation. Group home staff rarely placed any demands on Lorraine in an attempt to avoid her problem behavior.

Interpreting Information and Formulating Hypotheses

Some of Lorraine's problem behaviors seemed to be related to a dosage change in her medication. Because Lorraine's physician judged her medication to be at therapeutic levels, a decision was made to analyze the environmental events related to her problem behavior. Observations of problem behavior during the ABC assessment were limited because workshop staff placed minimal demands on Lorraine to avoid problem behaviors. However, Lorraine's noncompliance reportedly occurred when demands were placed on her. Therefore, it was hypothesized that these problem behaviors were maintained by escape from task demands. Aggression occurred during the ABC assessment when Lorraine was ignored. Although SIB was not observed during the ABC

assessment, group home staff reported that Lorraine often engaged in SIB during the same situations that evoked aggression. Therefore, it was hypothesized that both aggression and SIB were maintained by attention.

Testing Hypotheses

The functional analysis consisted of free play, contingent attention, and contingent escape conditions (see Figure 24.9). Because the problem behaviors may have served different functions, each problem behavior was coded and graphed separately. Noncompliance occurred most frequently during the contingent escape condition and rarely occurred during the free play or contingent attention conditions. SIB occurred most frequently during the contingent attention condition and rarely occurred during the free play or contingent escape conditions. These data suggested that noncompliance served an escape function, and SIB served an attention function. As is often the case for low-frequency, high-intensity behaviors, it was difficult to form hypotheses about the function of aggression because the behavior occurred rarely in any of the FBA conditions.

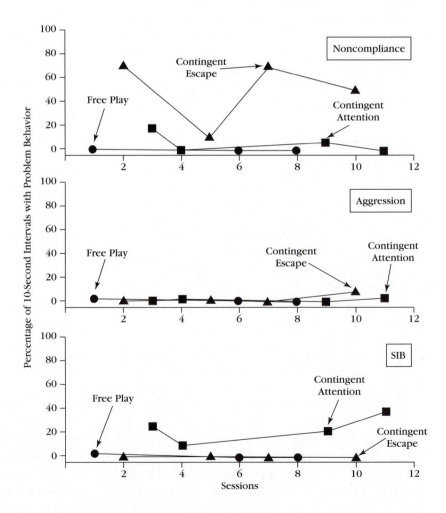

Figure 24.9   Results of Lorraine's functional analysis.

Functional analysis conducted by Corrine M. Murphy and Tabitha Kirby.

Developing an Intervention.

Different interventions were developed for the problem behaviors because results of the FBA suggested that the behaviors served different functions. To address noncompliance, Lorraine was taught to request breaks from difficult tasks. Tasks were broken down into very small steps. Lorraine was presented with only one step of a task at a time. Each time a task request was made, Lorraine was reminded that she could request a break (either by saying "Break, please" or by touching a break card). If she requested a break, the task materials were removed for a brief period of time. Then they were presented again. Also, if Lorraine engaged in noncompliance, she was *not* allowed to escape the task. Instead she was prompted through one step of the task and then another step of the task was presented. Initially, Lorraine was allowed to completely escape the task if she appropriately requested

a break each time the task was presented. Over time, however, she was required to complete increasing amounts of work before a break was allowed.

Intervention for aggression consisted of teaching Lorraine appropriate ways to gain attention (e.g., tapping someone on the arm and saying, "Excuse me") and teaching group home staff to regularly attend to Lorraine when she made such requests. In addition, because her articulation was so poor, a picture communication book was created to assist Lorraine in having conversations with others. This communication book could be used to clarify words that staff could not understand. Finally, staff were encouraged to ignore Lorraine's SIB when it did occur. In the past, staff had approached Lorraine and stopped her from engaging in SIB when it occurred. The functional analysis demonstrated that this intervention may have increased the occurrence of SIB, so this practice was discontinued.

Summary

Functions of Behavior

1. Many problem behaviors are learned and maintained via positive, negative, and/or automatic reinforcement. In this respect, problem behavior can be said to have a "function" (e.g., to gain access to stimuli or to escape stimuli).

2. The *topography,* or form, of a behavior often reveals little useful information about the conditions that account for it. Identifying the *conditions* that account for a behavior (its function) suggests what conditions need to be altered to change the behavior. Assessment of the function of a behavior can therefore yield useful information with respect to intervention strategies that are likely to be effective.

Role of Functional Behavior Assessment in Intervention and Prevention

3. FBA can lead to effective interventions in at least three ways: (a) it can identify antecedent variables that can be altered to prevent problem behavior, (b) it can identify reinforcement contingencies that can be altered so that problem behavior no longer receives reinforcement, and (c) it can help identify reinforcers for alternative replacement behaviors.

4. FBA can decrease reliance on default technologies (increasingly intrusive, coercive, and punishment-based interventions) and contribute to more effective interventions. When FBAs are conducted, reinforcement-based interventions are more likely to be implemented than are interventions that include a punishment component.

Overview of FBA Methods

5. FBA methods can be classified into three types: (a) functional (experimental) analysis, (b) descriptive assessment, and (c) indirect assessment. The methods can be

ordered on a continuum with respect to considerations such as ease of use and the type and precision of information they yield.

6. Functional analysis involves systematically manipulating environmental events thought to maintain problem behavior within an experimental design. The primary advantage of functional analysis is its ability to yield a clear demonstration of the variable(s) that relate to the occurrence of a problem behavior. However, this assessment method requires a certain amount of expertise to implement and interpret.

7. Descriptive assessment involves observation of the problem behavior in relation to events that are not arranged in a systematic manner and includes ABC recording (both continuous and narrative) and scatterplots. The primary advantages to these assessment methodologies are that they are easier to do than functional analyses and they represent contingencies that occur within the individual's natural routine. Caution must be exercised when interpreting information from descriptive assessments, however, because they can be biased and unreliable, and they provide correlations (as opposed to functional relations).

8. Indirect functional assessment methods use structured interviews, checklists, rating scales, or questionnaires to obtain information from persons who are familiar with the individual exhibiting the problem behavior (e.g., teachers, parents, caregivers, and/or the individual him- or herself) to identify possible conditions or events in the natural environment that correlate with the problem behavior. Again, these forms of FBA are easy to conduct, but they are limited in their accuracy. As such, they are probably best reserved for hypothesis formulation. Further assessment of these hypotheses is often necessary.

Conducting a Functional Behavior Assessment

9. Given the strengths and limitations of the different FBA procedures, FBA can best be viewed as a four-step process:

   a. Gather information via indirect and descriptive assessment.

   b. Interpret information from indirect and descriptive assessment and formulate hypotheses about the purpose of problem behavior.

   c. Test hypotheses using functional analysis.

   d. Develop intervention options based on the function of problem behavior.

10. A brief functional analysis can be used to test hypotheses when time is very limited.

11. When teaching an alternative behavior as a replacement for problem behavior, the replacement behavior should be functionally equivalent to the problem behavior (i.e., it should be reinforced using the same reinforcers that previously maintained the problem behavior).

Case Examples Illustrating the FBA Process

12. A person can display one problem behavior for more than one reason, as shown in Brian's case example. In such cases, intervention may need to consist of multiple components to address each function of problem behavior.

13. Functional analyses can be tailored to test specific and/or idiosyncratic hypotheses, as shown in Kaitlyn's example.

14. Undifferentiated problem behavior during a functional analysis may indicate an automatic reinforcement function and warrants further evaluation, as shown in DeShawn's case example. In such cases, alternative reinforcers can sometimes be identified and used effectively in an intervention to decrease problem behavior and improve adaptive responding.

15. Sometimes a person displays multiple topographies of problem behavior (e.g., self-injury and aggression), with each topography serving a different function, as shown in Lorraine's example. In such cases, a different intervention for each topography of problem behavior is warranted.

PART 10

Verbal Behavior

Chapter 25 is devoted to verbal behavior, a distinguishing feature of the human behavioral repertoire. Verbal behavior is at once the phenomenon that makes humans particularly interesting and the vehicle with which we express that interest. Verbal behavior makes progress possible from one generation to the next and enhances the development of sciences, technologies, and the arts. Building on Skinner's (1957) conceptual analysis, Mark Sundberg presents verbal behavior in the context of typical human development, with an emphasis on language assessment and intervention programs for children with autism or other developmental disabilities.

CHAPTER 25

Verbal Behavior

Key Terms

audience	generic (tact) extension	private events
autoclitic	impure tact	solistic (tact) extension
automatic punishment	intraverbal	speaker
automatic reinforcement	listener	tact
convergent multiple control	mand	textual
copying a text	metaphorical (tact) extension	transcription
divergent multiple control	metonymical (tact) extension	verbal behavior
echoic	multiple control	verbal operant
formal similarity	point-to-point correspondence	

Behavior Analyst Certification Board® BCBA® & BCABA® Behavior Analyst Task List,© Third Edition

	Content Area 3: Principles, Processes and Concepts.
3-15	Define and provide examples of echoics and imitation.
3-16	Define and provide examples of mands.
3-17	Define and provide examples of tacts.
3-18	Define and provide examples of intraverbals.

	Content Area 9: Behavior Change Procedures
9-25	Use language acquisition programs that employ Skinner's analysis of verbal behavior (i.e., echoics, mands, tacts, intraverbals).
9-26	Use language acquisition and communication training procedures.

This chapter was written by Mark L. Sundberg.

Why should applied behavior analysts be concerned with verbal behavior? A review of the definition of applied behavior analysis as presented in Chapter 1 can provide an answer to this question.

> Applied behavior analysis is the science in which tactics derived from the principles of behavior are applied to improve socially significant behavior and experimentation is used to identify the variables responsible for behavior change (p. 20).

Note the point *to improve socially significant behavior*. The most socially significant aspects of human behavior involve verbal behavior. Language acquisition, social interaction, academics, intelligence, understanding, thinking, problem solving, knowledge, perception, history, science, politics, and religion are all directly relevant to verbal behavior. In addition, many human problems, such as autism, learning disabilities, illiteracy, antisocial behavior, marital conflicts, aggression, and wars, involve verbal behavior. In short, verbal behavior plays a central role in most of the major aspects of a person's life, and in the laws, conventions, archives, and activities of a society. These topics are the main subject topics of most introductory psychology textbooks. These are socially significant behaviors that applied behavior analysts need to address. However, the verbal analysis of these topics has just begun, and a substantial amount of work has yet to be accomplished.

Verbal Behavior and Properties of Language

Form and Function of Language

It is important in the study of language to distinguish between the formal and functional properties of language (Skinner, 1957). The *formal properties* involve the topography (i.e., form, structure) of the verbal response, whereas the *functional properties* involve the causes of the response. A complete account of language must consider both of these elements.

The field of structural linguistics specializes in the formal description of language. The topography of what is said can be measured by (a) phonemes: the individual speech sounds that comprise a word; (b) morphemes: the units with an individual piece of meaning; (c) lexicon: the total collection of words that make up a given language; (d) syntax: the organization of words, phrases, or clauses in sentences; (e) grammar: the adherence to established conventions of a given language; and (f) semantics: what words *mean* (Barry, 1998; Owens, 2001).

The formal description of a language can be accomplished also by classifying words as nouns, verbs, prepositions, adjectives, adverbs, pronouns, conjunctions, and articles. Other aspects of a formal description of language include prepositional phrases, clauses, modifiers, gerunds, tense markers, particles, and predicates. Sentences then are made up of the syntactical arrangement of the lexical categories of speech with adherence to the grammatical conventions of a given verbal community. The formal properties of language also include articulation, prosody, intonation, pitch, and emphasis (Barry, 1998).

Language can be formally classified without the presence of a speaker or any knowledge about why the speaker said what he did. Sentences can be analyzed as grammatical or ungrammatical from a text or from a tape recorder. For example, incorrect use of word tense can be identified easily from a recording of a child saying, "Juice all goned."

A common misconception about Skinner's analysis of verbal behavior is that he rejected the formal classifications of language. However, he did not find fault with classifications or descriptions of the response, but rather with the failure to account for the "causes" or functions of the classifications. The analysis of how and why one says words is typically relegated to the field of psychology combined with linguistics; hence the field of psycholinguistics.

Theories of Language

A wide variety of theories of language attempt to identify the causes of language. These theories can be classified into three separate, but often overlapping, views: biological, cognitive, and environmental. The basic orientation of the biological theory is that language is a function of physiological processes and functions. Chomsky (1965), for example, maintained that language is innate to humans.[1] That is, a human's language abilities are inherited and present at birth.

Perhaps the most widely accepted views of the causes of language are those derived from cognitive psychology (e.g., Bloom, 1970; Piaget, 1952). Proponents of the cognitive approach to language propose that language is controlled by internal processing systems that accept, classify, code, encode, and store verbal information. Spoken and written language is considered to be the structure of thought. Distinguishing between the biological and cognitive views is often difficult; many are mixed (e.g., Pinker, 1994) and invoke cognitive metaphors such as storage and processing as explanations of language behaviors, or interchange the words *brain* and *mind* (e.g., Chomsky, 1965).

---

[1]For more detail see Mabry (1994, 1995) and Novak (1994).

Development of Verbal Behavior

Skinner began working on a behavioral analysis of language in 1934 as a result of a challenge from Alfred North Whitehead,[2] which Whitehead made when he was seated next to Skinner at a dinner at the Harvard Society of Fellows. Skinner (1957) described the interaction as follows:

> We dropped into a discussion of behaviorism which was then still very much an "ism" and of which I was a zealous devotee. Here was an opportunity which I could not overlook to strike a blow for the cause .... White-head ... agreed that science might be successful in accounting for human behavior provided one made an exception of verbal behavior. Here, he insisted something else must be at work. He brought the discussion to a close with a friendly challenge: "Let me see you," he said, "account for my behavior as I sit here saying 'No black scorpion is falling upon this table.'" The next morning I drew up the outline of the present study. (p. 457)

It took Skinner 23 years to fill in the details of his outline, which he published in his book *Verbal Behavior* (1957). The end result was so significant to Skinner (1978) that he believed *Verbal Behavior* would prove to be his most important work. However, Skinner's use of the phrase *prove to be* 20 years after the book was published indicated that his analysis of verbal behavior had not yet had the impact that he thought it would.

There are several reasons for the slow appreciation of *Verbal Behavior*. Soon after the book was published, it was met with immediate challenges from the field of linguistics and the emerging field of psycholinguistics. Most notably was a review by Noam Chomsky (1959), a young linguist from MIT who had published his own account of language (Chomsky, 1957) the same year *Verbal Behavior* was published. Chomsky maintained that Skinner's analysis was void of any value. Chomsky criticized every aspect of the analysis, but more so, he criticized the philosophy of behaviorism in general. However, a reading of Chomsky's review will reveal to those who comprehend *Verbal Behavior* that Chomsky, like many scholars, gravely misunderstood Skinner's radical behaviorism, which provided the philosophical and epistemological foundations for *Verbal Behavior* (Catania, 1972; Mac-Corqoudale, 1970).

Skinner never responded to Chomsky's review, and many felt this lack of response was responsible for the widely held conclusion that Chomsky's review was unanswerable and that Chomsky made valid criticisms. MacCorquodale (1970) pointed out that the reason no one challenged Chomsky's review was the condescending tone of the review, in addition to the clear misunderstandings of Skinner's behaviorism.

Skinner was not at all surprised by this reaction from linguists because of their emphasis on the structure of language rather than its function. More recently however, a favorable review of Skinner's book from within the field of linguistics was published, recognizing that Skinner has changed the history of linguistics (Andresen, 1991).

Although Skinner anticipated criticism from outside the field of behavior analysis, he probably did not expect the general disinterest and often outspoken negative reaction to *Verbal Behavior* from within the field. A number of behaviorists have examined this issue and have collectively provided a list of reasons behavior analysts did not immediately embrace *Verbal Behavior* (e.g., Eshleman, 1991; Michael, 1984; E. Vargas, 1986). Perhaps most troublesome to the behavior analysts of the time was that *Verbal Behavior* was speculative and did not contain experimental data (Salzinger, 1978).

The lack of research on verbal behavior continued to concern behavior analysts well into the 1980s (e.g., McPherson, Bonem, Green, & Osborne, 1984). However, this situation now appears to be changing, and a number of advances in research and applications directly relate to *Verbal Behavior* (Eshleman, 2004; Sundberg, 1991, 1998). Many of these advances are published in the journal, *The Analysis of Verbal Behavior.*

Defining Verbal Behavior

Skinner (1957) proposed that language is learned behavior, and that it is acquired, extended, and maintained by the same types of environmental variables and principles that control nonlanguage behavior (e.g., stimulus control, motivating operations, reinforcement, extinction). He defined **verbal behavior** as behavior that is reinforced through the mediation of another person's behavior. For example, the verbal response "Open the door" can produce the reinforcer of an open door mediated through the behavior of a listener. This reinforcer is indirectly obtained, but is the same reinforcer that could be obtained nonverbally by opening the door.

Skinner defined verbal behavior by the function of the response, rather than by its form. Thus, any response form can become verbal based on Skinner's functional definition. For example, the early differential crying of a 2-month-old infant may be verbal, as would other responses such as pointing, clapping for attention, gestures

---

[2]Whitehead was perhaps the most prominent philosopher of the time, known best for his landmark three-volume set coauthored with Bertrand Russell titled *Principia Mathematica* (1910, 1912, 1913).

such as waving one's arm for attention, writing, or typing. In other words, verbal behavior involves a social interaction between a speaker and a listener.

Speaker and Listener

The definition of verbal behavior makes a clear distinction between the behavior of the **speaker** and that of the **listener.** Verbal behavior involves social interactions between speakers and listeners, whereby speakers gain access to reinforcement and control their environment through the behavior of listeners. In contrast with most approaches to language, Skinner's verbal behavior is primarily concerned with the behavior of the speaker. He avoided terms such as *expressive language* and *receptive language* because of the implication that these are merely different manifestations of the same underlying cognitive processes.

The listener must learn how to reinforce the speaker's verbal behavior, meaning that listeners are taught to respond to words and interact with speakers. It is important to teach a child to react appropriately to the verbal stimuli provided by speakers, and to behave verbally as a speaker. These are different functions, however. In some cases learning one type of behavior (i.e., speaker or listener) facilitates learning another, but this must also be understood in terms of motivating operations, antecedent stimuli, responses, and consequences rather than in terms of learning the meanings of words as a listener and then using the words in various ways as a speaker.

Verbal Behavior: A Technical Term

In searching for what to call the subject matter of his analysis of language, Skinner wanted a term that (a) emphasized the individual speaker, (b) referred to behavior that was selected and maintained by consequences; and (c) was relatively unfamiliar in the professions of speech and language. He selected the term *verbal behavior.* However, in recent years *verbal behavior* has acquired a new meaning, independent from Skinner's usage. In the field of speech pathology, *verbal* behavior has become synonymous with *vocal* behavior. Also, in psychology, the term *nonverbal communication,* which became popular in the 1970s, was contrasted with the term *verbal behavior,* implying that verbal behavior was vocal communication and nonverbal behavior was nonvocal communication. The term *verbal* has also been contrasted with *quantitative* as in GRE and SAT tests for college admissions. This distinction suggests that mathematical behavior is not verbal. However, according to Skinner's definition, much of mathematical behavior is verbal behavior. Noting that verbal behavior includes *vocal-verbal behavior* and *nonvocal-verbal behavior* is sometimes confusing for those learning to use Skinner's analysis.

Unit of Analysis

The unit of analysis of verbal behavior is the functional relation between a type of responding and the same independent variables that control nonverbal behavior, namely (a) motivating variables, (b) discriminative stimuli, and (c) consequences. Skinner (1957) referred to this unit as a **verbal operant,** with *operant* implying a type or class of behavior as distinct from a particular response instance; and he referred to a set of such units of a particular person as a *verbal repertoire.* The verbal repertoire can be contrasted with the units in linguistics that consists of words, phrases, sentences, and the mean length of utterances.

Elementary Verbal Operants

Skinner (1957) identified six elementary verbal operants: mand, tact, echoic, intraverbal, textual, and transcription. He also included audience relation and copying a text as separate relations, but in this discussion the audience (or the listener) will be treated independently and copying a text will be considered a type of echoic behavior. Table 25.1 presents plain English descriptions of

Table 25.1   Plain English Definitions of Skinner's Six Elementary Verbal Operants

Mand	Asking for reinforcers that you want. Saying *shoe* because you want a shoe.
Tact	Naming or identifying objects, actions, events, etc. Saying *shoe* because you see a shoe.
Echoic	Repeating what is heard. Saying *shoe* after someone else says *shoe.*
Intraverbal	Answering questions or having conversations in which your words are controlled by other words. Saying *shoe* when someone else says, *What do you wear on your feet?*
Textual	Reading written words. Saying *shoe* because you see the written word *shoe.*
Transcription	Writing and spelling words spoken to you. Writing *shoe* because you hear *shoe* spoken.

these terms. Technical definitions and examples of each elementary verbal operant are provided in the following sections.

Mand

The mand is a type of verbal operant in which a speaker asks for (or states, demands, implies, etc.) what he needs or wants. For example, the behavior of asking for directions when lost is a mand. Skinner (1957) selected the term *mand* for this type of verbal relation because the term is conveniently brief and is similar to the plain English words *command, demand,* and *countermand.* The **mand** is a verbal operant for which the form of the response is under the functional control of motivating operations (MOs) and specific reinforcement (see Table 25.2). For example, food deprivation will (a) make food effective as reinforcement and (b) evoke behavior such as the mand "cookie" if this behavior has produced cookies in the past.

The specific reinforcement that strengthens a mand is directly related to the relevant MO. For example, if there is an MO for physical contact with one's mother, the specific reinforcement that is established is physical contact. The response form may occur in several topographical variations such as crying, pushing a sibling, reaching up, and saying "hug." All of these behaviors could be mands for physical contact if functional relations exist among the MO, the response, and the specific reinforcement history. However, the response form alone is insufficient for the classification of a mand, or any other verbal operant. For example, crying could also be a respondent behavior if it were elicited by a conditioned or unconditioned stimulus.

Mands are very important for the early development of language and for the day-to-day verbal interactions of children and adults. Mands are the first verbal operant acquired by a human child (Bijou & Baer, 1965; Novak, 1996). These early mands usually occur in the form of differential crying when a child is hungry, tired, in pain, cold, or afraid; or wants toys, attention, help, movement of objects and people, directions, or the removal of aversive stimuli. Typically developing children soon learn to replace crying with words and signs or other standard forms of communication. Manding not only lets children control the delivery of reinforcers, but it begins to establish the speaker and listener roles that are essential for further verbal development.

Skinner (1957) pointed out that the mand is the only type of verbal behavior that directly benefits the speaker, meaning that the mand gets the speaker reinforcers such as edibles, toys, attention, or the removal of aversive stim-

uli. As a result, mands often become strong forms of verbal behavior because of specific reinforcement, and this reinforcement often satisfies an immediate deprivation condition or removes some aversive stimulus. For example, young children often engage in a very high rate of manding because of its effects on listeners. In addition, much of the problem behaviors of children who have weak, delayed, or defective verbal repertoires may be mands (e.g., Carr & Durand, 1985). Eventually, a child learns to mand for verbal information with *who, what,* and *where* questions, and the acquisition of new verbal behavior accelerates rapidly (Brown, Cazden, & Bellugi, 1969). Ultimately, mands become quite complex and play a critical role in social interaction, conversation, academic behavior, employment, and virtually every aspect of human behavior.

Tact

The tact is a type of verbal operant in which a speaker names things and actions that the speaker has direct contact with through any of the sense modes. For example, a child saying "car" because he sees a car is a tact. Skinner (1957) selected the term *tact* because it suggests making contact with the physical environment. The **tact** is a verbal operant under the functional control of a nonverbal discriminative stimulus, and it produces generalized conditioned reinforcement (see Table 25.2). A nonverbal stimulus becomes a discriminative stimulus (S^D) with the process of discrimination training. For example, a shoe may not function as an S^D for the verbal response "shoe" until after saying "shoe" in the presence of a shoe produces differential reinforcement.

A wide variety of nonverbal stimuli evoke tact relations. For example, a cake produces nonverbal visual, tactile, olfactory, and gustatory stimuli, any or all of which can become S^Ds for the tact "cake." Nonverbal stimuli can be, for example, static (nouns), transitory (verbs), relations between objects (prepositions), properties of objects (adjectives), or properties of actions (adverbs); that is, nonverbal stimuli can be as simple as a shoe, or as complex as a cancerous cell. A stimulus configuration may have multiple nonverbal properties, and a response may be under the control of those multiple properties, as in the tact "The red truck is on the little table." Nonverbal stimuli may be observable or unobservable (e.g., pain), subtle or salient (e.g., neon lights), relational to other nonverbal stimuli (e.g., size), and so on. Given the variation and ubiquity of nonverbal stimuli, it is no surprise that the tact is a primary topic in the study of language.

Echoic

The echoic is a type of verbal operant that occurs when a speaker repeats the verbal behavior of another speaker. For example, a child saying "cookie" after hearing the word spoken by her mother is echoic. Repeating the words, phrases, and vocal behavior of others, which is common in day-to-day discourse, is echoic also. The **echoic** operant is controlled by a verbal discriminative stimulus that has point-to-point correspondence and formal similarity with the response (Michael, 1982) (see Table 25.2).

Point-to-point correspondence between the stimulus and the response or response product occurs when the beginning, middle, and end of the verbal stimulus matches the beginning, middle, and end of the response. **Formal similarity** occurs when the controlling antecedent stimulus and the response or response product (a) share the same sense mode (e.g., both stimulus and response are visual, auditory, or tactile) and (b) physically resemble each other (Michael, 1982). In the echoic relation the stimulus is auditory and the response produces an auditory product (echoing what one hears), and the stimulus and the response physically resemble each other.

Echoic behavior produces generalized conditioned reinforcement such as praise and attention. The ability to echo the phonemes and words of others is essential for learning to identify objects and actions. A parent might say, "That's a bear, can you say bear?" If the child can respond "bear," then the parent says "Right!" Eventually, the child learns to name a bear without the echoic prompt. This often occurs in a few trials. For example, if a child can say "bear" (or a reasonable approximation) after a parent says "bear," then it becomes possible to teach the child to say "bear" in the presence of a picture of a bear or a bear at the zoo. The echoic repertoire is very important for teaching language to children with language delays, and it serves a critical role in the process of teaching more complex verbal skills (e.g., Lovaas, 1977; Sundberg & Partington, 1998).

Motor imitations can have the same verbal properties as echoic behavior as demonstrated by their role in the acquisition of sign language by children who are deaf. For example, a child may learn to imitate the sign for cookie first, and then mand for cookie without an imitative prompt. Imitation is also critical for teaching sign language to hearing children who are nonvocal. For the many children who do not have an adequate echoic repertoire for vocal language instruction, time is spent teaching echoic behavior rather than more useful types of verbal behavior. A strong imitative repertoire permits a teacher to use sign language immediately to instruct more advanced forms of language (e.g., mands, tacts, and intraverbals). This allows a child to learn quickly to communicate with others without using inappropriate behavior (e.g., a tantrum) to get what he wants.

Skinner also presented **copying a text** as a type of verbal behavior in which a written verbal stimulus has point-to-point correspondence and formal similarity with a written verbal response. Because this relation has the same defining features as echoic and imitation as it relates to sign language, the three will be treated as one category, echoic.

Intraverbal

The intraverbal is a type of verbal operant in which a speaker differentially responds to the verbal behavior of others. For example, saying "the Buckeyes" as a result of hearing someone else say "Who won the game Saturday?" is intraverbal behavior. Typically developing children emit a high frequency of intraverbal responses in the form of singing songs, telling stories, describing activities, and explaining problems. Intraverbal responses are also important components of many normal intellectual repertoires, such as saying "Sacramento" as a result of hearing "What is the capital of California?"; saying "sixty-four" as a result of hearing "eight times eight"; or saying "antecedent, behavior, and consequence" when asked, "What is the three-term contingency?" The intraverbal repertoires of typical adult speakers include hundreds of thousands of such relations.

The **intraverbal** operant occurs when a verbal discriminative stimulus evokes a verbal response that does not have point-to-point correspondence with the verbal stimulus (Skinner, 1957). That is, the verbal stimulus and the verbal response do not match each other, as they do in the echoic and textual relations. Like all verbal operants except the mand, the intraverbal produces generalized conditioned reinforcement. For example, in the educational context, the reinforcement for correct answers usually involves some form of generalized conditioned reinforcement such as "Right!" or points, or the opportunity to move to the next problem or item (see Table 25.2).

An intraverbal repertoire facilitates the acquisition of other verbal and nonverbal behavior. Intraverbal behavior prepares a speaker to respond rapidly and accurately with respect to further stimulation, and plays an important role in continuing a conversation. For example, a child hears an adult speaker say "farm" in some context. If the stimulus farm evokes several relevant intraverbal responses, such as "barn," "cow," "rooster," or "horse," then a child is better able to react to other parts of an adult's verbal behavior that may be related to a recent trip to a farm. One might say that the child is now thinking about farms and now has relevant verbal responses at strength for further responses to the adult's verbal behavior. An intraverbal stimulus probes the listener's repertoire and gets it ready for further stimulation. Collectively, mands, tacts, and intraverbals contribute to a conversation in the following ways: (a) A mand repertoire allows a speaker to ask questions, (b) a tact repertoire permits verbal behavior about an object or event that is actually present, and (c) an intraverbal repertoire allows a speaker to answer questions and to talk about (and think about) objects and events that are not physically present.

Textual

Textual behavior (Skinner, 1957) is reading, without any implications that the reader understands what is being read. Understanding what is read usually involves other verbal and nonverbal operants such as intraverbal behavior and receptive language (e.g., following instructions, compliance). For example, saying "shoe" upon seeing the written word *shoe* is textual behavior. Understanding that shoes go on a person's feet is not textual. Understanding is typically identified as reading comprehension. Skinner chose the term *textual* because the term *reading* refers to many processes at the same time.

The **textual** operant has point-to-point correspondence, but not formal similarity, between the stimulus and the response product. For example, (a) the verbal stimuli are visual or tactual (i.e., in one modality) and the response is auditory (i.e., another modality) and (b) the auditory response matches the visual or tactual stimuli. Table 25.2 presents a diagram of the textual relation.

Textuals and echoics are similar in three respects: (a) They both produce generalized conditioned reinforcement, (b) both are controlled by antecedent verbal stimuli, and (c) there is point-to-point correspondence between the antecedent stimulus and the response. The important difference between textuals and echoics is that the response product of textual behavior (e.g., the spoken word) is not similar to its controlling stimulus (e.g., the written word evokes a spoken response or auditory response product). The textual operant does not have formal similarity, meaning that the S^Ds are not in the same sense mode and do not physically resemble the textual response. Words are visual and comprised of individual letters, whereas the reading response produces an auditory response product (which often is covert) comprising phonemes. The echoic response product, however, does have formal similarity with its controlling verbal stimulus.

Transcription

Transcription consists of writing and spelling words that are spoken (Skinner, 1957). Skinner also referred to this behavior as *taking dictation,* with the key repertoires involving not only the manual production of letters, but also accurate spelling of the spoken word. In technical terms, transcription is a type of verbal behavior in which a spoken verbal stimulus controls a written, typed, or finger-spelled response. Like the textual operant, there is point-to-point correspondence between the stimulus and the response product, but no formal similarity (see Table 25.2). For example, when asked to spell the spoken word "hat," a response h-a-t is a transcription. The stimulus and the response product have point-to-point correspondence, but they are not in the same sense mode or do not physically resemble each other. Spelling English words

Table 25.2   Antecedent and Consequent Controlling Variables for Six Elementary Verbal Operants

Antecedent Variables	Response	Consequence
Motivating operations (4 hours without water)	Mand ("water, please")	Specific reinforcement (glass of water)
Nonverbal stimulus (see toy truck)	Tact ("truck")	Generalized conditioned reinforcement (GCSR) (praise and approval)
Verbal stimulus with point-to-point correspondence and formal similarity (hear "book")	Echoic (say "book")	GCSR
Verbal stimulus without point-to point correspondence or formal similarity (hear "cats and . . .")	Intraverbal (say "dogs")	GCSR
Verbal stimulus with point-to-point correspondence, without formal similarity (see *apple* written)	Textual (say "apple")	GCSR
Verbal stimulus with point-to-point correspondence, without formal similarity (hear "apple")	Transcription (write *apple*)	GCSR

is a difficult repertoire to acquire. Because many words in the English language are not spelled the way they sound, shaping an appropriate discriminative repertoire is often difficult.

Role of the Listener

Skinner's analysis of verbal behavior focuses on the speaker, whereas most linguists and psycholinguistic accounts of language emphasize the listener. Skinner suggested that the listener's role is less significant than typically assumed because much of what is often described as listener behavior (e.g., thinking, understanding) is more correctly classified as speaker behavior. It is just that often the speaker and listener reside within the same skin (as we will see in the following discussion).

What role does the listener then play in Skinner's account of language? In his analysis of listener behavior, Skinner pointed out that a verbal episode requires a speaker and a listener. The listener not only plays a critical role as a mediator of reinforcement for the speaker's behavior, but also becomes a discriminative stimulus for the speaker's behavior. In functioning as a discriminative stimulus, the listener is an **audience** for verbal behavior. "An audience, then, is a discriminative stimulus in the presence of which verbal behavior is characteristically reinforced and in the presence of which, therefore, it is characteristically strong" (Skinner, 1957, p. 172). When Skinner (1978) wrote "very little of the behavior of the listener is worth distinguishing as verbal" (p. 122), he was referring to when the listener serves as a discriminative stimulus in the role of an audience.

A listener functions in additional roles, other than as a mediator of reinforcement and a discriminative stimulus. For example, verbal behavior functions as discriminative stimuli (i.e., stimulus control) when a speaker talks to a listener. The question is, What are the effects of verbal behavior on listener behavior? A verbal discriminative stimulus may evoke echoic, textual, transcription, or intraverbal operants of a listener. The listener becomes a speaker when this occurs. This is Skinner's point: The speaker and listener can and often do reside within the same skin, meaning that a listener behaves simultaneously as a speaker. The most significant and complex responses to verbal stimuli occur when they evoke covert intraverbal behavior from a listener who becomes a speaker and functions as her own audience. For example, a speaker's verbal discriminative stimuli related to Pavlov's work on respondent conditioning, such as, "What was Pavlov's technique?" may evoke a listener's covert intraverbal behavior such as

thinking, "He paired the sound of a metronome with meat powder."[3]

Verbal stimulus control may also evoke a listener's nonverbal behavior. For example, when someone says "Shut the door," the behavior of shutting a door is nonverbal, but shutting the door is evoked by verbal stimuli. Skinner (1957) identified this type of listener behavior as *understanding.* "The listener can be said to understand a speaker if he simply behaves in an appropriate fashion" (p. 277).

Verbal stimuli can become quite complex because separating the verbal and nonverbal behaviors of the listener is difficult (Parrott, 1984; Schoenberger, 1990, 1991). For example, in following a directive to buy a certain type and style of pipe fitting at the hardware store, success will involve both nonverbal behavior such as discriminating among pipe fittings and verbal behavior such as self-echoic prompts (e.g., "I need a three-quarter-inch fitting, three-quarter-inch"), tacts of the fittings (e.g., "This looks like three-quarter-inch"), and mands for information (e.g., "Can you tell me if this will fit a three-quarter-inch pipe?").

Identifying Verbal Operants

The same word (i.e., topography or form of the behavior) can appear in the definitions of all of the elementary verbal operants because controlling variables define verbal operants, not the form of the verbal stimuli. Verbal behavior is not classified or defined by its topography or form (i.e., by the words themselves). The classification of verbal operants can be accomplished by asking a series of questions regarding the relevant controlling variables that evoke a specific response form (see Figure 25.1). A sample of verbal behavior classification exercise is presented in Table 25.3

1. Does an MO control the response form? If yes, then the operant is at least part mand.
2. Does an S^D control the response form? If yes, then:
3. Is the S^D nonverbal? If yes, then the operant is at least part tact.
4. Is the S^D verbal? If yes, then:

---

[3]In three of his books, Skinner devoted a full chapter to the topic of thinking: *Science and Human Behavior* (1953, Chapter 16), *Verbal Behavior* (1957, Chapter 19), and *About Behaviorism* (1974, Chapter 7) with several sections dedicated to the topic of understanding (e.g., *Verbal Behavior,* pp. 277–280; *About Behaviorism,* pp. 141–142). A behavior analysis of thinking and understanding involves, in large part, situations in which both listener and speaker reside within the same skin.

Controlling variables   *Verbal relation*

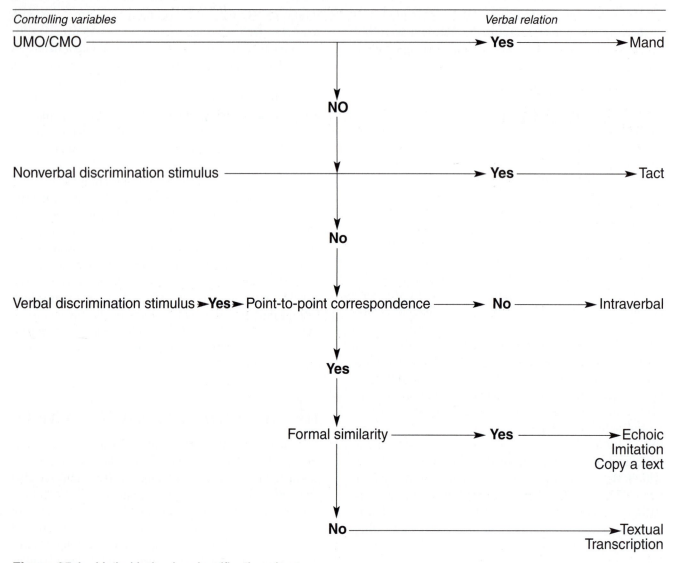

Figure 25.1 Verbal behavior classification chart.

5. Is there point-to-point correspondence between the verbal S^D and the response? If not, then the operant is at least part intraverbal. If there is point-to-point correspondence, then:

6. Is there formal similarity between the verbal S^D and the response. If yes, then the operant must be echoic, imitative, or copying a text). If not, then the operant must be textual or transcription.

Analyzing Complex Verbal Behavior

Analysis of more complex verbal behavior includes automatic reinforcement, tact extensions (generalization), and private events. These topics are presented in the following sections.

Automatic Reinforcement

A common misconception about reinforcement in the context of verbal behavior is that it occurs only when the listener mediates the reinforcer. When behavior occurs without the apparent delivery of reinforcement, it is often assumed that higher mental processes are at work (e.g., Brown, 1973; Neisser, 1976). Intermittent reinforcement can explain some behavior that occurs in the absence of an observed consequence, but not all such behavior. Some behavior is strengthened or weakened, not by external consequences, but by its *response products,* which have reinforcing or punishing effects. Skinner used the terms **automatic reinforcement** and **automatic punishment** in a number of his writings simply to indicate that an effective consequence can occur without someone providing it (cf., Vaughan & Michael, 1982).

Table 25.3 Verbal Behavior Classification Exercises

As a result of . . .	One has a tendency to . . .	This is a(n) . . .
1. seeing a dog	say "dog"	_____
2. hearing an airplane	say "airplane"	_____
3. wanting a drink	say "water"	_____
4. hearing "How are you?"	say "I'm fine"	_____
5. smelling cookies baking	say "cookies"	_____
6. tasting soup	say "pass the salt"	_____
7. hearing "book"	write *book*	_____
8. hearing "book"	sign "book"	_____
9. hearing "book"	say "book"	_____
10. hearing "book"	say "read"	_____
11. hearing "book"	sign "read"	_____
12. hearing "book"	finger-spell "book"	_____
13. seeing a book	write *book*	_____
14. wanting a book	write *book*	_____
15. signing "book"	write *book*	_____
16. hearing "color"	say "red"	_____
17. seeing a dog on the table	say "get off"	_____
18. seeing *stop* written	hit the brakes	_____
19. hearing "Skinner"	write *behavior*	_____
20. smelling smoke	say "fire"	_____
21. being hungry	go to a store	_____
22. seeing *apple* written	sign "apple"	_____
23. seeing *5*	say "five"	_____
24. wanting things	say "thanks"	_____
25. hearing "write your name"	write your name	_____
26. hearing "run"	finger-spell "run"	_____
27. seeing "home" signed	sign "Battle Creek"	_____
28. hearing a phone ring	say "phone"	_____
29. smelling a skunk	say "skunk"	_____
30. hearing "table"	say "mesa"	_____
31. being happy	smile	_____
32. hoping a pilot sees it	writing *SOS*	_____
33. wanting blue	say "blue"	_____
34. hearing "Red, white, and"	say "blue"	_____
35. tasting candy	say "mmmm"	_____

Provide examples of verbal behavior.

36. Give an example of a mand involving an adjective.

37. Give an example of a tact of a smell.

38. Give an example of a response that is part mand and part tact.

39. Give an example of a response that is part tact and part intraverbal.

40. Give an example of a tact involving multiple responses.

41. Give an example of an intraverbal using writing.

42. Give an example of receptive language using sign language.

Answers to verbal behavior classification exercises in Table 25.3:

1. T; 2. T; 3. M; 4. IV; 5. T/M; 6. M; 7. TX; 8. IV; 9. E; 10. IV; 11. IV; 12. TR; 13. T; 14. M; 15. IV; 16. IV/T; 17. M; 18. NV; 19. IV; 20. T/M; 21. NV; 22. IV; 23. IV; 24. M; 25. IV; 26. TX; 27. IV; 28. T/M; 29. T; 30. IV; 31. NV; 32. M; 33. M; 34. IV; 35. T; 36. "I want the red one."; 37. "Someone is smoking.";
38. "My throat is dry."; 39. "Macy's." When asked "Where did you buy that?"; 40. "That's a big burger!"; 41. A response to an e-mail; 42. Stopping when someone signs "stop."

Verbal behavior can produce automatic reinforcement, which has a significant role in the acquisition and maintenance of verbal behavior. For example, automatic reinforcement may explain why a typically developing infant engages in extensive babbling without the apparent delivery of reinforcement. Skinner (1957) pointed out that the exploratory vocal behavior of young children could produce automatic reinforcement when those exploratory sounds match the speech sounds of parents, caregivers, and others.

Skinner (1957) described a two-stage conditioning history in establishing vocal responses as automatic reinforcers. First, a neutral verbal stimulus is paired with an existing form of conditioned or unconditioned reinforcement. For example, a mother's voice is paired with conditions such as presenting food and warmth and removing aversive stimuli (e.g., medication on a diaper rash). As a result, the mother's voice, a previously neutral stimulus, becomes a conditioned reinforcer. The mother's voice will now strengthen whatever behavior precedes it. Second, a child's vocal response as either random muscle movement of the vocal cords or reflexive behavior produces an auditory response that on occasion may sound somewhat like the mother's words, intonations, and vocal pitches. Thus, a vocal response can function as reinforcement by automatically increasing the frequency of a child's vocal behavior.[4]

Automatic reinforcement also plays an important role in the development of more complex aspects of verbal behavior, such as the acquisition of syntax and grammatical conventions. For example, Donahoe and Palmer (1994) and Palmer (1996, 1998) suggested that a child's use of grammar produces automatic reinforcement when it sounds like the grammar used by others in the environment, but is automatically punished when it sounds odd or unusual. Palmer (1996) referred to this as *achieving parity.*

The stimulus conditions that evoke automatically reinforced behavior may be encountered everywhere because each time a response is automatically reinforced it may alter the evocative effect of any stimulus condition that might be present. For example, a person may persist in singing or humming a theme song from a movie while driving home from the movie because of the two-stage conditioning process described previously. However, the song may be periodically evoked several hours, or even days, after the movie because each time the song is re-

peated, a new stimulus such as a traffic light, a street corner, or a neon sign might acquire some degree of stimulus control. The next time the person comes in contact with, say, a red light, there could be some tendency to sing or hum the song. This effect might explain what is often termed *delayed echolalia* observed with children who have autism (Sundberg & Partington, 1998). At present, however, there have been no empirical investigations of the stimulus control involved in automatic consequences, although it certainly seems like an interesting and important area of study.

Tact Extensions

Contingencies that establish stimulus and response classes and generalization allow a variety of novel and different discriminative stimuli to evoke verbal behavior. Skinner (1957) said it this way:

> [A] verbal repertoire is not like a passenger list on a ship or plane, in which one name corresponds to one person with no one omitted or named twice. Stimulus control is by no means so precise. If a response is reinforced upon a given occasion or class of occasions, any feature of that occasion or common to that class appears to gain some measure of control. A novel stimulus possessing one such feature may evoke a response. There are several ways in which a novel stimulus may resemble a stimulus previously present when a response was reinforced, and hence there are several types of what we may call "extended tacts" (p. 91).

Skinner (1957) distinguished four types of extended tacts: generic, metaphorical, metonymical, and solistic. The distinction is based on the degree to which a novel stimulus shares the relevant or irrelevant features of the original stimulus.

Generic Extension

In **generic extension,** the novel stimulus shares all of the relevant or defining features of the original stimulus. For example, a speaker who learns to tact "car" in the presence of a white Pontiac Grand Am emits the tact "car" in the presence of a novel blue Mazda RX-7. A generic tact extension is evoked by simple stimulus generalization.

Metaphorical Extension

In **metaphorical extension,** the novel stimulus shares some but not all of the relevant features associated with the original stimulus. For example, Romeo was experiencing a beautiful, sunny, warm day, and the exceptional weather elicited respondent behaviors (e.g., good feelings). When Romeo saw Juliet, whose presence elicited

---

[4]Miller and Dollard (1941) were perhaps the first to suggest that a process like automatic reinforcement might be partially responsible for an infant's high rate of babbling. Since then, many others have discussed and researched the role of automatic reinforcement in language acquisition (e.g., Bijou & Baer, 1965; Braine, 1963; Miguel, Carr, & Michael, 2002; Mowrer, 1950; Novak, 1996; Osgood, 1953; Smith, Michael, & Sundberg, 1996; Spradlin, 1966; Staats & Staats, 1963; Sundberg, Michael, Partington, & Sundberg, 1996; Vaughan & Michael, 1982; Yoon & Bennett, 2000).

similar respondent behaviors like the sunny day, he said, "Juliet is like the sun." The sun and Juliet evoked a similar effect on Romeo, controlling the metaphorical tact extension "Juliet is like the sun."

Metonymical Extension

Metonymical extensions are verbal responses to novel stimuli that share none of the relevant features of the original stimulus configuration, but some irrelevant but related feature has acquired stimulus control. Simply, one word substitutes for another in metonymical tact extensions, meaning that a part is used for a whole. As examples: Saying "car" when shown a picture of a garage, or saying "the White House requested" in place of "President Lincoln requested."

Solistic Extension

Solistic extensions occur when a stimulus property that is only indirectly related to the tact relation evokes substandard verbal behavior such as malaprops. For instance, using the solistic tact extension, a person may say "You read good" instead of "You read well." Saying "car" when referring to the driver of the car is a solistic tact extension.

Private Events

In 1945 Skinner first described radical behaviorism, his philosophy. At the core of radical behaviorism is the analysis of private stimuli (see also Skinner, 1953, 1974). Verbal behavior under the control of private stimuli has been a main topic of theoretical and philosophical analyses of behavior ever since. In 1957 Skinner stated, "A small but important part of the universe is enclosed within the skin of each individual. . . . It does not follow that . . . it is any way unlike the world outside the skin or inside another's skin" (p. 130).

A significant amount of day-to-day verbal behavior is controlled in part by private events. What is commonly referred to as thinking involves overt stimulus control and private events (e.g., covert stimulus control). The analysis of private stimulation and how it acquires stimulus control is complex because of two problems: (a) The participant can directly observe the private stimuli, but the applied behavior analyst cannot (a limiting factor in the prediction and control of behavior), and (b) private stimulus control of verbal episodes in the natural environment will likely remain private, no matter how sensitive instruments will become in detecting private stimuli and behaviors. Skinner (1957) identified four ways that caregivers teach young persons to tact their private stimulation: Public accompaniment, collateral responses, common properties, and response reduction.

Public Accompaniment

Public accompaniment occurs when an observable stimulus accompanies a private stimulus. For example, a father may observe a child bump his head on a table while chasing a ball. The public stimuli are available to the father, but not the private and more salient painful stimuli experienced by the child. The father can assume that the child is experiencing pain because of his own history of bumping objects, and may say "Ouch," or "You hurt yourself." In this way, the father is using the bump (observable stimulus) as an opportunity to develop verbal behavior under the stimulus control of a private stimulus. This may occur with an echoic to the private event; later, the stimulus control transfers to the private stimuli. Specifically, the child may echo the father's "ouch" while the painful stimuli are present, and quickly (depending on the child's history of echoic to tact transfer) the painful stimuli alone evokes the tact "ouch."

Collateral Responses

Caregivers also teach young persons to tact their private stimuli by using collateral responses (i.e., observable behavior) that reliably occur with private stimuli. For example, the father may not observe the child bump his head, but may see the child holding his head and crying. These collateral behaviors inform the father that a painful stimulus is present. The same training procedures with public accompaniment can be used with collateral responses. Because the painful private stimuli are salient, only one trial may be needed for the private stimuli to acquire stimulus control of the tact relation.

Parents should use public accompaniment and collateral responses during the beginning stages of tact training. However, even after developing a repertoire of tacting private events, a parent or listener will have difficulty confirming the actual presence of the private event as in "My stomach hurts," or "I have a headache now."

Also, learning to tact private behaviors is acquired probably with public accompaniment and collateral responses; for example, private stimuli that evoke private emotions (behaviors) that we tact with words such as *happiness, sadness, fear,* and *being upset.* Learning to tact such private events is difficult if the private stimulation is not present during training. For example, procedures that use pictures of people smiling and frowning (i.e., public stimuli) for teaching children to tact emotions will be less effective than procedures that use variables to evoke pleasure or displeasure (i.e., private stimuli) during training.

Common Properties

The two procedures described earlier use public stimuli to establish tacting of private events. Common properties also involve public stimuli, but in a different way. A speaker may learn to tact temporal, geometrical, or descriptive properties of objects and then generalize those tact relations to private stimuli. As Skinner (1957) noted, "[M]ost of the vocabulary of emotion is metaphorical in nature. When we describe internal states as 'agitated,' 'depressed,' or 'ebullient,' certain geometrical, temporal, and intensive properties have produced a metaphorical extension of responses" (p. 132). Much of our verbal behavior regarding emotional events is acquired through this type of stimulus generalization.

Response Reduction

Most speakers learn to tact features of their own bodies such as movements and positions. The kinesthetic stimuli arising from the movement and positions can acquire control over the verbal responses. When movements shrink in size (become covert), the kinesthetic stimuli may remain sufficiently similar to those resulting from the overt movements that the learner's tact occurs as an instance of stimulus generalization. For example, a child can report imagining swimming, or can report self-talk about a planned conversation with someone, or can report thinking of asking for a new toy (Michael & Sundberg, 2003). Responses produced by private covert verbal behavior can evoke other verbal behavior and will be discussed later in further detail.

Multiple Control

All verbal behavior contains multiple functional relations among antecedents, behavior, and consequences. "[A]ny sample of verbal behavior will be a function of many variables operating at the same time" (Skinner, 1957, p. 228). The functional units of mands, tacts, echoics, intraverbals, and textual relations form the foundation of a verbal behavior analysis. A working knowledge of these functional units is essential for understanding the analysis of multiple control and complex verbal behavior.

Convergent Multiple Control

Michael (2003) used the term **convergent multiple control** to identify when the occurrence of a single verbal response is a function of more than one variable. The task of an applied behavior analyst is to identify the relevant sources that control an instance of verbal behavior. For example, saying "Why did the United States enter World War II?" may be evoked by (a) MOs (making it part mand), (b) verbal discriminative stimuli (making it part echoic, intraverbal, or textual), (c) nonverbal stimuli (making it part tact), or the presence of a specific audience. For example, it's possible that an audience with contempt for war (i.e., the MO) evoked a mand, "Why did the United States enter World War II?" The question may be more a function of this variable than an intraverbal related to the ongoing conversation or the nonverbal or textual stimuli that may be present in the room. On the other hand, the speaker may have no strong MO for the answer, but asks the question because of its relation to MOs for social reinforcement related to political involvement.

Divergent Multiple Control

Multiple control also occurs when a single antecedent variable affects the strength of many responses. For example, a single word (e.g., *football*) will evoke a variety of intraverbal responses from different people, and from the same person at different times. Michael (2003) used the term **divergent multiple control** to identify this type of control. Divergent multiple control can occur also with mand and tact relations. A single MO may strengthen a variety of responses, such as food deprivation strengthening the response "I'm hungry," or "Let's go to a restaurant." A single nonverbal stimulus can also strengthen several response forms, as when a picture of a car strengthens the responses "car," "automobile," or "Ford."

Thematic and Formal Verbal Operants

Skinner (1957) identified thematic and formal verbal operants that function as sources of multiple control. The thematic verbal operants are mands, tacts, and intraverbals and involve different response topographies controlled by a common variable. For an intraverbal example, the S^D "blue" can evoke verbal responses such as "lake," "ocean," and "sky." The formal verbal operants are echoic (imitation, copying a text) and textual (and transcription) and are controlled by a common variable, with point-to-point correspondence. For example, the S^D "ring" can evoke verbal responses such as "sing," "wing," and "spring."

Multiple Audiences

The role of the audience raises the issue of multiple audiences. Different audiences may evoke different response forms. For example, two applied behavior analysts talking (i.e., a technical speaker and a technical audience) will likely use different response forms than will a behavior analyst speaking with a parent (i.e., a technical speaker and a nontechnical audience). A *positive audience* has special effects, especially a large positive audience (e.g., as in a rally for a certain cause), as does a *negative audience.* When the two audiences are combined, the effects of the negative audience are most obvious: "[When a] seditious soapbox orator sees a policeman approaching from a distance, his behavior decreases in strength as the negative audience becomes more important" (Skinner, 1957, p. 231).

Elaborating Multiple Control

Convergent multiple control occurs in most instances of verbal behavior. An audience is always a source of stimulus control related to verbal behavior, even when a speaker serves as his own audience. In addition, it is also the case that more than one of the controlling variables related to the different verbal operants may be relevant to a specific instance of verbal behavior. Convergent control often occurs with MOs and nonverbal stimuli, resulting in a response that is part mand and part tact. For example, saying "You look great" may be partly controlled by the nonverbal stimuli in front of a speaker (a tact), but also by MOs related to wanting to leave soon or wanting to avoid potential aversive events (a mand). Skinner (1957) identified this particular blend of controlling variables as evoking **impure tacts** (i.e., impure because an MO affects the tact relation).

Verbal and nonverbal stimuli can also share control over a particular response. For example, a tendency to say "green car" may be evoked by the verbal stimulus "What color is the car?" and the nonverbal stimulus of the color green.

Multiple sources of control can be any combination of thematic or formal sources, even multiple sources from within a single verbal operant, such as multiple tacts or multiple intraverbals. Skinner pointed out that because these separate sources may be additive, the "multiple causation produces many interesting verbal effects, including those of verbal play, wit, style, the devices of poetry, formal distortions, slips, and many techniques of verbal thinking" (pp. 228–229). Additional sources of control often reveal themselves—for example, when a speaker in the presence of an obese friend who is wearing a new hat emits the "Freudian slip," "I like that fat on you." Multiple sources of control often provide the basis for verbal humor and listener enjoyment.

Autoclitic Relation

This chapter has emphasized that a speaker can, and often does, function as her own listener. The analysis of how and why a speaker becomes a listener of her own verbal behavior and then manipulates her verbal behavior with additional verbal behavior addresses the topic of the autoclitic relation. Skinner (1957) introduced the term **autoclitic** to identify when a speaker's own verbal behavior functions as an S^D or an MO for additional speaker verbal behavior. In other words, the autoclitic is verbal behavior about a speaker's own verbal behavior. The consequences for this behavior involve differential reinforcement from the ultimate listener, meaning that the listener discriminates whether to serve or not serve as a mediator of reinforcement for those verbal stimuli. A speaker becomes a listener, and observer, of his own verbal behavior and its controlling variables, and then in turn becomes a speaker again. This effect can be very rapid and typically occurs in the emission of a single sentence composed of the two levels of responses.

Primary and Secondary Verbal Operants

Michael (1991, 1992) suggested that applied behavior analysts classify verbal behavior about a speaker's own verbal behavior as *primary* (Level 1) and *secondary* (Level 2) verbal operants. In Level 1, MOs and/or S^Ds are present and affect the primary verbal operant. The speaker has something to say. In Level 2, the speaker observes the primary controlling variables of her own verbal behavior and her disposition to emit the primary verbal behavior. The speaker discriminates these controlling variables and describes them to the listener. A secondary verbal operant enables the listener's behavior as a mediator of reinforcement. For example, an MO or S^D evokes the response, "She is in Columbus, Ohio." It is important for listeners as reinforcement mediators to discriminate the primary variables controlling the speaker's behavior. The verbal operant "She is in Columbus, Ohio," does not inform the listener as to why the speaker said it. "I read in the *Columbus Dispatch* that she is in Columbus, Ohio," informs the listener of the primary controlling variable. The first level is "She is in Columbus, Ohio" (the primary verbal operant), and the second level is "I read in the *Columbus Dispatch*" (the autoclitic).

Autoclitic Tact Relations

Some autoclitics inform the listener of the type of primary verbal operant the autoclitic accompanies (Peterson, 1978). The *autoclitic tact* informs the listener of some nonverbal aspect of the primary verbal operant and is therefore controlled by nonverbal stimuli. For example, a child's statement, "I see Mommy" may contain an autoclitic tact. The primary verbal operant (i.e., the tact) is the nonverbal S^D of (a) the child's mother; (b) the response, "Mommy"; and (c) the associated reinforcement history. The secondary verbal operant (i.e., the autoclitic tact) is the speaker's tact informing that a nonverbal S^D evoked the primary verbal operant. In this case, the nonverbal S^D was the visual stimulus of the child's mother, and the response "I see" informs the listener of the source of control that evoked the primary tact. If the child heard his mother, but did not see his mother, the autoclitic tact "I hear" would be appropriate.

The listener may challenge the existence and nature of the autoclitic tact—for example, "How do you know it's mommy?" The challenge is one way that effective autoclitic behavior is shaped and brought under appropriate stimulus control.

Autoclitic tacts also inform the listener of the strength of the primary operant. In the examples of the verbal stimuli, "I think it is Mommy" and "I know it is Mommy," "I think" informs the listener that the source of control for the primary tact "Mommy" is weak; "I know" is strong.

Autoclitic Mand Relations

Speakers use autoclitic mands frequently to help the listener present effective reinforcers (Peterson, 1978). A specific MO controls the *autoclitic mand,* and its role is to mand the listener to react in some specific way to the primary verbal operant. "I know it is Mommy" may contain an autoclitic mand. For example, if "I know" is not a tact of response strength, it may be an MO in the same sense as "Hurry up."

Autoclitic mands occur everywhere, but listeners have difficulty recognizing the MO controlling the autoclitic mand because the sources of control are private. For example, hidden agendas as autoclitic mands often revel themselves only to the careful observer. For example, a primary intraverbal such as an answer to a question about the sale of a product may contain autoclitic mands, as in "I'm sure you will be pleased with the sale," in which "I'm sure you will be pleased" is controlled by the same MO that might control the response "Don't ask me for any details about the sale."

Developing Autoclitic Relations

Speakers develop autoclitic relations in several ways. For example, a father is wrapping a gift for his child's mother, and the child nearby says, "Mommy." The father may ask the child to identify the primary variables controlling the response by asking, "Did you see her?" The father may differentially respond to "I see" indicating that clearly "Mommy" is a tact and hide the gift; rather than a mand for "Mommy," in which case, he keeps wrapping the gift. The source of control for the response "Mommy" could be the gift, as in, "That is for Mommy." "That is for" (i.e., the autoclitic) informs the father that the gift is a nonverbal stimulus controlling the primary tact, "Mommy," and the father continues wrapping the gift. As Skinner (1957) pointed out, "[A]n autoclitic affects the listener by indicating either a property of the speaker's behavior or the circumstances responsible for that property" (p. 329).

Early language learners seldom emit autoclitic responses. Skinner was clear on this point: "In the absence of any other verbal behavior whatsoever autoclitics cannot occur. . . . It is only when [the elementary] verbal operants have been established in strength that the speaker finds himself subject to the additional contingencies which establish autoclitic behavior" (p. 330). Thus, early language intervention program should not include autoclitic training.

Applications of Verbal Behavior

Skinner's analysis of verbal behavior provides a conceptual framework of language that can be quite beneficial for applied behavior analysts. Viewing language as learned behavior involving a social interaction between speakers and listeners, with the verbal operants as the basic units, changes how clinicians and researchers approach and ameliorate problems related to language. Skinner's theory of language has been successfully applied to an increasing number of human areas. For example, the analysis has been used for typical language and child development (e.g., Bijou & Baer, 1965), elementary and high school education (e.g., Johnson & Layng, 1994), college education (e.g., Chase, Johnson, & Sulzar-Azaroff, 1985), literacy (e.g., Moxley, 1990), composition (e.g., J. Vargas, 1978), memory (e.g., Palmer, 1991), second language acquisition (e.g., Shimamune & Jitsumori, 1999), clinical interventions (e.g., Layng & Andronis, 1984), behavior problems (e.g., McGill, 1999), traumatic brain injury (e.g., Sundberg, San Juan, Dawdy, & Arguelles, 1990), artificial intelligence (e.g., Stephens & Hutchison, 1992), ape language acquisition (e.g., Savage-Rumbaugh, 1984), and behavioral pharmacology (e.g., Critchfield, 1993). The most prolific application of Skinner's analysis of verbal behavior has been to language assessment and intervention programs for children with autism or other developmental disabilities. This area of application will be presented in more detail in the following sections.

Language Assessment

Most standardized language assessments designed for children with language delays seek to obtain an age equivalent score by testing a child's receptive and expressive language abilities (e.g., Peabody Picture

Vocabulary Test III [Dunn & Dunn, 1997], Comprehensive Receptive and Expressive Vocabulary Test [Hammill & Newcomer, 1997]). Although this information is helpful in many ways, the tests do not distinguish among the mand, tact, and intraverbal repertoires, and important language deficits cannot be identified. For example, these tests assess language skills under the control of discriminative stimuli (e.g., pictures, words, questions); however, a substantial percentage of verbal behavior is under the functional control of MOs. Manding is a dominating type of verbal behavior, yet rarely is this repertoire assessed in standardized testing. It is quite common to find children with autism or other developmental disabilities who are unable to mand, but have extensive tact and receptive repertoires. If a language assessment fails to identify delayed or defective language skills that are related to MO control, an appropriate intervention program may be difficult to establish. A similar problem is the failure to adequately assess the intraverbal repertoire with most standardized assessments.

If a child with language delays is referred for a language assessment, the behavior analyst should examine the current effectiveness of each verbal operant in addition to obtaining a standardized test from a speech and language pathologist. The behavior analyst would start by obtaining information about the child's mand repertoire. When known motivating operations are at strength, what behavior does the child engage in to obtain the reinforcer? When the reinforcer is provided, does the mand behavior cease? What is the frequency and complexity of the various mand units? Information regarding the quality and strength of the echoic repertoire can reveal potential problems in producing response topographies that are essential for other verbal interactions. A thorough examination of the tact repertoire will show the nature and extent of nonverbal stimulus control over verbal responses, and a systematic examination of the receptive and intraverbal repertoires will show the control by verbal stimuli. Thus, a more complete understanding of a language deficit, and hence a more effective language intervention program, can be obtained by determining the strengths and weaknesses of each of the verbal operants, as well as a number of other related skills (e.g., Partington & Sundberg, 1998; Sundberg, 1983; Sundberg & Partington, 1998).

Language Intervention

Skinner's analysis suggests that a complete verbal repertoire is composed of each of the different elementary operants, and separate speaker and listener repertoires. The individual verbal operants are then seen as the bases for building more advanced language behavior. Therefore, a language intervention program may need to firmly establish each of these repertoires before moving on to more complex verbal relations such as autoclitics or multiply controlled responses. Procedures for teaching mand, echoic, tact, and intraverbal repertoires will be presented briefly in the following sections, which will also include some discussion of the relevant research.

Mand Training

As previously stated, mands are very important to early language learners. They allow a child to control the delivery of reinforcers when those reinforcers are most valuable. As a result, a parent or language trainer's behavior (especially vocal behavior) can be paired with the reinforcer at the right time (i.e., when the relevant MO for an item is strong). Mands also begin to establish a child's role as a speaker, rather than just a listener, thus giving the child some control of the social environment. If mands fail to develop in a typical manner, negative behaviors such as tantrums, aggression, social withdrawal, or self-injury that serve the mand function (and thereby control the social environment) commonly emerge. Therefore, a language intervention program for a nonverbal child must include procedures to teach appropriate manding. The other types of verbal behavior should not be neglected, but the mand allows a child to get what he wants, when he wants it.

The most complicated aspect of mand training is the fact that the response needs to be under the functional control of the relevant MO. Therefore, mand training can only occur when the relevant MO is strong, and ultimately the response should be free from additional sources of control (e.g., nonverbal stimuli). Another complication of mand training is that different response forms need to be established and brought under the control of each MO. Vocal words are of course the most common response form, but sign language, pictures, or written words can also be used.

The basic procedure for establishing mands consists of using prompting, fading, and differential reinforcement to transfer control from stimulus variables to motivative variables (Sundberg & Partington, 1998). For example, if a child demonstrates an MO for watching bubbles by reaching for the bottle of bubbles, then smiling and laughing as he watches the bubbles in the air, the timing is probably right to conduct mand training. If the child can echo the word "bubbles" or an approximation such as "ba," teaching a mand can be easy (see Table 25.4). The trainer should first present the bottle of bubbles (a nonverbal stimulus) along with an echoic prompt (a verbal stimulus) and differentially reinforce successive approximations to "bubble" with blowing bubbles (specific reinforcement). The next step is to fade the echoic prompt to establish the response "bubble" under

Table 25.4   Teaching a Mand by Transferring Stimulus Control to MO Control

Antecedent	Behavior	Consequences
Motivating operation ⟍		
Nonverbal stimulus ⟶ ⟶	"Bubbles" ⟶	Blow bubbles
Echoic prompt ⟋		
Motivating operation ⟍		
Nonverbal stimulus ⟶ ⟶	"Bubbles" ⟶	Blow bubbles
Motivating operation ⟶	"Bubbles" ⟶	Blow bubbles

the multiple control of the MO and the nonverbal stimulus (the bottle of bubbles). The final step is to fade the nonverbal stimulus to bring the response form under the sole control of the MO.

The easiest mands to teach in an early language intervention program are usually mands for items for which the MO is frequently strong for the child and satiation is slow to occur (e.g., food, toys, videos). It is always important to assess the current strength of a supposed MO by using choice procedures, observation of a child's behavior in a free operant situation (i.e., no demands), latency to contacting the reinforcer, immediate consumption, and so forth. The goal of early mand training is to establish several different mands by bringing different response forms (i.e., words) under the functional control of different MOs. It is important to note that MOs vary in strength across time, and the effects may be momentary. In addition, the response requirement placed on a child may weaken the strength of an MO, making mand training more difficult. Many additional strategies exist for teaching early mands to more difficult learners, such as augmentative communication, physical prompts, verbal prompts, and more careful fading and differential reinforcement procedures (see Sundberg & Partington, 1998).

Manding continues to be an important part of a verbal repertoire as other verbal operants are acquired. Soon after mands for edible and tangible reinforcers are acquired, a typical child learns to mand for actions (verbs), attention, removal of aversive stimuli, movement to certain locations (prepositions), certain properties of items (adjectives) and actions (adverbs), verbal information (WH-questions), and so on. These mands are often more difficult to teach to a child with language delays because the relevant MO often must be captured or contrived for training purposes (Sundberg, 1993, 2004). Fortunately, Michael's (1993) classification of the different types of MOs provides a useful guide for capturing or contriving MOs. For example, capturing a transitive conditioned motivative operation (CMO-T) in the natural environ-

ment involves capitalizing on a situation in which one stimulus increases the value of a second stimulus. A child who likes fire trucks may see a fire truck parked outside the window. This stimulus condition increases the value of a second stimulus condition, an opened door, and will evoke behavior that has resulted in doors opening in the past. A skilled trainer would be watchful for these events and would be quick to conduct a mand trial for the word "open" or "out." The work of Hart and Risley (1975) and their incidental teaching model exemplify this teaching strategy.

Transitive CMOs can also be contrived to conduct mand training (e.g., Hall & Sundberg, 1987; Sigafoos, Doss, & Reichele, 1989; Sundberg, Loeb, Hale, & Eigenheer, 2002). For example, Hall and Sundberg (1987) used a contrived CMO-T procedure with a deaf teenager with autism by presenting highly desired instant coffee without hot water. The coffee altered the value of hot water and thereby evoked behavior that had been followed by hot water in the past. During baseline this behavior consisted of tantrums. Appropriate mands (i.e., signing "hot water") were easy to teach when this CMO-T was in effect by using the transfer of control procedure described earlier. In fact, a number of mands were taught by using this procedure, and often the procedure led to the emission of untrained mands and a substantial reduction in negative behavior.

Mand training should be a significant part of any intervention program designed for children with autism or other severe language delays. Without an appropriate mand repertoire, a child cannot obtain reinforcement when MOs are strong, or have much control of the social environment. As a result, people who interact with the child may become conditioned aversive stimuli, and/or problem behaviors may be acquired that serve the mand function. These behaviors and social relationships can become hard to change until replacement mands are established. Teaching mands early in a language intervention program may help to prevent the acquisition of negative behaviors as mands. In addition, parents and teachers are paired with successful manding and can become conditioned reinforcers. If people become more reinforcing to a child, social withdrawal, escape and avoidance, and noncompliance may be reduced.

Echoic Training

For an early language learner the ability to repeat words when asked to do so plays a major role in the development of other verbal operants (as in the bubbles example earlier). If a child can emit a word under echoic stimulus control, then transfer of stimulus control procedures can be used to bring that same response form under the control of not only MOs, but also stimuli such as objects (tacts) and questions (intraverbal). Because many children with autism and other language delays are unable to emit echoic behavior, special training procedures are required to develop the echoic repertoire.

The first goal of echoic training is to teach the child to repeat the words and phrases emitted by parents and teachers when asked to do so. Once echoic control is initially established, the goal becomes to establish a generalized repertoire in which the child can repeat novel words and combinations. But the ultimate goal with the echoic repertoire is to transfer the response form to other verbal operants. This transfer process can begin immediately and is not dependent on the acquisition of a generalized repertoire. Several procedures will be described to achieve the first goal of establishing initial echoic stimulus control.

The most common form of echoic training is direct echoic training in which a vocal stimulus is presented and successive approximations to the target response are differentially reinforced. This procedure involves a combination of prompting, fading, shaping, extinction, and reinforcement techniques. Speech therapists commonly use prompts such as pointing to the mouth, exaggerated movements, physical lip prompting, and mirrors to watch lip movement. Successive approximations to a target vocalization are reinforced, and others are ignored. The prompts are then faded, and pure echoic responses are

reinforced. For many children these procedures are effective in establishing and strengthening echoic control and improving articulation. However, for some children the procedures are ineffective, and additional measures are necessary.

Placing an echoic trial within a mand frame can often be a more effective procedure for establishing echoic stimulus control. The MO is a powerful independent variable in language training and can be temporally used to establish other verbal operants (e.g., Carroll & Hesse, 1987; Drash, High, & Tudor, 1999; Sundberg, 2004; Sundberg & Partington, 1998). For echoic training, an MO and nonverbal stimulus can be added to the target echoic antecedent as a way to evoke the behavior (see Table 25.5). For example, if a child demonstrates a strong MO for bubbles, an echoic trial can be conducted while that MO is strong, and in the presence of the nonverbal stimulus of the bottle of bubbles. These additional sources of control can help to evoke the vocal response along with the echoic prompt "Say bubbles." The specific reinforcement of blowing bubbles is then contingent on any successive approximation to "bubbles." These additional antecedent variables must be faded out, and the reinforcement changed from the specific reinforcement to generalized conditioned reinforcement. For some learners, the transfer from MO to echoic control may occur more quickly if a picture of the object is used rather than the actual object (this reduces the MO evocative effect).

Children with a low frequency of vocal behaviors may have difficulty establishing echoic control. For these children procedures to simply increase any vocal behavior may facilitate the ultimate establishment of echoic control. One method is to directly reinforce all vocal behaviors. Taking this procedure one step further, if a child randomly emits a particular sound, the behavior analyst can reinforce this behavior and conduct an echoic trial with that sound immediately after the delivery of reinforcement. Some children will repeat what they initially emitted, and this interaction sets up some of the basic variables that may facilitate echoic control.

Table 25.5 Teaching Echoics by Using a Mand Frame and Transferring Control from Multiple Control to Echoic Control

Antecedent	Behavior	Consequences
Motivating operation		
Nonverbal prompt	"Bubbles"	Blow bubbles
Echoic stimulus		
Nonverbal prompt		
Echoic stimulus	"Bubbles"	Praise (GCR)
Echoic stimulus	"Bubbles"	Praise (GCR)

Automatic reinforcement procedures can also be used to increase the frequency of vocal behavior. By pairing a neutral stimulus with an established form of reinforcement, the neutral stimulus can become a conditioned reinforcer. For example, if just prior to blowing bubbles the trainer emits the word *bubbles,* bubbles can become a reinforcer. Research has shown that this pairing procedure can increase the rate of a child's vocal play and result in the emission of targeted sounds and words that had never occurred echoically (Miguel, Carr, & Michael, 2002; Sundberg, Michael, Partington, & Sundberg, 1996; Smith, Michael, & Sundberg, 1996; Yoon & Bennett, 2000). For example, Yoon and Bennett (2000) demonstrated that this pairing procedure was more successful than direct echoic training in producing targeted sounds. Individual children who have difficulty acquiring an echoic repertoire may benefit from this procedure or a combination of all the procedures described in this section.

Tact Training

The tact repertoire is extensive and often the primary focus of many language intervention programs. A child must learn to tact objects, actions, properties of objects and actions, prepositional relations, abstractions, private events, and so on. The goal of the teaching procedures is to bring a verbal response under nonverbal stimulus control. If a child has a strong echoic repertoire, then tact training can be quite simple. A language trainer can present a nonverbal stimulus along with an echoic prompt, differentially reinforce a correct response, and then fade the echoic prompt. However, for some children tact training is more difficult, and special procedures may be required.

A mand frame can also be used to establish tacting (Carroll & Hesse, 1987). The procedure is similar to that described for teaching an echoic response. Training begins with an MO for a desired object, the nonverbal object, and an echoic prompt (see Table 25.6). Using the bubbles example, the first and second steps are the same, with the goal being to free the response from motivational control by providing generalized conditioned reinforcement rather than specific reinforcement. As with echoic training, at this point in the procedure the transfer may occur more quickly if a picture of the object is used rather than the actual object. Also, with some children it may be more effective to fade the echoic prompt before the MO is faded. The third step in the procedure involves fading out the echoic prompt and bringing the response under the sole control of the nonverbal stimulus, thus a tact. Additional nonechoic verbal prompts may also be helpful, such as "What is that?," but these too are verbal prompts that are additional sources of control that need to be accounted for in the analysis of tact acquisition (Sundberg & Partington, 1998).

Methods for teaching more complex tacts can also make use of the transfer of stimulus control procedure. For example, teaching tacts of actions requires that the nonverbal stimulus of movement be present and a response such as "jump" be brought under the control of the action of jumping. Teaching tacts involving prepositions, adjectives, pronouns, adverbs, and so on, also involves the establishment of nonverbal stimulus control. However, these advanced tacts are often more complex than they appear, and frequently the type of stimulus control established in formal training may not be the same type of stimulus control that evokes similar tacts for typically developing children (Sundberg & Michael, 2001). For example, some training programs with early learners attempt to bring verbal behavior under the control of private stimuli, such as those involved in emotional states (sad, happy, afraid), pains, itches, a full bladder, hunger pangs, nausea, and so forth. Such verbal behavior is an important part of any person's repertoire, but because the controlling variables that are affecting the learner cannot be directly contacted by the teacher or parent, accurate tact relations are difficult to develop. An instructor cannot present the relevant private stimulus that is inside a

Table 25.6   Teaching Tacts by Using a Mand Frame and Transferring Control from Multiple Control to Nonverbal Control

Antecedent	Behavior	Consequences
Motivating operation		
Nonverbal prompt	"Bubbles"	Blow bubbles
Echoic stimulus		
Nonverbal prompt		
Echoic stimulus	"Bubbles"	Praise (GCR)
Nonverbal stimulus	"Bubbles"	Praise (GCR)

person's body, and therefore cannot differentially re-inforce correct tact responses in the same way that correct tacts to objects and actions can be reinforced. Teaching a child to correctly say "itch" with respect to a stimulus coming from a portion of the child's arm is trained indirectly as the teacher reacts to common public accompaniments of such stimuli (observing a skin rash) and collateral responses by the learner (observing the child's scratching). However, this method is fraught with difficulties (the rash may not itch, the scratching may be imitated), and such repertoires even in typical adults are often quite imprecise.

Intraverbal Training

Many children with autism, developmental disabilities, or other language delays suffer from defective or nonexistent intraverbal repertoires, even though some can emit hundreds of mands, tacts, and receptive responses. For example, a child may (a) say "bed" when hearing "bed" spoken by another person (echoic), (b) say "bed" when he sees a bed (tact), and even (c) ask for bed when he is tired (mand), but (d) may not say "bed" when someone asks, "Where do you sleep?" or says, "You sleep in a . . . ." In cognitive terms, this type of language disorder may be described as a child's failure to process the auditory stimulus, or explained in terms of other hypothesized internal processes. However, verbal stimulus control is not the same as nonverbal stimulus control, and a response acquired as a tact for an early language learner may not automatically occur as an intraverbal without special training (e.g., Braam & Poling, 1982; Luciano, 1986; Partington & Bailey, 1993; Watkins, Pack-Teixteiria, & Howard, 1989).

In general, verbal stimulus control over verbal responding is more difficult to establish than nonverbal control. This does not mean that all intraverbals are harder than all tacts. Some intraverbal behavior is simple and easy to acquire. However, formal training on intraverbal

behavior for a language-delayed child should not occur until the child has well-established mand, tact, echoic, imitation, receptive, and matching-to-sample repertoires (Sundberg & Partington, 1998). A common mistake in early intraverbal training is to attempt to teach intraverbal relations too early, or intraverbals that are too complex and out of developmental sequence such as personal information (e.g., "What is your name and phone number?"). Some of the easiest intraverbal relations are fill-in-the-blanks with songs (e.g., "The wheels on the. . .)" and other fun activities (e.g., Peek-a-). The goal of early intraverbal training is to begin to break verbal responding free from mand, echoic, and tact sources of control. That is, no new response topographies are taught; rather, known words are brought under a new type of stimulus control.

MOs can be helpful independent variables in facilitating the transfer of stimulus control, as in the Peek-a-Boo example, and the mand frame procedures described earlier for the echoic and tact. However, ultimately, a child needs to learn to emit intraverbal responses that are free from MO control. For example, if a child likes bubbles and the target intraverbal is for the verbal stimulus "You blow. . ." to evoke the verbal response "bubbles," then intraverbal training should involve the transfer of control from MOs and nonverbal stimuli to verbal stimuli (echoic prompts can also be used). The language trainer can present the verbal stimulus (e.g., "You blow . . .") when the MO is strong along with the nonverbal stimulus (e.g., a bottle of bubbles). Then, the trainer can begin providing generalized conditioned reinforcement rather than specific reinforcement, use a picture of the item rather than the actual item, and finally, fade the nonverbal prompt (see Table 25.7)

The intraverbal repertoire becomes increasing more valuable to a child as the verbal stimuli and related responses become more varied and complex. Common associations (e.g., "Mommy and . . ."), fill-in-the-blanks (e.g., "You bounce a . . ."), animal sounds (e.g., "A kitty goes . . ."), and eventually *what* questions (e.g., "What

Table 25.7 Teaching Intraverbals by Using a Mand Frame and Transferring Control from Multiple Control to a Verbal Stimulus

Antecedent	Behavior	Consequences
Motivating operation ⟶ Nonverbal prompt ⟶ Verbal stimulus ⟶	"Bubbles" ⟶	Blow bubbles
Nonverbal prompt ⟶ Verbal stimulus ⟶	"Bubbles" ⟶	Praise (GCR)
Verbal stimulus ⟶	"Bubbles" ⟶	Praise (GCR)

do you eat?") will help to strengthen intraverbal behavior by expanding the content and variation of the verbal stimuli and the verbal responses. In addition, these procedures can help to develop verbal stimulus and response classes and more fluent intraverbal responding that is free from tact and echoic sources of stimulus control. More advanced intraverbal training can be accomplished in a variety of ways (Sundberg & Partington, 1998). For example, the verbal stimulus can have multiple components involving conditional discriminations in which one verbal stimulus alters the evocative effect of another, as in "What do you eat for breakfast?" versus "What do you eat for dinner?" Expansion prompts can also be used, such as "What else do you eat for lunch?," as well as additional WH-questions, such as "Where do you eat lunch?," and "When do you eat lunch?" As with the other verbal repertoires, typical developmental sequences can be a helpful guide to the progression of increasingly complex intraverbal behavior, as can the task analysis of the verbal operants presented in the *Assessment of Basic Learning and Language Skills: The ABLLS* (Partington & Sundberg, 1998).

Additional Aspects of Language Training

In addition to these four basic repertoires, there are several other components of a verbal behavior program and curriculum, such as receptive language training, matching-to-sample, mixing and varying trials, multiple response training, sentence construction, conversational skills, peer interaction, reading, and writing (Sundberg & Partington, 1998). Although a description of these programs is beyond the scope of this chapter, many of the procedures for teaching these skills involve the same basic elements of the transfer of stimulus control methods described here.

 Summary

Verbal Behavior and Properties of Language

1. Verbal behavior is defined as behavior that is reinforced through the mediation of another person's behavior.

2. The formal properties of verbal behavior involve the topography (i.e., form, structure) of the verbal response.

3. The functional properties of verbal behavior involve the causes (i.e., antecedents and consequences) of the response.

4. Skinner's analysis of verbal behavior was met with strong opposition from the field of linguistics, and with indifference within the field of behavior analysis. However, Skinner predicted in 1978 that *Verbal Behavior* would prove to be his most important work.

Defining Verbal Behavior

5. Verbal behavior involves a social interaction between speakers and listeners, whereby speakers gain access to reinforcement and control their environment through the behavior of listeners.

6. The verbal operant is the unit of analysis of verbal behavior and is the functional relation between a type of responding and (a) motivating variables, (b) discriminative stimuli, and (c) consequences.

7. A verbal repertoire is a set of verbal operants emitted by a particular person.

Elementary Verbal Operants

8. The mand is a verbal operant in which the form of the response is under the functional control of motivating operations (MOs) and specific reinforcement.

9. The tact is a verbal operant under the functional control of nonverbal discriminative stimulus, and it produces generalized conditioned reinforcement.

10. The echoic is a verbal operant that consists of a verbal discriminative stimulus that has point-to-point correspondence and formal similarity with a verbal response.

11. Point-to-point correspondence between the stimulus and the response or response product occurs when the beginning, middle, and end of the verbal stimulus matches the beginning, middle, and end of the verbal response.

12. Formal similarity occurs when the controlling antecedent stimulus and the response or response product (a) share the same sense mode (e.g., both stimulus and response are visual, auditory, or tactile) and (b) physically resemble each other.

13. The intraverbal is a verbal operant that consists of a verbal discriminative stimulus that evokes a verbal response that does not have point-to-point correspondence.

14. The textual relation is a verbal operant that consists of a verbal discriminative stimulus that has point-to-point correspondence between the stimulus and the response product, but does not have formal similarity.

15. The transcription relation is a verbal operant that consists of a verbal discriminative stimulus that controls a written, typed, or finger-spelled response. Like the textual relation, there is point-to-point correspondence between the stimulus and the response product, but no formal similarity.

Role of the Listener

16. The listener not only mediates reinforcement, but functions as a discriminative stimulus for verbal behavior. Often, much of the behavior of a listener is covert verbal behavior.

17. An audience is a discriminative stimulus in the presence of which verbal behavior is characteristically reinforced.

18. Classifying verbal responses as mands, tacts, intraverbals, etc., can be accomplished by an analysis of the relevant controlling variables.

Analyzing Complex Verbal Behavior

19. Automatic reinforcement is a type of conditioned reinforcement in which a response product has reinforcing properties as a result of a specific conditioning history.

20. Automatic punishment is a type of conditioned punishment in which a response product has punishing properties as a result of a specific conditioning history.

21. In generic tact extension, the novel stimulus shares all of the relevant or defining features associated with the original stimulus.

22. In metaphorical tact extension, the novel stimulus shares some, but not all, of the relevant features of the original stimulus.

23. In metonymical tact extension, the novel stimulus shares none of the relevant features of the original stimulus configuration, but some irrelevant but related feature has acquired stimulus control.

24. In solistic tact extension, a stimulus property that is only indirectly related to the tact relation evokes substandard verbal behavior.

25. Private events are stimuli that arise from within someone's body.

26. Public accompaniment occurs when a publicly observable stimulus accompanies a private stimulus.

27. Collateral responses are publicly observable behaviors that reliably occur with private stimuli.

28. Common properties involve a type of generalization in which private stimuli share some of the features of public stimuli.

29. Response reduction is also a type of generalization in which kinesthetic stimuli arising from movement and positions acquire control over the verbal responses. When movements shrink in size (become covert), the kinesthetic stimuli may remain sufficiently similar to those resulting from the overt movements.

Multiple Control

30. Convergent multiple control occurs when a single verbal response is a function of more than one controlling variable.

31. Divergent multiple control occurs when a single antecedent variable affects the strength of many responses.

32. The thematic verbal operants are mand, tact, and intraverbal, and involve different response topographies controlled by a common variable.

33. The formal verbal operants are echoic (and imitation as it relates to sign language and copying a text), textual, and transcription, and involve control by a common variable with point-to-point correspondence.

34. Multiple audiences consist of two or more different audiences that may evoke different response forms.

35. Impure tacts occur when an MO shares control with a nonverbal stimulus.

Autoclitic Relation

36. The autoclitic relation involves two related but separate three-term contingencies in which some aspect of a speaker's own verbal behavior functions as an SD or an MO for additional speaker verbal behavior.

37. Primary verbal behavior involves the elementary verbal operants emitted by a speaker.

38. Secondary verbal behavior involves verbal responses controlled by some aspect of the speaker's own ongoing verbal behavior.

39. The autoclitic tact informs the listener of some nonverbal aspect of the primary verbal operant and is therefore controlled by nonverbal stimuli.

40. The autoclitic mand is controlled by an MO and enjoins the listener to react in some specific way to the primary verbal operant.

Applications of Verbal Behavior

41. The verbal operants can be used to assess a wide variety of language deficits.

42. Mand training involves bringing verbal responses under the functional control of MOs.

43. Echoic training involves bringing verbal responses under the functional control of verbal discriminative stimuli that have point-to-point correspondence and formal similarity with the response.

44. Tact training involves bringing verbal responses under the functional control of nonverbal discriminative stimuli.

45. Intraverbal training involves bringing verbal responses under the functional control of verbal discriminative stimuli that lack point-to-point correspondence with the response.

PART 11

Special Applications

Parts 4 through 10 described basic principles of behavior and behavior change tactics derived from those principles. In Part 11 we describe four special applications of behavior change technology. Each of these applications can be conceived as a strategic approach to changing behavior that entails multiple principles and tactics. Chapter 26 combines topical treatment of contingency contracting, token economy, and group contingencies. Chapter 27, Self Management, warrants chapter-length treatment due to the significant research literature demonstrating the effectiveness of a variety of self-management tactics across a wide range of subjects, settings, and behaviors.

CHAPTER 26

Contingency Contracting, Token Economy, and Group Contingencies

Key Terms

backup reinforcer
behavioral contract
contingency contract
dependent group contingency

group contingency
hero procedure
independent group contingency
interdependent group contingency

level system
self-contract
token
token economy

Behavior Analyst Certification Board® BCBA® & BCABA® Behavior Analyst Task List,© Third Edition

Content Area 9: Behavior Change Procedures	
9-18	Use contingency contracting (e.g., behavioral contracts).
9-19	Use token economy procedures, including levels systems.
9-20	Use independent, interdependent, and dependent group contingencies.

This chapter addresses contingency contracting, token economy, and group contingencies as special applications of behavioral procedures. Each application will be defined; its relationship to behavioral principles will be explained; requisite components of the procedure will be addressed; and guidelines for designing, implementing, and evaluating each will be presented. These topics are grouped because they have several features in common. First, they have an effective and robust literature supporting their inclusion. Second, they can be combined with other approaches in package programs to provide an additive effect. Also, each can be used in individual and group arrangements. The flexibility that these three special applications provide makes them an attractive option for practitioners.

Contingency Contracting
Definition of Contingency Contract

A **contingency contract,** also called a **behavioral contract,** is a document that specifies a contingent relationship between the completion of a specified behavior and access to, or delivery of, a specified reward such as free time, a letter grade, or access to a preferred activity.

Typically, contracts specify how two or more people will behave toward each other. Such quid pro quo agreements make one person's behavior (e.g., preparing dinner) dependent on the other person's behavior (e.g., washing and putting away the dishes by a prescribed time the night before). Although verbal agreements may be considered contracts in the legal sense, they are not contingency contracts because the degree of specificity in designing, implementing, and evaluating a contingency contract far exceeds what is likely to occur in a verbal arrangement between parties. In addition, the physical act of signing the contract and its prominent visibility during execution are integral parts of contingency contracts.

Contingency and behavior contracts have been used to modify academic performance (Newstrom, McLaughlin, & Sweeney, 1999; Wilkinson, 2003), weight control (Solanto, Jacobson, Heller, Golden, & Hertz, 1994), adherence to medical regimens (Miller & Stark, 1994), and athletic skills (Simek, O'Brien, & Figlerski, 1994). Indeed, a compelling advantage of contingency contracts is their ability to be implemented alone or in packaged programs that incorporate two or more interventions concurrently (De Martini-Scully, Bray, & Kehle, 2000).

Components of Contingency Contracts

There are three major parts in most contracts—a description of the task, a description of the reward, and the task record. Essentially, the contract specifies the person(s) to perform the task, the scope and sequence of the task, and the circumstances or criterion for task completion. Figure 26.1 shows a contingency contract implemented by the parents of a 10-year-old boy to help him learn to get up and get ready for school each day.

Task

The task side of the contract consists of four parts. *Who* is the person who will perform the task and receive the reward—in this case, Mark. *What* is the task or behavior the person must perform—in this example, getting ready for school. *When* identifies the time that the task must be completed—every school day. *How well* is the most important part of the task side, and perhaps of the entire contract. It calls for the specifics of the task. Sometimes it is helpful to list a series of steps or subtasks so that the person can use the contract as a checklist of what must be done. Any exceptions should be written in this part.

Reward

The reward side of a contract must be as complete and accurate as the task side (Ruth, 1996). Some people are very good at specifying the task side of a contract; they know what they want the other person to do. When it comes to the reward side, however, specificity is lost and problems arise. Reward statements such as "Can watch some television" or "Will play catch when I get a chance" are not explicit, specific, or fair to the person completing the task.

On the reward side, *Who* is the person who will judge task completion and control delivery of the reward. With Mark's getting-ready-for-school contract, those persons are his parents. *What* is the reward. *When* specifies the time that the reward can be received by the person earning it. With any contract it is crucial that the reward come *after* successful task completion. However, many rewards cannot be delivered immediately following task completion. In addition, some rewards have built-in, limited availability and can be delivered only at certain times (e.g., seeing the home-town baseball team play). Mark's contract specifies that his reward, if earned, will be received on Friday nights. *How much* is the amount of reward that

CONTRACT

TASK	**REWARD**
Who: Mark	Who: Mom and Dad
What: Get ready for school	What: Jimmy staying over and treat
When: Every school day	When: Friday night after perfect week
How Well: Mark will get out of bed, get dressed and finish his cereal by 7:15 each school morning. No more than 1 reminder from Mom or Dad. Must be ready for bus all 5 days to get reward.	How Much: Jimmy can come home with Mark after school and stay overnight. Boys can have night snack of pizza and ice cream.

Sign Here: *Mark Davidson* Date: Feb. 12, 2007

Sign Here: *Belinda Davidson* Date: Feb. 12, 2007

TASK RECORD

M	T	W	TH	F	M	T	W	TH	F	M	T	W	TH	F
★	★		★	★	★	★	★	★	★	★	★	★	★	★
		oops!	*Great*	*work,*		*Mark*			*reward!!*					*reward*

Figure 26.1 Example of a contingency contract.

From *Sign Here: A Contracting Book for Children and Their Parents* (2nd ed., p. 31) by J. C. Dardig and W. I. Heward, 1981, Bridgewater, NJ: Fournies and Associates. Copyright 1981 by Fournies and Associates. Reprinted by permission.

can be earned by completing the task. Any bonus contingencies should be included; for example, "By adhering to her contract Monday through Friday, Eileen receives an extra reward on Saturday and Sunday."

Task Record

Including on the contract a place to record task completion serves two purposes. First, recording task completion and reward delivery on the contract sets the occasion for all parties to review the contract regularly. Second, if a certain number of task completions are required to earn the reward (e.g., if a child must dress herself each morning before school for 5 days in a row), a check mark, smiley face, or star can be placed on the task record each time the task is completed successfully. Marking the contract in this manner helps the person remain focused until the assignment is completed and the reward is earned. Mark's parents used the top row of boxes in the task record to record the days of the school week. In the middle row of boxes they placed gummed stars each day Mark met the conditions of his contract. In the bottom row, Mark's parents wrote comments about the progress of his contract.

Implementing Contingency Contracts

How Do Contracts Work?

At first glance the principle of behavior behind contingency contracts seems deceptively simple: A behavior is followed by a contingent reward—surely a case of positive reinforcement. Yet, in most contracts the reward, although contingent, is much too delayed to reinforce the specified behavior directly; and many successful contracts specify a reward that would not, in fact, function as a reinforcer for the task even if it was presented immediately after the task completion. Further, behavioral contracting is not a single procedure with a single associated behavior and a single reinforcer. Contracting is more accurately conceptualized as an intervention package that combines several behavior principles and procedures.

So how do contracts work? Several principles, procedures, and factors are likely to apply. Certainly reinforcement is involved, but not in as simple or direct a fashion as it might seem at first. *Rule-governed behavior* is probably involved (Malott, 1989; Malott & Garcia, 1991; Skinner, 1969). A contract describes a rule: A specified behavior will be followed by a specified (and reasonably immediate) consequence. The contract serves as a response prompt to perform the target behavior and enables the effective use of a consequence (e.g., going to the movies Saturday night), too delayed in itself to reinforce certain behaviors (e.g., practicing the trumpet on Tuesday). Delayed consequences can help exert control over behaviors performed hours and even days before if they are associated with and linked by verbal behavior to the rule (e.g., "I've just finished my trumpet practice— that's another check mark toward the movies on Saturday"), or to interim token reinforcers (e.g., the check mark on the contract after practicing). The physical visibility of the contract may also function as a response prompt for escaping "guilt" (Malott & Garcia, 1991). At this stage of knowledge development within the field, it cannot be said that contracting is simply positive reinforcement loosely based on the Premack principle (see Chapter 11). It is more likely a complex package intervention of related positive and negative reinforcement contingencies and rule-governed behavior that operate alone and together.

Applications of Contingency Contracting

Contracting in the Classroom

The use of contracting in classrooms is well established. For example, teachers have employed contracting to address specific discipline, performance, and academic challenges (Kehle, Bray, Theodore, Jenson, & Clark, 2000; Ruth, 1996). Newstrom and colleagues (1999), for instance, used a contingency contract with a middle school student with behavior disorders to improve the written mechanics associated with spelling and written language. After collecting baseline data on the percentage of capitalization and punctuation marks used correctly across spelling and sentence writing, a contingency contract was negotiated and signed with the student that specified that improved performance would yield free time on the classroom computer. The student was reminded of the terms of the contract before each language arts class that included spelling worksheets and journal writing (i.e., sentences).

Figure 26.2 shows the results of the contingency contracting intervention. When baseline was in effect for spelling and written sentences respectively, mean scores for both variables were in the 20% correct range. When contracting was initiated, the student's performance for spelling and written sentences increased immediately to an average of approximately 84% correct. Because the percentage of correct performance increased

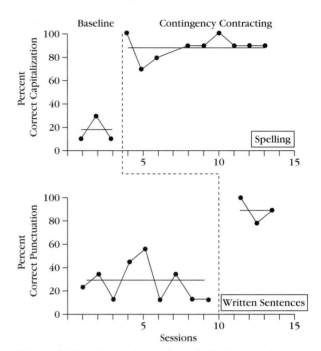

Figure 26.2   Percentage of capitalization and punctuation marks used correctly on spelling worksheets and journal writing during baseline and contingency contracting.

From "The Effects of Contingency Contracting to Improve the Mechanics of Written Language with a Middle School Student with Behavior Disorders" by J. Newstrom, T. F. McLaughlin, & W. J. Sweeney, 1999, *Child & Family Behavior Therapy, 21* (1), p. 44. Copyright 1999 by The Haworth Press, Inc. Reprinted by permission.

immediately when contingency contracting was implemented for spelling (Sessions 4 through 12), but did not increase for written sentences until Session 11, a functional relation was demonstrated between contracting and improved performance. The authors also reported positive anecdotal evidence related to spelling and written language from other teachers with whom this student interacted.

Wilkinson (2003) used a contingency contract to reduce the disruptive behavior of a first-grade student. Disruptive behaviors included being off-task, refusals to comply with work assignments and instructions, fighting with peers, and temper tantrums. A behavioral consultation effort was launched with the classroom teacher that included problem identification, analysis, intervention, and evaluation. Contingency contracting consisted of the student earning preferred rewards and social praise from the teacher for three behaviors: increased time on-task, appropriate interactions with other children, and compliance with teacher requests. Observations of her behavior over 13 sessions of baseline and contingency contracting showed a decrease in the percentage of intervals with disruptive behavior when the contingency contract was in effect. Wilkinson reported that the student's disruptive behavior decreased substantially and remained low during a 4-week follow-up period.

Ruth (1996) conducted a 5-year longitudinal study with emotionally disturbed students that blended contingency contracting with goal setting. After students negotiated their contracts with their teachers, a goal-setting component was added that included statements about their daily and weekly goals and the criterion levels for success. Results for the 37 out of 43 students who finished the program after 5 years showed that 75% of daily goals, 72% of weekly goals, and 86% of total goals were reached. Ruth summarized the beneficial effects of combining strategies: "When [goal-setting] methods are incorporated into a contract, the motivational aspects of behavior contracting and goal setting may combine to produce maximum effort and success" (p. 156).

Contracting in the Home

Miller and Kelley (1994) combined contingency contracting and goal setting to improve the homework performance of four preadolescent students with histories of poor homework completion and who were at risk for other academic problems (e.g., procrastination, being off-task, errors with submitted work). During baseline, parents recorded their children's homework time on-task, type and accuracy of problem completion, and number of problems completed correctly. Subsequently, parents and children entered into a goal-setting and contingency contracting phase that was preceded by parent training on how to set and negotiate goals and write contracts. Each night, parents and children established their respective goals and negotiated a compromise goal based on that interaction. Each week, renegotiations occurred for tasks, rewards, and sanctions should the contract not be met. A recording sheet was used to measure progress.

Figure 26.3 shows the results of the study. When goal setting was combined with contingency contracting, accuracy performance increased for all students. Miller and Kelley's findings reaffirm the notion that contingency contracting can be combined successfully with other strategies to produce functional outcomes.

Clinical Applications of Contracting

Flood and Wilder (2002) combined contingency contracting with functional communication training to re-

duce the off-task behavior of an elementary-aged student diagnosed with attention-deficit/hyperactivity disorder (ADHD) who had been referred to a clinic-based program because his off-task behavior had reached alarming levels. Antecedent assessment, functional communication training, and contingency contracting were conducted in a therapy room located in the clinical facility. Specifically, antecedent assessments were conducted to determine the level of off-task behavior when the difficulty of academic tasks varied from easy to difficult, and therapist attention varied from low to high. A preference assessment was also conducted. Using discrete trial training, the student was taught to raise his hand for assistance with tasks (e.g., "Can you help me with this problem?"). The therapist sat nearby and responded to appropriate requests for assistance and ignored other vocalizations. Once requesting assistance was mastered, the contingency contract was established whereby the student could earn preferred items, identified through the assessment, contingent on accurate task completion. The results showed that during baseline, off-task performance was high for math division and word problems. When the intervention was introduced, an immediate reduction in off-task behavior was noted for division and word problems. Also, the student's accuracy in completing the division and word problems improved as well. Whereas during baseline conditions he solved correctly 5% and 33% of the division and word problems, respectively, during intervention he solved 24% and 92% of the problems correctly.

Using Contracting to Teach Self-Management to Children

Ideally, contingency contracting involves the active participation of the child throughout the development, implementation, and evaluation of the contract. For many children, contracting is a first experience in identifying specific ways they would like to act and then arranging certain aspects of their environment to set the occasion for and reward those acts. If more of the decision making for all parts of the contracting process is turned over to children gradually and systematically, they can become skilled at self-contracting. A **self-contract** is a contingency contract that a person makes with herself, incorporating a self-selected task and reward as well as personal monitoring of task completion and self-delivery of the reward. Self-contracting skills can be achieved by a multistep process of having an adult prescribe virtually all of the elements of the task and reward and gradually shifting the design of the elements to the child.

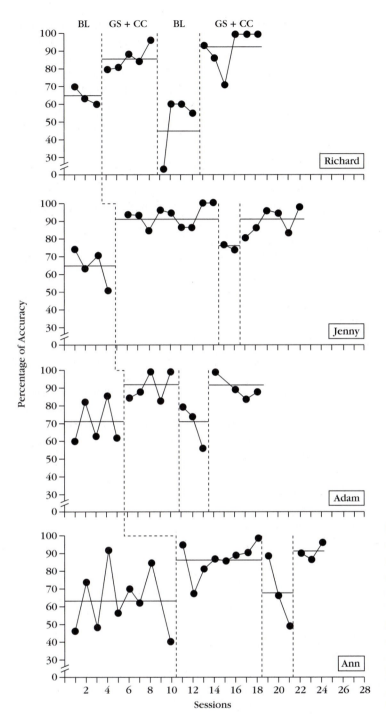

Figure 26.3   Percentage of homework problems completed accurately during baseline and a treatment condition consisting of goal setting and contingency contracting. Sessions correspond to sequential school days (i.e., Monday through Thursdays) on which subjects were assigned homework. Data were not collected on days on which homework was not assigned.

From "The Use of Goal Setting and Contingency Contracting for Improving Children's Homework Performance" by D. L. Miller & M. L. Kelley, 1994, *Journal of Applied Behavior Analysis, 27,* p. 80. Copyright 1994 by the Society for the Experimental Analysis of Behavior, Inc. Reprinted by permission.

Developing Contingency Contracts

Although teachers, therapists, or parents can unilaterally determine a contract for a child or client, contracting is usually more effective when all of the parties involved play an active role in developing the contract. Several methods and guidelines have been proposed for developing contingency contracts (Dardig & Heward, 1981;

Downing, 1990; Homme Csanyi, Gonzales & Rechs, 1970). Contract development involves the specification of tasks and rewards in a fashion agreeable and beneficial to each party. Dardig and Heward (1981) described a five-step procedure for task and reward identification that can be used by teachers and families.

Step 1: Hold a meeting.   To get the entire group (family or class) involved in the contracting process, a meeting should be held. At this meeting members can discuss how contracts work, how they can help the group cooperate and get along better, and how contracts can help individuals meet personal goals. Parents or teachers should emphasize that they will participate in all of the steps leading up to and including implementation of contracts. It is important that children view contracting as a behavior-exchange process shared by all members of the group, not as something adults impose on them. The field-tested list-making procedures described in the following steps provide a simple and logical framework for the selection of tasks and rewards for family and classroom contracts. Most groups can complete the procedure within 1 to 2 hours.

Step 2: Fill Out List A. Each member completes three lists prior to the actual writing of the contract. List A (see Figure 26.4) is designed to help each member identify not only those tasks he can perform within the context of a contract, but also those tasks he already does to help the group. In this way positive attention can be focused on appropriate behaviors that individual members are currently completing satisfactorily.

Each member should be given a copy of List A. Everyone should be careful to describe all tasks as specifically as possible. Then the completed lists can be put aside, and

the group can proceed to the next step. If a member is unable to write, that person's list can be completed orally.

Step 3: Fill Out List B. List B (see Figure 26.5) is designed to help group members identify possible contract tasks for other group members and helpful behaviors currently being completed by those persons. List B can also identify areas where disagreement exists between group members as to whether certain tasks are actually being completed properly and regularly.

Each member should be given a copy of List B and asked to write his or her name in all three blanks at the top. These lists can then be passed around the table so that everyone has a chance to write at least one behavior on each side of everyone else's list. Everyone writes on every List B except his or her own, and each person should be required to write at least one positive behavior on everyone else's List B. After completion, these lists should be set aside before moving to the next step.

Step 4: Fill Out List C. List C (see Figure 26.6) is simply a sheet with numbered lines on which each group member identifies potential rewards he would like to earn by completing contracted tasks. Participants should list not only everyday favorite things and activities, but also special items and activities they may have wanted for a long time. It is all right if two or more

Figure 26.4 A form for self-identification of possible tasks for contingency contracts.

List A Name: Jean	
Things I Do to Help My Family	Other Ways I Could Help My Family and Myself
1. Feed Queenie and Chippy	1. Be on time for supper
2. Clean up my bedroom	2. Turn off the lights when I leave a room
3. Practice my piano	3. Dust the living room
4. Wash dishes	4. Clean up the back yard
5. Help Dad with the laundry	5. Hang up my coat when I get home from school
6.	6.
7.	7.

From *Sign Here: A Contracting Book for Children and Their Parents* (2nd ed., p. 111) by J. C. Dardig and W. L. Heward, 1981. Bridgewater, NJ: Fournies and Associates. Copyright 1981 by Fournies and Associates. Reprinted by permission.

Figure 26.5   A form for identifying potential contracting tasks for others.

> **List B   Name:** <u>Bobby</u>
>
> THINGS <u>Bobby</u> DOES   OTHER WAYS <u>Bobby</u>
> TO HELP THE FAMILY   COULD HELP THE FAMILY
>
> 1. <u>Vacuums when asked</u>   1. <u>Put his dirty clothes in</u>
>   _____   <u>hamper</u>
> 2. <u>Makes his bed</u>   2. <u>Do homework at night</u>
>   _____   <u>without being asked</u>
> 3. <u>Reads stories to little</u>   3. <u>Make his own sandwiches</u>
>   <u>sister</u>   <u>for his school lunch</u>
> 4. <u>Empties trash</u>   4. <u>Clean and sponge off</u>
>   _____   <u>table after supper</u>
> 5. <u>Rakes leaves</u>   5. _____
>   _____   _____
> 6. _____   6. _____
>   _____   _____
> 7. _____   7. _____
>   _____   _____
>
> From *Sign Here: A Contracting Book for Children and Their Parents* (2nd ed., p. 113) by J. C. Dardig and
> W. L. Heward, 1981, Bridgewater, NJ: Fournies and Associates. Copyright 1981 by Fournies and Associates.
> Reprinted by permission.

Figure 26.6   A form for self-identification of possible rewards for contingency contracts.

> **List C Name:** <u>Sue Ann</u>
>
> MY FAVORITE THINGS, ACTIVITIES, AND SPECIAL TREATS
>
> 1. <u>Listening to records</u>
> 2. <u>Movies</u>
> 3. <u>Playing pinball</u>
> 4. <u>Miniature golf</u>
> 5. <u>Swimming</u>
> 6. <u>Ice skating</u>
> 7. <u>Ice cream sundaes</u>
> 8. <u>Aquarium and fish</u>
> 9. <u>Picnics</u>
> 10. <u>Coin collection</u>
> 11. <u>Riding a horse</u>
> 12. <u>Fishing with Dad</u>
> 13. _____
> 14. _____
> 15. _____
>
> From *Sign Here: A Contracting Book for Children and Their Parents* (2nd ed., p. 115) by J. C. Dardig and
> W. L. Heward, 1981, Bridgewater, NJ: Fournies and Associates. Copyright 1981 by Fournies and Associates.
> Reprinted by permission.

people indicate the same reward. After List C is completed, each person should collect his two other lists and read them carefully, talking over any misunderstood items.

Step 5: Write Contracts.   The final step begins with choosing a task for each person's first contract. Discussion should move around the group with members trying to help each other decide which task is the most important to start doing first. Everyone should write *who* is going to perform the task, exactly *what* the task is, *how well* and *when* it has to be done, and any possible exceptions. Everyone should also look at List C and choose a reward that is neither excessive nor insignificant but is fair for the selected task. Each member should write *who* will control the reward, *what* the reward is, *when* it is to be given, and *how much* is to be given. Everyone in the group should write one contract during the first meeting.

Guidelines and Considerations in Implementing Contracts

In determining whether contingency contracting is an appropriate intervention for a given problem, the practitioner should consider the nature of the desired behavior change, the verbal and conceptual skills of the participant, the individual's relationship with the person(s) with whom the contract will be made, and the available resources. The target behavior to be changed by a contingency contract must be in the person's repertoire already and must typically be under proper stimulus control in the environment in which the response is desired. If the behavior is not in the individual's repertoire, other behavior-building techniques should be attempted (e.g., shaping, chaining). Contracting is most effective with behaviors that produce permanent products (e.g., completed homework assignment, cleaned bedroom) or that occur in the presence of the person who is to deliver the reward (e.g., the teacher or parent).

Reading ability by the participant is not a prerequisite for successful contracting; however, the individual must be able to come under the control of the visual or oral statements (rules) of the contract. Contracting with nonreaders involves three types of clients: (a) preschoolers with good verbal skills, (b) school-aged children with limited reading skills, and (c) adults with adequate language and conceptual skills but who lack reading and writing skills. Contracts using icons, symbols, pictures, photographs, audiotapes, or other nonword characterizations can be developed to suit the individual skills of children and adults in all three nonreader groups (see Figure 26.7).

Persons who refuse to enter into a contingency contract are another consideration. Whereas many children are eager, or at least willing, to try a contract, some want nothing to do with the whole idea. Using contingency contracting in a collaborative approach (Lassman, Jolivette, & Wehby, 1999) may reduce the likelihood of noncompliance, and following a step-by-step method may help to ensure that consensus is reached at each decision point in the contract (Downing, 1990). However, the reality is that some nonsigners may not agree to participate in a contingency contract, even with the best of positive approaches built into the system. In such cases, another behavior change strategy would likely be a better alternative for dealing with the target behavior. Numerous lists of rules and guidelines for effective

Figure 26.7   A contingency contract for a nonreader.

Table 26.1   Guidelines and Rules for Contingency Contracts

Guidelines and rules for contracts	Comment
Write a fair contract.	There must be a fair relationship between the difficulty of the task and the amount of the reward. The goal is to achieve a win–win situation for both parties, not for one party to gain an advantage over the other.
Write a clear contract.	In many instances a contract's greatest advantage is that it specifies each person's expectations. When a teacher's or parent's expectations are explicit, performance is more likely to improve. Contingency contracts must say what they mean and mean what they say.
Write an honest contract.	An honest contract exists if the reward is delivered at the time and in the amount specified when the task is completed as agreed. In an honest contract the reward is *not* delivered if the task has not been completed as specified.
Build in several layers of rewards.	Contracts can include bonus rewards for beating the best daily, weekly, or monthly performance. Adding these bonuses increases the motivational effect.
Add a response cost contingency,	Occasionally, it may be necessary to incorporate a "fine"—the removal of rewards—if the agreed-upon task is not completed.
Post the contract in a visible place.	Public posting allows all parties to see progress toward achieving the goals of the contract.
Renegotiate and change a contract when either party is consistently unhappy with it.	Contracting is designed to be a positive experience for all parties, not a tedious endurance contest to determine survivors. If the contract is not working, reconsider the task, the reward components, or both.
Terminate a contingency contract.	A contingency contract is a means to an end, not the end product. Once independent and proficient performance is achieved, the contract can be terminated. Further, a contract can and should be terminated when one party or both parties consistently fail to live up to the terms of the contract.

contingency contracting have been published (e.g., Dardig & Heward, 1976; Downing, 1990; Homme et al., 1970). Table 26.1 provides a list of the frequently cited guidelines and rules.

Evaluating Contracts

The evaluation of a contingency contract should focus on the objective measurement of the target behavior. The simplest way to evaluate a contract is to record the occurance of task completion. Including a task record on the contract helps make evaluation a natural by-product of the contracting process. By comparing the task record with a precontract baseline of task completion, an objective determination can be made as to whether improvement has occurred. A good outcome is one that results in the specified task being completed more often than it was before the contract.

Sometimes the outcome data indicate that the task is being completed more often and more consistently than it was before the contract, but the parties involved are still not happy. In such cases, either the original problem or goal that prompted the development of the contract is not being attained, or one or more of the participants do not like the way in which the contract is being carried out. The first possibility results from selecting the wrong behavior for the task part of the contract. For example, let us suppose that John, a ninth-grader, wants to improve on the Ds and Fs he has been getting in algebra and writes a contract with his parents specifying as the task "studying his math" for 1 hour each school night. After several weeks John has failed to study for the required 1 hour on only two nights, but his in-school algebra performance remains unchanged. Has John's contract worked? The correct answer is both yes and no. John's contract was successful in that he was consistently completing the specified task—1 hour of study each day. However, in terms of his original objective—better algebra grades—the contract was a failure. John's contract helped him change the behavior he specified, but he specified the wrong task. Studying for 1 hour, for John at least, was not directly related to his goal. By changing his contract to require that he solve correctly 10 algebra equations each night (the behavior required to get good grades on algebra tests), his goal of obtaining better grades may become a reality.

It is also important to consider the participant's reactions to the contract. A contract that produces desired change in the specified target behavior but causes other maladaptive or emotional responses may be an unacceptable solution. Having the client in the negotiation development of the contract and jointly conducting regular progress checks helps to avoid this situation.

Token Economy

The token economy is a highly developed and researched behavior change system. It has been applied successfully in virtually every instructional and therapeutic setting possible. The usefulness of a token economy in changing behaviors that have been resistant to instruction or therapy is well established in the literature (Glynn, 1990; Musser, Bray, Kehle, & Jenson, 2001). In this section we describe and define token economy and outline effective procedures for using it in applied settings.

Definition of a Token Economy

A **token economy** is a behavior change system consisting of three major components: (a) a specified list of target behaviors; (b) tokens or points that participants receive for emitting the target behaviors; and (c) a menu of backup reinforcer items—preferred items, activities, or privileges—that participants obtain by exchanging tokens they have earned. Tokens function as generalized conditioned reinforcers for the target behaviors. First, behaviors to be reinforced are identified and defined. Second, a medium of exchange is selected; that medium of exchange is a symbol, object, or item, called a **token.** Third, **backup reinforcers** are provided that can be purchased with the token. Store-based or manufacturer coupons are analogous to a token economy. When a customer purchases an item from a participating store, the cashier provides the purchaser with the coupon—the medium of exchange—that serves as the token. The coupon is traded later for another item at a reduced price, or it is redeemed immediately for the backup reinforcer. Money is another example of a token that can be exchanged at a later time for backup objects and activities (e.g., food, clothing, transportation, entertainment).

As stated in Chapter 11, a token is an example of a generalized conditioned reinforcer. It can be exchanged for a wide variety of backup reinforcers. Generalized conditioned reinforcers are independent of specific states of motivation because they are associated with a wide variety of backup reinforcers. However, generalized conditioned reinforcement is a relative concept: Effectiveness depends to a large extent on the extensiveness of the backup reinforcers. Tokens exchangeable for a wide variety of backup reinforcers have considerable utility in schools, clinics, and hospitals where it is difficult for personnel to control the deprivation states of their clients.

Carton and Schweitzer (1996), for example, implemented a token economy to increase the compliance behavior of a 10-year-old boy who was hospitalized for severe renal disease and who required regular hemodialysis. The patient developed a noncompliant repertoire that affected his interactions with nurses and caretakers. During baseline, the number of 30-minute intervals of noncompliance was measured by dividing a 4-hour time block into eight, 30-minute segments. When the token economy was introduced, the boy was told that he could earn one token for each 30-minute period that passed without a noncompliant episode. Tokens were exchanged weekly for baseball cards, comics, and toys.

Carton and Schweitzer reported a functional relation between the onset of the token economy and the reduction in noncompliant behavior. When tokens were in effect, noncompliant behavior was virtually eliminated. Follow-up data collected 3 months and 6 months after termination of token reinforcement yielded continued evidence of low noncompliance to nurse and caretaker requests.

Higgins, Williams, and McLaughlin (2001) used a token economy to decrease the disruptive behaviors of an elementary-age student with learning disabilities. The student exhibited high levels of out-of-seat behavior, talking out, and poor sitting posture. After collecting baseline data on the number of out-of-seat, talking out, and poor posture responses, a token economy was implemented. The student earned a check mark that was exchangeable for free time after each minute if an alternative behavior was being emitted instead of the behaviors targeted for reduction. Maintenance checks were taken on two subsequent occasions to determine duration effects. Figure 26.8 displays the results of the study across the three dependent variables. A functional relation was established between the onset of the token economy and the reduction of the behaviors. Further, maintenance checks indicated that the behavior remained at low levels beyond the termination of the token economy.

Level Systems

A **level system** is a type of token economy in which participants move up (and sometimes down) a hierarchy of levels contingent on meeting specific performance criteria with respect to the target behaviors. As participants move "up" from one level to the next level, they have access to more privileges and are expected to demonstrate more independence. The schedule of token reinforcement is gradually thinned so that participants at the highest levels are functioning on schedules of reinforcement that are similar to those in natural settings.

According to Smith and Farrell (1993) level systems are an outgrowth of two major educational advances that began in the late 1960s and 1970s: (a) Hewett's *Engineered Classroom* (1968), and (b) Phillips, Phillips, Fixen, and Wolf's *Achievement Place* (1971). In both

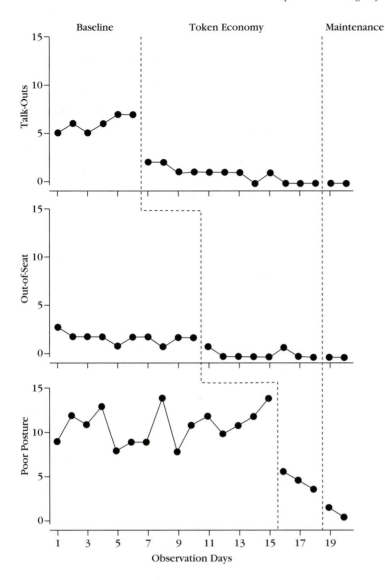

Figure 26.8   The number of talk-outs, out-of-seat behavior, and poor posture during baseline, token economy, and maintenance conditions.

From "The Effects of a Token Economy Employing Instructional Consequences for a Third-Grade Student with Learning Disabilities: A Data-Based Case Study" by J. W. Higgins, R. L. Williams, and T. F. McLaughlin, 2001, *Education and Treatment of Children, 24* (1), p. 103. Copyright 2001 by The H. W. Wilson Company. Reprinted by permission.

cases, systematic academic and social programming combined token reinforcement, tutoring systems, student self-regulation, and managerial arrangements. Smith and Farrell stated that level systems are designed to

> foster a student's improvement through self-management, to develop personal responsibility for social, emotional, and academic performance . . . and to provide student transition to a less restrictive mainstream setting. . . . Students advance through the various levels as they show evidence of their achievement. (p. 252)

In a level system, students must acquire and achieve increasingly more refined repertoires while tokens, social praise, or other reinforcers are simultaneously decreased. Level systems have built-in mechanisms for participants to advance through a series of privileges, and they are based on at least three assumptions: (a) combined techniques—so called "package programs"—are more ef-

fective than individual contingencies introduced alone, (b) student behaviors and expectations must be stated explicitly, and (c) differential reinforcement is necessary to reinforce closer and closer approximations to the next level (Smith & Farrell, 1993).

Lyon and Lagarde (1997) proposed a three-level group of reinforcers that placed less desirable reinforcers at Level 1. At this level, students had to earn 148 points or 80% of the 185 maximum points that could be earned during the week to purchase certain items. At Level 3, the highly desirable reinforcers could be purchased only if the students had accumulated at least 167 points, or 90% of the total points possible. As the levels progress, the expectations for performance increase.

Cavalier, Ferretti, and Hodges (1997) incorporated a self-management approach with an existing level system to improve the academic and social behavior of two adolescent students with learning disabilities for whom increased participation in a general education classroom was an individualized education program (IEP) goal. Basically, other students in the classroom were making adequate progress through the six-level point system that the teacher had devised, but the inappropriate verbalizations of the two target students during class stalled their progress at Level 1. After collecting baseline data on the number of inappropriate verbalizations, the researchers trained the students to self-record occurrences of these behaviors during two 50-minute intervals in the day. Inappropriate verbalizations were defined explicitly, and during mock trials the students practiced self-recording and received feedback based on teacher observations during the same interval. An emphasis was placed on the accuracy of the students' recording, and desirable reinforcers were awarded for accurate recording. During the intervention (level system plus self-recording), students were told that they would be observed during the two 50-minute intervals for accuracy. If they met the criterion for each level (e.g., a decrease of five inappropriate verbalizations from the previous session), a reinforcer was delivered. As the students progressed through the levels, the reinforcer changed to more highly desirable items. Results showed a high number of verbalizations during baseline; however, when the packaged intervention was initiated for Student 1, inappropriate verbalizations decreased. This outcome was replicated for Student 2, confirming a functional relation between the the intervention and the decrease in inappropriate verbalizations.

Designing a Token Economy

The basic steps in designing and preparing to implement a token economy are as follows:

1. Select tokens that will serve as a medium of exchange (e.g., points, stickers, plastic chips).

2. Identify target behaviors and rules.

3. Select a menu of backup reinforcers.

4. Establish a ratio of exchange.

5. Write procedures to specify when and how tokens will be dispensed and exchanged and what will happen if the requirements to earn a token are not met. Will the system include a response cost procedure?

6. Field-test the system before full-scale implementation.

Selecting Tokens

A token is a tangible symbol that can be given immediately after a behavior and exchanged later for known reinforcers. Frequently used tokens include washers, checkers, coupons, poker chips, points or tally marks, teacher initials, holes punched in a card, and strips of plastic. Criteria to consider in selecting the token itself are important. First, the token should be safe; it should not be harmful to the learners. If a very young child or a person with severe learning or behavioral problems is to receive the token, it should not be an item that can be swallowed or used to cause injury. Second, the analyst should control token presentation; learners should not be able to bootleg the delivery of the tokens. If tally marks are used, they should be on a special card or made with a special marking pen that is available only to the analyst. Likewise, if holes are punched in a card, the paper punch should be available only to the analyst to avoid counterfeiting.

Tokens should be durable because they may have to be used for an extended period of time, and they should be easy to carry, handle, bank, store, or accumulate. Tokens should also be readily accessible to the practitioner at the moment they are to be dispensed. It is important that they be provided immediately after the target behavior. Tokens should be inexpensive; there is no need to spend a large sum of money to purchase tokens. Rubber stamps, stars, check marks, and buttons are all inexpensive items that can be used as tokens. Finally, the token itself should not be a desirable object. One teacher used baseball cards as tokens, but the students spent so much time interacting with the tokens (e.g., reading about players) that the tokens distracted students from the purpose of the system.

For some students, the object of an obsession can serve as a token reinforcer (Charlop-Christy & Haymes, 1998). In their study, three children with autism who attended an after-school program served as participants. All three children were consistently off task during activities, preoccupied with some objects, and engaged in self-stimulatory behaviors. During baseline, the students earned stars for appropriate behavior. Inappropriate behaviors or incorrect responses were addressed by saying "try again" or "no." When the students earned five stars, the tokens could be exchanged for backup reinforcers (e.g., food, pencils, tablets). During the token condition, an "obsession" object (one the children had been previously preoccupied with) was used as the token. Once they had earned five obsession objects, children could exchange them for food items or other known reinforcers. Charlop-Christy and Haymes reported that the overall pattern of responding demonstrated that when the token was an obsession object, student performance improved.

Identifying Target Behaviors and Rules

Chapter 3 addressed the selection and definition of behavior change targets. The criteria presented in that chapter also apply to the selection and definition of rules and target behaviors for a token economy. Generally, the guidelines for selecting behaviors for a token economy include (a) selecting only measurable and observable behaviors; (b) specifying criteria for successful task completion; (c) starting with a small number of behaviors, including some that are easy for the individual to accomplish; and (d) being sure the individual possesses the prerequisite skills for any targeted behaviors (Myles, Moran, Ormsbee, & Downing, 1992).

After rules and behaviors that apply to everyone are defined, then criteria and behaviors specific to individual learners should be established. Many token economy failures can be traced to requiring the same behaviors and setting the same criteria for all learners. Token economies usually need to be individualized. For example, in a classroom setting the teacher may want to select different behaviors for each student. Or perhaps the token economy should not be applied to all students in the classroom. Perhaps only the lowest functioning students in the classroom should be included. However, students who do not need a token system should still continue to receive other forms of reinforcement.

Selecting a Menu of Backup Reinforcers

Most token economies can use naturally occurring activities and events as backup reinforcers. For example, in a classroom or school setting, tokens can be used to buy time with popular games or materials, or they can be exchanged for favorite classroom jobs such as office messenger, paper passer, teacher assistant, or media operator. Tokens can also be used for schoolwide privileges such as a library or study hall pass; a special period (e.g., physical education) with another class; or special responsibilities such as school patrol, cafeteria monitor, or tutor. Higgins and colleagues (2001) used naturally occurring activities and events as backup reinforcers for a token economy in their study (i.e., the students had access to computer games and leisure books). However, play materials, hobby-type games, snacks, television time, allowance, permission to go home or downtown, sports events, and coupons for gifts or special clothing could also be used as backup reinforcers because these objects or items tend to occur in many settings.

If naturally occurring activities and events fail, then backup items not ordinarily present in a particular program can be considered (e.g., pictures of movie or sports stars, CDs or DVDs, magazines, or edibles). Such items should generally be considered only when more naturally occurring activities have proven ineffective. Using the least intrusive and most naturally occurring reinforcers is recommended.

Selection of backup reinforcers should follow consideration of ethical and legal issues, as well as state and local education agency policies. Token reinforcement contingencies that would deny the learner basic needs (e.g., food) or access to personal or privileged information or events (e.g., access to mail, telephone privileges, attending religious services, medical care, etc.) should not be used. Furthermore, general comforts that are associated with basic rights afforded to all citizens should not be used in a token program (e.g., clean clothing, adequate heating, ventilation, hot water).

Establishing a Ratio of Exchange

Initially, the ratio between the number of tokens earned and the price of backup items should be small to provide immediate success for learners. Thereafter, the ratio of exchange should be adjusted to maintain the responsiveness of the participants. Following are several general guidelines for establishing the ratio between earned tokens and the price of backup items:

1. Keep initial ratios low.
2. As token-earning behaviors and income increase, increase the cost of backup items, devalue tokens, and increase the number of backup items.
3. With increased earnings, increase the number of luxury backup items
4. Increase the prices of necessary backup items more than those of luxury items.

Myles and colleagues (1992) provided guidelines for establishing and maintaining a token economy, including the distribution and redemption of tokens. The next section addresses frequently asked questions related to tokens.

What procedure will be used to dispense tokens? If objects such as tally marks or holes punched in a card are selected as the tokens, how the learner will receive them is obvious. If objects such as coupons or poker chips are used, there should be some container for storing the accumulated tokens before they are exchanged for the backup items. Some practitioners have learners construct individual folders or containers for storing their tokens. Another suggestion is to deposit the tokens through cut slots in the plastic tops of coffee cans. With younger learners tokens can be chained to form a necklace or bracelet.

How will the tokens be exchanged? A menu of the backup items should be provided with a given price for each item. Learners can then select from the menu. Many teachers have a table store with all the items displayed (e.g., games, balloons, toys, certificates for privileges). To avoid noise and confusion at shopping time, individual orders can be filled by writing in or checking off the items to be purchased. Those items are then placed in a bag with the order form stapled to the top and are returned to the purchaser. Initially, the store should be open frequently, perhaps twice per day. Lower functioning learners may need more frequent exchange periods. Later, exchange periods might be available only on Wednesdays and Fridays, or only on Fridays. As quickly as possible, token exchange should occur on an intermittent basis.

Writing Procedures to Specify What Happens if Token Requirements Are Not Met

Occasionally, token requirements will not be met for one reason or another. One approach is to nag the individual: "You didn't do your homework. You know your homework must be completed to earn tokens. Why didn't you do it?" A better approach is a matter-of-fact restatement of the contingency: "I'm sorry. You haven't enough tokens to exchange at this time. Try again." It is important to know whether the individual has the skills required to earn tokens. A learner should always be able to meet the response requirements.

What Should Be Done When a Learner Tests the System? How should a practitioner respond when a learner says she doesn't want any tokens or backup items? One approach is to argue, debate, or cajole the learner. A better approach is to say something neutral (e.g., "That is your decision") and then walk away, precluding any argument or debate. In this way a confrontation is avoided, and the occasion remains set for token delivery for the learner. Most learners can and should have input in selecting the backup items, generating the rules for the economy, establishing the price for the backup items, and performing general duties in managing the system. A learner can be a salesperson for the store or a bookkeeper to record who has how many tokens and what items are purchased. When learners are involved and their responsibilities for the economy are emphasized, they are less likely to test the system.

Will the Token Economy Include a Response Cost Procedure? Procedures for including response cost with a token economy were presented in Chapter 15. Most token economies do include a token loss contingency for inappropriate behaviors and rule infractions (Musser et al., 2001). Any behaviors subject to re-

sponse cost should be defined and stated clearly in the rules. Learners need to be aware of what actions will result in token loss and how much the behavior will cost. The more serious the inappropriate behavior is, the greater the token loss should be. Clearly, fighting, acting out, or cheating should result in greater token loss than minor infractions (e.g., out-of-seat behavior or talk-outs). Token loss should never be applied to a behavior if the learner does not have tokens. Students should not be allowed to go into debt, which would likely decrease the reinforcement value of the tokens. A learner should always earn more tokens than she loses.

Field-Testing the System

The final step before actually implementing a token system is to field-test it. For 3 to 5 days token delivery is tallied exactly as if tokens were being earned, but no tokens are actually awarded during the field test. Data from the field test are used for assessment. Are learners actually deficient in the targeted skills? Are some learners demonstrating mastery of behaviors targeted for intervention? Are some learners not receiving tokens? Based on answers to questions such as these, final adjustments in the system can be made. For some learners, more difficult behaviors may need to be defined; others may need less demanding target behaviors. Perhaps more or fewer tokens need to be delivered relative to the price of the backup reinforcers.

Implementing a Token Economy

Initial Token Training

The manner in which initial training is conducted to implement a token economy depends on the functioning level of the learners. For high-functioning learners and those with mild disabilities, initial training might require minimal time and effort and consist primarily of verbal instructions or modeling. Usually the initial token training for these individuals can be accomplished in one 30- to 60-minute session. Three steps are normally sufficient. First, an example of the system should be given. The practitioner might describe the system as follows:

> This is a token and you can earn it by [specify behavior]. I will watch your behavior; and when you accomplish [specify behavior], you will earn a token. Also, as you continue [specify behavior], you will earn more tokens. At [specify time period] you will be able to exchange the tokens you have earned for whatever you want and can afford on this table. Each item is marked with the number of tokens needed for purchase. You can spend only the tokens you have earned. If you want an

item that requires more tokens than you have earned, you will have to save your tokens over several [specify time period].

The second step is to model the procedure for token delivery. For instance, each learner might be directed to emit the specified behavior. Immediately following the occurrence of the behavior, the learner should be praised (e.g., "Enrique, I'm pleased to see how well you are working by yourself!") and the token delivered.

The third step is to model the procedure for token exchange. Learners should be taken to the store and shown the items for purchase. All learners should already have one token, which was acquired during the modeling of token delivery. At this time, several items should be able to be purchased for one token (the price may go up later)—a game, 5 minutes of free time, a pencil-sharpening certificate, or teacher helper privilege. Students should actually use their tokens in this exchange. Lower functioning learners may require several sessions of initial token training before the system is functional for them. Further response prompts may be needed.

Ongoing Token Training

During token reinforcement training, the practitioner and the students should follow the guidelines for effective use of reinforcement (see Chapter 11). For example, tokens should be dispensed contingently and immediately after the occurrence of the desired behavior. Procedures for delivery and exchange should be clear and should be followed consistently. If a booster session is needed to improve student understanding of how tokens are earned and exchanged, practitioners should do so early in the program. Finally, the focus should be on building and increasing desirable behaviors through token delivery rather than decreasing undesirable behaviors through response cost.

As part of the overall training, the behavior analyst may choose to take part in the token economy as well. For example, the analyst could pinpoint a personal behavior to be increased and then model how to act if her performance of that behavior does not meet the criterion to earn a token, how to save tokens, and how to keep track of progress. After 2 to 3 weeks, a revision in the token economy system may be needed. It is usually desirable to have learners discuss behaviors they want to change, the backup items they would like to have available, or the schedule of exchange. If some participants rarely earn tokens, a simpler response or prerequisite skill may be necessary. On the other hand, if some participants always earn all possible tokens, requirements may need to be changed to a more complex skill.

Management Issues During Implementation

Students must be taught how to manage the tokens they earn. For instance, once received, tokens should be placed in a safe, but accessible container so that they are out of the way, but readily available when needed. If the tokens are in clear view and readily accessible, some students might play with them at the expense of performing academic tasks assigned by the teacher. Also, placing the tokens in a secure location reduces the risk of other students counterfeiting or stealing them. Preemptive measures should be taken to ensure that tokens are not easily counterfeited or reachable by anyone other than the recipient. If counterfeiting or stealing occurs, switching to different tokens will help reduce the likelihood of these tokens being exchanged under false pretenses.

Another management issue, however, relates to students' token inventories. Some students may hoard their tokens and not exchange them for backup reinforcers. Other students may try to exchange their tokens for a backup reinforcer, but they lack the requisite number of tokens to do so. Both extremes should be discouraged. That is, students should be required to exchange at least some of their earned tokens periodically, and students without the requisite number of tokens should not be permitted to participate in an exchange. That is, they should not be permitted to buy backup reinforcers on credit.

A final management issue relates to chronic rule breakers or students who test the system at every turn. Practitioners can minimize this situation by (a) ensuring that the token does serve as a generalized conditioned reinforcer, (b) conducting a reinforcer assessment to determine that the backup reinforces are preferred by the students and function as reinforcers, and (c) applying response cost procedures for chronic rule breakers.

Withdrawing the Token Economy

Strategies for promoting generalization and maintenance of target behaviors to settings in which a token or level system is not used should be considered in the design and implementation of a token or level system. Before applying the initial token program, analysts should plan how they will remove the program. One goal of the token program should be to have the descriptive verbal praise that is delivered simultaneously with the token acquire the reinforcing capability of the token. From the beginning, a systematic goal of the token economy should be to withdraw the program. Such an approach, aside from having functional utility for practitioners (i.e., they will not have to issue tokens forever), also has advantages for the learner. For example, if a special education teacher is using a token economy with a student scheduled for full-time placement in a regular fourth grade classroom, the teacher wants to be certain that the student's responses can be maintained in the absence of the token economy. It is unlikely that the student would encounter a similar token system in the general education classroom.

Various methods have been used to withdraw token reinforcers gradually after criterion levels of behavior have been reached. The following six guidelines allow the practitioner to develop, and later withdraw, token reinforcers effectively. First, the token presentation should always be paired with social approval and verbal praise. This should increase the reinforcing effect of the social approval and serve to maintain behaviors after token withdrawal.

Second, the number of responses required to earn a token should be gradually increased. For instance, if a student receives a token initially after reading only one page, he should be required to read more pages later for token delivery.

Third, the duration the token economy is in effect should be gradually decreased. For example, during September the system might be in effect all day; in October the time might be 8:30 A.M. to 12:00 P.M. and 2:00 P.M. to 3:00 P.M.; and in November, 8:30 A.M. to 10:00 A.M. and 2:00 P.M. to 3:00 P.M. In December the times might be the same as those in November, but on only 4 days a week, and so on.

Fourth, the number of activities and privileges that serve as backup items and are likely to be found in the untrained setting should be increased gradually. For example, the analyst should start taking away tangible items in the store that might not be present in the regular classroom. Are edibles available at the store? They are usually not available for reinforcement in regular classrooms. Gradually, items should be introduced that would be common in a regular class (e.g., special award sheets, gold stars, positive notes home).

Fifth, the price of more desirable items should be increased systematically while keeping a very low price on less desirable items for exchange. For example, in a token system with adolescent girls with moderate to severe mental retardation, the price of candy bars and trips to the canteen and grooming aids (e.g., comb, deodorant) was initially about the same. Slowly, the cost of items such as candy bars was increased to such a high level that the girls no longer saved tokens to purchase them. More girls used their tokens to purchase grooming aids, which cost substantially less than candy.

Sixth, the physical evidence of the token should be faded over time. The following sequence illustrates how the physical evidence of the token can be faded.

- Learners earn physical tokens such as poker chips or washers.

- The physical tokens are replaced with slips of paper.

- The slips of paper are replaced with tally marks on an index card that is kept by the learners.

- In a school setting the index card can now be taped to the learner's desk.

- The index card is removed from the learner and is kept by the analyst, but participants can check their balance at any time.

- The analyst keeps tallies, but no checking is allowed during the day. Totals are announced at the end of the day, and then every other day.

- The token system is no longer operative. The behavior analyst does not announce point totals even though they are still kept.

Evaluating the Token Economy

Token economies can be evaluated using any number of reliable, valid, field-tested, best practice designs. Given that most token economy programs are conducted with small groups, we recommend that single-subject evaluation designs be used such that the participant serves as his or her own control. Further, we suggest that social validation data on the target participants and significant others who come into contact with the person be collected before, during, and after token intervention.

Reasons for the Effectiveness of the Token Economy

A token economy is often effective in applied settings for three reasons. First, tokens bridge the time gap between the occurrence of a behavior and delivery of a backup reinforcer. For example, a token may be earned during the afternoon, but the backup reinforcer is not awarded until the next morning. Second, tokens bridge the setting gap between the behavior and the delivery of the backup reinforcer. For instance, tokens earned at school could be exchanged for reinforcers at home, or tokens earned in a general education classroom in the morning could be exchanged in a special education classroom in the afternoon. Finally, as generalized conditioned reinforcers, tokens make the management of motivation less critical for the behavior analyst.

Further Considerations

Intrusive. Token systems can be intrusive. It takes time, energy, and resources to establish, implement, and evaluate token programs. Also, because most natural environments do not reinforce a person's behavior with tokens, careful thought must be given to how to thin the token schedule while simultaneously maintaining performance. In any case, token economy programs can have lots of "moving parts," and practitioners must be prepared to deal with them.

Self-Perpetuating.   A token economy can be an effective procedure for managing behavior, and analysts can be so encouraged by the results that they do not want to remove the system. Learners then continue working for reinforcement that is not normally available in the natural environment.

Cumbersome.   Token economies can be cumbersome to implement, especially if there are multiple participants with multiple schedules of reinforcement. The system may require additional time and effort from the learner and the behavior analyst.

Federal Mandates.   When tokens are introduced within the context of a level system, practitioners should exercise caution that the explicit and uniform requirements for students to earn a specific number of tokens before progressing to the next level does not violate the spirit or intent of federal mandates that call for individualized programs. Scheuermann and Webber (1996) suggested that tokens and other programs embedded within level systems be individualized and that self-management techniques be combined with the level system to increase the likelihood of a successful inclusion program.

Group Contingencies

Thus far in the text we have focused primarily on how contingencies of reinforcement can be applied to change the future frequency of certain behaviors of individual persons. Applied research has also demonstrated how contingencies can be applied to groups, and behavior analysts have increasingly turned their attention toward group contingencies in areas such as leisure activities for adults (Davis & Chittum, 1994), schoolwide applications (Skinner, Skinner, Skinner, & Cashwell, 1999), classrooms (Brantley & Webster, 1993; Kelshaw-Levering, Sterling-Turner, Henry, & Skinner, 2000; Skinner, Cashwell, & Skinner, 2000), and playgrounds (Lewis, Powers, Kelk, & Newcomer, 2002). Each of these applications has shown that group contingencies, properly managed, can be an effective and practical approach to changing

the behavior of many people simultaneously (Stage & Quiroz, 1997).

Definition of a Group Contingency

A **group contingency** is one in which a common consequence (usually, but not necessarily, a reward intended to function as reinforcement) is contingent on the behavior of one member of the group, the behavior of part of the group, or the behavior of everyone in the group. Group contingencies can be classified as dependent, independent, or interdependent (Litow & Pumroy, 1975).

Rationale for and Advantages of Group Contingency

There are a number of reasons for using a group contingency in applied settings. First, it can save time during administration (Skinner, Skinner, Skinner, & Cashwell, 1999). Instead of repeatedly administering a consequence to each member of a group, the practitioner can apply one consequence to all members of the group. From a logistical perspective, a practitioner's workload may be reduced. Group contingencies have been demonstrated to be effective in producing behavior change (Brantley & Webster, 1993). A group contingency can be effective and economical, requiring fewer practitioners or less time to implement.

Another advantage is that a practitioner can use a group contingency in a situation in which an individual contingency is impractical. For example, a teacher attempting to reduce disruptive behaviors of several students might have difficulty administering an individual program for each pupil in the classroom. A substitute teacher, in particular, might find the use of a group contingency a practical alternative because her knowledge of the students' previous histories of reinforcement would be limited, and the group contingency could be applied across a variety of behaviors, settings, or students.

A group contingency can also be used in cases in which the practitioner must resolve a problem quickly, as when serious disruptive behavior occurs. The practitioner might be interested not only in decreasing the disruptive behavior rapidly, but also in building improved levels of appropriate behavior (Skinner et al., 2000).

Furthermore, a practitioner can use a group contingency to capitalize on peer influence or peer monitoring because this type of contingency sets the occasion for peers to act as change agents (Gable, Arllen, & Hendrickson, 1994; Skinner et al., 1999). Admittedly, peer pressure can have a detrimental effect on some people; they may become scapegoats, and negative effects may surface (Romeo, 1998). However, potentially harmful or negative outcomes can be minimized by structuring the contingency elements randomly (Kelshaw-Levering et al., 2000; Poplin & Skinner, 2003).

Practitioners can establish a group contingency to facilitate positive social interactions and positive behavioral supports within the group (Kohler, Strain, Maretsky, & DeCesare, 1990). For example, a teacher might establish a group contingency for a student or a group of students with disabilities. The students with disabilities might be integrated into the general education classroom, and a contingency could be arranged in such a way that the class would be awarded free time contingent on the performance of one or more of the students with disabilities.

Independent Group Contingency Applications

An **independent group contingency** is an arrangement in which a contingency is presented to all members of a group, but reinforcement is delivered only to those group members who meet the criterion outlined in the contingency (see Figure 26.9) Independent group contingencies are frequently combined with contingency contracting and token reinforcement programs because these programs usually establish reinforcement schedules independent of the performance of other members of the group.

Brantley and Webster (1993) used an independent group contingency in a general education classroom to decrease the disruptive behavior of 25 fourth-grade students. After collecting data on off-task behavior, call-outs, and out-of-seat behavior, the teachers posted rules related to paying attention, seeking the teachers' permission before talking, and remaining in their seats. An independent group contingency was established whereby each student could earn a check mark next to his or her name on a list that was posted publicly in the room during any of the intervals that marked the observation periods during the day. When a student emitted an appropriate or prosocial behavior, a check mark was registered. The criterion for earning a reward was increased from four to six check marks over 4 out of 5 days per week.

Results showed that after 8 weeks, the total number of combined disruptions (e.g., off-task behavior, call-outs, and out-of-seat behavior) decreased by over 70%, and some off-task behaviors (e.g., not keeping hands to self) were eliminated completely. The teacher's satisfaction with the approach was positive, and parents reported that they were able to understand the procedures that were in place for their children at school. Brantley and Webster (1993) concluded:

> The independent contingency added structure for students by using clear time intervals and clarified teacher expectations by limiting and operationally defining rules to be followed, monitoring behavior consistently, and setting attainable criteria for students. (p. 65)

Dependent Group Contingency Applications

Under a **dependent group contingency** the reward for the whole group is dependent on the performance of an individual student or small group. Figure 26.10 illustrates the dependent group contingency as a three-term contingency. The contingency operates like this: If an individual (or small group within the total group) performs a behavior to a specific criterion, the group shares the reinforcer. The group's access to the reward depends on the individual's (or small group's) performance. If the individual performs below the criterion, the reward is not delivered. When an individual, or small group, earns a reward for a class, the contingency is sometimes referred to as the **hero procedure.**

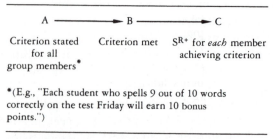

Figure 26.9 An independent group contingency.

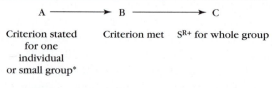

Figure 26.10 A dependent group contingency.

According to Kerr and Nelson (2002), the hero procedure can facilitate positive interactions among students because the class as a whole benefits from the improved behavior of the student targeted for the group contingency.

Gresham (1983) conducted a dependent group contingency study in which the contingency was applied at home, but the reward was delivered at school. In this study an 8-year-old boy who was highly destructive at home (e.g., set fires, destroyed furniture) earned good notes for nondestructive behavior at home. Billy received a good note—a daily report card—each day that no destructive acts took place. Each note was exchangeable for juice, recess, and five tokens at school the next day. After Billy received five good notes, the whole class received a party, and Billy served as the host. Gresham reported that the dependent group contingency reduced the amount of destructive behavior and represented the first application of a dependent group contingency in a combined home–school setting.

Allen, Gottselig, and Boylan (1982) used an interesting variation of the dependent group contingency. In their study eight disruptive third-graders from a class of 29 students served as target students. On the first day of intervention the teacher posted and explained classroom rules for hand raising, leaving a seat, disturbing others, and getting help. Contingent on reduced amounts of disruptive behavior during 5-minute intervals in math and language arts, the class earned 1 extra minute of recess time. If a disruptive behavior occurred during the 5-minute interval, the teacher cited the disrupter for the infraction (e.g., "James, you disturbed Sue") and reset the timer for another 5-minute interval. The teacher also posted the accumulated time on an easel in full view of the class. The results indicated that reduced disruptive behavior occurred under the dependent group contingency.

Interdependent Group Contingencies

An **interdependent group contingency** is one in which all members of a group must meet the criterion of the contingency (individually *and* as a group) before any member earns the reward (Elliot, Busse, & Shapiro, 1999; Kelshaw-Levering et al., 2000; Lewis et al., 2002; Skinner et al., 1999; Skinner et al., 2000). Theoretically, interdependent group contingencies have a value-added advantage over dependent and independent group contingencies insofar as they yoke students to achieve a common goal, thereby capitalizing on peer pressure and group cohesiveness.

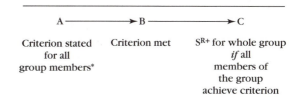

*(E.g., "Each student must complete at least four science projects by the 6th week in the term in order for the class to go on the field trip.")

Figure 26.11 An interdependent group contingency.

The effectiveness of dependent and interdependent group contingencies may be enhanced by randomly arranging some or all of the components of the contingency (Poplin & Skinner, 2003). That is, randomly selected students, behaviors, or reinforcers are targeted for the contingency (Kelshaw-Levering et al., 2000; Skinner et al., 1999). Kelshaw-Levering and colleagues (2000) demonstrated that randomizing either the reward alone or multiple components of the contingency (e.g., students, behaviors, or reinforcers) was effective in reducing disruptive behavior.

Procedurally, an interdependent group contingency can be delivered (a) when the group as a whole meets the criterion, (b) when the group achieves a mean group score, or (c) based on the results of the Good Behavior Game or the Good Student Game. In any case, interdependent group contingencies represent an "all or none" arrangement. That is, all students earn the reward or none of them do (Poplin & Skinner, 2003). Figure 26.11 illustrates the interdependent group contingency as a three-term contingency.

Total Group Meets Criterion

Lewis and colleagues (2002) used the *total group meets criterion* variation to reduce the problem playground behaviors of students enrolled in a suburban elementary school. After a faculty team conducted an assessment of problematic playground behaviors, social skill instruction in the classroom and on the playground was coupled with a group contingency. During social skills instruction, students learned how to get along with friends, cooperate with each other, and be kind. During the group contingency, students earned elastic loops that they could affix to their wrists. After recess, students placed the loops in a can on the teacher's desk. When the can was full, the group earned a reinforcer.

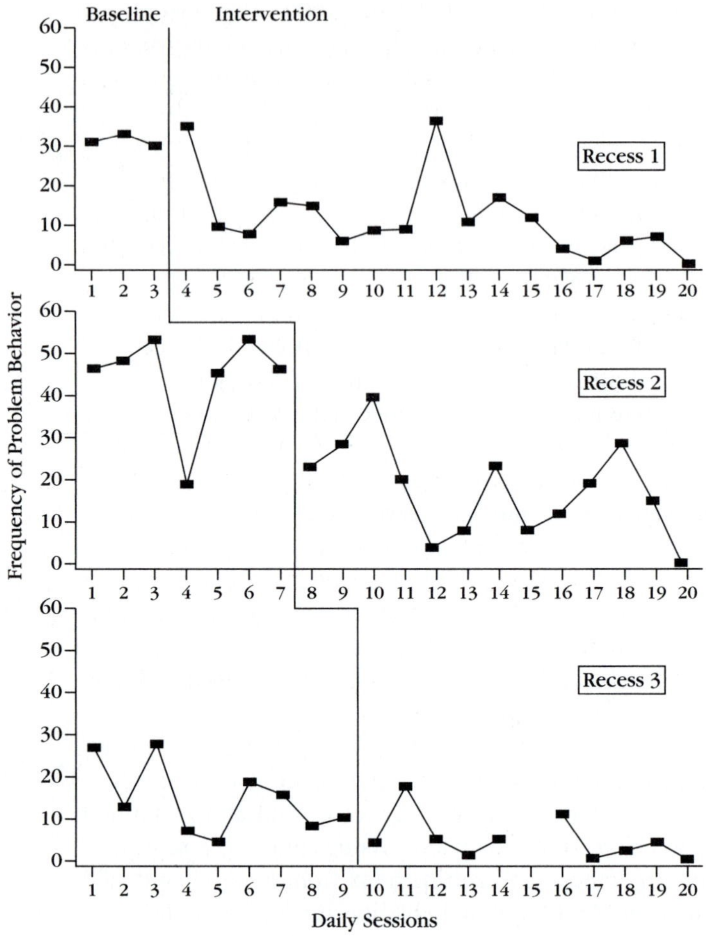

Figure 26.12 Frequency of problem behaviors across recess periods. Recess 1 was composed of second- and fourth-grade students, Recess 2 was composed of first- and third-grade students, and Recess 3 was composed of fifth- and sixth-grade students. Kindergarten students were on the playground across Recess 1 and 2.

From "Reducing Problem Behaviors on the Playground: An Investigation of the Application of School-Wide Positive Behavior Supports" by T. J. Lewis, L. J. Powers, M. J. Kelk, and L. L. Newcomer, 2002, *Psychology in the Schools, 39* (2), p. 186. Copyright 2002 by Wiley Periodicals, Inc. Reprinted by permission of John Wiley & Sons, Inc.

Figure 26.12 shows the results of the social skills plus group contingency intervention across three recess periods during the day.

Group Averaging

Baer and Richards (1980) used a group averaging interdependent group contingency to improve the math and English performance of 5 elementary-aged students. In their study all of the students in a class of 10, including the 5 target students, were told that they would earn 1 extra minute of recess for each point of class improvement beyond the previous weekly average. Also, all students were given a contract stating this same contingency. The extra recess was awarded every day of the following week. For example, if the students' weekly averages exceeded their previous weekly averages by 3 points, they would receive 3 minutes of extra recess every day of the following week. The results of this 22-week study showed that all students improved when the group contingency was in effect. Anecdotal data indicated that all students

participated and received extra recess time during the course of the study.

Good Behavior Game

Barrish, Saunders, and Wolf (1969) used the *Good Behavior Game* to describe an interdependent group contingency in which a group is divided into two or more teams. Prior to the game being played, the teams are told that whichever team has the *fewest* marks against it at the end of the game will earn a privilege. Each team is also told that it can win a privilege if it has fewer than a specified number of marks (a DRL schedule). Data reported by the authors show that this strategy can be an effective method of reducing disruptive behavior in the classroom. When game conditions were in effect during math or reading, talking-out and out-of-seat behaviors occurred at low levels. When game conditions were not in effect, disruptive behaviors occurred at much higher levels (see Figure 26.13).

In the Good Behavior Game teacher attention is directed toward observing and recording occurrences of

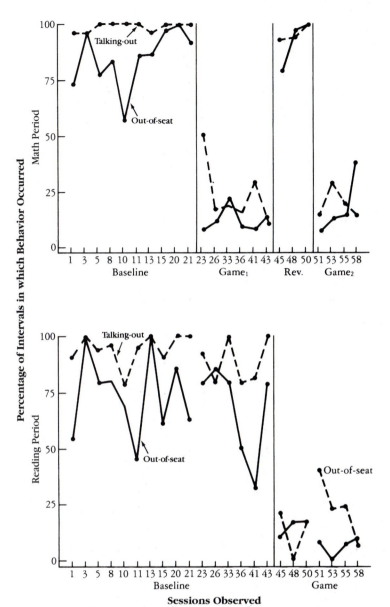

Figure 26.13   Percentage of 1-minute intervals containing talking-out and out-of-seat behaviors in a classroom of 24 fourth-grade children during math and reading periods.

From "Good Behavior Game: Effects of Individual Contingencies for Group Consequences on Disruptive Behavior in a Classroom" by H. H. Barrish, M. Saunders, and M. M. Wolf, 1969, *Journal of Applied Behavior Analysis, 2*, p. 122. Copyright 1969 by the Society for the Experimental Analysis of Behavior, Inc. Reprinted by permission.

misbehavior, with the incentive that if one or more teams have fewer than the criterion number of infractions, a reinforcer is delivered. The advantage of the Good Behavior Game is that competition occurs within teams and against the criterion, not across groups.

Good Student Game

The *Good Student Game* combines an interdependent group contingency (like the Good Behavior Game) with self-monitoring tactics (Babyak, Luze, & Kamps, 2000). Basically, the Good Student Game is intended for implementation during independent seatwork periods when problematic behaviors surface. In the Good Student

Game, the teacher (a) chooses target behaviors to modify, (b) determines goals and rewards, and (c) determines whether group or individual monitoring (or both) will occur.

Students are trained in the Good Student Game using a model-lead-test instructional sequence: students are arranged in clusters of four to five, the target behaviors are defined, examples and nonexamples are provided, practice occurs under teacher supervision, and one or more students record their own or the group's performance. Table 26.2 shows how the Good Student Game compares to the Good Behavior Game. Note that two distinctions relate to target behaviors, the delivery of rewards, and feedback.

Table 26.2   Components of the Good Behavior Game and the Good Student Game

Component	Good Behavior Game	Good Student Game
Organization	Students play in teams.	Students play in teams or as individuals.
Management	Teacher monitors and records behavior.	Students self-monitor and record their behavior.
Target behaviors	Behaviors are stated as rule breaking or rule following.	Behaviors are stated as rule following.
Recording	Teachers records incidents of rule-breaking behaviors as they occur.	Students record rule-following behaviors on a variable-interval schedule.
System of reinforcement	Positive.	Positive.
Criterion for reinforcement	Teams must not exceed a set number of rule-breaking behaviors.	Groups or individuals achieve or exceed a set percentage of rule-following behaviors.
Delivery of reinforcement	Dependent on group performance.	Dependent on individual or group performance.
Feedback	Teacher provides feedback when rule-breaking behaviors occur.	Teacher provides feedback at intervals. Praise and encouragement presented during the game to reinforce positive behaviors.

From "The Good Student Game: Behavior Management for Diverse Classrooms" by A. E. Babyak, G. J. Luze, and D. M. Kamps, 2000, *Intervention in School and Clinic, 35* (2), p. 217. Copyright 2000 by PRO ED, Inc. Reprinted by permission.

Implementing a Group Contingency

Implementing a group contingency requires as much preplanning as any other behavior change procedure. Presented here are six guidelines to follow before and during the application of a group contingency.

Choose an Effective Reward

One of the most important aspects of a group contingency is the strength of the consequence; it must be strong enough to serve as an effective reward. Practitioners are advised to use generalized conditioned reinforcers or reinforcer menus at every opportunity. Both of these strategies individualize the contingency, thereby increasing its power, flexibility, and applicability.

Determine the Behavior to Change and Any Collateral Behaviors That Might Be Affected

Let us suppose a dependent group contingency is established in which a class receives 10 minutes of extra free time, contingent on the improved academic performance of a student with developmental disabilities. Obviously, the teacher will need to collect data on the student's academic performance. However, data might also be collected on the number of positive interactions between the student and her classmates without disabilities within and outside the room. An additional benefit of using a group contingency might be the positive attention and encour-agement that the student with developmental disabilities receives from her classmates.

Set Appropriate Performance Criteria

If a group contingency is used, the persons to whom the contingency is applied must have the prerequisite skills to perform the specified behaviors. Otherwise, they will not be able to meet the criterion and could be subject to ridicule or abuse (Stolz, 1978).

According to Hamblin, Hathaway, and Wodarski (1971), the criteria for a group contingency can be established by using the average-, high-, or low-performance levels of the groups as the standard. In an average-performance group contingency, the mean performance of the group is averaged, and reinforcement is contingent on the achievement of that mean score or a higher score. If the average score for a math exercise were 20 correct problems, a score of 20 or more would earn the reward. In a high-performance group contingency, the high score determines the level of performance needed to receive the reward. If the high score on a spelling test was 95%, only students achieving a score of 95% would receive the reward. In the low-performance group contingency, the low performance score determines the reinforcer. If the low score on a social studies term paper were C, then students with a C or better would receive the reinforcer.

Hamblin and colleagues (1971) indicated that differential effects can be noted with these performance contingencies. Their data show that slow students performed worse under a high-performance contingency, whereas gifted students performed best under this contingency. The data of Hamblin and colleagues suggest that a group contingency can be effective in improving behavior, but it should be applied with the understanding that effectiveness may vary for different members of the group.

Combine with Other Procedures When Appropriate

According to LaRowe, Tucker, and McGuire (1980), a group contingency can be used alone or in combination with other procedures to systematically change performance. The LaRowe and colleagues study was designed to reduce the excessive noise levels in an elementary school lunchroom; their data suggest that differential reinforcement of low rates of behavior (DRL) can be incorporated easily into a group contingency. In situations in which higher levels of group performance are desired, differential reinforcement of high rates of behavior (DRH) can be used. With either DRL or DRH the use of a changing criterion design may facilitate the analysis of treatment effects.

Select the Most Appropriate Group Contingency

The selection of a specific group contingency should be based on the overall programmatic goals of the practitioner, the parents (if applicable), and the participants whenever possible. For instance, if the group contingency is designed to improve the behavior of one person or a small group of individuals, then perhaps a dependent group contingency should be employed. If the practitioner wants to differentially reinforce appropriate behavior, then an independent group contingency should be considered. But if the practitioner wants each individual within a group to perform at a certain level, then an interdependent group contingency should be chosen. Regardless of which group contingency is selected, the ethical issues discussed in Chapter 29 must be addressed.

Monitor Individual and Group Performance

With a group contingency practitioners must observe both group and individual performance. Sometimes the group's performance improves but some members within the group do not improve, or at least do not improve as fast. Some members of the group might even attempt to sabotage the group contingency, preventing the group from achieving the reinforcement. In these cases individual contingencies should be arranged for the saboteurs, in combination with the group contingency.

 # Summary

Contingency Contracting

1. A contingency contract, also called a behavioral contract, is a document that specifies a contingent relation between the completion of a specified behavior and access to, or delivery of, a specified reward such as free time, a letter grade, or access to a favorite activity.

2. Every contract has three major parts: a description of the task, a description of the reward, and the task record. Under task, who, what, when, and how well should be specified. Under reward, who, what, when, and how much should be specified. A task record provides a place for recording the progress of the contract and providing interim rewards.

3. Implementing a contract involves a complex package intervention of related positive and negative reinforcement contingencies and rule-governed behaviors that operate alone and together.

4. Contracting has been used widely in classroom, home, and clinical settings.

5. Contracts have also been used to teach self-management to children.

6. A self-contract is a contingency contract that an individual makes with herself, incorporating a self-selected task and reward as well as self-monitoring of task completion and self-delivery of the reward.

Token Economy

7. A token economy is a behavior change system consisting of three major components: (a) a specified list of target behaviors to be reinforced; (b) tokens or points that participants receive for emitting the target behaviors; and (c) a menu of items or activities, privileges, and backup reinforcers from which participants choose and obtain by exchanging tokens they have earned.

8. Tokens function as generalized conditioned reinforcers because they have been paired with a wide variety of backup reinforcers.

9. A level system is a type of token economy in which participants move up or down a hierarchy of levels

contingent on meeting specific performance criteria with respect to the target behaviors.

10. There are six basic steps in designing a token economy: (1) selecting the tokens that will serve as a medium of exchange; (2) identifying the target behaviors and rules; (3) selecting a menu of backup reinforcers; (4) establishing a ratio of exchange; (5) writing procedures to specify when and how tokens will be dispensed and exchanged and what will happen if the requirements to earn a token are not met; and (6) field testing the system before full-scale implementation.

11. When establishing a token economy, decisions must be made regarding how to begin, conduct, maintain, evaluate, and remove the system.

Group Contingencies

12. A group contingency is one in which a common consequence is contingent on the behavior of one member of the group, the behavior of part of the group, or the behavior of everyone in the group.

13. Group contingencies can be classified as independent, dependent, and interdependent.

14. Six guidelines can assist the practitioner in implementing a group contingency: (a) choose a powerful reward, (b) determine the behavior to change and any collateral behaviors that might be affected, (c) set appropriate performance criteria, (d) combine with other procedures when appropriate, (e) select the most appropriate group contingency, and (f) monitor individual and group performance.

CHAPTER 27

Self-Management

Key Terms

habit reversal	self-evaluation	self-monitoring
massed practice	self-instruction	systematic desensitization
self-control	self-management	

Behavior Analyst Certification Board® BCBA® & BCABA®
Behavior Analyst Task List,© Third Edition

Content Area 9: Behavior Change Procedures

9-27	Use self-management strategies.

Raylene used to be so forgetful, always failing to do the things she needed and wanted to do. Her days were just so busy! But Raylene is beginning to get a handle on her hectic life. For example, this morning a Post-It Note on her clothes closet door reminded her to wear her gray suit for her luncheon meeting. A note on the refrigerator prompted her to take her completed sales report to work. And when Raylene got into her car—sales report in hand and looking sharp in her gray suit—and sat on the library book she'd placed on the driver's seat the night before, the chances were very good that she would return the book to the library that day and avoid another overdue fine.

Almost a year has passed since Daryl collected the last data point for his master's thesis. It's a solid study on a topic Daryl enjoys and believes to be important, but Daryl is struggling mightily to get his thesis written. Although Daryl knows that if he could sit down and write for an hour or two each day his thesis would get written, the size and difficulty of the task are daunting. He wishes his ability to sit and write were half as good as his ability to avoid those behaviors.

 "Some people [self-manage their behavior] frequently and well, others do it rarely and poorly" (Epstein, 1997a, p. 547). Raylene has recently discovered self-management—behaving to alter the occurrence of other behaviors she wants to control—and feels on top of the world. Daryl, in sore need of some self-management, is feeling worse each passing week. This chapter defines self-management, identifies uses for self-management and the benefits of teaching and learning self-management skills, describes a variety of self-management tactics, and offers guidelines for conducting a successful self-management program. We begin with a discussion of the role of the self as a controller of behavior.

The "Self" as Controller of Behavior

A fundamental precept of radical behaviorism is that the causes of behavior are found in the environment (Skinner, 1974). Throughout the evolution of the human species, causal variables selected by the contingencies of survival have been transmitted through genetic endowment. Other causes of behavior can be found in the contingencies of reinforcement that describe behavior–environment interactions during the lifetime of an individual person. What role, then, if any, is left for the *self* to play?

Locus of Control: Internal or External Causes of Behavior

Proximate causes of some behaviors are apparent to anyone observing the events as they unfold. A mother picks up and cuddles her crying infant, and the baby stops cry-

ing. A highway worker leaps off the road when he sees a fast-approaching car not slowed by the warning signs. An angler casts his lure toward the spot where his previous cast produced a strike. A behavior analyst likely would suggest the involvement of escape, avoidance, and positive reinforcement contingencies, respectively, for these events. Although a nonbehaviorist might offer a mentalistic explanation for why the person in each scenario responded as he or she did (e.g., the infant's crying triggered the mother's nurturing instinct), most people, irrespective of their education and orientation, professional and layperson alike, would identify the same antecedent events—a baby cried, a speeding car approached, a fish struck the lure—as functional variables in the three scenarios. An analysis of the three episodes would reveal almost certainly that the immediately preceding events did have functional roles—the crying baby and speeding car as motivating operations that evoked escape or avoidance responses; the biting fish as a powerful reinforcer.

But much human behavior does not immediately follow such obviously related antecedent events. Nonetheless, we humans have a long history of assigning causal status to events that immediately precede behavior. As Skinner (1974) noted, "We tend to say, often rashly, that if one thing follows another, it was probably caused by it—following the ancient precept of *post hoc, ergo propter hoc* (after this, therefore because of this)" (p. 7). When causal variables are not readily apparent in the immediate, surrounding environment, the tendency to point to internal causes of behavior is particularly strong. As Skinner explained:

> The person with whom we are most familiar is ourself; many of the things we observe just before we behave occur within our body, and it is easy to take them as the causes of our behavior. . . . Feelings occur at just the right time to serve as causes of behavior, and they have been cited as such for centuries. We assume that other people feel as we feel when they behave as we behave. (pp. 7, 8)

Why does one college student maintain a regular study schedule from the first week of the semester, while her roommates are out partying night after night? When a group of people joins a weight-loss or a smoking cessation program in which each group member is exposed to the same intervention, why do some people meet their self-determined goals but many others do not? Why does a high school basketball player with limited physical abilities consistently outperform his more athletically gifted teammates? The hardworking student is said to have more willpower than her less studious roommates; the group members who lost weight or stopped smoking are thought to possess more desire than their peers who failed to meet their goals or dropped out; the athlete's superior play is considered a result of his exceptional drive. Although some psychological theories grant causal status to hypothetical constructs such as *willpower, desire,* and *drive,* these explanatory fictions lead to circular reasoning and bring us no closer to understanding the behaviors they claim to explain.[1]

Skinner's Two-Response Conceptualization of Self-Control

Skinner was the first to apply the philosophy and theory of radical behaviorism to actions typically considered to be controlled by the self. In his classic textbook, *Science and Human Behavior,* Skinner (1953) devoted a chapter to self-control.

> When a man controls himself, chooses a course of action, thinks out the solution to a problem, or strives toward an increase in self-knowledge, he is *behaving.* He controls himself precisely as he would control the behavior of anyone else—through the manipulation of variables of which behavior is a function. His behavior in so doing is a proper object of analysis, and eventually it must be accounted for with variables lying outside the individual himself. (pp. 228–229)

Skinner (1953) continued by conceptualizing **self-control** as a two-response phenomenon:

> One response, the *controlling response,* affects variables in such a way as to change the probability of the other, the *controlled response.* The controlling response may manipulate any of the variables of which the controlled response is a function; hence there are a good many different forms of self-control. (p. 231)

Skinner (1953) provided examples of a wide variety of self-control techniques, including using physical restraint (e.g., clapping a hand over one's mouth to prevent yawning at an embarrassing moment), changing the antecedent stimulus (e.g., putting a box of candy out of sight to reduce overeating), and "doing something else" (e.g., talking about another topic to avoid talking about a particular topic), to name a few. Since Skinner's initial list of techniques, a variety of taxonomies and catalogs of self-control tactics have been described (e.g., Agran, 1997; Kazdin, 2001; Watson & Tharp, 2007). All self-control—or self-management—tactics can be operationalized in terms of two behaviors: (a) the target behavior a person wants to change (Skinner's controlled response) and (b) the self-management behavior (Skinner's controlling response) emitted to control the target behavior. For example, consider the following table:

Target Behavior	Self-Management Behavior
• Save money instead of spending it on frivolous items.	• Enroll in a payroll deduction plan.
• Take garbage and recycling cans from garage to the curb on Thursday nights for pickup early Friday morning.	• After backing the car out of the garage for work Thursday morning, pull the trash and recycling cans onto the space in the garage where you will park the car in the evening.
• Ride exercise bike for 30 minutes each evening.	• Make a chart of the minutes you ride, and show it to a coworker each morning.
• Write 20-page paper.	• (1) Outline paper and divide it into five 4-page parts; (2) specify a due date for each part; (3) give roommate five $10 checks made out to a despised organization; (4) on each due date show a completed part of the paper to roommate and get one $10 check back.

A Definition of Self-Management

There is nothing mystical about self-management.[2] As the previous examples show, self-management is simply behavior that a person emits to influence another behavior. But many of the responses a person emits each day affect the frequency of other behaviors. Putting toothpaste on a toothbrush makes it very likely that tooth brushing will occur soon. But we do not think of squeezing toothpaste on a brush as an act of "self-management" just because it alters the frequency of tooth brushing. What gives some responses the special status of self-management? How can we distinguish self-management from other behavior?

Numerous definitions of self-control or self-management have been proposed, many of which are similar to the one offered by Thoresen and Mahoney (1974). They suggested that self-control occurs when, in the "relative absence" of immediate external controls, a person emits a response designed to control another behavior. For example, a man shows self-control if, when home alone and "otherwise free" to do whatever he wants, he forgoes his usual peanuts and beer and instead rides his

---

[1]Explanatory fictions and circular reasoning are discussed in Chapters 1 and 11.

[2]There is also nothing new about self-management. As Epstein (1997) pointed out, many of the self-control techniques outlined by Skinner were described by ancient Greek and Roman philosophers and have appeared in the teachings of many organized religions for millennia (cf. Bolin & Goldberg, 1979; Shimmel, 1977, 1979).

exercise bike for 20 minutes. According to definitions such as Thoresen and Mahoney's, self-control is not involved when immediate and obvious external events set the occasion for or reinforce the controlling response. The man would not be credited with self-control if his wife were there reminding him of his overeating, praising him for riding the exercise bike, and marking his time and mileage on a chart.

But what if the man had asked his wife to prompt, praise, and chart his exercise? Would his having done so constitute a form of self-control? One problem with conceptualizing self-control as occurring only in the absence of "external control" is that it excludes those situations in which the person designs and puts into place the contingencies entailing external control for a behavior he desires to change. An additional problem with the "relative absence of external controls" concept is that it creates a false distinction between internal and external controlling variables when, in fact, all causal variables for behavior ultimately reside in the environment.

Definitions of self-control such as Kazdin's (2001), "those behaviors that a person deliberately undertakes to achieve self-selected outcomes" (p. 303), are more functional for applied behavior analysis. With this definition self-control occurs whenever a person purposely emits behavior that changes the environment in order to modify another behavior. Self-control is considered *purposeful* in the sense that a person labels (or *tacts*) her responses as designed to attain a specified result (e.g., to reduce the number of cigarettes smoked each day).

We define **self-management** as the personal application of behavior change tactics that produces a desired change in behavior. This is an intentionally broad, functional definition of self-management. It encompasses one-time self-management events, such as Raylene's taping a note to her closet door to remind herself to wear her gray suit the next day, as well as complex, long-running self-directed behavior change programs in which a person plans and implements one or more contingencies to change his behavior. It is a functional definition in that the desired change in the target behavior must occur for self-management to be demonstrated.

Self-management is a relative concept. A behavior change program may entail a small degree of self-management or be totally conceived, designed, and implemented by the person. Self-management occurs on a continuum along which the person controls one or all components of a behavior change program. When a behavior change program is implemented by one person (e.g., teacher, therapist, parent) on behalf of another (e.g., student, client, child), the external change agent manipulates motivating operations, arranges discriminative stimuli, provides response prompts, delivers differential consequences, and observes and records the occurrence

or nonoccurrence of the target behavior. Some degree of self-management is involved whenever a person performs (that is to say, controls) any element of a program that changes his behavior.

It is important to recognize that defining self-management as the personal application of behavior change tactics that results in a desired change in behavior does not explain the phenomenon. Our definition of self-management is descriptive only, and then so in a very broad sense. Although self-management tactics can be classified according to their emphasis on a given component of the three- or four-term contingency, or by their structural similarity with a particular principle of behavior (e.g., stimulus control, reinforcement), it is likely that all self-management tactics involve multiple principles of behavior. Thus, when researchers and practitioners describe self-management tactics, they should provide a detailed statement of the exact procedures used. Behavior analysts should not ascribe the effects of self-management interventions to specific principles of behavior in the absence of an experimental analysis demonstrating such relations. Only through such research will a more complete understanding of the mechanisms that account for the effectiveness of self-management be attained.[3]

Terminology: Self-Control or Self-Management?

Although *self-control* and *self-management* often appear interchangeably in the behavioral literature, we recommend that *self-management* be used in reference to a person acting "in some way *in order to* change subsequent behavior" (Epstein, 1997, p. 547, emphasis in original). We have three reasons for making this recommendation. First, *self-control* is an "inherently misleading" term that implies that the ultimate control of behavior lies within the person (Brigham, 1980). Although Skinner (1953) acknowledged that a person could achieve practical control over a given behavior by acting in ways that manipulate variables that affect the frequency of that behavior, he argued that the controlling behaviors themselves are learned from the person's interactions with the environment.

> A man may spend a great deal of time designing his own life—he may choose the circumstances in which he is to live with great care, and he may manipulate his daily environment on an extensive scale. Such activity appears to exemplify a high order of self-determination. But it is also behavior, and we account for it in terms of other

---

[3]For a variety of conceptual analyses of self-control/self-management from a behavioral perspective, see Brigham (1983); Catania (1975, 1976); Goldiamond (1976); Hughes & Lloyd (1993); Kanfer and Karoly (1972); Malott (1984, 1989, 2005a, b); Nelson and Hayes (1981); Newman, Buffington, Hemmes, and Rosen (1996); Rachlin (1970, 1974, 1995); and Watson and Tharp (2007).

variables in the environment and history of the individual. It is these variables which provide the ultimate control. (p. 240)

In other words, the causal factors for "self-control" (i.e., controlling behaviors) are to be found in a person's experiences with his environment. Beginning with the example of a person setting an alarm clock (controlling behavior) so as to get out of bed at a certain time (controlled behavior) and concluding with an impressive instance of self-control by the main character in Homer's *Odyssey,* Epstein (1997) described the origin of self-control as follows:

> As is true of all operants, any number of phenomena might have produced the [controlling] behavior originally: instructions, modeling, shaping, or generative process (Epstein, 1990, 1996), for example. Its occurrence might have been verbally mediated by a self-generated rule ("I'll bet I'd get up earlier if I set an alarm clock"), and that rule, in turn, might have had any number of origins. Odysseus had his men tie him to his mast (controlling behavior) to lower the probability that he would steer toward the Siren's song (controlled behavior). This was an elegant instance of self-control, but it was entirely instruction driven: Circe had told him to do it. (p. 547)

Second, attributing the cause of a given behavior to self-control can serve as an explanatory fiction. As Baum (2005) pointed out, *self-control* "seems to suggest controlling a [separate] self inside or [that there is] a self inside controlling external behavior. Behavior analysts reject such views as mentalistic. Instead they ask, 'What is the behavior that people call "self-control"?'" (p. 191, words in brackets added). Sometimes *self* is synonymous with *mind* and "not far from the ancient notion of homunculus—an inner person who behaves in precisely the ways necessary to explain the behavior of the outer person in whom he dwells" (Skinner, 1974, p. 121).[4]

Third, laypeople and behavioral researchers alike often use *self-control* to refer to a person's ability to "delay gratification" (Mischel & Gilligan, 1964). In operant terms, this connotation of self-control entails responding to achieve a delayed, but larger or higher quality reward instead of acting to obtain an immediate, less-valuable reward (Schweitzer & Sulzer-Azaroff, 1988).[5] Using the same term to refer to a tactic for changing behavior and to a certain type of behavior that may be an

outcome of the tactic is at best confusing and logically faulty. Restricting the use of *self-control* to describe a certain type of behavior may reduce the confusion caused by using *self-control* as the name for both an independent variable and dependent variable. In this sense, self-control can be a possible goal or outcome of a behavior change program irrespective of whether that behavior is the product of an intervention implemented by an external agent or the subject. Thus, a person can use self-management to achieve, among other things, self-control.

Applications, Advantages, and Benefits of Self-Management

In this section we identify four basic applications of self-management and explain the numerous advantages and benefits that accrue to people who use self-management, to practitioners who teach it to others, and to society as a whole.

Applications of Self-Management

Self-management can help a person be more effective and efficient in his daily life, replace bad habits with good ones, accomplish difficult tasks, and achieve personal goals.

Living a More Effective and Efficient Daily Life

Raylene writing notes to herself and placing her library book on her car seat are examples of self-management techniques that can be used to overcome forgetfulness or lack of organization. Most people use simple self-management techniques such as making a shopping list before going to the store or creating "to-do" lists as ways to organize their day; but few probably consider what they are doing to be "self-management." Although many of the most widely used self-management techniques can be considered common sense, a person with an understanding of basic principles of behavior can use that knowledge to apply those common sense techniques more systematically and consistently in her life.

Breaking Bad Habits and Acquiring Good Ones

Many behaviors that we want to do more (or less) often and know that we should do (or not do) are caught in reinforcement traps. Baum (2005) suggested that impulsiveness, bad habits, and procrastination are products of

---

[4]In early biological theory, *homunculus* was a fully formed human being thought to exist inside an egg or spermatozoon.

[5]Behavior that fails to exhibit such self-control is often labeled "impulsive." Neef and colleagues (e.g., Neef, Bicard, & Endo, 2001; Neef, Mace, & Shade, 1993) and Dixon and colleagues (e.g., Binder, Dixon, & Ghezzi, 2000; Dixon et al., 1998; Dixon, Rehfeldt, & Randich, 2003) have developed procedures for assessing impulsiveness and for teaching self-control in the form of tolerance for delayed rewards.

naturally existing *reinforcement traps* in which immediate but smaller consequences have greater influence on our behavior than more significant outcomes that are delayed. Baum gave this description of a reinforcement trap for smoking:

> Acting impulsively leads to a small but relatively immediate reinforcer. The short-term reinforcement for smoking lies in the effects of nicotine and social reinforcers such as appearing grown-up or sophisticated. The trouble with impulsive behavior lies in long-term ill effects. It may be months or years before the bad habit takes its toll in consequences such as cancer, heart disease, and emphysema.
>
> The alternative to impulsiveness, refraining from smoking, also leads to both short-term and long-term consequences. The short-term consequences are punishing but relatively minor and short-lived: withdrawal symptoms (e.g., headaches) and possibly social discomfort. In the long run, however, . . . refraining from smoking reduces the risk of cancer, heart disease, and emphysema; ultimately, it promotes health. (pp. 191–192)

Reinforcement traps are two-sided contingencies that work to promote bad habits while simultaneously working against the selection of behavior that is beneficial in the long-term. Even though we may know the rules describing such contingencies, the rules are difficult to follow. Malott (1984) described weak rules as those with delayed, incremental, or unpredictable outcomes. An example of a hard-to-follow, weak rule is, *I'd better not smoke or I might get cancer someday and die.* Even though the potential consequence—cancer and death—is a major one, it is far off in the future and not a sure thing even then (we all know someone who smoked two packs a day since the age of 15 and lived to be 85), which severely limits its effectiveness as a behavioral consequence. So the rule *Don't smoke or you might get cancer* is hard to follow. The deleterious effect of any one cigarette is small, so small that it is not even noticed. Emphysema and lung cancer are probably years and thousands of puffs away. What will one more puff hurt?

Self-management provides one strategy for avoiding the deleterious effects of reinforcement traps. A person can use self-management tactics to arrange immediate consequences that will counteract the consequences currently maintaining the self-destructive behavior.

Accomplishing Difficult Tasks

Immediate outcomes that bring a person only "infinitesimally closer" to a significant outcome do not control behavior (Malott, 1989, 2005a). Many self-management problems are the result of outcomes that are small, but of cumulative significance.

Malott (2005a) argued that our behavior is controlled by the outcome of each individual response, not by the cumulative effect of a large number of responses.

> The *natural contingency* between a response and its outcome will be *ineffective* if the outcome of each individual response is too small or too improbable, even though the cumulative impact of those outcomes is significant. So, we have trouble managing our own behavior, when each instance of that behavior has only an insignificant outcome, though the outcomes of many repetitions of that behavior will be highly significant. And we have little trouble managing our own behavior, when each instance of that behavior has a significant outcome, though that outcome might be greatly delayed.
>
> Most obese people in the United States know the rule describing that contingency: *If you repeatedly overeat, you will become overweight.* The problem is, knowing the overweight rule does not suppress this one instance of eating that delicious fudge sundae topped with the whipped cream and the maraschino cherry, because a single instance of eating this dessert will cause no significant harm, and will, indeed, taste great. Knowledge of this rule describing the natural contingency exerts little control over gluttony.
>
> But the outcome of our behavior also needs to be probable. Many people have trouble following the buckle-up rule, even though they might get in a serious auto accident as soon as they pull onto the street. Even though the delay between the failure to buckle up and the accident could be only a few seconds, they fail to buckle up because the probability of the accident is so low. However, if they were driving in a dangerous auto race or a dangerous stunt-driving demonstration, they would always buckle up, because the probability of a serious accident would be fairly high. (pp. 516–517)

Just as a person who smokes another cigarette or eats just one more hot fudge sundae cannot detect that lung cancer or obesity is a noticeably closer outcome, graduate student Daryl does not perceive that writing one more sentence brings him closer to his long-term goal of a completed master's thesis. Daryl is capable of writing one more sentence but, like many of us, he often has trouble getting started and working steadily on difficult tasks where each response produces little or no apparent change in the size of the remaining task. He procrastinates.

Applying self-management to this type of performance problem involves designing and implementing one or more contrived contingencies to compete with the ineffective natural contingencies. The self-management contingency provides immediate consequences or short-term outcomes for each response or small set of responses. These contrived consequences increase the frequency of the target responses, which over time produce the cumulative effects necessary to complete the task.

Achieving Personal Goals

People can use self-management to achieve personal goals, such as learning to play a musical instrument, learning a foreign language, running a marathon, sticking to a schedule of daily yoga sessions (Hammer-Kehoe, 2002), or simply taking some time each day to relax (Harrell, 2002) or listen to enjoyable music (Dams, 2002). For example, a graduate student who wanted to become a better guitarist used self-management to increase the time he practiced scales and chords (Rohn, 2002). He paid a $1 fine to a friend for each day that he failed to practice playing scales and chords for a criterion number of minutes before going to bed. Rohn's self-management program also included several contingencies based on the Premack principle (see Chapter 11). For example, if he practiced scales (a low-frequency behavior) for 10 minutes, he could play a song (a high-frequency behavior).

Advantages and Benefits of Self-Management

A dozen potential advantages and benefits accrue to people who learn to use self-management skills and to practitioners who teach such skills to their clients and students.

Self-Management Can Influence Behaviors Not Accessible to External Change Agents

Self-management can be used to change behaviors with topographies that make them inaccessible to observation by others. Behaviors such as thoughts of self-doubt, obsessive thoughts, and feelings of depression are private events for which a self-managed treatment approach may be needed (e.g., Kostewicz, Kubina, & Cooper, 2000; Kubina, Haertel, & Cooper, 1994).

Even publicly observable target behaviors are not always emitted in settings and situations accessible to an external change agent. Sometimes the behavior a person wishes to change must be prompted, monitored, evaluated, or reinforced or punished on a day-to-day or even minute-to-minute basis in all of the situations and environments that the person encounters. Even though a person enrolls in a behavior change program planned and directed by others, most successful smoking, weight-loss, exercise, and habit-reversal programs rely heavily on participants using various self-management techniques when they are away from the treatment setting. Many behavior change goals brought to clinicians pose the same challenge: How can an effective contingency be arranged that follows the client at all times wherever she goes? For example, target behaviors designed to increase a secretary's self-esteem and assertiveness can be identified and practiced in the therapist's office, but implementation of an active contingency in the workplace is apt to require self-management techniques.

External Change Agents Often Miss Important Instances of Behavior

In most education and treatment settings, particularly in large group situations, many important responses go unnoticed by the person responsible for applying behavior change procedures. Classrooms, for example, are especially busy places where desired behaviors by students often go unnoticed because the teacher is engaged with other tasks and students. As a result, students invariably miss opportunities to respond, or they respond and receive no feedback because, in a behavioral sense, the teacher is not there. However, students who have been taught to evaluate their own performance and provide their own feedback in the form of self-delivered rewards and error correction, including seeking assistance and praise from their teacher when needed (e.g., Alber & Heward, 2000; Bennett & Cavanaugh, 1998; Olympia, Sheridan, Jenson, & Andrews, 1994), are not dependent on the teacher's direction and feedback for every learning task.

Self-Management Can Promote the Generalization and Maintenance of Behavior Change

A behavior change that (a) continues after treatment has ended, (b) occurs in relevant settings or situations other than the one(s) in which it was learned originally, or (c) spreads to other related behaviors has generality (Baer, Wolf, & Risley, 1968). Important behavior changes without such generalized outcomes must be supported indefinitely by continued treatment.[6] As soon as the student or client is no longer in the setting in which a behavior change was acquired, she may no longer emit the desired response. Certain aspects of the original treatment environment, including the person (teacher, parent) who administered the teaching program, may have become discriminative stimuli for the newly learned behavior, enabling the learner to discriminate the presence or absence of certain contingencies across settings. Generalization to nontreatment environments is also hampered when the naturally existing contingencies in those settings do not provide reinforcement for the target behavior.

---

[6]Producing generalized behavior change is a defining goal of applied behavior analysis and the focus of Chapter 28.

Such challenges to achieving generalized outcomes may be overcome if the learner has self-management skills. Baer and Fowler (1984) posed and answered a pragmatic question related to the problem of promoting the generalization and maintenance of newly learned skills.

> What behavior change agent can go with the student to every necessary lesson, at all times, to prompt and reinforce every desirable form of the behavior called for by the curriculum? The student's own "self" can always meet these specifications. (p. 148)

A Small Repertoire of Self-Management Skills Can Control Many Behaviors

A person who learns how to apply a few self-management tactics can control a potentially unlimited range of behaviors. For example, self-monitoring—observing and recording one's own behavior—has been used to increase on-task behavior (e.g., Blick & Test, 1987), academic productivity and accuracy (e.g., Maag, Reid, & DiGangi, 1993), employee productivity and job success (e.g., Christian & Poling, 1997), and independence (e.g., Dunlap, Dunlap, Koegel, & Koegel, 1991), and to decrease undesired behaviors such as habits or tics (e.g., Koegel & Koegel, 1991).

People with Diverse Abilities Can Learn Self-Management Skills

People of wide-ranging ages and cognitive abilities have successfully used self-management tactics. Preschoolers (e.g., Sainato, Strain, Lefebvre, & Rapp, 1990; DeHaas-Warner, 1992), typically developing students from primary grades through high school (e.g., Sweeney, Salva, Cooper, & Talbert-Johnson, 1993), students with learning disabilities (e.g., Harris, 1986), students with emotional and behavior disorders (e.g., Gumpel & Shlomit, 2000), children with autism (e.g., Koegel, Koegel, Hurley, & Frea, 1992; Newman, Reinecke, & Meinberg, 2000), and children and adults with mental retardation and other developmental disabilities (e.g., Grossi & Heward, 1998) have all used self-management successfully. Even college professors are capable of using self-management to improve their performance (Malott, 2005a)!

Some People Perform Better under Self-Selected Tasks and Performance Criteria

Most studies that have compared self-selected and other-selected reinforcement contingencies have found that under certain conditions self-selected contingencies can be as effective in maintaining behavior as contingencies determined by others (e.g., Felixbrod & O'Leary, 1973, 1974; Glynn, Thomas, & Shee, 1973). However, some studies have found better performance with self-selected

work tasks and consequences (e.g., Baer, Tishelman, Degler, Osnes, & Stokes, 1992; Olympia et al., 1994; Parsons, Reid, Reynolds, & Bumgarner, 1990). For example, in three brief experiments with a single student, Lovitt and Curtiss (1969) found pupil-selected rewards and contingencies to be more effective than teacher-selected performance standards. In the first phase of Experiment 1, the subject, a 12-year-old boy in a special education classroom, earned a teacher-specified number of minutes of free time based on the number of math and reading tasks he completed correctly. In the next phase of the study, the student was allowed to specify the number of correct math and reading items needed to earn each minute of free time. During the final phase of the study the original teacher-specified ratios of academic production to reinforcement were again in effect. The student's median academic response rate during the self-selected contingency phase was 2.5 correct responses per minute (math and reading tasks reported together), compared to correct rates of 1.65 and 1.9 in the two teacher-selected phases.

An experiment by Dickerson and Creedon (1981) employed a yoked-control (Sidman, 1960/1988) and between-group comparison experimental design with 30 second- and third-graders and found that pupil-selected standards resulted in significantly higher academic production of both reading and math tasks. Both the Lovitt and Curtiss and the Dickerson and Creedon studies demonstrated that self-selected reinforcement contingencies *can* be more effective than teacher-selected contingencies. However, research in this area also shows that simply letting children determine their own performance standards does not guarantee high levels of performance; some studies have found that children select too-lenient standards when given the opportunity (Felixbrod & O'Leary, 1973, 1974). But interestingly, in a study of student-managed homework teams by Olympia and colleagues (1994), although students assigned to teams who could select their own performance goals chose more lenient accuracy criteria than the 90% accuracy criterion required of students on the teams that worked toward teacher-selected goals, the overall performance of the student-selected-goal teams was slightly higher than that of the teams working toward teacher-selected goals. More research is needed to determine the conditions under which students will self-select and maintain appropriate standards of performance.

People with Good Self-Management Skills Contribute to More Efficient and Effective Group Environments

The overall effectiveness and efficiency of any group of people who share a working environment is limited when a single person is responsible for monitoring, supervising, and providing feedback for the performance of each group member. When individual students, teammates, band members, or employees have self-management skills that enable them to work without having to rely on the teacher, coach, band director, or shift manager for every task, the overall performance of the entire group or organization improves. In the classroom, for example, teachers traditionally have assumed full responsibility for setting performance criteria and goals for students, evaluating students' work, delivering consequences for those performances, and managing students' social behavior. The time required for these functions is considerable. To the extent that students can self-score their work, provide their own feedback using answer keys or self-checking materials (Bennett & Cavanaugh, 1998; Goddard & Heron, 1998), and behave appropriately without teacher assistance, the teacher is freed to attend to other aspects of the curriculum and perform other instructional duties (Mitchem, Young, West, & Benyo, 2001).

When Hall, Delquadri, and Harris (1977) conducted observations of elementary classrooms and found low levels of active student response, they surmised that higher rates of academic productivity might actually be punishing to teachers. Even though there is considerable evidence linking high rates of student opportunity to respond with academic achievement (e.g., Ellis, Worthington, & Larkin, 2002; Greenwood, Delquadri, & Hall, 1984; Heward, 1994), in most classrooms generating more student academic responses results in the teacher having to spend time grading papers. The time savings produced by students with even the most simple self-management skills can be significant. In one study a class of five elementary special education students completed as many arithmetic problems as they could during a 20-minute session each day (Hundert & Batstone, 1978). When the teacher graded the papers, an average of 50.5 minutes was required to prepare and conduct the session and score and record each student's performance. When the students scored their own papers, the total teacher time needed to conduct the arithmetic period was reduced to an average of 33.4 minutes, resulting in a greater than 50% savings of teacher time.

Teaching Students Self-Management Skills Provides Meaningful Practice for Other Areas of the School Curriculum

When students learn to define and measure behavior and to graph, evaluate, and analyze their own responses, they are practicing various math and science skills in a relevant way. When students are taught how to conduct self-experiments such as using A-B designs to evaluate their self-management projects, they receive meaningful practice in logical thinking and scientific method (Marshall & Heward, 1979; Moxley, 1998).

Self-Management Is an Ultimate Goal of Education

When asked to identify what education should accomplish for its students, most people—educators and laypeople alike—include in their reply the development of independent, self-directed people who are capable of behaving appropriately and constructively without the supervision of others. John Dewey (1939), one of this country's most influential educational philosophers, said that "the ideal aim of education is the creation of self-control" (p. 75). A student's ability to be self-directed, with the teacher as a guide or facilitator, and his ability to evaluate his own performance have long been considered cornerstones of humanistic education (Carter, 1993).

As Lovitt (1973) observed more than 30 years ago, the fact that systematic instruction of self-management skills is *not* a regular part of most schools' curricula is a paradox because "one of the expressed objectives of the educational system is to create individuals who are self-reliant and independent" (p. 139).

Although self-control is a social skill expected and valued by society, it is seldom addressed directly by the school curriculum. Teaching self-management as an integral part of the curriculum requires that students learn a fairly sophisticated sequence of skills (e.g., Marshall & Heward, 1979; McConnell, 1999). However, systematic teaching of self-management skills, if successful, is worthy of the effort required; students will have an effective means of dealing with situations in which there is little, if any, external control. Materials and lesson plans are available that help students become independent, self-directed learners (e.g., Agran, 1997; Daly & Ranalli, 2003; Young, West, Smith, & Morgan, 1991). Box 27.1 describes free software programs children can use to create self-management tools for use in school and at home.

Self-Management Benefits Society

Self-management serves two important functions for society (Epstein, 1997). First, citizens with self-management skills are more likely to fulfill their potential and make greater contributions to society. Second, self-management helps people behave in ways (e.g., purchasing fuel-efficient automobiles, taking public transportation) that forgo immediate reinforcers that are correlated with devastating outcomes that are so long deferred that only future generations will experience them (e.g., depletion of natural resources and global warming). People who have learned self-management techniques that help them to save resources, recycle, and burn less fossil fuel help create a better world for everyone. Self-management skills can provide people with the means of meeting the well-intentioned but difficult-to-follow rule, *Think globally but act locally.*

Box 27.1
Self-Management Software for Children

KidTools, KidSkills, and StrategyTools are software programs that help children create and use a variety of self-management tactics, organizational skills, and learning strategies. The programs enable children to take responsibility for changing and managing their own social and academic behaviors. eKidTools and eKidSkills are designed for children ages 7 to 10; iKidTools and iKidSkills are designed for children ages 11 to 14; Strategy Tools includes enhanced self-management and learning strategy tools, transition planning tools, and self-training modules for secondary students. All three programs feature easy-to-complete templates that let children be as independent as possible in identifying personal behaviors or academic learning needs, selecting a self-management tool to support the task, developing the steps of their personalized plan, and printing the tool for immediate use in the classroom or at home. The remainder of this essay provides additional information on the KidTools and KidSkills programs.

KidTools

The KidTools program supports children's self-management skills to identify behaviors, make plans, and monitor implementation of the plans. KidTools includes self-management interventions for three types, or levels, of control. In all three levels, there is an emphasis on what children say and think to themselves as they execute their behavior change plans.

External control procedures may be necessary to establish control over problematic behaviors before the child moves to shared control or self-control interventions. In these procedures, the adult provides direction and structure for appropriate behaviors. KidTools available for this level of intervention are point cards.

Shared control techniques provide a transition step for encouraging the child to develop self-control. There is an emphasis on problem solving and making plans to change or learn a behavior. The child and adult jointly participate in these procedures. KidTools available for this level of intervention are contracts, make-a-plan cards, and problem-solving planning tools.

Internal control techniques assist children through cues and structure provided by a variety of self-monitoring procedures.

KidSkills

KidSkills helps children be successful in school by getting organized, completing tasks, and using learning strategies. KidSkills provides computer-generated templates for getting organized, learning new stuff, organizing new information, preparing for tests, doing homework, and doing projects. KidSkills programs are complementary to the KidTools programs and operate the same in terms of selecting tools, entering content, recordkeeping, and adult supports.

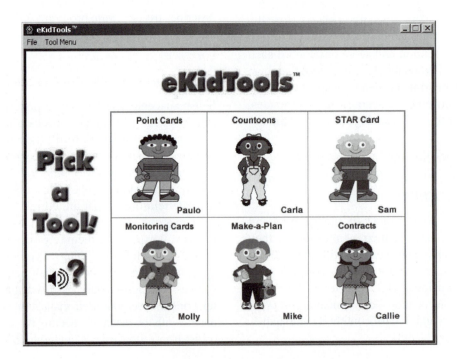

Tool Resources and Skill Resources

In addition to the computer programs for children, information databases about the tools and strategies are provided for parents and teachers who assist children with self-management and learning strategies. Each database includes guidelines and tips for each procedure, steps for implementation, age-appropriate examples for children, troubleshooting tips, and references to related resources. The user can navigate through the information, return to a menu to select new strategies, or search the entire database using the Find function.

Rationale for KidTools and KidSkills

KidTools and KidSkills encourage children to express their social and academic behaviors in positive terms. They focus on doing positive behaviors and being successful, rather than stopping negative behaviors and failure. For example, they decide "I will use my inside voice" rather than be reminded "Don't talk loudly in class." Children are taught organizational and learning strategies that can be used in general and special settings. The computerized tools serve as bridges to support students in behaving and learning. This form of assistive technology works because it provides direct instruction as well as scaffolds to support learning at the "right time, right form, and right place."

For these materials to be successful, teachers or parents must first provide instruction in behavior change techniques and self-monitoring. Children need to understand the concept of a behavior as something they do or think, be able to name behaviors, understand how to monitor whether behaviors occur or not, and assume some level of responsibility for their own behaviors. Children need to learn how and when to use organizational and learning strategies and to use self-monitoring techniques in applying the strategies across settings.

Helping Children Use KidTools and KidSkills

Children will need to be taught to use self-talk cues and inner speech to give themselves directions. Each self-management procedure in KidTools has variations that will need to be taught, demonstrated, and practiced with children before they can be used independently. The organizational and learning strategies in KidSkills are generic but require teaching, practice, and teacher help in applying the tools prior to independent use. Once children know the prerequisite skills, the computer program can be used with a minimal amount of teacher help. Ongoing support by the teacher or parent will ensure that the process remains effective and positive for children.

A teacher can use the following steps to help children learn to use KidTools and KidSkills.

Discuss behavioral and task expectations. The teacher can use setting or task demands to initiate discussion about expectations. Students can verbalize what they must do to be successful and identify challenges in meeting the expectations. Students should be able to demonstrate the behaviors and do the tasks prior to using the tools.

Introduce the software tools. The tool programs can be introduced to the whole class using a computer and

projection device. The teacher can demonstrate the menu of available tools and highlight a variety of them, including how to navigate the program, how to enter content into the tools, and how to save and print out completed tools.

Model and demonstrate use of the tools. Using preselected tools for specific purposes, the teacher can solicit student input while demonstrating how the software works. The finished tools can be displayed and printed out for students to have copies. A discussion of their actual use follows.

Provide guided practice. Using available computer equipment, in a lab for group practice or in the classroom for independent or small group practice, the teacher can guide and oversee student development of tools. It will be helpful to have students verbalize their content prior to filling in the tool. The purpose of the guided practice step is to ensure correct software usage.

Provide independent practice. The teacher can help students identify authentic uses for the tools and provide opportunities for creating and using tools. During independent usage, teachers should provide encouragement and reinforcement for student tool usage and successful outcomes in supervised situations.

Facilitate generalization. The teacher can help students identify authentic needs and uses of tools across school and home environments. The teacher can assist by prompting tool usage, problem solving, and communicating with other teachers and parents about the procedures.

Programs Available Free

The programs can be downloaded at no cost in Windows or Macintosh versions from the KTSS Web site at http://kidtools.missouri.edu. Training modules for teachers with video demonstrations and practice materials can also be downloaded at this site. All three programs are also available on CD-ROM at cost from Instructional Materials Laboratory at www.iml.coe.missouri.edu. The KTSS programs have been developed with partial funding by the U.S. Department of Education, Office of Special Education Programs.

Self-Management Helps a Person Feel Free

Baum (2005), noted that people caught in reinforcement traps who recognize the contingency between their addictive behavior, impulsiveness, or procrastination and the eventual consequence that is likely to occur as a result of that behavior are unhappy and do not feel free. However, "Someone who escapes from a reinforcement trap, like someone who escapes from coercion, feels free and happy. Ask anyone who has kicked an addiction" (p. 193).

Ironically, a person who skillfully uses self-management techniques derived from a scientific analysis of behavior–environment relations predicated on an assumption of determinism is more likely to feel free than is a person who believes that her behavior is a product of free will. In discussing the apparent disconnect between philosophical determinism and self-control, Epstein (1997) compared two people: one who has no self-management skills and one who is very skilled at managing his own affairs.

> First, consider the individual who has no self-control. In Skinner's view, such a person falls prey to all immediate stimuli, even those that are linked to delayed punishment. Seeing a chocolate cake, she eats it. Handed a cigarette, she smokes it. . . . She may make plans, but she has no ability to carry them out, because she is entirely at the mercy of proximal events. She is like a sailboat blowing uncontrollably in a gale. . . .

> At the other extreme, we have a skillful self-manager. He, too, sets goals, but he has ample ability to meet them. He has skills to set dangerous reinforcers aside. He identifies conditions that affect his behavior and alters them to suit him. He takes temporally remote possibilities into account in setting his priorities. The wind is blowing, but he sets the boat's destination and directs it there.

> These two individuals are profoundly different. The first is being controlled in almost a linear fashion by her immediate environment. The second is, in a nontrivial sense, controlling his own life. . . .

> The woman who lacks self-control skills *feels controlled.* She may believe in free will (in fact, in our culture, it's a safe bet that she does) but her own life is out of control. A belief in free will only exacerbate her frustration. She should be able to *will* herself out of any jam, but "willpower" proves to be highly unreliable. In contrast, the self-manager feels that *he is in control.* Ironically, like Skinner, he may believe in determinism, but he not only feels that he is in control, he is in fact exercising considerably more control over his life than our impulsive subject. (p. 560, emphasis in original)

Self-Management Feels Good

A final, but by no means trivial, reason for learning self-management is that being in control of one's life feels good. A person who arranges her environment in purposeful ways that support and maintain desirable behaviors will not only be more productive than she would otherwise be, but will also feel good about herself. Seymour (2002) noted her personal feelings about a self-management intervention she implemented with the objective of running for 30 minutes three times per week.

> The guilt I had been feeling for the past $2\frac{1}{2}$ years had been burning strong within me. [As a former scholarship softball player] I used to exercise 3 hours per day (6 days per week) because that exercise paid for my schooling. . . . But now the contingencies were missing, and my exercising had gone completely down the tubes. Since the start of my project, I've run 15 out of the 21 times; so I've gone from 0% during baseline to 71% during my intervention. I'm happy with that. Because the intervention's successful, the guilt I have felt for the past $2\frac{1}{2}$ years has been lifted. I have more energy and my body feels new and strong. It's amazing what a few contingencies can do to improve the quality of life in a big way. (p. 7–12)

Antecedent-Based Self-Management Tactics

In this and the three sections that follow we describe some of the many self-management tactics that behavioral researchers and clinicians have developed. Although no standard set of labels or classification scheme for self-management tactics has emerged, the techniques are often presented according to their relative emphasis on antecedents or consequences for the target behavior. An antecedent-based self-management tactic is one whose primary feature is the manipulation of events or stimuli antecedent to the target (controlled) behavior. Sometimes lumped under general terms such as *environmental planning* (Bellack & Hersen, 1977; Thoresen & Mahoney, 1974) or *situational inducement* (Martin & Pear, 2003), antecedent-based approaches to self-management encompass a wide range of tactics, including the following:

- Manipulating motivating operations to make a desired (or undesired) behavior more (or less) likely

- Providing response prompts

- Performing the initial steps of a behavior chain to ensure being confronted later with a discriminative stimulus that will evoke the desired behavior

- Removing the materials required for an undesired behavior

- Limiting an undesired behavior to restricted stimulus conditions

- Dedicating a specific environment for a desired behavior

Manipulating Motivating Operations

People with an understanding of the dual effects of motivating operations can use that knowledge to their advantage when attempting to self-manage their behavior. A motivating operation (MO) is an environmental condition or event that (a) alters the effectiveness of some stimulus, object, or event as a reinforcer and (b) alters the current frequency of all behaviors that have been reinforced by that stimulus, object, or event in the past. An MO that increases the effectiveness of a reinforcer and has an evocative effect on behaviors that have produced that reinforcer is called an establishing operation (EO); an MO that decreases the effectiveness of a reinforcer and has an abative (i.e., weakening) effect on the frequency of behaviors that have produced that reinforcer is called an abolishing operation (AO).[7]

The general strategy for incorporating an MO into a self-management intervention is to behave in a way (controlling behavior) that creates a certain state of motivation that, in turn, increases (or decreases as desired) the subsequent frequency of the target behavior (controlled behavior). Imagine that you have been invited to dinner at the house of someone known to be a first-rate cook. You would like to obtain maximum enjoyment from what promises to be a special meal but are worried you will not be able to eat everything. By purposively skipping lunch (controlling behavior), you create an EO that would increase the likelihood of your being able to enjoy the evening meal from appetizer through dessert (controlled behavior). Conversely, eating a meal just before going grocery shopping (controlling behavior) could serve as an AO that decreases the momentary value of ready-to-eat foods with high sugar and fat content as reinforcers and results in purchasing fewer such items at the supermarket (controlled behavior).

Providing Response Prompts

Creating stimuli that later function as extra cues and reminders for desired behaviors is one of the simplest, most effective, and most widely applied self-management techniques. Response prompts can take a wide variety of forms (e.g., visual, auditory, textual, symbolic), be permanent for regularly occurring events (e.g., entering "Put

---

[7]Motivating operations are described in detail in Chapter 16.

garbage out tonight!" each Thursday on one's calendar or PDA), or be one-time affairs such as when Raylene wrote, "gray suit today" on a Post-It Note and attached it to her closet door where she was sure to see it when dressing for work in the morning. Dieters often put pictures of overweight people, or perhaps even unattractive pictures of themselves, on the refrigerator door, near the ice cream, in the cupboard—anyplace where they might look for food. Seeing the pictures may evoke other controlling responses, such as moving away from the food, phoning a friend, going for a walk, or marking a point on an "I Didn't Eat It!" chart.

The same object can be used as a generic response prompt for various behaviors, such as putting a rubber band around the wrist as a reminder to do a certain task at some later time. This form of response prompt, however, will be ineffective if the person is unable later to remember what specific task the physical cue was intended to prompt. Engaging in some self-instruction when "putting on" a generic response prompt may help the person recall the task to be completed when seeing the cue later. For example, one of the authors of this text uses a small carabineer he calls a "memor-ring" as a generic re-

sponse prompt. When the thought of an important task that can only be completed in another setting later in the day occurs to him, he clips the carabineer to a belt loop or the handle of his briefcase and "activates the memor-ring" by stating the target task three times to himself (e.g., "borrow Nancy's journal at Arps Hall," "borrow Nancy's journal at Arps Hall," "borrow Nancy's journal at Arps Hall"). When he sees the "memor-ring" in the relevant setting later, it almost always functions as an effective response prompt for completing the targeted task.

Cues can also be used to prompt the occurrence of a behavior the person wants to repeat in a variety of settings and situations. In this case, the person might salt his environment with supplemental response prompts. For example, a father who wants to increase the number of times he interacts with and praises his children might put ZAP! cues like those shown in Figure 27.1 in various places around the house where he will see them routinely—on the microwave, on the TV remote control, as a bookmark. Every time he sees a ZAP! cue, the father is reminded to make a comment or ask a question of his child, or to look for some positive behavior for which he can provide attention and praise.

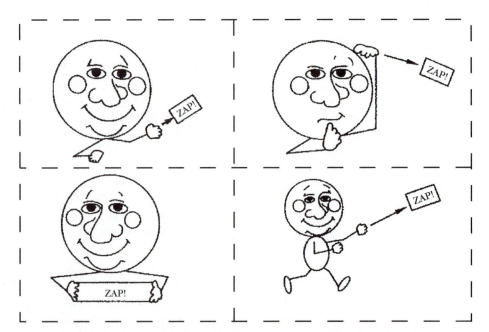

Instructions: Cut out these ZAP! cues and place them in conspicuous locations throughout your home or apartment, such as the refrigerator, bathroom mirror, TV remote control, and the door to your child's bedroom. Each time you see a ZAP cue, you'll be reminded to do one of your self-selected target behaviors.

Figure 27.1   Contrived cues used by parents to remind themselves to emit self-selected parenting behaviors.

Originally developed by Charles Novak. From *Working with Parents of Handicapped Children* by W. L. Heward, J. C. Dardig, and A. Rossett, 1979, p. 26, Columbus, OH: Charles E. Merrill. Copyright 1979 by Charles E. Merrill. Reprinted by permission.

Other people can also provide supplemental response prompts. For example, Watson and Tharp (2007) described the self-management procedure used by a man who had been off cigarettes for about 2 months and wanted to stop smoking permanently.

> He had stopped several times in the past, but each time he had gone back to smoking. He had been successful this time because he had identified those situations in which he had relapsed in the past and had taken steps to deal with them. One of the problem situations was being at a party. The drinks, the party atmosphere, and the feeling of relaxation represented an irresistible temptation to "smoke just a few," although in the past this usually led to a return to regular smoking. One night, as the man and his wife were getting ready to go out to a party, he said, "You know, I am really going to be tempted to smoke there. Will you do me a favor? If you see me bumming a cigarette from someone, remind me of how much the kids want me to stay off cigarettes." (pp. 153–154)

Performing the Initial Steps of a Behavior Chain

Another self-management tactic featuring manipulation of antecedent events entails behaving in a manner that ensures being confronted later with a discriminative stimulus (S^D) that reliably evokes the target behavior. Although operant behavior is selected and maintained by its consequences, the occurrence of many behaviors can be controlled on a moment-to-moment basis by the presentation or removal of discriminative stimuli.

A self-management tactic more direct than adding response prompts to the environment is to behave in such a way so that your future behavior makes contact with a powerful discriminative stimulus for the desired behavior. Many tasks consist of chains of responses. Each response in a behavior chain produces a change in the environment that serves both as a conditioned reinforcer for the response that preceded it and as an S^D for the next response in the chain (see Chapter 20). Each response in a behavior chain must occur reliably in the presence of its related discriminative stimulus for the chain to be completed successfully. By performing part of a behavioral chain (the self-management response) at one point in time, a person has changed her environment so that she will be confronted later with an S^D that will evoke the next response in the chain and will lead to the completion of the task (the self-managed response). Skinner (1983b) provided an excellent example of this tactic.

> Ten minutes before you leave your house for the day you hear a weather report: It will probably rain before you return. It occurs to you to take an umbrella (the sentence means quite literally what it says: The behavior of taking an umbrella occurs to you), but you are not yet able to execute it. Ten minutes later you leave without the umbrella. You can solve that kind of problem by executing as much of the behavior as possible when it occurs to you. Hang the umbrella on the doorknob, or put it through the handle of your briefcase, or in some other way start the process of taking it with you. (p. 240)

Removing Items Necessary for an Undesired Behavior

Another antecedent-based self-management tactic is to alter the environment so that an undesired behavior is less likely or, better yet, impossible to emit. The smoker who discards her cigarettes and the dieter who removes all cookies and chips from his house, car, and office, have, for the moment at least, effectively controlled their smoking and junk food eating. Although other self-management efforts will probably be needed to refrain from seeking and reobtaining the harmful material (e.g., the ex-smoker who asked his wife to provide response prompts if she saw him asking for cigarettes at a party), ridding oneself of the items needed to engage in an undesired behavior is a good start.

Limiting Undesired Behavior to Restricted Stimulus Conditions

A person may be able to decrease the frequency of an undesired behavior by limiting the setting or stimulus conditions under which he engages in the behavior. To the extent that the restricted situation acquires stimulus control over the target behavior and access to the situation is infrequent or otherwise not reinforcing, the target behavior will occur less frequently. Imagine a man who habitually touches and scratches his face (he is aware of this bad habit because his wife often nags him about it and asks him to stop). In an effort to decrease the frequency of his face touching, the man decides that he will do two things. First, whenever he becomes aware that he is engaging in face touching, he will stop; second, at any time he can go to a bathroom and touch and rub his face for as long as he wants.

Nolan (1968) reported the case of a woman who used restricted stimulus conditions in an effort to quit smoking. The woman noted that she most often smoked when other people were around or when she watched television, read, or lay down to relax. It was decided that she would smoke only in a prescribed place, and that she would eliminate from that place the potentially reinforcing effects of other activities. She designated a specific chair as her "smoking chair" and positioned it so that she could not watch TV or easily engage in conversation while sitting in it. She asked other family members not to approach her or talk to her while she was in her smoking chair. She followed the procedure faithfully, and her smoking decreased from a baseline average of 30 cigarettes per day to 12 cigarettes per day. Nine days after beginning the program, the woman decided to try to reduce her smoking even further by making her smoking chair less accessible. She put the chair in the basement, and her smoking decreased to five cigarettes per day. A month after beginning the smoking chair program, the woman had quit smoking completely.

Goldiamond (1965) used a similar tactic to help a man who continually sulked when interacting with his wife. The husband was instructed to limit his sulking behavior to his "sulking stool," which was placed in the garage. The man went to the garage whenever he felt like sulking, sat on his stool and sulked for as long as he wanted, and left when he was finished sulking. The man found that his sulking decreased considerably when he had to sit on a stool in the garage to do it.

Dedicating a Specific Environment for a Desired Behavior

A person may achieve some degree of stimulus control over a behavior that requires diligence and concentration by reserving or creating an environment where he will only engage in that behavior. For example, students have improved their study habits and professors their scholarly productivity when they have selected a specific place in which to study, free of other distractions, and have not engaged in any other behaviors such as daydreaming or letter writing in that place (Goldiamond, 1965). Skinner (1981b) suggested this kind of stimulus control strategy when he offered the following advice to aspiring writers:

> Equally important are the conditions in which the behavior occurs. A convenient place is important. It should have all the facilities needed for the execution of writing. Pens, typewriters, recorders, files, books, a comfortable desk and chair. . . . Since the place is to take control of a particular kind of behavior, you should do nothing else there at any time. (p. 2)

People who do not have the luxury of devoting a certain environment to a single activity can create a special stimulus arrangement that can be turned on and off in the multipurpose setting, as in this example provided by Watson and Tharp (2007):

> A man had in his room only one table, which he had to use for a variety of activities, such as writing letters, paying bills, watching TV, and eating. But when he wanted to do concentrated studying or writing, he always pulled his table away from the wall and sat on the other side of it. In that way, sitting on the other side of his table became the cue associated only with concentrated intellectual work. (p. 150)

Most students have a single personal computer that they use for their academic work and scholarly writing but also for completing administrative tasks, writing and reading personal e-mails, conducting family business, playing games, shopping online, browsing the Internet, and so on. In a manner similar to the man who sat on the other side of his table when studying and writing, a person could display a particular background on the computer's desktop that signals that only academic or scholarly work is to be done on the computer. For example, when he sits down to study or write, a student could replace the standard display on his computer desktop, a photo of his dog, let's say, with a solid green background. The green desktop signals that only scholarly work will be done. Over time the "scholarly work" desktop may acquire a degree of stimulus control over the desired behavior. If the student wants to quit working and do anything else on the computer, he must first change the background on the desktop. Doing so before he has fulfilled his time or productivity goal for a work session may generate some guilt that he can escape by returning to work.

This tactic can also be used to increase a desired behavior that is not being emitted at an acceptable rate because of competing undesired behaviors. In one case an adult insomniac reportedly went to bed about midnight but did not fall asleep until 3:00 or 4:00 A.M. Instead of falling asleep, the man would worry about several mundane problems and turn on the television. Treatment consisted of instructing the man to go to bed when he felt tired, but he was not to stay in bed if he was unable to sleep. If he wanted to think about his problems or watch television, he could do so, but he was to get out of bed and go into another room. When he again felt sleepy, he was to return to bed and try again to go to sleep. If he still could not sleep, he was to leave the bedroom again. The man reported getting up four or five times a night for the first few days of the program, but within 2 weeks he went to bed, stayed there, and fell asleep.

Self-Monitoring

Self-monitoring has been the subject of more research and clinical applications than any other self-management strategy. **Self-monitoring** (also called *self-recording* or *self-observation*) is a procedure whereby a person observes his behavior systematically and records the occurrence or nonoccurrence of a target behavior. Originally conceived as a method of clinical assessment for collecting data on behaviors that only the client could observe and record (e.g., eating, smoking, fingernail biting), self-monitoring soon became a major therapeutic intervention in its own right because of the reactive effects it often produced. As discussed in Chapters 3 and 4, *reactivity* refers to the effects on a person's behavior produced by an assessment or measurement procedure. In general, the more obtrusive an observation and measurement method, the greater will be the likelihood of reactivity (Haynes & Horn, 1982; Kazdin, 2001). When the person observing and recording the target behavior is the subject of the behavior change program, maximum obtrusiveness exists and reactivity is very likely.

Although reactivity caused by a researcher's measurement system represents uncontrolled variability in a study and must be minimized as much as possible, the reactive effects of self-monitoring are usually welcome from a clinical perspective. Not only does self-monitoring often change behavior, but also the change is typically in the educationally or therapeutically desired direction (Hayes & Cavior, 1977, 1980; Kirby, Fowler, & Baer, 1991; Malesky, 1974).

Behavior therapists have had adult clients use self-monitoring to reduce overeating, decrease smoking (Lipinski, Black, Nelson, & Ciminero, 1975; McFall, 1977), and stop biting their nails (Maletzky, 1974). Self-monitoring has helped students with and without disabilities be on task more often in the classroom (Blick & Test, 1987; Kneedler & Hallahan, 1981; Wood, Murdock, Cronin, Dawson, & Kirby, 1998), decrease talk-outs and aggression (Gumpel & Shlomit, 2000; Martella, Leonard, Marchand-Martella, & Agran, 1993), improve their performance in a variety of academic subject areas (Harris, 1986; Hundert & Bucher, 1978; Lee & Tindal, 1994; Maag, Reid, & DiGangi, 1993; Moxley, Lutz, Ahlborn, Boley, & Armstrong, 1995; Wolfe, Heron, & Goddard, 2000), and complete homework assignments (Trammel,

Schloss, & Alper, 1994). Classroom teachers have used self-monitoring to increase their use of positive statements during classroom instruction (Silvestri, 2004).

In one of the first published accounts of self-monitoring in the classroom, Broden, Hall, and Mitts (1971) analyzed the effects of self-recording on the behavior of two eighth-grade students. Liza was earning a D– in history and exhibited poor study behavior during the lecture format class. Using 10-second momentary time sampling for 30 minutes each day, an observer seated in the back of the classroom (Liza was not told she was being observed) produced a 7-day baseline showing that Liza exhibited study behaviors (e.g., faced the teacher, took notes when appropriate) an average of 30% of the observation intervals, despite two conferences with the school counselor in which she promised to "really try." Prior to the eighth session, the counselor gave Liza a piece of paper with three rows of 10 squares (see Figure 27.2) and directed her to record her study behavior "when she thought of it" during her history class sessions. Some aspects of study behavior were discussed at this time, including a definition of what constituted studying.

> Liza was instructed to take the slip to class each day and to record a "+" in the square if she was studying or had been doing so for the last few minutes, and a "−" if she was not studying at the time she thought to record. Sometime before the end of the school day she was to turn it in to the counselor. (p. 193)

Figure 27.3 shows the results of Liza's self-monitoring. Her level of study behavior increased to 78% (as measured by the independent observer) and stayed at approximately that level during Self-Recording 1, quickly

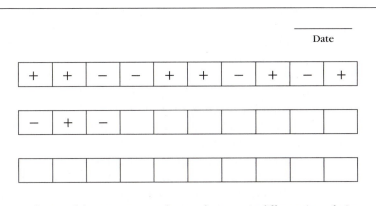

At the top of the page are several rows of squares. At different times during the period (whenever you think of it but don't fill them all in at the same time) put down a "+" if you were studying and a "−" if you weren't. If, for example, you were ready to mark a square, you would ask yourself if, for the last few minutes you had been studying and then you would put down a "+" if you had been studying or a "−" if you hadn't been studying.

Figure 27.2 Example of a self-recording form used by an eighth-grade girl.

From "The Effect of Self-Recording on the Classroom Behavior of Two Eighth-Grade Students" by M. Broden, R. V. Hall, and B. Mitts, 1971, *Journal of Applied Behavior Analysis, 4*, p. 193. Copyright 1971 by the Society for the Experimental Analysis of Behavior, Inc. Reprinted by permission.

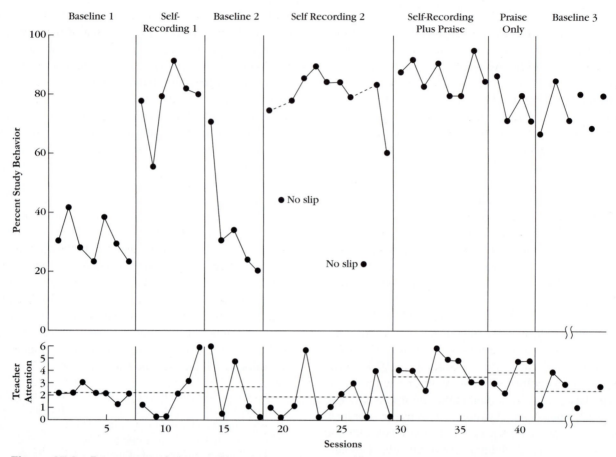

Figure 27.3   Percentage of observed intervals in which an eighth-grade girl paid attention in a history class.

From "The Effect of Self-Recording on the Classroom Behavior of Two Eighth-Grade Students" by M. Broden, R. V. Hall, and B. Mitts, 1971, *Journal of Applied Behavior Analysis, 4,* p. 194. Copyright 1971 by the Society for the Experimental Analysis of Behavior, Inc. Reprinted by permission.

decreased to baseline levels when self-recording was terminated during Baseline 2, and averaged 80% during Self-Recording 2. During Self-Recording Plus Praise, Liza's teacher attended to her whenever he could during history class and praised her for study behavior whenever possible. Liza's level of study behavior during this condition increased to 88%.

The bottom part of Figure 27.3 shows the number of times per session the observer recorded teacher attention toward Liza. The fact that the frequency of teacher attention did not correlate in any apparent way with Liza's study behavior during the first four phases of the experiment suggests that teacher attention—which often exerts a powerful influence on student behavior—was not a confounding variable and that the improvements in Liza's study behavior most likely can be attributed to the self-recording procedure. However, the effects of self-monitoring may have been confounded by the fact that Liza turned her self-recording slips in to the counselor before the end of each school day, and at weekly student–counselor conferences she received praise from the coun-

selor for recording slips with a high percentage of plus marks.

In the second experiment reported by Broden and colleagues (1971), self-monitoring was used with Stu, an eighth-grade student who talked out continually in class. Using a 10-second partial interval recording procedure to calculate the number of talk-outs per minute, an independent observer recorded Stu's behavior during both parts of a math class that met before and after lunch. Self-recording was begun first during the before-lunch portion of the math class. The teacher handed Stu a slip of paper on which was marked a 2-inch by 5-inch rectangular box and the instruction, "Put a mark every time you talk out" (p. 196). Stu was told to use the recording slip and turn it in after lunch. At the top of the recording slip was a place for the student's name and the date. No other instructions were given to Stu, nor were any consequences or other contingencies applied to his behavior. Self-recording was later implemented during the second half of the math class. During the prelunch portion of the math class, Stu's baseline rate of 1.1 talk-outs per minute was followed by a rate of 0.3 talk-outs per minute when he self-recorded. After lunch Stu talked out at an average rate of 1.6 times per minute before self-recording and 0.5 times per minute during self-recording.

The combination reversal and multiple baseline design showed a clear functional relation between Stu's reduced talk-outs and the self-monitoring procedure. During the final phase of the experiment, however, Stu talked out at rates equal to initial baseline levels, even though self-recording was in effect. Broden and colleagues (1971) suggested that the lack of effect produced by self-recording during the final phase may have resulted from the fact that "no contingencies were ever applied to differential rates of talking out and the slips thus lost their effectiveness" (p. 198). It is also possible that the initial decreases in talk-outs attributed to self-recording were confounded by Stu's expectations of some form of teacher reinforcement.

As can be seen from these two experiments, it is extremely difficult to isolate self-monitoring as a straightforward, "clean" procedure; it almost always entails other contingencies. Nevertheless, the various and combined procedures that comprise self-monitoring have often proved to be effective in changing behavior. However, the effects of self-monitoring on the target behavior are sometimes temporary and modest and may require the implementation of reinforcement contingencies to maintain the desired behavior changes (e.g., Ballard & Glynn, 1975; Critchfield & Vargas, 1991).

Self-Evaluation

Self-monitoring is often combined with goal setting and self-evaluation. A person using **self-evaluation** (also called *self-assessment*) compares her performance with a predetermined goal or standard (e.g., Keller, Brady, & Taylor, 2005; Sweeney et al., 1993). For example, Grossi and Heward (1998) taught four restaurant trainees with developmental disabilities to select productivity goals, self-monitor their work, and self-evaluate their performance against a competitive productivity standard (i.e., the typical rate at which nondisabled restaurant employees perform the task in competitive settings). Job tasks in this study included scrubbing pots and pans, loading a dishwasher, busing and setting tables, and mopping and sweeping floors.

Self-evaluation training with each trainee took approximately 35 minutes across three sessions and consisted of five parts: (1) rationale for working faster (e.g., finding and keeping a job in a competitive setting), (2) goal setting (trainee was shown a simple line graph of his baseline performance compared to the competitive standard and prompted to set a productivity goal), (3) use of timer or stopwatch, (4) self-monitoring and how to chart self-recorded data on a graph that showed competitive standard with a shaded area, and (5) self-evaluation (comparing their work against the competitive standard and making self-evaluative statements, e.g., "I'm not in the shaded area. I need to work faster." or "Good, I'm in the area."). When a trainee met his goal for three consecutive days, a new goal was selected. At that time all four trainees had selected goals within the competitive range.

The work productivity of all four trainees increased as a function of the self-evaluation intervention. Figure 27.4 shows the results for one of the participants, Chad, a 20-year-old male with mild mental retardation, cerebral palsy, and a seizure disorder. For the 3 months prior to the study, Chad had been training at two work tasks at the dishwashing job station: scrubbing cooking pots and pans and racking dishes (a six-step behavior chain for loading an empty dishwasher rack with dirty dishes). Throughout the study, pot scrubbing was measured during 10-minute observation sessions both before and after the daily lunch operation. Racking dishes was measured using a stopwatch to time to the nearest second how long a trainee took to load a rack of dishes; 4 to 8 racks per session were timed during the busiest hour of the lunch shift. After each observation session during baseline, Chad received feedback on the accuracy and quality of his work. No feedback was given during baseline on the productivity of his performance.

During baseline Chad scrubbed an average of 4.5 pots and pans every 10 minutes, and none of his 15 baseline trials were within the competitive range of 10 to 15 pots. Chad's pot scrubbing rate increased to a mean of 11.7 pots during self-evaluation, with 76% of 89 self-evaluation trials at or above the competitive range. During baseline it took Chad a mean of 3 minutes 2 seconds to load one rack of dishes, and 19% of his 97 baseline trials were within the competitive range of 1 to 2 minutes. During self-evaluation, Chad's time to load one rack improved to a mean of 1 minute 55 seconds, and 70% of the 114 self-evaluation trials were within the competitive range. At the end of the study, three of the four trainees stated that they liked to time and record their work performance. Although one trainee stated it was "too stressful" to time and record his work, he said that self-monitoring helped him show other people that he could do the work.

Self-Monitoring with Reinforcement

Self-monitoring is often part of an intervention package that includes reinforcement for meeting either self- or teacher-selected goals (e.g., Christian & Poling, 1997;

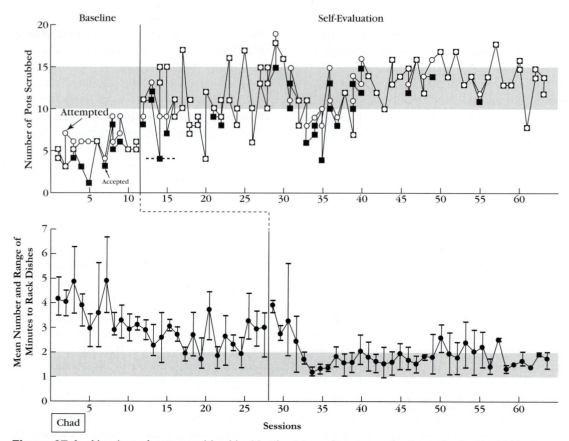

Figure 27.4 Number of pots scrubbed in 10 minutes and mean and range of minutes to load a rack of dishes in dishwasher during baseline and self-evaluation conditions. Shaded bands represent competitive performance range of restaurant workers without disabilities. Dashed horizontal line represents Chad's self-selected goal; no dashed line means that Chad's goal was within the competitive range. Vertical lines through data points on bottom graph show range of Chad's performance across 4 to 8 trials.

From "Using Self-Evaluation to Improve the Work Productivity of Trainees in a Community-Based Restaurant Training Program" by T. A. Grossi and W. L. Heward, 1998, *Education and Training in Mental Retardation and Developmental Disabilities, 33,* p. 256. Copyright 1998 by the Division on Developmental Disabilities. Reprinted by permission.

Dunlap & Dunlap, 1989; Olympia et al., 1994; Rhode, Morgan, & Young, 1983). The reinforcer may be self-administered or teacher delivered. For example, Koegel and colleagues (1992) taught four children with autism between the ages of 6 and 11 to obtain their own reinforcers after they had self-recorded a criterion number of appropriate responses to questions from others (e.g., "Who drove you to school today?").

Teacher-delivered reinforcement was a component of a self-monitoring intervention used by Martella and colleagues (1993) to help Brad, a 12-year-old student with mild mental retardation, reduce the number of negative statements he made during classroom activities (e.g., "I hate this #*%@! calculator," "Math is crappy"). Brad self-recorded negative statements during two class periods, charted the number on a graph, and then compared his count with the count obtained by a student teacher. If Brad's self-recorded data agreed with the teacher at a level of 80% or higher, he received his choice from a

menu of "small" reinforcers (items costing 25 cents or less). If Brad's self-recorded data were in agreement with the trainer's data and were at or below a gradually declining criterion level for four consecutive sessions, he was allowed to choose a "large" (more than 25 cents) reinforcer (see Figure 28.13).

Why Does Self-Monitoring Work?

The behavioral mechanisms that account for the effectiveness of self-monitoring are not fully understood. Some behavior theorists suggest that self-monitoring is effective in changing behavior because it evokes self-evaluative statements that serve either to reinforce desired behaviors or to punish undesired behaviors. Cautela (1971) hypothesized that a child who records on a chart that he has completed his chores may emit covert verbal responses (e.g., "I am a good boy") that serve to reinforce chore completion. Malott (1981) suggested that self-monitoring improves performance because of what he called guilt control. Self-monitoring less-than-desirable behavior produces covert guilt statements that can be avoided by improving one's performance. That is, the target behavior is strengthened through negative reinforcement by escape and avoidance of the guilty feelings that occur when one's behavior is "bad."

Descriptions of the self-monitoring techniques used by two famous authors apparently agreed with Malott's guilt control hypothesis. Novelist Anthony Trollope, writing in his 1883 autobiography, stated:

> When I have commenced a new book, I have always prepared a diary, divided into weeks, and carried on for the period which I have allowed myself for the completion of the work. In this I have entered, day by day, the number of pages I have written, so that if at any time I have slipped into idleness for a day or two, the record of that idleness has been there staring me in the face, and demanding of me increased labour, so that the deficiency might be supplied. . . . I have allotted myself so many pages a week. The average number has been about 40. It has been placed as low as 20, and has risen to 112. And as a page is an ambiguous term, my page has been made to contain 250 words; and as words, if not watched, will have a tendency to straggle, I have had every word counted as I went. . . . There has ever been the record before me, and a week passed with an insufficient number of pages has been a blister to my eye and a month so disgraced would have been a sorrow to my heart. (from Wallace, 1977, p. 518)

Guilt control also helped to motivate the legendary Ernest Hemingway. Novelist Irving Wallace (1977) reported the following extract from an article by George Plimpton about the self-monitoring technique used by the Hemingway.

> He keeps track of his daily progress—"so as not to kid myself"—on a large chart made out of the side of a cardboard packing case and set up against the wall under the nose of a mounted gazelle head. The numbers on the chart showing the daily output of words differ from 450, 575, 462, 1250, back to 512, the higher figures on days Hemingway put in extra work so he won't feel guilty spending the following day fishing on the gulf stream. (p. 518)

Exactly what principles of behavior are operating when self-monitoring results in a change in the target behavior is not known because much of the self-monitoring procedure consists of private, covert behaviors. In addition to the problem of access to these private events, self-monitoring is usually confounded by other variables. Self-monitoring is often part of a self-management package in which contingencies of reinforcement, punishment, or both, are included, either explicitly (e.g., "If I run 10 miles this week, I can go to the movies") or implicitly

(e.g., "I've got to show my record of calories consumed to my wife"). Regardless of the principles of behavior involved, however, self-monitoring is often an effective procedure for changing one's behavior.

Guidelines and Procedures for Self-Monitoring

Practitioners should consider the following suggestions when implementing self-monitoring with their students and clients.

Provide Materials That Make Self-Monitoring Easy

If self-monitoring is difficult, cumbersome, or time-consuming, at best it will be ineffective and disliked by the participant, and at worst it may have negative effects on the behavior. Participants should be provided with materials and devices that make self-monitoring as easy and efficient as possible. All of the devices and procedures for measuring behavior described in Chapter 4 (e.g., paper and pencil, wrist counters, hand-tally counters, timers, stopwatches) can be used for self-monitoring. For example, a teacher who wants to self-monitor the number of praise statements she makes to students during a class period could put ten pennies in her pocket prior to start of class. Each time she praises a student's behavior, she moves one coin to another pocket.

The recording forms used for most self-monitoring applications can and should be very simple. Self-recording forms consisting of little more than a series of boxes or squares such as the one shown in Figure 27.2 are often effective. At various intervals the participant might write a plus or minus, circle yes or no, or put an X through a smiling face or sad face, in a kind of momentary time sampling procedure; or he could record a count of the number of responses made during a just-completed interval.

Recording forms can be created for self-monitoring specialized tasks or a chain of behaviors. Dunlap and Dunlap (1989) taught students with learning disabilities to self-monitor the steps they used to solve subtraction problems with regrouping. Each student self-monitored his work by recording a plus or a minus next to each step on an individualized checklist of steps (e.g., "I underlined all the top numbers that were smaller than the bottom."; "I crossed out only the number next to the underlined number and made it one less." [p. 311]) designed to prompt the student from committing specific types of errors.

Lo (2003) taught elementary students who were at-risk for behavioral disorders to use the form shown in Figure 27.5 to self-monitor whether they worked quietly,

Figure 27.5 Form used by elementary school students to self-monitor whether they worked quietly and followed a prescribed sequence for recruiting teacher assistance.

From "Functional Assessment and Individualized Intervention Plans: Increasing the Behavioral Adjustment of Urban Learners in General and Special Education Settings" by Y. Lo, 2003. Unpublished doctoral dissertation. Columbus, OH: The Ohio State University. Reprinted by permission.

evaluated their work, and followed a prescribed sequence for obtaining teacher assistance during independent seat-work activities. The form, which was taped to each student's desk, functioned as a reminder to students of the expected behaviors and as a device on which they self-recorded those behaviors.

"Countoons" are self-monitoring forms that illustrate the contingency with a series of cartoon-like frames. A countoon reminds young children of not only what behavior to record, but also what consequences will follow if they meet their performance criteria. Daly and Ranalli (2003) created six-frame countoons that enable students to self-record an inappropriate behavior and an incompatible appropriate behavior. In the countoon shown in Figure 27.6, Frames F1 and F4 show the student doing her math work, appropriate behavior that is counted in Frame F5. The criterion number of math problems to meet the contingency—in this case 10—is also indicated in Frame F5. Frame F2 shows the student talking with a friend, the inappropriate behavior to be counted in F3. The student must not chat more than six times to meet the contingency. The "What Happens" frame (F6) depicts the reward the student will earn by meeting both parts of the contingency. Daly and Ranalli have provided detailed steps for creating and using countoons to teach self-management skills to children.

Self-monitoring forms can also be designed to enable self-recording of multiple tasks across days. For example, teachers working with high school-level students might employ the Classroom Performance Record (CPR) developed by Young and colleagues (1991) as a way to assist students with monitoring their assignments, completion of homework, points earned, and citizenship scores. The form also provides students with information about their current status in the class, their likely semester grade, and tips for improving their performance.

Provide Supplementary Cues or Prompts

Although some self-recording devices—a recording form taped to a student's desk, a notepad for counting calories carried in a dieter's shirt pocket, a golf counter on a teacher's wrist—serve as continual reminders to self-monitor, additional prompts or cues to self-monitor are often helpful. Researchers and practitioners have used a variety of auditory, visual, and tactile stimuli as cues and prompts for self-monitoring.

Auditory prompts in the form of prerecorded signals or tones have been widely used to cue self-monitoring in classrooms (e.g., Blick & Test, 1987; Todd, Horner, & Sugai, 1999). For example, second-graders in a study by Glynn, Thomas, and Shee (1973) placed a checkmark in a series of squares if they thought they were on task at the moment they heard a tape-recorded beep. A total of 10 beeps occurred at random intervals during a 30-minute class period. Using a similar procedure, Hallahan, Lloyd, Kosiewicz, Kauffman, and Graves (1979) had an 8-year-old boy place a checkmark next to *Yes* or *No* under the heading "Was I paying attention?" when he heard a tone played at random intervals by a tape recorder.

Ludwig (2004) used visual cues written on the classroom board to prompt kindergarten children to self-record

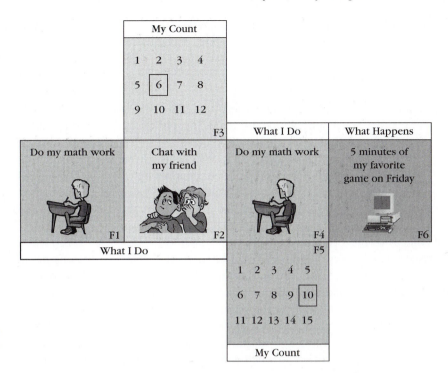

Figure 27.6 Example of a countoon that can be taped to a student's desk as a reminder of target behaviors, the need to self-record, and the consequence for meeting the contingency.

From "Using Countoons to Teach Self-Monitoring Skills" by P. M. Daly and P. Ranalli, 2003, *Teaching Exceptional Children, 35* (5), p. 32. Copyright 2003 by the Council for Exceptional Children. Reprinted by permission.

their productivity during a morning seatwork activity in which they wrote answers on individual worksheets to items, problems, or questions that the teacher had printed on a large whiteboard on the classroom wall. The work was divided into 14 sections by topic and covered a variety of curriculum areas (e.g., spelling, reading comprehension, addition and subtraction problems, telling time, money). At the end of each section the experimenter drew a smiley face with a number from 1 to 14. The numbered smiley faces drawn on the board corresponded to 14 numbered smiley faces on each student's self-monitoring card.

Tactile prompts can also be used to signal self-recording opportunities. For example, the *MotivAider* (www.habitchange.com) is a small electronic device that vibrates at fixed or variable time intervals programmed by the user. This device is excellent for signaling people to self-monitor or perform other self-management tasks, or to prompt practitioners to attend to the behavior of students or clients.[8]

Whatever form they take, prompts to self-monitor should be as unobtrusive as possible so they do not disrupt the participant or others in the setting. As a general rule, practitioners should provide frequent prompts to self-monitor at the beginning of a self-management intervention and gradually reduce their number as the participant becomes accustomed to self-monitoring.

[8]Flaute, Peterson, Van Norman, Riffle, and Eakins (2005) described 20 examples for using a MotivAider to improve behavior and productivity in the classroom.

Self-Monitor the Most Important Dimension of the Target Behavior

Self-monitoring is an act of measurement. But as we saw in Chapter 4, there are a variety of dimensions by which a given target behavior could be measured. What dimension of the target behavior should be self-monitored? A person should self-monitor the target behavior dimension that, should desired changes in its value be achieved, would yield the most direct and significant progress toward the person's goal for the self-management program. For example, a man wishing to lose weight by eating less food could measure the number of bites he takes throughout the day (count), the number of bites per minute during each meal (rate), how much time elapses from the time he sits down at the table to when he takes the first bite (latency), how long he pauses between bites (interresponse time), or the amount of time his meals last (duration). Although daily measures of each of these dimensions would provide the man with some quantitative information about his eating, none of the dimensions would be as directly related to his goal as would a count of the total number of calories he consumes each day.

Several studies have examined the question of whether students should self-monitor their on-task behavior or their academic productivity. Harris (1986) conducted one of the most frequently cited studies in this line of research. She taught four elementary students with learning disabilities to self-monitor either their on-task behavior or the number of academic responses they completed while practicing spelling. During the self-monitoring of attention condition, students asked themselves "Was I paying attention?" and checked their answer under *Yes* and *No* columns on a card whenever they heard a tape-recorded tone. During the self-monitoring of productivity condition, students counted the number of spelling words written at the end of the practice period. Both self-monitoring procedures resulted in increased on-task behavior for all four students. However, for three of the four students, self-monitoring of productivity resulted in higher academic response rates than did self-monitoring of on-task behavior.

Similar results have been reported in other studies comparing the differential effects of self-monitoring on-task behavior or productivity (e.g., Maag et al., 1993; Lloyd, Bateman, Landrum, & Hallahan, 1989; Reid & Harris, 1993). Although both procedures increase on-task behavior, students tend to complete more assignments when self-monitoring academic responses than when self-recording on-task behavior. Additionally, most students prefer self-monitoring academic productivity to on-task behavior.

In general we recommend teaching students to self-monitor a measure of academic productivity (e.g., number of problems or items attempted, number correct) rather than whether they are on task. This is because increasing on-task behavior, whether by self-monitoring or by contingent reinforcement, does not necessarily result in a collateral increase in productivity (e.g., Marholin & Steinman, 1977; McLaughlin & Malaby, 1972). By contrast, when productivity is increased, improvements in on-task behavior almost always occur. However, a student whose persistent off-task and disruptive behaviors are creating problems for him or others in the classroom may benefit more from self-monitoring on-task behavior, at least initially.

Self-Monitor Early and Often

In general, each occurrence of the target behavior should be self-recorded as soon as possible. However, the act of self-monitoring a behavior the person wants to increase should not disrupt "the flow of the behavior" (Critchfield, 1999). Self-monitoring target behaviors that produce natural or contrived response products (e.g., answers on academic worksheets, words written) can be conducted after the session by permanent product (see Chapter 4).

Relevant aspects of some behaviors can be self-monitored even before the target behavior itself has occurred. Self-recording a response early in a behavior chain that leads to an undesired behavior the person wants to decrease may be more effective in changing the target behavior in the desired direction than will recording on the terminal behavior in the chain. For example, Rozen-

sky (1974) reported that, when a woman who had been a heavy smoker for 25 years recorded the time and place she smoked each cigarette, there was little change in her rate of smoking. She then began to record the same information each time she noticed herself beginning the chain of behaviors that would lead to smoking: reaching for her cigarettes, removing a cigarette from the pack, and so on. She stopped smoking within a few weeks of self-monitoring in this fashion.

Generally, a person should self-monitor more often at the beginning of a behavior change program. If and as performance improves, the frequency of self-monitoring can be decreased. For example, Rhode and colleagues (1983) had students with behavioral disorders begin self-evaluating (on a 0- to 5-point scale) the extent to which they followed classroom rules and completed academic work correctly at the end of each 15-minute interval throughout the school day. Over the course of the study, the self-evaluation intervals were increased gradually, first to every 20 minutes, then every 30 minutes, then once per hour. Eventually, the self-evaluation cards were withdrawn and students reported their self-evaluations verbally. In the final self-evaluation condition, the students verbally self-evaluated their academic work and compliance with classroom rules on an average of every 2 days (i.e., a VR 2-day schedule).

Reinforce Accurate Self-Monitoring

Some studies have found little correlation between the accuracy of self-monitoring and its effectiveness in changing the behavior being recorded (e.g., Kneedler & Hallahan, 1981; Marshall, Lloyd, & Hallahan, 1993). It appears that accurate self-monitoring is neither a sufficient nor a necessary condition for behavior change. For example, Hundert and Bucher (1978) found that, even though the students became highly accurate in self-scoring their arithmetic, their performance on the arithmetic itself did not improve. On the other hand, in the Broden and colleagues (1971) study, both Liza and Stu's behavior improved even though their self-recorded data seldom matched the data from independent observers.

Nevertheless, accurate self-monitoring is desirable, especially when participants are using their self-recorded data as the basis for self-evaluation or self-administered consequences.

Although some studies have shown that young children can accurately self-record their behavior without specific external contingencies for accuracy (e.g., Ballard & Glynn, 1975; Glynn, Thomas, & Shee, 1973), other researchers have reported low agreement between the self-recordings of children and the data collected by independent observers (Kaufman & O'Leary, 1972; Turkewitz, O'Leary & Ironsmith, 1975). One factor that seems to affect the accuracy of self-scoring is the use of self-reported scores as a basis for reinforcement. Santogrossi, O'Leary, Romanczyk, and Kaufman (1973) found that, when children were allowed to evaluate their own work and those self-produced evaluations were used to determine levels of token reinforcement, their self-monitoring accuracy deteriorated over time. Similarly, Hundert and Bucher (1978) found that students who previously had accurately self-scored their arithmetic assignments greatly exaggerated their scores when higher scores resulted in points that could be exchanged for prizes.

Rewarding children for producing self-recorded data that match the data of an independent observer and spot-checking students' self-scoring reports are two procedures that have been used successfully to increase the accuracy of self-monitoring by young children. Drabman, Spitalnik, and O'Leary (1973) used these procedures in teaching children with behavior disorders to self-evaluate their own classroom behavior.

> Now something different is going to happen. If you get a rating within plus or minus one point of my rating, you can keep all your points. You lose all your points if you are off my rating by more than plus or minus one point. In addition, if you match my rating exactly you get a bonus point. (O'Leary, 1977, p. 204)

After the children demonstrated that they could evaluate their own behavior reliably, the teacher began checking only 50% of the children's self-ratings by pulling names from a hat at the end of the period, then 33%, then 25%, then 12%. During the last 12 days of the study she did not check any child's self-rating. Throughout this period of reduced checks and finally no checks at all, the children continued to self-evaluate accurately. Rhode and colleagues (1983) used a similar faded matching technique.

Self-Administered Consequences

Arranging to have specified consequences follow occurrences (or nonoccurrences) of one's behavior is one of the fundamental approaches to self-management. In this section we review some of the tactics people have used to self-reinforce and self-punish. First, we briefly examine some of the conceptual issues raised by the concept of "self-reinforcement."

Is Self-Reinforcement Possible?

Skinner (1953) pointed out that *self-reinforcement* should not be considered synonymous with the principle of operant reinforcement.

The place of operant reinforcement in self-control is not clear. In one sense, all reinforcements are self-administered since a response may be regarded as "producing" its reinforcement, but "reinforcing one's own behavior" is more than this. . . . Self-reinforcement of operant behavior presupposes that the individual has it in his power to obtain reinforcement but does not do so until a particular response has been emitted. This might be the case if a man denied himself all social contacts until he had finished a particular job. Something of this sort unquestionably happens, but is it operant reinforcement? It is roughly parallel to the procedure in conditioning the behavior of another person. But it must be remembered that the individual may at any moment drop the work in hand and obtain the reinforcement. We have to account for his not doing so. It may be that such indulgent behavior has been punished—say, with disapproval—except when a piece of work has just been completed. (pp. 237–38)

In his discussion of self-reinforcement, Goldiamond (1976) continued with Skinner's example and stated that the fact that a person "does not cheat, but engages in the task, cannot be explained simply by resort to *his* self-reinforcement by social contact, which he makes available contingent on his finishing the job" (p. 510). In other words, the variables influencing the controlling response—in this case not allowing oneself social contact until the job is complete—must still be accounted for; simply citing self-reinforcement as the cause is an explanatory fiction.

The issue is not whether procedures labeled as "self-reinforcement" often work to change behavior in ways that resemble the defining effect of reinforcement; they do. However, a careful examination of instances of self-reinforcement reveals that something more than, or different from, a straightforward application of positive reinforcement is involved (e.g., Brigham, 1980; Catania, 1975, 1976; Goldiamond, 1976a, 1976b; Rachlin, 1977). As a technical term, *self-reinforcement* (as also, *self-punishment*) is a misnomer, and the issue is not merely a semantic one as some writers have suggested (e.g., Mahoney, 1976). Assigning the effectiveness of a behavior change tactic to a well-understood principle of behavior when something other than, or in addition to, that principle is operating overlooks relevant variables that may hold the key to a fuller understanding of the tactic. Considering the analysis of a behavioral episode complete once it has been identified as a case of self-reinforcement precludes further search for other relevant variables.

We agree with Malott (2005a; Malott & Harrison, 2002; Malott & Suarez, 2004) who argued that performance-management contingencies, whether designed and implemented by oneself or by others, are best viewed as rule-governed analogs of reinforcement and punishment contingencies because the response-to-consequence delay is too great.[9] Malott (2005a) provided the following examples of self-management contingencies as analogs to negative reinforcement and punishment contingencies:

> [Consider the] contingency, *Every day I eat more than 1,250 calories, I will give someone else $5 to spend frivolously,* like a despised roommate or despised charity, though for many of us, the loss of $5 to a beloved charity is sufficiently aversive that the thought of it will punish overeating. [This] contingency is an analog to a penalty [punishment] contingency, an analog because the actual loss of the $5 will normally occur more than 1 minute after exceeding the 1,250 calorie limit. Such analog penalty contingencies are effective in decreasing undesirable behavior. And to increase desirable behavior, an analog to an avoidance [negative reinforcement] contingency works well: *Every day I exercise for one hour, I avoid paying a $5 fine.* But, if you have not finished your hour by midnight, you must pay the $5. (p. 519, emphasis in original, words in brackets added)

Self-Administered Consequences to Increase Desired Behavior

A person can increase the future frequency of a target behavior in a self-management program by applying contingencies that are analogs to positive reinforcement and negative reinforcement.

Self-Management Analogs of Positive Reinforcement

Several self-reinforcement studies with schoolchildren have involved positive reinforcement in which participants obtained a self-determined number of tokens, points, or minutes of free time based on a self-assessment of their performance (Ballard & Glynn, 1975; Bolstad & Johnson, 1972; Glynn, 1970; Koegel et al., 1992; Olympia et al., 1994).

The effects of treatments involving self-administered rewards are difficult to evaluate because they are typically confounded by self-monitoring and self-evaluation. However, in a study by Ballard and Glynn (1975), third-graders were taught after a baseline condition to self-score and self-record several aspects of their writing—number of sentences, number of describing words, and number of action words. Self-monitoring had no effect on any of the variables measured even though the students handed in their counting sheets with their writing each day. The children were then given a notebook in which to record their points, which could be exchanged

at the rate of one point per minute for each student's choice of activities during an earned-time period each day. The self-reinforcement procedure resulted in large increases in each of the three dependent variables.

Self-administered reinforcement does not have to be self-delivered: the learner could make a response that results in another person providing the reinforcer. For example, in studies on self-recruited reinforcement, students are taught to periodically self-evaluate their work and then show it to their teacher and request feedback or assistance (e.g., Alber, Heward, & Hippler, 1999; Craft, Alber, & Heward, 1998; Mank & Horner, 1987; Smith, & Sugai, 2000). In a sense, students administer their own reinforcer by recruiting the teacher's attention, which often results in praise and other forms of reinforcement (see Alber & Heward, 2000 for a review).

Todd and colleagues (1999) taught an elementary student to use a self-management system that included self-monitoring, self-evaluation, and self-recruited reinforcement. Kyle was a 9-year-old boy diagnosed with a learning disability and receiving special education services in reading, math, and language arts. Kyle's IEP also included several objectives for problem behavior (e.g., disrupting independent and group activities, teasing and taunting classmates, and saying sexually inappropriate comments). The classroom teacher's goal setting and daily evaluation had proven ineffective. An "action team" conducted a functional assessment (see Chapter 24) and designed a support plan that included the self-management system.

Kyle was taught how to use the self-management system during two 15-minute one-on-one training sessions in which he practiced self-recording numerous role-played examples and nonexamples of on-task and off-task behavior and learned appropriate ways to recruit teacher attention and praise. For self-monitoring, Kyle listened with a single earplug to a 50-minute cassette tape on which 13 checkpoints (e.g., "check one," "check two") had been prerecorded on a VI 4-minute schedule (ranging from 3- to 5-minute intervals between checkpoints). Each time Kyle heard a checkpoint, he marked a plus (if he had been working quietly and keeping his hands, feet, and objects to himself) or a zero (teasing peers and/or not working quietly) on a self-recording card.

Todd and colleagues (1999) described the recruitment of teacher praise and how Kyle's special program was integrated into the reinforcement system for the entire class:

> Each time Kyle marked three pluses on his card he raised his hand (during instruction) or walked up to the teacher (during group project time) and requested feedback on his performance. The teacher acknowledged Kyle's good work and placed a mark on his self-monitoring card to show where he should begin a new count of three pluses. In addition to these within-session contingencies, Kyle could earn a self-manager sticker at the end of each class

---

[9]The critical importance of immediacy in reinforcement is discussed in Chapter 11.

period if he had no more than two zeroes for the period. Stickers were earned by all students in the class for appropriate behavior and were pooled weekly for class rewards. Because these stickers were combined, Kyle's stickers were valued by all the students and provided opportunities for positive peer attention. (p. 70)

Procedures for the second self-management phase (SM2) were the same as the first phase; during the third phase (SM3) Kyle used a 95-minute tape on which 16 checkpoints were prerecorded on a VI 5-minute schedule (ranging from 4 to 6 minutes). When Kyle used the self-management system, the percentage of intervals in which he engaged in problem behavior was much lower than baseline levels (see Figure 27.7). Large increases in on-task behavior and completion of academic work were also noted. An important outcome of this study was that Kyle's teacher praised him more often. Significantly, the self-management intervention was initiated in Class Period B (bottom graph in Figure 27.7) at the teacher's request because she had noted an immediate and "dramatic change" in Kyle's performance when he began self-monitoring and recruiting teacher praise in Class Period A. This outcome is strong evidence for the social validity of the self-management intervention.

Self-Management Analogs of Negative Reinforcement

Many successful self-management interventions involve self-determined escape and avoidance contingencies that are analogous to negative reinforcement. Most of the case studies featured in Malott and Harrison's (2002) excellent book on self-management, *I'll Stop Procrastinating When I Get Around To It,* feature escape and avoidance contingencies in which emitting the target behavior enabled the person to avoid an aversive event. For example:

Target Behavior/Objective	Self-Management Contingency
Make a daily journal entry to be able to remember the interesting things that had happened to include in a weekly letter to my parents.	Each day I failed to make a journal entry, I had to do my friend's chores, including doing the dishes and laundry. (Garner, 2002)
Run 30 minutes, 3 times per week.	I had to pay the piper $3 at 10:00 P.M. Sunday for every day I'd run less than three times that week. I could count only one run per day. (Seymour, 2002)
Practice guitar for half an hour each day of the week before 11:00 P.M.	Do 50 sit-ups at 11:00 P.M. on Sundays for every day that I did not practice during the week. (Knittel, 2002)

In response to the uneasiness some people may feel about using negative reinforcement to control their behavior, Malott (2002) made the following case for building "pleasant aversive control" into self-management programs.

Aversive control doesn't have to be aversive! . . . Here's what I think you need in order to have a pleasant aversive control procedure. You need to make sure that the aversive consequence, the penalty, is small. And you need to make sure the penalty is usually avoided—the avoidance response needs to be one that the person will readily make, most of the time, as long as the avoidance procedure is in effect.

Our everyday life is full of such avoidance procedures, and yet they don't make us miserable. You don't have an anxiety attack every time you walk through a doorway, even though you might hurt yourself if you don't avoid bumping into the doorjamb. And you don't break out in a cold sweat every time you put the leftovers in the refrigerator, and thereby avoid leaving them out to spoil. So that leads us to the Self-Management Rule: Don't hesitate to use an avoidance procedure to get yourself to do something you want to do anyway. Just be sure the aversive outcome is as small as possible (but not so small it's ineffective) and the response is easy to make. (p. 8-2)

Self-Administered Consequences to Decrease Undesired Behavior

The frequency of an undesirable behavior can be decreased by self-administered consequences analogous to positive punishment or negative punishment.

Self-Management Analogs of Positive Punishment

A person can decrease the frequency of an undesired behavior by following each occurrence with the onset of painful stimulus or aversive activity. Mahoney (1971) reported a case study in which a man beleaguered by obsessive thoughts wore a heavy rubber band around his wrist. Each time he experienced an obsessive thought, he snapped the rubber band, delivering a brief, painful sensation to his wrist. A 15-year-old girl who had compulsively pulled her hair for $2\frac{1}{2}$ years, to the point of creating bald spots, also used contingent self-delivered snaps of a rubber band on her wrist to stop her habit (Mastellone, 1974). Another woman stopped her hair pulling by performing 15 sit-ups each time she pulled her hair or had the urge to do so (MacNeil & Thomas, 1976). Powell and Azrin (1968) designed a special cigarette case that delivered a one-second electric shock when opened. The controlling responses by a person using such a device as part of a self-management program is carrying the case and smoking only cigarettes that he has personally removed from it.

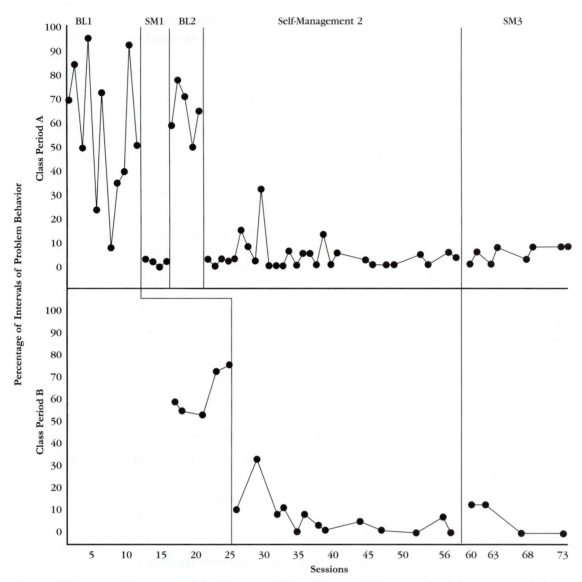

Figure 27.7 Problem behaviors by a 9-year-old boy during 10-minute probes across two class periods during baseline and self-management conditions.

From "Self-Monitoring and Self-Recruited Praise: Effects on Problem Behavior, Academic Engagement, and Work Completion in a Typical Classroom" by A. W. Todd, R. H. Horner, and G. Sugai, 1999, *Journal of Positive Behavior Interventions, 1,* p. 71. Copyright 1999 by Pro-Ed, Inc. Reprinted by permission.

Self-administering a positive practice overcorrection procedure also qualifies as an example of self-administered positive punishment. For example, a teenage girl who frequently said *don't* instead of *doesn't* with the third person singular (e.g., "She don't like that one") used this form of self-administered positive punishment to decrease the frequency of her speech error (Heward, Dardig, & Rossett, 1979). Each time the girl observed herself saying *don't* when she should have said *doesn't,* she repeated the complete sentence she had just spoken 10 times in a row using correct grammar. She wore a wrist counter that reminded her to listen to her speech and to keep track of the number of times she employed the positive practice procedure.

Self-Management Analogs of Negative Punishment

Self-administered analogs to negative punishment consist of arranging the loss of reinforcers (response cost) or denying oneself access to reinforcement for a specified period of time (time-out) contingent on the occurrence of the target behavior. Response cost and time-out contingencies are widely used self-management strategies. The most commonly applied self-administered response cost procedure is paying a small fine each time the target behavior occurs. In one study, smokers reduced their rate of smoking by tearing up a dollar bill each time they lit up (Axelrod, Hall, Weis, & Rohrer, 1971). Response cost procedures have also been used effectively with elementary school children who have self-determined the number of tokens they should lose for inappropriate social behavior (Kaufman & O'Leary, 1972) or for poor academic work (Humphrey, Karoly, & Kirschenbaum, 1978).

James (1981) taught an 18-year-old man who had stuttered severely since the age of 6 to use a time-out from speaking procedure. Whenever he observed himself stuttering, the young man immediately stopped talking for at least 2 seconds, after which he could begin speaking again. His frequency of dysfluencies decreased markedly. If talking is reinforcing, then this procedure might function as time-out (e.g., not allowing oneself to engage in a preferred activity for a period of time).

Recommendations for Self-Administered Consequences

Persons designing and implementing self-administered consequences should consider the following recommendations.

Select Small, Easy-to-Deliver Consequences

Both rewards and penalties used in self-management programs should be small and easily delivered. A common mistake in designing self-management programs is selecting consequences that are big and grand. Although a person may believe that the promise of a large reward (or threat of a severe aversive event) will motivate him to meet his self-determined performance criteria, large consequences often work against the program's success. Self-selected rewards and punishing consequences should not be costly, elaborate, time-consuming, or too severe. If they are, the person may not be able (in the case of grand rewards) or willing (in the case of severe aversive events) to deliver them immediately and consistently.

In general, it is better to use small consequences that can be obtained immediately and frequently. This is particularly important with consequences intended to function as punishers, which—in order to be most effective—must be delivered immediately every time the behavior targeted for reduction is emitted.

Set a Meaningful But Easy-to-Meet Criterion for Reinforcement

When designing contingencies involving self-administered consequences, a person should guard against making the same two mistakes practitioners often make when implementing reinforcement contingencies with students and clients: (1) setting expectations so low that improvement in the current level of performance is not necessary to obtain the self-administered reward, or

(2) making the initial performance criterion too high (the more common mistake), thereby effectively programming an extinction contingency that may cause the person to give up on self-management altogether. Keys to the effectiveness of any reinforcement-based intervention are setting an initial criterion that ensures that the person's behavior makes early contact with reinforcement and that continued reinforcement requires improvements over baseline levels. The criterion-setting formulae (Heward, 1980) described in Chapter 11 provide guidelines for making those determinations.

Eliminate "Bootleg Reinforcement"

Bootleg reinforcement—access to the specified reward or to other equally reinforcing items or events without meeting the response requirements of the contingency—is a common downfall of self-management projects. A person who obtains a comfortable supply of smuggled rewards is less likely to work hard to earn response-contingent rewards.

Bootleg reinforcement is common when people use everyday preferred activities and treats as rewards in self-management programs. Although everyday expectations and enjoyments are easy to deliver, a person may find it difficult to withhold things he is used to enjoying on a regular basis. For example, a man who is used to unwinding at the end of the day by watching *Baseball Tonight* with a beer and some peanuts may not be consistent in making those daily treats contingent on meeting the requirements of his self-management program.

One method for combating this form of bootleg reinforcement is to no longer make access to the activities or items the person routinely enjoyed prior to the self-management program contingent on meeting any performance criteria and provide alternative items or activities that are a cut above the usual. For example, each time the man in the previous scenario meets his performance criteria, he could replace his everyday brand of beer with his choice of a specialty beer from a collection reserved in the back of the refrigerator.

If Necessary, Put Someone Else in Control of Delivering Consequences

Most ineffective self-management programs fail, not because the controlling behavior is ineffective in controlling the controlled behavior, but because the contingencies that control the controlling behavior are not sufficiently strong. In other words, the person does not emit the controlling behavior consistently enough for its effects to be realized. What keeps a person from rationalizing that she did most of the behaviors she was supposed to and obtaining a self-determined reward anyway? What keeps a person from failing to deliver a self-determined aversive consequence? Too often, the answer to both questions is, nothing.

A person who really wants to change her behavior but has difficulty following through with delivering self-determined consequences should enlist another person to serve as performance manager. A self-manager can ensure that her self-designed consequences will be administered faithfully by creating a contingency in which the consequence for failing to meet the performance criterion is aversive to the her but a reinforcer for the person she has asked to implement the consequence. And, if the first person put in charge of the contingency fails to implement it as planned, the self-manager should find another person who will do the job. Malott and Harrison (2002) wrote,

> Christie wanted to walk on her dust-gathering treadmill 20 minutes a day, 6 days a week. She tried her husband as her performance contractor, but he wasn't tough enough; he always felt sorry for her. So she fired him and hired her son; she made his bed every time she failed to do her 20 minutes, and he showed no mercy. (p. 18-7)

Kanfer (1976) called this kind of self-management *decisional self-control:* The person makes the initial decision to alter her behavior and plans how that will be accomplished, but then turns over the procedure to a second party in order to avoid the possibility of not emitting the controlling response. Kanfer made a distinction between decisional self-control and protracted self-control, in which a person consistently engages in self-deprivation in order to effect the desired behavior change. Bellack and Hersen (1977) stated that decisional self-control "is generally considered to be less desirable than protracted self-control, as it does not provide the individual with an enduring skill or resource" (p. 111).

We disagree that a self-management program that involves the help of other people is less desirable than one in which the self-manager does everything. First, a self-management program in which the contingencies are turned over to someone else may be more effective than trying to "go it alone" because that other person is more consistent in applying the consequences. In addition, as a result of experiencing a successful self-management program in which he has chosen the target behavior, set performance criteria, determined a self-monitoring/self-evaluation system, and arranged to have someone else administer self-designed consequences, a person has acquired a considerable repertoire of self-management skills for future use.

Keep It Simple

A person should not create elaborate self-management contingencies if they are not needed. The same general rule that applies to behavior change programs designed on behalf of others—the least complicated and intrusive yet effective intervention should be employed—also applies to self-management programs. With respect to the use of self-administered consequences, Bellack and Schwartz (1976) warned that,

> Adding complicated procedures where they are not required is more likely to have negative than positive effects. Second, our experience indicates that many individuals find explicit self-reinforcement procedures to be tedious, childish, and "gimmicky." (p. 137)

There is no need for self-reinforcement procedures to be complicated. And in our experience, more people find creating and implementing their own performance management contingencies fun than find them tedious or childish.

Other Self-Management Tactics

Other self-management strategies have been the subject of behavior analysis research but are not so easily classified according to the four-term contingency. They include self-instruction, habit reversal, self-directed systematic desensitization, and massed practice.

Self-Instruction

People talk to themselves all the time, offering encouragement (e.g., "You can do this; you've done it before"), congratulations (e.g., "Great shot, Daryl! You just crushed that 5-iron!"), and admonishment (e.g., "Don't say that anymore; you hurt her feelings") for their behavior, as well as specific instructions (e.g., "Pull the bottom rope through the middle"). Such self-statements can function as controlling responses—verbal mediators—that affect the occurrence of other behaviors. **Self-instruction** consists of self-generated verbal responses, covert or overt, that function as response prompts for a desired behavior. As a self-management tactic, self-instructions are often used to guide a person through a behavior chain or sequence of tasks.

Bornstein and Quevillon (1976) conducted a study frequently cited as evidence of the positive and lasting effects of self-instruction. They taught three hyperactive preschool boys a series of four types of self-instructions designed to keep them on task with classroom activities:

1. Questions about the assigned task (e.g., "What does the teacher want me to do?")
2. Answers to the self-directed questions (e.g., "I'm supposed to copy that picture")
3. Verbalizations to guide the child through the task at hand (e.g., "OK, first I draw a line through here . . .")
4. Self-reinforcement (e.g., "I really did that one well")

During a 2-hour session the children were taught to use self-instructions using a sequence of training steps originally developed by Meichenbaum and Goodman (1971):

1. The experimenter modeled the task while talking aloud to himself.

2. The child performed the task while the experimenter provided the verbal instructions.

3. The child performed the task while talking aloud to himself with the experimenter whispering the instructions softly.

4. The child performed the task while whispering softly to himself with the experimenter moving his lips but making no sound.

5. The child performed the task while making lip movements but no sound.

6. The child performed the task while guiding his performance with covert instructions. (adapted from p. 117)

During the training session a variety of classroom tasks were used, ranging from simple motor tasks such as copying lines and figures to more complex tasks such as block design and grouping tasks. The children showed a marked increase in on-task behavior immediately after receiving self-instruction training, and their improved behavior was maintained over a considerable period of time. The authors suggested that the generalization obtained from the training setting to the classroom could have been the result of telling the children during training to imagine that they were working with their teacher, not the experimenter. The authors hypothesized that a behavioral trapping phenomenon (Baer & Wolf, 1970) may have been responsible for the maintenance of on-task behavior; that is, the self-instructions may have initially produced better behavior, which in turn produced teacher attention that maintained the on-task behavior.

Although some studies evaluating self-instruction failed to reproduce the impressive results obtained by Bornstein and Quevillon (e.g. Billings & Wasik, 1985; Friedling & O'Leary, 1979), other studies have produced generally encouraging results (Barkley, Copeland, & Sivage, 1980; Burgio, Whitman, & Johnson, 1980; Hughes 1992; Kosiewicz, Hallahan, Lloyd, & Graves, 1982; Peters & Davies, 1981; Robin, Armel, & O'Leary, 1975). Self-instruction training has increased the frequency of high school students' initiating conversations with familiar and unfamiliar peers (Hughes, Harmer, Killian, & Niarhos, 1995; see Figure 28.5).

Employees with disabilities have learned to self-manage their work performance by providing their own verbal prompts and self-instructions (Hughes, 1997). For example, Salend, Ellis, and Reynolds (1989) used a self-instruction strategy to teach four adults with severe mental retardation to "talk while you work." Productivity increased dramatically and error rates decreased when the women verbalized to themselves, "Comb up, comb down, comb in bag, bag in box" while packaging combs in plastic bags. Hughes and Rusch (1989) taught two supported employees working at a janitorial supply company how to solve problems by using a self-instruction procedure consisting of four statements:

1. Statement of the problem (e.g., "Tape empty")

2. Statement of the response needed to solve the problem (e.g., "Need more tape")

3. Self-report (e.g., "Fixed it")

4. Self-reinforcement (e.g., "Good")

O'Leary and Dubey (1979) summarized their review of self-instruction training by suggesting four factors that appear to influence its effectiveness with children.

> Self-instructions appear to be effective self-controlling procedures if the children actually implement the instructional procedure, if the children use them [the self-instructions] to influence behavior at which they are skilled, if children have been reinforced for adhering to their self-instructions in the past, and if the focus of the instructions is the behavior most subject to consequences. (p. 451)

Habit Reversal

In his initial discussion of self-control, Skinner (1953) included "doing something else" as a self-management tactic. In an interesting application of "doing something else," Robin, Schneider, and Dolnick (1976) taught 11 primary-aged children with emotional and behavioral disorders to control their aggressive behaviors by using the turtle technique: The children pulled their arms and legs close to their bodies, put their heads down on their desks, relaxed their muscles, and imagined they were turtles. The children were taught to use the turtle response whenever they believed an aggressive exchange with someone else was about to take place, when they were angry with themselves and felt they were about to have a tantrum, or when the teacher or a classmate called out, "Turtle!"

Azrin and Nunn (1973) developed an intervention they called *habit reversal,* in which clients are taught to self-monitor their nervous habits and interrupt the behavior chain as early as possible by engaging in behavior incompatible with the problem behavior (i.e., doing something else). For example, when a nail biter observes herself beginning to bite her fingernails, she might squeeze her hand into a tight fist for 2 or 3 minutes (Azrin, Nunn,

& Frantz, 1980) or sit on her hands (Long, Miltenberger, Ellingson, & Ott, 1999). As a clinical intervention, **habit reversal** is typically implemented as a multiple-component treatment package that includes self-awareness training involving response detection and procedures for identifying events that precede and trigger the response, competing response training, motivation techniques including self-administered consequences, social support systems, and procedures for promoting the generalization and maintenance of treatment gains (Long et al., 1999). Habit reversal has proven to be a highly effective self-management tactic for a wide variety of problem behaviors. For a review of habit reversal procedures and research, see Miltenberger, Fuqua, and Woods (1998).

Self-Directed Systematic Desensitization

Systematic desensitization is a widely used behavior therapy treatment for anxieties, fears, and phobias that features the self-management strategy of engaging in an alternative behavior (i.e., doing something else). Originally developed by Wolpe (1958, 1973), **systematic desensitization** involves substituting one behavior, generally muscle relaxation, for the unwanted behavior—the fear and anxiety. The client develops a hierarchy of situations from the least to the most fearful and then learns to relax while imagining these anxiety-producing situations, first the least fearful situation, then the next fearful one, and so on. Figure 27.8 shows a anxiety-stimulus hierarchy that a person might develop in attempting to control a fear of cats. When a person is able to go completely through his hierarchy, imagining each scene in detail while maintaining deep relaxation and feeling no anxiety, he begins to expose himself gradually to real-life (*in vivo*) situations.

Detailed procedures for achieving deep muscle relaxation, constructing and validating a hierarchy of anxiety- or fear-producing situations, and implementing a self-directed systematic desensitization program can be found in Martin and Pear (2003) and Wenrich, Dawley, and General (1976).

Massed Practice

Forcing oneself to perform an undesired behavior again and again, a technique called **massed practice,** will sometimes decrease the future frequency of the behavior.

Figure 27.8 Sequence of imaginary scenes concerning fear of cats that could be used for systematic self-desensitization.

Directions

1. You're sitting in a comfortable chair in the safety of your home watching TV.
2. You're watching a commercial for cat food—no cat is visible.
3. The commercial continues and a cat is now eating the food.
4. A man is now petting the cat.
5. A man is holding the cat and fondling it.
6. A woman is holding the cat, and the cat is licking her hands and face.
7. You're looking out the window of your home and you see a cat on the lawn across the street.
8. You're sitting in front of your house, and you see a cat walk by on the sidewalk across the street.
9. You're sitting in your yard, and you see a cat walk by on your sidewalk.
10. A cat walks within 15 feet of you.
11. A friend of yours picks the cat up and plays with it.
12. Your friend is 10 feet away from you, and the cat is licking his face.
13. Your friend comes within 5 feet of you while he's holding the cat.
14. Your friend stands 2 feet away and plays with the cat.
15. Your friend asks if you'd like to pet the cat.
16. Your friend reaches out and offers you the cat.
17. He puts the cat on the ground, and it walks over to you.
18. The cat rubs up against your leg.
19. The cat walks between your legs purring.
20. You reach down and touch the cat.
21. You pet the cat.
22. You pick up the cat and pet it. (p. 71)

From "Self-Directed Systematic Desensitization: A Guide for the Student, Client, and Therapist" by W. W. Wenrich, H. H. Dawley, and D. A. General, 1976, p. 71. Copyright 1976 by Behaviordelia, Kalamazoo, MI. Used by permission.

Wolff (1977) reported an interesting case of this form of treatment by a 20-year-old woman who engaged in a compulsive, ritualized routine of 13 specific security checks every time she entered her apartment (e.g., looking under beds, checking the closets, looking in the kitchen). She began her program by deliberately going through the 13 steps in an exact order and then repeating the complete ritual four more times. After doing this for 1 week, she permitted herself to check the apartment if she wanted to but made herself go through the entire routine five times whenever she did any checking at all. She soon quit performing her compulsive checking behavior.

Suggestions for Conducting an Effective Self-Management Program

Incorporating the suggestions that follow into the design and implementation of self-management programs should increase the likelihood of success. Although none of these guidelines has been rigorously examined through experimental analyses—research on self-management has a long way to go—each suggestion is consistent with procedures proven effective in other areas of applied behavior analysis and with "best practices" commonly reported in the self-management literature (e.g., Agran, 1997; Malott & Harrison, 2002; Martin & Pear, 2003; Watson & Tharp, 2007).

1. Specify a goal and define the behavior to be changed.
2. Begin self-monitoring the behavior.
3. Contrive contingencies that will compete with natural contingencies.
4. Go public with your commitment to change your behavior.
5. Get a self-management partner.
6. Continually evaluate your self-management program and redesign it as necessary.

Specify a Goal and Define the Target Behavior

A self-management program begins with identifying a personal goal or objective and the specific behavior changes necessary to accomplish that goal or objective. A person can use most of the questions and issues that practitioners should consider when selecting target behaviors for students or clients (see Chapter 3) to assess the social significance and prioritize the importance of a list of self-determined target behavior changes.

Begin Self-Monitoring the Behavior

A person should begin self-monitoring as soon as he has defined the target behavior. Self-monitoring prior to implementing any other form of intervention yields the same benefits as does taking baseline data described in Chapter 7:

1. Self-monitoring makes a person observant of events occurring before and after the target behavior; information about antecedent-behavior-consequent correlations that may be helpful in designing an effective intervention.
2. Self-monitored baseline data provide valuable guidance in determining initial performance criteria for self-administered consequences.
3. Self-monitored baseline data provide an objective basis for evaluating the effects of any subsequent interventions.

Another reason to begin self-monitoring as soon as possible without employing additional self-management tactics is that the desired improvement in behavior may be achieved by self-monitoring alone.

Create Contrived Contingencies That Will Compete with Ineffective Natural Contingencies

When self-monitoring alone does not result in the desired behavior changes, the next step is designing a contrived contingency to compete with the ineffective natural contingencies. A person who implements a contingency that provides immediate, definite consequences for each occurrence (or perhaps, nonoccurrence) of the target behavior greatly increases the probability of obtaining a previously elusive self-management goal. For example, a smoker who self-records and reports each cigarette smoked to his self-management partner, who provides contingent praise, rewards, and penalties, has arranged immediate, frequent, and more effective consequences for reducing his smoking behavior than those provided by the natural contingency: the threat of lung cancer and emphysema in the future, neither of which becomes appreciably more immediate or likely from one cigarette to the next.

Go Public

The effectiveness of a self-management effort may be enhanced by publicly sharing the intentions of the program. When a person shares a goal or makes a prediction to others about her future behavior, she has arranged potential consequences—praise or condemnation—for her success or failure in meeting that goal. A person should state in specific terms what she intends to do and her deadline for completing it. Taking the idea of public commitment a step further, consider the powerful potential of public posting (e.g., an untenured junior faculty member could post a chart of his writing where his department chair or dean could see and comment on it).

Malott (1981) called this the "public spotlight principle of self-management."

> A public statement of goals improves performance. But just how do the social contingencies engaged by public commitment produce change? They increase the rewarding value of success and the aversive value of failure, I presume. But those outcomes are probably too delayed to directly reinforce problem solving. Instead they must be part of the rules the student self-states at crucial times: "If I don't make my goal, I'll look like a fool; but if I do make it, I'll look pretty cool." Such rules then function as cues for immediate self-reinforcement of on-task behavior and self-punishment of off-task behavior. (Volume II, No. 18, p. 5)

Skinner (1953) also theorized about the principles of behavior that operate when a person shares his self-management goal with important others.

> By making it in the presence of people who supply aversive stimulation when a prediction is not fulfilled, we arrange consequences which are likely to strengthen the behavior resolved upon. Only by behaving as predicted can we escape the aversive consequences of breaking our resolution. (p. 237)

Get a Self-Management Partner

Setting up a self-management exchange is a good way to involve another person whose differential feedback about how a self-management project is going can be effective as a behavioral consequence. Two people, each of whom has a long-range goal or a regular series of tasks to do, can agree to talk to each other on a daily or weekly basis, as determined by the target behaviors and by each person's progress. They can share the data from their self-monitoring and exchange verbal praise or admonishments and perhaps even more tangible consequences contingent on performance. Malott (1981) reported a successful self-management exchange in which he and a colleague paid each other $1 every time either person failed to complete any one of a series of self-determined daily exercise, housekeeping, and writing tasks. Each morning they spoke on the telephone, reporting their performance during the previous 24 hours.

To help themselves and each other study for exams and complete research and writing tasks, one group of doctoral students created a self-management group they called the Dissertation Club (Ferreri et al., 2006). At weekly meetings each group member shared data on the "scholarly behaviors" she had targeted (e.g., graphs of words written each day or number of hours studied). Group members received social support from one another in the form of encouragement to continue working hard and praise for accomplishments, they served as behavioral consultants to one another on the deign of self-management interventions, and sometimes they administered rewards and fines to one another. All six members of the group wrote and successfully defended their dissertations within the timelines they had set.

Continually Evaluate and Redesign Program as Needed

> Your self-management project may not work the first time you try it. And it will certainly fall apart from time to time, so be prepared with some scotch tape and bubble gum to put it back together again.
> — Malott and Harrison (2002, p. 18-7)

The development and evaluation of most self-management programs reflects a pragmatic, data-based approach to personal problem solving more than it does rigorous research with an emphasis on experimental analysis and control. Like the researcher, however, the self-manager should be guided by the data. If the data show the program is not working satisfactorily, the intervention should be redesigned.

An A-B design is sufficient to evaluate the effects of most self-management projects. People who have learned to define, observe, record, and graph their own behavior can easily be taught how to evaluate their self-management efforts with self-experiments. A simple A-B design (Chapter 7) provides a straightforward accounting of the results in a before-and-after fashion that is usually sufficient for self-evaluation. Experimentally determining functional relations between self-managed interventions and their effects usually takes a back seat to the pragmatic goal of changing one's behavior. However, the changing criterion design (Chapter 9) lends itself nicely, not only to the stepwise increments in performance that are often a part of improving personal performance, but also to a clearer demonstration and understanding of the relation between the intervention and changes in the target behavior.

In addition to data-based evaluation, people should evaluate their self-management projects in terms of social validity dimensions (Wolf, 1978). A practitioner teaching self-management to others can aid his students' or clients' social validity assessments of their self-management efforts by providing checklists of questions covering topics such as how practical their intervention was, whether they felt their self-management program affected their behavior in any unmeasured ways, and whether they enjoyed the project.

One of the most important aspects of social validity for any behavior change program is the extent to which the results—measured changes in the target behavior—actually made a difference in the lives of the participants. One approach to assessing the social validity of the results of a self-management program is to collect data on what Malott and Harrison (2002) called *benefit measures.* For example, a person might measure:

- Number of pounds lost as a benefit measure of eating less or exercising more
- Improved lung capacity (peak airflow volume measured as cubic centimeters per second on an inexpensive device available at many pharmacies) as an outcome of reducing the number of cigarettes smoked
- Decrease in time it takes to run a mile as a benefit of number of miles run each day
- Lower resting heart rate and faster recovery time as a benefit of aerobic exercise
- Higher scores on foreign language practice exams as an outcome of studying

In addition to assessing the social validity of self-management interventions, the positive results of benefit measures can serve as consequences that reward and strengthen continued adherence to self-management.

An account of a self-management weight loss program that incorporated many of the tactics and suggestions described in this chapter is presented in Box 27.2, "Take a Load Off Me."

Behavior Changes Behavior

Referring to a book on self-management he wrote for a popular audience, Epstein (1997) wrote,

> A young man whose life is in disarray (he smokes, drinks, overeats, loses things, procrastinates, and so on) seeks advice from his parents, teachers, and friends, but no one can help. Then the young man remembers his Uncle Fred (modeled shamelessly after Fred Skinner), whose life always seemed to be in perfect harmony. In a series of visits, Uncle Fred reveals to him the three "secrets" of self-management, all *M*s: *Modify your environment, monitor your behaviors,* and *make commitments.* Fred also reveals and explains the "self-management principle": *Behavior changes behavior.* After each visit, the young man tries out a new technique, and his life is changed radically for the better. In one scene, he sees a classroom of remarkably creative and insightful children who have been trained in self-management techniques in a public school. It is fiction, of course, but the technology is well established and the possibilities are well within reach. (p. 563, emphasis in original)

Building upon Skinner's (1953) conceptual analysis of self-control more than 50 years ago, behavior analysts have developed numerous self-management tactics and methods for teaching learners with diverse abilities how to apply them. Underlying all of these efforts and findings is the simple, yet profound principle that behavior changes behavior.

Box 27.2
Take a Load Off Me:
A Self-Managed Weight-Loss Program

Joe was a 63-year-old man whose doctor had recently informed him that the 195 pounds on his 5-foot 11-inch frame must be reduced to 175 pounds or he was very likely to experience serious health problems. Although Joe obtained regular physical exercise by keeping up the lawn and garden, cutting and hauling firewood, feeding the rabbits, and doing myriad other chores that come with a farmhouse, his prodigious appetite—long considered one of the "best in the county"—had caught up with him. His doctor's warning and the recent death of a high school classmate had scared Joe enough to sit down with his son to plan a self-management weight-loss program.

Joe's program included antecedent-based tactics, self-monitoring, self-evaluation, contingency contracting, self-selected and self-administered consequences, and contingency management by significant others.

Goal

To reduce current weight of 195 pounds to 175 pounds at a rate of 1 pound per week.

Behavior Change Needed to Achieve Goal

Reduce eating to a maximum of 2,100 calories per day.

Rules and Procedures

1. Mount bathroom scale each morning before dressing or eating and chart weight on "Joe's Weight" graph taped to bathroom mirror.

2. Carry notepad, pencil, and calorie counter in pocket throughout the day and record the type and amount of *all* food and liquid (other than water) *immediately* after consumption.

3. Before going to bed each night, add total calories consumed during the day and chart that number on "Joe's Eating" graph taped to bathroom mirror.

4. *Do not waiver* from Steps 1–3, regardless of weight loss or lack of weight loss.

Immediate Contingencies/Consequences

- Calorie counter, notepad, and pencil in pocket provide continuously available response prompts.

- Recording all food and drink consumed provides immediate consequence.

- When you have not eaten any food you thought about eating, put a star on your notepad and give self-praise ("Way to go, Joe!").

Daily Contingencies/Consequences

- If the calories consumed during the day do not exceed the 2,100 criterion, put 50 cents in "Joe's Garden Jar."

- If total calories exceed the criterion, remove $1.00 from "Joe's Garden Jar."

- For each 3 days in a row that you meet the calorie criterion, add a bonus of 50 cents to "Joe's Garden Jar."

- Have Helen initial your contract each day that you meet the calorie criterion.

Weekly Contingencies/Consequences

- Each Sunday night write the calories consumed each day for the previous week on one of the predated, addressed, and stamped postcards. Helen will verify your self-report by initialing the postcard and mailing it to Bill and Jill on Monday.

- Each Monday, if total calories consumed met the criterion for at least 6 of the past 7 days, obtain an item or activity from "Joe's Reward Menu."

Intermediate Contingencies/Consequences

- Eat within the daily calorie limit often enough and there will be sufficient money in "Joe's Garden Jar" to buy seeds and plants for the spring vegetable garden.

- If weight during May visit to Ohio represents a loss of at least 1 pound per week, be a guest of honor at a restaurant of your choice.

Long-Term Consequences

- Feel better.
- Look better.
- Be healthier.
- Live longer.

Results

Joe often struggled with the rules and procedures, but he stuck with his self-management program and lost 22 pounds (achieving a weight of 173) in 16 weeks. As this report is being written, 26 years have passed since Joe's adventure in self-management. Joe can still hold his own at the dinner table, but he has retained his weight loss and enjoys gardening, singing in a barbershop choir, and listening to the Cubs on the radio.

Summary

The "Self" As Controller of Behavior

1. We tend to assign causal status to events that immediately precede behavior, and when causal variables are not readily apparent in the immediate, surrounding environment, the tendency to turn to internal causes is strong.

2. Hypothetical constructs such as willpower and drive are explanatory fictions that bring us no closer to understanding the behaviors they claim to explain and lead to circular reasoning.

3. Skinner (1953) conceptualized self-control as a two-response phenomenon: The *controlling response* affects variables in such a way as to change the probability of the other, the *controlled response.*

4. We define self-management as the personal application of behavior change tactics that produces a desired change in behavior.

5. Self-management is a relative concept. A behavior change program may entail a small degree of self-management or be totally conceived, designed, and implemented by the person.

6. Although *self-control* and *self-management* appear interchangeably in the behavioral literature, we recommend that *self-management* be used in reference to a person acting in some way *in order to* change his subsequent behavior.

   • Self-control implies that the ultimate control of behavior lies within the person, but the causal factors for "self-control" are to be found in a person's experiences with his environment.

   • Self-control "seems to suggest controlling a [separate] self inside or [that there is] a self inside controlling external behavior" (Baum, 1994, p. 157).

   • Self-control is also used to refer to a person's ability to "delay gratification" by responding to achieve a delayed, but larger or higher quality reward instead of acting to obtain an immediate, less valuable reward.

Applications, Advantages, and Benefits of Self-Management

7. Four uses of self-management are to
   • live a more effective and efficient daily life,
   • break bad habits and acquiring good ones,
   • accomplish difficult tasks, and
   • achieve personal lifestyle goals.

8. Advantages and benefits of learning and teaching self-management skills include the following:

   • Self-management can influence behaviors not accessible to external change agents.

   • External change agents often miss important instances of behavior.

   • Self-management can promote the generalization and maintenance of behavior change.

   • A small repertoire of self-management skills can control many behaviors.

   • People with diverse abilities can learn self-management skills.

   • Some people perform better under self-selected tasks and performance criteria.

   • People with good self-management skills contribute to more efficient and effective group environments.

   • Teaching students self-management skills provides meaningful practice for other areas of the curriculum.

   • Self-management is an ultimate goal of education.

   • Self-management benefits society.

   • Self-management helps a person feel free.

   • Self-management feels good.

Antecedent-Based Self-Management Tactics

9. Antecedent-based self-management tactics feature the manipulation of events or stimuli antecedent to the target (controlled) behavior, such as the following:

   • Manipulating motivating operations to make a desired (or undesired) behavior more (or less) likely

   • Providing response prompts

   • Performing the initial steps of a behavior chain to ensure being confronted later with a discriminative stimulus that will evoke the desired behavior

   • Removing the materials required for an undesired behavior

   • Limiting an undesired behavior to restricted stimulus conditions

   • Dedicating a specific environment for a desired behavior

Self-Monitoring

10. Self-monitoring is a procedure whereby a person observes and responds to, usually by recording, the behavior he is trying to change.

11. Originally developed as a method of clinical assessment for collecting data on behaviors that only the client could observe, self-monitoring evolved into the most widely used and studied self-management strategy because it often results in desired behavior change.

12. Self-monitoring is often combined with goal setting and self-evaluation. A person using self-evaluation compares her performance with a predetermined goal or standard.

13. Self-monitoring is often part of an intervention that includes reinforcement for meeting either self- or teacher-selected goals.

14. It is difficult to determine exactly how self-monitoring works because the procedure necessarily includes, and is therefore confounded by, private events (covert verbal behavior); it often includes either explicit or implicit contingencies of reinforcement.

15. Children can be taught to self-monitor and self-record their behavior accurately by means of a faded matching technique, in which the child is rewarded initially for producing data that match the teacher's or parent's data. Over time the child is required to match the adult's record less often, eventually monitoring the behavior independently.

16. Accuracy of self-monitoring is neither necessary nor sufficient to achieve improvement in the behavior being monitored.

17. Suggested guidelines for self-monitoring are as follows:
    - Provide materials that make self-monitoring easy.
    - Provide supplementary cues or prompts.
    - Self-monitor the most important dimension of the target behavior.
    - Self-monitor early and often, but do not interrupt the flow of a desired behavior targeted for increase.
    - Reinforce accurate self-monitoring.

Self-Administered Consequences

18. As a technical term, *self-reinforcement* (as also, *self-punishment*) is a misnomer. Although behavior can be changed by self-administered consequences, the variables influencing the controlling response make such self-management tactics more than a straightforward application of operant reinforcement.

19. Self-administered contingencies analogous to positive and negative reinforcement and positive and negative punishment can be incorporated into self-management programs.

20. When designing self-management programs involving self-administered consequences, a person should:
    - Select small, easy-to-deliver consequences.
    - Set a meaningful but easy-to-meet criterion for reinforcement.
    - Eliminate "bootleg reinforcement."
    - If necessary, put someone else in control of delivery consequences.

- Use the least complicated and intrusive contingencies that will be effective.

Other Self-Management Tactics

21. Self-instruction (talking to oneself) can function as controlling responses (verbal mediators) that affect the occurrence of other behaviors.

22. Habit reversal is a multiple-component treatment package in which clients are taught to self-monitor their unwanted habits and interrupt the behavior chain as early as possible by engaging in a behavior incompatible with the problem behavior.

23. Systematic desensitization is a behavior therapy treatment for anxieties, fears, and phobias that involves substituting one behavior, generally muscle relaxation, for the unwanted behavior—the fear and anxiety. Self-directed systematic desensitization involves developing a hierarchy of situations from the least to the most fearful and then learning to relax while imagining these anxiety-producing situations, first the least fearful situation, then the next fearful one, and so on.

24. Massed practice, forcing oneself to perform an undesired behavior again and again, can decrease the future frequency of the behavior.

Suggestions for Conducting an Effective Self-Management Program

25. Following are six steps in designing and implementing a self-management program:

    Step 1: Specify a goal and define the behavior to be changed.

    Step 2: Begin self-monitoring the behavior.

    Step 3: Create contingencies that will compete with natural contingencies.

    Step 4: Go public with the commitment to change behavior.

    Step 5: Get a self-management partner.

    Step 6: Continually evaluate and redesign the program as needed.

Behavior Changes Behavior

26. The most fundamental principle of self-management is that behavior changes behavior.

PART 12

Promoting Generalized Behavior Change

Socially important behavior can be changed deliberately. The preceding chapters describe basic principles of behavior and how practitioners can use behavior change tactics derived from those principles to increase appropriate behaviors, achieve desired stimulus controls, teach new behaviors, and decrease problem behaviors. Although achieving initial behavior changes often requires procedures that are intrusive or costly, or for a variety of other reasons cannot or should not be continued indefinitely, it is almost always important that the newly wrought behavior changes continue. Similarly, in many instances the intervention needed to produce new patterns of responding cannot be implemented in all of the environments in which the new behavior would benefit the learner. Nor is it possible in certain skill areas to teach directly all of the specific forms of the target behavior the learner may need. Practitioners face no more challenging or important task than that of designing, implementing, and evaluating interventions that produce behavior changes that continue after the intervention is terminated, appear in relevant settings and stimulus situations other than those in which the intervention was conducted, and/or spread to other related behaviors that were not taught directly. Chapter 28 defines the major types of generalized behavior change and describes the strategies and tactics applied behavior analysts use to achieve them.

Generalization and Maintenance of Behavior Change

Key Terms

behavior trap
contrived contingency
contrived mediating stimulus
general case analysis
generalization
generalization across subjects
generalization probe

generalization setting
indiscriminable contingency
instructional setting
lag reinforcement schedule
multiple exemplar training
naturally existing contingency

programming common stimuli
response generalization
response maintenance
setting/situation generalization
teaching sufficient examples
teaching loosely

Behavior Analyst Certification Board® BCBA® & BCABA® Behavior Analyst Task List©, Third Edition

Content Area 3: Principles, Processes, and Concepts	
3-12	Define and provide examples of generalization and discrimination.
9-28	Use behavior change procedures to promote stimulus and response generalization.
9-29	Use behavior change procedures to promote maintenance.

Sherry's teacher implemented an intervention that helped Sherry to complete each part of multiple-part, in-school assignments before submitting them and beginning another activity. Now, three weeks after the program ended, most of the work Sherry submits as "finished" is incomplete and her stick-with-a-task-until-it's-finished behavior is as poor as it was before the intervention began.

Ricardo has just begun his first competitive job working as a copy machine operator in a downtown business office. In spite of his long history of distractibility and poor endurance, Ricardo had learned to work independently for several hours at a time in the copy room at the vocational training center. His employer, however, is complaining that Ricardo frequently stops working after a few minutes to seek attention from others. Ricardo may soon lose his job.

Brian is a 10-year-old boy diagnosed with autism. In an effort to meet an objective on his individualized education program that targets functional language and communication skills, Brian's teacher taught him to say, "Hello, how are you?" as a greeting. Now, whenever Brian meets anyone, he invariably responds with, "Hello, how are you?" Brian's parents are concerned that their son's language seems stilted and parrot-like.

 Each of these three situations illustrates a common type of teaching failure insofar as the most socially significant behavior changes are those that last over time, are used by the learner in all relevant settings and situations, and are accompanied by changes in other relevant responses. The student who learns to count money and make change in the classroom today must be able to count and make change at the convenience store tomorrow and at the supermarket next month. The beginning writer who has been taught to write a few good sentences in school must be able to write many more meaningful sentences when writing notes or letters to family or friends. To perform below this standard is more than just regrettable; it is a clear indication that the initial instruction was not entirely successful.

In the first scenario, the mere passage of time resulted in Sherry losing her ability to complete assignments. A change of scenery threw Ricardo off his game; the excellent work habits he had acquired at the vocational training center disappeared completely when he arrived at the community job site. Although Brian used his new greeting skill, its restricted form was not serving him well in the real world. In a very real sense, the instruction they received failed all three of these people.

Applied behavior analysts face no more challenging or important task than that of designing, implementing, and evaluating interventions that produce generalized outcomes. This chapter defines the major

types of generalized behavior change and describes the strategies and tactics researchers and practitioners use most often to promote them.

Generalized Behavior Change: Definitions and Key Concepts

When Baer, Wolf, and Risley (1968) described the emerging field of applied behavior analysis, they included *generality of behavior change* as one of the discipline's seven defining characteristics.

> A behavior change may be said to have generality if it proves durable over time, if it appears in a wide variety of possible environments, or if it spreads to a wide variety of related behaviors. (p. 96)

In their seminal review paper, "An Implicit Technology of Generalization," Stokes and Baer (1977) also stressed those three facets of generalized behavior change—across time, settings, and behaviors—when they defined *generalization* as

> the occurrence of relevant behavior under different, non-training conditions (i.e., across subjects, settings, people, behaviors, and/or time) without the scheduling of the same events in those conditions. Thus, generalization may be claimed when no extratraining manipulations are needed for extratraining changes; or may be claimed when some extra manipulations are necessary, but their cost is clearly less than that of the direct intervention. Generalization will not be claimed when similar events are necessary for similar effects across conditions. (p. 350)

Stokes and Baer's pragmatic orientation toward generalized behavior change has proven useful for applied behavior analysis. They stated simply that if a trained behavior occurs at other times or in other places without it having to be retrained completely at those times or in those places, or if functionally related behaviors occur that were not taught directly, then generalized behavior change has occurred. The following sections provide definitions and examples of the three basic forms of generalized behavior change: response maintenance, setting/situation generalization, and response generalization. Box 28.1, "Perspectives on the Sometimes Confusing and Misleading Terminology of Generalization," discusses the many and varied terms applied behavior analysts use to describe these outcomes.

Response Maintenance

Response maintenance refers to the extent to which a learner continues to perform the target behavior after a portion or all of the intervention responsible for the

Box 28.1
Perspectives on the Sometimes Confusing and Misleading Terminology of Generalization

Applied behavior analysts have used many terms to describe behavior changes that appear as adjuncts or by-products of direct intervention. Unfortunately, the overlapping and multiple meanings of some terms can lead to confusion and misunderstanding. For example, *maintenance,* the most frequently used term for behavior changes that persist after an intervention has been withdrawn or terminated, is also the most common name for a condition in which treatment has been discontinued or partially withdrawn. Applied behavior analysts should distinguish between *response maintenance* as a measure of behavior (i.e., a dependent variable) and *maintenance* as the name for an environmental condition (i.e., an independent variable). Other terms found in the behavior analysis literature for continued responding after programmed contingencies are no longer in effect include *durability, behavioral persistence,* and (incorrectly) *resistance to extinction.**

Terms used in the applied behavior analysis literature for behavior changes that occur in nontraining settings or stimulus conditions include *stimulus generalization, setting generalization, transfer of training,* or simply, *generalization.* It is technically incorrect to use *stimulus generalization* to refer to the generalized behavior change achieved by many applied interventions. *Stimulus generalization* refers to the phenomenon in which a response that has been reinforced in the presence of a given stimulus occurs with an increased frequency in the presence of different but similar stimuli under extinction conditions (Guttman & Kalish, 1956; see Chapter 17). *Stimulus generalization* is a technical term referring to a specific behavioral process, and its use should be restricted to those instances (Cuvo, 2003; Johnston, 1979).

Terms such as *collateral* or *side effects, response variability, induction,* and *concomitant behavior change* are often used to indicate the occurrence of behaviors that have not been trained directly. To further complicate matters, *generalization* is often used as a catchall term to refer to all three types of generalized behavior change.

Johnston (1979) discussed some problems caused by using *generalization* (the term for a specific behavioral process) to describe any desirable behavior change in a generalization setting.

This kind of usage is misleading in that it suggests that a single phenomenon is at work when actually a number of different phenomena need to be described, explained, and controlled. . . . Carefully designing procedures to optimize the contributions of stimulus and response generalization would hardly exhaust our repertoire of tactics for getting the subject to behave in a desirable way in noninstructional settings. Our successes will be more frequent when we realize that maximizing behavioral influence in such settings requires careful consideration of *all* behavioral principles and processes. (pp. 1–2)

Inconsistent use of the "terminology of generalization" can lead researchers and practitioners to incorrect assumptions and conclusions regarding the principles and processes responsible for the presence or absence of generalized outcomes. Nevertheless, applied behavior analysts will probably continue to use **generalization** as a dual-purpose term, referring sometimes to types of behavior change and sometimes to behavioral processes that can bring such changes about. Stokes and Baer (1977) clearly indicated their awareness of the differences in definitions.

> The notion of generalization developed here is an essentially pragmatic one; it does not closely follow the traditional conceptualizations (Keller & Schoenfeld, 1950; Skinner, 1953). In many ways, this discussion will sidestep much of the controversy concerning terminology. (p. 350)

While discussing the use of naturally existing contingencies of reinforcement to maintain and extend programmed behavior changes, Baer (1999) explained his preference for using the term *generalization:*

> It is the best of the techniques described here and, interestingly, it does not deserve the textbook definition of "generalization." It is a reinforcement technique, and the textbook definition of generalization refers to unreinforced behavior changes resulting from other directly reinforced behavior changes. . . . [But] we are dealing with the pragmatic use of the word *generalization,* not the textbook meaning. We reinforce each other for using the word pragmatically, and it serves us well enough so far, so we shall probably maintain this imprecise usage. (p. 30, emphasis in original)

In an effort to promote the precise use of the technical terminology of behavior analysis and as a reminder that the phenomena of interest are usually products of multiple behavior principles and procedures, we use terms for generalized behavior change that focus on the type of behavior change rather than the principles or processes that bring it about.

---

*Response maintenance can be measured under extinction conditions, in which case the relative frequency of continued responding is described correctly in terms of *resistance to extinction.* However, using *resistance to extinction* to describe response maintenance in most applied situations is incorrect because reinforcement typically follows some occurrences of the target behavior in the post-treatment environment.

behavior's initial appearance in the learner's repertoire has been terminated. For example:

- Sayaka was having difficulty identifying the lowest common denominator (LCD) when adding and subtracting fractions. Her teacher had Sayaka write the steps for finding the LCD on an index card and told her to refer to the card when needed. Sayaka began using the LCD cue card, and the accuracy of her math assignments improved. After using the cue card for a week, Sayaka said she no longer needed it and returned it to her teacher. The next day Sayaka correctly computed the LCD for every problem on a quiz on adding and subtracting fractions.

- On Loraine's first day on the job with a residential landscaping company, a coworker taught her how to use a long-handled tool to extract dandelions, root and all. Without further instruction, Loraine continues to use the tool correctly a month later.

- When he was in the seventh grade, one of Derek's teachers taught him how to write down his assignments and keep materials for each class in separate folders. As a college sophomore, Derek continues to apply those organizational skills to his academic work.

These examples illustrate the relative nature of generalized behavior change. Response maintenance was evident in Sayaka's performance on a math quiz one day after the cue card intervention ended and also in Derek's continued use of the organizational skills he had learned years earlier. How long a newly learned behavior needs to be maintained depends on the importance of that behavior in the person's life. If covertly reciting a telephone number three times after hearing it enables a person to remember the number long enough to dial it correctly when he locates a telephone a few minutes later, sufficient response maintenance has been achieved. Other behaviors, such as self-care and social skills, must be maintained in a person's repertoire for a lifetime.

Setting/Situation Generalization

Setting/situation generalization occurs when a target behavior is emitted in the presence of stimulus conditions other than those in which it was trained directly. We define **setting/situation generalization** as the extent to which a learner emits the target behavior in a setting or stimulus situation that is different from the instructional setting. For example:

- While waiting for his new motorized wheelchair to arrive from the factory, Chaz used a computer simulation program and a joystick to learn how to op-

erate his soon-to-arrive chair. When the new chair arrived, Chaz grabbed the joystick and immediately began zipping up and down the hall and spinning perfectly executed donuts.

- Loraine had been taught to pull weeds from flowerbeds and mulched areas. Although she had never been instructed to do so, Loraine has begun removing dandelions and other large weeds from lawns as she crosses on her way to the flowerbeds.

- After Brandy's teacher taught her to read 10 different C-V-C-E words (e.g., *bike, cute, made*), Brandy could read C-V-C-E words for which she had not received any instruction (e.g., *cake, bite, mute*).

A study by van den Pol and colleagues (1981) provides an excellent example of setting/situation generalization. They taught three young adults with multiple disabilities to eat independently in fast-food restaurants. All three students had previously eaten in restaurants but could not order or pay for a meal without assistance. The researchers began by constructing a task analysis of the steps required to order, pay for, and eat a meal appropriately in a fast-food restaurant. Instruction took place in the students' classroom and consisted of role-playing each of the steps during simulated customer–cashier interactions and responding to questions about photographic slides showing customers at a fast-food restaurant performing the various steps in the sequence. The 22 steps in the task analysis were divided into four major components: locating, ordering, paying, and eating and exiting. After a student had mastered the steps in each component in the classroom, he was given "a randomly determined number of bills equaling two to five dollars and instructed to go eat lunch" at a local restaurant (p. 64). Observers stationed inside the restaurant recorded each student's performance of each step in the task analysis. The results of these generalization probes, which were also conducted before training (baseline) and after training (follow-up) are shown in Figure 28.1. In addition to assessing the degree of generalization from the classroom, which was based on the specific McDonald's restaurant used for most of the probes, the researchers conducted follow-up probes in a Burger King restaurant (also a measure of maintenance).

This study is indicative of the pragmatic approach to assessing and promoting generalized behavior change used by most applied behavior analysts. The setting in which generalized responding is desired can contain one or more components of the intervention that was implemented in the instructional environment, but not all of the components. If the complete intervention program is required to produce behavior change in a novel environment, then no setting/situation generalization can be claimed. However, if some component(s) of the training

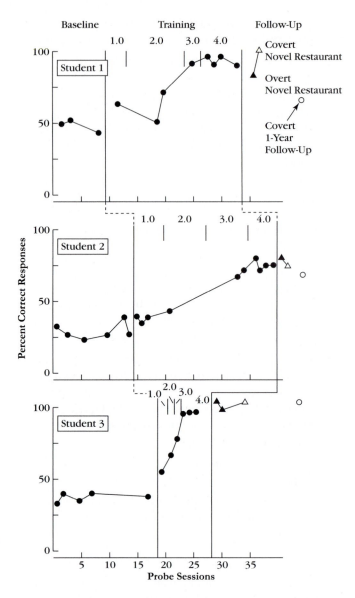

Figure 28.1 Percentage of steps necessary to order a meal at a fast-food restaurant correctly performed by three students with disabilities before, during, and after instruction in the classroom. During follow-up, the closed triangles represent probes conducted at a Burger King restaurant using typical observation procedures, open triangles represent Burger King probes during which students did not know they were being observed, and open circles represent covert probes conducted in a different McDonald's 1 year after training.

From "Teaching the Handicapped to Eat in Public Places: Acquisition, Generalization and Maintenance of Restaurant Skills" by R. A. van den Pol, B. A. Iwata, M. T. Ivanic, T. J. Page, N. A. Neef, and F. P. Whitley, 1981, *Journal of Applied Behavior Analysis, 14,* p. 66. Copyright 1981 by the Society for the Experimental Analysis of Behavior, Inc. Reprinted by permission.

program results in meaningful behavior change in a generalization setting, then setting/situation generalization can be claimed, provided it can be shown that the component(s) used in the generalization setting was insufficient to produce the behavior change alone in the training environment.

For example, van den Pol and colleagues taught Student 3, who was deaf, how to use a prosthetic ordering device in the classroom. The device, a plastic laminated sheet of cardboard with a wax pencil, had preprinted questions (e.g., "How much is . . . ?"), generic item names (e.g., large hamburger), and spaces where the cashier could write responses. Simply giving the student some money and the prosthetic ordering card would not have enabled him to order, purchase, and eat a meal independently. However, after classroom instruction that included guided practice, role playing, social reinforcement ("Good job! You remembered to ask for your change" [p. 64]),

corrective feedback, and review sessions with the prosthetic ordering card produced the desired behaviors in the instructional setting, Student 3 was able to order, pay for, and eat meals in a restaurant aided only by the card.

Distinguishing Between Instructional and Generalization Settings

We use **instructional setting** to denote the total environment where instruction occurs, including any aspects of the environment, planned or unplanned, that may influence the learner's acquisition and generalization of the target behavior.[1] Planned elements are the stimuli and

---

[1]Because the majority of the examples in this chapter are school based, we have used the language of education. For our purposes here, *instruction* can be a synonym for *treatment, intervention,* or *therapy,* and *instructional setting* can be a synonym for *clinical setting* or *therapy setting.*

events the teacher has programmed in an effort to achieve initial behavior change and promote generalization. Planned elements of an instructional setting for a math lesson, for example, would include the specific math problems to be presented during the lesson and the format and sequencing of those problems. Unplanned aspects of the instructional setting are elements the teacher is not aware of or has not considered that might affect the acquisition and generalization of the target behavior. For example, the phrase, *how much* in a word problem may acquire stimulus control over a student's use of addition, even when the correct solution to the problem requires a different arithmetic operation. Or, perhaps a student always uses subtraction for the first problem on each page of word problems because a subtraction problem has always been presented first during instruction.

A **generalization setting** is any place or stimulus situation that differs in some meaningful way from the instructional setting and in which performance of the target behavior is desired. There are multiple generalization settings for many important target behaviors. The student who learns to solve addition and subtraction word problems in the classroom should be able to solve similar problems at home, at the store, and on the ball diamond with his friends.

Examples of instructional and generalization settings for six target behaviors are shown in Figure 28.2. When a person uses a skill in an environment physically removed from the setting where he learned it—as with Behaviors 1 through 3 in Figure 28.2—it is easy to understand that event as an example of generalization across settings. However, many important generalized outcomes occur across more subtle differences between the instructional setting and generalization setting. It is a mistake to think that a generalization setting must be some*where* different from the place where instruction is provided. Students often receive instruction in the same place where they will need to maintain and generalize what they have learned. In other words, the instructional setting and generalization setting can, and often do, share the same physical location (as with Behaviors 4 through 6 in Figure 28.2).

Distinguishing between Setting/Situation Generalization and Response Maintenance

Because any measure of setting/situation generalization is conducted after some instruction has taken place, it might be argued that setting/situation generalization and response maintenance are the same, or are inseparable phenomena at least. Most measures of setting/situation generalization do provide information on response maintenance, and vice versa. For example, the post-training generalization probes conducted by van den Pol and colleagues (1981) at the Burger King restaurant and at the second McDonald's provided data on setting/situation generalization (i.e., to novel restaurants) and on response maintenance of up to 1 year. However, a functional distinction exists between setting/situation generalization and response maintenance, with each outcome presenting a somewhat different set of challenges for programming and ensuring enduring behavior change. When a behavior change produced in the classroom or clinic is not observed in the generalization environment, a lack of setting/situation generalization is evident. When a behavior change produced in the classroom or clinic has occurred at least once in the generalization setting and then ceases to occur, a lack of response maintenance is evident.

An experiment by Koegel and Rincover (1977) illustrated the functional difference between setting/situation generalization and response maintenance. Participants

Figure 28.2 Examples of an instructional setting and a generalization setting for six target behaviors.

Instructional Setting	Generalization Setting
1. Raising hand when *special education teacher* asks a question in the *resource room.*	1. Raising hand when *general education teacher* asks a question in the *regular classroom.*
2. Practicing conversational skills with *speech therapist at school.*	2. Talking with *peers in town.*
3. Passing basketball during a *team scrimmage on home court.*	3. Passing basketball during a *game on the opponent's court.*
4. Answering *addition problems in vertical format* at desk at school.	4. Answering *addition problems in horizontal format* at desk at school.
5. Solving *word problems with no distracter* numbers on homework assignment.	5. Solving *word problems* with *distracter numbers* on homework assignment.
6. Operating package sealer at community job site *in presence of supervisor.*	6. Operating package sealer at community job site *in absence of supervisor.*

were three young boys with autism; each was mute, echolalic, or displayed no appropriate contextual speech. One-to-one instructional sessions were conducted in a small room with the trainer and child seated across from each other at a table. Each child was taught a series of imitative responses (e.g., the trainer said, "Touch your [nose, ear]" or "Do this" and [raised his arm, clapped his hands]). Each 40-minute session consisted of blocks of 10 training trials in the instructional setting alternated with blocks of 10 trials conducted by an unfamiliar adult standing outside, surrounded by trees. All correct responses in the instructional setting were followed by candy and social praise. During the generalization trials the children received the same instructions and model prompts as in the classroom, but no reinforcement or other consequences were provided for correct responses in the generalization setting.

Figure 28.3 shows the percentage of trials in which each child responded correctly in the instructional setting and in the generalization setting. All three children learned to respond to the imitative models in the instructional setting. All three children showed 0% correct responding in the generalization setting at the end of the experiment, but for different reasons. Child 1 and Child 3 began emitting correct responses in the generalization setting as their performances improved in the instructional setting, but their generalized responding was not maintained (most likely the result of the extinction conditions in effect in the generalization setting). The imitative responding acquired by Child 2 in the instructional setting never generalized to the outside setting. Therefore, the 0% correct responding at the experiment's conclusion represents a lack of response maintenance for Child 1 and Child 3, but for Child 2 it represents a failure of setting generalization.

Response Generalization

We define **response generalization** as the extent to which a learner emits untrained responses that are functionally equivalent to the trained target behavior. In other words, in response generalization forms of behavior for which no programmed contingencies have been applied appear as a function of the contingencies that have been applied to other responses. For example:

- Traci wanted to earn some extra money by helping her older brother with his lawn mowing business. Her brother taught Traci to walk the mower up and down parallel rows that moved progressively from

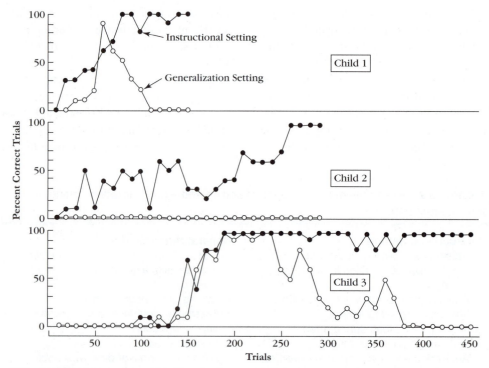

Figure 28.3 Correct responding by three children on alternating blocks of 10 trials in the instructional setting and 10 trials in the generalization setting.

From "Research on the Differences Between Generalization and Maintenance in Extra-Therapy Responding" by R. L. Koegel and A. Rincover, 1977, *Journal of Applied Behavior Analysis, 10,* p. 4. Copyright 1977 by the Society for the Experimental Analysis of Behavior, Inc. Reprinted by permission.

one side of a lawn to the other. Traci discovered that she could mow some lawns just as quickly by first cutting around the perimeter of the lawn and then walking the mower in concentric patterns inward toward the center of the lawn.

- Loraine was taught to remove weeds with a long weed-removal tool. Although she has never been taught or asked to do so, sometimes Loraine removes weeds with a hand trowel or with her bare hands.

- Michael's mother taught him how to take phone messages by using the pencil and notepaper next to the phone to write the caller's name, phone number, and message. One day, Michael's mother came home and saw her son's tape recorder next to the phone. She pushed the play button and heard Michael's voice say, "Grandma called. She wants to know what you'd like her to cook for dinner Wednesday. Mr. Stone called. His number is 555-1234, and he said the insurance payment is due."

The study by Goetz and Baer (1973) described in Chapter 8 of the block building by three preschool girls provides a good example of response generalization. During baseline the teacher sat by each girl as she played with the blocks, watching closely but quietly, and displaying neither enthusiasm nor criticism for any particular use of the blocks. During the next phase of the experiment, each time the child placed or rearranged the blocks to create a new form that had not appeared previously in that session's constructions, the teacher commented with enthusiasm and interest (e.g., "Oh, that's very nice—that's different!"). Another phase followed in which each repeated construction of a given form within the session was praised (e.g., "How nice—another arch!"). The study ended with a phase in which descriptive praise was again contingent on the construction of different block forms. All three children constructed more new forms with the blocks when form diversity was reinforced than they did under baseline or under the reinforcement-for-the-same-forms condition (see Figure 8.7).

Even though specific responses produced reinforcement (i.e., the actual block forms that preceded each instance of teacher praise), other responses sharing that functional characteristic (i.e., being different from block forms constructed previously by the child) increased in frequency as a function of the teacher's praise. As a result, during reinforcement for different forms, the children constructed new forms with the blocks even though each new form itself had never before appeared and therefore could not have been reinforced previously. Reinforcing a few members of the response class of new forms increased the frequency of other members of the same response class.

Generalized Behavior Change: A Relative and Intermixed Concept

As the examples presented previously show, generalized behavior change is a relative concept. We might think of it as existing along a continuum. At one end of the continuum are interventions that might produce a great deal of generalized behavior change; that is, after all components of an intervention have been terminated, the learner may emit the newly acquired target behavior, as well as several functionally related behaviors not observed previously in his repertoire, at every appropriate opportunity in all relevant settings, and he may do so indefinitely. At the other end of the continuum of generalized outcomes are interventions that yield only a small amount of generalized behavior change—the learner uses the new skill only in a limited range of nontraining settings and situations, and only after some contrived response prompts or consequences are applied.

We have presented each of the three primary forms of generalized behavior change individually to isolate its defining features, but they often overlap and occur in combination. Although it is possible to obtain response maintenance without generalization across settings/situations or behaviors (i.e., the target behavior continues to occur in the same setting in which it was trained after the training contingencies have been terminated), any meaningful measure of setting generalization will entail some degree of response maintenance. And it is common for all three forms of generalized behavior change to be represented in the same instance. For example, during a relatively quiet shift at the widget factory on Monday, Joyce's supervisor taught her to obtain assistance by calling out, "Ms. Johnson, I need some help." Later that week (response maintenance) when it was very noisy on the factory floor (setting/situation generalization), Joyce signaled her supervisor by waving her hand back and forth (response generalization).

Generalized Behavior Change Is Not Always Desirable

It is hard to imagine any behavior that is important enough to target for systematic instruction for which response maintenance would be undesirable. However, unwanted setting/situation generalization and response generalization occur often, and practitioners should design intervention plans to prevent or minimize such unwanted outcomes. Undesirable setting/situation generalization takes two common forms: overgeneralization and faulty stimulus control.

Overgeneralization, a nontechnical but effectively descriptive term, refers to an outcome in which the behavior has come under the control of a stimulus class that is too broad. That is, the learner emits the target behavior in the presence of stimuli that, although similar in some way to the instructional examples or situation, are inappropriate occasions for the behavior. For example, a student learns to spell *division, mission,* and *fusion* with the grapheme, *–sion.* When asked to spell *fraction,* the student writes *f-r-a-c-s-i-o-n.*

With *faulty stimulus control,* the target behavior comes under the restricted control of an irrelevant antecedent stimulus. For example, after learning to solve word problems such as, "Natalie has 3 books. Amy has 5 books. How many books do they have in total?" by adding the numerals in the problem, the student adds the numerals in any problem that includes the words "in total" (e.g., "Corinne has 3 candies. Amanda and Corinne have 8 candies in total. How many candies does Amanda have?").[2]

Undesired response generalization occurs when any of a learner's untrained but functionally equivalent responses results in poor performance or undesirable outcomes. For example, although Jack's supervisor at the widget factory taught him to operate the drill press with two hands because that is the safest method, sometimes Jack operates the press with one hand. One-handed responses are functionally equivalent to two-handed responses because both topographies cause the drill press to stamp out a widget, but one-handed responses compromise Jack's health and the factory's safety record. Or, perhaps some of her brother's customers do not like how their lawns look after Traci has mowed them in concentric rectangles.

Other Types of Generalized Outcomes

Other types of generalized outcomes that do not fit easily into categories of response maintenance, setting/situation generalization, and response generalization have been reported in the behavior analysis literature. For example, complex members of a person's repertoire sometimes appear quickly with little or no apparent direct conditioning, such as the *stimulus equivalence* relations described in Chapter 17 (Sidman, 1994). Another type of such rapid learning that appears to be a generalized outcome of other events has been called *contingency adduction,* a process whereby a behavior that was initially selected and shaped under one set of conditions is recruited by a different set of contingencies and takes on a

new function in a person's repertoire (Adronis, 1983; Johnson & Layng, 1992).

Sometimes an intervention applied to one or more people results in behavior changes in other people who were not directly treated by the contingencies. **Generalization across subjects** refers to changes in the behavior of people not directly treated by an intervention as a function of treatment contingencies applied to other people. This phenomenon, which has been described with a variety of related or synonymous terms—*vicarious reinforcement* (Bandura, 1971; Kazdin, 1973), *ripple effect* (Kounin, 1970), and *spillover effect* (Strain, Shores, & Kerr, 1976)—provides another dimension for assessing the generalization of treatment effects. For example, Fantuzzo and Clement (1981) examined the degree to which behavior changes would generalize from one child who received teacher-administered or self-administered token reinforcement during a math activity to a peer seated next to the child.

Drabman, Hammer, and Rosenbaum (1979) combined four basic types of generalized treatment effects— (a) across time (i.e., response maintenance), (b) across settings (i.e., setting/situation generalization), (c) across behaviors (i.e., response generalization), and (d) across subjects—into a conceptual framework they called the *generalization map.* By viewing each type of generalized outcome as dichotomous (i.e., either present or absent) and by combining all possible permutations of the four categories, Drabman and colleagues arrived at 16 categories of generalized behavior change ranging from maintenance (Class 1) to subject-behavior-setting-time generalization (Class 16). Class 1 generalization is evident if the target behavior of the target subject(s) continues in the treatment setting after any "experiment-controlled contingencies" have been discontinued. Class 16 generalization, which Drabman and colleagues (1979) called the "ultimate form" of generalization, is evidenced by "a change in a nontarget subject's nontarget behavior which endures in a different setting after the contingencies have been withdrawn in the treatment setting" (p. 213).

Although Drabman and colleagues recognized that "with any heuristic technique the classifications may prove arbitrary" (p. 204), they provided objectively stated rules for determining whether a given behavioral event fits the requirements of each of their 16 classifications. Regardless of whether generalized behavior change consists of such distinctly separate and wide-ranging phenomena as detailed by Drabman and colleagues, their generalization map provided an objective framework by which the extended effects of behavioral interventions can be described and communicated. For example, Stevenson and Fantuzzo (1984) measured 15 of the 16 generalization map categories in a study of the effects of teaching a fifth-grade boy to use self-management

---

[2]Examples of faulty stimulus control caused by flaws in the design of instructional materials, and suggestions for detecting and correcting those flaws, can be found in J. S. Vargas (1984).

techniques. They not only measured the effects of the intervention on the target behavior (math performance) in the instructional setting (school), but they also assessed effects on the student's math behavior at home, disruptive behavior at home and at school, both behaviors for a nontreated peer in both settings, and maintenance of all of the above.

Planning for Generalized Behavior Change

In general, generalization should be programmed, rather than expected or lamented.

—Baer, Wolf, and Risley (1968, p. 97)

In their review of 270 published studies relevant to generalized behavior change, Stokes and Baer (1977) concluded that practitioners should always "assume that generalization does not occur except through some form of programming . . . and act as if there were no such animal as 'free' generalization—as if generalization never occurs 'naturally,' but always requires programming" (p. 365). Of course, generalization of some type and degree does usually occur, whether or not it is planned. Such unplanned and unprogrammed generalization may be sufficient, but often it is not, particularly for many learners served by applied behavior analysts (e.g., children and adults with learning problems and developmental disabilities). And if left unchecked, unplanned generalized outcomes may be undesirable outcomes.

Achieving optimal generalized outcomes requires thoughtful, systematic planning. This planning begins with two major steps: (1) selecting target behaviors that will meet natural contingencies of reinforcement, and (2) specifying all desired variations of the target behavior and the settings/situations in which it should (and should not) occur after instruction has ended.

Selecting Target Behaviors That Will Meet Naturally Existing Contingencies of Reinforcement

The everyday environment is full of steady, dependable, hardworking sources of reinforcement for almost all of the behaviors that seem natural to us. That is why they seem natural to us.

—Donald M. Baer (1999, p. 15)

Numerous criteria have been suggested for determining whether a proposed teaching objective is relevant or functional for the learner. For example, the age-appropriateness of a skill and the degree to which it represents normalization are often cited as important criteria for choosing target behaviors for students with

disabilities (e.g., Snell & Brown, 2006). Each of these criteria was discussed in Chapter 3, along with numerous other issues that should be considered when selecting and prioritizing target behaviors. In the end, however, there is just one ultimate criterion of functionality: *A behavior is functional only to the extent that it produces reinforcement for the learner.* This criterion holds no matter how important the behavior may be to the person's health or welfare, or no matter how much teachers, family, friends, or the learner himself considers the behavior to be desirable. To repeat: A behavior is not functional if it does not produce reinforcement for the learner. Said another way: Behaviors that are not followed by reinforcers on at least some occasions will not be maintained.

Ayllon and Azrin (1968) recognized this fundamental truth when they recommended that practitioners follow the *relevance-of-behavior rule* when selecting target behaviors. The rule: Choose only those behaviors to change that will produce reinforcers in the postintervention environment. Baer (1999) believed so strongly in the importance of this criterion that he recommended that practitioners heed a similar rule:

> *A good rule is to not make any deliberate behavior changes that will not meet natural communities of reinforcement.* Breaking this rule commits you to maintain and extend the behavior changes that you want, by yourself, indefinitely. If you break this rule, do so knowingly. Be sure that you are willing and able to do what will be necessary. (p. 16, emphasis in original)

Programming for the generalization and maintenance of any behavior for which a natural contingency of reinforcement exists, no matter the specific tactics employed, consists of getting the learner to emit the behavior in the generalization setting just often enough to contact the occurring contingencies of reinforcement. Generalization and maintenance of the behavior from that point forward, while not assured, is a very good bet. For example, after receiving some basic instruction on how to operate the steering wheel, gas pedal, and brakes on a car, the naturally existing reinforcement and punishment contingencies involving moving automobiles and the road will select and maintain effective steering, acceleration, and braking. Very few drivers need booster training sessions on the basic operation of the steering wheel, gas pedal, and brakes.

We define a **naturally existing contingency** as any contingency of reinforcement (or punishment) that operates independent of the behavior analyst's or practitioner's efforts. This is a pragmatic, functional conception of a naturally existing contingency defined by the absence of the behavior analyst's efforts. Naturally existing contingencies include contingencies that operate without social mediation (e.g., walking fast on an icy sidewalk is often punished by a slip and fall) and socially mediated contingencies contrived and implemented by other people in the generalization setting. From the perspective of a special educator who is teaching a set of targeted social and academic skills to students for whom the general education classroom represents the generalization setting, a token economy operated by the general education classroom teacher is an example of the latter type of naturally existing contingency.[3] Even though the token economy was contrived by the teacher in the general education classroom, it is a naturally existing contingency because it already operates in the generalization setting.

We define a **contrived contingency** as any contingency of reinforcement (or punishment) designed and implemented by a behavior analyst or practitioner to achieve the acquisition, maintenance, and/or generalization of a targeted behavior change. From the perspective of the teacher in the general education classroom who designed and implemented it, the token economy in the previous example is a contrived contingency.

In reality, practitioners are often charged with the difficult task of teaching important skills for which there are no dependable naturally existing contingencies of reinforcement. In such cases, practitioners should realize and plan for the fact that the generalization and maintenance of target behaviors will have to be supported, perhaps indefinitely, with contrived contingencies.

Specifying All Desired Variations of the Behavior and the Settings/ Situations Where It Should (and Should Not) Occur

This stage of planning for generalized outcomes includes identifying all the desired behavior changes that need to be made and all the environments and stimulus conditions in which the learner should emit the target behavior(s) after direct training has ceased (Baer, 1999). For some target behaviors, the most important stimulus control for each response variation is clearly defined (e.g., reading C-V-C-E words) and restricted in number (e.g., solving multiplication facts). For many important target behaviors, however, the learner is likely to encounter a multitude of settings and stimulus conditions where the behavior, in a wide variety of response forms, is desired. Only by considering these possibilities prior to instruction can the behavior analyst design an intervention with the best chance of preparing the learner for them.

In one sense, this component of planning for generalized outcomes is similar to preparing a student for a fu-

ture test without knowing the content or the format of all of the questions that will be on the test. The stimulus conditions and contingencies of reinforcement that exist in the generalization setting(s) will provide that test to the learner. Planning involves trying to determine what the final exam will cover (type and form of questions), whether there will be any trick questions (e.g., confusing stimuli that might evoke the target response when it should not occur), and whether the learner will need to use his new knowledge or skill in different ways (response generalization).

List All the Behaviors That Need to Be Changed

A list should be made of all the forms of the target behavior that need to be changed. This is not an easy task, but a necessary one to obtain a complete picture of the teaching task ahead. For example, if the target behavior is teaching Brian, the young boy with autism, to greet people, he should learn a variety of greetings in addition to "Hello, how are you?" Brian may also need many other behaviors to initiate and participate in conversations, such as responding to questions, taking turns, staying on topic, and so forth. He may also need to be taught when and with whom to introduce himself. Only by having a complete list of all the desired forms of the behavior can the practitioner make meaningful decisions about which behaviors to teach directly and which to leave to generalization.

The practitioner should determine whether and to what extent response generalization is desirable for all of the behavior changes listed, and then, make a prioritized list of the variations of the target behavior he would like to see as generalized outcomes.

List All the Settings and Situations in Which the Target Behavior Should Occur

A list should be made of all the desired settings and situations in which the learner will emit the target behavior if optimal generalization is achieved. Will Brian need to introduce himself and talk with children his own age, to adults, to males and females? Will he need to talk with others at home, at school, in the lunchroom, on the playground? Will he be confronted with situations that may appear to be appropriate opportunities to converse but are not (e.g., an unknown adult approaches and offers candy) and for which an alternative response is needed (e.g., walking away, seeking out a known adult). (This kind of analysis often adds additional behaviors to the list of skills to be taught.)

When all of the possible situations and settings have been identified, they should be prioritized according to

---

[3]Token economies are described in Chapter 26.

their importance and the client's likelihood of encountering them. Further analysis of the prioritized environments should then be conducted. What discriminative stimuli usually set the occasion for the target behavior in these various settings and situations? What schedules of reinforcement for the target behavior are typical in these nontraining environments? What kinds of reinforcers are likely to be contingent on the emission of the target behavior in each of the settings? Only when she has answered all of these questions, if not by objective observation then at least by considered estimation, can the behavior analyst begin to have a full picture of the teaching task ahead.

Is the Pre-Intervention Planning Worth It?

Obtaining all of the information just described requires considerable time and effort. Given limited resources, why not design an intervention and immediately begin trying to change the target behavior? It is true that many behavior changes do show generalization, even though the extension of the trained behavior across time, settings, and other behaviors was unplanned and unprogrammed. When target behaviors have been chosen that are truly functional for the subject and when those behaviors have been brought to a high level of proficiency under discriminative stimuli relevant to generalization settings, the chances of generalization are good. But what constitutes a high level of proficiency for certain behaviors in various settings? What are all of the relevant discriminative stimuli in all of the relevant settings? What are all the relevant settings?

Without a systematic plan, a practitioner will usually be ignorant of the answers to these vital questions. Few behaviors that are important enough to target have such limited needs for generalized outcomes that the answers to such questions are obvious. Just a cursory consideration of the behaviors, settings, and people related to a child introducing himself revealed numerous factors that may need to be incorporated into an instructional plan. A more thorough analysis would produce many more. In fact, a complete analysis will invariably reveal more behaviors to be taught, to one person or another, than time or resources would ever allow. And Brian—the 10-year-old who is learning to greet people and introduce himself—in all likelihood needs to learn many other skills also, such as self-help, academic, and recreation and leisure skills, to name just a few. Why then create all the lists in the first place when everything cannot be taught anyway? Why not just train and hope?[4]

Baer (1999) described six possible benefits of listing all the forms of behavior change and all the situations in which these behavior changes should occur.

1. You now see the full scope of the problem ahead of you, and thus see the corresponding scope that your teaching program needs to have.

2. If you teach less than the full scope of the problem, you do so by choice rather than by forgetting that some forms of the behavior could be important, or that there were some other situations in which the behavior change should or should not occur.

3. If less than a complete teaching program results in less than a complete set of behavior changes, you will not be surprised.

4. You can decide to teach less than there is to learn, perhaps because that is all that is practical or possible for you to do.

5. You can decide what is most important to teach. You can also decide to teach the behavior in a way that encourages the indirect development of some of the other forms of the desired behavior, as well as the indirect occurrence of the behavior in some other desired situations, that you will not or cannot teach directly.

6. But if you choose the option discussed in number 5 above, rather than the complete program implicit in number 1, you will do so knowing that the desired outcome would have been more certain had you taught every desirable behavior change directly. The best that you can do is to encourage the behavior changes that you do not cause directly. So, you will have chosen the option in number 5 either of necessity or else as a well-considered gamble after a thoughtful consideration of possibilities, costs, and benefits. (pp. 10–11)

After determining which behaviors to teach directly and in which situations and settings to teach those behaviors, the behavior analyst is ready to consider strategies and tactics for achieving generalization to untrained behaviors and settings.

Strategies and Tactics for Promoting Generalized Behavior Change

Various authors have described conceptual schemes and taxonomies of methods for promoting generalized behavior change (e.g., Egel, 1982; Horner, Dunlap, & Koegel, 1988; Osnes & Lieblein, 2003; Stokes & Baer,

---

[4]Teaching a new behavior without developing and implementing a plan to facilitate its maintenance and generalization is done so often that Stokes and Baer 1977) called it the "train and hope" approach to generalization.

1977; Stokes & Osnes, 1989). The conceptual scheme presented here is informed by the work of those authors and others, and by our own experiences in designing, implementing, and evaluating procedures for promoting generalized outcomes and in teaching practitioners to use them. Although numerous methods and techniques have been demonstrated and given a variety of names, most tactics that effectively promote generalized behavior change can be classified under five strategic approaches:

- Teach the full range of relevant stimulus conditions and response requirements.

- Make the instructional setting similar to the generalization setting.

- Maximize the target behavior's contact with reinforcement in the generalization setting.

- Mediate generalization.

- Train to generalize.

In the following sections we describe and provide examples of 13 tactics applied behavior analysts have used to accomplish these five strategies (see Figure 28.4). Although each tactic is described individually, most efforts to promote generalized behavior change entail a combination of these tactics (e.g., Ducharme & Holborn, 1997; Grossi, Kimball, & Heward, 1994; Hughes, Harmer, Killina, & Niarhos, 1995; Ninness, Fuerst, & Rutherford, 1991; Trask-Tyler, Grossi, & Heward, 1994).

Teach the Full Range of Relevant Stimulus Conditions and Response Requirements

> The most common mistake that teachers make, when they want to establish a generalized behavior change, is to teach one good example of it and expect the student to generalize from that example.
> — Donald M. Baer (1999, p. 15)

To be most useful, most important behaviors must be performed in various ways across a wide range of stimulus conditions. Consider a person skilled in reading, math, conversing with others, and cooking. That person can read thousands of different words; add, subtract, multiply, and divide any combination of numbers; make a multitude of relevant and appropriate comments when talking with others; and measure, combine, and prepare numerous ingredients in hundreds of recipes. Helping learners achieve such wide-ranging performances presents an enormous challenge to the practitioner.

One approach to this challenge would be to teach every desired form of a target behavior in every setting/situation in which the learner may need that behavior in the future. Although this approach would eliminate the need to program for response generalization and setting/situation generalization (response maintenance would remain the only problem), it is seldom possible and never practical. A teacher cannot provide direct instruction on every printed word a student may encounter in the future, or teach a student every measuring, pouring, stirring, and sautéing movement needed to make every dish

Figure 28.4 Strategies and tactics for promoting generalized behavior change.

Teach the Full-Range of Relevant Stimulus Conditions and Response Requirements
  1. Teach sufficient stimulus examples
  2. Teach sufficient response examples
Make the Instructional Setting Similar to the Generalization Setting
  3. Program common stimuli
  4. Teach loosely
Maximize Contact with Reinforcement in the Generalization Setting
  5. Teach the target behavior to levels of performance required by naturally existing contingencies of reinforcement
  6. Program indiscriminable contingencies
  7. Set behavior traps
  8. Ask people in the generalization setting to reinforce the target behavior
  9. Teach the learner to recruit reinforcement
Mediate Generalization
  10. Contrive a mediating stimulus
  11. Teach self-management skills
Train to Generalize
  12. Reinforce response variability
  13. Instruct the learner to generalize

he may want to make in the future. Even for most skill areas for which it would be *possible* to teach every possible example (e.g., instruction *could* be provided on all 900 different single-digit-times-two-digit multiplication problems), to do so would be impractical for many reasons, not the least of which is that the student needs to learn not only many other types of math problems but also skills in other curriculum areas.

A general strategy called **teaching sufficient examples** consists of teaching the student to respond to a subset of all of the possible stimulus and response examples and then assessing the student's performance on untrained examples.[5] For example, the generalization of a student's ability to solve two-digit-minus-two-digit arithmetic problems with regrouping can be assessed by asking the student to solve several problems of the same type for which no instruction or guided practice has been provided. If the results of this **generalization probe** show that the student responds correctly to untaught examples, then instruction can be halted on this class of problems. If the student performs poorly on the generalization probe, the practitioner teaches additional examples before again assessing the student's performance on a new set of untaught examples. This cycle of teaching new examples and probing with untaught examples continues until the learner consistently responds correctly to untrained examples representing the full range of stimulus conditions and response requirements found in the generalization setting.

Teach Sufficient Stimulus Examples

The tactic for promoting setting/situation generalization called *teaching sufficient stimulus examples* involves teaching the learner to respond correctly to more than one example of antecedent stimulus conditions and probing for generalization to untaught stimulus examples. A different stimulus example is incorporated into the teaching program each time a change is made in any dimension of the instructional item itself or the environmental context in which the item is taught. Examples of four dimensions by which different instructional examples can be identified and programmed are the following:

- The specific *item* taught (e.g., multiplication facts: 7×2, 4×5; letter sounds: *a, t*)
- The *stimulus context* in which the item is taught (e.g., multiplication facts presented in *vertical format,* in *horizontal format,* in *word problems;* saying the sound of *t* when it appears at the beginning and end of words: *t*ab, ba*t*)

- The *setting* where instruction occurs (e.g., large-group instruction at school, collaborative learning group, home)
- The *person* doing the teaching (e.g., classroom teacher, peer, parent)

As a general rule, the more examples the practitioner uses during instruction, the more likely the learner will respond correctly to untrained examples or situations. The actual number of examples that must be taught before sufficient generalization occurs will vary as a function of factors such as the complexity of the target behavior being taught, the teaching procedures employed, the student's opportunities to emit the target behavior under the various conditions, the naturally existing contingencies of reinforcement, and the learner's history of reinforcement for generalized responding.

Sometimes teaching as few as two examples will produce significant generalization to untaught examples. Stokes, Baer, and Jackson (1974) taught a greeting response to four children with severe mental retardation who seldom acknowledged or greeted other people. The senior author, working as a dormitory assistant, used unconditioned reinforcers (potato chips and M&Ms) and praise to shape the greeting response (at least two back-and-forth waves of a raised hand). Then this initial trainer maintained the newly learned hand wave by contriving three to six contacts per day with each of the children in various settings (e.g., playroom, corridor, dormitory, courtyard). Throughout the study as many as 23 different staff members systematically approached the children during different times of the day in different settings and recorded whether the children greeted them with a hand waving response. If a child greeted a prober with the waving response, the prober responded with "Hello, (name)." Approximately 20 such generalization probes were conducted each day with each child.

Immediately after learning the greeting response with just one trainer, one of the children (Kerry) showed good setting/situation generalization by using it appropriately in most of her contacts with other staff members. However, the other three children usually failed to greet staff members most of the time, even though they continued to greet the original trainer on virtually every occasion. A second staff member then began to reinforce and maintain the greeting responses of these three children. As a result of adding the second trainer, the children's greeting behavior showed widespread generalization to the other staff members. Stokes and colleagues' (1974) study is important for at least two reasons. First, it demonstrated an effective method for continual assessment of setting/situation generalization across numerous examples (in this case, people). Second, the study showed that it is

---

[5]Other terms commonly used for this strategy for promoting generalized behavior change are *training sufficient exemplars* (Stokes & Baer, 1977) and *training diversely* (Stokes & Osnes, 1989).

sometimes possible to produce widespread generalization by programming only two examples.

Teach Sufficient Response Examples

Instruction that provides practice with a variety of response topographies helps to ensure the acquisition of desired response forms and also promotes response generalization in the form of untrained topographies. Often called **multiple exemplar training,** this tactic typically incorporates both stimulus and response variations. Multiple exemplar training was used to achieve the acquisition and generalization of affective behavior by children with autism (Gena, Krantz, McClannahan, & Poulson, 1996); cooking skills by young adults with disabilities (Trask-Tyler, Grossi, & Heward, 1994); domestic skills (Neef, Lensbower, Hockersmith, DePalma, & Gray, 1990); vocational skills (Horner, Eberhard, & Sheehan, 1986); daily living skills (Horner, Williams, & Steveley, 1987); and requests for assistance (Chadsey-Rusch, Drasgow, Reinoehl, Halle, & Collet-Klingenberg, 1993).

Four female high school students with moderate mental retardation participated in a study by Hughes and colleagues (1995) that assessed the effects of an intervention they called *multiple-exemplar self-instructional training* on the acquisition and generalization of the students' conversational interactions with peers. The young women were recommended for the study because they initiated conversations and responded to peers efforts to talk with them at "low or nonexistent rates" and maintained little eye contact. One of the students, Tanya, had recently been refused a job at a restaurant because of her "reticence and lack of eye contact during her job interview" (p. 202).

A key element of Hughes and colleagues' intervention was practicing a wide variety of conversation starters and statements with different peer teachers. Ten volunteer peer teachers recruited from general education classrooms helped teach conversation skills to the participants. The peer teachers were male and female, ranged in grade level from freshmen to seniors, and represented African American, Asian American, and Euro-American ethnic groups. Instead of learning a few scripted conversation openers, the participants practiced using multiple examples of conversation starters selected from a pooled list of conversation openers used by general education students. Additionally, participants were encouraged to develop individual adaptations of statements, which further promoted response generalization by increasing the number and range of conversational statements that were likely to be used in subsequent conversations.

Before, during, and after multiple exemplar training, generalization probes were conducted of each participant's use of self-instructions, eye contact, and initiating

and responding to conversation partners. The 23 to 32 different students who served as conversation partners for each participant represented the full range of student characteristics in the school population (e.g., gender, age, ethnicity, students with and without disabilities) and included students who were known and unknown to the participants prior to the study. The rate of conversation initiations by all four participants increased during multiple exemplar training to levels approximating those of general education students and was maintained at those rates after the intervention was terminated completely (see Figure 28.5).

General Case Analysis

Teaching a learner to respond correctly to multiple examples will not automatically produce generalized responding to untaught examples. To achieve an optimal degree of generalization and discrimination, the behavior analyst must pay close attention to the specific examples used during instruction; not just any examples will do. Optimally effective instructional design requires selecting teaching examples that represent the full range of stimulus situations and response requirements in the natural environment.[6] **General case analysis** (also called *general case strategy*) is a systematic method for selecting teaching examples that represent the full range of stimulus variations and response requirements in the generalization setting (Albin & Horner, 1988; Becker & Engelmann, 1978; Engelmann & Carnine, 1982).

A series of studies by Horner and colleagues demonstrated the importance of teaching examples that systematically sample the range of stimulus variations and response requirements the learner will encounter in the generalization setting (e.g., Horner, Eberhard, & Sheehan, 1986; Horner & McDonald, 1982; Horner, Williams, & Steveley, 1987). In a classic example of this line of research, Sprague and Horner (1984) evaluated the effects of general case instruction on the generalized use of vending machines by six high school students with moderate to severe mental retardation. The dependent variable was the number of vending machines each student operated correctly during generalization probes of 10 different machines located within the community. For a probe trial to be scored as correct, a student had to correctly perform a chain of five responses (i.e., insert the proper number of coins, activate the machine for the desired item, and so on). The researchers selected the 10 vending machines used to assess generalization because each student's performance on those machines would serve as an index of

---

[6]Siegfried Engelmann and Douglas Carnine's (1982) *Theory of Instruction: Principles and Applications* is one of the most thorough and sophisticated treatments of the selection and sequencing of teaching examples for effective and efficient curriculum design.

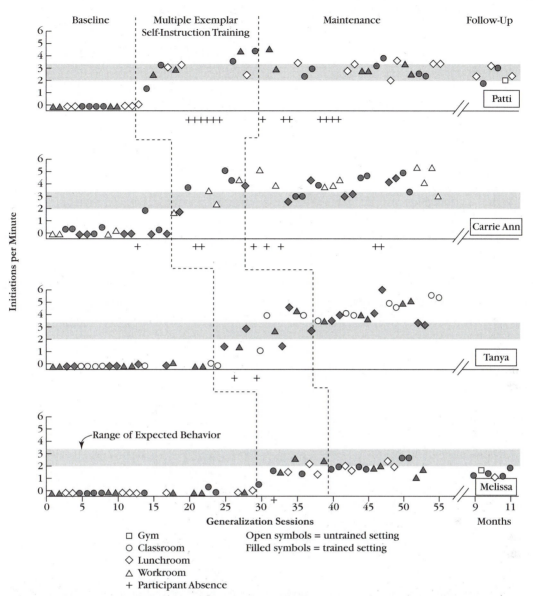

Figure 28.5   Conversation initiations per minute by four high school students with disabilities to conversation partners with and without disabilities during generalization sessions. The shaded bands represent typical performance by general education students.

From "The Effects of Multiple-Exemplar Training on High-School Students' Generalized Conversational Interactions" by C. Hughes, M. L. Harmer, D. J. Killina, and F. Niarhos, 1995. *Journal of Applied Behavior Analysis, 28,* p. 210. Copyright 1995 by the Society for the Experimental Analysis of Behavior, Inc. Reprinted by permission.

his performance "across all vending machines dispensing food and beverage items costing between $.20 and $.75 in Eugene, Oregon" (p. 274). None of the vending machines used in the generalization probes was identical to any of the vending machines used during instruction.

After a single-baseline probe verified each student's inability to use the 10 vending machines in the community, a condition the researchers called "single-instance instruction" began. Under this condition each student received individual training on a single vending machine located in the school until he used the machine independently for three consecutive correct trials on each

of two consecutive days. Even though each student had learned to operate the training machine without errors, the generalization probe following single-instance instruction revealed little or no success with the vending machines in the community (see Probe Session 2 in Figure 28.6). The continued poor performance of Students 2, 3, 5, and 6 on successive generalization probes that followed additional instruction with the single-instance training machine shows that overlearning on a single example does not necessarily aid generalization. Further evidence of the limited generalization obtained from single-instance instruction is the fact that seven of

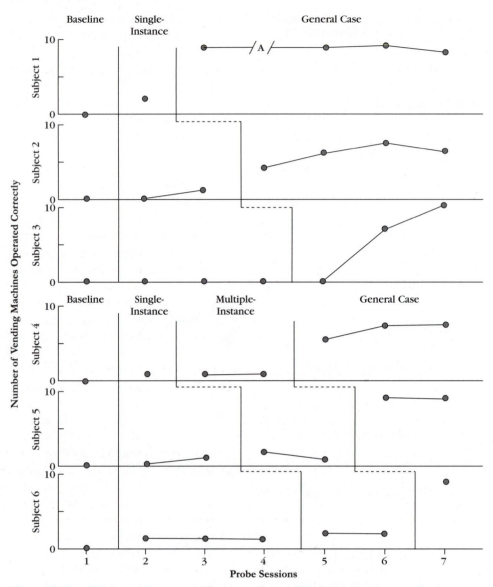

Figure 28.6   The number of nontrained probe machines operated correctly by students across phases and probe sessions.

From "The Effects of Single Instance, Multiple Instance, and General Case Training on Generalized Vending Machine Use by Moderately and Severely Handicapped Students" by J. R. Sprague and R. H. Horner, 1984, *Journal of Applied Behavior Analysis, 17,* p. 276. Copyright 1984 by the Society for the Experimental Analysis of Behavior, Inc. Reprinted by permission.

the eight total probe trials performed correctly by all students after single-instance instruction were on Probe Machine 1, the vending machine that most closely resembled the machine on which the students had been trained.

Next, multiple-instance training was implemented with Students 4, 5, and 6. The teaching procedures and performance criteria for multiple-instance training were the same as those used in the single-instance condition except that each student received instruction until he reached criterion on all three new machines. Sprague and Horner (1984) purposely selected vending machines to use in the multiple-instance instruction that were similar

to one another and that did not sample the range of stimulus variations and response requirements that defined the vending machines in the community. After reaching training criterion on three additional machines, Students 4, 5, and 6 were still unable to operate the machines in the community. During the six probe sessions that followed multiple-instance instruction, these students correctly completed only 9 of the 60 total trials.

The researchers then introduced general case instruction in multiple-baseline fashion across students. This condition was the same as multiple-instance instruction except that the three different vending machines used in general case training, when combined with the single-instance machine, provided the students with practice across the total range of stimulus conditions and response variations found in vending machines in the community. None of the training machines, however, were exactly the same as any machine used in the generalization probes. After reaching training criterion on the general case machines, all six students showed substantial improvements in their performance on the 10 untrained machines. Sprague and Horner (1984) speculated that Student 3's poor performance on the first generalization probe following general case instruction was caused by a ritualistic pattern of inserting coins that he had developed during previous probe sessions. After receiving repeated practice on the coin insertion step during a training session between Probe Sessions 5 and 6, Student 3's performance on the generalization machines improved greatly.

Negative, or "Don't Do It," Teaching Examples

Generalization across every possible condition or situation is rarely desirable. Teaching a student where and when to use a new skill or bit of knowledge does not mean that he also knows where and when *not* to use this newly learned behavior. Brian, for example, needs to learn that he should not say, "Hello, how are you?" to people that he greeted within the past hour or so. Learners must be taught to discriminate the stimulus conditions that signal when responding is appropriate from stimulus conditions that signal when responding is inappropriate.

Instruction that includes "don't do it" teaching examples intermixed with positive examples provides learners with practice discriminating stimulus situations in which the target behavior should not be emitted (i.e., S^Δs) from those conditions when the behavior is appropriate. This sharpens the stimulus control necessary to master many concepts and skills (Engelmann & Carnine, 1982).[7]

Horner, Eberhard, and Sheehan (1986) incorporated "don't do it" examples into training programs to teach four high school students with moderate to severe mental retardation how to bus tables in cafeteria-style restaurants. To correctly bus a table, the student had to remove all dishes, silverware, and garbage from tabletop, chairs, and the floor

under and around the table; wipe the tabletop; straighten chairs; and place dirty dishes and garbage in appropriate receptacles. In addition, the students were taught to inquire, through the use of cards, if a customer was finished with empty dishes. The three settings, one for training and two for generalization probes, differed in terms of size and furniture characteristics and configurations.

Each training trial required the student to attend to the following stimulus features of a table: (a) the presence or absence of people at a table, (b) whether people were eating at the table, (c) the amount and/or status of food on dishes, (d) the presence or absence of garbage at a table, and (e) the location of garbage and/or dirty dishes at a table. Training consisted of 30-minute sessions involving six table types that represented the range of conditions likely to be encountered in a cafeteria-style restaurant. A trainer modeled correct table bussing, verbally prompted correct responding and stopped the student when errors occurred, recreated the situation, and provided additional modeling and assistance. The six training examples consisted of four to-be-bussed tables and two not-to-be-bussed tables (see Table 28.1).

During generalization probe sessions, which were conducted in two restaurants not used for training, each student was presented with 15 tables selected to represent the range of table types the students could be expected to encounter if employed in a cafeteria-style restaurant. The 15 probe tables consisted of 10 to-be-bussed tables and 5 not-to-be-bussed tables. The results showed a functional relation between general case instruction that included not-to-be-bussed tables and "immediate and pronounced improvement in the percentage of probe tables responded to correctly" (p. 467).

Negative teaching examples are necessary when discriminations must be made between appropriate and inappropriate conditions for a particular response. Practitioners should ask this question: Is responding *always appropriate* in the generalization setting(s)? If the answer is no, then "don't do it now" teaching examples should be part of instruction.

Does the teaching setting or situation naturally or automatically include a sufficient number and range of negative examples? The teaching situation must be analyzed to answer this important question. Practitioners may need to contrive some negative teaching examples. *Practitioners should not assume the natural environment will readily reveal sufficient negative examples.* Conducting training in the natural environment is no guarantee that learners will be exposed to stimulus situations that they are likely to encounter in the generalization environment after training. For example, in the study on teaching table bussing described earlier, Horner and colleagues (1986) noted that, "on some days the trainer needed actively to

---

[7]Teaching examples used to help students discriminate when not to respond (i.e., S^Δs) are sometimes called *negative examples* and contrasted with positive examples (i.e., S^Ds). However, in our work in teaching this concept, practitioners have told us that the term *negative teaching example* suggests that the teacher is modeling or showing the learner *how* not to perform the target behavior. Instruction on the desired topography for some behaviors may be aided by providing students with models on how not to perform certain behavior (i.e., negative examples), but the function of "don't do it" examples is to help the learner discriminate antecedent conditions that signal an inappropriate occasion for responding.

Table 28.1 Six Training Examples Used to Teach Students with Disabilities How to Bus Tables in Cafeteria-Style Restaurants

Training Examples	Presence of People and Possessions	People Eating or Not Eating	Dishes: Empty/ Part/New Food	Garbage: Present or Not Present	Location of Garbage and Dishes	Correct Response
1	0 People + possessions	N/A	Partial	Present	Table Chairs	Don't Bus
2	0 People	N/A	Partial	Present	Table, Floor, Chair	Bus
3	2 People	Eating	New food	Present	Table, Chair, Floor	Don't Bus
4	0 People	N/A	Empty	Present	Table, Floor	Bus
5	1 Person	Not eating	Empty	Present	Chair, Floor	Bus
6	2 People	Not eating	Empty	Present	Table	Bus

From "Teaching Generalized Table Bussing: The Importance of Negative Teaching Examples" by R. H. Horner, J. M. Eberhard, and M. R. Sheehan, 1986, *Behavior Modification, 10,* p. 465. Copyright 1986 by the Sage Publications, Inc. Used by permission.

set up one or more table types to ensure that a student had access to a table type that was not 'naturally' available" (p. 464).

"Don't do it" teaching examples should be selected and sequenced according to the degree to which they differ from positive examples (i.e., S^{D}s). The most effective negative teaching examples will share many of the relevant characteristics of the positive teaching examples (Horner, Dunlap, & Koegel, 1988). Such *minimum difference negative teaching examples* help the learner to perform the target behavior with the precision required by the natural environment. Minimum difference teaching examples help eliminate "generalization errors" due to overgeneralization and faulty stimulus control. For example, the "don't bus" tables used by Horner and colleagues (1986) shared many features with the "bus" tables (see Table 28.1).

Make the Instructional Setting Similar to the Generalization Setting

> Fresno State coach Pat Hill expects Ohio Stadium to be a new experience for the Bulldogs, who will visit for the first time. For a practice last week in FSU's stadium, Hill hired a production company to blast the Ohio State fight song—at about 90 decibels—throughout the two-hour session. "We created some noise and atmosphere to give us a feel of a live game," Hill said.
> —*Columbus Dispatch* (August 27, 2000)

A basic strategy for promoting generalization is to incorporate into the instructional setting stimuli that the learner is likely to encounter in the generalization setting. The greater the similarity between the instructional environment and the generalization environment, the more likely the target behavior will be emitted in the generalization setting. The principle of stimulus generalization states that

a behavior is likely to be emitted in the presence of a stimulus very similar to the stimulus conditions in which the behavior was reinforced previously, but the behavior will likely not be emitted under stimulus conditions that differ significantly from the training stimulus.

Stimulus generalization is a relative phenomenon: The more a given stimulus configuration resembles the stimulus conditions present during instruction, the greater the probability that the trained response will be emitted, and vice versa. A generalization setting that differs significantly from the instructional setting may not provide sufficient stimulus control over the target behavior. Such a setting may also contain stimuli that impede the target behavior because their novelty confuses or startles the learner. Exposing the learner to stimuli during instruction that are commonly found in the generalization setting increases the likelihood that those stimuli will acquire some stimulus control over the target behavior and also prepares the learner for the presence of stimuli in the generalization setting that have the potential of impeding performance. Two tactics used by applied behavior analysts to implement this basic strategy are programming common stimuli and teaching loosely.

Program Common Stimuli

Programming common stimuli means including typical features of the generalization setting into the instructional setting. Although behavior analysts have attached a special term to this tactic, successful practitioners in many fields have long used this technique for promoting generalized behavior change. For example, coaches, music teachers, and theater directors hold scrimmages, mock auditions, and dress rehearsals to prepare their athletes, musicians, and actors to perform important skills in settings that include the sights, sounds, materials, people, and procedures that simulate as closely as possible those in the "real world."

Van den Pol and colleagues (1981) programmed common stimuli when they taught three young adults with disabilities how to order and eat in fast-food restaurants. The researchers used numerous items and photos from actual restaurants to make the classroom simulate the conditions found in actual restaurants. Plastic signs with pictures and names of various McDonald's sandwiches were posted on the classroom wall, a table was transformed into a mock "counter" for role-playing transactions, and the students practiced responding to 60 photographic slides taken in actual restaurants showing both positive and negative ("don't do it") examples of situations customers are likely to encounter.

Why go to all the trouble of simulating the generalization setting? Why not just conduct instruction in the generalization setting itself to ensure that the learner experiences all of the relevant aspects of the setting? First, conducting instruction in natural settings is not always possible or practical. Lots of resources and time may be necessary to transport students to community-based settings.

Second, community-based training may not expose students to the full range of examples they are likely to encounter later in the same setting. For example, students who receive *in situ* instruction for grocery shopping or street crossing during school hours may not experience the long lines at the checkout counters or heavy traffic patterns typical of evening hours.

Third, instruction in natural settings may be less effective and efficient than classroom instruction because the trainer cannot halt the natural flow of events to contrive an optimal number and sequence of training trials needed (e.g., Neef, Lensbower, Hockersmith, DePalma, & Gray, 1990).

Fourth, instruction in simulated settings can be safer, particularly with target behaviors that must be performed in potentially dangerous environments or that have severe consequences if performed incorrectly (e.g., Miltenberger et al., 2005), or when children or people with learning problems must perform complex procedures. If the procedures involve invading the body or errors during practice are potentially hazardous, simulation training should be used. For example, Neef, Parrish, Hannigan, Page, and Iwata (1990) had children with neurogenic bladder complications practice performing self-catheterization skills on dolls.

Programming common stimuli is a straightforward two-step process of (a) identifying salient stimuli that characterize the generalization setting(s) and (b) incorporating those stimuli into the instructional setting. A practitioner can identify possible stimuli in the generalization setting to make common by direct observation or

by asking people familiar with the setting. Practitioners should conduct observations in the generalization setting(s) and write down prominent features of the environment that might be important to include during training. When direct observation is not feasible, practitioners can obtain secondhand knowledge of the setting by interviewing or giving checklists to people who have firsthand knowledge of the generalization setting—those who live, work in, or are otherwise familiar with the generalization setting(s) in question.

If a generalization setting includes important stimuli that cannot be recreated or simulated in the instructional setting, then at least some training trials must be conducted in the generalization setting. However, as pointed out previously, practitioners should not assume that community-based instruction will guarantee students' exposure to all of the important stimuli common to the generalization setting.

Teach Loosely

Applied behavior analysts control and standardize intervention procedures to maximize their direct effects, and so the effects of their interventions can be interpreted and replicated by others. Yet restricting teaching procedures to a "precisely repetitive handful of stimuli or formats may, in fact, correspondingly restrict generalization of the lessons being learned" (Stokes & Baer, 1977, p. 358). To the extent that generalized behavior change can be viewed as the opposite of strict stimulus control and discrimination, one technique for facilitating generalization is to vary as many of the noncritical dimensions of the antecedent stimuli as possible during instruction.

Teaching loosely, randomly varying noncritical aspects of the instructional setting within and across teaching sessions, has two advantages or rationales for promoting generalization. First, teaching loosely reduces the likelihood that a single or small group of noncritical stimuli will acquire exclusive control over the target behavior. A target behavior that inadvertently comes under the control of a stimulus present in the instructional setting but not always present in the generalization setting may not be emitted in the generalization setting. Here are two examples of this type of faulty stimulus control:

* *Following teachers' directions:* A student with a history of receiving reinforcement for complying with teachers' directions when they are given in a loud voice and accompanied by a stern facial expression may not follow directions that do not contain one or both of those noncritical variables. The discriminative stimulus for the student's compliance with teacher directions should be the content of the teacher's statements.

- *Assembling bicycle sprocket sets:* A new employee at the bicycle factory inadvertently learns to assemble rear sprocket sets by putting a red sprocket on top of a green sprocket and a green sprocket on top of a blue sprocket because the sprocket sets on a particular bicycle model in production on the day she was trained were colored in that fashion. However, proper assembly of a sprocket set has nothing to do with the colors of the individual sprockets; the relevant variable is the relative size of the sprockets (i.e., the biggest sprocket goes on the bottom, the next biggest on top of that one, and so on).

Systematically varying the presence and absence of noncritical stimuli during instruction greatly decreases the chance that a functionally irrelevant factor, such as a teacher's tone of voice or sprocket color in these two examples, will acquire control of the target behavior (Kirby & Bickel, 1988).

A second rationale for loose teaching is that including a wide variety of noncritical stimuli during instruction increases the probability that the generalization setting will include at least some of the stimuli that were present during instruction. In this sense, loose teaching acts as a kind of catchall effort at programming common stimuli and makes it less likely that a student's performance will be impeded or "thrown off" by the presence of a "strange" stimulus.

Loose teaching applied to the previous two examples might entail the following:

- *Following teachers' directions:* During instruction the teacher varies all of the factors mentioned earlier (e.g., tone of voice, facial expression), plus gives directions while standing, while sitting, from different places within the classroom, at different times of the day, while the student is alone and in groups, while looking away from the student, and so on. In each instance, reinforcement is contingent on the student's compliance with the content of the teacher's direction irrespective of the presence or absence of any of the noncritical features.

- *Assembling bicycle sprocket sets:* During training the new employee assembles sprocket sets containing sprockets of widely varying colors, after receiving the component sprockets in varied sequences, when the factory floor is busy, at different times during a work shift, with and without music playing, and so forth. Irrespective of the presence, absence, or values of any of these noncritical factors, reinforcement would be contingent on correct assembly of sprockets by relative size.

Seldom used as a stand-alone tactic, loose teaching is often a recognizable component of interventions when generalization to highly variable and diverse settings or situations is desired. For example, Horner and colleagues (1986) incorporated loose teaching into their training program for table busing by systematically but randomly varying the location of the tables, the number of people at the tables, whether food was completely or partially eaten, the amount and location of garbage, and so forth. Hughes and colleagues (1995) incorporated loose teaching by varying the peer teachers and varying the locations of training sessions. Loose teaching is often a recognizable feature of language training programs that use milieu, incidental, and naturalistic teaching methods (e.g., Charlop-Christy & Carpenter, 2000; McGee, Morrier, & Daly, 1999; Warner, 1992).

Few studies evaluating the effects of using loose teaching in isolation have been reported. One exception is an experiment by Campbell and Stremel-Campbell (1982), who evaluated the effectiveness of loose teaching as a tactic for facilitating the generalization of newly acquired language by two students with moderate mental retardation. The students were taught the correct use of the words *is* and *are* in "wh" questions (e.g., "What are you doing?"), yes/no reversal questions (e.g., "Is this mine?"), and statements (e.g., "These are mine?"). Each student received two 15-minute language training sessions conducted within the context of other instructional activities that were part of each child's individualized education program, one during an academic task and the second during a self-help task. The student could initiate a language interaction based on the wide variety of naturally occurring stimuli, and the teacher could try to evoke a statement or question from the student by intentionally misplacing instructional materials or offering indirect prompts. Generalization probes of the students' language use during two daily 15-minute free-play periods revealed substantial generalization of the language structures acquired during the loose teaching sessions.

The learner's performance of the target behavior should be established under fairly restricted, simplified, and consistent conditions, before much "looseness" is introduced. This is particularly important when teaching complex and difficult skills. Only noncritical (i.e., functionally irrelevant) stimuli should be "loosened." Practitioners should not inadvertently loosen stimuli that reliably function in the generalization setting as discriminative stimuli (S^Ds) or as "don't do it" examples (S^Δs). Stimuli known to play important roles in signaling when and when not to respond should be systematically incorporated into instructional programs as teaching examples. A stimulus condition that may be functionally irrelevant for one skill may be a critical S^D for another skill.

Taking the notion of varying noncritical aspects of the instructional setting and procedures to its logical limit, Baer (1999) offered the following advice for loose teaching:

- Use two or more teachers.

- Teach in two or more places.

- Teach from a variety of positions.

- Vary your tone of voice.

- Vary your choice of words.

- Show the stimuli from a variety of angles, using sometimes one hand and sometimes the other.

- Have other persons present sometimes and not other times.

- Dress quite differently on different days.

- Vary the reinforcers.

- Teach sometimes in bright light, sometimes in dim light.

- Teach sometimes in noisy settings, sometimes in quiet ones.

- In any setting, vary the decorations, vary the furniture, and vary their locations.

- Vary the times of day when you and everyone else teach.

- Vary the temperature in the teaching settings.

- Vary the smells in the teaching settings.

- Within the limits possible vary the content of what's being taught.

- Do all of this as often and as unpredictably as possible. (p. 24)

Of course, Baer (1999) was not suggesting that a teacher needs to vary all of these factors for every behavior taught. But building a reasonable degree of "looseness" into teaching is an important element of a teacher's overall effort to program for generalization rather than train and hope.

Maximize Contact with Reinforcement in the Generalization Setting

Even though a practitioner is successful in getting the learner to emit a newly acquired target behavior in a generalization setting with a naturally existing contingency of reinforcement, generalization and maintenance may be short-lived if the behavior makes insufficient contact with reinforcement. In such cases the practitioner's efforts to promote generalization revolves around ensuring that the target behavior contacts reinforcement in the generalization setting. Five of the 13 tactics for promoting

generalized behavior change described in this chapter involve some form of arranging or contriving for the target behavior to be reinforced in the generalization setting.

Teach Behavior to Levels Required by Natural Contingencies

Baer (1999) suggested that a common mistake practitioners make when attempting to employ natural contingencies of reinforcement is failing to teach the behavior change well enough so that it contacts the contingency.

> Sometimes behavior changes that seem to need generalization may only need better teaching. Try making the students fluent, and see if they still need further support for generalization. Fluency may consist of any or all of the following: high rate of performance, high accuracy of performance, fast latency, given the opportunity to respond, and strong response. (p. 17)

A new behavior may occur in the generalization setting but fail to make contact with the naturally existing contingencies of reinforcement. Common variables that diminish contact with reinforcement in the generalization setting include the accuracy of the behavior, the dimensional quality of the behavior (i.e., frequency, duration, latency, magnitude), and the form (topography) of the behavior. The practitioner may need to enhance the learner's performance in one or more of these variables to ensure that the new behavior will meet the naturally existing contingencies of reinforcement. For example, when given a worksheet to complete at his desk, a student's behavior that is consistent with the following dimensions is unlikely to contact reinforcement for completing the task, even if the student has the ability to complete each worksheet item accurately.

- *Latency too long.* A student who spends 5 minutes "daydreaming" before he begins reading the directions may not finish in time to obtain reinforcement.

- *Rate too low.* A student who needs 5 minutes to read the directions for an independent seatwork assignment that his peers read in less than 1 minute may not finish in time to obtain reinforcement.

- *Duration too brief.* A student who can work without direct supervision for only 5 minutes at a time will not be able to complete any task requiring more than 5 minutes of independent work.

The solution for this kind of generalization problem, if not always simple, is straightforward. The behavior change must be made more fluent: The learner must be taught to emit the target behavior at a rate commensurate with the naturally occurring contingency, with more accuracy, within a shorter latency, and/or at a greater magnitude. Generalization planning should include identification of the levels of performance necessary to access existing criteria for reinforcement.

Program Indiscriminable Contingencies

Applied behavior analysts purposely design and implement interventions so the learner receives consistent and immediate consequences for emitting the target behavior. Although consistent and immediate consequences are often necessary to help the learner acquire new behavior, those very contingencies can impede generalization and maintenance. The clear, predictable, and immediate consequences that are typically part of systematic instruction can actually work against generalized responding. This is most likely to occur when a newly acquired skill has not yet contacted naturally existing contingencies of reinforcement, and the learner can discriminate when the instructional contingencies are absent in the generalization settings. If the presence or absence of the controlling contingencies in the generalization setting is obvious or predictable to the learner ("Hey, the game's off. There's no need to respond here/now"), the learner may stop responding in the generalization setting, and the behavior change the practitioner worked so hard to develop may cease to occur before it can contact the naturally existing contingency of reinforcement.

An **indiscriminable contingency** is one in which the learner cannot discriminate whether the next response will produce reinforcement. As a tactic for promoting generalization and maintenance, programming indiscriminable contingencies involves contriving a contingency in which (a) reinforcement is contingent on some, but not all, occurrences of the target behavior in the generalization setting, and (b) the learner is unable to predict which responses will produce reinforcement.

The basic rationale for programming indiscriminable contingencies is to keep the learner responding often enough and long enough in the generalization setting for the target behavior to make sufficient contact with the naturally existing contingencies of reinforcement. From that point on, the need to program contrived contingencies to promote generalization will be moot. Applied behavior analysts use two related techniques to program indiscriminable contingencies: intermittent schedules of reinforcement and delayed rewards.

Intermittent Schedules of Reinforcement. A newly learned behavior often must occur repeatedly over a period of time in the generalization setting before it contacts a naturally existing contingency of reinforcement. During that time, an extinction condition exists for responses emitted in the generalization setting. The current or most recent schedule of reinforcement for a behavior in the instructional setting plays a significant role in how many responses will be emitted in the generalization setting prior to reinforcement. Behaviors that have been under continuous schedules of reinforcement (CRF) show very limited response maintenance under extinction. When reinforcement is no longer available, responding is likely to decrease rapidly to prereinforcement levels. On the other hand, behaviors with a history of intermittent schedules of reinforcement often continue to be emitted for relatively long periods of time after reinforcement is no longer available (e.g., Dunlap & Johnson, 1985; Hoch, McComas, Thompson, & Paone, 2002).

An experiment by Koegel and Rincover (1977, Experiment II) showed the effects of intermittent schedules of reinforcement on response maintenance in a generalization setting. The participants were six boys diagnosed with autism and severe to profound mental retardation, ages 7 to 12 years, who had participated in a previous study on generalization and had showed generalized responding in the extra-therapy setting used in that experiment (Rincover & Koegel, 1975). As in Experiment I by Koegel and Rincover (1977) described earlier in this chapter, one-on-one training trials were conducted with each child and the trainer seated at a table in a small room, and generalization trials were conducted by an unfamiliar adult standing outside on the lawn, surrounded by trees. Two types of imitative response class consisted of (a) nonverbal imitation (e.g., raising arm) in response to an imitative model and the verbal instruction, "Do this" and (b) touching a body part in response to verbal instructions such as, "Touch your nose." After acquiring an imitation response, each child was given additional trials on one of three randomly chosen schedules of reinforcement: CRF, FR 2, or FR 5. Only after these additional training trials were the children taken outside to assess response maintenance. Once outside, trials were conducted until the child's correct responding had decreased to 0%, or was maintained at 80% correct or above for 100 consecutive trials.

Behaviors that were most recently on a CRF schedule in the instructional setting underwent extinction quickly in the generalization setting (see Figure 28.7). Generalized responding occurred longer for the FR 2 trained behavior, and longer still for behavior that had been shifted to an FR 5 schedule in the instructional setting. The results showed clearly that the schedule of reinforcement in the instructional setting had a predictable effect on responding in the absence of reinforcement in the generalization setting: The thinner the schedule in the instructional setting, the longer the response maintenance in the generalization setting.

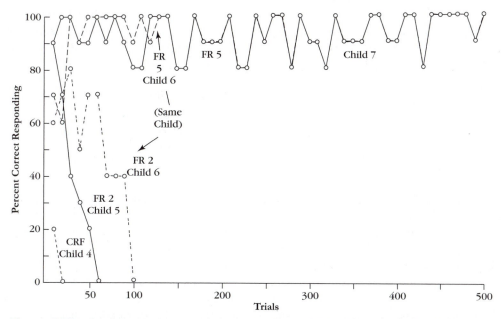

Figure 28.7   Percent of correct responses by three children in a generalization setting as a function of the schedule of reinforcement used during the final sessions in an instructional setting.

From "Research on the Differences between Generalization and Maintenance in Extra-Therapy Responding" by R. L. Koegel and A. Rincover, 1977, *Journal of Applied Behavior Analysis, 10,* p. 8. Copyright 1977 by the Society for the Experimental Analysis of Behavior, Inc. Reprinted by permission.

The defining feature of all intermittent schedules of reinforcement is that only some responses are reinforced, which means, of course, that some responses go unreinforced. Thus, one possible explanation for the maintenance of responding during periods of extinction for behaviors developed under intermittent schedules is the relative difficulty of discriminating that reinforcement is no longer available. Thus, the unpredictability of an intermittent schedule may account for the maintenance of behavior after the schedule is terminated.

Practitioners should recognize that although *all indiscriminable contingencies of reinforcement involve intermittent schedules, not all schedules of intermittent reinforcement are indiscriminable.* For example, although the FR 2 and FR 5 schedules of reinforcement used by Koegel and Rincover (1977) were intermittent, many learners would soon be able to discriminate whether reinforcement would follow their next response. In contrast, a student whose behavior is being supported by a VR 5 schedule of reinforcement cannot determine whether his next response will be reinforced.

Delayed Rewards. Stokes and Baer (1977) suggested that not being able to discriminate in what settings a behavior will be reinforced is similar to not being able to discriminate whether the next response will be reinforced. They cited an experiment by Schwarz and Hawkins (1970) in which each day after school a sixth-grade girl was shown videotapes of her behavior in that

day's math class and received praise and token reinforcement for improvements in her posture, reducing the number of times she touched her face, and speaking with sufficient volume to be heard by others. Reinforcement after school was contingent on behaviors emitted during math class only, but comparable improvements were noted in spelling class as well. The generalization data were taken from videotapes that were made of the girl's behavior in spelling class but were never shown to her. Stokes and Baer hypothesized that because reinforcement was delayed (the behaviors that produced praise and tokens were emitted during math class but were not rewarded until after school), it may have been difficult for the student to discriminate when improved performance was required for reinforcement. They suggested that the generalization across settings of the target behaviors may have been a result of the indiscriminable nature of the response-to-reinforcement delay.

Delayed rewards and intermittent schedules of reinforcement are alike in two ways: (a) Reinforcement is not delivered each time the target behavior is emitted (only some responses are followed by reinforcement), and (b) there are no clear stimuli to signal the learner which current responses will produce reinforcement. A delayed reward contingency differs from intermittent reinforcement in that instead of delivering the consequence immediately following an occurrence of the target behavior, the reward is provided after a period of time has elapsed (i.e., a response-to-reward delay). Receiving the delayed reward is contingent on the learner having performed the target behavior in the generalization setting *during an earlier time period.* With an effective delayed reward contingency, the learner cannot discriminate when (or where, depending on the details of the contingency) the target behavior must be emitted in order to receive reinforcement. As a result, to have the best chance to receive the reward later, the learner must "be good all day" (Fowler & Baer, 1981).

Two similar studies by Freeland and Noell (1999, 2002) investigated the effects of delayed rewards on the maintenance of students' mathematics performance. Participants in the second study were two third-grade girls who had been referred by their teacher for help with mathematics. That target behavior for both students was writing answers to single-digit addition problems with sums to 18. The researchers used a multiple-treatment reversal design to compare the effects of five conditions on the number of correct digits written as answers to single-digit addition problems during daily 5-minute work periods (e.g., writing "11" as the answer to "5 + 6 = ?" counted as two digits correct).

- *Baseline:* Green worksheets; no programmed consequences; students were told they could attempt as many or as few problems as they wanted.

- *Reinforcement:* Blue worksheets with a goal number at the top indicating the number of correct digits needed to choose a reward in the "goody box"; each student's goal number was the median number of correct digits on the last three worksheets; all worksheets were graded after each session.

- *Delay 2:* White worksheets with goal number; after every two sessions, one of the two worksheets completed by each student was randomly selected for grading; reinforcement was contingent on meeting highest median of three consecutive sessions up to that point in the study.

- *Delay 4:* White worksheets with goal number and same procedures as Delay 2 except that worksheets were not graded until four sessions had been completed, at which time one of each student's previous four worksheets was randomly selected and graded.

- *Maintenance:* White worksheets with goal number as before; no worksheets were graded and no feedback or rewards for performance were given.

The fact that different colored worksheets were used for each condition in this study made it easy for the students to predict the likelihood of reinforcement. A green worksheet meant no "goody bag"—and no feedback at all—no matter how many correct digits were written. However, meeting one's performance criterion on a white

worksheet sometimes produced reinforcement. This study provides powerful evidence of the importance of having contingencies in the instructional setting "look like" the contingencies in effect in the generalization setting(s) in two ways: (a) Both students showed large decreases in performance when baseline conditions were reinstated, and immediate drops during a second return to baseline; and (b) the students continued completing math problems at a high rate during the maintenance condition, even though no reinforcement was provided. (See Figure 28.8.)

When the delayed (indiscriminable) contingencies were implemented, all students demonstrated levels of correct responding at or above levels during the reinforcement phase. When the students were exposed to maintenance conditions, Amy maintained high levels of responding for 18 sessions with variable performance over the final six sessions, and Kristen showed a gradually increasing rate of performance over 24 sessions. The results demonstrated that behavior with an indiscriminable contingency can be maintained at the same rate as with a predictable schedule, and with greater resistance to extinction.

Delayed consequences have been used to promote the setting/situation generalization and response maintenance of a wide range of target behaviors, including academic and vocational tasks by individuals with autism (Dunlap, Koegel, Johnson, & O'Neill, 1987), young children's toy play, social initiations, and selection of healthy snacks (R. A. Baer, Blount, Dietrich, & Stokes, 1987; R. A. Baer, Williams, Osnes, & Stokes, 1984; Osnes, Guevremont, & Stokes, 1986), restaurant trainees' responding appropriately to coworkers' initiations (Grossi et al., 1994); and performance on reading and writing tasks (Brame, 2001; Heward, Heron, Gardner, & Prayzer, 1991).

The effective use of delayed consequences can reduce (or even eliminate in some instances) the learner's ability to discriminate when a contingency is or is not in effect. As a result, the learner needs to "be good" (i.e., emit the target behavior) all the time. If an effective contingency can be made indiscriminable across settings and target behaviors, the learner will also have to "be good" everywhere, with all of his or her relevant skills.

Following are four examples of classroom applications of indiscriminable contingencies involving delayed rewards. Each of these examples also features an interdependent group contingency (see Chapter 26) by making rewards for the whole class contingent on the performance of randomly selected students.

- *Spinners and dice.* A procedure such as the following can make academic seatwork periods more effective. Every few minutes (e.g., on a VI 5-minute

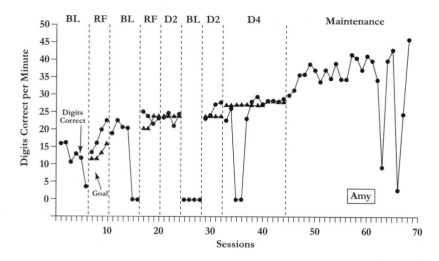

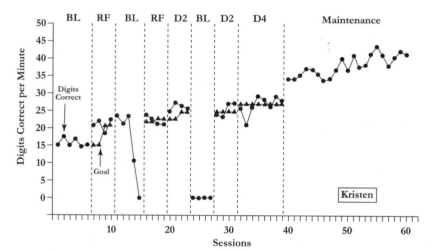

Figure 28.8 Number of correct digits per minute by two third-grade students while answering math problems during baseline (BL), reinforcement contingent on performance on one randomly selected worksheet after each session (RF), reinforcement contingent on performance on one randomly selected worksheet after every two (D2) or four (D4) sessions, and maintenance conditions.

From "Programming for Maintenance: An Investigation of Delayed Intermittent Reinforcement and Common Stimuli to Create Indiscriminable Contingencies" by J. T. Freeland and G. H. Noell, 2002, *Journal of Behavioral Education, 11*, p. 13. Copyright 2002 by Human Sciences Press. Reprinted by permission.

schedule), the teacher (a) randomly selects a student's name, (b) walks to that student's desk and has the student spin a spinner or roll a pair of dice, (c) counts backward from the worksheet problem or item the student is currently working on by the number shown on the spinner or dice, and (d) gives a token to the student if that problem or item is correct. Students who immediately begin to work on the assignment and work quickly but carefully throughout the seatwork period are most likely to obtain reinforcers under this indiscriminable contingency.

• *Story fact recall game.* Many teachers devote 20 to 30 minutes per day to sustained silent reading (SSR), a period when students can read silently from books of their choice. A story fact recall game can encourage students to read with a purpose during SSR. At the end of the SSR period the teacher asks several randomly selected students a question about the book they are reading. For ex-

ample, a student who is reading Chapter 3 of Elizabeth Winthrop's *The Castle in the Attic* might be asked, What did William give the Silver Knight to eat? (Answer: bacon and toast). A correct answer is praised by the teacher, applauded by the class, and earns a marble in a jar toward a reward for the whole class. Students do not know when they will be called on or what they might be asked (Brame, Bicard, Heward, & Greulich, 2007).

• *Numbered heads together.* Collaborative learning groups (small groups of students working together on a joint learning activity) can be effective, but teachers should use procedures that motivate all students to participate. A technique called numbered heads together can ensure that all students actively participate (Maheady, Mallete, Harper, & Saca, 1991). Students are seated in heterogeneous groups of three or four, and each student is given the number 1, 2, 3, or 4. The teacher asks the class a question, and each group discusses the problem and comes up with an answer. Next, the teacher randomly selects a number from 1 to 4 and then calls on one or more students with that number to answer. It is important that every person in the group knows the answer to the question. This strategy promotes cooperation within the group rather than competition. Because all students must know the answer, group members help each other understand not only the answer, but also the how and why behind it. Finally, this strategy encourages individual responsibility.

- *Intermittent grading.* Most students do not receive sufficient practice writing, and when students do write, the feedback they receive is often ineffective. One reason for this may be that providing detailed feedback on a daily composition by each student in the class requires more time and effort than even the most dedicated teacher can give. A procedure called intermittent grading offers one solution to this problem (Heward, Heron, Gardner, & Prayzer, 1991). Students write for 10 to 15 minutes each day, but instead of reading and evaluating every student's paper, the teacher provides detailed feedback on a randomly selected 20 to 25% of students' daily compositions. The students whose papers were graded earn points based on individualized performance criteria, and bonus points are given to the class contingent on the quality of the selected and graded papers (e.g., if the authors of four of the five papers that were graded met their individual criteria). Students' papers that were graded can be used as a source of instructional examples for the next lesson.

The success of a delayed reward tactic in promoting generalization and maintenance rests on (a) the indiscriminability of the contingency (i.e., the learner cannot tell exactly when emitting the target behavior in the generalization setting will produce a reward at a later time), and (b) the learner understanding the relation between his emitting the target behavior at an earlier time and receiving a reward later. A delayed rewards intervention may not be effective with some learners with severe cognitive disabilities.

Guidelines for Programming Indiscriminable Contingencies. Practioners should consider these guidelines when implementing indiscriminable contingencies:

- Use continuous reinforcement during the initial stages of acquiring new behaviors or when strengthening little-used behaviors.
- Systematically thin the schedule of reinforcement based on the learner's performance (see Chap-

ter 13). Remember that the thinner the schedule of reinforcement is, the more indiscriminable it is (e.g., an FR 5 schedule is more indiscriminable than an FR 2 schedule); and variable schedules of reinforcement (e.g., VR and VI schedules) are more indiscriminable than fixed schedules are (e.g., FR and FI schedules).

- When using delayed rewards, begin by delivering the reinforcer immediately following the target behavior and gradually increase the response-to-reinforcement delay.
- Each time a delayed reward is delivered, explain to the learner that he is receiving the reward for specific behaviors he performed earlier. This helps to build and strengthen the learner's understanding of the rule describing the contingency.

When selecting reinforcers to use during instruction, practitioners should try to use or eventually shift to the same reinforcers that the learner will acquire in the generalization environment. The reinforcer itself may serve as a discriminative stimulus for the target behavior (e.g., Koegel & Rincover, 1977)

Set Behavior Traps

Some contingencies of reinforcement are especially powerful, producing substantial and long-lasting behavior changes. Baer and Wolf (1970) called such contingencies **behavior traps.** Using a mouse trap as an analogy, they described how a householder has only to exert a relatively small amount of behavioral control over the mouse—getting the mouse to smell the cheese—to produce a behavior change with considerable (in this case, complete) generalization and maintenance.

> A householder without a trap can, of course, still kill a mouse. He can wait patiently outside the mouse's hole, grab the mouse faster than the mouse can avoid him, and then apply various forms of force to the unfortunate animal to accomplish the behavioral change desired. But this performance requires a great deal of competence: vast patience, super-coordination, extreme manual dexterity, and a well-suppressed squeamishness. By contrast, a householder with a trap need very few accomplishments: If he can merely apply the cheese and then leave the trap where the mouse is likely to smell that cheese, in effect he has guaranteed general(ized) change in the mouse's future behavior.
>
> The essence of a trap, in behavioral terms, is that *only a relatively simple response is necessary to enter the trap, yet once entered, the trap cannot be resisted in creating general behavior change.* For the mouse, the entry response is merely to smell the cheese. Everything

proceeds from there almost automatically. (p. 321, emphasis added)

Behavioral trapping is a fairly common phenomenon that everyone experiences from time to time. Behavior traps are particularly evident in the activities we "just cannot get (or do) enough of." The most effective behavior traps share four essential features: (a) They are "baited" with virtually irresistible reinforcers that "lure" the student to the trap; (b) only a low-effort response already in the student's repertoire is necessary to enter the trap; (c) interrelated contingencies of reinforcement inside the trap motivate the student to acquire, extend, and maintain targeted academic and/or social skills (Kohler & Greenwood, 1986); and (d) they can remain effective for a long time because students show few, if any, satiation effects.

Consider the case of the "reluctant bowler." A young man is persuaded to fill in as a substitute for a friend's bowling team. He has always regarded bowling as uncool. And bowling looks so easy on television that he does not see how it can be considered a real sport. Nevertheless, he agrees to go, just to help out this one time. During the evening he learns that bowling is not as easy as he had always assumed (he has a history of reinforcement for athletic challenges) and that several people he would like to get to know are avid bowlers (i.e., it is a mixed doubles league). Within a week he has purchased a custom-fitted bowling ball, a bag, and shoes; practiced twice on his own; and signed up for the next league season.

The reluctant bowler example illustrates the fundamental nature of behavior traps: easy to enter and difficult to exit. Some naturally existing behavior traps can lead to maladaptive behaviors, such as alcoholism, drug addiction, and juvenile delinquency. The everyday term *vicious circle* refers to the natural contingencies of reinforcement that operate in destructive behavior traps. Practitioners, however, can learn to create behavior traps that help students develop positive, constructive knowledge and skills. Alber and Heward (1996), who provided guidelines for creating successful traps, gave the following example of an elementary teacher creating a behavior trap that took advantage of a student's penchant for playing with baseball cards.

> Like many fifth graders struggling with reading and math, Carlos experiences school as tedious and unrewarding. With few friends of his own, Carlos finds that even recess offers little reprieve. But he does find solace in his baseball cards, often studying, sorting and playing with them in class. His teacher, Ms. Greene, long ago lost count of the number of times she had to stop an instructional activity to separate Carlos and his beloved baseball cards. Then one day, when she approached Carlos' desk to confiscate his cards in the middle of a lesson on alphabetization, Ms. Greene discovered that Carlos had already alphabetized all the left-handed pitchers in

the National League! Ms. Greene realized she'd found the secret to sparking Carlos' academic development.

> Carlos was both astonished and thrilled to learn that Ms. Greene not only let him keep his baseball cards at his desk, but also encouraged him to "play with them" during class. Before long, Ms. Greene had incorporated baseball cards into learning activities across the curriculum. In math, Carlos calculated batting averages; in geography, he located the hometown of every major leaguer born in his state; and in language arts, he wrote letters to his favorite players requesting an autographed photo. Carlos began to make significant gains academically and an improvement in his attitude about school was also apparent.

> But school became really fun for Carlos when some of his classmates began to take an interest in his knowledge of baseball cards and all the wonderful things you could do with them. Ms. Greene helped Carlos form a classroom Baseball Card Club, giving him and his new friends opportunities to develop and practice new social skills as they responded to their teacher's challenge to think of new ways to integrate the cards into the curriculum. (p. 285)

Ask People in the Generalization Setting to Reinforce the Behavior

> The problem may be simply that the natural community [of reinforcement] is asleep and needs to be awakened and turned on.
>
> —Donald M. Baer (1999, p. 16).

Sometimes a potentially effective contingency of reinforcement in the generalization setting is not operating in a form available to the learner no matter how often or well she performs the target behavior. The contingency is there, but dormant. One solution for this kind of problem is to inform key people in the generalization setting of the value and importance of their attention to the learner's efforts to acquire and use new skills and ask them to help.

For example, a special education teacher who has been helping a student learn how to participate in class discussions by providing repeated opportunities for practice and feedback in the resource room could inform the teachers in the general education classes that the student attends about the behavior change program and ask them to look for and reinforce any reasonable effort by the student to participate in their classrooms. A small amount of contingent attention and praise from these teachers may be all that is needed to achieve the desired generalization of the new skill.

This simple but often effective technique for promoting generalized behavior was evident in the study by Stokes and colleagues (1974) in which staff members responded to the children's waving response by saying,

"Hello, (name)." Approximately 20 such generalization probes were conducted each day with each child.

Williams, Donley, and Keller (2000) gave mothers of two preschool children with autism explicit instructions on providing models, response prompts, and reinforcement to their children who were learning to ask questions about hidden objects (e.g., "What's that?", "Can I see it?").

Contingent praise and attention from significant others can add to the effectiveness of other strategies already in place in the generalization environment. Broden, Hall, and Mitts (1971) showed this in the self-monitoring study described in Chapter 27. After self-recording had improved eighth-grader Liza's study behavior during history class, the researchers asked Liza's teacher to praise Liza for study behavior whenever he could during history class. Liza's level of study behavior during this Self-Recording Plus Praise condition increased to a mean of 88% and was maintained at levels nearly as high during a subsequent Praise Only condition (see Figure 27.3).

Teach the Learner to Recruit Reinforcement

Another way to "wake up" a potentially powerful but dormant natural contingency of reinforcement is to teach the learner to recruit reinforcement from significant others. For example, Seymour and Stokes (1976) taught delinquent girls to work more productively in the vocational training area of a residential institution. However, observation showed that staff at the institution gave the girls no praise or positive interaction regardless of the quality of their work. The much-needed natural community of reinforcement to ensure the generalization of the girls' improved work behaviors was not functioning. To get around this difficulty, the experimenters trained the girls to use a simple response that called the attention of staff members to their work. With this strategy, staff praise for good work increased. Thus, teaching the girls an additional response that could be used to recruit reinforcement enabled the target behavior to come into contact with natural reinforcers that would serve to extend and maintain the desired behavior change.

Students of various ages and abilities have learned to recruit teacher and peer attention for performing a wide range of tasks in classroom and community settings; preschoolers with developmental delays for completing pre-academic tasks and staying on task during transitions (Connell, Carta, & Baer, 1993; Stokes, Fowler, & Baer, 1978) as well as students with learning disabilities (Alber, Heward, & Hippler, 1999; Wolford, Alber, & Heward, 2001), students with behavioral disorders (Morgan, Young, & Goldstein, 1983), students with mental retar-

dation performing academic tasks in regular classrooms (Craft, Alber, & Heward, 1998), and secondary students with mental retardation for improved work performance in vocational training settings (Mank & Horner, 1987).

Craft and colleagues (1998) assessed the effects of recruitment training on academic assignments for which students recruited teacher attention. Four elementary students were trained by their special education teacher (the first author) when, how, and how often to recruit teacher attention in the general education classroom. Training consisted of modeling, role-playing, error correction, and praise in the special education classroom. The students were taught to show their work to the teacher or ask for help two to three times per work page, and to use appropriate statements such as "How am I doing?" or "Does this look right?"

Data on the frequency of student recruiting and teacher praise statements were collected during a daily 20-minute homeroom period in a general education classroom. During this period, the general education students completed a variety of independent seatwork tasks (reading, language arts, math) assigned by the general education teacher, while the four special education students completed spelling worksheets assigned by the special education teacher, an arrangement that had been established prior to the experiment. If students needed help with their assignments during homeroom, they took their work to the teacher's desk and asked for help.

The effects of recruitment training on the children's frequency of recruiting and on the number of praise statements they received from the classroom teacher are shown in Figure 28.9. Recruiting across students increased from a mean rate of 0.01 to 0.8 recruiting responses per 20-minute session during baseline to a mean rate of 1.8 to 2.7 after training. Teacher praise statements received by the students increased from a mean rate of 0.1 to 0.8 praise statements per session during baseline to a mean rate of 1.0 to 1.7 after training. The ultimate meaning and outcome of the intervention was in the increased amount and improved accuracy of all four of the students' academic work (see Figure 6.9).

For a review of research on recruiting and suggestions for teaching children to recruit reinforcement from significant others, see Alber and Heward (2000). Box 28.2, "Look, Teacher, I'm All Finished!" provides suggestions for teaching students to recruit teacher attention.

Mediate Generalization

Another strategy for promoting generalized behavior change is to arrange for some thing or person to act as a medium that ensures the transfer of the target behavior from the instructional setting to the generalization setting.

Box 28.2
"Look, Teacher, I'm All Finished!"
Teaching Students to Recruit Teacher Attention

Classrooms are extremely busy places, and even the most conscientious teachers can easily overlook students' important academic and social behaviors. Research shows that teachers are more likely to pay attention to a disruptive student than to one who is working quietly and productively (Walker, 1997). It is hard for teachers to be aware of students who need help, especially low-achieving students who are less likely to ask for help (Newman & Golding, 1990).

Although teachers in general education classrooms are expected to adapt instruction to serve students with disabilities, this is not always the case. Most secondary teachers interviewed by Schumm and colleagues (1995) believed that students with disabilities should take responsibility for obtaining the help they need. Thus, knowing how to politely recruit teacher attention and assistance can help students with disabilities function more independently and actively influence the quality of instruction they receive.

Who Should Be Taught to Recruit?

Although most students would probably benefit from learning to recruit teacher praise and feedback, here are some ideal candidates for recruitment training:

Withdrawn Willamena. Willamena seldom asks a teacher anything. Because she is so quiet and well behaved, her teachers sometimes forget she's in the room.

In-a-Hurry Harry. Harry is usually half-done with a task before his teacher finishes explaining it. Racing through his work allows him to be the first to turn it in. But his work is often incomplete and filled with errors, so he doesn't hear much praise from his teacher. Harry would benefit from recruitment training that includes self-checking and self-correction.

Shouting Shelly. Shelly has just finished her work, and she wants her teacher to look at it—right now! But Shelly doesn't raise her hand. She gets her teacher's attention—and disrupts most of her classmates—by shouting across the room. Shelly should be taught appropriate ways to solicit teacher attention.

Pestering Pete. Pete always raises his hand, waits quietly for his teacher to come to his desk, and then politely asks, "Have I done this right?" But he repeats this routine a dozen or more times in a

20-minute period, and his teachers find it annoying. Positive teacher attention often turns into reprimands. Recruitment training for Pete will teach him to limit the number of times he cues his teachers for attention.

How to Get Started

1. *Identify target behaviors.* Students should recruit teacher attention for target behaviors that are valued and therefore likely to be reinforced, such as writing neatly and legibly, working accurately, completing assigned work, cleaning up at transitions, and making contributions when working in a cooperative group.

2. *Teach self-assessment.* Students should self-assess their work before recruiting teacher attention (e.g., Sue asks herself, "Is my work complete?"). After the student can reliably distinguish between complete and incomplete work samples, she can learn how to check the accuracy of her work with answer keys or checklists of the steps or components of the academic skill, or how to spot-check two or three items before asking the teacher to look at it.

3. *Teach appropriate recruiting.* Teach students when, how, and how often to recruit and how to respond to the teacher after receiving attention.

   • *When?* Students should signal for teacher attention after they have completed and self-checked a substantial part of their work. Students should also be taught when not to try to get their teacher's attention (e.g., when the teacher is working with another student, talking to another adult, or taking the lunch count).

   • *How?* The traditional hand raise should be part of every student's recruiting repertoire. Other methods of gaining attention should be taught depending on teacher preferences and routines in the general education classroom (e.g., have students signal they need help by standing up a small flag on their desks; expect students to bring their work to the teacher's desk for help and feedback).

   • *How often?* While helping Withdrawn Willamena learn to seek teacher attention, don't turn her into a Pestering Pete. How often a student should recruit varies across teachers and activities (e.g., independent seatwork, cooperative learning groups, whole-class instruction). Direct observation in the classroom is the best way to establish an optimal rate of recruiting; it is also a good idea to ask the regular classroom teacher when, how, and with what frequency she prefers students to ask for help.

- *What to say?* Students should be taught several statements that are likely to evoke positive feedback from the teacher (e.g., "Please look at my work." "Did I do a good job?" "How am I doing?"). Keep it simple, but teach the student to vary her verbal cues so she will not sound like a parrot.

- *How to respond?* Students should respond to their teacher's feedback by establishing eye contact, smiling, and saying, "Thank you." Polite appreciation is very reinforcing to teachers and will increase the likelihood of more positive attention the next time.

4. *Model and role-play the complete sequence.* Begin by providing students with a rationale for recruiting (e.g., the teacher will be happy you did a good job, you will get more work done, your grades might improve). Thinking aloud while modeling is a good way to show the recruiting sequence. While performing each step, say, "Okay, I've finished my work. Now I'm going to check it. Did I put my name on my paper? Yes. Did I do all

the problems? Yes. Did I follow all the steps? Yes. Okay, my teacher doesn't look busy right now. I'll raise my hand and wait quietly until she comes to my desk." Have another student pretend to be the regular classroom teacher and come over to you when you have your hand up. Say, "Mr. Patterson, please look at my work." The helper says, "Oh, you did a very nice job." Then smile and say, "Thank you, Mr. Patterson." Role-play with praise and offer corrective feedback until the student correctly performs the entire sequence on several consecutive trials.

5. *Prepare students for alternate responses.* Of course, not every recruiting student attempt will result in teacher praise; some recruiting responses may even be followed by criticism (e.g., "This is all wrong. Pay better attention the next time."). Use role-playing to prepare students for these possibilities and have them practice polite responses (e.g., "Thank you for helping me with this").

6. *Promote generalization to the regular classroom.* The success of any recruitment training effort depends on the student actually using his or her new skill in the regular classroom.

Adapted from "Recruit it or lose it! Training students to recruit contingent teacher attention" by S. R. Alber and W. L. Heward, 1997, *Intervention in School and Clinic, 5,* pp. 275–282. Used with permission.

Two tactics for implementing this strategy are contriving a mediating stimulus and teaching the learner to mediate her own generalization through self-management.

Contrive a Mediating Stimulus

One tactic for mediating generalization is to bring the target behavior under the control of a stimulus in the instructional setting that will function in the generalization setting to reliably prompt or aid the learner's performance of the target behavior. The stimulus selected for this important role may exist already in the generalization environment, or it may be a new stimulus added to the instruction program that subsequently goes with the learner to the generalization setting. Whether it is a naturally existing component of the generalization setting or an added element to the instructional setting, to effectively mediate generalization, a **contrived mediating stimulus** must be (a) made functional for the target behavior during instruction and (b) transported easily to the generalization setting (Baer, 1999). The mediating stimulus is *functional* for the learner if it reliably prompts or

aids the learner in performing the target behavior; the mediating stimulus is *transportable* if it easily goes with the learner to all important generalization settings.

Naturally existing features of generalization settings that are used as contrived mediating stimuli may be physical objects or people. Van den Pol and colleagues (1981) used paper napkins, a common feature of any fast-food restaurant, as a contrived mediating stimulus. They taught students that a paper napkin was the only place to put food. In this way, the researchers eliminated the added challenge and difficulty of teaching the students to discriminate clean tables from dirty tables, to sit only at clean tables, or to wipe dirty tables and then programming the generalization and maintenance of those behaviors. By contriving the special use of the napkin, only one response had to be trained, and napkins then served as mediating stimulus for that behavior.

When choosing a stimulus to be made common to both teaching and social generalization setting(s), practitioners should consider using people. In addition to being a requisite feature of social settings, people are transportable and important sources of reinforcement for

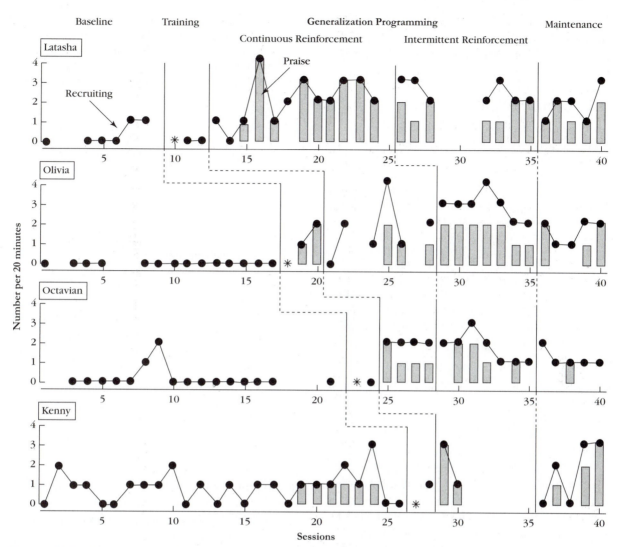

Figure 28.9 Number of recruiting responses (data points) and teacher praise statement (bars) per 20-minute seatwork sessions. Target recruiting rate was two to three responses per session. Asterisks indicate when each student was trained in the resource room.

From "Teaching Elementary Students with Developmental Disabilities to Recruit Teacher Attention in a General Education Classroom: Effects on Teacher Praise and Academic Productivity" by M. A. Craft, S. R. Alber, and W. L. Heward, 1998, *Journal of Applied Behavior Analysis, 31*, p. 407. Copyright 1998 by the Society for the Experimental Analysis of Behavior, Inc. Reprinted by permission.

many behaviors. A study by Stokes and Baer (1976) is a good example of the potential effects of the evocative effects of the presence of a person in the generalization setting who had a functional role in the learner's acquisition of the target behavior in the instructional setting. Two preschool children with learning disabilities learned word-recognition skills while working as reciprocal peer tutors for one another. However, neither child showed reliable generalization of those new skills in nontraining settings until the peer with whom he had learned the skills was present in the generalization setting.

Some contrived mediating stimuli serve as much more than response prompts; they are prosthetic devices that assist the learner in performing the target behavior. Such devices can be especially useful in promoting gen-

eralization and maintenance of complex behaviors and extend response chains by simplifying a complex situation. Three common forms are cue cards, photographic activity schedules, and self-operated prompting devices.

Sprague and Horner (1984) gave the students in their study cue cards to aid them in operating a vending machine without another person's assistance. The cue cards, which had food and drink logos on one side and pictures of quarters paired with prices on the other, not only were used during instruction and generalization probes, but also were kept by the students at the end of the program. A follow-up 18 months after the study was completed revealed that five of the six students still carried a cue card and were using vending machines independently.

MacDuff, Krantz, and McClannahan (1993) taught four boys with autism ages 9 to 14 to use photographic activity schedules when performing domestic-living skills such as vacuuming and table setting and for leisure activities such as using manipulative toys. Prior to training with photographic activity schedules, the boys

> were dependent on ongoing supervision and verbal prompts to complete self-help, housekeeping, and leisure activities. . . . In the absence of verbal prompts from supervising adults, it appeared that stimulus control transferred to photographs and materials that were available in the group home. When the study ended, all 4 boys were able to display complex home-living and recreational repertoires for an hour, during which time they frequently changed tasks and moved to different areas of their group home without adults' prompts. Photographic activity schedules, . . . became functional discriminative stimuli that promoted sustained engagement after training ceased and fostered generalized responding to new activity sequences and novel leisure materials. (pp. 90, 97)

Numerous studies have shown that learners across a wide range of age and cognitive levels, including students with severe intellectual disabilities, can learn to use personal audio playback devices to independently perform a variety of academic, vocational, and domestic tasks (e.g., Briggs et al., 1990; Davis, Brady, Williams, & Burta, 1992; Grossi, 1998; Mechling & Gast, 1997; Post, Storey, & Karabin, 2002; Trask-Tyler, Grossi, & Heward, 1994). The popularity of personal music devices such as "Walkman-style" tape players and iPods enables a person to listen to a series of self-delivered response prompts in a private, normalized manner that does not impose on or bother others.

Teach Self-Management Skills

The most potentially effective approach to mediating generalized behavior changes rests with the one element that is always present in every instructional and generalization setting—the learner herself. Chapter 27 described a variety of self-management tactics that people can use to modify their own behavior. The logic of using self-management to mediate generalized behavior changes goes like this: If the learner can be taught a behavior (not the original target behavior, but another behavior—a controlling response from a self-management perspective) that serves to prompt or reinforce the target behavior in all the relevant settings, at all appropriate times, and in all of its relevant forms, then the generalization of the target behavior is ensured. But as Baer and Fowler (1984) warned:

> Giving a student self-control responses designed to mediate the generalization of some critical behavior

changes does not ensure that those mediating responses will indeed be used. They are, after all, just responses: they, too, need generalization and maintenance just as do the behavior changes that they are meant to generalize and maintain. Setting up one behavior to mediate the generalization of another behavior may succeed—but it may also represent a problem in guaranteeing the generalization of two responses, where before we had only the problem of guaranteeing the generalization of one! (p. 149)

Train to Generalize

> If generalization is considered as a response itself, then a reinforcement contingency may be placed on it, the same as with any other operant.
>   —Stokes and Baer (1977, p. 362)

Training "to generalize" was one of the eight proactive strategies for programming generalized behavior change in Stokes and Baer's (1977) conceptual scheme (which also included the nonstrategy, train and hope). The quotation marks around "to generalize" signified that the authors were hypothesizing about the possibilities of treating "to generalize" as an operant response and that they recognized "the preference of behaviorists to consider generalization to be an outcome of behavioral change, rather than as a behavior itself" (p. 363). Since the publication of Stokes and Baer's review, basic and applied research has demonstrated the pragmatic value of their hypothesis (e.g., Neuringer, 1993, 2004; Ross & Neuringer, 2002; Shahan & Chase, 2002). Two tactics that applied behavior analysts have used are reinforcing response variability and instructing the learner to generalize.

Reinforce Response Variability

Response variability can help a person solve problems. A person who can improvise by emitting a variety of responses is more likely to solve problems encountered when a standard response form fails to obtain reinforcement (e.g., Arnesen, 2000; Marckel, Neef, & Ferreri, 2006; Miller & Neuringer, 2000; Shahan & Chase, 2002). Response variability also may result in behavior that is valued because it is novel or creative (e.g., Goetz & Baer, 1973; Holman, Goetz, & Baer, 1977; Pryor, Haag, and O'Reilly, 1969). Response variability may expose a person to sources of reinforcement and contingencies not accessible by more constricted forms of responding. The additional learning that results from contacting those contingencies further expands the person's repertoire.

One direct way to program desired response generalization is to reinforce response variability when it occurs. The contingency between response variability and reinforcement can be formalized with a lag reinforcement schedule (Lee, McComas, & Jawar, 2002). On a **lag reinforcement schedule,** reinforcement is contingent on a response being different in some defined way from the previous response (a Lag 1 schedule) or a specified number of previous responses (Lag 2 or more). Cammilleri and Hanley (2005) used a lag reinforcement contingency to increase varied selections of classroom activities by two typically developing girls, who were selected to participate in the study because they spent the vast majority of their time engaged in activities not systematically designed to result in a particular set of skills within the curriculum.

At the beginning of each 60-minute session, the children were told they could select any activity and could switch activities at any time. A timer sounded every 5 minutes to prompt activity choices. During baseline there were no programmed consequences for selecting any of the activities. Intervention consisted of a lag reinforcement schedule in which the first activity selection and each subsequent novel selection were followed by the teacher handing the student a green card that she could exchange later for 2 minutes of teacher attention (resulting in a Lag 12 contingency, which was reset if all 12 activities were selected within a session).

Activity selections during baseline showed little variability, with both girls showing strong preferences for stackable blocks (Figure 28.10 shows results for one of the girls). When the lag contingency was introduced, both girls

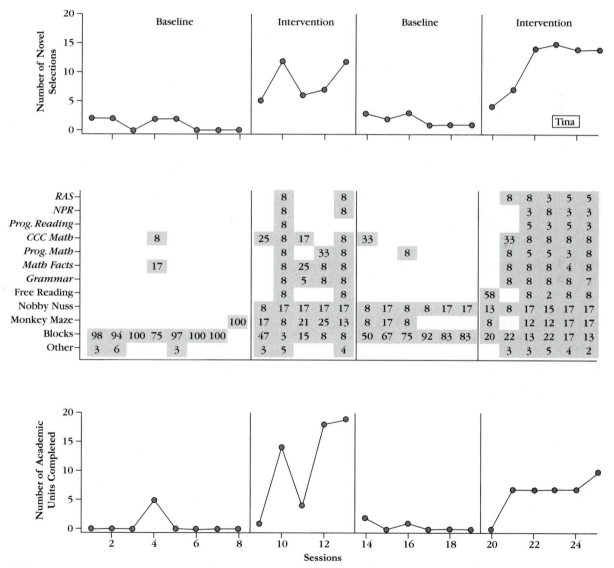

Figure 28.10   Number of novel activity selections (top panel), percentage of intervals of engagement in programmed (italicized) and nonprogrammed activities (middle panel; shaded cells indicate activities for which there was some engagement), and number of academic units completed (bottom panel).

From "Use of a Lag Differential Reinforcement Contingency to Increase Varied Selections of Classroom Activities" by A. P. Cammilleri and G. P. Hanley, 2005, *Journal of Applied Behavior Analysis, 38,* p. 114. Copyright 2005 by the Society for the Experimental Analysis of Behavior, Inc. Reprinted by permission.

immediately selected and engaged in more diverse activities. The researchers noted that "an indirect but important outcome of this shift in time allocation was a marked increase in the number of academic units completed" (p. 115).

Instruct the Learner to Generalize

The simplest and least expensive of all tactics for promoting generalized behavior change is to "tell the subject about the possibility of generalization and then ask for it" (Stokes & Baer, 1977, p. 363). For example, Ninness and colleagues (1991) explicitly told three middle school students with emotional disturbance to use self-management procedures they had learned in the classroom to self-assess and self-record their behavior while walking from the lunchroom to the classroom. Hughes and colleagues (1995) used a similar procedure to promote generalization: "At the close of each training session, peer teachers reminded participants to self-instruct when they wished to talk to someone" (p. 207). Likewise, at the conclusion of each training session conducted in the special education classroom on how to recruit assistance from peers during cooperative learning groups, Wolford and colleagues (2001) prompted middle school students with learning disabilities to recruit peer assistance at least two times but not more than four times during each cooperative learning group in the language arts classroom.

To the extent that generalizations occur and are themselves generalized, a person might then become skilled at generalizing newly acquired skills, or in the words of Stokes and Baer (1977), become a "generalized generalizer."

Modifying and Terminating Successful Interventions

With most successful behavior change programs it is impossible, impractical, or undesirable to continue the intervention indefinitely. Withdrawal of a successful intervention should be carried out in a systematic fashion, guided by the learner's performance of the target behavior in the most important generalization settings. Gradually shifting from the contrived conditions of the intervention to the typical, everyday environment will increase the likelihood that the learner will maintain the new behavior patterns. When deciding how soon and how swiftly to withdraw intervention components, practitioners should consider factors such as the complexity of the intervention, the ease or speed with which behavior changed, and the availability of naturally existing contingencies of reinforcement for the new behavior.

This shift from intervention conditions to the postintervention environment can be made by modifying one or more of the following components, each representing one part of the three-term contingency:

- Antecedents, prompts, or cue-related stimuli
- Task requirements and criteria
- Consequences or reinforcement variables

Although the order in which intervention components are withdrawn may make little or no difference, in most programs it is probably best to make all task-related requirements as similar as possible to those of the postintervention environment before withdrawing significant antecedent or consequence components of the intervention. In this way the learner will be emitting the target behavior at the same level of fluency that will be required after the complete intervention has been withdrawn.

A behavior change program carried out many years ago by a graduate student in one of our classes illustrates how the components of a program can be gradually and systematically withdrawn. An adult male with developmental disabilities took an inordinate amount of time to get dressed each morning (40 to 70 minutes during baseline), even though he possessed the skills needed to dress himself. Intervention began with a construction paper clock hung by his bed with the hands set to indicate the time by which he had to be fully dressed to receive reinforcement. Although the man could not tell time, he could discriminate whether the position of the hands on the real clock nearby matched those on his paper clock. Two task-related intervention elements were introduced to increase the likelihood of initial success. First, he was given fewer and easier clothes to put on each morning (e.g., no belt, slip-on loafers instead of shoes with laces). Second, based on his baseline performance, he was initially given 30 minutes to dress himself, even though the objective of the program was for him to be completely dressed within 10 minutes. An edible reinforcer paired with verbal praise was used first on a continuous schedule of reinforcement. Figure 28.11 shows how each aspect of the intervention (antecedent, behavior, and consequence) was modified and eventually withdrawn completely, so that by the program's end the man was dressing himself completely within 10 minutes without the aid of extra clocks or charts or contrived reinforcement other than a naturally existing schedule of intermittent praise from staff members.

Rusch and Kazdin (1981) described a method for systematically withdrawing intervention components while simultaneously assessing response maintenance that they called "partial-sequential withdrawal." Martella, Leonard, Marchand-Martella, and Agran (1993) used a partial-sequential withdrawal of various components of a self-monitoring intervention they had implemented to

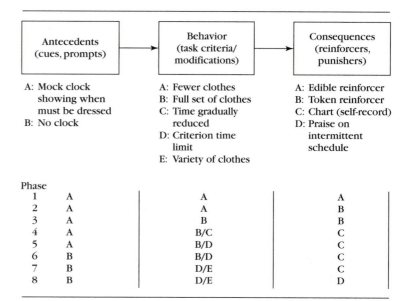

Antecedents (cues, prompts)	Behavior (task criteria/ modifications)	Consequences (reinforcers, punishers)
A: Mock clock showing when must be dressed B: No clock	A: Fewer clothes B: Full set of clothes C: Time gradually reduced D: Criterion time limit E: Variety of clothes	A: Edible reinforcer B: Token reinforcer C: Chart (self-record) D: Praise on intermittent schedule

Phase			
1	A	A	A
2	A	A	B
3	A	B	B
4	A	B/C	C
5	A	B/D	C
6	B	B/D	C
7	B	D/E	C
8	B	D/E	D

Figure 28.11   An example of modifying and withdrawing components of an independent morning dressing program for an adult with developmental disabilities to facilitate maintenance and generalization.

help Brad, a 12-year-old student with mild mental retardation, reduce the number of negative statements (e.g., "I hate this @#!%ing calculator," "Math is crappy") he made during classroom activities. The self-management intervention consisted of Brad (a) self-recording negative statements on a form during two class periods, (b) charting the number on a graph, (c) receiving his choice from a menu of "small" reinforcers (items costing 25 cents or less), and (d) when his self-recorded data were in agreement with the trainer and at or below a gradually reducing criterion level for four consecutive sessions, he was allowed to choose a "large" reinforcer (more than 25 cents). After the frequency of Brad's negative statements was reduced, the researchers began a four-phase partial-sequential withdrawal of the intervention. In the first phase, charting and earning of "large" reinforcers were withdrawn; in the second phase, Brad was required to have zero negative statements in both periods to receive a daily "small" reinforcer; in the third phase, Brad used the same self-monitoring form for both class periods instead of one form for each period as before, and the small reinforcer was no longer provided; and in the fourth phase (the follow-up condition), all components of the intervention were withdrawn except for the self-monitoring form without a criterion number highlighted. Brad's negative statements remained low throughout the gradual and partial withdrawal of the intervention (see Figure 28.12).

A word of caution is in order regarding the termination of successful behavior change programs. Achieving socially significant improvements in behavior is a defining purpose of applied behavior analysis. Additionally, those improved behaviors should be maintained and should show generalization to other relevant settings and behaviors. In most instances, achieving optimal gen-

eralization of the behavior change will require most, if not all, of the intervention components to be withdrawn. However, practitioners, parents, and others responsible for helping children learn important behaviors are sometimes more concerned with whether and with how a potentially effective intervention will eventually be withdrawn than they are with whether it will produce the needed behavior change. Considering how a proposed intervention will lend itself to eventual withdrawal or blending into the natural environment is important and consistent with everything recommended throughout this book. And clearly, when the choice is between two or more interventions of potentially equal effectiveness, the intervention that is most similar to the natural environment and the easiest to withdraw and terminate should be given first priority. However, an important behavior change should not go unmade because complete withdrawal of the intervention required to achieve it may never be possible. Some level of intervention may always be required to maintain certain behaviors, in which case attempts to continue the necessary programming must be made.

The Sprague and Horner (1984) study on teaching generalized vending machine use provides another example of this point. The six students with moderate to severe mental retardation who participated in the program were given cue cards to aid them in operating a vending machine without another person's assistance. The cue cards, which had food and drink logos on one side and pictures of quarters paired with prices on the other, not only were used during instruction and generalization probes, but also were kept by the students at the end of the program. Five of the six students still carried a cue card and were using vending machines independently 18 months after the study had ended.

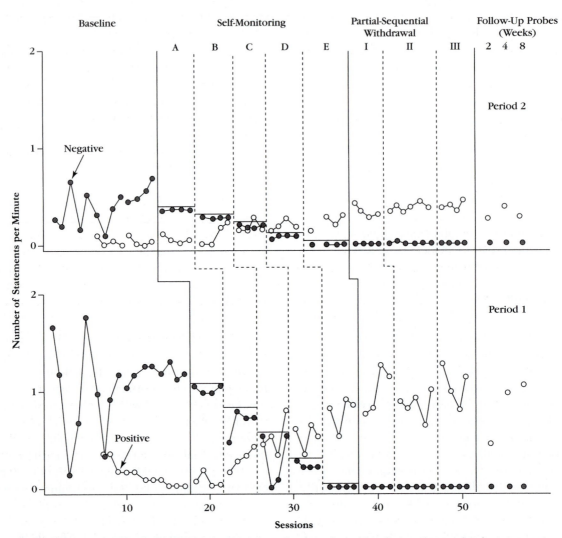

Figure 28.12   Number of negative (solid data points) and positive (open data points) statements in two class periods by an adolescent boy with disabilities during baseline, self-monitoring, and partial-sequential withdrawal conditions. Horizontal lines during self-monitoring condition show changing criteria for teacher-delivered reinforcement.

From "Self-Monitoring Negative Statements" by R. Martella, I. J. Leonard, N. E. Marchand-Martella, and M. Agran, 1993, *Journal of Behavioral Education, 3,* p. 84. Copyright 1993 by Human Sciences Press. Reprinted by permission.

Guiding Principles for Promoting Generalized Outcomes

Regardless of the specific tactics selected and applied, we believe that practitioners' efforts to promote generalized behavior change will be enhanced by adherence to five guiding principles:

- Minimize the need for generalization as much as possible.
- Conduct generalization probes before, during, and after instruction.
- Involve significant others whenever possible.

- Promote generalization with the least intrusive, least costly tactics possible.
- Contrive intervention tactics as needed to achieve important generalized outcomes.

Minimize the Need for Generalization

Practitioners should reduce the need for generalization to untaught skills, settings, and situations as much as possible. Doing so requires thoughtful, systematic assessment of what behavior changes are most important. Practitioners should prioritize the knowledge and skills that will most often be required of the learner and the settings and situations in which the learner will most often benefit from using those skills. In addition to the environment(s) in which the learner is currently functioning, practitioners should consider the environments in which the learner will function in the immediate future and later in life.

The most critical behavior changes should not be relegated to the not-for-certain technology of generalization. The most important skill-setting-stimulus combinations should always be taught directly and, when possible, taught first. For example, a training program to teach a young adult with disabilities to ride the public bus system should use the bus routes the person will take most often (e.g., to and from her home, school, job site, and community recreation center) as teaching examples. Instead of providing direct instruction on routes to destinations the learner may visit only occasionally after training, use those routes as generalization probes. Achieving a high level of response maintenance on the trained routes will still be a challenge.

Probe for Generalization Before, During, and After Instruction

Generalization probes should be conducted prior to, during, and after instruction.

Probe Before Instruction

Generalization probes conducted before instruction begins may reveal that the learner already performs some or all of the needed behaviors in the generalization setting, thereby reducing the scope of the teaching task. It is a mistake to assume that because a learner does not perform a particular behavior in the instructional setting, she does not or cannot do it in the generalization setting(s). Preinstruction generalization probe data are the only objective basis for knowing that the learner's performance of the target behavior *after instruction* is in fact a generalized outcome.

Probes before instruction enable observation of the contingencies that operate in the generalization setting. Knowledge of such information may contribute to a more effective treatment or instruction.

Probe During Instruction

Generalization probes during instruction reveal if and when generalization has occurred and if and when instruction can be terminated or shifted in focus from acquisition to maintenance. For example, a teacher who finds that a student can solve untaught examples of a particular type of algebraic equation after receiving instruction on just a few examples and shifts instruction to the next type of equation in the curriculum, will cover more

of the algebra program effectively than will a teacher who continues to present additional examples.

Results of probes during instruction also show whether generalization is not occurring, thereby indicating that a change in instructional strategies is needed. For example, when Sprague and Horner (1984) observed that one student's poor performance on the first generalization probe was caused by a ritualistic pattern of inserting coins, they incorporated repeated practice on the coin insertion step during a training session and the student's performance on the generalization task improved greatly.

Probing can often be made more efficient by contriving opportunities for the learner to use her new knowledge or skill. For example, instead of waiting for (and perhaps missing) naturally occurring opportunities for the learner to use her new conversational skills in the generalization environment, a practitioner could enlist the assistance of a "confederate" peer to approach the learner. Ninness, Fuerst, and Rutherford, (1991) used contrived generalization probes in which students were provoked or distracted to test the extent to which they used a set of self-management skills.

Contrived generalization probes can also be used as primary measures of acquisition and generalization. For example, Miltenberger and colleagues (2005) contrived opportunities to measure and teach children's use of gun safety skills by placing a gun in home and school locations where the children would find it. If a child did not execute the target safety skills when finding a gun (i.e., do not touch it, get away from the gun, and tell an adult), the trainer entered the room and conducted an *in situ* training session, asking the child what he should have done and rehearsing the entire sequence five times.

Probe After Instruction

Generalization probes after instruction has ended reveal the extent of response maintenance. The question of how long probes should be conducted after instruction has ended should be answered by factors such as the severity of the target behavior, the importance of the behavior change to the person's quality of life, the strength and consistency of the response maintenance obtained by probes to date, and so forth. The need for long-term assessment of maintenance is especially critical for severe behavior problems. In some cases, maintenance probes over many months and several years may be indicated (e.g., Derby et al., 1997; Foxx, Bittle, & Faw, 1989; Wagman, Miltenberger, & Woods, 1995).

If conducting systematic generalization and maintenance probes seems too difficult or too contrived, the practitioner should consider the relative importance of the target behavior to the student or client. If a behavior is important to target for intervention then assessing the generalized outcomes of that intervention is worth whatever effort that assessment requires.

Involve Significant Others

> All persons are potential teachers of all sorts of behavior changes. Just because you are designated as "teacher" or "behavior analyst" does not mean that you have an exclusive franchise on the ability to make deliberate behavior changes. In fact, there is no possibility of such a franchise. Everyone in contact contributes to everyone else's behavior, both to its changes and its maintenance.
> — Donald M. Baer (1999, p. 12)

Teaching for generalized outcomes is a big job, and practitioners should try to get as much help as they can. People are almost always around where and when important behaviors need to be prompted and reinforced; and when social behaviors are targeted, people are there by definition.

In virtually every behavior change program people other than the participant and the behavior analyst are involved, and their cooperation is crucial to the success of the program. Foxx (1996) stated that in programming successful behavior change interventions, "10% is knowing what to do; 90% is getting people to do it. . . . Many programs are unsuccessful because these percentages have been reversed" (p. 230). Although Foxx was referring to the challenge and importance of getting staff to implement programs with the consistency and fidelity needed for success, the same holds for the involvement of significant others.

Baer (1999) suggested identifying others who will or may be involved in a behavior change program as active supporters or tolerators. An active supporter is someone naturally present in the generalization setting who helps promote the generalization and maintenance of the target behavior by doing specific things. Active supporters help facilitate the desired generalized outcomes by arranging opportunities for the learner to use or practice the new skill, giving cues and response prompts for the behavior, and providing reinforcement for performance of the target behavior.

Active supporters for a behavior change program to teach independent eating to a child with severe disabilities might include one or two key people in the school's cafeteria, a volunteer or aide who works regularly with the child, the child's parents, and an older sibling. These people are vital parts of the teaching team. If optimal generalization is to occur, the active supporters must see to it that the learner has many opportunities to use the new skill in the generalization environments they share, and the natural reinforcers they control in those environments (e.g., praise, touch, smiles, companionship) must be used as consequences for the target behavior. It is not necessary, and probably not desirable, to limit an active

supporters list, to school staff, family members, and peers. They may not be regularly available in all the environments and situations in which generalization is desired.

A tolerator is someone in the generalization setting who agrees not to behave in ways that would impede the generalization plan. Tolerators should be informed that the learner will be using a new skill in the generalization environment and asked to be patient. In an independent eating program a list of tolerators would likely include some members of the child's family, school cafeteria staff, and peers. Beyond the home and school environments the behavior analyst should consider the possible role of the general public with whom the child may find herself sharing a table or dining area in a public restaurant. The learner's initial sloppiness and slowness (she may always be sloppier and slower than most people) as she makes the first attempts beyond the familiar contingencies of home and school might result in various responses from strangers that could punish the new eating skills. Being stared at, laughed at, talked about, told to hurry up, or even offered assistance could reduce the possibility of generalization. Certainly, the behavior analyst can inform various school staff and family members of the ongoing eating program and request that they not interfere with the child's attempts to eat independently. But the public at large is another issue. It is impossible to inform everyone of the program. However, by considering the types of intolerant behaviors that the learner may encounter in the generalization setting, the teaching program can be constructed to include practice under such intolerant conditions. Instructional trials might be contrived to reinforce the learner for ignoring rude remarks and continuing to eat independently.

Use the Least Intrusive, Least Costly Tactics Possible

Behavior analysts should use less intrusive and less costly tactics to promote generalization before using more intrusive and costly tactics. As noted previously, simply reminding students to use their new skills in the generalization setting is the easiest and least expensive of all methods that might promote generalization. Although practitioners should never assume that telling the learner to generalize will produce the desired outcomes, neither should they fail to include such a simple and cost-free tactic. Similarly, incorporating some of the most relevant features of the generalization setting into the instructional setting (i.e., programming common stimuli) often helps produce the needed generalization and is less costly than conducting instruction in the natural setting (e.g., Neef, Lensbower et al., 1990; van den Pol et al., 1981).

Not only is using less costly tactics good conservation of the limited resources available for teaching, but also less intrusive interventions with fewer moving parts are easier to withdraw. Systematic generalization probes will determine whether generalization has occurred and whether more elaborate and intrusive intervention and supports are needed.

Contrive Intervention Tactics as Needed to Achieve Important Generalized Outcomes

A practitioner should not be so concerned about intrusiveness that she fails to implement a potentially effective intervention or procedures that will achieve important outcomes for the learner. Therefore, if necessary, practitioners should disregard the previous guideline and contrive as many instruction and generalization tactics as necessary to enable the learner to generalize and maintain critical knowledge and skills.

Rather than lament the lack of generalization or blame the learner for his inability to show generalized behavior changes, the behavior analyst should work to arrange whatever socially valid contingencies may be needed to extend and maintain the target behavior.

Some Final Words of Wisdom from Don Baer

The most difficult and important challenge facing behavioral practitioners is helping learners achieve generalized change in socially significant behaviors. A behavior

change—no matter how important initially—is of little value to the learner if it does not last over time, is not emitted in appropriate settings and situations, or occurs in restricted form when varied topographies are desired.

Research during the past 30 years has developed and advanced the knowledge base of what Stokes and Baer (1977) described as an "implicit technology of generalization" into an increasingly explicit and effective set of strategies and tactics for promoting generalized behavior change. Knowledge of these methods, combined with knowledge of the basic principles and behavior change tactics described throughout this book, provides behavior analysts with a powerful approach for helping people enjoy healthy, happy, and productive lives.

We end this chapter with a dually wise observation by Don Baer (1999), in which he pointed out a fundamental truth about the relation between a person's experience (in this case, the nature of a lesson) and what is learned or not learned from that experience. Like Skinner before him, Baer wisely reminded us not to blame the learner for not behaving as we think he should.

> Learning one aspect of anything never means that you know the rest of it. Doing something skillfully now never means that you will always do it well. Resisting one temptation consistently never means that you now have character, strength, and discipline. Thus, it is not the learner who is dull, learning disabled, or immature, because all learners are alike in this regard: *no one learns a generalized lesson unless a generalized lesson is taught.* (p. 1) [emphasis in original]

 Summary

Generalized Behavior Change: Definitions and Key Concepts

1. Generalized behavior change has taken place if trained behavior occurs at other times or in other places without having to be retrained completely in those time or places, or if functionally related behaviors occur that were not taught directly.

2. Response maintenance refers to the extent to which a learner continues to perform a behavior after a portion or all of the intervention responsible for the behavior's initial appearance in the learner's repertoire has been terminated.

3. Setting/situation generalization refers to the extent to which a learner emits the target behavior in settings or situations that are different from the instructional setting.

4. The instructional setting is the environment where instruction occurs and encompasses all aspects of the environment,

planned or unplanned, that may influence the learner's acquisition and generalization of the target behavior.

5. A generalization setting is any place or stimulus situation that differs from the instructional setting in some meaningful way and in which performance of the target behavior is desired.

6. Response generalization refers to the extent to which a learner emits untrained responses that are functionally equivalent to the trained response.

7. Some interventions yield significant and widespread generalized effects across time, settings, and other behaviors; others produce circumscribed changes in behavior with limited endurance and spread.

8. Undesirable setting/situation generalization takes two common forms: overgeneralization, in which the behavior has come under control of a stimulus class that is too broad, and faulty stimulus control, in which the behavior

comes under the control of an irrelevant antecedent stimulus.

9. Undesired response generalization occurs when any of a learner's untrained but functionally equivalent responses produce undesirable outcomes.

10. Other types of generalized outcomes (e.g., stimulus equivalence, contingency adduction, and generalization across subjects) do not fit easily into categories of response maintenance, setting/situation generalization, and response generalization.

11. The generalization map is a conceptual framework for combining and categorizing the various types of generalized behavior change (Drabman, Hammer, & Rosenbaum, 1979).

Planning for Generalized Behavior Change

12. The first step in promoting generalized behavior changes is to select target behaviors that will meet naturally existing contingencies of reinforcement.

13. A naturally existing contingency is any contingency of reinforcement (or punishment) that operates independent of the behavior analyst's or practitioner's efforts, including socially mediated contingencies contrived by other people and already in effect in the relevant setting.

14. A contrived contingency is any contingency of reinforcement (or punishment) designed and implemented by a behavior analyst to achieve the acquisition, maintenance, and/or generalization of a targeted behavior change.

15. Planning for generalization includes identifying all the desired behavior changes and all the environments in which the learner should emit the target behavior(s) after direct training has ceased.

16. Benefits of developing the planning lists include a better understanding of the scope of the teaching task and an opportunity to prioritize the most important behavior changes and settings for direct instruction.

Strategies and Tactics for Promoting Generalized Behavior Change

17. Researchers have developed and advanced what Stokes and Baer (1977) called an "implicit technology of generalization" into an increasingly explicit and effective set of methods for promoting generalized behavior change.

18. The strategy of teaching sufficient examples requires teaching a subset of all of the possible stimulus and response examples and then assessing the learner's performance on untrained examples.

19. A generalization probe is any measurement of a learner's performance of a target behavior in a setting and/or stimulus situation in which direct training has not been provided.

20. Teaching sufficient stimulus examples involves teaching the learner to respond correctly to more than one example

of an antecedent stimulus and probing for generalization to untaught stimulus examples.

21. As a general rule, the more examples the practitioner uses during instruction, the more likely the learner will be to respond correctly to untrained examples or situations.

22. Having the learner practice a variety of response topographies helps ensure the acquisition of desired response forms and promotes response generalization. Often called multiple exemplar training, this tactic typically incorporates numerous stimulus examples and response variations.

23. General case analysis is a systematic method for selecting teaching examples that represent the full range of stimulus variations and response requirements in the generalization setting.

24. Negative, or "don't do it," teaching examples help learners identify stimulus situations in which the target behavior should not be performed.

25. Minimum difference negative teaching examples, which share many characteristics with positive teaching examples, help eliminate "generalization errors" due to overgeneralization and faulty stimulus control.

26. The greater the similarity between the instructional setting and the generalization setting, the more likely the target behavior will be emitted in the generalization setting.

27. Programming common stimuli means including in the instructional setting stimulus features typically found in the generalization setting. Practitioners can identify possible stimuli to make common by direct observation in the generalization setting and by asking people who are familiar with the generalization setting.

28. Teaching loosely—randomly varying noncritical aspects of the instructional setting within and across teaching sessions—(a) reduces the likelihood that a single or small group of noncritical stimuli will acquire exclusive control over the target behavior and (b) makes it less likely that the learner's performance will be impeded or "thrown off" by the presence of a "strange" stimulus in the generalization setting.

29. A newly learned behavior may fail to contact an existing contingency of reinforcement because it has not been taught well enough. The solution for this kind of generalization problem is to teach the learner to emit the target behavior at the rate, accuracy, topography, latency, duration, and/or magnitude required by the naturally occurring contingencies of reinforcement.

30. The use of intermittent schedules of reinforcement and delayed rewards can create indiscriminable contingencies, which promote generalized responding by making it difficult for the learner to discriminate whether the next response will produce reinforcement.

31. Behavior traps are powerful contingencies of reinforcement with four defining features: (a) They are "baited"

with virtually irresistible reinforcers; (b) only a low-effort response already in the student's repertoire is needed to enter the trap; (c) interrelated contingencies of reinforcement inside the trap motivate the student to acquire, extend, and maintain targeted skills; and (d) they can remain effective for a long time.

32. One way to wake up an existing but inoperative contingency of reinforcement is to ask key people in the generalization setting to attend to and praise the learner's performance of the target behavior.

33. Another tactic for waking up a natural contingency of reinforcement is to teach the learner how to recruit reinforcement in the generalization setting.

34. One tactic for mediating generalization is to bring the target behavior under the control of a contrived stimulus in the instructional setting that will reliably prompt or aid the learner's performance of the target behavior in the generalization setting.

35. Teaching a learner self-management skills with which he can prompt and maintain targeted behavior changes in all relevant settings at all times is the most potentially effective approach to mediating generalized behavior changes.

36. The strategy of training to generalize is predicated on treating "to generalize" as an operant response class that, like any other operant, is selected and maintained by contingencies of reinforcement.

37. One tactic for promoting response generalization is to reinforce response variability. On a lag reinforcement schedule, reinforcement is contingent on a response being different in some defined way from the previous response (a Lag 1 schedule) or a specified number of previous responses (Lag 2 or more).

38. The simplest and least expensive tactic for promoting generalized behavior change is to tell the learner about the usefulness of generalization and then instruct him to do so.

Modifying and Terminating Successful Interventions

39. With most successful behavior change programs it is impossible, impractical, or undesirable to continue the intervention indefinitely.

40. The shift from formal intervention procedures to a normal everyday environment can be accomplished by gradually withdrawing elements comprising the three components of the training program: (a) antecedents, prompts, or cue-related stimuli; (b) task modifications and criteria; and (c) consequences or reinforcement variables.

41. An important behavior change should not go unmade because complete withdrawal of the intervention required to achieve it may never be possible. Some level of intervention may always be required to maintain certain behaviors, in which case attempts must be made to continue necessary programming.

Guiding Principles for Promoting Generalized Outcomes

42. Efforts to promote generalized behavior change will be enhanced by adhering to five guiding principles:

- Minimize the need for generalization as much as possible.
- Conduct generalization probes before, during, and after instruction.
- Involve significant others whenever possible.
- Promote generalized behavior change with the least intrusive, least costly tactics possible.
- Contrive intervention tactics as needed to achieve important generalized outcomes.

PART 13

Ethics

Part 13 contextualizes the behavior change tactics and procedures addressed in the preceding chapters within the realm of ethical practice. In Chapter 29, Ethical Considerations for Applied Behavior Analysts, Jose Martinez-Diaz, Tom Freeman, and Matt Normand help researchers, practitioners, and caretakers address three fundamental questions concerning ethical practice: (1) What is the right thing to do? (2) What is worth doing? (3) What does it mean to be a good practitioner? The authors define ethical behavior, identify tactics for addressing potential ethical conflicts, describe guidelines and codes for professional conduct, and offer recommendations for how persons can achieve, maintain, and extend their professional competence as behavior analysts.

CHAPTER 29

Ethical Considerations for Applied Behavior Analysts

Key Terms

confidentiality

conflict of interest

ethical codes of behavior

ethics

informed consent

Behavior Analyst Certification Board® BCBA® & BCABA® Behavior Analyst Task List©, Third Edition

	Content Area 1: Ethical Considerations
1-1	Solicit or otherwise influence clients only through the use of truthful and accurate representations of intervention efficacy and one's professional competence in applied behavior analysis.
1-2	Practice within one's limits of professional competence in applied behavior analysis; obtain consultation, supervision, or training; or make referrals as necessary.
1-3	Maintain competence by engaging in ongoing professional development activities.
1-4	Obtain informed consent within applicable legal and ethical standards.
1-5	Assist the client with identifying lifestyle or systems change goals and targets for behavior change that are consistent with the following:
(a)	The applied dimension of applied behavior analysis (Baer, Wolf, & Risley 1968)
(b)	Applicable laws
(c)	The ethical and professional standards of the profession of applied behavior analysis.
1-6	Initiate, continue, modify, or discontinue behavior analysis services only when the risk–benefit ratio of doing so is lower than the risk–benefit ratio for taking alternative actions.
1-7	Identify and reconcile contingencies that compromise the practitioner–client covenant, including relationships among the practitioner, the client, and other parties.

This chapter was written by José A. Martinez-Diaz, Thomas R. Freeman, Matthew Normand, and Timothy E. Heron.

1-8	Use the most effective assessment and behavior change procedures within applicable ethical standards, taking into consideration the guideline of minimal intrusiveness of the procedure to the client.
1-9	Protect confidentiality.
1-10	Truthfully and accurately represent one's contributions and those of others to the practice, discipline, and profession of applied behavior analysis.
1-11	Ensure that the dignity, health, and safety of one's client are fully protected at all times.
1-12	Give preference to assessment and intervention methods that have been scientifically validated, and use scientific methods to evaluate those that have not yet been scientifically validated.

Content Area 8: Selecting Intervention Outcomes and Strategies

| 8-2 | Make recommendations to the client regarding target outcomes based on such factors as: client preferences, task analysis, current repertoires, supporting environments, constraints, social validity, assessment results, and best available scientific evidence. |
| 8-4 | Make recommendations to the client regarding intervention strategies based on such factors as: client preferences, task analysis, current repertoires, supporting environments, constraints, social validity, assessment results and best available scientific evidence. |

 Ethical dilemmas surface frequently in educational and clinical practice. Consider these situations:

- A person residing in a private, rural, for-profit community-based home for persons with developmental disabilities approaches the director and states that he wants to move to an apartment in a nearby town. Such a move would represent a loss of income to the agency, might generate additional transition costs (e.g., moving expenses, future on-site supervision), and has the potential to be dangerous to the resident given the area of town that the person could afford. How could the director respond ethically to the resident's inquiry about moving without being biased by a conflict of interest?

- Julian, a student with severe disabilities, engages in frequent and severe self-injurious behavior (SIB) (e.g., head banging, eye gouging). Many positive and positive-reductive approaches have been attempted to reduce his SIB, but none have been successful. The support coordinator recommends the Self-Injurious Behavior Inhibition System (SIBIS) as an option, but the parents object because they fear that electrical shock will hurt their son. Given that documented positive attempts have failed, is it an appropriate ethical course of action to recommend that SIBIS treatment be initiated?

- During the course of an annual individualized education program (IEP) meeting, Ms. Dougherty, a first-year teacher, perceives that a school district administrator is trying to "steer" the parents of a student with emotional disabilities into accepting a revised IEP without the provision of school-based applied behavior analysis services recommended by the majority of other team members. Ms. Dougherty hypothesizes that the administrator's position is based on the added costs the financially strapped school district would bear if it provided these services. As a first-year teacher, Ms. Dougherty is concerned that if she speaks up, she might lose the favor of her principal and maybe her job. If she remains silent, the student might not receive needed services. How might Ms. Dougherty serve as an advocate for the student, but not lose her position on the faculty?

Given each of these situations, how is the behavior analyst to respond ethically? This chapter addresses the issues surrounding and underlying these situations. We begin by discussing what ethics is and why it is important. Next, we present ethical behavior and behavior analysis standards for professional practice as a way for practitioners to navigate ethical dilemmas that arise in day-to-day practice. Finally, we discuss ethical issues within the context of client services (e.g., informed consent and conflict of interest).

What Is Ethics and Why Is It Important?

Definition of Ethics

Ethics refers to behaviors, practices, and decisions that address three basic and fundamental questions: What is the right thing to do? What is worth doing? What does it mean to be a good behavior analyst? (Reich, 1988; Smith, 1987, 1993). Guided by these questions, personal and professional practices are conducted for the principal purpose of helping others to improve their physical, social, psychological, familial, or personal condition. As Corey, Corey, and Callanan (1993) stated, "The basic purpose of practicing ethically is to further the welfare of the client" (p. 4).

What Is the Right Thing to Do?

Addressing the question of what is the right thing to do leads to an examination of several areas of influence: our personal histories of what is right and wrong, the context within which applied behavior analysis is practiced, including legal and illegal versus ethical and unethical issues, and codified ethical rules of conduct. Further, how to determine what is the right thing to do is derived from established principles, methods, and decisions that have been used successfully by other applied behavior analysts and professionals primarily to ensure the welfare of those entrusted to our care, the well-being of the profession, and ultimately the survival of the culture (Skinner, 1953, 1971).

At the outset, we would state that what is ethical (right) or unethical (wrong) behavior is ultimately related to cultural practices. Therefore, it is subject to differences across cultures and the passage of time. What might be acceptable in one culture may be unacceptable in other cultures. What might be acceptable at one time may be completely unacceptable 20 years later.

Personal Histories. When deciding how to proceed with an assessment or intervention, all applied behavior analysts are influenced by their personal histories of making decisions in similar situations. Presumably, the analyst's training and experiences will balance negative biases or predispositions that may carry over from his or her personal or cultural background. For example, assume that a behavior analyst has a sibling who engages in self-injurious behavior (SIB). Further, assume that the practitioner faces a decision on how to assist another family with a child who exhibits severe SIB. The practitioner may be influenced by his recollection of procedures his parents used (or did not use) to help his sibling. Did they use punishment? Include the sibling in family gatherings? Seek competent programs and services? However, given the analyst's training in a range of assessments and interventions, the potential influence of such personal experience is more likely to be overridden in favor of an unbiased exploration of clinically appropriate treatment alternatives.

Further, the practitioner's cultural or religious upbringing may influence decisions about the right course of action. Prior to formal training in behavior analysis, a practitioner reared in a family culture that supported "Spare the rod and spoil the child" may manage severe behavior differently than if that same practitioner was reared in a family culture that supported a "He'll grow out of it" philosophy. Subsequent to training, however, a more unbiased and informed set of principles is likely to surface.

Finally, a person's professional training and experiences with other cases involving severe behavior challenges will likely influence whether Method A (e.g., a differential reinforcement procedure) is favored over Method B (e.g., overcorrection). The behavior analyst must recognize that her personal history is likely to be a factor when making a decision. Still, the practitioner needs to be careful lest her personal background lead her to select inappropriate or ineffective interventions. To counteract this possibility and ensure that personal history and background will not influence decision making over professional knowledge and experience, the practitioner can seek help from supervisors or colleagues, review the research literature, consult case studies to determine past courses of successful action, or excuse herself from the case.

The Context of Practice. Applied behavior analysts work in schools, homes, community settings, job sites, and other natural environments. Rules within these environments cover a host of behaviors (e.g., attendance, use of sick time). Included in the rules are policy statements that are designed to help practitioners differentiate between legal issues and ethical issues. For example, some practices may be legal, but unethical. Breaking a professional confidence, accepting valued family "heirlooms" in lieu of payment for services, or engaging in consensual sexual relations with a client over age 18 serve as examples of behaviors that are legal but unethical. Other behaviors are both illegal and unethical. For instance, misrepresenting personal skills or promised services; stealing the belongings of a client while rendering services; abusing a client physically, emotionally, sexually, or socially; or engaging in consensual sexual interaction with persons under age 18 are all examples of behaviors that are both illegal and unethical (Greenspan & Negron, 1994). Behavior analysts who can discriminate between these legal and ethical distinctions are more likely to provide effective services, maintain a focused sensitivity toward clients, and not run afoul of the law or professional standards of conduct.

Ethical Codes of Behavior.   All professional organizations have generated or adopted **ethical codes of behavior.** These codes provide guidelines for association members to consider when deciding a course of action or conducting their professional duties. Also, these guidelines provide the standard by which graduated sanctions can be imposed for deviating from the code (e.g., reprimand, censure, expulsion from the organization). The Association for Behavior Analysis has adopted the American Psychological Association's Code of Ethics. More discussion of this point is found later in the chapter.

What Is Worth Doing?

Questions related to what is worth doing directly address the goals and objectives of practice. What are we trying to accomplish? How are we trying to accomplish it? Clearly, social validity, cost–benefit ratio, and existing exigencies enter into decision making about what is worth doing.

Social Validity.   Questions of social validity ask: Are the goals acceptable for the planned behavior change intervention? Are the procedures acceptable and are they aligned with best treatment practices (Peters & Heron, 1993)? Finally, do the results show meaningful, significant, and sustainable change (Wolf, 1978)? Most people would agree that teaching a child to read is a desirable goal. Using direct instruction, or another measurably effective instructional method, is procedurally sound, and outcomes that show improved reading are socially significant. In every sense, teaching a child or adult to read meets the ethical test for social validity. The new reading skill has a positive effect on the life of the individual. However, we cannot make the same claim for every skill in every situation. Does teaching street safety signs to a person who has mobility, sight, and hearing problems have true worth to the individual? How about teaching an Alzheimer's patient to recall the serial order of U.S. presidents? Why teach an adult with developmental disabilities to play with coloring books? Does a first-grade student with autism need to spend 20 minutes of one-on-one discrete trial instruction per day to learn to discriminate among pictures of women wearing fall and spring fashions? Does a child with

quadriplegia really need to learn to use a standard pencil to write? In each of these cases, the present and future "worth" of the treatment with respect to goals, procedures, and outcomes is not clear. Given adequate programming and technological advances, teaching street safety signage to a person with mobility, sight, and hearing challenges, or the order of presidents to an Alzheimer's patient, or coloring skills to an adult with developmental disabilities, seasonal fashions to a child with autism, or pencil-gripping skills to a person with quadriplegia could be accomplished. However, from an ethical standpoint, the questions are: Should it be accomplished? And is it worth doing?

Cost–Benefit Ratio.   Cost–benefit ratio decisions are contextual and involve a balance among planning, implementing, and evaluating a treatment or intervention (i.e., the cost side) and projecting future potential gain by the person (i.e., the benefit side). In other words, does the potential benefit to the individual justify the short- and long-term cost for providing the service? For instance, is it worth the time, cost, and emotional resources to transport a student with learning disabilities to an out-of-state private school with high-cost tuition when (a) comparable services can be provided free within the neighborhood public school system and (b) improved student learning and social behavior outcomes are uncertain at best? Is it worth the practitioner's efforts (i.e., financial cost plus time) to continue to maintain an 11th grade student with development disabilities in an academic, college-oriented program when switching to a functional curriculum program would likely enhance employability, self-sufficiency, and independence? Ethically, it is difficult to support a decision to spend school district dollars for outside private services that otherwise should be provided through public support. Likewise, it is difficult to defend a decision to subject a student to the continued reflexive establishing operations for negative reinforcement generated by an academic program, when a functional curriculum model would likely meet more appropriate short-term and long-term goals. To address the thorny issue of cost versus benefit, Sprague and Horner (1991) suggested that decisions should be made by committee, and that the perspectives of those with the highest stake in the outcome be given the greatest consideration. They also recommended that a hierarchy of opinions and inputs be sought to gain the widest possible viewpoint.

Existing Exigencies.   Some behaviors challenge practitioners to find effective solutions quickly. A child who engages in self-injurious behavior, a child with feeding problems, or a student who engages in severe disruptive behaviors present such cases. Most practitioners would agree that these behaviors are worth changing so that the potential for harm to the person or others is reduced. Further, most practitioners would agree that to not act might lead to an even worse condition. So from an ethical standpoint, behaviors that are more serious warrant intervention consideration before behaviors that are less problematic. However, that such behaviors may necessitate a quick and expedited treatment is not an invitation to adopt a *situational ethics* perspective in which the promise of fast results in the short term is compromised by not fully considering long-term ramifications. In short, important questions relative to effectiveness, intrusiveness, possible deleterious side effects of potential treatments, and independence also must be considered, even if that means delaying an intervention temporarily (Sprague, 1994).

What Does It Mean to Be a Good Behavior Analyst?

To be a good behavior analyst requires more than following professional codes of conduct. Although adherence to the codes of the Association for Behavior Analysis and the Behavior Analyst Certification Board is necessary, it is not sufficient. Even keeping the client's welfare at the forefront of decision making is not sufficient. Following the Golden Rule (Do unto others as you would have them do unto you), a code valued by virtually every culture and religion in the world, is also not sufficient (Maxwell, 2003). A good practitioner is self-regulating. That is, the ethical practitioner seeks ways to calibrate decisions over time to ensure that values, contingencies, and rights and responsibilities are integrated and an informed combination of these is considered (Smith, 1993).

Why Is Ethics Important?

Behavior analytic practitioners abide by ethical principles to (a) produce "meaningful" behavior change of social significance for the persons entrusted to their care (Hawkins, 1984), (b) reduce or eliminate harm (e.g., poor treatments, self-injury), and (c) conform to the ethical standards of learned societies and professional organizations. Without an ethical compass, practitioners would be adrift when deciding whether a course of action is morally right or wrong, or whether they have slipped into the realm of situational ethics in which decisions to act (or not to act) are based on expediency, pressure, or misplaced priorities (Maxwell, 2003). For instance, if the teacher mentioned in our earlier scenario acquiesced to the administrator's pressure to not support applied behavior analysis services, when she might have taken a firmer stand if other teachers voiced their positions, situational ethics may be at work.

Further, ethical practices are important because they increase the likelihood that appropriate services will be rendered to individuals. As a result, the individual and the culture will improve. Over time, practices that produce such improvement survive and become codified into ethical rules of conduct. These codes are selected and change over time in response to new environmental issues, dilemmas, or questions.

Standards of Professional Practice for Applied Behavior Analysts

What Are Professional Standards?

Professional standards are written guidelines or rules of practice that provide direction for conducting the practices associated with an organization. Professional societies and certification or licensing boards develop, refine, and revise the standards that govern their profession to provide members with parameters for appropriate behavior in a dynamic and changing environment. In practice, organizations initially form task forces to develop standards that are reviewed and approved by their respective boards of directors and members. In addition to prescribing rules of conduct, most professional organizations exact sanctions on members who do not follow the rules. Major code violations may result in expulsion from the organization, or revocation of certification or licensure.

Five complementary and interrelated documents describe standards of professional conduct and ethical practice for applied behavior analysts.

- *Ethical Principles of Psychologists and Code of Conduct* (American Psychological Association, 2002)

- *The Right to Effective Behavioral Treatment* (Association for Behavior Analysis, 1989)

- *The Right to Effective Education* (Association for Behavior Analysis, 1990)

- *Guidelines for Responsible Conduct for Behavior Analysts* (Behavior Analyst Certification Board, 2001)

- The *BCBA and BCABA Behavior Analyst Task List*—Third Edition (Behavior Analyst Certification Board, 2005)

Figure 29.1   Ethical principles of psychologists and code of conduct.

General Principles	Ethical Standards
Principle A: Beneficence and nonmaleficence Principle B: Fidelity and responsibility Principle C: Integrity Principle D: Justice Principle E: Respect for people's rights and dignity	1. Resolving ethical Issues 2. Competence 3. Human relations 4. Privacy and confidentiality 5. Advertising and other public statements 6. Record keeping and fees 7. Education and training 8. Research and publication 9. Assessment 10. Therapy

Adapted from "Ethical Principles of Psychologists and Code of Conduct," by the American Psychological Association, 2002. Retrieved November 11, 2003, from www.apa.org/ethics/code2002.html. Copyright 2002 by the American Psychological Association. Adapted with permission from the author.

Ethical Principles of Psychologists and Code of Conduct—American Psychological Association

The American Psychological Association first published its code of ethics in 1953 as *Ethical Standards of Psychologists* (American Psychological Association, 1953). Reflecting the changing nature of the field, eight revisions of the code were published between 1959 and 2002. In 1988 the Association for Behavior Analysis first adopted the American Psychological Association's code of ethics (American Psychological Association, 2002) to guide professional practice. The five general principles and 10 areas of ethical standards on which the code is based are shown in Figure 29.1.

The Right to Effective Behavioral Treatment

The Association for Behavior Analysis has published two position papers describing clients' rights. In 1986 the association established a task force to examine the rights of people receiving behavioral treatment and how behavior analysts can ensure that clients are served appropriately. After two years of study, the task force outlined six basic client rights as the basis for directing the ethical and appropriate application of behavioral treatment (see Figure 29.2) (Van Houten et al., 1988).

The Right to Effective Education

The Association for Behavior Analysis also adopted a position paper titled *The Right to Effective Education* (Association for Behavior Analysis, 1989). The full report of the task force (Barrett et al., 1991) was accepted by the ABA Executive Council. The abbreviated statement shown in Figure 29.3 was subsequently approved by majority vote of the general membership and now constitutes official ABA policy. This position statement essentially requires that assessment and educational interventions (a) rest on a foundation of solid research demonstrating effectiveness, (b) address functional relations between behavior and environmental events, and

Figure 29.2   The right to effective behavioral treatment.

1. An individual has a right to a therapeutic environment.
2. An individual has a right to services whose overriding goal is personal welfare.
3. An individual has a right to treatment by a competent behavior analyst.
4. An individual has a right to programs that teach functional skills.
5. An individual has a right to behavioral assessment and ongoing evaluation.
6. An individual has a right to the most effective treatment procedures available.

Adapted from "The Right to Effective Behavioral Treatment" by the Association for Behavior Analysis, 1989. Retrieved November 11, 2006, from www.abainternational.org/ABA/statements/treatment.asp. Copyright 1989 by the Association for Behavior Analysis. Adapted with permission.

Figure 29.3 The right to effective education.

1. The student's overall educational context should include:
   a. Social and physical school environments that encourage and maintain academic achievement and progress, and discourage behavior inconsistent with those goals;
   b. Schools that treat students with care and individual attention, comparable to that offered by a caring family;
   c. School programs that provide support and training for parents in parenting and teaching skills; and
   d. Consequences and attention at home that encourage and maintain success at school.
2. Curriculum and instructional objectives should:
   a. Be based on empirically validated hierarchies or sequences of instructional objectives and measurable performance criteria that are demonstrated to promote cumulative mastery and that are of long-term value in the culture;
   b. Specify mastery criteria that include both the accuracy and the speed dimensions of fluent performance;
   c. Include objectives that specify both long-term and short-term personal and vocational success, and that, once mastered, will be maintained by natural consequences in everyday living; and
   d. Include long-term retention and maintenance of skills and knowledge as explicitly measured instructional objectives.
3. Assessment and student placement should involve:
   a. Assessment and reporting methods that are sufficiently criterion-referenced to promote useful decision-making based on actual levels of skills and knowledge rather than on categorical labels such as "emotionally disturbed" or "learning disabled," and
   b. Placement based on correspondence between measured entering skills and skills required as prerequisites for a given level in a hierarchically sequenced curriculum.
4. Instructional methods should:
   a. Allow students to master instructional objectives at their own pace and to respond as rapidly and as frequently as they are able during at least some self-paced instructional session each day;
   b. Provide sufficient practice opportunities to enable students to master skills and knowledge at each step in the curriculum;
   c. Provide consequences designed to correct errors and/or to increase frequency of responding and that are adjusted to individual performance until they enable students to achieve desired outcomes;
   d. Be sensitive to and adjust in response to measures of individual learning and performance, including use of individualized instruction when group instruction fails to produce desired outcomes;
   e. Regularly employ the most advanced equipment to promote skill mastery via programs incorporating validated features described in this document; and
   f. Be delivered by teachers who receive performance-based training, administrative and supervisory support, and evaluation in the use of measurably effective, scientifically validated instructional procedures, programs, and materials.
5. Measurement and summative evaluation should entail:
   a. Decision-making via objective curriculum-based measures of performance, and
   b. Reports of objectively measured individual achievement and progress rather than subjective ratings, norm-referenced comparisons, or letter grading.
6. Responsibility for success should stipulate that:
   a. Financial and operational consequences for school personnel depend on objective measures of student achievement;
   b. Teachers, administrators, and the general educational program assume responsibility for student success, and change programs until students achieve their highest performance levels; and
   c. Students and parents should be allowed and encouraged to change schools or school programs until their educational needs are met.

(c) are monitored and evaluated on a systematic and ongoing basis (Van Houten, 1994). Interventions are considered only when they are likely to be effective, based on empirical evidence and assessment results.

Guidelines for Responsible Conduct for Behavior Analysts

The Behavior Analyst Certification Board's *Guidelines for Responsible Conduct for Behavior Analysts* (2004) describes specific expectations for professional practice and ethical conduct under 10 major areas (see Figure 29.4). The BACB's guidelines are based on, and consistent with, a variety of other ethical guidelines, including *The Belmont Report* (produced by The National Commission for the Protection of Human Subjects of Biomedical and Behavioral Research, 1979) and ethical codes developed and adopted by nine different professional organizations in behavior analysis and related fields (e.g., American Psychological Association, 2002; Florida Association for Behavior Analysis, 1988; National Association of School Psychologists, 2000; National Association of Social Workers, 1996).

BCBA and BCABA Behavior Analyst Task List

The *BCBA and BCABA Behavior Analyst Task List* describes the knowledge, skills, and attributes expected of a certified behavior analyst. The task list describes 111 tasks (some have multiple subtasks) across 10 content areas. Content Area 1, Ethical Considerations, consists of the 12 tasks listed at the beginning of this chapter.[1] We will address these tasks in the remainder of this chapter.

Three of the tasks relate to professional competence (i.e., what behavior analysts need to do to become and remain professionally capable); the remaining nine tasks in Content Area 1 focus on ethics associated with the provision of client services

Ensuring Professional Competence

Professional competence in applied behavior analysis is achieved through academic training that involves formal coursework, supervised practica, and mentored professional experience. Many excellent behavior analysts have been trained through university-based master's and doctoral-level programs housed in psychology, education, social work, and other human service departments.[2]

ABA accreditation and certification bodies have specified minimum curriculum and supervised experience requirements for behavior analysts. Both the Association for Behavior Analysis (1993, 1997) and the Behavior Analyst Certification Board have set minimum standards for what constitutes training in behavior analysis. The Association for Behavior Analysis accredits university training programs; the BACB certifies individual practitioners. Practitioners must not only meet the certification criteria, but also pass a certification examination. The BACB has conducted an extensive occupational analysis and developed the Behavior Analyst Task List (Behavior Analyst Certification Board, 2005), which specifies the minimum content that all behavior analysts should master (BACB, 2005; Shook, Johnston, & Mellichamp, 2004; cf. Martinez-Diaz, 2003).[3]

Obtaining Certification and Licensure

Potential consumers must be able to identify practicing behavior analysts who have demonstrated at least a minimum standard of training and competence (Moore & Shook, 2001; Shook & Favell, 1996; Shook & Neisworth, 2005). In the past, most behavior analysts in private practice were licensed in psychology, education, or clinical social work. The public had no way to determine whether the licensed professional had specific training in applied behavior analysis (Martinez-Diaz, 2003). In 1999 the BACB began credentialing behavior analysts in the United States and other countries with a certificate. The BACB certification program was based on Florida's long-standing innovative certification program (Shook, 1993; Starin, Hemingway, & Hartsfield, 1993).

Practicing Within One's Areas of Competence

Behavior analysts should practice within their areas of professional training, experience, and competence. For example, professionals with extensive experience with adults with developmental disabilities should restrict their services to this field. They should not suddenly begin working with young children diagnosed with autism-spectrum disorders. Likewise, analysts with extensive experience working with adolescents and young adults

---

[1]The entire Task List is reprinted on the inside front and back covers of this book.

[2]For a list of colleges and universities with graduate programs in behavior analysis, see the *ABA Directory of Graduate Training in Behavior Analysis*.

[3]Information on the certification requirements and process is available at the BACB Web site: www.BACB.com.

Figure 29.4 Behavior Analyst Certification Board® guidelines for responsible conduct for behavior analysts.

1.0 Responsible Conduct of a Behavior Analyst
    1.01 Reliance on Scientific Knowledge
    1.02 Competence and Professional Development
    1.03 Competence
    1.04 Professional Development
    1.05 Integrity
    1.06 Professional and Scientific Relationships
    1.07 Dual Relationships
    1.08 Exploitative Relationships
2.0 The Behavior Analyst's Responsibility to Clients
    2.01 Definition of Client
    2.02 Responsibility
    2.03 Consultation
    2.04 Third-Party Requests for Services
    2.05 Rights and Prerogatives of Clients
    2.06 Maintaining Confidentiality
    2.07 Maintaining Records
    2.08 Disclosures
    2.09 Treatment Efficacy
    2.10 Documenting Professional and Scientific Work
    2.11 Records and Data
    2.12 Fees and Financial Arrangements
    2.13 Accuracy in Reports to Those Who Pay for Services
    2.14 Referrals and Fees
    2.15 Interrupting or Terminating Services
3.0 Assessing Behavior
    3.01 Environmental Conditions that Preclude Implementation
    3.02 Environmental Conditions that Hamper Implementation
    3.03 Functional Assessment
    3.04 Accepting Clients
    3.05 Consent—Client Records
    3.06 Describing Program Objectives
    3.07 Behavioral Assessment Approval
    3.08 Describing Conditions for Program Success
    3.09 Explaining Assessment Results
4.0 The Behavior Analyst and the Individual Behavior Change Program
    4.01 Approving Interventions
    4.02 Reinforcement/Punishment
    4.03 Avoiding Harmful Reinforcers
    4.04 Ongoing Data Collection
    4.05 Program Modifications
    4.06 Program Modifications Consent
    4.07 Least Restrictive Procedures
    4.08 Termination Criteria
    4.09 Terminating Clients
5.0 The Behavior Analyst as a Teacher and/or Supervisor
    5.01 Designing Competent Training Programs
    5.02 Limitations on Training
    5.03 Providing Course Objectives
    5.04 Describing Course Requirements
    5.05 Describing Evaluation Requirements
    5.06 Providing Feedback to Students/Supervisees
    5.07 Providing Behavior Analysis Principles in Teaching
    5.08 Requirements of Supervisees
    5.09 Training and Supervision
    5.10 Feedback to Supervisees
    5.11 Reinforcing Supervisee Behavior

Figure 29.4 (continued)

6.0 The Behavior Analyst and the Workplace
   6.01 Job Commitments
   6.02 Assessing Employee Interactions
   6.03 Preparing for Consultation
   6.04 Employees Interventions
   6.05 Employee Health and Well-Being
   6.06 Conflicts with Organizations
7.0 The Behavior Analyst and Research
   7.01 Scholarship and Research
   7.02 Using Confidential Information for Didactic or Instructive Purposes
   7.03 Conforming with Laws and Regulations
   7.04 Informed Consent
   7.05 Deception in Research
   7.06 Informing of Future Use
   7.07 Minimizing Interference
   7.08 Commitments to Research Participants
   7.09 Ensuring Participant Anonymity
   7.10 Informing of Withdrawal
   7.11 Debriefing
   7.12 Answering Research Questions
   7.13 Written Consent
   7.14 Extra Credit
   7.15 Acknowledging Contributions
   7.16 Principal Authorship and Other Publication Credits
   7.17 Paying Participants
   7.18 Withholding Payment
   7.19 Grant Reviews
   7.20 Animal Research
8.0 The Behavior Analyst's Ethical Responsibility to the Field of Behavior Analysis
   8.01 Affirming Principles
   8.02 Disseminating Behavior Analysis
   8.03 Being Familiar with these Guidelines
   8.04 Discouraging Misrepresentation by Non-Certified Individuals
9.0 The Behavior Analyst's Responsibility to Colleagues
   9.01 Ethical Violations by Colleagues
   9.02 Accuracy of Data
   9.03 Authorship and Findings
   9.04 Publishing Data
   9.05 Withholding Data
10.0 The Behavior Analyst's Ethical Responsibility to Society
   10.01 Promotion in Society
   10.02 Scientific Inquiry
   10.03 Public Statements
   10.04 Statements by Others
   10.05 Avoiding False or Deceptive Statements
   10.06 Media Presentations
   10.07 Testimonials
   10.08 In-Person Solicitation

should not begin working with preschool clients, who would be outside of their expertise. A person whose entire career has been set in preschool or home-based settings with children should not start offering services in the area of organizational behavior management.

Even within one's competence area, practitioners who come upon a situation that exceeds their training or experience should make a referral to another behavior analyst or consultant. Where gaps in professional training exist, increased competence can be achieved by attending workshops, seminars, classes, and other continuing education activities. When possible, analysts should work with mentors, supervisors, or colleagues who can provide enhanced training and professional development.

Maintaining and Expanding Professional Competence

Behavior analysts have an ethical responsibility to stay informed of advancements in the field. For example, conceptual advances and technical innovations in the 1990s in areas such as antecedent interventions, functional analysis, and motivating operations have had profound implications for clinical and educational practice. Behavior analysts can maintain and expand their professional competence by earning continuing education credits, attending and participating in professional conferences, reading professional literature, and presenting cases to peer review and oversight committees.

Continuing Education Units

Behavior analysts can expand their professional competence and keep abreast of new developments by attending training events offering continuing education unit (CEU) credits. The BACB requires a minimum number of CEUs per three-year renewal period to maintain certification. CEU credits are available by attending workshops at national and local conferences such as those of the Association for Behavior Analysis and its local affiliates, or events sponsored by universities and other agencies approved as CEU providers by the BACB. Continuing education credits demonstrate that the behavior analyst has added relevant awareness, knowledge, and/or skills to his or her repertoire.

Attending and Presenting at Conferences

Attending and participating in local, state, or national conferences enhance every behavior analyst's skills. The axiom, "You never learn something so well as when you have to teach it" continues to have value. Hence, participating in a conference helps practitioners refine their skills.

Professional Reading

Self-study is a fundamental way to maintain currency in an ever-changing field. In addition to routinely reading the *Journal of Applied Behavior Analysis* (JABA) and *The Behavior Analyst,* all behavior analysts should study other behavioral publications specific to their areas of expertise and interest.

Oversight and Peer Review Opportunities

When behavior analysts approach a difficult problem, they apply skills and techniques within their repertoire to address the problem. For example, in a case of a child with a history of severe and frequent face-slapping, an intervention that involved the child wearing a helmet or protective device might be faded as differential reinforcement for appropriate object-holding becomes more effective. Fading the helmet presents no ethical problems as long as the technique remains conceptually systematic, is based in the basic principles of behavior, is tied to the published research literature in some way, and is effective in the present case. However, even the most technically proficient and professionally careful practitioner is subject to contingencies that can lead to treatment drift or error. This is where oversight and peer review come into play.

Many states have laws requiring that oversight be provided under specific circumstances, which are defined either by the type and severity of behaviors being addressed or the restrictiveness of the procedure(s) being proposed. The presence or absence of laws in a particular jurisdiction should not determine our dedication to a process of peer review and oversight, however these safeguards protect not only the consumers of behavior analytic services, but also behavior analysts themselves.

When findings are presented before a group of colleagues outside of the behavior analytic community, clear demonstrations of procedures that comply with clinical and professional standards must apply. Moreover, such presentations set the occasion for behavior analysts to clarify behavioral outcomes, present graphic displays that are easy to interpret, and explain in clear and rational language why various educational or clinical choices were made.

Making and Substantiating Professional Claims

Sometimes overzealous practicing behavior analysts are so certain of the superiority of operant and respondent principles that they make preemptive claims that are not realistic. For example, asserting, "I am certain I can help your son" borders on an unethical claim. A more ethical and appropriate statement may be, "I have had success working with other children who have profiles similar to your son's." Behavior analysts who are well acquainted with the professional literature on treatment effectiveness for the target behaviors, the functions that behaviors serve (e.g., attention, escape), and specific client populations are less likely to make unsubstantiated and far-reaching claims.

A second aspect of this professional standard relates to presenting oneself as having certifications, licenses, educational experiences, or training that one does not have.

Falsely claiming to have applied behavior analysis experiences or valid credentials is always unethical and may be illegal in many states.

Ethical Issues in Client Services

As stated earlier, although applied behavior analysis shares many ethical concerns with other disciplines, some ethical questions are specific to the choices posed when behavior analysis services are considered. For example, the decision to use an aversive procedure poses complex ethical questions that must be addressed prior to implementation (Herr, O'Sullivan, & Dinerstein, 1999; Iwata, 1988; Repp & Singh, 1990).

Although our discussion is limited to the most common areas of ethical concern related to the BACB standards, we strongly advise that students and practitioners read the BACB's guidelines and task-list objectives to maintain their ethical perspective and skills across a wide range of standards.

Informed Consent

Informed consent means that the potential recipient of services or participant in a research study gives his or her explicit permission before any assessment or treatment is provided. Informed consent requires more than obtaining permission. Permission must come after full disclosure and information is provided to the participant. Figure 29.5 shows an example of an informed consent letter in which such information is provided.

Three tests must be met before informed consent can be considered valid: (a) The person must demonstrate the capacity to decide, (b) the person's decision must be voluntary, and (c) the person must have adequate knowledge of all salient aspects of the treatment.

Capacity to Decide

To be considered capable of making an informed decision, a participant must have (a) an adequate mental process or faculty by which he or she acquires knowledge, (b) the ability to select and express his or her

Figure 29.5   Example of an informed consent form.

Informed Consent Form
A.B.A. TECHNOLOGIES, INC.

CLIENT: _____ DOB: _____

STATEMENT OF AUTHORITY TO CONSENT: I certify that I have the authority to legally consent to assessment, release of information, and all legal issues involving the above-named client. Upon request, I will provide A.B.A. Technologies, Inc., with proper legal documentation to support this claim. I further hereby agree that if my status as legal guardian should change, I will immediately inform A.B.A. Technologies, Inc., of this change in status and will further immediately inform A.B.A. Technologies, Inc., of the name, address, and phone number of the person or persons who have assumed guardianship of the above-named client.

TREATMENT CONSENT: I consent for behavioral treatment to be provided for the above-named client by A.B.A. Technologies, Inc., and its staff. I understand that the procedures used will consist of manipulating antecedents and consequences to produce improvements in behavior. At the beginning of treatment behavior may get worse in the environment where the treatment is provided (e.g., "extinction burst") or in other settings (e.g., "behavioral contrast"). As part of the behavioral treatment, physical prompting and manual guidance may be used. The actual treatment protocols that will be used have been explained to me.

I understand that I may revoke this consent at any time. However, I cannot revoke consent for action that has already been taken. A copy of this consent shall be as valid as the original.

PARENT/GUARDIAN: _____ DATE: _____

WITNESS: _____ DATE: _____

_____

From *ABA Technologies, Inc.,* by José A. Martinez-Diaz, Ph.D., BCBA, 129 W. Hibiscus Blvd., Melbourne, FL. Used with permission.

choices, and (c) the ability to engage in a rational process of decision making. Concepts such as "mental process or faculty" are mentalistic to behavior analysts, and there are no agreed-upon evaluative tools for testing preintervention capacity. Capacity is questioned only if the person "has impaired or limited ability to reason, remember, make choices, see the consequences of actions, and plan for the future" (O'Sullivan, 1999, p. 13). A person is considered mentally incapacitated if a disability affects his or her ability to understand the consequences of his or her actions (Turnbull & Turnbull, 1998).

According to Hurley and O'Sullivan (1999), "Capacity to give informed consent is a fluid concept and varies with each individual and proposed procedure" (p. 39). A person may have capacity to consent to participate in a positive reinforcement program that poses little or no risk, but may not have the capacity to understand the complexities that might be involved in a more complex treatment such as overcorrection combined with response cost. Hence, practitioners should not assume that a client capable of informed consent at one level can provide informed consent if the complexity of the proposed treatment changes.

Capacity must be viewed within a legal context as well as a behavioral one. Courts have held that capacity requires that the person "rationally understand the nature of the procedure, its risk, and other relevant information" (*Kaimowitz v. Michigan Department of Mental Health,* 1973, as cited in Neef, Iwata, & Page, 1986, p. 237). The determination of capacity by persons with developmental disabilities poses specific challenges, and the behavior analyst would benefit from consulting a legal expert whenever a question of capacity arises for such persons.

When a person is deemed incapacitated, informed consent may be obtained either through a surrogate or a guardian.

Surrogate Consent. Surrogate consent is a legal process by which another individual—the surrogate—is authorized to make decisions for a person deemed incompetent based on the knowledge of what the incapacitated person would have wanted. Family members or close friends most often serve as surrogates.

In most states, a surrogate's authority is limited. A surrogate may not authorize treatment when the client is actively refusing treatment (e.g., when an adult with developmental disabilities refuses to sit in a dentist's chair, a surrogate cannot consent to sedation); or for controversial medical procedures such as sterilization, abortion, or certain treatments for mental disorders (e.g., electroconvulsive therapy or psychotropic medication) (Hurley & O'Sullivan, 1999). The surrogate is required to consider specific information when making decisions. For a person who is incapacitated, the landmark case of *Superintendent of Belchertown State School v. Saikewicz* (1977) crystallized factors that surrogates must consider when making informed consent decisions for persons who cannot make their own decisions (Hurley & O'Sullivan, 1999). Figure 29.6 lists necessary information

Figure 29.6 Factors surrogates must consider when making informed consent decisions for persons who are incapacitated.

FOR A PERSON WHOSE WISHES MAY BE KNOWN OR INFERRED
1. The person's current diagnosis and prognosis.
2. The person's expressed preference regarding the treatment at issue.
3. The person's relevant religious or personal beliefs.
4. The person's behavior and attitude toward medical treatment.
5. The person's attitude toward a similar treatment for another individual.
6. The person's expressed concerns about the effects of his or her illness and treatment on family and friends.

FOR A PERSON WHOSE WISHES ARE UNKNOWN AND PROBABLY UNKNOWABLE
1. The effects of the treatment on the physical, emotional, and mental functions of the person.
2. The physical pain that the person would suffer from the treatment or from the withholding or withdrawal of the treatment.
3. The humiliation, loss of dignity, and dependency the person is suffering as a result of the condition or as a result of the treatment.
4. The effect the treatment would have on the life expectancy of the person.
5. The person's potential for recovery, with the treatment and without the treatment.
6. The risks, side effects, and benefits of treatment.

Adapted From "Informed Consent for Health Care" by A. D. N. Hurley & J. L. O'Sullivan, 1999, in R. D. Dinerstein, S. S. Herr, & J. L. O'Sullivan (Eds.), *A Guide to Consent,* Washington DC, American Association on Mental Retardation, pp. 50–51. Used by permission.

for the two primary areas of concern for surrogates: (a) decision making for a person who is incapacitated and whose wishes may be known or inferred, and (b) decision making for a person whose wishes are unknown and probably unknowable (e.g., a person with profound disabilities).

Guardian Consent. *Guardian consent* is obtained through a guardian, a person whom a court appoints as a legal custodian of an individual. Guardianship is a complex legal issue that varies from state to state. Hence, only two main points will be made. First, guardianship may be sought when treatment is deemed necessary but a surrogate is inappropriate because the client without capacity refuses treatment. The greater the degree of guardianship, the less legal control a person has over his or her own life. Because helping the person become more independent is a goal of behavior analysis, a decision to seek guardianship at any level should be considered only as a final option to be exercised in the most limited way that still resolves the issue.

Second, guardianship may be limited in any way that the court deems appropriate. In most states, a full guardian is responsible for essentially every important decision in a person's life. The court, in protecting the rights of the individual, may determine that limited or temporary guardianship is more appropriate. The guardianship may apply only to financial or medical concerns, and may remain in effect only so long as a very specific concern is at issue (such as a need for surgery). In all guardianship cases, the court is the ultimate decision-making body and may take any action including revoking guardianship or determining who should serve as the guardian (O'Sullivan, 1999).

Voluntary Decision

Consent is considered voluntary when it is given in the absence of coercion, duress, or any undue influence and when it is issued with the understanding that it can be withdrawn at any time. As Yell (1998) stated, "Revocation of consent has the same effects as an initial refusal to consent" (p. 274).

Family members, doctors, support staff, or others may exert strong influence over a person's willingness to grant or deny consent (Hayes, Adams, & Rydeen, 1994). For example, individuals with developmental disabilities may be asked to make major decisions during interdisciplinary team meetings. The way questions are posed to the prospective client may suggest that consent is not entirely voluntary (e.g., "You want us to help you with this intervention, right?").

To ensure that a person's consent is voluntary, a practitioner may want to discuss topics related to assessment and treatment privately and with an independent advocate present. Further, having discussions without severe time constraints reduces the pressure to evoke a response. Finally, anyone being asked to give consent should be given time to think, discuss, and review all options with a trusted confidant to ensure that consent is voluntary.

Knowledge of the Treatment

A person considering services or research participation must be provided information in clear, nontechnical language regarding (a) all important aspects of the planned treatment, (b) all potential risks and benefits of the planned procedure, (c) all potential alternative treatments, and (d) the right to refuse continued treatment at any time. The recipient must be able to answer questions correctly about the information he or she has been given, and should be able to describe the procedures in his or her own words. If, for example, a time-out procedure is part of the intervention package, the client should be able to describe all aspects of how time-out will operate and be able to say more than, "I'll get in trouble if I hit another person." Figure 29.7 outlines additional information that the potential client should have to ensure voluntary, informed consent (Cipani, Robinson, & Toro, 2003).

Treatment Without Consent

Most states have policies authorizing a course of action when a potential procedure is needed and informed consent by the individual is not possible. Typically, consent may be granted in the case of a life-threatening emergency, or when there is an imminent risk of serious harm. In educational instances in which the school district determines that services are needed or desired (e.g., special education programming), but the parents refuse, the district has progressive recourse through administrative review, mediation, and ultimately the court system (Turnbull & Turnbull, 1998). State statutes differ in instances in which consent is denied; thus, practitioners should consult current local or state statutes. Further, practitioners should recognize that rules and regulations associated with state laws may be subject to change and therefore require regular review.

Confidentiality

Professional relationships require **confidentiality,** meaning that any information regarding an individual receiving or having received services may not be discussed with, or otherwise made available to any third party, unless that individual has provided explicit authorization

Figure 29.7   Information for clients to ensure informed consent.

Documentation Required:
All forms indicating an understanding of information and agreement to various policies
listed below must be signed and dated.

Issues Presented/Discussed:
1. Confidentiality and its limits—how information will be used, with whom it will be shared
2. Provider qualifications
3. Risks/benefits of treatment
4. Nature of procedures and alternatives
5. Logistics of service
   • Monetary issues—Fee structure, billing, methods of payment, insurance issues, other
     fees
   • Communication—ways to contact between appointments by phone, pager, etc.
   • Cancellations and missed appointments
   • Termination of services
6. Responsibilities of client and behavior analyst

Adapted from "Ethical and Risk Management Issues in the Practice of ABA" by E. Cipani, S. Robinson, and
H. Toro (2003). Paper presented at the annual conference of the Florida Association for Behavior Analysis,
St. Petersburg. Adapted with permission of the authors.

---

for release of that information. Although confidentiality is a professional ethical standard for behavior analysts, it is also a legal requirement in some states (Koocher & Keith-Spiegel, 1998). Figure 29.8 shows a standard release of information (ROI) form. Note that the ROI form clearly specifies what can be shared and released, and the expiration date for such releases.

Limits to Confidentiality

When service to a client begins, the limits on confidentiality must be fully explained to the client. For instance, confidentiality does not extend to abusive situations and when knowledge of impending harm to the individual or others is known. All professionals must report suspected abuse of children in all states, and suspected abuse of elders in most states. Figure 29.9 shows a form typical for informing the client of abuse-reporting requirements.

As stated previously, in circumstances in which the practicing behavior analyst becomes aware of the possibility of imminent, severe harm to the individual or another person, confidentiality no longer applies. In such cases, it is ethical to inform supervisors, administrators, or other caregivers of the pending injury so that appropriate preventative action can be taken.

Breaches of Confidentiality

Breaches of confidentiality generally occur for two main reasons: (a) The breach is intentional to protect someone from harm, or (b) the breach is unintentional and is the result of carelessness, neglect, or a misunderstanding of the nature of confidentiality. An intentional

breach of confidentiality is warranted when credible information becomes available that imminent harm or danger is possible. For instance, if a reliable student approached a teacher after learning that another student brought a gun to school, confidentiality can be breached to protect potential victims. Such a breach is intended to serve the greater good (i.e., protect others from imminent harm). Unintentional breaches can occur when a teacher unwittingly provides confidential information to a parent about a child's performance, but fails to confirm that the parent who is requesting the information is the de facto legal guardian for the child. To avoid this second type of breach, practitioners must remain vigilant about information sharing throughout all phases of service delivery.

A good rule to follow with respect to confidentiality is: If uncertain whether confidentiality applies in a given situation, assume that it does. Some actions to protect confidentiality include locking file cabinets, requiring passwords to access computer files, avoiding the transmission of nonencrypted information across wireless systems, and confirming an individual's status as a surrogate or legal guardian before providing information concerning the client.

Protecting the Client's Dignity, Health, and Safety

Dignity, health, and safety issues often center on the contingencies and physical structures present in the environments in which people live and work. The behavior analyst should be acutely aware of these issues. Favell and McGimsey (1993) provided a list of acceptable characteristics of

Figure 29.8 Release of information form.

A.B.A. TECHNOLOGIES, INC.
RELEASE OF INFORMATION AND ASSESSMENT CONSENT FORM

CLIENT: _____ DOB: _____

PARENT/GUARDIAN NAME: _____

I consent for the above-named client to participate in an assessment through A.B.A. Technologies, Inc. I consent to have the assessment with the above-named individual conducted at the following locations (Circle relevant ones)

Home   School   Other: _____

I understand and consent to have the individuals responsible for care in the above-named locations involved in the assessment of the above-named client. In order to coordinate the assessment with these individuals, I authorize the release of the following confidential records to the individuals responsible for care in the above-named locations:

Evaluations/Assessments: _____

_____

IEP or Other Records: _____

Other: _____

I understand that these records may contain psychiatric and/or drug and alcohol information. I understand that these records may also contain references to blood-borne pathogens (e.g., HIV, AIDS). I understand that I may revoke this consent at any time; however, I cannot revoke consent for action that has already been taken. A copy of this release shall be as valid as the original. THIS CONSENT AUTOMATICALLY EXPIRES 30 DAYS <u>AFTER</u> TERMINATION OF SERVICES.

PARENT/GUARDIAN: _____ DATE: _____

From *ABA Technologies, Inc.*, by José A. Martinez-Diaz, Ph.D., BCBA, 129 W. Hibiscus Blvd., Melbourne, FL. Used with permission.

Figure 29.9 Example of abuse-reporting protocol form.

A.B.A. Technologies, Inc.
Confidentiality Act/Abuse-Reporting Protocol

Client: _____

I understand that all information related to the above-named client's assessment and treatment must be handled with strict confidentiality. No information related to the client, either verbal or written, will be released to other agencies or individuals without the express written consent of the client's legal guardian. By law, the rules of confidentiality do not hold under the following conditions:

1. If abuse or neglect of a minor, disabled, or elderly person is reported or suspected, the professional involved is required to report it to the Department of Children and Families for investigation.
2. If, during the course of services, the professional involved receives information that someone's life is in danger, that professional has a duty to warn the potential victim.
3. If our records, our subcontractor records or staff testimony are subpoenaed by court order, we are required to produce requested information or appear in court to answer questions regarding the client.

This consent expires 1 year after signature date below.

_____   _____
Parent/Legal Guardian   Date

From *ABA Technologies, Inc.*, by José A. Martinez-Diaz, Ph.D., BCBA, 129 W. Hibiscus Blvd., Melbourne, FL. Used with permission.

Figure 29.10   Defining an acceptable treatment environment.

1. The environment is engaging: Reinforcement is readily available; problem behaviors are reduced; reinforcement contingencies are effective; exploratory play and practice flourish; the environment is by definition humane.
2. Functional skills are taught and maintained: Environments are judged not by paperwork or records, but by observed evidence of training and progress; incidental teaching allows the natural environment to support skill acquisition and maintenance.
3. Behavior problems are ameliorated: A purely functional approach regarding both behaviors and procedures leads to effective interventions; arbitrary labels based on topographies are replaced by individualized definitions based on function.
4. The environment is the least restrictive alternative. Again, this is functionally defined, based on freedom of movement and activity engagement parameters; community settings may actually be more restrictive than institutional ones, depending on their behavioral effects.
5. The environment is stable: Changes in schedules, programs, peers, caregivers, etc., are minimized; skills are maintained; consistency and predictability.
6. The environment is safe: Physical safety is paramount; supervision and monitoring are adequate; peer review ensures that proper program procedures are based on function.
7. The client chooses to live there: Efforts are made to determine client choice; alternative environments may be sampled.

Adapted from "Defining an Acceptable Treatment Environment" by J. E. Favell and J. E. McGimsey, 1993. In R. Van Houten & S. Axelrod (Eds.), *Behavior Analysis and Treatment* (pp. 25–45). New York: Plenum Press. Copyright 1993 by Plenum Press. Used with permission.

treatment environments to ensure dignity, health, and safety (see Figure 29.10).

Dignity can be examined by addressing the following questions: Do I honor the person's choices? Do I provide adequate space for privacy? Do I look beyond the person's disability and treat the person with respect? Behavior analysts can help to ensure dignity for their clients by defining their own roles. By using operant principles of behavior, they teach skills that will enable learners to establish increasingly effective control over the contingencies in their own natural environments. Everyone has the right to say yes, no, or sometimes nothing at all (cf. Bannerman, Sheldon, Sherman, & Harchik, 1990).

Choice is a central principle in the delivery of ethical behavioral services. In behavioral terms, the act of making a choice requires that both behavioral and stimulus alternatives be possible and available (Hayes et al., 1994). Practitioners must provide the client with behavioral alternatives, and the person must be capable of performing the actions required by the alternatives. To leave a room, a person must be physically capable of opening the door, and the door must not be blocked or locked. The term *stimulus alternatives* refers to the simultaneous presence of more than one stimulus item from which to choose (e.g., choosing to eat an apple instead of an orange or pear). The point is that, to have a fair choice, a client must have alternatives, must be able to perform each alternative, and must be able to experience the natural consequences of the chosen alternative.

Helping the Client Select Outcomes and Behavior Change Targets

The term *outcomes* refers to the lifestyle changes a client has identified as the ultimate goals of behavior analysis services. In part, it refers to a quality of life issue for the individual (Felce & Emerson, 2000; Risley, 1996). Obtaining a job, establishing a loving relationship with a significant other, pursuing personal goals, engaging in community-based activities, and living independently are examples of outcomes. Ultimately, behaviors selected for change must benefit the individual, not the practitioner or caregiver. Peterson, Neef, Van Norman, and Ferreri (2005) expressed this point succinctly:

> One reason often cited for providing opportunities for choices is that it is consistent with social values such as self-determination and empowerment. . . . We also maintain that we can best "empower" students by arranging conditions to promote choices that benefit the student, and by helping students to recognize the factors that can influence their choices. (p. 126)

In the early days of the field, behavior analysts were criticized rightfully for targeting behaviors that mostly benefited staff (e.g., Winett & Winkler, 1972). For example, achieving a sheltered workshop of docile, compliant adults is not an appropriate goal if functional work-related or social skills are not addressed adequately. Compliance, although commonly identified in behavior programs, is not an appropriate goal by itself. Teaching compliant behavior becomes ethically justifiable when it facilitates the development of other functional or social skills that will, in turn, help the person achieve higher levels of independence.

To help people select appropriate outcomes and target behaviors within an ethical framework, practitioners need to have a thorough understanding of variables that affect reinforcer assessment, the function of stimuli identified as reinforcers in an assessment, and how these variables interact when a choice is made. As Peterson and colleagues (2005) stated:

> It may be that the act of choosing is effective only to the extent that it permits access to preferred reinforcers. We posit that assessment of the variables that affect preference contributes to efforts to promote choices that are beneficial. (p. 132)

Maintaining Records

In addition to data on behavior change, behavior analysts must keep records of their interactions with clients. Assessment data, descriptions of interventions, and progress notes are part of a client record that must be considered confidential. The following points on maintaining records comply with the APA *Ethical Principles of Psychologists and Code of Conduct* (2002):

- A release must be obtained from the client or his or her guardian (unless ordered otherwise by a judge) before records may be shared with anyone.
- Records must be kept in a secure area.
- Well-maintained records facilitate the provision of future services, meet agency or institutional requirements, ensure accurate billing, allow for future research, and may comply with legal requirements.
- Records disposal should be complete (shredding is probably best).
- Electronic transmission of confidential records across any unsecured medium (e.g., fax lines in public areas, e-mail) is prohibited under the Health Insurance Portability and Accountability Act (HIPAA) regulations (1996).

Advocating for the Client
Providing Necessary and Needed Services

Prior to initiating services, a behavior analyst has the responsibility to validate that a referral warrants further action. This poses the first ethical challenge to the practitioner: deciding whether to accept or reject the case. The decision to provide treatment may be divided into two sequential decisions: (1) Is the presenting problem amenable to behavioral intervention? and (2) is the proposed intervention likely to be successful?

Is the Problem Amenable to Behavior Treatment?

To determine whether behavioral intervention is necessary and appropriate, the behavior analyst should seek answers to the following questions:

1. Has the problem emerged suddenly?
   a. Might the problem have a medical cause?
   b. Has a medical evaluation been done?
2. Is the problem with the client or with someone else? (For example, a student who has done well through fourth grade suddenly exhibits "behavior problems" in fifth grade, although she remains well behaved at home. Perhaps a simple change of teachers will solve the problem.)
3. Have other interventions been tried?
4. Does the problem actually exist? (For example, a parent has serious concerns about a 3-year-old child who "refuses to eat" everything provided at every meal.)
5. Can the problem be solved simply or informally? (For example, the same 3-year-old "elopes" through a back door left wide open all day.)
6. Might the problem be better addressed by another discipline? (For example, a child with cerebral palsy may need adaptive equipment instead of behavioral treatment.)
7. Is the behavioral problem considered an emergency?

Is the Proposed Intervention Likely to Be Successful?

Questions to ask when considering whether the intervention is likely to be successful include the following:

1. Is the client willing to participate?
2. Are the caregivers surrounding the client willing or able to participate?
3. Has the behavior been successfully treated in the research literature?
4. Is public support likely?
5. Does the behavior analyst have the appropriate experience to deal with the problem?

6. Will those most likely to be involved in implementing the program have adequate control of the critical environmental contingencies?

If the answer to all of these questions is yes, then the behavior analyst can act. If the answer to any of these questions is no, the behavior analyst should seriously consider declining to initiate treatment.

Embracing the Scientific Method

General questions related to what constitutes science and how it applies to the study and improvement of behavior were addressed in Chapter 1. With respect to how the scientific method relates to ethics, practitioners use measurably effective, research-based methods and test emerging practices to assess their effectiveness before implementing them. As space engineer James Oberg once stated, "In science keeping an open mind is a virtue, but not so open that your brains fall out" (cited in Sagan, 1996, p. 187). Embracing the scientific method is important as claims of the effectiveness of treatment regimens and intervention methods become more widespread and accepted by the public without critical examination (Shermer, 1997). In Sagan's (1996) view, extraordinary claims require extraordinary evidence.

Heward and Silvestri (2005) elaborated further on the essential ingredients of extraordinary evidence.

> What constitutes extraordinary evidence? In the strictest sense, and the sense that should be employed when evaluating claims of educational effectiveness, evidence is the outcome of the application of the scientific method to test the effectiveness of a claim, a theory, or a practice. Evidence becomes extraordinary when it is extraordinarily well tested. . . . In addition, extraordinary evidence requires replication. A single study, anecdote, or theoretical article, no matter how impressive the findings or how complicated the writing, is not a basis for practice. (p. 209)

Applied behavior analysts should base their practices on two primary sources: the scientific literature and direct and frequent measurements of behaviors. Literature-based data inform initial decisions about intervention. However, practicing ethically also means that consultations with other professionals who have tackled similar problems is often necessary.[4]

Peer-reviewed scientific reports published in reputable outlets are a strong source of objective information concerning effective intervention strategies. When

confronted with data that differ from well-established, peer-reviewed literature, practitioners are obliged to investigate the situation further. By examining critical variables or combinations of interactions, the practitioner would be likely to determine differences that would benefit the individual.

There are almost as many ideas about instructional strategies and behavioral treatments as there are teachers and people treating problem behaviors. Unfortunately, many ideas have not been empirically validated. Take, for example, the popular notion in education that repeated practice of a skill is harmful to the student because it destroys his or her motivation to learn and ultimately results in unhappiness with school (e.g., Heron, Tincani, Peterson, & Miller, 2005; Kohn, 1997). Despite the popular appeal of this philosophy, it is simply unsubstantiated. Decades of carefully controlled and replicated research have demonstrated that repeated practice is a necessary ingredient to skill mastery (Binder, 1996; Ericsson & Charness, 1994).

The area of autism treatment offers another example of untested claims permeating the mainstream culture. In the 1990s a technique called facilitated communication was hailed as an amazing breakthrough for people with autism. Reports surfaced claiming that children who previously had no communication skills were now able to communicate, sometimes in very sophisticated language, with the aid of a facilitator. The facilitator guided the child's hand over a keyboard as he or she typed messages. The results of numerous experiments showed that it was the facilitators who typed the messages, not the children. (e.g., Green & Shane, 1994; Szempruch & Jacobson, 1993; Wheeler, Jacobson, Paglieri, & Schwartz, 1993).

Carefully controlled scientific studies debunked what had become a popular perception among desperate parents and teachers. For behavior analysts, the cornerstone of ethical practice is providing effective services based on solid, replicated research evidence.

Evidenced-Based Best Practice and Least Restrictive Alternatives.

An essential component of ethically driven behavior analysis is that interventions and related practices be evidence based, and that the most powerful, but least intrusive methods be used first. Further, intervention plans must be designed, implemented, and evaluated systematically. If the individual fails to show progress, data systems should be reviewed and if necessary interventions modified. If progress is made, the intervention should be phased out and assessed for generalization and maintenance. In all phases of an intervention, data and direct observations should drive treatment decisions.

---

[4]Remember that in applied behavior analysis parlance, *similarity* means likeness in function (i.e., controlling variables) as well as form (i.e., topography).

Conflict of Interest

A **conflict of interest** occurs when a principal party, alone or in connection with family, friends, or associates, has a vested interest in the outcome of the interaction. The most common form of conflict arises in the form of dual-role relationships. Conflicts arise when a person acting as a therapist enters into another type of relationship with the client, a family member, or a close associate of the client, or promises to enter into such a relationship in the future. These relationships may be financial, personal, professional (providing another service, for example), or otherwise beneficial to the therapist in some way.

Direct and frequent observations during assessment and intervention phases bring the behavior analyst into close contact with the client (and often family members, other professionals, and caregivers) in various natural settings. Personal relationships can be formed that cross professional boundaries. Family members may offer unsolicited gifts or make invitations to parties or other events. In every interaction, the behavior analyst must monitor her own behavior with vigilance and guard against crossing any personal or professional boundaries. This is especially true when treatment is provided within a private home. In service contexts, personal relationships of any kind can quickly develop ethical tangles, and are to be avoided.

Other professional conflicts of interest might arise as well. A teacher, for example, should not simultaneously be a student's employer outside of school because performance in one area can affect behavior in the other. A supervisee should be off limits as a potential romantic partner. A member of a peer review committee should not participate in reviews of his own work or the work of his supervisees. The general rule to follow with respect to conflict of interest is to avoid it. A practitioner in doubt should consult with a supervisor or trusted and experienced confidant.

Conclusion

Practicing ethically can be challenging and uncertain because anticipating the full ramifications of a decision or a given course of action is not always possible. Furthermore, it is hard work because practicing ethically requires vigilance, self-monitoring, and the application of dynamic guidelines and principles with virtually every case.

Returning to our scenarios at the beginning of the chapter, how might the director, the support coordinator, and the teacher proceed? Prescriptive, pat solutions are not possible. Yet these practitioners need not be at a loss as to what to do. In our view, ethical challenges, regardless of their sources, are best addressed by revisiting the three questions posed early in the chapter: What is the right thing to do? What is worth doing? What does it mean to be a good practitioner? Behavior analysts who use these three questions as the focal points for their decision making will have a foundation for responding to such dilemmas. Further, addressing these questions honestly, openly, and without prejudice will help practitioners avoid many potential ethical pitfalls and keep the client, student, or care recipient at the center of their efforts.

Finally, by practicing ethically, and by maintaining adherence to the scientific method and the principles, procedures, and dimensions of applied behavior analysis, practitioners will have a ready source of valid, accurate, reliable, and believable data to inform decision making. As a result, they will be more likely to achieve the original and continuing promise of applied behavior analysis: the application of the experimental analysis of behavior to problems of social importance.

 Summary

What Is Ethics and Why Is It Important?

1. Ethics describes behaviors, practices, and decisions that address three basic and fundamental questions: What is the right thing to do? What is worth doing? What does it mean to be a good behavior analyst?

2. Ethics is important because it helps practitioners decide whether a course of action is morally right or wrong, and it guides decisions to act irrespective of the demands of expediency, pressure, or priorities.

3. Ethical practices are derived from other behavior analysts and professionals to ensure the well-being of (a) clients, (b) the profession itself, and (c) the culture as a whole. Over time, practices become codified into ethical rules of conduct that may change in response to a changing world.

4. Personal histories, including cultural and religious experiences, influence how practitioners decide a course of action in any given situation.

5. Practicing behavior analysts must be aware of the particular settings in which they work and the specific rules and ethical standards applicable to those settings. Behavior might be illegal but ethical, legal but unethical, or illegal and unethical.

Standards of Professional Practice for Applied Behavior Analysts

6. Professional organizations adopt formalized statements of conduct, codes of professional behavior, or ethical standards of behavior to guide their members in making decisions. Also, standards exact sanctions when deviations from the code occur.

7. The client's welfare is at the forefront of ethical decision making.

8. Behavior analysts must take steps to ensure that their professional conduct is self-regulating.

9. Professional standards, guidelines, or rules of practice are written statements that provide direction for conducting the practices associated with an organization.

10. Behavior analysts are guided by five documents with respect to ethical behavior: *Ethical Principles of Psychologists and Code of Conduct (APA, 2002), The Right to Effective Behavioral Treatment (ABA, 1989), The Right to Effective Education (ABA, 1990), Guidelines for Responsible Conduct for Behavior Analysts (BACB, 2001),* and the *Behavior Analyst Task List (BACB, 2005).*

Ensuring Professional Competence

11. Professional competence in applied behavior analysis is achieved through formal academic training that involves coursework, supervised practica, and mentored professional experience.

12. Behavior analysts must be truthful and accurate in all professional and personal interactions.

Ethical Issues in Client Services

13. Three tests must be met before informed consent can be considered valid: capacity to decide, voluntary decision, and knowledge of the treatment.

14. Confidentiality refers to the professional standard requiring that the behavior analyst not discuss or otherwise release information regarding someone in his or her care. Information may be released only with formal permission of the individual or the individual's guardian.

15. Practicing behavior analysts have a responsibility to protect a client's dignity, health, and safety. Various rights must be observed and protected, including the right to make choices, the right to privacy, the right to a therapeutic treatment environment, and the right to refuse treatment.

16. The individual receiving services must be given the opportunity to assist in selecting and approve of treatment goals. Outcomes must be selected that are primarily aimed at benefiting the individual receiving services.

17. Records of service must be maintained, preserved, and considered confidential.

18. In deciding to provide services, the behavior analyst must determine that services are needed, that medical causes have been ruled out, that the treatment environment will support service delivery, and that a reasonable expectation of success exists.

19. All sources of conflict of interest, and in particular dual relationships, are to be avoided.

Advocating for the Client

20. The choice to provide treatment may be divided into two sets of decision rules: (1) determining that the problem is amenable to behavioral intervention, and (2) evaluating the likely success of an intervention.

21. A conflict of interest occurs when a principal party, alone or in connection with family, friends, or associates, has a vested interest in the outcome of the interaction.

Appendix

Textbook Coverage of the Behavior Analyst Certification Board® BCBA® & BCABA® Behavior Analyst Task List© – Third Edition

This appendix enables you to locate the page numbers where concepts, principles, or procedures related to each item of the Behavior Analyst Certification Board's Task List—Third Edition are discussed in the text. A complete listing of the BCBA® & BCABA® Behavior Analyst Task List—Third Edition is printed inside the front and back covers of this text. For the current requirements for taking the examination, go the Behavior Analyst Certification Board's website at www.BACB.com.

The organization and format of this appendix, when used in conjunction with the BACB® Task List grids on the first page of each chapter and the Subject Index, will aid you in determining where each task is discussed in the text.

This text covers most of the basic knowledge that a qualified behavior analyst must possess, and mastering this content will contribute to your attaining a passing score on the Behavior Analysis Certification Board's ex-

aminations to become a Board Certified Associate Behavior Analyst® (BCABA) or a Board Certified Behavior Analyst® (BCBA). However, two important qualifiers must be recognized. First, each of the Behavior Analyst Certification Board examinations requires some knowledge beyond what is included in this or any other single text. Knowing everything in this book will not guarantee a passing score on either of the BACB examinations. Second, no matter how accurate, extensive, and current any textbook and no matter how thoroughly a student masters that content, he or she will not be qualified to function as a behavior analyst as the result. Successful completion of the required coursework in behavior analysis is but one step in the preparation to become a BCBA or BCABA. For the current requirements for becoming a BCABA or BCBA, go to the Behavior Analyst Certification Board's website at http://www.BACB.com.

CONTENT AREA 1: ETHICAL CONSIDERATIONS

	Task	Relevant Textbook Content on These Pages
1-1	Solicit or otherwise influence clients only through the use of truthful and accurate representations of intervention efficacy and one's professional competence in applied behavior analysis.	• 665–669
1-2	Practice within one's limits of professional competence in applied behavior analysis, and obtain consultation, supervision, training, or make referrals as necessary.	• 665–668
1-3	Maintain competence by engaging in ongoing professional development activities.	• 665–668
1-4	Obtain informed consent within applicable legal and ethical standards.	• 669–671

1-5	Assist the client with identifying lifestyle or systems change goals and targets for behavior change that are consistent with:	• 48–71, 674–675
	a. the applied dimension of applied behavior analysis (Baer, Wolf, & Risley 1968).	• 50–69, 676
	b. applicable laws.	• N/A
	c. the ethical and professional standards of the profession of applied behavior analysis.	• 75, 186–187, 302, 349–352, 363, 662–665
1-6	Initiate, continue, modify, or discontinue behavior analysis services only when the risk-benefit ratio of doing so is lower than the risk-benefit ratio for taking alternative actions.	• 350–353
1-7	Identify and reconcile contingencies that compromise the practitioner-client covenant, including relationships among the practitioner, the client and other parties	• 677
1-8	Use the most effective assessment and behavior change procedures within applicable ethical standards, taking into consideration the guideline of minimal intrusiveness of the procedure to the client.	• 48–71, 350–353,362, 652–653
1-9	Protect confidentiality.	• 55, 671–672
1-10	Truthfully and accurately represent one's contributions and those of others to the practice, discipline, and profession of applied behavior analysis.	• 668–669
1-11	Ensure that the dignity, health and safety of one's client are fully protected at all times.	• 62, 351–352, 573, 672–674
1-12	Give preference to assessment and intervention methods that have been scientifically validated, and use scientific methods to evaluate those that have not yet been scientifically validated.	• 48–71, 275–285, 500–523

CONTENT AREA 2: DEFINITION AND CHARACTERISTICS

	Task	Relevant Textbook Content on These Pages
2-1	Explain and behave in accordance with the philosophical assumptions of behavior analysis, such as the lawfulness of behavior, empiricism, experimental analysis, and parsimony.	• 3–7, 15, 159
2-2	Explain determinism as it relates to behavior analysis.	• 5, 159, 161
2-3	Distinguish between mentalistic and environmental explanations of behavior.	• 5–6, 11–14
2-4	Distinguish among the experimental analysis of behavior, applied behavior analysis, and behavioral technologies.	• 10–11, 14–16, 20–21 (F 1.2)
2-5	Describe and explain behavior, including private events, in behavior analytic (non-mentalistic) terms.	• 7, 9–14, 25–45, 260–269, 537–538, 599–600
2-6	Use the dimensions of applied behavior analysis (Baer, Wolf, & Risley 1968) for evaluating interventions to determine if they are behavior analytic.	• 16–18
2-7	Interpret articles from the behavior analytic literature.	• 93–94, 149–155, 230–252 (see discussions that accompany various graphs throughout text)

CONTENT AREA 3: PRINCIPLES, PROCESSES AND CONCEPTS

	Task	*Relevant Textbook Content on These Pages*
3-1	Define and provide examples of behavior/response/response class.	• 25–26, 34, 429–430, 620–621
3-2	Define and provide examples of stimulus and stimulus class.	• 27–29, 41, 393–397
3-3	Define and provide examples of positive and negative reinforcement.	• 36–37, 255–289, 291–302, 501–502
3-4	Define and provide examples of conditioned and unconditioned reinforcement.	• 38–41, 269–274, 295
3-5	Define and provide examples of positive and negative punishment.	• 37–38, 42 (F 2.3), 327–331 (F 14.2), 338–345
3-6	Define and provide examples of conditioned and unconditioned punishment.	• 38–41, 331–332
3-7	Define and provide examples of stimulus control.	• 35, 41–42, 261, 393–408, 589–590
3-8	Define and provide examples of establishing operations.	• 39, 134, 261, 263–265, 292–293, 295, 300, 375–389, 394, 464, 487–488, 494–496, 502, 530, 533–534, 541–545, 587
3-9	Define and provide examples of behavioral contingencies.	• 35, 41–42, 258–259, 261, 263–265, 292–294, 331 (F 14.2)
3-10	Define and provide examples of functional relations.	• 4–6, 17, 38–39, 167–174, 177–179, 188–191, 201–204, 219–221, 230–237
3-11	Define and provide examples of extinction.	• 30–31 (F 2.1), 37, 283–285, 457–467
3-12	Define and provide examples of generalization and discrimination.	• 393–398
3-13	Describe and provide examples of the respondent conditioning paradigm.	• 29–31 (F 2.1), 30–31, 33 (T 2.3), 393, 606
3-14	Describe and provide examples of the operant conditioning paradigm.	• 31–36 (T 2.3)
3-15	Define and provide examples of echoics and imitation.	• 412–419, 531, 543–544
3-16	Define and provide examples of mands.	• 193–194, 530, 540–543
3-17	Define and provide examples of tacts.	• 530, 536–537, 539–540, 544–545
3-18	Define and provide examples of intraverbals.	• 531,532, 538–539, 545–546
3-19	Define and provide examples of contingency-shaped and rule-governed behavior and distinguish between examples of each.	• 259–260, 287

CONTENT AREA 4: BEHAVIORAL ASSESSMENT

	Task	Relevant Textbook Content on These Pages
4-1	State the primary characteristics of and rationale for conducting a descriptive assessment.	• 49–52, 506–509
4-2	Gather descriptive data.	• 48–71, 55, 506–509
	a. Select various methods.	• 48–71, 50–53, 55, 506–509
	b. Use various methods.	• 50–53, 55, 72–101, 506–509
4-3	Organize and interpret descriptive data.	• 72–101, 126–157, 506–509
	a. Select various methods.	• 72–101, 126–157, 499–524
	b. Use various methods.	• 72–101, 126–157, 506–509
4-4	State the primary characteristics of and rationale for conducting a functional analysis as a form of assessment.	• 26–27, 56, 501–506
4-5	Conduct functional analyses.	• 178–179 (F 8.3), 300, 335–336, 364–366, 457, 459–460, 501–524
	a. Select various methods.	• 504–511
	b. Use various methods.	• 300, 364–366, 511–524
4-6	Organize and interpret functional analysis data.	• 364–366, 511–524
	a. Select various methods.	• 364–366, 511–524
	b. Use various methods.	• 364–366, 511–524

CONTENT AREA 5: EXPERIMENTAL EVALUATION OF INTERVENTIONS

	Task	Relevant Textbook Content on These Pages
5-1	Systematically manipulate independent variables to analyze their effects on treatment.	• 162–167, 228–237, 504–506 (all of Chapters 7–10)
	a. Use withdrawal designs.	• 167–174, 177–187, 328 (F 14.1), 341 (F 14.6), 347 (F14.8), 365 (F 15.4), 366 (F 15.7), 460 (F 21.2), 461 (F 21.3), 472 (F 22.1), 477 (F 22.6), 478 (F 22.7), 592 (F 27.3), 647 (F 28.10)
	b. Use reversal designs.	• 129 (F 6.2), 172–173 (F 7.4 & 7.5), 177–187, 229–231 (F 10.2), 257 (F 11.1), 265 (F 11.5), 274 (F 11.8), 345 (F 14.7), 571 (F 26.13), 521 (F 24.8)

	Task	Relevant Textbook Content on These Pages
	c. Use alternating treatments (i.e., multielement, simultaneous treatment, multiple or concurrent schedule) designs.	• 133 (F 6.5), 187–197, 230–232 (F 10.3), 298 (F 12.5), 299 (F 12.6), 314 (F 13.6), 365 (F 15.5), 475 (F 22.4), 515 (F 24.4), 518 (F 24.5), 519 (F 24.6), 522 (F 24.9)
	d. Use changing criterion design.	• 218–223, 430 (F 19.5)
	e. Use multiple baseline designs.	• 131–132 (F 6.3 & 6.4), 201–219, 232 (F 10.3), 272 (F 11.7), 298 (F 12.5), 301 (F 12.8), 317 (F 13.7), 336 (F 14.4), 359 (F 15.1), 365 (F 15.4), 424 (F19.2), 443 (F 20.5) 445 (F 20.7), 489 (F 23.1), 490 (F 23.2), 493 (F 23.3), 495 (F 23.5), 553 (F 26.2), 555 (F 26.3), 561 (F 26.8), 570 (F 26.12), 594 (F 27.4), 602 (F 27.7), 629 (F 28.5), 630 (F 28.6), 645 (F 28.9)
5-2	Identify and address practical and ethical considerations in using various experimental designs.	• 168–169, 180, 182, 185–187, 195–197, 217–219, 222–223
5-3	Conduct a component analysis [.e., determining effective component(s) of an intervention package].	• 162, 166, 230, 359 (F 15.2)
5-4	Conduct a parametric analysis (i.e., determining effective parametric values of consequences, such as duration or magnitude).	• 166, 340 (F 14.5), 474 (F 22.3), 483 (F 22.9)

CONTENT AREA 6: MEASUREMENT OF BEHAVIOR

	Task	Relevant Textbook Content on These Pages
6-1	Identify the measurable dimensions of behavior (e.g., rate, duration, latency, or interresponse times).	• 75–87
6-2	Define behavior in observable and measurable terms.	• 25–27, 55–56, 65–69
6-3	State the advantages and disadvantages of using continuous measurement procedures and sampling techniques (e.g., partial- and whole-interval recording, momentary time sampling).	• 90–93, 161, 165
6-4	Select the appropriate measurement procedure given the dimensions of the behavior and the logistics of observing and recording.	• 75–100
6-5	Select a schedule of observation and recording periods.	• 90, 94–95, 106–108
6-6	Use frequency (i.e., count).	• 76, 85–87 (T 4.1), 88–89, 127 (F 6.1), 132 (F 6.4), 181 (F 8.4), 190 (F 8.10 & 8.11), 192 (F 8.12), 193 (F 8.13), 232 (F 10.3), 268 (F 11.6), 282 (F 11.12), 341 (F 14.6), 365 (F 15.4), 443 (F 20.5), 445 (F 20.7), 472 (F 22.1), 493 (F 23.3)

6-7	Use rate (i.e., count per unit time).	• 76–79, 85–87 (T 4.1), 127 (F 6.1), 129 (F 6.2), 133 (F 6.5), 140 (F 6.15), 142 (F 6.16), 182 (F 8.5), 265 (F 11.5), 272 (F 11.7), 281 (F 11.11), 301 (F 12.9), 308 (F 13.2), 328 (F 14.1), 334 (F 14.3), 336 (F 14.4), 340 (F 14.5), 345 (F 14.7), 359 (F 15.1), 365 (F 15.5), 460 (F 21.2), 463 (F 21.5), 474 (F 22.3), 475 (F 22.4), 478 (F 22.7), 481 (F 22.8), 489 (F 23.1), 490 (F 23.2)
6-8	Use duration.	• 79–80, 85–87 (T 4.1), 89–90, 133 (F 6.6), 317 (F 13.2), 459 (F 21.1)
6-9	Use latency.	• 80–81, 85–87 (T 4.1), 99
6-10	Use interresponse time (IRT).	• 80–81, 85–87 (T 4.1), 479, 481–484
6-11	Use percent of occurrence.	• 81–82, 85–87 (T 4.1), 127 (F 6.1), 131 (F 6.3), 132 (F 6.4), 134 (F 6.7), 135 (F 6.8), 136 (F 6.9), 145 (F 6.18), 185 (F 8.6), 187 (F 8.8), 194 (F 8.14 & 8.15), 231 (F 10.2), 241 (F 10.6), 257 (F 11.1), 274 (F 11.8), 298 (F 12.5), 300 (F 12.7), 314 (F 13.6), 318 (F 13.8), 336 (F 14.4), 347 (F 14.8), 359 (F 15.2), 395 (F 17.1), 444 (F 20.6), 446 (F 20.8), 461 (F 21.3), 474 (F 22.3), 477 (F 22.6), 490 (F 23.2), 495 (F 23.5)
6-12	Use trials to criterion.	• 82–83, 85–87 (T 4.1)
6-13	Use interval recording methods.	• 90–95
6-14	Use various methods of evaluating the outcomes of measurement procedures, such as interobserver agreement, accuracy, and reliability.	• 94–95, 97, 103–122

CONTENT AREA 7: DISPLAYING AND INTERPRETING BEHAVIORAL DATA

Task	Relevant Textbook Content on These Pages
7-1	Select a data display that effectively communicates quantitative relations.	• 127–155
7-2	Use equal-interval graphs.	• 129–136, 144–145
7-3	Use Standard Celeration Charts (for BCBA only – excluded from BCABA).	• 139–144
7-4	Use a cumulative record to display data.	• 133, 135–139, 192 (F 8.12), 268 (F 11.6), 297 (F 12.4), 299 (F 12.6)

7-5	Use data displays that highlight patterns of behavior (e.g., scatter plot).	• 142, 144, 150–155, 509
7-6	Interpret and base decision-making on data displayed in various formats.	• 115–122, 127–128, 149–155, 177–197, 206–219, 514–524 (plus descriptions accompanying numerous graphs throughout text)

CONTENT AREA 8: SELECTING INTERVENTION OUTCOMES AND STRATEGIES

	Task	Relevant Textbook Content on These Pages
8-1	Conduct a task analysis.	• 437–441, 444–446
8-2	Make recommendations to the client regarding target outcomes based upon such factors as: client preferences, task analysis, current repertoires, supporting environments, constraints, social validity, assessment results and best available scientific evidence.	• 55–65, 237–243, 623–624
8-3	State target intervention outcomes in observable and measurable terms.	• 65–69
8-4	Make recommendations to the client regarding intervention strategies based on such factors as: client preferences, task analysis, current repertoires, supporting environments, constraints, social validity, assessment results, and best available scientific evidence.	• 274–289
8-5	Make recommendations to the client regarding behaviors that must be established, strengthened, and/or weakened to attain the stated intervention outcomes.	• 55–61
8-6	When a behavior is to be weakened, select an acceptable alternative behavior to be established or strengthened.	• 283–285, 469–485
8-7	Determine and make environmental changes that reduce the need for behavior analysis services.	• 167
8-8	Identify the contingencies governing the behavior of those responsible for carrying out behavior change procedures and design interventions accordingly.	• 603–604, 607–609, 652

CONTENT AREA 9: BEHAVIOR CHANGE PROCEDURES

	Task	Relevant Textbook Content on These Pages
9-1	Use antecedent-based interventions, such as: contextual or ecological variables, establishing operations, and discriminative stimuli.	• 41, 374–409, 392–409, 587–590, 644–646
9-2	Use positive and negative reinforcement.	• 36, 256–290, 291–303, 463–464, 599–604, 635–642
	a. Identify and use reinforcers.	• 36, 274–285, 295, 551, 557, 560–567, 635–642
	b. Use appropriate parameters and schedules of reinforcement.	• 280–283, 287, 304–323, 636–640, 646–648
	c. Use response-deprivation procedures (e.g., Premack principle).	• 39, 271–273, 277
	d. State and plan for the possible unwanted effects of the use of reinforcement.	• 36, 266–267, 302, 640

9-3	Use positive and negative punishment.	• 37, 329–330, 338–345, 357–371, 601–604
	a. Identify and use punishers.	• 37–38, 40, 331–332, 338–345, 357–360, 367–368
	b. Use appropriate parameters and schedules of punishment	• 37–38, 304–323, 332–335, 361–363, 368–371
	c. State and plan for the possible unwanted effects of the use of punishment	• 37–38, 336–338, 349, 370–371
9-4	Use extinction.	• 456–468
	a. Identify possible reinforcers maintaining behavior and use extinction.	• 274–285, 458–461
	b. State and plan for the possible unwanted effects of the use of extinction.	• 461–463, 466–467
9-5	Use response-independent (time-based) schedules of reinforcement.	• 182–184, 284, 489–492
9-6	Use differential reinforcement.	• 284–285, 314–315, 392–409, 421–422, 469–485
9-7	Use discrimination training procedures.	• 395, 421–424, 426–427
9-8	Use prompt and prompt fading.	• 401–408, 417–418, 426
9-9	Use instructions and rules.	• 465, 604–605
9-10	Use modeling and imitation.	• 412–419
9-11	Use shaping.	• 420–433
9-12	Use chaining.	• 434–453, 589
9-13	Use incidental teaching techniques.	• 448 (F 20.10)
9-14	Use Direct Instruction.	• N/A
9-15	Use precision teaching.	• Standard Celeration Charts used by precision teachers shown on 139–144
9-16	Use personalized system of instruction (PSI).	• N/A
9-17	Use discrete trials.	• 78
9-18	Use contingency contracting (e.g., behavioral contracts).	• 550–559
9-19	Use token economy procedures, including levels systems.	• 14, 39 (B. 2.2), 145 (F 6.18), 166, 209–211 (F 9.7), 234–235, 239–241 (F 10.6), 261, 264, 270, 288–289, 367–368, 559–567
9-20	Use independent, interdependent, and dependent group contingencies.	• 567–573
9-21	Use stimulus equivalence procedures.	• 398–401
9-22	Plan for behavioral contrast effects.	• 337–338
9-23	Use behavioral momentum.	• 492–494
9-24	Use the matching law and recognize factors influencing choice.	• 318–319
9-25	Use language acquisition programs that employ Skinner's analysis of verbal behavior (i.e., echoics, mands, tacts, intraverbals).	• 525–547

9-26	Use language acquisition/communication training procedures.	• 494–496, 525–547
9-27	Use self-management strategies.	• 575–612
9-28	Use behavior change procedures to promote stimulus and response generalization.	• 614–655
9-29	Use behavior change procedures to promote maintenance.	• 614–617, 619–620 (F 28.3), 623–626, 635–642, 648, 655

CONTENT AREA 10: SYSTEMS SUPPORT

	Task	Relevant Textbook Content on These Pages
10-1	Use competency-based training for persons who are responsible for carrying out behavioral assessment and behavior change procedures.	• 108–110, 114
10-2	Use effective performance monitoring and reinforcement systems.	• N/A
10-3	Design and use systems for monitoring procedural integrity.	• 235–237
10-4	Establish support for behavior analysis services from persons directly and indirectly involved with these services.	• N/A
10-5	Secure the support of others to maintain the clients' behavioral repertoires in their natural settings.	• 641–642, 652
10-6	Provide behavior analysis services in collaboration with others who support and/or provide services to one's clients.	• 675–676

Glossary

A-B design   A two-phase experimental design consisting of a pre-treatment baseline condition (A) followed by a treatment condition (B).

A-B-A design   A three-phase experimental design consisting of an initial baseline phase (A) until steady state responding (or countertherapeutic trend) is obtained, an intervention phase in which the treatment condition (B) is implemented until the behavior has changed and steady state responding is obtained, and a return to baseline conditions (A) by withdrawing the independent variable to see whether responding "reverses" to levels observed in the initial baseline phase. (See **A-B-A-B design, reversal design, withdrawal design.**)

A-B-A-B design   An experimental design consisting of (1) an initial baseline phase (A) until steady state responding (or countertherapeutic trend) is obtained, (2) an initial intervention phase in which the treatment variable (B) is implemented until the behavior has changed and steady state responding is obtained, (3) a return to baseline conditions (A) by withdrawing the independent variable to see whether responding "reverses" to levels observed in the initial baseline phase, and (4) a second intervention phase (B) to see whether initial treatment effects are replicated (also called *reversal design, withdrawal design*).

abative effect (of a motivating operation)   A decrease in the current frequency of behavior that has been reinforced by the stimulus that is increased in reinforcing effectiveness by the same motivating operation. For example, food ingestion abates (decreases the current frequency of) behavior that has been reinforced by food.

ABC recording   See **anecdotal observation.**

abolishing operation (AO)   A motivating operation that decreases the reinforcing effectiveness of a stimulus, object, or event. For example, the reinforcing effectiveness of food is abolished as a result of food ingestion.

accuracy (of measurement)   The extent to which observed values, the data produced by measuring an event, match the true state, or true values, of the event as it exists in nature. (See **observed value** and **true value.**)

adjunctive behavior   Behavior that occurs as a collateral effect of a schedule of periodic reinforcement for other be- havior; time-filling or interim activities (e.g., doodling, idle talking, smoking, drinking) that are induced by sched- ules of reinforcement during times when reinforcement is unlikely to be delivered. Also called *schedule-induced behavior.*

affirmation of the consequent   A three-step form of reason- ing that begins with a true antecedent–consequent (if-A- then-B) statement and proceeds as follows: (1) If A is true, then B is true; (2) B is found to be true; (3) therefore, A is true. Although other factors could be responsible for the truthfulness of A, a sound experiment affirms several if-A- then-B possibilities, each one reducing the likelihood of factors other than the independent variable being respon- sible for the observed changes in behavior.

alternating treatments design   An experimental design in which two or more conditions (one of which may be a no- treatment control condition) are presented in rapidly alter- nating succession (e.g., on alternating sessions or days) independent of the level of responding; differences in re- sponding between or among conditions are attributed to the effects of the conditions (also called *concurrent schedule design, multielement design, multiple schedule design*).

alternative schedule   Provides reinforcement whenever the requirement of either a ratio schedule or an interval sched- ule—the basic schedules that makeup the alternative schedule—is met, regardless of which of the component schedule's requirements is met first.

anecdotal observation   A form of direct, continuous obser- vation in which the observer records a descriptive, tem- porally sequenced account of all behavior(s) of interest and the antecedent conditions and consequences for those behaviors as those events occur in the client's natural en- vironment (also called *ABC recording*).

antecedent   An environmental condition or stimulus change existing or occurring prior to a behavior of interest.

antecedent intervention   A behavior change strategy that manipulates contingency-independent antecedent stimuli (motivating operations). (See **noncontingent reinforce- ment, high-probability request sequence,** and **functional communication training.** Contrast with **antecedent con- trol,** a behavior change intervention that manipulates contingency-dependent consequence events to affect stimulus control.)

antecedent stimulus class   A set of stimuli that share a common relationship. All stimuli in an antecedent stimulus class evoke the same operant behavior, or elicit the same respondent behavior. (See **arbitrary stimulus class, feature stimulus class.**)

applied behavior analysis (ABA)   The science in which tactics derived from the principles of behavior are applied to improve socially significant behavior and experimentaton is used to identify the variables responsible for the improvement in behavior.

arbitrary stimulus class   Antecedent stimuli that evoke the same response but do not resemble each other in physical form or share a relational aspect such as bigger or under (e.g., peanuts, cheese, coconut milk, and chicken breasts are members of an arbitrary stimulus class if they evoke the response "sources of protein"). (Compare to **feature stimulus class.**)

artifact   An outcome or result that appears to exist because of the way it is measured but in fact does not correspond to what actually occurred.

ascending baseline   A data path that shows an increasing trend in the response measure over time. (Compare with **descending baseline.**)

audience   Anyone who functions as a discriminative stimulus evoking verbal behavior. Different audiences may control different verbal behavior about the same topic because of a differential reinforcement history. Teens may describe the same event in different ways when talking to peers versus parents.

autoclitic   A secondary verbal operant in which some aspect of a speaker's own verbal behavior functions as an S^D or an MO for additional speaker verbal behavior. The autoclitic relation can be thought of as verbal behavior about verbal behavior.

automatic punishment   Punishment that occurs independent of the social mediation by others (i.e., a response product serves as a punisher independent of the social environment).

automatic reinforcement   Reinforcement that occurs independent of the social mediation of others (e.g., scratching an insect bite relieves the itch).

automaticity (of reinforcement)   Refers to the fact that behavior is modified by its consequences irrespective of the person's awareness; a person does not have to recognize or verbalize the relation between her behavior and a reinforcing consequence, or even know that a consequence has occurred, for reinforcement to "work." (Contrast with **automatic reinforcement.**)

aversive stimulus   In general, an unpleasant or noxious stimulus; more technically, a stimulus change or condition that functions (a) to evoke a behavior that has terminated it in the past; (b) as a punisher when presented following behavior, and/or (c) as a reinforcer when withdrawn following behavior.

avoidance contingency   A contingency in which a response prevents or postpones the presentation of a stimulus. (Compare with **escape contingency.**)

B-A-B design   A three-phase experimental design that begins with the treatment condition. After steady state responding has been obtained during the initial treatment phase (B), the treatment variable is withdrawn (A) to see whether responding changes in the absence of the independent variable. The treatment variable is then reintroduced (B) in an attempt to recapture the level of responding obtained during the first treatment phase.

backup reinforcers   Tangible objects, activities, or privileges that serve as reinforcers and that can be purchased with tokens.

backward chaining   A teaching procedure in which a trainer completes all but the last behavior in a chain, which is performed by the learner, who then receives reinforcement for completing the chain. When the learner shows competence in performing the final step in the chain, the trainer performs all but the last two behaviors in the chain, the learner emits the final two steps to complete the chain, and reinforcement is delivered. This sequence is continued until the learner completes the entire chain independently.

backward chaining with leaps ahead   A backward chaining procedure in which some steps in the task analysis are skipped; used to increase the efficiency of teaching long behavior chains when there is evidence that the skipped steps are in the learner's repertoire.

bar graph   A simple and versatile graphic format for summarizing behavioral data; shares most of the line graph's features except that it does not have distinct data points representing successive response measures through time. Also called a *histogram.*

baseline   A condition of an experiment in which the independent variable is not present; data obtained during baseline are the basis for determining the effects of the independent variable; a control condition that does not necessarily mean the absence of instruction or treatment, only the absence of a specific independent variable of experimental interest.

baseline logic   A term sometimes used to refer to the experimental reasoning inherent in single-subject experimental designs; entails three elements: prediction, verification, and replication. (See **steady state strategy.**)

behavior   The activity of living organisms; human behavior includes everything that people do. A technical definition: "that portion of an organism's interaction with its environment that is characterized by detectable displacement in space through time of some part of the organism and that results in a measurable change in at least one aspect of the environment" (Johnston & Pennypacker, 1993a, p. 23). (See **operant behavior, respondent behavior, response, response class.**)

behavior-altering effect (of a motivating operation)   An alteration in the current frequency of behavior that has been reinforced by the stimulus that is altered in effectiveness by the same motivating operation. For example, the frequency of behavior that has been reinforced with food is increased or decreased by food deprivation or food ingestion.

behavior chain A sequence of responses in which each response produces a stimulus change that functions as conditioned reinforcement for that response and as a discriminative stimulus for the next response in the chain; reinforcement for the last response in a chain maintains the reinforcing effectiveness of the stimulus changes produced by all previous responses in the chain.

behavior chain interruption strategy An intervention that relies on the participant's skill in performing the critical elements of a chain independently; the chain is interrupted occasionally so that another behavior can be emitted.

behavior chain with a limited hold A contingency that specifies a time interval by which a behavior chain must be completed for reinforcement to be delivered.

behavior change tactic A technologically consistent method for changing behavior derived from one or more principles of behavior (e.g., differential reinforcement of other behavior, response cost); possesses sufficient generality across subjects, settings, and/or behaviors to warrant its codification and dissemination.

behavior checklist A checklist that provides descriptions of specific skills (usually in hierarchical order) and the conditions under which each skill should be observed. Some checklists are designed to assess one particular behavior or skill area. Others address multiple behaviors or skill areas. Most use a Likert scale to rate responses.

behavior trap An interrelated community of contingencies of reinforcement that can be especially powerful, producing substantial and long-lasting behavior changes. Effective behavior traps share four essential features: (a) They are "baited" with virtually irresistible reinforcers that "lure" the student to the trap; (b) only a low-effort response already in the student's repertoire is necessary to enter the trap; (c) once inside the trap, interrelated contingencies of reinforcement motivate the student to acquire, extend, and maintain targeted academic and/or social skills; and (d) they can remain effective for a long time because students shows few, if any, satiation effects.

behavioral assessment A form of assessment that involves a full range of inquiry methods (observation, interview, testing, and the systematic manipulation of antecedent or consequence variables) to identify probable antecedent and consequent controlling variables. Behavioral assessment is designed to discover resources, assets, significant others, competing contingencies, maintenance and generality factors, and possible reinforcer and/or punishers that surround the potential target behavior.

behavioral contract See **contingency contract.**

behavioral contrast The phenomenon in which a change in one component of a multiple schedule that increases or decreases the rate of responding on that component is accompanied by a change in the response rate in the opposite direction on the other, unaltered component of the schedule.

behavioral cusp A behavior that has sudden and dramatic consequences that extend well beyond the idiosyncratic change itself because it exposes the person to new environments, reinforcers, contingencies, responses, and stimulus controls. (See **pivotal behavior.**)

behavioral momentum A metaphor to describe a rate of responding and its resistance to change following an alteration in reinforcement conditions. The momentum metaphor has also been used to describe the effects produced by the **high-probability (high-*p*) request sequence.**

behaviorism The philosophy of a science of behavior; there are various forms of behaviorism. (See **methodological behaviorism, radical behaviorism.**)

believability The extent to which the researcher convinces herself and others that the data are trustworthy and deserve interpretation. Measures of interobserver agreement (IOA) are the most often used index of believability in applied behavior analysis. (See **interobserver agreement (IOA).**)

bonus response cost A procedure for implementing response cost in which the person is provided a reservoir of reinforcers that are removed in predetermined amounts contingent on the occurrence of the target behavior.

calibration Any procedure used to evaluate the accuracy of a measurement system and, when sources of error are found, to use that information to correct or improve the measurement system.

celeration The change (acceleration or deceleration) in rate of responding over time; based on count per unit of time (rate); expressed as a factor by which responding is accelerating or decelerating (multiplying or dividing); displayed with a trend line on a Standard Celeration Chart. *Celeration* is a generic term without specific reference to accelerating or decelerating rates of response. (See **Standard Celeration Chart.**)

celeration time period A unit of time (e.g., per week, per month) in which celeration is plotted on a Standard Celeration Chart. (See **celeration** and **celeration trend line.**)

celeration trend line The celeration trend line is measured as a factor by which rate multiplies or divides across the celeration time periods (e.g., rate per week, rate per month, rate per year, and rate per decade). (See **celeration.**)

chained schedule A schedule of reinforcement in which the response requirements of two or more basic schedules must be met in a specific sequence before reinforcement is delivered; a discriminative stimulus is correlated with each component of the schedule.

chaining Various procedures for teaching behavior chains. (See **backward chaining, backward chaining with leaps ahead, behavior chain, forward chaining.**)

changing criterion design An experimental design in which an initial baseline phase is followed by a series of treatment phases consisting of successive and gradually changing criteria for reinforcement or punishment. Experimental control is evidenced by the extent the level of responding changes to conform to each new criterion.

clicker training A term popularized by Pryor (1999) for shaping behavior using conditioned reinforcement in the form of an auditory stimulus. A handheld device produces a click sound when pressed. The trainer pairs other forms of reinforcement (e.g., edible treats) with the click sound so that the sound becomes a conditioned reinforcer.

component analysis Any experiment designed to identify the active elements of a treatment condition, the relative contributions of different variables in a treatment package, and/or the necessary and sufficient components of an intervention. Component analyses take many forms, but the basic strategy is to compare levels of responding across successive phases in which the intervention is implemented with one or more components left out.

compound schedule A schedule of reinforcement consisting of two or more elements of continuous reinforcement (CRF), the four intermittent schedules of reinforcement (FR, VR, FI, VI), differential reinforcement of various rates of responding (DRH, DRL), and extinction. The elements from these basic schedules can occur successively or simultaneously and with or without discriminative stimuli; reinforcement may be contingent on meeting the requirements of each element of the schedule independently or in combination with all elements.

concept formation A complex example of stimulus control that requires stimulus generalization within a class of stimuli and discrimination between classes of stimuli.

concurrent schedule (conc) A schedule of reinforcement in which two or more contingencies of reinforcement (elements) operate independently and simultaneously for two or more behaviors.

conditional probability The likelihood that a target behavior will occur in a given circumstance; computed by calculating (a) the proportion of occurrences of behavior that were preceded by a specific antecedent variable and (b) the proportion of occurrences of problem behavior that were followed by a specific consequence. Conditional probabilities range from 0.0 to 1.0; the closer the conditional probability is to 1.0, the stronger the relationship is between the target behavior and the antecedent/consequence variable.

conditioned motivating operation (CMO) A motivating operation whose value-altering effect depends on a learning history. For example, because of the relation between locked doors and keys, having to open a locked door is a CMO that makes keys more effective as reinforcers, and evokes behavior that has obtained such keys.

conditioned negative reinforcer A previously neutral stimulus change that functions as a negative reinforcer because of prior pairing with one or more negative reinforcers. (See **negative reinforcer;** compare with **unconditioned negative reinforcer**).

conditioned punisher A previously neutral stimulus change that functions as a punisher because of prior pairing with one or more other punishers; sometimes called *secondary* or *learned punisher*. (Compare with **unconditioned punisher.**)

conditioned reflex A learned stimulus–response functional relation consisting of an antecedent stimulus (e.g., sound of refrigerator door opening) and the response it elicits (e.g., salivation); each person's repertoire of conditioned reflexes is the product of his or her history of interactions with the environment (ontogeny). (See **respondent conditioning, unconditioned reflex.**)

conditioned reinforcer A stimulus change that functions as a reinforcer because of prior pairing with one or more other reinforcers; sometimes called *secondary* or *learned reinforcer*.

conditioned stimulus (CS) The stimulus component of a conditioned reflex; a formerly neutral stimulus change that elicits respondent behavior only after it has been paired with an unconditioned stimulus (US) or another CS.

confidentiality Describes a situation of trust insofar as any information regarding a person receiving or having received services may not be discussed with or otherwise made available to another person or group, unless that person has provided explicit authorization for release of such information.

conflict of interest A situation in which a person in a position of responsibility or trust has competing professional or personal interests that make it difficult to fulfill his or her duties impartially.

confounding variable An uncontrolled factor known or suspected to exert influence on the dependent variable.

consequence A stimulus change that follows a behavior of interest. Some consequences, especially those that are immediate and relevant to current motivational states, have significant influence on future behavior; others have little effect. (See **punisher, reinforcer.**)

contingency Refers to dependent and/or temporal relations between operant behavior and its controlling variables. (See **contingent, three-term contingency.**)

contingency contract A mutually agreed upon document between parties (e.g., parent and child) that specifies a contingent relationship between the completion of specified behavior(s) and access to specified reinforcer(s).

contingency reversal Exchanging the reinforcement contingencies for two topographically different responses. For example, if Behavior A results in reinforcement on an FR 1 schedule of reinforcement and Behavior B results in reinforcement being withheld (extinction), a contingency reversal consists of changing the contingencies such that Behavior A now results in extinction and Behavior B results in reinforcement on an FR 1 schedule.

contingent Describes reinforcement (or punishment) that is delivered only after the target behavior has occurred.

contingent observation A procedure for implementing timeout in which the person is repositioned within an existing setting such that observation of ongoing activities remains, but access to reinforcement is lost.

continuous measurement Measurement conducted in a manner such that all instances of the response class(es) of interest are detected during the observation period.

continuous reinforcement (CRF) A schedule of reinforcement that provides reinforcement for each occurrence of the target behavior.

contrived contingency Any contingency of reinforcement (or punishment) designed and implemented by a behavior analyst or practitioner to achieve the acquisition, maintenance, and/or generalization of a targeted behavior change. (Contrast with **naturally existing contingency.**)

contrived mediating stimulus Any stimulus made functional for the target behavior in the instructional setting that later prompts or aids the learner in performing the target behavior in a generalization setting.

copying a text An elementary verbal operant that is evoked by a nonvocal verbal discriminative stimulus that has point-to-point correspondence and formal similarity with the controlling response.

count A simple tally of the number of occurrences of a behavior. The observation period, or counting time, should always be noted when reporting *count measures.*

counting time The period of time in which a count of the number of responses emitted was recorded.

cumulative record A type of graph on which the cumulative number of responses emitted is represented on the vertical axis; the steeper the slope of the data path, the greater the response rate.

cumulative recorder A device that automatically draws cumulative records (graphs) that show the rate of response in real time; each time a response is emitted, a pen moves upward across paper that continuously moves at a constant speed.

data The results of measurement, usually in quantifiable form; in applied behavior analysis, it refers to measures of some quantifiable dimension of a behavior.

data path The level and trend of behavior between successive data points; created by drawing a straight line from the center of each data point in a given data set to the center of the next data point in the same set.

delayed multiple baseline design A variation of the multiple baseline design in which an initial baseline, and perhaps intervention, are begun for one behavior (or setting, or subject), and subsequent baselines for additional behaviors are begun in a staggered or delayed fashion.

dependent group contingency A contingency in which reinforcement for all members of a group is dependent on the behavior of one member of the group or the behavior of a select group of members within the larger group.

dependent variable The variable in an experiment measured to determine if it changes as a result of manipulations of the independent variable; in applied behavior analysis, it represents some measure of a socially significant behavior. (See **target behavior;** compare with **independent variable.**)

deprivation The state of an organism with respect to how much time has elapsed since it has consumed or contacted a particular type of reinforcer; also refers to a procedure for increasing the effectiveness of a reinforcer (e.g., withholding a person's access to a reinforcer for a specified period of time prior to a session). (See **motivating operation;** contrast with **satiation.**)

descending baseline A data path that shows a decreasing trend in the response measure over time. (Compare with **ascending baseline.**)

descriptive functional behavior assessment Direct observation of problem behavior and the antecedent and consequent events under naturally occurring conditions.

determinism The assumption that the universe is a lawful and orderly place in which phenomena occur in relation to other events and not in a willy-nilly, accidental fashion.

differential reinforcement Reinforcing only those responses within a response class that meet a specific criterion along some dimension(s) (i.e., frequency, topography, duration, latency, or magnitude) and placing all other responses in the class on extinction. (See **differential reinforcement of alternative behavior, differential reinforcement of incompatible behavior, differential reinforcement of other behavior, discrimination training, shaping.**)

differential reinforcement of alternative behavior (DRA) A procedure for decreasing problem behavior in which reinforcement is delivered for a behavior that serves as a desirable alternative to the behavior targeted for reduction and withheld following instances of the problem behavior (e.g., reinforcing completion of academic worksheet items when the behavior targeted for reduction is talk-outs).

differential reinforcement of diminishing rates (DRD) A schedule of reinforcement in which reinforcement is provided at the end of a predetermined interval contingent on the number of responses emitted during the interval being fewer than a gradually decreasing criterion based on the individual's performance in previous intervals (e.g., fewer than five responses per 5 minutes, fewer than four responses per 5 minutes, fewer than three responses per 5 minutes).

differential reinforcement of high rates (DRH) A schedule of reinforcement in which reinforcement is provided at the end of a predetermined interval contingent on the number of responses emitted during the interval being greater than a gradually increasing criterion based on the individual's performance in previous intervals (e.g., more than three responses per 5 minutes, more than five responses per 5 minutes, more than eight responses per 5 minutes).

differential reinforcement of incompatible behavior (DRI) A procedure for decreasing problem behavior in which reinforcement is delivered for a behavior that is topographically incompatible with the behavior targeted for reduction and withheld following instances of the problem behavior (e.g., sitting in seat is incompatible with walking around the room).

differential reinforcement of low rates (DRL)   A schedule of reinforcement in which reinforcement (a) follows each occurrence of the target behavior that is separated from the previous response by a minimum interresponse time (IRT), or (b) is contingent on the number of responses within a period of time not exceeding a predetermined criterion. Practitioners use DRL schedules to decrease the rate of behaviors that occur too frequently but should be maintained in the learner's repertoire. (See **full-session DRL, interval DRL,** and **spaced-responding DRL.**)

differential reinforcement of other behavior (DRO)   A procedure for decreasing problem behavior in which reinforcement is contingent on the absence of the problem behavior during or at specific times (i.e., momentary DRO); sometimes called *differential reinforcement of zero rates of responding* or *omission training*). (See **fixed-interval DRO, fixed-momentary DRO, variable-interval DRO,** and **variable-momentary DRO.**)

direct measurement   Occurs when the behavior that is measured is the same as the behavior that is the focus of the investigation. (Contrast with **indirect measurement.**)

direct replication   An experiment in which the researcher attempts to duplicate exactly the conditions of an earlier experiment.

discontinuous measurement   Measurement conducted in a manner such that some instances of the response class(es) of interest may not be detected.

discrete trial   Any operant whose response rate is controlled by a given opportunity to emit the response. Each discrete response occurs when an opportunity to respond exists. *Discrete trial, restricted operant,* and *controlled operant* are synonymous technical terms. (Contrast with **free operant.**)

discriminated avoidance   A contingency in which responding in the presence of a signal prevents the onset of a stimulus from which escape is a reinforcer (See also **discriminative stimulus, discriminated operant, free-operant avoidance,** and **stimulus control.**)

discriminated operant   An operant that occurs more frequently under some antecedent conditions than under others. (See **discriminative stimulus [S^D], stimulus control.**)

discriminative stimulus (S^D)   A stimulus in the presence of which responses of some type have been reinforced and in the absence of which the same type of responses have occurred and not been reinforced; this history of differential reinforcement is the reason an S^D increases the momentary frequency of the behavior. (See **differential reinforcement, stimulus control, stimulus discrimination training,** and **stimulus delta [S$^\Delta$].**)

double-blind control   A procedure that prevents the subject and the observer(s) from detecting the presence or absence of the treatment variable; used to eliminate confounding of results by subject expectations, parent and teacher expectations, differential treatment by others, and observer bias. (See **placebo control.**)

DRI/DRA reversal technique   An experimental technique that demonstrates the effects of reinforcement; it uses differential reinforcement of an incompatible or alternative behavior (DRI/DRA) as a control condition instead of a no-reinforcement (baseline) condition. During the DRI/DRA condition, the stimulus change used as reinforcement in the reinforcement condition is presented contingent on occurrences of a specified behavior that is either incompatible with the target behavior or an alternative to the target behavior. A higher level of responding during the reinforcement condition than during the DRI/DRA condition demonstrates that the changes in behavior are the result of *contingent reinforcement,* not simply the presentation of or contact with the stimulus event. (Compare with **DRO reversal technique** and **noncontingent reinforcement (NCR) reversal technique.**)

DRO reversal technique   An experimental technique for demonstrating the effects of reinforcement by using differential reinforcement of other behavior (DRO) as a control condition instead of a no-reinforcement (baseline) condition. During the DRO condition, the stimulus change used as reinforcement in the reinforcement condition is presented contingent on the absence of the target behavior for a specified time period. A higher level of responding during the reinforcement condition than during the DRO condition demonstrates that the changes in behavior are the result of *contingent reinforcement,* not simply the presentation of or contact with the stimulus event. (Compare with **DRI/DRA reversal technique** and **noncontingent reinforcement (NCR) reversal technique.**)

duration   A measure of the total extent of time in which a behavior occurs.

echoic   An elementary verbal operant involving a response that is evoked by a verbal discriminative stimulus that has point-to-point correspondence and formal similarity with the response.

ecological assessment   An assessment protocol that acknowledges complex interrelationships between environment and behavior. An ecological assessment is a method for obtaining data across multiple settings and persons.

empiricism   The objective observation of the phenomena of interest; objective observations are "independent of the individual prejudices, tastes, and private opinions of the scientist. . . . Results of empirical methods are objective in that they are open to anyone's observation and do not depend on the subjective belief of the individual scientist" (Zuriff, 1985, p. 9).

environment   The conglomerate of real circumstances in which the organism or referenced part of the organism exists; behavior cannot occur in the absence of environment.

escape contingency   A contingency in which a response terminates (produces escape from) an ongoing stimulus. (Compare with **avoidance contingency.**)

escape extinction   Behaviors maintained with negative reinforcement are placed on escape extinction when those behaviors are not followed by termination of the aversive stimulus; emitting the target behavior does not enable the person to escape the aversive situation.

establishing operation (EO) A motivating operation that establishes (increases) the effectiveness of some stimulus, object, or event as a reinforcer. For example, food deprivation establishes food as an effective reinforcer.

ethical codes of behavior Statements that provide guidelines for members of professional associations when deciding a course of action or conducting professional duties; standards by which graduated sanctions (e.g., reprimand, censure, expulsion) can be imposed for deviating from the code.

ethics Behaviors, practices, and decisions that address such basic and fundamental questions as: What is the right thing to do? What's worth doing? What does it mean to be a good behavior analytic practitioner?

event recording Measurement procedure for obtaining a tally or count of the number of times a behavior occurs.

evocative effect (of a motivating operation) An increase in the current frequency of behavior that has been reinforced by the stimulus that is increased in reinforcing effectiveness by the same motivating operation. For example, food deprivation evokes (increases the current frequency of) behavior that has been reinforced by food.

exact count-per-interval IOA The percentage of total intervals in which two observers recorded the same count; the most stringent description of IOA for most data sets obtained by event recording.

exclusion time-out A procedure for implementing time-out in which, contingent on the occurrence of a target behavior, the person is removed physically from the current environment for a specified period.

experiment A carefully controlled comparison of some measure of the phenomenon of interest (the dependent variable) under two or more different conditions in which only one factor at a time (the independent variable) differs from one condition to another.

experimental analysis of behavior (EAB) A natural science approach to the study of behavior as a subject matter in its own right founded by B. F. Skinner; methodological features include rate of response as a basic dependent variable, repeated or continuous measurement of clearly defined response classes, within-subject experimental comparisons instead of group design, visual analysis of graphed data instead of statistical inference, and an emphasis on describing functional relations between behavior and controlling variables in the environment over formal theory testing.

experimental control Two meanings: (a) the outcome of an experiment that demonstrates convincingly a functional relation, meaning that experimental control is achieved when a predictable change in behavior (the dependent variable) can be reliably produced by manipulating a specific aspect of the environment (the independent variable); and (b) the extent to which a researcher maintains precise control of the independent variable by presenting it, with-

drawing it, and/or varying its value, and also by eliminating or holding constant all confounding and extraneous variables. (See **confounding variable, extraneous variable,** and **independent variable.**)

experimental design The particular type and sequence of conditions in a study so that meaningful comparisons of the effects of the presence and absence (or different values) of the independent variable can be made.

experimental question A statement of what the researcher seeks to learn by conducting the experiment; may be presented in question form and is most often found in a published account as a statement of the experiment's purpose. All aspects of an experiment's design should follow from the experimental question (also called the *research question*).

explanatory fiction A fictitious or hypothetical variable that often takes the form of another name for the observed phenomenon it claims to explain and contributes nothing to a functional account or understanding of the phenomenon, such as "intelligence" or "cognitive awareness" as explanations for why an organism pushes the lever when the light is on and food is available but does not push the lever when the light is off and no food is available.

external validity The degree to which a study's findings have generality to other subjects, settings, and/or behaviors. (Compare to **internal validity.**)

extinction (operant) The discontinuing of a reinforcement of a previously reinforced behavior (i.e., responses no longer produce reinforcement); the primary effect is a decrease in the frequency of the behavior until it reaches a prereinforced level or ultimately ceases to occur. (See **extinction burst, spontaneous recovery;** compare **respondent extinction**)

extinction burst An increase in the frequency of responding when an extinction procedure is initially implemented.

extraneous variable Any aspect of the experimental setting (e.g., lighting, temperature) that must be held constant to prevent unplanned environmental variation.

fading A procedure for transferring stimulus control in which features of an antecedent stimulus (e.g., shape, size, position, color) controlling a behavior are gradually changed to a new stimulus while maintaining the current behavior; stimulus features can be faded in (enhanced) or faded out (reduced).

feature stimulus class Stimuli that share common physical forms or structures (e.g., made from wood, four legs, round, blue) or common relative relationships (e.g., bigger than, hotter than, higher than, next to). (Compare to **arbitrary stimulus class.**)

fixed interval (FI) A schedule of reinforcement in which reinforcement is delivered for the first response emitted following the passage of a fixed duration of time since the last response was reinforced (e.g., on an FI 3-minute schedule, the first response following the passage of 3 minutes is reinforced).

fixed-interval DRO (FI-DRO) A DRO procedure in which reinforcement is available at the end of intervals of fixed duration and delivered contingent on the absence of the problem behavior during each interval. (See **differential reinforcement of other behavior (DRO)**.)

fixed-momentary DRO (FM-DRO)   A DRO procedure in which reinforcement is available at specific moments of time, which are separated by a fixed amount of time, and delivered contingent on the problem not occurring at those moments. (See **differential reinforcement of other behavior (DRO)**.)

fixed ratio (FR)   A schedule of reinforcement requiring a fixed number of responses for reinforcement (e.g., an FR 4 schedule reinforcement follows every fourth response).

fixed-time schedule (FT)   A schedule for the delivery of non-contingent stimuli in which a time interval remains the same from one delivery to the next.

formal similarity   A situation that occurs when the controlling antecedent stimulus and the response or response product (a) share the same sense mode (e.g., both stimulus and response are visual, auditory, or tactile) and (b) physically resemble each other. The verbal relations with formal similarity are echoic, coping a text, and imitation as it relates to sign language.

forward chaining   A method for teaching behavior chains that begins with the learner being prompted and taught to perform the first behavior in the task analysis; the trainer completes the remaining steps in the chain. When the learner shows competence in performing the first step in the chain, he is then taught to perform the first two behaviors in the chain, with the training completing the chain. This process is continued until the learner completes the entire chain independently.

free operant   Any operant behavior that results in minimal displacement of the participant in time and space. A free operant can be emitted at nearly any time; it is discrete, it requires minimal time for completion, and it can produce a wide range of response rates. Examples in ABA include (a) the number of words read during a 1-minute counting period, (b) the number of hand slaps per 6 seconds, and (c) the number of letter strokes written in 3 minutes. (Contrast with **discrete trial**.)

free-operant avoidance   A contingency in which responses at any time during an interval prior to the scheduled onset of an aversive stimulus delays the presentation of the aversive stimulus. (Contrast with **discriminated avoidance**.)

frequency   A ratio of count per observation time; often expressed as count per standard unit of time (e.g., per minute, per hour, per day) and calculated by dividing the number of responses recorded by the number of standard units of time in which observations were conducted; used interchangeably with *rate*.

full-session DRL   A procedure for implementing DRL in which reinforcement is delivered at the end of the session if the total number of responses emitted during the session does not exceed a criterion limit. (See **differential reinforcement of low rates (DRL)**.)

function-altering effect (relevant to operant relations)   A relatively permanent change in an organism's repertoire of MO, stimulus, and response relations, caused by reinforcement, punishment, an extinction procedure, or a recovery from punishment procedure. Respondent function-altering effects result from the pairing and unpairing of antecedent stimuli.

function-based definition   Designates responses as members of the targeted response class solely in terms of their common effect on the environment.

functional analysis   (as part of **functional behavior assessment**)   An analysis of the purposes (functions) of problem behavior, wherein antecedents and consequences representing those in the person's natural routines are arranged within an experimental design so that their separate effects on problem behavior can be observed and measured; typically consists of four conditions: three test conditions—contingent attention, contingent escape, and alone—and a control condition in which problem behavior is expected to be low because reinforcement is freely available and no demands are placed on the person.

functional behavior assessment (FBA)   A systematic method of assessment for obtaining information about the purposes (functions) a problem behavior serves for a person; results are used to guide the design of an intervention for decreasing the problem behavior and increasing appropriate behavior.

functional communication training (FCT)   An antecedent intervention in which an appropriate communicative behavior is taught as a replacement behavior for problem behavior usually evoked by an establishing operation (EO); involves differential reinforcement of alternative behavior (DRA).

functional relation   A verbal statement summarizing the results of an experiment (or group of related experiments) that describes the occurrence of the phenomena under study as a function of the operation of one or more specified and controlled variables in the experiment in which a specific change in one event (the dependent variable) can be produced by manipulating another event (the independent variable), and that the change in the dependent variable was unlikely the result of other factors (confounding variables); in behavior analysis expressed as $b = f(x1), (x2), \ldots$, where b is the behavior and $x1$, $x2$, etc., are environmental variables of which the behavior is a function.

functionally equivalent   Serving the same function or purpose; different topographies of behavior are functionally equivalent if they produce the same consequences.

general case analysis   A systematic process for identifying and selecting teaching examples that represent the full range of stimulus variations and response requirements in the generalization setting(s). (See also **multiple exemplar training** and **teaching sufficient examples**.)

generalization   A generic term for a variety of behavioral processes and behavior change outcomes. (See **generalization gradient, generalized behavior change, response generalization, response maintenance, setting/situation generalization,** and **stimulus generalization**.)

generalization across subjects Changes in the behavior of people not directly treated by an intervention as a function of treatment contingencies applied to other people.

generalization probe Any measurement of a learner's performance of a target behavior in a setting and/or stimulus situation in which direct training has not been provided.

generalization setting Any place or stimulus situation that differs in some meaningful way from the instructional setting and in which performance of the target behavior is desired. (Contrast with **instructional setting.**)

generalized behavior change A behavior change that has not been taught directly. Generalized outcomes take one, or a combination of, three primary forms: response maintenance, stimulus/setting generalization, and response generalization. Sometimes called *generalized outcome.*

generalized conditioned punisher A stimulus change that, as a result of having been paired with many other punishers, functions as punishment under most conditions because it is free from the control of motivating conditions for specific types of punishment.

generalized conditioned reinforcer A conditioned reinforcer that as a result of having been paired with many other reinforcers does not depend on an establishing operation for any particular form of reinforcement for its effectiveness.

generic (tact) extension A tact evoked by a novel stimulus that shares all of the relevant or defining features associated with the original stimulus.

graph A visual format for displaying data; reveals relations among and between a series of measurements and relevant variables.

group contingency A contingency in which reinforcement for all members of a group is dependent on the behavior of (a) a person within the group, (b) a select group of members within the larger group, or (c) each member of the group meeting a performance criterion. (See **dependent group contingency, independent group contingency, interdependent group contingency.**)

habilitation Habilitation (adjustment) occurs when a person's repertoire has been changed such that short- and long-term reinforcers are maximized and short- and long-term punishers are minimized.

habit reversal A multiple-component treatment package for reducing unwanted habits such as fingernail biting and muscle tics; treatment typically includes self-awareness training involving response detection and procedures for identifying events that precede and trigger the response; competing response training; and motivation techniques including self-administered consequences, social support systems, and procedures for promoting the generalization and maintenance of treatment gains.

habituation A decrease in responsiveness to repeated presentations of a stimulus; most often used to describe a reduction of respondent behavior as a function of repeated presentation of the eliciting stimulus over a short span of time; some researchers suggest that the concept also applies to within-session changes in operant behavior.

hallway time-out A procedure for implementing time-out in which, contingent on the occurrence of an inappropriate behavior, the student is removed from the classroom to a hallway location near the room for a specified period of time.

hero procedure Another term for a dependent group contingency (i.e., a person earns a reward for the group).

high-probability (high-*p*) request sequence An antecedent intervention in which two to five easy tasks with a known history of learner compliance (the high-*p* requests) are presented in quick succession immediately before requesting the target task, the low-*p* request. Also called *interspersed requests, pretask requests,* or *behavioral momentum.*

higher order conditioning Development of a conditioned reflex by pairing of a neutral stimulus (NS) with a conditioned stimulus (CS). Also called *secondary conditioning.*

history of reinforcement An inclusive term referring in general to all of a person's learning experiences and more specifically to past conditioning with respect to particular response classes or aspects of a person's repertoire. (See **ontogeny.**)

hypothetical construct A presumed but unobserved process or entity (e.g., Freud's id, ego, and superego).

imitation A behavior controlled by any physical movement that serves as a novel model excluding vocal-verbal behavior, has formal similarity with the model, and immediately follows the occurrence of the model (e.g., within seconds of the model presentation). An imitative behavior is a new behavior emitted following a novel antecedent event (i.e., the model). (See **formal similarity;** contrast with **echoic.**)

impure tact A verbal operant involving a response that is evoked by both an MO and a nonverbal stimulus; thus, the response is part mand and part tact. (See **mand** and **tact.**)

independent group contingency A contingency in which reinforcement for each member of a group is dependent on that person's meeting a performance criterion that is in effect for all members of the group.

independent variable The variable that is systematically manipulated by the researcher in an experiment to see whether changes in the independent variable produce reliable changes in the dependent variable. In applied behavior analysis, it is usually an environmental event or condition antecedent or consequent to the dependent variable. Sometimes called the *intervention* or *treatment variable.* (Compare with **dependent variable.**)

indirect functional assessment Structured interviews, checklists, rating scales, or questionnaires used to obtain information from people who are familiar with the person exhibiting the problem behavior (e.g., teachers, parents, caregivers, and/or the individual him- or herself); used to identify conditions or events in the natural environment that correlate with the problem behavior.

indirect measurement Occurs when the behavior that is measured is in some way different from the behavior of interest; considered less valid than direct measurement because inferences about the relation between the data obtained and the actual behavior of interest are required. (Contrast with **direct measurement.**)

indiscriminable contingency   A contingency that makes it difficult for the learner to discriminate whether the next response will produce reinforcement. Practitioners use indiscriminable contingencies in the form of intermittent schedules of reinforcement and delayed rewards to promote generalized behavior change.

informed consent   When the potential recipient of services or participant in a research study gives his explicit permission before any assessment or treatment is provided. Full disclosure of effects and side effects must be provided. To give consent, the person must (a) demonstrate the capacity to decide, (b) do so voluntarily, and (c) have adequate knowledge of all salient aspects of the treatment.

instructional setting   The environment where instruction occurs; includes all aspects of the environment, planned and unplanned, that may influence the learner's acquisition and generalization of the target behavior. (Contrast with **generalization setting.**)

interdependent group contingency   A contingency in which reinforcement for all members of a group is dependent on each member of the group meeting a performance criterion that is in effect for all members of the group.

intermittent schedule of reinforcement (INT)   A contingency of reinforcement in which some, but not all, occurrences of the behavior produce reinforcement.

internal validity   The extent to which an experiment shows convincingly that changes in behavior are a function of the independent variable and not the result of uncontrolled or unknown variables. (Compare to **external validity.**)

interobserver agreement (IOA)   The degree to which two or more independent observers report the same observed values after measuring the same events.

interresponse time (IRT)   A measure of temporal locus; defined as the elapsed time between two successive responses.

interval-by-interval IOA   An index of the agreement between observers for data obtained by interval recording or time sampling measurement; calculated for a given session or measurement period by comparing the two observers' recordings of the occurrence or nonoccurrence of the behavior in each observation interval and dividing the number of intervals of agreement by the total number of intervals and multiplying by 100. Also called the *point-by-point* or *total interval IOA.* (Compare to **scored-interval IOA** and **unscored-interval IOA.**)

interval DRL   A procedure for implementing DRL in which the total session is divided into equal intervals and reinforcement is provided at the end of each interval in which the number of responses during the interval is equal to or below a criterion limit. (See **differential reinforcement of low rates (DRL).**)

intraverbal   An elementary verbal operant that is evoked by a verbal discriminative stimulus and that does *not* have point-to-point correspondence with that verbal stimulus.

irreversibility   A situation that occurs when the level of responding observed in a previous phase cannot be reproduced even though the experimental conditions are the same as they were during the earlier phase.

lag reinforcement schedule   A schedule of reinforcement in which reinforcement is contingent on a response being different in some specified way (e.g., different topography) from the previous response (e.g., Lag 1) or a specified number of previous responses (e.g., Lag 2 or more).

latency   See **response latency.**

level   The value on the vertical axis around which a series of behavioral measures converge.

level system   A component of some token economy systems in which participants advance up (or down) through a succession of levels contingent on their behavior at the current level. The performance criteria and sophistication or difficulty of the behaviors required at each level are higher than those of preceding levels; as participants advance to higher levels, they gain access to more desirable reinforcers, increased privileges, and greater independence.

limited hold   A situation in which reinforcement is available only during a finite time following the elapse of an FI or VI interval; if the target response does not occur within the time limit, reinforcement is withheld and a new interval begins (e.g., on an FI 5-minute schedule with a limited hold of 30 seconds, the first correct response following the elapse of 5 minutes is reinforced only if that response occurs within 30 seconds after the end of the 5-minute interval).

line graph   Based on a Cartesian plane, a two-dimensional area formed by the intersection of two perpendicular lines. Any point within the plane represents a specific relation between the two dimensions described by the intersecting lines. It is the most common graphic format for displaying data in applied behavior analysis.

listener   Someone who provides reinforcement for verbal behavior. A listener may also serve as an audience evoking verbal behavior. (Contrast with **speaker.**)

local response rate   The average rate of response during a smaller period of time within a larger period for which an overall response rate has been given. (See **overall response rate.**)

magnitude   The force or intensity with which a response is emitted; provides important quantitative parameters used in defining and verifying the occurrence of some response classes. Responses meeting those criteria are measured and reported by one or more fundamental or derivative measures such as frequency, duration, or latency. Sometimes called *amplitude.*

maintenance   Two different meanings in applied behavior analysis: (a) the extent to which the learner continues to perform the target behavior after a portion or all of the intervention has been terminated (i.e., response maintenance), a dependent variable or characteristic of behavior; and (b) a condition in which treatment has been discontinued or partially withdrawn, an independent variable or experimental condition.

mand An elementary verbal operant that is evoked by an MO and followed by specific reinforcement.

massed practice A self-directed behavior change technique in which the person forces himself to perform an undesired behavior (e.g., a compulsive ritual) repeatedly, which sometimes decreases the future frequency of the behavior.

matching law The allocation of responses to choices available on concurrent schedules of reinforcement; rates of responding across choices are distributed in proportions that match the rates of reinforcement received from each choice alternative.

matching-to-sample A procedure for investigating conditional relations and stimulus equivalence. A matching-to-sample trial begins with the participant making a response that presents or reveals the sample stimulus; next, the sample stimulus may or may not be removed, and two or more comparison stimuli are presented. The participant then selects one of the comparison stimuli. Responses that select a comparison stimulus that matches the sample stimulus are reinforced, and no reinforcement is provided for responses selecting the nonmatching comparison stimuli.

mean count-per-interval IOA The average percentage of agreement between the counts reported by two observers in a measurement period comprised of a series of smaller counting times; a more conservative measure of IOA than total count IOA.

mean duration-per-occurrence IOA An IOA index for duration per occurrence data; also a more conservative and usually more meaningful assessment of IOA for total duration data calculated for a given session or measurement period by computing the average percentage of agreement of the durations reported by two observers for each occurrence of the target behavior.

measurement bias Nonrandom measurement error; a form of inaccurate measurement in which the data consistently overestimate or underestimate the true value of an event.

measurement by permanent product A method of measuring behavior after it has occurred by recording the effects that the behavior produced on the environment.

mentalism An approach to explaining behavior that assumes that a mental, or "inner," dimension exists that differs from a behavioral dimension and that phenomena in this dimension either directly cause or at least mediate some forms of behavior, if not all.

metaphorical (tact) extension A tact evoked by a novel stimulus that shares some, but not all, of the relevant features of the original stimulus.

methodological behaviorism A philosophical position that views behavioral events that cannot be publicly observed as outside the realm of science.

metonymical (tact) extension A tact evoked by a novel stimulus that shares none of the relevant features of the original stimulus configuration, but some irrelevant yet related feature has acquired stimulus control.

mixed schedule (mix) A compound schedule of reinforcement consisting of two or more basic schedules of reinforcement (elements) that occur in an alternating, usually random, sequence; no discriminative stimuli are correlated with the presence or absence of each element of the schedule, and reinforcement is delivered for meeting the response requirements of the element in effect at any time.

momentary time sampling A measurement method in which the presence or absence of behaviors are recorded at precisely specified time intervals. (Contrast with **interval recording**.)

motivating operation (MO) An environmental variable that (a) alters (increases or decreases) the reinforcing effectiveness of some stimulus, object, or event; and (b) alters (increases or decreases) the current frequency of all behavior that have been reinforced by that stimulus, object, or event. (See **abative effect, abolishing operation (AO), behavior-altering effect, evocative effect, establishing operation (EO), value-altering effect.**)

multielement design See **alternating treatments design**.

multiple baseline across behaviors design A multiple baseline design in which the treatment variable is applied to two or more different behaviors of the same subject in the same setting.

multiple baseline across settings design A multiple baseline design in which the treatment variable is applied to the same behavior of the same subject across two or more different settings, situations, or time periods.

multiple baseline across subjects design A multiple baseline design in which the treatment variable is applied to the same behavior of two or more subjects (or groups) in the same setting.

multiple baseline design An experimental design that begins with the concurrent measurement of two or more behaviors in a baseline condition, followed by the application of the treatment variable to one of the behaviors while baseline conditions remain in effect for the other behavior(s). After maximum change has been noted in the first behavior, the treatment variable is applied in sequential fashion to each of the other behaviors in the design. Experimental control is demonstrated if each behavior shows similar changes when, and only when, the treatment variable is introduced.

multiple control (of verbal behavior) There are two types of multiple control: (a) *convergent multiple control* occurs when a single verbal response is a function of more than one variable and (b) what is said has more than one antecedent source of control. *Divergent multiple control* occurs when a single antecedent variable affects the strength of more than one responses.

multiple exemplar training Instruction that provides the learner with practice with a variety of stimulus conditions, response variations, and response topographies to ensure the acquisition of desired stimulus controls response forms; used to promote both setting/situation generalization and response generalization. (See **teaching sufficient examples.**)

multiple probe design   A variation of the multiple baseline design that features intermittent measures, or probes, during baseline. It is used to evaluate the effects of instruction on skill sequences in which it is unlikely that the subject can improve performance on later steps in the sequence before learning prior steps.

multiple schedule (mult)   A compound schedule of reinforcement consisting of two or more basic schedules of reinforcement (elements) that occur in an alternating, usually random, sequence; a discriminative stimulus is correlated with the presence or absence of each element of the schedule, and reinforcement is delivered for meeting the response requirements of the element in effect at any time.

multiple treatment interference   The effects of one treatment on a subject's behavior being confounding by the influence of another treatment administered in the same study.

multiple treatment reversal design   Any experimental design that uses the experimental methods and logic of the reversal tactic to compare the effects of two or more experimental conditions to baseline and/or to one another (e.g., A-B-A-B-C-B-C, A-B-A-C-A-D-A-C-A-D, A-B-A-B-B+C-B-B+C).

naive observer   An observer who is unaware of the study's purpose and/or the experimental conditions in effect during a given phase or observation period. Data obtained by a naive observer are less likely to be influenced by observers' expectations.

naturally existing contingency   Any contingency of reinforcement (or punishment) that operates independent of the behavior analyst's or practitioner's efforts; includes socially mediated contingencies contrived by other people and already in effect in the relevant setting. (Contrast with **contrived contingency.**)

negative punishment   A response behavior is followed immediately by the removal of a stimulus (or a decrease in the intensity of the stimulus), that decreases the future frequency of similar responses under similar conditions; sometimes called *Type II punishment.* (Contrast with **positive punishment.**)

negative reinforcer   A stimulus whose termination (or reduction in intensity) functions as a reinforcement. (Contrast with **positive reinforcer.**)

neutral stimulus (NS)   A stimulus change that does not elicit respondent behavior. (Compare to **conditioned stimulus (CS), unconditioned stimulus (US).**)

noncontingent reinforcement (NCR)   A procedure in which stimuli with known reinforcing properties are presented on fixed-time (FT) or variable-time (VT) schedules completely independent of behavior; often used as an an-

tecedent intervention to reduce problem behavior. (See **fixed-time schedule (FT), variable-time schedule (VT).**)

noncontingent reinforcement (NCR) reversal technique   An experimental control technique that demonstrates the effects of reinforcement by using noncontingent reinforcement (NCR) as a control condition instead of a no-reinforcement (baseline) condition. During the NCR condition, the stimulus change used as reinforcement in the reinforcement condition is presented on a fixed or variable time schedule independent of the subject's behavior. A higher level of responding during the reinforcement condition than during the NCR condition demonstrates that the changes in behavior are the result of *contingent reinforcement,* not simply the presentation of or contact with the stimulus event. (Compare with **DRI/DRA reversal technique, DRO reversal technique.**)

nonexclusion time-out   A procedure for implementing time-out in which, contingent on the occurrence of the target behavior, the person remains within the setting, but does not have access to reinforcement, for a specified period.

normalization   As a philosophy and principle, the belief that people with disabilities should, to the maximum extent possible, be physically and socially integrated into the mainstream of society regardless of the degree or type of disability. As an approach to intervention, the use of progressively more typical settings and procedures "to establish and/or maintain personal behaviors which are as culturally normal as possible" (Wolfensberger, 1972, p. 28).

observed value   A measure produced by an observation and measurement system. Observed values serve as the data that the researcher and others will interpret to form conclusions about an investigation. (Compare with **true value.**)

observer drift   Any unintended change in the way an observer uses a measurement system over the course of an investigation that results in measurement error; often entails a shift in the observer's interpretation of the original definitions of the target behavior subsequent to being trained. (See **measurement bias, observer reactivity.**)

observer reactivity   Influence on the data reported by an observer that results from the observer's awareness that others are evaluating the data he reports. (See also **measurement bias** and **observer drift.**)

ontogeny   The history of the development of an individual organism during its lifetime. (See **history of reinforcement;** compare to **phylogeny.**)

operant behavior   Behavior that is selected, maintained, and brought under stimulus control as a function of its consequences; each person's repertoire of operant behavior is a product of his history of interactions with the environment (ontogeny).

operant conditioning   The basic process by which operant learning occurs; consequences (stimulus changes immediately following responses) result in an increased (reinforcement) or decreased (punishment) frequency of the same type of behavior under similar motivational and environmental conditions in the future. (See **motivating operation, punishment, reinforcement, response class, stimulus control.**)

overall response rate   The rate of response over a given time period. (See **local response rate.**)

overcorrection   A behavior change tactic based on positive punishment in which, contingent on the problem behavior, the learner is required to engage in effortful behavior directly or logically related to fixing the damage caused by the behavior. Forms of overcorrection are restitutional overcorrection and positive practice overcorrection. (See **positive practice overcorrection, restitutional overcorrection.**)

parametric analysis   An experiment designed to discover the differential effects of a range of values of an independent variable.

parsimony   The practice of ruling out simple, logical explanations, experimentally or conceptually, before considering more complex or abstract explanations.

partial-interval recording   A time sampling method for measuring behavior in which the observation period is divided into a series of brief time intervals (typically from 5 to 10 seconds). The observer records whether the target behavior occurred at any time during the interval. Partial-interval recording is not concerned with how many times the behavior occurred during the interval or how long the behavior was present, just that it occurred at some point during the interval; tends to overestimate the proportion of the observation period that the behavior actually occurred.

partition time-out   An exclusion procedure for implementing time-out in which, contingent on the occurrence of the target behavior, the person remains within the time-in setting, but stays behind a wall, shield, or barrier that restricts the view.

percentage   A ratio (i.e., a proportion) formed by combining the same dimensional quantities, such as count (number ÷ number) or time (duration ÷ duration; latency ÷ latency); expressed as a number of parts per 100; typically expressed as a ratio of the number of responses of a certain type per total number of responses (or opportunities or intervals in which such a response could have occurred). A percentage presents a proportional quantity per 100.

philosophic doubt   An attitude that the truthfulness and validity of all scientific theory and knowledge should be continually questioned.

phylogeny   The history of the natural evolution of a species. (Compare to **ontogeny.**)

pivotal behavior   A behavior that, when learned, produces corresponding modifications or covariation in other untrained behaviors. (Compare to **behavioral cusp.**)

placebo control   A procedure that prevents a subject from detecting the presence or absence of the treatment variable. To the subject the placebo condition appears the same as the treatment condition (e.g., a placebo pill contains an inert substance but looks, feels, and tastes exactly

like a pill that contains the treatment drug). (See **double-blind control.**)

planned activity check (PLACHECK)   A variation of momentary time sampling in which the observer records whether each person in a group is engaged in the target behavior at specific points in time; provides a measure of "group behavior."

planned ignoring   A procedure for implementing time-out in which social reinforcers—usually attention, physical contact, and verbal interaction—are withheld for a brief period contingent on the occurrence of the target behavior.

point-to-point correspondence   A relation between the stimulus and response or response product that occurs when the beginning, middle, and end of the verbal stimulus matches the beginning, middle, and end of the verbal response. The verbal relations with point-to-point correspondence are echoic, copying a text, imitation as it relates to sign language, textual, and transcription.

positive practice overcorrection   A form of overcorrection in which, contingent on an occurrence of the target behavior, the learner is required to repeated a correct form of the behavior, or a behavior incompatible with the problem behavior, a specified number of times; entails an educative component. (See **overcorrection, restitutional overcorrection.**)

positive punishment   A behavior is followed immediately by the presentation of a stimulus that decreases the future frequency of the behavior; sometimes called *Type I punishment.* (Contrast with **negative punishment.**)

positive reinforcement   Occurs when a behavior is followed immediately by the presentation of a stimulus that increases the future frequency of the behavior in similar conditions (Contrast to **negative reinforcement.**)

positive reinforcer   A stimulus whose presentation or onset functions as reinforcement. (Contrast with **negative reinforcer.**)

postreinforcement pause   The absence of responding for a period of time following reinforcement; an effect commonly produced by fixed interval (FI) and fixed ratio (FR) schedules of reinforcement.

practice effects   Improvements in performance resulting from opportunities to perform a behavior repeatedly so that baseline measures can be obtained.

prediction   A statement of the anticipated outcome of a presently unknown or future measurement; one of three components of the experimental reasoning, or baseline logic, used in single-subject research designs. (See **replication, verification.**)

Premack principle   A principle that states that making the opportunity to engage in a high-probability behavior contingent on the occurrence of a low-frequency behavior will function as reinforcement for the low-frequency behavior. (See also **response-deprivation hypothesis.**)

principle of behavior   A statement describing a functional relation between behavior and one or more of its controlling variables with generality across organisms, species, settings, behaviors, and time (e.g., extinction, positive reinforcement); an empirical generalization inferred from many experiments demonstrating the same functional relation

procedural fidelity See **treatment integrity.**

programming common stimuli A tactic for promoting setting/situation generalization by making the instructional setting similar to the generalization setting; the two-step process involves (1) identifying salient stimuli that characterize the generalization setting and (2) incorporating those stimuli into the instructional setting.

progressive schedule of reinforcement A schedule that systematically thins each successive reinforcement opportunity independent of the individual's behavior; progressive ratio (PR) and progressive interval (PI) schedules are thinned using arithmetic or geometric progressions.

punisher A stimulus change that decreases the future frequency of behavior that immediately precedes it. (See **aversive stimulus, conditioned punisher, unconditioned punisher.**)

punishment Occurs when stimulus change immediately follows a response and decreases the future frequency of that type of behavior in similar conditions. (See **negative punishment, positive punishment.**)

radical behaviorism A thoroughgoing form of behaviorism that attempts to understand all human behavior, including private events such as thoughts and feelings, in terms of controlling variables in the history of the person (ontogeny) and the species (phylogeny).

rate A ratio of count per observation time; often expressed as count per standard unit of time (e.g., per minute, per hour, per day) and calculated by dividing the number of responses recorded by the number of standard units of time in which observations were conducted; used interchangeably with *frequency*. The ratio is formed by combining the different dimensional quantities of count and time (i.e., count time). Ratios formed from different dimensional quantities retain their dimensional quantities. *Rate* and *frequency* in behavioral measurement are synonymous terms. (Contrast with **percentage.**)

ratio strain A behavioral effect associated with abrupt increases in ratio requirements when moving from denser to thinner reinforcement schedules; common effects include avoidance, aggression, and unpredictable pauses or cessation in responding.

reactivity Effects of an observation and measurement procedure on the behavior being measured. Reactivity is most likely when measurement procedures are obtrusive, especially if the person being observed is aware of the observer's presence and purpose.

recovery from punishment procedure The occurrence of a previously punished type of response without its punishing consequence. This procedure is analogous to the extinction of previously reinforced behavior and has the effect of undoing the effect of the punishment.

reflex A stimulus–response relation consisting of an antecedent stimulus and the respondent behavior it elicits (e.g., bright light–pupil contraction). Unconditioned and conditioned reflexes protect against harmful stimuli, help regulate the internal balance and economy of the organism, and promote reproduction. (See **conditioned reflex, respondent behavior, respondent conditioning, unconditioned reflex.**)

reflexive conditioned motivating operation (CMO-R) A stimulus that acquires MO effectiveness by preceding some form of worsening or improvement. It is exemplified by the warning stimulus in a typical escape–avoidance procedure, which establishes its own offset as reinforcement and evokes all behavior that has accomplished that offset.

reflexivity A type of stimulus-to-stimulus relation in which the learner, without any prior training or reinforcement for doing so, selects a comparison stimulus that is the same as the sample stimulus (e.g., A = A). Reflexivity would be demonstrated in the following matching-to-sample procedure: The sample stimulus is a picture of a tree, and the three comparison stimuli are a picture of a mouse, a picture of a cookie, and a duplicate of the tree picture used as the sample stimulus. The learner selects the picture of the tree without specific reinforcement in the past for making the tree-picture-to-tree-picture match. (It is also called *generalized identity matching.*) (See **stimulus equivalence;** compare to **transitivity, symmetry.**)

reinforcement Occurs when a stimulus change immediately follows a response and increases the future frequency of that type of behavior in similar conditions. (See **negative reinforcement, positive reinforcement.**)

reinforcer A stimulus change that increases the future frequency of behavior that immediately precedes it. (See **conditioned reinforcer, unconditioned reinforcer.**)

reinforcer-abolishing effect (of a motivating operation) A decrease in the reinforcing effectiveness of a stimulus, object, or event caused by a motivating operation. For example, food ingestion abolishes (decreases) the reinforcing effectiveness of food.

reinforcer assessment Refers to a variety of direct, empirical methods for presenting one or more stimuli contingent on a target response and measuring their effectiveness as reinforcers.

reinforcer-establishing effect (of a motivating operation) An increase in the reinforcing effectiveness of a stimulus, object, or event caused by a motivating operation. For example, food deprivation establishes (increases) the reinforcing effectiveness of food.

relevance of behavior rule Holds that only behaviors likely to produce reinforcement in the person's natural environment should be targeted for change.

reliability (of measurement) Refers to the consistency of measurement, specifically, the extent to which repeated measurement of the same event yields the same values.

repeatability Refers to the fact that a behavior can occur repeatedly through time (i.e., behavior can be counted); one of the three dimensional quantities of behavior from which all behavioral measurements are derived. (See **count, frequency, rate, celeration, temporal extent**, and **temporal locus**.)

repertoire All of the behaviors a person can do; or a set of behaviors relevant to a particular setting or task (e.g., gardening, mathematical problem solving).

replication (a) Repeating conditions within an experiment to determine the reliability of effects and increase internal validity. (See **baseline logic, prediction, verification**.) (b) Repeating whole experiments to determine the generality of findings of previous experiments to other subjects, settings, and/or behaviors. (See **direct replication, external validity, systematic replication**.)

resistance to extinction The relative frequency with which operant behavior is emitted during extinction.

respondent behavior The response component of a reflex; behavior that is elicited, or induced, by antecedent stimuli. (See **reflex, respondent conditioning**.)

respondent conditioning A stimulus–stimulus pairing procedure in which a neutral stimulus (NS) is presented with an unconditioned stimulus (US) until the neutral stimulus becomes a conditioned stimulus that elicits the conditioned response (also called *classical* or *Pavlovian conditioning*). (See **conditioned reflex, higher order conditioning**.)

respondent extinction The repeated presentation of a conditioned stimulus (CS) in the absence of the unconditioned stimulus (US); the CS gradually loses its ability to elicit the conditioned response until the conditioned reflex no longer appears in the individual's repertoire.

response A single instance or occurrence of a specific class or type of behavior. Technical definition: an "action of an organism's effector. An effector is an organ at the end of an efferent nerve fiber that is specialized for altering its environment mechanically, chemically, or in terms of other energy changes" (Michael, 2004, p. 8). (See **response class**.)

response blocking A procedure in which the therapist physically intervenes as soon as the learner begins to emit a problem behavior to prevent completion of the targeted behavior.

response class A group of responses of varying topography, all of which produce the same effect on the environment.

response cost The contingent loss of reinforcers (e.g., a fine), producing a decrease of the frequency of behavior; a form of negative punishment.

response-deprivation hypothesis A model for predicting whether contingent access to one behavior will function as reinforcement for engaging in another behavior based on whether access to the contingent behavior represents a restriction of the activity compared to the baseline level of engagement. (See **Premack principle**.)

response differentiation A behavior change produced by differential reinforcement: Reinforced members of the current response class occur with greater frequency, and unreinforced members occur less frequently (undergo extinction); the overall result is the emergence of a new response class.

response generalization The extent to which a learner emits untrained responses that are functionally equivalent to the trained target behavior. (Compare to **response maintenance** and **setting/situation generalization**.)

response latency A measure of temporal locus; the elapsed time from the onset of a stimulus (e.g., task direction, cue) to the initiation of a response.

response maintenance The extent to which a learner continues to perform the target behavior after a portion or all of the intervention responsible for the behavior's initial appearance in the learner's repertoire has been terminated. Often called *maintenance, durability, behavioral persistence,* and (incorrectly) *resistance to extinction.* (Compare to **response generalization** and **setting/situation generalization**.)

restitutional overcorrection A form of overcorrection in which, contingent on the problem behavior, the learner is required to repair the damage or return the environment to its original state and then to engage in additional behavior to bring the environment to a condition vastly better than it was in prior to the misbehavior. (See **overcorrection** and **positive practice overcorrection**.)

reversal design Any experimental design in which the researcher attempts to verify the effect of the independent variable by "reversing" responding to a level obtained in a previous condition; encompasses experimental designs in which the independent variable is withdrawn (A-B-A-B) or reversed in its focus (e.g., DRI/DRA). (See **A-B-A design, A-B-A-B design, B-A-B, DRI/DRA reversal technique, DRO reversal technique, noncontingent reinforcement (NCR) reversal technique**.)

rule-governed behavior Behavior controlled by a rule (i.e., a verbal statement of an antecedent-behavior-consequence contingency); enables human behavior (e.g., fastening a seatbelt) to come under the indirect control of temporally remote or improbable but potentially significant consequences (e.g., avoiding injury in an auto accident). Often used in contrast to *contingency-shaped behavior,* a term used to indicate behavior selected and maintained by controlled, temporally close consequences.

satiation A decrease in the frequency of operant behavior presumed to be the result of continued contact with or consumption of a reinforcer that has followed the behavior; also refers to a procedure for reducing the effectiveness of a reinforcer (e.g., presenting a person with copious amounts of a reinforcing stimulus prior to a session). (See **motivating operation;** contrast with **deprivation**.)

scatterplot A two-dimensional graph that shows the relative distribution of individual measures in a data set with respect to the variables depicted by the x and y axes. Data points on a scatterplot are not connected.

schedule of reinforcement A rule specifying the environmental arrangements and response requirements for reinforcement; a description of a contingency of reinforcement.

schedule thinning Changing a contingency of reinforcement by gradually increasing the response ratio or the extent of the time interval; it results in a lower rate of reinforcement per responses, time, or both.

science   A systematic approach to the understanding of natural phenomena (as evidenced by description, prediction, and control) that relies on determinism as its fundamental assumption, empiricism as its primary rule, experimentation as its basic strategy, replication as a requirement for believability, parsimony as a value, and philosophic doubt as its guiding conscience.

scored-interval IOA   An interobserver agreement index based only on the intervals in which either observer recorded the occurrence of the behavior; calculated by dividing the number of intervals in which the two observers agreed that the behavior occurred by the number of intervals in which either or both observers recorded the occurrence of the behavior and multiplying by 100. Scored-interval IOA is recommended as a measure of agreement for behaviors that occur at low rates because it ignores the intervals in which agreement by chance is highly likely. (Compare to **interval-by-interval IOA** and **unscored-interval IOA.**)

selection by consequences   The fundamental principle underlying operant conditioning; the basic tenet is that all forms of (operant) behavior, from simple to complex, are selected, shaped, and maintained by their consequences during an individual's lifetime; Skinner's concept of selection by consequences is parallel to Darwin's concept of natural selection of genetic structures in the evolution of species.

self-contract   Contingency contract that a person makes with himself, incorporating a self-selected task and reward as well as personal monitoring of task completions and self-delivery of the reward.

self-control   Two meanings: (a) A person's ability to "delay gratification" by emitting a response that will produce a larger (or higher quality) delayed reward over a response that produces a smaller but immediate reward (sometimes considered *impulse control);* (b) A person's behaving in a certain way so as to change a subsequent behavior (i.e., to self-manage her own behavior). Skinner (1953) conceptualized self-control as a two-response phenomenon: The *controlling response* affects variables in such a way as to change the probability of the *controlled response.* (See **self-management.**)

self-evaluation   A procedure in which a person compares his performance of a target behavior with a predetermined goal or standard; often a component of self-management. Sometimes called *self-assessment.*

self-instruction   Self-generated verbal responses, covert or overt, that function as rules or response prompts for a desired behavior; as a self-management tactic, self-instruction can guide a person through a behavior chain or sequence of tasks.

self-management   The personal application of behavior change tactics that produces a desired change in behavior.

self-monitoring   A procedure whereby a person systematically observes his behavior and records the occurrence or nonoccurrence of a target behavior. (Also called *self-recording* or *self-observation.*)

semilogarithmic chart   A two-dimensional graph with a logarithmic scaled *y* axis so that equal distances on the vertical axis represent changes in behavior that are of equal proportion. (See **Standard Celeration Chart.**)

sensory extinction   The process by which behaviors maintained by automatic reinforcement are placed on extinction by masking or removing the sensory consequence.

sequence effects   The effects on a subject's behavior in a given condition that are the result of the subject's experience with a prior condition.

setting/situation generalization   The extent to which a learner emits the target behavior in a setting or stimulus situation that is different from the instructional setting.

shaping   Using differential reinforcement to produce a series of gradually changing response classes; each response class is a successive approximation toward a terminal behavior. Members of an existing response class are selected for differential reinforcement because they more closely resemble the terminal behavior. (See **differential reinforcement, response class, response differentiation, successive approximations.**)

single-subject designs   A wide variety of research designs that use a form of experimental reasoning called *baseline logic* to demonstrate the effects of the independent variable on the behavior of individual subjects. (Also called *single-case, within-subject,* and *intra-subject* designs) (See also **alternating treatments design, baseline logic, changing criterion design, multiple baseline design, reversal design, steady state strategy.**)

social validity   Refers to the extent to which target behaviors are appropriate, intervention procedures are acceptable, and important and significant changes in target and collateral behaviors are produced.

solistic (tact) extension   A verbal response evoked by a stimulus property that is only indirectly related to the proper tact relation (e.g., Yogi Berra's classic malapropism: "Baseball is ninety percent mental; the other half is physical."

spaced-responding DRL   A procedure for implementing DRL in which reinforcement follows each occurrence of the target behavior that is separated from the previous response by a minimum interresponse time (IRT). (See **differential reinforcement of low rates (DRL).**)

speaker   Someone who engages in verbal behavior by emitting mands, tacts, intraverbals, autoclitics, and so on. A speaker is also someone who uses sign language, gestures, signals, written words, codes, pictures, or any form of verbal behavior. (Contrast with **listener.**)

split-middle line of progress   A line drawn through a series of graphed data points that shows the overall trend in the data; drawn through the intersections of the vertical and horizontal middles of each half of the charted data and then adjusted up or down so that half of all the data points fall on or above and half fall on or below the line.

spontaneous recovery A behavioral effect associated with extinction in which the behavior suddenly begins to occur after its frequency has decreased to its prereinforcement level or stopped entirely.

stable baseline Data that show no evidence of an upward or downward trend; all of the measures fall within a relatively small range of values. (See **steady state responding.**)

Standard Celeration Chart A multiply–divide chart with six base-10 (or × 10, ÷ 10) cycles on the vertical axis that can accommodate response rates as low as 1 per 24 hours (0.000695 per minute) to as high as 1,000 per minute. It enables the standardized charting of celeration, a factor by which rate of behavior multiplies or divides per unit of time. (See **semilogarithmic chart.**)

steady state responding A pattern of responding that exhibits relatively little variation in its measured dimensional quantities over a period of time.

steady state strategy Repeatedly exposing a subject to a given condition while trying to eliminate or control extraneous influences on the behavior and obtaining a stable pattern of responding before introducing the next condition.

stimulus "An energy change that affects an organism through its receptor cells" (Michael, 2004, p. 7).

stimulus class A group of stimuli that share specified common elements along formal (e.g., size, color), temporal (e.g., antecedent or consequent), and/or functional (e.g., discriminative stimulus) dimensions.

stimulus control A situation in which the frequency, latency, duration, or amplitude of a behavior is altered by the presence or absence of an antecedent stimulus. (See **discrimination, discriminative stimulus.**)

stimulus delta (S$^\Delta$) A stimulus in the presence of which a given behavior has not produced reinforcement in the past. (Contrast with **discriminative stimulus (S^D).**)

stimulus discrimination training The conventional procedure requires one behavior and two antecedent stimulus conditions. Responses are reinforced in the presence of one stimulus condition, the S^D, but not in the presence of the other stimulus, the S$^\Delta$.

stimulus equivalence The emergence of accurate responding to untrained and nonreinforced stimulus–stimulus relations following the reinforcement of responses to some stimulus–stimulus relations. A positive demonstration of reflexivity, symmetry, and transitivity is necessary to meet the definition of equivalence.

stimulus generalization When an antecedent stimulus has a history of evoking a response that has been reinforced in its presence, the same type of behavior tends to be evoked by stimuli that share similar physical properties with the controlling antecedent stimulus.

stimulus generalization gradient A graphic depiction of the extent to which behavior that has been reinforced in the presence of a specific stimulus condition is emitted in the presence of other stimuli. The gradient shows relative degree of stimulus generalization and stimulus control (or

discrimination). A flat slope across test stimuli shows a high degree of stimulus generalization and relatively little discrimination between the trained stimulus and other stimuli; a slope that drops sharply from its highest point corresponding to the trained stimulus indicates a high degree of stimulus control (discrimination) and relatively little stimulus generalization.

stimulus preference assessment A variety of procedures used to determine the stimuli that a person prefers, the relative preference values (high versus low) of those stimuli, the conditions under which those preference values remain in effect, and their presumed value as reinforcers.

stimulus–stimulus pairing A procedure in which two stimuli are presented at the same time, usually repeatedly for a number of trials, which often results in one stimulus acquiring the function of the other stimulus.

successive approximations The sequence of new response classes that emerge during the shaping process as the result of differential reinforcement; each successive response class is closer in form to the terminal behavior than the response class it replaces.

surrogate conditioned motivating operation (CMO-S) A stimulus that acquires its MO effectiveness by being paired with another MO and has the same value-altering and behavior-altering effects as the MO with which it was paired.

symmetry A type of stimulus-to-stimulus relationship in which the learner, without prior training or reinforcement for doing so, demonstrates the reversibility of matched sample and comparison stimuli (e.g., if A = B, then B = A). Symmetry would be demonstrated in the following matching-to-sample procedure: The learner is taught, when presented with the spoken word *car* (sample stimulus A), to select a comparison picture of a car (comparison B). When presented with the picture of a car (sample stimulus B), without additional training or reinforcement, the learner selects the comparison spoken word *car* (comparison A). (See **stimulus equivalence;** compare to **reflexivity, transitivity.**)

systematic desensitization A behavior therapy treatment for anxieties, fears, and phobias that involves substituting one response, generally muscle relaxation, for the unwanted behavior—the fear and anxiety. The client practices relaxing while imagining anxiety-producing situations in a sequence from the least fearful to the most fearful.

systematic replication An experiment in which the researcher purposefully varies one or more aspects of an earlier experiment. A systematic replication that reproduces the results of previous research not only demonstrates the reliability of the earlier findings but also adds to the external validity of the earlier findings by showing that the same effect can be obtained under different conditions.

tact An elementary verbal operant evoked by a nonverbal discriminative stimulus and followed by generalized conditioned reinforcement.

tandem schedule A schedule of reinforcement identical to the chained schedule except, like the mix schedule, the tandem schedule does not use discriminative stimuli with the elements in the chain. (See **chained schedule, mixed schedule.**)

target behavior The response class selected for intervention; can be defined either functionally or topographically.

task analysis The process of breaking a complex skill or series of behaviors into smaller, teachable units; also refers to the results of this process.

teaching loosely Randomly varying functionally irrelevant stimuli within and across teaching sessions; promotes setting/situation generalization by reducing the likelihood that (a) a single or small group of noncritical stimuli will acquire exclusive control over the target behavior and (2) the learner's performance of the target behavior will be impeded or "thrown off" should he encounter any of the "loose" stimuli in the generalization setting.

teaching sufficient examples A strategy for promoting generalized behavior change that consists of teaching the learner to respond to a subset of all of the relevant stimulus and response examples and then assessing the learner's performance on untrained examples. (See **multiple exemplar training.**)

temporal extent Refers to the fact that every instance of behavior occurs during some amount of time; one of the three dimensional quantities of behavior from which all behavioral measurements are derived. (See **repeatability** and **temporal locus.**)

temporal locus Refers to the fact that every instance of behavior occurs at a certain point in time with respect to other events (i.e., when in time behavior occurs can be measured); often measured in terms of *response latency* and *interresponse time (IRT);* one of the three dimensional quantities of behavior from which all behavioral measurements are derived. (See **repeatability, temporal extent.**)

terminal behavior The end product of shaping.

textual An elementary verbal operant involving a response that is evoked by a verbal discriminative stimulus that has point-to-point correspondence, but not formal similarity, between the stimulus and the response product.

three-term contingency The basic unit of analysis in the analysis of operant behavior; encompasses the temporal and possibly dependent relations among an antecedent stimulus, behavior, and consequence.

time-out from positive reinforcement The contingent withdrawal of the opportunity to earn positive reinforcement or the loss of access to positive reinforcers for a specified time; a form of negative punishment (also called *time-out*).

time-out ribbon A procedure for implementing nonexclusion time-out in which a child wears a ribbon or wristband that becomes discriminative for receiving reinforcement. Contingent on misbehavior, the ribbon is removed and access to social and other reinforcers are unavailable for a specific period. When time-out ends, the ribbon or band is returned to the child and time-in begins.

time sampling A measurement of the presence or absence of behavior within specific time intervals. It is most useful with continuous and high-rate behaviors. (See **momentary time sampling, partial-interval recording,** and **whole-interval recording.**)

token An object that is awarded contingent on appropriate behavior and that serves as the medium of exchange for backup reinforcers.

token economy A system whereby participants earn generalized conditioned reinforcers (e.g., tokens, chips, points) as an immediate consequence for specific behaviors; participants accumulate tokens and exchange them for items and activities from a menu of backup reinforcers. (See **generalized conditioned reinforcer.**)

topography The physical form or shape of a behavior.

topography-based definition Defines instances of the targeted response class by the shape or form of the behavior.

total count IOA The simplest indicator of IOA for event recording data; based on comparing the total count recorded by each observer per measurement period; calculated by dividing the smaller of the two observers' counts by the larger count and multiplying by 100.

total duration IOA A relevant index of IOA for total duration measurement; computed by dividing the shorter of the two durations reported by the observers by the longer duration and multiplying by 100.

total-task chaining A variation of forward chaining in which the learner receives training on each behavior in the chain during each session.

transcription An elementary verbal operant involving a spoken verbal stimulus that evokes a written, typed, or finger-spelled response. Like the textual, there is point-to-point correspondence between the stimulus and the response product, but no formal similarity.

transitive conditioned motivating operation (CMO-T) An environmental variable that, as a result of a learning history, establishes (or abolishes) the reinforcing effectiveness of another stimulus and evokes (or abates) the behavior that has been reinforced by that other stimulus.

transitivity A derived (i.e., untrained) stimulus-stimulus relation (e.g., A = C, C = A) that emerges as a product of training two other stimulus-stimulus relations (e.g., A = B and B = C). For example, transitivity would be demonstrated if, after training the two stimulus-stimulus relations shown in 1 and 2 below, the relation shown in 3 emerges without additional instruction or reinforcement:
(1) If A (e.g., spoken word *bicycle*) = B (e.g., the picture of a bicycle) (see Figure 17.3), and
(2) B (the picture of a bicycle) = C (e.g., the written word *bicycle*) (see Figure 17.4), then
(3) C (the written word *bicycle*) = A (the spoken name, *bicycle*) (see Figure 17.5). (See **stimulus equivalence;** compare to **reflexivity, symmetry.**)

treatment drift An undesirable situation in which the independent variable of an experiment is applied differently during later stages than it was at the outset of the study.

treatment integrity The extent to which the independent variable is applied exactly as planned and described and no other unplanned variables are administered inadvertently along with the planned treatment. Also called **procedural fidelity.**

trend The overall direction taken by a data path. It is described in terms of direction (increasing, decreasing, or zero trend), degree (gradual or steep), and the extent of variability of data points around the trend. Trend is used in predicting future measures of the behavior under unchanging conditions.

trial-by-trial IOA An IOA index for discrete trial data based on comparing the observers' counts (0 or 1) on a trial-by-trial, or item-by-item, basis; yields a more conservative and meaningful index of IOA for discrete trial data than does total count IOA.

trials-to-criterion A special form of event recording; a measure of the number of responses or practice opportunities needed for a person to achieve a preestablished level of accuracy or proficiency.

true value A measure accepted as a quantitative description of the true state of some dimensional quantity of an event as it exists in nature. Obtaining true values requires "special or extraordinary precautions to ensure that all possible sources of error have been avoided or removed" (Johnston & Pennypacker, 1993a, p. 136). (Compare with **observed value.**)

Type I error An error that occurs when a researcher concludes that the independent variable had an effect on the dependent variable, when no such relation exists; a *false positive.* (Contrast with **Type II error.**)

Type II error An error that occurs when a researcher concludes that the independent variable had no effect on the dependent variable, when in truth it did; a *false negative.* (Contrast with **Type I error.**)

unconditioned motivating operation (UMO) A motivating operation whose value-altering effect does not depend on a learning history. For example, food deprivation increases the reinforcing effectiveness of food without the necessity of any learning history.

unconditioned negative reinforcer A stimulus that functions as a negative reinforcer as a result of the evolutionary development of the species (phylogeny); no prior learning is involved (e.g., shock, loud noise, intense light, extreme temperatures, strong pressure against the body). (See **negative reinforcer;** compare with **conditioned negative reinforcer.**)

unconditioned punisher A stimulus change that decreases the frequency of any behavior that immediately precedes it irrespective of the organism's learning history with the stimulus. Unconditioned punishers are products of the evolutionary development of the species (phylogeny), meaning that all members of a species are more or less susceptible to punishment by the presentation of unconditioned punishers (also called *primary* or *unlearned punishers*). (Compare with **conditioned punisher.**)

unconditioned reflex An unlearned stimulus–response functional relation consisting of an antecedent stimulus (e.g., food in mouth) that elicits the response (e.g., salivation); a product of the phylogenic evolution of a given species; all biologically intact members of a species are born with similar repertoires of unconditioned reflexes. (See **conditioned reflex.**)

unconditioned reinforcer A stimulus change that increases the frequency of any behavior that immediately precedes it irrespective of the organism's learning history with the stimulus. Unconditioned reinforcers are the product of the evolutionary development of the species (phylogeny). Also called *primary* or *unlearned reinforcer.* (Compare with **conditioned reinforcer.**)

unconditioned stimulus (US) The stimulus component of an unconditioned reflex; a stimulus change that elicits respondent behavior without any prior learning.

unpairing Two kinds: (a) The occurrence alone of a stimulus that acquired its function by being paired with an already effective stimulus, or (b) the occurrence of the stimulus in the absence as well as in the presence of the effective stimulus. Both kinds of unpairing undo the result of the pairing: the occurrence alone of the stimulus that became a conditioned reinforcer; and the occurrence of the unconditioned reinforcer in the absence as well as in the presence of the conditioned reinforcer.

unscored-interval IOA An interobserver agreement index based only on the intervals in which either observer recorded the nonoccurrence of the behavior; calculated by dividing the number of intervals in which the two observers agreed that the behavior did not occur by the number of intervals in which either or both observers recorded the nonoccurrence of the behavior and multiplying by 100. Unscored-interval IOA is recommended as a measure of agreement for behaviors that occur at high rates because it ignores the intervals in which agreement by chance is highly likely. (Compare to **interval-by-interval IOA, scored-interval IOA.**)

validity (of measurement) The extent to which data obtained from measurement are directly relevant to the target behavior of interest and to the reason(s) for measuring it.

value-altering effect (of a motivating operation) An alteration in the reinforcing effectiveness of a stimulus, object, or event as a result of a motivating operation. For example, the reinforcing effectiveness of food is altered as a result of food deprivation and food ingestion.

variability The frequency and extent to which multiple measures of behavior yield different outcomes.

variable baseline Data points that do not consistently fall within a narrow range of values and do not suggest any clear trend.

variable interval (VI) A schedule of reinforcement that provides reinforcement for the first correct response following the elapse of variable durations of time occurring in a random or unpredictable order. The mean duration of the intervals is used to describe the schedule (e.g., on a VI 10-minute schedule, reinforcement is delivered for the first response following an average of 10 minutes since the last reinforced response, but the time that elapses following the last reinforced response might range from 30 seconds or less to 25 minutes or more).

variable-interval DRO (VI-DRO)   A DRO procedure in which reinforcement is available at the end of intervals of variable duration and delivered contingent on the absence of the problem behavior during the interval. (See **differential reinforcement of other behavior (DRO)**.)

variable-momentary DRO (VM-DRO)   A DRO procedure in which reinforcement is available at specific moments of time, which are separated by variable amounts of time in random sequence, and delivered if the problem is not occurring at those times. (See **differential reinforcement of other behavior (DRO)**.)

variable ratio (VR)   A schedule of reinforcement requiring a varying number of responses for reinforcement. The number of responses required varies around a random number; the mean number of responses required for reinforcement is used to describe the schedule (e.g., on a VR 10 schedule an average of 10 responses must be emitted for reinforcement, but the number of responses required following the last reinforced response might range from 1 to 30 or more).

variable-time schedule (VT)   A schedule for the delivery of noncontingent stimuli in which the interval of time from one delivery to the next randomly varies around a given time. For example, on a VT 1-minute schedule, the delivery-to-delivery interval might range from 5 seconds to 2 minutes, but the average interval would be 1 minute.

verbal behavior   Behavior whose reinforcement is mediated by a listener; includes both vocal-verbal behavior (e.g., saying "*Water, please*" to get water) and nonvocal-verbal behavior (pointing to a glass of water to get water). Encompasses the subject matter usually treated as language and topics such as thinking, grammar, composition, and understanding.

verification   One of three components of the experimental reasoning, or baseline logic, used in single-subject research designs; accomplished by demonstrating that the prior level of baseline responding would have remained unchanged had the independent variable not been introduced. Verifying the accuracy of the original prediction reduces the probability that some uncontrolled (confounding) variable was responsible for the observed change in behavior. (See **prediction, replication.**)

visual analysis   A systematic approach for interpreting the results of behavioral research and treatment programs that entails visual inspection of graphed data for variability, level, and trend within and between experimental conditions.

whole-interval recording   A time sampling method for measuring behavior in which the observation period is divided into a series of brief time intervals (typically from 5 to 15 seconds). At the end of each interval, the observer records whether the target behavior occurred throughout the entire interval; tends to underestimate the proportion of the observation period that many behaviors actually occurred.

withdrawal design   A term used by some authors as a synonym for A-B-A-B design; also used to describe experiments in which an effective treatment is sequentially or partially withdrawn to promote the maintenance of behavior changes. (See **A-B-A-B design, reversal design.**)

Bibliography

Achenbach, T. M., & Edelbrock, C. S. (1991). *Manual for the Child Behavior Checklist.* Burlington: University of Vermont, Department of Psychiatry.

Adams, C., & Kelley, M. (1992). Managing sibling aggression: Overcorrection as an alternative to timeout. *Behavior Modification, 23,* 707–717.

Adelinis, J. D., Piazza, C. C., & Goh, H. L. (2001). Treatment of multiply controlled destructive behavior with food reinforcement. *Journal of Applied Behavior Analysis, 34,* 97–100.

Adkins, V. K., & Mathews, R. M. (1997). Prompted voiding to reduce incontinence in community-dwelling older adults. *Journal of Applied Behavior Analysis, 30,* 153–156.

Adronis, P. T. (1983). *Symbolic aggression by pigeons: Contingency coadduction.* Unpublished doctoral dissertation, University of Chicago, Department of Psychiatry and Behavior Analysis, Chicago.

Agran, M. (Ed.). (1997). *Self-directed learning: Teaching self-determination skills.* Pacific Grove, CA: Brooks/Cole.

Ahearn, W. H. (2003). Using simultaneous presentation to increase vegetable consumption in a mildly selective child with autism. *Journal of Applied Behavior Analysis, 36,* 361–365.

Ahearn, W. H., Clark, K. M., Gardenier, N. C., Chung, B. I., & Dube, W. V. (2003). Persistence of stereotypic behavior: Examining the effects of external reinforcers. *Journal of Applied Behavior Analysis, 36,* 439–448.

Ahearn, W. H., Kerwin, M. E., Eicher, P. S., Shantz, J., & Swearingin, W. (1996). An alternating treatments comparison of two intensive interventions for food refusal. *Journal of Applied Behavior Analysis, 29,* 321–332.

Alber, S. R., & Heward, W. L. (1996). "GOTCHA!" Twenty-five behavior traps guaranteed to extend your students' academic and social skills. *Intervention in School and Clinic, 31* (5), 285–289.

Alber, S. R., & Heward, W. L. (2000). Teaching students to recruit positive attention: A review and recommendations. *Journal of Behavioral Education, 10,* 177–204.

Alber, S. R., Heward, W. L., & Hippler, B. J. (1999). Training middle school students with learning disabilities to recruit positive teacher attention. *Exceptional Children, 65,* 253–270.

Alber, S. R., Nelson, J. S., & Brennan, K. B. (2002). A comparative analysis of two homework study methods on elementary and secondary students' acquisition and maintenance of social studies content. *Education and Treatment of Children, 25,* 172–196.

Alberto, P. A., & Troutman, A. C. (2006) *Applied behavior analysis for teachers* (7th ed.). Upper Saddle River, NJ: Merrill/Prentice Hall.

Alberto, P. A., Heflin, L. J., & Andrews, D. (2002). Use of the timeout ribbon procedure during community-based instruction. *Behavior Modification, 26* (2), 297–311.

Albin, R. W., & Horner, R. H. (1988). Generalization with precision. In R. H. Horner, G. Dunlap, & R. L. Koegel (Eds.), *Generalization and maintenance: Life-style changes in applied settings* (pp. 99–120). Baltimore: Brookes.

Alessi, G. (1992). Models of proximate and ultimate causation in psychology. *American Psychologist, 48,* 1359–1370.

Alexander, D. F. (1985). The effect of study skill training on learning disabled students' retelling of expository material.

Journal of Applied Behavior Analysis, 18, 263–267.

Allen, K, E., Hart, B. M., Buell, J. S., Harris, F. R., & Wolf, M. M. (1964). Effects of social reinforcement on isolate behavior of a nursery school child. *Child Development, 35,* 511–518.

Allen, K. D., & Evans, J. H. (2001). Exposure-based treatment to control excessive blood glucose monitoring. *Journal of Applied Behavior Analysis, 34,* 497–500.

Allen, L. D., Gottselig, M., & Boylan, S. (1982). A practical mechanism for using free time as a reinforcer in the classroom. *Education and Treatment of Children, 5* (4), 347–353.

Allison, J. (1993). Response deprivation, reinforcement, and economics. *Journal of the Experimental Analysis of Behavior, 60,* 129–140.

Altschuld, J. W., & Witkin, B. R. (2000). *From needs assessment to action: Transforming needs into solution strategies.* Thousand Oaks, CA: Sage.

Altus, D. E., Welsh, T. M., & Miller, L. K. (1991). A technology for program maintenance: Programming key researcher behaviors in a student housing cooperative. *Journal of Applied Behavior Analysis, 24,* 667–675.

American Psychological Association. (1953). *Ethical standards of psychologists.* Washington, DC: Author.

American Psychological Association. (2001). *Publication Manual of the American Psychological Association* (5th ed.). Washington, DC: Author

American Psychological Association. (2002). *Ethical principles of psychologists and code of conduct.* Washington, DC: Author. Retrieved November 11, 2003, from www.apa.org/ethics/code2002.html.

American Psychological Association. (2004). Ethical principles of psychologists and code of conduct. Retrieved October 21, 2004, from www.apa.org/ethics.

Andersen, B. L., & Redd, W. H. (1980). Programming generalization through stimulus fading with children participating in a remedial reading program. *Education and Treatment of Children, 3,* 297–314.

Anderson, C. M., & Long, E. S. (2002). Use of a structured descriptive assessment methodology to identify variable affecting problem behavior. *Journal of Applied Behavior Analysis, 35,* 137–154.

Andresen, J. T. (1991). Skinner and Chomsky 30 years later OR: The return of the repressed. *The Behavior Analyst, 14,* 49–60.

Ardoin, S. P., Martens, B. K., & Wolfe, L. A. (1999). Using high-probability instruction sequences with fading to increase student compliance during transitions. *Journal of Applied Behavior Analysis, 32,* 339–351.

Armendariz, F., & Umbreit, J. (1999). Using active responding to reduce disruptive behavior in a general education classroom. *Journal of Positive Behavior Interventions, 1,* 152–158.

Arndorfer, R. E., Miltenberger, R. G., Woster, S. H., Rortvedt, A. K., & Gaffaney, T. (1994). Home-based descriptive and experimental analysis of problem behaviors in children. *Topics in Early Childhood Special Education, 14,* 64–87.

Arndorfer, R., & Miltenberger, R. (1993). Functional assessment and treatment of challenging behavior: A review with implications for early childhood. *Topics in Early Childhood Special Education, 13,* 82–105.

Arnesen, E. M. (2000). *Reinforcement of object manipulation increases discovery.* Unpublished bachelor's thesis, Reed College, Portland, OR.

Arntzen, E., Halstadtrø, A., & Halstadtrø, M. (2003). Training play behavior in a 5-year-old boy with developmental disabilities. *Journal of Applied Behavior Analysis, 36,* 367–370.

Ashbaugh, R., & Peck, S. M. (1998). Treatment of sleep problems in a toddler: A replication of the faded bedtime with response cost protocol. *Journal of Applied Behavior Analysis, 31,* 127–129.

Association for Behavior Analysis. (1989). *The right to effective education.* Kalamazoo, MI: Author. Retrieved November 11, 2006, from www.abainternational.org/ABA/statements/treatment.asp.

Association for Behavior Analysis. (1990). *Students' right to effective education.* Kalamazoo, MI: Author. Retrieved November 11, 2006, from www.abainternational.org/ABA/statements/treatment.asp

Association for Behavior Analysis. (1993, 1997). *Guidelines for the accreditation of programs in behavior analysis.* Kalamazoo, MI: Author. Retrieved December 2, 2003, from www.abainternational.org/sub/behaviorfield/education/accreditation/index.asp.

Association for Persons with Severe Handicaps. (1987, May). Resolution on the cessation of intrusive interventions. *TASH Newsletter, 5,* 3.

Atwater, J. B., & Morris, E. K. (1988). Teachers' instructions and children's compliance in preschool classrooms: A descriptive analysis. *Journal of Applied Behavior Analysis, 21,* 157–167.

Axelrod, S. A. (1990). Myths that (mis)guide our profession. In A. C. Repp & N. N. Singh (Eds.), *Perspectives on the use of nonaversive and aversive interventions for persons with developmental disabilities* (pp. 59–72). Sycamore, IL: Sycamore.

Axelrod, S., Hall, R. V., Weis, L., & Rohrer, S. (1971). *Use of self-imposed contingencies to reduce the frequency of smoking behavior.* Paper presented at the Fifth Annual Meeting of the Association for the Advancement of Behavior Therapy, Washington, DC.

Ayllon, T., & Azrin, N. H. (1968). *The token economy: A motivational system for therapy and rehabilitation.* New York: Appleton-Century-Crofts.

Ayllon, T., & Michael, J. (1959). The psychiatric nurse as a behavioral engineer. *Journal of the Experimental Analysis of Behavior, 2,* 323–334.

Azrin, N. H. (1960). Sequential effects of punishment. *Science, 131,* 605–606.

Azrin, N. H., & Besalel, V. A. (1999). *How to use positive practice, self-correction, and overcorrection* (2nd ed.). Austin, TX: Pro-Ed.

Azrin, N. H., & Foxx, R. M. (1971). A rapid method of toilet training the institu-

tionalized retarded. *Journal of Applied Behavior Analysis, 4,* 89–99.

Azrin, N. H., & Holz, W. C. (1966). Punishment. In W. K. Honig (Ed.), *Operant behavior: Areas of research and application* (pp. 380–447). New York: Appleton-Century-Crofts.

Azrin, N. H., & Nunn, R. G. (1973). Habit-reversal for habits and tics. *Behavior Research and Therapy, 11,* 619–628.

Azrin, N. H., & Powers, M. A. (1975). Eliminating classroom disturbances of emotionally disturbed children by positive practice procedures. *Behavior Therapy, 6,* 525–534.

Azrin, N. H., & Wesolowski, M. D. (1974). Theft reversal: An overcorrection procedure for eliminating stealing by retarded persons. *Journal of Applied Behavior Analysis, 7,* 577–581.

Azrin, N. H., Holz, W. C., & Hake, D. C. (1963). Fixed-ratio punishment by intense noise. *Journal of the Experimental Analysis of Behavior, 6,* 141–148.

Azrin, N. H., Hutchinson, R. R., & Hake, D. C. (1963). Pain-induced fighting in the squirrel monkey. *Journal of the Experimental Analysis of Behavior, 6,* 620.

Azrin, N. H., Kaplan, S. J., & Foxx, R. M. (1973). Autism reversal: Eliminating stereotyped self-stimulation of retarded individuals. *American Journal of Mental Deficiency, 78,* 241–248.

Azrin, N. H., Nunn, R. G., & Frantz, S. E. (1980). Habit reversal vs. negative practice treatment of nail biting. *Behavior Research and Therapy, 18,* 281–285.

Azrin, N. H., Rubin, H., O'Brien, F., Ayllon, T., & Roll, D. (1968). Behavioral engineering: Postural control by a portable operant apparatus. *Journal of Applied Behavior Analysis, 1,* 99–108.

Babyak, A. E., Luze, G. J., & Kamps, D. M. (2000). The good student game: Behavior management for diverse classrooms. *Intervention in School and Clinic, 35* (4), 216–223.

Bacon-Prue, A., Blount, R., Pickering, D., & Drabman, R. (1980). An evaluation of three litter control procedures: Trash receptacles, paid workers, and the marked item techniques. *Journal of Applied Behavior Analysis, 13,* 165–170.

Baer, D. M. (1960). Escape and avoidance response of preschool children to two schedules of reinforcement withdrawal. *Journal of the Experimental Analysis of Behavior, 3,* 155–159.

Baer, D. M. (1961). Effect of withdrawal of positive reinforcement on an extinguishing response in young children. *Child Development, 32,* 67–74.

Baer, D. M. (1962). Laboratory control of thumbsucking by withdrawal and representation of reinforcement. *Journal of the Experimental Analysis of Behavior, 5,* 525–528.

Baer, D. M. (1970). An age-irrelevant concept of development. *Merrill-Palmer Quarterly, 16,* 238–245.

Baer, D. M. (1971). Let's take another look at punishment. *Psychology Today, 5,* 5–32.

Baer, D. M. (1975). In the beginning, there was the response. In E. Ramp & G. Semb (Eds.), *Behavior analysis: Areas of research and application* (pp. 16–30). Upper Saddle River, NJ: Prentice Hall.

Baer, D. M. (1977a). Reviewer's comment: Just because it's reliable doesn't mean that you can use it. *Journal of Applied Behavior Analysis, 10,* 117–119.

Baer, D. M. (1977b). "Perhaps it would be better not to know everything." *Journal of Applied Behavior Analysis, 10,* 167–172.

Baer, D. M. (1981). A hung jury and a Scottish verdict: "Not proven." *Analysis and Intervention in Developmental Disabilities, 1,* 91–97.

Baer, D. M. (1982). Applied behavior analysis. In G. T. Wilson & C. M. Franks (Eds.), *Contemporary behavior therapy: Conceptual and empirical foundations* (pp. 277–309). New York: Guilford Press.

Baer, D. M. (1985). [Symposium discussant]. In C. E. Naumann (Chair), *Developing response classes: Why reinvent the wheel?* Symposium conducted at the Annual Conference of the Association for Behavior Analysis, Columbus, OH.

Baer, D. M. (1987). Weak contingencies, strong contingencies, and too many behaviors to change. *Journal of Applied Behavior Analysis, 20,* 335–337.

Baer, D. M. (1991). Tacting "to a fault". *Journal of Applied Behavior Analysis, 24,* 429–431.

Baer, D. M. (1999). *How to plan for generalization* (2nd ed.). Austin, TX: Pro-Ed.

Baer, D. M. (2005). Letters to a lawyer. In W. L. Heward, T. E. Heron, N. A. Neef, S. M. Peterson, D. M. Sainato, G. Cartledge, R. Gardner, III, L. D. Peterson, S. B. Hersh, & J. C. Dardig (Eds.),

Focus on behavior analysis in education: Achievements, challenges, and opportunities (pp. 3–30). Upper Saddle River, NJ: Merrill/Prentice Hall.

Baer, D. M., & Bushell, Jr., D. (1981). The future of behavior analysis in the schools? Consider its recent pact, and then ask a different question. *School Psychology Review, 10*(2), 259–270.

Baer, D. M., & Fowler, S. A. (1984). How should we measure the potential of self-control procedures for generalized educational outcomes? In W. L. Heward, T. E. Heron, D. S. Hill, & J. Trap-Porter (Eds.), *Focus on behavior analysis in education* (pp. 145–161). Columbus, OH: Charles E. Merrill.

Baer, D. M., & Richards, H. C. (1980). An interdependent group-oriented contingency system for improving academic performance. *School Psychology Review, 9,* 190–193.

Baer, D. M., & Schwartz, I. S. (1991). If reliance on epidemiology were to become epidemic, we would need to assess its social validity. *Journal of Applied Behavior Analysis, 24,* 321–234.

Baer, D. M., & Sherman, J. A. (1964). Reinforcement control of generalized imitation in young children. *Journal of Experimental Child Psychology, 1,* 37–49.

Baer, D. M., & Wolf, M. M. (1970a). Recent examples of behavior modification in preschool settings. In C. Neuringer & J. L. Michael (Eds.), *Behavior modification in clinical psychology* (pp. 10–55). Upper Saddle River, NJ: Prentice Hall.

Baer, D. M., & Wolf, M. M. (1970b). The entry into natural communities of reinforcement. In R. Ulrich, T. Stachnik, & J. Mabry (Eds.), *Control of human behavior* (Vol. 2, pp. 319–324). Glenview, IL: Scott, Foresman.

Baer, D. M., Peterson, R. F., & Sherman, J. A. (1967). The development of imitation by reinforcing behavioral similarity of a model. *Journal of the Experimental Analysis of Behavior, 10,* 405–416.

Baer, D. M., Wolf, M. M., & Risley, T. R. (1968). Some current dimensions of applied behavior analysis. *Journal of Applied Behavior Analysis, 1,* 91–97.

Baer, D. M., Wolf, M. M., & Risley, T. (1987). Some still-current dimensions of applied behavior analysis. *Journal of Applied Behavior Analysis, 20,* 313–327.

Baer, R. A. (1987). Effects of caffeine on classroom behavior, sustained attention, and a memory task in preschool children. *Journal of Applied Behavior Analysis, 20,* 225–234.

Baer, R. A., Blount, R., L., Detrich, R., & Stokes, T. F. (1987). Using intermittent reinforcement to program maintenance of verbal/nonverbal correspondence. *Journal of Applied Behavior Analysis, 20,* 179–184.

Baer, R. A., Tishelman, A. C., Degler, J. D., Osnes, P. G., & Stokes, T. F. (1992). Effects of self- vs. experimenter-selection of rewards on classroom behavior in young children. *Education and Treatment of Children, 15,* 1–14.

Baer, R. A., Williams, J. A., Osnes, P. G., & Stokes, T. F. (1984). Delayed reinforcement as an indiscriminable contingency in verbal/nonverbal correspondence training. *Journal of Applied Behavior Analysis, 17,* 429–440.

Bailey, D. B. (1984). Effects of lines of progress and semilogarithmic charts on ratings of charted data. *Journal of Applied Behavior Analysis, 17,* 359–365.

Bailey, D. B., Jr., & Wolery, M. (1992). *Teaching infants and preschoolers with disabilities* (2nd ed). Upper Saddle River, NJ: Merrill/Prentice Hall.

Bailey, J. S. (2000). A futurist perspective for applied behavior analysis. In J. Austin & J. E. Carr (Eds.), *Handbook of applied behavior analysis* (pp. 473–488). Reno, NV: Context Press.

Bailey, J., & Meyerson, L. (1969). Vibration as a reinforcer with a profoundly retarded child. *Journal of Applied Behavior Analysis, 2,* 135–137.

Bailey, J. S. & Pyles, D. A. M. (1989). Behavioral diagnostics. In E. Cipani (Ed.), *The treatment of severe behavior disorders: Behavior analysis approach* (pp. 85–107). Washington, DC: American Association on Mental Retardation.

Bailey, S. L., & Lessen, E. I. (1984). An analysis of target behaviors in education: Applied but how useful? In W. L. Heward, T. E. Heron, D. S. Hill, & J. Trap-Porter (Eds.), *Focus on behavior analysis in education* (pp. 162–176). Columbus, OH: Charles E. Merrill.

Ballard, K. D., & Glynn, T. (1975). Behavioral self-management in story writing with elementary school children. *Journal of Applied Behavior Analysis, 8,* 387–398.

Bandura, A. (1969). *Principles of behavior modification.* New York: Holt, Rinehart & Winston.

Bandura, A. (1971). Vicarious and self-reinforcement processes. In R. Glaser (Ed.), *The nature of reinforcement.* New York: Academic Press.

Bannerman, D. J., Sheldon, J. B., Sherman, J. A., & Harchik, A. E. (1990). Balancing the rights to habilitation with the right to personal liberties: The rights of people with developmental disabilities to eat too many doughnuts and take a nap. *Journal of Applied Behavior Analysis, 23,* 79–89.

Barbetta, P. M., Heron, T. E., & Heward, W. L. (1993). Effects of active student response during error correction on the acquisition, maintenance, and generalization of sight words by students with developmental disabilities. *Journal of Applied Behavior Analysis, 26,* 111–119.

Barker, M. R., Bailey, J. S., & Lee, N. (2004). The impact of verbal prompts on child safety-belt use in shopping carts. *Journal of Applied Behavior Analysis, 37,* 527–530.

Barkley, R., Copeland, A., & Sivage, C. (1980). A self-control classroom for hyperactive children. *Journal of Autism and Developmental Disorders, 10,* 75–89.

Barlow, D. H., & Hayes, S. C. (1979). Alternating treatments design: One strategy for comparing the effects of two treatments in a single behavior. *Journal of Applied Behavior Analysis, 12,* 199–210.

Baron, A., & Galizio, M. (2005). Positive and negative reinforcement: Should the distinction be preserved? *The Behavior Analyst, 28,* 85–98.

Baron, A., & Galizio, M. (2006). The distinction between positive and negative reinforcement: Use with care. *The Behavior Analyst, 29,* 141–151.

Barrett, B. H., Beck, R., Binder, C., Cook, D. A., Engelmann, S., Greer, R. D., Kyrklund, S. J., Johnson, K. R., Maloney, M., McCorkle, N., Vargas, J. S., & Watkins, C. L. (1991). The right to effective education. *The Behavior Analyst, 14* (1), 79–82.

Barrish, H. H., Saunders, M., & Wolf, M. M. (1969). Good behavior game: Effects of individual contingencies for group consequences on disruptive behavior in a classroom. *Journal of Applied Behavior Analysis, 2,* 119–124.

Barry, A. K. (1998). *English grammar: Language as human behavior.* Upper Saddle River, NJ: Prentice Hall.

Barton, E. S., Guess, D., Garcia, E., & Baer, D. M. (1970). Improvement of retardates' mealtime behaviors by timeout procedures using multiple baseline techniques. *Journal of Applied Behavior Analysis, 3,* 77–84.

Barton, L. E., Brulle, A. R., & Repp, A. C. (1986). Maintenance of therapeutic change by momentary DRO. *Journal of Applied Behavior Analysis, 19,* 277–282.

Barton-Arwood, S. M., Wehby, J. H., Gunter, P. L., & Lane, K. L. (2003). Functional behavior assessment rating scales: Intrarater reliability with students with emotional or behavioral disorders. *Behavior Disorders, 28,* 386–400.

Baum, W. M. (1994). *Understanding behaviorism: Science, behavior, and culture.* New York: Harper Collins.

Baum, W. M. (2005). *Understanding behaviorism: Science, behavior, and culture* (2nd ed.). Malden, MA: Blackwell Publishing.

Bay-Hinitz, A. K., Peterson, R. F., & Quilitch, H. R. (1994). Cooperative games: A way to modify aggressive and cooperative behaviors in young children. *Journal of Applied Behavior Analysis, 27,* 435–446.

Becker, W. C., & Engelmann, S. E. (1978). Systems for basic instruction: Theory and applications. In A. Catania & T. Brigham (Eds.), *Handbook of applied behavior analysis: Social and instructional processes.* New York: Irvington.

Becker, W. C., Engelmann, S., & Thomas, D. R. (1975). *Teaching 2: Cognitive learning and instruction.* Chicago: Science Research Associates.

Behavior Analyst Certification Board. (2001). *Guidelines for responsible conduct for behavior analysts.* Tallahassee, FL: Author. Retrieved November 11, 2003, from http://bacb.com/consum_frame.html.

Behavior Analyst Certification Board. (2005). *Behavior analyst task list, third edition.* Tallahassee, FL: Author. Retrieved November 11, 2003, from http://bacb.com/consum_frame.html.

Belfiore, P. J., Skinner, C. H., & Ferkis, M. A. (1995). Effects of response and trial repetition on sight-word training for students with learning disabilities. *Journal of Applied Behavior Analysis, 28,* 347–348.

Bell, K. E., Young, K. R., Salzberg, C. L., & West, R. P. (1991). High school driver education using peer tutors, direct instruction, and precision teaching. *Journal of Applied Behavior Analysis, 24,* 45–51.

Bellack, A. S., & Hersen, M. (1977). *Behavior modification: An introductory textbook.* New York: Oxford University Press.

Bellack, A. S., & Schwartz, J. S. (1976). Assessment for self-control programs. In M. Hersen & A. S. Bellack (Eds.), *Behavioral assessment: A practical handbook* (pp. 111–142). New York: Pergamon Press.

Bellamy, G. T., Horner, R. H., & Inman, D. P. (1979). *Vocational habilitation of severely retarded adults.* Austin, TX: Pro-Ed.

Bender, W. N., & Mathes, M. Y. (1995). Students with ADHD in the inclusive classroom: A hierarchical approach to strategy selection. *Intervention in School & Clinic, 30* (4), 226–234.

Bennett, K., & Cavanaugh, R. A. (1998). Effects of immediate self-correction, delayed self-correction, and no correction on the acquisition and maintenance of multiplication facts by a fourth-grade student with learning disabilities. *Journal of Applied Behavior Analysis, 31,* 303–306.

Bicard, D. F. & Neef, N. A. (2002). Effects of strategic versus tactical instructions on adaptation to changing contingencies in children with ADHD. *Journal of Applied Behavior Analysis, 35,* 375–389.

Bijou, S. W. (1955). A systematic approach to an experimental analysis of young children. *Child Development, 26,* 161–168.

Bijou, S. W. (1957). Patterns of reinforcement and resistance to extinction in young children. *Child Development, 28,* 47–54.

Bijou, S. W. (1958). Operant extinction after fixed-interval schedules with young children. *Journal of the Experimental Analysis of Behavior, 1,* 25–29.

Bijou, S. W., & Baer, D. M. (1961). *Child development: Vol. 1. A systematic and empirical theory.* New York: Appleton-Century-Crofts.

Bijou, S. W., & Baer, D. M. (1965). *Child development: Vol. 2. Universal stage of infancy.* New York: Appleton-Century-Crofts.

Bijou, S. W., Birnbrauer, J. S., Kidder, J. D., & Tague, C. (1966). Programmed instruction as an approach to teaching of reading, writing, and arithmetic to retarded children. *The Psychological Record, 16,* 505–522.

Bijou, S. W., Peterson, R. F., & Ault, M. H. (1968). A method to integrate descriptive and experimental field studies at the level of data and empirical concepts. *Journal of Applied Behavior Analysis, 1,* 175–191.

Billings, D. C., & Wasik, B. H. (1985). Self-instructional training with preschoolers: An attempt to replicate. *Journal of Applied Behavior Analysis, 18,* 61–67.

Billingsley, F., White, D. R., & Munson, R. (1980). Procedural reliability: A rationale and an example. *Behavioral Assessment, 2,* 247–256.

Binder, C. (1996). Behavioral fluency: Evolution of a new paradigm. *The Behavior Analyst, 19,* 163–197.

Binder, L. M., Dixon, M. R., & Ghezzi, P. M. (2000). A procedure to teach self-control to children with attention deficit hyperactivity disorder. *Journal of Applied Behavior Analysis, 33,* 233–237.

Birnbrauer, J. S. (1979). Applied behavior analysis, service, and the acquisition of knowledge. *The Behavior Analyst, 2,* 15–21.

Birnbrauer, J. S. (1981). External validity and experimental investigation of individual behavior. *Analysis and Intervention in Developmental Disabilities, 1,* 117–132.

Birnbrauer, J. S., Wolf, M. M., Kidder, J. D., & Tague, C. E. (1965). Classroom behavior of retarded pupils with token reinforcement. *Journal of Experimental Child Psychology, 2,* 219–235.

Bishop, B. R., & Stumphauzer, J. S. (1973). Behavior therapy of thumb sucking in children: A punishment (time out) and generalization effect—what's a mother to do? *Psychological Reports, 33,* 939–944.

Bjork, D. W. (1997). *B. F. Skinner: A life.* Washington, DC: American Psychological Association.

Blew, P. A., Schwartz, I. S., & Luce, S. C. (1985). Teaching functional community skills to autistic children using nonhandicapped peer tutors. *Journal*

of Applied Behavior Analysis, 18, 337–342.

Blick, D. W., & Test, D. W. (1987). Effects of self-recording on high school students' on-task behavior. *Learning Disability Quarterly, 10,* 203–213.

Bloom, L. (1970). *Language development: Form and function in emerging grammars.* Cambridge, MA: MIT Press.

Bloom, M., Fischer, J., & Orme, J. G. (2003). *Evaluating practice: Guidelines for the accountable professional* (4th ed.). Boston: Allyn & Bacon.

Bolin, E. P., & Goldberg, G. M. (1979). Behavioral psychology and the Bible: General and specific considerations. *Journal of Psychology and Theology, 7,* 167–175.

Bolstad, O., & Johnson, S. (1972). Self-regulation in the modification of disruptive classroom behavior. *Journal of Applied Behavior Analysis, 5,* 443–454.

Bondy, A., & Frost, L. (2002). *The Picture Exchange Communication System.* Newark, DE: Pyramid Educational Products.

Boring, E. G. (1941). Statistical frequencies as dynamic equilibria. *Psychological Review, 48,* 279–301.

Bornstein, P. H., & Quevillon, R. P. (1976). The effects of a self-instructional package on overactive preschool boys. *Journal of Applied Behavior Analysis, 9,* 179–188.

Bosch, S., & Fuqua, W. R. (2001). Behavioral cusps: A model for selecting target behaviors. *Journal of Applied Behavior Analysis, 34,* 123–125.

Bourret, J., Vollmer, T. R., & Rapp, J. T. (2004). Evaluation of a vocal mand assessment and vocal mand procedures. *Journal of Applied Behavior Analysis, 37,* 129–144.

Bowers, F. E., Woods, D. W., Carlyon, W. D., & Friman, P. C. (2000). Using positive peer reporting to improve the social interactions and acceptance of socially isolated adolescents in residential care: A systematic replication. *Journal of Applied Behavior Analysis, 33,* 239–242.

Bowman, L. G., Piazza, C. C., Fisher, W., Hagopian, L. P., & Kogan, J. S. (1997). Assessment of preference for varied versus constant reinforcement. *Journal of Applied Behavior Analysis, 30,* 451–458.

Boyajian, A. E., DuPaul, G. J., Wartel Handler, M., Eckert, T. L., & McGoey, K. E. (2001). The use of classroom-based brief functional analyses with preschoolers at risk for attention deficit hyperactivity disorder. *School Psychology Review, 30,* 278–293.

Boyce, T. E., & Geller, E. S. (2001). A technology to measure multiple driving behaviors without self-report or participant reactivity. *Journal of Applied Behavior Analysis, 34,* 39–55.

Boyle, J. R., & Hughes, C. A. (1994). Effects of self-monitoring and subsequent fading of external prompts on the on-task behavior and task productivity of elementary students with moderate mental retardation. *Journal of Behavioral Education, 4,* 439–457.

Braam, S. J., & Poling, A. (1982). Development of intraverbal behavior in mentally retarded individuals through transfer of stimulus control procedures: Classification of verbal responses. *Applied Research in Mental Retardation, 4,* 279–302.

Braine, M. D. S. (1963). The ontogeny of English phrase structure: The first phrase. *Language, 39,* 1–13.

Brame, P. B. (2001). *Making sustained silent reading (SSR) more effective: Effects of a story fact recall game on students' off-task behavior during SSR and retention of story facts.* Unpublished doctoral dissertation, The Ohio State University, Columbus, OH.

Brame, P., Bicard, S. C., Heward, W. L., & Greulich, H. (2007). *Using an indiscriminable group contingency to "wake up" sustained silent reading: Effects on off-task behavior and recall of story facts.* Manuscript submitted for publication review.

Brantley, D. C., & Webster, R. E. (1993). Use of an independent group contingency management system in a regular classroom setting. *Psychology in the Schools, 30,* 60–66.

Brantner, J. P., & Doherty, M. A. (1983). A review of timeout: A conceptual and methodological analysis. In S. Axelrod & J. Apsche (Eds.), *The effects of punishment on human behavior* (pp. 87–132). New York: Academic Press.

Brethower, D. C., & Reynolds, G. S. (1962). A facilitative effect of punishment on unpunished behavior. *Journal of the Experimental Analysis of Behavior, 5,* 191–199.

Briggs, A., Alberto, P., Sharpton, W., Berlin, K., McKinley, C., & Ritts, C. (1990). Generalized use of a self-operated audio prompt system. *Education and Training in Mental Retardation, 25,* 381–389.

Brigham, T. A. (1980). Self-control revisited: Or why doesn't anyone read Skinner anymore? *The Behavior Analyst, 3,* 25–33.

Brigham, T. A. (1983). Self-management: A radical behavioral perspective. In P. Karoly & F. H. Kanfer (Eds.), *Self-management and behavior change: From theory to practice* (pp. 32–59). New York: Pergamon Press.

Brobst, B., & Ward, P. (2002). Effects of public posting, goal setting, and oral feedback on the skills of female soccer players. *Journal of Applied Behavior Analysis, 27,* 247–257.

Broden, M., Hall, R. V., & Mitts, B. (1971). The effect of self-recording on the classroom behavior of two eighth-grade students. *Journal of Applied Behavior Analysis, 4,* 191–199.

Brothers, K. J., Krantz, P. J., & McClannahan, L. E. (1994). Office paper recycling: A function of container proximity. *Journal of Applied Behavior Analysis, 27,* 153–160.

Browder, D. M. (2001). *Curriculum and assessment for students with moderate and severe disabilities.* New York: Guilford Press.

Brown, K. A., Wacker, D. P., Derby, K. M., Peck, S. M., Richman, D. M., Sasso, G. M., Knutson, C. L., & Harding, J. W. (2000). Evaluating the effects of functional communication training in the presence and absence of establishing operations. *Journal of Applied Behavior Analysis, 33,* 53–71.

Brown, R. (1973). *A first language: The early stages.* Cambridge, MA: Harvard University Press.

Brown, R., Cazden, C., & Bellugi, U. (1969). The child's grammar from I to III (pp. 28–73). In J. P. Hill (Ed.), *The 1967 symposium on child psychology.* Minneapolis: University of Minnesota Press.

Brown, S. A., Dunne, J. D., & Cooper, J. O. (1996) Immediate retelling's effect on student retention. *Education and Treatment of Children, 19,* 387–407.

Browning, R. M. (1967). A same-subject design for simultaneous comparison of three reinforcement contingencies. *Behavior Research and Therapy, 5,* 237–243.

Budd, K. S., & Baer, D. M. (1976). Behavior modification and the law: Implications of recent judicial decisions. *Journal of Psychiatry and Law, 4,* 171–244.

Burgio, L. D., Whitman, T. L., & Johnson, M. R. (1980). A self-instructional package for increasing attending behavior in educable mentally retarded children. *Journal of Applied Behavior Analysis, 13,* 443–459.

Bushell, D., Jr., & Baer, D. M. (1994). Measurably superior instruction means close, continual contact with the relevant outcome data. Revolutionary! In R. Gardner, III, D. M. Sainato, J. O. Cooper, T. E. Heron, W. L. Heward, J. Eshleman, & T. A. Grossi (Eds.), *Behavior analysis in education: Focus on measurably superior instruction* (pp. 3–10). Pacific Grove, CA: Brooks/Cole.

Byrd, M. R., Richards, D. F., Hove, G., & Friman, P. C. (2002). Treatment of early onset hair pulling as a simple habit. *Behavior Modification, 26* (3), 400–411.

Byrne, T., LeSage, M. G., & Poling, A. (1997). Effects of chlorpromazine on rats' acquisition of lever-press responding with immediate and delayed reinforcement. *Pharmacology Biochemistry and Behavior, 58,* 31–35.

Caldwell, N. K., Wolery, M., Werts, M. G., & Caldwell, Y. (1996). Embedding instructive feedback into teacher-student interactions during independent seatwork. *Journal of Behavioral Education, 6,* 459–480.

Cameron, J. (2005). The detrimental effects of reward hypothesis: Persistence of a view in the face of disconfirming evidence. In W. L. Heward, T. E. Heron, N. A. Neef, S. M. Peterson, D. M. Sainato, G. Cartledge, R. Gardner, III, L. D. Peterson, S. B. Hersh, & J. C. Dardig (Eds.), *Focus on behavior analysis in education: Achievements, challenges, and opportunities* (pp. 304–315). Upper Saddle River, NJ: Merrill/Prentice Hall.

Cammilleri, A. P., & Hanley, G. P. (2005). Use of a lag differential reinforcement contingency to increase varied selections of classroom activities. *Journal of Applied Behavior Analysis, 38,* 111–115.

Campbell, D. T., & Stanley, J. C. (1966). *Experimental and quasi-experimental designs for research.* Chicago: Rand McNally.

Campbell, R. C., & Stremel-Campbell, K. (1982). Programming "loose training" as a strategy to facilitate language generalization. *Journal of Applied Behavior Analysis, 15,* 295–301.

Carr, E. G., & Durand, V. M. (1985). Reducing behavior problems through functional communication training. *Journal of Applied Behavior Analysis, 18,* 111–126.

Carr, E. G., & Kologinsky, E. (1983). Acquisition of sign language by autistic children II: Spontaneity and generalization effects. *Journal of Applied Behavior Analysis, 16,* 297–314.

Carr, E. G., & Lovaas, I. O. (1983). Contingent electric shock as a treatment for severe behavior problems. In S. Axelrod & J. Apsche (Eds.), *The effects of punishment on human behavior* (pp. 221–245). New York: Academic Press.

Carr, J. E., & Burkholder, E. O. (1998). Creating single-subject design graphs with Microsoft Excel. *Journal of Applied Behavior Analysis, 31* (2), 245–251.

Carr, J. E., Kellum, K. K., & Chong, I. M. (2001). The reductive effects of noncontingent reinforcement: Fixed-time versus variable-time schedules. *Journal of Applied Behavior Analysis, 34,* 505–509.

Carr, J. E., Nicolson, A. C., & Higbee, T. S. (2000). Evaluation of a brief multiple-stimulus preference assessment in a naturalistic context. *Journal of Applied Behavior Analysis, 33,* 353–357.

Carroll, R. J., & Hesse, B. E. (1987). The effects of alternating mand and tact training on the acquisition of tacts. *The Analysis of Verbal Behavior, 5,* 55–65.

Carter, J. F. (1993). Self-management: Education's ultimate goal. *Teaching Exceptional Children, 25*(3), 28–32.

Carter, M., & Grunsell, J. (2001). The behavior chain interruption strategy: A review of research and discussion of future directions. *Journal of the Association for Persons with Severe Handicaps, 26* (1), 37–49.

Carton, J. S., & Schweitzer, J. B. (1996). Use of token economy to increase compliance during hemodialysis. *Journal of Applied Behavior Analysis, 29,* 111–113.

Catania, A. C. (1972). Chomsky's formal analysis of natural languages: A behavioral translation. *Behaviorism, 1,* 1–15.

Catania, A. C. (1975). The myth of self-reinforcement. *Behaviorism, 3,* 192–199.

Catania, A. C. (1976). Self-reinforcement revisited. *Behaviorism, 4,* 157–162.

Catania, A. C. (1992). B.F. Skinner, Organism. *American Psychologist, 48,* 1521–1530.

Catania, A. C. (1998). *Learning* (4th ed.). Upper Saddle River, NJ: Prentice Hall.

Catania, A. C., & Harnad, S. (Eds.). (1988). *The selection of behavior: The operant behaviorism of B. F. Skinner: Comments and controversies.* New York: Cambridge University Press.

Catania, A. C., & Hineline, P. N. (Eds.). (1996). *Variations and selections: An anthology of reviews from the* Journal of the Experimental Analysis of Behavior. Bloomington, IN: Society for the Experimental Analysis of Behavior.

Cautela, J. R. (1971). Covert conditioning. In A. Jacobs & L. B. Sachs (Eds.), *The psychology of private events: Perspective on covert response systems* (pp. 109–130). New York: Academic Press.

Cavalier, A., Ferretti, R., & Hodges, A. (1997). Self-management within a classroom token economy for students with learning disabilities. *Research in Developmental Disabilities, 18* (3), 167–178.

Cavanaugh, R. A., Heward, W. L., & Donelson, F. (1996). Effects of response cards during lesson closure on the academic performance of secondary students in an earth science course. *Journal of Applied Behavior Analysis, 29,* 403–406.

Chadsey-Rusch, J., Drasgow, E., Reinoehl, B., Halle, J., & Collet-Klingenberg, L. (1993). Using general-case instruction to teach spontaneous and generalized requests for assistance to learners with severe disabilities. *Journal of the Association for Persons with Severe Handicaps, 18,* 177–187.

Charlop, M. H., Burgio, L. D., Iwata, B. A., & Ivancic, M. T. (1988). Stimulus variation as a means of enhancing punishment effects. *Journal of Applied Behavior Analysis, 21,* 89–95.

Charlop-Christy, M. H., & Carpenter, M. H. (2000). Modified incidental teaching sessions: A procedure for parents to increase spontaneous speech in their children with autism. *Journal of Positive Behavioral Interventions, 2,* 98–112.

Charlop-Christy, M. H., & Haymes, L. K. (1998). Using objects of obsession as token reinforcers for children with autism. *Journal of Autism and Developmental Disorders, 28* (3), 189–198.

Chase, P. N. (2006). Teaching the distinction between positive and negative reinforcement. *The Behavior Analyst, 29,* 113–115.

Chase, P. N., & Danforth, J. S. (1991). The role of rules in concept learning. In L. J. Hayes and P. N. Chase (Eds.), *Dialogues on verbal behavior* (pp. 205–225). Reno, NV: Context Press.

Chase, P., Johnson, K., & Sulzer-Azaroff, B. (1985). Verbal relations within instruction: Are there subclasses of the intraverbal? *Journal of the Experimental Analysis of Behavior, 43,* 301–314.

Chiang, S. J., Iwata, B. A., & Dorsey, M. F. (1979). Elimination of disruptive bus riding behavior via token reinforcement on a "distance-based" schedule. *Education and Treatment of Children, 2,* 101–109.

Chiesa, M. (1994). *Radical behaviorism: The philosophy and the science.* Boston: Authors Cooperative.

Chomsky, N. (1957). *Syntactic structures.* The Hague: Mouton and Company.

Chomsky, N. (1959). Review of B. F. Skinner's *Verbal behavior. Language, 35,* 26–58.

Chomsky, N. (1965). *Aspects of a theory of syntax.* Cambridge, MA: MIT Press.

Christian, L., & Poling, A. (1997). Using self-management procedures to improve the productivity of adults with developmental disabilities in a competitive employment setting. *Journal of Applied Behavior Analysis, 30,* 169–172.

Christle, C. A., & Schuster, J. W. (2003). The effects of using response cards on student participation, academic achievement, and on-task behavior during whole-class, math instruction. *Journal of Behavioral Education, 12,* 147–165.

Ciccone, F. J., Graff, R. B., & Ahearn, W. H. (2006). Stimulus preference assessments and the utility of a moderate category. *Behavioral Intervention, 21,* 59–63.

Cipani, E. C., & Spooner, F. (1994*). Curricular and instructional approaches for persons with severe disabilities.* Boston: Allyn & Bacon.

Cipani, E., Brendlinger, J., McDowell, L., & Usher, S. (1991). Continuous vs. intermittent punishment: A case study. *Journal of Developmental and Physical Disabilities, 3,* 147–156.

Cipani, E., Robinson, S., & Toro, H. (2003). *Ethical and risk management issues in the practice of ABA.* Paper presented at annual conference of the Florida Association for Behavior Analysis, St. Petersburg.

Clark, H. B., Rowbury, T., Baer, A., & Baer, D. M. (1973). Time out as a punishing stimulus in continuous and intermittent schedules. *Journal of Applied Behavior Analysis, 6,* 443–455.

Codding, R. S., Feinberg, A. B., Dunn, E. K., & Pace, G. M. (2005). Effects of immediate performance feedback on implementation of behavior support plans. *Journal of Applied Behavior Analysis, 38,* 205–219.

Cohen, J. A. (1960). A coefficient of agreement for nominal scales. *Educational and Psychological Measurement, 20,* 37–46.

Cohen-Almeida, D., Graff, R. B., & Ahearn, W. H. (2000). A comparison of verbal and tangible stimulus preference assessments. *Journal of Applied Behavior Analysis, 33,* 329–334.

Cole, G. A., Montgomery, R. W., Wilson, K. M., & Milan, M. A. (2000). Parametric analysis of overcorrection duration effects: Is longer really better than shorter? *Behavior Modification, 24,* 359–378.

Coleman-Martin, M. B., & Wolff Heller, K. (2004). Using a modified constant prompt-delay procedure to teach spelling to students with physical disabilities. *Journal of Applied Behavior Analysis, 37,* 469–480.

Conaghan, B. P., Singh, N. N., Moe, T. L., Landrum, T. J., & Ellis, C. R. (1992). Acquisition and generalization of manual signs by hearing-impaired adults with mental retardation. *Journal of Behavioral Education, 2,* 175–203.

Connell, M. C., Carta, J. J., & Baer, D. M. (1993). Programming generalization of in-class transition skills: Teaching preschoolers with developmental delays to self-assess and recruit contingent teacher praise. *Journal of Applied Behavior Analysis, 26,* 345–352.

Conners, J., Iwata, B. A., Kahng, S. W., Hanley, G. P, Worsdell, A. S., & Thompson,

R. H. (2000). Differential responding in the presence and absence of discriminative stimuli during multi-element functional analyses. *Journal of Applied Behavior Analysis, 33,* 299–308.

Conroy, M. A., Fox, J. J., Bucklin, A., & Good, W. (1996). An analysis of the reliability and stability of the Motivation Assessment Scale in assessing the challenging behaviors of persons with developmental disabilities. *Education and Training in Mental Retardation and Developmental Disabilities, 31,* 243–250.

Cooke, N. L. (1984). Misrepresentations of the behavioral model in preservice teacher education textbooks. In W. L. Heward, T. E. Heron, D. S. Hill, & J. Trap-Porter (Eds.), *Focus on behavior analysis in education* (pp. 197–217). Columbus, OH: Charles E. Merrill.

Cooper, J. O. (1981). *Measuring behavior* (2nd ed.). Columbus, OH: Charles E. Merrill.

Cooper, J. O. (2005). Applied research: The separation of applied behavior analysis and precision teaching. In W. L. Heward, T. E. Heron, N. A. Neef, S. M. Peterson, D. M. Sainato, G. Cartledge, R. Gardner, III, L. D. Peterson, S. B. Hersh, & J. C. Dardig (Eds.), *Focus on behavior analysis in education: Achievements, challenges, and opportunities* (pp. 295–303). Upper Saddle River, NJ: Prentice Hall/Merrill.

Cooper, J. O., Kubina, R., & Malanga, P. (1998). Six procedures for showing standard celeration charts. *Journal of Precision Teaching & Celeration, 15* (2), 58–76.

Cooper, K. J., & Browder, D. M. (1997). The use of a personal trainer to enhance participation of older adults with severe disabilities in a community water exercise class. *Journal of Behavioral Education, 7,* 421–434.

Cooper, L. J., Wacker, D. P., McComas, J. J., Brown, K., Peck, S. M., Richman, D., Drew, J., Frischmeyer, P., & Millard, T. (1995). Use of component analysis to identify active variables in treatment packages for children with feeding disorders. *Journal of Applied Behavior Analysis, 28,* 139–153.

Cooper, L. J., Wacker, D. P., Thursby, D., Plagmann, L. A., Harding, J., Millard, T., & Derby, M. (1992). Analysis of the effects of task preferences, task demands, and adult attention on child be-

havior in outpatient and classroom settings. *Journal of Applied Behavior Analysis, 25,* 823–840.

Copeland, R. E., Brown, R. E., & Hall, R. V. (1974). The effects of principal-implemented techniques on the behavior of pupils. *Journal of Applied Behavior Analysis, 7,* 77–86.

Corey, G., Corey, M. S., & Callanan, P. (1993). *Issues and ethics in the helping professions* (4th ed.). Pacific Grove, CA: Brooks/Cole.

Costenbader, V., & Reading-Brown, M. (1995). Isolation timeout used with students with emotional disturbance. *Exceptional Children, 61* (4), 353–364.

Cowdery, G., Iwata, B. A., & Pace, G. M. (1990). Effects and side effects of DRO as treatment for self-injurious behavior. *Journal of Applied Behavior Analysis, 23,* 497–506.

Cox, B. S., Cox, A. B., & Cox, D. J. (2000). Motivating signage prompts safety belt use among drivers exiting senior communities. *Journal of Applied Behavior Analysis, 33,* 635–638.

Craft, M. A., Alber, S. R., & Heward, W. L. (1998). Teaching elementary students with developmental disabilities to recruit teacher attention in a general education classroom: Effects on teacher praise and academic productivity. *Journal of Applied Behavior Analysis, 31,* 399–415.

Crawford, J., Brockel, B., Schauss, S., & Miltenberger, R. G. (1992). A comparison of methods for the functional assessment of stereotypic behavior. *Journal of the Association for Persons with Severe Handicaps, 17,* 77–86.

Critchfield, T. S. (1993). Behavioral pharmacology and verbal behavior: Diazepam effects on verbal self-reports. *The Analysis of Verbal Behavior, 11,* 43–54.

Critchfield, T. S. (1999). An unexpected effect of recording frequency in reactive self-monitoring. *Journal of Applied Behavior Analysis, 32,* 389–391.

Critchfield, T. S., & Kollins, S. H. (2001). Temporal discounting: Basic research and the analysis of socially important behavior. *Journal of Applied Behavior Analysis, 34,* 101–122.

Critchfield, T. S., & Lattal, K. A. (1993). Acquisition of a spatially defined operant with delayed reinforcement. *Journal of the Experimental Analysis of Behavior, 59,* 373–387.

Critchfield, T. S., & Vargas, E. A. (1991). Self-recording, instructions, and public self-graphing: Effects on swimming in the absence of coach verbal interaction. *Behavior Modification, 15,* 95–112.

Critchfield, T. S., Tucker, J. A., & Vuchinich, R. E. (1998). Self-report methods. In K. A. Lattal & M. Perone (Eds.), *Handbook of research methods in human operant behavior* (pp. 435–470). New York: Plenum.

Cromwell, O. (1650, August 3). Letter to the general assembly of the Church of Scotland. Available online: http://en .wikiquote.org/wiki/Oliver_Cromwell

Crosbie, J. (1999). Statistical inference in behavior analysis: Useful friend. *The Behavior Analyst, 22,* 105–108.

Cushing, L. S., & Kennedy, C. H. (1997). Academic effects of providing peer support in general education classrooms on students without disabilities. *Journal of Applied Behavior Analysis, 30,* 139–151.

Cuvo, A. J. (1979). Multiple-baseline design in instructional research: Pitfalls of measurement and procedural advantages. *American Journal of Mental Deficiency, 84,* 219–228.

Cuvo, A. J. (2000). Development and function of consequence classes in operant behavior. *The Behavior Analyst, 23,* 57–68.

Cuvo, A. J. (2003). On stimulus generalization and stimulus classes. *Journal of Behavioral Education, 12,* 77–83.

Cuvo, A. J., Lerch, L. J., Leurquin, D. A., Gaffaney, T. J., & Poppen, R. L. (1998). Response allocation to concurrent fixed-ratio reinforcement schedules with work requirements by adults with mental retardation and typical preschool children. *Journal of Applied Behavior Analysis, 31,* 43–63.

Dalton, T., Martella, R., & Marchand-Martella, N. E. (1999). The effects of a self-management program in reducing off-task behavior. *Journal of Behavioral Education, 9,* 157–176.

Daly, P. M., & Ranalli, P. (2003). Using countoons to teach self-monitoring skills. *Teaching Exceptional Children, 35* (5), 30–35.

Dams, P-C. (2002). A little night music. In R. W. Malott & H. Harrison, *I'll stop procrastinating when I get around to it: Plus other cool ways to succeed in school and life using behavior analysis to get your act together* (pp. 7–3–7-4).

Kalamazoo, MI: Department of Psychology, Western Michigan University.

Dardig, J. C., & Heward, W. L. (1976). *Sign here: A contracting book for children and their families.* Kalamazoo, MI: Behaviordelia.

Dardig, J. C., & Heward, W. L. (1981a). A systematic procedure for prioritizing IEP goals. *The Directive Teacher, 3,* 6–8.

Dardig, J. C., & Heward, W. L. (1981b). *Sign here: A contracting book for children and their parents* (2nd ed.). Bridgewater, NJ: Fournies.

Darwin, C. (1872/1958). *The origin of species* (6th ed.). New York: Mentor. (Original work published 1872)

Davis, C. A., & Reichle, J. (1996). Variant and invariant high-probability requests: Increasing appropriate behaviors in children with emotional-behavioral disorders. *Journal of Applied Behavior Analysis, 29,* 471–482.

Davis, C. A., Brady, M. P., Williams, R. E., & Burta, M. (1992). The effects of self-operated auditory prompting tapes on the performance fluency of persons with severe mental retardation. *Education and Training in Mental Retardation, 27,* 39–50.

Davis, L. L., & O'Neill, R. E. (2004). Use of response cards with a group of students with learning disabilities including those for whom English is a second language. *Journal of Applied Behavior Analysis, 37,* 219–222.

Davis, P. K., & Chittum, R. (1994). A group-oriented contingency to increase leisure activities of adults with traumatic brain injury. *Journal of Applied Behavior Analysis, 27,* 553–554.

Davison, M. (1999). Statistical inference in behavior analysis: Having my cake and eating it too. *The Behavior Analyst, 22,* 99-103.

Dawson, J. E., Piazza, C. C., Sevin, B. M., Gulotta, C. S., Lerman, D. & Kelley, M. L. (2003). Use of the high-probability instructional sequence and escape extinction in a child with food refusal. *Journal of Applied Behavior Analysis, 36,* 105–108.

De Luca, R. B., & Holborn, S. W. (1990). Effects of fixed-interval and fixed-ratio schedules of token reinforcement on exercise with obese and nonobese boys. *Psychological Record, 40,* 67–82.

De Luca, R. B., & Holborn, S. W. (1992). Effects of a variable-ratio reinforce-ment schedule with changing criteria on exercise in obese and nonobese boys. *Journal of Applied Behavior Analysis, 25,* 671–679.

De Martini-Scully, D., Bray, M. A., & Kehle, T. J. (2000). A packaged intervention to reduce disruptive behaviors in general education students. *Psychology in the Schools, 37* (2), 149–156.

de Zubicaray, G., & Clair, A. (1998). An evaluation of differential reinforcement of other behavior, differential reinforcement of incompatible behaviors, and restitution for the management of aggressive behaviors. *Behavioral Interventions, 13,* 157–168.

Deaver, C. M., Miltenberger, R. G., & Stricker, J. M. (2001). Functional analysis and treatment of hair twirling in a young child. *Journal of Applied Behavior Analysis, 34,* 535–538.

DeCatanzaro, D., & Baldwin, G. (1978). Effective treatment of self-injurious behavior through a forced arm exercise. *Journal of Applied Behavior Analysis, 1,* 433–439.

DeHaas-Warner, S. (1992). The utility of self-monitoring for preschool on-task behavior. *Topics in Early Childhood Special Education, 12,* 478–495.

Deitz, D. E. D. (1977). An analysis of programming DRL schedules in educational settings. *Behavior Research and Therapy, 15,* 103–111.

Deitz, D. E. D., & Repp, A. C. (1983). Reducing behavior through reinforcement. *Exceptional Education Quarterly, 3,* 34–46.

Deitz, S. M. (1977). An analysis of programming DRL schedules in educational settings. *Behavior Research and Therapy, 15,* 103–111.

Deitz, S. M., & Repp, A. C. (1973). Decreasing classroom misbehavior through the use of DRL schedules of reinforcement. *Journal of Applied Behavior Analysis, 6,* 457–463.

Deitz, S. M. (1982). Defining applied behavior analysis: An historical analogy. *The Behavior Analyst, 5,* 53–64.

Deitz, S. M., & Repp, A. C. (1983). Reducing behavior through reinforcement. *Exceptional Education Quarterly, 3,* 34–46.

Deitz, S. M., Slack, D. J., Schwarzmueller, E. B., Wilander, A. P., Weatherly, T. J., & Hilliard, G. (1978). Reducing inappropriate behavior in special class-rooms by reinforcing average interresponse times: Interval DRL. *Behavior Therapy, 9,* 37–46.

DeLeon, I. G., & Iwata, B. A. (1996). Evaluation of a multiple-stimulus presentation format for assessing reinforcer preferences. *Journal of Applied Behavior Analysis, 29,* 519–533.

Deleon, I. G., Anders, B. M., Rodriguez-Catter, V., & Neidert, P. L. (2000). The effects of noncontingent access to single-versus multiple-stimulus sets on self-injurious behavior. *Journal of Applied Behavior Analysis, 33,* 623–626.

DeLeon, I. G., Fisher, W. W., Rodriguez-Catter, V., Maglieri, K., Herman, K., & Marhefka, J. M. (2001). Examination of relative reinforcement effects of stimuli identified through pretreatment and daily brief preference assessments. *Journal of Applied Behavior Analysis, 34,* 463–473.

DeLeon, I. G., Iwata, B. A., Conners, J., & Wallace, M. D. (1999). Examination of ambiguous stimulus preferences with duration-based measures. *Journal of Applied Behavior Analysis, 32,* 111–114.

DeLeon, I. G., Iwata, B. A., Goh, H., & Worsdell, A. S. (1997). Emergence of reinforcer preference as a function of schedule requirements and stimulus similarity. *Journal of Applied Behavior Analysis, 30,* 439–449.

DeLissovoy, V. (1963). Head banging in early childhood: A suggested cause. *Journal of Genetic Psychology, 102,* 109–114.

Delprato, D. J. (2002). Countercontrol in behavior analysis. *The Behavior Analyst, 25,* 191–200.

Delprato, D. J., & Midgley, B. D. (1992). Some fundamentals of B. F. Skinner's behaviorism. *American Psychologist, 48,* 1507–1520.

DeLuca, R. V., & Holborn, S. W. (1992). Effects of a variable-ratio reinforcement schedule with changing criteria on exercise in obese and nonobese boys. *Journal of Applied Behavior Analysis, 25,* 671–679.

DeMyer, M. K., & Ferster, C. B. (1962). Teaching new social behavior to schizophrenic children. *Journal of the American Academy of Child Psychiatry, 1,* 443–461.

Derby, K. M., Wacker, D. P., Berg, W., DeRaad, A., Ulrich, S., Asmus, J., Harding, J., Prouty, A., Laffey, P., & Stoner, E. A. (1997). The long-term effects of functional communication training in home settings. *Journal of Applied Behavior Analysis, 30,* 507–531.

Derby, K. M., Wacker, D. P., Sasso, G., Steege, M., Northup, J., Cigrand, K., & Asmus, J. (1992). Brief functional assessment techniques to evaluate aberrant behavior in an outpatient setting: A summary of 79 cases. *Journal of Applied Behavior Analysis, 25,* 713–721.

DeVries, J. E., Burnette, M. M., & Redmon, W. K. (1991). AIDS prevention: Improving nurses' compliance with glove wearing through performance feedback. *Journal of Applied Behavior Analysis, 24,* 705–711.

Dewey, J. (1939). *Experience and education.* New York: Macmillan.

Dickerson, E. A., & Creedon, C. F. (1981). Self-selection of standards by children: The relative effectiveness of pupil-selected and teacher-selected standards of performance. *Journal of Applied Behavior Analysis, 14,* 425–433.

Didden, R., Prinsen, H., & Sigafoos, J. (2000). The blocking effect of pictorial prompts on sight-word reading. *Journal of Applied Behavior Analysis, 33,* 317–320.

Dinsmoor, J. A. (1952). A discrimination based on punishment. *Quarterly Journal of Experimental Psychology, 4,* 27–45.

Dinsmoor, J. A. (1995a). Stimulus control: Part I. *The Behavior Analyst, 18,* 51–68.

Dinsmoor, J. A. (1995b). Stimulus control: Part II. *The Behavior Analyst, 18,* 253–269.

Dinsmoor, J. A. (2003). Experimental. *The Behavior Analyst, 26,* 151–153.

Dixon, M. R., & Cummins, A. (2001), Self-control in children with autism: Response allocation during delays to reinforcement. *Journal of Applied Behavior Analysis, 34,* 491–495.

Dixon, M. R., & Falcomata, T. S. (2004). Preference for progressive delays and concurrent physical therapy exercise in an adult with acquired brain injury. *Journal of Applied Behavior Analysis, 37,* 101–105.

Dixon, M. R., & Holcomb, S. (2000). Teaching self-control to small groups of dually diagnosed adults. *Journal of Applied Behavior Analysis, 33,* 611–614.

Dixon, M. R., Benedict, H., & Larson, T. (2001). Functional analysis and treatment of inappropriate verbal behavior. *Journal of Applied Behavior Analysis, 34,* 361–363.

Dixon, M. R., Hayes, L. J., Binder, L. M., Manthey, S., Sigman, C., & Zdanowski, D. M. (1998). Using a self-control training procedure to increase appropriate behavior. *Journal of Applied Behavior Analysis, 31,* 203–210.

Dixon, M. R., Rehfeldt, R. A., & Randich, L. (2003). Enhancing tolerance to delayed reinforcers: The role of intervening activities. *Journal of Applied Behavior Analysis, 36,* 263–266.

Doke, L. A., & Risley, T. R. (1972). The organization of day care environments: Required vs. optional activities. *Journal of Applied Behavior Analysis, 5,* 453–454.

Donahoe, J. W., & Palmer, D. C. (1994). *Learning and complex behavior.* Boston: Allyn and Bacon.

Dorigo, M., & Colombetti, M. (1998). *Robot shaping: An experiment in behavior engineering.* Cambridge, MA: MIT Press.

Dorow, L. G., & Boyle, M. E. (1998). Instructor feedback for college writing assignments in introductory classes. *Journal of Behavioral Education, 8,* 115–129.

Downing, J. A. (1990). Contingency contracting: A step-by-step format. *Teaching Exceptional Children, 26* (2), 111–113.

Drabman, R. S., Hammer, D., & Rosenbaum, M. S. (1979). Assessing generalization in behavior modification with children: The generalization map. *Behavioral Assessment, 1,* 203–219.

Drabman, R. S., Spitalnik, R., & O'Leary, K. D. (1973). Teaching self-control to disruptive children. *Journal of Abnormal Psychology, 82,* 10–16.

Drasgow, E., Halle, J., & Ostrosky, M. M. (1998). Effects of differential reinforcement on the generalization of a replacement mand in three children with severe language delays. *Journal of Applied Behavior Analysis, 31,* 357–374.

Drash, P. W., High, R. L., & Tudor, R. M. (1999). Using mand training to establish an echoic repertoire in young children with autism. *The Analysis of Verbal Behavior, 16,* 29–44.

Ducharme, D. W., & Holborn, S. W. (1997). Programming generalization of social skills in preschool children with hearing impairments. *Journal of Applied Behavior Analysis, 30,* 639–651.

Ducharme, J. M., & Rushford, N. (2001). Proximal and distal effects of play on

child compliance with a brain-injured parent. *Journal of Applied Behavior Analysis, 34,* 221–224.

Duker, P. C., & Seys, D. M. (1996). Long-term use of electrical aversion treatment with self-injurious behavior. *Research in Developmental Disabilities, 17,* 293–301.

Duker, P. C., & van Lent, C. (1991). Inducing variability in communicative gestures used by severely retarded individuals. *Journal of Applied Behavior Analysis, 24,* 379–386.

Dunlap, G., & Johnson, J. (1985). Increasing the independent responding of autistic children with unpredictable supervision. *Journal of Applied Behavior Analysis, 18,* 227–236.

Dunlap, G., de Perczel, M., Clarke, S., Wilson, D., Wright, S., White, R., & Gomez, A. (1994). Choice making to promote adaptive behavior for students with emotional and behavioral challenges. *Journal of Applied Behavior Analysis, 27,* 505–518.

Dunlap, G., Kern-Dunlap, L., Clarke, S., & Robbins, F. R. (1991). Functional assessment, curricular revision, and severe behavior problems. *Journal of Applied Behavior Analysis, 24,* 387–397.

Dunlap, G., Koegel, R. L., Johnson, J., & O'Neill, R. E. (1987). Maintaining performance of autistic clients in community settings with delayed contingencies. *Journal of Applied Behavior Analysis, 20,* 185–191.

Dunlap, L. K., & Dunlap, G. (1989). A self-monitoring package for teaching subtraction with regrouping to students with learning disabilities. *Journal of Applied Behavior Analysis, 22,* 309–314.

Dunlap, L. K., Dunlap, G., Koegel, L. K., & Koegel, R. L. (1991). Using self-monitoring to increase independence. *Teaching Exceptional Children, 23*(3), 17–22.

Dunn, L. M., & Dunn, L. M. (1997). *Peabody Picture Vocabulary Test—III.* Circle Pines, MN: American Guidance Service.

Durand, V. M. (1999). Functional communication training using assistive devices: Recruiting natural communities of reinforcement. *Journal of Applied Behavior Analysis, 32,* 247–267.

Durand, V. M., & Carr, E. G. (1987). Social influences on "self-stimulatory" behavior: Analysis and treatment application. *Journal of Applied Behavior Analysis, 20,* 119–132.

Durand, V. M., & Carr, E. G. (1992). An analysis of maintenance following functional communication training. *Journal of Applied Behavior Analysis, 25,* 777–794.

Durand, V. M., & Crimmins, D. (1992). *The Motivation Assessment Scale.* Topeka, KS: Monaco & Associates.

Durand, V. M., Crimmins, D. B., Caufield, M., & Taylor, J. (1989). Reinforcer assessment I: Using problem behavior to select reinforcers. *Journal of the Association for Persons with Severe Handicaps, 14,* 113–126.

Duvinsky, J. D., & Poppen, R. (1982). Human performance on conjunctive fixed-interval fixed-ratio schedules. *Journal of the Experimental Analysis of Behavior, 37,* 243–250.

Dyer, K., Schwartz, I., & Luce, S. C. (1984). A supervision program for increasing functional activities for severely handicapped students in a residential setting. *Journal of Applied Behavior Analysis, 17,* 249–259.

Ebanks, M. E., & Fisher, W. W. (2003). Altering the timing of academic prompts to treat destructive behavior maintained by escape. *Journal of Applied Behavior Analysis, 36,* 355–359.

Eckert, T. L., Ardoin, S., P., Daly, III, E. J., & Martens, B. K. (2002). Improving oral reading fluency: A brief experimental analysis of combining an antecedent intervention with consequences. *Journal of Applied Behavior Analysis, 35,* 271–281.

Ecott, C. L., Foate, B. A. L., Taylor, B., & Critchfield, T. S. (1999). Further evaluation of reinforcer magnitude effects in noncontingent schedules. *Journal of Applied Behavior Analysis, 32,* 529–532.

Edwards, K. J., & Christophersen, E. R. (1993). Automated data acquisition through time-lapse videotape recording. *Journal of Applied Behavior Analysis, 24,* 503–504.

Egel, A. L. (1981). Reinforcer variation: Implications for motivating developmentally disabled children. *Journal of Applied Behavior Analysis, 14,* 345–350.

Egel, A. L. (1982). Programming the generalization and maintenance of treatment gains. In R. L. Koegal, A. Rincover, & A. L. Egel (Eds.), *Edu-cating and understanding autistic children* (pp. 281–299). San Diego, CA: College-Hill Press.

Elliot, S. N., Busse, R. T., & Shapiro, E. S. (1999). Intervention techniques for academic problems. In C. R. Reynolds & T. B. Gutkin (Eds.), *The handbook of school psychology* (3rd ed., pp. 664–685). New York: John Wiley & Sons.

Ellis, E. S., Worthington, L. A., & Larkin, M. J. (2002). *Executive summary of the research synthesis on effective teaching principles and the design of quality tools for educators.* [available online: http://idea.uoregon.edu/~ncite/documents/techrep/tech06.html]

Emerson, E., Reever, D. J., & Felce, D. (2000). Palmtop computer technologies for behavioral observation research. In T. Thompson, D. Felce, & F. J. Symons (Eds.), *Behavioral observation: Technology and applications in developmental disabilities* (pp. 47–59). Baltimore: Paul H. Brookes.

Engelmann, S. (1975). *Your child can succeed.* New York: Simon & Shuster.

Engelmann, S., & Carnine, D. (1982). *Theory of instruction: Principles and applications.* New York: Irvington.

Engelmann, S., & Colvin, D. (1983). *Generalized compliance training: A direct-instruction program for managing severe behavior problems.* Austin, TX: Pro-Ed.

Epling, W. F., & Pierce, W. D. (1983). Applied behavior analysis: New directions from the laboratory. *The Behavior Analyst, 6,* 27–37.

Epstein, L. H., Beck, B., Figueroa, J., Farkas, G., Kazdin, A., Daneman, D., & Becker, D. (1981). The effects of targeting improvement in urine glucose on metabolic control in children with insulin dependent diabetes. *Journal of Applied Behavior Analysis, 14,* 365–375.

Epstein, R. (1982). *Skinner for the classroom.* Champaign, IL: Research Press.

Epstein, R. (1990). Generativity theory and creativity. In M. A. Runco & R. S. Albert (Eds.), *Theories of creativity* (pp. 116–140). Newbury Park, CA: Sage.

Epstein, R. (1991). Skinner, creativity, and the problem of spontaneous behavior. *Psychological Science, 2,* 362–370.

Epstein, R. (1996). *Cognition, creativity, and behavior: Selected essays.* Westport, CT: Praeger.

Epstein, R. (1997). Skinner as self-manager. *Journal of Applied Behavior Analysis, 30,* 545–568.

Ericsson, K. A., & Charness, N. (1994). Expert performance. Its structure and acquisition. *American Psychologist, 49* (8), 725–747.

Ervin, R., Radford, P., Bertsch, K., Piper, A., Ehrhardt, K., & Poling, A. (2001). A descriptive analysis and critique of the empirical literature on school-based functional assessment. *School Psychology Review, 30,* 193–210.

Eshleman, J. W. (1991). Quantified trends in the history of verbal behavior research. *The Analysis of Verbal Behavior, 9,* 61–80.

Eshleman, J. W. (2004, May 31). *Celeration analysis of verbal behavior: Research papers presented at ABA 1975–present.* Paper presented at the 30th Annual Convention of the Association for Behavior Analysis, Boston, MA.

Falcomata, T. S., Roane, H. S., Hoyanetz, A. N., Kettering, T. L., & Keeney, K. M. (2004). An evaluation of response cost in the treatment of inappropriate vocalizations maintained by automatic reinforcement. *Journal of Applied Behavior Analysis, 37,* 83–87.

Falk, J. L. (1961). Production of polydipsia in normal rats by an intermittent food schedule. *Science, 133,* 195–196.

Falk, J. L. (1971). The nature and determinants of adjunctive behavior. *Physiology and Behavior, 6,* 577–588.

Fantuzzo, J. W., & Clement, P. W. (1981). Generalization of the effects of teacher- and self-administered token reinforcers to nontreated students. *Journal of Applied Behavior Analysis, 14,* 435–447.

Fantuzzo, J. W., Rohrbeck, C. A., Hightower, A. D., & Work, W. C. (1991). Teacher's use and children's preferences of rewards in elementary school. *Psychology in the Schools, 28,* 175–181.

Farrell, A. D. (1991). Computers and behavioral assessment: Current applications, future possibilities, and obstacles to routine use. *Behavioral Assessment, 13,* 159–179.

Favell, J. E., & McGimsey, J. E. (1993). Defining an acceptable treatment environment. In R. Van Houten & S. Axelrod (Eds.), *Behavior analysis and treatment* (pp. 25–45). New York: Plenum Press.

Favell, J. E., Azrin, N. H., Baumeister, A. A., Carr, E. G., Dorsey, M. F., Forehand, R., Foxx, R. M., Lovaas, I. O., Rincover, A., Risley, T. R., Romanczyk, R. G., Russo, D. C., Schroeder, S. R., & Solnick, J. V. (1982). The treatment of self-injurious behavior. *Behavior Therapy, 13,* 529–554.

Favell, J. E., McGimsey, J. F., & Jones, M. L. (1980). Rapid eating in the retarded: Reduction by nonaversive procedures. *Behavior Modification, 4,* 481–492.

Fawcett, S. B. (1991). Social validity: A note on methodology. *Journal of Applied Behavior Analysis, 24,* 235–239.

Felce, D., & Emerson, E. (2000). Observational methods in assessment of quality of life. In T. Thompson, D. Felce, & F. J. Symons (Eds.), *Behavioral observation: Technology and applications in developmental disabilities* (pp. 159–174). Baltimore: Paul H. Brookes.

Felixbrod, J. J., & O'Leary, K. D. (1973). Effects of reinforcement on children's academic behavior as a function of self-determined and externally imposed systems. *Journal of Applied Behavior Analysis, 6,* 241–250.

Felixbrod, J. J., & O'Leary, K. D. (1974). Self-determination of academic standards by children: Toward freedom from external control. *Journal of Educational Psychology, 66,* 845–850.

Ferguson, D. L., & Rosales-Ruiz, J. (2001). Loading the problem loader: The effects of target training and shaping on trailer-loading behavior of horses. *Journal of Applied Behavior Analysis, 34,* 409–424.

Ferrari, M., & Harris, S. (1981). The limits and motivational potential of sensory stimuli as reinforcers for autistic children. *Journal of Applied Behavior Analysis, 14,* 339–343.

Ferreri, S. J., Allen, N., Hessler, T., Nobel, M., Musti-Rao, S., & Salmon, M. (2006). *Battling procrastination: Self-managing studying and writing for candidacy exams and dissertation defenses.* Symposium at 32nd Annual Convention of the Association for Behavior Analysis, Atlanta, GA.

Ferreri, S. J., Neef, N. A., & Wait, T. A. (2006). *The assessment of impulsive choice as a function of the point of reinforcer delay.* Manuscript submitted for publication review.

Ferster, C. B., & DeMyer, M. K. (1961). The development of performances in autistic children in an automatically controlled environment. *Journal of Chronic Diseases, 13,* 312–345.

Ferster, C. B., & DeMyer, M. K. (1962). A method for the experimental analysis of the behavior of autistic children. *American Journal of Orthopsychiatry, 32,* 89–98.

Ferster, C. B., & Skinner, B. F. (1957). *Schedules of reinforcement.* Englewood Cliffs, NJ: Prentice Hall.

Fink, W. T., & Carnine, D. W. (1975). Control of arithmetic errors using informational feedback and graphing. *Journal of Applied Behavior Analysis, 8,* 461.

Finney, J. W., Putnam, D. E., & Boyd, C. M. (1998). Improving the accuracy of self-reports of adherence. *Journal of Applied Behavior Analysis, 31,* 485–488.

Fisher, R. (1956). *Statistical methods and statistical inference.* London: Oliver & Boyd.

Fisher, W. W., & Mazur, J. E. (1997). Basic and applied research on choice responding. *Journal of Applied Behavior Analysis, 30,* 387–410.

Fisher, W. W., Kelley, M. E., & Lomas, J. E. (2003). Visual aids and structured criteria for improving visual inspection and interpretation of single-case designs. *Journal of Applied Behavior Analysis, 36,* 387–406.

Fisher, W. W., Kuhn, D. E., & Thompson, R. H. (1998). Establishing discriminative control of responding using functional and alternative reinforcers during functional communication training. *Journal of Applied Behavior Analysis, 31,* 543–560.

Fisher, W. W., Lindauer, S. E., Alterson, C. J., & Thompson, R. H. (1998). Assessment and treatment of destructive behavior maintained by stereotypic object manipulation. *Journal of Applied Behavior Analysis, 31,* 513–527.

Fisher, W. W., Piazza, C. C., Bowman, L. G., & Almari, A. (1996). Integrating caregiver report with a systematic choice assessment to enhance reinforcer identification. *American Journal on Mental Retardation, 101,* 15–25.

Fisher, W. W., Piazza, C. C., Bowman, L. G., Hagopian, L. P., Owens, J. C., & Slevin, I. (1992). A comparison of two approaches for identifying reinforcers for persons with severe and profound disabilities. *Journal of Applied Behavior Analysis, 25,* 491–498.

Fisher, W. W., Piazza, C. C., Bowman, L. G., Kurtz, P. F., Sherer, M. R., & Lachman, S. R. (1994). A preliminary evaluation of empirically derived consequences for the treatment of pica. *Journal of Applied Behavior Analysis, 27,* 447–457.

Fisher, W. W., Piazza, C. C., Cataldo, M. E., Harrell, R., Jefferson, G., & Conner, R. (1993). Functional communication training with and without extinction and punishment. *Journal of Applied Behavior Analysis, 26,* 23–36.

Flaute, A. J., Peterson, S. M., Van Norman, R. K., Riffle, T., & Eakins, A. (2005). Motivate me! 20 tips for using a MotivAider® to improve your classroom. *Teaching Exceptional Children Plus, 2* (2) Article 3. Retrieved March 1, 2006, from http://escholarship.bc.edu/education/tecplus/vol2/iss2/art3.

Fleece, L., Gross, A., O'Brien, T., Kistner, J., Rothblum, E., & Drabman, R. (1981). Elevation of voice volume in young developmentally delayed children via an operant shaping procedure. *Journal of Applied Behavior Analysis, 14,* 351–355.

Flood, W. A., & Wilder, D. A. (2002). Antecedent assessment and assessment-based treatment of off-task behavior in a child diagnosed with Attention Deficit-Hyperactivity Disorder (ADHD). *Education and Treatment of Children, 25* (3), 331–338.

Flora, S. R. (2004). *The power of reinforcement.* Albany: State University of New York Press.

Florida Association for Behavior Analysis. (1988). *The behavior analyst's code of ethics.* Tallahassee, FL: Author.

Forthman, D. L., & Ogden, J. J. (1992). The role of applied behavior analysis in zoo management: Today and tomorrow. *Journal of Applied Behavior Analysis, 25,* 647–652

Foster, W. S. (1978). Adjunctive behavior: An underreported phenomenon in applied behavior analysis? *Journal of Applied Behavioral Analysis, 11,* 545–546.

Fowler, S. A., & Baer, D. M. (1981). "Do I have to be good all day?" The timing of delayed reinforcement as a factor in generalization. *Journal of Applied Behavior Analysis, 14,* 13–24.

Fox, D. K., Hopkins, B. L., & Anger, A. K. (1987). The long-term effects of a token economy on safety performance in open-pit mining. *Journal of Applied Behavior Analysis, 20,* 215–224.

Foxx, R. M. (1982). *Decreasing behaviors of persons with severe retardation and autism.* Champaign, IL: Research Press.

Foxx, R. M. (1996). Twenty years of applied behavior analysis in treating the most severe problem behavior: Lessons learned. *The Behavior Analyst, 19,* 225–235.

Foxx, R. M., & Azrin, N. H. (1972). Restitution: A method of eliminating aggressive-disruptive behavior of retarded and brain damaged patients. *Behavior Research and Therapy, 10,* 15–27.

Foxx, R. M., & Azrin, N. H. (1973). The elimination of autistic self-stimulatory behavior by overcorrection. *Journal of Applied Behavior Analysis, 6,* 1–14.

Foxx, R. M., & Bechtel, D. R. (1983). Overcorrection: A review and analysis. In S. Axelrod & J. Apsche (Eds.), *The effects of punishment on human behavior* (pp. 133–220). New York: Academic Press.

Foxx, R. M., & Rubinoff, A. (1979). Behavioral treatment of caffeinism: Reducing excessive coffee drinking. *Journal of Applied Behavior Analysis, 12,* 335–344.

Foxx, R. M., & Shapiro, S. T. (1978). The timeout ribbon: A non-exclusionary timeout procedure. *Journal of Applied Behavior Analysis, 11,* 125–143.

Foxx, R. M., Bittle, R. G., & Faw, G. D. (1989). A maintenance strategy for discontinuing aversive procedures: A 52-month follow-up of the treatment of aggression. *American Journal on Mental Retardation, 94,* 27–36.

Freeland, J. T., & Noell, G. H. (1999). Maintaining accurate math responses in elementary school students: The effects of delayed intermittent reinforcement and programming common stimuli. *Journal of Applied Behavior Analysis, 32,* 211–215.

Freeland, J. T., & Noell, G. H. (2002). Programming for maintenance: An investigation of delayed intermittent reinforcement and common stimuli to create indiscriminable contingencies. *Journal of Behavioral Education, 11,* 5–18.

Friedling, C., & O'Leary, S. G. (1979). Effects of self-instructional training on second- and third-grade hyperactive children: A failure to replicate. *Journal of Applied Behavior Analysis, 12,* 211–219.

Friman, P. C. (1990). Nonaversive treatment of high-rate disruptions: Child and provider effects. *Exceptional Children, 57,* 64–69.

Friman, P. C. (2004). Up with this I shall not put: 10 reasons why I disagree with Branch and Vollmer on *behavior* used as a count noun. *The Behavior Analyst, 27,* 99–106.

Friman, P. C., & Poling, A. (1995). Making life easier with effort: Basic findings and applied research on response effort. *Journal of Applied Behavior Analysis, 28,* 538–590.

Friman, P. C., Hayes, S. C., & Wilson, K. G. (1998). Why behavior analysts should study emotion: The example of anxiety. *Journal of Applied Behavior Analysis, 31,* 137–156.

Fuller, P. R. (1949). Operant conditioning of a vegetative organism. *American Journal of Psychology, 62,* 587–590.

Fuqua, R. W., & Schwade, J. (1986). Social validation of applied research: A selective review and critique. In A. Poling & R. W. Fuqua (Eds.), *Research methods in applied behavior analysis* (pp. 265–292). New York: Plenum Press.

Gable, R. A., Arllen, N. L., & Hendrickson, J. M. (1994). Use of students with emotional/behavioral disorders as behavior change agents. *Education and Treatment of Children, 17* (3), 267–276.

Galbicka, G. (1994). Shaping in the 21st century: Moving percentile schedules into applied settings. *Journal of Applied Behavior Analysis, 27,* 739–760.

Gallagher, S. M., & Keenan, M (2000). Independent use of activity materials by the elderly in a residential setting. *Journal of Applied Behavior Analysis, 33,* 325–328.

Gambrill, E. (2003). Science and its use and neglect in the human services. In K. S. Budd & T. Stokes (Eds.), *A small matter of proof: The legacy of Donald M. Baer* (pp. 63–76). Reno, NV: Context Press.

Gambrill, E. D. (1977). *Behavior modification: Handbook of assessment, intervention, and evaluation.* San Francisco: Jossey-Bass.

Garcia, E. E. (1976). The development and generalization of delayed imitation. *Journal of Applied Behavior Analysis, 9,* 499.

Garcia, E. E., & Batista-Wallace, M. (1977). Parental training of the plural morpheme in normal toddlers. *Journal of Applied Behavior Analysis, 10,* 505.

Gardner, III, R., Heward, W. L., & Grossi, T. A. (1994). Effects of response cards on student participation and academic achievement: A systematic replication with inner-city students during whole-class science instruction. *Journal of Applied Behavior Analysis, 27,* 63–71.

Garfinkle, A. N., & Schwartz, I. S. (2002). Peer imitation: Increasing social interactions in children with autism and other developmental disabilities in inclusive preschool classrooms. *Topics in Early Childhood Special Education, 22,* 26–38.

Garner, K. (2002). Case study: The conscientious kid. In R. W. Malott & H. Harrison, *I'll stop procrastinating when I get around to it: Plus other cool ways to succeed in school and life using behavior analysis to get your act together* (p. 3-13). Kalamazoo, MI: Department of Psychology, Western Michigan University.

Gast, D. L., Jacobs, H. A., Logan, K. R., Murray, A. S., Holloway, A., & Long, L. (2000). Pre-session assessment of preferences for students with profound multiple disabilities. *Education and Training in Mental Retardation and Developmental Disabilities, 35,* 393–405.

Gaylord-Ross, R. (1980). A decision model for the treatment of aberrant behavior in applied settings. In W. Sailor, B. Wilcox, & L. Brown (Eds.), *Methods of instruction for severely handicapped students* (pp. 135–158). Baltimore: Paul H. Brookes.

Gaylord-Ross, R. J., Haring, T. G., Breen, C., & Pitts-Conway, V. (1984). The training and generalization of social interaction skills with autistic youth. *Journal of Applied Behavior Analysis, 17,* 229–247.

Gee, K., Graham, N., Goetz, L., Oshima, G., & Yoshioka, K. (1991). Teaching students to request the continuation of routine activities by using time delay and decreasing physical assistance in the context of chain interruption. *Journal of the Association for Persons with Severe Handicaps, 10,* 154–167.

Geller, E. S., Paterson, L., & Talbott, E. (1982). A behavioral analysis of incentive prompts for motivating seat belt use. *Journal of Applied Behavior Analysis, 15,* 403–415.

Gena, A., Krantz, P. J., McClannahan, L. E., & Poulson, C. L. (1996). Training and generalization of affective behavior displayed by youth with autism. *Journal of Applied Behavior Analysis, 29,* 291–304.

Gentile, J. R., Roden, A. H., & Klein, R. D. (1972). An analysis-of-variance model for the intrasubject replication design. *Journal of Applied Behavior Analysis, 5,* 193–198.

Gewirtz, J. L., & Baer, D. M. (1958). The effect of brief social deprivation on behaviors for a social reinforcer. *Journal of Abnormal Social Psychology, 56,* 49–56.

Gewirtz, J. L., & Pelaez-Nogueras, M. (2000). Infant emotions under the positive-reinforcer control of caregiver attention and touch. In J. C. Leslie & D. Blackman (Eds.), *Issues in experimental and applied analyses of human behavior* (pp. 271–291). Reno, NV: Context Press.

Glenn, S. S. (2004). Individual behavior, culture, and social change. *The Behavior Analyst, 27,* 133–151.

Glenn, S. S., Ellis, J., & Greenspoon, J. (1992). On the revolutionary nature of the operant as a unit of behavioral selection. *American Psychologist, 47,* 1329–1336.

Glynn, E. L. (1970). Classroom applications of self-determined reinforcement. *Journal of Applied Behavior Analysis, 3,* 123–132.

Glynn, E. L., Thomas, J. D., & Shee, S. M. (1973). Behavioral self-control of on-task behavior in an elementary classroom. *Journal of Applied Behavior Analysis, 6,* 105–114.

Glynn, S. M. (1990). Token economy: Approaches for psychiatric patients: Progress and pitfalls over 25 years. *Behavior Modification, 14* (4), 383–407.

Goetz, E. M., & Baer, D. M. (1973). Social control of form diversity and the emergence of new forms in children's block-building. *Journal of Applied Behavior Analysis, 6,* 209–217.

Goetz, L., Gee, K., & Sailor, W. (1985). Using a behavior chain interruption strategy to teach communication skills to students with severe disabilities. *Journal of the Association for Persons with Severe Handicaps, 10,* 21–30.

Goh, H-L., & Iwata, B. A. (1994). Behavioral persistence and variability during extinction of self-injury maintained by escape. *Journal of Applied Behavior Analysis, 27,* 173–174.

Goldiamond, I. (1965). Self-control procedures in personal behavior problems. *Psychological Reports, 17,* 851–868.

Goldiamond, I. (1974). Toward a constructional approach to social problems: Ethical and constitutional issues raised by applied behavior analysis. *Behaviorism, 2,* 1–85.

Goldiamond, I. (1976a). Self-reinforcement. *Journal of Applied Behavior Analysis, 9,* 509–514.

Goldiamond, I. (1976b). Fables, armadyllics, and self-reinforcement. *Journal of Applied Behavior Analysis, 9,* 521–525.

Gottschalk, J. M., Libby, M. E., & Graff, R. B. (2000). The effects of establishing operations on preference assessment outcomes. *Journal of Applied Behavior Analysis, 33,* 85–88.

Grace, N. C., Kahng, S., & Fisher, W. W. (1994). Balancing social acceptability with treatment effectiveness of an intrusive procedure: A case report. *Journal of Applied Behavior Analysis, 27,* 171–172.

Graf, S. A., & Lindsley, O. R. (2002). *Standard Celeration Charting 2002.* Poland, OH: Graf Implements.

Gray, J. A. (1979). *Ivan Pavlov.* New York: Penguin Books.

Green, C. W., & Reid, D. H. (1996). Defining, validating, and increasing indices of happiness among people with profound multiple disabilities. *Journal of Applied Behavior Analysis, 29,* 67–78.

Green, C. W., Gardner, S. M., & Reid, D. H. (1997). Increasing indices of happiness among people with profound multiple disabilities: A program replication and component analysis. *Journal of Applied Behavior Analysis, 30,* 217–228.

Green, G., & Shane, H. C. (1994). Science, reason, and facilitated communication. *Journal of the Association for Persons with Severe Handicaps, 19,* 151–172.

Green, L., & Freed, D. W. (1993). The substitutability of reinforcers. *Journal of the Experimental Analysis of Behavior, 60,* 141–158.

Greene, B. F., Bailey, J. S., & Barber, F. (1981). An analysis and reduction of disruptive behavior on school buses. *Journal of Applied Behavior Analysis, 14,* 177–192.

Greenspan, S., & Negron, E. (1994). Ethical obligations of special services personnel. *Special Services in the Schools, 8* (2), 185–209.

Greenwood, C. R., & Maheady, L. (1997). Measurable change in student performance: Forgotten standard in teacher preparation? *Teacher Education and Special Education, 20,* 265–275.

Greenwood, C. R., Delquadri, J. C., & Hall, R. V. (1984). Opportunity to respond and student academic achievement. In W. L. Heward, T. E. Heron, D. S. Hill, & J. Trap-Porter (Eds.), *Focus on behavior analysis in education* (pp. 58–88). Columbus, OH: Merrill.

Greer, R. D. (1983). Contingencies of the science and technology of teaching and pre-behavioristic research practices in education. *Educational Researcher, 12,* 3–9.

Gresham, F. M. (1983). Use of a home-based dependent group contingency system in controlling destructive behavior: A case study. *School Psychology Review, 12* (2), 195–199.

Gresham, F. M., Gansle, K. A., & Noell, G. H. (1993). Treatment integrity in applied behavior analysis with children. *Journal of Applied Behavior Analysis, 26,* 257–263.

Griffen, A. K., Wolery, M., & Schuster J. W. (1992). Triadic instruction of chained food preparation responses: Acquisition and observational learning. *Journal of Applied Behavior Analysis, 25,* 193–204.

Griffith, R. G. (1983). The administrative issues: An ethical and legal perspective. In S. Axelrod & J. Apsche (Eds.), *The effects of punishment on human behavior* (pp. 317–338). New York: Academic Press.

Grossi, T. A. (1998). Using a self-operated auditory prompting system to improve the work performance of two employees with severe disabilities. *Journal of The Association for Persons with Severe Handicaps, 23,* 149–154.

Grossi, T. A., & Heward, W. L. (1998). Using self-evaluation to improve the work productivity of trainees in a community-based restaurant training program. *Education and Training in Mental Retardation and Developmental Disabilities, 33,* 248–263.

Grossi, T. A., Kimball, J. W., & Heward, W. L. (1994). What did you say? Using review of tape-recorded interactions to increase social acknowledgments by trainees in a community-based vocational program. *Research in Developmental Disabilities, 15,* 457–472.

Grunsell, J., & Carter, M. (2002). The behavior change interruption strategy: Generalization to out-of-routine contexts. *Education and Training in Mental Retardation and Developmental Disabilities, 37* (4), 378–390.

Guilford, J. P. (1965). *Fundamental statistics in psychology and education.* New York: McGraw-Hill.

Gumpel, T. P., & Shlomit, D. (2000). Exploring the efficacy of self-regulatory training as a possible alternative to social skills training. *Behavioral Disorders, 25,* 131–141.

Gunter, P. L., Venn, M. L., Patrick, J., Miller, K. A., & Kelly, L. (2003). Efficacy of using momentary time samples to determine on-task behavior of students with emotional/behavioral disorders. *Education and Treatment of Children, 26,* 400–412.

Gutowski, S. J., & Stromer, R. (2003). Delayed matching to two-picture samples by individuals with and without disabilities: An analysis of the role of naming. *Journal of Applied Behavior Analysis, 36,* 487–505.

Guttman, N., & Kalish, H. (1956). Discriminability and generalization. *Journal of Experimental Psychology, 51,* 79–88.

Haagbloom, S. J., Warnick, R., Warnick J. E., Jones, V. K., Yarbrough, G. L., Russell, T. M., et al. (2002). The 100 most eminent psychologists of the 20th century. *Review of General Psychology, 6,* 139–152.

Hackenberg, T. D. (1995). Jacques Loeb, B. F. Skinner, and the legacy of prediction and control. *The Behavior Analyst, 18,* 225–236.

Hackenberg, T. D., & Axtell, S. A. M. (1993). Humans' choices in situations of time-based diminishing returns. *Journal of the Experimental Analysis of Behavior, 59,* 445–470.

Hagopian, L. P., & Adelinis, J. D. (2001) Response blocking with and without redirection for the treatment of pica. *Journal of Applied Behavior Analysis, 34,* 527–530.

Hagopian, L. P., & Thompson, R. H. (1999). Reinforcement of compliance with respiratory treatment in a child with cystic fibrosis. *Journal of Applied Behavior Analysis, 32,* 233–236.

Hagopian, L. P., Farrell, D. A., & Amari, A. (1996). Treating total liquid refusal with backward chaining and fading. *Journal of Applied Behavior Analysis, 29,* 573–575.

Hagopian, L. P., Fisher, W. W., Sullivan, M. T., Acquisto, J., & Leblanc, L. A. (1998). Effectiveness of functional communication training with and without extinction and punishment: A summary of 21 inpatient cases. *Journal of Applied Behavior Analysis, 31,* 211–235.

Hagopian, L. P., Rush, K. S., Lewin, A. B., & Long, E. S. (2001). Evaluating the predictive validity of a single stimulus engagement preference assessment. *Journal of Applied Behavior Analysis, 34,* 475–485.

Hake, D. F., & Azrin, N. H. (1965). Conditioned punishment. *Journal of the Experimental Analysis of Behavior, 6,* 297–298.

Hake, D. F., Azrin, N. H., & Oxford, R. (1967). The effects of punishment intensity on squirrel monkeys. *Journal of the Experimental Analysis of Behavior, 10,* 95–107.

Hall, G. A., & Sundberg, M. L. (1987). Teaching mands by manipulating conditioned establishing operations. *The Analysis of Verbal Behavior, 5,* 41–53.

Hall, R. V., & Fox, R. G. (1977). Changing-criterion designs: An alternative applied behavior analysis procedure. In B. C. Etzel, J. M. LeBlanc, & D. M. Baer (Eds.), *New developments in behavioral research: Theory, method, and application* (pp. 151–166). Hillsdale, NJ: Erlbaum.

Hall, R. V., Cristler, C., Cranston, S. S., & Tucker, B. (1970). Teachers and parents as researchers using multiple baseline designs. *Journal of Applied Behavior Analysis, 3,* 247–255.

Hall, R. V., Delquadri, J. C., & Harris, J. (1977, May). *Opportunity to respond: A new focus in the field of applied behavior analysis.* Paper presented at the Midwest Association for Behavior Analysis, Chicago, IL.

Hall, R. V., Lund, D., & Jackson, D. (1968). Effects of teacher attention on study behavior. *Journal of Applied Behavior Analysis, 1,* 1–12.

Hall, R. V., Panyan, M., Rabon, D., & Broden. D. (1968). Instructing beginning teachers in reinforcement procedures which improve classroom control. *Journal of Applied Behavior Analysis, 1,* 315–322.

Hall, R., Axelrod, S., Foundopoulos, M., Shellman, J., Campbell, R. A., & Cranston, S. S. (1971). The effective use of punishment to modify behavior in the classroom. *Educational Technology, 11* (4), 24–26.

Hall, R.V., Fox, R., Williard, D., Goldsmith, L., Emerson, M., Owen, M., Porcia, E., & Davis, R. (1970). *Modification of disrupting and talking-out behavior with the teacher as observer and experimenter.* Paper presented at the American Educational Research Association Convention, Minneapolis, MN.

Hallahan, D. P., Lloyd, J. W., Kosiewicz, M. M., Kauffman, J. M., & Graves, A. W. (1979). Self-monitoring of attention as a treatment for a learning disabled boy's off-task behavior. *Learning Disability Quarterly, 2,* 24–32.

Hamblin, R. L., Hathaway, C., & Wodarski, J. S. (1971). Group contingencies, peer tutoring and accelerating academic achievement. In E. A. Ramp & B. L. Hopkins (Eds.), *A new direction for education: Behavior analysis* (Vol. 1, pp. 41–53). Lawrence: University of Kansas.

Hamlet, C. C., Axelrod, S., & Kuerschner, S. (1984). Eye contact as an antecedent to compliant behavior. *Journal of Applied Behavior Analysis, 17,* 553–557.

Hammer-Kehoe, J. (2002). Yoga. In R. W. Malott & H. Harrison (Eds.), *I'll stop procrastinating when I get around to it: Plus other cool ways to succeed in school and life using behavior analysis to get your act together* (p. 10-5). Kalamazoo, MI: Department of Psychology, Western Michigan University.

Hammill, D., & Newcomer, P. L. (1997). *Test of language development—3.* Austin, TX: Pro-Ed.

Hanley, G. P., Iwata, B. A., & Thompson, R. H. (2001). Reinforcement schedule thinning following treatment with functional communication training. *Journal of Applied Behavior Analysis, 34,* 17–38.

Hanley, G. P., Iwata, B. A., Thompson, R. H., & Lindberg, J. S. (2000). A component analysis of "stereotypy and reinforcement" for alternative behavior. *Journal of Applied Behavior Analysis, 33,* 299–308.

Hanley, G. P., Piazza, C. C., Fisher, W. W., Contrucci, S. A., & Maglieri, K. A. (1997). Evaluation of client preference of function-based treatment packages.

Journal of Applied Behavior Analysis, 30, 459–473.

Hanley, G. P., Piazza, C. C., Keeney, K. M., Blakeley-Smith, A. B., & Worsdell, A. S. (1998). Effects of wrist weights on self-injurious and adaptive behaviors. *Journal of Applied Behavior Analysis, 31,* 307–310.

Haring, T. G., & Kennedy, C. H. (1990). Contextual control of problem behavior. *Journal of Applied Behavior Analysis, 23,* 235–243.

Harlow, H. R. (1959). Learning set and error factor theory. In S. Kock (Ed.), *Psychology: A study of science* (Vol. 2, pp. 492–537). New York: McGraw-Hill.

Harrell, J. P. (2002). Case study: Taking time to relax. In R. W. Malott & H. Harrison, *I'll stop procrastinating when I get around to it: Plus other cool ways to succeed in school and life using behavior analysis to get your act together* (p. 10-2). Kalamazoo, MI: Department of Psychology, Western Michigan University.

Harris, F. R., Johnston, M. K., Kelly, C. S., & Wolf, M. M. (1964). Effects of positive social reinforcement on regressed crawling of a nursery school child. *Journal of Educational Psychology, 55,* 35–41.

Harris, K. R. (1986). Self-monitoring of attentional behavior versus self-monitoring of productivity: Effects on on-task behavior and academic response rate among learning disabled children. *Journal of Applied Behavior Analysis, 19,* 417–424.

Hart, B., & Risley, T. R. (1975). Incidental teaching of language in the preschool. *Journal of Applied Behavior Analysis, 8,* 411–420.

Hart, B. M., Allen, K. E., Buell, J. S., Harris, F. R., & Wolf, M. M. (1964). Effects of social reinforcement on operant crying. *Journal of Experimental Child Psychology, 1,* 145–153.

Hartmann, D. P. (1974). Forcing square pegs into round holes: Some comments on "an analysis-of-variance model for the intrasubject replication design". *Journal of Applied Behavior Analysis, 7,* 635–638.

Hartmann, D. P. (1977). Considerations in the choice of interobserver reliability estimates. *Journal of Applied Behavior Analysis, 10,* 103–116.

Hartmann, D. P., & Hall, R. V. (1976). The changing criterion design. *Journal of Applied Behavior Analysis, 9,* 527–532.

Hartmann, D. P., Gottman, J. M., Jones, R. R., Gardner, W., Kazdin, A. E., & Vaught, R. S. (1980). Interrupted time-series analysis and its application to behavioral data. *Journal of Applied Behavior Analysis, 13,* 543–559.

Harvey, M. T., May, M. E., & Kennedy, C. H. (2004). Nonconcurrent multiple baseline designs and the evaluation of educational systems. *Journal of Behavioral Education, 13,* 267–276.

Hawkins, R. P. (1975). Who decided *that* was the problem? Two stages of responsibility for applied behavior analysts. In W. S. Wood (Ed.), *Issues in evaluating behavior modification* (pp. 195–214). Champaign, IL: Research Press.

Hawkins, R. P. (1979). The functions of assessment. *Journal of Applied Behavior Analysis, 12,* 501–516.

Hawkins, R. P. (1984). What is "meaningful" behavior change in a severely/profoundly retarded learner: The view of a behavior analytic parent. In W. L Heward, T. E. Heron, D. S. Hill, & J. Trap-Porter (Eds.), *Focus on behavior analysis in education* (pp. 282–286). Upper Saddle River, NJ: Prentice-Hall/Merrill.

Hawkins, R. P. (1986). Selection of target behaviors. In R. O. Nelson & S. C. Hayes (Eds.), *Conceptual foundations of behavioral assessment* (pp. 331–385). New York: Guilford Press.

Hawkins, R. P. (1991). Is social validity what we are interested in? *Journal of Applied Behavior Analysis, 24,* 205–213.

Hawkins, R. P., & Anderson, C. M. (2002). On the distinction between science and practice: A reply to Thyer and Adkins. *The Behavior Analyst, 26,* 115–119.

Hawkins, R. P., & Dobes, R. W. (1977). Behavioral definitions in applied behavior analysis: Explicit or implicit? In B. C. Etzel, J. M. LeBlanc, & D. M. Baer (Eds.), *New developments in behavioral research: Theory, method, and application* (pp. 167–188). Hillsdale, NJ: Erlbaum.

Hawkins, R. P., & Dotson, V. A. (1975). Reliability scores that delude: An Alice in Wonderland trip through the misleading characteristics of interobserver agreement scores in interval recording. In E. Ramp & G. Semp (Eds.), *Behavior analysis: Areas of research and application* (pp. 359–376). Upper Saddle River, NJ: Prentice Hall.

Hawkins, R. P., & Hursh, D. E. (1992). Levels of research for clinical practice: It isn't as hard as you think. *West Virginia Journal of Psychological Research and Practice, 1,* 61–71.

Hawkins, R. P., Mathews, J. R., & Hamdan, L. (1999). *Measuring behavioral health outcomes: A practical guide.* New York: Kluwer Academic/Plenum.

Hayes, L. J., Adams, M. A., & Rydeen, K. L. (1994). Ethics, choice, and value. In L. J. Hayes et al. (Eds.), *Ethical issues in developmental disabilities* (pp. 11–39). Reno, NV: Context Press.

Hayes, S. C. (1991). The limits of technological talk. *Journal of Applied Behavior Analysis, 24,* 417–420.

Hayes, S. C. (Ed.). (1989). *Rule-governed behavior: Cognition, contingencies, and instructional control.* Reno, NV: Context Press.

Hayes, S. C., & Cavior, N. (1977). Multiple tracking and the reactivity of self-monitoring: I. Negative behaviors. *Behavior Therapy, 8,* 819–831.

Hayes, S. C., & Cavior, N. (1980). Multiple tracking and the reactivity of self-monitoring: II. Positive behaviors. *Behavioral Assessment, 2,* 238–296.

Hayes, S. C., & Hayes, L. J. (1993). Applied implications of current JEAB research on derived relations and delayed reinforcement. *Journal of Applied Behavior Analysis, 26,* 507–511.

Hayes, S. C., Rincover, A., & Solnick, J. V. (1980). The technical drift of applied behavior analysis. *Journal of Applied Behavior Analysis, 13,* 275–285.

Hayes, S. C., Rosenfarb, I., Wulfert, E., Munt, E. D., Korn, D., & Zettle, R. D. (1985). Self-reinforcement effects: An artifact of social standard setting? *Journal of Applied Behavior Analysis, 18,* 201–214.

Hayes, S. C., Zettle, R. D., & Rosenfarb, I. (1989). Rule-following. In S. C. Hayes (Ed.), *Rule-governed behavior: Cognition, contingencies, and instructional control* (pp. 191–220). New York: Plenum Press.

Haynes, S. N., & Horn, W. F. (1982). Reactivity in behavioral observation: A methodological and conceptual critique. *Behavioral Assessment, 4,* 369–385.

Health Insurance Portability and Accountability Act (HIPAA). (1996). Washington, DC: Office for Civil Rights. Retrieved December 14, 2003, from http://aspe.hhs.gov/admnsimp/pl104191.htm>http://aspe.hhs.gov/admnsimp/pl104191.htm.

Heckaman, K. A., Alber, S. R., Hooper, S., & Heward, W. L. (1998). A comparison of least-to-most prompts and progressive time delay on the disruptive behavior of students with autism. *Journal of Behavior Education, 8,* 171–201.

Heflin, L. J., & Simpson, R. L. (2002). Understanding intervention controversies. In B. Scheuermann & J. Weber (Eds.), *Autism: Teaching does make a difference* (pp. 248–277). Belmont, CA: Wadsworth.

Helwig, J. (1973). *Effects of manipulating an antecedent event on mathematics response rate.* Unpublished manuscript, Ohio State University, Columbus, OH.

Heron, T. E., & Harris, K. C. (2001). *The educational consultant: Helping professionals, parents, and students in inclusive classrooms* (4th ed.). Austin, TX: Pro-Ed.

Heron, T. E., & Heward, W. L. (1988). Ecological assessment: Implications for teachers of learning disabled students. *Learning Disability Quarterly, 11,* 224–232.

Heron, T. E., Heward, W. L., Cooke, N. L., & Hill, D. S. (1983). Evaluation of a classwide peer tutoring system: First graders teach each other sight words. *Education and Treatment of Children, 6,* 137–152.

Heron, T. E., Hippler, B. J., & Tincani, M. J. (2003). *How to help students complete classwork and homework assignments.* Austin, TX: Pro-Ed.

Heron, T. E., Tincani, M. J., Peterson, S. M., & Miller, A. D. (2005). Plato's allegory of the cave revisited. Disciples of the light appeal to the pied pipers and prisoners in the darkness. In W. L. Heward, T. E. Heron, N. A. Neef, S. M. Peterson, D. M. Sainato, G. Cartledge, R. Gardner, III, L. D. Peterson, S. B. Hersh, & J. C. Dardig (Eds.), *Focus on behavior analysis in education: Achievements, challenges, and opportunities* (pp. 267–282), Upper Saddle River, NJ: Merrill/Prentice Hall.

Herr, S. S., O'Sullivan, J. L., & Dinerstein, R. D. (1999). *Consent to extraordinary interventions.* In R. D. Dinerstein, S. S. Herr, & J. L. O'Sullivan (Eds.), *A guide to consent* (pp. 111–122). Washington DC: American Association on Mental Retardation.

Herrnstein, R. J. (1961). Relative and absolute strength of a response as a function of frequency of reinforcement. *Journal of the Experimental Analysis of Behavior 4,* 267–272.

Herrnstein, R. J. (1970). On the law of effect. *Journal of the Experimental Analysis of Behavior 13,* 243–266.

Hersen, M., & Barlow, D. H. (1976). *Single case experimental designs: Strategies for studying behavior change.* New York: Pergamon Press.

Heward, W. L. (1978, May). *The delayed multiple baseline design.* Paper presented at the Fourth Annual Convention of the Association for Behavior Analysis, Chicago.

Heward, W. L. (1980). A formula for individualizing initial criteria for reinforcement. *Exceptional Teacher, 1* (9), 7, 9.

Heward, W. L. (1994). Three "low-tech" strategies for increasing the frequency of active student response during group instruction. In R. Gardner, D. M. Sainato, J. O. Cooper, T. E. Heron, W. L. Heward, J. Eshleman, & T. A. Grossi (Eds.), *Behavior analysis in education: Focus on measurably superior instruction* (pp. 283–320). Monterey, CA: Brooks/Cole.

Heward, W. L. (2003). Ten faulty notions about teaching and learning that hinder the effectiveness of special education. *The Journal of Special Education, 36* (4), 186–205.

Heward, W. L. (2005). Reasons applied behavior analysis is good for education and why those reasons have been insufficient. In W. L. Heward, T. E. Heron, N. A. Neef, S. M. Peterson, D. M. Sainato, G. Cartledge, R. Gardner, III, L. D. Peterson, S. B. Hersh, & J. C. Dardig (Eds.), *Focus on behavior analysis in education: Achievements, challenges, and opportunities* (pp. 316–348). Upper Saddle River, NJ: Merrill/Prentice Hall.

Heward, W. L. (2006). *Exceptional children: An introduction to special education* (8th ed.). Upper Saddle River, NJ: Merrill/Prentice Hall.

Heward, W. L., & Cooper, J. O. (1992). Radical behaviorism: A productive and needed philosophy for education. *Journal of Behavioral Education, 2,* 345–365.

Heward, W. L., & Eachus, H. T. (1979). Acquisition of adjectives and adverbs in sentences written by hearing impaired and aphasic children. *Journal of Applied Behavior Analysis, 12,* 391–400.

Heward, W. L., & Silvestri, S. M. (2005a). The neutralization of special education. In J. W. Jacobson, J. A. Mulick, & R. M. Foxx (Eds.), *Fads: Dubious and improbable treatments for developmental disabilities.* Mahwah NJ: Erlbaum.

Heward, W. L., & Silvestri, S. M. (2005b). Antecedent. In G. Sugai & R. Horner (Eds.), *Encyclopedia of behavior modification and cognitive behavior therapy, Vol. 3: Educational applications* (pp. 1135–1137). Thousand Oaks, CA: Sage.

Heward, W. L., Dardig, J. C., & Rossett, A. (1979). *Working with parents of handicapped children.* Upper Saddle River, NJ: Merrill/Prentice Hall.

Heward, W. L., Heron, T. E., Gardner, III, R., & Prayzer, R. (1991). Two strategies for improving students' writing skills. In G. Stoner, M. R. Shinn, & H. M. Walker (Eds.), *A school psychologist's interventions for regular education* (pp. 379–398). Washington, DC: National Association of School Psychologists.

Heward, W. L., Heron, T. E., Neef, N. A., Peterson, S. M., Sainato, D. M., Cartledge, G., Gardner, III, R., Peterson, L. D., Hersh, S. B., & Dardig, J. C. (Eds.). (2005). *Focus on behavior analysis in education: Achievements, challenges, and opportunities.* Upper Saddle River, NJ: Prentice Hall/Merrill.

Hewett, F. M. (1968). *The emotionally disturbed child in the classroom.* New York: McGraw-Hill.

Higbee, T. S., Carr, J. E., & Harrison, C. D. (1999). The effects of pictorial versus tangible stimuli in stimulus preference assessments. *Research in Developmental Disabilities, 20,* 63–72.

Higbee, T. S., Carr, J. E., & Harrison, C. D. (2000). Further evaluation of the multiple-stimulus preference assessment. *Research in Developmental Disabilities, 21,* 61–73.

Higgins, J. W., Williams, R. L., & McLaughlin, T. F. (2001). The effects of a token economy employing instructional consequences for a third-grade student with learning disabilities: A data-based case study. *Education and Treatment of Children, 24* (1), 99–106.

Himle, M. B., Miltenberger, R. G., Flessner, C., & Gatheridge, B. (2004). Teaching safety skills to children to prevent gun play. *Journal of Applied Behavior Analysis, 1,* 1–9.

Himle, M. B., Miltenberger, R. G., Gatheridge, B., & Flessner, C., (2004). An evaluation of two procedures for training skills to prevent gun play in children. *Pediatrics, 113,* 70–77.

Hineline, P. N. (1977). Negative reinforcement and avoidance. In W. K. Honig & J. E. R. Staddon (Eds.), *Handbook of operant behavior* (pp. 364–414). Upper Saddle River, NJ: Prentice Hall.

Hineline, P. N. (1992). A self-interpretive behavior analysis. *American Psychologist, 47,* 1274–1286.

Hobbs, T. R., & Holt, M. M. (1976). The effects of token reinforcement on the behavior of delinquents in cottage settings. *Journal of Applied Behavior Analysis, 9,* 189–198.

Hoch, H., McComas, J. J., Johnson, L, Faranda, N., & Guenther, S. L. (2002). The effects of magnitude and quality of reinforcement on choice responding during play activities. *Journal of Applied Behavior Analysis, 35,* 171–181.

Hoch, H., McComas, J. J., Thompson, A. L., & Paone, D. (2002). Concurrent reinforcement schedules: Behavior change and maintenance without extinction. *Journal of Applied Behavior Analysis, 35,* 155–169.

Holcombe, A., Wolery, M., & Snyder, E. (1994). Effects of two levels of procedural fidelity with constant time delay with children's learning. *Journal of Behavioral Education, 4,* 49–73.

Holcombe, A., Wolery, M., Werts, M. G., & Hrenkevich, P. (1993). Effects of instructive feedback on future learning. *Journal of Behavioral Education, 3,* 259–285.

Holland, J. G. (1978). Behaviorism: Part of the problem or part of the solution? *Journal of Applied Behavior Analysis, 11,* 163–174.

Holland, J. G., & Skinner, B. F. (1961). *The analysis of behavior: A program for self-instruction.* New York: McGraw-Hill.

Holman, J., Goetz, E. M., & Baer, D. M. (1977). The training of creativity as an operant and an examination of its generalization characteristics. In B. C. Etzel, J. M. LeBlanc, & D. M. Baer (Eds.), *New developments in behavioral research: Theory, method, and practice* (pp. 441–471). Hillsdale, NJ: Erlbaum.

Holmes, G., Cautela, J., Simpson, M., Motes, P., & Gold, J. (1998). Factor structure of the School Reinforcement Survey Schedule: School is more than grades. *Journal of Behavioral Education, 8,* 131–140.

Holth, P. (2003), Generalized imitation and generalized matching to sample. *The Behavior Analyst, 26,* 155–158.

Holz, W. C., & Azrin, N. H. (1961). Discriminative properties of punishment. *Journal of the Experimental Analysis of Behavior, 4,* 225–232.

Holz, W. C., & Azrin, N. H. (1962). Recovery during punishment by intense noise. *Journal of the Experimental Analysis of Behavior, 6,* 407–412.

Holz, W. C., Azrin, N. H., & Ayllon, T. (1963). Elimination of behavior of mental patients by response-produced extinction. *Journal of the Experimental Analysis of Behavior, 6,* 407–412.

Homme, L., Csanyi, A. P., Gonzales, M. A., & Rechs, J. R. (1970). *How to use contingency contracting in the classroom.* Champaign, IL: Research Press.

Honig, W. K. (Ed.). (1966). *Operant behavior: Areas of research and application.* New York: Appleton-Century-Crofts.

Hoover, H. D., Hieronymus, A. N., Dunbar, S. B. Frisbie, D. A., & Switch (1996). *Iowa Tests of Basic Skills.* Chicago: Riverside.

Hopkins, B. L. (1995). Applied behavior analysis and statistical process control? *Journal of Applied Behavior Analysis, 28,* 379–386.

Horner, R. D., & Baer, D. M. (1978). Multiple-probe technique: A variation on the multiple baseline design. *Journal of Applied Behavior Analysis, 11,* 189–196.

Horner, R. D., & Keilitz, I. (1975). Training mentally retarded adolescents to brush their teeth. *Journal of Applied Behavior Analysis, 8,* 301–309.

Horner, R. H. (2002). On the status of knowledge for using punishment: A commentary. *Journal of Applied Behavior Analysis, 35,* 465–467.

Horner, R. H., & McDonald, R. S. (1982). Comparison of single instance and general case instruction in teaching of a generalized vocational skill. *Journal of the Association for Persons with Severe Handicaps, 7* (3), 7–20.

Horner, R. H., Carr, E. G., Halle, J., McGee, G., Odom, S., & Wolery, M. (2005). The use of single-subject research to identify evidence-based practice in special education. *Exceptional Children, 71,* 165–179.

Horner, R. H., Day, M., Sprague, J., O'Brien, M., & Heathfield, L. (1991). Interspersed requests: A nonaversive procedure for reducing aggression and self-injury during instruction. *Journal of Applied Behavior Analysis, 24,* 265–278.

Horner, R. H., Dunlap, G., & Koegel, R. L. (1988). *Generalization and maintenance: Life-style changes in applied settings.* Baltimore: Paul H. Brookes.

Horner, R. H., Eberhard, J. M., & Sheehan, M. R. (1986). Teaching generalized table bussing: The importance of negative teaching examples. *Behavior Modification, 10,* 457–471.

Horner, R. H., Sprague, J., & Wilcox, B. (1982). Constructing general case programs for community activities. In B. Wilcox & G. T. Bellamy (Eds.), *Design of high school programs for severely handicapped students* (pp. 61–98). Baltimore: Paul H. Brookes.

Horner, R. H., Williams, J. A., & Steveley, J. D. (1987). Acquisition of generalized telephone use by students with moderate and severe mental retardation. *Research in Developmental Disabilities, 8,* 229–247.

Houten, R. V., & Rolider, A. (1990). The use of color mediation techniques to teach number identification and single digit multiplication problems to children with learning problems. *Education and Treatment of Children, 13,* 216–225.

Howell, K. W. (1998). *Curriculum-based evaluation: Teaching and decision making* (3rd ed.). Monterey, CA: Brooks/Cole.

Hughes, C. (1992). Teaching self-instruction using multiple exemplars to produce generalized problem-solving by individuals with severe mental retardation. *Journal on Mental Retardation, 97,* 302–314.

Hughes, C. (1997). Self-instruction. In M. Agran (Ed.), *Self-directed learning: Teaching self-determination skills* (pp. 144–170). Pacific Grove, CA: Brooks/Cole.

Hughes, C., & Lloyd, J. W. (1993). An analysis of self-management. *Journal of Behavioral Education, 3,* 405–424.

Hughes, C., & Rusch, F. R. (1989). Teaching supported employees with severe mental retardation to solve problems.

Journal of Applied Behavior Analysis, 22, 365–372.

Hughes, C., Harmer, M. L., Killian, D. J., & Niarhos, F. (1995). The effects of multiple-exemplar self-instructional training on high school students' generalized conversational interactions. *Journal of Applied Behavior Analysis, 28,* 201–218.

Hume, K. M., & Crossman, J. (1992). Musical reinforcement of practice behaviors among competitive swimmers. *Journal of Applied Behavior Analysis, 25,* 665–670.

Humphrey, L. L., Karoly, P., & Kirschenbaum, D. S. (1978). Self-management in the classroom: Self-imposed response cost versus self-reward. *Behavior Therapy, 9,* 592–601.

Hundert, J., & Bucher, B. (1978). Pupils' self-scored arithmetic performance: A practical procedure for maintaining accuracy. *Journal of Applied Behavior Analysis, 11,* 304.

Hunt, P., & Goetz, L. (1988). Teaching spontaneous communication in natural settings using interrupted behavior chains. *Topics in Language Disorders, 9,* 58–71.

Hurley, A. D. N., & O'Sullivan, J. L. (1999). *Informed consent for health care.* In R. D. Dinerstein, S. S. Herr, & J. L. O'Sullivan (Eds.), *A guide to consent* (pp. 39–55). Washington DC: American Association on Mental Retardation.

Hutchinson, R. R. (1977). By-products of aversive control In W. K. Honig & J. E. R. Staddon (Eds.), *Handbook of operant behavior* (pp. 415–431). Upper Saddle River, NJ: Prentice Hall.

Huybers, S., Van Houten, R., & Malenfant, J. E. L. (2004). Reducing conflicts between motor vehicles and pedestrians: The separate and combined effects of pavement markings and a sign prompt. *Journal of Applied Behavior Analysis, 37,* 445–456.

Individuals with Disabilities Education Act of 1997, P. L. 105–17, 20 U.S.C. para. 1400 *et seq.*

Irvin, D. S., Thompson, T. J., Turner, W. D., & Williams, D. E. (1998). Utilizing response effort to reduce chronic hand mouthing. *Journal of Applied Behavior Analysis, 31,* 375–385.

Isaacs, W., Thomas, I., & Goldiamond, I. (1960). Application of operant conditioning to reinstate verbal behavior in psychotics. *Journal of Speech and Hearing Disorders, 25,* 8–12.

Iwata, B. A. (1987). Negative reinforcement in applied behavior analysis: An emerging technology. *Journal of Applied Behavior Analysis, 20,* 361–378.

Iwata, B. A. (1988). The development and adoption of controversial default technologies. *The Behavior Analyst, 11,* 149–157.

Iwata, B. A. (1991). Applied behavior analysis as technological science. *Journal of Applied Behavior Analysis, 24,* 421–424.

Iwata, B. A. (2006). On the distinction between positive and negative reinforcement. *The Behavior Analyst, 29,* 121–123.

Iwata, B. A., & DeLeon, I. (1996). The functional analysis screening tool. Gainesville, FL: The Florida Center on Self-Injury, The University of Florida.

Iwata, B. A., & Michael, J. L. (1994). Applied implications of theory and research on the nature of reinforcement. *Journal of Applied Behavior Analysis, 27,* 183–193.

Iwata, B. A., Dorsey, M. F., Slifer, K. J., Bauman, K. E., & Richman, G. S. (1994). Toward a functional analysis of self-injury. *Journal of Applied Behavior Analysis, 27,* 197–209. (Reprinted from *Analysis and Intervention in Developmental Disabilities, 2,* 3–20, 1982).

Iwata, B. A., Pace, G. M., Cowdery, G. E., & Miltenberger, R. G. (1994). What makes extinction work: An analysis of procedural form and function. *Journal of Applied Behavior Analysis, 27,* 131–144.

Iwata, B. A., Pace, G. M., Dorsey, M. F., Zarcone, J. R., Vollmer, T. R., Smith, R. G., Rodgers, T. A., Lerman, D. C., Shore, B. A., Mazaleski, J. L., Goh, H., Cowdery, G. E., Kalsher, M. J., & Willis, K. D. (1994). The functions of self-injurious behavior: An experimental-epidemiological analysis. *Journal of Applied Behavior Analysis, 27,* 215–240.

Iwata, B. A., Pace, G. M., Kissel, R. C., Nau, P. A., & Farber, J. M. (1990). The Self-Injury Trauma (SIT) Scale: A method for quantifying surface tissue damage caused by self-injurious behavior. *Journal of Applied Behavior Analysis, 23,* 99–110.

Iwata, B. A., Smith, R. G., & Michael, J. (2000). Current research on the influence of establishing operations on behavior in applied settings. *Journal of Applied Behavior Analysis, 33,* 411–418.

Iwata, B. A., Wallace, M. D., Kahng, S., Lindberg, J. S., Roscoe, E. M., Conners, J., Hanley, G. P., Thompson, R. H., & Worsdell, A. S. (2000). Skill acquisition in the implementation of functional analysis methodology. *Journal of Applied Behavior Analysis, 33,* 181–194.

Jacobs, H. E., Fairbanks, D., Poche, C. E., & Bailey, J. S. (1982). Multiple incentives in encouraging car pool formation on a university campus. *Journal of Applied Behavior Analysis, 15,* 141–149.

Jacobson, J. M., Bushell, D., & Risley, T. (1969). Switching requirements in a Head Start classroom. *Journal of Applied Behavior Analysis, 2,* 43–47.

Jacobson, J. W., Foxx, R. M., & Mulick, J. A. (Eds.). (2005). *Controversial therapies for developmental disabilities: Fads, fashion, and science in professional practice.* Hillsdale, NJ: Erlbaum.

Jason, L. A., & Liotta, R. F. (1982). Reduction of cigarette smoking in a university cafeteria. *Journal of Applied Behavior Analysis, 15,* 573–577.

Johnson, B. M., Miltenberger, R. G., Egemo-Helm, K. R., Jostad, C., Flessner, C. A., & Gatheridge, B. (2005). Evaluation of behavior skills training for teaching abduction prevention skills to young children. *Journal of Applied Behavior Analysis, 38,* 67–78.

Johnson, B. M., Miltenberger, R. G., Knudson, P., Egemo-Helm, K., Kelso, P., Jostad, C., & Langley, L. (2006). A preliminary evaluation of two behavioral skills training procedures for teaching abduction-prevention skills to school children. *Journal of Applied Behavior Analysis, 39,* 25–34.

Johnson, K. R., & Layng, T. V. J. (1992). Breaking the structuralist barrier: Literacy and numeracy with fluency. *American Psychologist, 47,* 1475–1490.

Johnson, K. R., & Layng, T. V. J. (1994). The Morningside model of generative instruction. In R. Gardner, D. M., III, Sainato, J. O., Cooper, T. E., Heron, W. L., Heward, J., Eshleman, & T. A. Grossi (Eds.), *Behavior analysis in education: Focus on measurably superior instruction* (pp. 173–197). Pacific Grove, CA: Brooks/Cole.

Johnson, T. (1973). *Addition and subtraction math program with stimulus shaping and stimulus fading.* Produced pursuant to a grant from the Ohio Department of Education, BEH Act, P.L. 91-203, Title VI-G; OE G-0-714438(604). J. E. Fisher & J. O. Cooper, project codirectors.

Johnston, J. M. (1979). On the relation between generalization and generality. *The Behavior Analyst, 2,* 1–6.

Johnston, J. M. (1991). We need a new model of technology. *Journal of Applied Behavior Analysis, 24,* 425–427.

Johnston, J. M., & Pennypacker, H. S. (1980). *Strategies and tactics for Human Behavioral Research.* Hillsdale, NJ: Erlbaum.

Johnston, J. M., & Pennypacker, H. S. (1993a). *Strategies and tactics for human behavioral research* (2nd ed.). Hillsdale, NJ: Erlbaum.

Johnston, J. M., & Pennypacker, H. S. (1993b). *Readings for Strategies and tactics of behavioral research* (2nd ed.). Hillsdale, NJ: Erlbaum.

Johnston, M. K., Kelly, C. S., Harris, F. R., & Wolf, M. M. (1966). An application of reinforcement principles to the development of motor skills of a young child. *Child Development, 37,* 370–387.

Johnston, R. J., & McLaughlin, T. F. (1982). The effects of free time on assignment completion and accuracy in arithmetic: A case study. *Education and Treatment of Children, 5,* 33–40.

Jones, F. H., & Miller, W. H. (1974). The effective use of negative attention for reducing group disruption in special elementary school classrooms. *Psychological Record, 24,* 435–448.

Jones, F. H., Fremouw, W., & Carples, S. (1977). Pyramid training of elementary school teachers to use a classroom management "skill package." *Journal of Applied Behavior Analysis, 10,* 239–254.

Jones, R. R., Vaught, R. S., & Weinrott, M. (1977). Time-series analysis in operant research. *Journal of Applied Behavior Analysis, 10,* 151–166.

Journal of Applied Behavior Analysis. (2000). Manuscript preparation checklist. *Journal of Applied Behavior Analysis, 33,* 399. Lawrence, KS: Society for the Experimental Analysis of Behavior.

Kachanoff, R., Leveille, R., McLelland, H., & Wayner, M. J. (1973). Schedule induced behavior in humans. *Physiology and Behavior, 11,* 395–398.

Kadushin, A. (1972). *The social work interview.* New York: Columbia University Press.

Kahng, S. W., & Iwata, B. A. (1998). Computerized systems for collecting real-time observational data. *Journal of Applied Behavior Analysis, 31,* 253–261.

Kahng, S. W., & Iwata, B. A. (2000). Computer systems for collecting real-time observational data. In T. Thompson, D. Felce, & F. J. Symons (Eds.), *Behavioral observation: Technology and applications in developmental disabilities* (pp. 35–45). Baltimore: Paul H. Brookes.

Kahng, S. W., Iwata, B. A., DeLeon, I. G., & Wallace, M. D. (2000). A comparison of procedures for programming noncontingent reinforcement schedules. *Journal of Applied Behavior Analysis, 33,* 223–231.

Kahng, S. W., Iwata, B. A., Fischer, S. M., Page, T. J., Treadwell, K. R. H., Williams, D. E., & Smith, R. G. (1998). Temporal distributions of problems behavior based on scatter plot analysis. *Journal of Applied Behavior Analysis, 31,* 593–604.

Kahng, S. W., Iwata, B. A., Thompson, R. H., & Hanley, G. P. (2000). A method for identifying satiation versus extinction effects under noncontingent reinforcement schedules. *Journal of Applied Behavior Analysis, 33,* 419–432.

Kahng, S. W., Tarbox, J., & Wilke, A. (2001). Use of multicomponent treatment for food refusal. *Journal of Applied Behavior Analysis, 34,* 93–96.

Kahng, S., & Iwata, B. A. (1999). Correspondence between outcomes of brief and extended functional analyses. *Journal of Applied Behavior Analysis, 32,* 149–159.

Kahng, S., Iwata, B. A., Fischer, S. M., Page, T. J., Treadwell, K. R. H., Williams, D. E., & Smith, R. G. (1998). Temporal distributions of problem behavior based on scatter plot analysis. *Journal of Applied Behavior Analysis, 31,* 593–604.

Kahng, S., Iwata, B. A., & Lewin, A. B. (2002). Behavioral treatment of self-injury, 1964 to 2000. *American Journal of Mental Retardation, 107* (3), 212–221.

Kame'enui, E. (2002, September). *Beginning reading failure and the quantification of risk: Behavior as the supreme index.* Presentation to the Focus on Behavior Analysis in Education Conference, Columbus, OH.

Kanfer, F. H. (1976). *The many faces of self-control, or behavior modification changes its focus.* Paper presented at the Fifth International Banff Conference, Banff, Alberta, Canada.

Kanfer, F. H., & Karoly P. (1972). Self-control: A behavioristic excursion into the lion's den. *Behavior Therapy, 3,* 398–416.

Kantor, J. R. (1959). *Interbehavioral psychology.* Granville, OH: Principia Press.

Katzenberg, A. C. (1975). *How to draw graphs.* Kalamazoo, MI: Behaviordelia.

Kauffman, J. M. (2005). *Characteristics of emotional and behavioral disorders of children and youth* (8th ed.). Upper Saddle River, NJ: Merrill/Prentice Hall.

Kaufman, K. F., & O'Leary, K. D. (1972). Reward, cost, and self-evaluation procedures for disruptive adolescents in a psychiatric hospital school. *Journal of Applied Behavior Analysis, 5,* 293–309.

Kazdin, A. E. (1973). The effects of vicarious reinforcement on attentive behavior in the classroom. *Journal of Applied Behavior Analysis, 6,* 77–78.

Kazdin, A. E. (1977). Artifact, bias, and complexity of assessment: The ABCs of reliability. *Journal of Applied Behavior Analysis, 10,* 141–150.

Kazdin, A. E. (1978). *History of behavior modification.* Austin: TX: Pro-Ed.

Kazdin, A. E. (1979). Unobtrusive measures in behavioral assessment. *Journal of Applied Behavior Analysis, 12,* 713–724.

Kazdin, A. E. (1980). Acceptability of alternative treatments for deviant child behavior. *Journal of Applied Behavior Analysis, 13,* 259–273.

Kazdin, A. E. (1982). *Single case research designs: Methods for clinical and applied settings.* Boston: Allyn and Bacon.

Kazdin, A. E. (1982). Observer effects: Reactivity of direct observation. *New Directions for Methodology of Social and Behavioral Science, 14,* 5–19.

Kazdin, A. E. (2001). *Behavior modification in applied settings* (6th ed.). Belmont, CA: Wadsworth.

Kazdin, A. E., & Hartmann, D. P. (1978). The simultaneous-treatment design. *Behavior Therapy, 9,* 912–922.

Kee, M., Hill, S. M., & Weist, M. D. (1999). School-based behavior management of cursing, hitting, and spitting in a girl with profound retardation. *Education and Treatment of Children, 22* (2), 171–178.

Kehle, T. J., Bray, M. A., Theodore, L. A., Jenson, W. R., & Clark, E. (2000). A multi-component intervention designed to reduce disruptive classroom behavior. *Psychology in the Schools, 37* (5), 475–481.

Keller, C. L., Brady, M. P., & Taylor, R. L. (2005). Using self-evaluation to improve student teacher interns' use of specific praise. *Education and Training in Mental Retardation and Developmental Disabilities, 40,* 368–376.

Keller, F. S. (1941). Light aversion in the white rat. *Psychological Record, 4,* 235–250.

Keller, F. S. (1982). *Pedagogue's progress.* Lawrence, KS: TRI Publications.

Keller, F. S. (1990). Burrhus Frederic Skinner (1904–1990) (a thank you). *Journal of Applied Behavior Analysis, 23,* 404–407.

Keller, F. S., & Schoenfeld, W. M. (1950/1995). *Principles of psychology.* Acton, MA: Copley Publishing Group.

Keller, F. S., & Schoenfeld, W. N. (1995). *Principles of psychology.* Acton, MA: Copley Publishing Group. (Reprinted from *Principles of psychology: A systematic text in the science of behavior.* New York: Appleton-Century-Crofts, 1950)

Kelley, M. E., Piazza, C. C., Fisher, W. W., & Oberdorff, A. J. (2003). Acquisition of cup drinking using previously refused foods as positive and negative reinforcement. *Journal of Applied Behavior Analysis, 36,* 89–93.

Kelley, M. L., Jarvie, G. J., Middlebrook, J. L., McNeer, M. F., & Drabman, R. S. (1984). Decreasing burned children's pain behavior: Impacting the trauma of hydrotherapy. *Journal of Applied Behavior Analysis, 17,* 147–158.

Kellum, K. K., Carr, J. E., & Dozier, C. L. (2001). Response-card instruction and student learning in a college classroom. *Teaching of Psychology, 28* (2), 101–104.

Kelshaw-Levering, K., Sterling-Turner, H., Henry, J. R., & Skinner, C. H. (2000). Randomized interdependent group contingencies: Group reinforcement with a twist. *Psychology in the Schools, 37* (6), 523–533.

Kennedy, C. H. (1994). Automatic reinforcement: Oxymoron or hypothetical construct. *Journal of Behavioral Education, 4* (4), 387–395.

Kennedy, C. H. (2005). *Single-case designs for educational research.* Boston: Allyn and Bacon.

Kennedy, C. H., & Haring, T. G. (1993). Teaching choice making during social interactions to students with profound multiple disabilities. *Journal of Applied Behavior Analysis, 26,* 63–76.

Kennedy, C. H., & Sousa, G. (1995). Functional analysis and treatment of eye poking. *Journal of Applied Behavior Analysis, 28,* 27–37.

Kennedy, C. H., Meyer, K. A., Knowles, T., & Shukla, S. (2000). Analyzing the multiple functions of stereotypical behavior for students with autism: Implications for assessment and treatment. *Journal of Applied Behavior Analysis, 33,* 559–571.

Kennedy, G. H., Itkonen, T., & Lindquist, K. (1994). Nodality effects during equivalence class formation: An extension to sight-word reading and concept development. *Journal of Applied Behavior Analysis, 27,* 673–683.

Kern, L., Dunlap, G., Clarke, S., & Childs, K. E. (1995). Student-assisted functional assessment interview. *Diagnostique, 19,* 29–39.

Kern, L., Koegel, R., & Dunlap, G. (1984). The influence of vigorous versus mild exercise on autistic stereotyped behaviors. *Journal of Autism and Developmental Disorders, 14,* 57–67.

Kerr, M. M., & Nelson, C. M. (2002). *Strategies for addressing behavior problems in the classroom* (4th ed.). Upper Saddle River, NJ: Merrill/Prentice Hall.

Killu, K., Sainato, D. M., Davis, C. A., Ospelt, H., & Paul, J. N. (1998). Effects of high-probability request sequences on preschoolers' compliance and disruptive behavior. *Journal of Behavioral Education, 8,* 347–368.

Kimball, J. W. (2002). Behavior-analytic instruction for children with autism: Philosophy matters. *Focus on Autism and Other Developmental Disabilities, 17* (2), 66–75.

Kimball, J. W., & Heward, W. L. (1993). A synthesis of contemplation, prediction, and control. *American Psychologist, 48,* 587–588.

Kirby, K. C., & Bickel, W. K. (1988). Toward an explicit analysis of generalization: A stimulus control interpretation. *The Behavior Analyst, 11,* 115–129.

Kirby, K. C., Fowler, S. A., & Baer, D. M. (1991). Reactivity in self-recording: Obtrusiveness of recording procedure and peer comments. *Journal of Applied Behavior Analysis, 24,* 487–498.

Kladopoulos, C. N., & McComas, J. J. (2001). The effects of form training on foul-shooting performance in members of a women's college basketball team. *Journal of Applied Behavior Analysis, 34,* 329–332.

Klatt, K. P., Sherman, J. A., & Sheldon, J. B. (2000). Effects of deprivation on engagement in preferred activities by persons with developmental disabilities. *Journal of Applied Behavior Analysis, 33,* 495–506.

Kneedler, R. D., & Hallahan, D. P. (1981). Self-monitoring of on-task behavior with learning disabled children: Current studies and directions. *Exceptional Education Quarterly, 2* (3), 73–82.

Knittel, D. (2002). Case study: A professional guitarist on comeback road. In R. W. Malott & H. Harrison (Eds.), *I'll stop procrastinating when I get around to it: Plus other cool ways to succeed in school and life using behavior analysis to get your act together* (pp. 8-5–8-6). Kalamazoo, MI: Department of Psychology, Western Michigan University.

Kodak, T., Grow, L., & Northrup, J. (2004). Functional analysis and treatment of elopement for a child with attention deficit hyperactivity disorder. *Journal of Applied Behavior Analysis, 37,* 229–232.

Kodak, T., Miltenberger, R. G., & Romaniuk, C. (2003). The effects of differential negative reinforcement of other behavior and noncontingent escape on compliance. *Journal of Applied Behavior Analysis, 36,* 379–382.

Koegal, R. L., & Rincover, A. (1977). Research on the differences between generalization and maintenance in extra-therapy responding. *Journal of Applied Behavior Analysis, 10,* 1–12.

Koegel, L. K., Carter, C. M., & Koegel, R. L. (2003). Teaching children with autism self-initiations as a pivotal response. *Topics in Language Disorders, 23* (2), 134–145.

Koegel, L. K., Koegel, R. L., Hurley, C., & Frea, W. D. (1992). Improving social skills and disruptive behavior in children with autism through self-management. *Journal of Applied Behavior Analysis, 25,* 341–353.

Koegel, R. L., & Frea, W. (1993). Treatment of social behavior in autism through the modification of pivotal social skills. *Journal of Applied Behavior Analysis, 26,* 369–377.

Koegel, R. L., & Koegel, L. K. (1988). Generalized responsivity and pivotal behaviors. In R. H. Horner, G. Dunlap, &

R. L. Koegel (Eds.), *Generalization and maintenance: Life-style changes in applied settings* (pp. 41–66). Baltimore; Paul H. Brookes.

Koegel, R. L., & Koegel, L. K. (1990). Extended reductions in stereoptypic behavior of students with autism through a self-management treatment package. *Journal of Applied Behavior Analysis, 23,* 119–127.

Koegel, R. L., & Williams, J. A. (1980). Direct versus indirect response-reinforcer relationships in teaching autistic children. *Journal of Abnormal Child Psychology, 8,* 537–547.

Koegel, R. L., Koegel, L. K., & Schreibman, L. (1991). Assessing and training parents in teaching pivotal behaviors. In R. J. Prinz (Ed.), *Advances in behavioral assessment of children and families* (Vol. 5, pp. 65–82). London: Jessica Kingsley.

Koehler, L. J., Iwata, B. A., Roscoe, E. M., Rolider, N. U., & O'Steen, L. E. (2005). Effects of stimulus variation on the reinforcing capability of nonpreferred stimuli. *Journal of Applied Behavior Analysis, 38,* 469–484.

Koenig, C. H., & Kunzelmann, H. P. (1980). *Classroom learning screening.* Columbus, OH: Charles E. Merrill.

Kohler, F. W., & Greenwood, C. R. (1986). Toward a technology of generalization: The identification of natural contingencies of reinforcement. *The Behavior Analyst, 9,* 19–26.

Kohler, F. W., Strain, P. S., Maretsky, S., & Decesare, L. (1990). Promoting positive and supportive interactions between preschoolers: An analysis of group-oriented contingencies. *Journal of Early Intervention, 14* (4), 327–341.

Kohn, A. (1997). Students don't "work"—they learn. *Education Week,* September 3, 1997. Retrieved January 1, 2004, from www.alfiekohn.org/teaching/edweek/sdwtl.htm.

Komaki, J. L. (1998). When performance improvement is the goal: A new set of criteria for criteria. *Journal of Applied Behavior Analysis, 31,* 263–280.

Konarski, E. A., Jr., Crowell, C. R., & Duggan, L. M. (1985). The use of response deprivation to increase the academic performance of EMR students. *Applied Research in Mental Retardation, 6,* 15–31.

Konarski, E. A., Jr., Crowell, C. R., Johnson, M. R., & Whitman T. L. (1982). Response deprivation, reinforcement, and instrumental academic performance in an EMR classroom. *Behavior Therapy, 13,* 94–102.

Konarski, E. A., Jr., Johnson, M. R., Crowell, C. R., & Whitman T. L. (1980). Response deprivation and reinforcement in applied settings: A preliminary report. *Journal of Applied Behavior Analysis, 13,* 595–609.

Koocher, G. P., & Keith-Spiegel, P. (1998). *Ethics in psychology: Professional standards and cases.* New York, Oxford: Oxford University Press.

Kosiewicz, M. M., Hallahan, D. P., Lloyd, J. W., & Graves, A. W. (1982). Effects of self-instruction and self-correction procedures on handwriting performance. *Learning Disability Quarterly, 5* (1), 71–78.

Kostewicz, D. E., Kubina, R. M., Jr., & Cooper, J. O. (2000). Managing aggressive thoughts and feelings with daily counts of non-aggressive thoughts and feelings: A self-experiment. *Journal of Behavior Therapy and Experimental Psychiatry, 31,* 177–187.

Kounin, J. (1970). *Discipline and group management in classrooms.* New York: Holt, Rinehart & Winston.

Kozloff, M. A. (2005). Fads in general education: Fad, fraud, and folly. In J. W. Jacobson, R. M. Foxx, & J. A. Mulick (Eds.), *Controversial therapies in developmental disabilities: Fads, fashion, and science in professional practice* (pp. 159–174). Hillsdale, NJ: Erlbaum.

Krantz, P. J., & McClannahan, L. E. (1993). Teaching children with autism to initiate to peers: Effects of a script-fading procedure. *Journal of Applied Behavior Analysis, 26,* 121–132.

Krantz, P. J., & McClannahan, L. E. (1998). Social interaction skills for children with autism: A script-fading procedure for beginning readers. *Journal of Applied Behavior Analysis, 31,* 191–202.

Krasner, L. A., & Ullmann, L. P. (Eds.). (1965). *Research in behavior modification: New developments and implications.* New York: Holt, Rinehart & Winston.

Kubina, R. M., Jr. (2005). The relations among fluency, rate building, and practice: A response to Doughty, Chase, and O'Shields (2004). *The Behavior Analyst, 28,* 73–76.

Kubina, R. M., & Cooper, J. O. (2001). Changing learning channels: An efficient strategy to facilitate instruction and learning. *Intervention in School and Clinic, 35,* 161–166.

Kubina, R. M., Haertel, M. W., & Cooper, J. O. (1994). Reducing negative inner behavior of senior citizens: The one-minute counting procedure. *Journal of Precision Teaching, 11* (2), 28–35.

Kuhn, S. A. C., Lerman, D. C., & Vorndran, C. M. (2003). Pyramidal training for families of children with problem behavior. *Journal of Applied Behavior Analysis, 36,* 77–88.

La Greca, A. M., & Schuman, W. B. (1995). Adherence to prescribed medical regimens. In M. C. Roberts (Ed.), *Handbook of pediatric psychology* (2nd ed., pp. 55–83). New York: Guildford.

LaBlanc, L. A., Coates, A. M., Daneshvar, S. Charlop-Christy, Morris, C., & Lancaster, B. M. (2003). *Journal of Applied Behavior Analysis, 36,* 253–257.

Lalli, J. S., Browder, D. M., Mace, F. C., & Brown, D. K. (1993). Teacher use of descriptive analysis data to implement interventions to decrease students' problem behaviors. *Journal of Applied Behavior Analysis, 26,* 227–238.

Lalli, J. S., Casey, S., & Kates, K. (1995). Reducing escape behavior and increasing task completion with functional communication training, extinction, and response chaining. *Journal of Applied Behavior Analysis, 28,* 261–268.

Lalli, J. S., Livezey, K., & Kates, D. (1996). Functional analysis and treatment of eye poking with response blocking. *Journal of Applied Behavior Analysis, 29,* 129–132.

Lalli, J. S., Mace, F. C., Livezey, K., & Kates, K. (1998). Assessment of stimulus generalization gradients in the treatment of self-injurious behavior. *Journal of Applied Behavior Analysis, 31,* 479–483.

Lalli, J. S., Zanolli, K., & Wohn, T. (1994). Using extinction to promote response variability. *Journal of Applied Behavior Analysis, 27,* 735–736.

Lambert, M. C., Cartledge, G., Lo, Y., & Heward, W. L. (2006). Effects of response cards on disruptive behavior and participation by fourth-grade students during math lessons in an urban school. *Journal of Positive Behavioral Interventions, 8,* 88–99.

Lambert, N., Nihira, K., & Leland, H. (1993). *Adaptive Behavior Scale—School* (2nd ed.). Austin, TX: Pro-Ed.

Landry, L., & McGreevy, P. (1984). The paper clip counter (PCC): An inexpensive and reliable device for collecting behavior frequencies. *Journal of Precision Teaching, 5,* 11–13.

Lane, S. D., & Critchfield, T. S. (1998). Classification of vowels and consonants by individuals with moderate mental retardation: Development of arbitrary relations via match-to-sample training with compound stimuli. *Journal of Applied Behavior Analysis, 31,* 21–41.

Laraway, S., Snycerski, S., Michael, J., & Poling, A. (2001). The abative effect: A new term to describe the action of antecedents that reduce operant responding. *The Analysis of Verbal Behavior, 18,* 101–104.

Larowe, L. N., Tucker, R. D., & McGuire, J. M. (1980). Lunchroom noise control using feedback and group reinforcement. *Journal of School Psychology, 18,* 51–57.

Lasiter, P. S. (1979). Influence of contingent responding on schedule-induced activity in human subjects. *Physiology and Behavior, 22,* 239–243.

Lassman, K. A., Jolivette, K., & Wehby, J. H. (1999). "My teacher said I did good work today!": Using collaborative behavioral contracting. *Teaching Exceptional Children, 31* (4), 12–18.

Lattal, K. A. (1969). Contingency management of toothbrushing behavior in a summer camp for children. *Journal of Applied Behavior Analysis, 2,* 195–198.

Lattal, K. A. (1995). Contingency and behavior analysis. *The Behavior Analyst, 18,* 209–224.

Lattal, K. A. (Ed.). (1992). Special issue: Reflections on B. F. Skinner and psychology. *American Psychologist, 47,* 1269–1533.

Lattal, K. A., & Griffin, M. A. (1972). Punishment contrast during free operant responding. *Journal of the Experimental Analysis of Behavior, 18,* 509–516.

Lattal, K. A., & Lattal, A. D. (2006). And yet . . .: Further comments on distinguishing positive and negative reinforcement. *The Behavior Analyst, 29,* 129–134.

Lattal, K. A., & Neef, N. A. (1996). Recent reinforcement-schedule research and applied behavior analysis. *Journal of Applied Behavior Analysis, 29,* 213–220.

Lattal, K. A., & Shahan, T. A. (1997). Differing views of contingencies: How contiguous. *The Behavior Analyst, 20,* 149–154.

LaVigna, G. W., & Donnellen, A. M. (1986). *Alternatives to punishment: Solving behavior problems with nonaversive strategies.* New York: Irvington.

Layng, T. V. J., & Andronis, P. T. (1984). Toward a functional analysis of delusional speech and hallucinatory behavior. *The Behavior Analyst, 7,* 139–156.

Lee, C., & Tindal, G. A. (1994). Self-recording and goal-setting: Task and math productivity of low-achieving Korean elementary school students. *Journal of Behavioral Education, 4,* 459–479.

Lee, R., McComas, J. J., & Jawor, J. (2002). The effects of differential and lag reinforcement schedules on varied verbal responding by individuals with autism. *Journal of Applied Behavior Analysis, 35,* 391–402.

Lee, V. L. (1988). *Beyond behaviorism.* Hillsdale, NJ: Erlbaum.

Leitenberg, H. (1973). The use of single-case methodology in psychotherapy research. *Journal of Abnormal Psychology, 82,* 87–101.

Lenz, M., Singh, N., & Hewett, A. (1991). Overcorrection as an academic remediation procedure. *Behavior Modification, 15,* 64–73.

Lerman, D. C. (2003). From the laboratory to community application: Translational research in behavior analysis. *Journal of Applied Behavior Analysis, 36,* 415–419.

Lerman, D. C., & Iwata, B. A. (1993). Descriptive and experimental analysis of variables maintaining self-injurious behavior. *Journal of Applied Behavior Analysis, 26,* 293–319.

Lerman, D. C., & Iwata, B. A. (1995). Prevalence of the extinction burst and its attenuation during treatment. *Journal of Applied Behavior Analysis, 28,* 93–94.

Lerman, D. C., & Iwata, B. A. (1996a). Developing a technology for the use of operant extinction in clinical settings: An examination of basic and applied research. *Journal of Applied Behavior Analysis, 29,* 345–382.

Lerman, D. C., & Iwata, B. A. (1996b). A methodology for distinguishing between extinction and punishment effects associated with response blocking. *Journal of Applied Behavior Analysis, 29,* 231–234.

Lerman, D. C., & Vorndran, C. M. (2002). On the status of knowledge for using punishment: Implications for treating behavior disorders. *Journal of Applied Behavior Analysis, 35,* 431–464.

Lerman, D. C., Iwata, B. A., & Wallace, M. D. (1999). Side effects of extinction: Prevalence of bursting and aggression during the treatment of self-injurious behavior. *Journal of Applied Behavior Analysis, 32,* 1–8.

Lerman, D. C., Iwata, B. A., Shore, B. A., & DeLeon, I. G. (1997). Effects of intermittent punishment on self-injurious behavior: An evaluation of schedule thinning. *Journal of Applied Behavior Analysis, 30,* 187–201.

Lerman, D. C., Iwata, B. A., Shore, B. A., & Kahng, S. W. (1996). Responding maintained by intermittent reinforcement: Implications for the use of extinction with problem behavior in clinical settings. *Journal of Applied Behavior Analysis, 29,* 153–171.

Lerman, D. C., Iwata, B. A., Smith, R. G., Zarcone, J. R., & Vollmer, T. R. (1994). Transfer of behavioral function as a contributing factor in treatment relapse. *Journal of Applied Behavior Analysis, 27,* 357–370.

Lerman, D. C., Iwata, B. A., Zarcone, J. R., & Ringdahl, J. (1994). Assessment of stereotypic and self-injurious behavior as adjunctive responses. *Journal of Applied Behavior Analysis, 27,* 715–728.

Lerman, D. C., Kelley, M. E., Vorndran, C. M., & Van Camp, C. M. (2003). Collateral effects of response blocking during the treatment of stereotypic behavior. *Journal of Applied Behavior Analysis, 36,* 119–123.

Lerman, D. C., Kelley, M. E., Vorndran, C. M., Kuhn, S. A. C., & LaRue, Jr., R. H. (2002). Reinforcement magnitude and responding during treatment with differential reinforcement. *Journal of Applied Behavior Analysis, 35,* 29–48.

Levondoski, L. S., & Cartledge, G. (2000). Self-monitoring for elementary school children with serious emotional disturbances: Classroom applications for increased academic responding. *Behavioral Disorders, 25,* 211–224.

Lewis, T. J., Powers, L. J., Kelk, M. J., & Newcomer, L. L. (2002). Reducing problem behaviors on the playground: An intervention of the application of school-wide positive behavior supports. *Psychology in the Schools, 39* (2), 181–190.

Lewis, T., Scott, T. & Sugai, G. (1994). The problem behavior questionnaire: A teacher-based instrument to develop functional hypotheses of problem behavior in general education classrooms. *Diagnostique, 19,* 103–115.

Lindberg, J. S., Iwata, B. A., Kahng, S. W., & DeLeon, I. G. (1999). DRO contingencies: Analysis of variable-momentary schedules. *Journal of Applied Behavior Analysis, 32,* 123–136.

Lindberg, J. S., Iwata, B. A., Roscoe, E. M., Worsdell, A. S., & Hanley, G. P. (2003). Treatment efficacy of noncontingent reinforcement during brief and extended application. *Journal of Applied Behavior Analysis, 36,* 1–19.

Lindsley, O. R. (1956). Operant conditioning methods applied to research in chronic schizophrenia. *Psychiatric Research Reports, 5,* 118–139.

Lindsley, O. R. (1960). Characteristics of the behavior of chronic psychotics as revealed by free-operant conditioning methods. *Diseases of the Nervous System (Monograph Supplement), 21,* 66–78.

Lindsley, O. R. (1968). A reliable wrist counter for recording behavior rates. *Journal of Applied Behavior Analysis, 1,* 77–78.

Lindsley, O. R. (1971). An interview. *Teaching Exceptional Children, 3,* 114–119.

Lindsley, O. R. (1985). *Quantified trends in the results of behavior analysis.* Presidential address at the Eleventh Annual Convention of the Association for Behavior Analysis, Columbus, OH.

Lindsley, O. R. (1990). Precision teaching: By teachers for children. *Teaching Exceptional Children, 22,* 10–15.

Lindsley, O. R. (1992). Precision teaching: Discoveries and effects. *Journal of Applied Behavior Analysis, 25,* 51–57.

Lindsley, O. R. (1996). The four free-operant freedoms. *The Behavior Analyst, 19,* 199–210.

Linehan, M. (1977). Issues in behavioral interviewing. In J. D. Cone & R. P. Hawkins (Eds.), *Behavioral assessment: New directions in clinical psychology* (pp. 30–51). New York: Bruner/Mazel.

Linscheid, T. R, Iwata, B. A., Ricketts, R. W., Williams, D. E., & Griffin, J. C. (1990). Clinical evaluation of the self-injurious behavior inhibiting system (SIBIS). *Journal of Applied Behavior Analysis, 23,* 53–78.

Linscheid, T. R., & Meinhold, P. (1990). The controversy over aversives: Basic operant research and the side effects of punishment. In A. C. Repp & N. N. Singh (Eds.), *Perspectives on the use of non-aversive and aversive interventions for persons with developmental disabilities* (pp. 59–72). Sycamore, IL: Sycamore.

Linscheid, T. R., & Reichenbach, H. (2002). Multiple factors in the long-term effectiveness of contingent electric shock treatment for self-injurious behavior: A case example. *Research in Developmental Disabilities, 23,* 161–177.

Linscheid, T. R., Iwata, B. A., Ricketts, R. W., Williams, D. E., & Griffin, J. C. (1990). Clinical evaluation of SIBIS: The self-injurious behavior inhibiting system. *Journal of Applied Behavior Analysis, 23,* 53–78.

Linscheid, T. R., Pejeau C., Cohen S., & Footo-Lenz, M. (1994). Positive side effects in the treatment of SIB using the Self-Injurious Behavior Inhibiting System (SIBIS): Implications for operant and biochemical explanations of SIB. *Research in Developmental Disabilities, 15,* 81–90.

Lipinski, D. P., Black, J. L., Nelson, R. O., & Ciminero, A. R. (1975). Influence of motivational variables on the reactivity and reliability of self-recording. *Journal of Consulting and Clinical Psychology, 43,* 637–646.

Litow, L., & Pumroy, D. K. (1975). A brief review of classroom group-oriented contingencies. *Journal of Applied Behavior Analysis, 3,* 341–347.

Lloyd, J. W., Bateman, D. F., Landrum, T. J., & Hallahan, D. P. (1989). Self-recording of attention versus productivity. *Journal of Applied Behavior Analysis. 22,* 315–323.

Lloyd, J. W., Eberhardt, M. J., Drake, G. P., Jr. (1996). Group versus individual reinforcement contingencies with the context of group study conditions. *Journal of Applied Behavior Analysis, 29,* 189–200.

Lo, Y. (2003). *Functional assessment and individualized intervention plans: Increasing the behavior adjustment of urban learners in general and special education settings.* Unpublished doctoral dissertation. Columbus, OH: The Ohio State University.

Logan, K. R., & Gast, D. L. (2001). Conducting preference assessments and reinforcer testing for individuals with profound multiple disabilities: Issues and procedures. *Exceptionality, 9* (3), 123–134.

Logan, K. R., Jacobs, H. A., Gast, D. L., Smith, P. D., Daniel, J., & Rawls, J.

(2001). Preferences and reinforcers for students with profound multiple disabilities: Can we identify them? *Journal of Developmental and Physical Disabilities, 13,* 97–122.

Long, E. S., Miltenberger, R. G., Ellingson, S. A., & Ott, S. M. (1999). Augmenting simplified habit reversal in the treatment of oral-digital habits exhibited by individuals with mental retardation. *Journal of Applied Behavior Analysis, 32,* 353–365.

Lovaas, O. I. (1977). *The autistic child: Language development through behavior modification.* New York: Irvington.

Lovitt, T. C. (1973). Self-management projects with children with behavioral disabilities. *Journal of Learning Disabilities, 6,* 138–150.

Lovitt, T. C., & Curtiss, K. A. (1969). Academic response rates as a function of teacher- and self-imposed contingencies. *Journal of Applied Behavior Analysis, 2,* 49–53.

Lowenkron, B. (2004). Meaning: A verbal behavior account. *The Analysis of Verbal Behavior, 20,* 77–97.

Luce, S. C., & Hall, R. V. (1981). Contingent exercise: A procedure used with differential reinforcement to reduce bizarre verbal behavior. *Education and Treatment of Children, 4,* 309–327.

Luce, S. C., Delquadri, J., & Hall, R. V. (1980). Contingent exercise: A mild but powerful procedure for suppressing inappropriate verbal and aggressive behavior. *Journal of Applied Behavior Analysis, 13,* 583–594.

Luciano, C. (1986). Acquisition, maintenance, and generalization of productive intraverbal behavior through transfer of stimulus control procedures. *Applied Research in Mental Retardation, 7,* 1–20.

Ludwig, R. L. (2004). *Smiley faces and spinners: Effects of self-monitoring of productivity with an indiscriminable contingency of reinforcement on the on-task behavior and academic productivity by kindergarteners during independent seatwork.* Unpublished master's thesis, The Ohio State University.

Luiselli, J. K. (1984). Controlling disruptive behaviors of an autistic child: Parent-mediated contingency management in the home setting. *Education and Treatment of Children, 3,* 195–203.

Lynch, D. C., & Cuvo, A. J. (1995). Stimulus equivalence instruction of fraction-decimal realations. *Journal of Applied Behavior Analysis, 28,* 115–126.

Lyon, C. S., & Lagarde, R. (1997). Tokens for success: Using the graduated reinforcement system. *Teaching Exceptional Children, 29* (6), 52–57.

Maag, J. W., Reid, R., & DiGangi, S. A. (1993). Differential effects of self-monitoring attention, accuracy, and productivity. *Journal of Applied Behavior Analysis, 26,* 329–344.

Mabry, J. H., (1994). Review of R. A. Harris' *Linguistic wars. The Analysis of Verbal Behavior, 12,* 79–86.

Mabry, J. H., (1995). Review of Pinker's *The language instinct. The Analysis of Verbal Behavior, 12,* 87–96.

MacCorquodale, K. (1970). On Chomsky's review of Skinner's *Verbal behavior. Journal of the Experimental Analysis of Behavior, 13,* 83–99.

MacCorquodale, K., & Meehl, P. (1948). On a distinction between hypothetical constructs and intervening variables. *Psychological Record, 55,* 95–107.

MacDuff, G.S. Krantz, P. J., & McClannahan, L. E. (1993). Teaching children with autism to use photographic activity schedules: Maintenance and generalization of complex response chains. *Journal of Applied Behavior Analysis, 26,* 89–97.

Mace, F. C. (1996). In pursuit of general behavioral relations. *Journal of Applied Behavior Analysis, 29,* 557–563.

Mace, F. C., & Belfiore, P. (1990). Behavioral momentum in the treatment of escape-motivated stereotypy. *Journal of Applied Behavior Analysis, 23,* 507–514.

Mace, F. C., Hock, M. L., Lalli, J. S., West, B. J., Belfiore, P., Pinter, E., & Brown, D. K. (1988). Behavioral momentum in the treatment of noncompliance. *Journal of Applied Behavior Analysis, 21,* 123–141.

Mace, F. C., Page, T. J., Ivancic, M. T., & O'Brien, S. (1986). Effectiveness of brief time-out with and without contingency delay: A comparative analysis. *Journal of Applied Behavior Analysis, 19,* 79–86.

MacNeil, J., & Thomas, M. R. (1976). Treatment of obsessive-compulsive hairpulling (trichotillomania) by behavioral and cognitive contingency manipulation. *Journal of Behavior Therapy and Experimental Psychiatry, 7,* 391–392.

Madden, G. J., Chase, P. N., & Joyce, J. H. (1998). Making sense of sensitivity in

the human operant literature. *The Behavior Analyst, 21,* 1–12.

Madsen, C. H., Becker, W. C., Thomas, D. R., Koser, L., & Plager, E. (1970). An analysis of the reinforcing function of "sit down" commands. In R. K. Parker (Ed.), *Readings in educational psychology* (pp. 71–82). Boston: Allyn & Bacon.

Maglieri, K. A., DeLeon, I. G., Rodriguez-Catter, V., & Sevin, B. M. (2000). Treatment of covert food stealing in an individual with Prader-Willi Syndrome. *Journal of Applied Behavior Analysis, 33,* 615–618.

Maheady, L., Mallete, B., Harper, G. F., & Saca, K. (1991). Heads together: A peer-mediated option for improving the academic achievement of heterogeneous learning groups. *Remedial and Special Education, 12* (2), 25–33.

Mahoney, M. J. (1971). The self-management of covert behavior: A case study. *Behavior Therapy, 2,* 575–578.

Mahoney, M. J. (1976). Terminal terminology. *Journal of Applied Behavior Analysis, 9,* 515–517.

Malesky, B. M. (1974). Behavior recording as treatment. *Behavior Therapy, 5,* 107–111.

Maloney, K. B., & Hopkins, B. L. (1973). The modification of sentence structure and its relationship to subjective judgments of creativity in writing. *Journal of Applied Behavior Analysis, 6,* 425–433.

Malott, R. W. (1981). *Notes from a radical behaviorist.* Kalamazoo, MI: Author.

Malott, R. W. (1984). Rule-governed behavior, self-management, and the developmentally disabled: A theoretical analysis. *Analysis and Intervention in Developmental Disabilities, 6,* 53–68.

Malott, R. W. (1988). Rule-governed behavior and behavioral anthropology. *The Behavior Analyst, 11,* 181–203.

Malott, R. W. (1989). The achievement of evasive goals: Control by rules describing contingencies that are not direct acting. In S. C. Hayes (Ed.), *Rule-governed behavior: Cognition, contingencies, and instructional control* (pp. 269–322). Reno, NV: Context Press.

Malott, R. W. (2005a). Self-management. In M. Hersen & J. Rosqvist, (Eds.), *Encyclopedia of behavior modification and cognitive behavior therapy (Volume I: Adult Clinical Applications)* (pp. 516–521). Newbury Park, CA: Sage.

Malott, R. W. (2005b). Behavioral systems analysis and higher education. In W. L.

Heward, T. E. Heron, N. A. Neef, S. M. Peterson, D. M. Sainato, G. Cartledge, R. Gardner III, L. D. Peterson, S. B. Hersh, & J. C. Dardig (Eds.), *Focus on behavior analysis in education: Achievements, challenges, and opportunities* (pp. 211–236). Upper Saddle River, NJ: Merrill/Prentice Hall.

Malott, R. W., & Garcia, M. E. (1991). The role of private events in rule-governed behavior. In L. J. Hayes & P. Chase (Eds.), *Dialogues on verbal behavior* (pp. 237–254). Reno, NV: Context Press.

Malott, R. W., & Harrison, H. (2002). *I'll stop procrastinating when I get around to it: Plus other cool ways to succeed in school and life using behavior analysis to get your act together.* Kalamazoo, MI: Department of Psychology, Western Michigan University.

Malott, R. W., & Suarez, E. A. (2004). *Elementary principles of behavior* (5th ed.). Upper Saddle River, NJ: Prentice Hall.

Malott, R. W., & Trojan Suarez, E. A. (2004). *Elementary principles of behavior* (5th ed.). Upper Saddle River, NJ: Prentice Hall.

Malott, R. W., General, D. A., & Snapper, V. B. (1973). *Issues in the analysis of behavior.* Kalamazoo, MI: Behaviordelia.

Malott, R. W., Tillema, M., & Glenn, S. (1978). *Behavior analysis and behavior modification: An introduction.* Kalamazoo, MI: Behaviordelia.

Mank, D. M., & Horner, R. H. (1987). Self-recruited feedback: A cost-effective procedure for maintaining behavior. *Research in Developmental Disabilities, 8,* 91–112.

March, R., Horner, R. H., Lewis-Palmer, T., Brown, D., Crone, D., Todd, A. W. et al. (2000). *Functional Assessment Checklist for Teachers and Staff (FACTS).* Eugene, OR: University of Oregon, Department of Educational and Community Supports.

Marckel, J. M., Neef, N. A., & Ferreri, S. J. (2006). A preliminary analysis of teaching improvisation with the picture exchange communication system to children with autism. *Journal of Applied Behavior Analysis, 39,* 109–115.

Marcus, B. A., & Vollmer, T. R. (1995). Effects of differential negative reinforcement on disruption and compliance. *Journal of Applied Behavior Analysis, 28,* 229–230.

Marholin, D., II, & Steinman, W. (1977). Stimulus control in the classroom as a function of the behavior reinforced. *Journal of Applied Behavior Analysis, 10,* 465–478.

Marholin, D., Touchette, P. E., & Stuart, R. M. (1979). Withdrawal of chronic chlorpromazine medication: An experimental analysis. *Journal of Applied Behavior Analysis, 12,* 150–171.

Markle, S. M. (1962). *Good frames and bad: A grammar of frame writing* (2nd ed.). New York: Wiley.

Markwardt, F. C. (2005). *Peabody Individual Achievement Test.* Circle Pines, MN: American Guidance Service.

Marmolejo, E. K., Wilder, D. A., & Bradley, L. (2004). A preliminary analysis of the effects of response cards on student performance and participation in an upper division university course. *Journal of Applied Behavior Analysis, 37,* 405–410.

Marr, J. (2003). Empiricism. In K. A. Lattal & P. C. Chase (Eds.), *Behavior theory and philosophy* (pp. 63–82). New York: Kluwer/Plenum.

Marshall, A. E., & Heward, W. L. (1979). Teaching self-management to incarcerated youth. *Behavioral Disorders, 4,* 215–226.

Marshall, K. J., Lloyd, J. W., & Hallahan, D. P. (1993). Effects of training to increase self-monitoring accuracy. *Journal of Behavioral Education, 3,* 445–459.

Martella, R., Leonard, I. J., Marchand-Martella, N. E., & Agran, M. (1993). Self-monitoring negative statements. *Journal of Behavioral Education, 3,* 77–86.

Martens, B. K., Hiralall, A. S., & Bradley, T. A. (1997). A note to teacher: Improving student behavior through goal setting and feedback. *School Psychology Quarterly, 12,* 33–41.

Martens, B. K., Lochner, D. G., & Kelly, S. Q. (1992). The effects of variable-interval reinforcement on academic engagement: A demonstration of matching theory. *Journal of Applied Behavior Analysis, 25,* 143–151.

Martens, B. K., Witt, J. C., Elliott, S. N., & Darveaux, D. (1985). Teacher judgments concerning the acceptability of school-based interventions. *Professional Psychology: Research and Practice, 16,* 191–198.

Martin, G., & Pear, J. (2003). *Behavior modification: What it is and how to do it* (7th ed.). Upper Saddle River, NJ: Prentice Hall.

Martinez-Diaz, J. A. (2003). *Raising the bar.* Presidential address presented at the annual conference of the Florida Association for Behavior Analysis, St. Petersburg.

Mastellone, M. (1974). Aversion therapy: A new use of the old rubberband. *Journal of Behavior Therapy and Experimental Psychiatry, 5,* 311–312.

Matson, J. L., & Taras, M. E., (1989). A 20-year review of punishment and alternative methods to treat problem behaviors in developmentally delayed persons. *Research in Developmental Disabilities, 10,* 85–104.

Mattaini, M. A. (1995). Contingency diagrams as teaching tools. *The Behavior Analyst, 18,* 93–98.

Maurice, C. (1993). *Let me hear your voice: A family's triumph over autism.* New York: Fawcett Columbine.

Maurice, C. (2006). The autism wars. In W. L. Heward (Ed.), *Exceptional children: An introduction to special education* (8th ed., pp. 291–293). Upper Saddle River, NJ: Merrill/Prentice Hall.

Maxwell, J. C. (2003). *There's no such thing as "business" ethics: There's only one rule for decision making.* New York: Warner Business Books: A Time Warner Company.

Mayer, G. R., Sulzer, B., & Cody, J. J. (1968). The use of punishment in modifying student behavior. *Journal of Special Education, 2,* 323–328.

Mayfield, K. H., & Chase, P. N. (2002). The effects of cumulative practice on mathematics problem solving. *Journal of Applied Behavior Analysis, 35,* 105–123.

Mayhew, G., & Harris, F. (1979). Decreasing self-injurious behavior. *Behavior Modification, 3,* 322–326.

Mazaleski, J. L., Iwata, B. A., Rodgers, T. A., Vollmer, T. R., & Zarcone, J. R. (1994). Protective equipments as treatment for stereotypic hand mouthing: Sensory extinction or punishment effects? *Journal of Applied Behavior Analysis, 27,* 345–355.

McAllister, L. W., Stachowiak, J. G., Baer, D. M., & Conderman, L. (1969). The application of operant conditioning techniques in a secondary school classroom. *Journal of Applied Behavior Analysis, 2,* 277–285.

McCain, L. J., & McCleary, R. (1979). The statistical analysis of the simple interrupted time series quasi-experiment. In T. D. Cook & D. T. Campbell (Eds.), *Quasi-experimentation: Design and analysis issues for field settings.* Chicago: Rand McNally.

McClannahan, L. E., & Krantz, P. J. (1999). *Activity schedules for children with autism: Teaching independent behavior.* Bethesda, MD: Woodbine House.

McClannahan, L. E., McGee, G. G., MacDuff, G. S., & Krantz, P. J. (1990). Assessing and improving child care: A person appearance index for children with autism. *Journal of Applied Behavior Analysis, 23,* 469–482.

McConnell, M. E. (1999). Self-monitoring, cueing, recording, and managing: Teaching students to manage their own behavior. *Teaching Exceptional Children, 32* (2), 14–21.

McCord, B. E., Iwata, B. A., Galensky, T. L., Ellingson, S. A., & Thomson, R. J. (2001). Functional analysis and treatment of problems behavior evoked by noise. *Journal of Applied Behavior Analysis, 34,* 447–462.

McCullough, J. P., Cornell, J. E., McDaniel, M. H., & Mueller, R. K. (1974). Utilization of the simultaneous treatment design to improve student behavior in a first-grade classroom. *Journal of Consulting and Clinical Psychology, 42,* 288–292.

McEntee, J. E., & Saunders, R. R. (1997). A response-restriction analysis of stereotypy in adolescents with mental retardation: Implications for applied behavior analysis. *Journal of Applied Behavior Analysis, 30,* 485–506.

McEvoy, M. A., & Brady, M. P. (1988). Contingent access to play materials as an academic motivator for autistic and behavior disordered children. *Education and Treatment of Children, 11,* 5–18.

McFall, R. M. (1977). Parameters of self-monitoring. In R. B. Stuart (Ed.), *Behavioral self-management* (pp. 196–214). New York: Bruner/Mazel.

McGee, G. G., Krantz, P. J., & McClannahan, L. E. (1985). The facilitative effects of incidental teaching on preposition use by autistic children. *Journal of Applied Behavior Analysis, 18,* 17–31.

McGee, G. G., Morrier, M., & Daly, T. (1999). An incidental teaching approach to early intervention for toddlers with autism. *Journal of the Association for Persons with Severe Handicaps, 24,* 133–146.

McGill, P. (1999). Establishing operations: Implications for assessment, treatment, and prevention of problem behavior. *Journal of Applied Behavior Analysis, 32,* 393–418.

McGinnis, E. (1984). Teaching social skills to behaviorally disordered youth. In J. K. Grosenick, S. L. Huntze, E. McGinnis, & C. R. Smith (Eds.), *Social/affective interventions in behaviorally disordered youth* (pp. 87–112). De Moines, IA: Department of Public Instruction.

McGonigle, J. J., Rojahn, J., Dixon, J., & Strain, P. S. (1987). Multiple treatment interference in the alternating treatments design as a function of the intercomponent interval length. *Journal of Applied Behavior Analysis, 20,* 171–178.

McGuffin, M. E., Martz, S. A., & Heron, T. E. (1997). The effects of self-correction versus traditional spelling on the spelling performance and maintenance of third grade students. *Journal of Behavioral Education, 7,* 463–476.

McGuire, M. T., Wing, R. R., Klem, M. L., & Hill, J. O. (1999). Behavioral strategies of individuals who have maintained long-term weight losses. *Obesity Research, 7,* 334–341.

McIlvane, W. J., & Dube, W. V. (1992). Stimulus control shaping and stimulus control topographies. *The Behavior Analyst, 15,* 89–94.

McIlvane, W. J., Dube, W. V., Green, G., & Serna, R. W. (1993). Programming conceptual and communication skill development: A methodological stimulus class analysis. In A. P. Kaiser & D. B. Gray (Eds.), *Enhancing children's communication* (Vol. 2, pp. 243–285). Baltimore: Brookes.

McKerchar, P. M., & Thompson, R. H. (2004). A descriptive analysis of potential reinforcement contingencies in the preschool classroom. *Journal of Applied Behavior Analysis, 21,* 157.

McLaughlin, T., & Malaby, J. (1972). Reducing and measuring inappropriate verbalizations in a token classroom. *Journal of Applied Behavior Analysis, 5,* 329–333.

McNeish, J., Heron, T. E., & Okyere, B. (1992). Effects of self-correction on the spelling performance of junior high students with learning disabilities. *Journal of Behavioral Education, 2,* 17–27.

McPherson, A., Bonem, M., Green, G., & Osborne, J. G. (1984). A citation analysis of the influence on research of Skinner's *Verbal behavior. The Behavior Analyst, 7,* 157–167.

McWilliams, R., Nietupski, J., & Hamre-Nietupski, S. (1990). Teaching complex activities to students with moderate handicaps through the forward chaining of shorter total cycle response sequences. *Education and Training in Mental Retardation, 25* (3), 292–298.

Mechling, L. C., & Gast, D. L. (1997). Combination audio/visual self-prompting system for teaching chained tasks to students with intellectual disabilities. *Education and Training in Mental Retardation and Developmental Disabilities, 32,* 138–153.

Meichenbaum, D., & Goodman, J. (1971). The developmental control of operant motor responding by verbal operants. *Journal of Experimental Child Psychology, 7,* 553–565.

Mercatoris, M., & Craighead, W. E. (1974). Effects of nonparticipant observation on teacher and pupil classroom behavior. *Journal of Educational Psychology, 66,* 512–519.

Meyer, L. H., & Evans, I. M. (1989). *Nonaversive intervention for behavior problems: A manual for home and community.* Baltimore: Paul H. Brookes.

Michael, J. (1974). Statistical inference for individual organism research: Mixed blessing or curse? *Journal of Applied Behavior Analysis, 7,* 647–653.

Michael, J. (1975). Positive and negative reinforcement, a distinction that is no longer necessary; or a better way to talk about bad things. *Behaviorism, 3,* 33–44.

Michael, J. (1980). Flight from behavior analysis. *The Behavior Analyst, 3,* 1–22.

Michael, J. (1982). Distinguishing between discriminative and motivational functions of stimuli. *Journal of the Experimental Analysis of Behavior, 37,* 149–155.

Michael, J. (1982). Skinner's elementary verbal relations: Some new categories. *The Analysis of Verbal Behavior, 1,* 1–4.

Michael, J. (1984). Verbal behavior. *Journal of the Experimental Analysis of Behavior, 42,* 363–376.

Michael, J. (1988). Establishing operations and the mand. *The Analysis of Verbal Behavior, 6,* 3–9.

Michael, J. (1991). *Verbal behavior: Objectives, exams, and exam answers.* Kalamazoo, MI: Western Michigan University.

Michael, J. (1992). *Introduction I.* In *Verbal behavior* by B. F. Skinner (Reprinted edition). Cambridge, MA: B. F. Skinner Foundation.

Michael, J. (1993). *Concepts and principles of behavior analysis.* Kalamazoo, MI: Society for the Advancement of Behavior Analysis.

Michael, J. (1993). Establishing operations. *The Behavior Analyst, 16,* 191–206.

Michael, J. (1995). What every student of behavior analysis ought to learn: A system for classifying the multiple effects of behavioral variables. *The Behavior Analyst, 18,* 273–284.

Michael, J. (2000). Implications and refinements of the establishing operation concept. *Journal of Applied Behavior Analysis, 33,* 401–410.

Michael, J. (2003). *The multiple control of verbal behavior.* Invited tutorial presented at the 29th Annual Convention of the Association for Behavior Analysis, San Francisco, CA.

Michael, J. (2004). *Concepts and principles of behavior analysis* (rev. ed.) Kalamazoo, MI: Society for the Advancement of Behavior Analysis.

Michael, J. (2006). Comment on Baron and Galizio. *The Behavior Analyst, 29,* 117–119.

Michael, J., & Shafer, E. (1995). State notation for teaching about behavioral procedures. *The Behavior Analyst, 18,* 123–140.

Michael, J., & Sundberg, M. L. (2003, May 23). *Skinner's analysis of verbal behavior: Beyond the elementary verbal operants.* Workshop conducted at the 29th Annual Convention of the Association for Behavior Analysis, San Francisco, CA.

Miguel, C. F., Carr, J. E., & Michael, J. (2002). Effects of stimulus-stimulus pairing procedure on the vocal behavior of children diagnosed with autism. *The Analysis of Verbal Behavior, 18,* 3–13.

Millenson, J. R. (1967). *Principles of behavioral analysis.* New York: Macmillan.

Miller, A. D., Hall, S. W., & Heward, W. L. (1995). Effects of sequential 1-minute time trials with and without inter-trial feedback and self-correction on general and special education students' fluency with math facts. *Journal of Behavioral Education, 5,* 319–345.

Miller, D. L., & Kelley, M. L. (1994). The use of goal setting and contingency contracting for improving children's homework performance. *Journal of Applied Behavior Analysis, 27,* 73–84.

Miller, D. L., & Stark, L. J. (1994). Contingency contracting for improving adherence in pediatric populations. *Journal of the American Medical Association, 271* (1), 81–83.

Miller, N., & Dollard, J. (1941). *Social learning and imitation.* New Haven, CT: Yale University Press.

Miller, N., & Neuringer, A. (2000). Reinforcing variability in adolescents with autism. *Journal of Applied Behavior Analysis, 33,* 151–165.

Miltenberger, R. (2004). *Behavior modification: Principles and procedures* (3rd ed.). Belmont, CA: Wadsworth/Thomson Learning.

Miltenberger, R. G. (2001). *Behavior modification: Principles and procedures* (2nd ed.). Belmont, CA: Wadsworth/Thomson Learning.

Miltenberger, R. G., & Fuqua, R. W. (1981). Overcorrection: A review and critical analysis. *The Behavioral Analyst, 4,* 123–141.

Miltenberger, R. G., Flessner, C., Gatheridge, B., Johnson, B., Satterlund, M., & Egemo, K. (2004). Evaluation of behavior skills training to prevent gun play in children. *Journal of Applied Behavior Analysis, 37,* 513–516.

Miltenberger, R. G., Fuqua, R. W., & Woods, D. W. (1998). Applying behavior analysis to clinical problems: Review and analysis of habit reversal. *Journal of Applied Behavior Analysis, 31,* 447–469.

Miltenberger, R. G., Gatheridge, B., Satterlund, M., Egemo-Helm, K. R., Johnson, B. M., Jostad, C., Kelso, P., & Flessner, C. A. (2005). Teaching safety skills to children to prevent gun play: An evaluation of in situ training. *Journal of Applied Behavior Analysis, 38,* 395–398.

Miltenberger, R. G., Rapp, J., & Long, E. (1999). A low-tech method for conducting real time recording. *Journal of Applied Behavior Analysis, 32,* 119–120.

Mineka, S. (1975). Some new perspectives on conditioned hunger. *Journal of Experimental Psychology: Animal Behavior Processes, 104,* 143–148.

Mischel, H. N., Ebbesen, E. B., & Zeiss, A. R. (1972). Cognitive and attentional mechanisms in delay of gratification. *Journal of Personality and Social Psychology, 16,* 204–218.

Mischel, W., & Gilligan, C. (1964). Delay of gratification, motivation for the pro-

hibited gratification, and responses to temptation. *Journal of Abnormal and Social Psychology, 69,* 411–417.

Mitchell, R. J., Schuster, J. W., Collis, B. C., & Gassaway, L. J. (2000). Teaching vocational skills with a faded auditory prompting system. *Education and Training in Mental Retardation and Developmental Disabilities, 35,* 415–427.

Mitchem, K. J., & Young, K. R. (2001). Adapting self-management programs for classwide use: Acceptability, feasibility, and effectiveness. *Remedial and Special Education, 22,* 75–88.

Mitchem, K. J., Young, K. R., West, R. P., & Benyo, J. (2001). CWPASM: A classwide peer-assisted self-management program for general education classrooms. *Education and Treatment of Children, 24,* 3–14.

Molè, P. (2003). Ockham's razor cuts both ways: The uses and abuses of simplicity in scientific theories. *Skeptic, 10* (1), 40–47.

Moore, J. (1980). On behaviorism and private events. *Psychological Record, 30,* 459–475.

Moore, J. (1984). On behaviorism, knowledge, and causal explanation. *Psychological Record, 34,* 73–97.

Moore, J. (1985). Some historical and conceptual relations among logical positivism, operationism, and behaviorism. *The Behavior Analyst, 8,* 53–63.

Moore, J. (1995). Radical behaviorism and the subjective-objective distinction. *The Behavior Analyst, 18,* 33–49.

Moore, J. (2000). Thinking about thinking and feeling about feeling. *The Behavior Analyst, 23* (1), 45–56.

Moore, J. (2003). Behavior analysis, mentalism, and the path to social justice. *The Behavior Analyst, 26,* 181–193.

Moore, J. W., Mueller, M. M., Dubard, M., Roberts, D. S., & Sterling-Turner, H. E. (2002). The influence of therapist attention on self-injury during a tangible condition. *Journal of Applied Behavior Analysis, 35,* 283–286.

Moore, J., & Cooper, J. O. (2003). Some proposed relations among the domains of behavior analysis. *The Behavior Analyst, 26,* 69–84.

Moore, J., & Shook, G. L. (2001). Certification, accreditation and quality control in behavior analysis. *The Behavior Analyst, 24,* 45–55.

Moore, R., & Goldiamond, I. (1964). Errorless establishment of visual discrimi-

nation using fading procedures. *Journal of the Experimental Analysis of Behavior, 7,* 269–272.

Morales v. Turman, 364 F. Supp. 166 (E.D. Tx. 1973).

Morgan, D., Young, K. R., & Goldstein, S. (1983). Teaching behaviorally disordered students to increase teacher attention and praise in mainstreamed classrooms. *Behavioral Disorders, 8,* 265–273.

Morgan, Q. E. (1978). *Comparison of two "Good Behavior Game" group contingencies on the spelling accuracy of fourth-grade students.* Unpublished master's thesis, The Ohio State University, Columbus.

Morris, E. K. (1991). Deconstructing "technological to a fault". *Journal of Applied Behavior Analysis, 24,* 411–416.

Morris, E. K., & Smith, N. G. (2003). Bibliographic processes and products, and a bibliography of the published primary-source works of B. F. Skinner. *The Behavior Analyst, 26,* 41–67.

Morris, R. J. (1985). *Behavior modification with exceptional children: Principles and practices.* Glenview, IL: Scott, Foresman.

Morse, W. H., & Kelleher, R. T. (1977). Determinants of reinforcement and punishment. In W. K. Honig & J. E. R. Staddon (Eds.), *Handbook of operant behavior* (pp. 174–200). Upper Saddle River, NJ: Prentice Hall.

Morton, W. L., Heward, W. L., & Alber, S. R. (1998). When to self-correct? A comparison of two procedures on spelling performance. *Journal of Behavioral Education, 8,* 321–335.

Mowrer, O. H. (1950). *Learning theory and personality dynamics.* New York: The Ronald Press Company.

Moxley, R. A. (1990). On the relationship between speech and writing with implications for behavioral approaches to teaching literacy. *The Analysis of Verbal Behavior, 8,* 127–140.

Moxley, R. A. (1998). Treatment-only designs and student self-recording strategies for public school teachers. *Education and Treatment of Children, 21,* 37–61.

Moxley, R. A. (2004). Pragmatic selectionism: The philosophy of behavior analysis. *The Behavior Analyst Today, 5,* 108–125.

Moxley, R. A., Lutz, P. A., Ahlborn, P., Boley, N., & Armstrong, L. (1995). Self-recording word counts of freewriting in grades 1-4. *Education and Treatment of Children, 18,* 138–157.

Mudford, O. C. (1995). Review of the gentle teaching data. *American Journal on Mental Retardation, 99,* 345–355.

Mueller, M. M., Moore, J. W., Doggett, R. A., & Tingstrom, D. H. (2000). The effectiveness of contingency-specific prompts in controlling bathroom graffiti. *Journal of Applied Behavior Analysis, 33,* 89–92.

Mueller, M. M., Piazza, C. C., Moore, J. W., Kelley, M. E., Bethke, S. A., Pruett, A. E., Oberdorff, A. J., & Layer, S. A. (2003). Training parents to implement pediatric feeding protocols. *Journal of Applied Behavior Analysis, 36,* 545–562.

Mueller, M., Moore, J., Doggett, R. A., & Tingstrom, D. (2000). The effectiveness of contingency-specific and contingency nonspecific prompts in controlling bathroom graffiti. *Journal of Applied Behavior Analysis, 33,* 89–92.

Murphy, E. S., McSweeny, F. K., Smith, R. G., & McComas, J. J. (2003). Dynamic changes in reinforcer effectiveness: Theoretical, methodological, and practical implications for applied research. *Journal of Applied Behavior Analysis, 36,* 421–438.

Murphy, R. J., Ruprecht, M. J., Baggio, P., & Nunes, D. L. (1979). The use of mild punishment in combination with reinforcement of alternate behaviors to reduce the self-injurious behavior of a profoundly retarded individual. *AAESPH Review, 4,* 187–195.

Musser, E. H., Bray, M. A., Kehle, T. J., & Jenson, W. R. (2001). Reducing disruptive behaviors in students with serious emotional disturbance. *School Psychology Review, 30* (2), 294–304.

Myer, J. S. (1971). Some effects of noncontingent aversive stimulation. In R. F. Brush (Ed.), *Aversive conditioning and learning* (pp. 469–536). NY: Academic Press.

Myles, B. S., Moran, M. R., Ormsbee, C. K., & Downing, J. A. (1992). Guidelines for establishing and maintaining token economies. *Intervention in School and Clinic, 27* (3), 164–169.

Nakano, Y. (2004). Toward the establishment of behavioral ethics: Ethical principles of behavior analysis in the era of empirically supported treatment (EST). *Japanese Journal of Behavior Analysis, 19* (1), 18–51.

Narayan, J. S., Heward, W. L., Gardner R., III, Courson, F. H., & Omness, C. (1990). Using response cards to increase student participation in an elementary classroom. *Journal of Applied Behavior Analysis, 23,* 483–490.

National Association of School Psychologists. (2000). *Professional conduct manual: Principles for professional ethics and guidelines for the provision of school psychological services.* Bethesda, MD: NASP Publications.

National Association of Social Workers. (1996). The NASW code of ethics. Washington, DC: Author.

National Commission for the Protection of Human Subjects of Biomedical and Behavioral Research. (1979). *The Belmont Report: Ethical principles and guidelines for the protection of human subjects of research.* Washington, DC: Department of Health, Education, and Welfare. Retrieved November 11, 2003, from http://ohsr.od.nih.gov/mpa/belmont.php3.

National Reading Panel (2000). *Teaching children to read: An evidence-based assessment of the scientific research literature on reading and its implications for reading instruction: Reports of the subgroups.* (NIH Pub No. 00-4754). Bethesda, MD: National Institute of Child Health and Human Development. [Available at: www.nichd.nih.gov.publications/nrp.report/htm]

National Reading Panel. www.nationalreadingpanel.org. Retrieved November 29, 2005, from www.nationalreadingpanel.org

Neef, N. A., Bicard, D. F., & Endo, S. (2001). Assessment of impulsivity and the development of self-control by students with attention deficit hyperactivity disorder. *Journal of Applied Behavior Analysis, 34,* 397–408.

Neef, N. A., Bicard, D. F., Endo, S., Coury, D. L., & Aman, M. G. (2005). Evaluation of pharmacological treatment of impulsivity by students with attention deficit hyperactivity disorder. *Journal of Applied Behavior Analysis, 38,* 135–146.

Neef, N. A., Iwata, B. A., & Page, T. J. (1980). The effects of interspersal training versus high density reinforcement on spelling acquisition and retention. *Journal of Applied Behavior Analysis, 13,* 153–158.

Neef, N. A., Lensbower, J., Hockersmith, I., DePalma, V., & Gray, K. (1990). In vivo versus stimulation training: An interactional analysis of range and type of training exemplars. *Journal of Applied Behavior Analysis, 23,* 447–458.

Neef, N. A., Mace, F. C., & Shade, D. (1993). Impulsivity in students with serious emotional disturbance: The interactive effects of reinforcer rate, delay, and quality. *Journal of Applied Behavior Analysis, 26,* 37–52.

Neef, N. A., Mace, F. C., Shea, M. C., & Shade, D. (1992). Effects of reinforcer rate and reinforcer quality on time allocation: Extensions of matching theory to educational settings. *Journal of Applied Behavior Analysis, 25,* 691–699.

Neef, N. A., Markel, J., Ferreri, S., Bicard, D. F., Endo, S., Aman, M. G., Miller, K. M., Jung, S., Nist, L., & Armstrong, N. (2005). Effects of modeling versus instructions on sensitivity to reinforcement schedules. *Journal of Applied Behavior Analysis, 38,* 23–37.

Neef, N. A., Parrish, J. M., Hannigan, K. F., Page, T. J., & Iwata, B. A. (1990). Teaching self-catheterization skills to children with neurogenic bladder complications. *Journal of Applied Behavior Analysis, 22,* 237–243.

Neisser, U. (1976). *Cognition and reality.* San Francisco: Freeman.

Nelson, R. O., & Hayes, S. C. (1981). Theoretical explanations for reactivity in self-monitoring. *Behavior Modification, 5,* 3–14.

Neuringer, A. (1993). Reinforced variation and selection. *Animal Learning and Behavior, 21,* 83–91.

Neuringer, A. (2004). Reinforced variability in animals and people: Implication for adaptive action. *American Psychologist, 59,* 891–906.

Nevin, J. A. (1998). Choice and momentum. In W. O'Donohue (Ed.), *Learning and behavior therapy* (pp. 230–251). Boston: Allyn and Bacon.

Newman, B., Buffington, D. M., Hemmes, N. S., & Rosen, D. (1996). Answering objections to self-management and related concepts. *Behavior and Social Issues, 6,* 85–95.

Newman, B., Reinecke, D. R., & Meinberg, D. (2000). Self-management of varied responding in children with autism. *Behavioral Interventions, 15,* 145–151.

Newman, R. S., & Golding, L. (1990). Children's reluctance to seek help with school work. *Journal of Educational Psychology, 82,* 92–100.

Newstrom, J., McLaughlin, T. F., & Sweeney, W. J. (1999). The effects of contingency contracting to improve the mechanics of written language with a middle school student with behavior disorders. *Child & Family Behavior Therapy, 21* (1), 39–48.

Newton, J. T., & Sturmey, P. (1991). The Motivation Assessment Scale: Interrater reliability and internal consistency in a British sample. *Journal of Mental Deficiency Research, 35,* 472–474.

Nihira, K., Leland, H., & Lambert, N. K. (1993). *Adaptive Behavior Scale—Residential and Community* (2nd ed.). Austin, TX: Pro-Ed.

Ninness, H. A. C., Fuerst, J., & Rutherford, R. D. (1991). Effects of self-management training and reinforcement on the transfer of improved conduct in the absence of supervision. *Journal of Applied Behavior Analysis, 24,* 499–508.

Noell, G. H., VanDerHeyden, A. M., Gatti, S. L., & Whitmarsh, E. L. (2001). Functional assessment of the effects of escape and attention on students' compliance during instruction. *School Psychology Quarterly, 16,* 253–269.

Nolan, J. D. (1968). Self-control procedures in the modification of smoking behavior. *Journal of Consulting and Clinical Psychology, 32,* 92–93.

North, S. T., & Iwata, B. A. (2005). Motivational influences on performance maintained by food reinforcement. *Journal of Applied Behavior Analysis, 38,* 317–333.

Northup, J. (2000). Further evaluation of the accuracy of reinforcer surveys: A systematic replication. *Journal of Applied Behavior Analysis, 33,* 335–338.

Northup, J., George, T., Jones, K., Broussard, C., & Vollmer, T. R. (1996). A comparison of reinforcer assessment methods: The utility of verbal and pictorial choice procedures. *Journal of Applied Behavior Analysis, 29,* 201–212.

Northup, J., Vollmer, T. R., & Serrett, K. (1993). Publication trends in 25 years of the *Journal of Applied Behavior Analysis. Journal of Applied Behavior Analysis, 26,* 527–537.

Northup, J., Wacker, D., Sasso, G., Steege, M., Cigrand, K., Cook, J., & DeRaad, A. (1991). A brief functional analysis of aggressive and alternative behavior in an outclinic setting. *Journal of Applied Behavior Analysis, 24,* 509–522.

Novak, G. (1996). *Developmental psychology: Dynamical systems and behavior analysis.* Reno, NV: Context Press.

O'Brien, F. (1968). Sequential contrast effects with human subjects. *Journal of the Experimental Analysis of Behavior, 11,* 537–542.

O'Brien, S., & Karsh, K. G. (1990). Treatment acceptability, consumer, therapist, and society. In A. C. Repp & N. N. Singh (Eds.), *Perspectives on the use of nonaversive and aversive interventions for persons with developmental disabilities* (pp. 503–516). Sycamore, IL: Sycamore.

O'Donnell, J. (2001). The discriminative stimulus for punishment or S^{Dp}. *The Behavior Analyst, 24,* 261–262.

O'Leary, K. D. (1977). Teaching self-management skills to children. In D. Upper (Ed.), *Perspectives in behavior therapy.* Kalamazoo, MI: Behaviordelia.

O'Leary, K. D., & O'Leary, S. G. (Eds.). (1972). *Classroom management: The successful use of behavior modification.* New York: Pergamon.

O'Leary, K. D., Kaufman, K. F., Kass, R. E., & Drabman, R. S. (1970). The effects of loud and soft reprimands on the behavior of disruptive students. *Exceptional Children, 37,* 145–155.

O'Leary, S. G., & Dubey, D. R. (1979). Applications of self-control procedures by children: A review. *Journal of Applied Behavior Analysis, 12,* 449–465.

O'Neill, R. E. Horner, R. H., Albin, R. W., Sprague, J. R., Storey, K., & Newton, J. S. (1997). *Functional assessment for problem behavior: A practical handbook* (2nd ed.). Pacific Grove, CA: Brooks/Cole.

O'Reilly, M. F. (1995). Functional analysis and treatment of escape-maintained aggression correlated with sleep deprivation. *Journal of Applied Behavior Analysis, 28,* 225–226.

O'Reilly, M., Green, G., & Braunling-McMorrow, D. (1990). Self-administered written prompts to teach home accident prevention skills to adults with brain injuries. *Journal of Applied Behavior Analysis, 23,* 431–446.

O'Sullivan, J. L. (1999). Adult guardianship and alternatives. In R. D. Dinerstein, S. S. Herr, & J. L. O'Sullivan (Eds.), *A guide to consent* (pp. 7–37). Washington DC: American Association on Mental Retardation.

Odom, S. L., Hoyson, M., Jamieson, B., & Strain, P. S. (1985). Increasing handi-

capped preschoolers' peer social interactions: Cross-setting and component analysis. *Journal of Applied Behavior Analysis, 18,* 3–16.

Oliver, C. O., Oxener, G., Hearn, M., & Hall, S. (2001). Effects of social proximity on multiple aggressive behaviors. *Journal of Applied Behavior Analysis, 34,* 85–88.

Ollendick, T. H., Matson, J. L., Esvelt-Dawson, K., & Shapiro, E. S. (1980). Increasing spelling achievement: An analysis of treatment procedures utilizing an alternating treatments design. *Journal of Applied Behavior Analysis, 13,* 645–654.

Ollendick, T., Matson, J., Esveldt-Dawson, K., & Shapiro, E. (1980). An initial investigation into the parameters of overcorrection. *Psychological Reports, 39,* 1139–1142.

Olympia, D. W., Sheridan, S. M., Jenson, W. R., & Andrews, D. (1994). Using student-managed interventions to increase homework completion and accuracy. *Journal of Applied Behavior Analysis, 27,* 85–99.

Ortiz, K. R., & Carr, J. E. (2000). Multiple-stimulus preference assessments: A comparison of free-operant and restricted-operant formats. *Behavioral Interventions, 15,* 345–353.

Osborne, J. G. (1969). Free-time as a reinforcer in the management of classroom behavior. *Journal of Applied Behavior Analysis, 2,* 113–118.

Osgood, C. E. (1953). *Method and theory in experimental psychology.* New York: Oxford University Press.

Osnes, P. G., Guevremont, D. C., & Stokes, T. F. (1984). If I say I'll talk more, then I will: Correspondence training to increase peer-directed talk by socially withdrawn children. *Behavior Modification, 10,* 287–299.

Osnes, P. G., & Lieblein, T. (2003). An explicit technology of generalization. *The Behavior Analyst Today, 3,* 364–374.

Overton, T. (2006). *Assessing learners with special needs: An applied approach* (5th ed.). Upper Saddle River, NJ: Prentice Hall.

Owens, R. E. (2001). *Language development: An introduction* (5th ed.). Boston: Allyn & Bacon.

Pace, G. M., & Troyer, E. A. (2000). The effects of a vitamin supplement on the pica of a child with severe mental retardation. *Journal of Applied Behavior Analysis, 33,* 619–622.

Pace, G. M., Ivancic, M. T., Edwards, G. L., Iwata, B. A., & Page, T. J. (1985). Assessment of stimulus preference and reinforcer value with profoundly retarded individuals. *Journal of Applied Behavior Analysis, 18,* 249–255.

Paclawskyj, T. R., & Vollmer, T. R. (1995). Reinforcer assessment for children with developmental disabilities and visual impairments. *Journal of Applied Behavior Analysis, 28,* 219–224.

Paclawskyj, T., Matson, J., Rush, K., Smalls, Y., & Vollmer, T. (2000). Questions about behavioral function (QABF): Behavioral checklist for functional assessment of aberrant behavior. *Research in Developmental Disabilities, 21,* 223–229.

Page, T. J., & Iwata, B. A. (1986). Interobserver agreement: History, theory, and current methods. In A. Poling & R. W. Fuqua (Eds.), *Research methods in applied behavior analysis* (pp. 92–126). New York: Plenum Press.

Palmer, D. C. (1991). A behavioral interpretation of memory. In L. J. Hayes & P. N. Chase (Eds.), *Dialogues on verbal behavior* (pp. 261–279). Reno NV: Context Press.

Palmer, D. C. (1996). Achieving parity: The role of automatic reinforcement. *Journal of the Experimental Analysis of Behavior, 65,* 289–290.

Palmer, D. C. (1998). On Skinner's rejection of S-R psychology. *The Behavior Analyst, 21,* 93–96.

Palmer, D. C. (1998). The speaker as listener: The interpretations of structural regularities in verbal behavior. *The Analysis of Verbal Behavior, 15,* 3–16.

Panyan, M., Boozer, H., & Morris, N. (1970). Feedback to attendants as a reinforcer for applying operant techniques. *Journal of Applied Behavior Analysis, 3,* 1–4.

Parker, L. H., Cataldo, M. F., Bourland, G., Emurian, C. S., Corbin, R. J., & Page, J. M. (1984). Operant treatment of orofacial dysfunction in neuromuscular disorders. *Journal of Applied Behavior Analysis, 17,* 413–427.

Parrott, L. J. (1984). Listening and understanding. *The Behavior Analyst, 7,* 29–39.

Parsons, M. B., Reid, D. H., Reynolds, J., & Bumgarner, M. (1990). Effects of chosen versus assigned jobs on the work performance of persons with severe handicaps. *Journal of Applied Behavior Analysis, 23,* 253–258.

Parsonson, B. S. (2003). Visual analysis of graphs: Seeing *is* believing. In K. S. Budd & T. Stokes (Eds.), *A small matter of proof: The legacy of Donald M. Baer* (pp. 35–51). Reno, NV: Context Press.

Parsonson, B. S., & Baer, D. M. (1978). The analysis and presentation of graphic data. In T. R. Kratochwill (Ed.), *Single subject research: Strategies for evaluating change* (pp. 101–165). New York: Academic Press.

Parsonson, B. S., & Baer, D. M. (1986). The graphic analysis of data. In A. Poling & R. W. Fuqua (Eds.), *Research methods in applied behavior analysis* (pp. 157–186). New York: Plenum Press.

Parsonson, B. S., & Baer, D. M. (1992). The visual analysis of graphic data, and current research into the stimuli controlling it. In T. R. Kratochwill & J. R. Levin (Eds.), *Single subject research design and analysis: New directions for psychology and education* (pp. 15–40). New York: Academic Press.

Partington, J. W., & Bailey, J. S. (1993). Teaching intraverbal behavior to preschool children. *The Analysis of Verbal Behavior, 11,* 9–18.

Partington, J. W., & Sundberg, M. L. (1998). *The assessment of basic language and learning skills (The ABLLS).* Pleasant Hill, CA: Behavior Analysts, Inc.

Patel, M. R., Piazza, C. C., Kelly, M. L., Ochsner, C. A., & Santana, C. M. (2001). Using a fading procedure to increase fluid consumption in a child with feeding problems. *Journal of Applied Behavior Analysis, 34,* 357–360.

Patel, M. R., Piazza, C. C., Martinez, C. J., Volkert, V. M., & Santana, C. M. (2002). An evaluation of two differential reinforcement procedures with escape extinction to treat food refusal. *Journal of Applied Behavior Analysis, 35,* 363–374.

Patterson, G. R. (1982). *Coercive family process.* Eugene, OR: Castalia.

Patterson, G. R., Reid, J. B., & Dishion, T. J. (1992). *Antisocial boys. Vol. 4: A social interactional approach.* Eugene, OR: Castalia.

Pavlov, I. P. (1927). *Conditioned reflexes: An investigation of the physiological activity of the cerebral cortex* (W. H. Grant, Trans.). London: Oxford University Press.

Pavlov, I. P. (1927/1960). *Conditioned reflexes* (G. V. Anrep, Trans.). New York: Dover.

Pelaez-Nogueras, M., Gewirtz, J. L., Field, T., Cigales, M., Malphurs, J., Clasky, S., & Sanchez, A. (1996). Infants' preference for touch stimulation in face-to-face interactions. *Journal of Applied Developmental Psychology, 17,* 199–213.

Pelios, L., Morren, J., Tesch, D., & Axelrod, S. (1999). The impact of functional analysis methodology on treatment choice for self-injurious and aggressive behavior. *Journal of Applied Behavior Analysis, 32,* 185–195.

Pennypacker, H. S. (1981). On behavioral analysis. *The Behavior Analyst, 3,* 159–161.

Pennypacker, H. S. (1994). A selectionist view of the future of behavior analysis in education. In R. Gardner, III, D. M. Sainato, J. O. Cooper, T. E. Heron, W. L. Heward, J. Eshleman, & T. A. Grossi (Eds.), *Behavior analysis in education: Focus on measurably superior instruction* (pp. 11–18). Monterey, CA: Brooks/Cole.

Pennypacker, H. S., & Hench, L. L. (1997). Making behavioral technology transferable. *The Behavior Analyst, 20,* 97–108.

Pennypacker, H. S., Gutierrez, A., & Lindsley, O. R. (2003). *Handbook of the Standard Celeration Chart.* Gainesville, FL: Xerographics.

Pennypacker, H. S., Koenig, C., & Lindsley, O. (1972). *Handbook of the Standard Behavior Chart.* Kansas City: Precision Media.

Peters, M., & Heron, T. E. (1993). When the best is not good enough: An examination of best practice. *Journal of Special Education, 26* (4), 371–385.

Peters, R., & Davies, K. (1981). Effects of self-instructional training on cognitive impulsivity of mentally retarded adolescents. *American Journal of Mental Deficiency, 85,* 377–382.

Peterson, I., Homer, A. L., & Wonderlich, S. A. (1982). The integrity of independent variables in behavior analysis. *Journal of Applied Behavior Analysis, 15,* 477–492.

Peterson, N. (1978). *An introduction to verbal behavior.* Grand Rapids, MI: Behavior Associates, Inc.

Peterson, S. M., Neef, N. A., Van Norman, R., & Ferreri, S. J. (2005). Choice making in educational settings. In W. L. Heward, T. E. Heron, N. A. Neef, S. M. Peterson, D. M. Sainato, G. Cartledge, R. Gardner, III, L. D. Peterson, S. B.

Hersh, & J. C. Dardig (Eds.), *Focus on behavior analysis in education: Achievements, challenges, and opportunities* (pp. 125–136). Upper Saddle River, NJ: Merrill/Prentice Hall.

Pfadt, A., & Wheeler, D. J. (1995). Using statistical process control to make data-based clinical decisions. *Journal of Applied Behavior Analysis, 28*, 349–370.

Phillips, E. L., Phillips, E. A., Fixen, D. L., & Wolf, M. M. (1971). Achievement Place: Modification of the behaviors of predelinquent boys with a token economy. *Journal of Applied Behavior Analysis, 4*, 45–59.

Piaget, J. (1952). *The origins of intelligence in children.* (M. Cook, Trans.). New York: International University Press.

Piazza, C. C., & Fisher, W. (1991). A faded bedtime with response cost protocol for treatment of multiple-sleep problems in children. *Journal of Applied Behavior Analysis, 24*, 129–140.

Piazza, C. C., Bowman, L. G., Contrucci, S. A., Delia, M. D., Adelinis, J. D., & Goh, H-L. (1999). An evaluation of the properties of attention as reinforcement for destructive and appropriate behavior. *Journal of Applied Behavior Analysis, 32*, 437–449.

Piazza, C. C., Fisher, W. W., Hagopian, L. P., Bowman, L. G., & Toole, L. (1996). Using a choice assessment to predict reinforcer effectiveness. *Journal of Applied Behavior Analysis, 29*, 1–9.

Piazza, C. C., Moses, D. R., & Fisher, W. W. (1996). Differential reinforcement of alternative behavior and demand fading in the treatment of escape maintained destructive behavior. *Journal of Applied Behavior Analysis, 29*, 569–572.

Piazza, C. C., Roane, H. S., Kenney, K. M., Boney, B. R., & Abt, K. A. (2002). Varying response effort in the treatment of pica maintained by automatic reinforcement. *Journal of Applied Behavior Analysis, 35*, 233–246.

Pierce, K. L., & Schreibman, L. (1994). Teaching daily living skills to children with autism in unsupervised settings through pictorial self-management. *Journal of Applied Behavior Analysis, 27*, 471–481.

Pierce, W. D., & Epling, W. F. (1999). *Behavior analysis and learning* (2nd ed.). Upper Saddle River, NJ: Prentice Hall/Merrill.

Pindiprolu, S, S., Peterson, S. M. P., Rule, S., & Lignuaris/Kraft, B. (2003). Using web-mediated experiential case-based instruction to teach functional behavioral assessment skills. *Teacher Education in Special Education, 26*, 1–16.

Pinker, S. (1994). *The language instinct.* New York: Harper Perennial.

Pinkston, E. M., Reese, N. M., Leblanc, J. M., & Baer, D. M. (1973). Independent control of a preschool child's aggression and peer interaction by contingent teacher attention. *Journal of Applied Behavior Analysis, 6*, 115–124.

Plazza, C. C., Bowman, L. G., Contrucci, S. A., Delia, M. D., Adelinis, J. D., & Goh, H.-L. (1999). An evaluation of the properties of attention as reinforcement for destructive and appropriate behavior. *Journal of Applied Behavioral Analysis, 32*, 437–449.

Poche, C., Brouwer, R., & Swearingen, M. (1981). Teaching self-protection to young children. *Journal of Applied Behavior Analysis, 14*, 169–176.

Poling, A., & Normand, M. (1999). Noncontingent reinforcement: An inappropriate description of time-based schedules that reduce behavior. *Journal of Applied Behavior Analysis, 32*, 237–238.

Poling, A., & Ryan, C. (1982). Differential-reinforcement-of-other-behavior schedules: Therapeutic applications. *Behavior Modification, 6*, 3–21.

Poling, A., Methot, L. L., & LeSage, M. G. (Eds.). (1995). *Fundamentals of behavior analytic research.* New York: Plenum Press.

Poplin, J., & Skinner, C. (2003). Enhancing academic performance in a classroom serving students with serious emotional disturbance: Interdependent group contingencies with randomly selected components. *School Psychology Review, 32* (2), 282–296.

Post, M., Storey, K., & Karabin, M. (2002). Cool headphones for effective prompts: Supporting students and adults in work and community environments. *Teaching Exceptional Children, 34*, 60–65.

Potts, L., Eshleman, J. W., & Cooper, J. O. (1993). Ogden R. Lindsley and the historical development of Precision Teaching. *The Behavior Analyst, 16* (2), 177–189.

Poulson, C. L. (1983). Differential reinforcement of other-than-vocalization as a control procedure in the conditioning of infant vocalization rate. *Journal of Experimental Child Psychology, 36*, 471–489.

Powell, J., & Azrin, N. (1968). Behavioral engineering: Postural control by a portable operant apparatus. *Journal of Applied Behavior Analysis, 1*, 63–71.

Powell, J., Martindale, B., & Kulp, S. (1975). An evaluation of time-sample measures of behavior. *Journal of Applied Behavior Analysis, 8*, 463–469.

Powell, J., Martindale, B., Kulp, S., Martindale, A., & Bauman, R. (1977). Taking a closer look: Time sampling and measurement error. *Journal of Applied Behavior Analysis, 10*, 325–332.

Powell, T. H., & Powell, I. Q. (1982). The use and abuse of using the timeout procedure for disruptive pupils. *The Pointer, 26*, 18–22.

Powers, R. B., Osborne, J. G., & Anderson, E. G. (1973). Positive reinforcement of litter removal in the natural environment. *Journal of Applied Behavior Analysis, 6*, 579–586.

Premack, D. (1959). Toward empirical behavioral laws: I. Positive reinforcement. *Psychological Review, 66*, 219–233.

President's Council on Physical Fitness. www.fitness.gov.

Progar, P. R., North, S. T., Bruce, S. S., Dinovi, B. J., Nau, P. A., Eberman, E. M., Bailey, J. R., Jr., & Nussbaum, C. N. (2001). Putative behavioral history effects and aggression maintained by escape from therapists. *Journal of Applied Behavioral Analysis, 34*, 69–72.

Pryor, K. (1999). *Don't shoot the dog! The new art of teaching and training* (rev. ed.). New York: Bantam Books.

Pryor, K. (2005). *Clicker trained flight instruction.* Retrieved April 10, 2005, from http://clickertraining.com/training/humans/job/flight_training.

Pryor, K., Haag, R., & O'Reilly, J. (1969). The creative porpoise: Training for novel behavior. *Journal of the Experimental Analysis of Behavior, 12*, 653–661.

Pryor, K., & Norris, K. S. (1991). *Dolphin societies: Discoveries and puzzles.* Berkeley: University of California Press.

Rachlin, H. (1970). *The science of self-control.* Cambridge: Harvard University Press.

Rachlin, H. (1974). Self-control. *Behaviorism, 2*, 94–107.

Rachlin, H. (1977). *Introduction to modern behaviorism* (2nd ed.). San Francisco: W. H. Freeman.

Rachlin, H. (1995). *Self-control.* Cambridge: Harvard University Press.

Rapp, J. T., Miltenberger, R. G., & Long, E. S. (1998). Augmenting simplified habit reversal with an awareness enhancement device. *Journal of Applied Behavior Analysis, 31,* 665–668.

Rapp, J. T., Miltenberger, R. G., Galensky, T. L., Ellingson, S. A., & Long, E. S. (1999). A functional analysis of hair pulling. *Journal of Applied Behavior Analysis, 32,* 329–337.

Rasey, H. W., & Iversen, I. H. (1993). An experimental acquisition of maladaptive behaviors by shaping. *Journal of Behavior Therapy and Experimental Psychiatry, 24,* 37–43.

Readdick, C. A., & Chapman, P. L. (2000). Young children's perceptions of time out. *Journal of Research in Childhood Education, 15* (1), 81–87.

Reese, E. P. (1966). *The analysis of human operant behavior.* Dubuque, IA: Brown.

Rehfeldt, R. A., & Chambers, M. C. (2003). Functional analysis and treatment of verbal perseverations displayed by an adult with autism. *Journal of Applied Behavior Analysis, 36,* 259–261.

Reich, W. T. (1988). Experiential ethics as a foundation for dialogue between health communications and health-care ethics. *Journal of Applied Communication Research, 16,* 16–28.

Reid, D. H., Parsons, M. B., Green, C. W., & Browning, L. B. (2001). Increasing one aspect of self-determination among adults with severe multiple disabilities in supported work. *Journal of Applied Behavioral Analysis, 34,* 341–344.

Reid, D. H., Parsons, M. B., Phillips, J. F., & Green, C. W. (1993). Reduction of self-injurious hand mouthing using response blocking. *Journal of Applied Behavior Analysis, 26,* 139–140.

Reid, R., & Harris, K. R. (1993). Self-monitoring attention versus self-monitoring of performance: Effects on attention and academic performance. *Exceptional Children, 60,* 29–40.

Reimers, T. M., & Wacker, D. P. (1988). Parents' ratings of the acceptability of behavior treatment recommendations made in an outpatient clinic: A preliminary analysis of the influence of

treatment effectiveness. *Behavioral Disorders, 14,* 7–15.

Reitman, D., & Drabman, R. S. (1999). Multifaceted uses of a simple timeout record in the treatment of a noncompliant 8-year-old boy. *Education and Treatment of Children, 22* (2), 136–145.

Reitman, D., & Gross, A. M. (1996). Delayed outcomes and rule-governed behavior among "noncompliant" and "compliant" boys: A replication and extension. *The Analysis of Verbal Behavior, 13,* 65–77.

Repp, A. C., & Horner, R. H. (Eds.). (1999). *Functional analysis of problem behavior: From effective assessment to effective support.* Belmont, CA: Wadsworth.

Repp, A. C., & Karsh, K. G. (1994). Laptop computer system for data recording and contextual analyses. In T. Thompson & D. B. Gray (Eds.), *Destructive behavior in developmental disabilities: Diagnosis and treatment* (pp. 83–101). Thousand Oaks, CA: Sage.

Repp, A. C., & Singh, N. N. (Eds.). (1990). *Perspectives on the use of nonaversive and aversive interventions for persons with developmental disabilities.* Sycamore, IL: Sycamore.

Repp, A. C., Barton, L. E., & Brulle, A. R. (1983). A comparison of two procedures for programming the differential reinforcement of other behaviors. *Journal of Applied Behavior Analysis, 16,* 435–445.

Repp, A. C., Dietz, D. E. D., Boles, S. M., Dietz, S. M., & Repp, C. F. (1976). Differences among common methods for calculating interobserver agreement. *Journal of Applied Behavior Analysis, 9,* 109–113.

Repp, A. C., Harman, M. L., Felce, D., Vanacker, R., & Karsh, K. L. (1989). Conducting behavioral assessments on computer collected data. *Behavioral Assessment, 2,* 249–268.

Repp, A. C., Karsh, K. G., Johnson, J. W., & VanLaarhoven, T. (1994). A comparison of multiple versus single examples of the correct stimulus on task acquisition and generalization by persons with developmental disabiliteis. *Journal of Behavioral Education, 6,* 213–230.

Rescorla, R. (1988). Pavlovian conditioning: It's not what you think it is. *American Psychologist, 43,* 151–160.

Reynolds, G. S. (1961). Behavioral contrast. *Journal of the Experimental Analysis of Behavior, 4,* 57–71.

Reynolds, G. S. (1968). *A primer of operant conditioning.* Glenview, IL: Scott, Foresman.

Reynolds, G. S. (1975). *A primer of operant conditioning* (Rev. ed.). Glenview, IL: Scott, Foresman.

Reynolds, N. J., & Risley, T. R. (1968). The role of social and material reinforcers in increasing talking of a disadvantaged preschool child. *Journal of Applied Behavior Analysis, 1,* 253–262.

Rhode, G., Morgan, D. P., & Young, K. R. (1983). Generalization and maintenance of treatment gains of behaviorally handicapped students from resource rooms to regular classrooms using self-evaluation procedures. *Journal of Applied Behavior Analysis, 16,* 171–188.

Richman, D. M., Berg, W. K., Wacker, D. P., Stephens, T., Rankin, B., & Kilroy, J. (1997). Using pretreatment assessments to enhance and evaluate existing treatment packages. *Journal of Applied Behavior Analysis, 30,* 709–712.

Richman, D. M., Wacker, D. P., Asmus, J. M., Casey, S. D., & Andelman, M. (1999). Further analysis of problem behavior in response class hierarchies. *Journal of Behavior Analysis, 32,* 269–283.

Ricketts, R. W., Goza, A. B., & Matese, M. (1993). A 4-year follow-up of treatment of self-injury. *Journal of Behavior Therapy and Experimental Psychiatry, 24* (1), 57–62.

Rincover, A. (1978). Sensory extinction: A procedure for eliminating self-stimulatory behavior in psychotic children. *Journal of Abnormal Child Psychology, 6,* 299–310.

Rincover, A. (1981). *How to use sensory extinction.* Austin, TX: Pro-Ed.

Rincover, A., & Koegel, R. L. (1975). Setting generality and stimulus control in autistic children. *Journal of Applied Behavior Analysis, 8,* 235–246.

Rincover, A., & Newsom, C. D. (1985). The relative motivational properties of sensory reinforcement with psychotic children. *Journal of Experimental Child Psychology, 24,* 312–323.

Rincover, A., Cook, R., Peoples, A., & Packard, D. (1979). Sensory extinction and sensory reinforcement principles for programming multiple adaptive behavior change. *Journal of Applied Behavior Analysis, 12,* 221–233.

Rindfuss, J. B., Al-Attrash, M., Morrison, H., & Heward, W. L. (1998, May). *Using guided notes and response cards to improve quiz and exam scores in an eighth grade American history class.* Paper presented at 24th Annual Convention of the Association for Behavior Analysis, Orlando, FL.

Ringdahl, J. E., Kitsukawa, K., Andelman, M. S., Call, N., Winborn, L. C., Barretto, A., & Reed, G. K. (2002). Differential reinforcement with and without instructional fading. *Journal of Applied Behavior Analysis, 35,* 291–294.

Ringdahl, J. E., Vollmer, T. R., Borrero, J. C., & Connell, J. E. (2001). Fixed-time schedule effects as a function of baseline reinforcement rate. *Journal of Applied Behavior Analysis, 34,* 1–15.

Ringdahl, J. E., Vollmer, T. R., Marcus, B. A., & Roane, H. S (1997). An analogue evaluation of environmental enrichment: The role of stimulus preference. *Journal of Applied Behavior Analysis, 30,* 203–216.

Riordan, M. M., Iwata, B. A., Finney, J. W., Wohl, M. K., & Stanley, A. E. (1984). Behavioral assessment and treatment of chronic food refusal in handicapped children. *Journal of Applied Behavior Analysis, 17,* 327–341.

Risley, T. (1996). Get a life! In L. Kern Koegel, R. L. Koegel, & G. Dunlap (Eds.), *Positive behavioral support* (pp. 425–437). Baltimore: Paul H. Brookes.

Risley, T. (2005). Montrose M. Wolf (1935–2004). *Journal of Applied Behavior Analysis, 38,* 279–287.

Risley, T. R. (1968). The effects and side effects of punishing the autistic behaviors of a deviant child. *Journal of Applied Behavior Analysis, 1,* 21–34.

Risley, T. R. (1969, April). *Behavior modification: An experimental-therapeutic endeavor.* Paper presented at the Banff International Conference on Behavior Modification, Banff, Alberta, Canada.

Risley, T. R. (1997). Montrose M. Wolf: The origin of the dimensions of applied behavior analysis. *Journal of Applied Behavior Analysis, 30,* 377–381.

Risley, T. R. (2005). Montrose M. Wolf (1935–2004). *Journal of Applied Behavior Analysis, 38,* 279–287.

Risley, T. R., & Hart, B. (1968). Developing correspondence between the non-verbal and verbal behavior of preschool children. *Journal of Applied Behavior Analysis, 1,* 267–281.

Roane, H. S., Fisher, W. W., & McDonough, E. M. (2003). Progressing from programmatic to discovery research: A case example with the overjustification effect. *Journal of Applied Behavior Analysis, 36,* 23–36.

Roane, H. S., Kelly, M. L., & Fisher, W. W. (2003). The effects of noncontingent access to food on the rate of object mouthing across three settings. *Journal of Applied Behavior Analysis, 36,* 579–582.

Roane, H. S., Lerman, D. C., & Vorndran, C. M. (2001). Assessing reinforcers under progressive schedule requirements. *Journal of Applied Behavior Analysis, 34,* 145–167.

Roane, H. S., Vollmer, T. R., Ringdahl, J. E., & Marcus, B. A. (1998). Evaluation of a brief stimulus preference assessment. *Journal of Applied Behavior Analysis, 31,* 605–620.

Roberts-Pennell, D., & Sigafoos, J. (1999). Teaching young children with developmental disabilities to request more play using the behavior chain interruption strategy. *Journal of Applied Research in Intellectual Disabilities, 12,* 100–112.

Robin, A. L., Armel, S., & O'Leary, K. D., (1975). The effects of self-instruction on writing deficiencies. *Behavior Therapy, 6,* 178–187.

Robin, A., Schneider, M., & Dolnick, M., (1976). The turtle technique: An extended case study of self-control in the classroom. *Psychology in the Schools, 13,* 449–453.

Robinson, P. W., Newby, T. J., & Gansell, S. L. (1981). A token system for a class of underachieving hyperactive children. *Journal of Applied Behavior Analysis, 14,* 307–315.

Rodgers, T. A., & Iwata, B. A. (1991). An analysis of error-correction procedures during discrimination training. *Journal of Applied Behavior Analysis, 24,* 775–781.

Rohn, D. (2002). Case study: Improving guitar skills. In R. W. Malott & H. Harrison, *I'll stop procrastinating when I get around to it: Plus other cool ways to succeed in school and life using behavior analysis to get your act together* (p. 8-4). Kalamazoo, MI: Department of Psychology, Western Michigan University.

Rolider, A., & Van Houten, R. (1984). The effects of DRO alone and DRO plus reprimands on the undesirable behavior of three children in home settings. *Education and Treatment of Children, 7,* 17–31.

Rolider, A., & Van Houten, R. (1984). Training parents to use extinction to eliminate nighttime crying by gradually increasing the criteria for ignoring crying. *Education and Treatment of Children, 7,* 119–124.

Rolider, A., & Van Houten, R. (1985). Suppressing tantrum behavior in public places through the use of delayed punishment mediated by audio recordings. *Behavior Therapy, 16,* 181–194.

Rolider, A. , & Van Houten, R. (1993). The interpersonal treatment model. In R. Van Houten & S. Axelrod (Eds.), *Behavior analysis and treatment* (pp. 127–168). New York: Plenum Press.

Romanczyk, R. G. (1977). Intermittent punishment of self-stimulation: Effectiveness during application and extinction. *Journal of Consulting and Clinical Psychology, 45,* 53–60.

Romaniuk, C., Miltenberger, R., Conyers, C., Jenner, N., Jurgens, M., & Ringenberg, C. (2002). The influence of activity choice on problem behaviors maintained by escape versus attention. *Journal of Applied Behavioral Analysis, 35,* 349–362.

Romaniuk, C., Miltenberger, R., Conyers, C., Jenner, N., Roscoe, E. M., Iwata, B. A., & Goh, H.-L. (1998). A comparison of noncontingent reinforcement and sensory extinction as treatments for self-injurious behavior. *Journal of Applied Behavior Analysis, 31,* 635–646.

Romeo, F. F. (1998). The negative effects of using a group contingency system of classroom management. *Journal of Instructional Psychology, 25* (2), 130–133.

Romer, L. T., Cullinan, T., & Schoenberg, B. (1994). General case training of requesting: A demonstration and analysis. *Education and Training in Mental Retardation, 29,* 57–68.

Rosales-Ruiz, J., & Baer, D. M. (1997). Behavioral cusps: A developmental and pragmatic concept for behavior analysis. *Journal of Applied Behavior Analysis, 30,* 533–544.

Roscoe, E. M., Iwata, B. A., & Goh, H.-L. (1998). A comparison of noncontingent reinforcement and sensory extinction as treatments for self-injurious behavior. *Journal of Applied Behavior Analysis, 31,* 635–646.

Roscoe, E. M., Iwata, B. A., & Kahng, S. (1999). Relative versus absolute reinforcement effects: Implications for preference assessments. *Journal of Applied Behavior Analysis, 32,* 479–493.

Rose, J. C., De Souza, D. G., & Hanna, E. S. (1996). Teaching reading and spelling: Exclusion and stimulus equivalence. *Journal of Applied Behavior Analysis, 29,* 451–469.

Rose, T. L. (1978). The functional relationship between artificial food colors and hyperactivity. *Journal of Applied Behavior Analysis, 11,* 439–446.

Ross, C., & Neuringer, A. (2002). Reinforcement of variations and repetitions along three independent response dimensions. *Behavioral Processes, 57,* 199–209.

Rozensky, R. H. (1974). The effect of timing of self-monitoring behavior on reducing cigarette consumption. *Journal of Consulting and Clinical Psychology, 5,* 301–307.

Rusch, F. R., & Kazdin, A. E. (1981). Toward a methodology of withdrawal designs for the assessment of response maintenance. *Journal of Applied Behavior Analysis, 14,* 131–140.

Russell, B., & Whitehead A. N. (1910–1913). *Principia mathematica.* Cambridge, MA: University Press.

Ruth, W. J. (1996). Goal setting and behavioral contracting for students with emotional and behavioral difficulties: Analysis of daily, weekly, and total goal attainment. *Psychology in the Schools, 33,* 153–158.

Ryan, C. S., & Hemmes, N. S. (2005). Effects of the contingency for homework submission on homework submission and quiz performance in a college course. *Journal of Applied Behavior Analysis, 38,* 79–88.

Ryan, S., Ormond, T., Imwold, C., & Rotunda, R. J. (2002). The effects of a public address system on the off-task behavior of elementary physical education students. *Journal of Applied Behavior Analysis, 35,* 305–308.

Sagan, C. (1996). *The demon-haunted world: Science as a candle in the dark.* New York: Ballantine.

Saigh, P. A., & Umar, A. M. (1983). The effects of a good behavior game on the disruptive behavior of Sudanese elementary school students. *Journal of Applied Behavior Analysis, 16,* 339–344.

Sainato, D. M., Strain, P. S., Lefebvre, D., & Rapp, N. (1990). Effects of self-evaluation on the independent work skills of preschool children with disabilities. *Exceptional Children, 56,* 540–549.

Sajwaj, T., Culver, P., Hall, C., & Lehr, L. (1972). Three simple punishment techniques for the control of classroom disruptions. In G. Semb (Ed.), *Behavior analysis and education.* Lawrence: University of Kansas.

Saksida, L. M., Raymond, S. M., & Touretzky, D.S. (1997). Shaping robot behavior using principles from instrumental conditioning. *Robotics and Autonomous Systems, 22,* 231–249.

Salend, S. J. (1984b). Integrity of treatment in special education research. *Mental Retardation, 22,* 309–315.

Salend, S. J., Ellis, L. L., & Reynolds, C. J. (1989). Using self-instruction to teach vocational skills to individuals who are severely retarded. *Education and Training of the Mentally Retarded, 24,* 248–254.

Salvy, S.-J., Mulick, J. A., Butter, E., Bartlett, R. K., & Linscheid, T. R. (2004). Contingent electric shock (SIBIS) and a conditioned punisher eliminate severe head banging in a preschool child. *Behavioral Interventions, 19,* 59–72.

Salzinger, K. (1978). Language behavior. In A. C. Catania & T. A. Brigham (Eds.), *Handbook of applied behavior analysis: Social and instructional processes* (pp. 275–321). New York: Irvington.

Santogrossi, D. A., O'Leary, K. D., Romanczyk, R. G., & Kaufman, K. F. (1973). Self-evaluation by adolescents in a psychiatric hospital school token program. *Journal of Applied Behavior Analysis, 6,* 277–287.

Sarakoff, R. A., & Strumey, P. (2004). The effects of behavioral skills training on staff implementation of discrete-trial teaching. *Journal of Applied Behavior Analysis, 37,* 535–538.

Saraokoff, R. A., Taylor, B. A., & Poulson, C. L. (2001). Teaching children with autism to engage in conversational exchanges: Script fading with embedded textual stimuli. *Journal of Applied Behavior Analysis, 34,* 81–84.

Sasso, G. M., Reimers, T. M., Cooper, L. J., Wacker, D., Berg, W., Steege, M., Kelly, L., & Allaire, A. (1992). Use of descriptive and experimental analysis to identify the functional properties of aberrant behavior in school settings. *Journal of Applied Behavior Analysis, 25,* 809–821.

Saudargas, R. A., & Bunn, R. D. (1989). A hand-held computer system for classroom observation. *Journal of Special Education, 9,* 200–206.

Saudargas, R. A., & Zanolli, K. (1990). Momentary time sampling as an estimate of percentage time: A field validation. *Journal of Applied Behavior Analysis, 23,* 533–537.

Saunders, M. D., Saunders, J. L., & Saunders, R. R. (1994). Data collection with bar code technology. In T. Thompson & D. B. Gray (Eds.), *Destructive behavior in developmental disabilities: Diagnosis and treatment* (pp. 102–116). Thousand Oaks, CA: Sage.

Savage, T. (1998). Shaping: The link between rats and robots. *Connection Science, 10* (3/4), 321–340.

Savage-Rumbaugh, E. S. (1984). Verbal behavior at the procedural level in the chimpanzee. *Journal of the Experimental Analysis of Behavior, 41,* 223–250.

Saville, B. K., Beal, S. A., & Buskist, W. (2002). Essential readings for graduate students in behavior analysis: A survey of the JEAB and JABA Boards of Editors. *The Behavior Analyst, 25,* 29–35.

Schepis, M. M., Reid, D. H., Behrmann, M. M., & Sutton, K. A. (1998). Increasing communicative interactions of young children with autism using a voice output communication aid and naturalistic teaching. *Journal of Applied Behavior Analysis, 31,* 561–578.

Scheuermann, B., & Webber, J. (1996). Level systems: Problems and solutions. *Beyond Behavior, 7,* 12–17.

Schleien, S. J., Wehman, P., & Kiernan, J. (1981). Teaching leisure skills to severely handicapped adults: An age-appropriate darts game. *Journal of Applied Behavior Analysis, 14,* 513–519.

Schlinger, H., & Blakely, E. (1987). Function-altering effects of contingency-specifying stimuli. *The Behavior Analyst, 10,* 41–45.

Schoenberger, T. (1990). Understanding and the listener: Conflicting views. *The Analysis of Verbal Behavior, 8,* 141–150.

Schoenberger, T. (1991). Verbal understanding: Integrating the conceptual analyses of Skinner, Ryle, and Wittgenstein. *The Analysis of Verbal Behavior, 9,* 145–151.

Schoenfeld, W. N. (1995). "Reinforcement" in behavior theory. *The Behavior Analyst, 18,* 173–185.

Schumm, J. S., Vaughn, D., Haager, D., McDowell, J., Rothlein, L., & Saumell, L. (1995). General education teacher planning: What can students with learning disabilities expect? *Exceptional Children, 61,* 335–352.

Schuster, J. W., Griffen, A. K., & Wolery, M. (1992). Comparison of simultaneous prompting and constant time delay procedures in teaching sight words to elementary students with moderate mental retardation. *Journal of Behavioral Education, 7,* 305–325.

Schwartz, B. (1974). On going back to nature: A review of Seligman and Hager's *Biological Boundaries of Learning. Journal of the Experimental Analysis of Behavior, 21,* 183–198.

Schwartz, I. S., & Baer, D. M. (1991). Social validity assessments: Is current practice state of the art? *Journal of Applied Behavior Analysis, 24,* 189–204.

Schwarz, M. L., & Hawkins, R. P. (1970). Application of delayed reinforcement procedures to the behavior of an elementary school child. *Journal of Applied Behavior Analysis, 3,* 85–96.

Schweitzer, J. B., & Sulzer-Azaroff, B. (1988). Self-control: Teaching tolerance for delay in impulsive children. *Journal of the Experimental Analysis of Behavior, 50,* 173–186.

Scott, D., Scott, L. M., & Goldwater, B. (1997). A performance improvement program for an international-level track and field athlete. *Journal of Applied Behavior Analysis, 30,* 573–575.

Seymour, F. W., & Stokes, T. F. (1976). Self-recording in training girls to increase work rate and evoke staff praise in an institution for offenders. *Journal of Applied Behavior Analysis, 9,* 41–54.

Seymour, M. A. (2002). Case study: A retired athlete runs down comeback road. In R. W. Malott & H. Harrison, *I'll stop procrastinating when I get around to it: Plus other cool ways to succeed in school and life using behavior analysis to get your act to-gether* (p. 7-12). Kalamazoo, MI: Department of Psychology, Western Michigan University.

Shahan, T. A., & Chase, P. N. (2002). Novelty, stimulus control, and operant variability. *The Behavior Analyst, 25,* 175–190.

Shermer, S. (1997). *Why people believe weird things.* New York: W. H. Freeman.

Shimamune, S., & Jitsumori, M. (1999). Effects of grammar instruction and fluency training on the learning of *the* and *a* by native speakers of Japanese. *The Analysis of Verbal Behavior, 16,* 3–16.

Shimmel, S. (1977). Anger and its control in Greco-Roman and modern psychology. *Psychiatry, 42,* 320–327.

Shimmel, S. (1979). Free will, guilt, and self-control in rabbinic Judaism and contemporary psychology. *Judaism, 26,* 418–429.

Shimoff, E., & Catania, A. C. (1995). Using computers to teach behavior analysis. *The Behavior Analyst, 18,* 307–316.

Shirley, M. J., Iwata, B. A., Kahng, S. W., Mazaleski, J. L., & Lerman, D. C. (1997). Does functional communication training compete with ongoing contingencies of reinforcement? An analysis during response acquisition and maintenance. *Journal of Applied Behavior Analysis, 30,* 93–104.

Shook, G. L. (1993). The professional credential in behavior analysis. *The Behavior Analyst, 16,* 87–101.

Shook, G. L., & Favell, J. E. (1996). Identifying qualified professionals in behavior analysis. In C. Maurice, G. Green, & S. C. Luce (Eds.), *Behavioral intervention for young children with autism: A manual for parents and professionals* (pp. 221–229). Austin, TX: Pro-Ed.

Shook, G. L., & Neisworth, J. (2005). Ensuring appropriate qualifications for applied behavior analyst professionals: The Behavior Analyst Certification Board. *Exceptionality 13* (1), 3–10.

Shook, G. L., Johnston, J. M., & Mellichamp, F. (2004). Determining essential content for applied behavior analyst practitioners. *The Behavior Analyst, 27,* 67–94.

Shook, G. L., Rosales, S. A., & Glenn, S. (2002). Certification and training of behavior analyst professionals. *Behavior Modification, 26* (1), 27–48.

Shore, B. A., Iwata, B. A., DeLeon, I. G., Kahng, S., & Smith, R. G. (1997). An analysis of reinforcer substitutability using object manipulation and self-injury as competing responses. *Journal of Applied Behavior Analysis, 30,* 439–449.

Sideridis, G. D., & Greenwood, C. R. (1996). Evaluating treatment effects in single-subject behavioral experiments using quality-control charts. *Journal of Behavioral Education, 6,* 203–211.

Sidman, M. (1960). *Tactics of scientific research.* New York: Basic Books.

Sidman, M. (1960/1988). *Tactics of scientific research: Evaluating experimental data in psychology.* New York: Basic Books/Boston: Authors Cooperative (reprinted).

Sidman, M. (1971). Reading and auditory-visual equivalences. *Journal of Speech and Hearing Research, 14,* 5–13.

Sidman, M. (1994). *Equivalence relations and behavior: A research story.* Boston: Author's Cooperative.

Sidman, M. (2000). Applied behavior analysis: Back to basics. *Behaviorology, 5* (1), 15–37.

Sidman, M. (2002). Notes from the beginning of time. *The Behavior Analyst, 25,* 3–13.

Sidman, M. (2006). The distinction between positive and negative reinforcement: Some additional considerations. *The Behavior Analyst, 29,* 135–139.

Sidman, M., & Cresson, O., Jr. (1973). Reading and crossmodal transfer of stimulus equivalences in severe retardation. *American Journal of Mental Deficiency, 77,* 515–523.

Sidman, M., & Stoddard, L. T. (1967). The effectiveness of fading in programming a simultaneous form discrimination for retarded children. *Journal of the Experimental Analysis of Behavior, 10,* 3–15.

Sidman, M., & Tailby, W. (1982). Conditional discrimination vs. matching-to-sample: An expansion of the testing paradigm. *Journal of the Experimental Analysis of Behavior, 37,* 5–22.

Sigafoos, J., Doss, S., & Reichle, J. (1989). Developing mand and tact repertoires with persons with severe developmental disabilities with graphic symbols. *Research in Developmental Disabilities, 11,* 165–176.

Sigafoos, J., Kerr, M., & Roberts, D. (1994). Interrater reliability of the Motivation Assessment Scale: Failure to replicate with aggressive behavior.

Research in Developmental Disabilities, 15, 333–342.

Silvestri, S. M. (2004). *The effects of self-scoring on teachers' positive statements during classroom instruction.* Unpublished doctoral dissertation. Columbus, OH: The Ohio State University.

Silvestri, S. M. (2005). *How to make a graph using Microsoft Excel.* Unpublished manuscript. Columbus, OH: The Ohio State University.

Simek, T. C., O'Brien, R. M., & Figlerski, L. B. (1994). Contracting and chaining to improve the performance of a college golf team: Improvement and deterioration. *Perceptual and Motor Skills, 78* (3), 1099.

Simpson, M. J. A., & Simpson, A. E. (1977). One-zero and scan method for sampling behavior. *Animal Behavior, 25,* 726–731.

Singer, G., Singer, J., & Horner, R. (1987). Using pretask requests to increase the probability of compliance for students with severe disabilities. *Journal of the Association for Persons with Severe Handicaps, 12,* 287–291.

Singh, J., & Singh, N. N. (1985). Comparison of word-supply and word-analysis error-correction procedures on oral reading by mentally retarded children. *American Journal of Mental Deficiency, 90,* 64–70.

Singh, N. N. (1990). Effects of two error-correction procedures on oral reading errors. *Behavior Modification, 11,* 165–181.

Singh, N. N., & Katz, R. C. (1985). On the modification of acceptability ratings for alternative child treatments. *Behavior Modification, 9,* 375–386.

Singh, N. N., & Singh, J. (1984). Antecedent control of oral reading errors and self-corrections by mentally retarded children. *Journal of Applied Behavior Analysis, 17,* 111–119.

Singh, N. N., & Singh, J. (1986). Increasing oral reading proficiency: A comparative analyst off drill and positive practice overcorrection procedures. *Behavior Modification, 10,* 115–130.

Singh, N. N., & Winton, A. S. (1985). Controlling pica by components of an overcorrection procedure. *American Journal of Mental Deficiency, 90,* 40–45.

Singh, N. N., Dawson, M. J., & Manning, P. (1981). Effects of spaced responding DRI on the stereotyped behavior of profoundly retarded persons. *Journal of Applied Behavior Analysis, 14,* 521–526.

Singh, N. N., Dawson, M. J., & Manning, P. (1981). The effects of physical restraint on self-injurious behavior. *Journal of Mental Deficiency Research, 25,* 207–216.

Singh, N. N., Singh, J., & Winton, A. S. (1984). Positive practice overcorrection of oral reading errors. *Behavior Modification, 8,* 23–37.

Skiba, R., & Raison, J. (1990). Relationship between the use of timeout and academic achievement. *Exceptional Children, 57* (1), 36–46.

Skinner, B. F. (1938). *The behavior of organisms.* New York: Appleton-Century-Crofts.

Skinner, B. F. (1938/1966). *The behavior of organisms: An experimental analysis.* New York: Appleton-Century. (Copyright renewed in 1966 by the B. F. Skinner Foundation, Cambridge, MA.)

Skinner, B. F. (1948). *Walden two.* New York: Macmillan.

Skinner, B. F. (1948). Superstition in the pigeon. *Journal of Experimental Psychology, 38,* 168–172.

Skinner, B. F. (1953). *Science and human behavior.* New York: MacMillan.

Skinner, B. F. (1956). A case history in scientific method. *American Psychologist, 11,* 221–233.

Skinner, B. F. (1957). *Verbal behavior.* New York: Appleton-Century-Crofts.

Skinner, B. F. (1966). Operant behavior. In W. K. Honig (Ed.), *Operant behavior: Areas of research and application* (pp. 12–32). New York: Appleton-Century-Crofts.

Skinner, B. F. (1967). B. F. Skinner: An autobiography. In E. G. Boring & G. Lindzey (Eds.), *A history of psychology in autobiography* (Vol. 5, pp. 387–413). New York: Irvington.

Skinner, B. F. (1969). *Contingencies of reinforcement: A theoretical analysis.* New York: Appleton-Century-Crofts.

Skinner, B. F. (1971). *Beyond freedom and dignity.* New York: Knopf.

Skinner, B. F. (1974). *About behaviorism.* New York: Knopf.

Skinner, B. F. (1976). *Particulars of my life.* Washington Square, NY: New York University Press.

Skinner, B. F. (1978). *Reflections on behaviorism and society.* Upper Saddle River, NJ: Prentice Hall.

Skinner, B. F. (1979). *The shaping of a behaviorist.* Washington Square, NY: New York University Press.

Skinner, B. F. (1981a). Selection by consequences. *Science, 213,* 501–504.

Skinner, B. F. (1981b). How to discover what you have to say—A talk to students. *The Behavior Analyst, 4,* 1–7.

Skinner, B. F. (1982). Contrived reinforcement. *The Behavior Analyst, 5,* 3–8.

Skinner, B. F. (1983a). *A matter of consequences.* Washington Square, NY: New York University Press.

Skinner, B. F. (1983b). Intellectual self-management in old age. *American Psychologist, 38,* 239–244.

Skinner, B. F. (1989). *Recent issues in the analysis of behavior.* Columbus, OH: Merrill.

Skinner, B. F., & Vaughan, M. E. (1983). *Enjoy old age: A program of self-management.* New York: Norton.

Skinner, C. H., Cashwell, T. H., & Skinner, A. L (2000). Increasing tootling: The effects of a peer-mediated group contingency program on students' reports of peers' prosocial behavior. *Psychology in the Schools, 37* (3), 263–270.

Skinner, C. H., Fletcher, P. A., Wildmon, M., & Belfiore, P. J. (1996). Improving assignment preference through interspersing additional problems: Brief versus easy problems. *Journal of Behavioral Education, 6,* 427–436.

Skinner, C. H., Skinner, C. F., Skinner, A. L., & Cashwell, T. H. (1999). Using interdependent contingencies with groups of students: Why the principal kissed a pig. *Educational Administration Quarterly, 35* (Suppl.), 806–820.

Smith, B. W., & Sugai, G. (2000). A self-management functional assessment-based behavior support plan for a middle school student with EBD. *Journal of Positive Behavior Interventions, 2,* 208–217.

Smith, D. H. (1987). Telling stories as a way of doing ethics. *Journal of the Florida Medical Association, 74,* 581–588.

Smith, D. H. (1993). Stories, values, and patient care decisions. In C. Conrad (Ed.), *Ethical nexus* (pp. 123–148). Norwood, NJ: Ablex.

Smith, L. D. (1992). On prediction and control: B. F. Skinner and the technological ideal of science. *American Psychologist, 47,* 216–223.

Smith, R. G., & Iwata, B. A. (1997). Antecedent influences of behavior disorders. *Journal of Applied Behavior Analysis, 30,* 343–375.

Smith, R. G., Iwata, B. A., & Shore, B. A. (1995). Effects of subject-versus experimenter-selected reinforcers on the behavior of individuals with profound developmental disabilities. *Journal of Applied Behavior Analysis, 28,* 61–71.

Smith, R. G., Iwata, B. A., Goh, H., & Shore, B. A. (1995). Analysis of establishing operations for self-injury maintained by escape. *Journal of Applied Behavior Analysis, 28,* 515–535.

Smith, R. G., Russo, L., & Le, D. D. (1999). Distinguishing between extinction and punishment effects of response blocking: A replication. *Journal of Applied Behavior Analysis, 32,* 367–370.

Smith, R., Michael, J., & Sundberg, M. L. (1996). Automatic reinforcement and automatic punishment in infant vocal behavior. *The Analysis of Verbal Behavior, 13,* 39–48.

Smith, S., & Farrell, D. (1993). Level system use in special education: Classroom intervention with prima facie appeal. *Behavioral Disorders, 18* (4), 251–264.

Snell, M. E., & Brown, F. (2000). *Instruction of students with severe disabilities* (5th ed.). Upper Saddle River, NJ: Merrill Prentice Hall.

Snell, M. E., & Brown, F. (2006). *Instruction of students with severe disabilities* (6th ed.). Upper Saddle River, NJ: Prentice Hall.

Solanto, M. V., Jacobson, M. S., Heller, L., Golden, N. H., & Hertz, S. (1994). Rate of weight gain of inpatients with anorexia nervosa under two behavioral contracts. *Pediatrics, 93* (6), 989.

Solomon, R. L. (1964). Punishment. *American Psychologist, 19,* 239–253.

Spies, R. A., & Plake, B. S. (Eds.). (2005). *Sixteenth mental measurements yearbook.* Lincoln, NE: Buros Institute of Mental Measurements.

Spooner, F., Spooner, D., & Ulicny, G. R. (1986). Comparisons of modified backward chaining: Backward chaining with leaps ahead and reverse chaining with leaps ahead. *Education and Treatment of Children, 9* (2), 122–134.

Spradlin, J. E. (1966). Environmental factors and the language development of retarded children. In S. Rosenberg (Ed.), *Developments in applied psycholinguist research* (pp. 261–290). Riverside, NJ: MacMillian.

Spradlin, J. E. (1996). Comments on Lerman and Iwata (1996). *Journal of Applied Behavior Analysis, 29,* 383–385.

Spradlin, J. E. (2002). Punishment: A primary response. *Journal of Applied Behavior Analysis, 35,* 475–477.

Spradlin, J. E., Cotter, V. W., & Baxley, N. (1973). Establishing a conditional discrimination without direct training: A study of transfer with retarded adolescents. *American Journal of Mental Deficiency, 77,* 556–566.

Sprague, J. R., & Horner, R. H. (1984). The effects of single instance, multiple instance, and general case training on generalized vending machine used by moderately and severely handicapped students. *Journal of Applied Behavior Analysis, 17,* 273–278.

Sprague, J. R., & Horner, R. H. (1990). Easy does it: Preventing challenging behaviors. *Teaching Exceptional Children, 23,* 13–15.

Sprague, J. R., & Horner, R. H. (1991). Determining the acceptability of behavior support plans. In M. Wang, H. Walberg, & M. Reynolds (Eds.), *Handbook of special education* (pp. 125–142). Oxford, London: Pergamon Press.

Sprague, J. R., & Horner, R. H. (1992). Covariation within functional response classes: Implications for treatment of severe problem behavior. *Journal of Applied Behavior Analysis, 25,* 735–745.

Sprague, J., & Walker, H. (2000). Early identification and intervention for youth with antisocial and violent behavior. *Exceptional Children, 66,* 367–379.

Spreat, S., & Connelly, L. (1996). Reliability analysis of the Motivation Assessment Scale. *American Journal on Mental Retardation, 100,* 528–532.

Staats, A. W., & Staats, C. K. (1963). *Complex human behavior: A systematic extension of learning principles.* New York: Holt, Rinehart and Winston.

Stack, L. Z., & Milan, M. A. (1993). Improving dietary practices of elderly individuals: The power of prompting, feedback, and social reinforcement. *Journal of Applied Behavior Analysis, 26,* 379–387.

Staddon, J. E. R. (1977). Schedule-induced behavior. In W. K. Honig & J. E. R. Staddon (Eds.), *Handbook of operant behavior* (pp. 125–152). Upper Saddle River, NJ: Prentice Hall.

Stage, S. A., & Quiroz, D. R. (1997). A meta-analysis of interventions to decrease disruptive classroom behavior in public education settings. *School Psychology Review, 26,* 333–368.

Starin, S., Hemingway, M., & Hartsfield, F. (1993). Credentialing behavior analysts and the Florida behavior analysis certification program. *The Behavior Analyst, 16,* 153–166.

Steege, M. W., Wacker, D. P., Cigrand, K. C., Berg, W. K., Novak, C. G., Reimers, T. M., Sasso, G. M., & DeRaad, A. (1990). Use of negative reinforcement in the treatment of self-injurious behavior. *Journal of Applied Behavior Analysis, 23,* 459–467.

Stephens, K. R., & Hutchison, W. R. (1992). Behavioral personal digital assistants: The seventh generation of computing. *The Analysis of Verbal Behavior, 10,* 149–156.

Steuart, W. (1993). Effectiveness of arousal and arousal plus overcorrection to reduce nocturnal bruxism. *Journal of Behavior Therapy & Experimental Psychiatry, 24,* 181–185.

Stevenson, H. C., & Fantuzzo, J. W. (1984). Application of the "generalization map" to a self-control intervention with school-aged children. *Journal of Applied Behavior Analysis, 17,* 203–212.

Stewart, C. A., & Singh, N. N. (1986). Overcorrection of spelling deficits in mentally retarded persons. *Behavior Modification, 10,* 355–365.

Stitzer, M. L., Bigelow, G. E., Liebson, I. A., & Hawthorne, J. W. (1982). Contingent reinforcement for benzodiazepine-free urines: Evaluation of a drug abuse treatment intervention. *Journal of Applied Behavior Analysis, 15,* 493–503.

Stokes, T. (2003). A genealogy of applied behavior analysis. In K. S. Budd & T. Stokes (Eds.), *A small matter of proof: The legacy of Donald M. Baer* (pp. 257–272). Reno, NV: Context Press.

Stokes, T. F., & Baer, D. M. (1976). Preschool peers as mutual generalization-facilitating agents. *Behavior Therapy, 7,* 599–610.

Stokes, T. F., & Baer, D. M. (1977). An implicit technology of generalization.

Journal of Applied Behavior Analysis, 10, 349–367.

Stokes, T. F., & Osnes, P. G. (1982). Programming the generalization of children's social behavior. In P. S. Strain, M. J. Guralnick, & H. M. Walker (Eds.), *Children's social behavior: Development, assessment, and modification* (pp. 407–443) Orlando, FL: Academic Press.

Stokes, T. F., & Osnes, P. G. (1989). An operant pursuit of generalization. *Behavior Therapy, 20,* 337–355.

Stokes, T. F., Baer, D. M., & Jackson, R. L. (1974). Programming the generalization of a greeting response in four retarded children. *Journal of Applied Behavior Analysis, 7,* 599–610.

Stokes, T. F., Fowler, S. A., & Baer, D. M. (1978). Training preschool children to recruit natural communities of reinforcement. *Journal of Applied Behavior Analysis, 11,* 285–303.

Stolz, S. B. (1978). *Ethical issues in behavior modification.* San Francisco: Jossey-Bass.

Strain, P. S., & Joseph, G. E. (2004). A not so good job with "Good job." *Journal of Positive Behavior Interventions, 6* (1), 55–59.

Strain, P. S., McConnell, S. R., Carta, J. J., Fowler, S. A., Neisworth, J. T., & Wolery, M. (1992). Behaviorism in early intervention. *Topics in Early Childhood Special Education, 12,* 121–142.

Strain, P. S., Shores, R. E., & Kerr, M. M. (1976). An experimental analysis of "spillover" effects on the social interaction of behaviorally handicapped preschool children. *Journal of Applied Behavior Analysis, 9,* 31–40.

Striefel, S. (1974). *Behavior modification: Teaching a child to imitate.* Austin, TX: Pro-Ed.

Stromer, R. (2000). Integrating basic and applied research and the utility of Lattal and Perone's *Handbook of Research Methods in Human Operant Behavior. Journal of Applied Behavior Analysis, 33,* 119–136.

Stromer, R., McComas, J. J., & Rehfeldt, R. A. (2000). Designing interventions that include delayed reinforcement: Implications of recent laboratory research. *Journal of Applied Behavior Analysis, 33,* 359–371.

Sugai, G. M., & Tindal, G. A. (1993). *Effective school consultation: An interactive approach.* Pacific Grove, CA: Brooks/Cole.

Sulzer-Azaroff, B., & Mayer, G. R. (1977). *Applying behavior-analysis procedures with children and youth.* New York: Holt, Rinehart & Winston.

Sundberg, M. L. (1983). Language. In J. L. Matson, & S. E. Breuning (Eds.), *Assessing the mentally retarded* (pp. 285–310). New York: Grune & Stratton.

Sundberg, M. L. (1991). 301 research topics from Skinner's book *Verbal behavior. The Analysis of Verbal Behavior, 9,* 81–96.

Sundberg, M. L. (1993). The application of establishing operations. *The Behavior Analyst, 16,* 211–214.

Sundberg, M. L. (1998). Realizing the potential of Skinner's analysis of verbal behavior. *The Analysis of Verbal Behavior, 15,* 143–147.

Sundberg, M. L. (2004). A behavioral analysis of motivation and its relation to mand training. In L. W. Williams (Ed.), *Developmental disabilities: Etiology, assessment, intervention, and integration.* Reno, NV: Context Press.

Sundberg, M. L., & Michael, J. (2001). The value of Skinner's analysis of verbal behavior for teaching children with autism. *Behavior Modification, 25,* 698–724.

Sundberg, M. L., & Partington, J. W. (1998). *Teaching language to children with autism or other developmental disabilities.* Pleasant Hill, CA: Behavior Analysts, Inc.

Sundberg, M. L., Endicott, K., & Eigenheer, P. (2000). Using intraverbal prompts to establish tacts for children with autism. *The Analysis of Verbal Behavior, 17,* 89–104.

Sundberg, M. L., Loeb, M., Hale, L., & Eigenheer, P. (2002). Contriving establishing operations to teach mands for information. *The Analysis of Verbal Behavior, 18,* 14–28.

Sundberg, M. L., Michael, J., Partington, J. W., & Sundberg, C. A. (1996). The role of automatic reinforcement in early language acquisition. *The Analysis of Verbal Behavior, 13,* 21–37.

Sundberg, M. L., San Juan, B., Dawdy, M., & Arguelles, M. (1990). The acquisition of tacts, mands, and intraverbals by individuals with traumatic brain injury. *The Analysis of Verbal Behavior, 8,* 83–99.

Surratt, P.R., Ulrich, R.E., & Hawkins, R. P. (1969). An elementary student as a behavioral engineer. *Journal of Applied Behavior Analysis.* 85–92.

Sutherland, K. S., Wehby, J. H., & Yoder, P. J. (2002). An examination of the relation between teacher praise and students with emotional/behavioral disorders' opportunities to respond to academic requests. *Journal of Emotional and Behavioral Disorders, 10,* 5–13.

Swanson, H. L., & Sachse-Lee, C. (2000). A meta-analysis of single-subject-design intervention research for students with LD. *Journal of Learning Disabilities, 38,* 114–136.

Sweeney, W. J., Salva, E., Cooper, J. O., & Talbert-Johnson, C. (1993). Using self-evaluation to improve difficult-to-read handwriting of secondary students. *Journal of Behavioral Education, 3,* 427–443.

Symons, F. J., Hoch, J., Dahl, N. A., & McComas, J. J. (2003). Sequential and matching analyses of self-injurious behavior: A case of overmatching in the natural environment. *Journal of Applied Behavior Analysis, 36,* 267–270.

Symons, F. J., McDonald, L. M., & Wehby, J. H. (1998). Functional assessment and teacher collected data. *Education and Treatment of Children, 21* (2), 135–159.

Szempruch, J., & Jacobson, J. W. (1993). Evaluating the facilitated communications of people with developmental disabilities. *Research in Developmental Disabilities, 14,* 253–264.

Tang, J., Kennedy, C. H., Koppekin, A., & Caruso, M. (2002). Functional analysis of stereotypical ear covering in a child with autism. *Journal of Applied Behavior Analysis, 35,* 95–98.

Tapp, J. T., & Walden, T. A. (2000). A system for collecting and analysis of observational data from videotape. In T. Thompson, D. Felce, & F. J. Symons (Eds.), *Behavioral observation: Technology and applications in developmental disabilities* (pp. 61–70). Baltimore: Paul H. Brookes.

Tapp, J. T., & Wehby, J. H. (2000). Observational software for laptop computers and optical bar code readers. In T. Thompson, D. Felce, & F. J. Symons (Eds.), *Behavioral observation: Technology and applications in developmental disabilities* (pp. 71–81). Baltimore: Paul H. Brookes.

Tapp, J. T., Wehby, J. H., & Ellis, D. M. (1995). A multiple option observation system for experimental studies: MOOSES. *Behavior Research Methods Instruments & Computers, 27,* 25–31.

Tarbox, R. S. F., Wallace, M. D., & Williams, L. (2003). Assessment and treatment of elopement: A replication and extension. *Journal of Applied Behavior Analysis, 36,* 239–244.

Tarbox, R. S. F., Williams, W. L., & Friman, P. C. (2004). Extended diaper wearing: Effects on continence in and out of the diaper. *Journal of Applied Behavior Analysis, 37,* 101–105.

Tawney, J., & Gast, D. (1984). *Single subject research in special education.* Columbus, OH: Charles E. Merrill.

Taylor, L. K., & Alber, S. R. (2003). The effects of classwide peer tutoring on the spelling achievement of first graders with disabilities. *The Behavior Analyst Today, 4,* 181–189.

Taylor, R. L. (2006). Assessment of exceptional students: *Educational and psychological procedures* (7th ed.). Boston: Pearson/Allyn and Bacon.

Terrace, H. S. (1963a). Discrimination learning with and without "errors." *Journal of the Experimental Analysis of Behavior, 6,* 1–27.

Terrace, H. S. (1963b). Errorless transfer of a discrimination across two continua. *Journal of the Experimental Analysis of Behavior, 6,* 223–232.

Terris, W., & Barnes, M. (1969). Learned resistance to punishment and subsequent responsiveness to the same and novel punishers. *Psychonomic Science, 15,* 49–50.

Test, D. W., & Heward, W. L. (1983). Teaching road signs and traffic laws to learning disabled students. *Science Education, 64,* 129–139.

Test, D. W., & Heward, W. L. (1984). Accuracy of momentary time sampling: A comparison of fixed- and variable-interval observation schedules. In W. L. Heward, T. E. Heron, D. S. Hill, and J. Trap-Porter (Eds.), *Focus on behavior analysis in education* (pp. 177–194). Columbus, OH: Charles E. Merrill.

Test, D. W., Spooner, F., Keul, P. K., & Grossi, T. (1990). Teaching adolescents with severe disability to use the public telephone. *Behavior Modification, 14,* 157–171.

Thompson, R. H., & Iwata, B. A. (2000). Response acquisition under direct and indirect contingencies of reinforce-ment. *Journal of Applied Behavior Analysis, 33,* 1–11.

Thompson, R. H., & Iwata, B. A. (2001). A descriptive analysis of social consequences following problem behavior. *Journal of Applied Behavior Analysis, 34,* 169–178.

Thompson, R. H., & Iwata, B. A. (2003). A review of reinforcement control procedures. *Journal of Applied Behavior Analysis, 38,* 257–278.

Thompson, R. H., & Iwata, B. A. (2005). A review of reinforcement control procedures. *Journal of Applied Behavior Analysis, 38,* 257–278.

Thompson, R. H., Fisher, W. W., Piazza, C. C., & Kuhn D. E. (1998). The evaluation and treatment of aggression maintained by attention and automatic reinforcement. *Journal of Applied Behavior Analysis, 31,* 103–116.

Thompson, R. H., Iwata, B. A., Conners, J., & Roscoe, E. M. (1999). Effects of reinforcement for alternative behavior during punishment of self-injury. *Journal of Applied Behavior Analysis, 32,* 317–328.

Thompson, T. J., Braam, S. J., & Fuqua, R. W. (1982). Training and generalization of laundry skills: A multiple probe evaluation with handicapped persons. *Journal of Applied Behavior Analysis, 15,* 177–182.

Thompson, T., Symons, F. J., & Felce, D. (2000). Principles of behavioral observation. In T. Thompson, F. J. Symons, & D. Felce (Eds.), *Behavioral observation: Technology and applications in developmental disabilities* (pp. 3–16). Baltimore: Paul H. Brookes.

Thomson, C., Holmber, M., & Baer, D. M. (1974). A brief report on a comparison of time sampling procedures. *Journal of Applied Behavior Analysis, 7,* 623–626.

Thoresen, C. E., & Mahoney, M. J. (1974). *Behavioral self-control.* New York: Holt, Rinehart & Winston.

Timberlake, W., & Allison, J. (1974). Response deprivation: An empirical approach to instrumental performance. *Psychological Review, 81,* 146–164.

Tincani, M. (2004). Comparing the Picture Exchange Communication System and sign language training for children with autism. *Focus on Autism and Other Developmental Disabilities, 19,* 152–163.

Todd, A. W., Horner, R. W., & Sugai, G. (1999). Self-monitoring and self-recruited praise: Effects on problem behavior, academic engagement, and work completion in a typical classroom. *Journal of Positive Behavior Interventions, 1,* 66–76, 122.

Todd, J. T., & Morris, E. K. (1983). Misconception and miseducation: Presentations of radical behaviorism in psychology textbooks. *The Behavior Analyst, 6,* 153–160.

Todd, J. T., & Morris, E. K. (1992). Case histories in the great power of steady misrepresentation. *American Psychologist, 47,* 1441–1453.

Todd, J. T., & Morris, E. K. (1993). Change and be ready to change again. *American Psychologist, 48,* 1158–1159.

Todd, J. T., & Morris, E. K. (Eds.). (1994). *Modern perspectives on John B. Watson and classical behaviorism.* Westport, CT: Greenwood Press.

Touchette, P. E., MacDonald, R. F., & Langer, S. N. (1985). A scatter plot for identifying stimulus control of problem behavior. *Journal of Applied Behavior Analysis, 18,* 343–351.

Trammel, D. L., Schloss, P. J., & Alper, S. (1994). Using self-recording, evaluation, and graphing to increase completion of homework assignments. *Journal of Learning Disabilities, 27,* 75–81.

Trap, J. J., Milner-Davis, P., Joseph, S., & Cooper, J. O. (1978). The effects of feedback and consequences on transitional cursive letter formation. *Journal of Applied Behavior Analysis, 11,* 381–393.

Trask-Tyler, S. A., Grossi, T. A., & Heward, W. L. (1994). Teaching young adults with developmental disabilities and visual impairments to use tape-recorded recipes: Acquisition, generalization, and maintenance of cooking skills. *Journal of Behavioral Education, 4,* 283–311.

Tucker, D. J., & Berry, G. W. (1980). Teaching severely multihandicapped students to put on their own hearing aids. *Journal of Applied Behavior Analysis, 13,* 65–75.

Tufte, E. R. (1983). *The visual display of quantitative information.* Chesire, CT: Graphics Press.

Tufte, E. R. (1990). *Envisioning information.* Chesire, CT: Graphics Press.

Turkewitz, H., O'Leary, K. D., & Ironsmith, M. (1975). Generalization and maintenance of appropriate behavior through self-control. *Journal of Consulting and Clinical Psychology, 43,* 577–583.

Turnbull, H. R., III., & Turnbull, A. P. (1998). *Free appropriate public education: The law and children with disabilities.* Denver: Love.

Tustin, R. D. (1994). Preference for reinforcers under varying schedule arrangements: A behavioral economic analysis. *Journal of Applied Behavior Analysis, 28,* 61–71.

Twohig, M. P., & Woods, D. W. (2001). Evaluating the duration of the competing response in habit reversal: A parametric analysis. *Journal of Applied Behavior Analysis, 34,* 517–520.

Twyman, J., Johnson, H., Buie, J., & Nelson, C. M. (1994). The use of a warning procedure to signal a more intrusive timeout contingency. *Behavioral Disorders, 19* (4), 243–253.

U. S. Department of Education. (2003). *Proven methods: Questions and answers on No Child Left Behind.* Washington, DC: Author. Retrieved October 24, 2005, from www.ed.gov/nclb/methods/whatworks/doing.html.

Ulman, J. D., & Sulzer-Azaroff, B. (1975). Multi-element baseline design in educational research. In E. Ramp & G. Semb (Eds.), *Behavior analysis: Areas of research and application* (pp. 371–391). Upper Saddle River, NJ: Prentice Hall.

Ulrich, R. E., & Azrin, N. H. (1962). Reflexive fighting in response to aversive stimulation. *Journal of the Experimental Analysis of Behavior, 5,* 511–520.

Ulrich, R. E., Stachnik, T. & Mabry, J. (Eds.). (1974). *Control of human behavior (Vol. 3), Behavior modification in education.* Glenview, IL: Scott, Foresman and Company.

Ulrich, R. E., Wolff, P. C., & Azrin, N. H. (1962). Shock as an elicitor of intra- and inter-species fighting behavior. *Animal Behavior, 12,* 14–15.

Umbreit, J., Lane, K., & Dejud, C. (2004). Improving classroom behavior by modifying task difficulty: Effects of increasing the difficulty of too-easy tasks. *Journal of Positive Behavioral Interventions, 6,* 13–20.

Valk, J. E. (2003). *The effects of embedded instruction within the context of a small group on the acquisition of imitation skills of young children with disabilities.* Unpublished doctoral dissertation, The Ohio State University.

Van Acker, R., Grant, S. H., & Henry, D. (1996). Teacher and student behavior as a function of risk for aggression. *Education and Treatment of Children, 19,* 316–334.

Van Camp, C. M., Lerman, D. C., Kelley, M. E., Contrucci, S. A., & Vorndran, C. M. (2000). Variable-time reinforcement schedules in the treatment of socially maintained problem behavior. *Journal of Applied Behavior Analysis, 33,* 545–557.

van den Pol, R. A., Iwata, B. A., Ivancic, M. T., Page, T. J., Neef, N. A., & Whitley, F. P. (1981). Teaching the handicapped to eat in public places: Acquisition, generalization and maintenance of restaurant skills. *Journal of Applied Behavior Analysis, 14,* 61–69.

Van Houten, R. (1979). Social validation: The evolution of standards of competency for target behaviors. *Journal of Applied Behavior Analysis, 12,* 581–591.

Van Houten, R. (1993). Use of wrist weights to reduce self-injury maintained by sensory reinforcement. *Journal of Applied Behavior Analysis, 26,* 197–203.

Van Houten, R. (1994). The right to effective behavioral treatment. In L. J. Hayes, G. J. Hayes, S. C. Moore, & P. M. Gjezzi (Eds.), *Ethical issues in developmental disabilities* (pp. 103–118). Reno, NV: Context Press.

Van Houten, R., Axelrod, S., Bailey, J. S., Favell, J. E., Foxx, R. M., Iwata, B. A., & Lovaas, O. I. (1988). The right to effective behavioral treatment. *The Behavior Analyst, 11,* 111–114.

Van Houten, R., & Doleys, D. M. (1983). Are social reprimands effective? In S. Axelrod & J. Apsche (Eds.). *The effects of punishment on human behavior* (pp. 45–70). New York: Academic Press.

Van Houten, R., & Malenfant, J. E. L. (2004). Effects of a driver enforcement program on yielding to pedestrians. *Journal of Applied Behavior Analysis, 37,* 351–363.

Van Houten, R., Malenfant, J. E., Austin, J., & Lebbon, A. (2005). The effects of a seatbelt-gearshift delay prompt on the seatbelt use of motorists who do not regularly wear seatbelts. *Journal of Applied Behavior Analysis, 38,* 195–203.

Van Houten, R., Malenfant, L., & Rolider, A. (1985). Increasing driver yielding and pedestrian signaling with prompting, feedback, and enforcement. *Journal of Applied Behavior Analysis, 18,* 103–110.

Van Houten, R., & Nau, P. A. (1981). A comparison of the effects of posted feedback and increased police surveillance on highway speeding. *Journal of Applied Behavior Analysis, 14,* 261–271.

Van Houten, R., & Nau, P. A. (1983). Feedback interventions and driving speed: A parametric and comparative analysis. *Journal of Applied Behavior Analysis, 17,* 253–281.

Van Houten, R., Nau, P. A., Mackenzie-Keating, S. E., Sameoto, D., & Colavecchia, B. (1982). An analysis of some variables influencing the effectiveness of reprimands. *Journal of Applied Behavior Analysis, 15,* 65–83.

Van Houten, R., Nau, P. A., & Marini, Z. (1980). An analysis of public posting in reducing speeding behavior on an urban highway. *Journal of Applied Behavior Analysis, 13,* 383–395.

Van Houten, R., & Retting, R. A. (2001). Increasing motorist compliance and caution at stop signs. *Journal of Applied Behavior Analysis, 434,* 185–193.

Van Houten, R., & Retting, R. A. (2005). Increasing motorist compliance and caution at stop signs. *Journal of Applied Behavior Analysis, 34,* 185–193.

Van Houten, R., & Rolider, A. (1988). Recreating the scene: An effective way to provide delayed punishment for inappropriate motor behavior. *Journal of Applied Behavior Analysis, 21,* 187–192.

Van Houten, R., & Rolider, A. (1990). The role of reinforcement in reducing inappropriate behavior: Some myths and misconceptions. In A. C. Repp & N. N. Singh (Eds.), *Perspectives on the use of nonaversive and aversive interventions for persons with developmental disabilities* (pp. 119–127). Sycamore, IL: Sycamore.

Van Norman, R. K. (2005). *The effects of functional communication training, choice making, and an adjusting work schedule on problem behavior maintained by negative reinforcement.* Unpublished doctoral dissertation, The Ohio State University, Columbus.

Vargas, E. A. (1986). Intraverbal behavior. In P. N. Chase & L. J. Parrott (Eds.), *Psychological aspects of language* (pp. 128–151). Springfield, IL: Charles C. Thomas.

Vargas, J. S. (1978). A behavioral approach to the teaching of composition. *The Behavior Analyst, 1,* 16–24.

Vargas, J. S. (1984). What are your exercises teaching? An analysis of stimulus control in instructional materials. In W. L. Heward, T. E. Heron, D. S. Hill, & J. Trap-Porter (Eds.), *Focus on behavior analysis in education* (pp. 126–141). Columbus, OH: Merrill.

Vargas, J. S. (1990). B. F. Skinner–The last few days. *Applied Behavior Analysis, 23,* 409–410.

Vaughan, M. (1989). Rule-governed behavior in behavior analysis: A theoretical and experimental history. In S. C. Hayes (Ed.), *Rule-governed behavior: Cognition, contingencies, and instructional control* (pp. 97–118). New York: Plenum Press.

Vaughan, M. E., & Michael, J. L. (1982). Automatic reinforcement: An important but ignored concept. *Behaviorism, 10,* 217–227.

Vollmer, T. R. (1994). The concept of automatic reinforcement: Implications for behavioral research in developmental disabilities. *Research in Developmental Disabilities, 15* (3), 187–207.

Vollmer, T. R. (2002). Punishment happens: Some comments on Lerman and Vorndran's review. *Journal of Applied Behavior Analysis, 35,* 469–473.

Vollmer, T. R. (2006, May). *On the utility of automatic reinforcement in applied behavior analysis.* Paper presented at the 32nd annual meeting of the Association for Behavior Analysis, Atlanta, GA.

Vollmer, T. R., & Hackenberg, T. D. (2001). Reinforcement contingencies and social reinforcement: Some reciprocal relations between basic and applied research. *Journal of Applied Behavior Analysis, 34,* 241–253.

Vollmer, T. R., & Iwata, B. A. (1991). Establishing operations and reinforcement effects. *Journal of Applied Behavior Analysis, 24,* 279–291.

Vollmer, T. R., & Iwata, B. A. (1992). Differential reinforcement as treatment for behavior disorders: Procedural and functional variations. *Research in Developmental Disabilities, 13,* 393–417.

Vollmer, T. R., Marcus, B. A., Ringdahl, J. E., & Roane, H. S. (1995). Progressing from brief assessments to extended experimental analyses in the evaluation of aberrant behavior. *Journal of Applied Behavior Analysis, 28,* 561–576.

Vollmer, T. R., Progar, P. R., Lalli, J. S., Van Camp, C. M., Sierp, B. J., Wright, C. S., Nastasi, J., & Eisenschink, K. J. (1998). Fixed-time schedules attenuate extinction-induced phenomena in the treatment of severe aberrant behavior. *Journal of Applied Behavior Analysis, 31,* 529–542.

Vollmer, T. R., Roane, H. S., Ringdahl, J. E., & Marcus, B. A. (1999). Evaluating treatment challenges with differential reinforcement of alternative behavior. *Journal of Applied Behavior Analysis, 32,* 9–23.

Wacker, D. P., & Berg, W. K. (1983). Effects of picture prompts on the acquisition of complex vocational tasks by mentally retarded adolescents. *Journal of Applied Behavior Analysis, 16,* 417–433.

Wacker, D. P., Berg, W. K., Wiggins, B., Muldoon, M., & Cavanaugh, J. (1985). Evaluation of reinforcer preferences for profoundly handicapped students. *Journal of Applied Behavior Analysis, 18,* 173–178.

Wacker, D., Steege, M., Northup, J., Reimers, T., Berg, W., & Sasso, G. (1990). Use of functional analysis and acceptability measures to assess and treat severe behavior problems: An outpatient clinic model. In A. C. Repp & N. N. Singh (Eds.), *Perspectives on the use of nonaversive and aversive interventions for persons with developmentaly disabilities* (pp. 349–359). Sycamore, IL: Sycamore.

Wagman, J. R., Miltenberger, R. G., & Arndorfer, R. E. (1993). Analysis of a simplified treatment for stuttering. *Journal of Applied Behavior Analysis, 26,* 53–61.

Wagman, J. R., Miltenberger, R. G., & Woods, D. W. (1995). Long-term follow-up of a behavioral treatment for stuttering. *Journal of Applied Behavior Analysis, 28,* 233–234.

Wahler, R. G., & Fox, J. J. (1980). Solitary toy play and time out: A family treatment package for children with aggressive and oppositional behavior. *Journal of Applied Behavior Analysis, 13,* 23–39.

Walker, H. M. (1983). Application of response cost in school settings: Outcomes, issues and recommendations. *Exceptional Education Quarterly, 3,* 46–55.

Walker, H. M. (1997). *The acting out child: Coping with classroom disruption* (2nd ed.). Longmont, CO: Sopris West.

Wallace, I. (1977). Self-control techniques of famous novelists. *Journal of Applied Behavior Analysis, 10,* 515–525.

Ward, P., & Carnes, M. (2002). Effects of posting self-set goals on collegiate football players' skill execution during practice and games. *Journal of Applied Behavior Analysis, 35,* 1–12.

Warner, S. F. (1992). Facilitating basic vocabulary acquisition with milieu teaching procedures. *Journal of Early Intervention, 16,* 235–251.

Warren, S. F., Rogers-Warren, A., & Baer, D. M. (1976). The role of offer rates in controlling sharing by young children. *Journal of Applied Behavior Analysis, 9,* 491–497.

Watkins, C. L., Pack-Teixteira, L., & Howard, J.S. (1989). Teaching intraverbal behavior to severely retarded children. *The Analysis of Verbal Behavior, 7,* 69–81.

Watson, D. L., & Tharp, R. G. (2007). *Self-directed behavior: Self-modification for personal adjustment* (9th ed.). Belmont, CA: Wadsworth/Thomson Learning.

Watson, J. B. (1913). Psychology as the behaviorist views it. *Psychological Review, 20,* 158–177.

Watson, J. B. (1924). *Behaviorism.* New York: W. W. Norton.

Watson, P. J., & Workman, E. A. (1981). The nonconcurrent multiple baseline across-individuals design: An extension of the traditional multiple baseline design. *Journal of Behavior Therapy and Experimental Psychiatry, 12,* 257–259.

Watson, T. S. (1996). A prompt plus delayed contingency procedure for reducing bathroom graffiti. *Journal of Applied Behavior Analysis, 29,* 121–124.

Webber, J., & Scheuermann, B. (1991). Accentuate the positive . . . eliminate the negative. *Teaching Exceptional Children, 24* (1), 13–19.

Weber, L. H. (2002). The cumulative record as a management tool. *Behavioral Technology Today, 2,* 1–8.

Weeks, M., & Gaylord-Ross, R. (1981). Task difficulty and aberrant behavior in severely handicapped students. *Journal of Applied Behavior Analysis, 14,* 449–463.

Wehby, J. H., & Hollahan, M. S. (2000). Effects of high-probability requests on the latency to initiate academic tasks. *Journal of Applied Behavior Analysis, 33,* 259–262.

Weiher, R. G., & Harman, R. E. (1975). The use of omission training to reduce self-injurious behavior in a retarded child. *Behavior Therapy, 6,* 261–268.

Weiner, H. (1962). Some effects of response cost upon human operant behavior. *Journal of Experimental Analysis of Behavior, 5,* 201–208.

Wenrich, W. W., Dawley, H. H., & General, D. A. (1976). *Self-directed systematic desensitization: A guide for the student, client, and therapist.* Kalamazoo, MI: Behaviordelia.

Werts, M. G., Caldwell, N. K., & Wolery, M. (1996). Peer modeling of response chains: Observational learning by students with disabilities. *Journal of Applied Behavior Analysis, 29,* 53–66.

West, R. P., & Smith, T. G. (2002, September 21). *Managing the behavior of groups of students in public schools: Clocklights and group contingencies.* Paper presented at The Ohio State University Third Focus on Behavior Analysis in Education Conference, Columbus, OH.

West, R. P., Young, K. R., & Spooner, F. (1990). Precision teaching: An introduction. *Teaching Exceptional Children, 22,* 4–9.

Wetherington, C. L. (1982). Is adjunctive behavior a third class of behavior? *Neuroscience and Biobehavioral Reviews, 6,* 329–350.

Whaley, D. L., & Malott, R. W. (1971). *Elementary principles of behavior.* Englewood Cliffs, NJ: Prentice Hall.

Whaley, D. L., & Surratt, S. L. (1968). *Attitudes of science.* Kalamazoo, MI: Behaviordelia.

Wheeler, D. L., Jacobson, J. W., Paglieri, R. A., & Schwartz, A. A. (1993). An experimental assessment of facilitated communication. *Mental Retardation, 31,* 49–60.

White, A., & Bailey, J. (1990). Reducing disruptive behaviors of elementary physical education students with sit and watch. *Journal of Applied Behavior Analysis, 23,* 353–359.

White, D. M. (1991). *Use of guided notes to promote generalized notetaking behavior of high school students with learning disabilities.* Unpublished master's thesis. Columbus, OH: The Ohio State University.

White, G. D. (1977). The effects of observer presence on the activity level of families. *Journal of Applied Behavior Analysis, 10,* 734.

White, M. A. (1975). Natural rates of teacher approval and disapproval in the classroom. *Journal of Applied Behavior Analysis, 8,* 367–372.

White, O. (2005) Trend lines. In G. Sugai & R. Horner (Eds.), *Encyclopedia of behavior modification and cognitive behavior therapy, Volume 3: Educational applications.* Pacific Grove, CA; Sage Publications.

White, O. R. (1971). *The "split-middle": A "quickie" method of trend estimation* (working paper No. 1). Eugene: University of Oregon, Regional Center for Handicapped Children.

White, O. R., & Haring, N. G. (1980). *Exceptional teaching* (2nd ed.). Columbus, OH: Charles E. Merrill.

Wieseler, N. A., Hanson, R. H., Chamberlain, T. P., & Thompson, T. (1985). Functional taxonomy of stereotypic and self-injurious behavior. *Mental Retardation, 23,* 230–234.

Wilder, D. A., & Carr, J. E. (1998). Recent advances in the modification of establishing operations to reduce aberrant behavior. *Behavioral Interventions, 13,* 43–59.

Wilder, D. A., Masuda, A., O'Conner, C., & Baham, M. (2001). Brief functional analysis and treatment of bizarre vocalizations in an adult with schizophrenia. *Journal of Applied Behavior Analysis, 34,* 65–68.

Wilkenfeld, J., Nickel, M., Blakely, E., & Poling, A. (1992). Acquisition of lever press responding in rats with delayed reinforcement: A comparison of three procedures. *Journal of the Experimental Analysis of Behavior, 51,* 431–443.

Wilkinson, G. S. (1994). *Wide Range Achievement Test—3.* Austin, TX: Pro-Ed.

Wilkinson, L. A. (2003). Using behavioral consultation to reduce challenging behavior in the classroom. *Preventing School Failure, 47* (3), 100–105.

Williams, C. D. (1959). The elimination of tantrum behavior by extinction procedures. *Journal of Abnormal and Social Psychology, 59,* 269.

Williams, D. E., Kirkpatrick-Sanchez, S., & Iwata, B. A. (1993). A comparison of shock intensity in the treatment of long-standing and severe self-injurious behavior. *Research in Developmental Disabilities, 14,* 207–219.

Williams, G., Donley, C. R., & Keller, J. W. (2000). Teaching children with autism to ask questions about hidden objects. *Journal of Applied Behavior Analysis, 33,* 627–630.

Williams, J. A., Koegel, R. L., & Egel, A. L. (1981). Response-reinforcer relationships and improved learning in autistic children. *Journal of Applied Behavior Analysis, 14,* 53–60.

Williams, J. L. (1973). *Operant learning: Procedures for changing behavior.* Monterey, CA: Brooks/Cole.

Windsor, J., Piche, L. M., & Locke, P. A. (1994). Preference testing: A comparison of two presentation methods. *Research in Developmental Disabilities, 15,* 439–455.

Winett, R. A., & Winkler, R. C. (1972). Current behavior modification in the classroom: Be still, be quiet, be docile. *Journal of Applied Behavior Analysis, 5,* 499–504.

Winett, R. A., Moore, J. F., & Anderson, E. S. (1991). Extending the concept of social validity: Behavior analysis for disease prevention and health promotion. *Journal of Applied Behavior Analysis, 24,* 215–230.

Winett, R. A., Neale, M. S., & Grier, H. C. (1979). Effects of self-monitoring on residential electricity consumption. *Journal of Applied Behavior Analysis, 12,* 173–184.

Witt, J. C., Noell, G. H., LaFleur, L. H., & Mortenson, B. P. (1997). Teacher use of interventions in general education settings: Measurement and analysis of the independent variable. *Journal of Applied Behavior Analysis, 30,* 693–696.

Wittgenstein, L. (1953). *Philosophical investigations.* New York: Macmillan.

Wolery, M. (1994). Procedural fidelity: A reminder of its functions. *Journal of Behavioral Education, 4,* 381–386.

Wolery, M., & Gast, D. L. (1984). Effective and efficient procedures for the transfer of stimulus control. *Topics in Early Childhood Special Education, 4,* 52–77.

Wolery, M., & Schuster, J. W. (1997). Instructional methods with students who have significant disabilities. *Journal of Special Education, 31,* 61–79.

Wolery, M., Ault, M. J., Gast, D. L., Doyle, P.M., & Griffen, A. K. (1991). Teaching chained tasks in dyads: Acquisition of target and observational behaviors. *The Journal of Special Education, 25* (2), 198–220.

Wolf, M. M. (1978). Social validity: The case for subjective measurement or how applied behavior analysis is finding its heart. *Journal of Applied Behavior Analysis, 11,* 203–214.

Wolf, M. M., Risley, T. R., & Mees, H. L. (1964). Application of operant conditioning procedures to improve the behaviour problems of an autistic child. *Behavior Research and Therapy, 1,* 305–312.

Wolfe, L. H., Heron, T. E., & Goddard, Y. I. (2000). Effects of self-monitoring on the on-task behavior and written language performance of elementary students with learning disabilities. *Journal of Behavioral Education, 10,* 49–73.

Wolfensberger, W. (1972). *The principle of normalization in human services.* Toronto: National Institute on Mental Retardation.

Wolff, R. (1977). Systematic desensitization and negative practice to alter the after-effects of a rape attempt. *Journal of Behavior Therapy and Experimental Psychiatry, 8,* 423–425.

Wolford, T., Alber, S. R., & Heward, W. L. (2001). Teaching middle school students with learning disabilities to recruit peer assistance during cooperative learning group activities. *Learning Disabilities Research & Practice, 16,* 161–173.

Wolpe, J. (1958). *Psychotherapy by reciprocal inhibition.* Stanford, CA: Stanford University Press.

Wolpe, J. (1973). *The practice of behavior therapy* (2nd ed.). New York: Pergamon Press.

Wong, S. E., Seroka, P., L., & Ogisi, J. (2000). Effects of a checklist on self-assessment of blood glucose level by a memory-impaired woman with Diabetes Mellitus. *Journal of Applied Behavior Analysis, 33,* 251–254.

Wood, F. H., & Braaten, S. (1983). Developing guidelines for the use of punishing interventions in the schools. *Exceptional Education Quarterly, 3,* 68–75.

Wood, S. J., Murdock, J. Y., Cronin, M. E., Dawson, N. M., & Kirby, P. C. (1998). Effects of self-monitoring on on-task behaviors of at-risk middle school students. *Journal of Behavioral Education, 9,* 263–279.

Woods, D. W., & Miltenberger, R. G. (1995). Habit reversal: A review of applications and variations. *Journal of Behavior Therapy and Experimental Psychiatry, 26* (2), 123–131.

Woods, D. W., Twohig, M. P., Flessner, C. A., & Roloff, T. J. (2003). Treatment of vocal tics in children with Tourette syndrome: Investigating the efficacy of habit reversal. *Journal of Applied Behavior Analysis, 36,* 109–112.

Worsdell, A. S., Iwata, B. A., Dozier, C. L., Johnson, A. D., Neidert, P. L., & Thomason, J. L. (2005). Analysis of response repetition as an error-correction strategy during sight-word reading. *Journal of Applied Behavior Analysis, 38,* 511–527.

Wright, C. S., & Vollmer, T. R. (2002). Evaluation of a treatment package to reduce rapid eating. *Journal of Applied Behavior Analysis, 35,* 89–93.

Wyatt v. Stickney, 344 F. Supp. 387, 344 F. Supp. 373 (M.D. Ala 1972), 344 F. Supp. 1341, 325 F. Supp. 781 (M.D. Ala. 1971), *aff'd* sub nom, Wyatt v. Aderholt, 503 F. 2d. 1305 (5th Cir. 1974).

Yeaton, W. H., & Bailey, J. S. (1983). Utilization analysis of a pedestrian safety training program. *Journal of Applied Behavior Analysis, 16,* 203–216.

Yell, M. (1994). Timeout and students with behavior disorders: A legal analysis. *Education and Treatment of Children, 17* (3), 293–301.

Yell, M. (1998). *The law and special education.* Upper Saddle River, NJ: Merrill/Prentice Hall.

Yell, M. L., & Drasgow, E. (2000). Litigating a free appropriate public education: The Lovaas hearings and cases. *Journal of Special Education, 33,* 206–215.

Yoon, S., & Bennett, G. M. (2000). Effects of a stimulus–stimulus pairing procedure on conditioning vocal sounds as reinforcers. *The Analysis of Verbal Behavior, 17,* 75–88.

Young, J. M., Krantz, P. J., McClannahan, L. E., & Poulson, C. L. (1994). Generalized imitation and response-class formation in children with autism. *Journal of Applied Behavior Analysis, 27,* 685–697.

Young, R. K., West, R. P., Smith, D. J., & Morgan, D. P. (1991). *Teaching self-management strategies to adolescents.* Longmont, CO: Sopris West.

Zane, T. (2005). Fads in special education. In J. W. Jacobson, R. M. Foxx, & J. A. Mulick (Eds.), *Controversial therapies in developmental disabilities: Fads, fashion, and science in professional practice* (pp. 175–191). Hillsdale, NJ: Erlbaum.

Zanolli, K., & Daggett, J. (1998). The effects of reinforcement rate on the spontaneous social initiations of socially withdrawn preschoolers. *Journal of Applied Behavior Analysis, 31,* 117–125.

Zarcone, J. R., Rodgers, T. A., & Iwata, B. A., (1991). Reliability analysis of the Motivation Assessment Scale: A failure to replicate. *Research in Developmental Disabilities, 12,* 349–360.

Zhou, L., Goff, G. A., & Iwata, B. A. (2000). Effects of increased response effort on self-injury and object manipulation as competing responses. *Journal of Applied Behavior Analysis, 33,* 29–40.

Zhou, L., Iwata, B. A., & Shore, B. A. (2002). Reinforcing efficacy of food on performance during pre- and postmeal sessions. *Journal of Applied Behavior Analysis, 35,* 411–414.

Zhou, L., Iwata, B. A., Goff, G. A., & Shore, B. A. (2001). Longitudinal analysis of leisure-item preferences. *Journal of Applied Behavior Analysis 34,* 179–184.

Zimmerman, J., & Ferster, C. B. (1962). Intermittent punishment of S^Δ responding in matching-to-sample. *Journal of the Experimental Analysis of Behavior, 6,* 349–356.

Zuriff, G. E. (1985). *Behaviorism: A conceptual reconstruction.* New York: Columbia University Press.

Name Index

Subject Index